I am glad I had a
chance to meet you.

Sharee Rappe

1-27-2013

Letters of a desperate woman to her "OWN" God

By:

Shamci Rafani (Gharavi)

Ketab Corp.

Letters of a Desperate Woman to her "Own" God
Shamci Rafani (Gharavi)
First Edition-2009
Published by: Ketab Corp. USA
Printed in China

I S B N: 978-1-59584-172-8

Ketab Corp.
1419 Westwood Blvd.
Los Angeles, CA 90024 U.S.A.
Tel: (310) 477-7477
Fax: (310) 444-7176

I am proud and honored

to dedicate my autobiography

to my three children,

Maryam Rafani,

Maseeh Rafani,

and

Mojgan Rafani.

And also to my grandchildren

Samantha and Hana Scheiller,

who joined us at the ending of this book.

This piece was given to me by a gentleman whom I met on the plane coming from Iran. His name and the date are on the piece. The text is in Arabic and it reads , "In the name of God, the kind, the merciful."

WITH THE NAME OF GOD THE KIND AND MERCIFUL

When I wrote these lines, I was desperately seeking for some kind of recovery. Since I couldn't bring myself to committing suicide, and I was not able to become a murderer, nor could I talk to my children to make them understand what was going on in my mind at that desperate and mixed emotion times of my life, I decided to put myself into writing to my " OWN " God. I thought I must talk to someone or I will die. I needed someone to listen to me, to hear me out, to cry on his shoulder, and to be able to release my anger and frustration by putting myself in his hand so he can cure my disease one way or another. The more I searched, the more I couldn't find a human-being who has the answer to all my pains and agony. When I fell in love with Iraj, I thought he would be my best friend, my lover, my supporter, and someone who would also listen to my problems with much care and attention. But after I lost him and everything else connected to him, I was left alone in this whole wild world. So I realized that I must go to a higher power who once had found Iraj for me. That higher power was no one but my " OWN " God. I decided to write to him, talked to him about all my problems, and poured out all my anger and frustrations which were slowly destroying me year after year after year. And that's why I started writing to my "Own" God.

Those moments that I was trying to become my own doctor to my problems, I found the cure with the help of my " OWN " God in the typewriter, and soon opened my heart to him as truthfully and as innocently as possible. If in one way or the other I had offended anyone in my book or any group or organization for that matter, I sincerely and deeply apologize to each and every one of you. I have and had great respect for all the different religious groups and organizations, all races: a1l colors, and all professions and never meant to criticize anyone of them.

This writing brought back my sanity because of the help of the only super power known to us as our God.

And for the two ANIMALS who viciously ruined me, my children's happiness and destroyed our future I must say that "I searched the entire dictionary to look for the word to describe the kind of person you are but I couldn't find one. Maybe it's not in this world yet. But why waste my time when I know that you know better what "word" best described both of you".

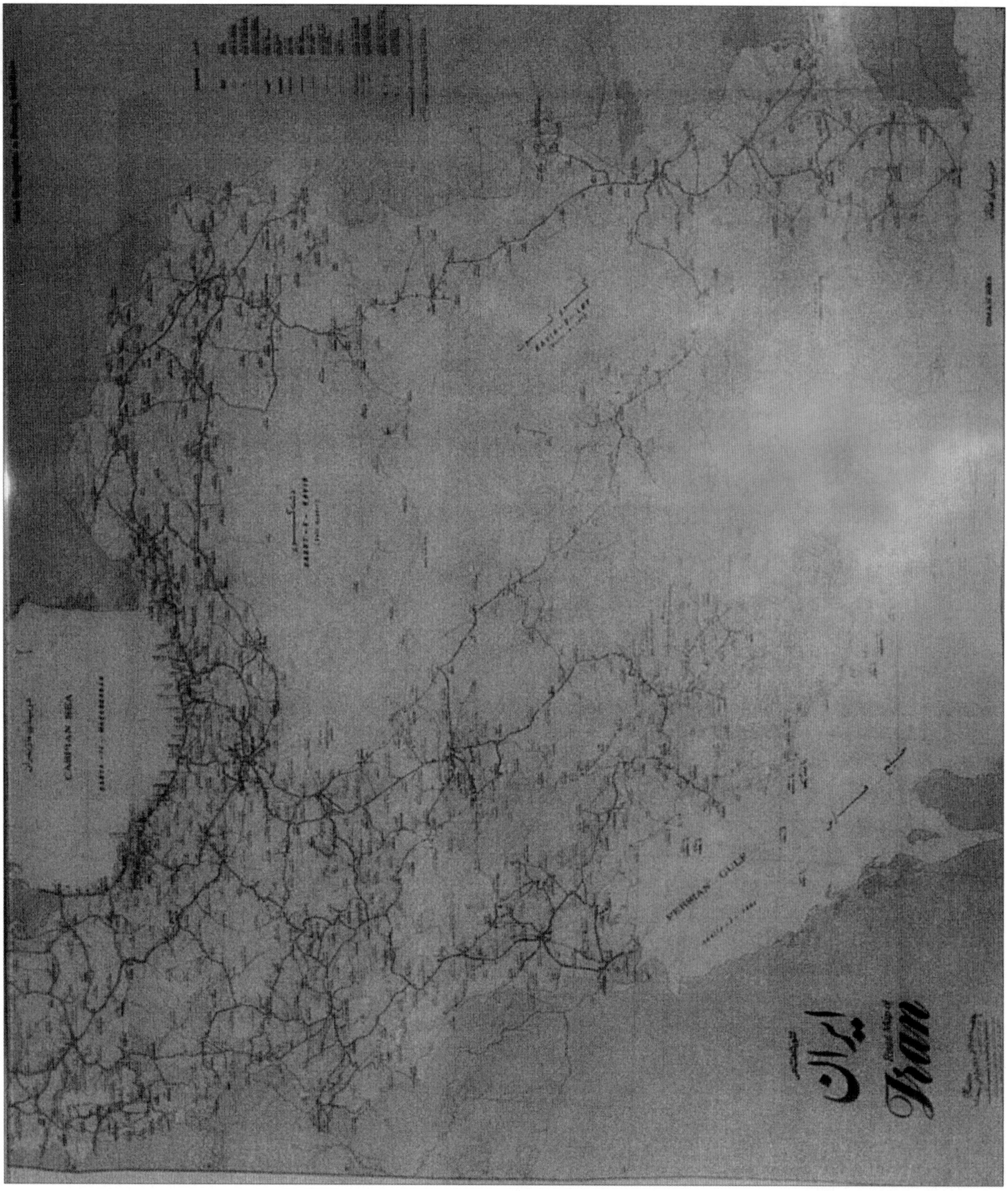

Here is the map of my beautiful country, Iran. This is where I was born and raised, where my ancestors descended from. I did not comprehend the meaning of the word "country" until I had to leave Iran. My country is like a mother or a father to me, and life is meaningless without it.

Norooz Mobarak
(Happy New Year)

سال نو مبارک

Long Live Iran

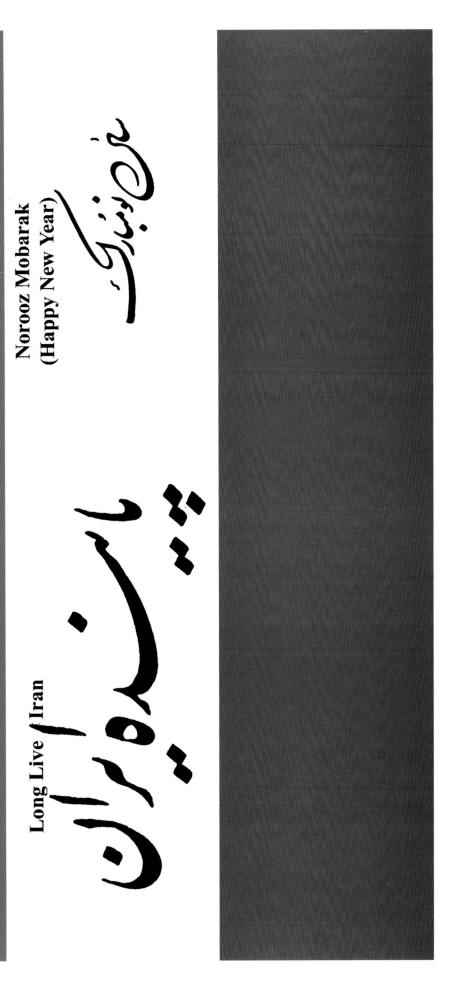

پاینده ایران

ای ایران، ای مرز پرگهر — ای خاکت سرچشمه هنر
دور از تو اندیشه بدان — پاینده مانی تو جاودان
ای دشمن ار تو سنگ خاره‌ای من آهنم — جان من فدای خاک پاک میهنم
مهر تو چون شد پیشه‌ام — دور از تو نیست اندیشه‌ام
در راه تو کی ارزشی دارد این جان ما — پاینده باد خاک ایران ما

This is our national anthem which we used to sing in elementary school.
It is about Iran and our promise to fight for it to the last drop of blood.

PREFIX

My Dear GOD:

You know, that I have been in touch with you all my life. I cannot recall a time of my life that I have been without you.

I have often blamed you for all that went wrong in my life, and sometimes I have even doubted your existence. I came to a realization that there was an unknown power within me, and that this power is you. I knew that you were watching over me then, just as you are now. I knew you were the one who knew all that was taking place then, all that is happening now, and all that will come to happen in the future. I knew that all is in your hands and that we have no say in it whatsoever. I just thought of talking to someone to be able to put my mind together, and help myself to get through the ordeal I was facing. I couldn't think of anyone else but you. Please help me, listen to me, and while you are listening, just help me to survive.

I am not a religious person. Many religious groups and organizations have turned me off from the thought of becoming religious, but I have never given up on you, your power, or your strength over me or within me.

One night while I had the Ghoran (Koran) in my hand, and in that way I was trying to hold my father in my arms asking him what I should do, a thought suddenly came to me, "You must start writing to GOD, to your GOD, and just leave everything up to him."

Since that day, I started to go to the library and write to you. Yes, I started writing to you, and I would then come home prepared to face whatever was awaiting me that day or any other day.

At that time, I had a huge responsibility of looking after my children. Mary was twenty-two, Maseeh was twenty, and my Mojgan was just turning thirteen.

I would walk around our indoor swimming pool, and ask you millions of times, "Should I drown myself in this pool, or could you give me strength and wisdom to be able to carry this heavy weight on my shoulders?" "No," you would say to me. "Don't do it. Your children need you. Even though they are confused and rebel against you, they still need you to support them and show them your strength. You are the only person in this world that cares for them. They don't have any relatives in this country to care for them as you do. Their father is busy with his love affair and his mid-life crisis and so you are the only person who can protect them". I don't remember who told me "NO", but I know for sure that you had something to do with the decision I had made, because I really heard you.

My Dear GOD:

I was suicidal. I wanted to kill myself many times. Now I believe that it was you who gave me the strength to be able to approach the unknown and take one thing at a time. It is easy to live and it is easy to die. But it is not easy to cope with the loss of the greatest love in your heart. It was easy to kill myself, but it was so difficult to kill that nasty love that persisted to live in my heart and followed me around all my life. So my goal was to do exactly that. I just wished to kill that love in my heart so that I was able to continue living.

Yes, my dear GOD, with your help I was able to kill the feelings within me. And then I started to live with complete emptiness. I felt hollow, I felt absolutely emotionless like a robot. I was certainly numb.

Yes, my dear GOD, at the time you had introduced me to some strangers who eventually became my friends. Each one of them played a significant role in helping me cope. They all became my angels.

Little by little I forgot about my own life, and I started concentrating solely on my children's lives and their well-being.

That was the time when I started to write to you and give you the complete information on that day and every day that followed. It wasn't that you didn't know it yourself; it was just that I wanted to inform you of the pain I was going through.

The more I wrote to you, the more I was able to handle things around me. I wrote to you during the day and cried to you at night in my bed. There were times that I imagined your hands around me. They were comforting me and telling me to calm myself down and go to sleep. I know it was you because, I would listen to you, and after a short while I would fell asleep.

Later, by holding a fulltime job at my friend's restaurant, moving from place to place and talking and writing to you on daily basis, I had regained my strength. Things started to come to my mind a little easier. While things were happening one after another, I did not know what to handle first. I was just trying to put myself together and be able to survive, pretending meanwhile that everything was all right.

Step by step my destruction took place. Like a linked chain, things would take place one after the other, each triggered it their turn by a previous disaster.

My latest decision was to buy a house together with my son Maseeh in Los Angeles, California. It was in this house that I decided to organize the letters I had written to you. It was then that I had thought of going back and talking to you, starting from the beginning of my life. It feels so good when I am talking to you. I feel very safe, and I go to bed at night, sleep comfortably with you and the thought of you. UNTIL TOMORROW, AGAIN AND AGAIN.

My letters to GOD
(because He knows everything.)
For my children to read
(because they don't know everything.)

Okay, My Dear God:

It is almost the year 1994, since we only have sixteen days left till the end of 1993. I am living with my son, Maseeh and his girlfriend Anna, in our new house that we decided to buy together. I have lived here for two months.

I don't know how to start my life story or why I should even start to talk about my life. The fact is that the things that happened to me were arranged step by step, and looking back now they look more like a set-up. I don't think that I or anyone else could have done anything to stop it. The events took place like a chain reaction; one caused the next one and so on.

Yes my dear GOD, whether by your will or by someone else everything took place in a planned manner. You are the only one who remember exactly how that day my life crashed in front of my eyes.

It was the night of March 1st, 1982, or perhaps it's more appropriate to identify as the day that he started to react strangely (now that I look back I think he had planned in his mind and wanted to let me know what was going on.)

March 1st was his birthday. His birthday has always been a big deal to me. I made sure that we all remembered his birthday. To me that day was a holy day. I loved him so much that I contributed the presence of the great love for him in my heart to his birthday. There were times that I would throw a big party, and other times I invited just a small group of friends (so-called friends). On the day of his birthday I have always made sure to do something that he liked the most, or cook his favorite dishes and care for him just as if he was my baby. My love was truly unconditional. I would let him walk all over my eyes instead of walking on the ground to make sure that he would never get hurt as long as he was alive. I didn't ever want him to get hurt. He was my doll. I wanted to keep him close to my chest forever.

My Dear GOD, you know all these things better than anyone else and you probably remember everything better than I do. I only am writing these letters for my children. I am writing them with a purpose of letting them know of what was happening to us before they had come into our lives.

Okay, on March 1st, 1982 we celebrated his birthday in a more private manner. My three children were home. We had a common room in the bedroom area that we called a TV room. That night we were all sitting in the TV room under the korsi (korsi is a square, short-legged table that was used as a heater in the old days in Iran. They would keep a fire pit under the table and use it to heat up the room. People would gather around this short table, which was covered with a heavy blanket or comforter, extend their legs under the table and make their back comfortable by lying down against big cushions that were arranged around the korsi). I had made all the cushions, as well as the table with the heater underneath it by myself for our house.

My Dear GOD:

You know how big the house was. I'll talk about it some other time. Keeping up the house by itself was a full-time job. With the added responsibility of taking care of and watching over my three children, I was carrying a heavy load. Despite all these responsibilities I have never let myself forget my husband's birthday. On that night, that special night, we were all sitting under the korsi. Each person talked about something funny that had happened to them recently. We were all laughing hard while watching TV. The warmth of the korsi and the comfort of lying down in front of the TV with the kids beside us had made me fall asleep. I don't remember how long I was asleep for; when suddenly someone kicking my feet gently awakened me. I opened my eyes and saw Iraj standing there beside my feet. He asked me to go into the bedroom with him.

Half asleep I replied, "I will be there." He went into the bedroom, but I fell asleep again under the korsi, right where I had been before.

In about five or six minutes I heard a door slam. It was our bedroom door. I got up quickly and went towards the bedroom. I attempted to open the door when I realized that it was locked. I kept knocking, asking him to open the door, but he wouldn't. I continued knocking because I thought he was teasing me like he always did. But there was no answer. He finally opened the door after almost five minutes. He had his pillow and his blanket in his hand. He passed by me, and rushed downstairs. We were all so shocked. We were looking at each other and wondering what could have possibly happened. This was the first time in 30-years of our marriage that he acted so strange. My son Maseeh looked at me and said, "I think he wanted you in the bedroom because it is his birthday". (GOD, my children were always smarter than I was.)

"Well what can I do?" I said. "I fell asleep under the korsi for just five minutes." I got up thinking that it was all a joke. I rushed downstairs but I couldn't find him in the family room. I kept searching for him around the house, and there he was, in the poolroom area. We had a large indoor pool. He put his pillow and blanket on the moist

floor beside the pool, he was planning to sleep there (a sort of stupidity that I never thought my husband would be capable of).

My Dear GOD:

I approached him, and just like we have been laughing before all this had happened, I tried to snatch the blanket from him. "Are you crazy?" I asked playfully. "Let's go upstairs to bed".

He paid no attention. I started to tickle him. He still did not react. And then suddenly, with a voice I hardly recognized, he started calling me bad names and screaming, "I never want or beg sex from you!" And he went on and on.

I was so shocked that if someone shot me at that time I probably wouldn't have felt it at all. I felt blood rushing to my head. I said to myself, "GOD, please not again".

After that night, my life at least everything I loved about it, became history.

I finally made him get up and go upstairs. But things didn't change back to the way they were before. All those actions were signals to warn me that something was wrong. As a matter of fact something was very wrong. (Later on the meaning of his words "I never want or beg any sex from you" became very clear to me. That was what she used to hypnotize him with.)

My dear GOD, my English is not very good. My children complained about it all the time. However, I am sure that you understand me no matter how poorly I speak it.

Exactly one year before that dreadful night, March 1st, 1982, I had held a very big surprise birthday party for him in Troy's Hilton hotel hall. It was March 1st 1981. That was his 50th birthday party. I always had a difficult time surprising him. He would usually find a way to catch me by surprise instead. I remember back in 1972, when we were still in our first house, located on 860 Helston Rd., in Bloomfield Hills, MI 48013. He had medical meetings for a few days in a row. He arrived back on the night of his birthday and I had asked some friends to come over to surprise him. I was expecting him to call me so that I would pick him up from the airport, when to my surprise he came in yelling, "Surprise!" He caught a taxi home to surprise us all. He was always so sure that I would have something planned for his birthday. So for his 50th birthday party I had to find a way to make sure that I surprised him. I decided to have two parties. I planned the first party for the night of his actual birthday, and the other one was to be held the following night. I had invited only a few of our friends the first night, and we had a cozy party. We all had a very joyful and pleasant time. They brought gifts, and my daughter Mary read a poem that she had written for him. He was expecting a bigger party.

This was Mary's poem:

Rush to work, rush home
Rush every day of the week
Pay the telephone man, the gasman
You're swimming in bills neck deep
Secretary goofs, nurse drops the SCALPEL, patient threatens to sue
Hospital calls: emergency, baby arrived too soon.
You trudge home, it's 3:00 am, your ravaged body aching, 6:00 am the clock screams out, are you alive or faking?
Breakfast burns, kids fight, wife hollers in frustration, yet so quiet and patient, you pay little attention.
Why work so hard and give so much, when you receive so little?
I don't know daddy, but I think it's why we all think you're so special.
We ask a lot
And you give it, and then you give even more.
It seems unfair
And it is, and I can't understand it at all.
Today you turn 50, the year went by too fast, and sometimes it all seems so meaningless, the youth and adventure all passed.
But daddy if I could
I'd give you the sun
And the sea and the sand
And all the flowers….
But oh …I can't, and I cry
Because I'm still selfish
And you still give more than you receive from us
But for what it is worth, let me just say
I love you Daddy because you are that way.

by Mary Rafani
March 1st 1981

Rush to work, rush home, rush everyday of the week,
Pay the telephone man, the gas man, you're swimming in bills neck deep.
Secretary goofs, nurse drops the scalpel, patient threatens to sue,
Hospital calls: emergency, baby arrived too soon.

You trudge home, it's 3:00 a.m., your ragged body aching,
6:00 a.m. the clock screams out, are you alive or faking?
Breakfast burns, kids fight, wife hollers in frustration,
Yet so quiet and patient, you pay little attention.

Why work so hard and give so much
When you receive so little?
I don't know daddy, but I think it's why
We all think you're so special.

We ask a lot
And you give it, and then you give even more.
It seems unfair
And it is, and I can't understand it at all.

Today you turn 50,
The years went by too fast,
And sometimes it all seems so meaningless,
The youth and adventure all passed.

But daddy, if I could
I'd give you the sun
And the sea and the sand and all the flowers...
But oh... I can't, and I cry

Because I'm still selfish
And you still give more
Than you receive from us
But, for what it's worth, let me just say
I love you daddy because you're that way.

Margit 1981

Mary Rafani wrote this poem for the fiftieth birthday of her father, Dr. Iraj Rafani Motlagh. She was very happy to read this poem to him. This was what she believed her father was. This was what she saw in her father. We all believed in it. We were all glad that he had reached his fiftieth birthday. This was my dream coming true. I felt lucky. I was lucky. My children were becoming adults. They were trying to get the grasp of life. They needed their father to be their leader, their mentor, their supporter, and their friend. This was what he was at that time.

But one day from all those days, one shotgun changed all of them. All of our lives were shambled. We couldn't see where it was coming from. Dr. Malakuti got shot with a gun in his office. That was the end of him, and the beginning of our desperation. As we saw that he was buried, my family's happiness was buried with him. Guess who came to life and gained from all this; Mrs. Malakuti whose husband wanted to divorce her and had acted so many times.

After all, it is true that whatever happens in this world, happens for a purpose. Yes, now I know the true meaning of this sentence.

My Dear GOD:

Yes, this poem, which brought tears to everybody's eyes was written and read by Mary. But the message conveyed what I believed and made sure that my children also became aware of. And that was exactly how much their father was worth in our lives. I wanted to feed them the love that I had for him, I wanted to make them realize that our restrictions are only for their best interest. That night I thought that my family and I were the luckiest and the happiest family in this world. I believed that Iraj really and truly loved us and as always he told and showed me that he lived only for our happiness and us. Indeed I believed him and loved him even more and more in return. I didn't know that just one year later my family would be pulled apart and crushed for the rest of our lives.

Now, after twelve years, when I look back I still can't believe that I am still alive after everything that has happened. No, I think, that this is not really I living. This is just a body with no feelings whatsoever. I wonder at time, "Why am I walking, why am I talking, why am I eating?" Oh, there are so many other whys!

Okay. So that night he really believed that was his birthday party. He was really happy.

Then there was the second night, which was a Sunday. He had no idea there might be another birthday party. I had asked his nephew, Arman Forghani (who is now deceased), to make up a story to his uncle about some meeting that he had to arrange with his partner. He had to convince Iraj that his presence at the meeting was very important. He thought that the rest of us were supposed to go to movies. So he was almost sure that he was just going to a meeting with his nephew, and he was not expecting anything else. It was so funny. He kept telling Arman, "How did you arrange a meeting in this hotel? Where are you going? There are only dining rooms here; they don't have any conference rooms". But Arman assured him that there was one conference room past the dining rooms.

So when he arrived to a darkened dining room and we turned the lights on and shouted, "Surprise! Surprise!" not only he was surprised but he was completely shocked. He wasn't dressed for the occasion. He had his winter coat and his Russian lambskin hat on. He was very surprised and thought it was great. I had arranged a telephone call from Iran. All his sisters talked to him and wished him a happy birthday. All my wishes came true at that time. It has been almost thirty years from the time we had fallen in love. I had dreamt of seeing him alive, healthy, successful and happy. He certainly was happy and at the peak of his joy and success.

This was my dream party, I was able to arrange it for him in Hilton Hotel in Troy, Michigan. Azeez, Badri, and Kashef were sitting to our left. Did Malakuti know what the future would bring him after that day? I don't believe so. Badri probably knew. I had arranged for Iraj's sister to call and talk to Iraj. After that party I thought I had made it. All my wishes would come true. I was dancing on top of the world. I thought my Iraj had hit fifty, and we had survived the existence of evil. Not knowing that the evil, the wicked witch of the Malakutis, was sitting next to her husband among our friends. How would any of us know that in a year or so, she, the evil of my life would get to work? Boy oh boy, who knew that Badri who was not allowed to talk in front of her husband, was capable of doing such an evil thing?

Here, my dear husband is excited about the party. He is giving his speech of "a million thanks".

What a fool I was! What a naive woman I was! And how loving and caring I was...

There were times when my children were happy. I was trying so hard to see their happiness last, but we were never aware of the unexpected. Here, Mary is helping herself with some good food.

Oh, how quickly life passes us! On his fiftieth birthday in Hilton Hotel in Troy, Michigan, he was blowing the candles out, not knowing that in fact our lives and happiness were being blown away as well.

Here is my happy Mary.
What a beautiful face!

My Dear GOD:

It was scary for me, but I never thought that he would do it again. I thought that he would have learned a lesson from his mistakes, and that no one in the world would ever be able to destroy him again. I thought, based on what he had said himself, that he had such a bitter experience that he would never allow for it to happen again.

At that time he welcomed everyone and we sat and had a wonderful dinner. I spoke a few words in his honor, and some other doctors joined me in praising him in their words to toast or roast him.

Yes, my dear GOD, that night, his health clinic partner, Dr. Azeez Malakuti and his family were sitting at our table to our right side.

Okay, my dear GOD, from here on you will see how events took place, like a circle of chains connected to each other.

After the party we all went to our house and we continued celebrating his birthday until morning. He thanked me so many times. He was so appreciative of my love and attention that he wanted to cry. (Or probably, my dear GOD, it was just that I was so busy with loving him that at the time I couldn't see what was going on.)

I don't know if that party had made him realize that he was getting old, or if he was on the verge of menopause, his mid-life crisis. But whatever it was, due to the death of his partner, Dr. Azeez Malakuti, our lives were crushed into million pieces. That was the end of our love and togetherness forever.

Okay my dear GOD, to get to know our families and how it all started, I have to go back to my childhood, as far back as I can remember.

Okay
Once upon a time,
And it was like this.

My Dear God:

I was born to a middle class family in Damghan, Iran. My father was very religious. He deeply believed in morality, and devoted his life to our well-being. He was the only child on his mother's side. He had a stepbrother and a stepsister, who were very much unlike him, and in fact they had absolutely nothing in common. He was twenty and my mother was fourteen when they got married (it must have been an arranged marriage). He was from a well-respected family with high morals and standards. He was very strict and opinionated. I heard from my mother that he had lost his mother at a very young age, and so he was cared for with much love by his aunt (his mother's sister).

We are at a party which we held for going back to Iran for a three-month visit. My older sister Ezzat, my younger sister Azar-holding my hands, and my youngest sister Saideh are in this picture.

Here, we were picnicking in Iran. Left to right: Moosavi, Ezzat, Hosain, Sina, my mother, Azar, Maseeh. Mary is in the front.

In front from left to right: Moosavi, Ezzat, Azar, Mamanjoon, Saideh In the back: Sina, Chirazi and Afsaneh.

We took the pictures on the right while we were in London, half way to our return to America. I was going back to Iraj to start life with him again,after his first affair. Mary, Maseeh and I were having fun spending time with my brother Javad in London. Although it was my brother's graduation and he needed one of us to be with him, Iraj stopped me from postponing my ticket for a few days. He said he had been expecting us for a long time and he could not wait any longer. I don't know why I listened to him. I think having to pay more money to postpone the ticket was why Iraj opposed the idea. And, poor my brother, who loved so much for us to be there, calmly accepted the idea.

Iraj in his pajamas

Iraj's father in his French coat

I am holding Saideh in my arms. Azar is walking away.

Iraj, Kamal, Jalal and Javad. I am under the umbrella, my skirt is showing. That day was the beginning of unknown.

Azar, uncle Ravan, my mother, Ezzat and Javad

Me, my father, my mother and Azar; In the front Javad, Saideh and Jalal are sitting.

This was the day that I gave my life forever. He was at the picnic with us.

Here, Pari is posing like a movie star.

Pari on the grass posing for a picture

Azar and I are looking down our bedroom window.

On the left is Neya

Pari, wearing my mother's drape, is going up the stairs acting like a movie star. My younger brother Jalal, is watching her from down the stairs.

This picture is very interesting. Ezzat sitting down on the right was complaining about how I was sitting with lack of confidence, while the girl on the right who was the maid in that house was looking very confident. Standing in the back are my brother Jamal, my mother in the sleeveless dress, and my father with the moustache behind her next to my uncle

Azar and I with a group of my students at the zoo in Tehran before I left Iran and my job to come to the United States for good.

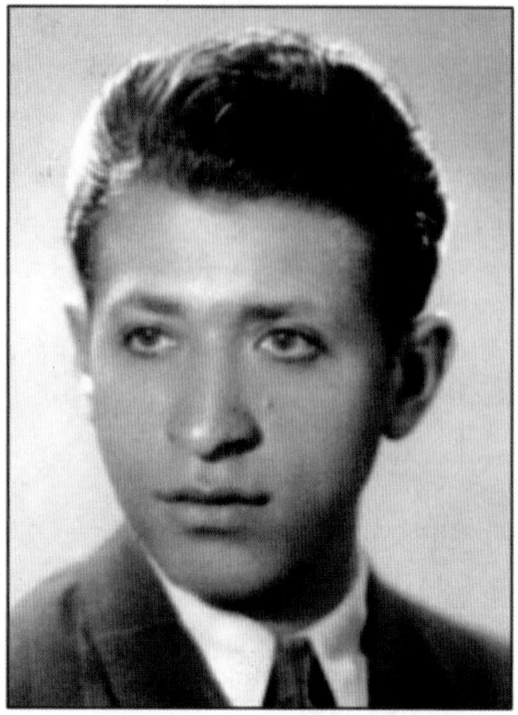

my brother Jamal, and Afsar's wedding

my brother Jamal

my sister Azar, and Shahab Gharavi's wedding

Masoomeh Hormozi, Shahab, Azar, Maseeh, Reza, Mary, and Rokhand Gharavi

Chirazi, Sina, and little Ehsan

Azar and Shahab Gharavi

Sina and Chirazi, Ali and Ehsan

Ali

Ehsan

Ezzat's Family:

Ezzat

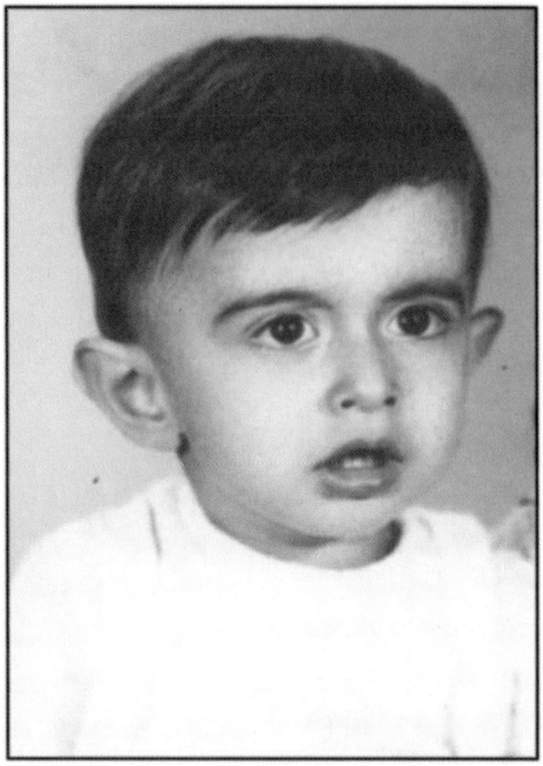

Nader

Ezzat, Afsaneh, and her father Mr. Moosavi

Afsaneh

Top left are my three brothers when I left Iran, from left to right Jalal, Jamal and Javad. This picture was taken long before Javad left to go to England to continue his education. This was the last time Javad and Jalal were together. On the left is Jalal before he died. On the top right is the two Tooman money that my father gave me as a gift on Norooz. On the top he wrote; "to commemorate this day, and hopefully to bring you more money, I will give to you as a gift." He signed it "Gharavi" and dated 3/1/1967.

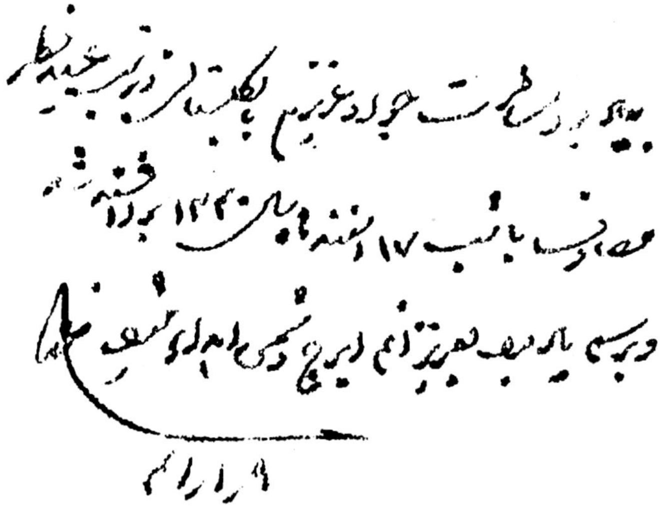

This is a picture of my father taken before Javad had to leave the country to go to England. On the back of the photo my father had written; "This picture is taken to the memory of Javad's departure to England on the night of Fetr holiday on 3/8/1961 and also to my dear children Iraj and Shamcy," Signature: Gharavi

This is a picture of my three brothers and my father before Javad's departure. Don't you think they were the most handsome young men alive? It is unfortunate that we had to lose the youngest one shortly after this picture was taken. After his death, no one in the family was able to live a normal life.

This picture was taken when I was separated from Iraj and he was having his first affair in Tehran. During the summer holiday, with the advice of my parents, I took Mary and Maseeh to Maygoon. Then, my sisters-in-law were very supportive of me. In this picture in Maygoon, Neya is visiting me with her children Arman and Nazy.

This very interesting picture was taken during Reza Shah, the founder of Pahlavi's dynasty. This was a celebration by the government when Reza Shah was trying to abolish the Islamic coverage for ladies (the veil) that was adopted from the Arab culture.

My mother is the second lady from right with a buttoned coat on. My father is the third man from right, right above my mother. Everyone from that office is there with their children. It was the most important time in Iran's history to be able to see Iranian women liberated after Arabs invaded Iran. What a picture! What a memory!

These are the Gharavi Family:

Javad Gharavi

Jamalaldeen Gharavi

Jalal Gharavi

Sina Gharavi

my mother, Behjat Saleh Gharavi

my father, Saied Nooraldeen Gharavi

Saiedeh Gharavi

Ezzat Gharavi

Shamci Gharavi

Azar Gharavi

His aunt has never been married, and she devoted herself and her love solely to my father. From what I understood his aunt was a lady of a very strong character. She was an educated, very intelligent woman. I don't know much about his mother or father, except that his father was both an Islamic leader and a teacher (ayatollah). He was a kind of person, who never cared for or valued the material aspect of life. He was a humanitarian and his life was completely devoted to others. I have always pictured him having all the characteristics of Mother Teresa.

My father, on the other hand, was a combination of both his father's and his aunt's characteristics. He had very strong beliefs, and he tried very hard to enforce them, his religious beliefs in particular, on his children. He was very much someone, who had molded his own character. He was born in Shiraz and graduated from Islamic school, where he received his degree, which was equivalent to a master's degree in philosophy. My father worked for the government, in the department of licensing and registry. He would generally be appointed as a chief of that department. We often had to move from one state to the other.

My father had lost his father and his aunt long before we were in the picture. The only family he ever had been his wife and his children for as long as I remember. He was devoted to his wife and his nine children. He lived and worked for us and he expected us to follow his ideals and be on our best behavior.

My Dear GOD:

He strongly believed in rewards and punishments. He would punish his children when they did wrong, and he rewarded them if they showed they knew the difference between right and wrong.

He believed that his children had to become useful people to themselves and to their society; otherwise he would not like to think of them as a part of his life. So he put all his efforts to teach us about life, the purpose of life, and what our responsibilities are in order to live fully in this world.

We all knew that working hard for the sake of having an average life, while trying to raise and teach nine children his idea of morality and culture would at some point create a lot of friction between the two generations.

I think I was the most difficult one because I always questioned everything, "Why? Why is GOD the way he is? And how can I find out where GOD is? Or why so many other questions that did not have any answer". So, as you see, I was very difficult to deal with.

During the times my father was appointed as chief of the department of a certain state, we would live a life of rich, upper class. We were able to have a chauffeur, cook, a

few housekeepers, and maids. We have so many memories of our loving and caring maids. Sometimes my father financially supported the families of our maids and nannies. We used to become so friendly with them that if and when we were separated from them, it would become an immense emotional disaster. These people were so loyal and devoted to us that they made us feel we were like their own family.

However when we lived in Shiraz, we led a more average lifestyle. My grandmother (my mother's mother) had four houses that were connected by one big room, the common room for us, the kids, to play in. My family lived in one of those houses.

I remember that my mother got sick when I was in fourth or fifth grade. The doctors said she had yellow fever, and she had to remain in quarantine. We needed someone to take care of the household and cook for us. My aunt found a lady with her eight-year old daughter to come and stay with us. We had a room at the other corner of the house, which was almost like a maid's quarter. We all had to keep away from our mother for almost a year. So my little brother, Jalal, who at that time was only four or five months old, lived with the nanny in her quarter. She became like his mother to him in a very short period of time.

My Dear GOD:

When my mother recovered, the nanny had to leave us because of some family matters. We were all depressed. My little brother Jalal believed that his mother had left him. One day my mother was wearing a dress that was made from the same fabric as a dress his nanny used to wear. He started crying and asking my mother to remove that dress. He thought the dress was his mom's (meaning his nanny's).

I never thought of this back then, but at this time of my life I wonder what my poor mother went through. Facing her son's rejection must have been a difficult blow for her.

This and many more similar incidents were part of our regular lives. As I remember, most of the maids were loyal, trustworthy, and played a big role in our family affairs. They taught us how to love and care for one another. They taught us not by words, but by their everyday actions.

Another incident I recollect was when I was five or six years old, and my sister Azar was three. We were living in Jahrom, a city near Shiraz. It was summertime. My father let us use a summerhouse near the mountains north of Jahrom for our vacation. With the help of the maids, the house was furnished before we arrived there. And we were all very excited.

Although the place wasn't too far away from our house, we still had to ride our horses in order to get there. My mother and the rest of the family left a day ahead of us. The next day my sister Azar and I rode a horse with Safar, one of the maids. He sat in the

middle while I sat in the back and my sister was in the front, hanging on to him. We were crossing a big farm. After we passed a few yards, suddenly we found ourselves going down towards a large ditch. The horse was desperately trying to hold onto the side of the ditch, which was very deep and full of water. In Iran they call this type of ditch a "ghanat". We were all screaming and crying for help. Safar knew how dangerous it was if we all fell in headfirst into the water. He knew that the water was stored there in order to water the crops in the farm. Although we screamed as loud as we could, no one was there to hear us. After a while, which seemed like a year to us, we had almost accepted that the end had come upon us. I remember so clearly how poor Safar tried to hold us with one hand while with his other hand he tried to keep the horse from falling into the ditch while clinging to the horse. He called to the shepherd, who had appeared in a distance, to come and save us. We were numb to the point that we were losing control.

My Dear GOD:

If I were to tell you how this man moved us from the top of the horse and how Safar was overjoyed at being able to save us, it would be a long story. But after what seemed like ages, we all got to the summerhouse. Everyone gathered around us and tried to comfort us. But I know for sure that Safar was the one who needed the most comforting and appreciation. Because he was the one who saved us and deserved a reward.

Well, my dear God, this is as much as I remember from that day. If I am not correct please correct me yourself.

This is why I think anything that happens in this world has been planned. I am sure that even if the shepherd didn't come to our rescue, we still would have been saved one way or another. Because I think it was meant for me to stay alive and see all the things that have happened to me until now and will happen in the future.

You see, my dear God, these were a few of the stories of the love and affection that surrounded us. These loyal servants always contacted us and stopped to see us even when we were older.

So until today I am still wondering why a horse with three people on its back could hold on while head down in the deep water and not fall in there for almost an hour. Except for believing that it had been foreordained, how could I explain it? For sure we all will go one day, no question about it. But the way that we are saved from going sometimes, when everything is provided for us to go, leads to a big question. And the way that someone could die without any sign of dying leads to a much bigger question.

***

Okay, so as far as I can remember and from all I've heard, my father's people were okay people. And now I would like to tell you about my mother. Her name was Behjat and she was born in Shiraz, Iran. As I was told, there were nine children in her family also. One of them died at a young age and the other eight, four girls and four boys, lived on till adulthood.

My Dear GOD:

My mother was her father's favorite. Her father was a businessman. They had a comfortable life. He died before I was born.

My mother was only fourteen when she got married, and she had her first child at the age of fifteen.

Those days parents were the ones to select their children's partners (meaning their spouses). Their reasoning was that they felt parents knew best who was most compatible to be with their child. They usually knew the spouses' families and believed that knowing the family from which the intended spouse was raised would help parents to be able to decide well for their children. According to their beliefs, they felt their children would understand and hopefully end up falling in love.

Believe it or not, most of the time this was true and the children would find a lasting love. That was why they started to wed their children at the age of thirteen or fourteen. They knew that both boys and girls were ready both physically and emotionally. Meanwhile, with the help from both sides, they would be able to learn the responsibility and the meaning of love.

Those days, the education was not really an issue, and especially not for girls. The structure and framework of a family was fixed and most people were in different businesses and used to involve their sons in that business as well. It was customary for newly married couples to live in the homes of one of the in-laws. Then, when they were ready, with the help of the parents they would establish their own households and move into their own homes. Even during the time when I was a student, many parents still insisted on this method for their children.

Many families helped their children to study while they were married. Many provided home teaching for their children, like my mother's family did.

My mother was a very hard-working woman. Her father died when she was very young and left my grandmother with eight children. At that time my grandmother was only thirty-two. She was married at the age of nine (this is permitted in Islamic religion). So a young woman with eight children knew how to raise all her children with all that was left for the family. She kept all of them under her wing and made sure that everyone did all right. She was a very faithful and devoted woman, and at the same time she was very

young and beautiful. She had never agreed to get involved with any young men, even though there were many who were interested in marrying her. She had never remarried until she died. So, in raising her children, she not only imbued a sense of diligence for hard work, but discipline, organization, and economy as well.

My Dear GOD:

It is clear my mother acquired all these traits from her mother. She had a plan and pattern for everything firmly set in her mind. Although my father had to travel often because of his job, my mother would manage to keep everything at home under control. There were times that we had it very good and sometimes just average. But still my mother was able to do her best and make us all comfortable. When one person has to play the role of mother and the other the role of father, with a little understanding, they can establish a very good sense of management. Although my parents had their differences, they still managed to raise their kids in a very full and disciplined manner. When they were alive I was not smart enough to be able to understand and thank them. But now I can say proudly, "Thank you father. Thank you mother. I have never recognized the value of your training back then. Now, after all these years, I will say with a loud voice, a million times, thank you".

I have heard so many stories of my mother's bravery that I think I should mention some of them here and now.

Once, when my older sister Ezzat was only six months old, while she was in my mother's arms together with her servant, they sat in a carriage with horses. These carriages did not have a door on either side. They were crossing a bridge to reach their destination. Those days they used to wrap their babies in fabric like mummies so that the babies were unable to move their hands or legs.

While the carriage was crossing the bridge, all of the sudden, with one quick move, the baby jumps out of my mother's hand and into the river.

My mother, who at that time was only seventeen and didn't know how to swim, jumps into the river and grabs the corner of her baby's blanket. That was an automatic impulse. Not knowing what would happen to both of them; she just reacted as fast as she could. If it wasn't for the army soldier that was standing nearby, both my mother and my sister would have sunk into the river and have died. Luckily he jumped into the river and grabbed both my mother and sister and swam to the bridge.

Another time my mother displayed her bravery when the same sister, Ezzat, was three-years-old. My mother was giving me medication and I wasn't being cooperative. She asked my sister to go and find something to play with me. So Ezzat started carrying the candle lamp with her. My mother heard her screaming within seconds. She leaves me

by myself, and runs toward the screams. To her horror she finds Ezzat in flames, running and screaming. Again, without any hesitation, she runs to her and jumps on top of her, in an effort to put the fire out. She rubbed her hands against the flames and put them out. My sister was saved. But my mother's palms were deeply burnt. She had her hands bandaged for a long time.

My Dear GOD:

As for my mother's family, they were more absorbed in money and material possessions. Although their mother was a lady of respect, compassion and a strong sense of togetherness, the children did not have a good relationship with each other.

After the loss of their father, some of the older children became very greedy and tried to take advantage of their younger siblings, particularly the boys over the girls. They did not show any respect or interest for each other's rights. I remember many of their family quarrels that always made me want to get as far away from them as possible (probably to flee to another state).

Actually, I remember when we were living in Shiraz in one of my grandmother's houses. I was six or seven years old. We used to go from that one central common room to each other's house any time of the day or night. One of my uncles had married a country girl when he was in the army. Her name was Tavangar. They loved each other so much. But the whole family was against the marriage from day one.

This story is about how they had given birth to five girls. In the Middle East, and especially in Iran, parents preferred to have boys instead of girls. Not only they were against Tavangar's marriage, but they were angered by her giving birth to all girls as well. At that time Tavangar and my uncle were living in my grandmother's house. I think Tavangar had epilepsy, and that particular day was having one of her attacks. From what I saw I think she was having a big quarrel with her sister-in-laws, which caused her to collapse. While she was lying there, her sister-in-laws, without paying any attention to her were still busy fighting. When I saw them act in that manner, I said to myself, "GOD, please help me. Don't ever let me be like them."

Another time I recollect was when my aunt Zeenat had some kind of gum disease, which caused her gums to be infected. For a long time she was in pain and very ill. Instead of helping her out, no matter what time of the day it was, I saw her siblings fighting with her. To me it was just embarrassing. I was just a kid then. But I hated them for not being considerate and causing each other agony. I was always the kind of person who felt sorry and wanted to support the underdog.

My Dear GOD:

I look back now and wonder how my father, at the age of twenty, and my mother at the age of fourteen, both of them came from very different kinds of rituals and backgrounds, did not see each other at all before their wedding night yet were still able to become the first and last partners in each other's lives. They went through the hardship of raising nine children, without having so much money, and they learned to love each other for the rest of their lives. I am really amazed at how they did it!

My father loved his wife so much that many of these modern lovers can ever come close to that kind of love. He remained faithful to my mother throughout his life, until he died. He loved his children so much that he thought of them as his world.

Earlier in my life, I always was against the idea of those kinds of marriages. I questioned my parents regarding their beliefs and their morals and culture. I was the "why?" girl all my life. And then I picked and chose my own lifestyle. (Whoopee).

Yes, my dear GOD, I did it my way. Yet at this time in my life, I do not have any judgment left for anything. I don't know what is good or bad. What is right or wrong? Who is telling the truth or who is not? At this time in my life, I do not know myself even. These things that I learned before and I believed for sure, all were correct, and now I have doubt and question what is really right or wrong. Who is really living and who is not?

We have learned that what goes around comes around. No way. I don't see myself being able to think or judge or give advice. I have lost my love of life one hundred percent. Nothing matters to me anymore. Things will take place whether we want them to or not. Things will take place whether we ask for them or not. Not only will the guilty pay the price always. Good will comes to us whether we are good or bad. And bad will come to us whether we are good or bad. It does not make any difference who we are and how we behave. In the long run, we all pay the same price and we will all be equal.

It is not what you do and it is not how you try. It is not how much you love or hate. I really don't know what it is, but I do know this, that if the way that my husband made me believe in myself is true, at this moment I should've been next to him, with my children around us, and I would've been the luckiest, happiest, and most successful woman in the world. According to my husband, there was no woman on Earth that would be able to love and care for him so much, and to also be so devoted, loyal, and fun. To him I was a very capable, smart, and trustworthy woman. I do not make these things up. I have many letters to prove his beliefs. In return, he showed me much love and affection in order to make me believe in him. He wanted me to trust in his love, and I did. So, my dear GOD, what happened?

***

Okay, so now we should talk about the time when my husband and I met. Obviously you were there and you know how it started but I have to write this for my children to know something about my life.

As I said before, we used to move from place to place because of my father's job. At that time we were living in Tehran, in a subdivision called Four Hundred Units (chahr sad dastgah). We owned one of those units. I was attending Daneshsara in order to receive my teaching certificate. Although I was a very smart kid with a high IQ, I unfortunately didn't apply myself as much as everyone else did. As much as my father was expecting from all of us to do well at school, still some of us, including myself, did not pay enough attention. He knew that with a little application and a minimum display of attention, I could have been an honor student. I was always competitive and liked challenge. I was always stimulated by the game that involved the most challenge. Unfortunately, an unfair experience that traumatized me during my maturing years made me turn my back on schoolwork.

The final ceremony of sixth graders in Iran, at that time, was comparable to getting a diploma. We were in Boushehr. All the six graders of the whole city would gather in one hall for the final exam.

My father was the chief of the department of licensing and registry. We were friends with all of the other chiefs of governmental departments. Their children had exams on the same day that I had mine. Before that exam we were required to take a primary exam in all subjects. By then all the teachers told me that I had made it to the top, and I was the number one triumphant competitor among the students. Everyone was congratulating me, everyone was certain that I would be the one. All the teachers were happy with the result during final exams, and promised me that I certainly had made it to be number one; they said I had the highest record after all.

During that time if you got a score of twenty on your paper that meant that you had received a 100% perfect score.

Yet one of the teachers, who was a close friend of one of the other influential families, decided to deduct one number from my best subject, Art and Creativity. That was the only subject which its grade depended on the teacher's taste rather than proof of excellence. By this one unfair act, I lost all the trust I had in any establishment and decided not to ever deal with the formalities of school again.

My Dear GOD:

All the teachers and members of faculty turned around and started congratulating the other student, who had achieved the title of the number one instead of me. That was

the end of it. With the brains and mentality of a twelve-year old student, I started to punish myself rather that deal with the situation. Instead of showing more interest in my studies, I just studied enough to get by. Unconsciously, I refused to go after achievements. It was the greatest disappointment in my life.

After facing that act of betrayal from the people who were assigned to teach me in good faith, I isolated myself from everyone. I cried for one week straight. I couldn't put myself together and come to my senses that this wasn't necessarily the end of the world.

Luckily it was the end of the school year and we had to leave to go to Shiraz for the summer. The city of Boushehr was on the Persian Gulf. We used to live outside of the city because of the heat. My father arranged for us to get out of the heated city of Boushehr and spend our summer break in Shiraz every summer. Yet all that crying gave me an eye infection that lasted throughout the whole summer. The city's heat was so intense that many people would die during the course of one night from heatstroke. I remember a particular night, exactly two nights before we left for Shiraz. The heat and the humidity were so severe that all of us, including Sina, who was only a year old, had to sit in the balcony naked, wetting ourselves all night.

So anyways, when I met my husband, I was in Daneshsara in Tehran in order to get my teaching certificate. My brother had many friends in chaharsad dastgah. We all used to invite our friends home to socialize. My brother Jamal and his friend Iraj were both starting their university studies. Iraj was going to medical school and Jamal was majoring in education and English. When his friends came to our house, they usually went upstairs in his room and my mother would prepare some snack or soft drink for them. Sometimes she asked us to take the food up to his room. It seems very funny that I never had a chance to meet Iraj until he was caught among demonstrators and put into jail.

My brother and Iraj were both political activists, like all the other young students in Iran. When Iraj was caught, nobody knew where he was for almost one week. He had refused to give his correct name to the police. So his poor mom and his sisters thought that he had died. I remember we went to Parvin's, Iraj's sister, apartment to comfort them. His mother was crying and mourning in a way that made everyone believe he had to be dead. Parvin was so sad for her mother and so mad at Iraj that she said, "I wish I didn't have a brother to begin with."

My Dear GOD:

Among all my brother's friends, who usually came to our house, he was the only one that I hadn't met.

My mother tried to bring to my attention many different instances where I might have met him. It didn't work. She was trying to refresh my memory by giving me some

characteristic signs and descriptions of the arrested friend, yet I couldn't remember whether I had ever met him. Then she even asked, "You don't remember him? He is very short, and he stutters very noticeably." I still didn't remember ever meeting this young man. As odd as it may seem, I met him right after he got out of prison.

That evening I was sitting with my sisters in our living room. His sister Pari, who was my friend, came to borrow something for his coming home party. She asked me to go to the party also. I didn't want to go at first but she assured me that there would only be a few guest, who were mostly Iraj's friends and one of them was my brother. "It is just to celebrate his freedom," she explained.

Their older sister Parvin was married to Mr. Safavi at the time, and they were living in our neighborhood. Iraj with his mother and sisters were renting a house nearby. So when Pari invited me to go to her house, and most importantly, my parents allowed me to go, I agreed. Again, it's funny that my parents actually allowed me to go to that party without making a big deal out of it. (Didn't I say, "Everything had to happen the way that it was planned?"?) My parents allowed me to go because first of all my brother was going to be there and second of all my parents knew his parents and his sisters.

Yes, my dear GOD, a very big YES. It was that night that I met Iraj for the very first time.

He was short; he stuttered noticeably, he acted as if he was very shy. He spoke of how he was arrested. The police under a stairway at the university building had cornered him. Then the policeman took his wristwatch from him, and so on.

Those days were the time that Iran was under cold fire and was caught between the so-called two big powers, communist (U.S.S.R.) versus right-wing countries like America (U.S.A.) and the United Kingdom (U.K.). The pressure from both rivaling sides was putting the Iranian people in the middle politically and squeezing them to the point of destruction.

My Dear GOD:

We were very young at that time. The only way to deal with life was to get involved with reading and try to understand what was going on. Reza Shah, father of Mohammad Reza Pahlavi, was selected and supported by the right wings. When he started to disobey his rulers, they decided to put him in exile. Those countries have made a decision to appoint his son, Mohammad Reza, in place of his father, after a world-famous meeting.

Okay my dear GOD, tell me, why should other countries come to my country and elect and appoint a ruler for the people of our country? Don't you think that we were and are smart enough to know what is best for our own people? Don't you think that by appointing these particular rulers, the powerful countries were expecting the rulers to

World

U.S. makes overture to improve ties with Iran

BY ROBIN WRIGHT
LOS ANGELES TIMES

Acknowledging past mistakes in U.S. policy toward Iran, Secretary of State Madeleine Albright on Friday launched a major overture to Tehran that could open up trade, expedite settlement of frozen assets and lead to a renewal of formal diplomatic relations after 20 years of hostility.

As an initial step toward normalized trade, Albright announced that the United States will lift sanctions that bar imports of Iranian carpets, caviar, pistachios and dried fruit, Iran's biggest export items after petroleum. But the move stops short of removing a similar prohibition on oil and gas that accounts for more than 80% of Iranian export revenue.

In an unprecedented gesture, Albright said the United States now understands Iranian anger over a 1953 CIA operation that toppled a nationalist government and allowed the last shah to return to Iran and preside over a "brutally repressive" regime for a quarter of a century. She acknowledged that the coup was "clearly a setback" for Iran's political development.

Albright also expressed regret for America's support of Baghdad during the eight-year Iran-Iraq war in the 1980s, the bloodiest modern Mideast conflict. She said Washington was "regrettably shortsighted ... especially in light of our subsequent experiences with [Iraqi President] Saddam Hussein."

Lifting of embargo concerns local nut growers.
Page C1

The Clinton administration's overture — both in substance and symbolism — is the boldest move yet in an accelerating process of rapprochement with an Islamic government that once allowed radical students to hold 52 Americans hostage for 444 days and excoriated the United States as "the Great Satan." Iran immediately welcomed the move.

"The United States must bear its share of responsibility for the problems that have arisen in U.S.-Iranian relations," Albright said in remarks delivered at a Washington conference on the eve of the Iranian new year.

Following the partial lifting of sanctions, a second step of the new U.S. policy is to "deepen the bonds of mutual understanding and trust" by removing impediments to "people-to-people contacts." Those contacts began after reformist Iranian President Mohammad Khatami called in January 1998 for cultural exchanges to help bring down the "wall of mistrust" between the United States and Iran.

As a third step, Albright announced that the United States is willing to expedite efforts to achieve a "global settlement" of outstanding legal and financial claims between the two countries since President Jimmy Carter's administration froze all Iranian assets after the Tehran hostage drama two decades ago.

The claims have been adjudicated by a tribunal in The Hague as part of the deal that won freedom for the U.S. hostages in 1981.

This newspaper article will tell my children that what they have read about the United States' foreign affairs regarding Iran, is the complete truth and nothing but the truth. I would like to tell Albright and the American government in general, that even if you pay the United States' budget for ten years for reparations to Iran you would not be able to cover all the damages you have cost, like all the people you have killed in Iran in war with Iraq, shooting down a civilian plane, and burning down a cinema with 400 civilians inside.

serve them rather than serving their own people? Anyways, with this political game going on, we the young people were busy reading and finding out what would be the future of our country.

To tell you the truth, my dear GOD, we will never be able to find anything out.

There were no drugs, alcohol or other wrong or sinful actions going on among the youth. We were all into reading magazines, newspapers and books. The more we read, the more we realized that our country was in deep trouble. Not only those big countries were after their own benefit, but some money hungry and power hungry Iranians were helping them to achieve their goals faster and with more ease. These Iranians, like Reza Shah and his son Mohammad Reza Pahlavi and many others made us, the young people, be able to recognize the truly honest people, who would work toward the welfare and prosperity of Iranians. We actually knew who those people were. But the country was under the influence of big and powerful countries.

We thought that we had it bad then. But we never knew what these countries had planned for us in later years. Ironically, after nearly forty years of struggle, just recently I read this column from the Fresno Bee on Saturday, March 18, 2000. The title is "U.S. Makes Overture to Improve Ties with Iran". I will attach a copy of that newspaper to the book. The reason that I bring it up now is to be able to show you this was the situation that we were growing up in. We were caught in the middle of a power struggle between two or three big countries.

My Dear GOD:

There was another important column written by Robin Wright from the Los Angeles Times. As I said, with all the studying that we did, we almost found the right person to govern our country, and that was the only true nationalistic ruler for our country. He was Dr. Mohammad Mossadegh.

Much to my surprise, Secretary of State Madeline Albright expressed regret for America's support of Baghdad during the eight-year Iran-Iraq war in the 1980s, which was the bloodiest modern Middle East conflict. She also expressed regret and said, "United States now understands Iranian anger over a 1953 CIA operation that toppled a nationalist government (meaning Dr. Mossadegh's government), and allowed the last Shah to return to Iran and preside over a "brutally repressive" regime for a quarter of a century. She acknowledged that the coup was clearly a "setback" for Iran's political development. She said Washington was "regrettably shortsighted ... especially in light of our subsequent experiences with (Iraqi President) Saddam Hussein." And many more excuses and mistakes.

The New York Times ON THE WEB

SECRETS OF HISTORY

The C.I.A. in Iran

"...the Shah requires special preparation. By nature a creature of indecision, beset by formless doubts and fears, he must be induced to play his role..." -TPAJAX Plan

Corbis / Bettmann

By JAMES RISEN

The Central Intelligence Agency's secret history of its covert operation to overthrow Iran's government in 1953 offers an inside look at how the agency stumbled into success, despite a series of mishaps that derailed its original plans.

Written in 1954 by one of the coup's chief planners, the history details how United States and British officials plotted the military coup that returned the shah of Iran to power and toppled Iran's elected prime minister, an ardent nationalist.

▶ C.I.A. DOCUMENT

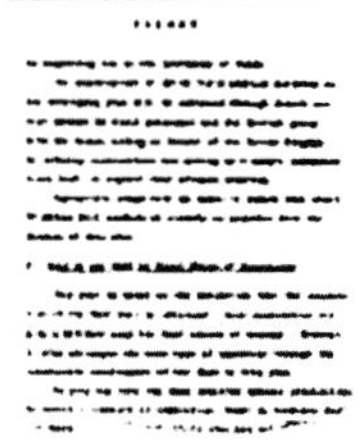

Requires Adobe Acrobat

Since I do not want to lie to my children or inform them of untrue statements, I decided to include thirty pages from the New York Times that I have collected via the internet. This way, I am hoping to clear people's mind regarding the American foreign policy especially in Iran and in the Middle East in general.

The document shows that:

• Britain, fearful of Iran's plans to nationalize its oil industry, came up with the idea for the coup in 1952 and pressed the United States to mount a joint operation to remove the prime minister.

• The C.I.A. and S.I.S., the British intelligence service, handpicked Gen. Fazlollah Zahedi to succeed Prime Minister Mohammed Mossadegh and covertly funneled $5 million to General Zahedi's regime two days after the coup prevailed.

- VI: THE MEDIA
- VII: THE SPY
- TIMELINES
- THE U.S. & IRAN
- THE COUP PERIOD
- TIMES ARCHIVES
- ARTICLES
- PAGE ONES
- PHOTOS
- DISCUSS
- ASK THE TIMES
- THE C.I.A.'S ROLE

• Iranians working for the C.I.A. and posing as Communists harassed religious leaders and staged the bombing of one cleric's home in a campaign to turn the country's Islamic religious community against Mossadegh's government.

• The shah's cowardice nearly killed the C.I.A. operation. Fearful of risking his throne, the Shah repeatedly refused to sign C.I.A.-written royal decrees to change the government. The agency arranged for the shah's twin sister, Princess Ashraf Pahlevi, and Gen. H. Norman Schwarzkopf, the father of the Desert Storm commander, to act as intermediaries to try to keep him from wilting under pressure. He still fled the country just before the coup succeeded.

• Send your comments to The New York Times on the Web

TO The New York Times ON THE WEB

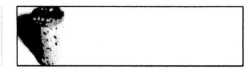

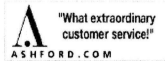

SECRETS OF HISTORY
The New York Times ON THE WEB

The C.I.A. in Iran

How a Plot Convulsed Iran in '53 (and in '79)

By JAMES RISEN

For nearly five decades, America's role in the military coup that ousted Iran's elected prime minister and returned the shah to power has been lost to history, the subject of fierce debate in Iran and stony silence in the United States. One by one, participants have retired or died without revealing key details, and the Central Intelligence Agency said a number of records of the operation — its first successful overthrow of a foreign government — had been destroyed.

But a copy of the agency's secret history of the coup has surfaced, revealing the inner workings of a plot that set the stage for the Islamic revolution in 1979, and for a generation of anti-American hatred in one of the Middle East's most powerful countries.

The document, which remains classified, discloses the pivotal role British intelligence officials played in initiating and planning the coup, and it shows that Washington and London shared an interest in maintaining the West's control over Iranian oil.

The secret history, written by the C.I.A.'s chief coup planner and obtained by The New York Times, says the operation's success was mostly a matter of chance. The document shows that the agency had almost complete contempt for the man it was empowering, Shah Mohammed Reza Pahlevi, whom it derided as a vacillating coward. And it recounts, for the first time, the agency's tortured efforts to seduce and cajole the shah into taking part in his own coup.

The operation, code-named TP-Ajax, was the blueprint for a succession of C.I.A. plots to foment coups and

C.I.A. DOCUMENT
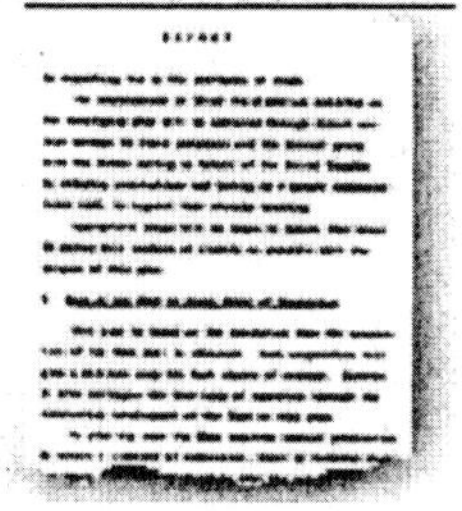
Acrobat Reader
INTRODUCTION
I: THE ROOTS
II: THE PRESSURE
III: THE COUP
IV: THE SUCCESS
V: THE PREMIER
VI: THE MEDIA
VII: THE SPY
TIMELINES
THE U.S. & IRAN
THE COUP PERIOD
TIMES ARCHIVES
ARTICLES
PAGE ONES
PHOTOS
DISCUSS

▶ ASK THE TIMES
▶ THE C.I.A.'S ROLE

destabilize governments during the cold war — including the agency's successful coup in Guatemala in 1954 and the disastrous Cuban intervention known as the Bay of Pigs in 1961. In more than one instance, such operations led to the same kind of long-term animosity toward the United States that occurred in Iran.

The history says agency officers orchestrating the Iran coup worked directly with royalist Iranian military officers, handpicked the prime minister's replacement, sent a stream of envoys to bolster the shah's courage, directed a campaign of bombings by Iranians posing as members of the Communist Party, and planted articles and editorial cartoons in newspapers.

But on the night set for Prime Minister Mohammed Mossadegh's overthrow, almost nothing went according to the meticulously drawn plans, the secret history says. In fact, C.I.A. officials were poised to flee the country when several Iranian officers recruited by the agency, acting on their own, took command of a pro-shah demonstration in Tehran and seized the government.

Two days after the coup, the history discloses, agency officials funneled $5 million to Iran to help the government they had installed consolidate power.

The outlines of the American role in the coup were disclosed in Iran at the outset and later in the memoirs of C.I.A. officers and other published accounts. But many specifics have remained classified, and the secret history obtained by The New York Times is the first detailed government account of the coup to be made public.

The C.I.A. has been slow to make available the Iran files. Two directors of central intelligence, Robert Gates and R. James Woolsey, vowed to declassify records of the agency's early covert actions, including the coup. But the agency said three years ago that a number of relevant documents had been destroyed in the early 1960's.

A C.I.A. spokesman said Friday that the agency had retained about 1,000 pages of documents related to the coup, besides the history and an internal account written later. He said the papers destroyed in the early 1960's were duplicates and working files.

The chief State Department historian said that his office received a copy of the history seven years ago but that no decision on declassifying it had yet been made.

The secret history, along with operational assessments written by coup planners, was provided to The Times by a former official who kept a copy.

It was written in March 1954 by Dr. Donald N. Wilber, an expert in Persian architecture, who as one of the leading planners believed that covert operatives had much to learn from history.

Photograph from "Adventures in the Middle East" by Donald N. Wilber, Darwin.

Donald Wilber

In less expansive memoirs published in 1986, Dr. Wilber asserted that the Iran coup was different from later C.I.A. efforts. Its American planners, he said, had stirred up considerable unrest in Iran, giving Iranians a clear choice between instability and supporting the shah. The move to oust the prime minister, he wrote, thus gained substantial popular support.

Dr. Wilber's memoirs were heavily censored by the agency, but he was allowed to refer to the existence of his secret history. "If this history had been read by the planners of the Bay of Pigs," he wrote, "there would have been no such operation."

"From time to time," he continued, "I gave talks on the operation to various groups within the agency, and, in hindsight, one might wonder why no one from the Cuban desk ever came or read the history."

The coup was a turning point in modern Iranian history and remains a persistent irritant in Tehran-Washington relations. It consolidated the power of the shah, who ruled with an iron hand for 26 more years in close contact with to the United States. He was toppled by militants in 1979. Later that year, marchers went to the American Embassy, took diplomats hostage and declared that they had unmasked a "nest of spies" who had been manipulating Iran for decades.

The Islamic government of Ayatollah Ruhollah Khomeini supported terrorist attacks against American interests largely because of the long American history of supporting the shah. Even under more moderate rulers, many Iranians still resent the United States' role in the coup and its support of the shah.

Secretary of State Madeleine K. Albright, in an address in March, acknowledged the coup's pivotal role in the troubled relationship and came closer to apologizing than any American official ever has before.

"The Eisenhower administration believed its actions were justified for strategic reasons," she said. "But the coup was clearly a setback for Iran's political development. And it is easy to see now why many Iranians continue to resent this intervention by America in their internal affairs."

The history spells out the calculations to which Dr. Albright referred in her speech.

Britain, it says, initiated the plot in 1952. The Truman administration rejected it, but President Eisenhower approved it shortly after taking office in 1953, because of fears about oil and Communism.

The document pulls few punches, acknowledging at one point that the agency baldly lied to its British allies. Dr. Wilber reserves his most withering asides for the agency's local allies, referring to "the recognized incapacity of Iranians to plan or act in a thoroughly logical manner."

Continue reading next section.

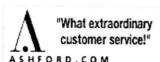

BACK TO MAIN PAGE

The New York Times on the Web

SECRETS OF HISTORY

The C.I.A. in Iran

THE ROOTS

Britain Fights Oil Nationalism

The coup had its roots in a British showdown with Iran, restive under decades of near-colonial British domination.

The prize was Iran's oil fields. Britain occupied Iran in World War II to protect a supply route to its ally, the Soviet Union, and to prevent the oil from falling into the hands of the Nazis — ousting the shah's father, whom it regarded as unmanageable. It retained control over Iran's oil after the war through the Anglo-Iranian Oil Company.

In 1951, Iran's Parliament voted to nationalize the oil industry, and legislators backing the law elected its leading advocate, Dr. Mossadegh, as prime minister.

Britain responded with threats and sanctions.

Dr. Mossadegh, a European-educated lawyer then in his early 70's, prone to tears and outbursts, refused to back down. In meetings in November and December 1952, the secret history says, British intelligence officials startled their American counterparts with a plan for a joint operation to oust the nettlesome prime minister.

The Americans, who "had not intended to discuss this question at all," agreed to study it, the secret history says. It had attractions. Anti-Communism had risen to a fever pitch in Washington, and officials were worried that Iran might fall under the sway of the Soviet Union, a historical presence there.

In March 1953, an unexpected development pushed the plot forward: the C.I.A.'s Tehran station reported that an Iranian general had approached the American

C.I.A. DOCUMENT

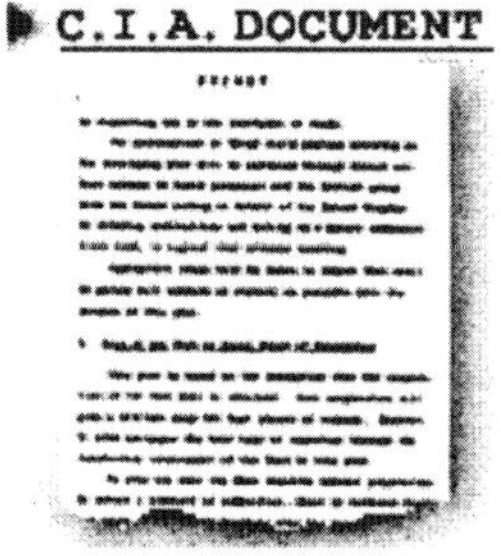

Acrobat Reader
INTRODUCTION
I: THE ROOTS
II: THE PRESSURE
III: THE COUP
IV: THE SUCCESS
V: THE PREMIER
VI: THE MEDIA
VII: THE SPY
TIMELINES
THE U.S. & IRAN
THE COUP PERIOD
TIMES ARCHIVES
ARTICLES
PAGE ONES
PHOTOS
DISCUSS

Embassy about supporting an army-led coup.

ASK THE TIMES
THE C.I.A.'S ROLE

The newly inaugurated Eisenhower administration was intrigued. The coalition that elected Dr. Mossadegh was splintering, and the Iranian Communist Party, the Tudeh, had become active.

Allen W. Dulles, the director of central intelligence, approved $1 million on April 4 to be used "in any way that would bring about the fall of Mossadegh," the history says.

"The aim was to bring to power a government which would reach an equitable oil settlement, enabling Iran to become economically sound and financially solvent, and which would vigorously prosecute the dangerously strong Communist Party."

Within days agency officials identified a high-ranking officer, Gen. Fazlollah Zahedi, as the man to spearhead a coup. Their plan called for the shah to play a leading role.

"A shah-General Zahedi combination, supported by C.I.A. local assets and financial backing, would have a good chance of overthrowing Mossadegh," officials wrote, "particularly if this combination should be able to get the largest mobs in the streets and if a sizable portion of the Tehran garrison refused to carry out Mossadegh's orders."

But according to the history, planners had doubts about whether the shah could carry out such a bold operation.

His family had seized Iran's throne just 32 years earlier, when his powerful father led a coup of his own. But the young shah, agency officials wrote, was "by nature a creature of indecision, beset by formless doubts and fears," often at odds with his family, including Princess Ashraf, his "forceful and scheming twin sister."

Also, the shah had what the C.I.A. termed a "pathological fear" of British intrigues, a potential obstacle to a joint operation.

In May 1953 the agency sent Dr. Wilber to Cyprus to meet Norman Darbyshire, chief of the Iran branch of British intelligence, to make initial coup plans. Assuaging the fears of the shah was high on their agenda; a document from the meeting said he was to be persuaded that the United States and Britain "consider the oil question secondary."

The conversation at the meeting turned to a touchy subject, the identity of key agents inside Iran. The British said they had recruited two brothers named Rashidian. The Americans, the secret history discloses, did not trust the British and lied about the identity of their best "assets" inside Iran.

C.I.A. officials were divided over whether the plan drawn up in Cyprus could work. The Tehran station warned headquarters that the "the shah would not act decisively against Mossadegh." And it said General Zahedi, the man picked to lead the coup, "appeared lacking in drive, energy and concrete plans."

Despite the doubts, the agency's Tehran station began disseminating "gray propaganda," passing out anti-Mossadegh cartoons in the streets and planting unflattering articles in the local press.

Continue reading next section.

BACK TO MAIN PAGE

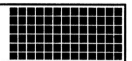

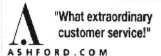

The New York Times ON THE WEB

SECRETS OF HISTORY

The C.I.A. in Iran

THE PLOTTING

Trying to Persuade a Reluctant Shah

The plot was under way, even though the shah was a reluctant warrior and Mr. Eisenhower had yet to give his final approval.

In early June, American and British intelligence officials met again, this time in Beirut, and put the finishing touches on the strategy. Soon afterward, the chief of the C.I.A.'s Near East and Africa division, Kermit Roosevelt, a grandson of Theodore Roosevelt, arrived in Tehran to direct it.

The shah was a problem from the start. The plan called for him to stand fast as the C.I.A. stirred up popular unrest and then, as the country lurched toward chaos, to issue royal decrees dismissing Dr. Mossadegh and appointing General Zahedi prime minister.

The agency sought to "produce such pressure on the shah that it would be easier for him to sign the papers required of him than it would be to refuse," the secret history states. Officials turned to his sister for help.

On July 11, President Eisenhower finally signed off on the plan. At about the same time, C.I.A. and British intelligence officers visited Princess Ashraf on the French Riviera and persuaded her to return to Iran and tell her brother to follow the script.

The return of the unpopular princess unleashed a storm of protest from pro-Mossadegh forces. The shah was furious that she had come back without his approval and refused at first to see her. But a palace staff member — another British agent, according to the secret history — gained Ashraf access on July 29.

C.I.A. DOCUMENT

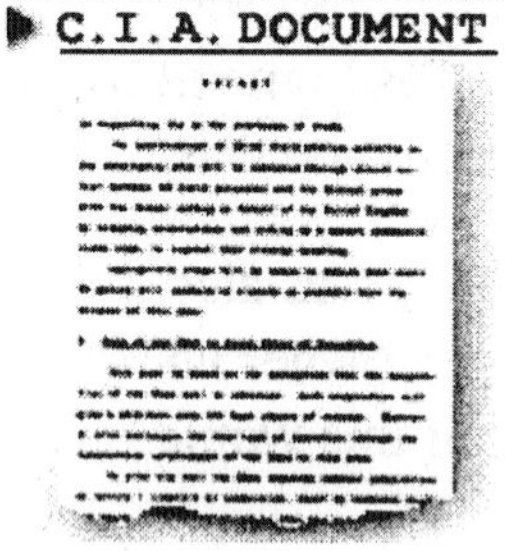

Acrobat Reader

INTRODUCTION
I: THE ROOTS
II: THE PRESSURE
III: THE COUP
IV: THE SUCCESS
V: THE PREMIER
VI: THE MEDIA
VII: THE SPY
TIMELINES
THE U.S. & IRAN
THE COUP PERIOD
TIMES ARCHIVES
ARTICLES
PAGE ONES
PHOTOS
DISCUSS

The history does not reveal what the siblings said to each other. But the princess gave her brother the news that C.I.A. officials had enlisted Gen. H. Norman Schwarzkopf in the coup campaign. General Schwarzkopf, the father of the Persian Gulf war commander, had befriended the shah a decade earlier while leading the United States military mission to Iran, and he told the agency "he was sure he could get the required cooperation."

▶ ASK THE TIMES
▶ THE C.I.A.'S ROLE

The British, too, sought to sway the shah and assure him their agents spoke for London. A British agent, Asadollah Rashidian, approached him in late July and invited him to select a phrase that would then be broadcast at prearranged times on the BBC's Persian-language program — as proof that Mr. Rashidian spoke for the British.

The exercise did not seem to have much effect. The shah told Mr. Rashidian on July 30 and 31 that he had heard the broadcast, but "requested time to assess the situation."

In early August, the C.I.A. stepped up the pressure. Iranian operatives pretending to be Communists threatened Muslim leaders with "savage punishment if they opposed Mossadegh," seeking to stir anti-Communist sentiment in the religious community.

In addition, the secret history says, the house of at least one prominent Muslim was bombed by C.I.A. agents posing as Communists. It does not say whether anyone was hurt in this attack.

The agency was also intensifying its propaganda campaign. A leading newspaper owner was granted a personal loan of about $45,000, "in the belief that this would make his organ amenable to our purposes."

But the shah remained intransigent. In an Aug. 1 meeting with General Schwarzkopf, he refused to sign the C.I.A.-written decrees firing Mr. Mossadegh and appointing General Zahedi. He said he doubted that the army would support him in a showdown.

During the meeting, the document says, the shah was so convinced that the palace was bugged that he "led the general into the grand ballroom, pulled a small table to its exact center" and got onto it to talk, insisting that the general do the same.

"This meeting was to be followed by a series of additional ones, some between Roosevelt and the shah and some between Rashidian and the shah, in which relentless pressure was exerted in frustrating attempts to overcome an entrenched attitude of vacillation and indecision," the history states.

▶ ASK THE TIMES
Find out more about this story. Send your questions to reporter James Risen.
▶ THE C.I.A.'S ROLE
What is the

Dr. Mossadegh had by now figured out that there was a

plot against him. He moved to consolidate power by calling for a national referendum to dissolve Parliament.

C.I.A.'s record abroad? Add your thoughts and see what other readers are saying in Abuzz.

The results of the Aug. 4 referendum were clearly rigged in his favor; The New York Times reported the same day that the prime minister had won 99.9 percent of the vote. This only helped the plotters, providing "an issue on which Mossadegh could be relentlessly attacked" by the agency-backed opposition press.

But the shah still wouldn't move against Dr. Mossadegh.

"On Aug. 3rd," the secret history says, "Roosevelt had a long and inconclusive session with the shah," who "stated that he was not an adventurer, and hence, could not take the chances of one.

"Roosevelt pointed out that there was no other way by which the government could be changed and the test was now between Mossadegh and his force and the shah and the army, which was still with him, but which would soon slip away."

Mr. Roosevelt told the shah "that failure to act could lead only to a Communist Iran or to a second Korea."

Still haunted by doubts, the shah asked Mr. Roosevelt if President Eisenhower could tell him what to do.

"By complete coincidence and great good fortune," the secret history says, "the president, while addressing the governors' convention in Seattle on 4 August, deviated from his script to state by implication that the United States would not sit by idly and see Iran fall behind the Iron Curtain."

By Aug. 10, the shah had finally agreed to see General Zahedi and a few army officers involved in the plot, but still refused to sign the decrees. The C.I.A. then sent Mr. Rashidian to say Mr. Roosevelt "would leave in complete disgust unless the shah took action within a few days."

The shah finally signed the decrees on Aug. 13. Word that he would support an army-led coup spread rapidly among the army officers backing General Zahedi.

Continue reading next section.

BACK TO MAIN PAGE

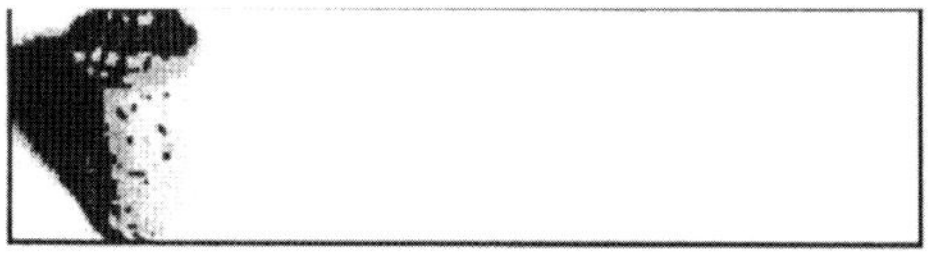

The New York Times ON THE WEB

SECRETS OF HISTORY
The C.I.A. in Iran

THE COUP

First Few Days Look Disastrous

The coup began on the night of Aug. 15 and was immediately compromised by a talkative Iranian Army officer whose remarks were relayed to Mr. Mossadegh.

The operation, the secret history says, "still might have succeeded in spite of this advance warning had not most of the participants proved to be inept or lacking in decision at the critical juncture."

Dr. Mossadegh's chief of staff, Gen. Taghi Riahi, learned of the plot hours before it was to begin and sent his deputy to the barracks of the Imperial Guard.

The deputy was arrested there, according to the history, just as pro-shah soldiers were fanning out across the city arresting other senior officials. Telephone lines between army and government offices were cut, and the telephone exchange was occupied.

But phones inexplicably continued to function, which gave Dr. Mossadegh's forces a key advantage. General Riahi also eluded the pro-shah units, rallying commanders to the prime minister's side.

Pro-shah soldiers sent to arrest Dr. Mossadegh at his home were instead captured. The top military officer working with General Zahedi fled when he saw tanks and loyal government soldiers at army headquarters.

The next morning, the history states, the Tehran radio announced that a coup against the government had failed, and Dr. Mossadegh scrambled to strengthen his hold on the army and key installations. C.I.A. officers

▸ C.I.A. DOCUMENT

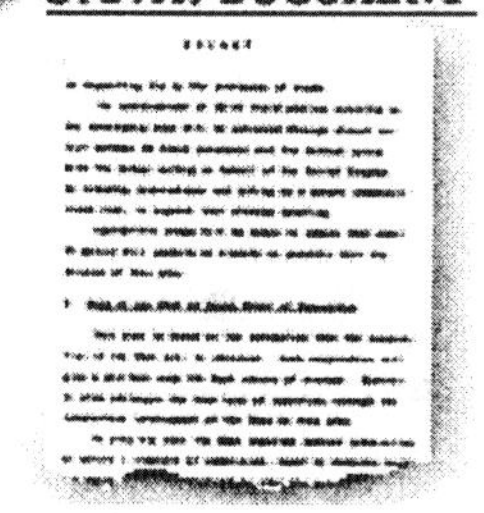

Acrobat Reader
▸ INTRODUCTION
▸ I: THE ROOTS
▸ II: THE PRESSURE
▸ III: THE COUP
▸ IV: THE SUCCESS
▸ V: THE PREMIER
▸ VI: THE MEDIA
▸ VII: THE SPY
TIMELINES
▸ THE U.S. & IRAN
▸ THE COUP PERIOD
TIMES ARCHIVES
▸ ARTICLES
▸ PAGE ONES
▸ PHOTOS
DISCUSS

inside the embassy were flying blind; the history says they had "no way of knowing what was happening."

▶ ASK THE TIMES
▶ THE C.I.A.'S ROLE

Mr. Roosevelt left the embassy and tracked down General Zahedi, who was in hiding north of Tehran. Surprisingly, the general was not ready to abandon the operation. The coup, the two men agreed, could still work, provided they could persuade the public that General Zahedi was the lawful prime minister.

To accomplish this, the history discloses, the coup plotters had to get out the news that the shah had signed the two decrees.

The C.I.A. station in Tehran sent a message to The Associated Press in New York, asserting that "unofficial reports are current to the effect that leaders of the plot are armed with two decrees of the shah, one dismissing Mossadegh and the other appointing General Zahedi to replace him."

The C.I.A. and its agents also arranged for the decrees to be mentioned in some Tehran papers, the history says.

The propaganda initiative quickly bogged down. Many of the C.I.A.'s Iranian agents were under arrest or on the run. That afternoon, agency operatives prepared a statement from General Zahedi that they hoped to distribute publicly. But they could not find a printing press that was not being watched by forces loyal to the prime minister.

On Aug. 16, prospects of reviving the operation were dealt a seemingly a fatal blow when it was learned that the shah had bolted to Baghdad. C.I.A. headquarters cabled Tehran urging Mr. Roosevelt, the station chief, to leave immediately.

He did not agree, insisting that there was still "a slight remaining chance of success," if the shah would broadcast an address on the Baghdad radio and General Zahedi took an aggressive stand.

The Associated Press
Protestors tore down a statue of Riza Shah, the father of Shah Mohammed Reza Pahlevi.
SLIDE SHOW

The first sign that the tide might turn came with reports that Iranian soldiers had broken up Tudeh, or Communist, groups, beating them and making them chant their support for the shah. "The station continued to feel that the project was not quite dead," the secret history recounts.

Meanwhile, Dr. Mossadegh had overreached, playing into the C.I.A.'s hands by dissolving Parliament after the coup.

On the morning of Aug. 17 the shah finally announced from Baghdad that he had signed the decrees — though he had by now delayed so long that plotters feared it was too late.

At this critical point Dr. Mossadegh let down his guard. Lulled by the shah's departure and the arrests of some officers involved in the coup, the government recalled most troops it had stationed around the city, believing that the danger had passed.

That night the C.I.A. arranged for General Zahedi and other key Iranian agents and army officers to be smuggled into the embassy compound "in the bottom of cars and in closed jeeps" for a "council of war."

They agreed to start a counterattack on Aug. 19, sending a leading cleric from Tehran to the holy city of Qum to try to orchestrate a call for a holy war against Communism. (The religious forces they were trying to manipulate would years later call the United States "the Great Satan.")

Corbis Bettmann

As the C.I.A.-backed royalist coup seemed to be failing in Iran, the shah and Empress Soraya arrived in Rome on Aug. 18, 1953.

Using travel papers forged by the C.I.A., key army officers went to outlying army garrisons to persuade commanders to join the coup.

Once again, the shah disappointed the C.I.A. He left Baghdad for Rome the next day, apparently an exile. Newspapers supporting Dr. Mossadegh reported that the Pahlevi dynasty had come to an end, and a statement from the Communist Party's central committee attributed the coup attempt to "Anglo-American intrigue." Demonstrators ripped down imperial statues -- as they would again 26 years later during the Islamic revolution.

The C.I.A. station cabled headquarters for advice on whether to "continue with TP-Ajax or withdraw."

"Headquarters spent a day featured by depression and despair," the history states, adding, "The message sent to Tehran on the night of Aug. 18 said that 'the operation has been tried and failed,' and that 'in the absence of strong recommendations to the contrary operations against Mossadegh should be discontinued.'"

Continue reading next section.

BACK TO MAIN PAGE

The New York Times ON THE WEB

SECRETS OF HISTORY

The C.I.A. in Iran

THE SUCCESS

C.I.A. and Moscow Are Both Surprised

But just as the Americans were ready to quit, the mood on the streets of Tehran shifted.

On the morning of Aug. 19, several Tehran papers published the shah's long-awaited decrees, and soon pro-shah crowds were building in the streets.

"They needed only leadership," the secret history says. And Iranian agents of the C.I.A. provided it. Without specific orders, a journalist who was one of the agency's most important Iranian agents led a crowd toward Parliament, inciting people to set fire to the offices of a newspaper owned by Dr. Mossadegh's foreign minister. Another Iranian C.I.A. agent led a crowd to sack the offices of pro-Tudeh papers.

"The news that something quite startling was happening spread at great speed throughout the city," the history states.

The C.I.A. tried to exploit the situation, sending urgent messages that the Rashidian brothers and two key American agents should "swing the security forces to the side of the demonstrators."

But things were now moving far too quickly for the agency to manage. An Iranian Army colonel who had been involved in the plot several days earlier suddenly appeared outside Parliament with a tank, while members of the now-disbanded Imperial Guard seized trucks and drove through the streets. "By 10:15 there were pro-shah truckloads of military personnel at all the main squares," the secret history says.

C.I.A. DOCUMENT

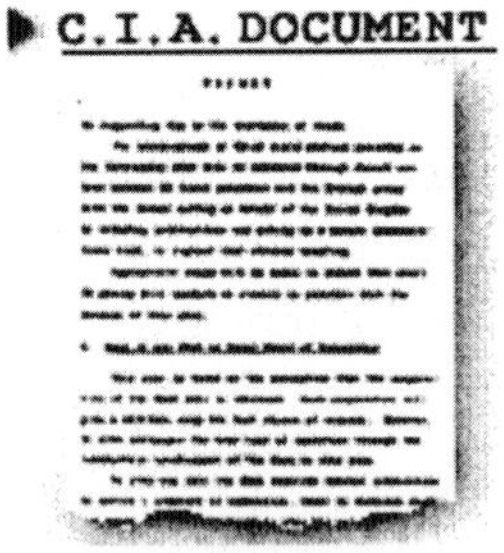

Acrobat Reader
INTRODUCTION
I: THE ROOTS
II: THE PRESSURE
III: THE COUP
IV: THE SUCCESS
V: THE PREMIER
VI: THE MEDIA
VII: THE SPY
TIMELINES
THE U.S. & IRAN
THE COUP PERIOD
TIMES ARCHIVES
ARTICLES
PAGE ONES
PHOTOS
DISCUSS
ASK THE TIMES
THE C.I.A.'S ROLE

By noon the crowds began to receive direct leadership from a few officers involved in the plot and some who had switched sides. Within an hour the central telegraph office fell, and telegrams were sent to the provinces urging a pro-shah uprising. After a brief shootout, police headquarters and the Ministry of Foreign Affairs fell as well.

The Tehran radio remained the biggest prize. With the government's fate uncertain, it was broadcasting a program on cotton prices. But by early afternoon a mass of civilians, army officers and policemen overwhelmed it. Pro-shah speakers went on the air, broadcasting the coup's success and reading the royal decrees.

At the embassy, C.I.A. officers were elated, and Mr. Roosevelt got General Zahedi out of hiding. An army officer found a tank and drove him to the radio station, where he spoke to the nation.

Dr. Mossadegh and other government officials were rounded up, while officers supporting General Zahedi placed "known supporters of TP-Ajax" in command of all units of the Tehran garrison.

The Soviet Union was caught completely off-guard. Even as the Mossadegh government was falling, the Moscow radio was broadcasting a story on "the failure of the American adventure in Iran."

A. Rashki / The Associated Press

Royalists, carrying a picture of the shah, rode a commandeered bus in Tehran on Aug. 19, 1953, when the coup became a success.

But C.I.A. headquarters was as surprised as Moscow. When news of the coup's success arrived, it "seemed to be a bad joke, in view of the depression that still hung on from the day before," the history says.

Throughout the day, Washington got most of its information from news agencies, receiving only two cablegrams from the station. Mr. Roosevelt later explained that if he had told headquarters what was going on, "London and Washington would have thought they were crazy and told them to stop immediately," the history states.

Still, the C.I.A. took full credit inside the government. The following year it overthrew the government of Guatemala, and a myth developed that the agency could topple governments anywhere in the world.

Iran proved that third world king-making could be heady.

"It was a day that should never have ended," the C.I.A.'s secret history said, describing Aug. 19, 1953. "For it carried with it such a sense of excitement, of satisfaction and of jubilation that it is doubtful whether any other can come up to it."

Continue reading next section.

BACK TO MAIN PAGE

TO The New York Times ON THE WEB

The New York Times ON THE WEB

SECRETS OF HISTORY
The C.I.A. in Iran

MOHAMMED MOSSADEGH

Eccentric Nationalist Begets Strange History

By ELAINE SCIOLINO

WASHINGTON, April 15 — Except for Ayatollah Ruhollah Khomeini, father of its revolution, no leader has left a deeper mark on Iran's 20th century landscape than Mohammed Mossadegh. And no 20th century event has fueled Iran's suspicion of the United States as his overthrow has.

An eccentric European-educated lawyer whose father was a bureaucrat and whose mother descended from Persian kings, Dr. Mossadegh served as a minister and governor before he opposed Reza Shah's accession in the 1920's.

He was imprisoned and then put under house arrest at his estate in the walled village of Ahmadabad west of Tehran. Eventually he bought the village, growing crops, founding an elementary school and beginning a public health project.

When Britain and Russia forced Reza Shah from power in favor of his son, Mohammed Reza Pahlevi, in 1941, Dr. Mossadegh became a member of Parliament. He was hailed as a hero for his fiery speeches on the evils of British control of Iran's oil industry. In 1951, when Parliament voted to nationalize the industry, the young shah, recognizing the nationalists' popularity, appointed Dr. Mossadegh prime minister.

In that job he became a prisoner of his own nationalism, unable to reach an oil compromise. Even as the British negotiated with Iran, they won the

C.I.A. DOCUMENT

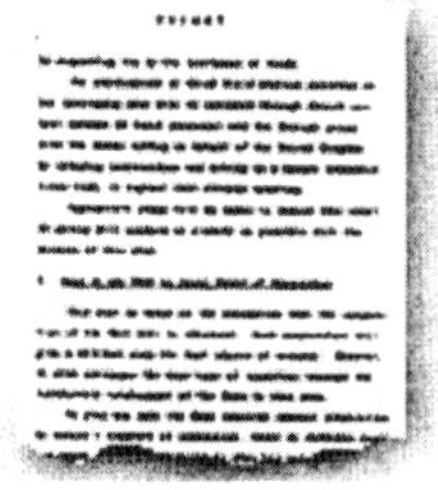

Acrobat Reader
INTRODUCTION
I: THE ROOTS
II: THE PRESSURE
III: THE COUP
IV: THE SUCCESS
V: THE PREMIER
VI: THE MEDIA
VII: THE SPY
TIMELINES
THE U.S. & IRAN
THE COUP PERIOD
TIMES ARCHIVES
ARTICLES
PAGE ONES
PHOTOS
DISCUSS

ASK THE TIMES
THE C.I.A.'S ROLE

support of the major oil companies in imposing an effective global boycott on Iranian oil.

Still, in the developing world Dr. Mossadegh became an icon of anti-imperialism. He was revered despite his odd mannerisms, which included conducting business in bed in gray woolen pajamas, weeping publicly and complaining perpetually of poor health.

He amassed power. When the shah refused his demand for control of the armed forces in 1952, Dr. Mossadegh resigned, only to be reinstated in the face of popular riots.

He then displayed a streak of authoritarianism, bypassing Parliament by conducting a national referendum to win approval for its dissolution. Meanwhile, the United States became alarmed at the strength of Iran's Communist Party, which supported Dr. Mossadegh.

In August 1953, a dismissal attempt by the shah sent Dr. Mossadegh's followers into the streets. The shah fled, amid fears in the new Eisenhower administration that Iran might move too close to Moscow.

Yet Dr. Mossadegh did not promote the interests of the Communists, though he drew on their support. Paradoxically, the party turned from him in the end because it viewed him as insufficiently committed and too close to the United States. By the time the royalist coup overthrew him after a few chaotic days, he had alienated many landowners, clerics and merchants.

The Associated Press
Mohammed Mossadegh, the ousted prime minister, entering court for his trial.

After a trial, he served three years in prison and ended up under house arrest at his estate. In March 1967, in his mid-80's and weakened by radium treatments for throat cancer, he died.

When the revolution brought the clerics to power in 1979, anti-shah nationalists tried to revive Dr. Mossadegh's memory. A Tehran thoroughfare called Pahlevi Avenue was renamed Mossadegh Avenue.

But Ayatollah Khomeini saw him as a promoter not of Islam but of Persian nationalism, and envied his popularity. So Mossadegh Avenue became Vali Asr, after the revered Hidden Imam, whose reappearance someday, Shiite Muslims believe, will establish the perfect Islamic political community. Still, even Ayatollah Khomeini was careful not to go too far. Ignoring Dr. Mossadegh, rather than excoriating him, became the rule.

Two decades later, the Mossadegh cult has been revitalized by resurgent nationalism and frustration with the strictures of Islam. Dr. Mossadegh inspires the young, who long for heroes and have not necessarily found them, either in clerics or kings.

In campaigns for local elections in February 1999 and parliamentary elections a year later, reformist advertising made use of Dr. Mossadegh's sad, elongated face. And every year since his death, his supporters have rallied at his estate.

His legacy still stirs considerable debate. In August, Parliament approved a bill to abolish a holiday marking the nationalization of the oil industry in 1951. The decision set off protests in the press.

"Alas! Parliament ignored the most apparent symbol of the struggle of the Iranian people throughout history against colonialism," the reformist daily Khordad said.

In November, legislators were forced to reinstate the holiday.

Continue reading next section.

BACK TO MAIN PAGE

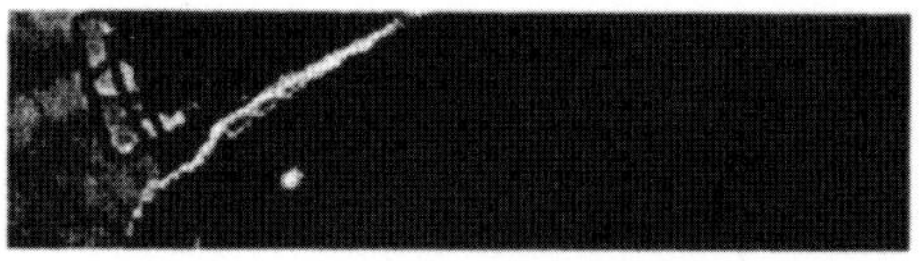

The New York Times
ON THE WEB

SECRETS OF HISTORY

The C.I.A. in Iran

C.I.A. Tried, With Little Success, to Use U.S. Press in Coup

By JAMES RISEN

WASHINGTON, April 15 — Central Intelligence Agency officials plotting the 1953 coup in Iran hoped to plant articles in American newspapers saying Shah Mohammed Reza Pahlevi's return resulted from a homegrown revolt against a Communist-leaning government, internal agency documents show.

Those hopes were largely disappointed. The C.I.A.'s history of the coup shows that its operatives had only limited success in manipulating American reporters and that none of the Americans covering the coup worked for the agency.

An analysis of the press coverage shows that American journalists filed straightforward, factual dispatches that prominently mentioned the role of Iran's Communists in street violence leading up to the coup. Western correspondents in Iran and Washington never reported that some of the unrest had been stage-managed by C.I.A. agents posing as Communists. And they gave little emphasis to accurate contemporaneous reports in Iranian newspapers and on the Moscow radio asserting that Western powers were secretly arranging the shah's return to power.

It was just eight years after the end of World War II, which left American journalists with a sense of national interest framed by six years of confrontation between the Allies and the Axis. The front pages of Western newspapers were dominated by articles about the new global confrontation with the Soviet Union,

▶ C.I.A. DOCUMENT

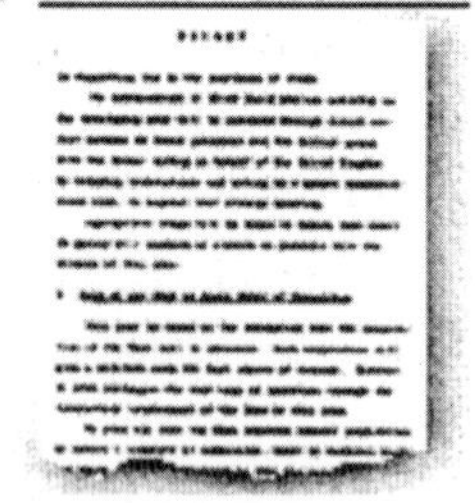

Acrobat Reader
▶ INTRODUCTION
▶ I: THE ROOTS
▶ II: THE PRESSURE
▶ III: THE COUP
▶ IV: THE SUCCESS
▶ V: THE PREMIER
▶ VI: THE MEDIA
▶ VII: THE SPY
TIMELINES
▶ THE U.S. & IRAN
▶ THE COUP PERIOD
TIMES ARCHIVES
▶ ARTICLES
▶ PAGE ONES
▶ PHOTOS
DISCUSS
▶ ASK THE TIMES

about Moscow's prowess in developing nuclear weapons and about Congressional allegations of "Red" influence in Washington.

THE C.I.A.'S ROLE

In one instance, the history indicates, the C.I.A. was apparently able to use contacts at The Associated Press to put on the news wire a statement from Tehran about royal decrees that the C.I.A. itself had written. But mostly, the agency relied on less direct means to exploit the media.

The Iran desk of the State Department, the document says, was able to place a C.I.A. study in Newsweek, "using the normal channel of desk officer to journalist." The article was one of several planted press reports that, when reprinted in Tehran, fed the "war of nerves" against Iran's prime minister, Mohammed Mossadegh.

The history says the Iran operation exposed the agency's shortcomings in manipulating the American press. The C.I.A. "lacked contacts capable of placing material so that the American publisher was unwitting as to its source."

The history discloses that a C.I.A. officer, working under cover as the embassy's press officer, drove two American reporters to a house outside Tehran where they were shown the shah's decrees dismissing the prime minister.

Kennett Love, the New York Times reporter in Tehran during the coup, wrote about the royal decrees in the newspaper the next day, without mentioning how he had seen them. In an interview, he said he had agreed to the embassy official's ground rules that he not report the American role in arranging the trip.

Mr. Love said he did not know at the time that the official worked for the C.I.A.

After the coup succeeded, Mr. Love did in one article briefly refer to Iranian press reports of American involvement, and The New York Times also published an article from Moscow reporting Soviet charges that the United States was behind the coup. But neither The Times nor other American news organizations appear to have examined such charges seriously.

In a 1960 paper he wrote while studying at Princeton University, Mr. Love explained that he "was responsible, in an impromptu sort of way, for speeding the final victory of the royalists."

Seeing a half-dozen tanks parked in front of Tehran's radio station, he said, "I told the tank commanders that a lot of people were getting killed trying to storm Dr. Mossadegh's house and that they would be of some use instead of sitting idle at the radio station." He added, "They took their machines in a body to Kokh Avenue and put the three tanks at Dr. Mossadegh's house out of action."

Mr. Love, who left The New York Times in 1962, said in an interview that he had urged the tanks into action "because I wanted to stop the bloodshed."

Months afterward, Mr. Love says, he was told by Robert C. Doty, then Cairo bureau chief and his boss, of evidence of American involvement in the coup.

But Mr. Doty, who died in 1974, did not write about the matter, and by the summer of 1954, Mr. Love decided to tell the New York office what he knew. In a July 26, 1954, letter to Emanuel R. Freedman, then the foreign editor, Mr. Love wrote, "The only instance since I joined The Times in which I have allowed policy to influence a strict news approach was in failing to report the role our own agents played in the overthrow of Mossadegh."

Mr. Love said he had hoped that the foreign editor would order him to pursue the subject. But he never received any response, he said.

"I wanted to let Freedman know that I knew there had been U.S. involvement in the coup, but that I hadn't written about it," he said. "I expected him to say, 'Jump on that story.' But there was no response." Mr. Freedman died in 1971.

Continue reading next section.

BACK TO MAIN PAGE

SECRETS OF HISTORY
The New York Times ON THE WEB

The C.I.A. in Iran

DONALD WILBER

'Gentleman Spy' at Helm

Donald Wilber, who planned the coup in Iran and wrote its secret history, was old-school C.I.A., a Princetonian and a Middle East architecture expert who fit neatly into the mold of the "gentleman spy."

C.I.A. DOCUMENT

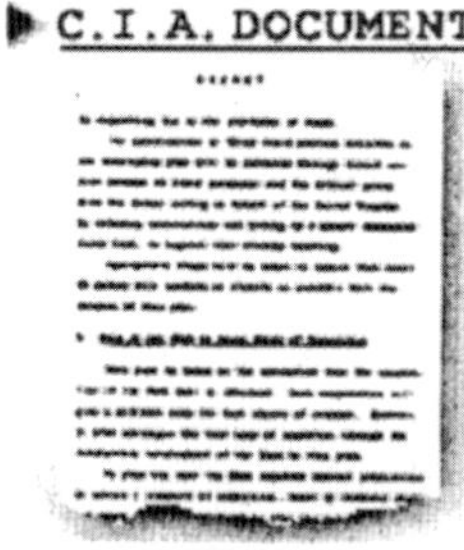

Acrobat Reader
INTRODUCTION
I: THE ROOTS
II: THE PRESSURE
III: THE COUP
IV: THE SUCCESS
V: THE PREMIER
VI: THE MEDIA

Years of wandering through Middle Eastern architectural sites gave him the perfect cover for a clandestine life. By 1953, he was an obvious choice as the operation's strategist.

The coup was the high point of his life as a spy. Although he would excel in academia, at the agency being part-time was a handicap.

"I never requested promotion, and was given only one, after the conclusion of Ajax," Dr. Wilber wrote of the Iran operation.

On his last day, "I was ushered down to the lobby by a young secretary, turned over my badge to her and left." He added, "This treatment rankled for some time. I did deserve the paperweight."

He died in 1997 at 89.

BACK TO MAIN PAGE

TO The New York Times ON THE WEB

The New York Times ON THE WEB

SECRETS OF HISTORY

The C.I.A. in Iran

Iran-U.S. Relations: A Chronology

1940

1941

• Britain and the Soviet Union invade western Iran to counter the threat of expanding Nazi influence.

1950

1951

• Mohammed Mossadegh, an ultranationalist, is elected prime minister, under the shah. He angers the British by trying to nationalize the oil industry.

Corbis / Bettman

1953

• American and British intelligence services overthrow Mossadegh. The coup consolidates power under the shah, ensuring cooperation on oil and discouraging Communist expansion.

Click here to view a magnified timeline of the coup period, with links to the original coverage from the Times.

1960

1963-64

• Ayatollah Ruhollah Khomeini, a religious leader, is exiled to Turkey after his arrest for speaking out against the shah's relationship with the United

States.

1978

1978

• Turmoil sweeps Iran. Khomeini establishes an opposition movement in Paris.

Corbis / Bettman - UPI

1979

• The Iranian revolution forces the shah to leave. A month later, he is allowed into the United States for cancer treatment in New York City.

Corbis/Bettman - UPI

1979

• Khomeini returns to proclaim an Islamic republic. With his support, Iranian students occupy the American Embassy in Tehran. Fifty-two Americans are held hostage for 444 days. The United States freezes Iranian assets.

1980

1980

• The United States breaks ties with Iran, bans American exports to the country and expels Iranian diplomats.

Corbis/Bettman - UPI

1980

• A secret American military mission to rescue the hostages is aborted because of bad weather. Eight servicemen die in a helicopter crash. The shah dies in Egypt at age

60.

1981

• The hostages are released minutes after President Carter's term ends. A United States-Iran claims tribunal is set up in The Hague.

1986

• Revelations emerge of an American deal to exchange arms for Iranian help in freeing hostages held in Lebanon.

1988

• The American cruiser Vincennes mistakenly shoots down an Iranian airliner over the Persian Gulf, killing all 290 aboard.

1989

• Ayatollah Khomeini dies and is replaced as the nation's spiritual leader by Ayatollah Ali Khamenei. The speaker of Iran's Parliament, Ali Akbar Hashemi Rafsanjani, is elected president.

1990

1993

• The Clinton administration starts a campaign to isolate Iran, accusing it of supporting terrorism, seeking nuclear arms and trying to derail Middle East peace.

1996

• President Clinton signs a law that imposes sanctions on foreign companies investing heavily in "terrorist" Iran or Libya.

Agence France Presse

1997

• Mohammad Khatami, a moderate cleric, wins Iran's presidential election. Clinton calls the election hopeful, but insists that ties are not possible until Iran renounces terrorism, opposition to the Middle East peace effort and weapons of mass destruction.

• Clinton asks Khatami for help in solving the 1996 bombing of a Saudi building in which 19 American servicemen died and

1998

• Khatami proposes cultural exchanges as a way to end mistrust, but rules out a government-to-government

American servicemen died and hundreds were wounded.

• The Clinton administration renews an offer for talks "on the basis of equality and mutual respect." Iran rejects the offer two days later.

• The United States agrees to let Boeing provide Iran's national airline with parts to ensure the safety of its 747's.

dialogue.

• Secretary of State Madeleine K. Albright invites Iranians to join with the United States in drawing up "a road map leading to normal relations." Iran responds that such a step must be followed up by acts.

1999

• The Clinton administration announces it will let American companies sell food and medical items to three countries off-limits as terrorist — Iran, Libya and Sudan.

2000

2000

• Albright announces the lifting of a ban on American imports of Iranian luxury goods. She acknowledges America's role in the 1953 coup, coming closer to apologizing for it than any American official ever has.

The Associated Press

▶ BACK TO MAIN PAGE

TO The New York Times ON THE WEB

Current View of the Bulletin

International News Circle

Bulletin Actions

Enter Response

Respond)))

Bulletin : Published and Discussed

Date: Sat Apr 15 7:25 PM EDT 2000
From: Stephen Miller, NYT
Subject: The C.I.A. in Iran
Body: A classified Central Intelligence Agency report, which the age
been destroyed, has resurfaced. The internal history describes the C
involvement in Iran's 1953 coup. It reveals for the first time the f
extent of the U.S. role in the rise of Shah Mohammed Reza Pahlevi, w
turn set the stage for the Islamic revolution in 1979, and for a gen
of anti-American hatred in one of the Middle East's most powerful co

Do you approve of the C.I.A.'s historical involvement in foreign cri
the U.S. inadvertently author its own misfortunes -- such as the 197
hostage crisis and the continuing growth of terrorism against the We
creating turmoil in Iran five decades ago?

Read more about the report in "Secrets of History: The C.I.A. in Ira
James Risen of The New York Times:
http://www.nytimes.com/library/world/mideast/041600iran-cia-index.ht

Discussion

top

edsigcat 0
(Sat Apr 15 11:59 PM EDT 2000)
Could someone get the Times to distill the PDF pages of CIA document
Those of us out here without high speed lines "time out" before thes
can be downloaded. How about a Web page listing the PDFs in sequenc
companion copy in HTML or even just text and a notice as to the size
files.
Any file over a megabyte should be broken up for digestion by reader

This could be bigger than last week's Rampage Killers piece which br
out a whole lot very different perspectives.

madcow2000 0
(Sun Apr 16 1:04 AM EDT 2000)
Well, the intervention of a foreign power in the internal affairs of
nation is shameful as many would undoubtedly say, however, the issue
as simple as it looks. What do you do when the government of a forei
country is killing its own people as in the Balkans and Africa (whic
course not too many people bother much about)? Obviously, there is a
factor here which must be taken into account and which justifies Ame
involvement. However, since this was a case in which a duly elected
minister was deposed in a coup (something that is totally against th

You see, my dear, dear GOD, their regret is not because of what they did to Iranian families. Their regret is not because they brought a nasty and bloody war upon us and provided the ammunition to the Iraqis. Their regret is not because they caused the death of one to four young girls or boys in every Iranian household. Their regret is not because they shot down the passenger airplane with 289 civilians, all children, women, and young adults, who were killed at once. Their regret is not because they burnt a movie theater with four hundred young people in it who all burned to ashes.

After all the regrets that Albright mentioned, she said that the United States is hoping it could open up trade and expedite settlement of frozen assets with Tehran in hopes that it would lead into a renewal of formal diplomatic relations after twenty years of hostility.

You see, my dear GOD, the asset that they were talking about on Friday the 17th of March in 2000. They were hoping to start a deal with Iran again. They changed their minds the next day on the Saturday AMC news.

In a very logical manner they announced that one of the journalists who was captured and being kept in Lebanon for seven years had issued a lawsuit against Iran's government for three hundred and forty some million dollars. They blamed Iran for being the cause of the kidnapping. And at the end of this statement, the newsman said, "If Iran does not agree to such a payment, the United States will take the money from their frozen assets." Oh yea, so what else is new? On one hand, they start apologizing and wishing to be able to deal with Iran again. And then on the other hand they already have the idea in their mind to spend Iranian assets, which have been frozen in their banks. You see, my dear GOD, to the government of America, this is called "democracy".

My Dear GOD:

So they don't regret what they had done to Iran and Iranians, but they have regret for helping Saddam Hussein (since he hasn't been a loyal servant to them), and they have regrets because Iran kept fifty-two Americans hostage for four hundred forty-four days.

Albright said, "The United States must bear its share of responsibility for the problems that have arisen in the U.S. – Iranian retaliations. She delivered this speech at a Washington conference on the eve of the Iranian New Year 2000.

You see, my dear GOD, I might not have enough knowledge to know the politic and what comes with it. But I know this much, if Iranians have to pay this amount for their defensive crime, the government of America must pay one billion dollars for each young man and woman who they killed either with their own guns or by the Iraqi guns (which were made by the United States and delivered by them anyways). If we have time to count all the young men and women who got killed only during the sixty years that we were

around and witnessed, the number would be so high that the United States would never be able to pay that amount, even if he wanted to pay the whole budget of the country for more than ten years.

I wish someone would ask Albright or Clinton, "What would you do if you had lost your child this way? Is there any amount that could bring back your child for you?"

Anyway, this was the situation we were growing up in. Our games and fun was reading books. From all that we read we realized exactly where Iran is located on the map and the great wealth and fortune stored within our country, the big countries would never leave us alone.

We learned that what Hitler did to the Jewish people was one of the worst things that could ever happen on the face of the Earth. Nobody could remember anything so horrible taking place in history. But since the United States and the United Kingdom decided to establish a country for Jews in the Middle East right next door to us, just so that they could support their position in the Middle East, life for us changed tremendously.

My Dear GOD:

The things that happened to them have been acknowledged by the whole world to be unbearable by any human being. But if what others did to them was wrong, they should not allow themselves to do the same thing to others. They have been doing the same kind of killing that Hitler did, but with a big support from the media, their activity never gets exploded like Hitler's did. For instance, they made Palestinians run away from their homes. Then they built new homes on their properties and told them that these had become their homes and that the Palestinians couldn't take it away from them.

Okay my dear GOD. Is this right? You accept what they are doing? I know you are aware of everything that is happening in this world. Then why don't you stop them? Why don't you make one of your miracles? Isn't this the time to speak up one way or another?

Anyway, my dear GOD, I have moved away from past to present like always. Now we have to go back to where we were before.

Yes my dear God, I met Iraj for the first time after he got out of prison. I admired his attitude and his political views. After that night we became friends. More and more often he and his family were coming to our house and were with us most of the time. They used to live in Zahedan.

***

My Dear GOD, now some words about his family. His father's name was Davood Gholi Rafani Motlagh. He was a retired army sergeant who had dealt with lots of unbearable difficulties in his life. From the time I met him, he was an alcoholic. His children acted embarrassed and very disturbed by this. Not only was his family embarrassed and ashamed by his destructive habits, but also he was more disturbed by it than anyone else. He was not one of those drunks who went home and broke things. Or probably he just never did that in front of me. But from what I got to know about him, I don't think he was a two-faced man. He did what he wanted to if he had to do it. To me his life story was very amazing. Please GOD, make me remember his exact words. He often liked to talk to me about his past.

My Dear GOD:

He told me that he was in the army. He was called Sarvan Rafani, which is a title that is given by the army. He had been a very tall and powerful young man. When he was in the army Reza Shah, the father of Mohammad Reza Pahlavi, was in power.

He always talked to us about the battles he won and received medals for. He told stories like, "Once Reza Shah was visiting the troops in Zahedan. When I shook his hand I shook it so hard that he asked my name. He asked me to see him in his office later on."

At that time, Reza Shah was trying to enforce Islam on everyone in the country. Sarvan Rafani was not Muslim. In the job application, which was sent out to all applicants, they had to write their faith and religion. When Sarvan Rafani filled out his application, he wrote that he was Bahaie. He felt he had to tell the truth because he was a Bahaie and could not lie about his faith. Reza Shah did not like it. He asked him to send another application, thinking that perhaps Sarvan Rafani might not have understood. But Sarvan Rafani again filled out the application marking his religion Bahaie. At this time Reza Shah ordered the army to fire Sarvan Rafani immediately.

He was fired from his job in the army the next day. Then he started to work any job that came along. At the same time, his wife started helping by sewing and doing other little jobs in order to earn some money.

Soon he found a way to go into business with one of his friends. Their business blossomed in no time at all. They started to live comfortably again. But before they started to enjoy the pleasures of a comfortable life, one of the jealous, fanatic Muslims reported to Reza Shah saying, "If people like Sarvan Rafani could go into private business and became very wealthy, it is not shocking if more people become Bahaei. In reply to this letter, Reza Shah ordered all the businessmen in Zahdan not to give Sarvan Rafani a job so that he would be punished and die.

Pari, Kamal, Fereshteh, Neya and me

On Pari's wedding; Fereshteh khagehnaseer, Neya, Mohandes Forghani, me and Iraj

Although it was Pari's wedding, that night was the best night of Neya's life. Her husband Mohandes Forghani was freed from prison for one night. On that night, Arman was conceived. As you see in this picture, I am as skinny as a toothpick. Do you know why? Because my parents had disowned me for marrying Iraj.

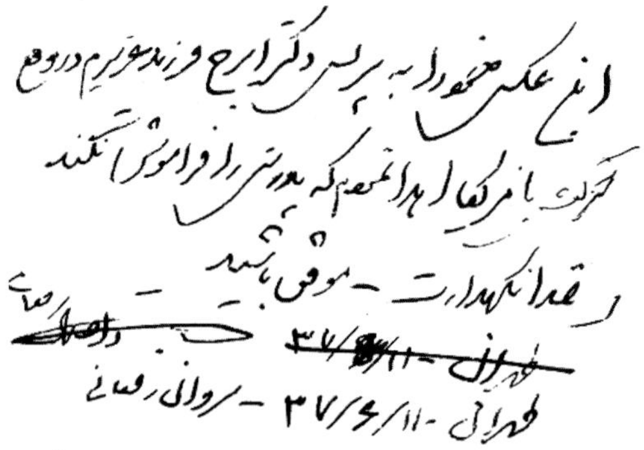

This is the picture of Sarvan Rafani, Iraj's father. On the back of the photo he writes, "I am presenting this pictrue of mine to my dear son, Prince Dr. Iraj Rafani, since he is leaving us to go to America. I hope he does not forget his father. God bless you, and good luck.
Tehran 9/2/1958
Signed: Sarvan Rafani

Poor Mr. Sarvan Rafani! He was the only alcoholic that I had a chance to live with for one whole year. I have never seen him mad, crazy, harsh or violent. He was especially nice to me. He was aware that my parents had disowned me for loving his son. He understood my hard life and had a lot of respect for me. He truly treated me like his own child. He was willing to help me in any way and anyhow he could. He was the most alert person that I have ever met. Although his children were ashamed of him and his drinking and they showed their resentment toward his actions, he tried to love them as much as he could. In any given situation, he would not give up his support for any of his children. The night that I was leaving to go to America to be with his son, he did not let himself fall sleep. He thought his children would not wake him up to come with us. He kept himself awake so he would be able to come to the airport to say good bye to me and wish me luck. I am sure that he did so because he knew my parents were not with me. God bless him indeed.

Pari

Kamal

Neya

Iraj

Parveen

This picture is very valuable. I don't know all of them. From left to right, I don't know the first lady, Pari, their uncle Mr. Hormozi, Neya, a lady holding her baby, Iraj, his Aunt Hormozi, his grandfather, his mother and his aunt. I think the other two are his uncle's wives. This was the uncle who Iraj thought had the same personality as he.

On the left, Neya is washing something while I am pumping water in their yard. Saideh is standing next to me.
On the right I am with three of my good students. God knows where they are now or what they are doing.

At this time his partner brought the bad news to him and told him that he had to break his partnership with him. And he added that, "Reza Shah has ordered all other businesses not to get involved with you."

You can imagine what happened to this active young man. After that, he stayed home and had nothing to do at all. Although in the Baha'i faith drinking is not allowed, he started drinking very heavily. This drinking became his habit and he never let go of for the rest of his life. He became an alcoholic to the point that his morning started with whisky or vodka and continued on until the next morning.

My Dear GOD:

You see, this man never knew that his life would end up this way. He never thought that one day his children would be ashamed to introduce him to their friends or show him to anyone. He was never prepared for his life to end like that. That is why I believe that certain things will happen that will make you change your way of life.

Sarvan Rafani wanted to accomplish much and make a good home for his family. He had been sure that his faith was one of the purest ones and went to great lengths in order not to lie about it. But in his case, and probably many more cases, being truthful cost him his life and his future.

So, while they were living in Zahedan, the whole family had many problems and difficulties.

Parveen, who was living with her husband Mr. Safari in our neighborhood was having problems with her marriage. She had fallen in love with Safari and her father had been against her marriage. I never found out what their problem was, but I knew that she wished to divorce him but her mother was against her divorce altogether. Her mother had asked Parvin, "If you love me, please don't divorce him while I am alive."

His parents were separated but they were living together in one house. Iraj and Pari had rented a room together two blocks away from our house. He had started his medical school studies and Pari was at high school near our house.

My father always gave him credit for working hard and continuing his education, and especially for looking after his sister Pari. They had become very close to us. Almost every day they were at our house. My parents treated them like they were their own children. They stayed over for lunch or dinner and sometimes slept over in our house.

Although my father was not a rich man, he and my mother always welcomed those friends of ours whom they thought were nice people.

Little by little, Iraj started to show interest in me. It was against my father's policy that someone should get close to his daughter to have a relationship with her. It was a big no-no in our home and within our society. They believed that their children could have a relationship only when they were ready for marriage. Nothing like a love affair could be permitted in our household, unless it was combined with marriage.

My Dear GOD:

The first New Year (Ayed) during our relationship, Iraj bought me a very beautiful watch. Obviously word got around and my parents found out about our relationship. That did it. The atmosphere of our house became cloudy. They were trying to make me understand that he was young and only trying to have fun. I never could understand them. The more they insisted on separating us, the more I drowned in him. When they found out about the watch, my father took the watch from me. While Iraj was standing in from of the house, my father threw the watch to him and said, "No one is ever allowed to bring a gift like this for my daughter. Take you gift and stay away from my daughter."

Oh, my dear GOD, do you remember what happened to me that day? I nearly died. I never expected him to do that. I worshiped the watch. Not because it was beautiful, but because it was from Iraj. After that act, I became more and more anxious. I wasn't able to stay away from him. We had a servant who brought his letters to me and took mine to him. We started secretly meeting each other in other places. He walked me to school. We went to restaurants. We tried to see each other one way or another.

I learned how to lie in order to see him. I'll never forget how all the times after seeing him I came home and was so afraid of what would happen if they found out about my lies. What would they do to me? I can still feel my quickened heartbeat and the loud noise of it. It seemed that my heart was in my hand. Many nights I felt that my heart would jump out of my chest and start rolling in front of me. I was so afraid of getting caught. No matter how much they punished me or how many times they stopped me, I still did my own thing. I don't think I could write the memory of seven years of challenge, but I will mention some of them.

Now that everything is in the past, when I look back I see why my parents were so concerned about my future. His behavior was telling them something that I couldn't see back then.

Fridays are holidays in Iran. One Friday afternoon he had asked me to go for a walk to a big farm behind our house. I was holding my little sister Saideh in my arms. I asked my parents if I could take her with me for a breath of fresh air. She was almost one year old. They agreed. I met Iraj at the corner of the road and we walked towards the meeting place. We talked about our life and our family and friends. The more I saw and spoke with him, the more I felt the chemistry between us. At that time I was seventeen and he was nineteen.

My Dear GOD:

He talked to me about everything. He talked about how much he loved his mother and how much she was abused in her married life. His mother had delivered fourteen children. Two of them were two sets of twins. From fourteen children she only had four of them left. The rest did not survive. The more he talked about sad things in his family, the deeper I drowned within him. One day I opened my eyes and found myself deeply in love with him. As the days and years went by I became madly in love with him. He kept himself so innocent and charming that I just couldn't resist him.

I wasn't the kind of girl that was after either marriage or sex. I thought that if I never found the person whom I could give my life for, I would never get married at all. At that time, I thought I had found my soul mate. To me it didn't matter if I could marry him or not, I wanted him and wanted to be faithful to him for the rest of my life. My feelings were so strong that I only needed to hear from his uncle's wife that, "Iraj had told his mother, "If I don't marry Shamci, I will commit suicide." When I heard how firmly he had expressed his feelings for me I felt even more sure and positive about loving him as much as I did.

Anyway, that Friday we walked and talked, laughed and cried and were so happy to be together. Long before sunset we started to head back home in order to make sure my parents would not become suspicious. All of the sudden Iraj turned around and pointed out three young men who were very far from us. He told me that if they asked us what we are doing here we would tell them that we are sister and brother and we were expecting our parents. Since we couldn't find them, we were going back home. And because my little sister Saideh was with us, it was easy for them to believe us. Soon the young men, each holding a stick in their hands, came toward us. They asked Iraj what he was doing there. He replied, "These are my sisters and we were looking for our parents. Since we didn't find them here, we are going back home."

For a moment I thought they were not going to buy that answer. Then they asked us where we were living and many more questions. After I talked to them, they became convinced that we were not lying. They asked us to go home before it got dark or something happened. When we started walking home, Iraj insisted that we take bus, incase they decided to follow us.

My Dear GOD:

On the bus I asked him how he knew that they were after us. He replied, "They thought that I took you out in order to harm you. They would have killed me if we didn't lie to them."

You see, my dear GOD, in my country and in our culture, men try to be protective of women. If they feel someone is harassing a girl or woman, they allow themselves to take the law in their own hands and do something about it.

The important part of this story is to display how quick and experienced Iraj was at recognizing danger. As soon as he saw them, he was prepared to deal with the problem. Smart, yes, but looking back he had to have been experienced in order to handle the situation so well. That was what my parents were aware of and why they were trying to tell me to "be careful". It took me many years to recognize who he really was.

Another friend of both my brother and Iraj was Hosain Shirazi. He was Iraj's friend from high school in Zahedon. In our household, the whole family always got together in order to sit, talk, eat or do something else. When Iraj was not allowed to come to our house Hosain was the one who brought Iraj's letters to me. With a signal he would tell me where to go to get his letters. If someone checked my heartbeat at that time, they would have thought I was going to have a heart attack. I was afraid that if my father were to find out, he would kill me for sure. He believed that Iraj was playing with my emotions and was incapable of marrying me. So, in order to save my name in the neighborhood and among his family and friends he was trying to keep us as far from each other as he could.

On the other hand, I never wanted to get married unless Iraj was sure that I was the one and only one, whom he wanted to marry. I knew that with the lifestyle that he had and the circumstances, which he was under at the time, the thought of marriage was out. I always thought that until he was ready to take up the responsibilities that would come with marriage, we must not even talk about it. But in my neighborhood and family this kind of relationship was a crime. No young couple could become intimate and continue a happy life living among all those people who felt that way.

Unfortunately, neither my father nor any other person could understand me or the kind of love that I had for Iraj. I myself couldn't understand what was happening to me. I was getting wild and out-of-hand. I wasn't seeing things right. Except Iraj, there was nothing else in my world. I had gotten to the point that I would do anything to be with him or see him. I was at the stage where I was capable of committing a crime just to be with him and have him. (Wasn't it a big crime that after all the love and devotion my parents and siblings had shown me, I left them all behind and even asked Iraj not to let me ever talk about them or think about them?) I worshiped the ground he walked on. I saw him as my GOD and I thought I should sacrifice my life or anybody else's life for him. I was in a dangerous situation. My parents could see that, and I was completely blind.

My Dear GOD:

You know better than I do that he pretended that he loved me even more than I loved him. The walk he did! The talk he did! The promises we made to each other! The things that he did for me at that stage of his life proved to me that he was sincerely in love with me. For example, there was the watch he gave me for New Years. He had put in so many hours of hard work selling pharmaceutical drugs door to door to doctors. Back then he did not have a car and usually had no money for the bus so he had to walk from his home to the university and other places to be able to make ends meet. And that watch was a very expensive watch, not only for the time period, but for now as well. I think that if he did not love me the way he wanted me to believe he did, he must have been very stupid indeed. Another example was also the first New Year when we were all going to their house. Before that day he gave me a gold coin as a gift. I was shocked because I knew he did not have any money.

That day, when we went to his parent's house for a visit, his father, who was very smart and clever, came into the room and with a loud voice asked his children if any of them had stolen a gold coin from them. Obviously everybody said no. I was the only person who knew where the coin was. I realized that the coin that Iraj had given me was the one that his father was looking for. But I never wanted to embarrass him. I never said anything about it and he never asked me anything. I pretended that I hadn't heard what his father had asked.

So you see my dear GOD, he also did wrong things in order to bring happiness to me. While I know that it was wrong, we both did it for each other anyways.

Because of all these things that he was doing for me and because of all the humiliation he dealt with from my parents but kept loving me nonetheless, I had promised myself that no matter what happened, I would never stop loving him. And I think I kept my promise to the end. Now that I look back, I see that I must have been sick to have not seen his true intentions. That kind of love truly is a destructive disease.

My Dear GOD:

I now think that this disease was getting worse because my father was acting very harsh with us. Whenever my father threw him out of our house, I became more and more determined to go after him. Whenever my father belted and embarrassed me, I made myself both tougher and stronger.

During the same time that I was going out with Iraj, his sister Pari started going out with a young man named Kamal Kamooneh. He was also a political activist who she met at the university. I was the only one who knew about their relationship. She too had to hide her relationship from her family, including Iraj. Once, when Kamal was arrested

during a student demonstration and thrown into jail, I decided to give Pari some emotional support by joining her when she went to visit him in jail. For me to lie to my parents and go visit the boyfriend of the sister of my boyfriend was the biggest crime anyone could commit. I don't remember how I lied to them, but I remember that we did go together to visit Kamal. She was feeling so sad and miserable that I didn't feel like I could leave her alone. When I got home, everything was all right and it seemed that no one had suspected anything.

One week later, my father questioned me, "Why have you been to jail and what were you doing there?"

I was able to make up a story. I knew he didn't buy it. Because of this he suspended me for one month from seeing anyone at all. Can you imagine what happened to my heart that night? I was going to die.

The worse part of this gap between my parents and I was that they had lost their trust in me and my everyday life had become a nightmare. When I look back, I believe that if, with the love that I had for my parents, had my father thought to deal with me by using reverse psychology, he probably would've been able to get rid of that nasty disease called, "love".

Fortunately, now that I am at this stage of my life, is easy to look and find a solution to my problem

But my dear GOD, as I have mentioned many times, it is not that we could have changed anything ever. This path of life had been there for me to follow. Not I, nor my father, nor anyone else could have changed anything of it or anything about it. This is what I believe. It does not mean that it is right.

My Dear GOD:

Another time, right after I had been grounded for the month, I snuck out with Iraj. This time my father not only belted me but also made me stay in the bathroom in the corner of the yard for one day.

As I said, none of these things ever worked for me or made me change my mind at all. At this time, not only my parents, but also my sisters and brothers, including Jamal who was Iraj's friend, were angry and mad at me. They didn't like people talking about me. Since I was their sister it was a big embarrassment for them. To other people I was considered a bad girl.

During the time when I was grounded, one evening, we were all sitting in the family room. It was one of those hopeless and sad evenings. I was almost giving up all my hopes. I had no one to turn to and no one to talk to at all. I was bad and I felt ugly. Then the doorbell rang. I saw Pari and Neia wearing veils (chadors) coming to visit. I had no idea

why they came or why they were wearing chadors. They sat with us and we talked and laughed at the present with my parents. Pari was always the comedian of the family. My father liked her a lot. She made everybody laugh. She made everyone forget about wearing their chadors, because we never wore chadors unless it was a funeral. Later I found out that they were trying to buy my father's trust that night. So after laughing and socializing for some time, she asked my father if he would allow me to go with her to buy fabric for her dress. Although he had doubts, he still let me go with them. When we walked out of the house they told me that Iraj had been missing me and that he wanted to see me. They told me he was at his sister Parvin's house. I was too shy and embarrassed to go to Parvin's house to strictly see and talk to Iraj. Although I was very uncomfortable, they assured me that it was no problem. Yet I wasn't afraid of any problem. I was worried that I might lose Parvin's respect for me. In their family as well this was a no-no, even though she had done this before I and Iraj had begun our secret relationship.

At first Iraj was not in sight. In a little while they took me to their yard and I saw him sitting on the steps of the living room. He did not seem happy. And I thought that he had been crying. My heart was coming to my mouth. I didn't know how to talk or what to say. I wanted to hold him in my arms, just as if he were a baby, and cure his wounds. I wanted to die so that I would not have to see him like that. I sat near him and we talked. He pretended that he had had a quarrel with his father.

My Dear GOD:

During those seven years I had never seen Iraj in the presence of his father. He was always avoiding him in public. He was embarrassed by his appearance. Many times people had to bring his father back home in a drunken bad shape. In both summer and winter he always wore his army coat and was very proud of it. To me he was a victim of society. He had done his part to be a good person. He had done his share to love and care for others. But, unfortunately, something went wrong and made him the kind of person that he became. With all his drinking and complete lack of awareness for what was going on, he was still very smart and intelligent in his own way. Although he knew that my parents were against my marriage with Iraj as well as Iraj's personality and character, he never cared or loved me the less for it. And when Iraj went to U.S.A. he was my strongest supporter at all times. I have heard that he himself had been in love with his wife and so he was very appreciative of my love for Iraj. And when Iraj was gone, he made sure to show me extensive love more during his absence.

After seven years of challenge and struggle with all the members of my family, just one month before his departure to the U.S.A., we were able to get married. It was a small wedding and the only guests were the members of his family, my family, and very few of our relatives. Molla presided over the ceremony in a very cold and bitter gathering of some unhappy people. The marriage took place on June 14th 1958.

My dear GOD, do you remember that day? Please help me to remember everything exactly the way it happened.

There were many things to be sad and unhappy about. During the seven years we all went through many drastic and painful experiences. One of them was sudden death of Iraj's mother. The second one was I saying goodbye forever to my only family I have ever known and much more besides that. Most of all the marriage took place with the disapproval and disagreement of both families. It looked more like a funeral than a wedding.

***

As I mentioned earlier, Iraj had started medical school in Tehran University. When he got free from prison I got to meet him. Then there had been no problem for any of us to sit and talk to each other. I remember once he came over and asked my parents to permit me to go to an amusement park with him. He showed two tickets to my father and it was my parents who asked me if I would like to go with him. At that time they were sure that it was merely a simple invitation. They had enough understanding to allow their daughter to be seen with a young man in an amusement park. I think as long as it was a clean friendship they did not mind it.

My Dear GOD:

That was the first time that I fell in love with his character. He talked all about his family. He talked about his father's alcoholism. He talked about his mother and how she had suffered going through that ordeal. He told me that his mother had delivered fourteen children but only four survived. He said that his mother was

Muslim and his father, coming from Muslim family, now is Baha'i. He told me that all the children were Baha'i until they were in ninth grade. Then they were allowed to change their religion. He said that he had converted to Moslem. Obviously it was because of their mother that they all became Muslim.

He told me that once his parents couldn't stand each other anymore and they decided to separate. But in Baha'i faith, a wife and husband who want to split up must live in one house but in separate sections of the house. The reason is that many husbands and wives might come to their senses and realize that divorce is not the answer to their problem. I especially fell in love with this method of reconciliation between a man and wife, and especially for those with children who would then be able to keep the family together.

Anything he talked about that night was completely what I had always harbored in my mind. The way he loved his mother made me believe that he was a good man and he could be a good father and probably a good husband.

That night we were two individuals expressing ourselves and discussing the facts of life and understanding the rule of existence. Although neither of us was thinking of being involved with a love affair or even getting married, it was so obvious that both of us were drowning within one another. We were mesmerized by each other and happy to spend a beautiful evening together.

By the time Pari and Iraj were living in our neighborhood and sharing one room together, Iraj and I had already had started our relationship. Once I went there and I saw him ironing, I noticed that he was ironing Pari's clothes as well. I said to myself, "He's such a gentleman!" Because they used to come to our house very often, in an effort to impress my father, one evening Iraj invited my family visit Pari and him. When we went over there he had set-up the table with all kinds of fruits and sweets. I knew that he didn't have money to spend so much just on fruit and sweets in one night, but it seemed to me that he wanted to treat my family with respect and made them understand that he appreciated their respect for him as well.

My Dear GOD:

After few years, they bought a small house not too far from us in Khiabaneh Delgosha. Due to their parents' relationship, they were on the move most of the time. During that same time, Parvin was having problems with her husband. Before they moved into that house, Niea, who was only sixteen, got married to Mr. Abbass Forghani. He was an agricultural engineer; he was twelve years older than her. Mr. Forghani was a very handsome and prestigious man, and he loved Niea very much. He was politically involved in the city of Zahedan. Their marriage took place in the city of Khash. While the father was in Zahedan, they rented an apartment, and Neia and Pari both attended Ghavam School near our house.

This was all during the Shah's reign and at that time the earliest a girl could get married was eighteen. So Neia kept her marriage a secret until she turned eighteen. While she was busy going to school in Tehran, her husband Mohandess was still working in Khash. Once we heard that he was captured and sent to prison because of his political activities. They were all so worried, especially her mother. One day I went to their house after school, I did not find them well. I did not want to interfere so I decided to leave them alone. But they asked me to stay. After awhile I found out that they read in the papers that

Mohandess was convicted, and he was supposed to be executed. I couldn't believe what I had heard. That was impossible. But I read about it myself in the newspaper. He was among forty men to be executed. Boy oh boy. What now?

Their mother had a very strong will. She was well respected among many influential army leaders in Khash. So she began visiting them all, one by one. She would leave her house at six in the morning, and at times she would come back as late as six or seven at night. They were not sure if anyone could do anything for them. But it couldn't hurt to try. She had never thought of giving-up.

The reason that she was hopeful was because she knew that the Shah would pardon a few prisoners every year on his birthday. She knew that any and every effort to free her son in-law from prison had to be made prior to the Shah's birthday. And guess what, my dear GOD? When that time came, we couldn't wait to see the newspaper. We found the list of pardoned prisoners and there was his name, Mr. Abbas Forghani. Wow, really Wow! It was time to celebrate. He was pardoned from execution. That meant that he could live again, but only GOD knew how long would he have to stay in prison.

My Dear GOD:

Now, don't forget that my partaking in all this was considered a crime. I had to make sure that I wouldn't get punished for everything I did. I had to be visiting them carefully, and then return stealthily.

Ok my dear GOD, I'm sure that anyone who reads this book is probably wondering why it was that everyone in this family ended up going to jail. The answer is quiet simple. During the Shah's regime the educated and intelligent people were aware of what was really going on in his government, and so they deserved to be punished and put into prison. And if they were even more intelligent and educated then they deserved to be put to death.

Ok, my dear GOD, as I said before and I will say this again, things that happen in the world happen for a reason, just like everything was planned ahead of time and no one could have changed them. You see, my dear GOD, just one year after his imprisonment his sentence was reduced to four years.

The prisoners were allowed to come home and spend a night with their family on special occasions. Since Pari had arranged a party for her wedding one week before Iraj's departure, they let him come home on the night of their wedding.

My dear GOD, you know what happened that night. They had conceived their first child, Arman. Mr. Forghani returned to prison the next morning. He was pardoned once again in a year, and he was freed on the Shah's birthday (Chaharomeh-Aban.)

While Mr. Forgani was in prison, Neia's mom started having some spotting. Iraj suggested that she must go and see a gynecologist. He knew many doctors that were his teachers since he was in medical school. So he asked his mom to go and see Dr. Mossadegh. He was the son of Dr. Mohammad Mossadegh. The doctor diagnosed her with D.&C. after the check-up.

I am not sure what the procedure is for a D.&C. But I do know that it is an easy procedure. It is as easy as an abortion. When Iraj was in practice, he would perform multiple D.& C's per day.

My Dear GOD:

So one Friday Iraj's mom said goodbye to all the neighbors and with a smile on her face she left for the hospital. She went to the hospital this one Friday, and her body was carried out from that hospital the next Friday. She was only forty-three years of age. When she was at the hospital I went to visit her (again without my parents' permission). We were not close enough to be discussing private matters. But before I said goodbye to her, she pulled her sleeve up and showed me her arms. It looked like she had a third degree burn. Part of her muscle was gone. She told me that after bringing fourteen children into this world and going through many painful times in her life, she had never felt that that was the end. But this time she didn't think she would make it. I walked all the way home from the hospital and I thought to myself, "Is this all there is?" I had never thought that she might die.

At that time, although I was a teacher, I still wasn't very good at finding my way to and from places. The only way we knew was from school to home, and vice versa. We never went anywhere by ourselves, unless we were with our parents. So that day, when I was walking home from the hospital, I got lost a few times. I think it was mostly because I was worried about Iraj's mom, and at the same time I was worried that my parents would find out, and I was worried for my own life and future.

I'll never forget the day that I was in their house, when Iraj told me that he wished to discuss something with me. I was uncomfortable to be alone with Iraj in front of his parents. I was very shy and did not want to do something foolish. Their house would open to a hallway with four bedrooms. His mother led me to the first room on the left, and after a few minutes she left and did not return. The rest of the time Iraj and I were alone in that room.

A few days later Iraj told me that the reason that his mother left us alone in that room was to allow Iraj to make a pass on me. He believed that his mother thought that by making me available for him she could stop him from marrying me. At the time my ideas

about life and our parents were completely different from the way they are now. Now that I look back, knowing Iraj's cleverness, I think that by putting this thought in my mind, he was able to take advantage of me first, and second he wanted to prove to me that against all the odds, he loved me enough to marry me. I really don't know what to believe. Please, my dear GOD, help me to know some truth about this man.

My Dear GOD:

Anyway, Iraj's dear mother, whom he loved so very much, died. It was needless for her to be seeing doctors. She was not sick. She was living happily with her children in that house. Iraj was at medical school, Pari and Neia were in high school, and Parveen, although married, was going to school as well. So you see, my dear GOD, was it her time to die? Was it necessary for her to leave her children when they needed her most? Was it necessary for you to take her life in the beginning of her happiness?

Am I right when I say that our lives are already arranged and planned? Because if they are not, why did she even think of going to a doctor? She was healthier than all the people around her. I think she wanted to take advantage of Iraj's privileges at the hospital. She wanted to make Iraj feel proud of himself. And Iraj wanted to do a big favor for his Mom. I don't know. I don't know anything at all, except that our lives have been planned for us.

Anyways, disasters started taking place one after the other. Their household economy was in bad shape as well. Their father was always drunk. Their mother, who had been the only source of strength in the family, was gone. Parveen did not want to see the very sight of her husband. Neia's husband was still in prison. Pari was in love with Kamal. And Iraj was supposedly in love with me. GOD, you think it was easy to handle this life? I don't know. I don't know at all.

After all the screaming, pulling of hair, beating themselves and going completely crazy for a few days, each one started to mourn in their own way. Iraj was trying not to show-up around home. He was afraid to face his sisters. He was the one who suggested that his mother saw a doctor, and I think in a way he blamed himself for what had happened.

I know he felt especially guilty when Parveen, while mourning, shook her head back and forth and said "You did your work, you killed her!" I don't know what state of mind she was in when she made that harsh statement, but I am sure she didn't know what she was really saying.

Pari was in the stage of denial. She was laughing, dancing and pretending that nothing had happened. Finally they had to take her to a psychiatrist. So she was not

present at the time of the ceremony and the funeral. At the time some of our mutual friends believed that she was faking it all. Oh well, people will talk.

Neia was the most innocent of all. She was the youngest, and she was very close to her mother. I have heard that she was still sleeping next to her Mom, not only because her husband was in prison, and not because she was the baby of the house, but because in Iran it is not unusual to sleep next to your mother. She was quiet and remained very introvert. She kept everything within herself. Most of the times when she was laughing very hard, all of a sudden her laugher would turn into harsh sobs, and she would shed tears like you'd never believe. I always thought that because she was hiding all her problems that her pain would unconsciously wrench out of her like that. I don't know how she did it but it seemed like it worked for her.

My Dear GOD:

And as for Iraj and I, things were all up in the air. We didn't see each other except during the time of the ceremonies. My parents paid their respects to Mrs. Maryam Rafani as well. Obviously, after that tragedy, my parents and Iraj were talking to each other again. I was feeling very sorry for Iraj. I didn't know how to approach him or comfort him. This was the last thing on earth that Iraj was expecting to happen. It was not on his list for another hundred of years. But again we fall back on the conclusion that things have to happen in a certain way, it is not up to us to change them. And we have to continue living.

As I said, Iraj loved his mother so much, that we decided to call our daughter Maryem after his mother. I remember this one day when we were all sitting in our living room, and like always we played some kind of game. Iraj found a questionnaire in one of the magazines, and he read it to me. It went like this, "If you are in a boat with your lover and your mother, and you have last piece of bread, which is supposed to save only one person's life, which person would you give the bread to and thus save? Is it your mother or is it your lover?" Obviously, without any doubt I answered, "Your mother".

He replied, "No, you give it to your lover". I was shocked and I didn't think that he was serious. I asked him to repeat his answer again or to explain it to me. How come you do not feed your mother and feed your lover? He explained it to me in a humanitarian way. He said, "Just because she has lived a longer life, and your lover is starting to live right then".

So Iraj decided to go to the USA to continue his education. On one hand he was concerned about my life and my future. I made him believe in my love and be sure that I would never betray him. I asked him to go ahead and that we would wait to see what was there for us. He didn't know what to do with me. He didn't have the opportunity to get married, and he wasn't able to provide me with necessary housing. He was telling me to do some research and find out how I would be able to join him after he was gone. He was so poor and broke that he didn't know how to provide the money for his own ticket.

My Dear GOD:

After he got his acceptance from DePaul Hospital in St. Louis Missouri, he arranged for a very small and private wedding. He told me that to make our lives easier, we had to get married there. And he said that he had discussed it with his sisters, and they had all agreed that after the wedding I would move in with them until we established what we should do with our future. The reason that I had to move in with his sisters was that my parents had agreed that I would not be able to stay in their house after I was married to Iraj.

So two weeks before Iraj left for the U.S.A., we got married in the presence of a Molla in a very cold and unhappy atmosphere. And one day later I moved in Iraj's parents' house with just my clothes and personal belongings.

No one even said a goodbye to me the day I moved out. My brother Jamal, who was Iraj's friend, threw the rest of my stuff out and told me to never come back.

I could cry now for myself and berate myself, "Shame on you Shamci! Indeed, shame on you. Who did you sell your parents and your family for? How could you have done it? Didn't you consider that they were the ones who were there for you all throughout? Weren't you ashamed and embarrassed to look your parents in their eyes?"

Anyhow, not only did I do it at that time, but also I blamed my parents for all, and I had even asked Iraj not to let me think of my parents or to mention their names.

My sisters were so mad at me that in order to avoid speaking to me, they ignored me when they would see me on the streets. They believed that I had ruined their reputation in the neighborhood and within society. Although I had reached my goal and nothing else was supposed to matter to me, I didn't know why I felt like I was the most lost person on Earth.

After one week Pari and Kamal had a we dd eremo ra made s re t at they got married before he left Iran. At this time we were all in his parents' house. His father was there, Parveen who had left her husband was there, Neia whose husband was in prison was there, and Pari and Kamal who had just gotten married were there. And Iraj and I were living in their house for two weeks.

My Dear GOD:

Iraj had to leave Iran in two weeks. Because he did not have any money for his ticket, he decided to go by boat, which was more economical. Even then I offered to pay the half, and Parveen paid the other half.

It was such an embarrassing state to be in. I had never had the experience of sleeping with someone in such a crowd. Every morning it was a drag to just come out of our room. Actually, I was relieved when Iraj left.

Ok my dear GOD. You were there with me at all times, and I don't have to explain anything for you. You were completely aware of my feelings and the activities of my heart. You were there, whatever we did and wherever we went. You saw the situation I was in. It wasn't easy to overcome all those obstacles at once.

On top of everything, Iraj was asking me to get pregnant. That was out of the question for me. I had no home, no money, no certainty, and most of all, I did not have any relationship with the only family I have ever known. I didn't want to bring a child in this world, just for the sake of being a mother. That any woman can do. The way that I fell in love, I just wanted to love my husband forever and ever. And I wanted to raise my children under one and only one flag. That was the flag of love, the flag of honesty, the flag of togetherness, and the flag of loyalty, and under the supervision of both parents as well. Iraj's idea was that he wanted to have a child in case something happened to him. That way there would be a memory left of him. But I did not agree with him. I thought that a child needs both father and a mother to be able to grow up happy and healthy. If they lose any of their parents with the force of nature, it is a different story. But to raise a child with uncertainty and lack of happiness, just for the sake of memory is not wise. Although I was the one, who wanted so badly to have a child from Iraj before I died, I still wasn't willing to go through it with all the uncertainty that I had. Finally I was able to convince him that it was not the right time or the right place to be conceiving a child.

On the other hand, those who knew I had gotten married to Iraj, when he was leaving me in two weeks to go to USA, were hounding me. Why had I done such a thing? Why did I let him to go to blond American? Or why aren't you getting pregnant so that in case he wants to leave you he has to take responsibility for his child? These people were all out of their minds. They didn't have the slightest idea about the kind of love that I had for Iraj. I didn't intend to put a chain around Iraj's neck by marrying him, or try to keep him next to me by means of rules and regulations. The only thing that I was expecting from Iraj was simply pure love, the same kind of love that I had for him. As a matter of fact, I was happy that if it happened that he would change his mind about us when he got to the

USA, then it would be the right time for him to do so. Otherwise, after having a child or two, it would be very difficult to handle separation.

My Dear GOD:

Anyway, in the two weeks that we spent together, he made me promise him to get active and go after my Visa in order to be able to join him after the school year was over. And he promised me that he would write me two letters per week, no matter how busy he might be.

My dear GOD, I wonder what had happened to the feelings that he professed during those days! He told me that he couldn't live a single day without me. He was telling me that something was telling him to change his mind and stay in Iran with me. He promised to make me a queen of his time. He promised me that in order to make my parents sorry for what they did to me, he would make me the happiest woman on Earth.

There was no question about how much I loved him. He had been testing me. Once, when my parents were not allowing me to see him, he sent me a message that he had to see me immediately. When I saw him in his own apartment, he was out of shape. It seemed he had been crying. He seemed so hopeless that I wished I could die so that I wouldn't have to see him like that. He told me that something had happened at the university and that the authorities were after him. The only way that he could survive would be by giving up school. And in that case he would have to escape to go to the mountains of Tabreez.

I believed him. I thought it might be due to something political that he was not telling me about. I started to comfort him. I told him it was not the end of the world. "If you have to go by yourself, it's another story. But I am willing to come with you wherever you go. I will go home and bring some of my stuff in my school bag and no one will ever find out where we went", I comforted him.

After he realized that I was willing to go with him, even if he were to give up his medical school, he told me the truth. He said that he was trying to see whether I loved him so much for his medical school or truly for himself. That day he realized that I was not a fake lover. I was so in love with him that I would've given my heart or my eyes for him. Now that I look back, I see how lucky I have been. He could have been one of those, who fool their lovers. He could have been one of those men who take their willing lover to the mountain of Tabreez in order to get rid of her once and for all. But obviously such a thing did not befall me at that time.

My Dear GOD:

So Iraj and I spent the first two weeks of our married life with his father and his sisters in their house. I think we lived a life of very civilized people. We all had respect for each other, and we were responsible for our own actions. Although it was very painful for me to experience being disowned by my parents like that, I was glad that I was living with people who were worthy of loving.

Since there were four of us, ladies, in the house, each day we took turns to cook. We shared everything, and we tried to go to movies together. So, like Kamal always teased me, I spent half of my honeymoon in Iran, and the other half GOD knows where. We used to laugh at our accomplishments and ourselves. Often we played Rummy, and Kamal collected the winning pennies in his socks.

Iraj's father was the one, who cared the most for me. He was aware that I had left my family for Iraj. Although he was drunk all the time, he never forgot his respect for me. He treated me as an equal among his other daughters. For instance, anytime he wanted to give his daughters money, he would call me first and give me the same amount of money. He knew that my parents were everything to me, and that I gave them up for Iraj. He didn't want me to get hurt more than I had already been hurt. Coming from an alcoholic, that kind of care was something to talk about and appreciate.

Anyway, after two memorable weeks, Iraj left. I started a new life with the rest of the family in their house. Look, my dear GOD, I was a person who loved my family. But then I was living in a new house with a new family, new environment, plus I didn't even have Iraj around. It was not easy. But the way they treated me, especially Sarvan Rafani, brought some comfort into my life.

As I promised Iraj, right after he left I started to go about getting my Visa. As the time was passing by, Sarvan Rafani was getting impatient. He was missing his only son and did not want him to stay away forever. He was telling me that if I didn't go to America, maybe Iraj would come back someday. I felt so sorry for him. He didn't want to admit that he was missing Iraj. But he wanted to stop me from going, so that perhaps Iraj could turn around and come back. It had been almost four years that he had lost his young wife whom he had loved so much. Now his only son had departed from him, almost forever. His girls did not have enough respect for him and the only thing that made him happy was his alcohol. But even with that, his children and especially Iraj were always asking me to add water to his drink. As if he wouldn't notice. You put one drop of water in his drink and he would go after you.

My Dear GOD:

As I said, he was aware of my painful relationship with my parents. One day he saw them passing by on the street. They stopped and talked to each other. They talked about everything, but they never mentioned my name. Then one day while Sarvan Rafani told me this, he asked me, "Why do you think your parents dislike your marriage, and hate Iraj?" I, who was mad at my life, and myself answered with an unhappy voice, "I really do not want to talk about it. Probably they had in mind for me to marry the prince of Iran. I really don't know at all". He didn't say anything about my parents to me after that.

Parveen was the type of lady, who always minded her own business. She never interfered with other people's affairs. To me she was a very quiet, lady-like, and respectable woman. Although we never became close friends, and although she probably never wanted me to marry her brother, I never heard or saw anything from her that made me believe that she didn't like me. She was very polite and had much respect for me. Not only the first year that I lived with them, but for as long as I can remember. I always thought of her to be a great lady.

Pari was my friend. At times I thought that I was her closest friend. I remember one incident that indicates how close we were. When Pari first started to go out with Kamal, no one, not even Iraj, knew anything about it. Kamal had given her a few of his pictures. Pari was afraid that someone would find the pictures in her bag. She gave me the pictures to hide. The best and the safest place I could think of was on top of the dresser I shared with my sister Azar. The dresser was six or seven feet tall. I thought that no one would ever be able to find them there. To everyone's surprise, and especially mine, Azar found them up there. Not only did she find them, but also she showed them to everyone. Oh my, oh my, oh my! What now? How do I fix this? Anyway, I made up a story. Nonetheless, from what I recall, I was still punished. I had to stay away from all my friends for a month.

During those days Iraj and Pari shared a one-bedroom apartment in our neighborhood. My parents liked them a lot and they were welcome to our house for lunch, dinner, or even to sleep over. Pari and my sister Azar were the family clowns. They were very talented, smart, and outspoken. When they were among a group, they took control over the party. They dressed in funny and unusual clothes and put-up a show for the whole family. Not only did we have fun, but my parents were very amused as well. The way I saw it, our house was their second home, and they felt comfortable coming to our house at anytime. So it would make us all very unhappy whenever I was punished, and forced to stay away from them. I don't know about Pari, but I considered her to be my best friend. I was truthful with Pari in exact same way I was truthful with Iraj. She was a good friend; she was a very easy going and funny girl. I had as much fun with her as I had with Iraj. The year that I stayed in their house, she really acted as though she was my sister. Both of us could sew, knit, cook, and play backgammon. We also enjoyed going to movies together and as well as each other's company. After she got married, her husband Kamal became a good friend of mine as well. We used to tease each other and joke around and have fun together. I have always felt a deep sense of closeness to them and I truly enjoyed their company. After Iraj was gone, they teased me more than ever. He joked that I had spent half of my honeymoon in Iran, and would have to spend the second half in the U.S.A in a year. He believed that I would not be able to find some of our native food products in the U.S.A. He asked me to eat much more than usual so that I was able to keep the taste of that food within myself. He used to laugh at his own jokes more than all of us.

My Dear GOD:

I remember many incidents that took place before I left for the USA. Once, Neia had bought herself a piece of fabric so that Pari made her a dress. I don't exactly remember what the topic of their argument was. We were all in the living room, when all of a sudden Neia got her new fabric and ran to the kitchen. Within seconds I started smelling something burning. As I ran to the kitchen I found the fabric in flames. We got there and put the flame out, but amazingly everybody forgot about the incident right after.

In our household we were not allowed to have physical fights, or for that matter any fights. We had to settle down before it became a fight; otherwise, we would get severely punished. But every other family that I knew would get into both verbal and physical fights.

My Dear GOD:

Once, when Iraj was away, his cousin, Mehdi Gangee, invited us to go with him to his house, which was located in Kordestan. He was married to Hadgee Khanoom from that area. They had a son named Syamak.

It was a long weekend, and we all had agreed to go. It was four of us. Parveen, Pari, Neia, and I. Mehdi had an old station wagon with no windows. We had no idea what kind of the road we were going to ride on.

I didn't want to go at first, because I used to get carsick. But they talked me into it. We all packed and got ready to go. During those days our cars were not equipped with fancy accessories. The car did not have operable windows, it had no cooling or heating.

The cars and even homes were not equipped with phones. So we decided to just go and have fun. I don't even know if Hadgee Khanoom knew that we were all going to stay in their house. In Iran even if you have only one room, you would still make room for guests.

It was a long trip. I know it took more than one day to get there. I lay down on the car floor the whole way there. Neia covered herself with a (chadore) veil to protect herself from dust, and so did Pari and Parveen. We stopped to rest in the middle of the way. The moment that we stepped out and looked at each other was the funniest moment of all. Everybody's hair and eyelashes were completely covered with heavy coat of dust. Neia looked worse than all of us. We realized how dusty we were without even looking at each other. At once we all started to laugh at ourselves loudly and we couldn't stop. We laughed for half an hour. It was the funniest scene anyone could see. We laughed to a point that we got a stomachache. Since that trip anytime we talk about that incident we laugh so hard. Many things happened during that short trip.

Part of the road was winding up and down the mountains. It was evening time, and it was starting to get dark. I was sitting next to Mehdi Agha. I felt there was something that he was not telling us. Twice he talked to the passing trucks and he told them something we did not understand. Later on we figured out why. There was a big car driving in front of us and there was a car behind us throughout. Everyone was driving very slowly. After almost an hour of slow driving we got to a very small coffee shop. Although it did not look like a place appropriate for ladies, Mehdi Agha asked us to stay there for a while. We still did not know what was going on. After having some tea and freshening up, we sat in a cool area to relax. Then we found out that the car's brake had been out of order, and Mehdi Agha couldn't stop the car when he had to. So the two cars were there to help him to slow down. I don't remember exactly if we had to stay there overnight, but by the following day we got to Mehdi Agha's house safe and sound. Poor Mehdi Agha, he must have been so worried. He had kept thinking to himself that if he would not be able to bring the car to stop on such a steep road, the car would have rolled down the mountain. There would have been no hope for any of us to survive.

My Dear GOD:

This is just the story of getting up there. Once again something strange happened while we were staying with them. Hadgee Khanoom was very nice; she had welcomed us with open arms. We were enjoying the beauty of Kordestan and the hospitality of our hosts. We did our share of help as needed.

One afternoon we were sitting in the room. Pari and Parveen started arguing over a telephone call to Kamal. I don't remember the whole story. But I know that their voices got higher and higher. They started calling each other names and blaming each other for all sorts of nasty things. I tried to stay out of the room so as not to embarrass them, but they got louder and louder. I think Parveen had said something bad about Kamal, which made Pari really mad. So they were at each other's throat for sometimes.

Anyway, they were really telling each other off. I have never seen such a bad fight between them. These two sisters did not talk to each other for almost five or six months until another disaster took place in their lives almost immediately after that incident.

And meanwhile, my dear GOD, you remember how happy I was with receiving Iraj's letters. He had kept his promise to me. He would send me two letters a week. I did not want to miss any of his letters, and for that reason I didn't want to go to Kordestan. Those letters were worth more than ten million to me. I would eat them, drink them, walk with them and sleep with them. They were the most precious gift I could have ever received. Although he would send letters to me every three days, sometimes I wouldn't get any, and other times I got three or four all at once. Those letters were my tranquilizers. When I got three of them in one day, I would smell them, I would put them on my heart, they made me very happy. But, GOD forbids, if I did not get them within a week. I felt like I was lost in the world. I would even blame Iraj for the delay.

My Dear GOD:

He wrote me three letters from the boat, while he was traveling. He would tell me in all those letters how sorry he was that he had left me behind. He explained to me that being away from me was making him crazy. He was worried, he was wondering if it was right for me to be staying at his house. He tried to explain to me how big the boat was, and the way the passengers interacted. He couldn't get any letters from me because I was sending them to his address at his hospital. He felt the same need and impatience I had for those letters. He was upset as to why he hadn't heard from us, even though he knew for fact that we were sending our letters to the hospital. His last letter from the boat was a bit happier. He was glad that the five-day trip had finally come to the end, and that had arrived to New York after all. He still had to wait to go to the hospital to get our letters. I think he received a big stack of letters from all of us when he first arrived at the hospital. I wrote to him almost every day. He reacted to my letters the same way I did to his. When he got many of them he sounded very happy, and when he got them late he was upset with me. Anyhow, that was the one section of my life that I still and will always cherish for the rest of my life. That was a period of truth, honesty, loyalty and pure love for both of us (although today I have doubts about him even about that period).

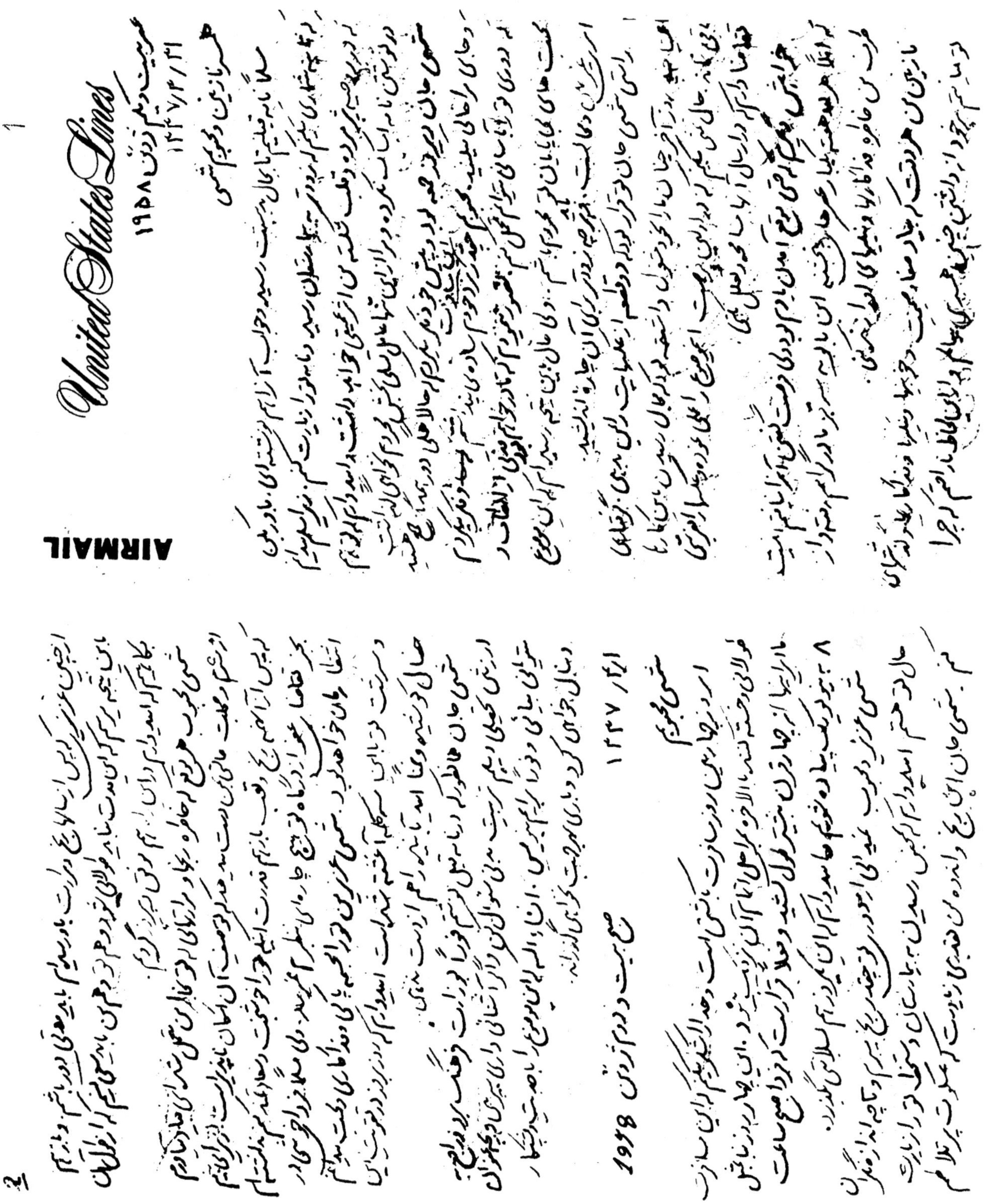
United States Lines

AIRMAIL

This was written to me on June 21st, 1958 from his ship going to New York. Wouldn't it be nice if my children paid attention to find out about their father's feelings for their mother? It is so nice that he had to skip the "bedroom words" in these letters; otherwise I would not be able to publish it. He wrote those words in different letters that no one could read. Isn't he clever?

اقیانوس عظیم و انواع سرگرمیها و تفریحات مشغول کننده کشتی توانسته اند
اندکی از آن را در خود حل کنند حال امیدوارم که دنیای پرجوش و خروش

عصر بیست و سوم ژوئن

شاید فکر کنی چگونه هیچ نامه را نیم تمام گذاشته ام باقیش را بخواهی دانست
که در حین نوشتن نامه حالت ضعف من دست داد و دیگر قادر بادامه آن نبودم
لذا بسرعت تا آسانسور با خانم رفتم و تا حال دراز کشیده بودم و حتی ظهر نهار
هم نخوردم. خواهی گفت که از کجا با این حالت رفتی مگر در اطاقت نامه نمی نوشتی
باید عرض کنم که نه در اینجا یک پستخانه دارد که دارای صندلی و میزهای متعدد
و قلم و دوات و کاغذ و پاکت که همه اش مجانی است در اینجا می نشینند و نامه
ها را می نویسند. و بعد هم پول را به پستچی داده او تمبر میکند.

عزیزم حال الحمدالله کاملا بهتر است بعد از آنکه این مسافرت کشتی
پایان می پذیرد خوشحالم که [illegible]. شمی جان راستش را بخواهی خودم هم
از این مسافرت پشیمان شده ام و اگر پول داشتم بمحض رسیدن به نیویورک
با هواپیما برمیگشتم ولی چکنم راهی را پیش گرفته ام که علی الاجبار باید تا پایان
آن را طی کنم فقط یک دلخوشی دارم آنهم اینکه تو زودتر کارهایت را
انجام داده و نزد من بیائی. شمی عزیزم تمام رنجها و ناراحتی های من
بواسطه دوری از توست تو تنها مونس و امید و آرزوی من در زندگی هستی
ولی بی تو زندگی برایم غیر مقدور است.

شمی من اگر بدانی امروز که در رختخواب دراز کشیده بودم چه افکاری
بمغزم هجوم آورد. گاهی بقدری وحشتناک بود که فکر میکردم دیوانه شده ام

[illegible]

و تومانی جان را در آرزوهای طلائی غوطه ور بودم که از خود بیخود شده ام درست
پیروزی [illegible]

شمی عزیزم حالا فکر میکنم که این تقصیر تو بود که باین مسافرت اقدام کردم زیرا تو نه تنها
یکدفعه مرا منع نکردی بلکه همیشه تشویقم هم نمودی و اگر واقعا مانع مسافرت من میشدی
الان از لذت زندگی در کنار تو برخوردار بودم. فکر میکنم که تو چقدر خوبی که همه
رنجها را بدون هیچگونه شکوه و شکایتی بر اثر خودت تحمل کردی. تو چقدر نازنینی که
از اینهمه مرارت در راه من کشیدی ولی هیچگاه بروی من نیاوردی و ابرو ترش نکردی
تو چه اندازه باوفا و فداکاری با اینقدر رنج و اذیت باز با روی باز خوب
وفاداری. شمی عزیزم تنها امید من همین نکته یعنی وفاداری و فداکاری است
من تنها بامید دلخوشم و اگر این نمیبود فکر میکنم که این مسافرت [illegible]
شمی عزیز و محبوب از خانواده ات از پدر و مادرت برای من
بنویس که چگونه آیا سلامتند آیا برگشته اند و با تو چگونه رفتار میکنند
آقای [illegible] و عزت خانم از قول من سلام برسان و عذر بخواه که در موقع
آمدنم با ایشان [illegible]

دست پدر بزرگوارم از طرف من ببوس و هرچه مهربانی درباره من داری
از او دریغ و مضایقه نکن. خواهر مهربانم پروین خانم دیگر دنیای عزیزم را از طرف
من سلام برسان آقای [illegible] را سلام برسان و هر کاری داری فقط با ایشان
مراجعه کن و مستحق باش که در صورت امکان انجام خواهند داد. مادر جان
و خانم را از قول من سلام برسان. خدمت آقای صفوی [illegible] سلام بعد عرض
شمی عزیز فردا صبح ساعت ۸ به نیویورک وارد خواهیم شد و پس از یک روز
توقف بطرف بیمارستان حرکت میکنم و از آنجا برایت درد دلهایم را خواهم
نوشت

قربان شمی مهربان دنیا کلام — دست را از راه دور می بوسم — ایرج

نازنین و وفادار همسرم شمسی

دست زیبایت را از راه دور میبوسم. هرچند که تا کنون من چهار نامه و ۲ کارت پستال برایت فرستاده‌ام و هنوز جوابی دریافت نکرده‌ام باز برخود واجب میدانم که درد دل باز بگویم تا شاید عقده‌ای از عقده‌هایم باز شود.

همسر عزیزم مدت سه روز است که وارد ایالت میسوری Missouri شهر St. Louis شده‌ام البته ممکن است سرزنشم کرده و از اینکه چرا تا کنون عریضه‌ای برایت نفرستاده‌ام گله نمائی. ولی نمیدانم خدا یا طبیعت یا قضا و قدر خلاصه هرچه که بخواهی فرض کنی نمیخواهند آب خوشی از گلوی من پائین برود و یک روز را اقلاً با اضطراب و دلهره‌ای کمتر از روز قبل بشام برسانم. نازنینم بیش از این تفصیل نمیدهم و ماحصل کلام اینست و با کمال خجالت باید عرض کنم که چمدانم که کلیه وسائل زندگی حتی اسباب اصلاح می‌بود در ایستگاه نیویورک گم کردم. و تا امروز حیران و سرگردان دنبال آن گشتم و با پلیس و آن متوسل شدم ضمناً چون امیدوار بودم که شاید پیدا شود لذا نمیخواستم با اطلاع دادن این خبر ترا که از آن ناراحتی باز هم ناراحت ترکنم. بهرحال امروز ساعت ۴ بعد از ظهر از ایستگاه ترن بمن خبر دادند که چمدانم پیدا شده و با ترن آورده‌اند.

نمیدانی در این چند روز چه کشیدم فکر کن در مرحله اول از طرف تو ناراحت بودم از آنطرف هم تمام اثاثیه و لوازم زندگی حتی پیراهن و زیرشلوارم را از دست داده بودم نزدیک بود دیوانه بشوم. عزیزم درست است که پول ارزشی ندارد ولی فکر کن شخصی مثل من که از نظر خانوادگی بهایت در حال اضطراب و نگرانیست در اول ورود به یک کشور غریب چنین حادثه‌ای یا بی پولی برایش اتفاق بیافتد چه خواهد شد. حال یکی از رفقایم وعده داده که با اسب و [illegible] فردا صبح با ماشینش عقب من آمده تا باتفاق برویم و چمدان را بگیریم و فکر میکنم که در داخل آن دخل و تصرفی شده باشد باز هم نتیجه را یا در همین نامه و یا نامه بعدی باطلاعت برسانم.

شمسی جان روز یکشنبه ساعت ۲½ از نیویورک با ترن حرکت کردم روز بعد یعنی ساعت ½۱ بعد از ظهر به این شهر وارد شدم. در بین راه مناظر زیبا و دیدنی بسیار بود و در این مدت تقریباً ۲۴ ساعت تمام راه همه‌اش سبزی و درخت و جنگل بود و یک کوه یا تپه مانند جنوب زمین بایر و بیمصرف در تمام راه ندیدم. خود شهر سنت لوئی شهر بسیار زیبا و جالب و دیدنیست. تا کنون من شهرهای زیبائی ندیده‌ام بقدری پارک و سبزکاری و درختکاری دارد که انسان از سبزی سیر میشود. کلیه خانه‌ها و آپارتمانها مردم یک طبقه و حداکثر دو طبقه بوده و دیوار نداشته و اطراف آنها چمن کاری و گلکاریست تمام خیابانها در دو طرف و وسط آن چمن کاری و درختکاری است و در هر گوشه‌ای پارکی زیبا و وسیع قرار دارد شهر بسیار بزرگ به بزرگی شهر تهرانست ولی تعداد ماشینهای سواری آن شاید بیش از ده الی سه برابر اتوبوسهای سواری تهران باشند و همه لوکس و آخرین سیستمند. تاکسی بسیار کم در اینست بطوریکه روز یکشنبه که وارد شدم از ایستگاه ترن تا هتل که تقریباً یک ربع راه بود یک دلار و پنجاه سنت یعنی نزدیک ۱۲ تومان دادم جای تعجب در اینجاست که شهرهای وسعت و عظمت مغازه بسیار کم دارد بطوریکه از چندین خیابانی

که من تا حال عبور کرده‌ام بیش از چند مغازه ندیده‌ام که آنها هم نه تنها اجناس عالی نداشتند بلکه گران هم بوده است
ولی شنیده‌ام که در یک قسمت شهر که بنام downtown نامیده میشود (در امریکا قسمتهائی از شهر را که شلوغ
و بازار و اسلامبول مانند جاهای بنام سیتی مینامند) دارای مغازه‌های زیادتری است و حال که من از موضوع حمل و نقل فراغت
یافته‌ام خیال دارم فردا آنجا بروم. بعد از آن دیگر کمترم رسد که بروم زیرا از سه روز دیگر یعنی اول جولای
کارم شروع میشود و بایستی شروع بکار کنم
از اوضاع و احوال بیمارستان هنوز خوب وارد نشده‌ام بعداً آشنا شده و حتماً برایت مینویسم.
شمسی عزیز و مهربانم خواهشی را که میخواستم برای چندمین بار از تو بکنم اینست که بهیچوجه غصه نخور و در سلامتی خودت حداکثر
بکوش زیرا تمام امید و دلخوشی من اینست که اگر خدای نخواسته تو اندک کسالتی پیدا کنی من چه حالی پیدا میکنم و چگونه
میتوانم از اینجا بتو دسترسی پیدا کنم و هرچند که امیدوارم که خواهرانم حداکثر کوشش را در شادی و سلامتی تو میکنند
ولی باز هم احتیاط را از دست مده و بیخود خودت را ناراحت نکن. شمسی جان تو تنها امید و آرزو و ایده‌آل
من در زندگی هستی. هرچه کوشش و کار میکنم فقط بخاطر شخص تو است من میخواهم تو را در آسایش و نعمت ببینم بلی دارم
میتوانم تو را سعادتمند و خوشبخت کنم. امیدوارم که قدرت آنرا داشته باشم که تو را در برابر دشمنانت موفق و
کامیاب بدارم. شمسی محبوب من، شمسی عزیز من، اینها موقتی و روزهای رنج و درد را تحمل میکنیم خواهش میکنم که
بجای غصه خوردن و غم خوردن دل قوی دار و کوشش کن تا هرچه زودتر وسائل حرکت خودت را فراهم کنی و مرا هم
از این تنهائی وحشت آور نجات دهی. بهم غصه میخورم ولی چون چاره‌ای ندارم غصه نخورم بخاطرم با این هم که در
اینجا بمانم و اگر باراده خودم بود به هیچوجه نرسیده برگشتیم ولی تو عزیزم چاره داری میتوانی بجای غم و اندوه
خوردن کوشش را برای آمدن در پیش گیری.
شمسی جان اولاً برو وزارت فرهنگ و راجع به مدارک تحصیلی خود سرپرس و ببین اگر من میتوانم در اینجا کاری
بکنم فوراً برایم بنویس تا اقدام کنم البته تنها رفتن فایده ندارد و سعی کن هروقت که میروی یک پارتی چه از طرف
خودت و چه از طرف ما به همراهت دنبال وسیله برو (راستی شوهر خواهر ناظم دبستان پروین خانم بنام
آقای شمس در وزارت فرهنگ است و شاید او بتواند کاری انجام دهد یا بتو وسیله شناسائی زیرا او خیلی
آشنا در وزارت فرهنگ دارد و من برایش نامه خواهم نوشت و یا کس دیگر) و همچنین با اداره لندن نامه رفته
(اینها هم بهتر است که پارتی شناسا) و بپرسی که چون شوهرم امریکا رفته آیا من میتوانم با لندن نامه عادی
(نه تحصیلی) بروم و اگر از این راه درست نشد برود ولو مختصر خرجی هم داشته باشد زودتر و راحت‌تر
میتوانی بنتیجه برسی. خلاصه این کار را ول نکن و فکر خرجش را هم نکن و با اینجا را امکن. زیرا برای خرج راحت
اگر تو تا ۴-۵ ماه دیگر میتوانی بیائی اولاً حقوق من در خودت میتوانی مقداری ذخیره کنی و ثانیاً کسانت که
بهتر است در اینموقع کمکی بکنند و اگر نتوانست بکنند بنویس تا من فوراً از اینجا ذخیره بکنم

راجع به نوشتم خلاف شانس در موضوع خرج اینجا هم شمسی اولاً امیدوارم که بیمارستان موافقت کند که اطاقی با دو نفری بدهد
و تازه اگر موافقت نکرد تو فعلاً با خودمان می‌توانی بخوبی زندگی کنی و در این بعد هم کاری پیدا کرده و کمکی باشی.
عزیزم زندگی ارزشی اینقدر ندارد که برای چند ریال هزاران کیلومتر از یکدیگر دور باشیم و ثانیاً اگر در اینجا بمانی
زبان یاد بگیری و شاید بتوانی به تحصیلت ادامه دهی و از نظر فردای فرزندانمان بسیار خوب خواهد بود.
لذا برای آخرین مرتبه تقاضا میکنم که از کوشش در این راه دست برنداشته و مرتباً نتیجه را اطلاع دهی.
ظاهراً موضوع حقوق شمسی دوم و یا سوم مرداد به اداره اجرائی کل قسمت حسابداری (خیابان سوم اسفند
جنب تدارکات) نزد جناب سرهنگ وحید رفته و کاملاً نامه را باو نشان میدهی و منهم تا آن وقت
برایش نامه خواهم نوشت و امیدوارم که در اینباره اشکالی پیش نیاید.
راجع به تغییر نام شناسنامه خودت نامه‌ای نوشته‌ام که نزد آقای شیرازد رفته و اولاً از اینکه برای مراسم
عقد دعوتش نکرده‌ایم عذرخواهی کنی و جریان را بگوئی و ثانیاً بگوئی ایرج حرکتش جلو افتاد و بنابراین عجله داشت
و نتوانست برای خداحافظی بیاید. این نامه را نزد ایشان برده و خواهش کنی که جریان را درست کنند.
نامه دیگر هم جوف است که راجع به رونوشت سال تحصیلی ششم شمسی همراه با دو قطعه عکس و یک برگ رونوشت
شناسنامه‌اش (که هر دو آن نزد خودت است) به اداره دبیرخانه دانشگاه خیابان شاهرضا روبروی
دالبرزا برده و به دفتر میدهی و پس از یکهفته الی ۱۰ روز با دادن ۵۰ ریال آنرا بگیری.
در نامه قبلی برایت عکس نوشتم که حتماً برایم یکی دوتا از عکسهایت را بفرستی البته تاکنون که نامه‌ای از تو نرسیده
امیدوارم که با اولین نامه این خواهش مرا انجام داده باشی.
باز هم توصیه میکنم هر وقت کار اداری داشتی که خودت از انجام آن عاجز بودی به جمال مراجعه کنی و از او
کمک بخواه سلامتی‌ام الحمدلله در خصوص حالا که سه ماه تعطیلی است بتو کمک خواهد کرد. و راستی کمال هم شاید در وزارت
فرهنگ یا اداره لندر نامه آشنا و کسی داشته باشد بنابراین برای اینموضوع باز هم مراجعه کن. خلاصه کمال هم
شمس هست و هرچه که بخواهی با دیگر و هیچ رودربایستی نکن و باو اعتماد و اطمینان داشته باشی.
شمسی حال خواهش دیگری از تو دارم و آن اینست که پس از اینکه حقوق گرفتی باداره روزنامه اطلاعات
رفته و سه ماه یا شش ماه اطلاعات هوائی را آبونه شده و بگوئی که با آدرس من در اینجا بفرستند زیرا
فکر میکنم اگر مرتب از اخبار آنجا با اطلاع باشم بهتر است. اگرچه آن زیاد نبود فعلاً سه ماه آبونه
شو تا بعداً وجه فرستاده و ششماهه یا یکسال آبونه بشویم.
شمسی عزیز و محبوب من آخرین تقاضایم اینست که مرتباً برایم نامه بنویسی. هر چند که تاکنون خبری نرسیده

من امیدوار بودم که بمحض رسیدن به پاریس آن چشمم با دیدن دستخط زیبای تو و قلبم با خواندن نغمه‌های
روحپرور و امیدبخش تو روشن و شاداب خواهد شد ولی متأسفانه چیزی نرسید.
تقاضا میکنم که هفته‌ای دو نامه بنویسی البته اگر بخواهی بطور معمولی بنویسی و تو بنویسی گران تمام خواهد شد و
بهتر است که به پستخانه رفته و از نامه‌هائی که دانه‌ای ۸ ریال است بخری و بنویسی و بفرستی البته انجام
از این نامه‌ها هست و قیمت آن در حدود همان ۸ ریال است من هم گاهی روی آنها برایت نامه مینویسم
و نامه‌هائی که با پست هوائی معمولی مینویسیم مال مملکت ایران یعنی در حدود ۲۵ ریال خرج برمیدارد.
شمسی جان تمام چشمم بطرف تو است که میدانی وقتی یاد من میکنی دلم [illegible] کلمه روحم را شاد میکنی بنابراین
تقاضا میکنم که از این فرصت مرا محروم نکنی و همانطور که گفتم مرتب برایم نامه بنویسی.

شمسی عزیز دیگر از اوضاع خانه ما برایم بنویس که آیا بتو خوش میگذرد در نامه از من چیزی پوشیده
و پنهان نکن و هرچه هست بنویس. از همه بنویس که آیا سلامت هست یا نه و بجای من از او
خداحافظی مواظب و پرستاری کن و دلش را بدست بیاور (البته نه با خوردن الکل و غیره)

حضور مادر بزرگوارم عرض دست بوسی تقدیم. خواهران مهربان و عزیزم پروین و [illegible] و [illegible] سلام زیاد
برسانید و سفارش کن که جواب نامه‌هایم را زودتر بدهند. خدمت آقای [illegible] و کمال و ناصر و کاظم
و خانواده آقای محمدزاده و قریب و سماطی و آقای [illegible] و عزت خانم سلام مرا ابلاغ کن.
از آقاجان و ملاقات و داداشت و حال زاهدیان و وضع زندگی آنها و در رابطه خودت تا الان هر دو را
برایم بنویس تا کاملاً روشن باشم ضمناً آیا اصلاح [illegible] که پیش از این نامه‌ای نوشتیم یا نه.

لبان زیبایت را میبوسم — دوستدار ابدی تو
ایرج

راستی شمسی جان ساعت را بالاخره من نتوانستم و حیف را از ساعت‌ساز
بگیرم و سرگرمی هم از یادم رفت که بتو بگویم بنابراین پس از رفتن او هرچه که فروخته تو و حیف را بگیر و ضمناً مبلغ هم
اطلاع بده که آیا وجه را داده است یا نه
قربان تو — ایرج

This four-page letter was written to me by Iraj on June 27th of 1958, the month in which he left me to go to America. It is not possible for me to translate these letters, nor are there more words to describe all this. I just hope for those who cannot read Farsi, especially my children, to get help from an Iranian friend who can read and understand it well. It is important for my children to know what their parents meant by marrying each other.

5-7-1958 غروب چهاردهم تیرماه ۱۳۳۷

همسر گرامم و عزیزم شمسی

جملات زیبا، عبارات نغز، کلمات دلنشین و امیدبخش نامه‌ات هنوز در نظرم مجسم است
هر آن آنها را بیاد میآورم درباره‌اش فکر میکنم و گاهی با آهنگی شاد زمزمه میکنم. عیدی ای امروز صبح دریافتم چشمم بنامه،
به دستخط زیبا و آشنای تو دوخته شد نمیدانم چه حالی شدم. اگر دقت کرده باشی من کمتر اخلاق کودکانه‌ام را
حفظ کرده‌ام ولی در این لحظه شادی بچگانه‌ای که حاکی از حال ساده دلیم است حس کردم. با خواندن نامه‌هایت
در عالم رؤیا و طرب انگیزی فرو رفته بودم. هر جمله‌ای، هر کلمه از آنها منزله منبع نیروئی از آرزوی و قوت قلب برایم بود.
شمسی عزیز باور کن که داشتم از بیخبری دیوانه میشدم امروز بیست و یکمین روز است که از شماها جدا شده بودم.
در این مدت من هر لحظه که دقیقه‌ای پیدا میکردم یا بهر نقطه تازه‌ای که وارد میشدیم نامه‌ای می‌نوشتم و ارسال میکردم
آگاهیتان میکردم مثلاً انتظار پاسخ داشتم. نامه نامرتبی خوب دیر میرسد واقعاً در تسکین اعصاب و روح
پر التهاب من اثر معجزآسائی داشت. امیدوارم که بعد مرتباً برایم نامه بنویسید و از کل وقایع زندگی مطلعم نمائید
شمسی عزیز نوشته بودی که تاکنون فقط یک نامه دریافت داشته‌اید (بجز این هم) در هر صورت نامه‌هائی را که برایتان نوشته‌ام
مینویسم تا ببینید کدامیک رسیده و کدامیک نرسیده برای ... یک نامه (پاریس - درون کشتی - سویس) - آنجا
دو نامه (پاریس - سویس) بیرون ... سه نامه (پاریس - نیویورک - سویس) برای ... نامه (درون کشتی - سویس)
بنابراین یک نامه و یکی هم همین روزها ارسال میکنیم) حال هر نامه (درون کشتی - سویس) ... که خاطره‌ها را با صورتی همه بیست
نامه البته برای عده‌ای دیگر مثل لطفی و دکتر نوری هم نوشته‌ام. حال مثل اینکه نامه‌های پاریس بدستتان نرسیده نمیدانم
علت آن چیست. خلاصه بعد از این هر نامه‌ای که میرسد در جوابش بنویسید که نامه چه تاریخی رسیده تا من بدانم
کدامیک رسیده و کدامیک نرسیده. و این نامه تو هم مورخ ششم تیرماه است که امروز صبح زیارت کردم.
شمسی عزیز از اینکه عکس زیبایت را فرستاده بودی بسیار ممنون و سپاسگزارم کردی فوراً آنرا با عکس خودم در
قابی که ... خریده و هدیه داده بود گذاشتم بدین ترتیب که یکی از آنها را در یک طرف قاب و دیگری را پهلوی عکس خودم در
بالای تخت قرار دادم و حال هر لحظه که بآن نگاه میکنم چشمم روشن میشود. امیدوارم که همانطور که در نامه قبلی نوشته‌ام
بزیارت عکس خواهران عزیز و مهربانم و مادر گرامم هم نائل شوم. از این محبتشان بی اندازه ممنون و متشکر خواهم شد
اگر خواسته باشند در اینمورد امروز و فردا نکنند تو دادرسان من که اینکار را زودتر انجام دهند.
از اینکه از ماندن در منزل ما اظهار رضایت و خرسندی نموده و از خواهرانم تعریف نموده بودی واقعاً دلشاد و مسرور
شدم. تو شمسی عزیزم میدانستم که در آنجا به خوشی ... میدانستم که آنها خیلی بهتر از من (البته تاکنون که این لیاقت را
نداشته‌ام) از تو نگهداری و حفظ و حراست میکنند. آنها خواهران من مثل من و تو ساده دل و ساده زندگی میکنند
آنها از هر گونه کینه توزی و عداوت و دشمنی بدورند و اگر گاهی برخی احساسات سطحی در نزد دیگر ... بین ایشان
رد و بدل شود از روی هیچگونه غرض درونی نیست. چون حباب صابونی که بر روی سطح آب پدید آید و باد بشود در دیگر قسمتها
در بخشهای آنها هم بی هیچ اثری از بین میرود. واقعاً من با همه ... خواهرانی افتخار میکنم بسیار ... را ابدی
و آنوقت به صفا و سادگی و صمیمیت خودتان بیشتر واقف میشود. سعی کنید که هر روز این رشته‌ها محکمتر و کاملتر و
پردوامتر کنید تو هم هر چه لطف و محبت درباره من داری از آنها مضایقه نکن. تو هم خوب میشناسم و در جواب
وار دهم میدانم که عاشق ... هستی و بیار این احتیاجی نیست بیش از این ...
شمسی عزیزم از اول جدائی یعنی پنج روز قبل شروع شده است واقعاً کار سختی است ... دلم تنگ است بخصوص

This was written to me on May 7th, 1958. It is amazing for someone who hated to write short notes, to write a four-page letter to his love while being sorry that the paper is finished and his words are not. Yes, I think he loved me enough to sit down and wish he was with me. Unfortunately, he didn't know how to make his dreams come true.

که در این محیط ما باید دو نفر باشیم و چون دیگری نیامده پس باید کار او را انجام دهم سی و شش ساعت کار متوالی که اگر ۲ یا ۳ ساعت
خواب داشته باشیم و ۱۲ ساعت استراحت را کسر کنیم این سی و شش ساعت کشیک پشت سر هم نیست بلکه باید راه رفت و کار
کرد و توی اطاق عمل مرتب مشغول عمل کرد بخصوص که آنها هم را برای عمل شسته ام و زخم شده است. البته منهم چون ادعا
میکنم که از زیر کار در بروم همه دوستم دارند و کارها را مرجوع میکنند و الا استراحتم که نصف این کشیک را تحمل کنم از آنجائیکه
میخواهم چیز یاد بگیرم دنبالش نمیخواهم سابقه ام بد شود ولذا از انجام هیچگونه کاری شانه خالی نمیکنم و با کمال میل انجام میدهم
بطور کلی امریکائیها از کسیکه کار بکند خوششان می آید و او را دوست دارند و باید بدنبال سرمشق بنابراین بنحو احسن از این نقطه ضعف
حداکثر استفاده میکنیم

اما راجع بوضع زندگی من البته با رسیدن نامه هایتان حالم خیلی راحت شد و اگر کاملاً رفع نگرانی نشد ولی باید بگویم نگرانی بسیار زیادی تخفیف
یافته که بقیه آن فقط با آمدن تو میسر است. با وضع کاری که خلاص دارم انجام هر گونه تفریح و غیر از آنکه برایم غیر مقدور است
بخصوص که پولی نیست و از اینجا میتوان از این غلط ها رد یک سینما حتی اقلاً ۵ دلار خرج برمیدارد (سه دلار کرایه رفتن و
برگشتن تاکسی و دو دلار بلیط سینما) رفتن به این جشن ها و غیر از آنکه رها خرج دارد مثلاً همینها در روز ۴ جولای روز
جشن استقلال امریکا بود. در هر گوشه ای مسابقه ورزشی و هر جائی کارناوالی برپا بود دلم رفتن آنجا برایم غیر مقدور
زیرا محتاج خرج دو دلار بود (البته وقت داشتم زیرا از ساعت ۵ بعد از ظهر کشیکم تمام شده بود) منهم با مردی یکروز یک
تفریح کم خرجی را انتخاب کردم با پای پیاده رفتن تا نزدیک بیمارستان ما (مقصودم از نزدیک فاصله منزل ما تا کجا است زیرا با پای
پیاده و سه ربع ساعت در راه بودم) پارکی قرار دارد بنام Forest park که از بزرگترین و قشنگترین پارک
این شهر است عرض این پارک ۲/۵ کیلومتر و طول آن هفت کیلومتر (این اندازه ها از روی نقشه حساب کرده ام) که
مدت یک ساعت و سه ربع درون این پارک راه رفتم تازه قسمت اندکی از آنرا دیدم ولی چون بیشتر ساختمانها در این
آن یعنی بفاصله تقریباً دو کیلومتری از جنب خیابان فاصله دارند نتوانستم ببینم. اولا این پارک تپه و ماهورها و
پستی و بلندیهای آن هیچگونه دست کاری نشده و همان شکل و فرازهای طبیعی خود را دارد و در تمام وسعت پارک عظمت
چمن کاری و درخت کاری شده و بطوریکه بجز جاده ها که موجب زیبائی کثیری است پیدا نیست. خیابانها هیچوقت راست و
مستقیم نیستند بلکه خیلی مرتب و کج و معوج (بقول بریکها مدرن) هستند و سعی شده است از هر لحاظ
حالت طبیعی خودش را حفظ کند. در درون این پارک بیش از ۱۰ استخر نظیر استخرهای تهران پارک وجود دارد که
رودهائی که از هم زیر یک سقف زده و تمام سقف پوشیده از چراغهای الکتریکی است و بخصوص تماشات البته
بلیطی است. یک اپرای بسیار مجلل و بزرگ که ساختمان اپرائی را که میخواستند در تهران بسازند نیمی آن چیزی
در کنار این پارک قرار دارد. یک باغ وحش به وسعت ۲۰۰ متر مربع وجود دارد در اطراف این باغ وحش انواع درختهای
بزرگ چون خرما و غیره وجود دارد و در وسط آن ساختمان یک دهکده قدیمی با تمام اوضاع و آداب آن را از آن
نشان داده شده مثلاً آسیاب بادی یا با دست چرخاندن آسیاب احتمالاً آب سیم و غیره. بقدری میدان ورزشی
با تمام ادوات ورزشی در این پارک موجود است که حساب آن مشکل است و چون جشن استقلال امریکا
بود در هر گوشه یک شیء آمده بودند. در یکجا عده ای نفر پرستار دور هم جمع شده و شبیه یک شب نشینیهای دسته جمعی
ما را تشکیل داده بودند (ولی باید اعتراف کرد که آن روح خلوص و صفا و گرمی که در آن جمع بود در این شهر هیچ
اصلا وجود نداشت). و در گوشه ای دیگر ... پرستار اجتماع کرده و همان ساعت آنها را که اضافه کرده (از اینجا
کاملاً اختلاف بین سیاه و سفید پوستان بچشم میخورد) درست است که سیاهان هم از همه وسائل زندگی
ثروت و اتومبیل و یخچال و غیره برخوردارند ولی تا کامل سیاه پوست و سفید پوست را با هم در حال معاشرت

وحتی حرف زدن نه بوده‌ام) خلاصه عبور و مرور در دل این پارک از لحاظ آدم صفر بلکه من تنها آدمی بودم که پیاده میرفتم ولی
از نظر وسائل نقلیه تردد فوق العاده زیاد بود (دقیقه‌ای سه عیب بزرگ آنهم همین است زیرا آن محیط ساکت دارایم را از بین
میبرد). خلاصه ساعت ۹ ½ خسته و کوفته پس از ۲ ½ ساعت پیاده روی به خانه مراجعت کردم. برای در دل این
پارک یک باغ وحشی وجود دارد که ساختمان و غارهای بتونی آنرا عینا کوه‌ها درست کرده ساخته‌اند و انسان از دور خیال
میکند که در وسط این باغ چند کوه از کجا آمده است ولی در وسط آن قفس‌ها نیست. البته امروز چون تعطیل بود
باغ وحش هم بسته بود والا بلیط آنجا را میگرفتم و میرفتم به بینم زیرا گویا به دیدنش بسیار می‌ارزد
تمام دکترهائی که توی این بیمارستان کار میکنند ماشین دارند و هیچیک هم بعد از ساعت ۵ (بجز آنهائی که کشیک هستند) در بیمارستان
نمی‌مانند و فقط من تنها بوده‌ام و گاهی عصری یک گردش نیم ساعتی در جاهای اطراف میکنم البته برای من هم مسلم هست که ماشین بخریم
ولی با این زودی و حد اکثر تا یکسال دیگر چنین تصمیمی ندارم و خرید اتومبیل را موکول با آمدن تو میکنم
اما از نظر مادی وضع من فعلا چندان رضایت بخش نیست زیرا همانطور که نامه برای تو نوشتم چهل دلار از پلیس را تقاضای قرض
کردم و علاوه بر آن بیمارستان برای ما [illegible] خریده (دو دست کت و شلوار سفید و یک شلوار اضافه با پیراهن)
که قرار است پول آنرا از حقوق ماهانه کسر کنند بنابراین تمام آنچه که از حقوق این ماه من چیزی باقی نمانده زیرا ما هر دو هفته به دو هفته
حقوق میگیریم و با ۸۰ هر دو هفته‌ای ۷۰ دلار میگیریم (که ماهی ۱۴۰ دلار میشود) ولی از این ۷۰ دلار ۱۴ دلار آنرا
بابت مالیات کسر میکنند و ۵۵ دلار باید بدهند البته میگویند که آخر سال این مالیات را پس میدهند و فقط مقدار
ناچیزی از آن را برنمیدارند و من هنوز این موضوع را سالم نمیدانم زیرا اگر اینطور باشد خیلی خوب است و اکثرا پولها پس داده شده است
البته من اینجا هیچگونه خرجی نداشته‌ام و فقط خیال دارم که یک مقداری سیگار بگیرم ولی از کجا تا اول پول خواهم داشت و اینکه در هر صورت بایستی
و شاید یک ذخیره‌ای داشته باشم که شاید برای روزهای بیاید بدرد بخورد. اما برای ۵۰ تومان تا روز اول قرار گذاشته خودم از آقای
صفوی بگیرم و حتی ساعت ۱۰ ½ در بانک قرار داشتیم که ایشان را ببینم که نیامدند و همین ۵۰ تومان دیگرم هم از پیش
نداده چون میگفت مثلا ما ۲۴۰ دلار از محمودهم بابت بیمه و با ۲۵ تا ۲۴۰ دیگر بیمه ۴۰ تومان گرفتم و نقشه پولها را بر اساس و غیره کردم
خلاصه بعد از ظهر آقای صفوی سر رفتن گفت که پول را به شما میدهم من چون دیگر تا چند روز دیگر حقوق میگیرم و احتیاجی
ندارم از خرجی خواهرم پیدا این برای ۲۴۰ تومان قسط دادم و بسیار [illegible] ۲۰۰ تومان بابت آن به هم کارم گفتم نه
بابت قرضم نخواهم داد که اصلا نفهمید سرش شلوغ شده که از یادم رفت ولی هم نمیشود هم نخواهم این موضوع را بگویم
البته اسم عوض کنیش برادرم حال اگر لازم داری و خواهم پول داشته باشم هر چه زودتر از ایشان بگیرد اگر لازم نداری که بگذار بابت
قرضشان باشد البته نتیجه را من اطلاع بده. در ثانی شما حال تو هم حدا‌کثر سعی کن که سعی کنید را در صرف خرجی نکنی زیرا
آمدنت فقط ۲۰۰۰ تومان کرایه میخواهد و سعی کن که بتوانی این پول را تا آنجا که مقدور است در جائی نگهداری و خرج نکنی و
ضمنا پولی را که من در اینجا ذخیره میکنم برای روز مبادا باشد البته اگر توانستی بنویسی تا کمبود را هر چه که هست برایت
فوری بفرستم خلاصه از نظر پول برای آمدنت تأخیر نکن
برای آمدنت سفارشهائی در نامه قبلی کردم که دیگر اینجا تکرار نمیکنم فقط میگویم که خودت بخشید در این مورد اگر صلاح بدانی
از دائی جانت و آقای شهرستانی کمک بخواه و اگر لازم شد از جانب من بنویس تا من برای آنها نامه بنویسیم و حتی المقدور نظرشان
را جلب کن. و راستی اول ماهی ۵۰۰ تومان پول بگیری و ۱۰۰ تومان منزل بدهی و بقیه را باید پس‌انداز کنی و هیچگونه خرجی
نکنی و حتی لباسی برای خودت نخری و تا موقع آمدنت از همان لباسهائی که داری استفاده کن زیرا که اینجا تو خواهی خرید
[illegible] لازم نیست که کلاس انگلیسی بروی زیرا اولا همانطور که من چیزی یاد نگرفتم تو هم یاد نخواهی گرفت و آنچه که
انگلیسی اینجا بخوانی اینجا هیچ بدرد نمیخورد و از زمینی تا آسمان با هم فرق دارند و باید برای پاک کردن را پیدا کنی

دیروز عزیز، خواهرم هم از رفتن و آمدن به اینجا را از نامه‌ات شان بگو بجای رفتن کلاس انجمن ایران امریکا برنامه را هم گرفته
بهتر است زیرا آنچه را که در ظرف ۳ سال یاد بگیرند و هیچ به دردشان نخورد در اینجا در ظرف ۳ ماه یاد بگیرند.
از وضع ترتیل و رفتاری که آنها با تو کرده بودی نوشته بودی واقعاً شرم‌آور و خجالت‌آور است ولی با این حال بروی خودت نیاور
و هر دقیقه که به محض مراجعت از شیراز اول مرتب به برنامه‌ات برو و در نامه‌ای برای من بنویس که چه نوع مراجعت کرده‌ای با آنان
نامه بنویسیم. همین نقشه را هم از برای آقای لوسوی نامه بنویسیم و چون از رستاخیز آمده‌ام با دیدن تو خواهم نوشت لطفاً
با ایشان در سال ... موضوع عزت را هم با زبرد بخواب بیاور و با اگر از همین باشی دنیا همین جور است مردم از زمان
همینطور هستند و اگر انسان نخواهد با هم بنشیند و بجنگد دائم با همه‌شان در جنگ است با این آدمها خوب بودن و دنیا و زندگی
لعنتی همین ارزش این حرفها را ندارد. مثلاً که تو راحت در کار سالش هی بگذار هرچه میخواهند بگویند هرچه بگویند بگو
درست میگوئید من اشتباه کردم ولی بعد از این سعی میکنم که اشتباه نکنم. خلاصه اگر آنها نفهم و نادان هستند تو عاقل و دانا باش
و بیخود و بیجهت روزگارت را ضایع مکن و غصه مخور و خودت را ناراحت مکن.
راستی درباره آمدنت سعی کن که بتوانی از حقوقت استفاده بکنی یعنی با یک نقشه حساب شده ... بتوانی خرج معاش خود
خدمت باشد ... البته مشکل است و باری طاقت میخواهد ولی تو هم جدیت کن که بتوانی انجام دهی و اگر هم نتوانستی
مانعی ندارد و شاید این موضوع باعث انصراف از آمدنت بشود. میبینی که خواهم ... و موضوعات را یک دفعه
ولی حالا نتوانستم بنویسم و تکه تکه می‌نویسیم. در موقع جواب دادن به نامه‌هایم لطفاً آنها را جلویت بگذار و یک یک موضوعاتی که
اشاره کرده‌ام جواب بده تا در مرتبه مجبور نباشم در نامه‌های بعدی آنها را تکرار کنم. البته طبیعه آقدامات را که برای
آمدنت میکنی و نتیجه آنها را از کل و جزء بنویس و مرا مطلع کن.
از اینکه نتوانسته‌ام هدیه خوب و جالب توجهی برایتان بفرستم ... میخواهم ترا خلاف تصور عموم اینجا هیچ چیز جالب
توجه و خوبی وجود ندارد و همین اشیاء هم به قدری گران است که ... البته میدانستم که از پارس با پیروزی ... ترا ... کرده‌ام
مخصوص پارس چیزهای خوب و ارزان هست ولی متأسفانه ... قرض بدهد. امیدوارم که ... بتوانم ... را
جبران نمایم. بسته را روز پنجشنبه ۱۲ تیرماه به پست انداختم و البته اینجا کمی رسید تا آنجا ... رسیده
و در نامه‌ای میخواستم ... در همین موضوع هم ... آنها را ... ولی آنها ... و ... ها
را فقط ... داخل امریکا ... اگر میدانستم ... اصلاً ... آنها را ... تا شما ... حال
... خاطرم ... اینجا ... هر وقت رسید ... روی دیگری ... است ... اینجا
... خوش شود.
نوشته بودی که ... هرچه ... کدام ... هیچ چیز ... رسید ... از آمدن ... در
... درست ... سبیل خود ... کردم همان ... سبیل ... اینجا ... بیرون ... سبیل ... اعتبار
درست است ... سبیل ... حال ... آنها
... است ... هم ... حال ... عمل
عمل است ... فردا ... اشتغال به تحصیل ... سبیل بگذارم
ببر ... (سهم ... کاغذ خواهم نوشت) دیگر ... اداره ... امریکا ... اصفهان
... اداره ... بدهد ... اگر شد ... اداره ... کدام اشتغال به تحصیل ... تعریف
... اطلاع ... موضوع با سایر موضوعهائی که در نامه‌های قبل ... ام ... نتیجه
... عزیز ... خودت ... بچه‌ها ... اگر ... باشی ... ارزانتر
... بیشتر ... بنویسیم ... ساعت
... ساعت ۶ ... خواهران عزیز ... را از طرف من ببوس. جناب
... عزیز ... کلمه ... را از طرف من سلام برسانید. از ... و خدیجه خانم و ... آقای
علاءالدین ... سلام ... حضرت ... صفوی ...
و ناصر خان ... سلام ... آقای ... حضرت خانم ... از طرف من سلام برسانید

... عزیز ... از ... نامه ... امضاء

Neia's husband was still in prison. And even though I knew all along that she was against my marriage to her brother, she had never been rude to me. And as the year went by and she realized that my love for her brother was genuine, she became much nicer, and she acted more respectfully towards me. I believe that Neia was a very loving wife, good mother, and a good-hearted person. And I knew that she didn't get what she had really deserved.

Okay, my dear GOD. I know you been a witness to everything, and that there is no need to explain anything for you. But I have to admit to you that there were times that I doubted your existence. And the reason for my doubts mainly was that if GOD created us, he had obviously created our characters as well. Correct me please if I am wrong. I think we were born with our characters as part of our physical existence. But personality I think that it is the learning and adapting ourselves within the world in which we live. I hope I am right about this. So if you create us with a specific character, how do you expect people to be able to change it.

My Dear GOD:

Anyway, I've come to a conclusion that since I can't change things that I have been born with, then it is not my fault the way that I think sometimes. That way of thinking is your creation also. But one thing is so obvious to me that I can swear on it and that's that, if it wasn't for your support and guidance that came to my rescue and kept me from wrongdoing, I wouldn't be where I am today. You stopped me from falling on my face and I thank you for that.

So the first year of my marriage circumstances brought me my father-in-law and my three sisters-in-law under one roof. They each had completely different personalities and different characters. As a teacher I had some of my own income. Sarvan Rafani had his retirement money, which wasn't much. Pari and Neia were both teaching and going to school at the same time. And Parveen, while she was going to school to become a teacher, was knitting baby clothes for sale. We all recognized our responsibilities, and we were very committed to them.

There was another funny incident had happened to us as on our way back from Kordestan. We saw an older man hitchhiking. Mehdi Agha asked us if it was okay to pick the poor man up. And although there was no more room in the car, we decided to make room for him. So we stopped, and he jumped in the front seat next to window. He had a suit and tie on. We realized the moment we started talking to him that the poor guy was drunk. He wasn't just drunk but he was acting very funny. We didn't travel very far yet, when this poor guy's hat blew out of the window, which did not have any glass on. Our

laughter, which had began when he first got into the car became completely out of control at that point. He tried to get his hat back through the window but it was too late. When we stopped to see if we could find his hat, we realized that it had already flown over the mountains. We felt very sorry for him but that didn't help him out at all. He got out of the car and refused to ride with us after that. But thanks to him we laughed so much that day that we will never forget it.

Pari and Kamal were both teaching and going to university at the same time. They were thinking to rent a house near the university and move out. But before they moved out, Pari started bleeding heavily. Pari and I were very close and she could talk to me openly. I found out that she was pregnant, and that her bleeding was a sign of a miscarriage. I tried to inform Parveen, who was not talking to Pari, and asked her to call Kamal and get a doctor. They did not want their father to find out. Although she was married, he still did not allow her to get pregnant while she was in her father's house. So I tried to keep it as quiet as possible. But Sarvan Rafani was no dummy; you couldn't fool him easily. Pari's bleeding was so heavy that no matter how many sheets we changed, the next one would be covered with blood in no time. We had to take her to the hospital or else she would have died. Thanks GOD Parveen decided to come and help Pari, and decided to forget about the fight they had in Kordestan. Anyway we put her in a taxi and took her to the hospital.

My Dear GOD:

You can imagine what was going on through our minds after what had happened to her mother in the hospital, Luckily the intern, who had examined her knew Iraj, so he paid special attention to her. Between him and the doctor on call, they took care of her problem and sent her home later.

While she was still at the hospital, I came home. Her father was standing by the door. I am sure he had heard everything that happened in the room next to his bedroom. He even realized that we had taken her to the hospital. When I saw him he was talking to himself in a very loud voice. He asked me what hospital I had taken her to. I pretended that I didn't know, since they had all asked me earlier to not let their father know anything about Pari's bleeding. So I simply answered, "I don't know".

At that time he became furious. He started calling everybody bad names and was getting ready to go to the hospital to kill someone. By then they all came home and they were able to calm him down. Parveen immediately started questioning me as to whether I had told him what had happened. I told her that there was no reason for me to tell him. He had heard everything from his room and he was the one who asked me which hospital she was at.

Anyway, they quieted him down and promised him that they were in the process of moving into their own house. They did move into their own apartment shortly after. Pari was raised in the same manner in which I was raised. She was used to a house full of people. In her new apartment, even during the daytime she was scared to be alone. I went there to see her one afternoon after school. I found her under a blanket when I came in. It seemed like she was hiding under that cloth. I started joking around with her, we made tea and like always we made my visit a happy one. This was near the time that I was preparing to go to the U.S.A. We used to spend lots of time together. We both were very talented and creative. We didn't have enough money to buy everything for ourselves. So we tried to make many of the things we wanted. For instance Pari used to make lipstick and rouge using Vaseline, turmeric and other stuff. We used to tailor together and make our own clothes. I decided to make a bedspread for her wedding because she was my best friend. I bought soft yellow satin with yellow ribbon for the edges and finishing seams. Not to be modest, I believe that I did a fantastic job.

My Dear GOD:

My feelings for Pari were genuine. And I truly believed that her feelings for me were mutually deep. Not only did we have so much in common, but also we always had so much fun when we were together. I remember that when I was in their apartment and they wanted me to spend the night; they would ask me to sleep in their bed. There was only one bedroom and one king size bed. (In Iran it is customary to treat your guests better than you treat yourself.) They continued to insist adamantly no matter how much I denied their offer. (Again, in Iran, sleeping in the sleeping bag or just a mattress on the floor is very common.) I didn't want to sleep on the bed with Pari while Kamal would sleep on the floor. And it was so obvious that I didn't want Pari to sleep on the floor because then Kamal and I would have to sleep on the bed together and that was a no-no. They didn't want me to go home that late at night. And they didn't want me to sleep on the floor. So after much laughter and thanks to their persistence, we had all agreed to share the bed. I slept on one side of Pari and Kamal slept on the other side. There was enough space for all of us to sleep comfortably. But this subject later became a good source for Kamal's teasing material. For the rest of our lives, he told everyone that he had slept with me on one bed. He was right about the sleeping on one bed. But he was wrong about me sleeping with him. He used to tease Iraj a million times with, "I have slept with your wife in one bed!"

Pari was the only person in my life that I called a friend. Not only I loved her as a friend, but also when she became my sister-in-law, I loved her even more. I'll never forget the times when I was in the USA I was feeling very homesick for the first few months. And

one day I started crying to Iraj wondering why Pari had not written to me. Iraj started laughing and said, "Are you crazy? She might not be even thinking of you and here you are crying for her". He didn't understand that Pari was not just my sister-in-law; she was a real sister to me as well. And yet as good as she was, there were times I couldn't understand her behavior towards me. Some people might call it jealousy, but I didn't understand why there would be any reason for her to be jealous of me.

My Dear GOD:

Once, when we were all living in Iran with Iraj and our children, Mary and Maseeh, Iraj got me a salon quality hair dryer for my birthday. That was quite an expensive item back then. When Pari saw the gift she said, "Iraj didn't want to pay for you to go to beauty salons, so he got you this gift to get rid of all other beauty expenses he would have to make later". I didn't get her reasoning, because I continued to go to beauty salons any time I wanted to. So what she said wasn't a joke, and it wasn't some sort of pleasantry either. I felt like she was trying to instigate a conflict between Iraj and me. I did not respond to her comment, and I have never mentioned it to anyone else.

These sorts of statements and events took place quite often. These emotions seemed very strange, especially coming from Pari, since she was the one who did many nice things for me. In particular, she would usually buy me many lovely gifts. I generally felt very lucky to have her as my sister-in-law and a friend. Even if in the end she did things that I would have never expected from her. I have no idea why she did those things.

While I was living in their house, at one point I heard that my father was sick. One afternoon I went to see him. My whole family acted as if they didn't know me. My father was lying down on his bed. I kissed his hand and sat by his side. He was angry with me and complained, "Why didn't you wait to come after I was dead!" I was very embarrassed and didn't want to argue with him. I didn't want to tell him that it was he who had thrown me out of his house. So I just sat there and apologized.

Okay, my dear GOD, I have been trying to put all my memories behind me and not to ever think about such times. But when I talk about it, all the memories start to flood back. When I left home my sister Saideh was only six years old. She was so dear to me because I took care of her as if she was my own baby. When we were having a good relationship, and Iraj was still welcome to visit, he would let Saideh play with his hair. She would bring a comb and water to style it. I used to make her dresses and take her shopping and to school. So when I was separated from her like that, it was a disaster for me. I wasn't allowed to go near that house. Better yet, after all the humiliation they put me through when they threw me out of that house, why should I want to go and visit? And yet I sat there and didn't say anything. Many years later Saideh told me how much she had

missed Iraj and me. And she didn't understand why we never came by after our marriage.

Anyway, so I ended up going there at that time, and I paid my respect to my father because I felt it was my duty after all. My family knew something about Iraj that I didn't know at the time. Good or bad, that was my destiny and I didn't have any choice but to follow. And when I follow something it does become my choice.

With each letter I received from Iraj, I realized that it was getting closer and closer to my departure from my home/my life/my family and I was supposed to replace all those things with Iraj and only Iraj. He was my whole life at that time. I was blind and couldn't see. I was deaf I couldn't hear. I was mute and couldn't talk. There was nothing in the world but Iraj. I used to read stories about kings who gave up their kingdoms just to get to their lover. I wasn't in-love to be just romantic. I was in love to give my whole existence to him. Nothing mattered to me but Iraj. So, while in the back of my mind it was very painful to give up everything, the desire of having Iraj was still worth giving my life for. Whether it was right or wrong, I was ready to do it. I didn't know where I was going or what was happening to me. I was following Iraj, and his promises were the only assurance that I counted on. And because I was completely honest with him, I thought there was no reason for Iraj to be dishonest with me.

My Dear GOD:

I remember some stories that make me laugh. I think my father ran out of ideas to try and stop me from marrying Iraj. One day he asked Iraj, "Why are you interested in Shamci?" And then, in front of me, he started to list my handicaps to Iraj. He said, "Shamci doesn't know how to cook, she doesn't know how to treat people, or how to be a housewife. And she is not even beautiful".

Then Iraj, whose face had turned red said, "You might be right, but I want to marry her and not you". I can only imagine now what my poor father went through that night.

Anyways, Iraj continued to persist that I join him in America. In every letter he asked me to go and get my visa. He showed extensive concern in me. He asked me to go to the same person who did his visa. He wanted to know whether my parents had changed their minds and had accepted me. He wanted to make sure that I was comfortable. His letters were always full of understanding, passion, love, and concern. While he wanted so badly for me to reconcile with my parents, he still tried to make up for the place of my father, mother, and the rest of my family. Although he made very little money with his internship, he promised me that he would make my life the happiest it could be.

At that time I was supporting myself with my teaching money and I hated the idea of losing my job. I was supposed to leave my country, my job, my home and my family to go to a life of uncertainty. I was going to go to the other side of the world just to be with Iraj, the person who I thought was my GOD.

My dear GOD, please forgive me if I say things that are not proper. The same goes for the fact that I always used to ask improper questions like, “Where is GOD and why does he do what He does?” Or other similar questions, “Where am I and where am I going? How do I leave my family? What will happen to me when I leave?” I was in such a state of uncertainty that I didn’t know what to do or what to think. And just as Iraj worried about me, I would also worry about something horrible happening to him. I was afraid that he would be utterly overworked. In those days hospitals didn’t get enough residents, and so all the residents, including Iraj, sometimes had to work up to thirty-two hours straight. One time he got a severe chest pain, and was hospitalized. Of course he didn’t tell me any of this at the time. They ran some E.K.G. on him; they did a blood test, along with some other necessary tests. Luckily it was nothing to be concerned about. He got back to work after few days of rest. By the time he informed me about the incident, he was feeling well again, and he was back to work. He said his illness had been caused by the stress of continuous work.

My Dear GOD:

Despite all the uncertainties involved, I was still determined to go and be with Iraj for the rest of my life. I took the steps to go see the same agent who got Iraj his visa. He started to work on my file and asked me to provide him with the necessary paperwork. The funny thing about men is that they would try to take advantage of you once they feel your vulnerability. That agent knew that we were victims of circumstances. He started off by being friendly with me and promising me that there wouldn’t be any problems involved with me getting my visa. But when it got closer to the time when I was due to receive my visa he began offering me rides home. At first I didn’t think it was a big deal but after two or three rides, I realized that he was trying to find a way to get something in return. Besides, I was afraid it would be a source of gossip for my neighbors and I didn’t like that prospect. I wrote to Iraj and told him that I knew what the agent had in his mind, but I assured him that without hurting the agent’s feelings I had stopped taking rides from him. And meanwhile I made him understand that I was not one of those girls that would make myself easily available for a guy. But Iraj started worrying and sending me letter after letter telling me what to do or where to go or how to act or do things. I assured him that I had taken care of everything, and that there was nothing to worry about.

Summer was approaching, and I was supposed to get ready to leave. The school district asked me for my resignation. Although the amount of money from my teaching job was not substantial, it was still enough to support me. I had experienced for the first time what it was like to make money for myself from my own job. It was thoroughly satisfying and I was enjoying the feeling of self-reliance. Now I had to let it go. I had to officially put it in writing that I did not want to have that job anymore. I had to let go of both my pride and my security. I had so many doubts in my mind. In our culture and within Iranian society, teaching was the most respectful job a woman could hold. I kept wondering, "What should I do?" What could I possibly do? It was with that money that I had been able to pay for Iraj's ticket.

Anyway, I had to resign and so I did. After the school season was over, I bought a one-way ticket to go to U.S., and to look for my destiny. The last few letters from Iraj were all orders to do this or that, to go here or go there. He would remind me not to forget this or that. On top of that he would send me a storehouse full of love and kisses and tell me that he couldn't wait to see me. Iraj's sisters and his father had been so good to me. I hated the very thought of leaving them.

The night that I left Tehran, Iraj's father came to the airport with me. Iraj's sisters did not want to bring him along. Since the plane was leaving at around 5 a.m., Sarvan Rafani knew that if he fell asleep no one would have awoken him. So, in the same manner that he would keep his army coat on, he lie down and put his arms under his head so as not to fall asleep. He stayed that way all night in our room, and at three a.m. he was ready to go to the airport with us. Unfortunately that was the last time I ever saw Sarvan Rafani. Every time I think of him, his memory is always delightful and greatly appreciated.

* * *

We got married in June of 1958, and he left for US two weeks later. The last few letters I had received from him before I left Iran were all about renting a house away from troubled areas. He was trying so hard to make me feel at home when I joined him. His last letters were always very apologetic for all that he had made me go through. He admired my loyalty, patience, devotion and pure love for him. He promised me that soon there would never be any suffering in store for me again.

My Dear GOD:

He was telling me that no one in the world can love as much as you do. He wanted me to believe him that he will do anything in his power to make me comfortable for the rest of my life. Most of the times I would get mad at myself, why do I make him feel this way. The more he apologized for problems and discomfort he made me, the more I loved him to death.

In one of his letters he said, "if it wasn't for your encouragement, probably I am with you at this time and never thought of going away from you again". Or on the other letter

he said, " you have been a friend and lover to me that with all the troubles that I caused you during all those years of friendship, you never complained, or made me feel bad about myself".

I didn't know any English word except the classic English that I learned in High School. He was worried about me that I might miss my plane by not understanding the pilot and his crew. With all the recommendation and guidance, still the unexpected happened.

I always get sick in any motion, especially airplane. Not only do I have to take pills, but I could not understand any single word of what they were saying inside the plane. We had one exchange in Chicago but we were delayed. The flight attendant had explained to the passengers that because of the delay, we have missed the connecting flight. So the passengers for St. Louis, Missouri, will be taking the later plane which is leaving in the evening flight.

Obviously, I didn't hear one word of what has been said. Either I was asleep or I just could not understand one word of their English. It was such a horrible feeling for me. All this time Iraj was trying to tell me to be sure not to get lost. And here I am lost after all. I didn't know where I was. I didn't understand anybody and no one could understand me. The flight attendants gathered around me to inform me what was going on. And because I was so tired and sick from the flight I couldn't open my eyes. Finally, with the little English that I knew, I told them that I couldn't understand what they were trying to tell me and that I only speak Farsi. One of the flight attendants thought of something and went to the information desk to call one of the employees who can speak Farsi. And the employee talked to me in Farsi so I understood what happened.

The man explained to me that I was already late for my connecting flight so the next flight will be in the evening. He also told me that they have informed my husband of everything. They booked to the nearest hotel so I can take a nap while waiting for my evening flight. Then they will come again to take me to the airport.

Oh my GOD. I was so relieved. I was able to think again. I knew that Iraj was very worried but when I was informed that he got the news of my late arrival I felt better and fell asleep.

My dear GOD, after what I went through for almost seven years, this incident was only a sweet topping on my cake. As they said they came on time and woke me up to go to my next flight. As usual, I didn't remember the whole trip because I was sleeping. When I arrived there, my Iraj, my love, my life, and my destiny was waiting for me. At last we were together again, and no one but no one could ever separate us from each other. (Well this was my feelings at that moment).

My Dear GOD:

You know my dear GOD, I think life is just a simple joke. All the time that we were together, Iraj was dreaming of having a black car. Guess what? He drove me home in his black Dodge built in 1938, I think. He was feeling like a king in his limousine. He was so proud of what he had done for me in our one year of separation. As he promised me, he rented a nice one-bedroom apartment on the sixth floor of the building complete with bathroom, kitchen, living room and other amenities. At that time, it was the greatest achievement in our lives. With the money that he was making, renting a house like this was very important to him. There were a couple of married doctors who were living a few blocks from us, who were both earning money, but, they had only rented one small room with the standing up bed, and they had to share the bathroom with the other occupants. Every morning, they had to line outside the bathroom with their towels on their arm and wait for their turn. Iraj was very glad that was able to rent this house for me. Obviously, I was happy and proud to see my dearest and sweetest person of my life; had appreciated my love and had tried to keep me dignified in our married life. And then I tried to show him my appreciation too. I loved him in a way that I worshipped my GOD.

We were the only married couple among twelve Iranian residents and interns. While I have been lucky to be able to get what I wished for, I was becoming homesick, and feeling very lonely. I used to be in a society of teachers and be with people. What happened to my large family? Where are the people who knew me? Please GOD help me. Iraj was the only person I wanted to be with. He is here next to me. He is doing everything in his power to make me happy. Why am I feeling this way? Why can't I put myself together?

I started to cook and do things to keep my mind off the homesickness. But there was not much to do. All those Iranian residents came to our house almost every night to get rid of our homesickness. Most of them get drank, and some of them used drugs also. But thanks GOD, my Iraj was not involved with any of those things. I remember once in Iran he was supposed to meet me and when I sat next to him I smelled cigarettes on his clothes. I questioned him and he said, "this evening, I hanged up my coat where people were smoking that's why it smelled like cigarette". I told him to stay away from these things because they can ruin his or my life. He promised me that it won't ever happen. I had great trust on him and I wanted to keep it like that for the rest of our lives together. I believed that the only essential rule for lasting love between two people is trust and only trust. And if once one of them lied and trust was broken, automatically love will die. So I knew that Iraj would not lie to me. And this made my love for him stronger.

Like us, those residents were lonely and homesick too. After work, they went from place to place to look for Iranian food and Farsi language. Although Iraj was younger than some of them, they respect him and most of the time they went to him for help. He was always there for them, and tried so hard to guide them in any way especially about

alcohol and drugs. I was truly proud of him.
And I was always proud of my selection of the best husband in the world.

My Dear GOD:

Ok my dear GOD. These are what I was feeling then. You remember the whole thing. You remember the kind of fulfillment that I had with having Iraj next to me and being his wife. Did I ever think of Iraj becoming a different man in my life? Never! We did not have anything at all, but we had each other and we felt that we were the richest couple on earth. We had the whole world in our hands.

He bought his Dodge for fifty dollars and it was running good. Yes my dear GOD. Fifty big dollars!

It was very expensive to pay fifty dollars for a car when your whole income in a month was one hundred dollars only. That car was worth more than the other car that he bought years later when his income was two hundred thousand dollars per year.

During the time that I was in war with my parents over getting married to Iraj, I could never picture the reality of being away from my parents. I could never picture the emptiness that I was facing at that time. I was drained and lifeless. Probably, if it wasn't for way that I separated from my parents, I would have been able to handle my homesickness differently.

For the first six months of my arrival to the U.S, every morning I would sit by the breakfast table and cried so hard. I didn't know what I wanted. I didn't know what to do; I didn't know why those tears were not drying up. I started to see the image of my family at night or in the day. Once when Iraj was at work, I heard my sister Ezzat calling. I ran to the door thinking she was behind the door. I opened the door but no one was there. I looked around but I didn't see anyone. I swear I heard her voice and saw her shadow. I started to getting worried. What was happening to me? The only family I used to write and had relationship with was my sister, Ezzat. I was writing about my feelings and my sadness. At the time of craziness and foolishness, I had asked Iraj that, "even if I wanted to get in touch with my family, you must stop me". He knew that my problem was my family so he asked me if agree to reconcile with them. He told me that, "now that we already made it, it is okay to write your father a letter of friendship". I agreed. Later on, I got a letter from Ezzat who opened my mind.

Her letter came after I wrote her my idea of returning to Iran. She was very upset with me. She told me that, "for eight years you fought your parents and your sisters and brothers. You wanted so much to be with Iraj, even if takes you to hell. Now that he has been taking you to heaven, please start thinking and understand your situation. At this time in Iran, you don't have your job anymore. Your parents disowned you and you don't have any place to stay. And I don't think with no money, you would be welcome to you sister-in law's house. So please think about it. Stop being negative! Your family does not

always stay with you. And for that matter, no one stays with you forever. Even if they don't want to leave you, most of the time nature will separate them from you. If you do not wake up now, the time will come that you will be sorry and find out that the door of all possible opportunities on you have closed.

My Dear GOD :

The move of Iraj towards, friendship with my parents, and the letter of my sister Ezzat, was enough to teach me a lesson. It was good enough to open my eyes.

Although Iraj was doing everything in his power to make me happy I remember two sentences that he told me during those times. Once we were walking in a park and talking about life and our happiness. When we lay down on the grass he sighed and said "it is so funny. People might think I have reached my ultimate goal in life." I asked "do you think you are not?" He did not say anything. And once we were talking while he was shaving. He turned to me and said "you can't have a baby also". To me that meant, I had other problems, plus not being able to bear him a baby. Now that I think back, I think that he wasn't too truthful with his feelings. Another time we were in Iran walking me home from school. He told me that he was going home and said good bye and walked toward his house. When the bus passed me, I recognized Iraj in the bus sitting next to the window, and for me not to be able to see him, he had cover, his face with the newspaper. Next day when I questioned him, he made up a story, but I realized that he had something to hide from me and he was not truthful to me. Then it didn't look important at all. But when later on, you run into other lies you will find out that lying has been part of his character.

Iraj was very patient during my homesickness. Before I completely get a nervous breakdown he decided to do something about it. He knew that, before, I get to know him, my relationship with all the, members of my family was happy and great. He knew that deep down inside I love each and every one of them. He knew that my parents were concerned about me and my future. He had knowledge if that if it wasn't for Iraj and my love for him, my parents would never liked to disown me the way that they did. Besides,

,just the fact that I came from a large family of nine children, and now a prisoner was cooped up in a house as big as one room he was very concerned about me. That was the reason that he was paying a little more money for the rental house in a less crime neighborhood.

It was year 1958. Blacks were considered dangerous in the eye of many white American. Actually those white American weren't used to seeing Black people anything else but slaves. Blacks on the other hand, were trying to find their freedom. I don't want to go to details about the history of slavery and racism in the world and in the United States of America specially. There are many books of pure facts that explains how Blacks were tortured by whites during the history of mankind, in all the libraries in the world. But in the city of St. Louis Missouri where we were residing ,were no peace among whites and

blacks. They brought as many bodies in one night at the hospital as possible. That is why Iraj had rented the house away from hospital, and away from town. It was less crime out of the city. Iraj had to drive to work forty five minutes to one hour each way. He would leave me in the morning with hug and kisses, and come home in the evening at five P.M. exact. He was first year resident at De Paul Hospital. He would tell me the stories about injured at the hospital every night. He was pathology resident and at nights he worked in the emergency room. One night he told me that, they had a pregnant woman at the hospital that she was stabbed with knife sixty times. Many times he came home with white uniform full of blood.

My Dear GOD:

We had a hole in our door as big as a silver quarter. It was covered with pressing newspaper in it. Every time there was a knock at the door, first we removed that paper to see who was at the door and then we opened the door.

Every morning he made sure that I know what to do in his absence. He made sure that I know my address, my telephone number, and the hospital number. We paid half of his monthly income which was fifty dollars for the rent and another fifty dollars for our all other expenses. We did everything together and we shopped together. I still didn't know the American money. You can imagine how hard it was to just have fifty dollars for all our expenses including the payment for the car.

After three months I realized that I am pregnant. Obviously he didn't have to worry about that subject any more. He was watching and caring for me like a baby. But I wasn't well enough to be able to get used to all those things. At that time the homesickness, the penniless, the loneliness, and the morning sickness combined together made me desperately scared for my life and my future.

It was one cold and rainy evening. My dinner was ready on the table. It was after five. I was expecting him any minute. When he was almost forty five minutes late, I called the hospital. I see that my telephone was out of order. I went downstairs to the first floor to ask the manager to allow me to make a call to my husband at the hospital. First, because I didn't understand English, they didn't open the door on me. I tried again. He opened the corner of the door and tried to listen to me. With so many movement and little bit of English I made him understand me just enough to let me call the hospital. The hospital told me that he has gone home. I got more worried and didn't know what to do. I tried the phone again, there was no sound at all. I started crying, mourning for Iraj and my baby without father. Two blocks away from our house, lived another Iranian couple, Dr. Jabbari and her husband. I got dressed and went to her house to tell her what happened. They told me that he had been home. since he couldn't find me at home, he goes to their house. And when he does not find me over there, he walks around the neighborhood to find me. We went home and waited for him. When he got home he was furious. He was so upset,

that almost he was crying, He always had asked me not to get out of the house without him. He was afraid that some one find out that I do not speak English, and they might do something to me. He said that when they left the hospital, his car got stuck in a pile of mud. They tried to push it out, but it didn't moved. So he goes to the hospital to call me and he will find out that it was out of order. So he goes back to the car and with the help of his friends, they pull the car out and he drove home. When he gets home, he does not see me at home and he goC5 to Dr. Jabbari's house. Actually, when he came home and couldn't find me, I was at the manager's house trying to call him. Boy oh boy. It was one of those experiences that I could never forget. I felt so alone, with no money, no language, no friend, no family, and a baby in my stomach.

With Such a lost in life. Such a emptiness. I am glad that it didn't last for more than three hours. After it was over I kiss -ed the ground, and thanked GOD, for not letting it to be rea1.I kissed Iraj and apologized and we had a wonderful time together.

My Dear GOD:

My morning sickness was killing me. I couldn't hold my head up. I was throwing up every second. GOD, please help me. When I was young and we traveled with my parents, instead of being excited about my trip, always I was sad. I was worried about my throwing up in the car. I always hated the feeling of nausea. Now I am having it all the times. It was awful feeling. I was trying to sleep as much as I could.

Once one of his friend came to visit him. He was in the U.S. for a seminar. Iraj brought him home without calling me. He said I told him when we go home Shamci will be sleep for sure and I was sleep. In all these/Iraj was very understanding. He wrote a very warm and apologetic letter to my father and we received warm and loving letters from them. We never thought of calling them, because it was so expensive and we couldn't afford it ever. So the only business that I had was to write to them, and wait two weeks, if not more for their answer.

Pari and Kamal wrote to me often. Kamal did his letters in poem.,) Any time I received a letter from him, it kept me laughing and happy for a long time. It is so funny. I made an album for the cards which I received from them. It is funny, because when I look at them now, I realized how much we have changed from that time, And how much we have grew apart from those who we loved once so much.

They wrote to us about things that were happening in Iran. One of the strangest thing that happened was the news of committing suicide of one of their friend who I knew also. He was a young man very handsome who started joining army. He was in love with this gir1.I think he will find out that his lover had betray him. He had gone to her house, first he shoot her and then turned the gun to himself and kill himself.

We decided for me to start some learning somewhere. Iraj believed that I might be able to start learning in the Lab. I did go with Iraj in the morning and come home with him after

work. I couldn't continue this. Because every day as soon as I started to do or go somewhere, I started throwing up. After that I had to go in the car and wait for Iraj to come and help me. I not only was suffering myself, but I saw that I was destroying Iraj also. So I stopped going to 'the hospital and started reading and writing for myself at home.

During those days, Iraj was doing his best to comfort me and keep his promises to me. His special care and attention was so greatly admired by me, that I could never forget such a love and devotion and affection.

Iraj knew that I have never been alone by myself ever. And you know that Dr.'s job requires night calls. He started working extra in the Lab at nights. 0ur house was one hour away from the hospital, Because of me being alone at home, he came home every night and waited for the hospital to call him if there was a case for him. One night he came home and they called him right after dinner. He drove one hour to the hospital. Almost two hours he worked on the case, and one hour drove back. By then it was nine O'clock. After he removed his cloths and his shoes to rest for a while, he got another call from hospital. He got ready and left again. When he came back it was past two A.M. We got ready to go to bed. After an hour they called him again. He got ready and left right away. When he came home it was six A.M.

My Dear GOD:

Although, I was alone, I was afraid, I was homesick and I have never been by myself ever at night, still I couldn't see Iraj suffer like that. He was thinking of not leaving me alone at night and himself was driving and working all night without any sleep. Loving him gave me such a strength, that I asked him please try to stay at the hospital, when you are on call. First he was uncomfortable to do that. But when I stayed few nights, we both got used to it. It was hard to be able to adopt myself with the loneliness in the strange country and on the top of that, not being able to speak English. It was awfully hard. But I didn't have any other choice. I had to learn rules and regulations of life. It didn't help any of us if he had to come home and back to work. That decision was the beginning of my surviving in the strange country and away from my family. The, things that Iraj did for comforting me in this country is unbelievable. I thanked GOD always for finding Iraj for me, to love the way I did. I was be1ieving that if I give the moon and stars to him, is not enough. If I give my heart and my eyes, for him still is not enough. I was hoping one day, I will find a big bulk of money and Iraj does not have to work this hard. I don't know, if it was him who made me love him so much, or I was sick and stupid to figure out what was wrong with me. Was it possible for me, after the kind of love that Iraj was giving to me, not to love him the way that I did ?.Was it possible to doubt his love and care and kindness toward me and ignore his love and attention for me? No way, I always thought to myself, If my love for

him could be fake, which is not, his love for me can not be fake So I followed my heart and loved him more and more as the time went by.

I had a very bad pregnancy. He was aware of the medical term for my kind of pregnancy. To get rid of my depression, sometimes he tried to put me to sleep with giving me some medication.

I never forget one night I was sick. We both went to the bedroom and he tried to give me medication, and put me to sleep. While we were sitting up in bed, after I took the medicine, I put my head on his shoulder and in no time I fell asleep. When I opened my eyes, it was morning and time for Iraj to go to work. I think he slept just sitting up. He didn't want to wake me up. If this is not love, what else could called love ?

You see my dear GOD. This was a kind of love that only mothers will give to their babies. He always told me that, no matter how much I do for you, still I haven't done anything compare to what you have done for me.

On the other hand, there were times that he did things that annoyed me completely.

Some of these Iranians for fun and laugh they did some shop1lfting.Sometimes a piece of gum. Sometimes a piece of candy. I think most people have done it once in a while. Once we went shopping with another couple. The husband paid at the cashier, and we went to their house. The husband who was an honest Dr. opened the bag. Then he said, “I didn't pay for this spool of tread” His wife said “just leave it in there. We did pay for it!” I realized that she had snatched the spool and put it in the bag afterward. So many people have done it. And I have done a little thing like that also.

As I said, all those Iranian residents and interns were coming to our house four or five nights of the week and sometimes for dinner.

My Dear GOD:

We didn't have that much income to entertain them as many times as they came. Iraj loved to have them all the times. One night when we went shopping, I had my big white hand bag with me.A1l of the sudden, he opened my bag and put the big size beef in it. I was shocked. I couldn't believe my eyes. If they caught us I was the blame. All my body was shaking and I was going to faint. This happened many times. Until one day I thought somebody saw him without any hesitation, I opened my hand bag, and I removed the meat and put it back. That was the last time that happened. After that I never was worried to go shopping with him. You won't believe how I felt with the baby in my stomach, my heart was coming in my mouth. Thank you GOD for saving me from that disaster. I was thinking that if we get arrested, for sure I will miscarriage and start bleeding right in the store. As many time I told him no, he asked me to be quiet and keep your cool, so no one will suspect anything. Once I remember one of his friends questioned him and said "with the money we make is hard to buy any meat. How come you are using this much meat in your food ?.Do

you have money that we don't know of, or you are a rich person ?~'I thought those people might have suspected something.

Ok my dear GOD, you were there and you know everything. You might say, you are as guilty as charge/as Iraj was. True. But you remember so well that I tried to stop him. We did argue a lot. And I stop his act when the time came. Thanks GOD that it was over.

I figured out that Iraj was a kind of a person who wanted to look nice and kind in the eyes of people around him. He was able to keep his innocence and make people to love him. He took that meat not for himself, but for his friends who were homesick and out of their country. I know that this does not make his act right, But for him to act innocent and caring toward his friends was very important.

Unfortunately, because of my bad pregnancy I had to stay home. When I was in Iran, I was advising to other ladies, not to ever let yourself to be needing someone or something. I used to teach extra hours in the evenings illiterate woman classes. I was trying to teach them how to read and write, And I wanted to open their eyes on the situation around them. We talked and discussed life, husband, children, more than what we studied. It is so easy to talk about a subject, when you are not involve yourself. Like American say, talk is sweet but when it comes for me to face the same thing, then it is different story.

I stayed home just depending on Iraj. It seemed that I was able to do everything, But circumstances put you in a position of either or neither nor. There are times that you find yourself in a situation that, you have to let yourself go with the flow of water. At any moment you have to find out, which way is more proper and wiser for you to follow. Different people select different path according to their benefit and desire. Although I had the whole world in my hand, just by finding and having Iraj in my life, Still I was nobody. I had lost my identity. I wasn't Shamci Gharavi. I didn't have anyone around me to even recognizes me. I always thought that, any woman who chooses to become a mother, to her, every other things must be secondary. A1l my life I thought a woman must think of herself first and her career first and all other things last.

My Dear GOD:

Now that I am becoming mother, nothing can take the place of my motherhood. That duty is first, and every thing else is last. In no time, my opinion about things that I believed had turned three hundred and sixty degrees. I had to learn who I was at that time. So I decided to put my child first and design everything else around it.

Many important things happened when we were in St. Louis. The saddest and most unwanted incident, was the death of Sarvan Rafani. We heard that he was in the city of Mashhad, and he passed away there. I think this was the biggest lost in Iraj's life. He never got to know his real father, because of his drinking habit. He didn't talk enough about it, but he suffered inside. This happened before my Maryem was born. Another thing was the unlucky accident that happened to one of the residents.

One Saturday evening I was in Dr. Jabbari's house. We were waiting for Iraj to come too. He was very late. Then we received a call from him, from hospital. It was a very cold and snowy night .He told us that, while they were walking to Dr. Jabbari's house from our house, his friend slipped and landed on his elbow. When they helped him to stand up, he kept saying my arm, my arm. Everybody was laughing, not knowing what he was telling them. When they look close and exam his elbow, they will find out that, his elbow was broken and separated from his upper arm. Soon they drive him to his hospital. They did X ray on his arm, and all other cautionary measures for his safety. When Iraj came to Dr. Jabbari's house, was very sad and unhappy for his friend. He was very homesick and was depending on Iraj and his friendship. He was younger than us, and in his first year of his internship.

He wasn't at the same hospital with Iraj. Next morning when Iraj goes to see him, he will not find him in his room. When he asked the faculty, they said "he was transferred to such and such hospital. He was shocked, because that hospital was a mental institution. Boy oh boy. I cried so hard for that young man, that I will never forget it. We decided to go and look for him. Iraj was working all day, and the only time we had was after five P.M. or week ends. We drove to that institution, which was two hours away from our house. Once they did not permit us to go and see him. They allowed only his immediate family. Since he did not have any family at all, nor he had any immediate family, Iraj got approval from his hospital to go and visit him.

Next day I cooked Iranian food hoping to be able to see him. They only allowed Iraj to go and see him. But I saw him from far. The scene was like a scene in the movie Over the Coocoo's Nest.

I cried and cried. I was seeing myself in that position, and couldn't stop from crying. I think Iraj had the same feeling. He was trying to find out, why they took him to that institution to begin with. And he was trying to relocate him to his own hospital. We were there almost every day after his work. Iraj had contacted his father in Iran, and assured them, that he will do everything in his power to get to the bottom of his case.

What we found out was that, the year before this happened at that hospital, one young Filipino intern commit suicide over the lost of his girl friend, and he died next morning.

My Dear GOD:

The reason that they transferred him to that institution was, that the night that Iraj drove him to the hospital, he has been under tremendous pain. He was asking for more pain killer, and while under severe pain, he was talking to himself; I want to die, I want to die, a nurse who heard him, reported to the staff of the hospital. The staff took preventing measure and right away they sent him to that institution. What an unlucky young man.

What an unfortunate thing to happen to any one. Seeing him in the middle of hundreds real crazy people was a night mare.

These twelve residents were so attached to Iraj that they were in our house almost every night. We rented that apartment for one year. Iraj had applied for residency at Boumont Hospital, in Royal Oak Michigan to become obstetrician and gynecologist. Thanks GOD he got accepted there. If not, we didn't have a place to stay. The reason was that, the manager of the building had asked us to leave the building as soon as our contract was over. He said that every family in that building complained about your friends coming here every night and make a lot of noise late at night when they are leaving. Obviously we promise them that we will move at the end of the year.

Maryem was born at De Paul Hospital in St. Louis Missouri. If I remember correctly, she was born at six O'clock in the morning, on June forth 1960.At all black hospital a girl with long curly blond hair and white skin with two big green eyes was born. She was one of the most beautiful girls on earth.

I have seen a lot of babies in my life. I had held my younger sisters and brothers in my arms. I fed them, changed them, and I bathe them so many times. But to hold my baby in my hand and be responsible for her life was a complete different story. I was so nervous that I thought I might drop my baby any time. I was shaking all over. The baby was mine and only mine and no one else could touch her. I was there/where I always wanted to be. I had my Iraj my only love. I had Maryem the fruit of my long lasting love. And I thought that all my dreams came true. What else did I need from God to give it to me ? I was complete. I had the whole world in my hand

When I was in Iran most of the times Pari and I would talk and discussed our future children's name. She liked the name Maryem for her daughter, and I said I like the name Maryem for my daughter. We repeated this for so many times. Then we laughed and said whoever gets the girl first she wins this name for her daughter. Not only we liked this name, Maryem was her mother's name also. (Actually this name must be spelled "Maryam" but we just spelled it like they do here).

The house at Boumont Hospital's complex was not ready for us until July first 1960.He had to start his residency by July 1st. and we could have the house by July 15th.There were three weeks between the time of our arrivals and the time that our house was ready for us. One of his friends who was sharing his house with two other doctors gave him a favor and asked Iraj to stay in his hous2 for that extra three weeks.

My Dear GOD:

That Dr.'s name was Dr. Talebzadeh. He called himself for short Zadeh. The other two, one was Dr. Anooshfar who was from Esfahan, and the other one was Dr. Mohammad Rabbani, who was with Iraj the same year at Tehran University. Non of them were married. I remember one funny story from living there.

This is probably the second or third week after I arrived to St. Louis, Missouri. The only couple we knew was Dr. Jabbari and her husband who was a doctor at the same hospital with her. They lived three blocks down from us in our street. We were the only married couples. The rest of the group were all bachelors.

Here are the rest of the group that we always associated with, some of whom we never saw again. We continued our friendship with some until now.

This picture was taken when I was pregnant with Mary. All the other doctors at that time were bachelors. Left to right: Dr. Irom, Dr. Mohammad Rabbani,and Dr. Anooshfar. I am heavy and cold standing next to Iraj. Those days he was full of promises. He was hoping to be a good father and a great husband. I don't know what happened to those promises.

Mary at six months old

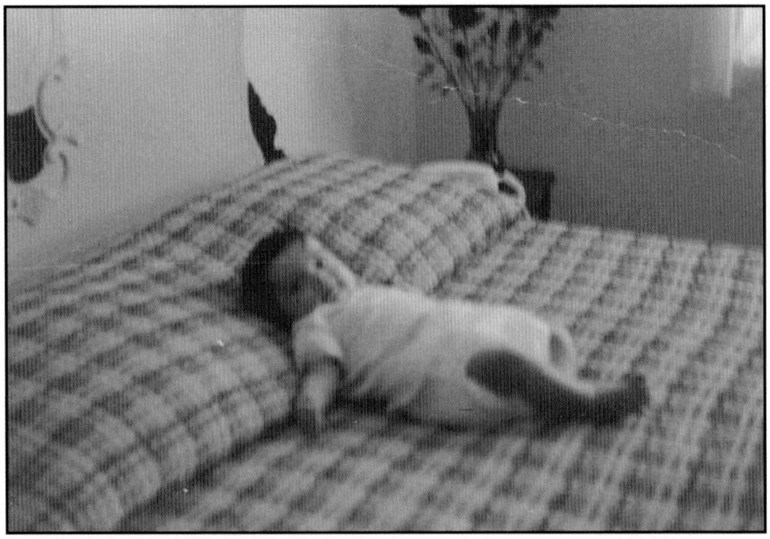

Mary is on her father's lap, next to me. I look happy and young sitting on the furniture purchased from the Salvation Army. Boy oh boy, we were so happy with the furniture. We didn't know what money or big houses were. I wonder if Iraj remembers those days at all. Or, was it just part of a game, a plan to collect money for his later years? I am glad I didn't know what he had in mind then. At least I spent some time with his love.

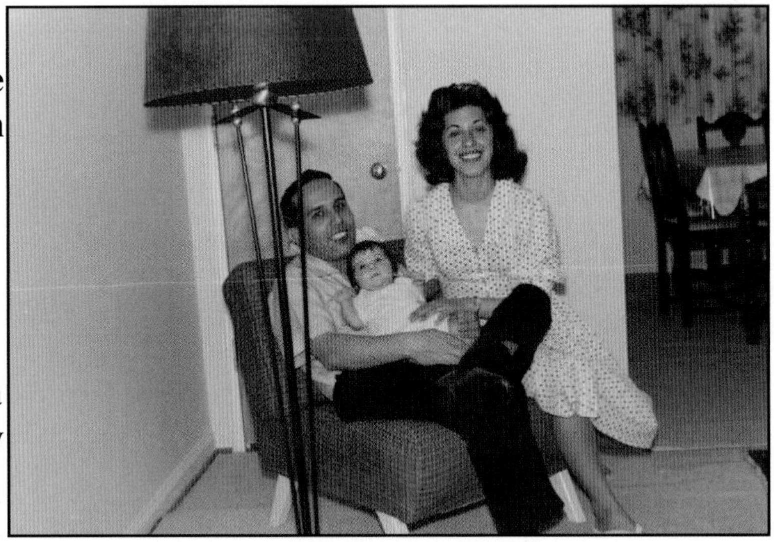

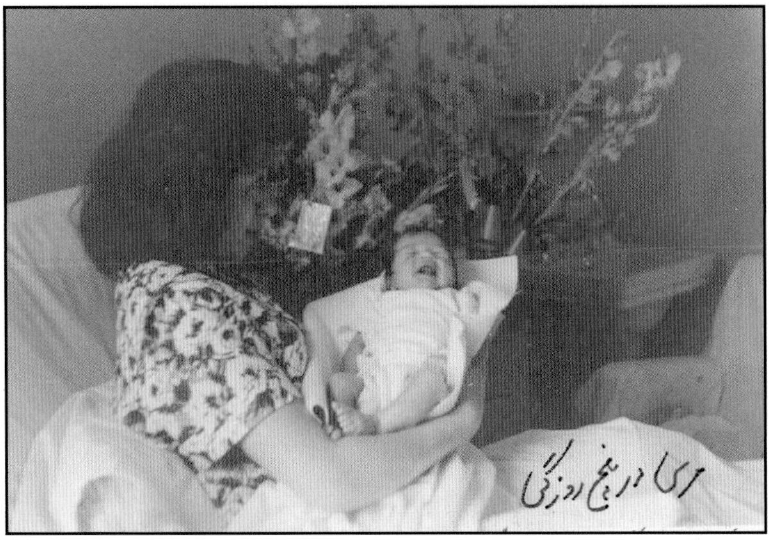

At the hospital with the robe I had made for myself. You see when I said we didn't have money, I was telling the truth. So I had to make my own clothes for the sake of love. In later years, he spent the money on someone else, also for the sake of love.

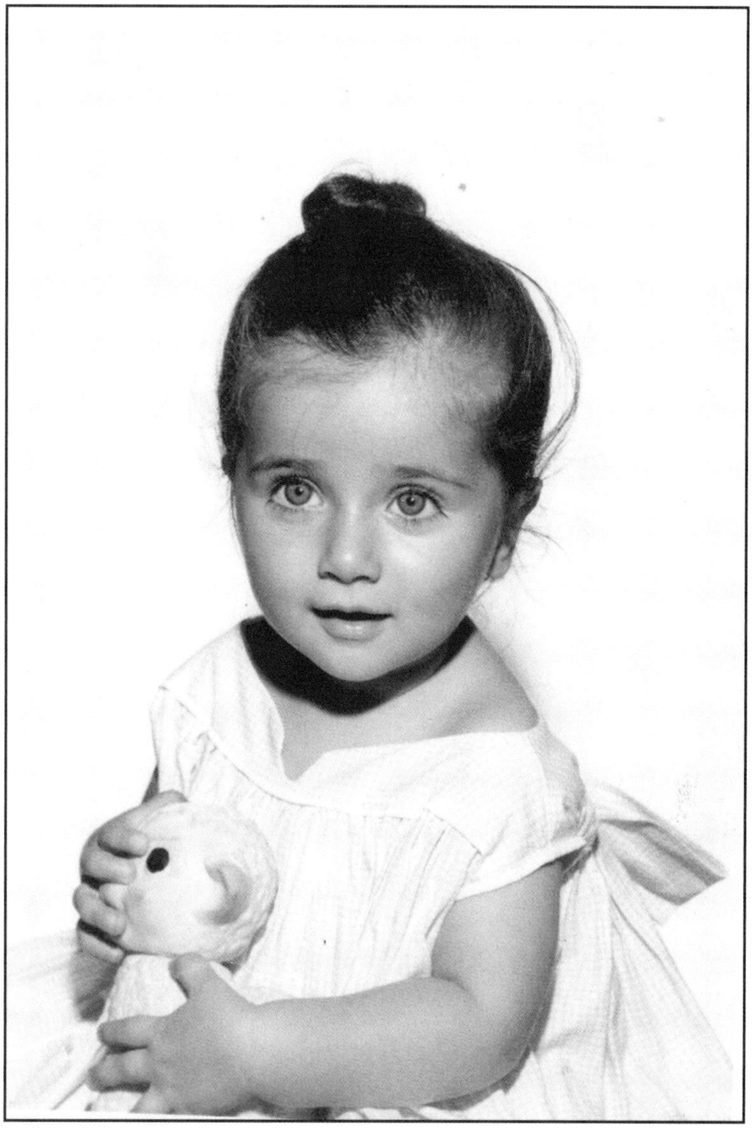

The most beautiful baby on the planet; my beautiful Maryam at age one

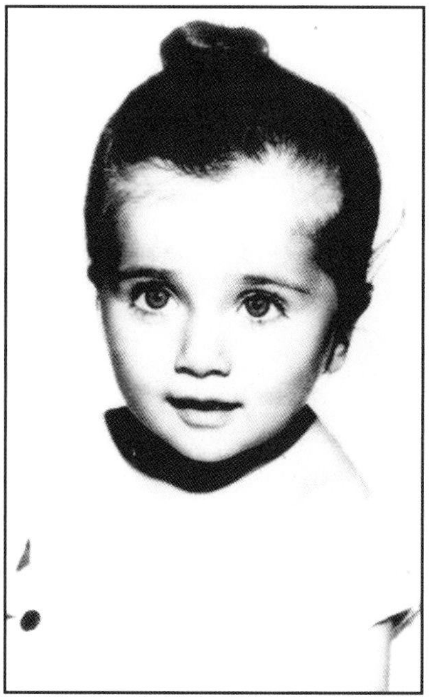

my beautiful Maryam

We were staying at the Grand Hotel in Mackinaw Island when Mary was three years old. At the time I thought we were a happy family, but what happened? I really don't know.

The group from left to right: Iraj, Maheen Anooshfar, Dr. Anooshfar, Sue Zadeh (holding her dog), Susan Barkhaordari, Dr. Barkhordari, and Dr. Zadeh. In the front I am sitting on Maseeh's stroller, while Mary is watching the dog.

Obviously these boys had girl friends. They used to bring their girl friends home every night. Probably they didn't know if we stayed in their house, they couldn't bring their girl friends whenever they wanted to.
I remember one night we were invited in Dr. Zadeh'S girlfriend house. I didn't want to go. Dr. Anooshfar was trying so hard to convince me to go. He was begging me to go. I saw him he was almost crying and begging me to go. I couldn't understand why he was insisting on sending me out of the house. Later on, when we had closer relationship he told me that, he wanted to bring his girl home and couldn't do it in front of me. So he was begging me to go out to be able to bring his girl home and do his own thing.

I don't remember what was the reason that we traveled with train rather than plane. I don't think it was money. I think Iraj liked to experience the feeling of the train ride, while we had enough time to waste.
He sold the car for fifty dollars, the same price he had bought it. And I think we sold whatever we had, just took baby's stuff with us. At that time to me things were not the object, money was not the object, his work and my little family were important to me. Again I had the whole world in my hand.
Few of those residents came to say good by to us in the train station. In the train was hot enough but I remember that I had covered my little baby with so many stuff that a lady came to me and said "this baby is suffocating under all these covers. I think I wanted to be cautious not to let her catch a cold in that hot June weather.

So we stayed in Dr. Zadeh's house until our house was available for us. I was breast feeding Mary. I thought she was a good baby because I was breast feeding her. while she was sleep I used to get up every second and check her breathing.

My mother always said to me "you are such a heavy sleeper that if you ever have a baby, you will never be able to wake up, when your baby cries ". Before Mary was born I was afraid myself, also.
But to my amaze from the first moment she was born, I became like a hawk. I was up all day, and I woke up with her littlest movement she made. I was shocked myself. How could this happen. I even didn't get tired of what I was doing. She was my real doll.Thanks GOD she was a good baby. Because she was a good baby and didn't cry, I thought she was fine. But when I took her to doctor for her first check up, he told me that she had lost weight .And the reason was that the quality of my milk was not good for her. So I had to start to give her formula. Doing this, created an abscess in my breasts. I had to go through pumping my breasts which was the most painful thing.

After three weeks living in Dr. Zadeh's house, our house was ready for us. Without any furniture, or any appliances, and without all the necessities for a basic living we moved into our house. Iraj have heard of this place, Salvation Army. He bought a bed, a crib, a chair and many more things from that place.

My Dear GOD:

Yes my dear GOD, my children cannot even imagine what kind of life we had. My children did not have any idea, what childhood we had, or how we grew up. My children didn't know how we started our lives together. And my children never knew about our promises and relationship for building the family nest together. They never knew how I managed to get over my homesickness. With nothing at all I learned to live with love and devotion to my family. They didn't know who I was when I met their father and who he was when he met me.

We started to decorate our house so it will look like a real house. He bought some cans of gray and black tinted colors, blended them, and painted our bed. These were all his ideas and I went along with it just to make him enjoy his life as long as he could. I was happy to see him happy. So I didn't disagreed with what color...he wants to make the bed, or what he wants to buy for the bathroom. I knew those were temporary. Those were not our furniture for life. Let him do his business and I will do my business which was watching over my beautiful family.

I made covers for the chairs. Made tablecloth with the cheapest fabric and made everything in my own design for that time of our life, we were all set. We had nice and good looking bed to sleep on, We had nice and clean furniture to live by. And we had all the necessities for starters. Again we had the whole world in our hand.

Because I didn't know how to speak English, I was so shy. I didn't want to meet any one at all. Even if people came toward me, I tried to avoid speaking to them. There were an older couple living in that complex. The lady came to visit me with a pie in her hand. I embarrassly welcomed her and offered her a cup of tea. She tried to make me understand that, there is nothing wrong with not knowing how to speak English. It will take time to become familiar with words. You must watch T V. And listen to radio to be able to separate the words from each other. She asked me not to stay home. Come out, and start talking to the neighbors. She was very nice and classy lady. I did listen to her. After I cooked an Iranian dish one day, I took it to her. It was so difficult to make people to understand you. Some people were very understanding, and some made fun of you. Some thought because you don't understand their language, you must be dumb. They didn't know that we know more than them, only in another language.

So I tried to get to know the neighbors. All the town houses in that complex belonged to Beaumont Hospital and were given to all residents and interns of the hospital. It was only five minutes walk to the hospital. We actually didn't need a car, except for going shopping or to go to our friends house. A big shopping center was near by. I had a stroller for Mary. Going shopping was not a big deal at all. It was fun to put her in her stroller and walk to shopping center.

All our neighbors were doctor's wives. We all needed baby sitters and we did not have enough money to get one. We decided to exchange babysitting for each other when we

can. It was working so well. To do something to boost my English, I signed up for a tailoring class at night when Iraj was home to watch the baby. The time of my absence was almost two hours, while Mary was sleep. Iraj always agreed to anything I wanted to do, or any decision I wanted to make. We had loving trust for each other's ideas. I thought he really loved me.

My Dear GOD:

The wives in our neighboring area and I decided to fulfill our staying home Mom's dreams, get together once every other week, and each one of us represents one talent. That was also working very we11. I learned more than what I was supposed to teach them. The reason was my ability not to be able to explain things to them in a simple language.

Ok my dear GOD, I have been known as a smart girl with high IQ all my life. I knew how to handle things around me, and I knew how to create relationship with others. I knew how to have money, how to keep money or how to spend money. But when I came here and start living with Iraj, I didn't know my way around at a11. I didn't know what was the money in this country, or many other simple things around me. And because I thought of Iraj being my GOD, I trusted him and allow him to take over completely, until I be ready and have enough knowledge to be able to handle everything in a proper way. But the trust between us was so great, that I never needed to say yourself or myself. As a matter of fact, I hated the talk of material between a husband and wife. I thought they are one person, and everything they have is equally theirs.

My dear GOD, you might say, haven't you seen people around you or haven't you read the stories about the separation of husbands and wives? Haven't you seen the results of trusting wives after their separation? Shouldn't you open your eyes and learn from other people's mistake?

Yes you are right. But I never wanted to be just any woman. Nor I thought of Iraj being any other man. I wanted to live with such a love and trust, that I never wanted that our relationship build on material and selfishness. That kind of life, does not have a true - meaning. It is not love, if there is no such a trust. I had a kind of love for Iraj, that I loved that loving. I never wanted to change my way of loving, otherwise ,just marriage did not have any meaning for me.

So I loved my loving, and put all my trust in his hand. And for this reason, he was honest with me, and the check books and every other thing in our household, was on both our names at that time

I was watching him. And I knew that, he liked the way that I was trusting him. We were open and clear with each other to a point that I always thought we were just one person. I really loved that feeling. This way with complete trust and communication, I was able to have control over our budget and prevent over spending before it was too late. To me no company, no organization, no home, and no country could ever survive without a

thoughtful budget management. Otherwise they will go bankrupt in no time. Budget planning in any company requires honesty, thoughtfulness and togetherness among the co-workers. If the co-workers consist of only a husband and wife, If they don't have one voice in all aspect of life, no one will benefit anything at all through their married life.
Those days not only we agreed on most everything, but each one of us tried to do the thing that it was other person's favorite.
Oh my GOD, do you remember how we tried to do things to make the other person happy? Do you remember how we enjoyed each other's happiness ? And do you remember how hard Iraj was working to build a great future for all of us, and was very happy to do it?

My Dear GOD:

Iraj was working on three different shifts, according to the hospital's schedule. The day shifts was from eight to four. Evening shifts was from four to twelve. And midnight shifts, from twelve to eight O'clock in the morning. I had to adopt my living style with his schedule. Not only with his work schedule, but with his studying also. For him to be able to sleep during the day, I had to keep Mary in the kitchen all day, and stay in there until he wakes up. Not that he ever asked me to do it, but only because I wanted him to have his sleep. The kitchen was so small that we couldn't move in there. In reality I treated Iraj like my baby. I wanted the whole world for him and because of him. This was true about him also.

The first year of our marriage that I was in Iran, he arrange a trip with four other friends to Florida. He spoke of that trip all the times. Five young poor doctors in an old car, with no money, shared bread and cheese and walnut, seemed to be the best vacation he could ever have. He never stopped talking about it.

These people were so poor, that they used to cut each other's hair. To me, although they were poor, but they never had a better life than those days.
Between the pictures that he showed me from first year he was here, there was a lady doctor among them. All his friends used to tease him and somehow connect him with her. It never was in open that there was something going on between them. But looking at the pictures any one could see that they were having fun.
But is this against the law that people have fun and take picture together ?. No, I don’t think so. You can not make a case of that and accuse Iraj from wrong doing. But if he had something going on with her that I didn't know of, it was the start of distrusting Iraj's truthfulness towards his lasting love for me. But I never wanted to think about it and put Iraj in the category of men in general. I always thought that, if I can love Iraj in such a special way, For sure Iraj is truthful to me, and his love for me could be special also. So although we were teasing him for those pictures, I never allow myself to think wrongly about Iraj and his trustworthy.

You see my dear GOD,I raised three very smart and intelligent children. They told me once "we always see the things the way we want to see them. And we believe on things the way we want to believe them." Looking back in to my past I realize that, what a true statement. Because in my dreams I always pictured Iraj loving me the way I wanted him to love me, so in reality I believed his truthfulness and I thought that his love for me is as pure as he show it to me. I completely believed in his words and trusted him.
Maryem, the fruit of our love had brightened our lives much more than we ever dreamed of. She was the most beautiful baby in the world. I am not exaggerating at a11.She had two big greenish-gray eyes, she had long curly thick blonde hair and lightest pink rosy skin you have ever seen. She was a real living doll. You see my dear GOD, after going through what I had gone for eight years of struggle to marry Iraj. Now I am having my Iraj and I am having my Mary, the most beautiful baby on earth, don't you see yourself in heaven, if you were me ? Don't you please? Don't you?

My Dear GOD:

I had promised myself, that I will never get married unless I love that person to death. Ok, I found that person to love at the age of seventeen. It was him, or no one else in the world. Luckily he loved me the same way that I did love him. So, I not only was very happy, but I was flying on the top of clouds.
I was spending all my life only with Mary and only with her. It was her, it was me, and it was me. We did not have any one else around us. She just knew me and only me. At that time I felt so proud to be stay home mother. I thought my every moment with her worth more than millions of dollars. I didn't want to exchange my life with anything else. I had the whole world in my hand.

Iraj was either working, sleeping, or studying for E.C.F.M.G. Mary even didn't have a chance to see her father regularly. It seemed that I was raising Mary in a glass house away from the rest of the world. I was everyone to Mary, and she was everyone to me. Except the times that we were with our friends, the rest of the times it was she and I. To try to teach her English, I used to read all the nursery books to her all the times. At the age of three, she memorized at least ten books by heart. She even put her finger on the words when she read them. Some of the doctors of our friends were insisting in the idea that, Mary not only has been memorizing the words, but for sure she can read those words. I knew that wasn't true. All our friends were bachelor doctors. They loved to play with Mary, and, because she was so sweet, they used to kiss her a lot I had to put a sign on her apron(please do not kiss me). Her face was sensitive to their harsh skin. She was my delightful joy. I was having fun with her.

Then in that house in Bell court avenue, I got pregnant for the second time. I had the same kind of pregnancy as the first one, only this time I couldn't sleep. I had Mary to

At Holland, Michigan's Tulip Festival; Iraj is wearing the sweater I had knitted for him. As you see, there were times that Iraj was laughing.

I am pregnant with Maseeh in this picture. Mary hadn't turned two yet.

It was Maseeh's birthday, and I was pregnant with Mojgan.

Going back to Iran, we were at a hotel in Paris, France.

my beautiful children
Maryam and Maseeh at
the ages three and one

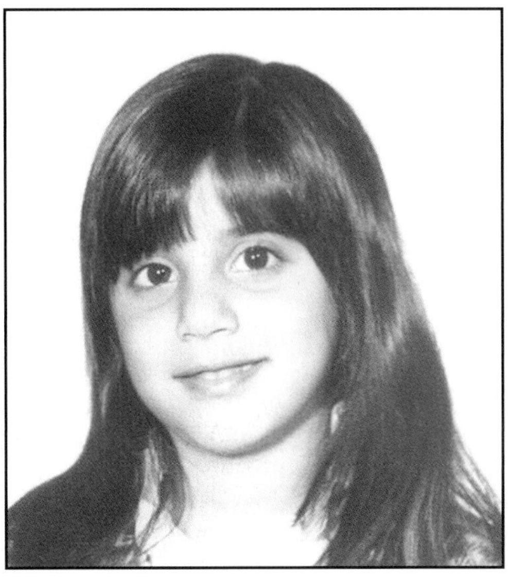

This is my beautiful Mojgan at the
age five.

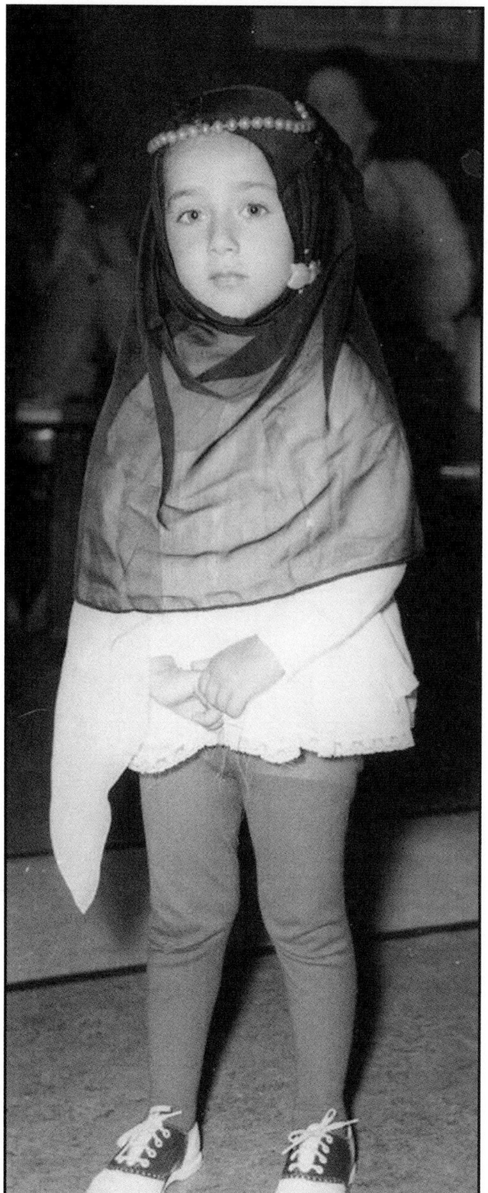

Above, at the board of Queen Elizabeth, going back to Iran People are admiring our million-dollar family. Oh, how I wish it stayed that way!

Left, at Queen Elizabeth's, I was able to dress up Mary this way for the contest among the children.

keep me real busy. Iraj was busy with his work, and I was busy with mine. I think it is proper to talk about some of the incidents that happened during those years.
As I said with all the experience that I had with babysitting I was worried that I might make a mistake, or not have enough knowledge to take care of Mary. Iraj was OBGYN, and knew about women and their pregnancy.
One day, for only few second, a strange feeling came to me, that I thought I was going to hurt my baby. With out any hesitation I called Iraj and asked him to come home. And I told him what happened. He tried to calmly talk to me and told me that these are one of many fazes that women go through after having a baby. You should not think about it. Just leave Mary in her room and start doing something to occupy your mind. I will finish my duty, and will be home in no time". That helped me a lot, and thank GOD, it never came back to me.
Another thing was that, I was a crazy mother. When Mary started to walk she started like a normal baby. But I was so afraid that if she falls while walking, she might hurt herself. So I was holding my hands around her like a cage not to let her get hurt. Years later, still my neighbors were asking me, if I am putting my hands around her to protect her from falling. That was embarrassing to see that I was such an over protective mother.

My Dear GOD:

Mary was almost a year old. I decided to remove a broken bone in my nose, a childhood injury. I was not aware of the fact that my face would have to remain covered with bandages for a long time. I thought that it would take a week, maybe two weeks at the most. And I never thought that it might affect Mary to such an extent. I had the surgery as an outpatient. When I returned home, Mary, whom I left with my neighbor for a few hours, was asleep. I always fed her in the middle of the night without waking her up. I entered Mary's room in the morning when she woke up. She didn't want me to touch her. She started to scream, she asked me to leave her room. So I did. And I called my neighbor, a mother of three. Her girls were at school at the time. I asked her to come over, and help me figure out what was going on with Mary. When my neighbor came over, and Mary went to her with no objections, I realized that she was afraid of my bandages. So I started to cry. I blamed myself for all the lack of knowledge. I blamed myself for not understanding a child of that age. I had to hire a lady to care for Mary for the time being, while I was in bandages. I remained in Mary's presence only when the lady was holding her to change her diaper. When my bandages were off, everything went back to normal.

Life can be so funny. Life has proved to me that history repeats itself. My thoughts went as far back as to the times when my little brother Jalal started to reject my mother. My mother was seriously ill for about a year. And she had to hire a Nanny to help her to care for the children. Meanwhile Jalal considered the Nanny to be his mother. And so after she left, he did not want my mother to even hold him.

The same thing happened to me after the surgery. Mary did not want me to touch her. Fortunately, unlike my poor mother, I had to deal with my child's rejection only for a little while. Nevertheless, what a misfortune that is to happen to any mother.

I never wanted to leave Mary alone with anybody. Even though it was very common to exchange baby-sitting services in our neighborhood, we would only use this source after we put the kids to bed. There were times when we had to attend parties. I knew that it was important to Iraj. But I didn't want to go anywhere. I wanted to stay home with my baby.

When Mary was six months old, we got invited to a party. We absolutely had to be there. And again I wanted to stay home with Mary. Dr. Zadeh and his girlfriend Betty came over and insisted that I would be letting Iraj down if I didn't go to the party. So they volunteered to baby-sit for us in their home. She was such a good baby, that anyone would love to have her over. When we came back from the party, we called Dr. Zadeh so that we could pick Mary up. But they told us to go to bed, and let Mary sleep over at their house. They said that Mary has been very good. "Why don't you call us in the morning and come and get her then."

My Dear GOD:

That was the first time that I left Mary with a baby sitter. It's probably just me, but I have never trusted anyone with my children.

There was another scary incident. It took place while Iraj was resting after a night shift. It was a hot summer day. I let Mary play in the large backyard that was shared among many other doctors. It was a mid day and all the kids were playing outside. I was frying eggplants. I kept an eye on the kids at all times. All of a sudden I turned around to see that the frying pan was in flames. I had no time to think, so without any further hesitation I got the frying pan by its handle and threw it out in the yard.

My dear, dear GOD. Can you believe what could have happened to Mary and all other children if you were not there? If those kids would happen to be near the kitchen, the flames of the frying oil would burn them. I was so lucky. I sat on the grass while I had Mary in my arms and the rest of the kids sitting around me. I thanked you my GOD million times and kissed the ground. GOD, you have been with me through so many disasters in my life. I don't know how to thank you. My children could have been dead, burnt, or drowned if it wasn't for your mercy. And I know that only your kindness has kept me alive till now.

My son Maseeh was born on March 28th 1962 at Beaumont Hospital in Royal Oak, Michigan. Mary & Maseeh were almost two years apart.

Since Mary was our first child, and she was used to receiving all the special attention, I became worried that she would get jealous of her baby brother. I knew that Maseeh was not really aware of many things at that age. So I never held him in front of Mary. I made her believe that the baby was hers. I let her feed the baby. She helped me change the baby.

She held the baby on her lap, and she even helped me bathe Maseeh. She was having so much fun. She treated Maseeh like her favorite doll. She would instruct me what to do with him; she would teach us how to hold him right. She pushed his stroller on the road, while watching carefully over him. She enjoyed Maseeh's babyhood so much.

In America a family with a baby girl and a baby boy is called a one million dollar family. Now I was a millionaire of love. Since Iraj was making more money, we started saving for our future. The relationship between our parents and us was beautiful. I was counting days to go back home. Iraj's three- year residency was almost over. We had always planned on having our beautiful family in Iran. We had never considered staying here, in America. Although I continued living here, on the inside I always remained in Iran with our families and friends. There was more to that. I was missing the roads, the shops, the culture, the people who knew me and most of all my country. I could not explain the love for my country.

My Dear GOD:

This brings up a special memory. This one Mexican doctor was returning to his country, Mexico. He was questioned by many why he was going back to Mexico. It's good to be here. You have all the freedom. You could and you will make more money than in your country. He listened to everybody for a while. And then he said, "I want to go to my country to become the head of a mouse. No matter how long I stay here, I will always be the tail of a lion. I would rather be the head of a mouse, than the tail of a lion." These feelings are very common when you are in a foreign country. It's not that you don't love the people. And neither it's a matter of lacking respect for that country, and it's not that you find anything wrong with their way of living. But you just miss the place of your birth, that place where you were brought up.

Iraj's friends were advising him to try to stay in U.S. if he could. I must say that he was very tempted to do so. It is so funny how we change every day depending on circumstances. Iraj was getting used to his surroundings, and having started his family here, he was pinning down the idea of staying in the U.S.A. A lion, on the other hand, would never consider the thought of staying away from home. Right or wrong, I couldn't imagine the possibility of staying here. For me that was out of the question. So I simply told Iraj, "No. I will never stay here". And we decided to go back to Iran, and live happily ever after. Now that I look back, I wish that I didn't.

He was done with his residency by July 1963. He tried to get a job for the remainder of his Visa in the U.S. He had almost four months to save some money before we go back. We had to vacate the house by July 1st for new residents. We didn't know where to move for four months with two children. So we asked the hospital to let us use another unit for only four months. To our surprise they did. We sold most everything, and we moved in to the new unit, which was next door to our first one. Everything seems so easy when I write

about all these events in just a few sentences. But the reality of it was a different story.

* * *

Mary was a beautiful girl. As a child she loved dressing up like a lady. She would wear her jewelry set: a ring, a bracelet, earrings, and a necklace. I would put her hair in a ponytail with a fancy hairpin. She would put on her glasses. Then she carried her handbag just like a lady, and walked around the yard. It was so much fun to watch her. She lost her necklace somewhere in the grass one of those days that she played dress up. We couldn't find it no matter what. It became our every day duty to search for Mary's necklace. I contribute her fashion preferences later in life to the loss of that necklace (this is just for laughs).

My Dear GOD:

On the night of Iraj's graduation the hospital presented each graduate with a diploma. And every wife of a graduate received a medallion with Beaumont Hospital logo along with a diploma for assisting our husbands during their residency with patience and cooperation. I think I deserved that diploma more than anyone else. Besides being patient and cooperative with my husband, I couldn't turn to any one for moral support; I had neither friends nor family here. They gave us a flying carpet also to fly to Iran with no problem.

We did not speak English at the time. Therefore we would seize the opportunity of starting a friendship with the first and any Iranians we have met along the way. It's obvious that we would never be able to know who is who right of the bet. One will never know what kind of people one's dealing with unless one starts socializing, and somehow gets to become friends.

We would get together with our new friends as often as it was possible at the time. One of the couples that we befriended also had a baby girl. Her name was Roksana. She was a year younger than Mary.

Nearly a year went by, when a friend of ours came over and asked us to accompany them to a party held by some Iranian doctors at a hall. Once again I didn't want to attend the party. I tried to reason with everybody by saying that I did not feel comfortable attending the party, since we didn't know anybody. I didn't think it was proper to take my baby with me to a dance party. But my reasoning didn't work. They still made me go. I guess we were not going to stay too long. Our friends were curios to see what kind of party it was, and how many Iranians were there.

I had to go, partially because if I had not gone, Iraj would end up staying home as well. In all fairness to Iraj, he has been working long hours at the hospital, and he deserved a break, especially on the weekend. So I got ready in a hurry. I threw some

William Beaumont Hospital

Royal Oak, Michigan

Presents To

Mrs. IRAJ RAFANI

this special award of appreciation and distinction in recognition of her contributions made toward the graduate medical education of her husband in Obstetrics and Gynecology from July 1, 1960 to June 30, 1963

In witness whereof, this certificate is given at Royal Oak, Michigan

on the twenty ninth day of June 1963

L. B. Babcock
PRESIDENT BOARD OF TRUSTEES

Harold W. Longyear M.D.
CHIEF OF DEPARTMENT

This award proves that I had helped Iraj to graduate with good honors. Besides this, the hospital staff gave a gold medallion of Beaumont Hospital to all the graduates' wives.

clothes on, nothing fancy.

When we finally got to the hall, all the ladies were dancing while dressed in party clothes, and it seemed like it was the end of the party. We didn't want to go in because of the baby. But Mrs. Avaregan, who was one of the organizers of the party, came to the door and asked us to go in. There were many Iranian doctors there who came from all over, but we did not know any of them. We met a new couple, Dr. Varjovandi and Maneejeh his wife. As we understood the organizers of the group, were Baha'is, and so were many of those attending doctors. We didn't stay long. Toloo Avaregan got our telephone number and contacted us later on. We got to know Dr. Saeed and Minoo Khadem, Dr. Moghtassed and his wife Khadigeh, Dr. Kashef and his wife Parvaneh, and many others through her.

My Dear GOD:

We were trying to adapt to the idea of being away from home by communicating and socializing with as many Iranians as we could. We arranged parties and picnics as often as it was possible. We tried to comfort and help one another when in need. Each couple had one or two kids, and when we were together every member of the family had the most enjoyable time.

As I have mentioned before, Iraj and myself are both great practical jokers. And we like bringing excitement to our daily life. We played jokes on each other, and we did it to others too.

We were just getting to know Dr. and Minoo Khadem. Minoo has recently arrived to U.S.A. One day Iraj decided to call Minoo one morning, but she wasn't home. She finally answered the phone when he tried her back later in the afternoon. Iraj changed his voice and said, "Where were you today? I saw you". Minoo hung up on him. She thought somebody must have been following her. People and especially her husband advised her to be very careful with strangers. Iraj realized that Minoo didn't recognize him, so this time he calls back to introduce himself. But as soon as he said hello, she immediately hung up. Iraj tried to call many times to clear the problem that he had created. But she finally stopped answering the phone.

Meanwhile her husband was trying to reach her as well. But she wouldn't answer the phone, fearing that some serial killer was stalking her. Dr. Khadem had become so worried that he rushed home. He found his wife extremely concerned, she told all about the disturbing phone calls. And even after we had paid them a visit with apologies and explanations, they would not believe us that Iraj was the one who had been calling Minoo. And although she was ready to kill us, we laughed about it for the rest of our life.

While we were here in U.S., we missed many pleasurable occasions. We missed wedding, birthdays, graduations, and many more celebrations in Iran. We found ways to brighten up our lives in order to survive and not allow our life and our children's life to be wasted.

The most pleasurable thing for us was to hear from someone we knew, or to see someone we knew from Iran. Once, his sister Neia wrote me a letter to inform us that her friend's husband was moving to Michigan to attend the East Lansing University. I was not familiar with her friend; I only knew that she had a friend who was not interested in ever getting married. I thought I was like her too, but love had made me change my mind completely. So we were anxious to meet this gentleman.

My Dear GOD:

His name was Morteza Alavinejad. He was working on his engineering degree in East Lansing. There was an obvious connection from the first time we met each other. He felt right at home, and it seemed like we knew each other forever. He came to our house on weekends. We made Iranian food and spoke Farsi. Then I realized that Neia's friend, who never wanted to get married, had fallen in love with this gentleman. Her name was Fereshteh Khajehnaseer. She attended the same high school with Neia and my sister Azar. She actually fell in love so deeply. She never thought she was capable of such feelings. They didn't get married while he was in Iran. They had to do it by proxy. The ceremony was held in Iran, without the presence of the groom. So we both felt to be in the same shoes. We had so much to laugh, and so much to talk about. We knew each other's families from my hometown Shiraz, since his family also came from Shiraz. He was a real clown and I was no less of a clown than him. We had such a great time every time we were together, that even forty years later we have something to laugh about. I wouldn't even know where to begin writing what went on every time we were together. It would take hundreds and hundreds of pages. But I can write about just a few incidents.

We got to meet Fereshteh in a few months when she came to U.S. Morteza and Fereshteh had rented an apartment in the University's housing complex, just like we did. We alternated house visits over the weekends. I asked them over more often since I had Mary. Morteza loved children a lot. He had really special feelings for Mary. Boy, he would kill himself over Mary. I have never met a man, who likes kids so much.

Morteza loved to watch sports like every man in the U.S.A. He particularly liked football. Oh God, God forbids if someone interfered with his football on Sundays. He would kill you. We, on the other hand, didn't like watching football. Many times when we were in their house there was a better show to watch. Iraj would turn off the TV and Morteza would turn it back on. Then Iraj would block Morteza's view by standing in front of the TV, and Morteza would get up and try to knock Iraj down in turn. This would go on and on. Meanwhile they had us all in fits of laughter. The show would continue until eventually one of them won. These gatherings were so much fun.

In another party, left to right: Kaveh Kamooneh, Nazi Forghani, Arman Forghani, Keyvan Kamooneh, Maryam Rafani, Maseeh Rafani, and Ameer who was living with us, with his mother, full time. These pictures are full of memories for me. When Iraj escaped Iran after his first affair, I tried so hard to fill out his empty place for my children. I tried to let them know that their father's absence is just temporary. I tried to make them understand that soon we would be back together. I knew because I had gotten back together with him with the advice of my father. Only and only a lady and a friend like Shahnaz was able to hold her husband's hand and bring him to a birthday party for Maseeh, so that he would have the satisfaction of being with the friend of his father, Dr. Toosi. No one ever understands the meaning of this action except me, being in the middle of the struggle of life.

Left to right: Minoo Khadem whose Marjaneh was the same age as Maseeh, Marjaneh, Maseeh, Layla Toosi, Dr. Toosi, Rokhand, Reza, Mary, Shahnaz, and Jahanshah Khadem.

The same party with the Toosis; from left to right: Reza, Maseeh, Jahanshah, Minoo, Mary, me, Layla, Rokhand, and Marjaneh. Standing at the back are Azar and Shahab.

Dr. Gangi with Mojgan in our living room

My friend Shahnaz; a very kind, talented, beautiful, and unique lady.

My brother Javad and my mother, in one of his visits from England. This picture was taken before he got married.

Morteza in Mojgan's bedroom, holding Mojgan and Maseeh Mary is standing on the bed, when we were living in Helston Rd.

We are all happy and laughing except Iraj. I wonder why.

Maseeh is holding Fereshteh and I close to his heart.

My Dear God:

Once we were invited to their house along with another Iranian couple whom we haven't met before. While we were being introduced, almost immediately Iraj and the other guest both started thinking. His name was Parvize Tehrani, and his wife was Parveen Tehrani. They looked at each other, seeking answers for all the questions they had in their eyes. They asked about each other's elementary school. Iraj has been raised in Zahedan, Kubol, Khash and the cities around. So were the Tehranis. They hugged each other and kissed each other again and just sat there. Then they looked at each other again. Iraj said, "No, I don't think you are the same Tehrani that we went to school with". Then in a few minutes Iraj said, "That was Vaheed Tehrani we knew". They jumped up again and screamed, "We are Vaheed Tehrani". So this time they hugged each other tighter and kissed each other warmer. By then we were all rolling on the floor from laughter. But they did not stop there. Once again they took up the kissing and hugging, and thought they were not who they thought they were. But after the tenth time of knowing and not knowing one another they confirmed that they did go to the same elementary school after all. And they remembered that they were all Baha'is at the time. That scene was enough for Morteza to have a subject to clown around all day, and for many, many years to come.

Oh my GOD. I have so many of these memories that when I think about them, they take me back to yet another scene. At this time that I am writing, I laughed so much that I cried.

These two couples did not have any kids and were free to do anything or go anywhere they pleased. When they came to my house, I had Mary to take care of, plus many other duties and chores. I was very disciplined and organized with my time and my schedule.

One of the Saturdays we had dinner together, we had so much fun. I had prepared Ghormeh Sabzi, a vegetable dish with meat and rice, for the next day, which was Sunday. This meal is hard to make just because it takes time and patience to make it right. After I put Mary to bed and we all went to our rooms to sleep, I could hear, and I could sense that these three men were up to something. After a while I got up to see what was going on. I caught them stealing Sunday's food and eating it out of one dish while sitting on the stairs. Well, you can imagine what has happened after they were caught. They started hiding from me. GOD knows we laughed so much. None of us can ever forget that day.

My Dear GOD:

Morteza knew how sensitive I was about everything, especially Mary. He knew that I would kill him if he ever bothers Mary. We were all riding in the car once. Iraj and I were in the front with Mary On my lap. Fereshteh and Morteza were sitting in the back. We were all quiet for a little while when that Morteza called my name in a very genuine voice. Obviously, I thought he needed to ask me something. I turned my face quickly to see what

he wants. Morteza's big toe was right in my face. He had extended his leg from behind Iraj's seat; he placed it on the back of my seat just so as to put his toe in my face. Well, I got mad at him and was ready to kill him. But GOD knows how much we laughed each time we were together. Fereshteh was the one who laughed more than everyone else. I said to Fereshteh that Morteza was doing all this just to entertain her.

We were poor, but so innocent; we were full of energy. And, most of all, we were honest and loyal to each other. These memories are so valuable; they cannot be exchanged for anything else.

While we were here, our families in Iran were also going through changes. I had two children, Pari had two children, and Neia had two children. Ezzat, Azar and Sina each had two children. My brother Jamal had two kids as well. Reminiscing on what my sister-in-law, Afsar, has always said, I was responsible for their marriage. Jamal and all of our family went to Afsar's house to introduce her to my brother one week before my departure. It was just a simple visit for the first time. Everyone knew why we were there, except for poor Afsar. She didn't know that we were there to see if my brother approves of Afsar to be his new bride. Their marriage took place after I left, and they had a daughter. They named her Negeen.

Mohandess Forghani was out of prison and he had his first child Arman. They built a big house in Shemiran. They were pretty well off among the rest of us.

Parveen went to England to study midwifery. And she divorced her husband, Mr. Safavi, after her mother died.

Pari and Kamal were both still teaching, while attending university in Tehran. Pari was studying French and Kamal took up a major in architecture. Financially they were not doing well back then. On many occasions they had to borrow money from Neia and Mohadess just to carry on.

Kamal built a beautiful house in Semiran after he graduated from university. That was his first project. Things started to go well for him after that. He even got involved with building a house for Ashraf Pahlavi, the twin sister of Mohammad Reza Pahlavi, Shahanshahe of Iran at the time.

My Dear GOD:

Everyone was doing well, and I was looking forward to getting ready to return to live among my siblings some day. We made sure to always exchange photographs to keep up with all that has changed throughout the years we've been apart. There were pictures from weddings and graduations. There was a particular photo I had once received. It was of my three brothers Jamal, Javad, and Jalal. I couldn't believe my eyes. My little brother Jalal, who was in sixth grade then, had a shaved head. It was accustomed for boys to have their heads shaved. The reasoning was that the kids of his age would concentrate on studying verses hairstyle or fashion. In that picture Jalal was taller than Jamal and Javad.

He had a mustache so handsomely groomed. I was so happy to see my three handsome, beautiful brothers that it brought tears to my eyes. They were tears of happiness, and not of sadness. I said to myself, "GOD! You have given it all to us. Thank you." I was so delighted with that picture that I carried it with me everywhere and showed it to everyone.

Then slowly, just simply by reading between the lines of their letters, and by gathering little hints from here and there, I sensed that something was wrong. I started asking everybody "Is there anything wrong with my family in Iran?" But no one knew anything.

But I knew for sure that something was wrong. Thoughts of possibility of loosing one of my parents were lingering in my mind. Now that I was gone for almost four years I was returning to them anticipating their forgiveness. I wanted to kiss their hands and apologize. But what if they were no longer there to hear my apology. Oh GOD. I have thought of worse, and the worst that could have happened to my family, except for what has taken place in reality. I was walking around like a zombie, and I was talking like a zombie. And I remained in that state for almost a year. Then I decided that I have to stop these negative thoughts, or they will eventually drive me insane.

We found out that we were allowed to take two cars home with us that particular year. We already had one car and so we bought the second one.

It was a long and a beautiful car. It was so great to be able to drive such a car for someone who has never owned a car. I didn't know how to drive since I didn't need a car. We had planned to live a fairly good life in Iran. Iraj intended to start big. He bought the most expensive things in Germany. We bought gifts for everyone. When I was choosing a gift for Jalal, Iraj helped me buy the most appropriate gift for his age. We decided to travel by ship first, and then take a journey through many countries all the way to Iran in our car. We shipped the smaller car to New York and we drove the bigger car ourselves. We decided to stay in New York for a little while to visit some of Iraj's resident friends from Iran.

My Dear GOD:

Once, before this trip, we drove to New York. We took Mary along with us. While we were sight seeing, a car rear-ended us. As a result Iraj's neck was hurt badly, and Mary, who was sitting in my lap, fell under the seat. Thanks GOD nothing serious happened. But we were all very scared.

After that accident I knew better to furnish the back seat of the car with pillows, blankets, and soft cushions for Mary and Maseeh so that they were able to play in the car. I packed books, coloring books and crayons, colored paper and baby scissors. I had to make sure my children were comfortable. The trip was supposed to last two and a half months, considering that everything went as planned.

Queen Elizabeth was still running at the time. It was a huge ship, and it was so

beautiful. I could have never imagined such a beauty even in my dreams. Each floor was like a city. The deck was at the top floor. It was amazing to observe the ocean from out there. And at the same time it was very scary. There was water all around as far your eyes could see. I don't know how to swim, and I get motion sick. So I was not having much fun.

The dance room was huge and all the guests were anticipating the evening. The dining room was clean and very well designed. Altogether it was a significant voyage, especially for us. Mary and Maseeh though were very confused. My poor children did not know why and where on earth they were.

Maseeh was still in diapers. I used to use fabric ones. I did not want to waist money. I wish I wasn't such a considered wife, a kind of a woman who thinks of her husband's pocket as of her own pocket, and tries to save money at all times. So I used fabric diapers to save money for my family. Naturally I had to wash the diapers by hand. I didn't know though that they used the seawater on the ship. Maseeh started feeling very uncomfortable.

My Dear GOD:

During the last two days in the ship, I was ok. And thank GOD, I was able to solve Maseeh's problem too.

So when we got to London, we got our car and we saw Parveen who was studying Midwifery in England. I knew my brother Javad was in England on a scholarship for his continuous education. We were supposed to see him there also. We stayed in England for two weeks. There was not enough time for us to drive around and see all the places that was there to see. Parveen was with us all the time. But for some reason, we did not find Javad when we got there. Every day I asked Iraj, what should we do to be able to find Javad? And he promised me, "don't worry we will find him". So one day we were sitting in Tehran Restaurant in London, we got a telephone call. When Iraj came back, he said "it was Javad, and he is coming here to join us. It was only two days before we leave England. I was so happy to see him.

When I left Javad, he was a young boy. Now he has grown up. He was always a gentleman, handsome and chic. From the moment I saw him, I asked him, "How is everybody in Iran"? He answered me in a way that I felt he did not want to talk about it. He never looked into my eyes and he was drain from complete happiness. No matter how many times I asked him, "what was wrong", he didn't answer me. He just said: "Nothing. Nothing".

That night that he was with me in the hotel, he laid down on my bed, while he was holding Mary in one arm and Maseeh in another; sadly, he stared at the ceiling. I sat by his side to talk to him. But his face never opened up to a smile. I kept asking him, is my mother dead? Is my father dead? Is anyone of your sisters or brothers dead? He kept looking at the ceiling and said "No". That night we were up till three in the morning, and I couldn't

make him talk.

Next morning we all went sightseeing, and it was around after noon that we said good bye to him, without finding out what was so bad that took all his happiness away from him.

With Parveen we traveled to Paris. They carried the car in the ship as well. The time that we spend in Paris, Parveen stayed with us. We did all the sightseeing together.

It was funny. One night we wanted to go to a nightclub called FOLLI BURJEH (I don't know if I spelled it right). I never left my children with a baby sitter in the U.S.A., how do I do it here? Not only was I afraid to leave them with the baby sitter but in the hotel there was no one who could speak English. My GOD, how do I do it? How do I leave them with some one who could not understand them? None of us can understand French as well. After all, the manager assured Iraj that taking care of your children for few hours is not that difficult, even if the baby sitter does not understand English. But when we were leaving the baby sitter came. Guess what? The baby sitter was a man. I was going to change my mind and stay in the hotel, but Iraj who wanted me to have fun in that trip insisted that, it is ok. Besides, the baby sitter speaks very little English, Overall, in that trip, Iraj did his best that I have the most fun. He did anything in his power to make me happy. He spent so much money on few very expensive fabrics. He bought two beautiful Indian Sarys. He bought two sets of dress with overcoat and one very beautiful suit. He did so much that it embarrassed me.

My dear GOD:

So I talked to my children and I sat on the bed with them and took some pictures with them. And I explained to them that I and their father were going somewhere and that we couldn't take them with us. I think they understood me, because neither of them cried. When we went to the club, as always I took my camera. I couldn't read French, so obviously I didn't know that I wasn't allowed to take pictures inside. Soon a gentleman came and wanted to get the camera from me. I told him that I don't understand French and that I didn't know taking pictures was forbidden. He did not take my camera, but he advised me not to take any more pictures.

After few days that we were in Paris, Parveen left for London and we continued our journey.

In all the times that we were in the U.S.A. and through out the journey, every second, Iraj stopped us to take our pictures. It seemed to me that he was the happiest man with his little family. If someone is not happy with his wife, he will never continue being so nice to her all the time. Why does someone have to pretend for such a long time? Why will anyone pretend to love his wife, if he is not really in love with her? Or why should a woman like me, who loves her husband more than anything else in the world, allow herself to doubt her husband's love to begin with? How does a woman know that her husband love

her? Aren't all the things that he was doing for her, the sign of loving a person? I don't know. I really don't know.

We traveled from country to country. In some countries, we stayed longer the others. We did a lot of shopping especially in Germany. We went to see Mr. Bagher Forhani, who is the brother of Mohandess Forghani, Iraj's brother-in-law. We went to meet Iraj's friend in high school days in Zahedan, Mr. Hosain Shirazi, who became our mutual friend. In Iran, he was the letter carrier from Iraj to me. Hosain was in Germany for continuous education. He got his degree in Mine Engineering. They knew each other from seventh grade and they were both friends of my brother, Jamal.

We did most of our sightseeing with these two gentlemen. We did such a stupid thing that I don't think any one is capable of doing that. I think, because from the beginning of my life with Iraj, I started in a strange country that I wasn't familiar with the language or any thing else, so I began to listening and following Iraj by all means. And when you started your life like that, it will become a habit that would be difficult to get rid of it. He was trying to be noticeable when we were in Iran. He bought a big Hi Fi set and was planning to take it to Iran over our car. To ship it to Iran was easy, but cost money. Iraj had never driven through the roads in Europe. Since he had only driven in the USA, he has forgotten that driving in England is on the other side of the road. So my opinion was dismissed, and we put the huge Hi Fi on the top of the car wrapped it tightly with lots of ropes, thinking that we are safe that way. We haven't gone fifty miles yet, when we noticed that the Hi Fi is sliding down. Thanks GOD, we were not in a place where we couldn't control the car. We tightened the ropes again and drove to the nearest big city so we can just ship the Hi Fi to Iran and drove continuously the rest of the way in peace and harmony.

My Dear GOD:

In the meantime my family kept up the pretence of normality. I chose to let everyone to carry on with their lives. I tried to block the unpleasant thoughts of bad news from back home; I kept them all to myself. And only in my solitude I kept moaning and groaning. The words, "Nothing bad has happened" kept ringing in my ears. I must have been out of my mind. I worked hard on reasoning with myself so that I could make sure that everyone lived a happy and healthy life.

Reflecting on couples' relationships every now and then, I came to a conclusion that while in love and dating or throughout years of marriage one of us will always try to mold, try to shape the other to our own liking. During the time that Iraj and I were in U.S., I felt very misplaced. I was overwhelmed by many responsibilities, and I lived a trivial life in my own trivial world. Those were the years when Iraj tried to reshape my character according to his own believes and desires. I have never been into pretentious lifestyle. And for that reason I chose to fall in love prior to getting married. Iraj's happiness has always

been of a greater significance to me than anything else. Iraj dreamt of living the life of a movie star in Iran. He wanted to glow in the eye of public. I, on the other hand, wanted to live a normal, happy, truthful and a genuine life full of love. (Keep dreaming Shamci).

So before we left Michigan Iraj was adamant about buying me a fur coat. It was right before we left. We were living in our second house. We had no furniture, no carpet, not even money, except for some savings for our return to Iran. We went to downtown where we saw a beautiful Chinchilla cape. And of course it looked beautiful on me when I tried it on. No doubt about that. But in addition to the immense price of the cape, we had to pay a fee to the customs as well. I would never hurt his feelings, so I never rubbed it in. I knew that he wanted to buy that fur cape to show me how much he loved me. But I always believed that one's lifestyle should go with one's means. The equation of having a fancy cape for my shoulders at the time when we couldn't afford first necessities did not make sense to me. I am sure there are other women who would love such an effort. But I was not just any other woman.

Morteza and Fereshteh came along when we went to get the cape. We got the cape and paid a fifty dollars deposit. The owner of the store advised us that they could ship the cape to us so that we avoid paying additional fees at customs.

My Dear GOD:

That day Morteza made fun of me and said, "You make your husband buy you a Chinchilla, and spend all his money in order to stop him from shopping for his sisters. I will tell them all that you have done."

So I was able to convince him this time that we need the money for our children more than the fur cape. So I made him return the cape. And meanwhile we had lost the fifty-dollar deposit, which was quite a substantial expense at the time. But despite this episode I went along with all his ideas in later years, I became the constant blame in the eyes of my children, especially Mary who was always looking for something to blame me for.

We are confronted by many occasions, and incidents in our daily life. And a lot of times we will simply let them pass by reason of being unaware of facts and/or circumstances.

Iraj and Hosain went to high school together, and they were roommates for a while. Iraj was a Baha'i and he became an object of ridicule among Muslim students. Hosain who was a Muslim went to his rescue and they became very close friends. They exchanged a lot of letters when we were away. We used to always read Hosain's letters together. That was one of the proofs that there was nothing to hide in our relationship. Good or bad, we knew everything about each other. I thought of us as of one person but in two bodies.

They discussed everything, even sex in their letters. I remember that there was a particular letter I couldn't make much sense of. Hosain was complaining about Iraj's way of sleeping in such and such place and that it bothered him a lot. Many times he would

discuss his sexual capabilities with Iraj. Iraj always advised him on how to handle different situations. This one letter was about a girl. She was a teacher. Hosain was writing that they made out in the movie theater. I was shocked. I knew that girl.

At one instance Hosain told Iraj, that he liked my sister Sina. But he wasn't sure if Sina was interested in him. So while we were still in Michigan, Hosain went back to Iran for a visit. He visited my family, but he didn't get to see Sina. In his letter that followed his visit to Iran he expressed to Iraj that he didn't believe that Sina cared for him, since every time he went to our house Sina was nowhere to be found. He felt like she was avoiding him. But once again Iraj recommended that if Hosain liked Sina so much, he should have asked Akram, who was our second cousin, and a good friend of Hosain, to step in the middle and ask my parents for their marriage. By then Hosain was done with his education in Germany, where he got his degree in Mine Engineering. So he followed Iraj's advice. But to our delight and surprise we found later on, that Sina would leave the house every time Hosain appeared only because she had feelings for him, and she did not want anyone to find out. When Hosain went back to Iran, they got married and they had two boys Ali, who was working on his PHD in physics in London, England and Ehsan, who got his Master in Electronic Engineering from a university in Belgium.

My Dear GOD:

I always wondered if all the talk of sleeping in such and such way, that was kicked around in Hosain's and Iraj's letters had anything to do with homosexuality. But anyway Iraj broke their relationship, just like the rest of his relationships. They had such great friendship, and yet they never contacted each other again.

We drove from one country to the other, from sunrise to sundown. One day we were passing through Yugoslavia, a communist country, driving a plum color Chevrolet, an American car. We were driving through some farms, when all of a sudden we came across some locals, who were screaming, "Yankees go home. Yankees go home". They started throwing rocks at us while running after our car. I asked Iraj to pass that area as fast as he could. While he was trying to make a safe escape through a farm he hit a hen that was running in the middle of the road. Oh GOD, we thought that was the end of us. We wanted to stop and pay for the damage, but that wouldn't be very wise. I think they would have killed us. So we just kept driving until they were out of sight. I couldn't help imagining what would have happened to us have we had that huge Hi-Fi on top of our car.

There was yet another obstacle in our way through the mountains of Turkey. We have heard about it from others before we went on this trip. "Every other car crashes down the hill", so we were told. It was described to be the most challenging road, and Iraj still wanted to attempt it.

So as we started on the road in those rocky mountains, we said our (Besmellah) with the name of GOD. It was a narrow unpaved road at the most outer edge of the highest

mountain you have ever seen. We drove up a sharp hill for miles and miles and miles. On one side there was a rocky mountain hovering over our heads, and on the other side, a long way down was a road with numerous cars. The cars looked so tiny from up there. I kept an eye on Iraj throughout, and I could sense his fear. I tried to talk and joke around to make him feel better. But when we got to the sharpest edge, where we had to make a turn he stopped the car and got out. I got out of the car as well. Even though it was hard for Iraj to admit that he was afraid he said, "That's it. I don't think I can do this". You can picture what I went through at that moment. I kept thinking, "What if there is a car behind us?" So I started clowning around and told him, "Come on. You have done things much harder than this and you have never complained. This is not a big deal. I will stay outside, and you take the wheels back and forth". After talking to him for few minutes, and boosting his ego by reminding him of all his abilities, he started to smile. It took him a few minutes, but followed my advice, and we passed the highest and most dangerous curve on that rocky mountain.

My Dear GOD:

This takes me back to his letters, where he always told me, "If it wasn't for you and your encouragement, I would never be able to achieve as much as I have".

And at the moments of cruelty towards me, when I asked him about his letters to me, he answered, "I didn't know any better those days. I was wrong if I wrote you those letters".

So we passed the rocky mountains of Turkey safe and sound. We were supposed to call Dr. Alkar and his wife, who left U.S. one year before we did. Mrs. Alkar was the one who took care of Mary after I have had nose surgery. They made us promise to call them and stay with them in Turkey.

They gave us a royal treatment, talking about being nice. They took care of my children, they included us in their family gatherings. They drove us all around Istanbul and Ankara. They took on scenic tours, and bought us sweets (Pashmak, a kind of sugar candy). Although neither of us smoked a tobacco pipe, they made sure to provide it just to make us feel at home. My GOD, they were a nice family. I heard later on that Dr. Alkar passed away. I wonder why he died; he was so young.

While in U.S., we agreed that my parents would meet us at the border of Turkey to welcome us home. I asked Iraj, "Where are they? How come no one is here?" He smiled and said, "There has been a slight change in our schedule. We are supposed to drive to Ghazveen to my uncle Mr. Hormozi, and we will find out everything then". I was going to visit his uncle's house for the first time, so I didn't want to come across as an impatient person. I found out that his uncle lived on his own. His family was living in Tehran. And he lived in Ghazveen because of his job.

We talked and laughed, and we played with Mary and Maseeh, but no one brought

up my parents. And each time I tried to ask about them, Iraj's uncle would bring up some funny story, and change the subject. After a while they said," We will drive to Tehran, and you will see your parents there". I started questioning Iraj. I wanted to know why I wasn't aware of all these changes. Once again his uncle started telling a funny story, so I forgot about my worries.

My Dear GOD:

It's been becoming more and more obvious that some disastrous news were awaiting me. How awful could it be that no one dared to talk about it? I have met all these people for the first time, and yet I kept asking them about what had happened. Everyone I turned my face to, kept repeating, "Nothing had happened at all." I was very embarrassed, and so I apologized and just sat there quietly for a while. I was holding both Mary and Maseeh in my arms. I knew how miserable they felt. They didn't know Farsi. And even though they were surrounded by family, in reality these people seemed like strangers to them. They were glued to me, as if they would never be able to hug me again. They could sense that there was something wrong with me, but they didn't know what to do about it. They couldn't understand anybody, and they didn't want to separate from me. I kept talking to Iraj's cousins and his aunt. I told them that I was glad to see them. But I wasn't expecting to meet them under such circumstances for the first time. Once again I tried to find out what had happened to my family. And yet again they answered, "Nothing. Nothing at all". And at the same time they never looked me in the eyes, as they answered "Nothing." So I apologized over and over for my behavior. I assured them that I didn't know why I had these feelings that there was something wrong with my family. I asked them to forgive me, and I promised that I am usually not like this at all.

Then in a little while Iraj was called out of the room by his uncle. He came back to let me know that he was going to get my parents. He was so pale and frightened. That look on his face made me feel very sad and worried. At that point I was sure that he was going to bring me the news, no matter what. I sat there and yet again apologized for my strange behavior. I was so impatient. I tried to distract myself by introducing everyone to Mary and Maseeh. Maseeh was more frightened than Mary. Mary was trying to keep him entertained by talking, and trying to engage him in a play.

I was very concerned about my children. We were on the road for two months. We were challenged by many changes. For instance going to the bathroom for Mary was disastrous. She didn't want to use bathrooms that had toilet with no seats. Maseeh did not have that problem, since he was still in diapers. So Mary stopped urinating and going to the bathroom altogether since we got to Turkey. I tried to take her to the bathroom at every stop, but she refused to go. She complained about bad odor and the toilet seat. She was afraid of getting dirty. It wasn't until we got to my parents' house, three days later, when she was finally able to use the bathroom. I always wondered how she did it. The consequences of this and many other similar incidents worried me. I tried so hard to help my children to make sense of everything that went on.

My Dear GOD:

When my parents did not come to Tabreez to welcome us, Iraj tried to reason with me by saying that it was because of the rough roads. I always wished that Mary and Maseeh were older during those two months of our exciting trip. If they were a little older they would retain memories of all the countries we traveled through starting with New York and the Queen Elizabeth, London, England and many European countries, and then our trip through Turkey to Iran. It must have been such an experience for them, if only they were older. But they were too little. I couldn't expect too much from them.

Iraj's family members, the ones that spoke some English were trying so hard to comfort my children with their kind words. But they were too shy to converse.

I worked hard to conceal my emotional distraught. I forced myself stay focused and polite. I made myself to talk to each and every person in the room. I thanked everyone for their hospitality.

It took almost one hour for Iraj to come back. He came inside with my sister Ezzat. And while I was holding her in my arms, I asked her if Moosavi was dead? She said, "No". Everyone looked at me as if I was crazy. Once again I went along with my apologies. My Mother and my sisters Azar and Sina arrived next. I held them all in my arms and asked them if my father was dead? "No, no" everybody kept saying. I already knew that my older brother Jamal was in Kerman with his family. I realized at that instance that the only person missing was my younger brother Jalal. Then I heard my own solemn voice say, "Perhaps you wish to tell me that Jalal is in Kerman with Jamal". I looked around the room. Everyone was looking down. I was in a state of shock. I kept asking, "Why Jalal, why Jalal? He was too young to die." My sister Saideh took my children away from me. I got up and went to the bedroom and sobbed and sobbed. I must have sobbed continuously for that whole year. I didn't want to talk to any one. I was dead myself. And yet I didn't want to cry in front of my children. I knew it was killing them. God, please give me strength to be able to deal with this without hurting my children. Please GOD, please help me.

It was then that I realized why my mother and my sisters showed up wearing wrinkled dresses. I had never seen my family dress so improperly. In our country a family continues wearing black for a whole year when somebody of a young age dies. So when Iraj caught them by surprise showing up at my parents' house, they had to remove their black dresses in a hurry, and throw on the first thing they found in their suit cases.

My Dear GOD:

I knew now why Javad was so lifeless. He wanted to cry on his sister's shoulder, but he couldn't. My family told him, "Shamci doesn't know anything about Jalal's death. Make sure not to tell her". GOD, what a tragedy! How did you take Jalal from us? He was such a handsome man. Girls would hand him flowers on his way home from school. Why did he have to die? I didn't know how he died.

Iraj didn't want to tell me, because he was afraid I would go crazy, and/or do harm to my children. I can't say that he wasn't right. I can't even imagine what could have happened to my children or me had I found out about Jalal's death while we were in Michigan. I loved Jalal so much. He was our baby. We fed him, we bathed him, and we held him in our arms and put him to sleep. Why must he die at the age of seventeen and a half? Why, why?

Alas my questions remained unanswered. I had to put myself together. I had to take care of my poor children before they died too.

So after all the sobbing and weeping, I came back from the bedroom. I apologized for all the inconvenience. I wished farewell to Iraj's family, and we went back home to my parents' house.

Okay my dear GOD. Was that all there was? Did we deserve a punishment as immense as Jalal's death? Or was it a punishment at all? I don't think you consider death a punishment. You take us away from this world the same way you bring us into here. If death is a punishment, then every single person, no matter good and bad, will be punished. This cannot be true by any means. We, the rest of the family, the so-called survivors, were the ones who were punished. All of us had to carry, and be forced to bear this tragic loss in our hearts for the rest of our lives.

That night I had to watch over my children. I introduced them to my family first. I finally fed them, bathed them, and put them to sleep. My grandmother was visiting from Shiraz. I was happy to see her. It's been a while.

I have accepted the fact that Jalal was dead, but I didn't know of the circumstances. I figured I had plenty of time to discuss this matter with my family. And I decided to get some rest. But I couldn't sleep that night. I awoke early next morning with a shrill howl. My GOD, I sounded like a wounded animal. I couldn't recognize my own voice. But I couldn't control myself any longer. I really didn't know how to stop. It took me half an hour before I could start to reason with myself.

Every single day, while in U.S., I dreamt of going back to Iran to see my dear brothers and sisters. At the time when I left Jalal, we were not able to keep in touch with one another due to circumstances. I can't even recall the last time we spoke.

I was very much aware of the fact that my mother always preferred Javad to Jalal. Everybody knew that, even Javad himself. I always had quarrels with my mother about her favoritism. And even Javad was trying to stop my mother from discriminating Jalal.

But she would never listen to us. I remember that right before I left for U.S., there was an instance when I thought my mother treated Jalal rather harshly. I sat next to him and asked him to ignore what my mother's doing. I tried to show him my support.

My Dear GOD:

Had Jalal been a kind of son who has always been in the wrong, my mother's preference of Javad to Jalal would be of a non-issue. But he was not. The College Alborz never accepted anyone lesser than great. And Jalal was great to be able to join that school. He was the friendliest and the funniest at home. And the most ambitious kid within our family. Although Jalal and Javad had very different characters, one funny and the other serious, they loved each other, and in addition they were best friends.

I knew that when Javad left for England, they exchanged letters more than twice a week. It's a fact that Javad was an A+ student, but Jalal's academics were excellent as well. Two people are never completely alike. I don't know why my mother has done what she has done. She probably didn't see it herself.

Jalal was my father's toy. He was my father's favorite when he was a baby. He actually was everyone's favorite. He was so beautiful that our home address was known as a house with the most beautiful baby. He was very chubby; he had fair skin, blond hair, and big green eyes. I savored those moments of having him in my arms.

When Jalal was almost five years old, my mother had my little sister Saideh. She was also a very cute baby. At the time none of us was aware of the fact how much attention Saideh got in comparison to Jalal. And later on during Jalal's teenage hood, my father did everything against his will. He had created such a great gap between the two of them that their relationship was impossible to repair.

When I got to Tehran, it was one week before Jalal's one year death anniversary. My GOD, I was hoping to be able to celebrate his wedding anniversary. In the meantime I found myself mourning his death anniversary. My dear GOD, how was that fair? How is it fair now?

For a long time I didn't know the circumstances of his death. When I found out that he had committed suicide by hanging himself in our green house, I was so furious with my parents that I wanted to kill them. I couldn't live a normal life any longer. I knew that one of these days this would happen to one of us. I blamed my mother the most for Jalal's death. His death was a big lesson in raising my own children. My parents were not willing to, or maybe simply couldn't adapt themselves to changes around them. They had always followed the rules and regulation of (Ghoran) Koran. They didn't know any better. As time went by I became more and more distressed with my parents. My anger and frustration was further directed towards my mother. I couldn't forgive or forget her deeds during the years of my own youth.

My Dear GOD:

Please don't forget my dear GOD. My children were still very young within that time period. I didn't know what life was all about; I didn’t know that eventually I would have to face the hardship of dealing with my children’s teenage hood. I had very poor judgment, therefore I was merciless. I was pushing my poor parents to the limits.

Jalal has been having emotional problems due to his environment. He was seeing a psychiatrist, who was a friend of the family. The psychiatrist had warned my family that he was in a dangerous state of emotional distress.

My father always tried to control us. In my case there was a power struggle between him and Iraj over giving me up to Iraj. And when it came down to Jalal, it would start with not allowing him to wear certain clothes and accessories, such as hats or T-shirts.

Nobody ever commits a suicide if the problem is not acute enough to drive the person to the edge. All the nagging and harassment over an extended period of time had become so severe and unbearable for Jalal that on that special Friday he said, "That is it. I am not going to take this humiliation any more. Goodbye forever."

It was Friday. My father has been nagging at Jalal about insignificant little things as usual. They were all supposed to go to Ezzat's house for dinner. She lived a few houses away from my parents. They were all waiting for Jalal to arrive. I expect that when he arrived my father yet again insulted him in front of everybody. So Jalal left and went back home. Ezzat ran after him and begged him to come back. She pleated him to ignore my father. But he wouldn’t go back. He didn’t go back.

It was while everyone was still having dinner, when my mother started to be concerned. She went back home to ask Jalal to come back. When she got to the house and opened the door, she found her son hanging from the ceiling. She ran toward Ezzat’s house screaming. Everyone ran to the house. When they got there my mother realized that she had locked herself out of the house. Moosavi broke the window. He cut the rope and took Jalal in his arms while they drove to the hospital. Jalal’s body still was warm. Moosavi tried to give him mouth-to-mouth resuscitation. It didn't work. It was a Friday evening, and there was not a single doctor on call in the entire hospital. By the time they found a hospital with a doctor on duty Jalal was announced dead upon arrival.

My Dear GOD:

You were there. You know how it happened and why it happened. You know what happened to the whole family. Every one of us died both on the inside and on the outside. Oh GOD, could there be any worse disaster than this? Was it fair for you to take away his beautiful life? How did you do it, GOD? How could you do it? Everybody thought that if the door did not get locked or if the doctor was there Jalal would have survived. But I say “No”. I said it once, I said it twice, and I will be saying it over and over again for as long as I am alive. Everything in the world is preplanned already. We can never change what it

has been planned before. Jalal had to die that day. Otherwise the door wouldn't get locked, and there would be a doctor on duty at the first hospital, at the first time round. So we lost my dear brother Jalal and the mourning remained with us for the rest of our lives.

And guess what, my dear GOD, Jalal left this world, and he is sleeping peacefully forever and ever. But those who didn't or couldn't understand him had to stay alive and suffer for the rest of their lives.

My poor parents, aside from having to deal with all these complex emotions of grief and guilt over loosing their son, they were faced with a very difficult accusation of killing our brother. My father became lifeless after Jalal's death. All the meaning has been leached from his life. He lost so much weight. He would really punish himself till the day he died. My mother could not get over Jalal's death. But the worst yet was that she couldn't talk to any one of us, she had no one to share in her grief. We were so much alike, always away from the siblings. Her children could never comprehend her loneliness. Jalal's death took away her liveliness, his death had turned her life upside down. Many times she wished to be dead instead of Jalal. But we all know that these wishes would never come true. My poor, poor mother. What a destiny, what a life.

I had no idea what my mother had gone through, until I was faced with sufferings of my own. I always recall her telling us, "You will never understand what I am going through until your time comes." This is true for any parent. Your age doesn't really count. Unless you have children of your own, you will never experience what your mother has gone through. Iraj's older sister Parveen doesn't have any kids. My youngest sister doesn't have kids either. I am sure that both of them don't comprehend what we, the parents, go through.

My mother has always been superstitious. She believed that we should be careful about sharing in our happiness, since apparent happiness of one person could provoke envious and dark thoughts and deeds of others. Then somehow the happiness shatters.

My Dear GOD:

She became a grandmother of four within three months: my son Maseeh, Azar's son Reza, Ezzat's son Nader, and Jamal's daughter Negeen. She asked us not to tell anybody that she had four grandchildren all in three months. She said, "Some people can't accept my happiness." When she lost her son, she blamed it on the powers of the evil eye. I don't know that I believe that. But there is a certain weird power of the phenomenon. My mother's life was filled with happiness, pride and joys of becoming a grandparent, and then suddenly she looses her seventeen-year-old son.

My sister Ezzat, in a moment of fury, shouted so loud in Nader's ears that he became deaf for a long time. She had to deal with the consequences for years to come. Azar dropped her son Reza from her arms and she had to pay for the consequences for years as well. My brother Jamal sought solitude for a very long time. There is so much to talk about. But in short, we all lost our soles.

We stayed with my parents for two months. I wanted to share my beautiful children with them. I wanted them to see what a happy life I had. I wanted to let the whole world know that I have made the right decision by choosing Iraj as my husband. But instead we were mourning for my brother.

Iraj had to start looking for a job at the hospital. He had to make himself known among physicians. We had to start looking for a house and move out.

Iraj and my father were getting along fine. They had respect for each other and looked forward to establishing a good relationship. Iraj had to go to Abadan to receive our shipment from U.S. My father was very knowledgeable about laws in government offices. So Iraj asked him to join him on a trip to Abadan together with his cousin Mehdi Agha. It was six to seven hour drive. It was an excellent and a very stimulating trip for both of them. My father needed to talk to a friend away from the subject of Jalal's death, and Iraj needed a father figure to talk to.

On the morning of their visit to customs office, Iraj realized that they were trying to give him a hard time. They were requesting paper work, and more paper work. They asked one question after the other. We had shipped quite a few items. There was a car, a hi-fi, and much more. He could have been in trouble had they decided to proceed with all the formalities. So Iraj requested to speak to the supervisor. As soon as he entered the room he recognized the supervisor. They happened to be classmates from high school. Iraj used to tutor this gentleman in math. And once he recognized Iraj, they both hugged each other, and they sat down for some tea and sweets, a typical Iranian tradition. So the subject of customs was resolved in a friendly manner.

My Dear GOD:

While they were in Abadan, Iraj received a job offer at one of the best hospitals in town. He knew that I wasn't ready to live away from my family then. So when he asked me if it was okay to accept the job offer, I told him that if I wanted to live away from my family, I would have rather stayed in U.S.A., and not go through all the trouble of getting back to Iran.

We rented two floors of a four-story apartment building on Kakh Avenue, near the Kakh Square. The building was located in a well-known, wealthy neighborhood. Very distinguished people like senator Moosavi and doctor Lashkari lived there. We set up Iraj's office on the lower level, somewhat a basement. And as always I got to use my talent of sewing for creating his office. This way, not only we saved money, but also we were able to realize our own special design ideas. We chose the light green color for his surgical room. I helped him save enough money to bring two cars to Iran and buy all the necessary furniture for his office and our house. We furnished our living and dining rooms, the bedrooms, the family room and the kitchen. In addition, with all the money I refused to spend on myself, I was able to assist on paying rent for a two-story building. I believe that we all learned great way of managing and spending money wisely from my mother. She always lived the best, spent the least, and enjoyed the most. We did learn this lesson from my mother.

The yard belonged to our residential level. At the far end of the yard there was a maid quarter of a fair size. It was a great yard with a shallow pool in the middle.

Well, a young doctor returns to his country. He finished his residency and he specializes in Obstetric and Gynecology. He possesses knowledge, good looks and lots of money (it just looked like that on the surface). Did he make a good name for himself or what? Did he make himself noticeable or what?

Iraj's plan was working. He was a family man, who was in love with his wife; he had two most beautiful children. My GOD, what else do you want Shamci? "Aren't you the luckiest woman on earth?" I asked myself. "Isn't this more than what Iraj had promised you?" Of course I thought that I was the luckiest woman on earth, but many people did not want to see me that fortunate.

One of the cases that I remember vividly was the life of our friend, Doctor and Minoo Khadem in Iran. They too returned from Michigan and started their life in Tehran. But their life was by far not anything close to ours.

I've got to know Minoo more than just any other doctor's wife. She felt very close to me. And most of the times she opened up to me with her private matters. I think she had trust in me. She was a Baha'i and had many Baha'i friends. While back in Michigan she had difficulty to accept and communicate with her sister in-law, Mulook. I always tried to make her understand that she had to find ways to deal with it because she was not going to share the rest of her life with her sister-in-law. But she always allowed herself to be bothered. Things got worse for her in Iran. She had a little girl Marganeh who was two weeks younger than Maseeh. They had rented a small apartment. They converted it into both living and office space with a simple room divider. All those limited living arrangements along with many other factors have eventually made a great contribution to Minoo's unhappiness with her overall life. She started talking of divorcing her husband. And at the same time Dr. Khadem would discuss his family matters with me on regular basis. Somehow I found myself in the middle of a very delicate situation. Mulook, who was very much in favor of Khadems' happiness, tried to assist in every way she could.

My Dear GOD:

God knows how many times I asked Khadems to come over and discuss the situation openly. There were times when I tried talking to them individually to get to the root of their problems. I tried to convey to them the idea that in reality all it would take is just a little understanding. They didn't have major issues. I made sure to talk to Minoo as often as needed to make her understand the core of life. I remember one very special day when

Dr. Khadem was on his knees begging Minoo not to let their baby face separation of her parents. This poor doctor with his tears running down his cheeks was asking Minoo not to jump into hasty, wrong conclusions. Khadem promised to me that he would do any thing that Minoo asked of him. So after a few days of discussions and a few weeks of problem solving, Minoo questioned me, "Why should I have this deprived life, while both our husbands came from Michigan with equal credentials?" Dr. Khadem's specialty was pediatrics. "Why must you possess two cars, a two-story building, and all this furniture? Don't you think that this is not fair to me? Don't you think that I deserve a better life than this? All of my sisters are having a good life. Why shouldn't I have a life like they do?"

I respected her honesty. I knew that many others went through unspoken speculations on this subject matter. But I liked Minoo very much for her honesty.

I would tell her about the times when we first got married. I told her how we didn't spend any money on our wedding. How Iraj didn't have any money to pay for his own ticket to go to U.S.A. And I told her that I loved him all the same, if not more, even though he had no money. "But your husband has spent so much money on your wedding only. And at this time he is spending all his money on you and your baby. He has plans to do good in a few years. Besides, you did not make a promise him to marry him for his money only."

My Dear GOD:

So we talked and talked, until one day she came to her senses and accepted my point of view. She realized that getting divorce for such a childish reason was not suitable for a real mother, and a real lady.

So they kissed and made up. They never thought of getting divorced again. And they lived happily ever after. Not only they were able to buy a house, but also they bought many other houses. They bought out Dr. Khadem's office space as well. They had a son, named Jahanshah two years later. My children and my entire family's children were Dr. Khadem's patients. Years later they moved back to U.S.A. We always kept remained in touch. Jahanshah became a doctor, and Marganeh was a teacher. She got married and had three children. But later I heard they got divorced at their old age.

So we started our life in Iran according to Iraj's expectations. He found a good job at the hospital and was very busy with promoting his practice.

I didn't see Iraj much while we were in Michigan. My children saw him even less. Obviously, we were never at the hospital to know for sure where he was or what he was doing. His words were the words of Ghoran. I believed every single word he told me. There was no reason for me not to believe him. He was mostly home when he needed to rest. It could have been during the day, or when we were going to a party, and/or when we have had company in our house. The rest of the time, be that day or night, he was at the hospital. I have always felt sorry for him that he had to work so hard. And although the load of my work and responsibilities was not any less than his, I still thought to myself that I owe him. I always felt that he deserves the best. There was no reason for me to ever doubt his words. I trusted him to an extent that I would readily cause harm to anyone who had ever doubted him.

He gave several lectures at the University of Tehran in front of medical students and Dr. Mossadegh, who operated on his mother years back. His lectures were very successful. They made him well recognized among the students. One of the lectures was on cancer, with a focus on specifically breast cancer. That was an important topic to discuss for women. Iraj also started to write a book on this subject with help of my sister Sina. In no time it caught attention of many women. That was his intention to begin with. He was arranging a good future for himself.

Although we were not among the rich and famous, Iraj for sure was acting like one. We arranged an open house party for his office. Besides many other gifts, he received hundreds of big baskets of flowers. We couldn't believe it. Our life style was changing rapidly. We were frequenting more and more night parties. There were months and months when we were going out at night. Our nights always started after nine P.M. I had to take my poor children to my sister Ezzat, who volunteered to take care of them while we were gone. We would normally pick them up around two A.M. I was so embarrassed to wake my sister up every night. I knew that she had to get up early in the morning to go to work. I was feeling really awkward. I didn't have any help. I had to entertain a lot and attend many parties. This crazy schedule was unfair to my poor sister, who has never complained, but it was also very excessive for my children. They had to get up early the following morning, and get ready to go to school. What could we do? What should we do?

My Dear GOD:

At the time Iraj was thinking of finding a girl to assist him with office work. One day he brought a girl home to introduce her to me. "This is Farkhondeh. She will be working for me in the office" he said. Well, I had no problems with that. She seemed nice and presentable. She was married to her cousin and had a little girl. Once or twice we asked her to baby-sit for my children at night, while we were at a party. It felt good not to take my children out of their beds, and drive them back home in the middle of the night.

Then Iraj started to take advantage of circumstances. He knew how hard I was working. He knew that I was getting tired of staying home day in and day out. I was thinking of going back to work if I could, even if it was just part time. We were trying to find help for me at home at the same time. I had interviewed many ladies, but I couldn't trust them with my children. We had to resolve this dilemma.

That was the time when Iraj came up with a splendid idea. He said, "Since that little maid quarter in the backyard is vacant, we can kill two birds with one stone. We can ask Farkhondeh and her family to move in there, and in return she will help you with your

work and baby-sit for the children at night as needed." At the time it was not a bad idea. But the building didn't have a separate entrance. The only access to it was through our living room. It seemed so odd to give away our privacy, and allow access to our house to all these strange people at any given time of the day or night.

There were two more levels above us. There was a Jewish family living right above us. They had four children. The husband was trading Persian rugs. They were quite, well-mannered, and very nice people. There was another Jewish family, who had two boys, living at the top level on the forth floor. They were very nice and quite people as well.

My Dear GOD:

We just greeted each other, and we were respectful to each other. Our neighbor on the fourth floor was a young lady. She enjoyed talking to me from time to time. I was so surprised when she told me her life story. Her husband was a blue-collar worker, who always worked late at night. They had a small apartment with a minimal life style.

This was the story of her life. When she was three and her brother was five they were vacationing with their parents in Europe. Her parents got into an awful fight one day on the train. They were very rich, and they always traveled. That day her mother was wearing an elegant dress, she had a beautiful feathered hat on, and white gloves. She was holding a colorful fan in her hand. Her father was wearing a magnificent suit. They started hitting each other and calling each other bad names. It was all because her mother found out that her father had his mistress with him everywhere they traveled. Her mother left the train that day, and they never saw her again.

Wow, what a story. She blamed her parents for all the unjustness that happened to her and her brother. And she was trying so hard to be an excellent mother to her two boys.

Iraj's schedule was completely different from the one in Michigan. In Tehran he came home for lunch and I had to have lunch ready at around one P.M. Many times he came home with a friend or his cousins. After lunch they took a short nap and later they would have tea and/or fruit. And at four P.M. he would go back to his office and work till nine or nine thirty. So the lady's schedule in Iran was much fuller. I was looking forward to finding someone to assist me.

At the same time our friends and family were going through changes as well. Mohandess and Neia bought a big house in Shemiran. They lived a comfortable life. They had two children, Arman and Nazi. Neia was a good mother. She was a very calm and quite person. Although she never told me that she loved me, I remember days when she showed me her love in her actions. Once we were sitting in her living room. Spring time people in Iran like to eat fresh walnuts. I had barely opened my mouth to say that I love fresh walnuts. Next thing I know we didn't see Neia for about ten minutes. When she came back in the room, she served me fresh walnuts that she bought within the ten minutes

time. I remember many cases like that. Not only was she a good mother to her own children, but also she took care of Pari's children when Pari was away, namely shopping in Paris. How odd it is that our destiny dictates our lives. It will always remain a mystery.

Pari had two boys Keyvan and Kaveh. They were still working on their college degrees. And Parveene returned home from England with her diploma in midwifery. While she was working as a teacher, she was trying to establish an office for her practice.

My Dear GOD:

I can't stop thinking of this other unfortunate episode. We were acquainted with a doctor who was taken in to a mental institution while we were still in St. Louis. Thanks to Iraj's tremendous performance the doctor was freed from the institution. But he couldn't pass the ECFMG test, and so he decided to return to Iran. We were informed of his sudden death shortly after. By that time we were back in Iran. Iraj has remained in contact with his father, we were told that he died of Hepatitis B. Iraj asked the doctor's father to accompany him to the cemetery. His gravestone was carved as an incomplete book. This was another example of how destiny works mysteriously.

While we were in America, my children did not have the opportunity to see their father too often. Iraj's schedule didn't improve when we moved back to Iran, and again the children didn't get to spend time with their father as often as they needed to.

He left the house around seven o'clock every morning, the kids had to rush to school at the same time. Then in the evenings he stayed at his office until nine. And by then the kids were in bed. So the interaction between them and their father was limited to simply exchanging greetings. It was just I and they, and they and I over and over. He would leave for the hospital in the mornings, and he stayed at the office in the evenings. I, on the other hand, was cooking, cleaning, shopping, and entertaining my husband, whom I loved so much. I would entertain others as well because I wanted to keep him happy. He was a good husband, a good provider, and a big spender. Many people envied me. He always showed his love and attention for me in front of my family, and particularly in front of his family. I was very flattered by his love and attention, I was proud of it, and I expressed and showed my love for him in return.

He had finally convinced me to allow Farkhondeh and her family to move in to the maids' quarter in our backyard. Farkhondeh was tall and pretty. She seemed very humble. I would never suspect a trap, not for a million years. I loved the idea of having her around; I was convinced at the time that she loved her husband as much as I loved mine. My baby-sitting problem would be solved. My dear God, what was wrong with that? Farkhondeh and her family would be staying in the maids' quarter for free, and in return they would watch my children when we were gone.

She would come in sometimes to just talk to me. And although I never wanted to become that close to her, I never wanted to be rude.

Then little by little I started noticing changes in Iraj's behavior. It wasn't that he all of a sudden stopped loving me, or that he started being rude. But I could sense that there was something between Iraj and Farkhondeh just by catching the glimpse of the way they looked at each other, that sly and sneaky way. That was not something I could ignore.

My Dear GOD:

To ensure that I loved him the way that he wanted me to, Iraj had always has kept his promises to me since the day I got to know him. There were times before we were married, when we frequently got into arguments for this particular reason. So he never wanted to make me mad or upset. His office was on the first level, and we lived on the second level. Whenever he mentioned to me a specific time that he would be home, he meant it. He knew that the dinner would be served on the table at that time.

I noticed that time after time he came up late. I was trying not to allow myself to be getting wrong ideas; I was trying to get the dreadful images out of my mind to prevent these ideas from ruining others and myself. I kept reminding myself that I was there to show my parents that Iraj was not and is not that wrong man that they always thought he was. I wanted to tell my father that my choice was not a bad one. My God, please tell me what to do.

She was working in his office with him in the evenings, during the best part of the day. And she always found excuses to come to our house throughout the rest of the day. I knew that he wanted to find help for me, and that he wanted to make it easy on me when we were going out at night. What should I tell him now? How should I deal with this ordeal?

It was only four months that we moved in that house. I was still in the midst of putting up the curtains. I started loosing weight. I couldn't talk to any one. I was feeling embarrassed in front of my family, relatives and friends.

By now we have made quite a few friends in Iran. Some of them we knew from U.S., and there were others that we met here in Iran. Among them were Morteza and Fereshteh, Dr. and Minoo Khadem, and Dr. and Naheed Naghshineh, Dr. and Froogh Azimi and Dr. Toosi. They came back from U.S. and they were living in Iran now. The couples that we have befriended in Iran were Dr. Toosi, and his wife Shahnaz, Dr. Pazandeh and his wife Farideh, and Mr. Hosaini and his wife Moneer. We would get together as a group every once in a while.

I have mentioned Fereshteh and Morteza previously. Naheed Naghshine and Froogh Azimi used to live in East Lansing, Michigan with them as well. Dr. Azimi was a psychiatrist. He was a designated doctor for Shah's family, namely Shah's brothers. Dr. Azimi has written numerous books on psychology. And besides giving lectures in universities, he had his own radio talk show. So he was doing very well. His wife Froogh was the daughter of a well-known businessman, Mr. Ghandehari, one of Iran's tea magnates. Froogh had the worst stuttering problem. She has had a few surgeries in England but the stuttering problem was still there. I heard through the grapevine that Froogh used to work for Dr. Azimi, and then he asked her to marry him. Obviously he was completely aware of her speech problem. Froogh's father was very wealthy. And while he was alive, he had given each of his children a house, and many other things. All the houses were located in Shemiran, the best part of Tehran.

My Dear GOD:

Froogh, was a very good-natured person and a very talented lady. She always liked to work. And while she worked, she liked to help others.

Dr. Toosi received his PHD in East Lansing, Michigan. His wife, Shahnaz, was a beautiful, talented, full of enthusiasm, but most importantly good-natured, and a very classy lady. She had studied fashion design in England. She was a great seamstress. Her father was an engineer and her mother was the first successful businesswoman in Iran. She owned the Skyway Company, plus she was involved in many other business affairs. When I first met her I had the impression that she was an intelligent, a trustworthy, and a classy lady. I never heard her talk badly or act mean, even to those who deserved it. She had respect for everyone and tried to be helpful to everyone. She always stood out among other ladies for her exceptional beauty. I cared for her a lot.

Dr. Naghshineh and Naheed were first cousins. This kind of marriage is allowed in Muslim religion. They had two children. He had received his PHD in Lansing, Michigan as well.

There was a time when Parveen started to look for a job. Iraj & Parveen were both in the medical field. He was an OBGYN and Parveen was a midwife. So it made sense that she would work with Iraj in his office.

I was busy with the housework: cooking, cleaning, entertaining, and taking care of my children at the same time. And after I would put my children to bed, I had to be ready to go out with Iraj for more parties.

I was completely drained. I didn't know who to talk to, I kept thinking in the meantime. I realized that before it gets too late, I should put stop to whatever was going on between Iraj and Farkhondeh. I thought that asking Iraj to get rid of her and at the same time asking her to move out was the best plan.

My Dear GOD:

One night he told me that he would be home for dinner at eight o'clock. When he didn't show up on time I walked down in the yard to see if there were any more patients waiting out there. To my shocking surprise I saw Farkhondeh through the corner of the curtain. She was pulling Iraj's hand as to keep him there with her. And Iraj was showing her his watch, telling her that it was time for him to go upstairs to his family.

Oh my GOD, I couldn't tolerate watching them any longer. I flew upstairs; I tried to stop myself from shivering. But how could I do control my emotions? So; everything I had sensed was true. There was something going on between them. I wasn't ready to face the reality. It all became very apparent to me. I was sure at that time that he has been having affairs all along while he was away, or even when I was around. The fact that he started having affairs within three months of living in this house, right under my nose, was a solid proof that he wouldn't have a problem with doing so while he was away from me. Now I remember the way the nurses were treating him. It was not just a doctor and nurse association. I couldn't make out their chats, but the body language accompanied by the laughter made the intentions very clear.

Parveen was visiting that night. I am sure she saw my desperation when I came in. I was able to calm myself down, at least for the moment. I set the table and waited for him. When he came in I asked him how come he was late. I don't remember his answer, but I was so convulsed with rage that I could have killed him. I am sure he saw it on my face. I assume Parveen noticed it too.

I believe, for those who were not aware of what was going on behind the closed doors, I would have come across as one ungrateful wife, who did not value her husband's hard work, the one who treated her husband with bad mood and angry behavior. The observers typically only see your façade, your face. They don't know anything about the killer turmoil inside of you. If they were to choose between a husband and a wife, they would vote for the one who is always in a good mood. And in my case it was my dear husband, who had his wife to love him in bed at home, and his mistresses outside of home. Don't you think that he would be in a good mood all the times?

After I confronted him, I asked him to get rid of Farkhondeh, and I insisted that he asked her to move out of the house. He made up many excuses and he warned me of very dangerous consequences. All I cared for is that she moved out of our house. All that I wanted at the time was to be able to live day by day and save my children from the disaster that I have always feared, the disaster of having a broken home. I had seen children from broken homes all my life. I have read the stories about their lives. I did not want my children to join them.

My Dear GOD:

One of the disturbing cases was the life story of his aunt. I heard this story from one of his cousins who was telling it as it really happened.

When I got to know this family I thought that this woman was their maid. I found out later that she was their aunt, the sister of their father. She did all the shopping, the cooking and the cleaning for them. I never questioned them openly, why this woman was living with them, or why she didn't have any family.

As time went by I found out that she had two sons. When she was young, her brother

Mr. Sarvan Rafani made her divorce her husband and took her children away from her. Her brother and his family justified their doings by accusing this woman in fooling around. In Islamic religion a brother could even kill his sister for being involved in extramarital affairs. So Iraj's aunt had to stay with her brother in his house, while others raised her children. One of her son's was raised by his paternal grandmother, and the second one was raised somewhere else.

No one ever called her by her name. Instead she was referred to as Ammeh, which means aunt in Farsi. Ammeh started conversations with me on several occasions, but never openly. She would always shake her head, and with tears in her eyes she would say, "It passed then and it will pass now".

Her two sons grew up to be so different. One of them never completed his education. He married a simple and uneducated girl. They had two children. He was the one who came to see his mother on rare occasions. Ammeh's older son, who was raised by his grandmother, continued his education through college, and became an engineer. He was also married to an educated girl. And they had a good life together with three children. He never asked about his mother and he never wanted to see her. His wife though would call Ammeh once in a while and she would invite her to their house. But even there, at her son's house, there was no respect for her. As if she really deserved it.

These two brothers were so distant. Neither of them cared about each other existence or well being.

I was invited to go to Ammeh's older son's house together with Pari and everybody else. Ammeh was there, I guess visiting for few days. I observed everyone around me, and especially the host, Ammeh's son. Despite all the wealth and success, along with all the academic and financial achievements, the so-called happiness, there was no sight of self-confidence or any real happiness in him. His mother was in front of his eyes to remind him what he had gone through in his childhood. And most of all to remind him that she has been the enslaved by all these people, her own family, and her entire life.

My Dear GOD:

He could neither change his past, nor the present. And he wouldn't even be able to change the future. All that I could as an observer was to feel sorry for all of them. I couldn't help contemplating that if Sarvan Rafani did not separate this family of four. If he would have let them run their own life. I am positive that the power of love and togetherness would have made a greater person of all of them.

In my opinion, to kill a person emotionally is much worse of a crime than killing someone physically. This family was destroyed; it was completely ruined at its inception. There were no ways of healing those mental bruises. When love disappears from hearts, we might continue living, but a loveless life can not ever be mended by success or money. Success and achievements cannot bring happiness to fulfill a person. No one knew what

had really happened to this family. They were all just victims.

Ammeh was very young at the time. She had neither education nor money to be able to escape her brother's ego. He would have killed her. Her children were too young to understand what was going on with their parents. They had to listen to the people around them and they had to believe them. Their mother was never allowed to explain to them her side of the story, so that they saw the truth. And so the entire family was put through tremendous sufferings. Each one of them blamed the other, while neither of them was a winner, except for those who used and abused them.

This was not the only case of injustice that I have witnessed or heard of. I have met so many children from broken homes that all these stories and incidents made me aware that once you become a mother, you better be responsible for the rest of your life. You can't give up on your children for no reason.

Once, when I was a little girl, I read an article in a magazine about a four year-old boy that was taken to the hospital. The doctors had to remove more than hundreds of needles from his body. The boy's stepmother pressed a needle inside his body when she wanted to punish him. That did it for me. I said to myself that I would never get married or have a child unless I was able to love my life, my husband, and my children to a point that I never had to leave them. I didn't want to get married unless I was absolutely sure that I would love that person forever.

My Dear GOD:

Okay my dear, dear GOD. You have been a witness to what my children had to go through from the very beginning of their lives. I delivered Mary in a strange country with no friends or family around us. Then, when she was barely two-weeks-old, I put her in the train and brought her to even stranger place. When I had that nose surgery, she was so scared of my bandaged face, that she wouldn't let me hold her. Maseeh was born when Mary was twenty-two-months-old, and I had to leave her with a neighbor who was a complete stranger to her. We had to move from one house to the other. Then to add to all the instability we put them through a two months trip from Michigan by ground and by water to Iran. And then I had to face the news of my brother's death in front of many strange people. And at the time that I was ready to show them some stability in our own house, it didn't last for even four months. They were faced with their father's infidelity and their mother's sadness and struggle. They were at the age of discovering the meaning of love.

One of the most significant ages in child's life is the period between two to five. Our actions will affect and/or infect their emotions in either positive or negative way. And in my children's case everything was negative according to psychological studies.

Since we have arrived to Iran things were happening so fast, one after another. We were so preoccupied with renting a house, furnishing it, and preparing the office for open house, that we didn't consider what was going on with our children. We never recognized their fears and emotional agitation caused by their parents and their surroundings. What a pity! I have always thought that if I fall in love and get married the way that I did, I would be able to raise my children right, according to the book. I was not aware that my own promise and devotion alone were not a solution to the problem. It takes two parents to be devoted and loyal to their promises. And naturally when one parent starts having an affair, the other parent would go crazy and do things that are not suitable to him or her. All of a sudden I found myself in a situation that I would have never thought of. All those dreams and all those hopes disappeared in no time. I had to face the fact that I was the one who must make sure that my children do not get destroyed. I had to be able to survive first, but how? Was it possible? Please, GOD, who should I turn to? Please help me. Please help me.

My Dear GOD:

As I said before I was working as a teacher before I got married. When I moved to USA, I had to resign from my work. I realized that I need something to hang on to at this point of my life. It was best for me go back to work to be able to stay away, even if it was temporarily, from that disaster that was facing me. I got my job back with Dr. Toosi's help. I started to go to work part time. I had signed up my children to a preschool. An American couple ran it. The wife, Miss Guss, was running the school. This couple was in Iran by assignment. They fell in love with Iran and Iranian culture, and decided to stay in Iran. And since they had no children, they ended up adopting an Iranian girl. We became friends. I invited them to my house on several occasions.

Mary and Maseeh took the bus to school. They came home after two p.m. I was working at the same time, and I was home before them.

I have finally found a lady that I liked a lot after many interviews. She agreed to live in our house and work for us. She was a tall, strong lady. Her name was Soltan. She did everything around the house, including the ironing, which I never liked to do. She had one day off during the week. Then all of a sudden, after three weeks, she told me that she had to leave. She said that she had a personal problem. But since I liked her a lot, and I also felt that she was happy to work and live with us, I had tried to find out what her problem was.

She explained to me that she had been "sigheh". Sigheh is a temporary marriage in Islamic religion. This marriage could be for twenty-four hours or longer, depending on the agreement. The purpose of this kind of marriage is that if a child is conceived within that time, he or she will have a father and a name. According to Iranian law the father has the responsibility for that child while he is living or deceased.

My Dear GOD:

Anyway, she had been "sigheh", and she had a child from that man. He eventually took her child away, and put him in the hands of social workers.

She was planning to go get him. But she was not sure if she could bring him to our house. She didn't even know how to get to that building, or how to ask for permission to see her son. I asked Iraj to help her make it possible for her to see her son. As a matter of fact, Iraj was the one who drove her to that place for the first time. He helped her find her son.

She was so furious when she came back that day. The story she told was hard to believe. After all the bureaucratic hassle of numerous paper works, the opportunity of seeing her son was getting closer and closer. Finally she was able to go in and hold her three-year-old son Ameer in her arms. She realized that something was bothering Ameer. She started to observe his body to find out what the matter was. To her complete surprise, she finally discovered that the elastic of his pants right above his knees has been awfully tight. It almost looked like the elastic has grown into his skin. Those social workers! Not only they did not change the little boy's clothes, but they never give him a bath either. This was beyond belief, but whenever he cried or asked for help, they punished him and tortured him to a point that he kept quiet and stopped crying all together. There was also a possibility that they sedated him at night with strong tranquilizers. There was no other way for someone to survive in these horrifying life conditions day in and day out.

My heart kept palpitating while I was listening to her story. I couldn't believe what I was hearing. I felt so sorry for that poor woman. I didn't know how to comfort her in that situation. The only thing I could think of was to offer that she brings her son to our house once he was released from that institution. And he will be like a brother to Maseeh. I think my idea helped her feel much better. She decided to stay with us, and bring Ameer in our house too.

Iraj followed his case persistently to make sure he was released from the institution. The whole process took a long time, but it was worth it. When they brought him home, it became very apparent to me how bad it has been. The little boy had marks of ruffled fabric around his legs, above his knees. Those marks remained on his legs forever. I had something to look forward when she accepted my offer to stay with us.

I am able to write about all these events with such ease now that it's all behind us. But it is very difficult to relate how I felt then.

My Dear GOD:

I was a very skinny girl to begin with. I was shy of five feet tall; I weighed ninety-six pounds. The hardship of dealing with Iraj's affairs made me loose more weight. Everyone could tell that I was having problems. At the same time my children were getting sick quite often. Dr. Khadem, who was our pediatrician, suggested that it would be better that

we had their tonsils removed.

Both operations were done at the hospital on the same day. I took one week off work to stay home with them. I sat in the middle of their beds for three days until they got better. Iraj was never around. He was not there at the time of the surgery. He wasn't there to comfort them while they were recovering. He was too busy achieving his goals, which I could never understand.

I didn't know how to handle this loveless life. I couldn't discuss my situation with anyone. I knew that my family would ridicule me. They have already disowned me once when I decided to marry Iraj. The only person I was close with, and the only person I could talk to was my sister Ezzat. She was very concerned about my children and me. And my only true friend was Pari, my sister in-law. She held my hand from the beginning to the end.

Iraj was on the rise. He has made a promise to make me the happiest woman ever. I wanted the best for him. I wished that all his dreams came true. I wanted him to sustain his prestige and image. GOD, please, how could I make him understand?

Now that I had Soltan as a living maid, I did not need Farkhondeh to baby sit for me. But when I wasn't home she still came to my house snooping around my closets, and admiring my clothes. Soltan would tell me, "I can't stop her from coming to the house". She had the key and she could come any time she wished.

When I insisted that she had to move out, Iraj was more offended than she was. Naturally, he had found himself a cheap and easy affair, and he did not want to get rid of it. She was quite brave to do all this, and mingle with a married man in his house, in front of her husband. In fact she was showing off to her husband that she was so good that this doctor, who had a wife and children, was coming after her.

Iraj was not ready to loose this battle. He told me that she does not want to move out of the house. And by law we cannot make her.

What can I say? At this time I was upset, I was mad, I was beyond being angry, I was furious. I remembered what my poor father was trying to tell me. He said he has never questioned my innocent love for Iraj. It was Iraj's feelings and honesty that he doubted.

My dear GOD, why didn't you let me have that knowledge at the beginning? Was it important to you to make me experience all this?

Farkhondeh had sent her mother once to beg me to let her stay in the house. I told her, "This house didn't have a separate door. We made a mistake and we apologized for our mistake".

My Dear GOD:

I am really not sure if it was that girl who was so daring, or if it was Iraj's encouragement that made her so courageous. In any event that girl had to leave the house, it was out of question.

By this time, I think that most neighbors knew that something was going on with us. From Moosavi's house, that was exactly across her apartment, they could observe her making gestures to Iraj. I was going crazy. Overflowing with desperation, my emotions and my actions were beyond control. I have threatened him with a big knife on one occasion. He was really scared. This other time I hid myself under his desk in the office to try to catch him in action. He checked around the office when he first came in. He opened the door of his desk to find me there. Thanks GOD, this took place before any patients got there. We both started laughing. But in reality there wasn't anything to laugh about. This was a very serious matter. There was a time when I took a whole bottle of aspirin. I don't remember who had found me first. They took me to the hospital, where Iraj and Parveen gave me an internal wash. I remember one day, while I was still in bed, Parveen was telling Iraj, "Why don't you divorce her and get rid of her?"

My family was not aware of what was going on in my house. They could sense that something was very wrong, but they did not interfere. I don't even remember if my sister Ezzat knew anything about me trying to commit suicide. Parveen was the only one who knew.

The worst part of it all was when he wanted to prove to everyone that I was loosing my mind, and there was nothing wrong with our lives.

This one night a whole group of us was invited to Froogh Azimi's house for dinner. Froogh was an artist and she arranged some of her artwork for sale. She presented all her artwork for sale after dinner. Her art was so beautiful. Everyone admired her pieces. None of the guests volunteered to buy anything for their wives. My dear GOD, you were there, and you know who bought the most beautiful and the most expensive black rose for his wife. It was Iraj. He, who was having an affair with his nurse under his wife's nose. Isn't he really something? Wasn't he really something? All the wives looked at each other, I knew that what they we re thinking. They thought what a nice husband Iraj was. What a big spender. Some of them started talking to their husbands. Oh my GOD, what a show off. If this man really loved me, like all other husbands loved their wives, he would not be involved in an extramarital affair. And he wouldn't be buying me flowers either. But no, he had to make a point of buying that flower for me in front of all those people. So that if I ever brought up his behavior, no one would ever believe me. He always wanted to make himself look good in the public eye.

My Dear GOD:

This man was so rootless. He wanted to portray me to those who knew us, as a woman with psychological problems. There was a time, while we were still completely in love that I wanted to go back to work. I had to come up with a reason for my resignation. That was an agreement between us. We made up a story that it was due to some psychological disorder. I would have never imagined that at some point he would try to

use that against me. I understand now why my father was against my marriage. He must have sensed these malicious trends of his personality.

I became pregnant right around those times. As if my children were not suffering enough. I have always been, and I still am against abortion. But this time around I did not want to bring a child into this world under those circumstances. I chose to be destructive at inception rather than killing my baby emotionally and physically when he/she is in my arms as a living being. GOD, you were there, and you were the judge of all that.

So, he performed the abortion with the help of his friend doctor Razzi.

Abortions are against the law in Iran. So he did not want to do it in his own office. Instead he drove me to this other office one day; he brought me back home in about half an hour.

It wasn't only his affair that was destroying me. I could never conceive how he could have done the things he did in that office. I was turning to look like a walking skeleton. Soltan told me one day, "The way that you are suffering in this house makes me forget about my own sufferings for my son".

Iraj would do everything in his power to earn more money and popularity. He had many ideas. American dollar was equal to seven Iranian toomans at that time. Iraj wanted to live his life within the rich and famous. He began with entertaining important and very well known people, whom, by the way, we had nothing in common with. He had to hire a chef to make himself live up to their expectations. He has never been a good dancer; he had no sense of rhythm. And yet he was arranging fancy dance parties. It was embarrassing for me to be involved with all his doings. But while he was on the go, I could do nothing to stop him. He was trying hard to fit in this new life style. It made many people ridicule him, more than enjoy him. I was very confused, trying to fit into his ideas and adapt myself to my surroundings. It was important to me to find a way to save my life and my children from destruction, while Iraj only gave importance to becoming rich and surrounding himself by the rich and famous. He was going out of way to be nice to me in front of people. He acted like a loving and caring husband. But that would only make me grow madder. I was at a point of being ready of either a murder or a suicide. That was why I acted so stupid many times. I am so thankful to you my dear GOD; it was you who kept me away from becoming a criminal. No one had ever witnessed what was going on behind the closed doors. I never talked about my problems. So people thought that he was a good and loving husband, while I was an unappreciative, scandalous wife.

My Dear GOD:

Many times when I watched soap operas on TV, I thought to myself, "How is it that some people have to go through such rough life, and just come across obstacles one after another?" But when my own life started to resemble one of these episodes, I realized that, yes, these stories were based on real life.

Before I hired Soltan to work for us, we found a young village boy to assist me. He was either fifteen or sixteen. It's been only a few months since he started to work for us. One day I was talking and playing with Maseeh. My little son in his childish way tried to show me that the young servant has been trying to molest him. I knew that my son, being only three, would never be able to make up such story. I decided to fire the boy immediately. Parveen, who did not have any children, decided to hire the boy. But then later on I heard that my accusation was assumed to be one of my hallucinations. Well, let it be, as long as my son was safe, I did not care what others thought of me. It was my son who was important to me, and not their gossip.

Mary and Maseeh were getting sick more than usual. So I called Dr. Khadem to ask him to check them once again. This was after they had their tonsils out. He told me, "These kids need attention. The lack of attention from one or both parents creates this kind of fatigue and sickness". It was around lunch time, and Iraj came home. Dr. Khadem told Iraj the same thing. But he just kept laughing as usual, and he said nothing. As if they weren't his children or as if doctor Khadem didn't know what he was talking about?

She was not afraid of anything at all. She was trying to take advantage of the situation. In Iran, if a man has an affair with a married woman, he deserves to be put to death, particularly by the woman's husband. She was using the law to manipulate Iraj.

After I insisted that Farkhondeh had to leave our house, she made Iraj to rent a house for her elsewhere.

I don't know if she was still with her husband. But after he rented out the house for her, he was not home for the most part. We would usually spend our weekends together as a family. But Iraj no longer joined us. My children, and especially Mary, who was a little older, knew what was going on.

My Dear GOD:

Pari was a real friend to me at that time. She would never leave us alone. We spent most of the evenings and every weekend at her house.

One weekend when we came home, Iraj was in the house with Farkhondeh, and they were in my bedroom. He sent her away as soon as he heard us, so that the children didn't see her. When I approached my bedroom, I saw a dish with fresh walnuts on the nightstand. And I noticed her shoes near my bedside. I did not say a word. I just threw her shoes out the window to make her realize that I was not bothered at all. Meanwhile, I did not want my children to think that their father would rather spend his weekends with another woman than being with them.

And so when Mary cheerfully asked her father if he bought the fresh walnuts for her, I interrupted him by saying, "Yes". Your daddy loves you so much, so he bought them for you".

One weekend we were having picnic together with Pari, Neia and their children.

While we were sitting around the table Mary asked me, "How come everybody's daddies are always here? But my daddy is never with us". I answered her, "Mary jon, your daddy is a doctor. His schedule is very different from other daddies' schedules. He has to work late or work on the weekends most of the time. That is why he can't be with us all the time". Mohandess knew by now that Iraj was having an affair, and so he made a sarcastic comment, "This is another advantage to be a doctor. He can do anything he wants, and get away with it".

I became fully aware at that moment that I made a big mistake by marrying Iraj, and I dragged my children into this mess. I realized that my father was right all along. But what could I do now? How could I correct my mistake, and could I prevent my children from suffering the consequences? I had no other choice but to lie to them to cover up for Iraj. Although I was dying inside, I had to keep them happy with my lies and let them be among others. Yes my dear GOD, after I have witnessed my husband in my bed with his mistress; I lied to them and made them believe that their father was working. And that he bought fresh walnuts for them because he loved them so much. Then I took them to their bedroom. And I read bedtime stories to them until they fell asleep. Then I slept on the floor next to their beds, and I prayed to GOD to give me strength, knowledge and understanding to help me overcome my problems. I knew that next morning I would have to resume my awful, miserable and sorrowful existence. And it was only you, my dear GOD, whom I could turn to; it was only you, whom I could ask for help.

My Dear GOD:

When doctor Khadem contributed Mary's frequent illnesses to the lack of her father's attention, there was nothing else I could have done except for taking his place and trying to give my both children love and attention. Pari was helping me to make this possible. But no matter what they wanted their father. They saw that all the other kids had their daddies, and they didn't have theirs. Iraj loved Mary so much that he named her Maryam after his mother. And now that he was having an affair, he had forgotten completely about his mother and his children. What a pity. GOD, have mercy.

I heard from some sources that not only he rented a house for Farkhondeh, but also he had furnished it in an identically with my house. He was living with her while she was married. He bought her as many clothes as I had. He spent most of his time and money with her. But on the surface, we were a husband and wife. We appeared together to social gatherings. And he stayed home when we had company. He made sure to keep his title and prestige among the doctors and the co-workers. He was playing it safe.

When I started to ignore his behavior, she started to make obscene calls. She made other people call me and inform me of my husband's whereabouts. Something inside me was telling me that she was trying hard to get a confession from me and record my voice to use it to convict Iraj.

One night after Iraj had left to go to her house a woman called me. She pretended to be my friend. She started complementing me and she was admiring my relationship with my husband. Then she told me where my husband was at that time. She wanted me to go and do something about it before it was too late.

I answered her, "My dear lady. You have the wrong person. You are confusing me with someone else. My husband is sleeping in bed next to me and I don't know what you are talking about". And while I was shivering I went to my bed, where I slept every night between my two children. I didn't let them wake up. I just let my tears roll down my cheeks until I fell asleep.

All these incidents led me to the assumption that Farkhondeh was after Iraj to marry her. In Iran and Muslim religion men are allowed to marry up to four wives, and hundred Sigheh. I think Iraj was refusing to marry her. So she was after me to get a confession to be able to take him to court, and make him marry her by government force. I, on the other hand, was waiting to find a way to be able to keep my children, and save them from possible destruction.

By this time I was so worn out, I was so drained and exhausted that everybody knew what was going on with my life and me. I had to talk to my father to find out about my chances to keep my children. He was very knowledgeable about Islamic and governmental laws. He informed me that there was no such law that would protect me from loosing my children to their father. "If he wants to keep his children and separate from you, there would be no law to stop him, even if he is a murderer, and you are the nicest woman and a wife on earth. That is the law in Iran, and you can't avoid it". But I wasn't satisfied with his answer; I wanted to do my own research. I decided to talk to my friend Molook Khadem. She had some lawyer friends. She helped me schedule an appointment with a lawyer. Once again I was told the same things my father told me word to word. He assured me that men have been using this law to be able to control their wives and at the same time have their extramarital affairs. If a man decided to leave the children with their mother that would be a different story. But if a man decided to hurt and harm his wife by taking the children away from her, no law could ever stop him. So I realized that I was trapped within my own web. What do I do now, GOD? It was I who told my parents "I will make sure that my children, have a wonderful life" It was I that told my parents, "I know that the man I fell in love with is the one and only gentleman on earth". It was I who wanted to make a love castle for my children. My dear GOD, how foolish can one be? I trusted in Iraj's love so much, that I thought our love is completely different from everyone else's. And just because some lovers did not make it, it does not mean that we can't make it. Our love is and must be different from all other loves.

My Dear GOD:

So the subject of divorce was completely discarded. He had warned me, that if I ever mentioned divorce, he would take my children away from me as far as he could go. And that he would never let me to see my children again. I knew that he meant it. I neither had the ability nor the money to go after my children. Besides, in such cases one parent should give up for the sake of her or his children. In our case I was the one who had to make up my mind and think of the best for my children, and become selfless.

It was summer. I was at home with my children. It was not possible for me to stay home and witness Iraj's behavior. I wouldn't even dare to put in words the things that went on in that house and in his office. I would be too embarrassed. He was obsessed with making money. It didn't matter to him how he earned it.

One day Iraj asked me to talk to the garbage man and ask him if he would donate his sperm. He said that he could use it for the ladies who need to get pregnant by artificial insemination. He also mentioned that he couldn't sleep with all of them, or use his own sperm. I almost fainted. I was thinking of whom to kill first. Should I kill myself first? Or was it going to be Iraj, or should I kill everyone at the same time and just put an end to this ugly life altogether? I did not have any answers for all those questions.

My Dear GOD:

I said to myself, "If he sleeps with all those women, he will bring me all kinds of venereal diseases. The sperm donation creates thousands of children in many strange homes. He never kept the records of sperm donors. And as for the husbands of all those ladies, they would never find out when or how their wives got pregnant. He sold his child for less than a hundred dollars, which was equivalent with seven hundred toomans, he sold a child to each one of those woman. So after thinking it through, I made myself strong enough to talk to the garbage man. I was so embarrassed to approach him. After I explained it all to him, and I told him that he could make easy money that way, he looked at me, and he asked me completely astonished, "You mean for me to sell my babies? Oh no, never, not me. I love my children with all my heart. I will never do such a thing. I'd rather be poor than ever give my children away". And he added, "If from now I find parts of bodies in the office trash, I will refuse to take your trash any more".

This conversation with a plain garbage man made me realize that it is not the education, money or the success which gives us the essence of inward nature of being. That man, who did not have any degree, money or prestige, was not willing to sell his sperm for any price. Bravo, bravo.

I knew that Iraj was performing abortions in his office with the help of Dr. Razi, who was an anesthesiologist. They kept it a secret to fool the public. Once I remember they were in our living room. Dr. Razi was complaining to Iraj about the way they were handling some abortion cases. He was telling him, "I don't have the heart to witness the

dismembering of babies from their mother's womb. I don't think it is right to give an abortion to a woman after eight weeks of conception. I can't watch the dismembered parts of babies. I can't sleep at night. I am having nightmares. I have to quit now".

I thought to myself, "Even this doctor can not accept Iraj's act of criminality. He aborted women at five or six months of pregnancy. He dismembered babies, wrapped them in surgical sheets, and then placed them in the garbage. That was why the garbage man complained, and refused to remove the garbage after my conversation with him".

He dismembered babies from their mothers' womb for as little as a hundred dollars. He sold his own sperm for as little as a hundred. I remember meeting some of his patients. They would announce to me happily, "This is Dr. Rafani's baby". I didn't know if he had slept with them, or if he had inseminated with his sperm. Or, maybe it was just a case of delivering that baby. Only GOD knows what the mother meant by saying, "This is Dr. Rafani's Baby".

My Dear GOD:

Okay, what did I really expect from a person who had given up thousands of his sperms in return for a very little money? How could I expect him to love my children and want the best for them? And in the end all the sperms that he sold to women, they all became young men or young women. The only difference was that they did not know who their father was.

My dear God, you were there while all this was happening. You might think that I was as guilty as anyone else. But you remember that I had to find the right solution to my problems. My children's life and happiness was at stake. I was only concerned about protecting my children from what was approaching them. So, yes, in a way I am guilty. But you were there, and you saw that I had no other choice. I had to do what I had done at the time. Had there been any other way, you would have probably shown it to me.

And then one day, almost around noon, he came home. He was acting very strange. After he removed his professional suit, he wore baggy clothes. He put on big round sunglasses, a very unusual hat, so that no one could ever recognize him. And he left the house in a hurry. I realized that something was wrong. I was sure that he was following Farkhondeh. He did admit to it later. But instead of hating him, I hated myself. Was he the person that I gave up my parents for? How could I give up my parents for him? Was it me who was so proud of having him as my husband? GOD, what did I do to myself? He was completely crazy.

That summer, after consulting with my father and the lawyer, I decided to take my children out of town. Although my teaching job didn't provide much money, I still chose to leave town. I didn't have enough funds to rent a place or be able to afford all other expenses. So my parents offered to help me move to Maygoon, a village near Tehran. Mary and Maseeh were my entire life. GOD forbids if I let them get hurt or be unhappy. I tried so hard to keep them happy, but they knew that something was not right. Maygoon was a resort town and many people spent their summer there. It was a very beautiful place to observe the nature. I would spend all day with Mary and Maseeh, and in the evenings we went out to eat. We often walked around the city. I kept the kids very busy so that they don't find out what was going on. My family visited us from time to time. Once it was Neia and her children, Arman and Nazi, who paid us a visit. We were very happy to see them. We had a great day together. And this other time my sister Ezzat came with her daughter Afsaneh. Afsaneh was either six or seven years old at the time. We thought that Afsaneh could stay with us and spend the weekend with Mary and Maseeh. Unfortunately she started feeling homesick as soon as her parents left. Boy, oh boy. We didn't know what to do. We could not stop her from crying no matter what. She wanted her parents so bad. So I had to go to the telephone station and call them to come and get her. We were almost five hours away from Tehran. Mind you that the road to Maygoon was very rough and rocky. I thought that Mary and Maseeh could keep her company. But it didn't work. She had to go home, and that was her decision.

My Dear GOD:

There was a little Bazaar in the middle of village. In the evenings everyone would go there to shop and look around. I was holding my children's hands at all times. Once in a while they wanted to let go of my hands. But this place was very crowded and I had to be very cautious. In just a blink of an eye, Maseeh jerked his hand and disappeared in the crowd. I kept looking for him. I zigzagged through the crowd. But there was no sight of Maseeh. I thought of a kidnapping possibility considering our circumstances. My dear GOD, you remember what happened to me, and how crushed I was. While I held on tight to Mary's hand, I started running around and asking people if they had seen a little boy. They all said, "No". It was getting dark, so I decided to start walking towards the house. I ran into a local housemate on my way. He said that he had seen a boy that fit my descriptions in front of my house. I couldn't believe it. The house was way too far from the Bazaar. And it would be very complicated for Maseeh to find his way home in the dark. But to my surprise, when I got home we saw him standing in front of our house talking to a housemate. I was so happy to find him there that I didn't even bother to ask him why he had run off the way he did. I was actually proud of Maseeh since he was able to find way home all by himself at the age of three and a half. He was very happy to see us as well.

One of our housemates was doctor Rastegar, who had a PHD in education. She was there with her son and her daughter-in-law. Her daughter-in-law was a beautiful young lady. She was a pure replica of young Sophia Loren, with same type of body. At first I was sad being cooped up in one room with my two children. I felt much more relaxed when I realized that they were living next to us in the same house. They were very nice.

I always thought that any mother would be ready to give up her rights for the sake of

her children. But I had to rethink my assumptions after meeting this one young mother. This woman had left both her husband and her child behind and came to Maygoon to have fun. She would tell me that she had a good, handsome, and caring husband. He was in the army, and did everything for her and her baby. He fed the baby at night and changed her and put her to sleep most of the times. I could not conceive that after all this she was still happy to leave her baby and her husband. She knew that her baby would be in safe hands with her father. I realized after I met that woman that not all mothers are alike. Some like themselves, and think of themselves before anyone else. It is not the culture or the upbringing that makes us the mothers we are. Not two mothers are alike. The seed of motherhood is not and cannot be planted with the expectations of the same result. I was learning life lessons day by day.

My Dear GOD:

In our room in Maygoon we had two portable beds, one for Mary and one for Maseeh. I used the sleeping bag in between those two beds for myself. I had one small burner and few small pots and pans with me. I knew that the children would like to help me with cooking and cleaning. Usually after we ate, I took the children by the stream in front of our house. The water was ice cold and Mary liked to walk around barefooted. We enjoyed our days in Maygoon. It made my children very happy when my family visited us. My parents came to visit us once and we went out to a restaurant for chelo kabab. My sister in-laws were very supportive and understanding. They also came to Maygoon to visit us, and they took us to Tehran to stay with them for a while.

As I have mentioned before, my sister in-laws were very supportive of me, they stood by me hundred percent. Parveen stopped working with Iraj after she had witnessed his hideous and shameful behavior. She chose to stay away from him, and she even stopped talking to him. That was very honorable of her. She didn't want to be part of his humiliating actions towards his wife and children. She couldn't endure the idea of Iraj's affair with a married woman. This sort of behavior of someone who was married was not acceptable in any society, and above all in an Islamic country like Iran. It was an immense shame to any family, and especially to a so-called prestigious doctor, who claimed to be the backbone of the female society.

I don't think Parveen did that only to please me. She did it because she loved her own name and had respect for her own actions while she was supporting me and my children.

Iraj and Parveen were very close all their lives. And I suppose that this punishment must have been very painful for Iraj. Most women would be jealous to see the closeness and the friendship between husband and in-laws. But, my dear GOD, you are the witness, and you know that the only reason that I admired Iraj and loved him was because he loved and respected his sisters and his mother in particular. I have always believed that

any man who valued his own family would have the capability to love and admire his wife and his children.

My Dear GOD:

Although my sister-in-laws were doing everything to keep us in high spirits, I have never heard them say “I love you”. Their actions were full of love and care. And while they never put their feelings into words, they always gave so much. I loved them back dearly. In fact, it is not vary customary to say “I love you” frequently in my culture. But at the same time you will see a lot of love and respect for one another through actions.

After my parents gave me up and disowned me, Iraj's sisters and their families became my true family. I loved them dearly and I always wanted to be with them. I enjoyed having them over at our house more than Iraj did. And after living with them one year, I considered them part of my life. The more support I received from them, the more determined I became to keep my children. I have decided that if anyone was to get hurt, GOD, please let it be me.

That summer I heard that Iraj was having troubles with the law. I become suspicious one day when he came home and changed his clothes to disguise himself. There must have been a good reason for doing so. I thought that he used the disguise to follow Farkhondeh. They must have had a fight, and most probably he was mixed up in some big mess. Unlike Iraj that woman had nothing to lose. He assumed that the women he was having affairs with would be as naïve, patient and bountiful as I was. I would not say a word about all the abuse he put me through. Alas he was just dreaming. There was not a single human being in this world that would continuously remain at his side. There was not a single human being in this world that would lend him a hand physically and emotionally in all the matters and circumstances. So he was in trouble and I have never found out why. Considering all the obscene phone calls, I knew that sooner or latter Farkhondeh would find a way to grab him by his neck and show him what life was all about.

There was another instance when he made a complete fool out of himself. He accused me of reporting him to police. I told him that I would never do that, and that I was the one who has been covering up for him. Meanwhile I had all the rights and reasons to do so. But of course he didn't believe me. To tell you the truth my dear GOD, at that moment I was only concerned about my children. Many times I thought that because he is part of my children's life, and they loved him so much, I had to support him no matter what.

Once I was in his uncle's, Mr. Hormozi’s, house. Mrs. Hormozi was a very good friend. She always had so much to say about Iraj and his family. She shared her very personal feelings about each and everyone of his family. I have always despised gossip and gossipers. People always shared their problems with me. And I am proud to admit that I have never spread any rumors throughout my entire life.

My Dear GOD:

That day I had to make a quick trip to my house. Their daughter Masoomeh (Havas) decided to come along. When we got there we saw a young soldier standing right in front of my door. I though he wanted to talk to one of my neighbors. I had asked him whom he wanted to talk to while I was opening my door. He mentioned my name.

He said he had something for me. It was a hot day. I asked him to go in the living room and wait for me. Then I took my children inside their room, and asked Massoomeh to make herself comfortable with them. I went to the living room to see what that gentleman had for me.

Ok, my dear GOD. Almost forty years have passed, and I still get shivers just thinking of what I had to put up with. He introduced himself as an ex-fiancé of Farkhondeh. He talked about her dishonesty and betrayal. He said, "We have been witnesses to what she has done to you and your husband, and we have noticed that your love for your husband is so great that you would not allow anyone to find out about their relationship".

At that time I thought that he might have been sent by Farkhondeh in order to record my voice. They didn't succeed to record my voice over the phone, and so they thought of coming to my house. Next he handed me a letter, and said, "My cousin sent you this letter to ask you if you could meet her at such and such address. She would like to talk to you about Farkhondeh and her viciousness". I was really afraid that something horrible must have happened.

I got the letter and said politely, "I don't know what you are talking about. I think you are in a wrong house. You have the right address, but you have the wrong person. I am sorry, I trust my husband and our relationship is perfect". He kept repeating, "You are a wonderful wife. And I hope that you will be able to bring shame to her, and so on". I opened the door and gestured for him to get out.

I said to myself after he left, "Boy, oh boy. It was stupid of me to ask him to come in to begin with. If my presumption was accurate, Farkhondeh sent him. I could have been in a big trouble. I never found out who he was or who sent him to talk to me. I was so glad that Massoomeh was in the house with me. She kept my children busy until he left. I was so shocked that I didn't know how to get a grip on myself. I talked to Massoomeh, who was only fourteen at the time. I expressed my sorrow and my desperation to her. I never talked to anyone on these issues. I knew that Iraj was under Farkhondeh's influence and most likely he would accuse me of lying.

My Dear GOD:

The letter, which I still have in my possession, was mostly about the same things he had told me. His sister was giving me a date to meet her in such and such place. She wanted to get to know me and talk to me more about Farkhondeh and her family. As if I

سیمین خانم

پس از تقدیم عرض سلام امیدوارم در زندگانی پیروز و موفق باشید و سعادتمند شده خود را بازیافته باشید

از اینکه آن روز بدون مقدمه منزل شما آمدم و جریان دوستی شوهر شما را با خنده به زبان می‌آوردم

نه دلبسته خداشناسان او بودم تعریف کردم معذرت می‌خواهم لو شما درباره من اشتباه کرده بودید باید

تصمیم با شما بود جای دیگر رو بیرون رفتم من هم بی‌اندازه خوشحال شدم از اینکه دیدم زنی مانند شما این‌قدر شوهر

خود را عشق می‌ورزد و حاضر نیست شوهری که روحش متعلق به دیگری است و حقیقتاً زن باید مانند شما

دانسته باشد بله خانم عزیز مثل شما و امثال شما در این دوره کمتر وجود دارند که این‌قدر فدا

کنند به خاطر شوهرشان به خاطر فرزندشان به این خاطر عقیده را به شما تبریک می‌گویم و امیدوارم

همیشه در زندگی موفق باشید تا بتوانید فرزندان خوب و تحصیل کرده تحویل جامعه دهید

دلم می‌خواست وقتی در تهران بودم برای شما تلفن کنم ولی با آن تصادف آن روز راضی

نشدم دلم می‌خواست از خداوند می‌خواهم تمام آن شایعه‌ها دروغ باشد و شوهرت متعلق به خودت

باشد اکنون که از طهران و شما دور هستم مایل بودم از نقشه‌های شما بیشتر بهره‌مند می‌شدم

برای اینکه این خبر خوش را زودتر بشنوم مایل بودم شما برایم قبل از هر کسی دیگر این

جمله را می‌نوشتید (خوشبختی را بازیافتم و آن موضوع دروغ بود)

در صفحه ۲

برای اینکه منظور که شما بتوانید بیشتر به من اطمینان کنید و من شرح زندگانی خودم بیان کنم
از یکی از دوستانم در طهران خواهش کرده‌ام در تاریخ ۴۵/۱/۲۸ ساعت ۱۰ الی ۱۱
صبح با تلفن به شما تماس بگیرد و آدرس مرا در اختیار شما بگذارد و از اینکه نتوانستم در روز یکشنبه ۵/۱/۲۹
هر چند من از طهران دور هستم ولی اگر خدمتی از دستم برآید با کمال میل حاضرم انجام دهم و برای اینکه
عشق از دست رفته شما کمک کنم امیدوارم همیشه شاد و خرم باشید

MA

This letter is presumably from an anonymous young soldier who once came to my door in Tehran, when Iraj was living with Farkhondeh and having an affair with her. In my book, I have talked about the day that this soldier came to my house and started talking about Farkhondeh's relationship with Iraj. He told me that he himself had been one of her lovers. On that day I never admitted to my husband's relationship with anyone, including Farkhondeh. I thought that he was there to tape my voice, admitting that Iraj was living with Farkhondeh, while she was married to her husband. So I asked him to leave and I pretended like I had a great time with my husband; like he was coming home to me every night. (At that time Farkhondeh was trying to take Iraj to the police and cause problems, or force him to divorce his wife to marry her.) After he left, he sent me this letter, congratulating me for loving my husband to a point that I would cover up for him to keep my family together. In the letter he also asked me to wait for his friend's telephone call on Sunday, 7/4/1966 to receive his address because he was out of Tehran. I wrote back that, "I would like to hear from you, but this really was a rumor and there was no truth behind it." At that time I was almost sure that there was a conspiracy and a plot against Iraj. I never paid attention to it, and I waited to see what would happen. Now, at this point of my life, I would like this person to come forward and talk to me. I would like to know who he was and what the real story was behind all this. Meanwhile, I could tell him that Farkhondeh wasn't as rootless, sneaky, and promiscuous as Badri was. I don't think there is a woman anywhere in the world who could be as rootless as Badri.

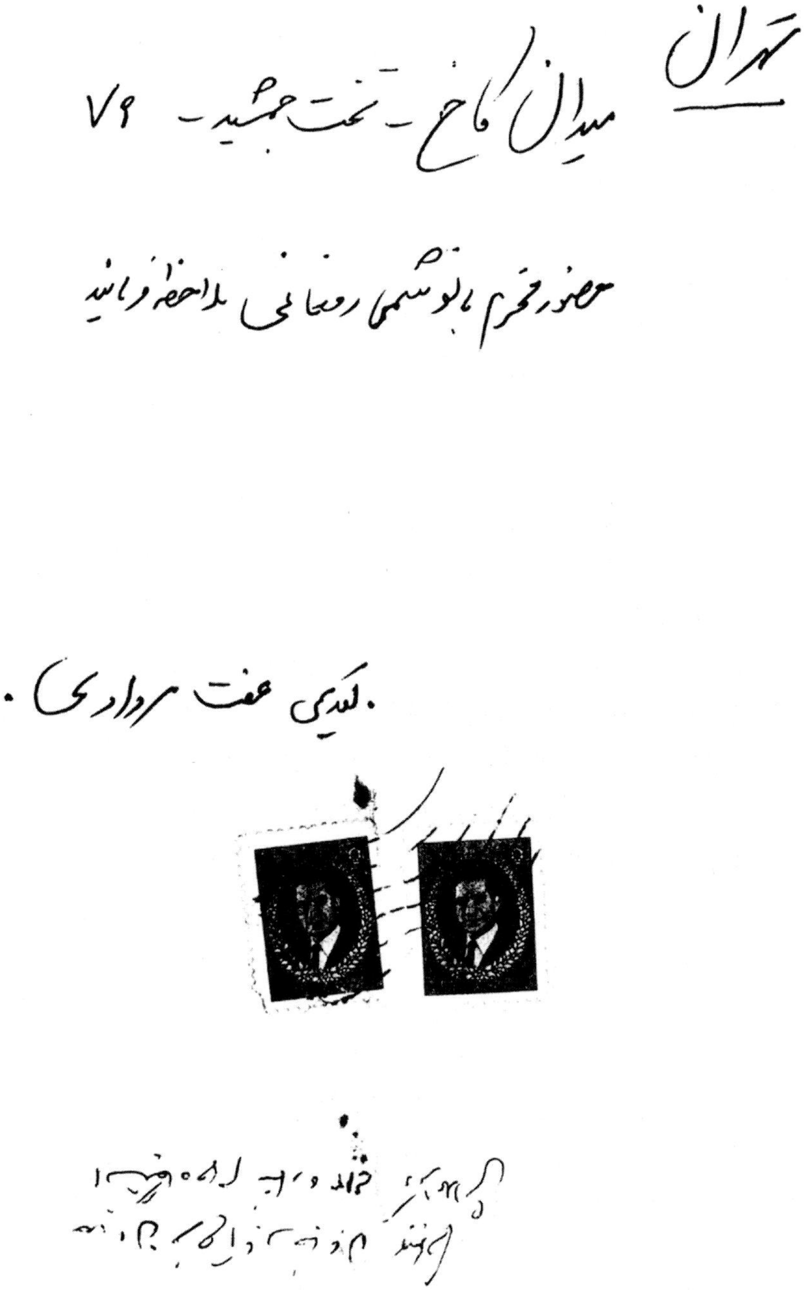

تهران
میدان کاخ - تخت جمشید - ۷۹
حضور محترم بانو شمسی رمضانی ملاحظه فرمایند

This is the envelope in which the letter from an anonymous person was. I don’t recognize the address, the name, or the handwriting. I wonder who he was, and what he had in mind for me.

ever cared. I am still wondering who that person was. Was he really who he said he was, or he just was sent by Farkhondeh? Who was that letter from? Why did they want to meet me somewhere out of my house? Any way that letter is one of the unsolved mysteries. I will attach the original copy to these pages.

I knew by now that Iraj was in trouble with the law. I was realizing that he was trapped, and most likely he wasn't going to be able to get out of this situation easily. I was glad to be able to stay out of it. And since I had established in my mind the idea of not divorcing him, I tried to live my life in a more comfortable way. With my head up, and everyone's support I tried to make my children happier by letting go of Iraj and all his activities. He was free to do anything he wished. I couldn't stop him by myself or by law. It was his choice. All his sisters had turned their backs on him, while they loved him a lot. I think it was the first time that Parveen wasn't talking to him.

One thing I got to give credit to Iraj is that he has always enjoyed being a family man. Or could it be that he was just pretending? Most American men, who are proud to be good husbands, keep their wives' portraits on their desks in the office. Iraj had one of my nice pictures enlarged, and framed. He kept it on his desk. This contributed a lot to his reputation and popularity. My photograph vanished from his desk when he started having an affair. That was the time when Farkhondeh started being difficult. I was not sure of what was going on between them, but whatever it was it must have been pretty terrible.

We were in Iran for only three year, and then "BOOM" I was faced by one disaster after the other. I truly believe that those disasters meant to happen.

My brother had to die due to circumstances on that particular Friday afternoon. There was absolutely no way of preventing it.

Certain life conditions, such as our property, the need for assistance, etc., have lead to my husband's extramarital affair.

I wonder what happened to all the wonderful plans we had. What happened to all those dreams? Where and how will our story end?

My dear GOD, what did I do to deserve this? Was it because I refused to listen to my parents when they were warning me? Do I have to pay this price for disobeying my parents for the rest of my life?

My Dear GOD:

I found out that he was trying to get rid of her. But I had doubts. That woman was getting comfortable with the idea of being the wife of a Doctor. She was getting the taste of having fancy clothes, and beautiful furniture. She had Iraj under her thumb; he was very threatened by her.

Although my family had no desire of associating with Iraj, one day he had asked my father if he could meet him. He made my father feel sorry for him that day. He convinced my father that he had no intentions or plans of falling into such trap. He tried to reason with my father. He said, "Shamci was not smart enough to handle the situation without letting it get too far and out of hand". He confessed to my father that Farkhondeh was trying to ruin him by any means. "She has been going through my wallet and stealing money from my pockets. She demands a marriage, a wedding, a ring and more". He almost broke down in the presence of my father.

My father decided to help him with anything he could. The only way to rid Iraj of Farkhondeh was for him to leave the country quietly. How was he going to do that? I wasn't sure. He was the "planner", and he had to get himself out of the hole he dug for himself. How was he going to sell his office furniture and other items? I didn't know. I was hoping that whatever happened would not cause my children and me more frustration and devastation.

Mary and Maseeh were really missing him. I was trying so hard to keep them busy so that they could forget about him. It was then that my father reminded me of my duties toward my children's happiness, he advised that I reconciled with Iraj. So one weekend he decided to come to Maygoon and spend some time with us.

My dear, dear GOD, I wish I was able to put my children's feelings in writing while they were put on that wild ride of torments. No words can describe the way that they felt that day. I wish I had a video camera at hand to record what these two little children went through.

That Thursday after Iraj called to say that he was coming to visit us, I announced it to the children. Witnessing my children's happiness prompted me to reconsider our reconciliation. It would have been worthwhile.

He drove our Comet to Maygoon. There was not enough parking in that narrow alley by our place. And, as always, Iraj put himself above the local villagers. So when he decided to park right in front of one of the homes. I warned him that just the other day a man was killed on the streets of Maygoon for being disrespectful and obnoxious. I was not kidding. He proceeded to park the car, and right when he was locking the door a man came out of the house and told him not to park his car there. He was a big man, and Iraj looked like a little boy next to him. Iraj started to say that was not blocking anyone's entry. The man did not let him finish his sentence and grabbed him by his neck. I came out of the car at that point and tried to calm the man down. I asked him to guide us where to park. I said, "Sorry, we are not familiar with the Maygoon". Then I asked Iraj to get in the car and get out of there before he was killed. This time, thanks GOD, he listened. We found a parking spot that wouldn't disturb anyone's privacy. Then he came up to our room to see where we have been living all that time.

My Dear GOD:

We did not discuss anything but the children. He had a shoe on one of his feet, and a sandal on the other. He said he had done a surgery on his toe. It was wrapped with bandages. We decided to go out with the children. It felt like the old days.

Next morning, which was Friday he decided to drive us to a nice restaurant located in a beautiful garden half way between Tehran and Maygoon. He wanted to convince me that he had all the intentions to get out of that trap. Kids were holding his hands. They were so happy. He was listening to their stories, and he paid attention to all their needs and desires. I haven't seen them this happy for the past three years. They had the whole world in their hands.

As I have mentioned, the restaurant was situated in a fenced off garden. Iraj parked next to all the other cars on the side of the road near the fence. We asked to be seated at the table next to the fence so that we could see the road and the car. Kids were walking around, playing and talking to Iraj. We ran into Mr. Moosavi, our neighbor. Mr. Moosavi was in the senate. He was having dinner at a table next to us. What a great opportunity for Iraj to show off himself and his family.

We have just ordered our food; it was less than half an hour, when I noticed that Iraj's face was turning yellow. He kept repeating, "Shamci she is coming, Shamci she's coming". He saw her car turn into the street; he saw her park in front of the restaurant across the street. It seemed that she had seen Iraj's car and she came to look for him. Iraj continued, "I had to lie to her in order for me to be able to come here. I told her that I am going to Ghazveen to see my uncle who was sick. I'll be in trouble if she finds out that I lied to her". I had to come up with an idea. And so I told him, "When she gets here, I will tell her that we were visiting your uncle as well. And so the children asked you to take them out. I will apologize for taking you away from her". I did not have my purse with me, so I had no money. And Iraj left his briefcase and his jacket in our house. He gave me some money and said, "Make sure no one follows you. Ask a police officer to follow you home. And then call me tomorrow. I will tell you what happened". All this took place right after they brought our food, and so we didn't get a chance to eat.

My Dear GOD:

Okay, my dear GOD, do you remember what position I was in? Do you remember the time that I had to come face to face with her? Do you remember the thoughts that went through my mind? Iraj was worried about being embarrassed in front of our neighbor Mr. Moosavi. While I was thinking that I had to face this promiscuous woman and instead of killing her I had to be nice to her.

She had finally arrived to the restaurant. While she had her hands on her hips she said, "Iraj, I thought you were going to your uncle in Ghazveen". But before Iraj got a chance to answer her, I got up and asked my children to follow me. Then I said, "I am sorry. It was my fault. We were at his uncle's house, and the children wanted to be with their father. I really apologize." And I started to leave.

Now she wanted me to stay. She tried to stop me every time I attempted to leave. She

followed me, and finally she pointed her finger at me and said, "Well, you are his wife, but so am I". I pulled myself away and I told her, "No madam, you are the one and I am none. I will never sit in the same place with you. Either you must sit down, or I will. Please let me go". She followed me to the door, asking me sit down with her. And I insisted that she must go and join Iraj, and not me. So I left the restaurant.

My children were very quiet. They were hanging on me. All their dreams went down the drain so unexpectedly. I took them to the shop across the road. They were looking for their father. I bought what they asked for, and tried to tell them that we will talk to their father the next day.

Maseeh was three and Mary was five. It was a very emotional age for both of them. Mary kept very quiet. I was very concerned about her. I did not let go of their hands. I kept promising them that they would talk to their father soon.

While I was making promises, we watched Farkhondeh and their father pass the shop. They went to the restaurant next door. But they immediately came back out. Iraj came in the store. He had his black sunglasses on. His voice was shaking, while he was crying under those glasses. He kept telling us, "I am sorry for what I have done to you. I can never forgive myself for destroying you. How can I make it up to you? Will you ever forgive me?" His voice almost disappeared. I tried to stop him. My children were falling apart. I had to push him to go with her so that she doesn't make our lives more complicated. And I promised him that the kids would call him the next day.

Meanwhile I have talked to a police officer, and asked him to follow us home.

The police followed our taxi to our house. I was so puzzled. I didn't know how to explain Farkhondeh's visit to my children. Once we got home they removed their shoes, and they went and lay on each side of the room, each in their own bed. Maseeh was looking at Mary and he repeated everything she did. I sat on a chair between them. Mary brought her hands up and under her head and stared at the ceiling. After a short period of silence I noticed that Mary's tears were rolling down her cheeks. Not a single muscle moved on her face. Just like an old, mature lady who is mourning the loss of a loved one, she kept saying in Farsi, "DIGEH RAFT, DIGEH RAFT. BORDESH DIGEH, BORDESH DIGEH. He is gone. He is gone. She took him away. She took him away". And the tears were rolling down her cheeks endlessly. Maseeh started to cry quietly as well. I didn't know what to do. Mary, at her age, was acting like a grown-up. I never expected that she knew so much about her father's affair.

My Dear GOD:

I wish I had someone to hold my hand and give me hope at that moment. Unfortunately I had no one to turn to. I sat at the corner of Mary's bed and held her hands and started to talk to her. I got her father's jacket and showed it to her and I said, "Mary jon, he is not gone. As a matter of fact he is here more than before. His briefcase is

here too. We have to go and call him tomorrow afternoon, and you will find out for yourself. You must believe me. You must tell Maseeh that we will talk to Daddy tomorrow and we will become happy. I wiped out their tears. I put them on my lap and started kissing them. They loved my kisses at that age. I kept talking and showing them their father's jacket and the briefcase. I promised them that we would go to the telephone station tomorrow after five to talk to him. It took me more than an hour to comfort them.

It was Friday afternoon, the loneliest time of the week. I wished I could cry a river. But instead I had to laugh and entertain my children. They were all that I had. They were all my heart, my eyes, my breath, and my whole life. I had to make it good for them.

Thank you my dear GOD for being with me every step of the way. Thank you for giving me enough thoughtfulness, whenever it was needed. With your help I learned to handle my life, at any given circumstance.

We went out to dinner that evening. Then we went by the water stream that Mary liked so much. And we talked about tomorrow and what each one was going to tell their father.

I think that that was the most damaging day in my children's life. I couldn't sleep all night. I visualized my children's sadness of that afternoon, and I cried for them in the silence of the dark night. I was embarrassed of the choices I've made. Something that was very hard to admit to my parents, especially because I would always tell them, "Because we love each other our children will be the happiest kids on earth". What was I really thinking? Didn't I know better that it takes two to tango? And wasn't it stupid of me to believe that just because I loved him so much he would be honest about his love for me. Not only I was disappointed, not only I felt like the biggest looser, but I was so embarrassed in front of my family that I would never be able to discuss my humiliation in the society that I was living in. Shame on me for my stupidity! There was no way out of it. I had already given life to the two most beautiful creatures on earth.

My Dear GOD:

It was our responsibility as parents to give our children the best life possible. They didn't ask us to bring them into this world. It was us who were anxious to have them. I remember the times when I did not get pregnant for three months when we first came to America. Iraj was questioning my ability to be able to bear a child for him. It reminded me of Mohammad Reza, the Shahanshah of Iran, who divorced Soraya for the reason of not being able to bear a son, the only way to keep monarchy among the Pahlavi dynasty.

Iraj has always surprised me. All those promises that he made were broken one by one. It was ruining me. I was very disturbed by that. But what about my children? No, no. What about our children? We can't send them back. We can't kill them. We can't sell them. So either both or one of us had to stand by them. Obviously with the lifestyle he had, he couldn't think of his children and their future. So it had to be me. The funniest part of all was that I was the blame for all his actions. And just like millions of women in Iran I was supposed to sit there and rub his feet as a gratitude for him having an affair. But since I refused to do that, I was considered a bad wife. I was considered to be the destroyer of my children's life because I did not cooperate with his extramarital affairs. Boy, oh boy, what a bad wife and a bad companion.

So this is why I have chosen to do what I did, when I had to do it. Besides, this man was so indecent that he sold his own sperm at his clinic. How could I expect his love for my children? The only difference was that my children were recognized as his children. And the children that were procreated with his sperm remained unrecognized. The only things that made a difference to him were the love for himself, and his name and prestige.

So I was responsible for the life and the happiness of my children regardless of whether their father loved them or not. Obviously I was to blame for what was happening to them because I was the one who brought them into this world. So during those ugly years, while my heart was constantly bleeding, my mouth was full with laughter to prevent my children from losing their father.

My Dear GOD:

By now everybody knew that Iraj was remorseful, and that he was trying to come back to his wife and the children. One day we were in his uncle's house. I was having a conversation with one person and there were many subjects that we discussed. That person said when Iraj asked me to go and pick up a prostitute, I thought he must have left that woman already. That is so embarrassing. He has a wife, he has a mistress, and he still picks up a prostitute." How could he consider himself a prestigious, respected doctor after all this? What a shame, what a shame. I don't know if he was aware of all that he has done. He obviously did. I still have his letters from America where he asked for my forgiveness. I still have all those letters where he talked about his losses, all the humiliation, and the loss of success and his prestige.

My dear GOD, once again I was fooled by all those letters. I really believed that he had learned his lesson. His letters were full of sorrow, mourning, and affliction. He was begging for forgiveness. Anyone who had read those letters would think of him as of the most innocent man on earth. That was why my father took his side and asked me to forgive him. He said, “He had made a mistake. He is admitting to his own mistake. It takes a big man to admit to his own mistakes and ask for his wife’s forgiveness. If you do not forgive him, it is you who is trying to destroy the children”. So it was my duty to forget and forgive.

I saw this movie in the theater years later,” Fatal Attraction". The difference between the scenario of that movie and my life was that the husband in the movie was really innocent. He only slept with that woman once. He never intended to harm his wife and his child. There was nothing to blame the husband for in the beginning. It was the

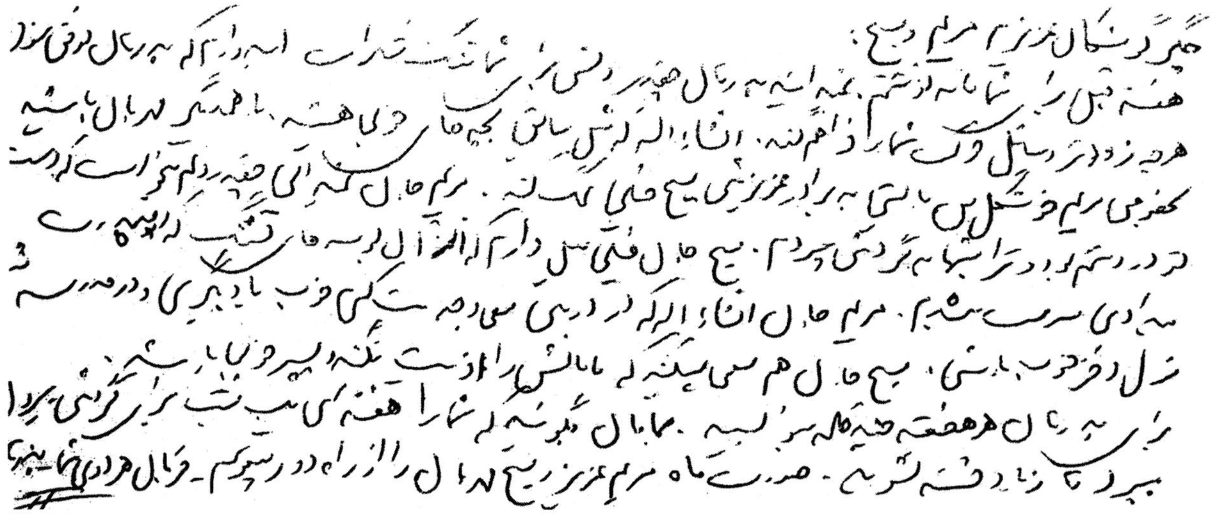

This letter is from Iraj to his love of life, Maryam and Maseeh, after he escaped from Iran. If you could read it, you would think that it is from a father who could never do wrong, a father who loved his children very much. I read this to them and it made them happy. We were looking forward to a new and a better life that he had promised. He cried for what he had done to them. I thought he would never do it again. That was why I was the only one who found out about his involvement with Badri, eight months after Malakuti's death.

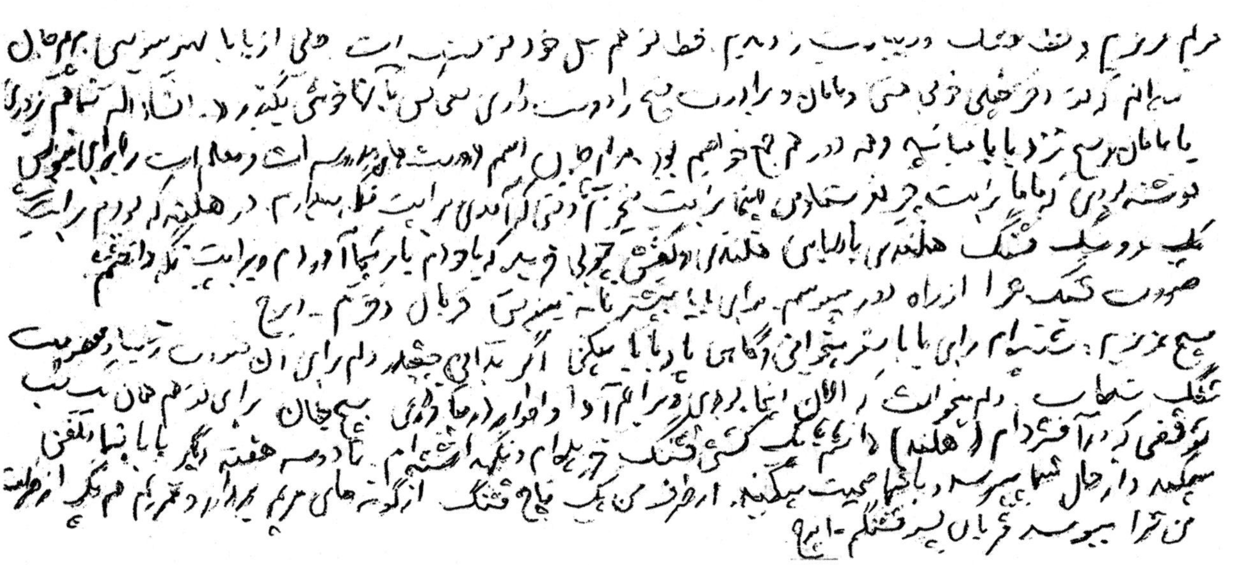

When I read the top letter to Mary and Maseeh, Mary wanted to write to her father herself. This is her father's answer to her letter. Although she had finished the first year of school, she did her best to write the letter. But in my opinion, Mary never forgot her father's first affair. She was an age that she could not believe her father's lack of love. She even remembers the night that we came home; he had the mistress in my bedroom and he had bought her walnut which Mary loved a lot. Well, everything is in the past now. We must stop thinking about it, because we won't get anything out of thinking.

[illegible]

شمسی عزیزم [illegible]

دو نامه ات پشت سر هم رسید. البته باز خوب و خوش نکته و آه و فغان راه انداخته بودی. دلم میخواست که جای من میبودی
تا معشوق آنچنانی میدیدی که در دل خونین من چه میگذرد که باز این حرفها را هم باید تحمل کنم و لب برنیاورم. آری شمسی عزیز منکه تمام
زندگی را داشته ام فدا کرده ام آرزوئی جز سعادت تو و بچه ها ندارم. فقط از خدا میخواهم که آنقدر زنده باشم همه و تکلیف بچه ها که بتوانم
۵-۶ سال اگر برای تامین سعادت شما زحمت بکشم. دفعه اگر از بین رفتم دیگر نگران جگر گوشه هائی که بی خانمان و بی سرپرست شده اند
نباشم. شاید تصور کنی که من دست جلو بگیرم که با اصطلاح پس نیفتم. ولی به روح مادرم قسم میخورم که این حرفها را از روی
کمال خلوص نیت دارم و از ته قلب میگویم. تصور میکنم که اگر هر کس دیگر جای من بود تا حال با [illegible] (۱۰) سال [illegible]
زحمت کشیدم و تحمل کردم و زندگی را درست کردم در مقابل [illegible] محصول دو جا [illegible] گرد بادی شدم که هر دو را
از جا میکنند و هر آدم صبوری در مقابل آن [illegible] بهترین زندگی که [illegible] کردم [illegible]
سر و همه آبرو و اعتباری داشتم و آشیانه خوبی را [illegible] خوابم [illegible] [illegible] [illegible] ولی تمام رشته ها و
[illegible] شده و تمام [illegible] [illegible] از آن کاخ [illegible] سعادت و خوشبختی جز یک خاکستر از تنگ
بدنامی و فقر چیزی باقی نمانده. حال در چنین حالتی [illegible] خانه های قدیم بنائی تازه برپا نمایم و اکنون [illegible] آخر [illegible]
نما شاید چون ابتدا کاخی پر شکوه پر سعادت درست نمایم. ولی تصور میکنم که دیگر صبر و تحمل تمام [illegible] و دیگران
[illegible] و [illegible] اگر برای [illegible] زندگی داشتم [illegible] [illegible] [illegible] پس باید [illegible] [illegible] کنم که [illegible] [illegible]
[illegible] [illegible] چرا [illegible] [illegible] میخواهم. آری از تو فقط میخواهم که در [illegible] جگر گوشگان عزیزم [illegible]
همکاری کنی. به هر حال قلم از دستم در رفت و آنچه را که نباید بگویم باز گو کردم ولی جز تو کسی دیگر را برای [illegible] [illegible]
امیدوارم که در [illegible] خودت و فرزندانمان و آسایش فکر خودتان تا حد امکان بکوشید. منهم سعی میکنم که [illegible] [illegible]
گرنه [illegible] آسایش شما را تا آنجا که مقدور است تامین کنم که کسی از درد [illegible] نباشد
راجع به پول همانطور که در نامه قبل بطور مفصل نوشتم از اول آذر ماه تنها ماهی ۱۸۰۰ تومان [illegible] [illegible] پول [illegible] [illegible]
و [illegible] تا حال جا گرفته ای [illegible] باید دقت کنی که اگر [illegible] پول در میان باشد [illegible] [illegible] پول [illegible] را
[illegible] [illegible] و [illegible] [illegible] اگر [illegible] [illegible] [illegible] [illegible] [illegible] [illegible] [illegible] [illegible] از آن
خودداری. اولاً مطابق حساب [illegible] [illegible] [illegible] بکند و ثانیاً [illegible] خواهران من [illegible] [illegible] [illegible] [illegible]
تو و بچه هایم هستند. راجع به لوازم جراحی هم [illegible] [illegible] [illegible] [illegible] [illegible] [illegible] [illegible] [illegible] [illegible]
[illegible] [illegible] [illegible] [illegible] [illegible] [illegible] [illegible] [illegible] [illegible] [illegible] [illegible] [illegible] [illegible]
[illegible] [illegible] اگر [illegible] خوب [illegible] لازم نیست [illegible] [illegible] [illegible] [illegible] [illegible] [illegible] [illegible] [illegible]
انجام بدهم. [illegible] [illegible] [illegible] [illegible] [illegible] [illegible] [illegible] [illegible] [illegible] [illegible] [illegible] [illegible] [illegible] راجع به [illegible] البته
خودت به اخلاق ایشان [illegible] [illegible] [illegible] [illegible] [illegible] [illegible] [illegible] [illegible] [illegible] [illegible] [illegible] [illegible] [illegible]
حال [illegible] [illegible] حال [illegible] البته ایشان [illegible] [illegible] [illegible] [illegible] [illegible] [illegible] [illegible] [illegible] [illegible] [illegible] همانطور که
[illegible] [illegible] [illegible] [illegible] [illegible] [illegible] [illegible] [illegible] [illegible] [illegible] [illegible] [illegible] [illegible] [illegible] [illegible]
راجع به [illegible] بچه ها [illegible] [illegible] [illegible] [illegible] [illegible] [illegible] ایران [illegible] [illegible] [illegible] بچه های بد اخلاق

[illegible]

SECOND FOLD

[illegible]

This is his answer to one of my letters which I wrote to him after he had escaped Iran from his first mistress. Obviously it is not a love letter. He is attacking me for not understanding his problem. Because it is impossible to translate this, a person who cannot read it should find an Iranian who can read Farsi very well, to be able to explain every word of this and how he was trying to make me feel guilty for the mistakes he had made. I have underlined the important sentences which made me want to kill him. But again with my father's advice, I decided to give it up. I learned to cope with him and everything regarding him. I thought I did the right thing. I thought my children are more important to me than my life. So, I tried to forgive him, and let him find himself again. He did, and he tried so hard to be number one. And he was number one until the day that Malakuti died.

woman who kept fantasizing about him. In my case my husband was the one who started the whole affair, and he put the wrong idea in his mistress's mind. Then later for whatever reason he was trying to get rid of her. I have never found out why, and I have never asked.

My dear GOD, I have always wondered why is it that we are so strong only when we are under tremendous amount of pressure. Is it possibly because at the time we are so busy fighting and coping with the pain that our body is numb to pain? Maybe it is better that I just keep wondering.

Okay, my dear God. How about the day that I was in Ezzat's house and Iraj called me? He was begging me to come home. He was telling me that Farkhondeh had put gasoline all over him, his house, and his clothes. She wanted to burn the whole building. Please hurry, please. I didn't have time to say anything. I just asked Mr. Moosavi to drive me home as fast as he could. I told him on the way there what had happened. When we got there, everything was under control. He had run up to the neighbors and they saved him from her.

My Dear GOD:

I found out later that they had a fight. So Iraj went home and cut up all the beautiful clothes that he bought for her. In return she came over to set him, and his house on fire. The neighbors told me so. I didn't even ask Iraj what had happened. I didn't need to know. I knew the story from beginning to the end. He hurt her, and she wanted to hurt him back. When I look back, I wonder why he had called me. What could I have done for him? Was it possible for me to solve their problems? I just wonder.

You see my dear GOD, when we moved into that building we had so much respect. After the open house for his office he had even more respect. We were one of the nicest families in the neighborhood. Look at him now. He had to run to the neighbors' house in his underwear to beg them to rescue him from his mistress. What a shame, what a shame. They say, "We are the ones who make our own life". That is very true in this case. Iraj had a choice of either continuing that respectful life or getting all that he deserved for all his actions.

In one of his letters to me from America he wrote, "I was a successful doctor with lots of dreams. I had worked so hard to get there. I had a home, a wife, and beautiful children; I had a very bright, full of success future ahead of me. Now I am back to where I started with my residency.

Didn't we promise each other ever lasting love? Weren't we both smart enough to recognize our desires and to be responsible for our actions? Weren't you always telling me that we have the best and the most affectionate intimacy? Then why did you have to look for extramarital affairs? Weren't you looking for trouble? Weren't you going after the destructive and heavy storm to hit you and destroy you?

Please my dear GOD, picture this, my dear lover and husband. A young, successful

doctor, who has made the front page of the newspapers; an intelligent and educated doctor who was supposed to earn the respect and trust of people, was now like a little mouse under the powerful paw of a big lion begging for his life. What a terrible embarrassment. What an ugly scene. What did the neighbors think when they had to save the Doctor from his mistress? How could I live with this shame? My dear GOD, please help me, please.

A person who kept loving me and pretending that he loved me so much, why did he have to put himself in such a disastrous situation? He had everything that a young doctor could ever ask for. These were his words, "I have got everything I have ever asked for".

That woman was so dangerous and brainless that she was willing to do anything to destroy him. He told my father that she was determined to harm my children by throwing ACID on them. That was why he asked me to get help from the police after I left the restaurant at Mygoon to take the children home.

My Dear GOD:

I figure Iraj has a multiple personality syndrome. There was one, who loved truly and acted out lovingly; and the other, the complicated destroyer, who was influencing him from inside. He was able to control the bad one with my influence on many occasions. Like the time when we were getting ready to go to Iran. I was aware that going to Iran with two little children was not only costly, but there was also the possibility of having great emergencies on our hands. He bought me a Chinchilla cape two months prior to our departure. After we got home I realized that the Chinchilla does not match my normal life style. At that time I did not realize that he had purchased it to show off. I thought he loved me so much that he wanted to buy me the most beautiful things. I talked to him about the possibilities of emergencies. Although we had paid a fifty-dollar deposit, I still asked him to return the cape, I asked him to cancel the deal. When I reasoned with him, he agreed with me and appreciated my concern.

Later, after he was having an affair, he accused me of not loving him enough just to put the blame on me. His reason was that I always returned the things that he bought for me.

On another occasion he bought a Mercedes Benz, 450 SL, hardtop convertible, black exterior and gray interior. It was a very beautiful car. Someone who could afford to spend that much money on that car should have been able to spend on other necessities at home. Once again I was able to convince him to take the car back and cancel the deal. He had lost five hundred on that occasion. This was the same man who dared question me about twenty-five dollars that I had spent on a new mailbox.

Unfortunately, there were times that I didn't go against his will. Those were the times that I thought we had enough money to splurge.

This time Parveen was in our house. He decided to buy me a Mink coat. He has been teasing me for a while that as a wife of a doctor I should be doing everything that made me

happy. I should have been going out with my friends every day; I should have been buying anything I liked. I should have been taking advantage of all the opportunities I had. I was very disappointed with him. I thought he was judging me wrongfully. I did not expect that from him. I didn't know he was looking for that kind of a woman.

So one day we went to a fur store by appointment. He introduced me to the owner and asked him about every design there was. Finally we ordered a long, floor length white mink coat with a matching hat and a matching belt with a big, beautiful buckle. Okay, my dear GOD. I went along with his desires. But wasn't I dumb? The lower part of the coat was connected by four zippers. Each zipper made a different length coat. And the lower part became a cape. At least I was able to wear it for different occasions as needed. Now, if this coat was black, I wouldn't mind it that much. But a floor length white Mink coat. Where was I able to wear it? Since I had many other coats, I decided to satisfy his ego and let him get his way. His sister Parveen was with us the day we got the coat. He was happy to show her what a good husband he has been for me.

My Dear GOD:

While he was showing off with that coat, I was often embarrassed to wear it.

In real life a person must be happy and in love with his wife to try to do so much for her and spend so much money on her. This was what I believed and so did many others. But this was only one side of the story. We were not aware of the other side. We have never met that other person inside him, the one who was telling him to go ahead and have affairs. I would have never imagined that after showing all the love for me, he would be having an affair with someone else. How foolish some of us, the ladies, are? How vulnerable most of us are?

So this young doctor who had all the success and happiness in the world decided to have an affair, and he wanted me to stay quiet and take it. Obviously this proves that he had two different personalities. And separating these two from each other was not an easy task.

I was ready to cry for him the day that I saw him in front of the neighbors' house so weak and helpless. I wanted to hold him in my arms and like in the old days kiss him and comfort him. But I was afraid that I would have made him more embarrassed in front of my brother-in-law. I am sure he wouldn't want that either.

When I fell in love with him I never knew these things about him. I never knew that he might abort a pregnant woman near the end of the term. That was killing life and normal babies. In the USA doctors would try to save the life of a baby even during very early pregnancy. It was very hard to recognize the other person within Iraj.

I was so relieved and happy to find out that Doctor Razi was not going to accompany him with the abortions any longer. It was like a wish came true. If I couldn't stop him from his doings, you, and only you, my dear GOD came to my rescue. Thank you.

I was dressed up to go out.

Surie Ghaemi in Azar's suit and hat

I am in my full-length white mink coat that had become a hot topic for gossipers. What a mistake I made by letting him buy that coat for me! It became his show off and a big headache for me.

Mary and I are in front of our house. Yes, there were times that we loved each other.

In our living room; Mojgan is wearing the lower part of my mink coat which could become a stole.

Here, we were ready to go out. I was teasing him to make him happy. I think I succeeded at the end.

I would have never imagined that this lover, who was ready to commit suicide if couldn't marry me, now very clearly, was trying to use the Islamic laws against my rights and me. He was probably completely unaware that if I ever asked for divorce, he would have used all that was in his power to stop me. But I am sure that he knew that I would not tolerate his unfaithfulness, and that I would protest loudly. I am sure that, just like many other lovers, neither of us truly and completely knew ourselves. We were only talking from our hearts for the moment.

My Dear GOD:

That was why my father was trying so hard to wake me up from the sweet dreams I have had within that period of my life. Unfortunately, myself, and even more so Iraj were not in the position to understand much. The one thing I've learned is that even though it is recognized that in theory we are the makers of our own lives, for the most part the real life circumstances are that which contributes to a drastic change of our plans.

I would like to talk about an incident somewhat unrelated to the subject matter. It took place long before Iraj and I became lovers. One day my entire family, accompanied by our friend Mansooreh went to the mountain of Shemiran, the northern part of Tehran. We were going up the mountain, through a narrow rocky pathway, when, out of nowhere, we ran into Sarvan Rafani and his family. Everybody stopped to exchange greetings. After that Sarvan Rafani proceeded to shake hands with everyone. I was waiting for my turn. And Sarvan approached me, we shook hands, and then he leaned over kissed my hand. After we all said good-bye, my family couldn't wait for Rafani's to leave so as to start making fun of me. Mansooreh was more excited than the rest of them. They were shocked about the way I was treated. They teased me all the way. They were saying that kissing a hand was very appropriate while at a black tie party, but not on the top of a mountain. I tried not to pay attention, but eventually that kissing of a hand contributed to the course of our relationship took place years later. It was obvious that he chose me among all the ladies for some unapparent reason.

Anyway, my dear, dear GOD, Iraj has ruined his name, his prestige and his life for no reason at all. Not to mention the damage to my children's emotion, the damage so great that the scars will never heal.

He was trying to rid himself of his mistress. And he was planning to keep it a secret, knowing that woman. He was sure that she would ruin his life before he could do anything about it. He was determined to go back to his family. That, which was once his only love. He was lost, confused, and helpless. Besides my compassion, my father was planning to help him in any way. He decided to carry on his relationship with her in order to keep her in the dark. Everyone, even the ones who chose to resent him for his actions, was trying to help Iraj out as much as they could. He knew that if Farkondeh ever suspected anything she would have undoubtedly destroyed us all. He was assuring her meanwhile that he

This picture was taken at the goodbye party given by Pari and Kamal Kamooneh for us when we were visiting Iran in the summer of 1947.
From left to right: Mrs. Mansoor Froozan (who was missing her daughter Susan, and didn't want to look at the camera), me, Azar, Ezzat, my friend Akram Yaghoobi, and Iraj's aunt Mrs. Hormozi.
This was the time that we had forgotten Iraj's first affair in Iran, and everyone was welcoming us with open arms and a lot of respect. And Iraj was trying to show everyone that there is no love greater than his love for me in the whole world. Believe it or not, everyone including I, was falling for it.

At the same party, from left to right: Parveen, Kamal, Fareedeh Pazandeh, me, Iraj, Naheed Naghshineh, Shahnaz Toosi, Dr. Mohammad Toosi, Dr. Pazandeh, and in the back, Mr. Mehdi Gangi.
In the front: Neya, Pari, and Minoo Khadem. These people all took him serious and believed that Iraj was a nice guy and loved his family dearly, especially Dr. Toosi who drove him to the airport when he was running away from his first mistress. Dr. Toosi said, "Iraj was so lost that he didn't know where his ticket was, or what he was doing. He just wanted to jump in the plane and leave the country." He was afraid that his mistress would find him, and cause him more embarrassment in front of his friends. My comment is that people like Iraj really deserve these kinds of women who can handle them well. Ladies like me, are not good for them. They need someone to really give it to them. And, at that time he had one.

Iraj had become somebody. He repeatedly said, "I had a great future. Everyone was looking up to me. I had a reputation among my friends. I don't know why whenever I am at the peak of my success and happiness,

somehow, something drastically happens to completely destroy me." But after what he did this time I would like to ask him, "My dear Iraj, isn't it you who creates this complexity in your life? Aren't you the one who is asking for it?"

At a wedding in Tehran; Pari, Iraj, Kamal, Parveen, and me. As you see, I am in a dress that I tailored for myself by Sari fabric which he had bought for me from London, England.

First time he was having an affair in Tehran, his sisters were supporting me to the full extend. Neya, me, Iraj, Arman, Nazy, Maseeh, Mary, and Keyvan

We are at Dr. Gangi's party held for a group of teachers in Tehran. From left to right: I don't know the first two people, Iraj, me, Mr. Gangi's wife, Mr. Gangi, Mr. Tahery's wife, Mr. Tahery.

would be leaving me soon. And so she was thrilled with the idea of becoming Mrs. Rafani among other doctors' wives.

My Dear GOD:

At the same time he was planning to sell everything and move back to U.S.A. We bought all our appliances in the U.S.A. and shipped them to Iran. We bought our huge Hi-Fi set with television and so on from Germany. We got a very expensive camera, all kinds of lenses and accessories, with a very beautiful case from Germany as well. We had all our savings at the time. I was planning to start a decent life in Iran. I assisted him not to waste money on unnecessary things, and only on basic and absolutely necessary items. Now we had to get rid of everything in a hurry. That meant throwing it all away. Still he did not mind to do so, as long as he could have his wife and his children back. With the help of his friends he put a lot of thought into planning his escape.

There were many doctors returning from America to start there practice in Iran at the time. Doctor Mohtadi happened to be one of them. They had agreed on a price for Iraj's office furniture over the phone. Iraj did not want anyone to know what was going on in his life. So Mohtadi had no idea why Iraj was returning to States. Mohtadi tried to bargain with Iraj for a lesser price when he got there. Suddenly Iraj got so mad that asked him to get out of his house. They didn't contact each other for many years until Mohtadi's came back to America, and I invited them to my house.

The funniest thing of all was that Iraj was completely oblivious of his surroundings and the results of his own deeds. He did not expect people to be aware of his affairs. I am sure that everyone had seen them together in his car, in many restaurants, in the parks and public places. But still, he was trying to cover up and pretend that he was the sweetest and nicest man among his friends. I don't know if he is foolish in general, or if he was naive and vulnerable. Today, having gained the experience and knowledge of what has passed on us, I strongly believe that, in a very stupid way, he was his own enemy. I really feel sorry for that person that he was.

There were days that he would come home from the hospital in the middle of the day. He would change his clothes into rags. He would put on a strange hat, with big black eye glasses, and then he would go out to follow his mistress, desperately trying to find out where she was going, what she was doing, or whom she was with.

Oh, my GOD, what a low, low person he was! What did he think of himself? Wasn't I stupid to fall in love with such a dumb and foolish person? I don't think that he had to attend a medical school to become such a worthless bum. No, there is no such a school that would train a bum like him. And then he cries, and he tries to put the blame for the ruined relationship on his wife for returning his gifts. What a lost and useless creature!

My Dear GOD:

My father wasn't a doctor, my brothers were not doctors, but never in their lifetime had they thought of such an ugly act. I will never forget what my father once told me. He said, "It might be easy to study to become a doctor, but it is not easy at all to learn how to become a worthy human being”. I understand now what he meant.

I spent most of my time with his family then. I became particularly close with Pari. She was more than just a sister-in-law to me, she was my best friend.

After that big fight between Iraj and his mistress, she started going to Pari's house and complain about Iraj. She had been crying on her knees, begging Pari to help her fix the things between them. Pari was feeling sorry for her. It was very strange for me to find out that Pari felt sorry for her. But she was free to feel what she felt.

One day after school my children and I were at Pari's house. While we were there, Farkhondeh came over to see Pari. Knowing that she had always planned throwing Acid on us, Pari rushed us up the stairways, and on to the roof. Farkhondeh was there for a whole hour. Meanwhile we had no time to put our shoes on. My poor, innocent children! They didn’t know what was going on. They knew that I had to hide them from something dangerous. We came down and started to have fun again after she left. We made up a story for my children in order to conceal the ugly truth.

As I’ve mentioned before, Pari was my best friend. She was always very supportive of us. She did everything in her power to keep us company at all times; we were together every weekend. My children were fully aware of their father’s absence. I had to lie to them and tell them that their father was working at the hospital. I didn't want them to feel embarrassed in front of their cousins. Although I knew that they knew of everything, I still preferred to see them believe otherwise.

My dear, dear GOD, you know how I passed those days. You are the only one who remembers how I felt those days. You remember how difficult it was for me to keep my children and myself happy. You know that I would never even attempt to explain my feelings those days. But I am very thankful to you for allowing me to gather my strength so that I was able to keep running.

My Dear GOD:

He sold most of the furniture; I only kept a few items. He said that when they were up north, his mistress dropped our expensive camera and the case in the water. What a pity. Now I know in reality that he deserved to have that kind of women in his life

We decided that I would rent an apartment. And so I rented an apartment next to my sister Azar, so that I was not alone. By then he left the country to go back to America. He was so scared, worried, and confused those days that he had mismanaged everything he was involved with. Thanks GOD I wasn't around him to witness what was going on. Doctor Toosi, who accompanied him to the airport, was very worried about him. He said that Iraj was so scared that he thought he had lost both his ticket and his passport. He was afraid that somehow she would follow him to the airport and make a terrible scene. He was so desperately confused that he did not say good-bye to his children. Actually he had asked Dr. Toosi to keep his ticket and his passport for him. And then he thought later that he had lost them. He wrote to me from Michigan about all this.

He was gone, leaving me with a load of unfinished business, and practically no money. And even though I did have income those days through my teaching job, which was not sufficient to cover our expenses. But he was expecting me to leave off of the sales of our furniture until we go back to U.S.A. I am embarrassed to even mention that he was counting on money for our used cassettes and records that we sold to our relatives naming Kamal.

I had the decency to know that it was not right to ask Kamal to be paying for those worthless records, especially after all the care and the attention they gave me and my children. But Iraj left me in such an awkward financial satiation. I was depending on every penny I could get my hands on. Later on Kamal teased my stinginess and me. He would always bring this subject up. He told everyone, "Shamci is so stingy that she charged me for a few ripped tapes and broken records". Kamal was right. I was not supposed to be charging him. I actually owed Kamal and Pari for their support and kindness. Kamal was right, but he didn't know that Iraj had left me with virtually nothing. And, as I said, I had to count every penny.

When he got to Michigan he immediately called his sister Parveen. Our phone in the new apartment was not connected yet. So he started writing to me again on weekly basis. We had to buy a telephone number under our own name in Iran, considering that it takes ten to fifteen days to exchange letters. On many occasions you would be put on a waiting list. There were agents who would speed up the process for a fee, like Mr. Shogaee, my sister in-law's brother in-law. He got us a phone within a few months.

My Dear GOD:

He wrote to me on a weekly basis. His letters would make me cry for him for weeks to follow. He would express much remorse and sorrow. He wasn't sure that he could get through all this. He wrote in one of the letters, "I had a great life. I had my wonderful wife, two most beautiful children, and my family. I had success, and a great future ahead of me. And now I am where I was four years ago, working so hard trying to find a job as a resident again. I don't know who to blame or what to think at all. It seems that whenever I am at the peak of my success and happiness, some huge storm arises and hits me so bad that it destroys all that I had built up before. I don't believe that I will be able to stand up on my feet again. But I only have one hope, and that is you and my two children. I am only counting on you and your forgiveness. I expect from you to cooperate and help me get back on my feet, and help me make my dreams come true. I just need your complete

support, please".

My dear, dear GOD, wouldn't you feel sorry for him at that time. Wasn't I supposed to feel sorry for him, wasn't I supposed to cry for the beautiful love of my life? He was so desperately in need of my help. He was my strong man, my main support. I was so proud to be his wife. I thought he had everything in the world to make me happy. I have disowned my entire family to be with him, I have chosen to depend on his love. How could I abandon him at this hard and crucial time of his life? He would say, "I know that you might not believe me, but with your help I am going to make it up to you and my children". He said, "You won't believe this, but when I see all other children alongside their parents, and then I think of my own beautiful children who are so far from me, I start melting away from all the embarrassment. I am praying to GOD that you allow me the chance to give you the happiness that I had promised you".

Those were the letters that he wrote to me. Although my children didn't know how to read or write then, he would still include a few paragraphs just for them. His letters not only made me feel sorry for him, but on many occasions I thought of myself as guilty of not being very encouraging. All that I did was shielding my children from suffering by concealing the ugliness of their father's behavior.

He started asking me to get ready to go back to Michigan the moment he left. In every letter he would instruct me what, where and how to go, or do.

He had a single aunt. We all called her Ammeh. She would alternate living between Pari & Neya's homes. He asked me to ask Ammeh to move in with us. It was a great idea; my children wouldn't feel so lonely at home without their father. Meanwhile my sister Azar, her husband Shahab and her two children Reza and Rokhand were living in the next-door apartment, in the same complex. It worked out for all of us. Kids especially were very happy.

My dear GOD:

I would like to tell again about Ammeh's life. I would like to share with you why I never wished that my children had a broken home. Ammeh was the sister of Sarvan Rafani. I heard her life story from Ammeh herself as well as from other very close relatives. Ammeh was a very beautiful girl. Her family made her to get married at a very young age according to Islamic rules, which would be the age of nine, ten or eleven. And naturally she shortly gave birth to two boys. I am not aware of what had happened next. But her family, her brother Sarvan Rafani in particular, had separated Ammeh from her husband. He made her to get a divorce.

I have no idea how much truth was in this statement.

My dear, dear GOD, once again this was a classic case of life circumstances prevailing over our will. Ammeh was married at the age of ten or eleven by the force of her parents; she was not given a chance to find out the value of money and/or education.

She was divorced at the age of thirteen or fourteen, she was not given an alternative.

Ninety nine percent of marriages in Iran are arranged by parents, of which approximately twenty percent continue a happy, loving life. The rest end up with life-long sufferings of extramarital affairs and divorces.

My Dear GOD:

It was because of these unfair and forceful laws that I never wanted to get married, unless I was so in love that I would be willing to end my life for the sake of my lover. The one thing that I was oblivious about was that the absolute love had to be mutual. But that was my foolishness. My beliefs were that when I am so deeply and truly in love, my partner would love me the same way. And I would be able to have control over every life circumstance. Once again I was very foolish.

Anyway, Ammeh stayed with us for that whole year. I liked her a lot, even though she was sad most of the time. I had so much respect for her. I knew that she had the right to be sad, and even to be mad at the world around her. Although she never talked about her life, one could tell that she didn't like living.

In 1993, the year that I was visiting Iran, Ammeh was living in Neya's house, in a room, smaller than a doghouse, under the stairway. I went to visit Ammeh there.

That year was another experience for me, yet another lesson learned. Azar was teaching and she was taking up a few courses at the university at the same time. Our children were happy to be together in the evenings and on the weekends. Ammeh has moved in with us. I was getting very comfortable with my new life. I had a great support from my family as well as my sisters-in-law. Azar was the one who disowned me when I was insisting on marrying Iraj. She went as far as turning her back on me and changing the side of the street when we ran into one another. Now they were all helping deal with my problems. For the first time, after all those disastrous years I was feeling free of pain. I was no longer suffering at every moment of my existence. I was hoping that my life stays that way for good.

You know, my dear GOD, life is very ironic. I have only dreamt of being together with Iraj before all this had happened. I would give/do anything just to be with him, and love him, and kiss him, and make him comfortable. But now I was very happy to be away from him. It took me four years of suffering to recognize what life was all about. I had to experience pain to understand my parent's words of wisdom.

He assigned me to be receiving money from the people whom he had sold the furniture to. He was asking me to get ready to return to U.S.A. He wanted me to sell all the remaining furniture for my spending money. He was asking me to be very conservative with spending money. Our "Groudnik" Hi-FI, which he gave to Parveen, was one of our most expensive possessions. I assume that it must have been in exchange for something.

My Dear GOD:

I came across as a stingy merchant on many occasions trying to collect money from all those we sold our belongings to. I would have never put myself through all that humiliation if I didn't have to. I remember I had to deal with my sister's complaints over the set of furniture she had purchased from me. She was not happy.

He wrote to me every week and asked me to get ready to come to Michigan. He thought that it would be so easy for me. He didn't know that our love for each other has been damaged. He was probably thinking that I was the same person I had been before. The more persistent he became about me returning to America, the more worried I grew.

On one hand I was very happy that my children were going to gain their father and family again. On the other hand I had lost all my trust on him. Deep down I was very scared to give up my job and my family. I have rediscovered them after many years, and now I had to go back to him. I was really terrified. I tried to ignore his requests for months. I tried to live a happy life with my children. As the time passed, he was getting impatient. His letters became more demanding.

After seven months he wrote to my father. He asked my father to intervene and find out, "What are Shamci's plans? It seems that she is trying to avoid my request".

My father called to talk to me one of the evenings. I told him how I felt, and how terrified and worried I was. And I asked him, "What if he does it again in the country that I have no job, no family, and no money?" My father said, "Marriage is a big risk for everyone. No one is ever promised a great result. We all try to do things right. But sometimes we might run into unforeseen circumstances that will change the direction of our lives. Many times these circumstances come our way in such manner that we don't have any control over them. I understand that in Iraj's case, he was not the initiator. It had just happened and he fell into that trap. He did try to pull himself out of it, and he did. It was not easy, but he was determined to do so, and he did." Then he continued, "We all are somebody before we get married. We can choose what we want to do. But after we had our children, our lives are not ours any more. We have to think of those little children that we have created. They did not come in to this world at their own will. They are our responsibility. We owe them their life, their happiness, and their success. From now on you have to give up many of your rights to be able to protect your children from possible destruction." Then he continued, "Iraj has done his job to save the family and bring them under one roof again. Now it's your turn to forget about the past and bring all the broken pieces together again. The decision is yours. If you don't pick up from here, you would be the one who destroyed the happy family".

My Dear GOD:

What was I supposed to tell him after that warning? He said, "Our parents did it for us, we do it for you, and you have to do it for your children. No questions asked".

It was then and only then that I had realized that there was no way out. Then he asked me to write to Iraj and let him know that I would be on my way right after the school year was over. That was what Iraj had asked me to do. He was insisting that I began with all the planning before the school was over. He would not accept any further delays.

After this long discussion with my father, I realized that I have one most difficult mission ahead of me, and that there was no way out of it. I had to either make it or break it.

And the most difficult part of all was that I had to love him the same way I did before, otherwise I couldn't be a wife to him. The thought of intimacy with a man that I wasn't deeply in love seemed impossible. So I had to find a reason to love him the same way I did before. Although he wasn't willing to spend money, his letters were still very promising. I decided to listen to my father and leave the rest to my GOD, and my luck. I wrote him a letter informing him that I was getting ready to join him.

It was a very difficult task since I didn't have enough money, my children got sick quite often, and there were lots of expenses anticipated for the preparation of passports, visas among many other things.

Since I was leaving Iran indefinitely, I had to resign from my teaching job, which by the way I liked a lot. This matter was a major drawback for me. I was very scared to lose my job; I was terrified thinking about the moment. But I had no other choice. I had to think of my children's life and accept the oncoming future.

I informed Iraj that I was ready to return to Michigan. And with his guidance through his letters I began the process of our departure. Sometimes we talked on the phone. But because long distance calls were costly for both of us he tried to avoid making them.

After the school was over they made me resign in order for me to be able to obtain my visa.

This incident is important to be mentioned. The gentleman, who was signing my visa at the embassy, asked me a personal question. He asked why I was leaving the country to go back to the U.S.A. He was working in a very small room, with used, and damaged furniture. I answered him, "I have to go. My husband is there and I have to take my children to be with their father". He paused for a moment and said, "I don't want to put wrong ideas in your mind. I myself had spent most of my life out of the country studying. I have been a professor at Boston University and U of M for many years. I had lived in France. I have had very good positions and a good income. But I was never able to adapt myself to their lifestyle. Now I am in my middle age, I prefer this little room, this broken furniture and my now days modest income. I am very happy here, and I could never be this happy when I was there". Obviously he didn't know why I was going back. I wished that I could scream, and tell him, "My dear friend, I tried so hard to come back to my

Afsaneh, Mary, Maseeh, Nader, Keyvan, Arman, Nazy, Kaveh. My cousin Koorosh is standing.

Before I leave to come to the U.S.A. for the second time, I am sitting between my two beautiful innocent children who did not know what was happening in their lives. Why should they go to Iran and rush back in a few years? The most difficult part was that I had to cover up for his act to not let my children get hurt.

My picture with Mary and Maseeh for our passport

country for the same reason. But I don't know what it is, it could be the circumstances, my destiny, or maybe it is my GOD who wants me to live in that country, away from all my loved ones". Instead I just shook my head and thanked him for his advice. "I completely understand your feelings", I said.

My Dear GOD:

I sold everything. I said goodbye to my job and my future. I got my visa, and bought our tickets. I said goodbye to my family and friends, and we flew to Michigan, toward the unknown future. We arrived at the Detroit Airport just one week before the riots of 1967. Many people showed up to the Tehran Airport to wish us farewell. Among them were my parents. That day I saw tears in my father's eyes for the first time in my whole life. He wished me good luck. Members of both of our families: all my sisters and their husbands, Iraj's three sisters and their husbands, his uncle and his wife with their children were there. Mehdi Agha and his wife, and last but not least, good friends of ours, Dr. Toosi and his wife Shahnaz had come to the airport.

Almost everyone, who really cared for us, was there. These were all very important people to our faith, and our future. I will never forget their support, their respect, and kindness for the rest of my life. Many people brought us boxes of different goodies. There was so many of them that I couldn't take everything with me on the plane. Keep in mind that I only have two hands that I had to hold Mary's and Maseeh's hands with. And I had a few handbags over my shoulders. But it was not proper to give them back to those who brought them for me. And most of all I was in such disarray at that time, I wouldn't know how to make a rational decision. So I gave all those boxes to our security, and asked him to take them to his family. He was so shocked. He kept asking, "Don't you want them for yourself?" When I got to Michigan, I felt sorry that I gave them all away.

He was at the Airport to drive us home.

NEW CHAPTER AND NEW LIFE AGAIN IN THE U.S. AND A.

My Dear GOD:

It was very awkward for the children to see him. It was more like meeting a stranger and not their father, especially for Mary. She was two years older than Maseeh, and she was able to understand, more than Maseeh, what was happening. She told me once, "I didn't know that he was my father". I realized then why she was trying to pull herself away from him. Iraj had noticed it himself as well. I don't know and I don't precisely remember my feelings at that time. I just know that I felt like I was meeting a new person in my life.

He was able to rent a town house in the same neighborhood that we used to live before. Those houses were only for the interns and residents of Beaumont hospital. They actually did him a favor. He was able to rent that house for only a year.

When we got home, Iraj tried to hold Mary's hand. She was hesitant to go to him. I thought that maybe she was shy. But she told me later on, "I was not shy. I just didn't know him. He looked different". He had somewhat furnished the house. He bought a pink bedroom set for Mary. It was a complete set with a dresser, a chest, a queen bed with canopy, all in pink, and a desk with a chair. There was hardly any room left for movement.

He placed a brown twin bed, a chest, a dresser, and a desk with a chair in Maseeh's room.

There was a bedroom set for us, and some other simple furniture for living room and the kitchen. I don't remember how or when we got intimate again. But I remember that I was expecting him talk about the issues from our recent past, and hopefully relieve my mind. But that did not happen. He was probably assuming that he had said enough in his letters, and there was no need to open wounds. I can't recall when and how we began being intimate again. Our life had resumed, and I had to make the best of it. I kept in mind that what my father had told me, and so I focused on my life and my children's happiness.

To tell you the truth, my dear GOD, I never wanted to talk about our past. It would have been more of a hurtful process rather than a healing one. He really was doing his best. Without having his affair, he was the best. Together, we put the past completely behind us. Although most of the times I felt embarrassed thinking that the whole world knows what he has done to me, still my father's words of wisdom always rang in my ears. I had to work on myself and become my own psychotherapist. I kept telling myself that I

had to start on the right foot; otherwise I would destroy everything again, especially when he was trying so hard to mend the feelings that have gone sour for many years. I must recognize his great effort for making our life lovable again. I made myself to understand the situation and work on my feelings little by little. With Iraj's effort, soon I found myself comfortable with him, and life started to go on.

My Dear GOD:

We lived in that town house for one year. I made contact with everyone in Iran and assured them that everything was fine, and that everything was getting back to normal. Mary and Maseeh started to go to school in that neighborhood. Mary had finished the first grade in Iran. So I asked the school faculty to place her in second grade. They agreed to put her in second grade after she successfully passed a few tests. Maseeh was in kindergarten; he was having a hard time with the new language. Even though I read a lot, I don't know much about psychology. I believe that kids establish their personality at the ages of two to six. In my children's case such a drastic change of environment, difficulties of learning a new language, and in particular all that had happened to them in Iran, had made them so insecure. Consequently they lost their ability of handling life issues. Each child reacts differently to oncoming situations. According to their character they take the bad, understand it and change themselves to good or they take the bad and follow it. The time period between the ages of one to five is the pick-up time, the most crucial learning time for a child. That is why special education trainers agree that kids who were disturbed and/or damaged physically, psychologically or emotionally will eventually become very difficult and uncontrollable. In many cases they will either become self-destructive or enjoy harming others.

In a society where marrying for love did not mean much, I wanted to get married only for love. I wished to live my entire life with love. I wanted to raise my children with love and at the end die with love. Yes, my dear GOD. It has been done. People had given up the throne to be able to keep the LOVE in their life forever. So my dream was not unreachable. As a matter of fact, this is the only correct way of living and raising kids. Loveless marriage is just a mistake, I am glad it didn't last for me. When I fell in love with him, I was ready to follow the ancient rule of when a husband dies, he must be buried along with his living wife. I loved Iraj to a point that I was ready to die with him. But unfortunately after seven years of struggle with my parents over him, and after only four years of marriage, my love broke into million pieces because of his affairs.

You see my dear GOD; this is the reason why I always say I feel guilty for bringing my children into this world. If they go through good times I don't mind it at all. But I will keep blaming myself for not being able to correct things for them when they go through bad times. I know that I have to put every effort into raising them as strong and capable individuals, so that they are able to handle every difficult matter on their own. It is my responsibility to create a healthy environment for them, and when I fail I shall be deemed to be guilty. They didn't ask me to bring them into this world. After all it was me who had procreated them for my own pleasure and then put them through such a misfortunate and miserable childhood. Although I was not the creator of that misfortunate situation, still they were the ones who got to suffer and pay for it. And when I am the only one who recognizes my children's emotions I have to learn how to relief their pain by giving up all my rights.

My Dear GOD:

The second year in Michigan we had to move into an apartment in Troy, Michigan near his new office. He wanted to have his solo practice. He was trying so hard to bring my emotions back. He tried to bring my trust back. He would get me involved with any and all decision-making, at least that's what I thought at the time.

You see my dear GOD, when I had left everybody behind in Iran and I had come to this country, I always missed my family, my friends, my culture, my food and all the familiar places. I always felt lonely in this country. Iraj felt the same way. We wanted to meet other Iranians in this country. We wanted to socialize with other doctors. Some of his friends, Dr. Mohammad Rabbani, Dr. Saeed Khadem, and Dr. Mohtadi had returned to Iran, but had been planning to eventually come back to U.S. So we knew very little Iranian doctors. We were always looking forward to meeting other Iranians. So we would accept with open arms anyone who came along and said "SALAM".

In a long run we were coming along so well. We were doing fine and I could say that we were involved again. My trust was back again, I had no reason for having doubts. Although every once in a while I did get the flashbacks of his actions, I never allowed for that grief to take over my life.

Marriage means oneness to me. Oneness is pure love, complete trust, and great togetherness. Without these I could never get intimate with my husband. Thanks GOD that Iraj made it possible to bring back those feelings in me.

Our children had to change their school again. We had to enroll them to a school in Troy. We lived in that apartment for one year. After that we decided to buy a house. He had good enough credit to get a mortgage loan. After searching for some time, we found a house in Bloomfield Hills, one of the finest neighborhoods.

Well, my dear GOD, listen to this. As much as I made myself guilty for bringing two children into this world, I got pregnant again in 1968. Just two weeks before I delivered Mojgan, we moved into our new house.

My Dear GOD:

It was located at 860 Helston Road, Bloomfield Hills, Michigan. It was a tri-level house with four bedrooms, three bathrooms, a living room, a dinning room, a family

In a hotel's restaurant at a convention
Left to right: me, Rohan Panah, Louise Neelfrooshan, Jalal Panah, Hassan Neelfrooshan and Iraj Rafani
I lost my leather coat which I had bought in Germany, at their parking, just because we gave them the key.

room, and a very big kitchen. The lot size was close to an acre. We had a big yard, and neighbors with children. The school was within a walking distance, and there was a Fire Station near us.

By this time Mary was nine, and Maseeh was seven. I was so happy to see that their life of emotional roller coaster was coming to an end, and soon they were going to feel right at home. At least I was hoping so. Now was the time to take advantage of everything good and beautiful around us. We had a few Iranian friends, and we also met a few new ones.

The birth of Mojgan brought special joy and happiness to our lives. We were a complete family now. We all enjoyed the fireplace in the family room during the winter. Maseeh loved the fire and the fireplace the most. Kids roasted marshmallows; we had such a great time with them. Our house was filled with sounds of laughter and giggles.

Due to the nature of his job, and his schedule, I was taking care of our children solely. He was either at work, or on-call. Even when he was home he had to sleep to make up for the night shifts, I couldn't count on him. I was so happy when on rare occasions he would make some time to spend with the children. Even when we entertained at nights, or went to a picnic he was busy playing cards or backgammon with his friends. I never allowed myself to depend on him or anyone else for any sort of help. I was doing everything by myself because I knew that I was responsible, and I would do it right.

To make my life a little more exciting, I had signed up for English and sewing courses on the evenings that he was home. I found a somewhat fulfillment in my studies, and at the same time I kept myself busy away from housework and my nostalgia. And at my spare time I did sewing for the children and myself, I knitted, crochet and read. I was thinking that marriage is all about cooperation and the awareness of our responsibilities. I always thought that we each must take the responsibility to do our work right. And because he was always away from home, I took the responsibility for everything. I always tried to make things by myself in order to have some savings . For instance he had bought a dinette set. The chair upholstery would get ripped from just sitting on them. I ordered a piece of leather through the yellow pages, and made covers for the six chairs. They actually lasted forever. I did not have a machine for sewing leather, so I stitched it all by hand. Because I was a stay home mother, I was always looking for something to do. I did everything starting from sewing clothes to painting and wall papering the rooms, and so on in order to save money for the future of our children. All the work that I was doing would cost a lot of money if someone else did it. But no one has ever given me a credit. I admit that I was trying to keep myself busy, but my primary goal was to save money for our future. You know, my dear GOD, I had a dream. And I would do anything to make my dream come true. I had always believed that with sincere love we could make that wish come true, and we would live happily ever after.

My Dear GOD:

My children were my career and my income was the well being of my family. Unfortunately my plan did not work, and pretty soon I had to open my eyes, and I said to myself, "Kay sera, sera. What will be will be".

As my children were growing up, I had to learn to understand them more and more. And after what Mary and Maseeh had gone through in the past, I was anticipating challenges, in Mary's case in particular.

When Mary had finished the sixth grade, we enrolled her in to a private Catholic school. Right after she turned ten, she started talking about boys. Step by step she did unusual things. So I had to sign up for a PTE (parents' teaching effectiveness) class. The class was held at a church near our house. It dealt with handling the changes in teen-agers. I needed to learn what my duty was to her strange behavior. You see my dear GOD; I've always been the one who thought of my children and their well-being. I was the one who took the PTE course. On the other hand he never even thought of taking it, it didn't seem important to him. He thought he knew everything just because he was a doctor. He was either at work, or buried in the Wall Street Journal studying how to become a millionaire when he was home.

The girl, who until yesterday was so loving and affectionate, the same girl, who didn't mind loving me, started hating me all of a sudden. I tried to talk to her about my culture, my morals and the respect that we have to have for ourselves. I had to tell her that in our country no girl ever thinks of having a boyfriend before she gets married. But because of the changes in the world and the vulnerability of girls in general, not only I would stop her from having a boyfriend at the age of sixteen, but also I would even help her meet good young boys. I would tell her that it was okay to have friends, who were boys, but they had to be just friends. She never had ears to listen to me. I was her only enemy in the world. She was telling me, "Girls my age at school can have boyfriends and their parents have nothing against it. I told her, "My dear Mary, kids are free to do anything their parents approve of. But in our household rules are different and we must follow those rules".

My Dear GOD:

From playing Barbies she went to making herself into one. She bought make-up, and used plenty of it. She locked herself in the bathroom one Saturday and plucked all her eyebrows. Obviously, she was embarrassed to go to school the next morning. I was so shocked that day that I decided to take the PTE course. I really needed help.

My sister Azar was visiting us during that time. She was separated from her husband and needed some time away from home. Her two children Reza and Rokhand were in Iran, and she was very worried. I had to learn to understand what Mary and Maseeh had gone through. I had a difficult time with them. I was especially concerned about Mary being teased by the school kids.

After taking the PTE class I learned to approach the matters differently. I was ready to change my beliefs, my attitude, and my reaction towards everything she did. I tried to talk to her about any and all subjects, especially the subject of sex. I bought her a set of four books about sex. They were written very clearly, specifically for kids of her age. The books had many illustrations on the anatomy of both male and the female. Although I was born in Muslim faith, I made sure that they had the freedom to study other faiths as well. I have been a liberated woman from the beginning to the end. I have never had a bone of prejudice in my body. The whole world is beautiful unless that is proven to me otherwise.

We had a few Baha'i friends who were very active in preaching and promoting their ideas. One of them was Dr. Rahmat and Parvaneh Kashef. Their children Fariba and Rameen were friends with Mary and Maseeh. I thought that if I would send her to a summer school with Fariba, not only she would be happy but she would also learn to behave. I drove her to the camp, which was more than an hour away from home. I checked the place and talked to most of the teachers. Tolue Avaregan, Fariba's aunt was one of the camp managers. Many parents were involved with teaching. So it seemed like a safe place to me. But to my bad luck, she met a fourteen-year-old boy who was there to find himself in Baha'i faith. She liked him and they become acquainted. When Mary talked to him about her problems at home, and how her parents won't let her do anything, he advised her to run away from home. He said, "I did it and it worked for me". She seemed to be very happy when she returned home in three weeks. I was so glad that I sent her there.

We got up to have breakfast one Saturday morning. I looked for Mary in her room, but she wasn't there. I looked all over the house. I knew that I had checked her room before I went to bed, and I found her sound asleep. I called everyone while I kept looking for her in her room. Then Maseeh found a note that said, "I couldn't take it any more, so I am leaving home". I just dropped dead. I got in the car and drove around, thinking that she might have been around the neighborhood. Oh GOD, my dear, dear GOD. What time did she get away? Where should I look for her? Please, my dear GOD, help me. Where did I go wrong? I certainly wasn't ready for this. At the same time Iraj drove his car, he got as far as Detroit. No, there was not a sign of her. I started mourning helplessly.

My Dear GOD:

We decided to call Dr. Jalal and Rohan Panah when Iraj came back home. Their daughter Roksan was Mary's friend. And after they came over, we decided to call the police. When the police officer arrived, he said, "This is happening to most families who have teenagers. She might not be too far away, and we might be able to find her". When he found out that Mary had just recently returned from a summer camp, he immediately requested more information about it. I called Parvaneh and asked her about the camp.

Then Fariba told us that there was a runaway boy who was at the camp and he had become friends with Mary. We gave his name, and whatever else information we had to the officer, and he left to follow-up with the case. He said, "These girls are so naïve that if not found they will get killed, or they will end up in the hands of pimps for the rest of their lives".

My dear, dear GOD, you know what had happened to me at that time. I felt as if I have lost everything: the baby that I cared, the one I watched over every second of my life was now lost forever and ever. I loved her so much; I lived for her life. Maseeh was very sad. Mojgan was just a baby, she couldn't understand much.

At the time that Mary decided to run away, there was no fight or any kind of disagreement between us. I was wondering what had triggered her to do so. There were no apparent alarming signs. The only thing that we could do at that point was to sit impatiently by the phone and wait for the news. Every one of us, including Iraj, started to give up hope. We were getting ready for the worst-ever news.

It was not until later that evening that police was able to track her down in Chicago. She was kept at the youth center there. We must have all died a million times.

The next day, which was Sunday, Iraj drove to Chicago and brought her back. I don't know what Iraj did or said to her, but I know that she would not allow me to look at her or talk to her. You see, my dear GOD, Mary was a kind of girl who wanted to put her foot down from the beginning, someone who demanded the things she wanted. My dear GOD, what language would you choose to speak to a girl that says, "Either do what I ask, or I will runaway"? With the help of that boy from the summer camp she got a bus ticket and took off to Chicago. Police found her at the bus station when she got off. How lucky she was. And how lucky we were!

My Dear GOD:

Now what? How do I approach a girl that runs away? I was worried how to have control over Maseeh and Mojgan. Mary was a product of the sixties. Could I get any luckier than that?

I remembered the day that my father told me, "You are spoiling this child to a point that not only she will destroy herself, but she will destroy you for sure". It was true. She had started already.

At this time I had to be very careful with Mary. I made sure that she understood me hundred percent that there would never be a second time. I gave her an ultimatum that if it ever happened again, I would not no longer be looking for her. She had to choose between either enjoying a happy, comfortable life, or destroying her life and having no life at all.

My father always believed that his children were raised to be normal human beings, who will be beneficial to their society and understand their duties with the acknowledgment of the responsibilities toward human race. “Otherwise”, he would say, “I am proud to announce that they are not my children, and I would not care if they are dead or alive. It is very easy to have children, but bringing them up as a right person is not that easy".

Anyway, my priority at that time was to learn the teen-age language. Now that we were back to having a peaceful and loving life together, we had to take the first step towards our children's well being. I think this was the most difficult chapter of our lives.

Okay, my dear GOD, looking back now I see that without you, who held my hands during those desperate times and guided me toward being hopeful and going forward, what would I have done?

I was nine months pregnant when we moved to that neighborhood. In order to save money I did all the packing myself. Everything was new to us. We all had to adapt to our new surroundings. We didn’t know our neighbors. I was ready to entertain friends in our new home a week after we had moved in. It was important that our children had their friends around. I didn’t want them to be feeling isolated.

There was still two weeks before my due date. I was having people over at my house. Everybody was talking about my delicious food. After dinner I went to the bathroom, and I found myself wet. I thought it was just a discharge. I mentioned it to Iraj after everybody had left. He immediately examined me in the bedroom. He said, "My God, your waters broke, and you are dilated. We decided not to go to the hospital yet, since I had no pain. I did not have anyone to stay with my children. He checked me once again in the morning before he went to the hospital. I was more dilated, but still no pain. He had four surgeries schedule for that morning. He said, "If your pain starts call my nurse at the office, she will drive you to the hospital”.

My Dear GOD:

Maseeh and his friend Jimmy Zadeh had a sleep over at our house. I had to find someone to leave my children with. I went to our neighbors, but there was no one home. Even simply walking to the neighbors was quite a distance for me. My pain started to come rapidly. I called Sue, Jimmy's mother, and told her about my situation. I asked her to come and get both Jimmy and Maseeh. Then I called Iraj's office and told his nurse that my pains are only three minutes apart. I picked up some personal stuff and packed my suitcase. Sue was not there yet. I called her again and I said, “I will leave Maseeh and Jimmy all alone waiting for you on the steps in the front door. If you don't get there quick, I don’t know what will happen to them”.

It was hot July day, 23rd of July 1969. At this time my pains were so close that I thought the baby will be in my hands any moment. Iraj’s nurse showed up at that time. I took Mary along so that she stayed with Iraj’s nurse until Iraj was free. I said goodbye to Maseeh and Jimmy, who were waiting for Sue to pick them up any time soon. Mary and I got in the car, and quickly we were driven away. She put her flashing red lights on for police to know that she had an emergency, and she had to drive faster than the speed limit.

They had informed my doctor, Dr. Longyear. He was at the hospital when I got there. There was no time to prepare or shave me. The baby was out in no time. But the placenta was still stock. It did not move at all. I think they put me to sleep to be able to remove the placenta. I woke up in about seven or eight hours. For some reason I woke up crying hard. Iraj had given up two surgeries to be there with me. He was holding my hand, and he said, "Why are you crying now? You must have been crying while seven interns and residents were working on you to save your life. You should be happy, because you are fine. Mojgan is fine and kids are all okay too".

You see, my dear GOD, don't think that I am complaining. I was very lucky comparing to that poor lady, who had delivered her baby on the top of a tree trying to survive from drowning in a disastrous mudslide. But let me tell you that having baby is one emotional process of our life. I felt very lonely; I wished I could have cried on my mother's shoulder, I wished I could have whispered to her, "My dear mother, how did you do it? How did you go live through nine pregnancies?" Yes, I wanted to have someone to talk to. But you were there, my dear GOD, and everything was okay.

My Dear GOD:

Once Iraj brought the children to the hospital to visit me. I felt great.

I was discharged from the hospital on the fifth day after delivering Mojgan. Mary and Maseeh were sitting in the back seat. For a few minutes we were all quite. Then Maseeh said, "From that big stomach, this little baby?"

Mojgan had a problem with her blood count right after birth. They had to make an incision at her heel to find out what the problem was, and so they were able to cure it.

Iraj always thought that no one knew about his life in Iran. We never talked about it, and that period of our life had completely disappeared from our minds.

We decided to take Mary to psychiatrist because of her behavior. Iraj thought that if necessary we would all go to therapy to rid ourselves of the ugly tumor that had been planted in all of our hearts. He was aware what a great damage had been done to my children. He found a group of psychiatrists after a long research. He had made an appointment for Mary. But soon I found out that he had changed his mind. His reason was that the group worked with an Iranian Doctor, Dr. Vaziri. I realized that while he believed that no one knew about his life in Iran, he did not want to volunteer the information about what he had done in Iran. So he had postponed taking Mary to psychiatrist all together. When I asked him to find another group, he refused to do so.

Another drawback for him was the money. Iraj had always been notorious for being too stingy to spend money on important matters, but at the same time being a very big spender when it came to showing off to his fellow doctors.

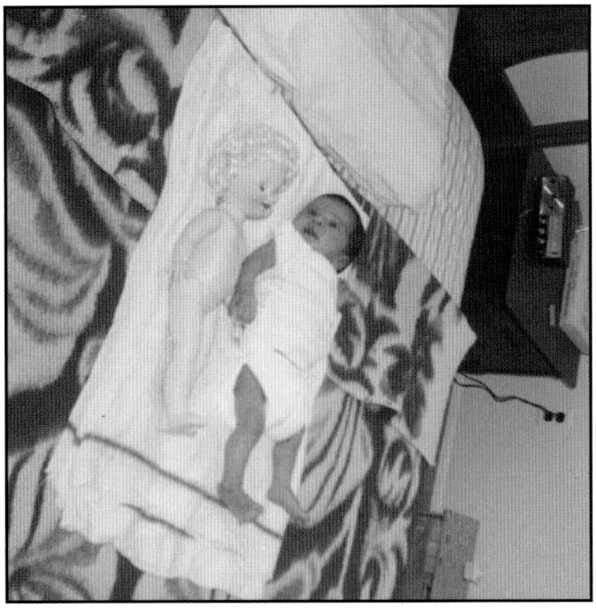

Mojgan is as big as her little doll. **Mojgan at six months old**

Indeed at the time Mary and Maseeh enjoyed to play with their little sister Mojgan .

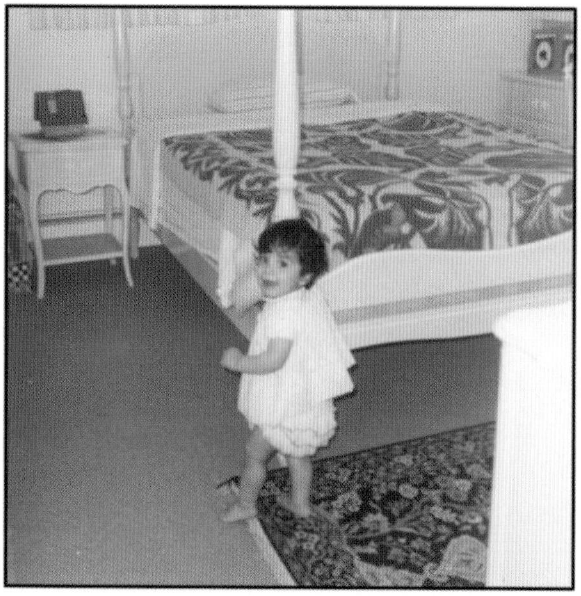

Mojgan started walking.

Mary was talking to her little sister.

Just living a happy life for some time

Mary, Maseeh, and Mojgan

Mojgan, the clown

Mojgan, with her favorite figure

Here, the three of them are enjoying life. Guess who the photographer was. It was nobody but me.

Maseeh at age ten and
Mojgan at age three

Walking and having fun

Mary at her High School Graduation

Daddy was walking his little
girl Mojgan, at age five.

I don't remember how he ended up convincing me not to go to a psychiatrist, but I knew that we had made a big mistake in Mary's case. That was the best time for trying to open Mary's wounds and putting a healing pad on them. Unfortunately he had the control of spending money. And I did not want to cloud the atmosphere more than it already was. I am not sure, but I think that had we have succeeded in helping Mary at that age, we would have probably not run into the difficulties that we ran into later in life.

In sixties hippies, drugs and alcohol were glamorized by the media. Means of parental control over children were limited, or in many cases impossible. Smoking cigarettes was another peer pressure for teenagers that I was very afraid of. Some kids are more prone to experiment and explore. I am afraid to admit that Mary was one of those.

My Dear GOD:

I was planning to give my children enough freedom that thy do whatever they want in front of me. I wanted to be able to show them the ugliness of their actions. I was trying to make them understand what it would do to them.

I don't know when Mary started to smoke cigarettes. But when we went to Iran for a visit, she would smoke there. On the summer of 1972, we went to Iran for a visit. Mary was turning thirteen, Maseeh was ten and a half, and Mojgan was three. After their school was over for summer holiday children and I flew to Iran, and Iraj joined us on the first of July. That visit was so important for all of us. My children got to know their cousins, aunts and uncles all over again. It seemed that they did not know that they had so much love waiting for them in Iran. They were so amused by all the love and attention that they fell in love with the idea of staying there. They didn't know that all that attention would only last for a little while, and then they would again start fighting with each other.

We would be invited to someone's house practically every day. Among all the children that were together at all times were Ezzat's two children, Neya's three children, Pari's three children, and mine. Azar's children and Jamal's daughter would join them sometimes as well. Afsaneh was the oldest, and Kasra was the youngest of all.

I took my children to Iran first of all so that they would get to know their close relatives. Second of all I wanted them to have a change of environment. I didn't know what was going on with raising teenagers in Iran. My children began to feel the sense of belonging. It felt wonderful. They walked together, talked together, ate together and played together. Some of them got friendlier than the others. It had been very lonely and depressing for my children to have always been alone for occasions like Thanksgiving and Christmas. Although I had always arranged parties with their friends, still nobody could take the place of their Grandmas, Grandpas, aunts, uncles, or all the cousins. In addition they had few dozens of second cousins.

Because this trip was after our reconciliation everyone from my family to his family, and all our friends had welcomed us with open arms. Every one of them made sure that

we had a great time. They adored the children. Everyone welcomed us at the airport. We all went to my parents' house. Both mine and Iraj's families were invited for all the occasions. After that we arranged to stay for a few days at Pari's house, then at Neya's house, next at Ezzat's house and so on.

Arman, Neya's son, and Mary became very close. He was fifteen at the time. I knew that they must have a puppy love. I did not want to make a big deal out of it. I made sure that hopefully nothing went wrong, while I was watching them.

My Dear GOD:

Mary was a thirteen-year-old going to twenty-two. I found out that she had been smoking with Arman. I made sure to let her know that I knew, and asked her to come to me if she had to smoke. I told her, "If you don't know what cigarettes will do to you, I will bring you a brochure to inform you of this deadly habit. I am not the one who can stop you from doing it. I don't want to put pressure on you, because you will still do it behind my back. But I am asking you not to start. I am sure one day you will be sorry, but it might be too late then". Although she did not smoke too often, still she would smoke when she was around other kids trying to act as if she was an adult.

While Mary and Arman were enjoying their teenage hood, Kayvan, who was very fond of Mary and was trying to get her attention, was very disturbed by their closeness. Every night while we were attending one party or the other, he would come to me, he would take me to a private place and he would talk to me about Arman. He would tell me how Arman did this and that. There was a big competition over winning Mary's friendship. I knew that Mary had her eye on Arman. But at the same time I didn't want to hurt Kayvan's feelings. Somehow I had to convince him that I believed in him, and that he was allowed to just keep watching Mary and try to have fun together while it lasted. But it didn't matter how much I talked to him, still the next day he would seek me out at a party, and he would tell me the same story. He would warn me of a possible harm to Mary. I started getting frustrated. We were going to stay in there for only two months. I did not want to put restriction on any of them. I wouldn't have been able to even if I tried. We were in Iran to be with everybody, and enjoy our stay together. I would have never considered staying home so that I would keep my children away from everybody. I came to realize that there was more to all Kayvan's words than I could see. He was insisting that Mary and Arman should not be together.

Arman was an explorer. He always acted much older than his own age. I know for a fact that Mary had gotten accustomed to frequent smoking by then. At that time I didn't know that he had been involved with drugs. But there were days that I saw him at Bazare-Safaviyeh, a shopping center, mingling with some strange looking adults, who didn't look trustworthy.

Iraj joined us a month later. Now we were having more parties, more invitations, and

more happy times together. They were treating us like Rafani's dynasty. It felt good while it lasted.

My dear, dear GOD, I have to talk about this. Just like at the time of my arrival, every member of our family was at the Tehran airport. The waiting room was too crowded. I knew that his family should have greeted him first, since they had been apart for a while; and then it would be my turn. Every one jumped to kiss him and hug him as soon as he appeared. He started pushing them all away, and he kept asking for me. They told him, “Shamci is here”. And they gave way for him to see me. He held me up in the air in front of all those people and started kissing me. His brother-in-law, Mr. Forghani said, "You should talk to us and kiss us first. We are the ones who haven't seen you for a long time. Shamci was away from you for just three weeks". While that was the truth, he said it in a funny way. Okay, my dear GOD, not only his actions made me believe in his love for me, but they made others wonder about his love as well. What he did that day at the airport, he did not even have to do it, had made me believing in his love for me more and more every day.

My Dear GOD:

It was impossible to keep an eye on that group of children every second. There were more than thirteen kids together at all times from ages of two and a half to seventeen. I was hoping that older ones would keep an eye on the little ones. I didn't want to separate the kids from each other because I knew that soon they would be separated by force of the compelling power of circumstances. So it was not fair to spoil their summer and ruin everybody's happiness.

Many accidents happened while we were there. They wanted to go to the movies together. They wanted to go to have ice cream together or go for a walk together, and so on. We, as mothers, had made sure to know where exactly they were going, at what time they were leaving, what time they would be back, and what transportation they were using. One day the older kids wanted to go to a movie. Neya drove them to the movies and they were supposed to come back right after the movie was over by themselves. While they were walking to get a taxi they all decided to jump over the park's iron fence. They were all able to jump the fence except for Afsaneh. Her throat got ripped on the sharp point of the iron fence. All other kids were younger than Afsaneh. She was bleeding so heavily that they thought she was going to die right then and there. They told me later that some of them put their hands over the cut to stop the bleeding. Arman called his Mom, Neya, right away. Neya left the house without mentioning anything to anyone. We thought she left to get something. She managed to take Afsaneh to a nearby clinic. Fortunately the cut was not life threatening. I had found out about all this later when they were already home celebrating that nothing serious had happened to Afsaneh.

Thank you GOD, for saving Afsaneh from a possible death. Another time we were all

out. All the kids were in Pari's house with the housekeeper. When we got back, they told us that Kasra got hold of a jar of Naft (Gasoline) and drank it by mistake. He didn't look that bad. But when we took him to the hospital they had to keep him overnight in isolation. He was at the hospital for a few days.

My Dear GOD:

Okay, GOD, Pari had a living made, which lived in the finished private basement of their house with her family. They were in the house all the time. Gasoline was in a jar at the entrance to the yard. Kasra had gotten thirsty, and without asking anyone he picked up the jar and drank out of it. I think this was the second blessing that you had sent our way. It could have been much worse. Thank you, and thank you again.

There was another strange accident that took place in Pari's house. It is well worthwhile listening to. That night everyone gathered at Pari's for dinner. Some of Pari's cousins, who were older than Arman and Kayvan were also there. Kayvan had always been into wrestling. It was before dinnertime, and all the kids were playing upstairs. All of a sudden we heard a loud boom above our heads. Then there was silence. And afterwards we had to take Pari's cousin to the hospital with a broken arm. While Kayvan and his cousin were playing, his cousin fell on his arm and broke it. He had to remain in a cast for a long time. We were thanking GOD for letting it be a minor accident. Meanwhile we carried on with our normal every day activities.

There were so many other incidents that happened within those two-months, which made our trip to Iran the most memorable visit for every one of us. We will never forget those days.

Parveen was practicing midwifery in Ghazveen, a small city near Tehran. Certain parts of the road from Ghazveen to Tehran were still unpaved. My entire family and her own sisters with their families were invited to her house. There was about fifty of us in her house. It is an Iranian tradition to have the whole family for lunch or dinner. We all drove from Tehran, following each other's cars, to Ghazveen. It was Friday, a very pleasant, sunny day. We liked each other, and everyone was pleased to be there. Parveen was serving Chello Kabab catered by a well-known restaurant atop a large Sofreh (table cloth). We were having so much fun; no one wanted to leave. It is hard to describe everyone's emotions that day; all I can say is that it was a heavenly day.

Iraj was trying so hard to show his love for me in front of his sisters on that trip. He did love me the same while in States, but it's just that he loved me respectfully all together. He loved me unconditionally, and in reality he made me forget what had happened in past. I loved him even more than when we had first met. He made me happy by all means. He always voluntarily bought me very expensive gifts. He never forgot my birthdays. He gave me funny and cute cards. He was so good to me that the thought of loosing him would make me crazy. He showed me so much love in the presence of his sisters that I was afraid

of their potential reaction. Iraj's affectionate behavior had made me worry that they might start thinking of me as a "sister-in-law". I truly loved his sisters, and I had a lot of respect for them. I spent that whole first year of my marriage with them. I have always considered them my true family.

My Dear GOD:

I thought his sisters had so much understanding in recognizing their brother's behavior. One night we were in Neya's house when they were in Michigan. Iraj and three others were playing Blot, a French card game. I was sitting next to him watching the game. I liked Blot a lot. Neya called me and asked me to leave Iraj alone. At that instance he pulled my chair closer to him, and said, "To those who can not see us close, I wish blindness" (ta koor shavad har-ankeh nat -vanad deed.) One can sense the meanness of the saying when said in Farsi. No one said a word. Neya did not say anything either. I felt so bad that right away I got up and went in the kitchen to help her.

Not only were we good together when we were among others, but we also were very good in our bedroom. He was very considerate and affectionate with me in private and in front of others. He showed me great appreciation when I did things to make him happy. And with this kind behavior, he had made me believe in his love for me. And if anyone had told me then that Iraj was having an affair, I would have never believed them. After witnessing the incident at Maygoon, I trusted in his love in such way that I sincerely believed that all other men in the world, but Iraj, might have the affairs. He could not have been such a great actor. I thought that this time he was sincere about his love for his family. I couldn't see any reason for him to play a trick on us. No one was in our bedroom to witness our love for each other. If his love for me was not sincere, it would have been so obvious behind the closed doors. He was thankful to me for being a good sex partner. I was happy to see him feeling great.

Ok, my dear, dear GOD. Was it smart of me to have doubted him after all that care and attention? Do you think it was right to still hold grudges against him because of what had happened in Iran? No, I didn't think it was right. That is why I answered his love with my love. Anyway, that trip to Iran was the most memorable one. Iraj had earned everyone's respect. This time we left the country with the memory of love, admiration, and understanding. At that time Iraj found himself to be the luckiest, and the happiest man on earth. Most of all, he had earned my father's trust and respect.

My Dear GOD:

That trip gave my children an idea of how we were and how we lived in Iran. Every one of my sisters and brothers gave a big party for us at the best and the most exotic places in Iran. Even some of our friends went through so much trouble to arrange big parties for us.

As I talked about our wedding before, we had no wedding at all. On this trip Pari, who had also owed her friends and family a get together, arranged a big party at the garden of a restaurant, combining it with our goodbye party. That was one celebration; it could have been a wedding.

My children were amused and mesmerize by all the happenings in Iran. I was worried about taking them away from all that attention. After two months of all the excitement of living among relatives and friends, I had to take them back to those empty rooms, and make them get used to the ordinary routine every day life. But my concerns were not limited to how difficult it would be for my children to adapt themselves to that boring and lifeless existence. It was very difficult for me to part from my family for an indefinite period.

It is obvious that circumstances play a big role in all aspects of our lives. What could I have done, or anyone else could have done to change anything? It was meant to be that way.

The only and the last time I saw my father's tears was at the airport, saying goodbye to me forever. I was afraid of saying goodbye at the time. I just said, "So 1ong. I will see you soon".

My dear GOD, don't you think that everyone's future is a big mystery? We have seen time after time that the ones who try the hardest to become rich would never get there. And in contrary to those who have never expected to get wealthy, the circumstances would bring them a lot of money. Time and time again it has so happened that a person got famous overnight, while many others did right and tried their best, but they never got it. Many famous and wealthy people are even surprised by oncoming fame and fortune. Yes, my dear GOD, our future is a big mystery, and no one can be certain of the outcome.

Once again we turned around, got on a plane, said goodbye to all our people and we flew back toward our destiny. Iraj's left a day before we did. We flew with British Airways. We had seven hours transit in London Heathrow airport. Mary and Maseeh were feeling miserable on the plane. Mary was hiding herself under her seat, and she did not eat, drink, or talk to anyone. Mary never wanted to show weakness in public. After her father's affair in Iran, I rarely saw her tears. Not only was she leaving all those cousins behind, but also she was being separated from her first love, ARMAN. I was aware of all those things, but she did not want to share her feelings with anyone. After all, that was her puppy love, and it was very important to her. She was departing from her love, and she wasn't sure that what was going to happen next.

My Dear GOD:

I wasn't feeling any better myself. I wasn't crying, I was just weeping. I felt lifeless without my family being near me. I started my days with them in my thoughts, and I went to sleep with them in my thoughts. I have always questioned myself, "What a powerful and

strong love I have had for Iraj that I was able to leave them all behind!"

Mary locked herself in her room for a week. No one was allowed to go in, or talk to her. I know that she was crying in privacy. Maseeh, on the other hand, did not loose special love, so he was able to go through the adjustment a little better than Mary. I was afraid that he would keep that pain inside and become depressed. While he was only three when that incident happened in Iran, he could understand everything. I never forget the look of his face, the look that told me everything. He never said a word, but I had felt his pain with the look in his big brown eyes. There were many questions in his eyes, but that particular look that had made me wish that the whole world disappeared, and let my baby free of those painful feelings. Then I held him in my arms and hugged him so tight, and I kissed those eyes. That was the best medicine to cure him.

Looking at my children would make me forget my own feelings. The old-fashioned mothers in Iran believed that when a woman becomes a mother she should learn to give up all her rights for the benefit of her children. In practice the husbands in front of their children beat the mothers. But even then they would go on pretending that nothing had happened, and they would provide their children with love and security. And to everyone's surprise those children would make beautiful individuals thanks to their mothers' absolute love.

So when I looked at Maseeh's beautiful eyes, I would forget my own sadness. I would try to cheer him up.

Years ago, after establishing the Muslim religion in Iran, they set-up a rule that girls were physically and mentally ready to get married at the age of nine. This rule was also followed in India. It was customary to take the bride to her in-laws house after the wedding. She was lucky if they were nice and had understanding. Some were able to move out after the husband acquired a job and income. Family was everything and anything to them. This way the girl matured and learned many things from her in-laws. While she was growing up, she was sexually satisfied and there was no need to look for sex elsewhere. She had many children, and she was the lady of the house at very early age. If everything worked out, the husband was a nice and faithful person, and everyone got along with each other, there was no better life than that. But the ratio was a million to one. And what about those for whom it didn't work?

My Dear GOD:

At that time I was not just against this philosophy, but I strongly felt that it was killing girls at the age of nine, especially the way it was executed. They would send a girl in a room with a boy or a man, it didn't matter what age, and they would lock the door on them. That poor girl has never even met the guy before. And just like a hungry Lion in one room with his prey, one can only imagine what would happen.

To everyone's surprise many of these marriages lasted forever, and they raised many

beautiful children, and learned to love one another for the rest of their lives.

I had a relative that was married this way. He was an Ayatollah and had four children. They both lived a long life. Right after the husband died, and before they even got a chance to bury him, his wife died also. Her children believed that their mother was so connected to their father emotionally that she wanted to die with him. And when she died they buried her next to her husband at the same time.

This kind of marriage was accepted neither by me nor by my sisters. When my sister Ezzat was in high school, there were families that started expressing interest in coming for KHASTEGARY (to visit with a purpose to see if a family likes a girl to marry their son). We would always help her hide; we wouldn't allow them to see her. Obviously we got in to deep trouble with my father, but my mother was the one who believed that we have to continue our education. We didn't want to be fruits in a basket, and then one day someone could come and pick the best.

But after living in the U.S.A. for a long time, and having witnessed the things that were happening to the society and the families of America, and seeing that girls were becoming pregnant at such a young age, I had realized that the Islamic law must have had something to say to the whole world. A girl could have sex under protective law, and therefore be able to satisfy her desire for motherhood, which is the most desirable need in any woman's life. She would become the lady of the house; she would not have the time to be looking elsewhere for other kinds of satisfaction. And if a girl was lucky, she would end up continuing her education while she was at her husband's side. Although this didn't happen too often, that was still one way to stop millions of unwanted pregnancies. Meanwhile the children had both a father and a mother, and a place to call "my parent's home".

My Dear GOD:

Unfortunately or maybe fortunately women of the world wanted to become liberated to keep control of their own destiny. There isn't anything wrong with that. Personally, I am all for it. But I think they were not able to introduce that freedom in a right way. The mess they left behind was not what they had expected.

I have read, and I have heard of women who had earned both fame and fortune, and had a healthy life. But they had always lacked something very important, a warm and loving place they could call home. After they would gain success and money, they were not able to find the right person to share those with. Some of them said that they were so unhappy that they went to bars to look for the right partner. And even then they were not able to find one. Or if they did find him, it would have either not lasted, or he would have end up being the wrong person.

Obviously there is no right answer to all these questions. And there is no guarantee that the choices we make in life are right. There is no right answer. But when we analyze

all the facts around us, we can at least see which outcome has provided the best results.

We always judge by what we see and what we hear. My grandmother and my mother are the examples of girls getting married at a very young age. My grandmother got married at nine, without seeing her husband before their wedding night. Her husband was a businessman and they had a good life. When my grandfather died, my grandma was only thirty-eight. They had eight children, four boys and four girls. I think he died before I was born. She never remarried. With the means of her wealth she raised them all, and she kept them together.

My mother got married at the age fourteen, also without ever seeing her husband before. She gave birth to nine children. One died at two, and the second one died at the age seventeen and a half. She worked so hard to raise us. She did go through very difficult times in her life, but she was in love with her family and gave up many of her rights to protect her children from disasters. She missed my father after he died, and she always said, "He was my only life I could remember".

Another example of getting married early was one of my cousins. I was so furious when I heard that she got married at the age of thirteen. I thought her parents had destroyed her by giving her away at that young age. Years later when I went to Iran for a visit, she had invited me to her house. And to my surprise, she had eight children: two girls and six boys, and she was also a grandmother. All of children were well educated, well behaved, and they all had respect and love for their mother. They all were taller than their mother, and they looked more like her friends than her children. She had a great life while she was enjoying her family. It was obvious that she must have worked very hard for it. She must have gone through many difficult times. Giving birth to eight children by itself is very difficult. But she was happy with the result. While at that same time I was the one who was lonely.

My Dear GOD:

That was the time when I realized that my judgment was completely wrong forty years ago. She had the life and the family that I have always dreamt of. Her children had always obeyed their parents. The word of a parent for them was that of equal to God's. They all were for each other, and helped each other when it was needed. Parents were for children, and children were for parents. They were happy with each other's happiness. They held each other's hands at the time of need. She had sent the girls to medical school. One became a dentist, and the other one was a pharmacist. I would laugh at myself for being so judgmental forty years ago, when I compared her life to mine. And who knows, years later I might still be laughing at some of my today's judgments.

I look at the new generation in America, and I see how wrongly they are involved with many different sexual activities at a very young age whether married or not married, they do it all in the name of freedom. I realized then that there must be a solution found to

this problem. Maybe and only maybe the solution is to be getting married at an early age under the right conditions. But then what do I know? Who am I to be able to solve the problems of the world? Oh well.

Now I am back in the United States of America, and I have to get ready for all the challenges ahead of me. I said YAHOO (in our language means, calling GOD), and I had proceeded what I thought would be the best.

Mary was my most difficult child. I was wrong if I kissed her, and I was still wrong if I didn't. I was wrong if I talked to her, and I did wrong if I didn't. I had to find a way to be able to speak her language, but I had no idea how. That was the time that I joined the P.T.E. class to be able to find a solution to my problem. I had learned that fads and fashion have an immense power over our children. It didn't matter what the fashion was. We, the parents, had to keep up with it. Being a HIPPIE was the most stylish fashion at that time. It was considered fashionable to be walking around in ripped clothes and no shoes, and smoking cigarettes or dope. Oh please, GOD, help me. How do I deal with all these problems?

Mary wanted to try it all. That was the time that she tried to run away from home. She wanted to show us where she had been standing with us. The other problem was that she was my oldest child, and the rest would have followed her footsteps. GOD, please come to my rescue.

My Dear GOD:

I was sure that she was smoking cigarettes in Iran. But I was not aware of what else she had been involved with.

We were socializing with many Iranian families, whose children were almost the same age with my children. We all watched our children like watchdogs. It was not simply the issue of a generation gap, but there was also a big cultural gap. Every time we gathered in someone's house, the kids would try to avoid us; they would stay in a different room so that they could speak English. They didn't like to mingle with us, the grown-ups. I wasn't able to teach them Farsi language, even though I brought many elementary books from Iran. Once Mrs. Mohajer (Pooneh and Dineh's mother) got to listen to a telephone conversation between Mary and Raxana Panah. She found out that their subject was Marijuana. That was it.

Dr. and Mrs. Rohan Panah were the couple that came to our house at the time that Mary ran away from home. From that moment on Mary and Roxana, their daughter, had stopped interacting. We had to impose harsher restrictions on our children. We were thinking of transferring them to a private school. It was right around the time when Mary was still in ninth grade, that we had found out that Detroit Country Day became a co-ed high school. We decided to enroll her there almost immediately.

When her visitations with Iranian children became so limited, she found her own

friends. I didn't know them or their parents. Sometimes she would introduce them to us, and if she didn't, I had to go out of my way to find out what kind of kids they were. Still we could never know what was going on behind the closed doors.

I had to make an effort to learn how to approach Mary. I had to give her all the freedom, while I carefully watched her every movement. I made sure that she knew what I liked, and what I didn't. Many times I knew what was going on with some of her friends, but I would let it pass. My plan was to teach her to be able to make the right decision, while she was among wrong people. Knowing myself, and remembering my own childhood, I had always rebelled against forceful law. So I never intended force her into or out of anything. So as she was growing up, I had to teach myself how to handle her, and how to watch her carefully. I did become the bad guy, who was watching Mary not with just one or two eyes, but with probably ten eyes, I was watching her not forcefully, but carefully. While Iraj and I agreed on the disciplinary rules, still in her eyes I was the disciplinary, the restrictor, and the controller.

My Dear GOD:

Thanks GOD; those days Iraj and I spoke the same language when it came to disciplining our children. He never was against my actions, and I wouldn't question his. We actually followed up each other's rules. But because of his schedule, I could never expect on him to be around. He was either at the hospital, or in his office, or he was delivering babies. So I had to borrow his eyes as well in order to have control over my children. He belonged more to people and his job, than to his own family. I had to realize my duties and responsibilities towards the well being of my children.

But, of course, my children had never recognized my duties, they, especially Mary, did not appreciate my restricted supervision over them. She showed her resentment towards me by just hating me all the time. But I wasn't there for her to love me. I believed that I was there to raise her right, so that she would love herself later.

As I had mentioned before, since we didn't have anybody in this country, and because of my shyness, Mary was so attached to me that I couldn't stay away from her for even a second. Mary was four when we went to Iran. I had signed her up for ballet classes. She was so attached to me that she did not want to let go of my skirt. Her teacher, who was an Armenian, got seriously mad at me one day for raising my child in a way that she wasn't able to stay away from me for even half an hour. She said with her Armenian accent, "You thought you are the only mother on the face of the earth who had a child? You must raise your child in a way that she enjoys playing with children of her age". I just became embarrassed. I couldn't explain my life conditions to her. So I let it be.

After that incident in Iran, her father having an affair, she had witnessed her Goddess of love being broken, crushed, shattered, and destroyed in front of her eyes. She had witnessed the possibility of loosing love eternally at the age of five. At the age of ten

she practically started to kill and destroy any and every kind of love around her so that she never had to deal with loosing it all over again. Because of the fear of loosing her loved ones, she chose to pretend that they were gone already. She didn’t want to either love, or to be loved.

I knew what she was going through, she was trying to resist to ever love or be loved. But I wasn't able to do anything for her. She kept things piled up inside her, and she would never allow anyone to get close to her feelings. She just had closed all the doors on herself and on others.

My dear GOD, you know how much I loved and cared for her. You remember how I was suffering for not being able to help her. With you in my mind at all times, I kept doing and running to find a closer way to the best result. I loved her so much that one day she told me, "You are suffocating us with your love". She had become a self-destructive person. She would do anything to hurt herself just to be able to see me suffer. She loved her brother and her sister so much that I was not able to punish them if it was ever needed. She would always defend them, no matter what.

My Dear GOD:

When Mojgan was five years old, we decided to have a reunion in England with my sisters. We wanted to meet in England, because my niece Afsaneh and my nephew Nader were living there. And the other reason was that it was closer to Iran and it was possible for my sisters to come there.

I took Mojgan with me. And my sister Sina had her two sons Ali and Ehsan with her. Together we had rented a flat in London, and we tried to have the most possible fun. Mojgan didn't know how to speak Farsi. Afsaneh was trying to teach Mojgan some nursery rhymes in Farsi. Once she recorded her singing. She sang it so beautifully, that we laughed so hard listening to it. Unlike Mary and Maseeh, Mojgan did not like Iranian food. Once, when she was a baby, she got sick from eating some Iranian food. That incident had some psychological effect on her, so since then she never wanted to even try Iranian food. She was afraid to get sick and throw up. She used to love steak, hamburgers, especially from McDonald’s, and pizza. While in London, every time we wanted to go out to dinner we had to go out of our way to find the nearest McDonald’s, because of Mojgan.

That was yet another subject of our jokes. My sister in-law Afsar and her daughter Negeen had joined us after a week. We all spent the rest of the time in London together. We all went shopping once. Although we were hanging on to our purses, all of a sudden Sina had realized that her purse was stolen from her shoulder. She was rubbed out of all her spending allowance. That made us all very sad. Another time we all went to a restaurant for dinner. We sat around a big table. No one spoke fluent English. In the meantime our waiter realized that he could pretend that he had made a mistake on our bill. I had already calculated the amount, which we must pay, so I was shocked when I received the bill. He had added many extra items to our bill. He was shocked in turn when he was questioned about the bill. He probably didn't think that we knew how to count. So they corrected the bill, and apologized for the mistake.

That was a memorable trip since we all had such a wonderful time. Being away from them for all those years made me appreciate every second of our togetherness.

Iraj was trying very hard to make up for those three awful and terrifying years. I had accepted all his love and kindness, and I never tried to look back. He had spent so much money on whenever he pleased. All together he wanted to prove to me that he was the man that I wished to marry.

My Dear GOD:

On the other hand there were times that he made me wish I had never met him. I always wished to be very conservative in my spending. Once I had fifty guests for dinner. I always did everything by myself in order to save money, and besides I liked to do creative cooking. One of our guests hit our mailbox when leaving. After being without a mailbox for a whole week, I went to the lumber store and ordered a nice mailbox to be installed in front of our house.

Iraj happened to be home on the day of installation. He started questioning me in the presence of the installer. I felt like a servant, who had disobeyed her master. I was ready to kill him. Oh well.

Another time I bought a beautiful suit for Mary from Saks Fifth Avenue. I wanted to introduce a proper way of clothing to her. Although Country Day School was a private school for advanced children, all the rich parents made their children dressed up like models. I wanted Mary to look decent among her peers.

But When Iraj find out that we bought the suit from Saks, once again like a master questioning his servant, he made a big deal out of my spending for Mary. I knew that if Mary started to look good, it would have had an effect on her attitude about herself and would have boosted her self-confidence. On one hand he spent many unnecessary dollars just to hear the "Wow" from people. On the other hand he would embarrass me for spending little money for a very important matter. Many times I stopped the dispute to end a quarrel. Especially I didn't like to be humiliated in front of my children. After all I was an equal partner, and I was not wasting money.

Ok my dear, dear GOD. You tell me, what kind of a person was he? Why did he have to act the way he did? The amount of work that I was putting in that house was worth much more than half of the share. I was a mother, a wife, a driver, a cook, a tailor, a housekeeper, and above all I was an entertainer of all the times, nights or days. It didn't matter. If he wanted to pay for each one of those duties separately, it would have added up to half of his salary. And if he wanted to prove to me that he loved me, he had to have respect for my actions and me. Spending money on jewelry or mink coat was not my desire.

Such incidents made me wonder why I shouldn't have had my own earnings, so that I could spend them whenever I wanted on whatever I wanted. But then again when I looked back I realized that even then we might have had other kinds of disagreements. I remember one evening before we returned to U.S.A. my sisters Ezzat and Sina and I went shopping. I remember we had to go to the pharmacy to purchase medication for my children. We saw a young poor man there, who was crying. He had a prescription in his hand for his baby; he was asking people for help. Sina volunteered to pay for his medicine. We offered to join together, but Sina did it anyway. We were very happy that we could help him. When we got home, they were finished eating. My father was sitting around the table with all the other family members. We were so sorry for the guy at the pharmacy that we kept discussing the incident among ourselves. Shirazi got very angry when he found out that Sina had paid for the poor guy's medication. He asked with a very negative attitude, acting as if somebody had stolen his money, " Why did you do that?" I didn't want to interfere, or cause a fight between them. But I got so mad that I wanted to attack him. I wanted to tell him, "It is none of your business. She didn't do it with your money. She is a teacher, and she has her own money. It is up to her how or when she wants to spend it. You do not, and I mean do not ever allow yourself to mind my sister this way". I wanted to scream and throw something at him. But I forced myself to keep my cool and stay calm. I just said that it was her money and she was very happy to help that poor guy.

My Dear GOD:

My sister Sina didn't said anything either. So you see my dear GOD, even if I had my own earnings, Iraj might still have done the same thing that Hosain did. Men always have something against women's independence. They always believe that they must be the masters of their wives.

While we were putting our lives together, and manage to deal with the changes around us, our sisters were putting their lives together as well.

During the years we were apart Pari and Kamal had built a house. She was teaching, and he was a successful architect. He worked for a firm along with three other well-known architects. They were doing fine and had good earnings, so they were able to come and visit us in US. I was very happy to have them around. Pari was not just a best friend and a sister in-law, she was funny, talented, kind and very generous. They were my second family; they became closer than my first family during those years. She did so much for me that I had always considered her my only and best friend. The kindness, the support and the friendship that they had provided throughout all those years weren't something to deny. I really and truly loved them. Every time I heard that they were going to visit us I would celebrate, I felt life within me. When they were with us, Pari and I had the most fun together. We cooked together, sewed together, went shopping together, and at the end

of the night when everyone was sleeping, we would seat in the kitchen and play Backgammon. We had a lot in common.

My Dear GOD:

While we were in Iran, I had heard that they were planning to send their children to United States to finish their education. I was so excited. I knew that was the beginning of a hopeful life for me. I had never had anybody in this country. But if and when they moved to US, I would have had a family and a best friend beside me for change. Kaveh, one of their sons, was already attending an American school in Iran. He was studying in English. Kayvan, the oldest, was enrolled in Iranian school. And Kasra was not at school yet. So they did not have any problems.

The political situation during that period was unpredictable. Shah had serious troubles in the relationship with United States. People of Iran were not comfortable. Most people were aware that United States would soon have instigated a revolution in Iran. Many people, rich or poor, fled Iran long before the revolution started. Please, my dear God, guide my children to educate themselves about the reasons of U.S.A.'s involvement with the revolution in Iran. I am aware of the fact that they would rather turn to more reputable source of information than their mother. Please, GOD, make it possible for them. Thank you.

So Pari and Kamal, like everyone else in Iran, were thinking of escaping as soon as possible. We had already applied for their Green Cards. Once we had heard that they were coming to stay with us in the summertime. We were very excited to have them around. We were impatiently awaiting the news of their arrival. I was thinking that my days in exile would be over with their arrival. We were all very anxious to have our family with us after these many years.

When I had asked Iraj about the anticipated time of their arrival, he answered, "Parveen had told me that they will inform you as soon as their tickets and passports are ready. Telephone calls to Iran were very expensive those days. Or maybe it was stingy Iraj who had made me believe so. So we would only make phone call in case of emergency).

We were waiting for their telephone call in eager anticipation. Our doorbell rang one night after we had all gone to bed. In America it happens to be alarming when someone appears unannounced at your door in the middle of the night. We rushed downstairs to find the whole group at our door. They had surprised us immensely. I was planning to cook for them, and fill the house with flowers and beautiful music, but instead I found myself just sitting at the foot of the stairs tremendously shocked. I forgot even to say hello.

We would always pick them up from the Metropolitan Airport. Just the drive form the airport in itself had always been a great pleasure. I was asking repeatedly, "What is this? Why did you come without any news? You never did that". They were very tired and did not want to deal with our questions. It almost seemed like they must have sent us a

letter with all the information, which we had never received. And when they got to the airport, they tried to call us, but our phone must have been accidentally off. So they had ended up taking a taxi to our house, and there they were. I had no food to offer, but we arranged a sleeping area for them.

My Dear GOD:

We were expecting Kamal, Pari and their three sons, Kayvan, Kaveh, and Kasra. But to our surprise Neya and her three children Arman, Nazi and Baharak also came along. Mary and Arman, more than anyone, were very excited to see each other.

For the first time in the United States I felt the pleasure of having my family with me.

Next day, while Pari and I were in the kitchen, she told me, "I wasn't aware that Neya is also coming with us. Until just recently she announced to me that she would like to bring her children to United States for continuation of their education". It seemed like she wasn't very happy with Neya's decision. At that time I didn't know why. But later on it became obvious to me why Pari was displeased with Neya's decision.

It seemed to me as if neither Pari nor Neya believed us telling them we had no correspondence from them informing us about their arrival. These doubts would hurt my feelings tremendously. I don't know what they were thinking. They did mention to me what they really thought of that night later on. In these accusations, their brother Iraj was witness that I was truthful. Actually it was Pari's idea to catch the taxi to surprise us. Anyway we started off that summer very good. And during that time we started to research into schools for their children.

There were two good private schools in our area. One of them was Detroit Country Day School, which my children were attending. And the second one was Cranbrook, a boarding school. The all-girls section was called Kingswood. After several summers they had spent with us, they decided to enroll the boys, Arman and Kayvan, to Cranbrook, and Nazi to Kingswood. I had heard that Arman had very poor grades. But with the assistance of some teachers, and some of their family friends, they provided him with a decent report card so that he would get accepted to Cranbrook.

The arrangement was that we would be carrying the role of their absent parents. They remained at school for five days of the week, and they stayed with us over the weekends. Ironically their major holiday breaks didn't fall on the same days with my children's breaks. So I had to be at home and available for all of them four times a year instead of only twice. We couldn't arrange any vacations during those years. And it was only summertime that their parents would come to visit and supervise their children.

My Dear GOD:

I was watching Iraj's nephews and nieces carefully like my own children while they were with us. I did not want to have any hanky-panky around my house.

Kayvan was raised under his grandmother's supervision, a very faithful Moslem woman. Pari had always been into fashion, and she would spend most of her time shopping in Europe, mainly in Paris. So when the children were still back in Iran, their grandmother and their live-in maid were the ones taking care of them in their mother's absence. Neya was the second important supervisor in their lives. Not only when Pari was out of the country but even when she was there. She took care of Pari's children just like her own regardless of Pari's traveling plans.

You know, my dear GOD, during the Shah's regime people were trying to become free and "Americanized", especially ladies. They were acting irresponsible, trying to forget their priorities, obligations and duties toward their families. They were arranging all sorts of parties trying to imitate the Hollywood movie stars. You would see women drinking, smoking, and in many cases the ones who wanted to outshine the others would even smoke pot. This was destroying the culture and morality of Iranian families. Many women would sell their household furniture and use the money to go to Europe, and join the first class society. It was embarrassing to think of Iranian women becoming all movie star-like and forgetting about their priorities in life.

My Dear GOD:

Ok, my dear GOD, not only it was hard to take care and watch over five different teenagers, but listening to Kayvan's stories every weekend was a very scary thing. My problem was that I wouldn't even believe him at that time. I believed that he was purposely exaggerating the stories because of his interest in Mary.

Every weekend when he would come home, seat on a chair in the kitchen at the countertop where I was preparing dinner, and he would talk to me about Arman's activities at school.

One night when he told me, "Arman is dealing drugs at school", I couldn't bear it any more. I asked him, "Why don't you personally go to your uncle and tell him everything? I am afraid if I step in and say something, he might think that I am trying to instigate a conflict. While if you tell him, he might take it serious and do something about it". But I don't know why he was afraid to talk to Iraj. On the other hand, I was very careful not to allow anything to ruin our friendship. What if he wouldn't believe me, and what if he thought that I was trying to get rid of those children? I asked Kayvan to talk to Iraj as a witness, "Then he will believe you and will talk to Arman before it is too late. I was very concerned about Arman and specially Mary. She was the one who had idealized Arman. It didn't matter what I said or did, she wanted to be accepted and loved by Arman.

Please, my dear GOD, come to my rescue. I need you more than anything at this moment. I cannot survive by myself. Please help me, PLEASE. I'd rather my children had safe sex than used drugs or alcohol, or even smoked cigarettes. Sex is a natural element of

our life. If it is done lovingly and safely, it does not cause a health hazard. Marriage is a man-made, fabricated law to protect the identity of a newborn. Those, who have safe sex will never get sick or die of it. While anyone, who drinks regularly, or uses drugs will become addicted in no time, and soon they will get sick and 1oose the health of all the related organs and the result will obviously be death. So in my children's case I preferred safe sex to the use of drugs. Not that I ever wanted them to get involved with sex at the wrong age. I just preferred sex if they ever wanted to do it. That wouldn't damage brain, and even too much of it, if it was done wisely, would never cause an overdose. It's the pressure of the society, which makes the sex look ugly on one hand, and on the other hand, tries to sell it in every aspect of life. What can I say, my dear GOD? You know more than I do, what's being done in this world by the creatures that you had created. I really wouldn't know.

So you see my dear GOD, I was caught in the middle of a forced situation, and I wasn't able to get out. At first I was afraid for Arman and thought that Mary would get involved with drugs outside of the house. Now the drugs had made their way into my house, right into Mary's hands. What could I do? What should I have said? Besides you, besides talking to you, and besides asking you for help, I knew no other way of handling the situation I was in. Knowing Mary, how motivated she was to experiment everything, specially if it comes from Arman.

My Dear GOD:

When I asked Kayvan to talk to his uncle before it was too late, he answered, "My mother had warned me not to interfere with Arman's personal life".

Then one day Kayvan told me something that I was completely unaware of. He said that Arman had escaped from his bedroom window and came back in the morning.

I talked to Iraj and asked Kayvan to talk to him as well, so that he didn't think that I was trying to wrongfully accuse his nephew. I did not allow them to go out of the house on the weekend that followed. I asked Arman and Nazi to stay in their rooms and try to get some work done. After an hour or so I heard strange noises. It sounded like heavy foot traffic. I went upstairs to find out if they were all right. I found them weeping, they were throwing things around the room.

They were desperately looking for a way to get out of their room, and somehow out of the house. They knew that I was not easy to be fooled. That was when I realized that their urge for drugs was so strong that they were crying like babies. I was embarrassed to be straightforward and talk to them about their involvement with drugs. But I still tried to talk to them. I said, "Your parents are not here. I have a responsibility to make sure that you follow the right path. You are here to study and do what your parents are expecting from you. They are spending a fortune on you to make sure you become somebody very valuable for yourselves. It is my duty to know where you are going, and what you are

doing". Ok, my dear, dear GOD. You were a witness in the house that day, and you saw them. One would have thought that I had abused these two; they were trying to run away.

With all the information from Kayvan, and my own observation, I was tangled within a "What to do, what to do ..." situation. Consequently my life had turned-out to a big disaster. After all I was only the uncle's wife. When my own children allowed themselves to tell me, "It is my life, and it is none of your business". What was I expecting from my husband's nephews and nieces? It was apparent that they did not want me to be running their business for them.

But that was what they had believed. I believed that my children's lives were in danger, along with the lives of Iraj's nephews and nieces. I felt it was my duty to step in whether they liked it or not. My children and their cousins were the ones being destroyed. It was my house that was being contaminated with wrong ideas and behavior. And after all it was my life that was being destroyed by circumstances.

My Dear GOD:

I was beginning to realize why Neya was so determined to take her children out of Iran. Too bad she didn't realize that she had saved them from drowning in a pool, and instead they might end up drowning in a big sea, and she would not be able to rescue them. I was feeling very sorry for her. I knew for sure that she must have been so desperate that she thought the change of environment would be the best answer. Although she was right in that matter, she should have considered a better environment, and not the filthiest of all. I don't think she was aware of many factors. She was planning to just keep him away from the wrong friends in Iran..

She thought that all the problems would vanish once he moved away. She did not recognize that the problems would escalate with his parents' absence. They were not aware that they were destroying their children unintentionally.

I tried to stay strong; I tried to keep up with my motherly duties as best as I could. After I have had a long discussion with Iraj about all this, I offered him my opinion regarding saving Arman from the disaster. I said, "Before it is too late, we have to inform Neya of the situation here with Arman. We should ask his parents to take him back to Iran". He never said anything. As always he continued reading his newspaper without agreeing or disagreeing. It was the same as speaking to a wall. I think he was confused himself and didn't know what to do. The idea of his niece and nephew coming in the United States was imposed on him. We have had many difficulties with our own children to begin with. And now we had to learn to deal with their children and their responsibilities. It was not a joke. It was a very serious matter. Although we loved to have them stay with us, but the responsibility was enormous and I was determined to be able to help Arman before it was too late.

Those days many Iranian families sent their children to US to stay with their uncles

or aunts. Those who did well at school and by all means were the achievers would get accepted to the best universities, and they graduated with honors. But there were others that had made disasters for themselves and their families, be that here or across the boarder.

My Dear GOD:

One very sad and a heart breaking accident happened with one of doctors in Bloomfield Hills, Michigan. It was very disturbing for all of us, Iranians. Dr. Minooie's nephew, who was a very bright and advanced student both in Iran and United States, had moved here attend a university. For the first few months before the school started, he was taking an advanced English course to improve his English. Their house was located on a lake in a wooded area. It was snowing and he was embarrassed to call Barbara, his aunt, to drive him to school, like she did every other day. He had thought to himself, "Since I have learned the way, it is better that I walk to the street (which was a very long distance) and not bother Barbara that morning".

He was gone for two days. No one found a trace of him. There were small bridges from their house to the road. On the third day they found his body hidden under the dirt by one of the bridges near the house. It must have been a car that hit him in the dark. Or, who knows, he might have slipped on the ice, and never got out of it. You can imagine what had happened to his parents. And most of all what the entire family must have gone through after that accident.

Barbara spoke to me on many occasions. She couldn't get over the feeling of guilt. She would say, "I didn't mind driving him to his classes. He was just a pleasure to be with. Why wouldn't he wake me up that morning? As if this was his destiny".

I had noticed after my conversation with Iraj that he talked to Arman time to time to make him realize that we knew what was going on. Meanwhile he made sure that he knew that we didn't appreciate his way of handling his life in general. I tried not to interfere with their communication. It was enough for me that he was aware that I was watching him like a hulk.

I have always had a very friendly and close relationship with them. I have always had fun playing cards or backgammon with them. I would cook their favorite food, I took them shopping if they needed anything. We talked about past and present and about everybody we knew in Iran. But he would never open up to me to talk about his personal problems. And I never wanted to make him uncomfortable. Arman was very nice young man by nature. I really wanted to find a way to keep him away from drugs and wrong people. But I didn't know how. Many times I wished that I could keep them inside the house like prisoners, and prevent their interactions with the rest of the world to save them from obvious destruction. But that was only a dream.

My Dear GOD:

Time and again I thought that it is not our children who are guilty of getting involved with drugs. For when we take a closer look, we will see that it is the high rank individuals like senators, politicians, police officers, and FBI who are behind all this, harvesting a greater market for drugs.

I remember when I had first started to worry about Mary, I immediately took a course to learn more in-depth about teenagers, and I read as many books on the subject as I could.

Once I heard that Mr. Art Linkletter had written a book about his daughter's overdose. Anxiously I went to the library and got the book. His daughter was an achiever and a very responsible girl. She tried joining the movie industry after graduating from school. At the time she was working for governmental offices. One of them, which she was very devoted to, was an organization for the rehabilitation of the drug addicts.

I don't recall the course of the story but she ended using drugs herself. The night that she killed herself, she had called her brother from the hundred and some-story high-rise building in New York City. She told him that she had to fly away somewhere. Her brother tried to stop her, and asked her not to do anything until he gets there. When he got there, he found her on the pavement, hopelessly dead.

In his book Mr. Art Linkletter said, "I wanted to find out how my beautiful daughter became the kind of person to do what she did? I found out about the person who made the drugs available to my daughter. Then I researched it more to find out who was responsible to deal the drug to him. Then I went farther to find out who was that person's connection. So I did all my research until I got to high rank police officers and FBI. I soon realized that I had to drop my research, or it was going to be the end of my story and me. They visibly and vividly made sure that I dropped the subject right there".

Obviously drugs are there for some users like our children. Guns are there for people to kill each other. Cigarettes are there to be sold to young and old, it doesn't matter what they will do to them.

The law says that a capitalist has to make money. If you don't buy it, they will find a buyer elsewhere. The companies that manufacture guns and ammunitions do not intend to sell those to a bride and a groom for their wedding celebration. They make them to be sold to people for the purpose of "just killing each other". And if and when they do not have enough market in this country, they have to find other countries to sell them to. And to make sure that those guns were used they have to find another country to fight with the first country, which they sold their guns to. If this is not a fact, please, my dear GOD, tell me what other purpose is behind making them? And funnier than this is that after those countries had fought and killed each other, they will go and offer them a helping hand in rebuilding their racked country. Don't you find this funny, my dear GOD? Oh well.

My Dear GOD:

Yes, my dear GOD, we have to follow all these man-made laws and we are not supposed to question anything. Then we simply put the blame on our children, and try so hard to make a better person of them.

So like Mr. Linkletter said, "We should never question the authorities, especially the higher rank ones if you want to be on the safe side".

Let's imagine that we found out who sold the drug to mine and your child. And let's say that we found the dealer above him. But if I can't find out who are the dealers above that dealer, what good will it do? Unless we push and pull our children to help them reason, until then whatever comes in the market, we must be careful how to get involved.

The saddest part was that all those advertising campaigns made sure to glamorize the drug use; they made a point of making it look like a high fashion activity among teenagers. They had gone so far those days that they started using drugs as the age eight or nine. And they would even use guns. What a shame! What a pity!

As I had mentioned before I had eight siblings. Most of us had either two or three children each. None of us has ever been involved with drugs, alcohol, or even cigarettes for as long as I remember. It was not that we were raised in an isolated environment.

We actually had a few uncles who would openly smoke opium in front of the whole family. It was considered a fashion in Iran, while we all knew that it was actually a poisonous killer. They would also drink. They never intimated us, but we had witnessed the ugliness and the danger of their actions. The same goes for my children, nieces and nephews. Thanks God, none of them has ever been involved with any of these. Even the ones who had to get out of the country at the age of fourteen had never thought of these kinds of activities. We all tried to raise our children in the most fruitful way.

My older brother Jamal has two girls, Negeen and Negar. Negeen is a pharmacist practicing in Canada. Negar is also a pharmacist, and she will soon move to Canada.

My Dear GOD:

My sister Ezzat has two children, a girl and a boy. Afsaneh and Nader had both graduated from a college in London, England. They have good jobs, and they reside in London.

My younger sister Azar has two children: Reza, whom I will talk about in time, and her daughter Rokhand, who is in Iran. She has got her Masters Degree in Art and Directing. She has a very good and reputable life next to her mother Azar.

And my sister Sina has two sons, Ali and Ehsan. Ali was seventeen and Ehsan was fourteen when they had to leave the country. They both studied and graduated with honors. And they would even tutor the native Belgians in math and their own French language, so that they spent their time wisely, and made extra money.

As my father said, "All and all, parents are responsible for the well-being of their children ". Even when children are away from their parents, their words and teaching will follow them wherever they go. When my parents said something to us, they expected it to be done. No questions to be asked. Unless they were unreasonable on enforcing wrong rules, which had never happened in our case, except for my marriage, and I did do it in a very revolutionary way. And this method had established in all of us as a basic rule, “Either our children will be smart enough to distinguish right from wrong, and choose to do what is right, or they will choose not to be a part of our family”. This way we all knew that good or bad, the choice was ours, and only ours.

So you see, my dear GOD, between the Mary’s telephone conversation about drugs with her friend Raxana, and the existence of the drug users, Arman and Nazi living in our house, you can imagine the kind of life I was having. The American- style sentence, "It is my life, leave me alone", was really killing me. “No, No, No”, I said, “As long you are under my roof, and you are eating my food, and mostly I am responsible for your actions, your life belongs to me. I don't care what American society is teaching you. But as your mother I wi1l either make it, or break it. I will try my best to see what will happen at the end.

I will never forget the day when I was kneeling in front of Mary, I was crying and begging her to open her eyes, and be aware of the danger of drugs and wrong friends. I did this because I knew that with kids who have something against the establishments, force would not be effective whatsoever. I tried every possible way of effectiveness. While I knew that smoking cigarettes would cause cancer, I would still allow them to smoke if they chose to do so. I preferred that they smoked in front of me. There were times when I would even buy her cigarettes. I wanted to leave the door open for her to do things in front of us and not behind our back.

Once, years later, Mary and I were having lunch. She was in a good mood and she was being herself. She told me then, “Mom, don't worry too much about us. If I wanted to get drugs, the easiest way was the school library. It gets easily hand to hand from teachers to students, and vice versa. And it is so easy, because no one ever suspected that the library would be the point of connection. Everything you have taught us is very important, and one day it will come back to us. Then it will be up to me to either still do it or not. At least you did your work".

My Dear GOD:

I always knew that Mary was very smart and very intelligent. Aside from being very beautiful, she had a very good head on her shoulders. I would hate to see all those qualities and abilities go to waste.

That kind of response was what had given me hope to continue with my duties, that was what had kept me going.

Those days I was very happy to see Iraj, and I used the same voice for directing our children. I tried not to say anything over his words, and he never tried to talk against mine. It is very important for children to know that both their father and their mother agree on their education. It came to a point that he left me with making most decisions on my own.

Many memorable events had taken place during the summers that our families visited with us.

Kamal had to go through a surgery on one of their trips. They had to remove his kidney stones; he has had them for a while. He would always talk about many painful experiences that he had to go through. He was absolutely ready to go under the surgeon's knife.

That day Iraj washed hand with his surgeon also. He was so worried for him. It seemed that everything was on his shoulders. He felt responsible for him and his family. I remember the time that the doctor gave us the good news. He said, "Everyone can relax now. He is no longer in danger. It is time to celebrate". When I looked at Iraj, I had noticed that he had tears in his eyes. I was feeling so sorry for him that he had to deal with, those emotional moments so quietly. I cried as well at that time. I kept looking at Iraj, I was admiring how giving and caring he was. I loved him so much; I never wished to see him unhappy. He had always shown so much responsibility towards his family, his sisters, and their families. That was the time that I had placed him above all mankind.

Many years later Pari and I were once reminiscing about those days. She was saying, "You were crying for Kamal". I was too embarrassed to tell her that I wasn't crying for Kamal, I was crying for Iraj, who had always suffered innocently and would never talk about it.

My Dear GOD:

I took many pictures while he was at the hospital. I had a very good relationship with all of them, especially Kamal. I was trying so hard to see that everything went well and nothing happened to him after the surgery.

There was a funny case that still keeps me wonder. Pari was his wife, and I was only a sister in-law. When he came home from the hospital, the doctor told him, "You must be very careful and try not to pick-up heavy things. We don't want you to return to the hospital".

On the first day Pari left him alone at home to go shopping. I was the one who was worried, and I stayed home just in case something happened. And the most important part was when Pari had to go away; Kamal was the one packing for her. Not only that, but he carried her big suitcase up the stairs. I couldn't stand it any longer, and I asked Pari not to let him to carry the heavy suitcase. But Pari answered calmly, "It's okay, doctors say many things. Don't pay too much attention". Obviously when I look back to compare our

lives, I believe that it was not her, who was wrong. It was me, who cared too much and worried for no reasons. She always knew that she had to think of herself first.

Before Kamal had his surgery, Mohandess Forghani had to go through a heart by-pass surgery. Both Kamal, and Mohandess Forghani had their surgeries at Beaumont hospital where Iraj was working. Before the surgery they had to take Mr. Forghani to Cleveland Clinic for more extensive observation. Iraj used to tease him, and said to Mr. Forghani while they were at a restaurant, "This is your last supper".

He had a triple by-pass heart surgery. It was very successful. And again Iraj was the one who worried and cared the most. In all these happenings I was hundred percent behind him. I did not lack any of my duties, if I didn't do more. I felt so sorry for Iraj and all those responsibilities. I was going to support him all the way to the end.

While they were with us, we took them everywhere and we saw most places together. We went to Boblo Island on a boat. Neya had prepared some Iranian rice, which she served from the pot.

It was so funny, that I took many pictures. These three sisters were completely different from each other. Neya was very quiet, and kept everything inside. No one could ever get into her private, inner world. I remember since the times that Arman was a baby; she had put all of herself into her home and her family. She was a great mother to her own children as well as Pari's children. She was helpful to Parveen, who was going to school at that time. I remember once she had to go to Parveen's house and prepare dinner. It had to be done before Mr. Safari, Parveen's husband, would get home. They didn't want him to get mad at Parveen, or pick on her. So Neya just made the dinner and left so that Mr. Safari thought that Parveen was the one who had cooked the dinner all by herself. She also was so helpful to Pari, who was going to college while she was raising her children.

My Dear GOD:

Both Kamal's mother and Neya had helped out Pari raising her children. There were many occasions when Pari had to spend a night over at a friend's house to study for exams, while Neya and Kamal's mother took care of her children. All and all I remember how sad and unexpected her mother died, as well as how right after she got married, even before they had a chance to celebrate their wedding, her husband was imprisoned. Then he was schedule to be executed, and on and on. She had faced all the obstacles and challenges in her life, and she had always tried to keep herself from falling apart.

Although I wasn't the favorite sister in-law, she had never lost respect for me. I had treated her in the same manner, and we had a very friendly relationship. I think she was more of a mother to her children than anyone else. During one of the summers that they were visiting America, while Arman was still at school, she bought him a motorcycle. I think she wanted to plea bargain with him. She was probably hoping to entice him material possessions so that he would reconsider his behavior, and would hopefully stop

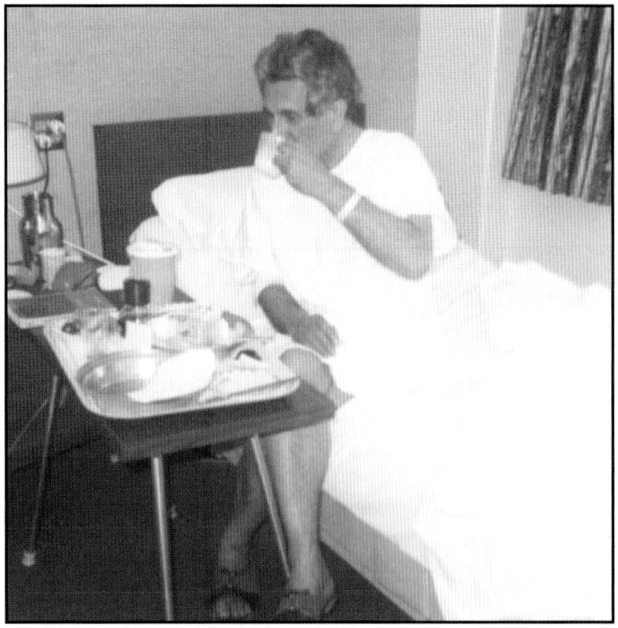

Mojgan and I are in the Madame Tussaud's
Wax Museum in London, England.

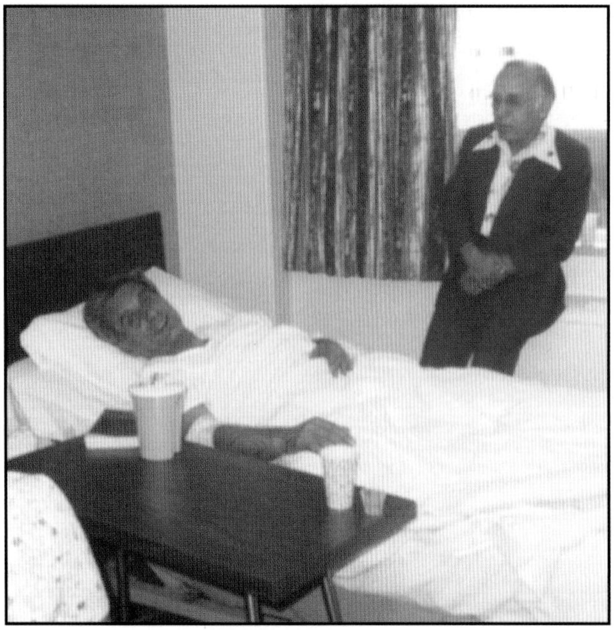

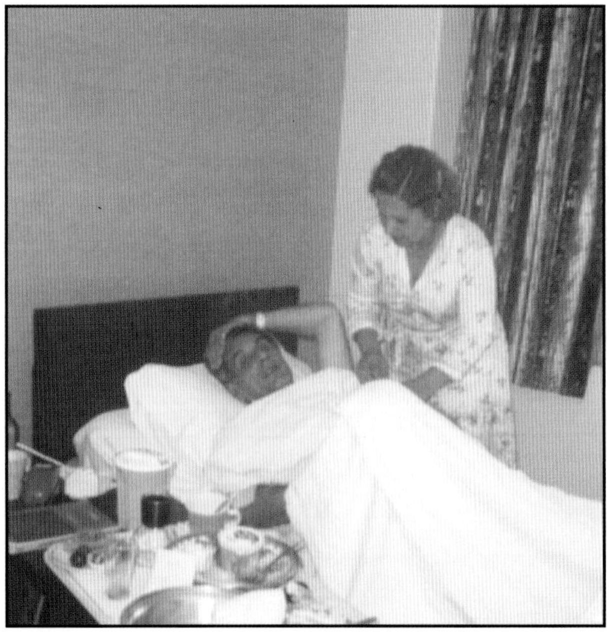

When Mr. Forghani had his heart surgery, Iraj was feeling responsible for his health. On the top right, after the surgery had been successfully done at the Beaumont Hospital, he is enjoying the food. Down on the right, Neya was visiting him. On the left, Iraj was visiting him.

This day was around our New Year, Norooz and I was visiting my family in Iran. People came to Saideh's house to welcome me home. Left to right: Zari, Saideh, Maryam- behind the flowers, Mr. Mohandess Forghani, me, and Neya. They were all there to visit me.

Here, my sister-in-law, Neya and Mr. Forghani had come to Azar's house to visit me. As you see, we are sitting under Reza's picture.

Here, I was painting Rokhand's fingernails with nail polish on the eve of her engagement party.

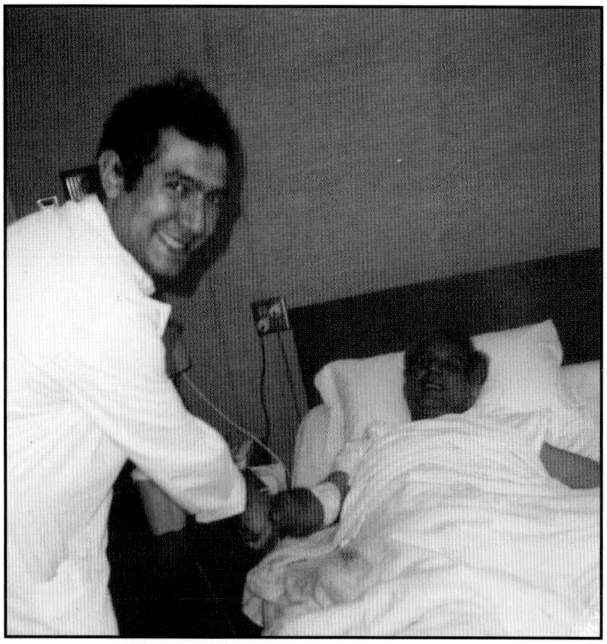

The doctor is examining Mr. Mohandes Forghani, my bother-in-law. He had a quadruple heart transplant at Beaumont Hospital in Royal Oak, Michigan.

Mojgan and I are standing next to Shah's figure at Madame Tussaud's Wax Museum in London, England.

My brother Javad who had a seminar in Paris, France, came to visit and stayed with us for one week.

Mojgan and Maseeh are standing in front of Hotel Holt in Iceland. Our plane had some mechanical problems.

What a day, what a lunch, and what a beautiful host! On that day Dr. Toosi and Shahnaz drove us to Parveen's house in Ghazveen. It was a long way, but we had fun. Around the table, left to right: Fereshteh, Parveen Rafani, Dr. Mohammad Toosi, me, and Shahnaz Toosi. I am sure Neya was taking the picture. Who in the world is so lucky to have her sister-in-law prepare such a beautiful luncheon and go through this much trouble to invite them? Don't you think I have been very lucky? Well, I think so.

We were all invited to Zahra-Neya's sister-in-law and Parveez Oryani's place. They sent us to go and take a boat ride on the ocean. We did listen to their advice, but my God it was cold, so cold that we didn't want to continue our fun. As you see, we all wrapped ourselves in our shawls in a way that my face is almost hidden. The gentleman is our leader. Left to right: Neya, me, the leader, Parveen, and Fereshteh.

I think this was a special day. As I remember, it was a celebration of some kind. We were invited to Mr. Mehdi Gangi and Haji Khanoom's place. We had lots of fun as usual. Left to right: Mr. Ghazvini- Mehdi Agha's son-in-law, Haji Khanoom, Mrs. Hormozi- Iraj's aunt, Homa Hormozi, Mr. Gangi, and Nasreen Ghazvini. Sitting around the table: happy me, Daryaneh Ghazvini, and Shahrooz, the birthday boy.

using drugs. Again, she was completely unaware that the motorcycle by itself would only contribute to his further involvement with drugs. Deep down I was feeling very sorry for her. Poor girl, she didn't know what to do, or which way to turn.

As I had previously mentioned we had a very friendly relationship. Parveen and I had a very formal kind of relationship. When it came to Neya I had a special kind of friendly respect. And for the longest time I had been convinced that Pari and I were best friends. I would typically never give this title to just anybody. I had many things in common with Pari. We had such good times when we were together; she brought laughter to everyone's life. During all those years we had never, not even once, gotten sour with each other.

This was a very funny trend. Almost every Iranian family had been receiving guests from Iran while residing in Michigan. But when the guests would have decided to prolong their visit, the hostesses would become very anxious, especially when the visitors happened to be from the husband's side. But my feelings for my in-laws were the exact opposite of what everyone expected. When my sister in-laws were visiting, I would tell everyone that I was very happy that they stayed in our house. But nobody would believe me; everyone thought I was crazy. They were not aware of the kind of relationship we had.

My Dear GOD:

But unfortunately it didn't last. On one of their trips, while they were staying in our house, there was a day when one of their children was checking the refrigerator to find a particular kind of cheese. I don't know what kind of mood I was in. I just remember that I said, "I can swear that I bought it yesterday when I went shopping". Right after I said that, I saw Pari rushing downstairs. She started accusing me of being rude and impolite in a harsh and very angry voice. While she was crying, she ran upstairs to Neya and said, "We are not going to stay in this house any more. We must pack our bags and get out of here". I tried to reason, "What did I say or do?" But no matter how much I tried to stop them, it didn't work. We have never had this kind of face-to-face argument. What was all this fuss about? Then I said a few words, and they said a few words back, and things just got out of hand.

I was blamed for not treating them well. They said that I made it sound as if I was tired of shopping, and spending money on them. I was so shocked. But knowing Pari and her hot temper, I should have known better that there would come a day when she turned on me.

In the past Pari and Iraj had spent most of their time in our house. My parents thought of them as of their own children. Whether we had little or enough to eat, we had always shared it without any doubt. And when I was in their house I felt like being in my own house. I had always felt so comfortable that I would help myself with food from their refrigerator; I would even tell them if they needed to get more groceries. We had never

considered it a big deal. Why then, all of a sudden, one simple sentence had made such an impact on them?

I used to go shopping as often as it was needed. We had always helped each other out with the chores inside or outside our homes; it had never made a difference which one of us needed. They were helpful to me, and I never hesitated to help them. Why then Pari was doing that to me, why was she making Neya and the rest get involved? So they decided to move out of our house and get a room at some nearby hotel, in Birmingham City. They were gone by the time Iraj and Kamal got back home. And they made me look like a devil. I was almost sure that Neya was not at fault. It was Pari, who, for whatever reason, had decided to explode that way. They humiliated me in front of everyone, especially our children.

Later on Kamal came to talk to me. I was not aware of what they told him, but I told Kamal, "I wish I knew why they were doing this". I went to the hotel later that evening, and tried to tell them everything that was on my mind and we apologized and made up.

My Dear GOD:

I have previously mentioned Pari's hot temper. And I have already told the stories of her quarrel with Parveen in Mehdi Agha's house, as well as her fights with Neya. It was obvious that it must have been my turn then. After all I had to have a share of her hot temper.

I had worshiped the friendship between us, and I hated to see it destroyed by Pari's wrong judgment. Well, this was yet another unexpected, unplanned, and unavoidable situation.

Although I have been quite daring throughout my whole life, I have been very conservative in many ways, especially when it came to my children's future. Since Iraj was making enough money, he started thinking of remodeling the house. The further we researched, the more we realized that it would be very costly, and besides we were not able to get the results that we were expecting. I had always prioritized the security and comfort of my family; everything else was secondary. I wanted to always travel in the moderate speed of life, and I never wanted to go overboard for the sake of being a show-off.

I remember while I was a very little girl when my mother and my aunts were trying to purchase rice and flour in large quantities so that they could make bread at home during the world war two. That memory had a serious effect on me. My parents were worried to run out of food, and not be able to feed us. So we have learned that there would be many unexpected and surprising days in our lives.

I believe that we will never be able to predict what is going to happen next. We must be ready for things as they come. I cannot recall a single day in my life that I was envious of anyone because of their material possessions. It has never occurred to me that having money would make you a better person. Deep down I believed that I was Okay. And "You are OK" is the answer to a better living. I felt that I was okay regardless of my finances or material possession. And I felt the same about others as well. I consider people who seek respect by gaining wealth are very limited. And even though this kind of individuals, people that would try to own and control the wealth of the world, make twenty percent of the world population, they will never be able to earn as much worldwide prestige and respect as Mother Teresa or Nelson Mandela, who are simple and not even wealthy. If it weren't for this greedy and money-hungry people in the world the other eighty percent would have the opportunity to live a simple and comfortable life. So it was with this belief that I wished for just a comfortable life, and nothing more. Being a show off or trying to prove that I was better than others was not my purpose of living.

But the sad part of this is that some people in reality do become wealthy and they do show it off. And there are others who go on with their existence of portrayal of the rich and famous while they are thinking of their worthlessness.

My Dear GOD:

Anyway, Iraj wanted to make changes in his house, and probably his lifestyle. We always discussed everything in a friendly manner. Many times he would ask for my advice. And there were times that he pretended that he did.

You see, my dear GOD, everything that I am writing with regards to my past, our relationship and his feelings for me, is and was my interpretation of what was going on at the time. Those days I was so certain that his love for us was real, and that his actions were pure and free of any kind of pretense. Don't you think, my dear GOD that it would have been foolish to doubt his love and care for us, while he was acting so lovingly and doing everything so right towards the children and me? I thought it was even unhealthy for me to doubt his love, and believe that beneath all that was a big lie and dishonesty. NO, I could never live like that. Everything and anything I say about his love and care appeared true to me, and, as a matter of fact, I might not be able to express facts as they really were. Don't forget, I am writing these notes at a time that when the love does not exist any more. So I could say that in reality his love was much greater than I am describing it. I am still wondering, "How could a person, who was so in love with his wife; how could someone who, according to his own words, shared the greatest intimacy with his wife, all of a sudden decide to break it all, and pretend that there was never anything there?"

We were very happy while we were living in that house. I believed that our love was genuine. Even the trouble with our teenagers could become easy when we handled it in the right way. Every evening we all gathered after dinner to watch family TV shows like "I love Lucy", and "Red Skilton", while I made them some snacks, and we laughed all night. For me, who was raised among a large family of nine, that was a meaningful life. I never wanted to exchange it for anything.

During the time that Iraj met my family, we would always gather in one room at the end of the day. Each one of us talked about our daily activities. We laughed at the funny things that happened to us, and we made fun of each other. We had the greatest time together. Every one of our family friends would become part of our family. That was how we had befriended Iraj and Pari. For us the idea of family was simple love and togetherness. And now I was witnessing it within my own little family, we were happy together. It was a wonderful feeling.

I don't remember if I had brought up Iraj's special attention toward me. Once he had a seminar in San Francisco. I had arranged a big party for the night that he was coming home. All the guests were already there when he arrived. He came in with carrying a big bucket in his hand. He said, "Here Shamci, this is Paloodeh Shirazy for you". All the ladies remained in their places wide-eyed. They kept saying, "My God, what a thoughtful husband". He was very happy to hear that. He felt great to be considered a loving husband. Some ladies said, "Our husbands don't even remember of our existence. Moreover to remember to buy us anything, especially something like Paloodeh Shirazy. Wow, you are a lucky woman".

My Dear GOD:

There was this other time when we were vacationing in San Francisco with the children. We were staying in Hyatt hotel. In the evening we were walking in the lobby. He stopped in front of one jewelry store and asked me to go in. He picked up an oval shaped onyx ring. It was black and beautiful. After observing it on my finger, he asked me if I liked it. Naturally I said, "Yes". He bought it without hesitation. Then he picked up yet another ring. While he was admiring it, I said to myself, "What is going on? Is he crazy, or is in love with me this much?" When he saw it on my finger, he asked the salesman to wrap it for us. And as usual he was happier than me.

Next weekend we were at Dr. Reza and Nazzi Mahager's house. I wore my rings. Nazzi immediately noticed the rings on my fingers, and after she found out that he bought them for me, she turned to Iraj and said jokingly, "Iraj, what has Shamci done for you that we can't do for our husbands?" You know, my dear GOD, I still don't know which one to believe. Should I choose the love he had for me, or my own passionate hatred for him? Anyway, I think I had all the right to be happy and feel great during that period of my life.

Like in many cases, my children were completely different from each other. My son Maseeh was very enthusiastic about nature, mostly animals. He wanted to have as many pets as he possibly could. I have gotten a couple Parakeets for him. Then it was a Jerboa. You should have seen how much fun we had when it got away from its cage. Personally, I had more fun when I got it back in the cage again. When he came across a little turtle he would make a close contact with it. In grade school his teachers would often catch him drawing sharks in his notebooks.

One day he came home with such an excitement. I realized that he had something to tell me while he was putting his books away. He got some food, and ran off to the garage. I soon found out that he brought a street cat home. I never liked having pets around the house because of the hair. He tried to hide the cat in the garage, where he would feed her. It was actually a little kitten, so he was able to feed her in a big box. For a while I didn't pay attention to everything he was doing. Obviously I was pretending that I didn't notice anything.

When I questioned him about the cat, he said, "She followed me home from school, I just couldn't ignore this poor little kitten and leave her alone on the street". I allowed him to keep her in the garage for a while. Then I realized that she was pregnant. I brought her in the house. And just as I always knew, she became my cat. No one showed enough responsibility to take care of the cat, or change her basket. The entire dispute over cat's responsibilities would make me very unhappy, up to a point that the cat officially became my responsibility. I named her Mitten and took care of her on a regular basis. Had I known that she was able to get pregnant in such an early age, I would have spayed her when she first came to our house. I set up a big bassinet for the kittens in the bathroom near the kitchen entrance. I was hoping she would deliver them there. One morning I went to the bathroom to check on her right after I woke up. I found four most beautiful kittens in that bassinet. They were all cleaned up, and lovingly waiting to be fed by their poor mother. I was so amazed by all the cleanliness and neatness. The first thing I did after she had her babies; I spayed and de-clawed her to make her a real house pet. I proceeded with taking care of her babies next. I had to make their box bigger and higher every few weeks to prevent them from getting out and destroying the furniture. Mitten's paws were all white while the rest of her body was black. One of the kittens was pure white. So I called her Snow White. She had green eyes that looked just like two big Emeralds. She had the longest hair I have ever seen on a cat. She was the most beautiful kitten I have ever seen. Another kitten was just pitch black with light brown eyes. The other one was completely gray with white paws. The forth one was just like any other cat. They were so beautiful that I had hard time parting with them.

My Dear GOD:

Dr. Rabbani's wife, Nayer, who had recently moved into a new house, wanted to adopt the white one. I warned her of her sharp paws, and I asked her to de-claw and spay her as soon as she could. Alas she wouldn't believe me. It was only a day after that she blamed me for the loss of her drapes. The kitten had ripped all her new drapes with her paws.

We took the other three to school to be adopted by other families. Although Mary was allergic to cats, and her doctor prohibited her to be anywhere around cats, we were not able to give up Mitten. She became my personal pet. At the end of the day when I sat

In our Helston Rd. house, Mojgan is standing next to Maseeh, holding Mittens.

Mojgan at a birthday party

Our famous Mittens

Mojgan and her friend are playing around my plants.

Mojgan and her friend posing for a picture

Mojgan is trying to look like a lady in big boots and high hills.

Mojgan and her friend at a dinner table

My beautiful wondering Mojgan

This picture was taken in Neya's house when they were moving to Michigan to stay with their children, Arman and Nazy. On that special night Parveen was there too. We were happy teasing each other and playing with our children. We were trying to make it fun no matter what. Of course, this was before Malakuti's death, if you know what I mean.

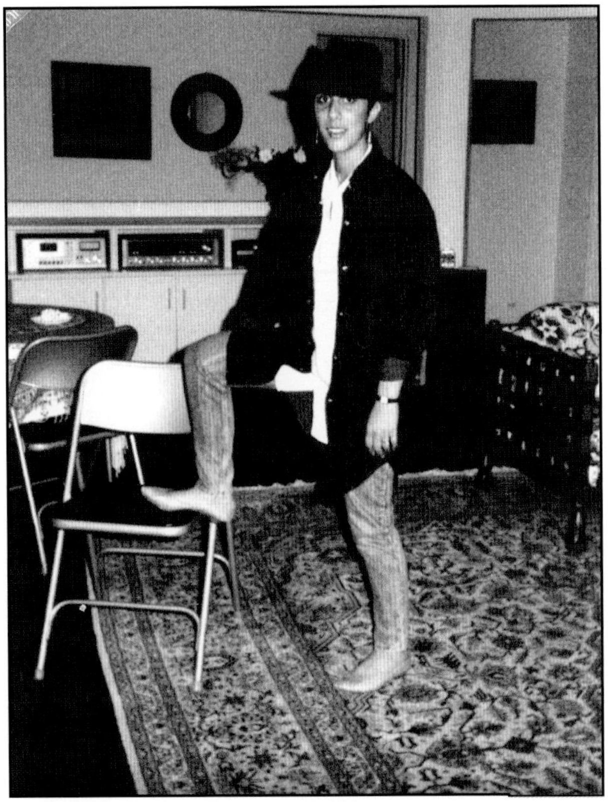

In our room, Mojgan was in her artistic mood to perform a role in high hills and a hat. Isn't she gorgeous?

Here, she is completing her act.

Mojgan and me

Iraj and Kamal are having a cup of coffee in our house. I wonder what they were talking about.

I didn't know before, when I used to look at this picture that even at this time Badri and Iraj had something going on between them. We were not the kind of people to have eyes on another person's spouse. We were trying to trust all of our friends. Neither of us was supposed to cheat on our husbands or wives. I wonder how these two were able to fool around with each other while they knew that Azeez would kill both of them if he ever found out. So Badri thought of a wise idea, "What if Azeez is dead?" And then, bang! Azeez got shot. Oh well. Left to right: Nazy Mahajer, me, Badri, Louise, and Iraj.

Pari and I are together. She was my best friend and I loved her dearly. She was beautiful, talented, generous, and she was helpful to me and my children at any time. I indeed miss her friendship. It was nice to have a sister-in-law who was also my friend.

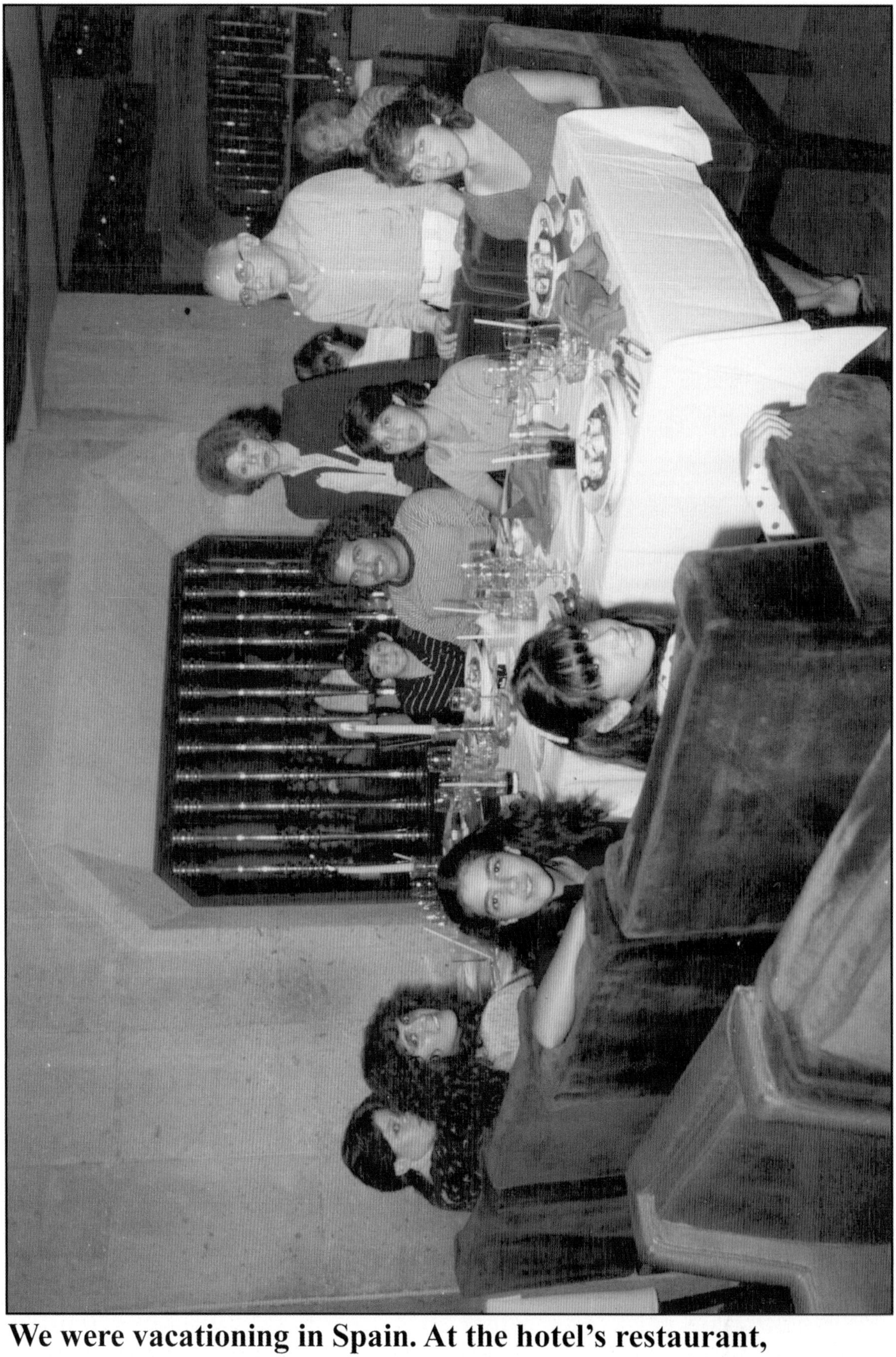

We were vacationing in Spain. At the hotel's restaurant, in the left side: Pooneh Mahajer, Kathy Fassihi, and Dineh Mahajer in the right side: Cyrus Fassihi, Maseeh, Mojgan, and Mary. Iraj and I are standing. At this time that we had money, it seems as if we didn't have happiness. I don't know what he had in mind.

We are at Vale, Colorado around a dinner table after a long hard skiing. Obviously Mary, Maseeh and Mojgan were the most tired.

down to rest, she would come and sat on my lap, and she would play with the ball of yarn. She was so smart and so playful, I felt like I was actually playing with a child.

The funniest thing happened while we were away visiting Iran. We made sure to provide her with everything she would need inside the garage. And we asked our neighbor, who also had children, to keep an eye on her after Iraj would have left. Iraj assumed that the cat ran away. He didn't know how to tell our children. But shortly before he left for Iran, our neighbor came to him and said, "Do you know that your cat has been living with us since your family had left?" Iraj was relieved. Mittens had chosen a family with children, rather than staying home alone. Funnier than that was when we came back home, she stormed into the house and started running all around the house. And to just punish me, she was crawling under furniture cover. She was running up and down, I have never seen her like that before. It was the saddest scene at the same time. She was punishing us for leaving her alone for two months.

My Dear GOD:

Parveen and Pari visited us in America once while Mojgan was still a little girl, and Mary and Maseeh were not teenagers yet. Iraj had always felt that he owed his sisters. He dedicated four weeks of his vacation time to them. He was authorized to a two-week vacation every year. So he spent two years of his off time in order to satisfy his sisters' desires. We drove to New York, Niagara Falls, Windsor, Toronto, and Montreal in Canada.

On this trip we were lucky to get a chance to see the EXPO sixty-seven, which was held in Canada. Every evening we stopped at a motel to rest for the night. Like always, Iraj being that person who spent money whenever and wherever he wished, he would leave a few hundreds of dollars in the checking accounts for all necessaries. And at the end of each month he would check to see where the money was spent. It would always embarrass me that I wasn't able to buy things for my children on my own. Many times I had to make it look like I was against that spending. And they were always under the impression that I was a stingy mother. They were not aware of the fact that I did not want their father to be making a big deal out of nothing.

When we were in New York, we went to see the Statue of Liberty. I only had my checking book with me, but I had no change in my pocket. Everyone decided to go up and see the city from up there. Since I had seen it before, and it would be difficult to take the big stroller up, I decided to stay down there until they come back. It took them so long to return. Mojgan's formula was finished, and she started crying. It was hot and she was very thirsty. I could neither leave her with a stranger to go and get her something, nor could I take the stroller up the stairs with me. In my poor English I was asking people around me to cash a check for me. But no one could understand me, and they wouldn't cash a check for me. So until late afternoon that they returned, Mojgan remained

screaming in my arms, she made my day so miserable, all because I couldn't have any cash with me. Obviously if I could have thought of that, I would have cashed the check before we got there.

My Dear GOD:

Anyway city to city, place to place we saw everything. It was a long and exciting trip. But having to watch over three children at all times, at the end of each night I was so tired that I couldn't move. It was my system to take my children with me wherever I went. I couldn't enjoy my life without them. No wonder they were tired of being with me in later years. And at the same time people, who spent most of their time away from their children, leaving them in care of grandmothers, aunts, or living maids, would not be rejected by their children. And since they were hardly ever around, they were wanted and needed by their children.

We entertained many visiting friends and relatives while we lived in Michigan. We took them sightseeing on many occasions. One of our favorite destinations was Niagara Falls. I remember once I took Azar and another time Saideh and Mojgan to Niagara Falls. We ended up taking the train at least half of the way. It was such a great experience.

It was the times before my children were teenagers. We had decided to spend our summer vacation on Sunnybrook Farm, north of Michigan, together with my sister Azar, some friends like Panah, Kasef, Nefrooshan and all the children.

There were Dr. Panah and Rohan and their three girls Roxana, Marganeh, and Lisa. There were Dr. Kashef, his wife Parvaneh, his daughter Faribba, and their son Rameen. Then there were Dr. Neelfrooshan, his wife Louise, and their three girls, the twins Suzzi and Sandi, and the youngest one, Nancy.

Depending on the size of the family, we rented one or two rooms. It was bed and breakfast. We stayed there for two weeks. Breakfast was set up in the yard from eight to eleven, where were served with great varieties of food each time. It was enough to be considered lunch, or even brunch.

Most Iranians are known for their eagerness of getting large amounts of anything that becomes available to them. Every morning there was plenty of food prepared for hundreds of guests, who were staying on the farm. It was actually too much of everything. They made sure that you would never run short on one thing. Even if we all filled our plates with food, it was more than enough for every one of us. But no, each parent had to fill two separate plates. And then children would bring their own plates as well. One condition though was that no one was allowed to take food in their rooms. So every morning our group would put a lot of food to waste. And even though they did recognized, they repeated the same thing over and over again. The good thing was that we didn't have to stay there for more than two weeks. Otherwise we would have made the poor hostesses go bankrupt.

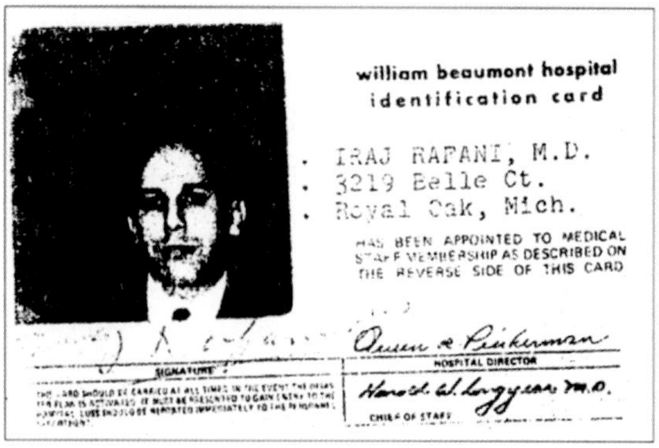

william beaumont hospital
identification card

IRAJ RAFANI, M.D.
3219 Belle Ct.
Royal Oak, Mich.

HAS BEEN APPOINTED TO MEDICAL STAFF MEMBERSHIP AS DESCRIBED ON THE REVERSE SIDE OF THIS CARD

SIGNATURE

HOSPITAL DIRECTOR

CHIEF OF STAFF

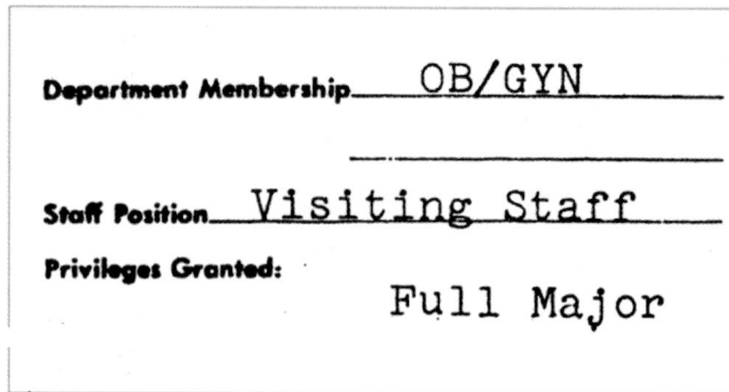

Department Membership OB/GYN

Staff Position Visiting Staff

Privileges Granted: Full Major

This was his ID card to enter the hospital at any time.

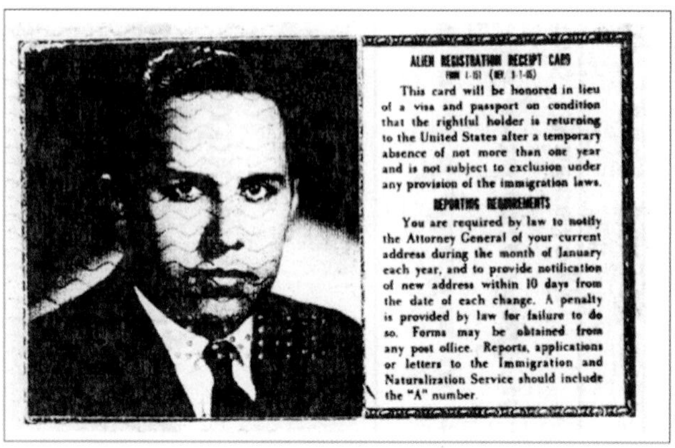

ALIEN REGISTRATION RECEIPT CARD

This card will be honored in lieu of a visa and passport on condition that the rightful holder is returning to the United States after a temporary absence of not more than one year and is not subject to exclusion under any provision of the immigration laws.

REPORTING REQUIREMENTS

You are required by law to notify the Attorney General of your current address during the month of January each year, and to provide notification of new address within 10 days from the date of each change. A penalty is provided by law for failure to do so. Forms may be obtained from any post office. Reports, applications or letters to the Immigration and Naturalization Service should include the "A" number.

This was his Green Card.

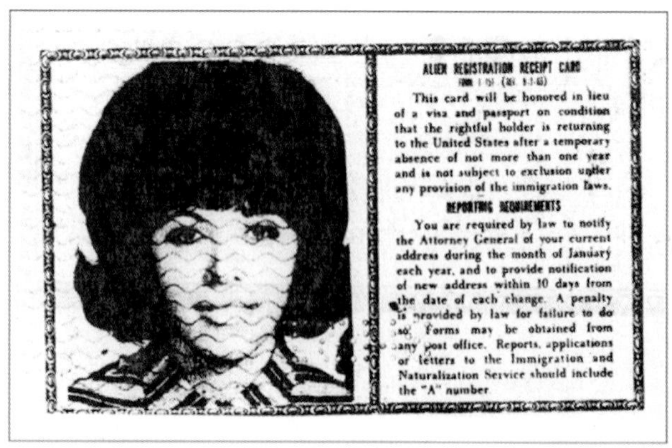

ALIEN REGISTRATION RECEIPT CARD

This card will be honored in lieu of a visa and passport on condition that the rightful holder is returning to the United States after a temporary absence of not more than one year and is not subject to exclusion under any provision of the immigration laws.

REPORTING REQUIREMENTS

You are required by law to notify the Attorney General of your current address during the month of January each year, and to provide notification of new address within 10 days from the date of each change. A penalty is provided by law for failure to do so. Forms may be obtained from any post office. Reports, applications or letters to the Immigration and Naturalization Service should include the "A" number.

This was my Green Card.

Dr. Baker and his wife, me, Dr. Joseph and his wife, and Iraj at a restaurant

Nazy, Mary, Baharak, Maseeh, and Mojgan in Ezzat's swimming pool in Tehran.

I am wearing a sweater which I had knitted and designed myself, sitting at the metropolitan beach.

Minoo Kadem was visiting us in our house in Bloomfield Hills, Michigan.

My Dear GOD:

In the evenings the hostess arranged activities for us. They had swimming, tennis, shuffleboard, and table tennis for the young adults, and dance and music for adults.

In the evenings young people would gather around the fire pit near the lake, and they would light a nice fire. We were watching our children very closely. One evening we went by the lake to see what was going on. Obviously we did not like the fact that the boys were getting close to our daughters. We all decided to take them away from the fire scene to their rooms. It wasn't easy to make them understand why we were doing what we were doing. They were mad at us, and they did not want to be with us any more.

There was this other time when we, the ladies, were playing shuffleboard. We were speaking Farsi, and we never thought that any of the other visitors would be able to understand us. There was an American gentleman there talking to us. In the middle of the discussion, Louise said something about him in Farsi. He answered her in English right away. We were so shocked. He answered when we asked him if he understood Farsi, "Not at all. I figured it by your body language". Again we laughed so much that we almost cried. We had wonderful time together during those two weeks. And even though there was both good and bad, we made an effort to enjoy our time together.

Each family took care of their own bill at the end of the trip. I noticed that Iraj did not want me to be present with him at the office. But I got curious, and I went in later on. I found out from the conversation that he had paid for only five people instead of six. And I realized that he didn't want me to find out about it. He wanted me to be grateful for paying for Azar. I was grateful to him anyway, and I never brought it up. I thought that whatever was done was done. There was no need to embarrass him.

Anyway, we had many good times in our first house where Mojgan was born. We also had a few crucial incidents that made us worry for a long time. Our children were growing up, and they were trying to get to know the world they were living in. But their world was completely different from our world, which caused a lot of friction between us. We had to learn how to talk to them, and how to understand their point of view. It wasn't easy, but I tried hard to learn their language.

My Dear GOD:

No matter how big the difficulty was, Iraj tried to be a good father and a great husband. We were happy, and he wanted to show his happiness to all his friends. Or I must say that was my belief at the time. Not only had he expressed his happiness to his friends, but to his sisters. He had embarrassed me many times. Those days he acted as if I was everything to him, and that he couldn't have survived without me.

How can a person do all the right things at all times, against what he is really feeling inside him? Is it possible that he did not love me, while he did every loving thing for me? Can a person live two different lives at the same time, and why? He didn't have to show me that much love. Not all other husbands did what he did for me for their wives. He did it with sincerity and lovingly. His love and attention for his family was to a point that I never allowed myself to ever question his love. Even at the time that he was cheating on me, he still wanted to love me by doing things for me that he knew I liked. He never gave me a signal to doubt his love. I don't know, my dear GOD, I must have either been very stupid, or he was very clever to be able to keep me fooled at all times.

In that first house some of our friends from Iran came to visit us. Among them were Dr. and Mrs. Shahnaz Toosi. Dr. Toosi was the friend who helped Iraj at the Mehrabad airport to escape from his mistress in Iran. They stayed with us for two weeks. There were times that Shahnaz and I went shopping, and Dr. Toosi baby-sat for Mojgan. Shahnaz was a good friend for me. I remember she was advising me to think of myself first. When she saw me constantly busy with housework and children, she made me go out shopping with her. And she even asked her husband to stay home and take care of Mojgan. She had a living made in Iran, and she knew how hard it would have been if she didn't have any help.

My Dear GOD:

Another person who came to visit was Dr. Syrous Azimi. He was the Psychologist who was treating Shah's brothers.

Dr. Gangi, who was related to Iraj, came next. During his first visit he was assigned by Iranian university to complete his research in Meteorology at Michigan University. He stayed with us for just one week. Second time he came here for a complete checkup. Because of Iraj's schedule, I had to drive him places. Sometimes he offered that I leave the children with him while I was running errands. He stayed with me enough to notice how busy my daily life was.

Because I didn't like to be forced into doing anything, I tried in my turn not to force my children. So I would always ask them. And if they did it, that was fine. Otherwise I did it myself. Dr. Gangi had noticed that children didn't help me in any way. One day he questioned Mary, "Why don't you help your mother?" That made Mary so mad that she got more upset with me.

As usual I drove him to the Metropolitan Airport, because Iraj had to be at the hospital. On the way there he asked me if Iraj had given his message to me. I told him, "No". Then he told me, "I was telling Iraj that he has been very lucky to have you as his wife. And that he owes all his success and happiness to your pure love for him. I believe that he couldn't be where he is now without you". I thanked him, and I told him I was very flattered. I knew that Iraj would not admit to all my contributions, or give me credit for all my efforts so that I don't get ahead of myself.

Top left: Dr. Gangi who brought the science of meteorology to Iran, and started the weather forecast broadcasting on the news. Dr. Pear is talking to him. Next to Dr. Pear are Iraj, and me.
Top right: At the dinner table, Gretchen Pear is listening to Dr. Gangi discussing his work.

Dr. Gangi, and Mojgan at five years old.

Anyway, Dr. Gangi had a lot of respect for me, and he wanted to tell me personally. After Dr. Gangi had that conversation with Mary asking her to help her mother, I looked back and I realized in our household that everyone at home had to help. We all were scheduled to do our daily chores, from washing the dishes to taking care of our siblings, and everything else that involved the family. I believe that it was our parents' training that made each one of us a responsible person.

My Dear GOD:

I came to realize that my children's behavior and attitude were the consequences of my poor training. I knew then that giving too much of anything, even love, if not practiced in right manner, would create bad results. In this case I was the target of my own training.

Okay, my dear GOD, I am sure I didn't have enough knowledge to train my children properly. And because I did not want to be forceful with my children, I always tried to do everything by myself. I wouldn't even take my parents' advice. I wish I had handled it in a different way to make life easier for all of us.

Another person who visited us in that house was my cousin Ali Akbar Mozzaffar. He was on a mission in Russia for two years. That summer he had a convention in New York. Fortunately when he came to visit us, we were going up north vacationing with few other families. He ended up joining us; we had a wonderful time together. It was Dr. Barkhordari, his wife Susan, and his children Parto, Farzad, and Roozbeh. Another family was Dr. Mohammad Rabbani, his wife Nayer, and their children Roya, and Rameen. The third family was Dr. Kashef, his wife Parvaneh, their children Fariba, and Rameen.

Each family took turns to prepare dinner. Akbar decided to take over when it was our turn. He decided to make Khoroshe Kadoo with rice (squash and meat sauce with rice). Everyone, and especially Dr. Rabbani, said, "I don't like that food, and I am not going to eat it". We all knew that he was joking. Not only he ate more than others, but also he was eating the squash while it was still in the frying pan, plus the shish kabab that he had requested. That day we had more fun than ever teasing Dr. Rabbani.

Another visitor was my brother Javad. He had a seminar in Paris, France. He arranged to come and spend one week with us in Michigan. It was the time that my children started locking the doors of their rooms behind them. Javad didn't like what he saw in my children. He felt sorry for me to have to raise my children in a country without any guidance or respect for parents. Because it was school season, I couldn't entertain him the way I wished I would. Seeing him here after the sad visit we had in London years ago was a very good experience for both of us.

Many times we took our guests to a nightclub in Windsor, Canada. It was called Elmwood Casino. One night we had invited a few of the doctors and their wives from the hospital. Believe it or not, we were watching Mr. Tom Jones. Well, what else is new? I had

followed him everywhere and did many things in our married life that were completely against my own wishes. This kind of entertainment was to repay the doctors. One of the wives passed out at our dinner table after drinking. And all the doctors rushed her to the backroom. She told me, “It was very embarrassing. All these doctors had to remove my clothes in order to remove my corset. Then they had to hold my head down for several minutes”. They all agreed that because she had no food during the course of the day, as soon as she had alcohol all her blood rushed to her stomach, which then caused her to become light headed to a point that she fainted. She said she was lucky that all the doctors were there to save her.

My Dear GOD:

You see, my dear GOD, this is one of the things that comes our way in life, and later on will connect us to something that was planned for us. One night we were in that same casino with a few of friends. That night Ann Margaret was performing. We went to use the bathroom during the intermission. Coming back we noticed a few Iranian families on our way back. It seemed that they got there too late to get their tickets. Iraj shook hands with one of the gentlemen. We found out that he was also a doctor. He was entertaining his wife's sisters.

Yes, my dear GOD, he was that Dr. Azeez Malakuti, whom we had never met before. And even that night I did not get to talk to them. When we went to our table our friends who knew them said, “He is a psychiatrist, and he is practicing in Michigan now”.

Some time later we got to meet them through our mutual friend Dr. Naser Barkhordari. We had heard so much about this doctor, and how crazy and funny he was. Dr. Jalal Panah, and Dr. Vaziri were the ones who knew him well.

Some other night that we were going to see yet another Ann Margaret show at the same casino, Dr. Malakuti and his wife were among the group. That night Rohan Panah who was so amused by Dr. Malakuti's wittiness, kept asking Azeez to talk about the times that he went to Badri's house (for “khastegari”) to meet Badri, and decide if he wants to marry her. That night I found out what they meant when they said he was funny, silly, and/or crazy.

You know, my dear GOD, in Iran it is customary that parents arrange the marriage for their children. They believe that they have enough knowledge to find the right match for their children. On the surface it is always the family of the groom that initiates the visit. But in reality when the family of bride gets to like an eligible young man, they will go after him by sending a mediator to arrange that special visit. In this case the mediator was Badri's sister, who knew Azeez well, and had made-up her mind to make this marriage possible.

That night by Rohan's request Malakuti started telling us about the first time that he had gone to Badri's house to see her. It was the first time for us to listen to his story. While

Rohan and others had heard it many times, and made him believe that he was a comedian. First he talked about many other (khastegarys) wife hunting occasions before he met and married Badri.

My Dear GOD:

Once he went to meet one of the brides to be. He was saying that the girl was so big and ugly that he was afraid to even look at her. They served tea, and everyone was sitting around the table. While he was spreading the napkin on his lap he had squeezed the tablecloth under his belt instead. When they were ready to leave, he got up in a hurry, while he pulled the tablecloth with him all the way to the door. He said he made a full of himself in front of that family.

He made up many stories like that, and made everyone, especially Rohan, laugh and be entertained. The second story was, "My mother, my sister and I were supposed to go and see this girl. After we got introduced, the girl served us hot tea in a tray. When she came to serve me I was so nervous and shaky, that I spilled the hot tea all over my hands and my new suit. I was so embarrassed; I couldn't hold my head up. The visit was over so quickly that we almost ran out of their house, and we never looked back again".

Everyone laughed, and laughed, and applauded him again and again as if he was the entertainer of the night. No matter how many times they had heard those stories, still they laughed and laughed. He was getting the pleasure of being a comedian. After hearing many stories like that, Rohan still kept asking for the story of Badri's "khastegary". Then with such a pride, he started to talk. He said, "My sister knew that Badri was near marrying age. Badri's sister, who was from a different father, knew that I was the most eligible bachelor. I was a doctor, and very handsome. Somehow we were related to each other, but because I have been away and out of the country, I was not aware of how the kids in our family had grown and developed during all those years. Anyway, my sister, and especially her sister, was after me to go and look at Badri. As I insisted that I didn't want to go, they insisted that I must go, even if it was just for a simple visit. I agreed, and one day we went to their house to visit. Because I was with her sister, we went unexpectedly. And then he continued, "When we rang the doorbell and went in I saw a girl with long hair, ruffled shirt, and barefoot who started running away from us like a gypsy girl. I asked who she was. Her sister said, "This is Badri. You have not seen her for fifteen years". Then he continued, "I was very amazed thinking that she was the same girl, and that when she was a baby I held her in my arms when I was ten or eleven years old. My, oh my, she had grown to be a beautiful lady. Then he added, "She was gorgeous, dazzling, wild, and gypsy looking girl". Then he turned to us and said, "You all know the rest of the story. Now I got stuck with this devilish and snaky woman that I don't know what to do with her".

My Dear GOD:

At this time again everyone applauded for a psychiatrist who loved to be the center of attention, and attraction was the most pleasant time of his life.

This doctor and his wife became part of our group that we regularly entertained and socialized with.

Ok, my dear GOD, this was one of those cases that we never chose or planned for, and we had no idea what was being planned for us later on. Only you and you only knew what was going to be planned for us by that visit later on.

Like any intelligent person we accepted them with open arms, and started socializing with them regularly.

You see, my dear GOD, the more I think about my life, the more I realize that actions and occurrences during those years would have taken their course regardless of our plans, dreams and desires. I have never been interested in forming close friendships; I knew that none of them were capable of comprehending the true meaning and value of friendship.

So I never allowed myself to get that close to anyone so as to be expecting anything from them. I knew that one day I would be disappointed. So I always created work and hobbies for myself in order to spend my time wisely. I didn't need anyone to be around me and entertain me. Not only was I able to entertain myself, but I made sure that my visits with others were somehow productive as well.

With all these, I got stock with their friendship and at the end the result was what we had never expected. Now you tell me, my dear GOD, why did it have to happen the way it did?

THE NEW HOUSE AND A NEW CHAPTER.

My Dear GOD:

By now everything was beautiful. Mary, Maseeh, and Mojgan were going to Detroit Country Day School, the best private school in Detroit. The school was for advanced students who wanted to achieve more. We believed that we were in this country to provide better education for our children. Although the school was very expensive, we decided that it was worth it.

At the age twelve Maseeh entered the seventh grade at Detroit Country Day. During that same year the school became co-ed. So Mary could join the school as well. We had enrolled Mary in a Catholic School prior to that. Mojgan started kindergarten the same year. That year the tuition started at thirty five hundred and up. Many children of low-income families were able to attend the school with scholarships. And many rich people sent their children there only for the sake of its name and the prestige. It wasn't easy to get accepted to that school, there was a waiting list. The school held tests for different entry levels, including the kindergarteners. The kids were encouraged to be compatible. The school was very strict about their rules and regulations.

I particularly loved it. I was raised in a very strict environment. No, I am not trying to say that I was wise enough to accept it and appreciate it when I was little. But I came to realize later on that it was the only way to raise a child. Especially when my children didn't accept any restrictions at home, that was the best answer to my problems.

At that time the headmaster was Dr. Schlagel. He believed that students who came from comfortable homes were completely sheltered from the real world. And we as parents were obligated to inform them through our teachings. He believed that they must be aware of what was going on in the rest of the world. So our children were required to finish the food on their plates, and they were not allowed to say, "I don't like it". He believed that not too many children were fortunate to have a comfortable life.

His belief was that we owe it to the whole world to teach our children, and that the rest of the children in the world are not lucky enough to have enough food to eat or clothes to wear.

Dr. Schlagel had come up with a dress code, and if a student did not follow the rule, he or she would send home. Meanwhile the student would lose points in their academics. To me this meant a two-way punishment. After all it had some embarrassment for the students also.

The boys had to wear blue suits, which were specifically made for Detroit Country Day School students. They had to wear white shirts and a Country Day School ties, white

socks and black shoes every day of the week, except for one day. On Thursdays they were free to wear anything they liked within the limits of school's prestige. Jeans or short sleeve shirts were not allowed.

My Dear GOD:

Mary had good grades in her sophomore year. She got a summa cum laude that year. I felt that she was happy to be in that school. She became friends with her English teacher Mr. Ronnie Clemmer. We even invited him a few times to our house for dinner. I was glad to be able to know her teachers personally. I felt that it could have been helpful to her behavior.

Maseeh was doing okay, but he was not applying himself to his full potential. At that time we were spending nearly ten thousand dollars a year on their education to make sure that they became advanced students. Otherwise if they chose to study the same way, they could have gone to the public school near our house. There was no need of attending Country Day School in order to be an average student, who would be barely making a passing grade.

When Mary started to smoke, Maseeh had developed allergies to the tobacco smoke, so one would assume that he would never get involved with smoking. Unfortunately he did start to smoke at the age fourteen. And in fact he became so addicted that I couldn't do anything to make him stop. He kept it private for the first few years. He actually wanted to show some respect for us. But I preferred that he smoked in front of us rather than doing it behind our back. And the same went for when and if he wanted to meat a girl; I would ask him to bring her home. Luckily he did end up introducing them all to me, and he would invite all his friends home for dinner. The only occasions that made me very unhappy were when he started giving big open parties. I would be so worried that I couldn't go to bed, and so I would just keep an eye on them at all times.

Each of my children had their own schedule, and they each got off school at different times. Then they joined the after school sport programs. It was a different program each term. So I would end up driving back and forth to schoo1 six or seven times within one day. That did not include the times that they were sent home to change their clothes, or when they would forget something important. And all those were besides their extracurricular activities. It was guitar classes for Maseeh, it was gymnastics for Mojgan, and it was piano lessons for all three of them, and so on. We had arranged it so that they take the bus at first. Unfortunately I was responsible for picking them up afterwards. When I realized that school bus only served during the regular school hours, for the second year I had decided to be their designated driver from morning till night.

My Dear GOD:

It was so funny, or better yet, it was ironic, that in reality, all those school rules and

regulations were imposed on me. If one of them broke the school dress code, he or she would have been sent home, and I would have to drive them back. If one of them forgot something, I was the one who had to deliver it to them. There were times that two of them would call in one day at different times to ask me to take their stuff to them. And GOD forbids if I said something regarding their self-discipline or being more organized, I would be the guilty one, the one who had to be punished.

Yes, my dear GOD, you might tell me that these are the children that I raised. What could I expect? You are right. But between the society, the school, the media, and my background and my culture I was trying to find the best way to succeeding. I was just hoping that it would happen sooner or later, that one day they would achieve it. In theory they should have been the ones to worry about their academics. But in reality I was the one who had to do something about it. These were the subjects of the disputes in our house, plus other involvements that occupied my entire life, even while I was asleep in my bed.

Speaking of bed, it reminded me of my craziness about my children. We would hear of fires every day in the news. On some occasions there would be residents trapped in their burning homes. That was my nightmare. I knew that Maseeh was very afraid of natural disasters. So on stormy nights I would tie three sheets together, I would tie one end to their beds, and I asked them to wrap themselves in those sheets and jump out from the window in case of fire. And I have always believed that if all other parents would think of taking necessary precautions, in many cases they could have eliminated injuries and fatalities in their homes. Well, I have never allowed myself to think, "What if they die from the smoke before they wake up from the heat. But as I said, I was a crazy mother, and I did that to be able to go to bed with a peace of mind, and so that I would fall asleep till next morning to start all over again.

Anyway, I was on call every minute of my life, and twenty-four hours a day. But my duties didn't end there. I had to borrow two extra eyes, and keep them at the top of my fingers just to be able to watch them and their behavior carefully. And for that reason when I came back from Iran I had made a promise not to engage myself with a regular job. I believe that if you cannot be around, you have to have someone like yourself to watch over your children the same way you would. I was raised that when I accepted a duty I had to do it well to the best of my abilities. You cannot get a job and not pay attention to what was requested from you. You cannot ignore the responsibilities that are yours and only yours.

My Dear GOD:

Iraj was just a father. He would spend most of his time at the hospital, or at his office, and then he studied at home. And at his leisure time he would stay in his room reading Wall Street Journal, while I carried on the role of a wife, a mother, a cook, a

housekeeper, a driver, a shopper, and most of all I was a lover and entertainer. This way absolutely everything was always taken care of. I was so tired at times that I would fall asleep behind the wheel. Then on weekends we would either entertain others, or be entertained by other so-called friends.

When you are single you only think of yourself, and how to satisfy your own needs. But when you are married, and especially if you have children, besides yourself you must satisfy everyone else. Oh, no, I am sorry, let me rephrase myself. If and when you have children, you must not think of yourself whatsoever. Just forget who you are, or what your needs are. With all this activity if things go well life is beautiful and enjoyable. Although I was so tired at the end of the night, in general I found myself to be a lucky woman. Iraj was trying to keep me happy. And I was trying to keep him happy in return. And we both tried to keep our children happy to the best of our ability.

I knew my children well. As the years went by, they started complaining about the school's management, and its army-like structure. They were tired of the rules and regulations both at home and at school. They were nagging at the faculty; they were seeking an easy way out. After the first year that Mary made summa cumlaude, neither one of them was even trying to become an above average students. Although they didn't do great at Detroit Country Day School, while we were spending great amount of money, I still preferred that they stayed at that school, because I preferred the management system.

Many times when Maseeh disappointed me, I would tell him, "Oh, I should have sent you to a military school so that you grow up to be an organized person". Most of the times we would just laugh, he knew I did not meant it.

The main reason for sending our children to that school was that we thought we could keep them away from the filthy environment. Alas that was a wishful thinking. Both Cranbrook Boarding School, the best private school in Detroit, and the Country Day School were as filthy as anywhere else.

I think I have mentioned this before. Once when I was begging Mary to stay away from drugs, and the kids who are involved with drugs, she told me, "Mom, please don't worry about us. We know what you want from us. If I want to use drugs, it would be so easy to do so, without even you suspecting anything. Kids and teachers are exchanging drugs hand-to-hand in the library, without anyone noticing. So don't worry. It is up to me to realize what I want to do. Or which way and direction I want to take". My GOD, how right she was. I just had to keep her at it, hoping that she became wise enough to recognize the right direction for herself. When she told me that, I felt very sorry for her. Again I blamed myself for bringing my innocent children into this world, and getting them involved with these complicated matters that made their lives so difficult. The only thing that gave me hope was to ask you, my dear God, to save my children from going in a wrong direction. And to tell you the truth, I have never felt like you ever left me. Thank you.

My Dear GOD:

Things were going so well, and Iraj moved into a new office near Beaumont Hospital on 13 Mile Road. He was gaining back his confidence, and we were thinking that we had made it after all. He thought he had made it by bringing his family together. Despite all the struggles of raising our children, I was happy to see that he was trying to make us happy. Then one day, after we had already changed our minds about remodeling our house, he started discussing his plans of building a new house.

He decided to buy a property. And when the right time came he would build it according to our taste. Then he said, "It has been my dream to build my dream house. But in order to build a house and to do it right we need more money. The advantage of doing so will be that our house will be built the way we like it". I said, "There is nothing wrong with that, as long as you don't go overboard, or put yourself under a lot of pressure". And I said, "As long as we could continue our normal life, it is going to be okay. We do not want to have more stress than we already do".

Then I told him, "We must approach this idea very carefully". Then I reminded him of the stock market deal that he had once made. Since he would always read the Wall Street Journal, he felt like he knew more than his agent. Taking a chance of losing money is not an issue for people who have the means. But in our case, when we had to take every dollar into account, it might have end up being a bad experience. And even though his only hobby was reading the Wall Street Journal and the book "How to become a millionaire", still we had lost a great amount of money at the time that we were so broke.

So I warned him that leaving a life in a fast lane does not always bring good results. I just wanted him be careful, I didn't want him to get hurt again. And I prayed to God to help him make the right decision.

My Dear GOD:

Another reason for my worries was that it seemed like he was competing with his ex-friend Dr. Talebzadeh. All these doctors, the so-called friends, were competing with one another. It would have been nice if they competed with each other in medical field. But no, it was only about money.

My Dear GOD:

So after many years when Iraj decided to build a house on the Wabeek Lake, the newest part of Bloomfield Hills, I realized that he had won the competition. But the race didn't end there, a year or two later Dr. Naser Barkhordari and Dr. Mohammad Rabbani each built themselves homes on both sides of our house. These three doctors were same year medical school graduates in Iran. They weren't simply competing; they were trying to damage each other's reputation by spreading rumors.

We were still on Helston Road when we decided to buy a property on Long Lake in Wabeek area. It was near closing the deal that I had to go to England to visit my sister. When I came back he told me, "We had to drop the deal because of some errors". Then he bought the property on the Wabeek Lake, and we started to build on it later.

It was a new subdivision, and we were one of the first families to build a house there. We selected the best property between Upper Long Lake and Wabeek Lake. I was thinking at that time that we made it after all. Iraj had done his best to provide a good and happy life for all of us.

He was trying to do everything to my needs and desires. We were so happy and excited. We found an architect, Mr. Jim Conn, and we found builders through him. We began with visiting some of the houses that Mr. Conn's had designed. That had become a big job for us. We would visit the houses that he had built a few times during the week and at times on Sundays. He was a single man who lived across the "BIJUE" restaurant on Thirteen Mile Road. He actually owned the property of that restaurant. He loved his mother who lived in California, and he would talk about her all the time. He liked our food, and so we often ate together. His office was behind his living area. Although he had built many big houses for others, he himself was living in a small studio. He was a very simple and a humble man. He became our friend, and I didn't mind having him over for dinner as many nights as it was possible for him.

It took us two years to build that house. We borrowed ideas from more than fifty houses we saw, and put them all together to build our house to our liking. We got to learn about almost every finish material on the market: all kinds of marbles, tiles, woods and many more.

Iraj was the happiest person at that time. One would have thought he had the whole world in his hands. He did not take a single step without consulting me. Furthermore it seemed that he wanted to build the house for me solely, he wanted everything to be done to my desires. We sat together and drew our plans on a piece of paper. Many times he would draw, and then I would correct the plan, and we would go back and forth. We were so happy and amused by doing that. And even though in reality he was making his own dreams come true, at the same time he tried to satisfy me by doing exactly what I would want and need in the house. We went everywhere together, and we did everything together. And while we were out, we had lunch together most of the times. That was besides Wednesdays, which was his day off that we were always together. I was having the time of my life. It seemed to me that he was trying to fulfill all my dreams just like he had promised. He was trying to take the place of my father, my mother, my sisters and brothers, and anything he thought I was missing in my life. He didn't hesitate to spend money on me. He was a husband that every woman dreams of. And I had him, and I enjoyed him thoroughly and lovingly. But above all he showed so much intimate satisfaction that would really amazed me. It made me very happy to see him coming out of

bed so happy.

My Dear GOD:

Once he told me a funny story about a patient of his, which had made him laugh in the surgical room. He said, "The lady asked me if I had a fight with my wife this morning, or did I have a good night with my wife. And she continued, "If you didn't have a good night, or if you had a fight this morning, I don't think I will come out of the surgery alive". And everyone laughed so hard".

Once we decided to go on a vacation to Spain with two other families, Dr. Naser and Susan Barkhordari and their children, and Dr. Reza and Shahnaz Mahajer and their children Pooneh and Dineh. They had suggested that the weather was nice, and that we didn't need warm clothing. But as a habit I took some coats for my children anyway. No one else had thought of bringing coats. It turned out that it was very cold and stormy. It was impossible to walk to a restaurant.

After the first day of shivering, and absolutely not enjoying our time, we were so cold that we didn't want to go anywhere; we just wanted to stay in the hotel. The next day while we were sightseeing in the midtown Bazzar, Iraj took me to a leather boutique. They had the best leather coats. I found a full length, light brown suede coat, which to my surprise fit me so well. Iraj bought for me without hesitating. Then we went to a shoe store, and he bought the first brown boots that were my size. He didn't want me to be cold on that vacation. No one else bought anything for their wives or their children. They were very cold as well, and probably they needed more than I did. Ok, my dear GOD, do you think he did all these just because he loved me? Or did he want to just prove to everyone that he was a big spender not having any passion for me? I have no answer, my dear GOD. You might know better than me why he did what he did. Altogether he made many of those ladies envious of me, up to a point that most of them would question him in a friendly manner.

My Dear GOD:

Our excitement was overwhelming. Building our first new house was really Iraj's dream. I was happy first of all to have him, and my beautiful children. And my comfortable home and life were the signs of my absolute happiness. I never asked for more. But okay, he wanted to build his dream house, and it wouldn't be right to go against his wish. After all I was the one who was going to enjoy it more than others. The only thing that worried me was that too much pressure might have ruined our peace and harmony that we have finally gained. So when he was ready, I went along with it.

The day of the ground breaking we were there with our cameras taking pictures of the bare ground. Step by step we took pictures of our house going up.

Those who have done it before had warned him of possibility of running into

One of those trips together; on the right: Iraj, Mojgan, me, Mary, and Maseeh. On the left: Roozbeh, Susan, Farzad, and Partow

Here, I am dressed up to go out.

Here, sitting on the edge: Badri, Susan, her mom, Mrs. Froozan, me, and Jila Mohtadi.

On the right side of this picture: Iraj, Reza, Mr. Mansoor Froozan, and Mrs. Froozan. I am on the left.

Lovingly, he has his hand on my shoulder. We walked on the streets of Spain and took a picture with a horse. Left to right: Iraj, Susan, the horse, and Naser

The same day and the same place, this time I have the hand of my so-called friend on my shoulder. Left to right: me, Susan, Naser, and Iraj.

On the same day, we are at the same place, except that my dear husband had bought his wife whom he pretended to love a lot, an ice cream cone. Don't you think I had to love him and stand by him during his hard times? I think so.

Nazy Mahajer, Badri, Marjon, Maseeh, and Roozbeh, watching carefully

All of us are picnicking with our families at Cedar Point. If you look carefully, you will see how Iraj and Badri were having their own fun while neither of their spouses suspected anything at all. I am sure if Azeez had ever suspected that something was going on between the two of them, he would have killed both of them right there without any hesitation. I think Mojgan was wondering what is going on.

Yes, I was always happy. There was nothing bad to make me unhappy. That was why after Badri got rid of her husband, she decided to get the husband that could make her happy. And, he did indeed.

I think Badri did anything she wanted while her husband was looking the other way. Here in this picture, Susan, Badri, Azeez-looking the other way, Iraj, and Naser

We are at Cedar Point, Michigan. The person whose hand was always on my shoulder or in my hand, and looked happy, was unhappy to do so after Malakuti's death. In this picture, he is the only husband who did so. Left to right: Naheed, Louise, Susan, Aghdass Shushtari, me, Iraj, Naser, Aghdass Barkhordari, and Dr. Shushtari

Please pay attention. In the next picture everyone is happy and laughing except Iraj. If I truly write about how I feel when I see these pictures, you will probably laugh at me. But you do not understand my feelings for Iraj to know that even then I was upset to see him that way. I always wanted the best for him. How could I sit and see him suffer this way? He was as dear as my children to me. I had given up all my siblings and my parents to be with him and make him happy. Why must he suffer like this? Why? This was a New Year's Eve party in Dr. Panah's house. Left to right: Nancy Neel, Roshanak, Badri, Louise, Mojgan, me, and Mary. In the front: Partow, Farzad, and Masseh. In the back: Roshanak, Roozbeh Malakuti, Iraj, Aghdass Shushtari, Dr. Shushtari, Jalal, Rohan, Lisa, Dr. Neel, Roozbeh B., Susan, and Marjon We had become so Americanized that on this night Iraj kissed Badri on her lips, who then said, "Can't Iranians learn?"

Reza Mahajer, Susan, Rohan, Jalal, me, Iraj, and Nazy. I wonder what happened to the days that we didn't know the Malakutis. Those days the people were all nice. No one was after anyone's wife or husband. Why did they come to Michigan? Why?

Yes, Azeez is sitting at the table and watching Badri next to Iraj. Then, no one knew that these two were cheating on their spouses. We all were happy that in a strange country we could have friends. Isn't it nice to have friends like Badri? Doesn't anyone wish they had a friend like her?

Here, the same night, all our children were there with us. I decided to take a picture of them. Left to right, first row: Negin, Marjon, Maseeh, Farzad, Partow, Fariba, Roozbeh. Second row: Nader, Lisa, Roshanak, and Pooneh. Third row: Roozbeh Barkhordari, Deeneh, Mojgan, Mary, Ramin, Rozan, and Roxana Panah. If we were sisters and brothers, obviously these kids would be cousins. To my shocking surprise, my children wanted me to look at everything this way when we were friends. They didn't realize that I had been destroyed emotionally and mentally. They didn't realize what had happened to me. I was the wife, and you were the children. You might be able to forget and forgive, but not me. Until I die, I wish the maximum level of unhappiness in the world for both of them, as long as they live.

This is from the night that I invited the group to my condo to talk about their involvement in connecting Badri and Iraj. Then, I realized that they were not even worth talking to. It was too late to tell them to cancel it. So I just entertained them.

My son, Maseeh

We are at a convention. They are Dr. Aryani, Louise, Masoodeh, Ramin, and me.

My daughter, Maryam

With Mary on the Florida Beach

As you see this group were always together. Before Malakuti's death I could have said that we were fortunate for that, but now I think that was unfortunate. Here, we are at Barkhordari's yard, across our house.
Left to right: Badri, Shushtari, Partow, Aghdass Shushtari, Naser, Susan, Iraj, me, and a few of their friends. All the ladies in the group were afraid of Badri being alone in bed. They were sure that she would take one of their husbands. So to make sure to not let that happen to them, they pushed Iraj who was partners with Azeez to go in bed with Badri so she would not feel the absence of Azeez. After all, what are good friends for?

Me, Susan, Rohan, Farzad, Jalal Panah, Iraj, and Naser

I had invited a belly dancer on Iraj's birthday. Actually, I should have left it to Badri to entertain Iraj as she was already doing so on Tuesdays, his day off. (I have talked about the day that I saw them together returning from their date.) Hushmand is in the picture.

Iraj really didn't know what to do with me. I was living my life taking care of him and my children, not interfering with his life. I was neither nagging nor talking to anyone. Look at this picture. I am happy and delighted to celebrate his birthday. But he cannot even smile. Left to right: Kashef, Rohan, Hassan, Iraj, Sally, happy me, Parvaneh, and Louise.

Look at this one. I invited Sara's parents to welcome them from Iran. Left to right: Iraj- the saddest person on Earth, Badri, Mr. Tofigh, Sara, Parvaneh, Susan, me, Mahmud, Roozbeh Barkhordari, and Roshanak Front row: Rahmat, Farzad, Maseeh, and Partow

We are celebrating Badri's birthday in Aghdass's house. Badri's family never did this for her. But Mr. Shushtari was nice enough to gather us together to have fun.

Left to right: Masoodeh, Minoo, me, Nayer, Badri, Louise, Sara, and Roozbeh Malakuti. This is when she was mourning for her lost husband.

difficulties with the builders. Some of them had to deal with courts and lawsuits, which interrupted the construction for a year or two.

At the beginning we didn't plan to build a large indoor pool. But Iraj would come up with new ideas every day. It got to a point that I gave up and let him go through it. At first it was the idea of building a swimming pool, next it was, "Why not an indoor pool?" And it went on and on like that. After the swimming pool came the whirlpool. If only any one of us was a great swimmer, or we have ever had the time to sit in the whirlpool there would be absolutely nothing wrong with that. But that was not the case. Okay, it might have been for our children. But they only used it when I invited their friends over. They never showed any interest to use it themselves.

At that time doctors and their offices were under a lot of pressure. The subject of HMO was spreading around, and doctor's offices were very slow, they didn't have many patients. During the nights that we all got together every one of the doctors would express their concerns about the future of the medicine in the United States. So I had all the rights to question him, and try to stop him from drowning himself under a heavy load of responsibilities. But every time that I tried to discuss to bring up the subject; he would answer me," Don't worry, I know what I am doing". I knew where he was going, and I knew that he was dragging us with him. But he wasn't willing to acknowledge that someone else might see the things that he was not able to see.

Even my children knew that he was under a lot of pressure, and they knew that he was going to the extreme. One day, when the house was almost half way done, and they had just dug out the area for the pool, Mary came home for lunch. I will never forget her face. While she was moving her head back and forth, and she held her books in her arms against her chest, she walked at the edge of the big hole, she turned to Iraj and with a big wonder in her voice she asked, "Do you know what you are putting yourself into? Do you really know?"

My Dear GOD:

It was so obvious that he had a big bite for his mouth. The problem was that he didn't want to admit that I knew more than he did. He wanted to believe that he was the one who knew everything. He accused me of being negative and unsupportive most of the time. But I couldn't be a show-off, and I just wanted to have a comfortable and normal life, and to him I was a backwards and a negative person. So because of this I had to mostly stay quiet.

Between Iraj and Mr. Conn we ended up with seven thousand square feet, tri-level, and a very contemporary house. We were hoping that this house might have enticed our children to return home after they graduated from college. They were welcome to stay in our house for as long as they wished whether married or unmarried. We had many dreams, and we would often talk about them.

Meanwhile he had entered into a partnership with three other doctors to build a community hospital. They were Dr. Mehrabian, Dr. Darian, and Dr. Farah, who were the three main partners at the hospital. Right after that he started talking about building their office. The office was shared with Dr. Mehrabian.

He was so wrapped up with numerous responsibilities. He was like a spider trapped in his own web. Someone who planned project after a project should have been able to provide a secure backup. Such person should not be hard on his children for spending insignificant amount of money. This person should not complain about the size of the lawnmower that his son had to be able to mow the lawn of our one and a half acre property. At the same time he didn't mind paying seven or nine hundred dollars to the interior decorator. The designer fee for choosing the wallpaper for a small guest bathroom would have cost us more than a large size lawn mower.

But after I watched my son struggling in that yard mowing the lawn with that little hand lawn mower, I couldn't take it any more, and I questioned him about his double standard behavior. He didn't like it, and again he accused me of being negative and destroying his spirit at the time that he needed it the most.

The difference between us was that I liked to spend money to bring comfort and happiness. And he wanted to spend money where it showed the most. Our first dispute was over spending excessive money on that little piece of the wallpaper, and ordering the most exotic and expensive furniture that was not that important or necessary. He knew that the logic of my argument was undeniable, but at the same time he was so wrapped up in the competition with other doctors. Nothing and nobody could have stopped him. One big mistake we made was that we had sold our first house on Helston Road. We had a choice to sell it to Neya, who needed a place to stay with her children every year. Not only it would have solved many of her problems, but also at that time they were able to pay for it, and her children could have had a safe and secure place. But unfortunately we thought of it after we had sold the house. We were lucky that the house was sold right before we wanted to move into our new house in Wabeek.

My Dear GOD:

Landscaping was the only part that remained unfinished. The landscapers were not easy to get along with. Iraj was assuming that just because they were bound by the contract he could take them to court, and clear out the whole thing. When he came home, he was so sorry for doing so. He told me, "There were many people in court against me whom I have never met before. They were all friends of the judge. They put me in the middle, and started attacking me with wrong words, so I preferred to leave the court, and let them win".

After living in the house for a few months, and not even having furnished it, we gave an open house party. And we invited all our friends, the so-called friends.

Private Lives

A Michigan Residence to Nurture Family Life

ROLLING LAWNS in Bloomfield Hills harbor a residence created to offer family life amid glorious views of a picturesque Michigan lake. The house was formulated to allow the various family members the freedom with which to enjoy their individual pursuits in privacy.

A two-level plan incorporates a series of bedrooms and elegant entertainment rooms on the main floor, and then devotes the lower level to informality and recreation. Two stairways, one off the foyer and one off the laundry, conveniently access the areas.

On the main level, a marble foyer handsomely introduces the focal point of the floor—a capacious great room with a beautiful high ceiling and wall of windows. Beyond lie the dining room, library, kitchen, and four bedrooms, including the master complex.

A gigantic indoor pool is the focus of the lower level. Glass doors join the pool to the lawns outside, while interior doorways tie the lighthearted area to a greenhouse, kitchen and bar area, and an octagonal family room that is similar in mood to the great room. A large game room adjoins the family room.

Throughout the house, large expanses of glass draw the eye to beautiful green lawns that carpet the gentle hills surrounding the house and tranquilly showcase the quiet lake beyond.

—$545,000

HANNETT, INC. REALTORS (John Hannett/DeChantel Alaimo) ● 2523 WEST MAPLE ● BIRMINGHAM, MICHIGAN 48009 ● (313) 646-6200; (313) 258-684(

As you see this ad was printed in the real estate magazine. The house was built to bring happiness to our children; unfortunately, it took away all our happiness instead. Actually this is the house that Iraj had built.

MY DEAR GOD :

That house that JACK BUILT was built for my children's happiness. Instead not only they did not had fun in that house,but it became the cause of their separation from their father's love,and their whole family all together.

Today I believe that Iraj had never loved anyone including himself. When you read his letters before his first affair,after his first affair,you will realize that,this person can not have no love in his heart for his family. Yet you see that,he had done so much damage to his children,to his wife,to himself in a way that if he did killed them all,at least it was less torture for them. Shame on you for destroying my children. Shame on you for being a worthless father who brought shame and embarrassment in his children's life. You thought your father was your embarrassment for you because he was only an alcoholic. Yet,you did something to answer his question from me one day.He asked me " SHAMCI why do you think your parents are this much against you marrying Iraj?" At that time I was so naive that I answered him," I really don't know. Probably they were expecting a prince to marry me." I now wish that he was alive to see for himself,what Iraj had done to destroy his children's home and happiness for a promiscuous worthless woman. Shame on you and million times more shame on you I helped my children to the best of my ability to put my humpty dumpty together again. Yet,there was no way to make them happy. One day Mojgan took me to lunch befor one of my trips to Iran. She looked at me and with tears in her eyes she told me " Mom I know that,I will die and I never get my wish for my parents to love each other again."
I held her hand and kissed her and I said," my dear Mojgan I tried and I did my best for eight years,if it didn't worked it was not my fault. Then,when I got home I cried for the lost of love and happiness that we had just a year befor Malakuti died. Many times I got mad at poor Malakuti who himself became Badri's victom and asked him in a hursh tone " why did you have to marry this no good woman who you knew yourself she was no good. you said many times yourself that,she was a crook and phony. Why, why did you have to marry her and this way make us her victom too."
Anyway,I was lucky in some ways,and her wedding was one of them. She was able to have Rute to help her and be with her at my absent. Then when I came back from my trip,they had duties for me to prepare the rehersal dinner for them,and I was glad to do it.

Mary's birthday

Pari and I are in my living room. Pari knew my problems, so she was trying to cheer me up. Look at my indoor plants. They had grown so much. Unfortunately, they were destroyed like the rest of us.

I am in a dress which I had made myself with a five-dollar fabric, standing in front of my expensive house which Iraj had built for our happiness.

With Mary in our living room when we were doing fine. Mary had come back home from the university to spend time with her parents.

Pari's house, California. My sad Maseeh is holding me in his arms thinking we might be able to survive one day.

Maseeh and Beth, his high-school sweetheart whom he loved a lot. After their break up, Maseeh broke into pieces. That was exactly the time that Dr. Malakuti got killed, and we all became emotionally servant to his family. Then, Roshanak who had always loved Maseeh found the right time to approach him. With the loss of her father, my son fell for her and the rest is history. I stood by my son and even held an engagement party for them.

Before we talk about the open house, I have to give you a tour to describe the house. In reality the house looked magnificent to those who loved modern and very contemporary design. Altogether it was a unique and special custom-built house. As we all know everything is relative. This house was big, and it looked magnificent only among the doctors who had similar lifestyles. And if you took one step farther, you would see that not only our house was not a big or a beautiful house, but also it was a very common and ordinary house. But among the people that we knew, this house looked big and beautiful.

The two big entrance doors, which were designed with heavy two feet clear glass at both sides, opened into a large foyer covered with beige and brown color marble called travertine. The foyer, the hallways, around the living room, dinning room and the kitchen were covered with one-foot square blocks of Italian travertine. The fireplace in the living room, including the entire wall was covered with three by one foot of the same travertine. The living room was octagonal shape, with a high ceiling of fifteen or sixteen feet.

All across the living room, dinning room, and the kitchen, there were wall-to-wall sliding glass doors and windows that made you feel like you were outdoors. The light in the living room came from two standing portable six feet high lamps two smoked glass shades. They sent the light upward to the ceiling, and at night they made the room very romantic, as if it was lit with candles. The rest of the house was furnished with the dimmer system.

My Dear GOD:

As you came in there was a guest closet on your right. Above the closet there was a fluorescence lamp hidden in the back with a purpose of lighting up a large hand-made bowl with colorful stones as big as a penny. Iraj brought it back with him from Iran. Those semi-precious stones added so much beauty to the room.

As you walked away from, you found a sliding door closet to your right leading to the Laundry Room. It was furnished with wall-to-wall cabinets. The carpets continued here from the kitchen. There was a wall cabinet for ironing board, and on the left you opened a door to the carport, on the right there was a closet for winter coats.

Right next to the sliding door on the right, there was a carpeted stairway leading to the lower level. Opposite the door to the pool room there was a wine cellar made of cedar wood. There was a bathroom in the laundry room. The entrance door from this room opened to the carport, and from carport to the garage. The two-car garage was heated, and it had wall-to-wall aluminum cabinets all the way around to keep my children organized in one way or another. There was a plan that after our children left home, we would enclose the carport with tall sliding glass doors, and turn it into a Florida room and enjoy the view of the lake and the beautiful scenery.

Our kitchen was right pass the laundry room. It was a very spacious and large kitchen. Because I always liked to cook and we would entertain on many occasions, Iraj

had made sure that I had everything I needed in the kitchen.

The same blocks of travertine were around the kitchen as well. Our appliances were by Kitchen-aid, Sub-Zero, and Corning. Even though my range was made by Corning, I didn't find it very accommodating for Iranian cooking. All my cabinets were wall to wall with sliding drawers and shelves. They all had the same beige color finish, just like my appliances.

There was five-foot square granite counter top in the middle of the kitchen. It had built-in toaster and bread warmer. And all the drawers were on rails.

I had two ovens: the big one was by Corning, and the other one was by Kitchen-aid. On the counter top next to the Corning cook top there was a pop-up section for a complete set of blender, mixer, and knife sharpener with all the necessary attachments. There was a cabinet to display and store all the attachments right underneath. It was really convenient, practical, and very beautiful. In one corner I had a Jen-Air grill with three convertible cook tops. One was for Bar-B-Q, one for frying meats and vegetables, and the other one for various cooking purposes. Underneath there was a cabinet for displaying all the equipment, and two jars to collect all the cooking oils and keep the kitchen area smokeless, and odorless. This was done by a special fan, which pulled the smoke in through the vents provided for pollution purposes.

My Dear GOD:

Iraj knew that I liked to have lots of lights around me, which kept me happy while I was cooking. So after consulting me he arranged to put as many lights in the kitchen as it was possible. Since it was done professionally, it made my performance immensely acceptable to me.

I told him once, "I am just like my mother. She likes lights around her to a point that she wished to have lights in her grave just to avoid darkness. And I am just like her. I do not like darkness at all". I know that must have been the reason behind the kitchen lighting.

The dinette's ceiling in the kitchen area was covered with six 150-volt recessed lamps which made the night look like a day. There were two twelve inch round smoked glass bulbs located on both walls overlooking the granite counter top. Each upper cabinet had an undercounter fluorescent strip lighting. It was phenomenal to cook in that kitchen. A long balcony stretched across the whole length of the kitchen all the way to the bedrooms. The balcony was looking out to the lake. From kitchen you walked into the dining room. There was a modern five-foot rectangular chandelier mounted over the dining table.

Across the dining room in the living room there was a fireplace surrounded with three-foot triangular travertine.

These were on your right when you entered to the foyer from the entrance door. On the left first there was a guest bathroom finished with travertine just like the rest of the house. Across that bathroom there was a space for displaying a very tall statue. It was finished with triangular travertine as well. And behind that there was a closet connected to our master bedroom.

There were two entrances to the bedroom area. One of the entrances took you to our bedroom by means of three steps. And the second one was the main entrance to our bedroom area. Another set of three steps up took you to our TV room.

Many years ago people in Iran used "KORSI" as a source of heat during the winter. "Korsi" wasn't simply a source of heat, but more so it was a source of family gathering. It contained a square table, the size of which varied upon the lifestyle and the wealth of the families, starting anywhere from two feet up to ten feet. Underneath "korsi" they would set up a small fire pit to burning charcoal. The table then was covered with either thick blankets or comforters. The covers would extend three or four feet on each side of the table. They would set up cushions all around the room, and especially around the korsi. It was a custom to sit on the floor, which was carpeted with Persian rugs. Everyone would extend their legs under the table. It was the most comfortable position anyone could be on cold winter days. Nothing can compare to the warm sensation of the mild heat while covering yourself with blankets reclining on those cushions around the korsi.

My Dear GOD:

This heating method served mostly the low-income families, and or those who loved that custom. Whenever you entered a korsi room in a house, you could have guessed their income just by the appearance of their furnishings.

The downside of this heater was that many poor families were not aware, or many times had no choice, that sleeping under that korsi with their heads under the blankets would cause slow suffocation of carbon monoxide produced by burning charcoal under the korsi. And for as long as I remember every year many poor families would lose their children to that heating system.

We never got the chance to have a korsi in our household since my father had to move from place to place. And many times we moved to areas with warmer climate. But we couldn't wait to sneak under a korsi and have the time of our lives whenever we were around those who had one. And for older kids korsi was the source of sneaking around to get involved with many unlawful things under there, if you know what I mean.

So I decided to set up a korsi in that TV room. I bought the wood for a short-legged table, and I made the table by myself. I made big cushions from the Persian rugs we brought from Iran. I got a small electric burner. And I attached a metal basket to the underside of the table, where I placed the burner. And I covered the table with large blankets. I wanted to first keep our big house warm, and I wanted to add warmer atmosphere to the cold contemporary design. But the most important of all I wanted to create a gathering room for my children.

It worked. Every year, before the real cold arrived, kids, and Maseeh in particular, would ask for korsi. I had so much fun observing them. They would be sitting under the korsi discussing the routine matters of their lives.

It was a spacious area, which lead to the all the bedrooms. We had a breakfast nook area, where we placed a small refrigerator to keep cold drinks and milk. Only the master bedroom door opened in the TV room area. The other three bedroom doors opened in a hallway behind separate from the korsi room.

My Dear GOD:

Our children each had their own shower or a bathtub in their bedrooms. They had a built-in desk and bookshelves, a big closet, their own telephone and stereo system. Come to think of it, what was the purpose of having that TV room equipped with a refrigerator? They did not need to come out of their private studio if they didn't want to.

Iraj blamed me for being unhappy with the house. But the main reason for my concerns was that when my children had way too much comfort, they actually had their own private houses within our house. I was afraid they would detach themselves from us more and more every day. And most of all they would never know the other side of the world, they wouldn't know of people trying to just meet the ends, or just plain surviving. That was my concern. And it did happen after all.

We weren't rich and famous, and I never wished to be. I have always wished to raise my three children to be proud of themselves. They were faced with fads and fashions of 1960s, along with the popularity of a hippy existence, including widespread drugs, and alcohol. Don't you think my dear GOD that I had the right to be concerned? Shouldn't I have been worried about the house, which made it possible for my children to distance themselves from us?

The funny thing was that Mary, who favored hippies, not only was unhappy to live in such a house, but she was ashamed and embarrassed to show her house to people she associated with. So it turned out to be a complete drawback for me to be raising teenagers in an environment of complete freedom and separation from their family.

Iraj was right. Because after all the running and caring for them day after day, I never saw them or their faces in the evenings when they were home. They spent most of their time talking on the phone with their friends. I couldn't see or hear what was going on behind the closed doors of my children's rooms, even though they were living with me, in my own house

Indeed Iraj was right, I was not happy. So, anyway, our master bedroom had two entrances: one that opened to the TV room and the second one that opened across the guest bathroom. We had a gas fireplace in our bedroom, clad in the same rectangular

Maseeh, me, Iraj, Mary, Mojgan and Kasra who were always at each other

Maseeh and me

Pari is sitting under the "korsi" in our TV room, looking at the gift I had bought for Iraj.

blocks of travertine. The fireplace was in an extended den-like area within our bedroom. One side of the wall was furnished with a wall-to-wall built-in desk, cabinets, and shelves for his home office.

We both were short, so we agreed to have our bed built-in with our comfort in mind. There was a huge linen cabinet two feet above the bed, atop which we displayed decorative objects. There were two beautiful wall sconces overhanging at each side of the bed.

My Dear GOD:

I will never forget about the night that I will tell about next. It was the night after I had given a big party. It was very late when everyone left. He would always help me with the clean up. He went to bed, and I joined in a little while. He was still up. Without any words he held me in his arms, and we kissed for a while. Then he kissed my hands, and said, "Good night". He turned around, covered his head and fell asleep. You remember, my dear GOD. I talked to you a lot that night. My side of bed was the one overlooking the lake. I turned around on my left side, as I always did, and attempted to go to sleep. But I couldn't fall asleep. I saw the reflection of the Moon in the lake. I observed the calmness and the beauty of the lake and the greenery around me. I perceived the beauty in my innocent husband. I perceived the beauty of my house, my children, my health, and their health. I became aware of the beauty of having happy and healthy family across the seas. All and all I had it all. I thanked you, and talked to you. I looked at the reflection of the moon in the water, and I cried and cried and cried. I cried because that night, I felt that I was floating above the clouds, and because I was the happiest person at that time. I thanked you, and thanked you again and again. I talked to you, and I said, "My dear GOD, you have given me the whole world. You have given me so much that I do not think that I deserve it. Please, my dear GOD, if you ever decided that I am not worthy of all these, and you decided to take something away from me, please take away my house, my furniture, take away our money, but please keep my husband, and my three children for me. I will still be happy. I will still thank you for your support and your forgiveness. I just cried and talked to you as I felt you were sleeping next to me. I know that you remember that night, and I know that you know that I will never forget that night".

Okay, when you came in from the entrance door to the foyer, on the left, before you got to the guest bathroom there was a carpeted stairway leading down to the pool and family room. On the left again there was a heavy iron and glass door to the pool area. The floor was covered with outdoor/indoor dark gray carpet. The depth of the pool at the high point was nine feet. There was a heavy diving board there. In the corner there was a room for the utilities and the pool supplies. The built-in vacuum for the entire house was also located there. There were side-to-side iron and glass doors around the poolroom. At the end of the room there was a glass green house. Outside, across the green house there was a covered area for the Bar-B-Q grill that my poor Maseeh cooked on during cold winter

nights to entertain his father's guests.

My Dear GOD:

There was a whirlpool at the corner of the pool. It was big enough to seat eight people.

We had five different furnaces in the house: one for pool area, one for family room, one for living room area, one for all the bedrooms, and a small one for the garage. But even then it was difficult to keep the house warm in Michigan. Actually the indoor pool was a better idea for Michigan weather.

Everyone else but me was enjoying these facilities. I was there to look over and take care of them. It seemed as if it was solely my responsibility. And even when I asked for a helping hand, they would either refuse to help, or they would do it all wrong. One would always see me walking around with various tools and supplies in my hands.

Coming down the stairway there was a large hallway on the right. On the right there was a huge opening for art display and decorative stuff, next to that there was a door to under-stair storage. The door next to storage opened to the family room. The entire lower level was covered with charcoal gray carpet. On the lakeside we had iron and glass sliding doors. There we had a full kitchen connecting the poolroom to the family room by means of two big sliding doors. On one side was a wet bar furnished with Sub-Zero refrigerator and freezer, built -in cabinets with glass doors, sinks and other stuff. On the other side were the sink and the counter top, and next to that there was a Jen-Air Bar-B-Q grill with the same attachments I had in the living room kitchen, plus Corning appliances. It was fantastic place for parties.

In front of the kitchen in the family room there was a wood fireplace. Maseeh was the one that had the most fun with that fireplace.

Maseeh was full of talents and splendid ideas. He had dug out a big fire pit in the grass in the yard. During the wintertime when the ground was covered with snow, he would light up big fire, and roast marshmallows with our neighbor's children, Parto and Farzad, and others. And so if you were sitting in front of the fireplace in the family room, you would see the fire outside in the middle of white snow. My god, it was a fantastic view. Many times I joined Maseeh and his friends, and they would share their marshmallows with me.

There was not a single time that I had seen Iraj observing his children's activities or joining them. He remained in bed, under a blanket reading the Wall Street Journal at all times. Not even once he had taken Maseeh to his baseball, soccer, wrestling, football, or any other activities he was involved in. He was sure that I was on top of all my duties, and that there was no need for him to even acknowledge his son's achievements. Now, if he wouldn’t participate in his son’s activities, you can only reason what he had done for his daughters.

My Dear GOD:

To tell you the truth, I never trusted anyone else ever with my duties. I knew that my children were my duty, and I had to be there for them at all times.

Okay, on the other side of the family room we had yet another bedroom. The area beneath the dining room was assigned for a pool or a billiard table. Next to the bedroom there was an opening for all its assembly. Then there was a door going to another utility room. From there you opened another door to a huge boat room. There was a heavy iron door to the back yard. I had made sure to build a workshop in that utility room to be able to keep the people in the house organized; alas it still didn't work. We never had a chance to do the things that we were supposed to do in that house. As I said before, this house was for show only and not for our comfort. None of us was a swimmer; neither did we care for boats. But we did not have the decency to admit it. And our children, who wanted to find a way to go around it, they couldn't. From the beginning the lake frontage was not ready for use. And it was too late when we were able to make it ready. My children were out of the house attending colleges.

There were two showers to serve the family room. They each had a big dressing room. Altogether we had eight bathrooms in the house: six full baths and two half baths, in addition to many other luxuries. This was the house, the house that "Jack built".

Many people thought that our master bathroom was done very tastefully. The walls, as well as the floors were covered with three-foot blocks of travertine, just like our fireplace. It was mirrored all around. We had extra heaters and lights. The design was not extremely elaborate; it looked very elegant, and it was very practical at the same time, with his and her separate sinks.

Iraj and I were so excited about building this house. So in effort to do it right, we had to perform extensive researches. Any little change to the original plan cost us a lot of money. We would still proceed with changes because we knew that we were building the home of our dreams. We studied many different houses, and we gathered many different ideas. Then we would ask our architect, Mr. Conn, to implement them on paper. We treated the dream of our house in the same manner we treated our love for one another, we were anticipating to live in that house forever.

At the end of the day Iraj and I would sit down to draw the type of wood that we were going to use in the poolroom. We chose the same kind of cut wood for the ceiling of the family room, which brought the same tone and continuity from the poolroom to the living part of the family room. We had lots of fun doing that. We would keep drawing over each other's plans, until we came up with a design that would suit both of us.

My Dear GOD:

Although we had hired a landscape contractor, we did much of the planting ourselves. We created a small island in the middle of our circle driveway in front of the entrance door to the foyer. It was a mixture of short trees, big rocks, and beautiful exotic plants and flowers, which made it look like a Japanese garden. It was indeed beautiful. Everyone else would plant small trees at their property lines, but Iraj wanted to build a wall. So he bought eight to ten feet tall trees, and asked Maseeh and I to plant those trees. Poor Maseeh and I carried those trees from place to place not even having the proper tools. We did that with the hope that we would live in the house forever.

One day Dr. Barkhordari, who became our neighbor later, was there. When he saw me working so hard, he teased me and said, "If you come and work for me, I will pay you much more than Iraj does". I believed that this house was ours, mine, my children's, and my husband's, forever. And I believed that we would have lots of happiness in it. If I wouldn't see it that way, I would never do what I had done. I put all of myself into my home, my children, my husband, and my family. Those were the only things in the world that mattered to me. And because Iraj was all for us, without a doubt, I was so certain that I had it made. So did Iraj, and so did our children.

My dear GOD, it is so funny that each time, and at each age we always think that what we live and witness at the moment is going to last forever. We won't allow ourselves to think that things could change at any given time. And that even those changes won't last forever either. And that basically nothing lasts forever. I wonder who made this law of marriage that states, "For all our lives till death do us apart". There is no bigger lie than this sentence. They only practice it in India. They bury the wife alive with her deceased husband.

From the beginning we, Iraj and I, had pinned these word in our minds, "Forever and ever". You are mine, and I am yours forever and ever. We didn't want it any other way. Without that belief I could have never stayed married, or devote myself to my family the way I did. I felt I was hundred percent theirs, and that feeling kept me going.

So that was our dream house, and we both, especially Iraj, were happy with the outcome. He wanted to make it big, and he did. He wanted to plant all-grown trees, and he did. He wanted to build an indoor pool, and he did. He wanted to become the example of a great husband, and he did. He wanted to show his friends that he could do better than them, he did. He wanted to become the topic of conversations among his friends, he did. He wanted to beat all other doctors he was competing with, he did. And most of all he wanted to prove to me that he loved me the most and he would do anything to make me happy, he did. So you see, my dear GOD, at that time we both believed that we had it made. The only thing we would have never imagined was that our happiness might not have lasted forever. And, yes, it didn't.

My Dear GOD:

Obviously after a few months of living in our new house we had decided to throw a house warming party. We invited all the doctors along with their wives, our so-called friends, to celebrate and share our happiness with them. By then everyone had heard about the house, and they had plenty of time to talk and gossip behind our backs. I had heard on many occasions their friendly criticism, which only proved their absolute jealousy. But so what? They were all competitors, and they were envious when one of them moved forward faster then they did, or if someone achieved more than they did. It was and is obvious to all of them that they couldn't see anyone else doing better than they did. Their jealousy was very destructive though. They were so anxious and eager to destroy that one succeeding doctor by damaging his reputation at his place of work. While they were attending each other's parties, and while they welcomed each other with words such as, "I love you, or I want you, or you are the best friend I have ever had", they still turned around and wished death for that person. I knew them all. They all recognized it as well, but still they went to each other's homes, and they would still pretend that they loved each other.

So having to know all this, I still gave a house warming party, and I was absolutely ready to be hearing their mind from most of them.

I am so amazed with the possibility of such a large group of doctors and their wives finding each other so far away from home, in one far away corner of the world, Michigan. And while they had so many similarities in thoughts, ideas, acts, and their characters, in general most of them, not all, were such a ... holes.

The things these people did to each other, or the things they would say behind each other's backs, or fights that went on between these so-called educated individuals, the scholars. All these deserve to be published in a book. I am sure and positive that it would make a great bestseller. It was surprising that I was the one who never took sides, or spread gossip, and yet each and every one of them brought their words of gossip to me. That was the reason that I arranged and established card game gatherings. I wanted all of us to be able to be together and have fun, and not talk too nonsense.

My Dear GOD:

I knew who was who from the beginning. I never referred or thought of any of them as "my friend". I only intended to associate with them from a distance; I never wished to get close with them.

It was such a revelation when they would talk to me about their best friends in a nasty, unpleasant, unkind, spiteful way, I knew better not to ever trust their friendship. What could I possibly expect from such people? I have always felt like an outsider among them with the acknowledgement of who they really were I was happy to realize that I wasn't one of them. So I have always tried to keep my distance, and just keep our so-called friendship on surface.

This group came from different parts of Iran. Each of them had different

backgrounds and upbringing; they had come together by the force of nature. And since they ended up being so far away from their country, their homes, their food and their language they were assuming that they would automatically have things in common with all other Iranians. But in reality they all were miles away from having anything in common. It was only the food and the language factor that had pulled them together, while intellectually they were millions of miles away from each other.

All other minority groups, but Iranians, that migrated to this country would form active communities in this country in effort to help each other away from home. Not even two of them could get along, or be of any help to one another. Not that there are no such an Iranian in general. I was just amazed that none of them were among this group of doctors in Michigan. As a matter of fact just recently it was officially announced on the evening news by Peter Jennings that among notable citizens of the United States "A young man named Tabatabai, who came to United States during Iranian revolution, had made it so big that in twenty years he owned a seven million dollar company". It was also said that he had donated millions and millions of computers to third world countries so that children had access to the world's technology and general sciences. There are so many people like him in Iran and abroad. I don't know why there weren't any among the Iranians in Michigan.

Not only this group was not able to come together and represent a useful community for Iranians away from home, but also in reality some of them wished death and destruction to their friends. I would like to talk about a few incidents that I had personally witnessed, on the other hand, I think I better not.

My Dear GOD:

We had invited fifty to sixty guests to that house warming party. Iraj gave a house tour to each group that came in. He explained the purpose behind having a house like that. Right in the middle of the tour all the lights went off. That was the first time that all the lights were on at the same time. We realized that circuit was not prepared to carry that heavy load. So we turned off the lights in certain parts of the house to continue the party. After that night we made all the necessary changes to the circuit.

The alarm system had a panic button on every level of the house. Right when Iraj was explaining to everybody what that button was for, Azeez Malakuti pressed on it. The police arrived before we had a chance to turn it off.

The pool, the hot tub, the central vacuum, the central intercom system, and the alarm system were all the subject of laughter that evening. There was a lot for our guests to talk about, especially with the alarm and the lights going off.

One can tell who is who and what is really bugging people by observing their faces, and their comments. That night some of them talked with both their eyes, and faces. Some of them whispered mischievously, and others spoke out loud questioning me.

The funny thing was that this house was not that big of a deal in comparison to other big houses. The only strange thing about it was the fact that it was mine. And Iraj made sure to explain to everyone of them that he had built every part of it to Shamci's satisfaction. Not in exactly in these words, but when he said, “We used these large double sinks to make the Iranian cooking and the washing of the big pots easier”, that alone proved to them that Iraj had taken my comfort into consideration. And many other things like that.

My Dear GOD:

When we reached the kitchen, and some ladies started opening the large wall- to-wall cabinets, and they pulled out the sliding drawers to see my white corning dishes there, they all looked at each other. Finally one of them said in a very loud voice, “Shamci, was there anything else in the market that you didn't buy?” I laughed and answered, “In fact there was much more, but I ran out of room”. I thought I had to answer her in her own language.

Although due to the dispute over the guest bathroom wallpaper we did not order new furniture, still they thought I had spent a lot for my comfort. The subject of Iranian bidets in our bathrooms was my favorite.

Although I had explained to them that there was a three or four foot hose, and it could be connected to the water pipe at one end, while the other end would be hanging from a hook on the wall, they still didn't do it.

Then Iraj decided to solve that problem by asking Kamal, his brother-in-law, to bring eight of those stainless steel hoses from Iran to install them here. That idea didn't work as well. Their excuse was that the diameter of the hose does not fit the diameter of the pipe. Well, the story starts here. Kamal blamed me for bugging him to bring those heavy metals from Iran, and that he had to carry them from airport to airport, and we were still not able to use them. Not only that, but he said, “First of all I had spent a lot of money. Second, I had to break my shoulders carrying the hoses here and there. And third, you are not using them after all”. He was telling this to everyone, asking for their sympathy.

Obviously those who were jealous of me were then hurt even more, since they realized that I have been getting attention from everyone, including Iraj’s brother-in-law.

Our house warming party made everyone aware of my comfortable life and happiness. My dinner table that night was very colorful. The food was delicious as always. That was what everyone was mumbling about while eating. Some of them were so excited with my food that they said, “We haven’t had anything to eat since last night so that we can eat as much as we want”. And they were not joking, because they refilled their plates more than twice. After all they all agreed that I was the best in everything I did.

My Dear GOD:

You see my dear GOD, they were right. I did my best in anything I put my mind to. I did well when I cooked. I did well when I sewed. I did well when I knitted. I did well when I crocheted. I did well as a hairdresser. I was a great mother. And I was good when it came to loving and caring for my husband and my family. I knew my own abilities, and I was aware of all my weaknesses. I didn't hesitate to research or get help when and if I needed improvement. I knew who I was, and what I was doing. As long as I stayed on top of all my duties, and Iraj showed his appreciation, I was happy to continue my life that way. I was never seeking other people's approval. And I was never discouraged by other peoples' disapproval. Like in ZOROASTRIAN religion, I just wanted to think right, say right, and act right. The rest is all nonsense. Don't take me wrong, please. I am not trying to act conceded. I just try to recognize my values and act accordingly.

Anyway that night went so well. I heard all their teasing, and I joined them with my own teasing. We cleaned up the place after they left, and we went to bed. He talked about some doctor's comments that proved their jealousy. It has always amazed me how similar our judgments about each one of these friends were. Although he was the one who went through years of Medical School with a few of them, and he knew more about their family life than I did, I was able to recognize their true characters behind the masks they put on. I have always believed that we cannot change a person. So it's better to try to find the good in them and ignore all that is bad in order to live a comfortable life.

I didn't want to make others behavior my problem. It was their problem, and they should have been bothered by it. Iraj felt the same way; only he recognized their devilish minds more than I did. His accurate judgment was quite shocking in many instances.

From the moment that I arrived in St. Louis, Missouri in June of 1959, I have met many of the doctors who were working with him, or he was acquainted with from Iran. Being away from Iran, the country that I was so adapted to, it felt like being reborn. I had to rediscover myself in a new country, among new people, and new surroundings. Who was I? Shamci Rafani. Who was she? She was the wife of Dr. Iraj Rafani. I was only identified as Mrs. Shamci Rafani, and no longer Shamci Gharavi. Nothing was familiar to me except Iraj.

When you are born, everything around you is new, and you will easily pick up things that surround you. But being reborn after you were past twenty was not easy. You have to disconnect yourself from whatever you have seen, or learned during those years, and then connect yourself with the new things, new people, and your new surroundings.

My Dear GOD:

At DePaul Hospital in St. Louis, Missouri he knew twelve bachelor doctors. They were all residents. They were all Iranian young doctors away from their homes, parents, and their country. Some were at the same hospital with Iraj, and some were working at other hospitals.

While all other doctors were living in one room, or they were sharing a room with another doctor, Iraj had rented a full unit for us. We all were feeling homesick. Every single night after work they came to our apartment to visit and talk about home. I was so happy to see them, and talk to them about familiar subject, IRAN.

Dr. Hotan was a young doctor whom Iraj knew from Iran. He was from Esfehan Iran. His family was among rich people. He was a young activist, who had a drug addiction. Everyone efforts of trying to help him to give up the addiction were in vain. Iraj, even more than anyone else, tried to help him. He had the advantage of being a doctor, and he could get his drugs easily, and sometimes for free.

Besides a few times that he was drunk, and he tried to make a pass at me, he did something very funny in one way and very embarrassing in another way. There was a nurse at his hospital that was after him to marry her. He had finally promised her to marry her after she pressured him for a while. She made her parents and her friends believe that she was getting married to doctor Hootan after all. They agreed on the wedding day, and she sent out invitations to everyone. When everyone was at the church, and they were ready to start the ceremony, the groom didn't show up. No matter how long they waited for him, there was no sight of him. He went into hiding, and soon enough he became the favorite object of ridicule among the group of twelve doctors. That was the funniest and the same time the most embarrassing incident. Hotan eventually returned to Esphehan his hometown in Iran. We heard later that his father was trying to help him snap out of his addiction. But while he was under full watch and treatment, he threw himself out from a high-rise building. His death brought sorrow to all who knew him.

I have never heard from any of those twelve doctors who used to come to our house every night for a year. I just remember the names of few of them: Dr. Kazemi, Dr. Kaboli, Dr. Sarram, and Dr. Anooshfar. I don't remember the names of the rest.

My Dear GOD:

There were many doctors that I met and socialized with once in a while. And then we would never see them again. And there were many of them that we continued friendship with forever. Unfortunately, the ones that we continued friendship with were the ones that we should have abandoned years ago. Only if at that time we knew how far they would go to hurt and destroy us. But no, no my dear God, never, we were not capable of knowing what the future held for us. We were supposed to face things as they came our way, without being aware of the outcome. And most of all we had to trust you in handling our lives, my dear GOD, the way you do it. It seems you know what is best for us, so you will bring upon us what we should go through. Then later we will recognize what was the reason that you brought upon us what you thought was the best.

As I said before we were very susceptible to get to know anybody who was from Iran.

As the case is for everyone, we never knew anything about them, except that we knew they spoke Farsi, and they cooked Iranian food. That was it. Then after the first or second meeting we would start seeing certain trends of their characters. Right or wrong, we were able to tell a thing or two about that person. Although we have learned to follow our intuition, we still made mistakes in our judgments. Whoever knew about Jeffrey Duhmer, Ted Bundy?

My Dear GOD:

So we got to know many Iranian whom we thought we could socialize with. We either met them at parties, or they happened to be friends of a friend. Our gatherings were usually divided into few groups. One was the group of his co-workers from the hospital. That was an annual party, and it was very formal. Except those who were friends, the rest were just Hi and Bye.

The second group was a group from the second hospital, which was owned and established by three Iranian doctors, Dr Edward Mehrabian, Dr. Jalil Farah, and Dr. Barkhordarian, also known as Dr Darian. Dr. Mehrabian and Shafiza his wife, and Dr. Darian and his wife were Iranian Armenians. And Dr. Farah was Iranian with his wife Elizabeth, who was American. These doctors were older than Iraj, and after he joined the staff of that hospital, we got to see them more than once a year. Besides going to each other's houses, some nights we would go out to dinner, just the four couples. Although these annual parties were not as exciting for me, they were completely harmless. We just went out, ate and chatted a little, and that was it. We then went home.

Then it was a group of Iranian doctors that got bigger and bigger as the time passed. This group later got divided into two separate groups. One was a group of Blot players, and the other group only met once or twice a year. Even with the group of Blot players, whom we played cards with once or twice a week, we did not establish too personal friendship. We would just play cards in the evenings as couples, and have dinner together.

I remember that at some of the parties we wouldn't see or even say hello to some of the guests until we left the party. Although I gave many parties myself, I remember that I hated attending those parties. At least men had something to talk about. It was the hospital, the patients or anything related to that matter. But ladies did not have anything to talk about. They were always in groups. One was friends with the other one day, and they had something to talk about others: who bought more clothes than others, or who had a fight with her husband, or whose husband spent more money on his wife, and other things like this. On many occasions they brought the issues they had with each other to those parties. The things that they were fighting about were so nasty and bad. You would not witness them even at parties in Hollywood. In one of those fights I had witnessed a scene that brought shame to all Iranian women. One of the doctor's wives, I don't think it would be right to mention her name here, was standing by the front door. While she was telling other ladies the reason of her fight with the yet another wife of a doctor, she realized that her friend was entering the building. She removed her high heel shoe, and she went toward her friend with the shoe in her hand saying, "Now you tell your husband to give me a finger from his car when I was driving my children to school. I am going to show you now." Thanks God there was enough people around them, to be able to stop her. Otherwise the party would have turned into a fighting ring that night. It would have been a very unique boxing match, where the contestants were all Iranian doctors' wives. But this was only one of the scenes. I would have to dedicate a whole book to all the scandals if I decided to tell about them all. And astonishingly you would see those two ladies together in the next party laughing and having great time.

My Dear GOD:

I usually enjoyed attending parties outside that circle. I would always find someone I could talk to, and I would leave the party without feeling like I had wasted my time.

Mary was only two weeks old when we first moved to Michigan. I met Dr. and Tolou Avaregan at an Iranian Norooz party. Dr. Anooshfar and Dr. Rabbani came to our house to ask us to accompany them to a party. I didn't have anybody to leave Mary with, so I didn't want to go. I knew this much that I wasn't supposed to take a baby to a party like that. But they insisted that we would not even go inside. They were just curious to see who was there. There were many doctors at that party, which was held in Flint Michigan. But I only met Tolou and her husband, Dr. Varjavandi and his wife Manijeh, and Dr. Moghtassed and his wife Khadijeh. We exchanged telephone numbers with Tolou, and she asked us to get in touch with her.

Tolou and Manijeh were both active Baha'is. Active means to be holding classes to teach Baha'i faith, it also means following all the Baha'i rules and regulations, as well as introducing the Baha'i faith to the rest of the world. After that visit we started socializing, and I had created a good relationship with Tolou until the time that we moved away from Michigan. They had two children, their son Ameen, and their daughter Naheed. They were very nice people, and they were much respected among friends. Their son Ameen had a rare liver disease that kept Tolou worried at all times. I would often see her crying, and worrying about losing him. But years went by, and Ameen got married and had a child. Naheed become a teacher and moved away from Michigan.

As a hobby Dr. Avaregan used to play violin. For some time he played with Detroit symphony orchestra. Tolou was involved with fund raising for the orchestra. Most of the time I would either accompany her to fund raisings, or to orchestra performances.

My Dear GOD:

Tolou was into arts and she also painted herself. She had donated many of her paintings to the symphony, and she had many of them in her house.

Sadly, right before we left Michigan, Dr. Avaregan lost his hearing, and he had to quit the orchestra. Tolou was one of the ladies whom I was interested to spend time with. She always had something to offer. After I left Michigan, I didn't hear from them.

Then through mutual friends, we met Dr. Minuie with his American wife Barbara. He was a psychiatrist. They had three girls and a boy. The oldest daughter, Maryan, became a doctor. The other three did not do well after their parents got divorced. Years later Dr. Minuie went to Iran for a visit. He had a massive heart attack in Iran, where he passed away. As he always wished, they buried him in Tehran near his parents. After I left Michigan, I never heard from them.

Day after day the number of Iranians whom we met and socialized with was increasing.

There were also doctors Mafee. They had four girls, and they lived in Annarbor Michigan. They were very nice people, and we used to get together at least once a year.

Then we met Dr. Jalal and Elizabeth Farah. Dr. Farah was a radiologist at Beaumont Hospital. I remember inviting them to my house once. They called to cancel the party that day. And their excuse was that they were expecting a guest from Iran. I insisted that it was okay to bring their guest along. They finally gave in. When they arrived that evening, it was Dr. Farah, his wife Elizabeth, and another lady, who was his brother's wife. Her name was Pari Farah.

As soon as they came in, I realized that I have met that lady before. I went in the kitchen, but I kept looking back trying to figure out where I had seen her. All of a sudden I remembered that we used to attend the same high school in Tehran. As soon as I turned around to tell her that we were together at Assadi high school, she came after me in the kitchen to tell me the same thing. Again we hugged each other and started talking about things that we each remembered from high school. It turned out to be a very pleasant evening. At that time Dr. Farah and Elizabeth had two children: a boy, named Micheal, and a girl, named Susan.

Pari was married to Mr. Mohandess Farah, who was the older brother of Dr. Farah. She got married right after she graduated from ninth grade. I think her husband was an architect. They had three children: two boys and a girl Nazaneen.

Pari and her family were working on moving to the USA. When they moved here they first settled in California. Her husband had his business both in Iran and in California. He used to travel back and forth. At that time Pari was very homesick, and she was making herself very close to me. She was having difficulty getting along with her sister-in-law, Elizabeth.

My Dear GOD:

Unfortunately, she lost her husband few years after that. While he was in Iran, he died of a heart attack in a city out of Tehran. The dispute between Pari and Dr. Farah's family got worse after her husband's death.

We went to visit her during one of our visits to California. We spent a nice day together. She also invited us to her house for dinner.

Nazaneen had twins first, and then later she had one more baby. We talked on the phone, and wrote to each other once in a while. Then we just stopped communicating for good.

On the other hand Dr. Farah and his wife Elizabeth were still doing fine. We contacted each other at least once a year, during the Christmas time. They were very nice people, and a very reputable family.

I was invited to the wedding of their oldest son Michael, who became a doctor. He specialized in radiology just like his father. And he started working at the same hospital where his father was a chief of the department of radiology, at Beaumont hospital. They had two children while I was there.

I was invited to their daughter's wedding as well. Susan was a nice young girl, and she was happy with her husband. They did not have any children, but she was on the waiting list to adopt a child.

Their youngest son Kamran (Kim) moved to Washington after he graduated from college.

My Dear GOD:

Dr. Farah was the second owner in partnership with the other two doctors at the Community Medical Center.

The third partner was Dr. Darian. His wife was a dentist, who was a stay-home mother. They had two children, a boy and a girl. They both became doctors. And soon after their graduation they got married and started families. We would keep in touch with them once a year as well. They were Iranian Armenians who treated the Armenian culture very seriously. They were very family oriented with close bounds.

Another doctor who graduated with Iraj from Tehran Medical School, besides Dr. Mohammad Rabbani, was Dr. Naser Barkhordari. I got to know him in Detroit among other friends. At that time neither he, nor Dr. Rabbani were married. After a few years of dating all American girls, he decided to go to Iran and marry a girl, whose parents, better yet his older sister, Aghdass Soltanpoor, had introduced to him. They told him all about the girl and her family in a letter, and they enclosed her picture. I am sure that he found that a subject to follow.

He went to Iran for two weeks. He saw the girl. After one week they got married, and soon he returned to Michigan. His wife, Susan Froozan, who had finished her high school

in London, England, was supposed to join him in a few months.

Susan's father, Mr. Mansoor Froozan, was working for an Iranian oil company, while Shah was in power.

Mr. and Mrs. Froozan had two boys and one girl. I don't know about the two boys, but I know that they had sent Susan to a catholic boarding school since the first grade. I don't know of the reason that they had to separate their child from her home and send her to a boarding school far away from their own country, unless it was for the sake of prestige within high-class society. Usually in Iran people are very family oriented, and they like to have their children under their own wings.

They raised her in a catholic school, and they visited her once or twice a year. She returned to Iran after graduating from high school. It was soon after that they arranged her marriage to Dr. Naser Barkhordari, a radiologist residing in Michigan. Susan eventually joined Naser in U.S. When she first arrived all by herself, she was not able to get in touch with Naser. So she stayed all alone at a hotel in Chicago that night. And Iraj always found an excuse to tease her, "If Susan was able to find Naser the very first night, their son Parto would have been born in nine months and a day". Obviously she ended up finding him the next day. But this was the topic of Iraj's jokes at our gatherings.

My Dear GOD:

I had met Mrs. Froozan for the first time when we were all going to a brunch. She was there to visit Susan when her son Parto was born. At that time I had two children, Mary and Maseeh. She seemed very nice, and she was very pretty. She had married her cousin Mansoor Froozan. Years later they decided to move to America. That was near the Shah's fall. They knew they couldn't get along with the upcoming regime. As I heard they bought an apartment in Washington, and they didn't even look back. Mrs. Froozan had her mother with her, who was the aunt of Mansoor Froozan. She was a very wise and respectful lady. I liked her a lot. I also enjoyed the presence of Mr. and Mrs. Froozan at our gatherings. It was very enjoyable for me to talk to them. I have never heard from them since I left Michigan. Only recently I heard from a friend in Michigan that their older son had committed suicide. As I had heard, he was a doctor, a scholar, and he was married, but had no children. The painful news had made me very sad and sorry. I wished I could send my condolences to them at times like that. I never found the reason why, or what the problem was that in almost thirty years that we were in Michigan, Susan's brothers, especially the older one, never came to visit her. And mind you, he was living in the U.S.A. This seemed very strange to me, as well as to many other friends.

Susan and Naser had three sons: Parto, Farzad, and Roozbeh. Naser was attending the Tehran Medical School at the same time with Iraj. Later on they ended up buying the property on our right. Although we socialized and partied together frequently, still I never thought of them as friends.

I remember one day I got into a car accident right at the corner of our street. I was returning home after taking my children to school. I was wondering on the side of the road while waiting for the police to arrive. I saw Dr. Barkhordari driving right pass by me. He even did not bother to stop. I could not believe that a friend could have done that. So I never felt like I was among friends. And in reality, they were very competitive with Iraj. When one of them would do something, the other ones immediately wanted to do more and better. They were one of the principal members of the Blot game club. Susan and I once decided to take a Bridge class at a high school near our house. And to our surprise, our husbands joined us. All four of us took the class together, but only Susan and I made it to the very end.

We had actually joined a group of bridge players in Cobo Hall in Detroit. We didn't even know that we were playing duplicate bridge. Had we known, we would be very intimidated. But our team became number one in that competition. We couldn't believe it even after seeing our names on the board. How was it possible that we became first among five hundred players? We though they made a mistake. We had never played duplicate before. It was only after we had received our trophy, that we realized we were not dreaming. It was true; Susan and I were number one in our bidding.

My Dear GOD:

Susan's parents were very good bridge players, and they had always encouraged me to go after it. I thank them for that, and I will always remember them as a nice couple.

Dr. Mohammad Rabbani also graduated from Tehran Medical School at the same time with Iraj. He was one of the three doctors who were sharing the house with Dr. Zadeh, when we first moved to Michigan. After dating American girls, he also married an Iranian girl that his parents had selected for him. Her name was Nayer Moghadass. She was in ninth grade at that time. Dr. Rabbani, just like Barkhordari, went to Iran with a letter of introduction and a picture of Nayer in his hand.

Nayer told me a funny story one day. She said, "I told my parents that I will never marry this man. He is married, and he has his child in his arms. I wonder how he dared to send a picture like that". Then later they found out that the baby in his arms was his friend's baby. Dr. Rabbani had sent one of his pictures with my Mary in his arms to his future wife. I thought it was funny.

Since Dr. Rabbani was older than Nayer, he took the responsibility of her father. He sent her to a high school to graduate. Meanwhile she got pregnant and had her first child Roya. They had returned to Iran at the same time we did. We would see each other in Iran as well. His parents took care of his wife and their baby while he served in the army. And while everything was taken care of for her, she went back to school and finished the high school. Then she got pregnant with the second child. When we returned to America after Iraj's messy encounters in Iran, they returned to America also. We rented a house in summerset neighborhood. And again they rented a house in summerset neighborhood. It seemed like they followed us around all the way through. And at the end they bought a property on our left side, and become our neighbors once and for all.

I could not believe how competitive these people were. Until one day the story of our lives came to an end.

Dr. Mohammad Rabbani was in pathology. I don't know if they ever told Nayer or her parents that he had tuberculosis. After a few months that Nayer was in Michigan he underwent a big surgery. I am not sure if Nayer knew what to expect, and what was going to become of her.

I went to visit him at the hospital after the surgery. I couldn't believe my eyes; I didn't think he would pull through. He had lost so much weight, and he could hardly breathe. I told Iraj when I came home, "I don't think he is going to make it". And I cried for poor Nayer.

My Dear GOD:

But Dr. Rabbani did survive, and he went back to Iran to serve in the army. They had the most beautiful children, Roya and Rameen. Roya became an optometrist. Rameen also became a doctor. Nayer had another son, while Roya and Rameen were in college. Rameen and his baby brother were seventeen years apart. Those who didn't know them thought that he was Rameen's son, which made Dr. Rabbani the grandfather.

Dr. Rabbani was great person in general. He was a great husband and a great father. Although I was not one of his favorites, I should speak the truth. Besides being a good husband, he provided Nayer with the utmost fatherly care. He took over all her responsibilities after he sent her to school in America. Her education became his primary concern. He made sure that Nayer concentrated on her studies at home, or at the library. He would first drop off Nayer at school, next he drove the kids to their school, and then he went to work. And he followed the same route on the way back home. His children were attending the Detroit Country Day School. They were among the advanced students. Rameen's classes would end earlier than Roya's. So he had arranged for him to stay in the school library to finish his homework. He cooked, he did the dishes and laundry, and he fed the baby, and did most of the shopping, while Nayer was at school. He actually raised Nayer just like one of his children.

Rabbanis' were from Hamedan. I got to know four brothers, and one sister of theirs. Their father was an Islamic Mullah. One of his brothers, Mehdi Rabbani, married an Iranian girl, and moved to Canada.

The youngest brother, Hadi, got his PHD. He went to Iran and married Nayer's sister, Gitty. She was a dentist. As far as I remember they had two children.

Ali Rabbani on the other hand, after he got his degree in pediatrics, went to Iran and married a girl from a nice family. He came back to America, and brought his bride here

as well. I heard from mutual friends that in less than a year he divorced her, and sent her back to Iran. They said she was emotionally destroyed.

All this happened while we were in Iran. Once Iraj arranged a dance party in our house. This was before Ali married that girl. He was there with a girlfriend. You can only imagine, my dear GOD, what it's like when a person who does not have a sense of rhythm throws a dance party. And to top it off he had invited people who didn't know how to dance. Don't you find this is very odd? They wanted to act civilized, they wanted to be line Americans, and they wanted to look fashionable among friends. Oh well, Ali was a bachelor for a few years after that. He had a reputation of having flings with some of the doctors' wives.

My Dear God:

Ali married a lady-doctor later on. Her name was Dokhie. Dr. Azeez Malakuti introduced them to one another. She was a very beautiful, well mannered, and a prestigious girl. We saw each other at parties, and we visited each other at least once a year. Her mother, who was separated from her father, was living with her. She was a very nice as well. They had two children, and it seemed like they had a happy home.

Rabbani had a younger sister, Ozra. Her brothers provided her with a full support, while keeping a watchful eye on her. She was wed to a young doctor, Salehi, by arrangement right after she graduated from college. I still recall the day of her wedding. Sury, who was very close friends with them, did her make-up, and helped get dressed her for the occasion.

We had a very casual friendship. We made sure to see each other once a year. Dokhie was a nice girl. They had two sons, and they lived a comfortable life with their children. Okay, my dear GOD, some might wonder why I am writing about all these families. I have to talk about them, because some of these characters were the main contributors to the cause of our separation. I am not trying to justify Iraj's faulty character, but their persuasion and selfishness were a big factor as well. And after you get to know them one by one, you will start recognizing who's who when I refer to them.

We were introduced to Dr. and Sury Ghaemi at one of the dinner parties. Suri had just arrived from Iran that night. She was very pregnant. Dr. Ghaemi was friends with Dr. Mohammad Rabbani from Tehran University. He had married Sury in Tehran. They came to socialize with Iranians in America.

We talked for a little while that night. My heart felt for her. She reminded me of myself being away from home and pregnant for the first time. We exchanged telephone numbers. I was willingly wanted to help her in any way I could.

She was much younger than me. She was nice, beautiful, and very talented girl.

My Dear God:

Mojgan was almost three at that time. She enjoyed playing with Suri's son Afsheen, who was a year old. Although it was expected that was friends with Nayer, it seemed that she was more interested in my friendship. We grew closer and closer, we saw each other two or three times a week.

I remember once Suri called me crying, shortly after she had Afsheen. She was experiencing a lot of pain while breastfeeding. And at the same time she came down with a bad feverish cold. I put everything at home aside, and I rushed to her rescue. I made her soup, I took care of the baby, and I even cried with her a little. And I left when her husband got home. We became very close. My children liked her a lot. We visited them, and we went picnicking together on many occasions. We had so much fun together when my sister Azar was visiting. Just like me Sury had many hobbies. She drew, she painted, she made designer-like clothing. And all in all she was capable of doing anything and everything.

One day Azar and Sury decided to have a make over and act like they were movie stars. They worked on each other's hair and make-up. They dressed in a very unique fashion. I took pictures of them that day to show them that they could have been stars.

Sury would always talk to Azar and me about her family. There seemed to be many hidden issues with her upbringing.

One night I had a party in my house. Sury had an excellent figure. She made everyone's eyes just freeze on herself that night. She made her own dress with matching shoes and a purse. She looked so beautiful that all the ladies hated her, and all the men loved to look at her.

Iraj made a comment after they left, "Did you notice that she wasn't wearing any underwear?" To tell you the truth, my dear GOD, I wasn't paying much attention, especially to Sury's underwear.

Sury would tell me that some of the married doctors tried calling her at home and to speak to her husband, while they knew that he was at work. She said she was positive that they wished to engage themselves into an affair with her. But she would always talk about Ali, who was at the time among the bachelor doctors. And every time she brought his love and attention for her, I would question, and at times even blamed her for her willingness. Their flirtatious affair got to a point that he asked her to divorce her husband and marry him. I tried to convince her that he would not keep his promises, and that he would not marry you. Unfortunately she never took my advice.

My Dear God:

At that time she was very close with Naheed.

Naheed was single then, and nobody was concerned with her personal life and affairs. While in Suri's case, she was married with a child, it was considered to be

adultery. Azar and I wanted to talk to her, and try to help her see that it was her who allowed the doctors to call her behind her husband's back. But we decided that we had no place getting involved with such delicate matters. But then a big fight broke out between Suri and Naheed. And they started giving out each other's secrets. They were both my friends, and they both sleeked my opinion. They both got a fare share of my criticism for their actions. But I couldn't believe everything I was hearing about them. With this Naheed was able to ruin Sury's reputation among all the mutual friends. And since all the ladies were threatened by Sury's beauty, they decided to exclude her from all the parties and gatherings.

Suri then befriended the younger group. There were many of them, and their parties were getting bigger. Although they were supposed to be friends, still all the ladies were afraid of her beauty. I would hear on many occasions from here and there of a big fight between those doctor's wives around a dinner table. It was very embarrassing to hear about it. One of the wives kicked Suri out of her house with screams, and the worst swearing. And she warned Suri, "If I ever see you near my house or my husband, not only I will kill you, but I will kill all of you". And then she asked other Iranian ladies to boycott her visitations. She warned them of the possibility of a relationship between each and every one of their husbands with Sury.

I usually did not listen to other people's gossip, unless they had a solid proof. I believed that Sury was innocent and naive. I always thought that she needed attention. And I even thought that she made up stories of all those pursuits.

Then one afternoon Suri called me desperately asking if I could watch Afsheen. I didn't mind it at all, especially knowing that Mojgan would be happy to play with Afsheen. I asked her to bring Afsheen over. I don't recall what she was planning to do. I just accepted her request with open arms.

I think her husband was getting suspicious. He came home, off his regular schedule, to find out that she wasn't home. He called me to ask if she was with me. I told him, "Afsheen is with me, and Suri had a doctor's appointment". He came to our house to get Afsheen.

My Dear God:

About an hour later Suri came to pick-up Afsheen. I saw her going out of her mind when she realized that her husband had already picked Afsheen up. It looked like she was not expecting that.

Their separation was the topic of everyone's conversation in town. And even after all those happenings her husband was not the one who wanted to break it. Suri was the one that did not want to continue her life with him.

I realized that day that she had been using me to assist her with her affairs. And I despised myself for that. But what could I have done to stop her? She needed my help as a

friend and I gave it to her. To this day I don't know where she went or what happened that day. But I saw her less and less. I heard that she got a job at Summerset Mall as a model to represent designer clothing and make-up.

I remember one Saturday she called me asking if she could see me again. Iraj happened to be in the kitchen also, and he was listening to our conversation. She was begging me to let her come to my house again. I was very upset with her, especially after I had realized that she's been taking advantage of our friendship and me. I had mentioned it to her many times that all the doctor's wives couldn't stand her just because of her talents and her beauty. But she would never listen to me. Every one of those so-called friends wanted to destroy her, they wanted to get rid of her.

Anyway I never thought that there was anything between them. Only GOD and those two would know.

After that Suri went from one job to the other. And she finally got a degree in cosmetology. She was good in everything. I am sure that she was good in that field also.

There were many things said behind her back, and there were many boys at her service. At the end she married a rich young Arab man. And when years later she opened a couple of jewelry stores, all those same Iranians were willing to be her friends again.

My Dear God:

I went to see her during my crisis. I was very happy for her. She had another child, and she seemed very happy. Her ex never left their side, and he was still providing for Suri and Afsheen with his attention. Afsheen became a doctor, and had a good relationship with his father.

After my divorce once she came to the restaurant with her old mother, who was here for a visit. I didn't want to talk about my life to anyone, so we just had a friendly visit. I never heard from her afterwards.

Naheed, on the other hand, was a strange girl. She was a physiotherapist. Before she started practicing in Michigan, she wanted to get married so badly. She was interested in any and every bachelor doctor around. She always wanted me to set her up with one of them. Then once she went on a trip to Washington, where she met a tall, handsome, young man. He came from a very good family in Iran. He really deserved marrying royalties, like Princess Diana. We found out that besides being good looking, he was working at the embassy of Iran in Washington. Her uncle arranged a big party for her in his house. I don't remember if this was her first or second marriage. Everyone bought her expensive gifts, with hopes for their everlasting marriage. Alas there were barely six months into it when we heard they were getting divorced. We have never learned why he married her to begin with. Some said he needed a green card, while others thought he was crazy. But we were all in unanimous agreement that he deserved much better. Naheed, herself, whispered to me at her wedding, "Shamci, look at him. I told you I would find a husband

there. Do you believe what you see? I cannot believe it myself. It is a miracle". I am sure everyone else saw it as a miracle.

She returned to Michigan, where she started to work at the hospital. Her uncle had a few bachelor friends, who often came to the house.

Nasser Froozan was another classmate of Iraj from the Medical University of Tehran. Nasser was also Susan's uncle. Nasser had a brother, whose name was Mansoor. These two brothers were just like day and night both in their appearances and characters. Mansoor was this handsome, charming, intelligent, and very well mannered man. Although he was a follower of Shah, I never found his behavior to be problematic. I then again didn't really know what was going on behind the scenes.

His brother Nasser on the other hand was nothing like him. He was married to an American girl, Sandy. They had three sons: John, Jimmy, and Nader. He was a gynecologist. He thought the whole world revolved around him. At least this was our impression. He would always talk about himself; he wanted to be in the spotlight.

My Dear God:

Then there were Dr. and Mrs. Rahmat and Parvaneh Kashef. They had two children: Fariba, and Rameen Kashef. Fariba and Maseeh were of same age. And since they enjoyed each other's company, it brought our families closer together. We made a point getting together more often.

Parvaneh was a nurse. I think she met Rahmat, who was a radiologist in England. They bought a small and a very modest house after they moved to Michigan.

Luckily I had a chance to meet people like Sara Fassihi, who was married to Mahmood Fassihi. He was a radiologist, and she was a radiotherapist. First time I met her in a party, at Dr. Vaziri's house. She had come from Iran, and they had a little girl, Katty

Sara was at medical school in Tabreez. And Mahmood, who got his degree in Michigan, had just returned to Iran. He was assigned to teach at Tabreez University, where he met Sara. Despite many disagreements they end up getting married.

She was very beautiful young girl, whose parents were both teachers from Rasht. At that time they were living in Tehran, and I think they got married there.

I had a lot of respect for her from day one. Although they didn't care for cards game, our friendship still grew to a meaningful one. She was beautiful, young, intelligent, loyal, and truthful. She was a hard working mother, and a great wife. You can imagine that she would have many enemies among all those jealous ladies. They had another child, a son, called Cyrous.

My Dear God:

She was the only Iranian friend, who stood by me all the way through my hardship. There were times that she had problems, and I made sure that I was there for her. And likewise she was there when I needed her.

Mahmood was also a nice person in his own way. But I could never understand the way he treated Sara. She deserved much more attention and love than she was getting from Mahmood. He either didn't want to admit his love for her, or he was jealous of her success and beauty.

He was brought up in a Muslim family. His parents were completely unaware of what he was planning to do with his life. These were his own words, “My mother used to go to Mosques or other Islamic gatherings. And once in a while she asked me if I was still going to school”. The same went for his father. Besides not knowing that Mahmood was attending a medical school, he didn't know if he was going to school, period.

These subjects were mentioned only when we started to worry about our children's future. He would tell us about his neighborhood he was raised at, and the difficulties that we were surrounded by. He was trying to tell us that it is up to our kids to want to do something with their lives, or become someone important.

They had major troubles with Katty's health before I got to know them. They found out that she had stomach cancer when she was three. They went through so much during that period. They almost lost her to cancer. But miraculously she was saved, and it brought back hope into their lives.

Although she was a good mother and a good caretaker for her children, she always planned to be successful in her career. She hired a Nanny while she was studying to finish her residency. She always made sure that her children came first, and that they were well cared for. I remember the times that she had to be at the office with her patients, she had to be at school to pick up a sick child, she had to cook for her dear husband, and do the shopping all by herself all at the same time. I am not making this up. It happened that I have been with her on many of those occasions. Not only she was devoted to her husband and her children, but she was devoted to her work and her career as well.

Sara and I frequently went out to lunch together. We discussed the things that were happening around us. We discussed our friends’ comments and criticisms of our lives, be that in front of us or behind our backs.

My Dear God:

This was one of the cases. Sara was staying home to assure the well being of her children. During one of the dinner parties one of the ladies said with a very caring voice, “My dear Sara, you should not stay home and watch your future pass by. Your kids will grow up, and things will be fine. You must go and do what you have to do”. As if Sara didn't know it herself.

On the other hand, when Sara did find a living made and went back to work, the same lady, started expressing her concerns around another dinner table, “My dear Sara, this is our children’s budding age. If we do not spend time with them now, we will regret it

later".

You see, my dear GOD, we were involved with this kind of people all those years, and we thought we were having fun. What a waste!

I often think of this one funny fact. As I have mentioned previously I knew that Sara and Louise came from the same city, and for the longest time I was convinced that they knew each other from Iran. I had no idea that Mahmood and Hassan were the ones who knew each other since college. They were same year graduates. And that was what brought the two families closer.

I asked Sara one day, "Were you and Louise friends in Rasht? She looked at me and she said, "No way, please bite your tongue. I have never been her friend; I didn't even know her then. I saw her at this party once, and I saw that she was kissing all these men while she talked so openly about private parts. I said to myself, "Oh boy, who is this woman?" I was hoping that all other women were not like her". But later on Sara had accepted Louise's odd way of entertaining. They became very good friends.

Sara was my only hope. She was hundred percent behind me. She would always advise me if I needed. And she gave me medicine when she thought it was necessary. Many things happened which I will talk about when the time comes. But there was one very disturbing, and at the same time significant episode that took place after I was divorced. Someone told Sara, "Shamci has been talking behind your back that if your children get hurt, you deserve it". Not only I was shocked to hear such obscenity, but also I was shocked to hear it coming from Sara. Sara knew me very well, and she knew them very well. How could she believe such a thing coming from them?

I told Sara, "You can believe what they told you, but I will never lose respect for you. You were my friend when I needed you, and I value that. I will let you find out for yourself who is who and what is behind all this".

My Dear God:

After a while we continued our friendship, and while we lived far apart from each other, we still arranged to see one another and talk about older days.

Another funny, or sad in a way, relationship was to know Dr. Ghandchi and his American wife Pat. We used to see them in different parties, mostly at Sara or Louise's houses. I think he graduated from medical school with Mahmood and Hassan. So these three families were very close. Patty Ghandchi had a daughter from her previous marriage and two girls from Ghandchi. He was a successful hand surgeon. They bought a house in Bloomfield Hill with an outdoor swimming pool.

One day we heard that young Dr. Ghandchi had drowned in his own pool. Okay, my dear GOD, a young doctor, a strong, educated and an intelligent man, who had no signs of illness or weakness, has drowned in his own back yard. Don't you find it was strange?

Well, Patty had lost the love of her life in the spring of her life. Now she had three

girls to handle. It wasn't easy to be in her place. All the Iranians gathered, in effort to support Patty and her children. They buried him, and people went their own ways. Little by little Patty's close friends started spreading rumors. No one was sure how it had happened, but they always had to have something to talk about. Some said, "He didn't know how to swim, and Patty made him build this pool so that she could enjoy it after their fight over girls". While others said, "Their older daughter had something to do with it to gain freedom". And these rumors went on and on. I was shocked of this kind of friendship all over again. Why did people have to make up stories? How could they possibly benefit from hurting their old friends?

But Patty still considered them friends. She remarried her neighbor from a few doors down. It seemed that she got her happiness back.

We met another couple through the Community Medical Hospital. They were Dr. Shahideh and his wife Almass. He was an allergist, and Almass was studying to become a psychologist. My children and I had always suffered of allergies, so eventually we all became his patients. They had three children: Shideh, Babak, and Ameer.

A few years later Dr. Shahideh started his own practice together with Dr. Ghaemi. Dr. Ghaemi was practicing Dermatology. He remarried an Iranian girl who did not associate with other Iranians. She was an intelligent woman, I gather. She started working with her husband, alongside Shahidehs'. After Almass got her degree, she shared same office with her husband and Ghaemis.

My Dear God:

Then they bought a house in Wabeek, in the same place where we had our house. Almass was an Iranian Turkish, so she was a good cook. After we sold our house, Almass and I saw each other more often. I would usually be the one visiting, since I was trying to fill the emptiness of my own family. She was nice, and she always welcomed me. Her children were also very nice. I haven't heard from them since I left Michigan.

Then there was the family of Farah Shushtari, whom I met at Dr. Fassihi's housewarming. She was staying with her brother-in-law, Kazem, and Aghdass Shushtari, when they first came to Michigan. She was still living with Aghdass when I met her. But these two old friends got into a bad fight after a month or so. And Farah and her family had to move. They rented an apartment nearby our subdivision. Their fight was huge, and it had deep roots. When this happened I had realized that Farah didn't know English, and she didn't have friends. My heart fell for her. And as always I tried putting myself in her position, and I felt her pain. So I tried calling her more often, and I assured her that everything will be all right. She used to cry me a river. I was mad at myself that I couldn't help her enough. But she was happy even with my telephone calls, and she was very appreciative.

She was here in United States with her two sons Fariborz and Farsheed. Her

daughter, Ghazaleh, who was married to Mohsen Ameenlary, and who had two sons: Ali Reza and Abdi, was in Iran at the time. They were trying to come to America. Farah told me that a few years after her marriage, she went to Germany to get her degree in cosmetology. Since then she started to run a beauty salon out of her house. She was telling me that she had made a lot of money, and at the same time she got to meet very important women.

Fariborz and Farsheed were finishing their school here. And with their help Farah got a job in a salon. I guess they gave her the job because she was very experienced, and she didn't need much training.

Meanwhile the boys got a job in a pizza place by their house. The owner of the pizza place immediately promoted them to a supervising position. She recognized their capabilities from the very beginning. And besides they were both very good looking, and they had good manners. Soon they started thinking of opening a pizza place of their own.

They didn't have money at first, so they went into partnership with a lawyer. That didn't last for some reason.

Then they opened their own pizza place near Nine Mile and Telegraph road. Their business took off right a way. All these times they were thinking of opening their own restaurant. They made their mother open her own beauty salon. They helped her pass the cosmetology test. They even helped her furnish her store as much as they could. Even though she still didn't speak much English, she was able to gather many clients.

My Dear God:

I never left her side, or forgot about her. That was the time that my life was on fire, and I was trying to keep it quiet. I used to go and see her at her shop. She had so many problems to talk about, and I was glad to be there for her. Meanwhile it helped me forget my own problems for a little while.

Many times she brought lunch to the shop, and she insisted that I stay with her. After a while it started to feel more like psychological therapy session for both of us. I figured out that her life from the beginning to the end was full of different kind of stories that by all means she had to let it out. She was away from her only daughter, who was indeed her whole life. I remember she called her every Monday morning, at a certain time. And she would not stop worrying until she was sure that her daughter and her family were all right.

Because of the involvement with Aghdass and others, she was suspecting that something was very wrong with my life. But I did not want to open up to her then because of my past experience.

Farah's parents got divorced after she was born. She stayed with her father, and her aunt raised her. Her mother remarried, and had her own children. Her father remarried, and had his own children as well. Her childhood memories of her mother were so bitter

that she could never talk about her without hatred. For this reason she was trying to keep her family together at all times.

I don't know what her husband had done when they were in Iran. She would always say, "I want my children to have ambitions in life. I want them to be achievers, and accomplish something in their lives. Not something like their father, who was by no means ambitious. She was proud of her children. She did anything and everything to make them happy, especially because of the times that they were in their uncle's house, where they were treated like nobodies. It was hard for her to witness her children get hurt.

Her husband came from a large Muslim family. Their father was against musical education. Kazem had to secretly save money to get himself a Violin. And in order to practice he had to use a dark room, at the far end of their yard. He made sure that no one saw or heard him. But despite all the precautions he took, his father still found the Violin and broke it in half.

My Dear God:

Although Farah put her husband down quite often, she still made sure that he was dressed well, and looked okay around family and friends.

Farah was determined to bring her daughter Ghazaleh along with her family to America. So on one of her trips to Iran she brought her first grandson, Alireza, back with her. She kept him here until the rest of his family was able to move here. She took him to school and raised him among her own children.

They bought a house with a swimming pool in Waterford, Michigan. It was a four-bedroom house. She was looking for a wife for her son Fariborz. Many times she asked me if she could bring Fariborz to our house to get to know Mary. I never agreed to that idea. First of all I didn't believe in arranged marriages, and I was sure that my Mary would not appreciate me telling her what to do. So I told Farah that I was very sorry because I could never make Mary stay home. So that subject was forgotten.

Then she arranged a marriage with the daughter of one Iranian army officer, who was residing in the U.S.A. with his family. Her name was Marjon. They arranged their wedding in Shushtari's house. We were all there. After the wedding they stayed with Farah in one of their rooms, until they were able to buy their own house. They were all working together at the restaurant, while living together in one house, under the same roof.

Then she decided to bring a wife for Farsheed, daughter of Farah's cousin, who was a retired army officer. He lived in their neighborhood. He had two children: a girl and a boy. They had bought a Xerox business, where the whole family was working. Both children were ready for a married life. So Shushtari decided to proceed to ask for their daughter Mojgan to become Farsheed's wife. Both families, and obviously the boy and the girl, had agreed to the marriage.

Again there was another wedding in Shushtari's house. And again the couple stayed in a room of Shushtari's house. But this particular marriage did not look like a real marriage to begin with. After the wedding the groom decided to go out with his friends, and he left his bride to find her own way. They were acting more like a sister and a brother. Or if I could explain it any better, it was like an old-fashioned wedding in Iran.

Farah's half sister, who was then living in Germany, had a girl named Sudabeh. Years ago in Iran, when Sudabeh was still very little, Farah wanted her for her son Farsheed. But that was just a thought. Now that she was living in Germany with her mother and her brother, she was of a marrying age. While her father was in Khomaini's prison after the revolution, they decided to engage Sudabeh with Mr. Arshi's son, the brother of Mojgan, Farsheed's wife. So Mr. Arshi's family flew to Germany happily, and they brought back with them their new bride Sudabeh. The wedding was held in Germany with the presence of her mother, her brother and the rest of Iranians.

My Dear God:

Now that Mojgan was living with her husband in Shushtari's house, Sudabeh also was supposed to live with her husband in Mr. Arshi's house, which was only a few blocks away from Shushtari's.

It must have been a happy occasion for both families. All their children were wedded. They were almost done with their school, and they all owned their businesses.

But that was not the reality. I don't remember all the details, but I remember Farah telling me that within a month Sudabeh couldn't see herself being married to Arshi's son. So one night, after a big fight she packed her stuff and walked a few blocks to her Aunt Farah's house.

At this time Fariborz and Marjon had bought their own house. They had started the restaurant business together with two Iranian families, Khosro and Simin. They referred to him as Mr. K. The reason that they got him as their partner was that they needed the cash, which he did have. This was what Farah had told me.

Once or twice my whole family went there for dinner, and we enjoyed it very much. They served Italian food, and the name of the restaurant was ALFOCCINO, some Italian name.

Iranians have a habit of treating their friends. So those few times that we dined there, they would not accept money from us, no matter how much Iraj insisted to pay. They treated us as guests, especially when Farah was there.

So after a month or two Sudabeh came to Farah's house since she decided to get divorced and go back to her mother. But it didn't happen that way. While Farsheed was trying to comfort his cousin Sudabeh, his wife Mojgan, now Sudabeh's sister in-law, packed her bags and went back home to her Mama and Papa. Now both Arshi's daughter-in-law and son-in-law were in Farah's house.

Both Farsheed and Sudabe tried to comfort each other in each other's arms in privacy of their bedrooms, while Arshi's children were both without a husband or a wife.

Three months later, after their divorces were final, Sudabeh gave a party for celebration of her marriage with Farsheed.

My Dear God:

Okay, my dear GOD, can you tell me who arranged Sudabeh and Farsheed's wedding? Who sent Mr. Arshi's son to Germany to make the impossible possible? Not in a million years Farsheed would have known that somebody would bring his wife to him all the way from Germany. Did anyone, especially Farah know that what had happened was the best for all of them? Isn't this funny, that after all those sufferings everything would be all right, and things would fall into their places? Well, if we all knew as much as you do, we would all be called GODS.

Farsheed and Sudabeh also lived in Farah's house, until they bought their own house.

Then luckily Ghazaleh, her husband Mohsen, and their other son Abdi came to U.S.A. Now the whole family was in Michigan, and they all lived close to one another. Ghazaleh had a baby girl, Rana, after a year or so. Fariborz has four children now, and Farsheed has none.

As far as Arshi's family, I had recently heard from Farah that they are doing very well. Mojgan had a chance to go back to school and she got her degree in Dentistry. She found a very nice husband. Her brother also found a very beautiful girl, and they all are doing fine,

My friendship with this family became so eminent, that at the time they became my lost family. I will tell you how, when I get there.

Then we met Dr. and Mrs. Maliheh Zamiri. Years ago, even before we met each other, before we build our new house, a lady once called me and started talking about my parents in Iran. I realized soon after listening to her that her husband and my father were second cousins. Then I found out that her daughter, whom I have not met then, was married to Dr. Zamiri. They were living in Michigan as well. She gave me a telephone number to contact them. But I was so busy with my children that I had put it aside, and completely forgot about it.

But then we met them at Mahajers once. We talked about her mother's call, and we talked about our parents and our families in Iran. She was younger than me, and I didn't remember meeting any of them while we were in Iran. But I could recall the times when her mother used to visit my Mom dressed in her Islamic uniform, Chadoor. From early on I never liked that uniform, especially knowing that Chadoor was not the original uniform of Islam. This was brought upon Muslim people by fanatic followers of Islam.

Islam dictates that ladies are to cover their hair and their bodies. And altogether the purpose of these rules is that ladies must cover and hide their beauty from the opposite sex. Ironically men created all these rules. They knew themselves very well; they knew how bad and uncontrollable they were. This way they wanted to make women responsible for their own responsibilities. And as we know, at the inception of Islam ladies would wear various kinds of head covers, and any other kind of fashionable clothing that was suitable to Islamic laws. There was no Chadoor at the beginning, and I don't know who had come up with it.

My Dear God:

As I'm writing now, I recall an incident when Mary confronted me by saying, "My Mom has to have an opinion on anything and everything, even when it is not any of her concern". I answered her, "Mary jon, you are right. Anything in the world must be of our concern. Automatically all things in the world we live in are and must be of our concern.

If you were among the women who had to follow those kind rules, and you would be expected to live happily ever after against your will, you then would and should have an opinion, and you must never stay undecided.

So this was the way I felt about Chadoor my entire life. And when someone came to our house with Chadoor, or Abba, an Islamic uniform for men, we tried not to associate with them.

So this way Mrs. Zamiri Maliheh, was almost my second cousin. She had three children: one boy and two girls. They all were very nice.

At that time Iraj's niece and nephew, Nazi and Arman, were here in the U.S.A. One was enrolled in Cranbrook Boarding School, and the other one was attending Kingswood Boarding School. They were both hungry for attention. We were trying so hard to make these kids snap out of it. Their poor parents did everything in their power to teach them right from wrong. They got to meet Maliheh's brother, who was living with them at that time.

Soon they started talking about going into business together. Their parents provided them with money to open up a gas station together. They lost all the money in no time, and they each started to blame one another for it. And before we got to find out what exactly was happening, Nazi drove to Maliheh's house to defend Arman. She had arrived there screaming. She attacked Maliheh and her brother for trying to destroy Arman.

I went over to Maliheh's house to apologize after I found out about all these happenings. I found Maliheh in a state of shock. She thought I knew about Nazi's visit and everything else that had happened. But I told her, "I didn't even know much about the business and especially about these violent actions of Nazi". It seemed that she didn't believe me at first. But then eventually she came to realize that neither I, nor my immediate family members ever took part in those doings. Our relationship remained friendly till the end. They were not part of the Blot group, but we saw each other here and there, and we paid visits to each other every once in a while.

My Dear God:

Another couple, whose lifestyle made many member of the group mad, was Dr. and Mrs. Rameen Radson. They had two children: a boy and a girl. This family, although they did intermingle with Iranians, they did their own thing. They knew where and how they want to live. They were not influenced by others to do anything against their own will. Things like moving to a newer neighborhood, or sending their children to a prestigious private school, or getting involved with wrong Iranians.

They lived in Michigan, two hours away from where most of us had lived. They built a beautiful house of a very comfortable size on a body of water. It was located near his work. They sent their children to a public school in their neighborhood. They didn't have to spend unnecessary thousands of dollars to become the best achievers among us all.

Rameen was a tennis player. Her both children, Afsheen and Azeen, were playing tennis with the school team as well as out of school. She would never disregard their tennis tournaments, despite of how many parties she had to miss, or what occasions she left unattended. Her children's tennis always came first. She was a good cook, and she baked beautifully. What I loved the most about her was that she was never afraid to say what was on her mind. And for this reason many ladies had some kind of resentment towards her. Oh my, Oh my.

It was a real show when Mrs. Radsan was sitting at there table, while talking about her children's achievements. Everyone else was spending so much money on their children in effort of them getting good grades, while her children were doing great without any monetary investment. On the contrary they made money.

It seemed that there was a race going on between the parents not the children. They each wanted to prove that their children, as well as their houses, and/or their husbands were the best. And when someone like Rameen came about, who was really genuine, they didn't like it. They wanted to hurt her, or ruin her in one way or another.

Afsheen was an honor student and he got accepted to Harvard University to study law. I am sure he will be a good lawyer. Azeen was an honor student as well and she got accepted to Stanford University.

Rameen used to play bridge at their club. One day she asked me join her as a partner. She showed me a copy of Azeen's school newspaper while I was there. There was a beautiful picture of her wearing a beautiful dress on the talent page. That column was mentioning her beauty, along with her selection of that inexpensive fashion. I think that was the best advertisement for Kmart. She won a prize for selecting that dress for a very minimal price at Kmart.

My Dear God:

I was really amazed. I showed that newspaper to some of those Iranians, who always were badmouthing that family. I was hoping it would make them realize how wrong they were. But instead they got more jealous, and they really wanted to destroy them. Luckily they were smart enough not to allow anyone to interfere with their family life. I lost contact with them after I left.

Rameen had a cousin who was married to Dr. Aryani. Her name was Massoodeh. They had two children, a girl and a boy. They were both very bright and good children. They were a nice family, and we used to see each other at least once a year at parties.

They lived in Gross Pointe shore, which was one-hour drive from our house. Massoodeh and I kept in touch by sending cards to each other for a few years after I left. Then I didn't hear from her.

One of the ladies that I personally made friends with was Dr. Golnar Kashefi. She was pregnant with her second child when I first met her at Dr. Shahideh's house. She was a psychiatrist. They lived in the same neighborhood with Dr. Aryani's. We hit it off from the first moment. We talked and exchanged telephone numbers. She was very nice, and I was happy that I had met her.

I usually didn't like going out to lunch with just anyone. Even though she lived far from us, every once in a while Sara and I would make plans to go out to lunch with her. And we would talk about our childhood. Although there was an age difference between us, we had plenty in common. Unfortunately we both had to go through many troubles in our lives at the same time. They had three children at that time. Her children were very young, and it was very difficult for them to face that difficulty. The only hope she had was that her mother came and stayed with her for some time. Her main problem was that her husband was trying to manipulate her young children. It was an enormous pressure for a working mother like her, the mother who had the responsibilities of both home and office. But she was a lady, and she didn't stop short.

We kept contact. And until now we exchange greeting cards for the New Year, and we talk about our families.

Then there was a group of Iranians that we met here and there.

We kept our relationship with this group very casual, limiting it to occasional invitations. We either saw each other at weddings, or funerals, or some other Iranian gatherings for the most part of it. I even forgot some of their names. There were people like Dr. and Mrs. Mahmoodzadeh, Dr. and Mrs. Malekhedayat, Dr. and Mrs. Kaffee, Dr. Najmabadi and his wife, and Dr. Babaoff and his wife Ansari, and Hariri and his wife, and many others.

Mirror, mirror Downriver

Her mother taught her fine points of coordinating clothes and especially how to pick out real bargains from the sale racks of the better stores and boutiques. Every day is a fashion experience for Grosse Ile's Azin Radsan and the color cognizant high school senior has started her own vocabulary of style on the island as she haunts second hand stores and places like Loehmanns and T.J. Maxx for "Boy George" or "Indiana Jones" looks.

Radsan's naturally curly hair was recently braided into 100 hanging locks which took 4½ hours to create. She'll be wearing a Marilyn Monroe-style gown with a pillbox hat to the high school prom and can't wait for the senior trip to Toronto in June, where bizzare looks like hers are more common.

An outstanding athlete in tennis and track, Radsan appears on the court or the oval in traditional uniform—accented by feathered earrings or orange "glo" socks. "I love clothes and like to have people take a second look," she assesses. Beautiful, she also is brainy. The valedictorian of her graduating class, she heads for Stanford this fall and studies in economics and business.

—Pat Andrews

This is Dr. and Mrs. Ramin Radson's daughter. I just added this to my notes to show you that although Dr. and Mrs. Radson did not send their two children to private schools, they became more successful than the ones who paid a lot to private schools.

My Dear God:

One incident I remember with Aazam took place on the day I drove Mojgan to YMCA for her swimming lesson. Aazam's son was enrolled in that same class. We started talking while our children were swimming. She had her two-year- old daughter with her. That was the first time I met her daughter. She was a very beautiful, talkative, and bright girl. We connected so quickly. She sat next to me in her beautiful dress, and we started exchanging ideas. We got warmer and warmer, and pretty soon she didn't want to separate from me. It was time to go home, and Aazam was in a hurry. Despite all her effort she couldn't make the little girl let go of me. She told her Mom, "You go home. I will go home with Shamci". Her mother was getting really mad at her.

My Dear God:

I thought it was my fault. I didn't want Aazam to punish her and make her cry, so I thought of an idea. We all went to her car, and we talked for a while. Then I gave her a quarter so that she could study it, and told her, "I have to go get my daughter". And soon after I closed the door behind me, I asked Aazam to take off. It was one of those beautiful memories I had with kids. I will never forget it

Then obviously of all the people in the world we got to meet Dr. Azeez Malakuti and his wife Badri. First time we met them was during the intermission at Elmwood Casino, where we were attending the Ann Margaret Show.

We heard some people speaking Farsi on our way back from the bathroom. And they were not part of our group. Then one of the doctors who knew Azzez introduced him to us. Our fried told us that they wanted to bring his sister-in-laws to see Ann Margaret, but they got there too late and all the tickets were sold out.

That was the first time we met Dr. and Mrs. Azeez Malakuti. They were friends of Dr. Barkhordari and Dr. Panah. That night Rohan told us all about Azeez and his wife. He was a psychiatrist who had just come to Michigan that year. They had three children: one boy and two girls.

Okay, my dear GOD, I don't know even how to begin writing about meeting this family. You must help me, and please help me well.

I find it very interesting that there are times that throughout your lifetime you meet certain people that leave a distinct mark in your memory. These memories could at times be good or bad. And then there is others who you wont' even remember meeting. So the night that we met Malakutis' for a brief second in that Casino, they left an impression of a chaotic, provincial family that had just moved from a remote rural area of the world. They didn't even know that they could make a simple phone call to find out the show times. I had no recollections of them. They were standing right in the middle of the hallway. Disregarding people around them, they were loudly discussing their problems. I didn't even take a note of their faces to remember anything about them.

The only thing I remember is the silliness of Azeez, and passiveness of Badri at parties. I can't remember how we started inviting visiting each other's homes

Azeez always made sure to be the center of attention, and in that effort he would always clown around. He would tell many stories, true and false, about himself, his wife, or his work.

As I have mentioned before most marriages in Iran are arranged by either parents or friends. Azeez always considered his the most entertaining. He repeated that story more than several times.

My Dear God:

Then once again we all went to see Ann Margaret at the Elmwood Casino. There were Panahs, Barkhordaris, Malakutis and us. From the moment we sat Rohan began asking Azeez to tell us about his wife hunting, khastegary, in Iran. He liked to talk, and everyone would give him a good review on his performance by laughing.

True or not that night he talked about three or five of them. His family or relatives arranged them all. At times there were agents from different neighborhoods.

My Dear God:

So you see my dear GOD, the whole night turned out to be about him and his wife. I can't remember that anyone else did anything or said anything. I don't think Iraj had met him before that night. But all and all he didn't think him to be a very wise person. Even after that night it took us some time to start socializing with them. I still don't remember the first time that we invited them to our house. I think they invited us first for some occasion.

I could never figure out what kind of background Azeez came from. It was my understanding that he had it hard, which had made him very bitter. He never spoke openly about his past or his family, but some of his comments were speaking up so clearly. Once we all were in their house. After dinner the discussion was about children in general. I don't remember what or how the discussion started. But I remember that he wanted to prove his point of view. I said something that he did not agree with. Then while we were standing in the doorway to say goodbye, he answered me in a very bitter way, "You have never been hungry, have you?" I said, "No, I have not. But neither were you". Then he turned around and said, "Oh yes I have. Oh yes I have". I felt embarrassed, so I stopped our discussion, and I said goodbye and left. That comment and many others made me to think twice about him. And I believe that behind all his clowning around must have been a serious bruise from childhood, which always hurt. Although he made himself look like an Iranian macho man, in reality he was very sensitive, seeking the truth. He was very concerned about his children. He was especially very sensitive about the females in his life. He was among those Iranian men, who were very protective of their wife, mother, sisters,

and especially their daughters. He hated those men who fooled around.

My Dear God:

I remember so clearly the time that he was thinking of buying a house. Most Sundays he called us to go house hunting. He had a property, and I knew that he was not going to buy a house. One Sunday we all got into our car, while Iraj was driving. The subject of a doctor and one doctor's wife came up. He was so disturbed by it that he was expecting all Iranian doctors to boycott that doctor, and not have any relationship with him. While I was saying that it might have been the work of some storyteller, and that there was no proof of such a thing, he didn't want even to listen to me. He said, "I will never invite him in my house, and I will never have respect for him". Then I said, "If once our spouses are away, aren't you suppose to talk if we see each other in a shopping center? Would that be considered to be the sign of unlimited relationship between us?" Still he wasn't listening to me. He was really furious with him, and he refused to accept that he might have been innocent.

When Badri and Iraj looked at each other in the mirror, and they both were quiet just listening, it never occurred to me that there was something going on between them at that time. And neither Azeez, in a million years, could have suspected that his wife at that same moment had something going on with Iraj. If he did, he would have killed both of them, without any hesitation. No one ever knew except the two of them, who quietly were watching Azeez in the mirror, and probably being scared to death. Now that I look back, I see that they both knew exactly how to act to have their fling under our noses, without any causing suspicions at that time they were already partners.

Once we heard that Azeez had lost his young sister in Iran. One night the whole group went there to condole him. He was so affected by her death that he seemed to be loosing his mind. He told everyone how it had happened, and how he remembered the place that she had fallen from. She was attending Tehran University, studying for the last year of her degree. There was a four-foot concrete wall around the university campus. Behind that wall there was a body of swirling water. The wall was three foot wide. She thought it was a comfortable place to sit and study. But for whatever the reason, with just one move, she lost control, and fell into that swirling water. No one ever could go after her. The waters swallowed her immediately. Azeez was very familiar with that special spot. He had studied there many times himself. It seemed that the loss of his younger sister had crushed him immensely.

My Dear God:

By this time our group of doctors, mainly the Blot players, spent our vacations together. This time we all went to Las Vegas. Our group consisted of Barkhordaris, Neelfrooshans, Mahajers, Malakutis, and us.

As I said Azeez was very sensitive about women in his life. At that time Roshanak was developing as a woman. First our children went to breakfast at a restaurant at Caesars Palace, where we were staying. While we were gathering in the lobby to go to the restaurant, the kids were already done with their breakfast waiting for us in the lobby. All of a sudden we noticed that all other doctors were holding screaming Azeez away from a young man, who attempted to either talk, or touch Roshanak in the lobby. He kept repeating, "I am going to kill him if he approaches my daughter again".

We were used to those scenes on the streets of Iran, but it was very awkward to be witnessing it in the hotel lobby. Poor Azeez, he didn't really know his daughter. He would have murdered many boys by then. He was hoping to raise his daughters the same way they were raised in Iran.

Ok, my dear GOD. How am I doing so far? You were there with us every step of the way. You remember the details of every incident that I am describing. The only difference is that unlike me you knew precisely what was going on.

Azeez was always the noisy one of the couple. He made sure that his presence was obvious. Many of us didn't think him to be a good husband, just by judging by what we knew of him. We felt sorry for Badri, and we sided with her on many occasions.

One night we were playing cards in his house. We had our dinner, and he had his when he got home, usually at eleven o'clock. Badri had his dinner ready for him and she tiptoed around him to make sure that everything was fine. And then with a great big smile she just sat there watching him eat. She looked like a servant, who was also providing good sex. But it did not end there. Azeez turned to Badri and said, "Close your crooked mouth. Don't laugh". And then turned to us and said, "You have no ides what she is doing to me, and then covers it up with her smile. You think she is nice, but she is not. Close your crooked mouth". But Badri always acted as if he was joking. She kept laughing, and he got more irritated. But she calmed him down. She was treating him like a baby.

My Dear God:

That night Minoo Panah and I were talking about that episode. She said, "I would never allow my husband to treat me this way". I said the same. As a matter of fact I said, "Iraj never asks me to do anything for him. If he wants something he will go get it himself, be that in public or in private". But I found out later that Badri was not taking all the abuse from Azeez out of simply being nice. And I had discovered the reason after Azeez's death. It was because he didn't love her, and he had no respect for her. But she gave him good sex to keep him quiet. Besides not trusting her, he was also very unhappy with her family.

On the outside everyone, including myself, thought that Azeez was the bad guy. The same judgment was ruled about Iraj and me. Only in our case Iraj was the one who looked like a good husband in the eye of the public, and I was the one who was the noisy, demanding wife. None of us were our true inner self in the eyes of the people around us. In reality those quiet ones were the ones who instigated the noise and unwillingness in both of us.

The real SOAP OPERA starts after Azeez's death. Boy, oh boy. My dear GOD, how did you give me this strength to be able to talk about them as a narrator? Thank you for giving me the power to be able to describe these two characters, and let loyal, intelligent, knowledgeable, and unbiased people to get to know them and their true characters. Obviously every one of us had to find our own way of living. One way or the other we are the makers of our lives. But it's how we make it, and what people remember us by.

My dear GOD, you know that my Iraj is dead. He is dead because he was not the joke of Iranian's gatherings. My Iraj is dead because he never wanted to be remembered by the kind of a father that he had become. My Iraj is dead because he had promised me to be a loyal husband. My Iraj is dead because he never dreamt of breaking our children's home, and he is dead because of a sensual, promiscuous woman. My Iraj is dead because he hated men who acted that way; he hated men that made their children to lose their dignity. And I proclaim that my Iraj is dead, my dear GOD, because Iraj that is living is all of the above.

I was the kind of a woman, who always took my children's needs into consideration before anything else. One day we all were in Nayer Rabbani's house. There was a long weekend coming up. Everyone was talking about going to Las Vegas for three days. And although my children were old enough, I said from the beginning, "Please don't count me in, I am not going. I do not want to leave my children by themselves". Then Iraj said hesitantly, "Don't include me, I am not coming either". Mohammad and Ali Rabbani and their wives agreed to go. Barkhordari and Susan and others agreed to go. Azeez was against the trip and he wouldn't allow Badri to go either, even though she really wanted to go. When I saw that Badri wanted to go, I told Azeez, "I will stay with your children either in my house or yours". He would not accept my offer, and he refused to leave his children alone for the sake of his own pleasure. He did exact same thing I had done.

My Dear God:

But the irony of it all was that a fire broke out in the hotel on the second night, and people were trapped in flames and smoke. They were showing men and women on TV in either their pajamas underwear, who were trying to escape from that inferno in a high-rise building. A few people died in that fire and some got injured.

My dear GOD, can you imagine being in that situation. We had seen the movie with Paul Newman. But that was just a movie, where this was a reality. Everyone returned home very regretful. We, on the other hand, were very happy that we had decided not to go.

Although Azeez and Badri were related, they had very different upbringing.

According to the way Badri had introduced her family to me, they were not only unintelligent, but they were all vicious enemies.

Like many other arranged marriages in Iran two of her sisters arranged for their children to get married. They were cousins, and in Iran this is allowed. The sister who had the son was wealthy, and the other one wasn't. The young couple had a baby girl. By the time the baby was two the matters between the two sisters gore more and more complicated. And it got to a point that they would not allow the father to see his child.

You know, my dear GOD, Badri was able to spread rumors better than the newspaper. And she was capable of exaggerating like no one else in our group. So I got so emotional when she told me the story that I cried for the father. How vicious can you be not to let your nephew, the father of your grand child, to see his daughter?

Azeez always complained about Badri's family. He actually didn't want them around. Every time he started complaining about them, Badri said, as Azeez would always say it, with that smile at the corner of her crooked mouth, "Well, they are your relatives also".

Her mother had been married, and she had five children. She fell in love with this other guy while she was still married. She ended up marrying that guy shortly after her husband died. Her older sister's husband died leaving three children behind. She soon remarried a younger and wealthy guy. Then the second sister's husband died leaving her with three children as well. And again her sister married a young guy. I have no idea how they found husbands so fast. They were neither beautiful, nor did they have nice figures. They were neither intelligent, nor talented. And yet the mother along with all her daughters followed exactly the same pattern. Did they have these husbands line-up, ready for them before their husbands died? Was it possible that they all died of natural causes? Is it possible that this custom of husband dying after having three children runs in the family? Or am I that stupid, my dear GOD, that this is the only explanation I can find? I really don't know, my dear GOD. It is only you, who could make me understand. And that is it.

My Dear God:

And then there was Badri who was able to outdo the rest of them. She was the one who took her mother's advice, and then elaborated on it. Years before her husband died, she had selected the best husband among all other husbands. And she had saved him for the right time. Boy, oh boy, my dear GOD. You are the creator of all these people, and yet you want us to recognize all of your creatures as well as you know them. This is too much to expect from us. I personally cannot believe the kind of creature Badri was. I think she was the one and only who was capable of fooling Iraj. It got to a point that there was nothing left of Iraj's image.

This kind of women, and this kind of families, whose only pride is their vanity and promiscuity are very rare in Iran. They are considered very low class women. That is why divorces are not common. And even when a woman is widowed, she will not remarry for the sake of her children. Women, who were brought up on a philosophy of grabbing any man if you can, are not among those who believe in morals and principals.

So this was the reason behind Azeez's disliking, and in many cases hating that family. None of them had anything to offer except for their sexual parts.

I remember she used to tell me, "I am not smart, so I can't learn something easily". And it was true, she was only taught one thing, and she was good at it. Smile, even at the time you are committing a crime, even if you are killing your husband. I do not remember even once that Azeez didn't ask Badri, "Close your crooked mouth, it is making me sick". She obviously pretended that it was just a joke.

And there were many more families that we got to know and socialized with once in a while. I don't know if I remember all of them, but I remember Dr. Kaffee and his wife, and his wife's sister and her husband and their mother. Then there were Dr. Malekhedayat and his wife, Dr. Mahmoodzadeh and his wife, Mr. Ansari and his wife, Mr. Hariri and his wife, and many, many others.

My Dear God:

We used to see some of them at parties, but we were not socializing with at that time. But later I continued my friendship with them, and they provided me with great emotional support.

They were Mary and Viki, two sisters, who had come to America years ago from Shiraz to continue their education. They were friends of Dr. and Betty Farah, who were also from Shiraz. I would always see them at Dr. Farah's house. We talked, we exchanged ideas, and I always enjoyed their company. Both sisters married out of Iranian descent.

Mary was married to Dr. Enrique Boquin, who, if I am not mistaken, was from Paraguay. They had three most beautiful and advanced children, all very bright and great achievers. And Viki was married to Mr. Zacharek Casimer, who I think was from Poland. They had four children: one set of twins, and two more. All of them were very advanced academically. They both had nice families, and I think the secret to their success laid in not to be mingling with Iranians just because they were Iranian themselves. They were able to arrange their family life that way because their husbands were not Iranian. I think that was a plus for both sisters, and I am sure they had taken it into consideration from the beginning.

I even kept my contact with Mary and Viki, and their families after I left Michigan. Viki's first son became a doctor and he got married to a lady doctor from India. I was invited to their wedding, but I was in Iran at that time, and missed their beautiful ceremony.

* * *

So these were the people we knew more or less. We were very involved with some. I had nearly sixty guests at our housewarming. Some were part of our original card group, and others were just friends. And like it always was at my parties, everyone had a great time. We laughed and joked around, and at the end, those who played cards sat around the table, and started their games, and those who didn't would carry on conversations of all kinds.

The great thing about our parties was that most of us did not consume alcohol. And the ones that did would drink moderately. I personally had lots of fun just having tea and playing cards. That game of cards kept us away from gossiping. I can't speak for all of us, but it kept some of us away from gossiping.

The card group consisted of Barkhordaris', Panahs', Shushtaris', Minoo and Foad Panah, Malakutis, Khodadadehs', Rahmat Kashef, sometimes Nazi Mahajer, Joorabchis', Louise Neelfrooshan, and us. The main reason of us getting together was to break the daily routine, and share a moment of fun and relaxation together.

My Dear God:

Since our children were being raised in this country, each one of us did our best to raise them according to our traditions, and upbringing. And obviously it wasn't easy.

My life was a dream at that time. Despite all the hard time we had with Mary, she got accepted to the University of Michigan majoring in history. Everything was perfect, and Iraj was proud and happy that he was able to finish his dream house without any major disappointments. Again he was happy that he had started a big project and was able to succeed.

Iraj was telling me that Dr. Mohammad Rabbani, who went to Medical School at the same time with him, seemed to be competing with him throughout. And because of the similarity of their names, they were after each other even in the classroom. They were good friends, and I had respect for him also because of his moral and family background. He knew his priorities in life, and he would go after them no matter how hard or impossible they seemed.

I don't know if it was a coincidence, or if he was really following us around. When we decided to go to Iran in 1964, they followed us there. When we returned to America in 1967, they came back also.

We rented an apartment in Summerset, Troy Michigan for one year, and they did the same. When we moved to Alding Brooks Apartments in Bloomfield, they did too. And just around the time that we had to sell our house, they had finished building their property next to our house on Upper Long Lake in Wabeek, on Shore View Court, Bloomfield Hills, Michigan.

My dear GOD, could it really be a coincidence that someone followed you around the world for that many years? But anyway whether it was a coincidence or not, or even if it was just a competition against one another, Dr. Rabbani not only won the competition, but he was able to put Iraj out of the race for the rest of his living life. And while Iraj's reputation, mind you with their assistance, turned out to be one of the worst, he became the number one leader in humanity and the symbol of good will of all times.

You see, my dear GOD, Iraj was a great man before Azeez had passed away. He was helpful to everyone, and he was very successful in everything he did. He had made a good name for himself. He was the love of my life as well as his children's. He was well respected by everyone. Just as he had promised me he was trying to be a great husband, a great father, a great doctor, and all in all a great human being.

My Dear God:

After Azeez's death he became exactly the opposite of what he had been in the eyes of everyone who knew him. This would have never happened if it wasn't for the jealousy of his competitors. They used his innocence and helpfulness, and made him look like nothing. Then by spreading a very destructive and sarcastic poem around all Iranian houses, they made him a joke of all Iranian parties.

You see, my dear GOD, killing a person with a gun puts him away and ends his sufferings. But destroying his name, his goodness and his reputation is a lifetime conviction with torture.

Some people might say, “Poor Shamci, she still believes this nonsense, and tries to blame others”. But they don't know Iraj. I know what he was aiming for. I know how he hated the man that he had become. I know how happy he was with the prestige he had created for himself. I know how happy he was to see his children entering college. And I know how happy he was to be able to see that he had made it after all. Please, GOD, if he was pretending all the time, he must have been a hell of a good actor.

Another person who was always in competition with Iraj was Dr. Nasser Barkhordari. He had also graduated from medical school the same year Iraj did. After a few years that we have lived in our new house, he bought the property above us, and built an outdoor swimming pool. Now we were sandwiched between Barkhordaris and Rabbanis.

Nasser used to tease me by saying, “If you people misbehave, we will make sure to overflow our pool water into your yard and your house”. Although they didn't do that, they made sure that Badri got what she wanted after Malakuti's death, the way they threw the red carpet for Badri. My dear GOD, you remember how they were poisoning her mind by giving her “Go get it, you can do it” idea. That devilish mind of hers that Azeez always complained about.

Besides, my dear GOD, I don't know who was the author of that sarcastic poem that

ایرج نامه

ایرج که رهبر ماست   بزرگ و سرور ماست
در ماتم و عروسی   معین و یاور ماست

فلفل نبین چه ریزه
بشکن ببین چه تیزه

این شاه پسر بلائی است   حکم و رأیش نهائی است
گر میرود در بسیجه   در اصل او بهائی است

اشکش اگر میریزه
از مردن عزیزه

این جانور چه ماری است   هر دم بفکر یاری است
در فعل و انفعالات   همچون خروس لاری است

اگر که ریزه و پیزه
غوره نشده مویزه

بدری که شوخ و شنگه   با عشوه و ملنگه
آهو صفت لقرگوش   در حلقوم پلنگه

دنیا براش پشیزه
ایرج خیلی عزیزه

دانی چرا که شمس   دائم به غر و تیزه
شمس به پیش بدری   الحق که چون کنیزه

بر سر ایرج ستیزه
ای خدا یک موش بریزه

ایرج و شمس با بدره*   رفتند بسوی ایل را
هرچند بهم پیوستند   قلب ما را شکستند

بدری بسر گل ریزه
شمس به جست خیزه

---

* بدره = بدری بلهجه شیرین ترکی

I don't know how I can translate this poem which was written by an anonymous person to humiliate Iraj in front of his colleagues, and the whole world. I never talked about this letter to any of my children. It was too hurtful to let them know, the father that they loved and had respect for, was introduced as a monster crook, cheater, disloyal, dishonest, robber, and sneaky womanizer to the whole world. This anonymous person, whoever he or she was, put himself into mailing this letter to all the Iranians in Michigan.

I have two guesses about this guy. One, he was one of the people around Badri, who had his heart and his eyes to get to her for free, but he had found Iraj in his way. My second guess is that, Badri was afraid that Iraj would dump her like he had dumped Farkhondeh. So, to put Iraj in a do-or-don't situation, she made sure that this poem was written by one person in her family or friends, to spread the word of her relationship with Iraj. This one is closer to the reality than my first guess.

Since Badri couldn't make me humiliate my husband in front of our friends, she decided to act on it herself. She could have never found a way better than this, to let Iraj know that someone else did it, or Shamci did it after all.

She was not smart enough to know that if Shamci wanted to do it, she would have done it on the anniversary of Azeez's death, when everyone had gathered around his grave, and Iraj was giving his speech. Due to his excitement, he said Behrooz instead of Roozbeh Malakuti. Shamci was planning to keep you from marrying Iraj, to keep you as his mistress for the rest of your life if necessary. Shamci knew what she wanted from life from the beginning to the end. It was Badri who had to find a sneaky way to make Iraj embarrassed enough to force him into divorcing Shamci. Without this sarcastic poem about Iraj, you Badri, could have never gotten your wish which was marrying Iraj.

Badri you were supposed to humiliate Iraj to be able to make him divorce me. I am sure you will never be what I was for him. You showed him good sex while he was in his mid-life crisis. You got help from your children and your family to find the right way, and you did it. Otherwise, Iraj was not ever ready to destroy his wife and his children, and as Mary said, "make them lose their dignity". As you have said it yourself, you did what your mother and all your sisters did in their marriage. I think this runs in your family. You must all be rewarded for your efforts to find husbands right after each of your husbands died.

To this day, I don't know if my children have had any knowledge regarding this sarcastic poem. Anyway, I had to write it here for you to know that I will never forgive these two people who stabbed me in the back. I just wish they get what they deserve until the end of their lives.

And to the poet whoever he was, your tactlessness regarding me proves that you have come from a household just like Badri. Otherwise, no one in their right mind could judge me the way you did. If only you are still around, and only if you have the nerve, you can contact me to discuss this in a civilized way.

was sent anonymously to every Iranian in Michigan.

As far as I know there were only few poets among us who were very familiar with Iraj's background, and who were able to use the Turkish accent. They were Nasser Barkhordari and his sister Aghdass Khanoom. But I don't believe that she would have done that. I know that she didn't have any part in that. It was too vicious of an act to be done by Aghdass Khanoom. I can't think of anyone else but Nasser. And even if he didn't do it, I am sure he knew who did. If the poet was from our group, Nasser, more than anyone else, would have obviously learned by then of his background.

My Dear God:

Anyway it was obvious that the author was a very tasteless person. Or probably he just had something against me personally. Badri was too stupid to be able to absorb any intellectual conversation. And someone who preferred her to me must have been of a similar intellect, unless her breasts were what had triggered his interest. This was Azeez's weak point, and it was so obvious to everyone, especially Iraj. Iraj always thought of Azeez as a fool and he always said that his wife fooled him. And I am sure that others thought of her the same way as well.

So the more I think about this poem, the more I become convinced that it must have been written either by Nasser or by one of his acquaintances. Anyway he must be a complete coward. This coward that remained anonymous during all those years is the one who opened the door for Badri, and he is the one who put Iraj in a position where he was forced to make the decision to pursued Badri.

For eight consecutive years Badri had made every effort to ensure that I lost control of my emotions and made scenes, but I still didn't. Even that night that I had told her, "I do not want you to come to my house and interact with my friends". While we were all getting ready to serve the dinner, she appeared at my door holding Rozan in her arms, accompanied by the other two, Roozbeh and Roshanak.

My dear GOD, you were there, and you witnessed what I had to go through. I opened the door, and just like in old times, I let her and her children in, and I did not make a scene. The poet was probably there too wondering, what was going on, "Why don't you scream and throw this ugly woman out of your house? Are you crazy?" Then he wrote that poem, and he mailed to every Iranian in effort to unveil what was going on in our life. Those who knew of their affair were already assisting Badri to get that weak and stupid man, to make sure that she left their own husbands alone. And the one's that knew nothing of the affair began wondering how Shamci could be so stupid? And, on the other hand, some of them were looking forward that Shamci lost her fortunate lifestyle. So they were actually glad that it was happening.

Those who thought Shamci was stupid didn't know that after his first affair in Iran, I didn't want for the same thing to happen again if I could help it. I wanted to keep my family together by my intellect and not scandalous scenes, for I have witnesses them on many occasions. Not only it didn't them any good, but also it kept them behind the bars. I was not out of my mind; I decided to let time bring back Iraj that I knew. I was trying to maintain and protect my children's dignity, and I wanted to teach them the importance of sacrificing in effort to keep the family together. No, I wasn't stupid at all. With help of my dear GOD I have learned how to become tolerant and broadminded to be able to keep everything under control. And I have succeeded.

My Dear God:

Anyway until that cowardly and anonymous creature comes out of his hiding, I am still convinced that it was Nasser who wanted to ruin Iraj's image. Otherwise if he is not the one, but he has knowledge of who had done this, come forward and reveal the anonymous poet.

Okay, my dear GOD, it is time for you to tell me if I am right or wrong? Do you think that it was the circumstances that brought Iraj and Azeez closer together, or do you think that Badri and Iraj arranged those circumstances beforehand?

Iraj after the partnership that he had with Dr. Zadeh did not want to go into partnership with just anybody. He was very careful about choosing a partner. Except for Dr. Edward Mehrabian, whom he trusted simply because his wife was not involved with his business, no one else had ever appealed to him. Once in a while he joined an obvious partnership with doctors Mohammad and Ali Rabbani, Nasser Barkhordari, including their wives. Unfortunately all of them were so knowledgeable about investing that even after twenty-five years the property still remains in its original, residential, use. Their goal was to change it to commercial use, and then sell it with a profit. Four doctors together were not able to do anything about it. This proves how much more knowledge they have over their wives. So Iraj was not ready to go into a partnership, especially with someone, whom he didn't think so highly of. I don't know why, but I know that in general he thought of Azeez as a silly and thoughtless individual. And in general his opinion about Badri was that she was the sneaky, devious, indirect and shifty by all means.

There were times that Reza Mahajer had asked Iraj to go to a partnership with him. But he knew that first of all Nazi was involved with Reza's business, and second of all he knew that she was very smart and she couldn't be fooled by anyone. And the main factor was that she was in love with her husband, and she was not a type of woman who would fool around. So he refused to be partners with Reza. At that time Nazi opened her own weight loss clinic, right next door to Reza's office. And I think she had asked Iraj to join her in partnership. But Iraj was in the establishing business partnership with someone, who was the least expected, Dr. Azeez Malakuti.

We all had a wonderful life. Our children were doing fine at school, and we were having fun getting together and playing cards. Little by little in the morning or evening news you would hear about the medicine and organized HMOs all around the country. Doctors were loosing their certainty about income and future of medicine. The most worried among them were those with hefty expenses on their shoulders. And the one, whose load was heavier than that of many others was yours truly, Iraj Rafani.

My Dear God:

Our children's private education alone accumulated to an enormous expense of fifteen thousand dollars annually. The matter of pulling the kids out of that school was out of question, he would have not agreed to that in a million years. It would have probably been okay to do that if they were not doing well at school. But no, that was not a good enough reason, not for the sake of weakening economy. It would ruin his prestige, and destroy his image among friends.

He had obtained bank loans for the office he built with Dr. Mehrabian. He built a huge house based on his projected income. And now he was desperately searching for the way out. Right around that time the revolution was taking place in Iran. Numerous people were dying every second. Every one of us was worried about our families in Iran. Our children were lost between the two cultures. At this time Azeez, who always liked to be the center of attraction, came up with an idea. He thought that apart from all other parties, which our children try to avoid, we should arrange weekly gatherings in our houses on Sundays in effort to teach our children where we come from, and what it meant to be an Iranian.

At the beginning Azeez and many others thought that that change was the answer to Iran's problems. They thought they were the one who would bring Iran back to the hands of Iranians. We were all lost trying to figure out what was really going on in Iran. Thousands and thousands of young Iranians who were enrolled at universities around the world were returning to Iran hoping that they could save Iran from further destruction. They thought that it was the right time to introduce Iran, its culture, and the way our ancestors lived to our children.

Azeez thought of it first, and then he introduced the idea to Iraj. Iraj, like always, just listened to him quietly; it was almost as if he could not hear him. He always seemed to be absorbed with his own world. Then he agreed, and said that it was a good idea.

As I said before they have both been involved in political activism during their college years. They had a lot in common, so they always had something to share and talk about politically, and bring back the memories of their younger years.

I don't think these two remembered the rules of Islam themselves. And now Azeez was going to teach our children the rules of Islam to our children who have been away from our country, religion, and culture since they were born. Many of our children were born here. None of them were of toddler age, so nourishing new and foreign ideas in them would be quite a challenge. Many families, including myself, were in disagreement with

At Arman and Julie's wedding; they are cutting the cake. Their parents were not there at that moment. But, Julie's parents were dancing while Arman's parents were far away in Iran. Poor Arman had to go through a lot.

It is one day before we go to the Malakutis' house, with my cousin Lily. Left to right: Iraj, Lily, Mojgan, and Mary

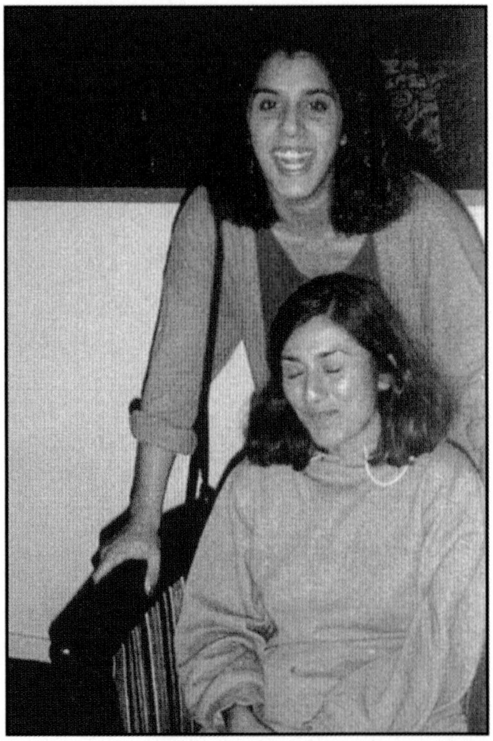

Mojgan and Mary were teasing me for taking pictures of them.

Nazy Forghani and her husband are at a party held for them by Pari and Kamal Kamooneh. Kamal and Pari are also in the picture. Nazy's parents were not present at their wedding.

Here, Arman is dancing. He was so young that he did not know what was going on. Pari and Kamal are also dancing.

The happy bride and the groom were entertaining their guests.

this gathering. How could I be teaching my children something that I didn't believe in? But since beyond all this laid the importance of out togetherness with our children we had all agreed.

My Dear God:

But in reality the children were not the problem. Our children knew exactly what they wanted. And they were very intelligent. The adults were the ones who needed to learn how to get along, and simply how to behave. They were in constant competition with each other. They always wanted to prove their superiority over the rest. I have no idea how they were planning to organize a group of young and old Iranians under one roof, and not have any friction among them?

They knew that the Baha'is had formed a Sunday school for their children, and they had monthly gatherings in each neighborhood for the conversion of their faith. These gatherings were established at the inception of the Baha'i faith. They had established rules and regulations.

The Baha'is reaction to the news that Muslims are trying to teach their children about Islam was the following, "Just wait, it will only last for a few weeks. For pretty soon they will get into a big fight, and there goes their Sunday school". Those were Parvaneh's words, and I was afraid that she was completely right.

The fights between these doctors were so shameful, despite the fact that they were absolutely over nothing. They were acting so infantile. They were so foolish that many times their own children questioned, "Why are we not seeing that doctor whose children are my friends?" So I had many doubts about the whole concept from the very beginning. I knew that success of any development is based on the management. And I was sure that the combination of Azeez and Iraj for this purpose could not end up in victory. But again I had to stay out because Azeez never considered Badri's opinion. And I didn't want Iraj to accuse me of being negative.

Azeez and Iraj were two completely opposites. Although Azeez was the sole decision maker at home, yet watch his mind change after he came out of his bedroom. When it came to organizing this Muslim group he obviously was the leader. Some families were delighted to see their children learn all about Iran, and its culture and history. But would they be able to convince them to join the group once a week in order to learn about Iran, that was the big question.

Azeez and Iraj met almost every night. Besides all the difficulties that they had to address, now they had to find the time to educate themselves about Iran and everything else that came along. That actually wasn't easy.

My Dear God:

They have been away from Iran and its politics for many years. They didn't know what was going on at that time. Even through studying it would not be possible to have the answers to all those children's questions.

They had come up with a list of families that would consider joining the group: Dr. Mahajer's two children, Dr. Radsan's two children, Dr. Aryani's two children, Dr. Neel's three children, Dr. M. Rabbani's two children, Dr. Barkhordari's three children, Dr. Malakuti's three children, and our three children. These are all I can remember.

All the parents agreed, and the group started getting together on Sundays. The subject was not just religion. The conversations were on any subject. But the kids were way too intelligent. Having all the freedom and a particular lifestyle it was impossible for them to accept the cultural philosophy of Iran and Islam.

Their intelligence however was not the only reason; it was their upbringing and their parents that they did not want to continue. Just like their parents, some were thinking that they were better and smarter than others. They would tease those who went to private schools, and many were offended by it.

Although these gatherings did not last long, they did contribute to a closer relationship between Azeez and Iraj or I must say Badri and Iraj.

In my opinion Azeez and Reza were more likely to establish close friendship. They both were sincere in their own way, honest with their own feelings, and very funny. They both had interest in collecting antiques and artwork. They had fun antique shopping together. They would bring home various pieces of art. Then they would evaluate for days that followed the merchandise they have purchased. And then all of a sudden, over something very childish, they would get upset with each other, and they would stop talking to one another for a long time.

Meanwhile, just like a group of teenagers, all the other doctor friends would intervene by taking sides. One would say, "You are right" to Azeez. And the other would say, "You are right" to Reza. It all depended on who that friend was, and how devious he was. What kind of children could you expect from this kind of parents? Who do you think they would learn from? If the fight was over an important issue that would have been a different story, but it was practically over nothing. They stopped seeing each other for months or at times for a whole year.

Then after a while when they got together again they would become much closer than before. This time no one could get close to them, no way. They belonged to each other. No one could touch that friendship. All this seemed so infantile to me They would fight over their toys, and after a few minutes they would started kissing up and sharing their toys again.

My Dear God:

I found out later that Malakuti came to Michigan with the help of Dr. Vaziri, who had a good position in Psychology department. I had heard this from Dr. Habeeb Vaziri when I saw during one of my visits. Azeez and Habeeb were good friends, while their wives, Rakhshi and Badri, were also good friends. Since Malakutis didn't know anyone in town, Vaziris introduced them to as many people as he could.

As soon as they found their ways around, got jobs and found new friends, they started gossiping about Vaziris. To begin with Vaziris' were not the type of people who would get involved with just anybody. They had their own class, and they had their own life style. They didn't care much what Malakutis' were doing. They just ended the friendship, and only once in a while they had to face each other at the hospitals, or other Psychology clinics.

When we met them, they were good friends of Barkhordaris'. They were such good friends that when Barkhordaris' were moving in to their new house to become our next-door neighbor, Azeez helped them move all their furniture upstairs into their tri-level house.

Nasser was telling us that they had packed all their furniture in the truck but the movers did not show up. Nasser had no choice but to finish moving that weekend". He was discussing his problem with Azeez when he offered his help. But because of Nasser's back ache Azeez had to carry the big dressers on his back, just like porters in Iran.

My Dear God:

I had come to a conclusion after Malakuti's death that those among us who seemed to be stingy at first appeared to be the real gentlemen. Those who did not go overboard spending their family money on Badri's family were true gentlemen. They did not take up any personal interest in Badri, and therefore they were not trying to prove that they care more than what they should do.

Iraj had the eyes to see other people's wrongdoings. But his insight had failed him when it came to his own behavior. He assumed for some reason that the eyes of others were not capable of watching him. And they were watching him closely. They had the eyes to see through him. They even wrote a poem about him, and they made sure that the rest of the Iranians saw him with through eyes also.

Our life couldn't get any better at that time. Despite all the pressure we managed to live a happy life. We both thought that we had made it through.

Parri and Kamal had finally gotten their green cards. The revolution had started in Iran by then, so they decided to move to America. They bought a house in Encino by Los Angeles CA, while staying with us to be able to be with their children. They were among those revolutionary people on the streets of Tehran, and so they gave us the first hand news. They knew how it started, but they didn't know how it was going to end. They chose to move to United States due to all the uncertainties in the country.

Parri was far more than just a sister in-law to me. When I left my family behind, she was able to take their place in my heart. She was my sister in-law, my sister, my friend, and my confidant. The news of them moving to America brought lots of joy and hope to my life.

It always felt like both Parri and Kamal were my family, more than they were Iraj's. We had so much in common. I was sure that our feelings for each other were mutual. The fact that they were going to live in the U.S.A. was very significant. For the first time in many years I felt like I had my own family by me.

We knew absolutely everything about each other's families, be that good or bad. There was no need to keep secrets or feel uncomfortable. It was thanks to these genuine feelings within me that I was feeling content and very happy.

We made it a custom to go away for Christmas holidays every year, to Parri and Kamal's house, and have the time of our life. Every once in a while our friends from Iran would stay with us. Among them were Mr. and Mrs. Parveez and Parveen Tehrani. This was the couple that I had mentioned meeting at Alavinejads' in East Lansing, Michigan. There was an important football game going on that day, and Morteza had to watch the game, or else. On the other hand Iraj was not too fond of football. We spent the whole day watching those two fighting over the TV channels. That afternoon there was another couple among the invitees. Almost immediately after we were introduced both Iraj and Parveez said, "oh, we have been at one school in Zahedan".

My Dear God:

So when they came to our new house this time, they said as they were looking around, "This is Rafani's Holiday Inn". They couldn't believe that he had built this such a big, show off house. They were remembering the times when we were still on Bell Court Road, next to Beaumont Hospital, and we barely possessed anything. We had some furniture there, which we got from thrift store. I had to refinish and reupholster it by myself. She was comparing lifestyle now with the good old days, when we possessed nothing but a happy life.

They were Baha'is, they had three children: two girls and a boy. Their children were raised and complied with all the rulings of Baha'i faith. During their one-week stay they had noticed that my children were trying to gain independence, and develop minds of their own. Also one day, when Soury was visiting, Parveen, who was very observant of her surroundings, pulled me aside and said, "Can I ask you why are you friends with this woman? And why do you let her feel like this is her own house?" My sister Azar was there, and they were washing dishes together. When I asked her what she meant by that, she said, "Well, nothing". Then she said, "She is too young and too beautiful to have her in your house all the time".

You know, my dear GOD, I think that most of the time people do not know what they are talking about. Don't these people understand that if a husband does not fool around is not because you are on a look out. People don't understand that it is their nature that would stop them from thinking of having affairs and not their watchful wives. Don't these people know that even when you watch and try to control your husband at home, if he is the unfaithful type he will engage himself elsewhere, outside his home? Any husband, or for that matter any wife, who wants to cheat on their partners, they will find ways to do it, and they will make sure to keep it undisclosed. While the ones who are faithful to their marital obligations no matter where and who they are with, they will never make themselves involved with anybody.

My Dear God:

I happened to watch a movie called “Doctor's wives”. The story was about doctors. These doctors were mostly working out of the house for extended hours. Meanwhile the wives stayed home, bored out of their wits. These women drank, and they slept with other men, they used drugs, and so on all in the name of loneliness. And their husbands did the same thing out side of their homes. These people knew nothing about the marriage constitution. You are predisposed for failure if you consider succeeding by simply watching your husbands, and keeping him behind thick bars of suspicions. You cannot alter a character.

So I told Parveen, “So you think that if I stop inviting people to my house, he won't look for them elsewhere? Do you think I should keep the doors to his office locked, and try to keep him away from going to the hospital? What will my life be like if I only think of him fooling around with every woman who came to my house?

You can watch your husband just enough to know what is going on. You are lucky if he is not the type, otherwise you can not change him to an honest and faithful man”.

I was pregnant with Maseeh when we were living in Bell Court. Iraj was always working either for himself, or he was moonlighting elsewhere. It was one of the nights near my due date when I heard a knock on my window. Then I heard someone knocking on my door. I kept looking around, but I didn't see anyone. I was so scared. I was very heavy, I could barely walk. Then all of a sudden I heard a loud laughter. Guess who was there, my dear GOD? Yes, you are right. It was Parveez and Parween Fereshteh and Morteza, who were trying to play a joke on me.

Neither of the couples had children at that time. They were free to go anywhere and do anything they wanted. That late at night they traveled all the way from Lansing that night just to scare me. They stayed with us for few days, and we had the loveliest time together.

My Dear God:

After giving up the Sunday school gatherings, I decided to organize a weekly Blot party. These kinds of gatherings were great for me. I liked to get together with others, but I did not want to just talk about shopping or gossip. And I think this was what the group of card players appreciated the most.

My Dear God:

The funnies thing about these two couples, Rafanis and Malakutis, was that Iraj was not found of Azeez, they had no similarities in their characters. And Shamci in her turn had no common interests with Badri. But something was making us closer and closer. At the time it was impossible to figure the source of this unknown power that was pushing us together. But now it is so clear that Badri and Iraj were playing their role beautifully, while Azeez and I were falling for it.

You see, my dear GOD, after some twenty years of socializing with many Iranians from this group, after all the joking and teasing that went on between us, how was I supposed to suspect anything between them? You can only imagine that if Azeez had suspected anything, he would have killed both of them.

Among the Blot players were Shushtaris, Barkhordaris, Rohan and Jalal Panah, Malakutis, and Rafanis. Then it was Khodadadeh and Sally, Rahmat Kashef, Louise Neel, and sometimes Dr. Joorabchi and Zari, and Minoo and Foad Panah. Of course it wasn't always that all these people were able to join the party. Everyone was really looking forward to the night of the card game. Actually those nights were a source of tranquility and time passing for all of us. Many of us liked to stay up and play till five o'clock in the morning. Some of us were able to make up, and sleep in on the following day, which was Sunday.

Most of us were away from our extended families and homes. So those evenings brought back the sense of unity and family. We were becoming closer and closer. We began having these gatherings more frequently, at times two or three times a week. That was our only source of fun and relaxation. Despite of all our differences, we have remained friends for over twenty years. We tried to make a good life for our children and us.

But our children refused to look it that way. They were neither comfortable being Iranians nor Americans. Each one of them had a different opinion about how to relate to their Iranian ethnicity.

They were Americans, because they were born and raised here. They carried American birth certificates and American passports. Their parents were working in a very high ranked profession, and they were paying their taxes, with the exception that their parents were born in Iran. They had no reason not to consider themselves Americans. But the society and the peer pressure they were surrounded by have made their existence uncomfortable. They had to make a choice between the two cultures.

My Dear God:

My children retained a very painful memory of their father's affair in Iran. This horrific experience that they were put through at a very young age left a big emotional scar on them.

Mary rebelled against everything, especially me. She was against my authority and me at the age of ten. She had made me a target no matter how I tried to approach her. My first child, who was supposed to be the role model for my other kids, had started rebelling at the age of ten. Thanks GOD, I was able to recognize her emotions at that time. I always made sure to find out how to deal with her. I thought of possibility that she was blaming me for what had happened; otherwise she had absolutely no reason to hate me so much. She was inseparable from me for that first ten years of her life. How could she switch one hundred and eighty degrees in an instance? I couldn't stop wondering. I was certain that the hurt of those four years of her life was so tremendous that she didn't know how to deal with it. It didn't help that it happened during the most sensitive years of her life, ages three to six. After we came back to U.S.A. neither Maseeh nor Mary have ever tried to bring up the subject of their father's affair.

Mary had so much love for her father and me, and I was sure that she was dying to keep that love forever and ever. And yet she acted completely the opposite on the surface. I had a feeling that she was trying to kill that love in her heart before we took it away from her again. So she tried to do anything that was a no-no in our book.

My Dear God:

Mary wanted to keep the control of her life.

One morning I went to her room, and I found out that she had put her mattress on the floor, and kept her chest and drawers inside her closet. Her father purchased that bedroom set for her before we came back from Iran. It was the beginning of our new life together after his affair. He wanted to prove to us that he cared for us a lot. He had ordered a complete set, a queen size bed with a very beautiful canopy, a chest, a desk with a chair, and a dresser with a big mirror all in pure pink. She was almost seven years old then. Now she was turning thirteen, and she did not like the style, the color, or the size of the whole bedroom set. So she wanted them out of her room, and that was it.

To tell you the truth, I never liked that bedroom set either. I recognized that sleeping on the floor was one of the sixty's fashions. And since that was her room, she wanted everything out of there.

I was able to convince her to at least keep the desk in her closet to use its drawers, and then I got rid of the rest.

Something funny happened when I placed an ad in the newspaper. One man called to find out what was the condition of the set. He asked many questions regarding the safety

and comfort of the bed. Then he asked me if I could sleep on the bed. I said, "Yes". He asked if he could sleep on the bed. I said, "Yes, why not?" And then he asked if I could sleep on the bed together with him? At that time I realized that he was trying to make a fool of me, and he wasn't interested in buying the bedroom set at all. After that I decided to give the bedroom set away to Salvation Army and altogether forget about selling it.

My Dear God:

So like always Mary got what she wanted. I believed that I should not force my children into anything. And even though it was my obligation to make them aware of things, I wanted them to decide for themselves.

I just could not understand why my children, who had so much freedom at home, and who acted very aggressive, were not aggressive beyond the boundaries of their home or among their friends? All in all Mary while a child, and then a teenager had a hard time finding herself among her peers.

Mary was very beautiful. I was not the only one who noticed that, but there was not one person who did not believe that strongly. And even in this case if I ever admired her beauty, for whatever the reason she reacted very harshly, and showed her resentment towards me.

While my children were growing up, we, the parents, were approaching the period of excruciating changes in our lives.

With the situation in Iran, and weak economy and oil crises in America, the creation of HMOS, and the huge expenses, he had woven a thick web around himself, he didn't know how to get out of it.

My Dear God:

It was during this time that Arman became partners with one other Iranian. His name was Naser Zarghami, who was the brother of Maliheh Zamiry. Their father was related to my father. They were third cousin or something. They had another American partner. These partners owned a gas station, and they consulted their partnership with Iraj. Iraj agreed that Arman would pay ten thousand dollars, and become one-third partner. Not long after the deal was done we heard that the money was gone. And the American partner was blaming Arman and Nasser for mismanaging the gas station and losing all the money. And he was opening a lawsuit against them.

At this time you can imagine what Iraj was going through. He was trying so hard to keep his niece and nephew out of trouble. His office income was decreasing, and he was stuck in the middle of all these problems without any help. But the more complicated his problems got, the harder he looked for more.

With all the mess around us, Arman had decided to get married. He wanted to marry Julie Meier, who was the sister of Mary's friend Sue Miere.

It was during or around this time that Nazi went to Maliheh's house and started a big physical fight. She even attacked Maliheh, and created a big mess. It was too late to correct anything by the time I found out what had happened. I immediately went to Maliheh's house, and I apologized profusely, I told her that I was not aware of all that had happened, and asked for her forgiveness.

Arman's marriage took place while his parents were in Iran. Mr. and Mrs. Claudett Miere were very nice people. Although they knew that Arman was not the right candidate for Julie, they still did their best to make their daughter and Arman happy.

Arman and Julie both were right out of high school when they decided to get married. I thought it was a joke at first. But when we were invited to the bridal shower, I realized it was real. While I was the one who was so sad for the Mieres family, Claudett was happy and was cheering for them. I thought that perhaps she didn't know as much as I knew about Arman. I heard later on that not only they didn't know much about him, but also Mr. Miere had given Arman six thousand dollars thinking that he was going to use the money on his gas station business. Obviously that money went to the same place where the other money had gone.

My Dear God:

Their wedding night was the coldest and iciest night ever in Michigan. Parri, Kamal, and their children were present from our side as a family. And among friends there were Barkhordaris, the Rabbanis, and obviously Dr. Malakuti and his family. The saddest part was that Arman's parents couldn't be there, and his aunt Parri was trying to cover for them. And above all Mr. and Mrs. Mieres did their best to make him happy.

It wasn't till after a few months that Julie started to come over and cry on our shoulders. She loved him, and she didn't want to believe that she couldn't live with the real Arman. She complained that he was always with his male friends, and that he treated her like his servant. "He wants me to do everything by myself, while he is always out with strange people". Although it really was not our problem, it had eventually become our problem. All of us were sad and unhappy to see that we were not able to do anything for her, or to change Arman.

I could see so vividly at that time that Iraj didn't know how to get out of that strong web that he had woven around himself. On the surface he did not show any signs of depression or anger, especially to me. He never complained about the things that were happening, because he did not want to admit that he had caused all those things by just being quiet and passive. I wish I was a courageous woman at that time to be able to send Arman to Iran. Probably, he would still be alive today.

At this time of our lives things were happening so fast that it felt like we were in a spinner, turning around, and around.

My children were not applying themselves at school as they were expected to do.

They were sent to Country Day School to be among advanced students. But neither of them tried to be better than average. It was only first year that Mary made Summa Cum Laude. Obviously she could have continued it, but unfortunately she was preoccupied being a sixty's teenager, so she did not apply herself to her full capacity.

I could never understand Mary's behavior towards me. There were times that I thought she loved me to death, and there were times that I felt her hatred for me.

Once she came home and gave me a piece of art that said, "GOD could not be everywhere, so he created mothers". Another time, while I knew she didn't have much money, she sent me a dozen roses on my birthday from Los Angeles, while she was visiting a friend. Another time, while she knew that I didn't smoke, she bought me a beautiful ashtray with an engraving, which said, "From one NUT to another".

Coming from Mary, who never wanted to show love to me, these acts were signs of pure love. And on the other hand the things that she did purposely to hurt me were countless. I wouldn't know where to begin.

Sometimes I wondered if Mary was jealous of her father's love for me. It so happened that on many occasions Mary spoke to me in a very harsh manner. Then Iraj stopped her and he told her, "You must know whom you are talking to". This was probably the reason behind her disliking me so much. Anyway I could never figure out the reason for her resentment for me.

My Dear God:

Both Iraj and I tried so hard to show our children that we must have respect for each other. I also never allowed my children to talk down to their father. We wanted to show our children that we both agreed to the ways of raising them. Our objective was to become one voice, and not to ever contradict one another.

I think kids are much smarter than their parents. Many times it happened that they tested us for our vulnerability.

Once Maseeh had asked us to get him something very expensive. He knew that I was completely against it. He knew that if he did not do exceptionally well at school, I would not agree to buy him an expensive gift. So he went to Iraj, and asked him in private to buy him that gift. I think it was a camera. Iraj, knowing that I was against it, told Maseeh, "I should ask your Mom. If she agrees, I will not have anything against buying it". This time Maseeh, who was very upset, told his father, "You always say let me ask your Mom. Don't you ever have a mind of your own to say yes to anything we ask you?"

Iraj came to me, and told me what happened between him and Maseeh. Thanks GOD those days we were very truthful to each other, and life was as good as it could be. We both performed our duties according to the book. We tried to open our eyes, and ears, and create a happy life for our children and ourselves. We were trying to live a respectful life, and we made sure that our children get our message. He was a great husband and a great father. And as I understood from his actions, I was a great wife, and a great mother. What else did we need to make us happy? When I look back, I see that he did everything in his power to show our children and I that he was proud of us, and that he was very happy. He knew that I was hundred percent for my family, and nothing could take their place. He was happy with my absolute loyalty to him.

Mary got accepted to University of Michigan majoring in history. For us, Iranians, the idea of sending our children away was a disaster at first. Although we got her a private room, she was never out of my mind. I was worried about how she was going to adapt. Soon we found out that some other Iranians, like Dr. Minooie, had purchased an apartment in Chapple Hill, Ann Arbor, Michigan for his daughter Maryam, who was attending a medical school there. She was renting out some of the rooms to other students, while it was a little help for the mortgage payment. On the other hand she had the opportunity of choosing a roommate that she was fond of.

My Dear God:

We jumped on to that splendid idea instantly. We discussed it with Mary first. She knew that many other Iranian doctors had done it, and their children were following the same routine that Maryam did.

So after we got the apartment, she would not move in right away. That was another mortgage on Iraj's shoulders. Then after she finally decided to move in, she did not agree to have a housemate for some time.

Being Mary, who approached things differently, she told her father once, "You only bought this apartment, one, for your tax shelter, and two, for your own investment. You were not really thinking of only my comfort".

Such harsh behavior brought tears to my eyes. It was very difficult to watch Iraj getting demolished this way. But who could say anything to Mary at that time? She was a teenager, who was determined to first destroy us, and then destroy herself.

Although later on Iraj blamed this and all her other acts on me, still I can say that we both were very tolerant.

We put that apartment on both Mary's and Iraj's name. In case something happened to Iraj, Mary would have been the sole owner. We always tried to do the best for all of us, because I never thought that there was any other way. I thought we were one for all, and all for one.

The house we built was an embarrassment to Mary. Living in a beautiful suburb was a crime. Everything we did was against the sixty's revolution.

Maseeh on the other hand was doing his own thing without getting into collisions with us. He was mainly with his friends, and he liked to give open parties at home. He would openly invite his girl friend from school. I was watching him like a hulk, and according to him I had made his life miserable.

I had asked all his teachers to make sure that he does not miss any of his classes. He was completely against the establishment of the school. He hated their lunch rules. And the way that I kept a watchful eye on everything he did made him mad.

The more discipline there was at school, the happier I was. Maseeh hated to be forced to finish food in his plate. But there was a rule to finish their food in their plates enforced by the school. Their headmaster at the time, Dr. Schlagle, believed that most children who were attending the Country Day School came from very comfortable and well-off families. He believed those children had no idea how children of the world were living day by day. He wanted them to know that there were many children around the world that wished for a piece of bread. He said that our children must learn that they can't get everything and anything they wanted. As much as my children hated that idea, I loved it. Iraj and I could remember seeing those children in Iran. We were raised in a way that we would get one pair of shoes a year if we were lucky. And we were very limited on selections. We were raised in a way that if we didn't like the food that was served on the dinner table, they would tell us, "There is nothing else for you, so you must go to bed without food". It hurt us then, but the result of the disciplinary action was great, and it made us tolerant of pain.

My Dear God:

My children would laugh at us when we told them about our lifestyle in Iran. They would even tease us. Those disciplinary measures might have been painful for us then, but they made us who we are now. Again, my children might laugh at me reading this sentence, but that is okay. They haven't lived in my shoes anyway to know what I am talking about.

Many people believed that we had spoiled our children. There were times that I did not want to believe that. But as the time passed, I realized that they were right. Although I was trying to discipline them in many ways, I had spoiled them in many other ways. And I can't go back and correct it now.

Maseeh had decided to go into arts and advertising. His art teacher at school believed that he was very talented, and therefore he would be successful in that field. Once, speaking of spoiling our kids, he took me aside and said, "Mrs. Rafani, I am a hard working teacher, and my wife is a hard working teacher also. The other day your son Maseeh brought his new camera to school to show it to me. He had so many different expensive lenses. I don't think I will ever be able to buy one like that". He was trying to tell me that when things came to them so easily, \they did not need to work hard for anything. Or when they had everything available for them, they would loose the excitement of receiving something great in their lives. I believe that he was absolutely right. And I had nothing to say.

Another time his aunt Niya brought a gold medallion for Maseeh. The medallion was more than one inch in diameter. It was very heavy, on a heavy chain. I noticed in a short while that he no longer wore it. When I asked him where the medallion was, he answered, "I had melted it at school to make a ring". When I asked him what he did with the rest of that heavy medallion, he told me, "I left it with my teacher". I guess that medallion, or the beauty of it did not mean anything to him. Oh well.

My Dear God:

Mojgan, who started attending the Country Day School in kindergarten, decided one day to no longer go there. This was a school that had a waiting list for kids to be enrolled. Now, because one of her friends wanted to transfer to Andover School near our house, she decided to do the same.

I have talked about Mojgan's stubbornness before. She was one girl you could not say "No" to. She joined the Andover School in Jr. High. I thought to myself that after all if she just wanted to be an average student, she might as well be one at Andover. At least it meant one less heavy tuition for us.

Iraj was under a lot of pressure, and he started blaming me for everything. I was to blame if Maseeh didn't want to become a doctor. It was my fault if Mary was getting involved with drugs, mind you due to the presence of his nieces and nephews. It was my fault if Mojgan wanted to change schools. And it still was my fault if his office didn't make enough money.

If at the times that he was getting involved with all those projects, I tried to advice him, and stop him from getting involved. He always said I was the negative factor of his life. I was more and more worried after each big project that he started. Sometimes listened to my opinion, and did what I had asked him to do.

Like the time that I stopped him from buying that Mercedes Benz 450 SL. Or like the time that I asked him not to spend money on an expensive chinchilla cape, or many other cases like that. But even then, while he was happy that we didn't proceed with the deal, still he found a reason to take those cases against me, and put the blame on me.

Neither of us was against having a big and beautiful house. But only if that big and beautiful house and it's up keep did not create uncomfortable daily routine life for people who lived there. I wasn't ready to give up our happiness for the price of being rich and famous. I married that person with or without money. And I wanted him to continue to be the same person for as long as we belonged to each other. But no, he wanted to become number one among his friends. He wanted to look great in the eyes of his friends, and he was not paying attention to the amount of the pressure that he was creating for himself. Although he was trying to prove to my children and me that everything he did was to make us happy, deep down, I think he had other plans.

We were both very excited that when our children graduate from college, they will have a home to come back to. We were dreaming to celebrate our children's weddings, while we were living in that house. Iraj was the one who was the most excited about all these dreams. To me he had become the lover that he was when we first met. He was telling me that after our children left for college, he would take me around the word for our silver anniversary. Those were all his ideas. I have never even mentioned our silver anniversary. He was excited that our relatives could come and visit us. I knew that my family members were not able to come because it would have been a very costly trip for them. But my relationship with his sisters was so good that I always thought of them as my own family. Even after the time that Parri created that big fight over nothing, still I always was excited when we were together. They were our only family that came to visit us and stayed with us in this country. I loved all of them truly and dearly, and I was the only person that looked forward to have them in my house.

My Dear God:

When Parri, Kamal, and their children moved to California after the revolution in Iran, we all looked forward to making up for all the lost times.

Being with Parri was like being among my family in Iran. We had many memories of my parents' house together. Besides the memories that I had with them, the friendship that I had with Parri and Kamal was so important to me that I would not exchange it with the world. Obviously these were all my feelings for them at that time. I really don't know if they had the same feelings or not. I always felt lucky to be able to have Parri's family in this country.

Once, Rohan was talking to me about our trips to California. She was surprised that when we were in California, we stayed with Parri instead of going to a hotel. In a way she was telling me that we were staying in Parri's house to save money.

Actually I did not expect her to understand my feelings. I said to her that the only reason that we go to California was to be with Parri and her family. If we didn't want to stay with Pari we would not go to California. We would have gone other places in America. I loved staying with my sister-in-law, because it reminded me of my parents, my home in Tehran, and all the fun we had together when we were a teenagers. I think she was not able to believe that someone might love her sister-in-law to a point that staying with her meant everything for her. And I was that person.

Sometimes I think that even Parri and Kamal were unaware of how important and valuable their visits were to me. I always looked forward to see them, and I enjoyed every minute of it.

That is why when Parri created that one time commotion between us, I felt so sorry for our greatest friendship that got damaged after thirty years of happy and peaceful relationship. I am sure that Parri was also sorry. Because after we got back together again, she was complaining to me once, "If Neya wouldn't decide to come to America with me, things could have been different, and I could have been more relaxed and cooperative".

My Dear God:

You see, my dear GOD, life is so funny at times. It just leaves us wondering. Or maybe I am the one who is funny.

As I said my parents disowned me when I decided to marry Iraj. I really hurt by choosing Iraj over them. If I was supposed to pay for the hurt I caused my parents, I would have been the unluckiest person on earth. But I became one of the luckiest women on earth.

One night when Iraj and I were driving home, I started crying from happiness. I said to Iraj, "I love my husband, I love my children, I love my sisters- in-law, I love my happiness. I love the whole world, and I know that I am considered to be one of the luckiest and happiest women on earth. How come I am not paying for what I have done to my parents? Do you think GOD had forgiven me?" Iraj laughed at me, and said something silly in Farsi, that he always used to say, "You know you deserve it". And then he started teasing me and said, "Now, are you crying for the wonderful life that GOD had given to you, or you are crying because you hurt your parents?"

Those were the days that we both thought we had made it. We noticed that those dark days were gone, and each one of us performed our duties to our full potential. He was recognizing his fatherhood, and I was aware of what was expected from me as a full time mother. It was his dream to complete his duty to be known as a great father.

And I would get so emotional when I saw my happiness in front of my eyes. I would get emotional because I remembered my mother's comment after my brother Jalal's death. She said, "When I got four grandchildren within three months, and I felt too lucky, I was expecting a disaster to happen. Life is never complete, unless we experience joy and sadness, happiness and unhappiness together". She always felt that she lost Jalal because she had received so much joy through getting four grand children at once. They were Maseeh, Negeen, Nader, and Reza. She celebrated the birth of each and every one of them one by one. And then losing one of her own children destroyed her.

So you see, my dear GOD, while I was very happy, and I knew that I had everything to be thankful for, still in the back of my mind I was begging you to save me from those disastrous times.

I really don't know what to say. Iraj was the happiest, when he saw me happy. He did anything and everything that made me happy. He bought me things that I liked. We ate at restaurants that I liked. We ordered the food that I liked. He always remembered my birthdays. He was nice in the house, in the bedroom, and everywhere else. I don't know. Why would he do all these things if he didn't love me? Those were the signs of love to me. And he must have needed my love for him. For I loved him with all my heart. I would give my heart, my eyes for him at any time. If he wasn't really in-love with me; then

probably my love and my devotion to him had made him so nice and thankful to me. I really don't know.

My Dear God:

You remember, my dear GOD, how often I thanked you for giving the kind of happiness that you had given me. You remember how often I thanked you for giving us more than we deserved. You remember how many times I asked you to take the excessive materials that you had given us, and keep my husband and my children healthy and happy. And you remember the night that we had a big party in our house. Like always the party went so well. The food was colorful and delicious. And everyone had a great time. After everyone left, as always he helped me to clean up. I went to bed after he did. He was still up. It was almost three o'clock in the morning. He turned to me and kissed me so lovingly, and he thanked me for the beautiful time we had. You remember, my dear GOD, I could never forget that night. I couldn't fall asleep that night. I was sleeping on the side overlooking the lake. I saw the moon in the lake. The reflection of the moon in the water was so great and beautiful, and Iraj's love and respect for me was so wonderful that tears started uncontrollably rolling down my cheeks.

For some reason I felt that I was at the peak of my happiness. I knew with all my heart that I was one of the luckiest women on earth. Besides having everything I had asked for, I had a husband that I loved dearly. And I was willing to exchange my whole life for him. And he knew it too. You remember, my dear GOD, at that moment I asked you, "Please, my dear GOD, if you ever wanted to punish me please take my house, my furniture, our money, but please keep my husband and my three children happy and healthy for me". I talked to you and begged you to bless my family for me. I know that you remember. There was no one else in our conversation, except you and I.

Yes, my dear GOD, we had our differences. Yes, we had our difficult moments in our marriage life. Yes, we went through many years of maturing, but the way that he showed his love for us was so great that I could never believe that he could have faked that love, or I would be the most stupid wife on earth.

Anyway it was with that idea of having a loving home, and loving children that we continued dealing with our children's development, and we tried to learn how to handle them.

My Dear God:

Although we were doing fine, we were not in debt, and we did not owe anybody anything, I somehow realized that Iraj was trying to get involved with more business affairs. And in reality he was trying to win the competition with other doctors, Dr. M Rabbani and Dr. Naser Barkhordari. His desire was to become number one. He wished to reach the unreachable star that was so high that it was out of human sight. And even then

he didn't mind to complicate his life getting involved with many business and many people. Money was his ultimate goal. Obviously this race was not for the comfort of the family, but to feed his ego.

A person whose dream was to own beautiful cars, a beautiful home, and a beautiful family, now that he had it all he wasn't feeling fulfilled at all. It seemed that he was not satisfied, and he was looking for satisfaction outside. In other words he was completely lost, and he was going through a severe case of menopause, meaning his mid life crisis.

Once he discussed with me that he was thinking of opening a weight loss clinic. There was a product in the market called Optifast. He was studying it very carefully. He was attending as many seminars as possible. He was planning to go into partnership with Dr. Malakuti. After a few discussions and some research they took the matter seriously. They thought if Nazi Mahajer could open a weight loss clinic successfully, why couldn't we? Soon they started gathering more information. He asked me to join him for one of the seminars for Optifast. He had planned that we would go to lunch together, while learning about Optifast at the same time.

Iraj, who from the very beginning wanted to have his solo practice, and who never wanted to have a partner, a person who had passed many offers for a partnership, now all of a sudden was willing to go into partnership with the most unexpected person, Azeez Malakuti.

Iraj was a very private person. He would never reveal his other side. He rarely expressed his opinion. When I suspected something, I had to literally pull it out of him.

I remember the times of revolution in Iran. Families were forced to sell their houses and leave the country in order to survive. One day while everyone was sharing many disastrous incidents, Iraj turned to me and said, "The hard days might come. We should be ready when it comes. Yes, it is coming". I looked at him to see if I heard him right. I felt that he was trying to tell me everything, while he was not saying much. What did he mean by "Yes, it is coming"? Why was this person, who never thought or talked negative, talking so hopelessly? I wondered if he really knew something that I didn't know. To me it seamed that he was at the end of his rope. He was afraid of dying.

My Dear God:

It was after the news of Dr. Ghandchi drowning in his own pool that both Iraj and Azeez were going crazy. It seemed to them that they were both at their own funerals.

That day after the funeral we were all standing around the pool that he drowned in. Azeez, who always had a kind of sadness in him, was talking about his funeral, and how or where it would take place. He always had a strong opinion about each and every one of us.

Or I remember one day at the dinner table Maseeh mentioned that one of his friend's uncle had passed away. Luckily he left him a great amount of money. Maseeh did not mean that the boy was lucky that his uncle died. He only meant that he was lucky that he

left him money. At this time Iraj, who never talked, expressed his opinion about anything, looked at Maseeh and asked, "Oh, he is lucky because his uncle died?" And then he remained quiet.

The thing that was surprising coming from him was that before he always saw the full part of the glass, and not the empty part. How did he become such a person who looked for the wrong meaning of the sentence? Maseeh tried to explain to him what he really meant. But he wasn't listening as usual. Deep down he thought his children were only after money, but he never talked about it.

The more I saw him being mad about things that didn't matter to him before, the more I arranged parties with our friends to be able to keep his mind occupied with fun and laughter. Although he did not like going to movies frequently, he went along with us anyway. But he fell asleep in the middle of the movie any way. And later he was embarrassed of being a sleepy head.

He never went anywhere without me. We always appeared together at all Iranian, American, and hospital gatherings. He was always home on time after his office hours. If for some reason he was going to be late, even for one hour he made sure to call me. At the time of our peaceful coexistence he never raised his voice on me, or allowed any of my children to do so. He never, not even once forgot my birthdays. And when he bought me expensive gifts, he was always happier than I was. Between the two of us he was the one who made promises to me for our happier future. He was the one who promised me that after we would sell the house, we would take a trip around the world. Would any woman in a right mind doubt her husband's love, and think of him as a trader? Could a wife ask for a better husband?

I don't remember if I mentioned this before. Every Wednesday, which was his day off, we went to lunch together. We would run errands together at first, and then after we went to lunch.

My Dear God:

That one Wednesday, after having lunch in Summerset Mall, we went window-shopping. We didn't need or want anything. We stopped at a handbag shop, and we decided to go in. A large snakeskin purse with a very beautiful handle soon attracted his attention. When he asked me if I liked it, I said, "Yes, but not for myself". He kept asking me, "Why don't you like it? " I said, "It is too big for my little figure, and the head does not get open wide enough". While we were discussing this, a sales lady approached us since she overheard our conversation. With a surprise in her voice she said, "Did I hear you right? All the ladies that come to this store with their husbands beg their husbands to buy something for them, and still they don't buy anything. And if I am correct, your husband is trying to convince you to buy this very expensive purse, yet you don't let him? I am really surprised". That did it for Iraj. Anyway he bought the purse for me, and he paid

four hundred dollars, only because he liked to be perceived as a generous husband.

At that time he was so proud of himself that I think I just said, "I am not against him buying a gift for me. I am only against the size of the purse for my figure".

That day specifically he told my children, "Your mom does not appreciate what I do for her. Even the sales lady today complained about your mother's reaction to my usual kindness". I had nothing to say except "I am sorry".

But obviously my children were more confused than ever. They thought, "How come you are willing to pay such large sum of money for just a handbag, which is not even necessary to have, and then you make a big fuss about spending little money on other things that are important". But of course none of them said anything except for Mary, who kept saying, "Wow, wow, four hundred dollars for a useless purse?"

Anyway that woman was a smart sales person, and with one assertive comment she sold an expensive purse to my husband, and made her day.

This was one of many cases that I was guilty of not recognizing my husband's kindness. And with this later he made a case against my loving him.

Meanwhile he was not aware that my love for him was much stronger than his love for himself. I wanted him not to waste his money, and I wanted him to keep that money for more important objects that were necessary to have. This way he didn't have to go into partnership with people that he didn't know or didn't trust.

My husband was a doctor. He was working hard to make our life happy, and I worked very hard to do my share of duties to keep our family happy. And in the same manner that we did not want our children to get involved with wrong people, I did not want Iraj to get involved with wrong people, or wrong business. He was a nice person, he had a nice image among his friends, and most of all he was a prestigious doctor. I wanted him to continue that way. Money was good to have, but it wasn't important enough not for the price of loosing your respect among your friends. Because I was against some of his involvement with certain businesses, he accused me of being negative. He was saying that I was trying to stop him from his achievements.

My Dear God:

Although he was not much of a talker, we always discussed things concerning our family. He used to accept, and most of the times follow my advice. He was sure that I was there hundred percent for him and his success. He really believed in me. He used to call me his lucky charm.

One evening a young doctor came to our house, which I haven't met before. His name was Hossaini. He was from Tabreez, the Turkish part of Iran. I knew that because he hadn't passed his ECFMG exams, he was not able to receive the certificate, which would allow him to practice medicine. So he was working temporarily at Community Medical center, which was originated and owned by three Iranian doctors, Dr.

Mehrabian, Dr. Farah, and Dr. Darian.

Iraj had invited him to our house. When I found out that he was planning to open a nightclub, I could smell the bad news. I asked myself, "Why would a doctor get involved with a night club business?" I know what nightclubs were all about. It was the business of medicine; it didn't have anything to do with a nightclub. And it was a nightclub located around the Six Mile Road, the most dangerous part of Detroit, Michigan. How could I stay quiet, and not say anything? Why was he insisting to get involved with wrong doings? How could I make him understand that his selection of that business was not the right choice? Or does he ever want to hear me out, and listen to me?

My Dear God:

Yes, I did become negative again. True that it was his business, and true that he thought he knew what he was doing. But obviously he did not know, or he chose not to know that he was not that type. And he didn't want to hear from me what kind of involvement he had to have to be able to become a nightclub owner, yet at the corner of the Six Mile Road, in Detroit. What a wife must do in these circumstances to help her husband out of wrong involvement remains an unsolved mystery.

After all a marriage consists of two equal partners. Both good and bad must be controlled by both sides in order to avoid disasters. If the man is a captain, the woman must be assistant and his guide. She must be able to instruct him all the way. Marriage does not mean that two people only become intimate with each other. They have responsibility to save each other from any possible destruction. And I felt that time was the time for me to stop Iraj from going to wrong business.

Hossaini was promising Iraj that they will be making millions of dollars just the first year. The surprising part of this was that Iraj would believe him. I didn't know what to do except to tell him my opinion, and to warn him of the dangerous trap that he was falling into. When he started to go into partnership with Azeez, the partnership with Hossaini was forgotten for a while. I thought he had heard me. I thought he was going to take my advice, and forget about it. But it didn't happen that way.

His partnership with Dr. Malakuti became final. He was promising that this clinic will bring him lots of money.

Think about it, my dear GOD, a doctor, who had spent many hours at the hospital, and he had his office hours five days a week. And he spent many hours of the nights in the delivery room. We know that there are only twenty-four hours in every day and night. And if we calculated the hours that he was spending out of the house, we would see that there were no more hours available for him to engage himself into any other activity. This was the reason that I had put my whole life into my children's involvement, so that I could keep them away from wrongdoing.

And yet Iraj wanted to involve himself with more and more work, as if he had any time for it. True, that money was good, but can we extend the hours of the day to more than twenty-four hours? In order to spend extra hours on the new business, we have to fail our day job, which in his case was good.

The busier he got with creating different businesses for himself, the more I got involved with my children's activities. Mary was the most difficult to understand. I had to find a way to deal with each and every one of her moves. I knew she was carrying a large amount of resentment against any kind of love for her family after witnessing her father's affair. And what hurt me the most was that we did not try to open her wound and talk about it. She kept it all within, and instead she started rebelling strongly against whatever we had asked her to do. She had become self destructive by approaching unwise and forbidden activities. It began with the way she chose her clothes and made sure to keep them dirty, and the way she chose her boyfriends. She continued smoking openly in front of us, and doing other things behind our backs. I knew what was going on with her. By reading books and talking to other mothers, and my own experiences from my childhood, I never wanted to force her towards giving up her bad behavior. I knew the results would have been devastating. I knew that wearing a dirty coat was a signal to her friends that she was part of their movement. I thought this was something that she would eventually get over one day. I didn't try to clean it against her will. Because of my own brother's suicide, I wasn't trying to create a suicidal case over little things. I knew that she was smart, intelligent, and beautiful. I knew that she was an achiever if she wanted to be one. While I was growing with her, I tried so hard to learn how to make steps forward without stepping on her sensitive rebellious feelings. I tried to get to her sometimes by crying on her knees, sometimes by a quarrel, sometimes with ignorance, and most of the time by proving to her that I would be there for her no matter what. Many times it happened that she tried to test my reaction to shocking news that she would prepare for us.

My Dear God:

Once she called me from the University to say that she wanted us to meet two of her friends. I made myself ready for something important. She was at U of M, majoring in History.

They came and waited in the family room. Iraj and I came down to welcome them. After the introduction I realized what that meeting was about.

Both gentlemen were U. of M. students. One was Mary's friend, and the other one was his friend. He was from Turkish part of Iran Tabreez, Azarbaijon. He was in the process of deportation to Iran. If this happened, he would be sent to war, and he would be among those who got killed in the war between Iran and Iraq at that time. Mary didn't know that young man. And if she could help it, she would have stopped the war completely. But since she couldn't, she had decided to marry that young man at least to be able to stop the war for him.

At this time she was over eighteen years of age. She was responsible for her own actions and decision-making. What could any of us have done to change her mind in that shocking moment? Iraj was more shocked than I was. I gave myself few minutes to be able to find myself in my own body. If I knew about it in advance, I wouldn't be that shocked. But the way she approached it was so sudden that I needed to absorb her decision, and then react.

My Dear God:

Soon I found myself, and I knew at that point that it was Mary who was talking to me. Not only I didn't try to go against her decision, but also I welcomed it with open arms. I felt that if I was her, and I had as much freedom as she did, I would have chosen to marry as many men as I could in order to save them from going to war, where they would either to get killed, or kill many people. So, I welcomed the idea.

The young man was tall, handsome, and polite, with very likeable manners. He was studying to become an electrical engineer, a great beneficial to American society. I thought to myself, "Obviously her desire of marrying him was nothing but a humanitarian act. I knew that she was completely aware of the possible consequences. She told us, "We all have to take many dangerous steps in our lives, and this looks like one of them".

I am sure that she was more shocked than I was. She was expecting a very harsh reaction from me, and she didn't get it. I passed her test, and let her know that I would like to raise a child with a healthy mind.

Another time she had invited us to her apartment in Ann Arbor Mi. She had prepared a very delicious dinner. After discussing many subjects, she announced that she has been living with an African American man for some time now.

She was expecting me to pass out, or scream with a huge disappointment. I remember that Iraj had turned red and blue. I was afraid that he might get a heart attack. While he sat there quietly, I started my reverse psychology. I told her that I was glad that she had found a person that she liked enough to live with. And I let her know that she was mature enough to know the right from wrong. I told her, "What makes us a good person is not our color, or our religion. As long as the person you love is the right person for you, and as long as he loves you the same, I am all for it. It is your life, and your decision. You are the one who must live with the man. I do not like to dictate to you who to love, or whom to marry".

I thought the way that Iraj was quiet; he was ready to kill me, "Why was I even discussing it?" But I knew Mary, and that was the way to approach her.

It wasn't long before she broke the news to me. She had gotten rid of him. After she started complaining about him, and wanted to blame his color for all his wrong behavior, it was the time for me to stop her right there. I asked her to sit down and listen to me. I said, "You see Mary, you have dated many men. Every one of them had their own faults

that were not acceptable by you. So you decided to leave them, and not to have to do anything with them. Neither of them had a special color to be blamed for. You cannot blame this one for his color either. Each individual is born with some unique characteristics, regardless of their skin color. If you didn't find this young man suitable to continue your friendship, you cannot, and you will not allow yourself to take it on his skin color, and consider it "guilty of sin".

My Dear God:

Anyway dealing with Mary alone was a learning experience for me. I knew that I was there for her to make it, and not to break it. By all means raising Mary for me was the most difficult learning, and the most challenging of all.

The most difficult time of my life was when I found between her throwaway scrap papers very sad and depressing poems, or life ending stories. Those made me like an egg in a frying pan, jumping up and down, to be able to find the right solution.

She used to read lots of books, and she encouraged me to read them too. Most of the books she read were by writers like Kafka. They were all sad, depressing, and they ended in hopeless situations. I read them to be able to discuss them with her, and try to change her mind about the conclusion of the book. This was never easy. I knew that I wasn't supposed to say anything against her beliefs. So I had to take her own words, add some humor, and then slowly deliver it to her. After reading each book like that I was expecting a new reaction from her. And I just prayed to GOD not to let her practice the conclusion of that book. I knew that the word "NO" had a very strong negative reaction on her. I had to avoid that word, and go around it to be able to find a meaningful word to do the job of a "No".

I was an ordinary person, and an ordinary mother. I did not have a degree of a psychology or psychiatry. I was just trying to keep her alive, healthy minded, and a useful person for her own society. I was trying to let her know that all those hormonal changes will end, and life will become easier.

Most of her writings were about the family, and the sufferings among the families. She had always feared losing LOVE, and those feelings were reflected in all her writings. No one in this world, even Mary herself, who had been in that situation of loosing her father's love, knows more than I do, my dear GOD. It was only you and I who witnessed her suffering, when she was only five years old. Yes, my dear GOD, it was you and it was me who saw everything.

I am talking about the day in Maygoon. I have talked about it before. You know how my Mary became Humpty Dumpty, and I had to be able to put her back together again. I am sure and positive my dear GOD, without your presence I couldn't have done it at all.

My Dear God:

From the beginning I was trying so hard to go by the book, and take every right step possible. When my second child Maseeh was born, I tried not to instigate jealousy in her. I let her think that Maseeh was her doll. I let her fed him, hold him, play with him, and put him to sleep. She not only did not become jealous of him, but she loved him so dearly until he went to high school. Until then he was her little brother, and she felt proud having her brother following her. Although they were only twenty-one months apart, at the beginning Maseeh liked to be Mary's little brother. He followed her everywhere, and did whatever she had asked him to do But soon, while at high school, Maseeh grew bigger, and stronger. He actually became a big brother to Mary.

When I look back, I see that the only real happy life that these two kids had was the first three years of their lives. That was the time that Iraj was doing his residency, and my only occupation was taking care of Mary and Maseeh. And it was the most enjoyable time of my life. Whenever someone said to me, you have a million dollar family". I felt like a real millionaire. Then after their father's affair in Iran, at the age of five and three, everything changed completely. That was the age that kids are supposed to learn about love and togetherness. Instead they had to face the fear of loosing their father, and the complication between their parents. When I look back, and I remember the look in Maseeh's big beautiful eyes, which was looking at me, with a big question in his mind, I really feel like I was melting. When I held him in my arms, he wanted to stay there forever. I felt guilty any time that one of my children was badly hurt, and I couldn't help them. I believe that had I not chosen Iraj to be their father, they would not be suffering that way. I felt I was the guilty one. After all I was the one who had made the only and the biggest mistake of my entire life.

If I had listened to my parents, and did not marry Iraj, today my children would not suffer like this. But I did allow myself to accept the fact that I might have been married to any other man and still find him promiscuous. How many men in the world were like my father, and believed in monogamy like my father did? Oh well.

After that first affair when we got back together, he did his best to make it up to them. He tried to be the best father, and the best husband ever, to a point that I completely forgot the past, and started loving him more than ever.

But I knew for sure that Mary and Maseeh have never completely recovered from those deep emotional scars. And I was hoping that when the time comes, they would talk about it, and clear their feelings with us. The way that our life was going at that time, and the trust that I had in Iraj made me believe that one day in the near future we would be able to cure our children's deep scar.

IT WAS TOO GOOD TO BE TRUE.

My Dear God:

Despite all the difficulties we were working side by side, each of us in our own way, and we had a great understanding of each other. And then with Iraj's great attention and interest in me, I was dancing over the clouds. I felt that Iraj was becoming more attached to me than ever. He made me believe that my dreams had come true. He made me believe that I would have him next to me for the rest of my life to love and to worship. To my understanding he took every step to bring more happiness to my children and me. We were becoming one. I could swear to you, my dear GOD, that no husband could have been nicer than him both in public and in our private life. I actually do not need to swear to you. You were there yourself, and you have seen it yourself. I refuse to believe that he could have been playing a role. No man could hate his wife, and act so lovingly toward her every day of his life.

With everything that happened later on, people might think that I was dreaming, and I didn't let myself to see his wrong side. But believe me, he was the greatest husband any woman could have. He wanted the best for me. He wanted to see a smile on my face at all times. He never went anywhere without me, even for an hour. I have never heard of a husband who thanks his wife after each intimacy in their private bedroom. Which husband could put up a show like that day after day after day? I thought the kind of love, understanding, and trust that we felt for each other was the kind of marriage that I was once dreaming of. And at that time I felt I had it. There were times that I wasn't in the mood for sex because of my children's behavior. He would talked to me, and try to put me in the mood by helping me forget the problem, and clear my mind from discrepancies. He was never harsh or forceful with me. How could all these be a big lie? He was sure that I loved him like my God. He was sure that I was his home, his security, his luck, and I was the complete base of his success. These are the things he was telling me. But he didn't really have to. I wasn't a kind of a woman, who demanded those things. I have never asked him to buy me anything extraordinary, which he still did. Just to be with him was my whole world.

This was why I was so lost when the incident happened. I was looking back to see where I missed to see his dishonesty in his actions. But there was no explanation what so ever. He never left a sign for me to become suspicious. He knew that I was too smart and focused on everything to be fooled. Sometimes I think that it was the way that I loved him, with purity and innocence that he never wanted to lose it. Probably if he was having a fling here and there, which I am sure he did, he covered it up so carefully.

My Dear God:

The only thing that he did not like doing was going to movies. Sometimes we went with some of our friends. And even then he fell asleep in the middle of the movie. If I asked him to go to a movie with me, he always rejected the idea, and asked me to accompany someone else.

Many times we have heard from people, "Those who do too much for their wives are trying to hide something from them. They are trying to cover up their acts and rid themselves of guilt by buying expensive things".

Even if this is true, should a woman hire an investigator to spy on her husband, who is so nice, kind, and a giving? Wouldn't that be kind of stupid? Do you think I could have done that, and then call myself a smart woman? I think every woman, or in this matter any man is liable to know each and every move of his or her partner in marriage. But it shouldn't be by means of being suspicious all their lives. Marriage would be doomed, and set for unhappiness and torment. Where there is no trust, there is no life, and that is it.

Besides, a woman would typically be the first to feel changes in their intimacy. She might not know the details, but she would know that there is something going on in her husband's mind that no longer lets him be himself.

In my case, during his loving time, there was nothing that I could pinpoint at. He was a great lover any woman could have. And that was it.

He was home every day after his office hours, between five and six o'clock. If he had a delivery at the hospital, or he was going to be late for one hour, he would call to notify me. On Wednesdays, his day off, he would stand by my bedside planning our day together. We would first run errands together, and then go to lunch. It reminded me of the days we spent together in Iran behind my parents' backs. There was a restaurant, called Park, which was our meeting place. Even after we got married, we would go there every time we had a chance. That's where we once ran into my cousin. I remember being scared to death, and while we had no money to spare, we decided to treat my cousin. Iraj's gesture served a dual purpose, where he was trying to let my cousin know that he didn't care if he told on us, while he acted as a gentleman. We went out together on Saturdays as well. It really wasn't me who asked him to give all his free times to me. He was the one who initiated and executed the idea. He knew that I didn't like going out with other ladies frequently. And he also knew that except Pari, his sister, I wasn't really close enough with anyone to enjoy their company. So he spent almost all his free time during the day with me.

My Dear God:

He was all of the above, how could I believe that he was fooling around? Or maybe he was wrapping me around his activities in such a way that I wouldn't ever get suspicious. But anyway, what do I know?

I am talking to you, my dear God, because I know that you were there, and you know that all these were true. Now, the things that went on behind the scenes that I was not aware of, I could not possibly be writing about. That would be only and only Iraj who knew. All that I am writing about is the absolute truth, and nothing but the truth. Or at least this was my understanding.

Once we went to Spain with two other families, Nazi and Reza Mahajer, and their children, Susan and Nasser Barkhordari with their children.

I don't remember if it was on this trip that our plain was experiencing some mechanical problems, and we had to land in Iceland Airport. We were informed that they were not able to obtain certain parts there, and they had to get It from New York. So we had to spend the night in a hotel that was provided for us. They transferred us to that hotel by a shuttle bus. It was cold. And the whole experience was strange, scary, and very unexpected. Our kids, who were used to a comfortable life, couldn't accept the fact that there would be times like that in our life. They passed around some small sandwiches. And if we didn't push our way through, we would not be able to get any. We stayed in the hotel until the next day. Then they took us back to the airport in the same shuttle bus, and we were supposed to leave that evening. We were so glad when that trip was over.

We were expecting the temperatures to be in mid-seventies. So we were not ready for freezing cold weather conditions. It turned out to be so cold that we were not able to get out of the hotel to even go to a restaurant. I had some warm clothing for my children, but others did not. And even when we borrowed our husband's coats, it still wasn't very satisfying. I already talk about it before. He did his best and spend so much money on me.

Well, I was happy with his thoughtfulness. But other ladies were not that happy. Not that they were not able to purchase things themselves, but it was their husband's lack of sensitivity and feelings that they were upset with. In a marriage this sort of attention is vital. Because of everything that he had always done for me, I had more enemies than friends. Many of them would ask me jokingly, "Why is Iraj doing this much for you?" And many others talked behind my back, wondering why he loved me so much. I think these people were the happiest individuals after our separation.

My Dear God:

Another wise thing I did when we were in Spain was that I decided not to go with everyone to watch the bullfights. They tried so hard to convince me to go and have fun, but I wouldn't agree. I stayed in the hotel all by myself. They were not very happy upon their return. They did regret going after all.

There was one couple among our friends that did not get involved with our card game, Drs. Sara and Mahmood Fassihi. They preferred outdoor activities. Mahmood started playing golf first, and then later Sara and her children joined him.

When Iraj was dealing with all the confusion of getting involved with different businesses, Mahmood had asked him join him for a golf game on many occasions. Mahmood believed that if Iraj got involved with playing golf, he would become less interested on running around complicating his life. But Iraj was never into playing golf. The game was too slow for him. At least that was what he thought.

So the only way of entertaining ourselves was to play Blot on the weekends. It had become such a custom that when anyone outside our Blot group wanted to invite us, all they had to check with my Blot schedule first to make sure we were available that night. Some of us had known each other for more than twenty-five years. We knew all about each other's life, and we were like family. We were thinking that when our children moved away, we would be able to enjoy each other's companionship. We all spoke the same language, cooked Iranian food, and humored each other by telling Iranian jokes. Then we played cards and fulfilled ourselves with the only amusement we had, which was just playing Blot.

We traveled together, we picnicked together, and we teased each other a lot. Once we were on our way back from Cedar Point in Michigan. We were in many cars following each other. Barkhordari's car was following ours. We both stopped somewhere midway to enjoy our last watermelon. We got back on the road, and in a little while we couldn't see them anywhere. We started wondering where they went. We got home in about fifteen minutes, when our phone rang. Iraj answered the phone, and I watched him turn black and blue as he was asking questions. I was getting panicky. I overheard that somebody was in a fatal accident. When I questioned him, he said, "Barkhordaris were involved in an accident. But the person on the phone didn't give enough information before she hung up. It wasn't after five minutes that Susan called. Iraj anxiously answered the phone. I heard Susan's laughter from the other side. She was able to change her voice, and fool Iraj. We were relived that they were not in an accident.

My Dear God:

Good or bad, we were friends and we had fun together. Our friendship was pure and simple. There was no hanky panky going on between anyone in our group at that time. We were getting closer thanks to that Blot game. That was what our gatherings were based on.

Iraj had never made suspicious remarks about any of our lady friends. We would discuss specific characteristics on each individual, but he had never made suspicious remarks, even about Louise, who always used verbal intimations.

One Saturday morning, while Iraj was shaving to get ready to go to the hospital for his round, we were talking about the Friday night game in Malakuti's house. We were talking about the game, and about everyone and their characters. Iraj was talking about Malakuti. I said, "Well, he is a psychiatrist". Iraj stopped and looked at me, and then he said in a very puzzled voice, "You think he is a Psychiatrist? Badri is the real Psychiatrist.

Those days, with Malakuti being alive, and being an Iranian macho man, I couldn't think that Badri might consider having a hanky panky with anyone. Considering that Malakuti was so crazy about his family and especially about the women in his life, such an act would have been a disaster. He would have killed Badri, and the people around her. So when in my mind I couldn't find anything, I thought that what Iraj meant was that Badri was a sneaky snake, a pretentious and monopolistic woman. I thought, "Well, that is what most of us think about her. But she probably chose to survive through life this way". How could I possibly think at that time that there must have been something between them, and Iraj was trying to tell me all about it in that one sentence?

It was the first time in more than twenty years, that I heard Iraj making such a comment about one of the doctors' wives.

True that we might not be able to know everyone from inside out. But when you interact with the same people as frequently as we did, you would start noticing certain traits of each individual character.

My Dear God:

At that time Iraj was very observant. One night Suri wore a dress that she had designed to wear at a party in our house. It was tailored for her elegant body, and she was not wearing any underwear. I was too busy to notice that. But at the end of night Iraj came up to me and said, "Did you notice she did not have any underwear on?" I was shocked to find that Iraj had been undressing his guests with his naked eyes. But then I thought about it, and I realized that true that we are husbands and wives. But that didn't mean that we had to lose our ability to recognize the beauty when we saw it.

There was a poet, named Hafez, from Shiraz, my parents' hometown. His book was like Ghoran in most Iranian homes. They believed that if they closed their eyes and wished for something while they open the book, the content of that page would describe their fortune. And even though not everyone believed in it, it was yet another opportunity for Malakuti to be the center of attraction, telling fortune from Hafez, and bring laughter to his audience. He made every body believe that he could read palms. Susan and Rohan were amused by his performances more than others. They made him believe that he was good, so he would get even more excited.

After we moved into our new house, Azeez started to talk to Iraj about his interest in building his own house. Meanwhile every Sunday he called us to go with him house hunting. We knew that he was not interested to buy a house, but he thought it was fun to go look at various new buildings with an agent.

You see, my dear GOD, those days we thought, oh no, I must correct myself, I thought, "Why should we waste our time, and do something unnecessary?" At that time I didn't know, and Azeez didn't know what was going on. This thought comes to my mind now that everything is in the past. Otherwise if we knew the truth, none of us would have been alive today.

Knowing Badri now, I am sure that it was Badri who wanted to spend her day with Iraj. So she was the one who initiated the idea of house hunting on Sundays. And in her own sneaky way asked Azeez to go and look for houses.

We were able to continue our peaceful life not knowing the truth. Isn't this ironic that I am glad that I was stupid enough not to know anything about their relationship then? Isn't it, my dear GOD? I wish you could answer me.

You see, my dear GOD, the way that I see it now, we were partying mostly twice a week, and Badri was able to arrange their third visit on Sundays without any one of us realizing anything.

All these kind of activities, and the involvement with the joined business opened the doors for us, the Rafanis and the Malakutis, to become closer. And, considering the fact that I knew nothing about what was going on, I became a devoted friend.

My Dear God:

As I said before, Iraj and Azeez had no temperamental similarities. In fact they were like day and night. Azeez was very noisy, restless, uneasy, emotional, sensitive, and very susceptible to lose his temper with any external disturbance. Whereas Iraj was quiet, very much into himself, non-emotional, patient, calm, not edgy, and rarely responsive to any kind of external conditions. In my mind these two were like oil and water. They could never stay mixed, unless there was one person, who would arrange that mixing. It took me years after Malakuti's death to find out that Badri was the one who arranged the mixing all that time.

He was a type of a man who was capable of killing someone for even looking at his wife the wrong way. He always talked to his wife as if she was lightheaded, and ready to give enjoyment of any kind. The funny thing about it was that she pretended that he was joking, and she continued her lightheadedness and just kept smiling. And then Azeez, in a very disrespectful way, would tell her, "Don't laugh, I mean it. Shut your crooked mouth". The left corner of her mouth was lower than the right side. So her mouth looked crooked when she laughed.

Malakuti's behavior offended many of us, ladies. But Badri, being such a pretentious woman, would never allow herself to say anything to Azeez. I know now who she really was then. One day she was in my kitchen, while we were cooking something. She was talking about herself, and she said, "I have always been dumb, and so I was afraid of learning. My family thought that, if I am not capable of learning, I should stay home". I felt really bad for her. I told her, "This is not true at all. You must never let anyone make you believe that you are dumb. You are smart, and I am sure you will be able to learn anything that you choose to learn".

My Dear God:

I really don't know if there was something going on between them at that time, and she just wanted to get closer to me. Only GOD knows when they started their relationship. But by telling me these kinds of things about herself, she made me get closer with her. And that made me believe that she was nice to her husband. She made sure to have his dinner every day for him at eleven o'clock at night, when he got home from the office.

I remember one very disturbing incident. It was our regular Friday night game at Malakuti's house. As usual he got home after eleven. We were sitting around the table in the kitchen when he came in. Badri jumped up immediately to serve his food. She lost one of her slippers, while she tried to run. Malakuti raised his voice and said, "This woman is no good, she is waiting for me to die, and she has her own fun. She is always after having fun".

Badri again started to laugh, and turned it into a joke. Then Azeez said again and again, "Close your crooked mouth. Don't laugh, I said".

Minoo and I were sitting next to each other. We stopped playing for a while, and then Minoo looked at me and said, "My GOD, I would never allow my husband to act this way towards me. I won't tolerate that". I said the same thing. And I remember that I said, "Iraj never asked me to do things for him. He always does it himself, unless I volunteer to do it for him". And then we all felt sorry for her, and we did our best to help her and keep her happy.

He always talked about her family. She would usually answer him laughing, "Don't you know that they are your family too?" They were somehow related to each other.

Malakuti would be furious, every time her sisters were visiting. I will never forget that one particular Thursday that I took Mojgan to Burger King at Fifteen Mile and Telegraph Road. I saw Malakuti there with his children. I knew that his sisters-in-law were visiting at the time. When I congratulated him on their arrival, he looked at me with a sad expression on his face, and said, "If you like them come and take them to your house. Please don't congratulate me on this disaster in my house. Although I wanted to think that he was joking, I found out after he passed away that he was sincere then. He really wanted them out of his house. And he continued, "Please come and save my life and the life of my children from these no good people. I promise you that you won't be sorry; you will be a great help to us. I don't want any part of them, so you can have them. I wish they would stop coming here to visit us".

My Dear God:

I found myself laughing by this time, and I thought he was teasing me. I just laughed, and found a place to sit down, and I kept analyzing him that he was never straightforward with me to tease and joke. Then I realized that the poor guy was telling the truth, but no one would believe him. No wonder Azeez always talked about them in a disrespectful way.

The poor guy really meant what he was saying about them.

Well, my dear GOD, guess who is having the pleasure of dealing with this strange family now? The person who hated them even before Azeez began talking about them. And I am very glad. He really deserves them. I know how much he hated them. And you know it, my dear GOD, as well.

My Dear God:

Azeez was very hurt by them, because they were asking the rest of the family to take sides and to be part of their mess. Badri was telling me this because she was disturbed by it too. She too was hoping that her sisters would stop visiting them.

I remember once she brought her older stepsister to a party in my house. Her son who was studying to becoming a doctor was with them also. She was talking about her escape from Iran. It was right after the revolution, and many people were trying to get out of the country. She had sold her house for a very high price. And she had wrapped herself in a shawl containing six million toomans, Iranian currency. This woman walked through the mountains of Azarbaijon, and she traveled by bus. While she was trying to show everyone that she was a brave woman, I realized that even in my wildest dream I would not imagine entertaining such people in my house. She would smile in my face, and she would turn around and say something about me and make the rest laugh. She was looking all around the house, and she would start talking to me about some things, and after I answered her, she would turn around and start laughing again. Her body language, her way of talking made me pity myself. Why was I put in a position that I had to meet and interact with someone like her? Her jealousy was to such degree that I thought to myself it was better to let her and her companions be, and let them talk about my happiness and die of jealousy.

I didn't simply dislike her, I hated her manners, and I hated her character. And the least enjoyable of all was the fact that in our culture we must thank our guests for visiting, and we must express how much we have enjoyed having them at the time of farewell. I wished I could say to her, "I wish you never came". And once again I felt sorry for Azeez, who had to deal with them all the time.

Can you imagine, my dear GOD, that this type of people who somehow get their hands on little money, would put themselves in the first class category. What a pity, really, what a pity.

When I said, "We lose our identity after marriage" I meant it. If I wasn't married to Iraj, I would never invite those people to my house. Not that Iraj ever forced me to do anything, but along with forming friendships, we built trust and respect. And so we welcomed everybody's sisters, mothers, and brothers in my house, and those were the results.

It really was a jungle. Iranians from different backgrounds had gathered, and they were competing with each other. The degree of a person's popularity was measured by the number of people you could invite to your house, regardless of who they were. For instance, if the people who were visiting me would run into one another, they would probably not even greet each other. With the exception of one or two, the rest of them didn't even know you. Now, can you imagine relying on such individuals? No, forget it.

My Dear God:

Some of you might question me, "Why did you do it?" I'll tell you why. First of all I always loved to cook. I liked to experiment. I wanted to create new things. And most of all I loved my husband, and I wanted to keep him happy. I believed he was working hard to keep us happy, so I felt obligated to make his life joyous. My life didn't turn out this way because I gave many parties. As they say, it takes one dirty, rotten apple in a large basket to destroy the rest of the apples. So this was the case of my happy life.

Another very important factor is that when something wrong becomes a norm in our society, we follow that norm without ever questioning. Such habits as drinking and smoking, our hairstyles and clothing are all fads and fashion that we follow without acknowledging their consequences. If throwing parties is considered a pleasure, why not I get involved with pleasurable stuff?

All that I had gathered that night from talking to Badri's sister was that I found her illiterate, jealous, and a low class woman. I feared her, and I no longer wanted to be around her.

There is an Iranian saying, "If a person has a low mentality, never bring yourself down to his or her level. I began to realize more and more after meeting the rest of her family that poor Azeez was right. And from what Badri has been telling me I felt that even she was disturbed by her family. But because of our husbands partnership our families were getting more involved. Besides at that time there was nothing about Badri or anyone else that would have stopped me from what I was doing. I couldn't be suspicious, and non-cooperative with Iraj for the rest of my life because of his affair in Iran. It was in the past, and I never wanted to think about it or go back to it. At that time everything was fine, and there was no need for me to turn my shinny life into a cloudy one. That was no-no. That pretentious Badri had made sure that none of us found out what was going on between them. So we were very happy together. We traveled and partied together year, after year. As they say, "Never judge the book by its cover".

At this time of our lives Iraj was so loving and caring. It is impossible to explain that kind of love. He had our house built to my liking. He never failed any of his duties as a great husband. He was always respectful with my needs and me. I cannot express the amount of love that I had for him. I was always looking to find a way to bring the greatest happiness to his life.

My Dear God:

One summer, when his sisters were staying with us, Parveen, his older sister, had mentioned something that gave me a great idea. She was talking about her life and how successful she was in achieving her goal. She said that she was hoping to be able to have a huge Birthday party on her fiftieth birthday, and she was hoping to be able to invite the whole world.

That was her dream. But she gave me an idea for Iraj's fiftieth Birthday. He still had a few years before his fiftieth Birthday. I didn't know how to go about celebrating it without creating a large bill for him to pay. We always had joined accounts. I always thought that we were like one person. I knew there must have been a way to collect money that would pay for his party. I gave the idea a lot of thought. And I came up with an idea of arranging some kind of an allowance for myself. That way I could save enough to arrange a Birthday party for him without giving him a shock of a large payment.

I have always been against the idea of allowance. I believed it would create the separation of the oneness of husband and wife. But I was ready to give up that principal in order to afford his Birthday celebration.

I was very surprised when I asked him for an allowance for our clothing that he welcomed the idea. I was delighted. Now I would be able to pay for the party without touching his checkbook. We had many credit cards and bank accounts, but just the fact that the funds for the party would come from money that he thought he had already spent would have been great news to him. My only concern was that if I didn't collect enough money for that Birthday, most probably he would disagree with that kind of expense. And instead of having a great birthday, we might have a great fight. I thought afterwards that the idea of having some savings elsewhere would be a great idea.

Then I remembered that during the revolution, the hostage crisis in Iran, and the oil crisis in America there was no certainty among many of us. I could recall a few times that Iraj, who never showed weakness, brought bundles of money home. He asked me to hide it somewhere safe in case of emergency. So with this thought in mind I felt that it was not a bad idea to have some money elsewhere besides the bank. As long as we didn't have any secrets from each other, our life together was very trustworthy and meaningful. This was what I have always wanted to happen in my married life, and I was glad to see it was there. So I started to save money for his Birthday.

My Dear God:

By this time they were getting serious about the clinic. Iraj did his homework in his office, and Azeez did his at his own office. And at the end of the night they would get together in our house to share their ideas and research. He would always show up after eleven, and I felt obligated to offer him dinner. But after a few nights he decided to go home and have his dinner there. Because he would always get home very late, he would sleep in till late morning. Iraj had to call him at eight o'clock every morning before he left home. Badri answered the phone every day, and they would discuss their daily schedule. Badri didn't want to wake Azeez up, so their conversations were becoming a routine task.

My dear, dear GOD, please pay attention to what I am trying to tell you. Before it was the friendship that brought us together. Now it was their partnership that brought them together. And the way that everything was arranged there was no way out of it. I had no room to tell him to stop calling their house at eight o'clock in the morning because he would be speaking to Badri and not Azeez. I didn't know, and I didn't even think that their conversations were not just about business. How could I stop any of those activities that were taking place right in front of me in the name of a partnership? Especially when Iraj would involved me with everything that was going on, starting from paper work, to office, to furniture, and legal papers. How could I see any hanky panky behind those moves? So you see, my dear GOD, I am not a stupid person. I am a person who just loves to love. And that is my only problem.

They were whispering and laughing while talking to each other. She was in bed with her husband, while Iraj in my arms. They would begin with just talking of anything and everything, and then they would switch to the messages for Azeez. What could possibly go wrong?

They rented an office next to Dr. Mehrabian's office for the weight loss clinic. I was with Iraj while he was ordering everything for the clinic, and not even once Badri was present. He asked for my opinion about the style, the color, and the sizes. He shared with me all the information that I had to know. I offered my help in any way I could. Maseeh was the most helpful. He had designed their Logo and advertising frames. He helped out with lighting, and many other things. Maseeh has always been helpful to him. He wanted to make his father happy.

They had to borrow money from the bank for all those expenses. He showed me the agreement between them. It stated that all the expenses and benefits would be divided equally between the partners, no question asked and if God forbid one of the partners passed away, the other partner is obligated to pay the deceased family one hundred thousand dollars.

My Dear God:

Once I asked Iraj, "Why didn't you accept Mahajer's offer to become your partner?" He answered me, "Malakuti suggested to be in a partnership with those whose wives are not interfering with their business. And with Mahajer this was impossible".

Then I remembered that once Iraj gave me a card. The card contained a headless woman and a writing that said, "Headless woman entertainment". I got really offended, and I said to him, "I am sorry, you were looking for a woman with no head. I hope you don't think that you got one". And now he was telling me that he agreed with Malakuti

who didn't want any involvement of their wives.

Seeing how Malakuti was treating Badri, and knowing that he bought many things on his name only, I knew what kind of a man we were dealing with.

We were no longer just friends; we were partners. They each had their share of working one late night at the clinic. Some nights that Azeez was on call, we were playing Blot. So when Badri wanted to take his dinner to him to the clinic, I would accompany her.

Malakuti was acting like a child in a body of a man. While he was convinced that he was the one wearing pants around the house, in reality it was Badri who was running the show.

I will never forget the night that we were in Barkhordari's house. Susan was arranging a trip for the whole group to go to Cidar Point in Michigan. She got everyone's okay to go ahead and pay for the tickets. Everyone had agreed including Badri. Susan mentioned the trip again after the game, when everyone started leaving. She said and in front of Malakuti, "At last everyone has agreed, and we bought the tickets". Oh, my GOD, all of a sudden Azeez started screaming. And Badri, who knew what was going on, jumped up and with a smile on her face she said, "No, we didn't agree, not for us". Susan became so furious with Badri and said, "My, oh my, what a liar". But before Susan had a chance to say another word, Badri stopped her, and with her regular body movement asked Azeez to leave. She completely dropped the subject at that time. Obviously when she took him home, she solved the problem in bed as usual. But Susan was still furious. She said, "Badri says something first, and then changes it the next minute". And she continued, "And she pretends like nothing has happened".

Although Badri had been able to run her life that way, she had created a lack of trust and respect for herself. She allowed Malakuti to look at her as a worthless woman, with the only capability of providing a good sex. At least this was what I saw.

My Dear God:

However I believe it is true about men in general that they prefer headless women in their beds. It is very rare that a man would enjoy an intelligent, studious, and loyal woman in his bed lovingly and passionately. These types of men must be very secure and self-confident. I always thought Iraj was one of them. We were getting closer and closer without knowing what was awaiting us. There was a musical festival every year on the Medow Brook Yard.

Naheed and her mother Aghdass Khanom, were with us that day. We had provided some sandwiches and other goodies for the picnic. Malakuti had bought a little white dog for his children. We ran into difficulties when we found out that dogs were not allowed on the grass in the concert area. That was way too big of a deal for Azeez to handle.

It is known that men like to think of their wives as their personal possessions. And as a habit they want to show off with their preferred stuff.

After we spread out our blankets on the grass, we all tried to make ourselves comfortable. It was before the concert started. Badri was lying on a blanket on her back. Suddenlv Azeez came towards her, with his two hands ready to grab her breasts, and then he pulled himself back and said, "Sometimes you want to squeeze them in wrong places". That kind of behavior might have been okay for teenagers, who he wasn't. We all blushed, and felt embarrassed in front of our children. This act coming from a doctor, who was raised in our culture, was not only childish, but it was a very stupid. True that sex is good, and we all like it, but there are some acts that are only allowed in our own private bedrooms. Aghdass Khanom and I looked at each other, and we were puzzled what was that act all about? Was he trying to show off his wife's breasts to Iraj, and my young son? This act, coming from Azeez, who was so sensitive about his wife and all the women in his family, was very, very strange. He was actually advertising his wife's breasts in public. What a shame! I just wonder.

My son Maseeh, who was eighteen at the time, was born and raised in America. He was away from our culture, and the way we were respectful to ladies, I cannot remember that he ever acted so childish in front of us, or for that matter in front of anyone else. He was such a gentleman, that even at his age he knew which acts belonged to the bedroom.

That was the time that Maseeh was in-love with his high school sweetheart, Beth. She came from Italian background, and was raised by her strict single mother. Their visitations were very limited and restricted. Many times they were in my house. I have never seen them doing something silly, or acting stupid in front of us. Both of them were very well behaved and polite. They both were raised in families that were far away from that mixed up class of the society. I was always proud of Maseeh to be my son. It wasn't that they didn't have feelings, or they didn't love each other, but they had enough understanding to know what to do and where to do it.

* * *

My Dear God:

From the moment that I met Iraj and his family I felt that they were for each other all the time. I think that was the main reason that I fell in love with him. I was thinking if a person could be so devoted to his family, he would have the capability to remain loyal and devoted to his wife.

At the time that I met them, all of them had a pretty mixed up life. Parveen was married to Mr. Safari. They didn't have any children, and she was in the process of getting divorced.

During that period they didn't have their basic needs. Parveen used to make children's clothes with the knitting machine that Iraj bought for her. And Iraj used to take those clothes door to door to sell them for her.

While Iraj was a medical student, he got the opportunity to work for a pharmaceutical company. He was delivering medicine to doctors' offices.

While their mother was in Tehran, living with Parveen, their father, who was a chronic alcoholic, was by himself in Zahedan. Pari and Niya were still in high school. There was no money coming in from anywhere.

When Iraj was leaving Tehran to go to America, he did not have enough money for a ticket. So he decided to take a boat. It took him many days to get there. And even then, he didn't have money to buy his ticket. So his sister and I volunteered to each pay half of the price to make his journey possible.

So when I saw their relationship, and the way they helped each other, I was happy to marry a man, who understood the feeling of the responsibility. I was the same way with my sisters, but we were never in need like that.

Years, after years they helped each other in a friendly way. I never questioned him. The thing that bothered me was that if I ever wanted to do anything for my sisters I couldn't because I did not have any official income. That really hurt. But at least I was glad that my sisters were not in need.

As I said before Iraj had applied for his citizenship so that he could bring his sisters to America. My children were American born. I was the only one who was left out.

It was after the revolution in Iran that we all were traveling to Canada. They let my husband and my children to go through at the American border, but they stopped me for more search and evaluation. They took me to the back room like a criminal. They checked my suitcase over and over, and they even performed a body search. That experience was not only embarrassing, but it was very humiliating. They had to wait for me more than one hour, until they let me free.

My Dear God:

Iraj and my children, especially Maseeh, had been after me to get my citizenship. That day they were so mad that I decided to apply for it. For some unknown reason I did not want to change my citizenship. At that time to me changing citizenship felt like loosing virginity. I didn't want to do it. But Iraj was insisting that if I didn't change my citizenship, we would never be able to travel comfortably. And since he was planning to take me around the world, he found a reason to show me the importance of the American citizenship. Then one night I watched on the news how some Iranians were thrown out of Iraq by force, while they had lived in that country for a long time.

Maseeh was very depressed watching that scene. He turned to me and said, "If you don't want to get your citizenship for yourself, you must get it because of your children. What if the American government does this to you? There are times that we don't have a choice, and that time is now".

They required two witnesses at that time. Guess what, my dear GOD. The only two

friends who came to my rescue were Sara Fassihi, and yes, Badri herself. I guess she was considered my best friend that day.

One day Badri asked me if I had a sawing machine. She wanted to hem Roozbe's pants. My sewing machine was in my bedroom. It was on a Sunday afternoon. Iraj was in bed reading his Wall Street Journal. She sat in the middle of the room with me, and I helped her with the hem. She started telling me that her mother could do that kind of sewing, and she had never done anything in her life.

GOD, please forgive me for my stupidity. Everything was so obvious that day: Iraj didn't move from his bed in front of her, and the way that she was talking with her body movement. I should have been more alert than that, but I wasn't. Today I see it vividly that it was their Sunday fling. Then again I am glad that I didn't know what was going on between them. Otherwise having Malakuti around, we would have been history.

Another thing I remember was that once their family was going out of town. They needed someone to watch over their birds. I volunteered to take care of them while they were gone. Well, my children had birds, and I knew what was like to have a bird in the cage. But I don't know what happened. I found one of the two birds dead the next morning. "Oh, my GOD. What can I do now? Is it possible to find one exactly like it?" I started to drive from one bird shop to the other. After all I found one just like it, and I replaced the dead bird. At first they didn't find out, but later Roshanak admitted that she knew something was different. I told them, "I did not want to disappoint you by returning one bird instead of two, so I felt replacing it was a better idea".

My Dear God:

Although for many reasons we were getting closer and closer, still my friendship with Badri wasn't based on having common grounds. And my children had no common grounds with their children. And for Azeez and Iraj, they were like day and night. How could these two families become so close together, and even become partners in business? I am still wondering.

I am asking you, my dear GOD. Please tell me, did you have to do anything with it? Did you arrange all those things without our knowledge? Don't you think it was Badri, and her influence on Azeez that brought us so close together? Don't you think, she was a woman, who married her husband without love, and then she found her fling here and there? Please, my dear GOD, you tell me what is happening in this world. You tell me what is right, or what is wrong. I wish I had a very strong English to be able to describe the real Badri to the world. Like Azeez said, "She was one person who will cut throat with a soft cotton, without anyone suspecting it". He knew her well indeed.

Now that I think back, I can see killing her own husband, friends, and then look, act, and monopolize you in a way that you would believe in her innocence.

Among Iranians that we knew we were able to categorize them for the most part of

it: a nice person, a truthful and sincere person, a creative person, and an achiever, a manipulative and vicious person, or a jealous person. But in Badri's case you could never guess who she really was. To me she was like a simple, helpless, powerless woman, who had to monopolize, and play games with her husband in order to get what she wanted from him, especially in bed.

What bothered me the most was that she talked to me about her lack of intelligence and mental abilities. It really made me feel sorry for her. And I always tried to talk her out of it. Now that I look back, I realize that she has been making fun of me. She was trying to tell me in her own language, "Stupid woman, I am trying to have an affair with your husband, and you still think you know him?"

She never had any opinion about politics, education, art, music, or anything related to that matter.

Once we were in DR. M. Rabbani's house. It was after dinner, and before the game. We all were sitting around the table discussing little matters. We got to the subject of Psychiatry and handling difficult patients.

My Dear God:

It was Parvaneh, Nayer, Badri, Rohan, and I around that table. Badri started to talk and said, "Treating this kind of patients is so easy that even I can do that". Parvaneh, who was always outspoken, and very straight forward turned to Badri ,and answered her sarcastically, "Oh really". Your husband and other psychiatrists had gone to universities for many years, and had worked so hard to be able to figure out how to treat each and every one of them, and yet they are still wondering. But you, without any kind of schooling, or knowledge, are capable of treating them so easily? I just wonder. So, Badri khanom, what else is new that we haven't discovered about you?"

So, Parvaneh, if you ever get to read these notes, do you remember that she was able to answer your question so clearly after she buried Malakuti? She answered you loud and clear, "This is the way that I could handle difficult cases. Do you believe in my ability now, Parvaneh khanom? DO YOU REALLY?"

She was so afraid of Malakuti. She was never allowed to speak-up or wear something improper. She knew that he would have insulted her in front of everyone.

One night at a party in M. Rabbani's house we were all sitting around a table discussing many aspects of life, when the subject came to clothing. Aghdass, who just like Badri's older sister was very proud of her body, and made all her dresses herself, wore very low cut neck lines. And like some women in Hollywood she was happy to show her big bosom. Not only she wore those embarrassing clothes, but also she allowed herself to make fun of those who didn't. Her comments to those who dressed conservatively, like myself, were as follows, "They always look like teachers", while she was aware that I was a teacher. But I never paid attention to her comments. I was thinking, "Let her enjoy

advertising for herself. She was embarrassing herself that way, she did not need my help".

They each were expressing their opinions about liking or disliking exotic types of clothing, and low cut neckline dresses.

This time Badri said, "If I was to ever wear this kind of a low cut top Azeez would kill me for sure. I'd love to try them, but I am really afraid that Azeez will really kill me". Then Minoo told her, "So even what you wear is not up to you. Because it seems like if it was up to you would wear low cut neckline to show off certain parts of your body to others. And if that is the case, I am glad that you have someone to watch you and keep you under control". Then she continued, "Boy, aren't we lucky to have someone like Azeez around, otherwise you would be walking around naked showing off all that you've got". All of us, including Badri, laughed.

There are many things that one can learn about a person just by paying attention to their comments about themselves. There obviously will be many other traits that will remain unrevealed for a while, until one day by chance or a mere coincidence everything will come into the open. And then we will be left to wonder, "What were we thinking?"

* * *

GIVING AN OPEN HOUSE FOR THE CLINIC.

My Dear God:

There were many activities taking place prior to the opening. They were working day and night to ensure that everything was handled right. Iraj's schedule was jammed as is. He looked tiered, but what was scaring me the most was the extent of his worries. I was very concerned about his health. It seamed that he was afraid of getting old, or maybe even dying. During one of our regular walks in our neighborhood we ended up at a court next to our street. There was an unfinished house overlooking on the lake at the end of the court. He stopped there. And while he kept shaking his head with sadness he said, "The owner of this house was a Greek business man. He went to Greece with his wife and children to visit the family during the summer. The poor man had an accident and died there. Now his wife will be returning to either finish the house or sell it just the way it is". The way that he was talking about them, I sensed so much sorrow within as he was telling me our neighbor's story. I thought I even saw tears in his eyes. I could not remember Iraj being so sensitive. I felt that his age was scaring him.

By then I was even more scared than he was. I told him, "What an awful and painful incident. How can his poor wife survive such a hurtful accident? GOD forbids if this was to happen to me. I would prefer to be buried with my husband. I can't imagine living even a day longer than my husband".

I was not telling him all these to just make him feel good. It was my dream to be able to die before Iraj did. I couldn't bear the thought of being alive after Iraj was dead for even a minute. His walking, talking, and breathing were gifts from GOD to me. I only saw the world with Iraj in it, for without him there was no world.

There were times that I wondered if there would ever come a day that I was put in a position to choose between my children, whom I loved and adored so much, and Iraj, who was considered my entire life. Whom would I choose? I never had an answer. I was just crazy about him.

The more he complicated his life, the more I became concerned about his health. Although when he got home, he was so comfortable and happy. He would lie in bed near the phone with his Wall Street Journal in his hand. He knew that everything else around him has been taking care of. He seamed so comfortable. One would have thought that he has not been working at all.

When he came in with his mail in his hands and a smile on his face, he would kiss the children and me. Then he would go to his room to change. The dinner would be served on the table by the time that he came down. The kids were ready around the table. And we would all watch the news while eating.

My Dear God:

Maseeh said one day after Iraj came home, "My Dad is so calm when he gets home. One would have never guessed that he has been working all day".

I think he had all the right to feel that comfortable. He knew that he had done his duties perfectly, and I have done mine. He was sure that I would never fail my responsibilities.

It was funny. One Saturday morning he was getting ready to go to the hospital. While he was shaving he told me, "Yesterday I had a surgery. While they were taking her to the room, she said, "Doctor I want to ask you a question". I asked her what was. She said, "Please tell me the truth. Did you have a fight with your wife this morning? And if you did, I must say my last good byes to my family". He continued, "She wanted to make sure that I had a good night. She wanted to be assured that I wouldn't make mistakes".

In my household and under my supervision things had to be done, and they had to be done on time. I never left anything for tomorrow.

I was on my feet all the time, even in the middle of the night. And yet I was considered a housewife who did not have a job.

On the day of the open house for the clinic I was dressed up welcoming all the guests. The clinic was introducing and promoting the Optifast for weight reduction. I was so fit and slim that most people thought I was a product of Optifast. They were asking me if I kept my figure by using Optifast. And I had to lie.

The clinic started and it seamed like everything was going well. Iraj had to attend Optifast seminars every once in a while. He always asked me to accompany him.

That same year Iraj decided to take us to Canada for Mojgan's twelfth Birthday, which was only two days after my birthday. We stayed at the Four Seasons. It was his gift to us, and we both were very happy. He made sure to make that birthday so special for Mojgan. It was just like a dream. She was extremely happy to be able to spend the whole weekend with her father without Mary or Maseeh. And for me it was another honeymoon. I was treated like a queen.

Actually that was the first time in our lives that Iraj took us out of the country just to entertain us on our birthdays.

He took Mojgan to the fair in the mornings. He dressed very casual, and turned into a twelve-year-old. He did anything and everything to make Mojgan happy. Their laughter and giggling brought tears in my eyes. I couldn't believe our happiness at the time.

My Dear God:

That weekend made me think about Iraj's promise to me. He had promised me that when the children were gone, we would sell the house, and we would travel around the world. That weekend made me dream of that day. I was feeling the happiness already. It wasn't just me who loved Iraj as my baby; it was indeed Iraj who watched me as his baby too. He made me believe in that happiness.

When I look back I see that every act of Iraj was an act of a real and genuine love. I couldn't find a reason for being even a bit suspicious about his daily love and care at that time.

Was it really wise of me, my dear GOD, to think of his loving acts as a guilty conscious prize? Would a smart woman ruin her beautiful life in effort of seeking where and what her husband was doing wrong? I really don't know. I just keep wondering. Obviously I didn't know him at all.

Malakuti on many occasions would start the conversations about human behavior in general after he came home late at night. One night he was talking about LOVE. He was saying, "There is no such a thing as love. Love is a voluntary action which was created by a selfish human being". That night I tried to challenge him. I would not agree with such statement. I was in love at that time, and I would not allow myself to doubt the existence of love. So I didn't believe him then. But today, with my new feelings, I believe in his statement hundred percent. Too bad he is no longer alive, and I can't admit to him that he was right. Oh, well.

I would frequently have the same nightmare, where Iraj had either died, or he was dying. He would gently wake me up by saying, "You are dreaming. Wake up. Whatever it was, it is not really happening". Sometimes he had to wake me up. Few times I wonder why I was going back to the same dream over and over again.

When I told him what my nightmares were about, he just laughed and said, "You are a silly woman. I don't intend to die, and no one is planning to kill me".

Now I know why my father was so worried about me. He knew that my love for Iraj was a fatal disease. And the reason that it had become incurable was because Iraj had continued his loving and caring to a point that I could never have gotten free of loving him. Had he not been loving, I would have left him years ago.

This reminds me of the times when we had just started seeing each other. We had a serious argument, and I told him, "I don't want to see you again". I wrote a six-page letter, and handed it to him in the bus coming home from school. I was so mad at him that I refused to sit next to him. I asked myself to forget him before I got any farther with my love for him. And I walked home so firmly. It felt like I had won a Nobel Prize. I thought to myself, "I made it. I left him for good, and his love cannot hurt me any more".

My Dear God:

But that only lasted till the next day. He found a reason, which I can't recall, to invite me to his house. After I heard his story, I felt so terrible for hurting him. And we kissed and made up. After all I think it was meant to be this way. Anyway, as they say, "Every good thing comes to an end one day". I could probably have left him if he wasn't so caring.

I only know that this very hand that is writing these very words now, this very heart that is beating gracefully at this moment, and these very eyes that could see the beauty of the world will stop all her activities one day. And then it will be the end of her. But I do not worry about it now. I thought this life was too precious to be wasted then.

Now, it was time for celebration of his fiftieth Birthday. My dear GOD, what was I thinking then, and what am I thinking now? What was in my heart for the preparation of his birthday? I cannot even put it into words, or describe it in any possible way. For people who had never experienced this kind of crazy love it would be hard to understand my feelings, even if I tried putting them into words. It will be the same as talking to someone about your terminal cancer condition, and expect them to feel the pain and agony you are experiencing. It's impossible to either explain or conceive.

I tried so hard to prove to my parents that he was the right person for me after all. I wanted to tell the whole world that my decision on loving Iraj was the right decision. So with these thoughts in my mind, and having arranged my monthly allowance, I made it possible. I thought that most important day of my life, Iraj's fiftieth birthday, had arrived. And I was trying to celebrate it abundantly.

What a lucky woman! I had my wonderful husband in good health; I had my children matured, intelligent, beautiful, and healthy. I had my beautiful house. I was in a perfect shape. And we were well off to have a very comfortable life. And it was time for me to celebrate Iraj's birthday. I wished to show him my admiration, my love and devotion, and everything that he was expecting from me all those years. I thought and felt that we were both at the peak of our happiness. I wished to thank him for the many years of his effort to be a good husband and a good father.

It wasn't a very big party, maybe around fifty people. I had invited those whom he had more contact with. Many of them we knew for more than twenty-five years.

I was only concerned of how to surprise him. I had to beg everyone to remain mute, but keeping fifty people quiet for two weeks was quite a challenge.

My Dear God:

At first I wanted to assign Malakuti to bring him to the hotel. But then I realized that it was likely that he would either forget or be late. So I changed my mind, and asked Arman, his nephew who is deceased now, to bring Iraj to the hotel. That wouldn't be too hard to handle since Iraj was involved with Arman's business. We decided that Arman made up a story that he had to meet with his partner and his lawyer in one of the conference room at Hilton Hotel in Troy, Michigan.

I had arranged a small dinner party at home on the Saturday, before that Sunday, to make sure that he did not suspect anything. Our friends showed up with their gifts. My children gave him their gifts. And Mary read him a poem that she dedicated to him.

For some reason I had a feeling that he was expecting a grand fiftieth birthday. And he seemed rather disappointed.

The next day was Sunday. I told Iraj, "Now that you are going out with Arman, I am going to see a movie with the kids". It appeared to be quite normal to him. I knew he was not suspecting anything.

The hotel had arranged two connecting rooms for us. The table settings were in a rectangular L-shape. Our families were sited in the middle of the long rectangle. The guests started to arrive, and they were being entertained. Dr. Azeez Malakuti, his partner and friend, was placed at Iraj's left. It was March, and it was very cold in Michigan. They arrived exactly on time. We had turned all the lights off and everyone remained very quiet.

Arman had a hard time convincing Iraj that the room that he was heading for was a conference room and that it was not a mistake. Iraj knew that hotel very well. He knew that those were all dining rooms. But Arman told him that there was a small room behind the dinning room. "Don't worry. I know where I am going".

Anyway they opened the door to a dark room, when everyone screamed "HAPPY BIRTHDAY", and we turned the lights back on. I have never seen him so surprised. He still had his lambskin Russian-style hat on. He had his heavy coat on. And he was so shocked and surprised that, he was lost for a second. He removed his hat and coat and hurried to shake hands with everyone and welcoming them.

And I was the happiest of all. I was happy and proud celebrating his birthday, as well the twenty-five years of our togetherness. That was one achievement that I have always dreamt of. And the older he got, the greater and stronger my love and respect for him grew. To me a husband and a wife who were able to make it through all the hardships of life were worth of all the respect in the world. And there we were.

My Dear God:

Today when I look back I see that I was having a really nice dream. And when I opened my eyes, there was nothing there. There was nothing real about it. It was all gone forever.

Everyone was having a great time. On my right were my children, Mary Maseeh, and Mojgan. Next to them were Arman, Kayvan, and other friends and on his left were Azeez, his partner, and his family. Since, his sisters couldn't be here for his birthday, I had arranged a phone call from Iran so that they could congratulate him on his fiftieth birthday. He was so excited that he was ready to cry.

First I had a toast to Iraj. And I said, "We have had our good times and bad times together. We have had many difficulties, and we had managed to overcome them all. We have had our differences. But today I could honestly say that Iraj has been a good husband, a good father, the best uncle, and a very gracious human being".

Then Arman said a few words about his uncle. Dr. Mehrabian toasted him next, and there were a few more who also teased him. The arrangement was that we all went to our house after dinner, and enjoyed each other's company for as long as we desired, and maybe play Blot. He opened his gifts. Some gifts were funny. But then there were some who brought a gift they had previously received from someone else. I know this because the old greeting cards were still attached. Our children seemed to be proud and happy; they were having a wonderful time.

Iraj almost had a heart attack when he saw the bill. But I calmed him down by disclosing the real purpose of my monthly allowance. He still wanted to pay with his credit card in front of his friends. So I reimbursed him after the party.

Only a few were happy for me, whereas many others were jealous. They couldn't help gossiping behind my back. I was never bothered by their actions. I have always believed that bad people will burn in the fire they had started.

Iraj was a big spender in general. He didn't ever mind spending money on me. And he didn't mind borrowing money for that purpose at the times that we were broke. But there had been several incidents that he made a big deal over something so insignificant. It would make me so mad.

My Dear God:

My idea of requesting a monthly allowance had a dual purpose. Number one was to save money for his party. And I also wanted to be able to buy things for my children without his interference. I wanted to be able to buy whatever I needed whenever I needed. It was our money, and I was a very conservative spender.

I remember once before our salary arrangement his sister Niya and I went gift shopping for her friends in Iran. She was asking me to get something for my Mom in Iran. When she realized that I was hesitant to spend money, she told me that I had to get something for my Mom. "I promise to take it to her, and I am sure that she will be happy". Then she held up a black jacket and said, "This is her. She will love it". I am sure that Niya was aware of what was behind my hesitations to buy that jacket. But we just left it as that. Although the money came from the same source, there were no disagreements after the arrangement for monthly salary.

Like once, while we were visiting Spain, I came across a beautiful figurine of Mary, the holy mother. It was made out of silver and seashells. I wanted to buy it for his birthday. We had our American Express card with us, knowing that it was acceptable everywhere in the world. But to our surprise and disappointment they did not accept our card. My money became handy that day, and I was able to pay for the statue right then and there.

He thanked me for the surprise party. He did admit that he believed that the party on Saturday was the celebration of his fiftieth birthday, and that he was completely surprised. He was especially glad about receiving the check from me the following day.

As the time went by, and our children grew older and went away to college, Iraj was becoming more withdrawn. But at the same time he was spending more of his free time with me so that I wouldn't get depressed.

Once he said very unexpectedly, "I had made an appointment with the Cleveland Clinic for a check up". He asked me if I was going with him. I said, "Yes, but why a check up? Is there anything wrong?" He said, "No, it's just the time for a full check up".

I knew that he had some problems with his bladder for many years. He used to urinate frequently. So I felt much better when he said he was going for a check up. I always worried if he had prostate Cancer, which was, and still is very common among men.

Early in the morning we went from building to building and from room to room for various tests. Many times I captured Iraj's glance, which made me very nervous. I felt as if he was hiding something from me. Although I was right by him most of the time, I couldn't understand what they were talking about. It seemed like they were using some sort code language. But there was one particular young doctor who told Iraj, "It might happen, but it is too early for you". And he continued to question him.

My Dear God:

By then I had made every effort to give in to my instincts, and start believing in what I did not want to believe.

Having considered how withdrawn he had been, and his dubious glances, I had come to conclusion that there was something he would rather not discuss with me. And after hearing that young doctor's comment, I felt that I have guessed it right. He has been worried aging, and his concern was about impotency. Although I have never experienced that, I knew that he was worried he was getting there. We still were having a great love affair.

Something funny happened while we were at the clinic one morning. We were sitting in the waiting room among many men and women waiting for their turns. I always dressed nice, but to some people I wore fashionable. First of all I knew how to sew, and I was creative in my sewing. So that day, while I was walking down the waiting room, a lady approached me and said, "You are a movie star. Yes, I have seen you in a movie. Am I right? Yes, am I right?" I just laughed. I sat next to Iraj and said, "I think she is mistaking me for someone else". People told me on many occasions that I look like Rita Morena in "West Side story", or Marisa Tomei in "My Cousin Vinny". But it was funny that she insisted that I was a movie star. To tell you the truth at the time my life was even better than one of a movie star.

Okay, my dear GOD, please tell me how many men are there who would take their

wives along for a physical check up, and then would make it as a short honeymoon? And if he hated me enough to be planning to end our marriage, why was he getting more and more attached to me, and why did he make sure that I had a happy life? Was he crazy, or am I the one who is crazy? I don't know what to say, or how to explain his character. God, you knew him well then, and you know him well now. I thought he loved his wife and his children. And I felt that he deserved to be loved by us. So if he fooled me, or if I did not possess wisdom to recognize his true character, I don't think I should be blamed. I was just human and I only judged by what I saw and what I felt. And I have enough understanding to recognize niceness apart from viciousness. I couldn't think of looking for his betrayal and disloyalty behind his loving and caring. My dear GOD, this is your job to reveal his true nature to me. That is why everyone turns to you and says, "Please God, help me, please". During that time I would not have doubted Iraj even if someone tried to convince me that they saw him in bed with another woman. After what had happened in Iran, and after him showing so much remorse, I believed that every man in the world was capable of cheating and betraying his wife, but not Iraj. I thought that never again in his lifetime he would be capable of ruining his own life. So you see, my dear GOD, with everything that happened; I have no choice but to believe that I was one emotional dumb woman, who couldn't tell right from wrong.

My Dear God:

I had decided to keep myself occupied during those times when my children were away. I didn't want to be feeling sorry for myself because I had nobody in this country. Now that my children were leaving to go to college and I would have more time to myself, I had to find different activities, and not cry over the spilled milk.

And Once Mojgan started going to school, I had arranged to be attending the college of beauty in Bloomfield Hills for a license in Cosmetology. I thought I had to keep myself busy while doing something that I enjoyed. The final test was taking place in Lansing, Michigan. Iraj drove me there.

I volunteered to work at hospitals. I joined a group of Bridge players in our neighborhood. Those ladies have been playing together for many years. And I was fortunate to be able to play with them.

This group took turns playing in each member's house. They were intelligent and talented ladies. Most of them were involved in different organizations, such as American Cancer Society, American Heart Association, and Bloomfield Birmingham Symphony Orchestra.

The host would prepare a very tasty, colorful and unique lunch, along with delicious desserts. I loved playing Bridge. It occupied my mind with numbers and decision-making. There was no time for gossiping or talking nonsense.

While I was playing Bridge, I decided to take some classes at Birmingham

Bloomfield Community Center. That helped me a lot. It was at that center that I met yet another group of ladies who were taking the class with me. After the classes were over, we decided to start getting together for a game once a week.

We took a Bridge class together with our husbands long time ago. It was Susan and Naser Barkhordari, and Iraj and I. It was an evening class at Lasher High School near our house. The teacher made it look so difficult that I thought I would never be able to learn this game. I thought that game was so important for my mental development. I needed to be able to play it so badly, and I wanted to play it right. But Iraj would fall asleep during the lessons. We were supposed to review our lessons by playing together. The only way to learn was to practice and practice. But the men no longer wished to apply themselves. It was easy for Susan and Naser, because Susan's parents were there to play with them, whereas I had to look for a way to practice. Later on I introduced Susan to our neighbors. We would call her when we needed a sub. Soon she became a member, and she played with us once a week.

My Dear God:

Although Blot was an interesting game, and I learned it quickly, but bridge was something else. It was very challenging for me. I wasn't one of those women who liked luncheons and shopping, let alone gossiping and bragging. So I was happy to discover activities that would keep me occupied at all the times. I was one happy person to become the number one in Bridge tournament.

By now we played Blot two to three times a week. That game was for couples. Some, like Fasihis and Dr. Mahajer, who didn't play would either go home early, or involve themselves with other activities. We got together without the Blot players on many occasions. It would typically be a quiet and pleasant evening at either of our houses.

My Dear God:

The men chose their own partners, and the ladies played with ladies, unless there was shortage.

And as usual there was much disagreement, nagging, and gossiping going on throughout the game. Once it would be that one didn't like the other one, and next time it would be that one said something nasty about the other one. There was not one time that these people got along. It was pathetic to be caught in the middle. At times we didn't know if we should be laughing at them, or should we cry for them?

Although Azeez and Reza had very similar characters, they both were also very vulnerable. And some took advantage of their vulnerability and instigated a fight between them.

This one fight, which I am going to talk about, was over nothing. As I remember their fight was over bidding over Azeez's bid at the antique shop, or it was over wrong

accusation that Reza had made.

Azeez was so mad at Reza. It was unbelievable. He would discuss Reza's faults with everyone every day. He had made it such a big deal. It seemed to him that was the end of the world. After weeks and weeks of speaking of him furiously, he asked a few of his friends to his house one night in effort to discuss the matter with them. It was Jalal and Rohan Panah, Naser and Susan Barkhordari, Iraj and I, with Badri and Malakuti himself. He was complaining about Reza All night. After dinner he suggested that everyone listened to him seriously. We were all ears.

He was talking with such an emotional exaggeration that we thought the discussion to be about World War III. While I was physically there, I didn't want to be any part of discussion. I knew that they would fight one day, and would be friends again the next day. Besides, the subject was so childish that it would have been a big mistake to get involved. And besides I knew Reza and Nazi, and I liked them both. I might not have liked their behavior at times, but I never had any clashes with them.

I turned into an observer that night, and I just paid attention to the silliness of the group of educated doctors and their wives, who were acting like a group of kids with no guide what so ever.

Malakuti was able to get the approval of Jalal, Rohan, Naser, and Susan to break up with Mahajers for supporting him. He said, "If you believe in me and my words, you must back me up in my decision and stay away from Rezas". Just like a little kid he was asking, "You have to choose between him and me". It seemed to me that they were all trying to find a way to stay out of this contract. The only person among them, who did not say a word of either approval or disapproval of his contract, was Iraj himself. Like always he sat there awaiting for the final result.

My Dear God:

I was not at all surprised to see Susan and Rohan go along with Azeez's idea. I just shook my head and laughed to myself and thought, "What a bunch of wrong people! How did these people manage to become doctors?"

Next evening Naser and Susan asked us to come over for a while. I knew that the subject must have been about Malakuti's decision. I was right. We sat in the living room, and talked about the previous night.

Naser was very upset with Malakuti's decision. He was complaining, "Why does Azeez try to put us in the middle of a situation which has nothing to do with us?" And then both husband and wife came to the conclusion that, "We don't have to go along with everything that Azeez wants us to do".

Although I did not interfere the night before, and I did not want to get involved at all, I couldn't help interfering now. I thought that I had to say something to those people who thought they knew everything, and who talked before they thought.

I said, "Last night I was wondering how can you all sit and listen to what he had to say? And how come you all agreed to his offer? If any one of you said something against his offer, maybe he could have come to his senses, and possibly he would have realized that he was over the board, that he was asking for an impossible, and that he was just plain acting childish". And then I continued, "But now, after you have given him a complete support, you realized that boycotting Reza was not a wise act". And I continued, "And if at this time you decide to break your promise to him, it would hurt him much more than before. If last night you all told him, "Although we have had problems with Reza and Nazi in the past, we think it is very childish to be creating such a big fight among a group of educated adults virtually over nothing", it would have been possible to calm him down and get rid of his anger".

So we talked. And they decided that it was not their business to get involved with such a matter, and they should mind their own business.

What has left me wondering was that this group of Iranians was trying to look good in the public eye. They were supposed to be an example of knowledge and intelligence. They were supposed to be the peaceful members of their own community. But not only were they not that, but also they had become the subject of jokes among their own children.

My Dear God:

There were fights over gifts and invitations. There were fights about serving wrong food, and many other subjects, which are quite embarrassing to be talking about.

I truly believe that our children blamed these uncivilized acts on our race and culture. I remember that one day during one of those fights between Susan and Nazi, Nazi came to our house. My sister-in-law, Parween, was visiting at the time. While Nazi was expressing her anger over Barkhordaris' behavior, she started experiencing difficulty breathing. And as always I gave her a paper bag to blow into it to help her release her frustration. And even though she was feeling much better within a few minutes, she appeared hopeless and overwhelmed.

After she left Parween, who doesn't usually say much, turned to me and said, "How come these people keep reconciling after all these difficulties? Can't they learn that these people will not be their friends? When do they want to, learn to stay away from troubles is the only way to happiness?"

Most member of this group of Iranians were so consumed by their own selfishness that they never took a moment to observe themselves in the mirror to find out where the problems were rooted. And the only way I was able to deal with them was by ignoring their friendship, as well as their animosity. And I chose to practice that philosophy till the end.

It was even more embarrassing that our relatives, who visited us occasionally, could

recognize the ugliness of their acts. In one of the parties Mrs. Moghaddass, the mother of Nayer Rabbani, told me, "Your party is so lifeless. It looks like everyone is avoiding one another. There is no dancing, no laughter, and not even communication. These people would have had more fun going out to a restaurant. Why do they bother inviting one another when they can't stand each other?" I laughed in response and said, "I have been asking this same question years now, and I haven't found the answer".

The fight between Azeez and Reza became a subject among many Iranians. Reza threw a party at his house once. And it so happened that it was also Azeez's birthday that day. And obviously Azeez was not invited.

Azeez, who was known for being easily bothered, became very depressed. Although they were not very close with Dr. M. Rabbani, these two families went out to dinner that night. It seemed that Rabbanis' were not invited also. They went back to Rabbani's house after dinner. Azeez has been very disappointed with his close friends Barkhordaris, and Panahs, who broke their promises to him. Rabbanis, who sympathized with Azeez, had gotten a cake for him. They celebrated his birthday, and tried to cheer him up. Azeez was so sensitive and depressed that most of the time you wouldn't know how to handle him.

My Dear God:

I remember one night when the Blot group was over at our house. I threw a party for Iraj. I started taking pictures after dinner. There was a moment that Iraj sat in the loveseat with Jalal and Rohan on each side. Azeez and Badri were standing right there. Rohan asked Badri to join them on the loveseat. Badri said, "No, there is no room". But Rohan pulled her by her hand and said, "Come on, sit on our laps". And while she had one hand around Iraj, she pushed Badri on Iraj's lap with the other hand. At that time Badri began moving on Iraj's lap with such sensuality, while saying, "No, no please no, Azeez will kill me". And at the same time she was looking at Azeez with bedroom eyes. I took a snap shot. Azeez was saying, "You, you are not afraid of me. You are enjoying it". Badri knew well how and when to excite Azeez, or how to fool him.

Okay, my dear GOD, we were supposed to be like sisters and brothers to each other at that time. We had respect for the morality among us. We were grateful that we had each other, and we had always tried to be there for each other. We had acted like that with each other many times. And no one ever suspected that there would be adulterous relationships taking place among best friends. How could I have possibly noticed the fling between Iraj and Badri? How could I have recognized her flirting with Iraj when Azeez didn't see it? Anyway I think we were just fools.

While Iraj was focused on how to earn more money, our children were growing. They had left home to attend college.

It is common in America that children are considered to be adults as soon as they turn eighteen. And by law they are entitled to do whatever they want with their lives.

This picture was taken on the night that everyone was asking Badri to sit on Iraj's lap and she was pretending to be too shy to do it. But her husband told her, "Don't be too shy, you know you wish to do it." As you see, we were like sisters and brothers, but not sisters and brothers who cannot marry each other. These sisters and brothers had already proven that they could get married after she could get rid of her husband. Isn't that nice?

Fereshteh and I are at Cranbrook School in Michigan.

Iraj's birthday. Take a good look at Badri in red. This was long before Malakuti's death. Doesn't the way Badri is looking at Iraj make you think they had something going on between them, even when Malakuti was alive? How stupid could I be? From left to right: Iraj, me, Nayer, and Badri, the evil of all evils

The same night, Iraj, Roozbeh Malakuti, Mary, and Maseeh. Kaveh Kamooneh is in the back row. Poor Iraj was trying to look happy standing next to Roozbeh. What a life! He wasn't happy with his own children. Now, he can be happy standing to someone else's child. Isn't that ironic?

While we were in the twilight zone, we arranged things to occupy our mind in a good way. It is somebody's birthday and we are trying to have fun. Maseeh, Mojgan, and Mary

At my house before I found out that Iraj and Badri were cooking something for me. In our TV room, Mary, Mojgan, Roshanak, Maseeh, and me. I am sitting with my children, the love of my life, and talking to them. Oh well.

In Pari's house, poor Iraj is confused. But, we were happy at least.

Here, although Pari had asked us not to look serious, Iraj was not able to stop thinking about the trap he was in.

Kasra, Mojgan, and Maseeh who was holding Pari and me in his arms

At Shushtary's house, they announced my birthday and we had to kiss. Sara and Azeez are very excited, I think.

I am happy. Mary is happy. I don't know what is wrong with the man in the middle (Iraj).

In here, we were waiting for our table. No wonder Mary is so happy on the top picture, because we were finally seated. Me, Iraj, Mojgan, Maseeh, and Mary. I don't know who the other two girls are. As you see here, he was upset with me holding his hand.

Mary had her own apartment in Ann Arbor in Michigan. Maseeh was attending the Center for Creative of Studies in Detroit Michigan. He was sharing an apartment with a roommate.

It had been quite challenging for Maseeh to adapt to the lifestyle in Detroit. It was difficult for him to be away from home. And on the top of everything he had to deal with the separation from his high school sweetheart, Beth.

I remember he called me one evening. He said, "Hi Mom". I knew immediately that something was very wrong. It seemed as if he was waiting for me to ask what was wrong. He began to cry. He was saying, "I lost my Beth. I lost her".

My Dear God:

I said, "Please talk to me. Tell me what happened". He said with much desperation in his voice, "Since she had to join out of Detroit College, and with her mother's influence, she had decided to end our relationship for good".

I let him to talk for a while. Then I told him, "It is not easy for me to comfort you from a distance, and it is easy for me to say, but you must believe me that these things will happen. The only thing that we can do at times like these would be to try and figure out how to deal with the situation". I didn't want to be lecturing him. I just wanted to assure him that we loved him, and we were expecting him to love himself as well. I asked him if he wanted me to stay with him for a while. But he said he would be okay. Besides he had a roommate, and he didn't want to be invading his privacy. I just asked him to be patient, and leave everything to GOD. I asked him to give it some time and see what happened. I offered him to come home for few days. I even mentioned that I could talk to Beth's mother to find out why she was so concerned about their relationship. But he refused all my offers. He wanted to handle it by himself.

Beth was Maseeh's first love. That feeling was very serious and precious for him. He was very handsome, quite popular, and most importantly a gentleman. There were many girls who wanted to be with him. He had much respect for a girl he chose to date. Even though many approached him, he wouldn't have sex with just any girl. I knew all these, because I watched him closely.

One evening after he got home, he was wondering around in his room. I went in there, and asked him what was wrong.

He did not want to say anything at first. But he opened up after I insisted, and with such a disappointment told me, "I don't know what is wrong with these girls. What do they think of themselves and their lives? They expect you to marry them as soon as they say hello to you. How stupid can they be? Why are they like this?"

I knew that he wasn't going out with any girl. But it was obvious that one of the seventeen year old girls had asked him to marry her. That had upset him so much that he decided to refuse going out with any girl. I congratulated myself after hearing his point of

view with the achievement of having such a son. I felt very proud to see that my son knew best. I said, "Bravo Shamci. You have raised a son with a good head on his shoulders". It was so common to run into someone whose daughter got pregnant, or her son impregnated a girl under aged. It was a great pleasure for me to see how thoughtful my son was.

So now that he had met Beth, whom he loved so much, I wanted him to be able to continue his friendship with her until the day that both of them were to decide on marriage or otherwise.

My Dear God:

It was during this time Rohan told me, "Do you know who is deeply in love with your son? It is Roshanak Malakuti. She has been telling everyone that she is in love with Maseeh". I told her, "I am sorry. Did you know that Roxana's friend Beth, who loves him very much, has already taken Maseeh? And as far as I know, there is no room for another girl".

One day we were joking around with Maseeh, and I told him, "Do you know that Roshanak had spread a rumor that she is in love with you?" With a funny face he looked at me grimacing and said, "Oh boy that would be the day. Tell me, who else is in love with me?" And we all laughed.

Maseeh's break-up with Beth was one of the saddest experiences in his life. Although now that I'm thinking; he did go through yet another horrible experience before that. It was the death of his best friend since the second grade. His name was Jeff. He was only seventeen. It was very interesting the way those two became friends.

Maseeh was a very family-oriented boy. He felt so sad for kids who did not have loving homes. Maseeh and Jeff were Boy Scouts. They were going camping that special summer. All kids were driven to school by their parents except for Jeff. He arrived all by himself on a bicycle. He had his sack over his shoulder and a smile on his face. Maseeh had asked him few times to either take him home or bring him to our house. He was the only child who had no one to greet him or drive him home upon their return. He politely refused our offer to take him home. That day Maseeh told me about Jeff's life.

When Jeff was three years old, once his mother came home from work unexpectedly to find her husband with her mother in her bed. She divorced her husband with an unbelievable commotion. She ended up remarrying several times after that, but her children, especially Jeff, accepted neither of her husbands. So while he loved his mother, he didn't really have a home to go to. He always felt like he didn't have anybody to turn to.

Despite all that was happening in his life, you would never see him sad or gloomy. Most of his good friends came from loving homes, and he chose to associate with them for the most part. Maseeh was one of them. He always welcomed Jeff to our house. I was happy to see my children were sharing their happiness with their friends. My house was

open, and my dinner table was ready to serve my children's friends. This was the tradition in my parents' home. My parents were very happy to provide home to our friends, especially to my brother's friends. They were welcome to share meals with us whenever they visited. Both Iraj and Pari were among our friends.

My Dear God:

On Maseeh's sixteenth birthday we took a few of his closest friends out to a Japanese restaurant. All the boys got dressed up that night. I was very proud to be accompanied by them. We were having a great time. They were talking about future, while teasing one another. Many of them were acting shy in front of us except for Jeff. He was talking about his great future, "I will graduate with honors, then I will become an executive of all the companies in the world. And if you guys, especially Maseeh, come to see me, I will make a point of dedicating a few seconds of my busy schedule to talk to you. But remember not to be asking me for any favors, for I will make sure not to recognize you then". He shook the dust of his suit pretending to be an executive. He certainly was the center of attention that night. He made us all laugh so much, while we all knew what a horrible life he had at home.

Jeff was a good boy, and he was Maseeh's best friend. I was happy when they were in my house under my supervision, and I didn't mind it at all. But as they grew older, Jeff began to seek dangerous life, particularly riding a motorcycle. I had no objections to many of their ideas, such as camping in our front yard, or picnicking in my back yard. I didn't mind if they stayed up all night giggling. But I did mind Maseeh's involvement with bike riding at that age.

My children have always believed that I was a strict mother with a nasty attitude. But I didn't mind them. They were not aware of where I was standing, and what my responsibilities were towards them. All they knew was that everyone else did it, and why couldn't they? I knew that as a mother I had to step forward to prevent my children from doing wrong whether they liked it or not.

It was Sunday. Iraj was in bed reading his Wall Street Journal. I was working around the yard, while watching my children like a hulk. I saw Jeff on his motorcycle in front of our house talking to Maseeh. I was very nervous and scared, and worried. I didn't know how to face the difficulty, when Maseeh told me he wanted to go with Jeff. I was determined not to let him go. And at the same time there was nothing I could do to stopping Jeff from persuading Maseeh to go with him. So I got into a big fight with Maseeh. He told me, "Then I will follow him in my car". By then I couldn't say anything to him. Except for I asking him to come home soon.

As we found out later, Maseeh took Jeff to a gas station, and he returned home shortly. He was very upset with me for not letting him ride with Jeff. But in a few hours he received a call that he wished he never received. Jeff was found dead by a huge tree near

their house.

He was driving at hundred and twenty miles per hour on a curvy road, when he hit the tree. He died instantly. Maseeh knew that had I not stopped him that day, his body would have been found next to Jeff's.

My Dear God:

I believe that Maseeh had died emotionally with this news. It was then that for the first time he had experienced the loss of someone whom he cared for. His life and his attitude changed that instance. They were four friends, who mourned for Jeff more than others. I still regret that I wasn't able to stop Jeff from riding his motorcycle that day.

The four friends, all dressed in black suits, carried his casket on their shoulders. Jeff's mother and siblings spoke of him serenely and lovingly. They all were missing him. They were missing his liveliness, his ambitions and eagerness. And I missed Jeff every time I came across his picture, for I had many of them. There were pictures of him and Maseeh from the very beginning of their friendship to the end. His memory stayed with us forever. I think Jeff's death haunted Maseeh for a long time. It was very difficult for him to accept that he was gone forever. Jeff's accident was Maseeh's first serious taste of reality.

And after that was the bitter taste of separation from his real love Beth. I don't think he ever got over it. After they both learned to cope with it, they remained friends. They would contact each other once in a while. The last he heard from her was that poor Beth was diagnosed with multiple sclerosis at such a young age. He felt very sad and helpless.

Although Maseeh would do everything other teenagers did, he kept it pretty low profile. While he did what he had to, he made sure to be a good son. I had a few clashes with Maseeh over things and ideas he wanted to force on me. One of them was the dog. I knew that Maseeh had to get over his fear of animals one day. And acquiring a dog was probably the best way accomplish it. But on the other hand, I used to be a human being before my children born. And I had my preferences. I did not like to having dogs, with their hair and saliva around my carpet and furniture, and in general around my living area. Maseeh was entitled to his own likings, but so was I.

We had a heated garage to accommodate the dog when it was cold, otherwise he had to stay outdoors. I was expecting Maseeh, the ultimate animal-lover, to care for the dog. While all that Maseeh cared for was to own a dog, I wanted him to also embrace the responsibilities that came along with it. It was a large size dog, I know for fact it was heavier than I was. The dog needed to be walked at least three times a day, fed regularly, and groomed.

My Dear God:

We had a huge fight over keeping the dog outdoors, and then eventually Maseeh started neglecting his responsibilities. So I was stuck with yet another set of duties: I had

to walk and feed, and, yes, I had to like the dog. It got loose and escaped from the yard on many occasions. I spent hours contacting police, and our neighbors.

There came a day when I've had enough of the dog business. I said to Maseeh, "You will either take over the responsibilities of this dog, or the dog has to go. It will be either the dog or me". He answered me sincerely, "Well, I choose the dog ". I will never forget that day.

From then on I decided to leave the dog's responsibilities to Maseeh, I stayed completely out of it. It didn't take him too long to come to a realization that the level of responsibility of having a dog equals that of having a child. It was an enormous responsibility to be able to keep that dog. The dog escaped more than once following this episode. We had to look for it for hours. So finally one day we all felt sorry for the poor neglected animal, and we decided to turn it in to the humane society. We came across a couple of farmers there, who were in need of a farm dog. It all turned out to be pretty fortunate.

Maseeh had his own special way of dealing with animals. He took great interest in sharks from very early age, which he articulated by drawing them, mainly during his classes at school. At some point he had birds, hamsters, cats, and dogs. He had turtles and frogs. And he even had pet snakes in Detroit. He enjoyed them all; he had special connection with each and every one of them. He loved any and every creature, be that from the bottom of the ocean, or from mountains and the deserts. It seemed that he was able communicating with them. He also collected rocks. Even though he was in love with nature in general, his main interest remained to be sharks I used to believe that he would become an oceanographer, just like Jaque Cousteau and his son, who had created amazing world for children.

Maseeh was a shy and sensitive little boy. He was my delight. I would always say to my children, "I have one heart, and that is Maseeh. And I have two eyes, they are Mary and Mojgan".

Although Maseeh did his share of things, and even though he mostly followed Mary's footsteps, for some reason he was not a bother to me. Yes he did put monster wheels on his car to make it stand out; yes he did remove the street signs along with some of his friends, which he got punished for. And he did other things that most teenagers do. But he didn't hate, and he was never hurtful.

Then again Mary and I were inseparable until she was ten. But I could never figure out what she had against me in later years. What was it that made her to go against my wishes? Why did she want to hurt me so badly? Why did she want to destroy me? She even said it herself that I never failed in loving her. But for some reason she blamed me for everything. Not that she told me, but she acted on hating me.

My Dear God:

I suspect she wanted me to stay out of her life forever, and I was not ready to do that. I had to stay on top of things, even if she didn't like it.

She would ask me not to ever visit her at the university. But when I did go there, she would after all proudly introduce me to her friends, "This is my Mom. She drove a long way to come and see me". She told me later, "Some of these girls have not seen their mothers for a while, although they live just a few blocks away". I could not understand her. On one hand she was rejecting me, and on the other hand I was one of her desirable assets.

When Mary was in her junior year at Country Day School, she got a chance to go to Spain for her internship for six weeks. She was insisting to wear her dirty snow jacket, with long sleeves down to her knees. And since I didn't allow her to wear the jacket she would not talk or say a good bye to me at the airport. Although I was very hurt, I kept smiling and waving good-bye. And only after I got home, I cried in the privacy of my bedroom. And I begged my dear GOD to help her and guide her.

There was a time when Mary decided to volunteer for international legal services in Harlingten Arizona. It was summer time, and I wasn't going to let her drive all by herself from Michigan to Arizona on such a hot day. So I thought of helping as well, and we decided that I drove with her to Harlingen, and stay with her for one week.

And on our way from Pennsylvania we decided to pick up one other girl. I have a letter from Kitty Ufford's father, and the copy of the newspaper that showed their appreciation of all the hard work that these three girls did that summer. I will include them in this book.

Those three girls, each from a different family, and a different state, all studying law, were trying to take the matters in their hands. Mary Lisa and Kitty volunteered for direct involvement with deportation proceedings of Central American refugees.

Kitty was very excited to be driving with us. And it seemed like she didn't mind that I stayed with them for one week. Then I met Lisa. She was a very nice and intelligent girl. They all had good heads on their shoulders. I got to meet many other volunteers, who were there trying to bring justice to the unjust world.

The girls were sharing a small townhouse, which was barely furnished. Each girl brought some necessities to get by. I would stop by the local grocery store during my morning walks. I cooked for them few times; they seemed to like it. They worked from sunrise to dawn. Among the group were students, teachers, writers, and nuns. Some brought their children along. They were living in houses full of ants, bugs, cockroaches, and all kinds of insects. I slept on the sofa in the living room.

My Dear God:

They arranged a picnic once when I was still there. They all were well-educated, intelligent people. Even the nun, who appeared to be their leader, had a PHD in philosophy. I realized as I was watching this group that they had given up their comfort, and they had gathered to change the wrong and the unjust. I felt so little. I knew at that moment why Mary was always embarrassed of our big and beautiful house. She seemed to be much happier sleeping on the ground in that heat, in a place full of insects. Thinking she'll be able to help some people if she could.

Although deep down Mary was pleased that I was proud of her, she still kept her distance. It so happened that I was there on Mary's birthday. They worked really hard that day, and so Mary went straight to bed when she got home. Lisa and Kitty were going to the other volunteer's house, which was a walking distance from ours. And since Mary was asleep, they asked me to join them. I didn't want to go at first. But then I went into Mary's room to ask her if it was okay to buy a cake, and celebrate her birthday with her friends. She was sound asleep, and I did not bother to wake her up. Then I decided to go with the girls, and give Mary her gift later.

Mary joined us soon after. I was glad that she came. But she left shortly saying that she wanted to go to bed. I stayed with the girls for a while, and then went home to see if she was up to wish her a happy birthday and give her a gift. As soon as I opened her door, she started shouting. She was throwing things around and calling me names. I remember that I thought she was not a normal person. I thought she was on something. I tried to tell her that I didn't forget her birthday. I told her that I came home so I could wish her a happy birthday. I told her that I thought she was asleep when I came home, so I did not wake her up. But she was out of control. Although I haven't noticed any misbehavior among other girls, I was positive that Mary was under influence that day.

I got ready to go for my daily walk, and did my prayers and cries while I was walking. And then I felt good, knowing that I did not have to spend the whole summer with her.

This act of Mary reminded me again of what my father warned me of, "You are doing too much for these kids. They are growing up with an idea that the whole world owes them something. But you are the closest target for them".

My Dear God:

When I managed to put myself together, I realized that I had done wrong. There are millions of people in this world who occasionally forget each other's birthdays. We didn't celebrate our birthdays with my family. We were not aware that when it passed. There wasn't more significance in the days we were born in comparison to any other days of the year. We were still the same children, and we were treated the same way. Our parents did not have to prove their love for us with material objects.

Brownsville Herald
6-14-87

Herald photo by Cathy Corman

From left, Lisa Carmona, Kitty Ufford and Maryem Rafani are working for Proyecto Libertad in Harlingen this summer to learn how to help Central American political refugees

Students seek justice for refugees

By CATHY CORMAN
Herald Staff Writer

Three young women, aged 20, 22 and 27, have come to The Valley this summer to get a taste of revolution.

It's not that they've come down here from Pennsylvania, Michigan and Indiana to carry guns or overthrow a government. They've come "to help people who are fleeing from the battle," they said — people who are tired of guns and governments.

They've traveled thousands of miles to work for Proyecto Libertad, a public interest legal organization dedicated to defending Central American refugees in deportation proceedings.

"When I'm in Michigan, it's all on paper... It's all written in black and white," said Maryem Rafani, a third-year law student at Wayne State University.

The refugees "aren't statistics any more. They're telling me 'my house was bombed,' and 'my brother was tortured.' It makes you feel a little bit ...well, it makes you reevaluate yourself," she said.

The three women arrived in Harlingen in early June and are sharing an apartment for the

All had worked on various political initiatives at home and had avidly followed news of civil unrest in Nicaragua and El Salvador.

Unlike many students with a political conscience, these three wanted to become directly involved with the news — if not at the "front line" in Central America, then as geographically and spiritually close as they could get.

Rafani, 27, was born in [illegible] and has been active in many Third World "liberation" campaigns. She is interested in immigration law and hopes her summer internship with Proyecto will familiarize her with the nuts and bolts of the legal process.

Lisa Carmona, a 22-year-old second-year law student at Indiana University at Bloomington, was raised in San Juan, Puerto Rico. Growing up there sensitized her to problems Hispanic Americans face, she said, and she specifically looked for a summer job which would allow her to use her Spanish and work with immigrants.

Younger than her two housemates, Kitty Ufford is a 20-year-old senior at Haverford College in Pennsylvania. Her trip south is sponsored by the Pennsylvania Yearly Meeting of the Society of Friends.

The Pennsylvania Society of Friends organized a program to sponsor students to study the sanctuary movement. It decided it wanted more information on legal work along the border and agreed to send Ufford here to work at Proyecto. In return, Ufford will make presentations about her experiences next year to Quaker meetings in the Pennsylvania area.

Ufford is unsure how much she'll be able to contribute at Proyecto since she has no legal training, but she says: "It's more like me trying to learn a lot so I can talk when I get back and raise consciousnesses."

All three expressed admiration for their co-workers at Proyecto. "I don't think I've ever seen people work as hard for a cause," said Carmona. "They work so hard, and yet at the same time... they keep really collected about it all," Ufford said.

They described their first trip to the detention center at Port Isabel, nicknamed *"El Corralon,"* as deeply disturbing.

"People come across the border after long, hard treks, and they wind up in detention centers where they're treated like criminals," Ufford said.

"When we left *El Corralon*, we were driving away, and I wondered where they went. They went through that door. I mean, even down here your life is still different... You can never really understand their experience," Ufford said.

"You can't understand it completely, I guess, unless you go to El Salvador and get yourself arrested," said Rafani.

As you see there is no need for any explanation. This is a copy of a newspaper article.

150 MERCER STREET
PRINCETON, NEW JERSEY 08540

June 26, 1987

Dear Mrs. Rafani,

Mrs. Ufford and I would like to thank you for your kindness to Kitty during your trip from Ohio to Texas.

It was a great comfort to us to know that she had some traveling companions for such a long trip. We realize it was an intrusion upon your plans that you and Maryem had worked out together to suddenly have to accomodate another voyager on short notice, but it was a true blessing for Kitty and she has spoken many times of how much she enjoyed your company and the many kindnesses that you showed her along the way.

It is quite a challenge that Kitty and Maryem have undertaken this Summer. It will be an experience that they will long remember and will draw on in many ways in the future for insights and understanding.

If you or Maryem or your family should ever find yourself coming to New York or New Jersey, we hope you will let us know as we would be pleased indeed to have you visit and stay with us. Princeton is a quiet university town within an hours train ride from New York, so please do come and see us when you can.

Again, many thanks for your generosity and kindness to Kitty.

Sincerely yours,

Charles Ufford

I think this letter speaks for itself. There is no need for writing.

Then I started to think, "Let's say for a minute that I had forgotten your birthday. Who gives you the right to attack your mother like that?"

Yes, GOD blesses your soul, wherever you are, my dear father, who knew much more than people with doctorate degrees. You were right, and I was wrong. I had gone too far to satisfy my children's desires. Indeed, by spoiling them I have done more harm than help.

And besides acknowledging someone's birthday is an act of love. If someone would not give it to me, I am not supposed to demand it from him or her by force and abuse.

Her behavior was unacceptable. But since she was under influence, she can't even remember the thing she did and said that day. But meanwhile she kept the hatred for me in her heart. I wouldn't be surprised if she tried to get rid of me one day. And the more I tried to make her understand what had happened, the more she refused to communicate.

Although I was fully aware that she was not conscious of what she was doing at the time, it still hurts to even think about that day. And I can't rid my heart from that pain.

The outbursts of Mary's emotions were very unpredictable. I had a hard time figuring out her mood patterns. Her behavior would alternate between ugly scenes and acts of pure love.

There was a tine when she would send artwork with, "God couldn't be everywhere, so he created mothers". There was this other time when she was visiting her friend Roxan in California, and she sent me a dozen of roses and a card, "No one is as lucky as I to have a mother like you". And many more little things like that. So considering all her mood swings, I had to come up with a balanced way of dealing with her. It was very difficult then, and it still is very difficult now.

I tried to give her as much love as I could, because I recognized my own mistakes, and her innocence. At times of my madness I told my children on many occasions, "I wish I did not have children". It was not because they did something wrong, but it was because I brought them into this world for my own pleasure. I brought then into this world not knowing that I would be introducing them to the world of hate, crime, drugs, and such uncertainty that neither of us could have ever helped it. But obviously my children interpreted it all wrong.

My Dear God:

I had read many books on PTE, parents training effectiveness, so that I knew that my children were conditioned to follow certain trends to some extend. While among those trends there were alcohol, drugs, hippies, boys, girls, cars, and speed, I had to learn how to deal with them. Since I was not able to keep them in the jar, I had to learn how to deal with the trends of their society. And in the process I felt obligated to teach them how to differentiate the right and wrong despite of the morals and values of their society. I wanted them to learn the humanitarian facts of life, and not the monopolistic abuse of their society. I wanted to teach them if killing a person was an act of crime, so were the killings of millions of innocent civilians in a war. I wanted them to know that respecting other's rights and ideals was the only way of respecting themselves, no matter what color or religious beliefs.

I remember that right at the time when Maseeh was graduating, young people were supposed to register with military. There was a possibility that they would be sent off to Middle East. Many young people were against the war, and they decided to flee to Canada to avoid killing in the name of defending the humanity". I was in absolute agreement with them. One had to obey orders when one joined the army. Then later on he or she would be proclaimed a Hero. But in reality in order for one to become a war hero, he or she would have to kill thousands of young soldiers from the opposite, the enemy's side. And God forbids if a soldier does not follow orders. We all know what would happen to him or her.

I was never afraid to express to my children how I felt about wars. I would tell him that there was not a good enough reason to justify wars, and that it relay did not matter who started them, and in who's name. Even now, when we refer to various history books mostly written by bystanders, it becomes apparent that none of the wars we had fought were necessary. Those wars could have been easily avoided if it wasn't for the selfishness and the cruelty of rulers.

I wanted my children to know that if they had humanitarian beliefs, they should study them carefully. If killing one person is considered a crime, then killing thousands of people could not possibly be an achievement. And in the end result no one deserved a Medal. We cannot, and must not have double standards when it came to accepting and practicing the rules of life. If killing human beings was acceptable in our society for our own defense, then the killing of a person should not be considered a murder either. But when the law makes you a murderer if you kill someone, even when it was not done intentionally, then ordering to bomb cities and/or countries should be considered a much greater crime. And it should not make any difference simply because one powerful ruler has ordered to do so. No matter how you look at it, the act of war means murdering young, hopeful people. Thanks God Maseeh was not called upon.

My Dear God:

Our children's behavior was the only problem we had to deal with, and at times quarrelled over. It was Mary's behavior and lifestyle that worried us the most. And since she was the oldest, the other two were looking up to her.

Mojgan was born while we were still living in our first house in Bloomfield Hills. She was born into comfort. She attended a private school from the beginning. We moved to our new luxurious house on Wabeek Lake when she was seven. So Mojgan couldn't really relate to the childhood of Mary and Maseeh.

Meanwhile Iraj and I were very happy in our relationship both as spouses and lovers. And except for the struggles we had to face while our children were maturing, we did not have anything to worry about. Iraj was a devoted, affectionate, and passionate husband at that time.

Excessive sweating, especially in the summertime, always bothered me. I wished I would never have to wear bras again. Then one day I came across a discussion of breast implants on TV. I knew I found the answer to my prayers. At first Iraj seemed to be very skeptic about this idea of mine. He was concerned about the safety of the procedure. But after a little persuasion on my part he agreed to arrange the surgery for me. I must admit that I was quite hesitant myself over the whole controversy of breast implants. But then I thought I would go for it anyway. Thanks God I was done breast feeding and having children. There was practically nothing to stop me.

I was a little embarrassed, and meanwhile I did not want to worry my children. So I decided to keep the surgery private. Iraj and I were like friends who trusted each other's opinion, and depended at each other's decisions. Or at least that was my understanding of our life together at that time.

He scheduled the appointment, and introduced me to the doctor. And then he said, "Now the decision is yours". We went over the details of the procedure, after which I decided to proceed with the surgery. We set up the date, and Iraj drove me to and from. Everything went well, and I was happy as one could be.

As I was suspecting Mary's behavior had a great impact on Maseeh and Mojgan. While I had never touched cigarettes in my life, they all were smoking. They drank on occasions, they did drugs to belong. My duty as a mother, who never was influenced by wrong doings of others, was to let them know that I was against all of their acts. And meanwhile I made sure to remind and make them aware of the consequences of their actions. I watched them like a hulk. I expressed my hatred towards their involvements. And then I asked them to think about it carefully.

My Dear God:

I always knew that one cannot stop the other from doing what they intend to do by sheer force. Therefore I chose to use educating techniques, communication, and guidance. They would either get it one day, or they would proceed with their own ways.

There were times that I cried would get on my knees begging them to straighten their acts. I wanted them to understand that the whole purpose of us moving to this country was to obtain great education. I tried to explain to them that their father and I had left our country and families for greater achievements. I was telling them that I did not expect to run into these kinds of difficulties. I have given all of myself to them, and I was not ready to settle for less than a simple respect. I have always been very understanding about everything that they were going through in order to adapt to their surroundings. And I have given them enough freedom, but not enough to get lost in. I wanted them to recognize the extent of their involvements. I wanted them to be aware that if my children chose to be menaces to their society, I would not hesitate to dishonor them. And I did mean it. I wanted them to know that I would never support their wrong actions, and that I would be the first person to turn them to authorities.

Mojgan and I were talking about drugs once. She was telling me about some of the Iranian kids who used them. I asked Mojgan if one special person was one of them. She told me then, "Oh no, he loves his mother too much, and he does not want to hurt her". That statement made me think, "Would that then mean that my children do not love me?"

Mary was very bright. And she was an activist. She had a whole lot to offer to the world. She had always taken special interest in writing. She was hoping to become a famous writer one day. I appreciated the direction that she was taking. I would not want her to grow up to be indifferent to the affairs of the society, and for that sake of the world. I wanted her to possess eyes to see with, and a heart to feel the pain with.

I knew that it was impossible for anybody to resolve the problems of the world. But I also knew that to recognize, to discuss, and to write about those issues would be as beneficial as resolving them. So despite of Mary's challenging personality, I was proud of her achievements, and I was happy that she was striving to make a difference. I have always dreamt of a glorious future for Mary, regardless of our relationship.

My Dear God:

The only person who actually enjoyed our house was Maseeh. He threw many grand parties there. I would be on guard during those nights, while Maseeh made sure that things didn't get out of hand. And even then they were able to sneak in alcohol. It seemed that the rowdier the party, the more fun they had.

I had agreed to Maseeh's parties at the house as long as I could intervene when necessary. There was this one particular party. Everything was going well, when Maseeh came to me desperately asking for help. I followed him to the family room, where I found most of the kids had surrounded Joe. I knew that his father was a lawyer, and I couldn't help it not to think of a potential lawsuit. While some were playing pool, others were jumping over the chairs. Joe had jumped so high that he hit his head on the wooden board above the pool table. There was no blood, but he was throwing up.

He was feeling better by the time I got there. The kids were hesitant about notifying his father. He seemed to be afraid of his father. And Maseeh feared the lawsuit. I told him, "We have to notify his father the sooner the better. They might have to take him to a doctor. But leave it to me, I will handle it". So I called Joe's father, Mr. Rebenwitz. I asked him to come to our house, since I had to discuss an important matter with him. He came over right away.

Joe was feeling much better and he was walking around by the time his father got there. I prayed to God that nothing happen to him. It was the first time that I met Mr.

Rebenowitz. We sat down to explain how it had happened. He agreed that such accidents were likely to happen at any gathering, be that among adults or teenagers. We were glad to have met each other.

I wasn't so worried when Maseeh's parties were by invitation only. But I went out of my mind every time that I heard that he was planning an open party.

I had asked Maseeh to keep all the sliding doors around locked. That way I knew who came to my house, and I knew what they brought along. You should have seen all the strange faces I saw that night. It was unbelievable. That was the last time Maseeh was allowed to have an open party in that house. They kept me up all night. I was so relieved that there were no casualties, and that everyone left the house safely.

Mojgan, on the other hand, being raised in prosperity, had acquired a mind of her own from early on. Once she set her mind to doing something, you could not have stopped her from doing so. I always thanked God for not letting her insist on extremely destructive matters. Otherwise I would have been in a real trouble.

My Dear God:

Mojgan was a joyful and delightful kid. We had so much fun with her when she was little. Alas it didn't last. Her parents eventually destroyed her.

She was a very interesting girl. She never fancied Iranian food. Between ages of nine and eleven Mojgan started experiencing severe pain in her legs, especially at night. Her pediatrician, Dr. Cooper, believed that those were growing pains. And there was nothing we could do, except for giving painkillers. I would stay with her through the night. I would wrap her legs in a wool shawl. I would not go to sleep until she felt better. Another particular habit of hers was that if she did not have a full meal at a certain time, and she just had some snacks instead, she would get sick, and started vomiting. There were nights that I walked with her for hours until her stomach settled down, and she fell asleep.

She turned into a compulsive shopper next. I will not forget the day that asked me to take her shopping for a coat. I tried to convince her that she didn't need a coat, but it didn't work. She was in the "I must" mood. I knew that I had no choice at the time. I was assuming that she must have had a bad day at school and she wanted to release her frustration this way. I was hoping to talk her out of it when we get there. But that didn't work either.

We drove to Jacobson. But we did not find anything that would suit her. We shopped around for a while, and after all she picked a long gray coat. I knew that it was not her style at all. But she kept insisting on buying it. I was positive that she would never wear that coat. But she kept saying that she really wanted it, and she wanted me to buy it for her. I even thought that the coat was not appropriate for my age. But once again she insisted that she wanted it. So I bought her that coat. I was absolutely right. She never wore that coat; she didn't even remove the price tag from it. And every time I asked her,

"When are you going to wear that coat?" She answered, "Tomorrow". I ended up giving it away.

You see, my dear GOD, you might blame me for such behavior. And it is possibly the truth. But at that time, of the age that she was, and the circumstances around us, I had to give in. I had to learn when to go along with their desires, and when not to. It was important to me.

Or speaking of this other time, when she was taking piano lessons. I had heard a lot of this one piano teacher. Everyone spoke highly of his teaching methods. I decided to give it a try, since I went through many teachers without any outcome. But I received a phone call form him only after a few lessons. The teacher said, "Mojgan does not want me to teach her any longer. She said she doesn't like to practice, and does not like me to teach her". That was the end of her piano practice.

My Dear God:

She talked me into signing her up for gymnastics. I ignored her requests at first. But I thought later that maybe it would be a better idea to involve her with activities that she was interested in, rather than imposing my own ideas. Her eagerness for gymnastics had only lasted for a couple of years. And of course I was very upset at that point. But I didn't think it was right to be forcing her to do something she didn't care for. I also contribute her failures to the fact that her older siblings helped her realize that she could get away with many things.

Yet again my father's words of wisdom came back to me as a reminder that when we spoil our children to a point that they believe the whole world must be at their service we would run into many difficulties later in life. Having three strong-minded children each possessing a different character; I had to come up with ways getting through each one of them. And as if that was not enough, I had to deal with their cousins, whom I had already talked about.

Then there was one day when Nazi brought a young friend home. I have never seen him before. They locked themselves in Mary's room. I went to check on them shortly after. A strange smell stopped me at the door. I rushed back to speak to Iraj. He demanded that Nazi immediately left our house with her friend. And he asked her not to ever come back until she was off her act, as soon as he recognized the smoke of drug.

I knew about many outstanding students that did drugs, in which case most parents did not want to believe in their involvement. They remained in the state of denial until it was too late. And by the time these kids were in college the chances were that they would commit suicide, kill someone, or develop drug addiction that was beyond any help.

So I had no choice but to keep a watchful eye on my children and I prayed to God to give me knowledge, patience, and understanding to guide them in the right direction.

Iraj wanted his children to pursue the field of medicine. He was very disappointed

when neither of them showed no interest. And as usual I was to be blamed when things went wrong. As he got involved with various businesses, he became more and more detached from the family affairs. So I, on the other hand, had to get more and more involved. I was the one. Obviously, it was more contact among us, and they saw me as a bad guy who was trying to control them. This made them mad.

My Dear God:

My idea of raising my children was that as a human being I had to make them or break them. Doctor, lawyer, teacher, or a writer I was trying to make a sincere human being of them. I wanted to make a person of them who can make a difference in whatever they decided or choose to do. That is why I was very proud of Mary who was trying to understand the problems of the world, and while she studied about it, she tried to talk about it clearly. I was hoping that she could continue, and never forget why she had existed in this world to begin with.

Some of our arguments were around acting and reacting wrongly about raising our children. Many times we both were complaining about Maseeh being too spoiled. I believed that we shouldn't have been buying things for our children just because they asked for them. And in Maseeh's case I preferred using the rewards technique. But no, Iraj had to go along with his requests, and he bought him that rather expensive photo camera. I was hurt, and I was demanding that he justified his act. The only thing that concerned Maseeh at that instance was that I was preventing his father from buying him gifts. That consequentially led to conflicts between us. He didn't like me, and he despised my actions. By no means am I implying that it was an issue of power struggle between Iraj and me. On the contrary we always tried to support each other's ideas.

I remember the day that Maseeh asked for a camera. I promised to get it for him in exchange for better grades. But he decided to approach his father instead. Iraj naturally told him, "Let me ask your Mom first", to which Maseeh confronted him, "You always say, "Let me ask your Mom, let me ask your Mom". Don't you have a mind of your own? Can't you decide by yourself for once?"

We laughed about that incident afterwards with Iraj. We knew that kids in general would attempt manipulating their parents given the chance.

At this time of our life we both knew what we wanted for our children, and we were trying to make the best of it. He was doing his job as a father, and I was doing what I knew best: caring, doing, running, shouting, laughing, crying, and above all just pure living.

* * *

HUGE, UNEXPECTED DISAPPOINTMENT

My Dear God:

It was one hot July Saturday morning that followed one of our Friday night Blot games. We would usually stay in bed longer on the weekend mornings. We had a great night, and we were in each other's arms.

Then the telephone rang. Iraj answered it. He began to shout, "What, what? Is he dead? Is he dead?" He jumped out of bed. I watched him walking around in his underwear. He could not speak clearly. He was on fire. I kept asking him, "What happened? Who is dead?" Then finally he muttered with uncertainty and confusion, "AZEEZ WAS SHOT IN HIS 0FFICE. AND HE IS DEAD".

Although I was very worried about Azeez's family, Iraj's well being was my main concern at that moment. It was barely eight months that they had started the weight lost clinic together. It was his only hope to get back on the track. They put themselves through great indebtedness. Oh GOD, please help him. He looked so lost and confused. He didn't react like this when he heard the news about his father's death. I was so worried about him. I did not want him to drive by himself, so I offered him a ride. But he just said, "I will be okay", and then he got dressed and left.

Susan called to let me know that they were taking Badri to Rohan's house, while men went to find out what had happened to Azeez. I joined everyone at Rohan's house. We were all feeling pretty awkward, none of us was able to speak or even move. No one knew what had happened, or how it had happened. The only thing that we have heard was that Azeez had been shot by one of his patients.

We had never before experienced such tragedy; except for I guess when that young hand surgeon, Dr. Ghandchi, had drowned in his own pool.

My Dear God:

Azeez's death was the most shocking incident that had ever taken place among us. He was one of us, and we were all falling apart.

That Saturday we all gathered at Rohan's house. We were not sure how to break the news to his children. It was later in the evening, and the children were playing outside. It almost seemed like Roozbeh could sense something. We had finally decided that Farzad would be the one to inform Roozbeh of his Father's death. Farzad quietly pulled Roozbeh aside. Next we saw Roozbeh jumping up and down, screaming and rolling on the grass. He kept repeating, "He did it. I knew he would do it. I knew he was going to do it. He finally did it, he did it, and he did it".

We were all standing by him, not knowing what to do next. We just left him alone to grief for a while. That was the first time that I felt the closeness and sincerity among us. Although every one of us was hurting, I felt the most hurt and confused of all.

We didn't know whom Roozbeh was talking about. He was still crying, screaming and blaming that person. It appeared to be Roshanak's boyfriend. Roshanak was not allowed to date. So when Azeez found out that she had a boyfriend, he naturally forbad her to see him.

Two weeks prior Azeez and Roozbeh paid Roshanak's boyfriend a visit. They asked him stay away from Roshanak. They ended up getting into an argument. The boy pulled out a knife as a warning to leave them alone. Roozbeh got between them. He did all he could to insure that his father didn't go back to that house again.

A single mother raised Roshanak's boyfriend. He did not want any trouble in his house. So he told Azeez to stay away, otherwise he would kill him.

This had happened two weeks ago. Roozbeh was almost certain that Roshanak's boyfriend killed his father. He became so angry at some point that he started running towards his house to kill him. But the rest of the boys prevented him from doing so.

Azeez was seeing a patient diagnosed with schizophrenia at that time. The gentleman was suicidal most of the time. He came to see Azeez on Friday night. Azeez scheduled him in for Saturday, and he took his chart home. I even heard him speak to his patient while we were playing cards. That night Azeez seemed to be very concerned about him.

Azeez took the station wagon to his office on Saturday morning. His in-laws were in town, and they had a doctor's appointment. Badri came by the office for a brief visit and to exchange cars.

My Dear God:

She returned to his office after she was done with the chores to once again exchange the cars. But she found the whole building taped and surrounded by police. They would not allow her to get through. Badri kept insisting that she was the doctor's wife and that she had to see him. That was when they told her, "The doctor was shot". And they took her to the crime scene. He was lying down face down in his own blood in the hallway, between the doors to his office and the exit.

I was always known for being very emotional. But this tragedy was too close to home. All of a sudden he became a big part of our lives. It was very foolish but this loss of Malakuti became equal of the loss of someone from my family. No wonder my children were the way they were. I became the master of the ceremony. I cried more than others, and did more than others.

Despite of all these happenings Iraj was still my main concern, "What will he do now? How can he help himself? Who is going to take care of all those expenses?" I was feeling hopeless. I would put myself in Badri's place, and I gave more and more to my

friendship. I was thinking that if Iraj died I would kill myself to be buried with him. I could not see myself living without Iraj. How could poor Badri go through this? How could she make her children understand the death of their father? I was completely lost, I was furious with the injustice in the world. I did not want anyone to be bothering her, even if it was her family. My sorrow for her was inexplicable. I spent all my time with her: I took walks with her and I talked to her, I cooked for her. I believed she felt for her husband the same way I did for mine. I was feeling as if it was my loss. I made the pain of others into my own pain.

While we all stood by Badri for the first few weeks preparing food and taking care of many other things, it was ironic to observe her sisters' behavior. These were the same whom Malakuti always complained about. They continued their arguments in his house, whi1e his body was still in the casket.

People flooded Malakuti's house to condole with Badri on the loss of her husband. I realized that the house was a mess. I didn't even consider that it was her sisters' responsibility to clean up and prepare the food. I proceeded with cleaning the house. I asked everyone to help preparing meals.

Rohan was shocked to see the house so orderly. She laughed and said, "This house wouldn't look like this if you were not here. Gosh, how did you do it? Don't work too hard Shamci". I am sure that her sisters were thinking at the time, "What a weirdo. What a foolish woman". And I am sure that gave them the idea of pushing Badri to succeed in her schemes later on.

My Dear God:

It was just the Thursday before he died that I ran into him at Burger King. He spoke to me about his sister-in-laws. He was furious with them. Poor guy, he really suffered in their presence.

I cleaned that house, so cluttered with dirt and clothes, thinking that those who visited knew that we were partners, and was not appropriate to have her house in that condition. Oh boy, oh boy, oh boy, what a brainless woman!

As I said before Azeez and Reza got into a fight shortly before he died. Now Azeez's death really crushed Reza and Nazi. Nazi came shopping with me, and she contributed to cold cuts, drinks, fruits, and much more. I assigned the ladies to provide different dishes every night. Everyone was working hard. Everyone felt responsible to do something for his family. It was a big loss for all of us. He was too young to die. He had many hopes and ideas for the future. He was always concerned about his children. Now he left without saying goodbye. Roozbeh was only seventeen. They were acting mature shocked by the death of their father.

While we were busy taking care of crowds of people, Iraj and others were trying to handle Azeez's funeral and the expenses that came with it.

Azeez didn't really need donations for his funeral. But due to the unusual circumstances of his death, his friends decided to take part in his burial. Their weight loss clinic had been operating for only eight months when Azeez passed away, and now Iraj had become the sole owner. He wanted to make sure that his partner's family didn't loose in this deal. He believed that he must stand by them. Both Iraj and I dealt with Azeez's death in the same manner; it was a great loss. There were times when Badri couldn't get hold of Iraj, so I made sure provide all his contact information to her.

One day Iraj asked M. Rabbani, Ali Rabbani, Naser Barkhordari, Jalal Panah, Foad Panah, Mahmood Fassihi, Kazem Shushtari, and Reza Mahajer to get together in our house to discuss how to handle the situation. Hassan and Louis Neelfrooshan were vacationing in California at the time.

Okay, my dear GOD, let's talk in private. You were with us everywhere during those times. I don't have to explain my intensions to you. You know they were good. You were with me in my heart, and you supported my actions. I was convinced that Iraj's intentions were on the same wavelength. Then please tell me, where did I go wrong?

We all agreed to share in our contributions towards the expenses of Malakuti's funeral and his household until the matters with estate and IRS were resolved. The only couple that didn't participate was Louis and her husband, Azeez's best friends. And even after they returned from California, they showed up with a box of donuts in their hands and sorrow on their faces.

My Dear God:

I have never considered Louise intelligent. But she appeared to be very wise in her ways of handling both Ghandchi's and Malakuti's deaths. She made sure to keep her involvement with their families, especially their wives, to a minimum. I realized, only a little too late, that she knew exactly what she was doing. She assured from the beginning that neither Patti nor Badri had a chance of getting near her husband. Even though I never thought that her husband Hassan would be their first choice. But all and all she kept her husband away from these two women.

She played her role well, seemingly acting that she was very sorry for them. She would arrange "khatme Ghoran" group of prayers for him. But she never allowed their problems become hers. Many other ladies did the same, while they were not aware that Badri had already chosen someone, and she was not willing to change her mind.

Looking back now. I think Iraj was seeking a miracle that would have saved him from drowning under such a tremendous pressure. As is he was torn apart between the responsibilities of his office, the two hospitals, home, the new clinic, the troubles caused by his niece and nephews or by our own children. And now he had to deal with the huge unexpected disaster. We knew that it was very important that he could find a partner or two for the new clinic. That would assist with paying the mortgage and the other bills.

Someone had to take Azeez's place, before it was too late.

I will never forget the day of Azeez's funeral. It was raining hard. We had just bought a new car, a hardtop Thunderbird with a sunroof. It was very beautiful. We took our new car out for the first time that day. Everyone was getting ready for the funeral procession. We were unpleasantly surprised by being showered when we got in the car. What an embarrassing scene! We had no idea that there was a leak in the sunroof. Although the fabric seat were soaking wet, we had to get going. I found some plastic in the trunk, I covered the seats, and we drove to the cemetery.

Iraj was very happy when he bought that car. He thought it was an executive car. It was a pre owned vehicle with very little miles, so he paid much less. But when Mahmood asked him about the car, Iraj told him that it was brand new. Then Mahmood asked if he could take it for a ride. Iraj felt embarrassed about lying. He said to me then, "I never lie. But this time I told Mahmood that this was a brand new car. Now he will know that I lied". He was very upset at himself.

While all these activities were going on, Iraj had to get to work. He had to find a replacement for Azeez. It didn't seem like the Iranian doctors wanted to take part in it. He was finally able to find two doctors from the Beaumont Hospital who were interested in becoming partners in the clinic.

My Dear God:

One of them was an internist, who had left his wife for his secretary, his present wife. They didn't have children together. But his wife had few sons. The other doctor was a psychiatrist, whose life was a story within a story.

Once we were invited to doctor Pear's house among many other doctors and their wives. Iraj pointed out two couples on the dance floor. He told me in disgust, "This psychiatrist first was married to the other doctor's wife. And this, his present wife, was the other doctor's ex-wife. They had exchanged their exes. And then above all that the psychiatrist had buried his twelve-year-old son last week. He died of an incurable cancer". He turned to me and held my hand. He told me, while we were leaving, "How strange some people are! How can these people live with themselves?"

After few years that they became partners, his present wife, whom I have met only once, and I found rather very strange, committed suicide.

Iraj was beginning to see himself as a hero among all. He was the one giving all of his time, money to the Malakutis. I was doing even more than that to prevent Badri from breaking down. Anywhere she wanted to go, I was with her. I did anything and everything she wanted. I never saw Badri shed a single tear over her loss. I wanted to believe that she cried privately. But what I didn't know at the time was that she was not mourning, but she was celebrating Azeez's passing away. You will find out later on why she was the happiest of all.

It was just a few weeks prior to Azeez's death. We were at his house one night. He was telling us about a patient who was widowed. Then he began telling us about women in general who fell into that category. He told us about all the stages that they would go through. There was the initial period of denial. Then he said, "A woman that loses her husband, thinks at first, "Why did this happen to me, and not to someone else? Why should I go through this, and not someone else? Why am I the one suffering, and not any of my friends?" And the answer to all these questions will naturally lead to trying to lure a husband of a friend into an affair". And he continued, "She will start believing that he is her husband. And she will work on him by all means, until she snatches him away".

I should have seriously considered this educated statement about widowed women. But instead I saw Badri as a weak little angle, she had kept Azeez's coat which was worn by him at the time he was shot on a chair in her living room all this time, and my dear Iraj as a loving and affectionate husband and father to help her. And especially in Iraj's case I believed that he had learned from his first mistake, and he would never again commit adultery. Despite of how many psychiatrists swore by it, that was my understanding of these two individuals at that time

My Dear God:

Badri played her cards very well, with the face that Azeez would often describe; she was acting like someone who was suffered a great loss. She made us all fall for it. She was able to make everyone in the world mourn for her. She wore her black dress with a black lace scarf over her head, and her sorrowful eyes.

Azeez's body remained in an open casket in an Islamic masque for two days. Hundreds of people came to pay their respect to the family.

As I said before I had lots of respect for Reza. But when Ali Rabbani was talking to Iraj and told him "we have to keep Reza away from Badri," such a comment by someone who was after his best friend's wife, only proved to me that he was a Muslim extremist and a backwards person.

At that time I didn't know where my life was going. I didn't know that Iraj had his eyes on Badri. I didn't know that it was Iraj who should have been kept away from Badri. Now I would like to tell Dr. Ali Rabbani, "If you knew Iraj, and you pushed him towards Badri, you should be ashamed." It has been wrong all along to be expecting Iraj to take Azeez's place. It was wrong to be pushing him to take on so much responsibility. You should all know by now that you have nurtured the impossible. I don't know if you ever thought of it that way".

And by the way Dr. Mahajer was a family man who loved his wife and his daughters. I am sure that if he was in charge of Malakuti's affairs nothing like this would have ever happened.

Reza was absolutely crushed when Azeez died. He lost a very dear friend, and on the

top of all, he lost him at the time that they were mad at each other. That really hurt him. That was why he was trying to do his best to bring comfort to that family. What hurt me the most was that Ali found the right time to come forward and accuse Reza of being an unreliable, while in reality they were the unreliable ones.

Azeez was buried in a cemetery in Troy, MI. His grave happened to be right in front of the great artwork "THE LAST SUPPER". We visited his grave for seven consecutive days, while we prepared dinner for everyone. Every night we set up the most colorful table filled with most delicious Iranian meals and desserts. Everyone was involved with the serving, cleaning, washing.

Then again Badri's family never thought of helping out in any way. It seemed as if they were there to be entertained. They kept themselves occupied by fighting with one another. Fortunately Azeez was no longer there.

My Dear God:

Every day more and more doctors, whom we never met before, came by the house to pay their respect. After the fortieth ceremonial day they started inviting Badri and her children to their house. For the most part of it we were included as well. Those invitations became so frequent that they didn't have time to think about Azeez any longer.

While Iraj was busy selling Azeez's properties, I was busy with Badri's affairs. We had found out that the IRS would be imposing taxations over art works and other valuable possessions, at which point Badri and I decided to transfer them all to my house. We asked Roozbeh to give us a hand with moving. I decided to keep everything in our wine cellar. Pretty soon both Roozbeh and Badri got tired walking up and down the stairs. But I didn't stop, and did most of the carrying by myself in an effort to lessen their pain. I stored her belongings in my wine cellar long after the inspection.

I dedicated all my time to Badri and her needs. I was at her house at the day of the inspection. Like a steadfast soldier I remained at her side. I did everything in my power to help her cope with her husband's death.

Badri and her family never had this much care and attention even when Azeez was still alive. All the doctors made sure to provide them with treatment and medications free of charge.

I got so carried away dealing with all her problems that I completely forgot about my routine calls to Pari in California. She called me one day, and when she found out how busy Iraj had been with Badri's affairs, she said to me, "What is this? Many people die. This happens to many families every day, but no one gets as involved as Iraj is. Why don't you put an end to it? Enough is enough. He should be embarrassed of not finding enough time to make a phone call to his sister. I really wonder. If you really care about this family, then you must let them accept what had happened, and let them go on with their lives". And she went on and on.

My dear GOD, I should have paid attention to what she was trying to tell me. I should have trusted her intuition. I knew she meant good, and she was as concerned about Iraj as I was. I assume the embarrassment of Iraj's affair in Iran was still haunting her, and she wanted to make sure that nothing of that sort took place again.

But you see, my dear GOD, there was some unknown power behind the way the events were unfolding. Maybe that power was your will, but it seemed as if the outcome was inevitable.

The conditions of the partnership agreement between Iraj and Azeez provided the grounds for the closeness of Iraj and Badri. The agreement stated that when and if one partner was survived by the other, he had to pay to the family of the deceased one hundred thousand dollars. And top of it we were friends, so Iraj felt responsible for many additional moral activities that came along.

My Dear God:

But, my dear, dear GOD, you know how Iraj felt about partnerships in general. He would never consider it unless there was something in it for him. And there was the proof. It was thanks to Badri's influence that Azeez convinced Iraj to that partnership. And soon you will see the rest of their arrangements.

Led by our example our children made every effort to comfort Malakuti's children. Roshanak proclaimed her love for Maseeh years ago. Maseeh was in love with Beth at the time. But then they broke up right around the time that Azeez passed away, and Maseeh was feeling very vulnerable.

Roshanak slowly got closer and closer with Maseeh. She made him believe that he was the only person who could save her from falling apart. So Maseeh was feeling very proud that he was able to help Roshanak. He, at such a young age, felt that he must take the place of her father, help her solve all her problems, and bring back hope to her life.

Although Roshanak was in love with Maseeh, she loved boys in general. I remember once we got together in our house for Thanksgiving dinner. Among our guests were Malakuti, Barkhordari, Froozan, and M. Rabbani families. It was right before dinner when I came in the living room. Susan was there and she was trying to show me something. She looked worried. She pointed out Roshanak to me. While the rest of the kids were in the TV room, she was sitting on John Froozan's lap. Susan and I were hoping that Malakuti never found out about that.

Iraj had made every effort to prove to me that his involvement with the Malakuti family was a gesture of goodwill. He was the knight in a shining armor. He condemned those who claimed to be friends, and did nothing. He often made fun of Louise and Hassan Neel whose generosity was limited to a box of donuts. His vigorous involvement with late Azeez's affairs had alienated all the other doctors.

At this time no one, including myself, was suspecting anything unusual. Badri and

her family were showered with everyone's attention and kindness. They were much happier and freer than before. I can't recall noticing a single tear in Badri's eyes through this ordeal.

Iraj delivered the eulogy at all the ceremonial days that followed Azeez's burial. Badri's nephew Bijan, who was a doctor, delivered the eulogy at his funeral. Roozbeh said a few words about his father as well. Meanwhile Aghdass Shushtari and Susan Barkhordari held Badri by her arms during each ceremony.

My Dear God:

Some faithful Muslim members of our community decided to set up a khatme-Ghoran, the reading of Ghoran, and prayers. It was to be held on Tuesday. Aghdass Barkhordari was a believer. She had a degree in law from Iran. She was very intelligent, and everyone assumed that we should listen to what she said. I believe she could read between the lines. Although I never believed in such groups, still I accompanied Badri.

I was sitting next to Louise. She turned to me; she held my hand and said, "We are no longer strangers to each other. We are not just friends; we are more like sisters who care for each other. Thanks God we have each other in this country".

It wasn't until five weeks later that I started noticing that Badri escaped right in the middle of those meetings. She would and usually leave Rozan with us, and she returned around three o'clock. That seemed strange to me. Badri was the reason behind those gatherings, but every Tuesday she came up with an excuse to miss them. Azeez's business was her usual excuse.

I was talking to Aghdass Barkhordari one day, when she said to me, "It seems like Badri is trying to leave Rozan with us and meet that person particularly on Tuesdays. I wonder what the arrangement is that she cannot change the days." And then to my surprise she said, "I wonder where she is going. Because wherever it is, she cannot take Rozan along".

There were times that she would just leave her in a hurry, and make one of us to stay with her daughter. Such behavior caused a few raised eyebrows. But who could have possibly known what she was after? We believed it was too soon for Badri to be having affairs. So we canceled our Tuesday prayers. I did not go anywhere without her. Many times she wanted to drive to Detroit to take care of some business. Once we went to a restaurant in downtown. We had so much fun. She found a penny that day. She picked it up and said, "This is my lucky penny. I will keep it until I get my wish". I wish I would have known then that her wish was to marry my husband.

Mrs. Shushtari had arranged a birthday party for Badri, something her family had never done. Then once we all went on a vacation with our children. We have tailored the whole trip with a sole purpose of pleasing the Malakuti family. One day, while having breakfast outside, we were approached by a gypsy fortuneteller. Badri accepted her offer.

Among many other things the fortuneteller told her, "You had lost one husband. Don't worry. Soon you will marry another one, and you will survive the other one too".

My Dear God:

Iraj asked for his fortune to be read next. I tried to stop him, but he continued anyway. It was quite shocking to observe the kind of person Iraj was turning to. I didn't hear Iraj's fortune. But the way he was acting around Badri put many unanswered questions in my mind. It was almost like I didn't know this new Iraj.

Even when no one else was around, we had Badri and her children in our house. Or we went out together. It was on Sunday when we once were picnicking with Badri and Naheed. Iraj was acting very strange. I decided to take a walk by myself. I am sure Naheed was conspiring with them.

One day Badri was in our house. She stayed after dinner to play Backgammon with Iraj. They set up in the kitchen. Mary came down to get something from the refrigerator. She shook her head while she was watching Iraj and Badri. She mumbled with a smile on her face, "I don't know. Badri is a clever woman". And she left. I was caught in the middle of something that was completely unaware about.

Iraj had always celebrated my birthday. And he never forgot the mother's day. That year, 1981, the year of Azeez's death, he arranged a big surprise mother's day for me and all other mothers. There was no doubt that he did it for me. He had discussed that celebration with other men. And they all believed they were preparing a big surprise for their wives. They probably had no idea what was on Iraj's mind. But in reality he was having a celebration for Badri.

He had arranged a fancy brunch for ten families, together with our children, at the Hilton Hotel. He ordered corsages for every one of us. We were waiting for the rest of the group to join us when Badri arrived. Iraj immediately started applauding her. Then everyone else, including myself, joined him. He dedicated the entire mother's day celebration to her. It was natural for everyone to be appreciative of such an arrangement. Badri's husband was not around to celebrate the day with her.

You see, my dear GOD, I believe that we are only able to conceive of what our eyes are able to see. Those two were able to fool all of us. They made me look like a fool in the eyes of our friends. I didn't even suspect that there had been strong ties between them.

Iraj and I helped ourselves to our food, and sat down at the same table with Minoo Panah, her sister Zari Joorabchi, Nayer Rabbani, Susan Barkhordari, Badri. He was the only man sitting next to his wife. He had always been good at making others believe that he was doing everything for me. And therefore he was always praised for being a great husband. That day he began by saying, "Although I am this kind of a husband, and I do everything for her just to please her, still she never appreciates me, and she is always suspicious of me".

What a memory! What a day! Both of us look worn out. I was wondering what was going on in Iraj's life. Iraj had arranged this Mother's Day party for Badri and he was trying to show that he had done it for me. I was reading lies from his face. He held a big surprise party on the first Mother's Day after Malakuti's death. The reason that he was so confused was that he thought he had a good life. He had a good and loving wife. He had three great children. Why should he destroy them? How can he destroy them? These questions in his mind were destroying him. Well, he got what he wanted.

In a restaurant in Detroit, Mi. It was all-you-can-eat shrimp before dinner. We ordered so many times that we were not hungry any more. We were all amused by this except you know who, Iraj. Left to right: Mojgan, Kaveh, Maseeh, Ali Elhaj- Mary's friend whom I met at the airport, Mary, Iraj, and me

We are posing for this picture while all of us are in big trouble. Because of Iraj's action, we knew that we would no longer be a happy family. Each one of us had different thoughts in mind. Neither of us was sure of what was coming next. I think the only person who knew his plan was Iraj.

This picture speaks for itself. It was taken when Iraj was confused between keeping his family together, and going after his mistress Badri. He is discussing his problems with Morteza Alavinejad who had come from Madrid, Spain to become Iraj's partner in the Hollywood Live Club in Los Angeles, Ca. At the end I got cheated on, and Mr. Alavinejad got robbed. It serves him right not to help someone who is cheating on his wife, especially the one who has been his good friend for years. In this picture both are in deep trouble. Too bad, you both deserved it.

On the left, poor suicidal Shamci is next to her confused husband and my dear Mojgan who was hoping to be able to correct the situation between her parents. She didn't know Badri at all. She didn't know we were dealing with a dangerous cobra that was getting support from her Iranian friends pushing them together to be able to have someone to laugh at, at their parties and gatherings. Yes, Iraj was confused at that time until Badri forced him to make his decision, by preparing that poem by an anonymous person.

This is my handsome and wonderful Maseeh involved in his father's discrepancies regarding Hollywood Live, hoping that his father could one day wise up and make it right. Unfortunately our children have no power over their parents' behavior, which is directly related to their future and happiness. My dear son is smoking his frustration out.

Morteza is bugging me in our living room. Left to right: Mary, Maseeh, Morteza, me and Mojgan. Iraj is taking the picture.

Morteza and Iraj crying for their loss

Now, Morteza is taking the picture and I am trying to make Iraj laugh. But as you see it didn't work.

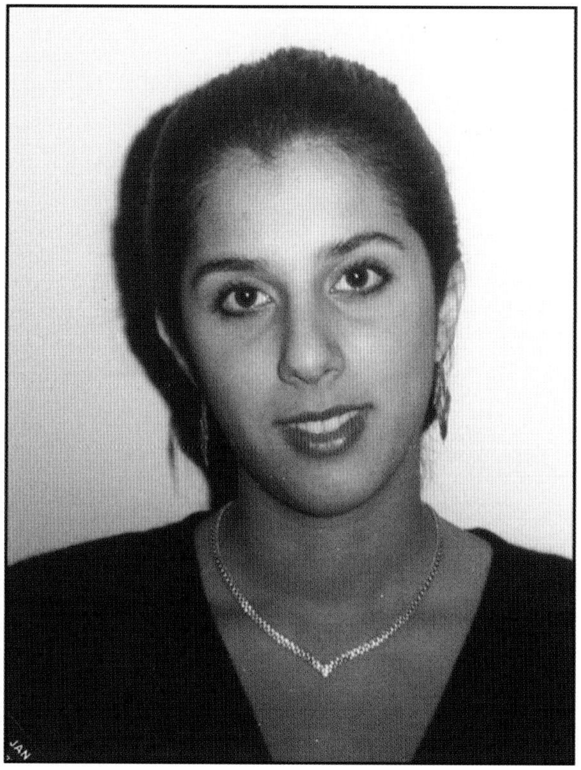

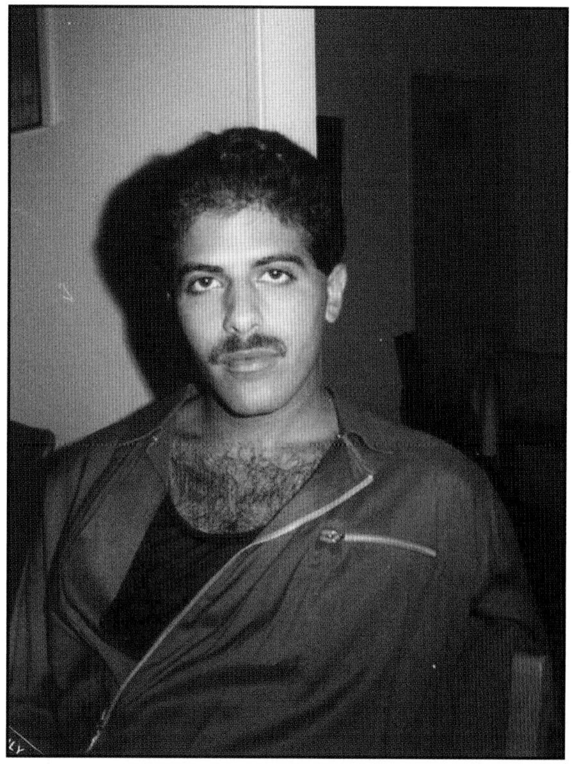

When I look at this picture of Maseeh, I just want to cry. At the age of eighteen, he had to first be a teenager, and second save his parents from wrong-doing. That was the reason that right after graduating from college, he left to go to California to help and watch over his father's business. It is too bad that no matter how hard my children tried, they couldn't stop their father from wrongdoing. Then, in his apologetic letters he wrote, "I don't know why whenever I am at the peak of my success and happiness, there comes a disastrous misfortune to demolish me and what I have accumulated through my hard work". The only thing he does not admit to is that he did it all by himself, without anyone's help. Even when his sisters and his children and especially I tried to stand by him to help him recuperate and wise up, he never understood us to a point that he destroyed all of us, mainly himself.

In the picture above you will see, all of us are trying to cheer him up, but his guilt is killing him, and does not allow him to smile. Poor Iraj!

Fereshteh visited me during my troubled times. We were walking in the yard of Cranbrook School.

I was in my own thoughts while everyone else was talking and laughing.

We are at Shushtari's house while he was sad and unhappy and I didn't care one way or another. Not because I didn't care for him, but because I wanted to be with him and stay with him as long as we were married. It was he, who had to make a move, not I. It was he who wanted to end my children's happiness, not I. So I was trying to be myself and not pay attention to his behavior one way or another.

When I look at my pictures in which I look so good, I am amazed. We were at a wedding and I remember I was thinking of committing suicide. Look at me! How and where did I get my strength?
Left to right: Sally Khodadadeh, and Dr. Khodadadeh (These two practically pushed Badri in Iraj's arms.), Badri, Jalal Panah, Shamci, and Iraj who was starting to look like a zombie.

The title of this picture must be, A Woman among Enemies. We are at a wedding again. Left to right: Mrs. Moghadass, Naheed Soltanpoor, Aghdass Barkhordari, Mrs Mansoor Froozan, and me. Standing at the back: Nayer Rabbani, Dr. Rabbani, Naser and Susan Barkhordari, and Iraj Rafani. Look at these two pictures. At the top, Badri was happy that she had been able to convince Iraj to get rid of Shamci. And at the bottom, Iraj is so sad and confused. I, on the other hand, was sitting and waiting for him to find a solution to his problem.

Look at this picture. How were we sticking to each other? This was happening because I was not able to show any reaction towards them whatsoever. I didn't want to destroy my husband's image among his friends. And they were sure the more they provide closeness for Badri and Iraj, the more their husbands will be safe from Badri. They knew that she wanted to find a strong man for her bed, so they pushed her away from their husbands. Not knowing that these two had already signed an agreement, and their push just made it easier.
Left to right: me, Aghdass, Badri, Rohan, Louise, Susan, and Rohan's mother sitting

My Dear God:

And while everyone was sympathizing with him, he continued by telling them about an incident that took place years ago. It was shortly after we had gotten back together. He just wanted to assure them that I had a suspicious mind. But he never told them that it happened after he had an affair.

This was what had happened then. It was my birthday. We had not planned anything special that day. Usually we would either go out to dinner at a restaurant, or he would give me a special card. I asked him that day where he was going to be all day. He said he was going to be at the hospital and at the office. Rohan called me that same day, "I saw Iraj with another woman in Summerset Mall". I knew it must have been a joke, because if it was true, she would never tell me. She would have tried to hide it from me. But I was still a little puzzled. I couldn't help not to wonder why Iraj didn't tell me that he would go to Summerset Mall.

And obviously I was upset when I mentioned it to him. He said Rohan had ruined his surprise. He brought the gift that he had bought for me and said, "Here, I wanted to surprise you. Now that you know it, forget about the whole thing".

Then he expressed his disappointment with me for actually believing Rohan's story. He blamed me for years, and years that I didn't trust him. "Don't you think that when a husband like me has a suspicious wife, I would suffer emotionally?" He almost made all those ladies cry for him. They all accused me of being an unappreciative, and evil wife.

I knew from the beginning that Iraj was a politician with a great diplomatic mind. I always called him a great politician. But this time he had outdone himself. He was having an extramarital affair with Badri long since, before Azeez had passed away. And now he was securing his grounds by portraying me as a suspicious wife. Oh, my dear God, how ingenious! Indeed, my father knew him so well.

I could not refuse her visitations for many reasons. Their involvement was to a certain point bound by the terms of the partnership agreement. And now he was accusing me of having a suspicious mind. Oh, my dear God, you are the one who created these creatures. I don't have anything to say to you, but I will say, "Well done!"

He always tried to make me jealous, thinking that will keep me interested in him. Both Iraj and Badri were under impression that Iraj had replaced Azeez. He took Azeez's place. He tried acting like Azeez; he wanted to have the same appeal. He made many funny remarks about my suspicions and me.

My Dear God:

I couldn't read his mind for the most part of it. We always teased each other that way. But I was able to put two and two together as time went by. I slowly started recognizing what was going on. Iraj would not leave Badri's sight on that special mother's

day. It really made me start wondering.

ANOTHER UNEXPECTED DISASTER.

My Dear God:

It was almost three months after Azeez's death. It was Friday evening, and I was at Badri's house comforting her. It was around nine o'clock when Iraj came over. He threw himself in my arms as soon as I opened the door. He was asking, "Where have you been? I have been looking all over for you." Then he told me that Mrs. Mehrabian was found dead in her house". He was like a scared child seeking comfort in my arms. Then he threw himself in Badri's arms, and back again in my arms, while he was telling us the story.

It was so strange. Mehrabians were not among our Blot group. They only knew Malakutis through us. They came to give their respect to the family. Shafizeh Mehrabian asked us to accompany her to Malakutis on the night of fortieth. I remember her saying while we were driving, "I wonder who is next". Although she did not know Malakuti, she was still very affected by his death.

You see, my dear God, life is so strange. It's a plane joke. We have been friends with Mehrabians for a long time. We visited each other frequently; we went out to dinners and opera always as couples, not even once without our husbands.

On Thursday morning, the day before she died, I decided to call her. The sun was out by the time I called her, and I wanted to get out of the house. She didn't sound too happy. So I told her, "It is a nice day, and I'd like to get out of the house". I'll come and get you". She did not want to go anywhere because she had to clean the pool, and take care of all the chores that she was not able to get to. I insisted that she put everything aside and get ready. I told her I was on my way to pick her up to go out to lunch". I told her, "All those things can be done tomorrow, but we might not have a sunny day like this tomorrow". When I went to pick her up, she had set the most beautiful table so that we had coffee and desserts when we got back from lunch.

She was used to going out to nice restaurants by reservations. That day I asked her to go to Tally Hall located on Orchard Lake road. It was a big hall that served international food. We could pick any food from the shops there, and then sit at any table we liked. It seemed to me that she had never been there before. She was feeling awkward at first. We walked around talking. Then we got our food and enjoyed every bite of it. By then she was happy to be there, and she started thanking me for insisting on getting her out of the house. When I offered to get ice cream, she was really against it. She thought the whole world was watching her. She was not used to live simple and be easy on herself.

My Dear God:

We got the ice cream after all. We walked, talked and laughed while eating it. She was holding my hand. Like two schoolgirls we were sharing secrets. She kept thanking me for giving her the happiness of that day. We drove to Summerset Mall, where she got herself shoes from Saks Fifth Avenue. We drove to her house, and she served desserts that she had prepared in advance. We talked about her hometown, Shiraz. She talked about the love she had for that city. She started showing me how to make the pastry she serves. I had to pick up Mojgan from school at three thirty. She had so much fun that she did not want to let me go. She was begging me that we must do this again. She thanked me so many times that I saw tears in her eyes. She had two daughters; they were both away. I felt very good for taking her out that day.

I realized that she forgot her sweater in my car when I got home. I called her to let her know that I had her sweater. She said, "Don't worry. I will get it next time we go out together". But I promised her to take it to her on Saturday. I did not know then that I had said good-bye to her for good.

She was a perfectionist. She was a much disciplined lady. On that Friday afternoon she set the table for dinner after all her work around the house was done. The soup was on the stove ready to be served. She took shower, and started putting on make-up, dressed in her lingerie. She was in her dressing when she started experiencing extreme pain in her chest. The phone was only ten feet away. She barely touched the phone, and that was it. She fell on her face on their shaggy carpet. She was dead.

That happened around four o'clock. Dr. Mehrabian got home around six o'clock. He kept calling her. And when she didn't answer, he went down to the basement where she had her sewing machine. He finally went upstairs, where he found her dead. He called the hospital immediately. Police and help got there soon, and they took the body to the hospital.

We got in the car soon after Iraj told us what had happened. And we drove to their house. Poor Dr. Mehrabian was devastated. He was all by himself. He was telling us about Shafizeh and her excessive smoking. He said, "She was trying to change her medication to help her smoke less". He was wondering around like a wounded animal. He was mumbling, "Why was she the one to have a massive heart attack?"

I knew that she was always worried, about something happening to her husband. She didn't have to worry any longer. She died in just a few seconds. There was no pain, no hospitalization. And although she was very young to die, I thought she was very lucky to die that way. She was buried a few blocks away from Azeez. She got her answer to, "I wonder who is next". She was next in line, and she even died before her time came up.

My Dear God:

She often talked to me about her daughter Margarett. Now, Margarett was at her mother's funeral together with her husband. She always was so wrapped up being rebellious. She never got a chance to know her mother.

As years went by I got to know Margarett better. We would go out just to talk about her Mom. She was very regretful for not having a relationship with her. And although she became a professor herself, still she wanted to put her foot where her mother's was.

My Dear God:

I remember how upset Dr. Mehrabian was to find out that Margarett decided to go into the restaurant business. He told me, "This girl has a PHD, and she is writing for a very prestigious science magazine. And she is planning to give it all up". I knew I was right when I heard that. Her Mom was a woman of so many talents. She was excellent in cooking and baking. So she was looking for a way to reconnect with her mother. I knew she would be searching for the rest of her life.

Dr. Mehrabian had another daughter, Dezireh, who was attending college at the time. She was also very talented. She was a good pianist, a good artist, and she possessed many other talents.

While the entire Iranian community was making such a big deal about Azeez's death, these two girls were acting so mature. They put us all to shame.

Badri and I decided to visit them one day to see if we could be of any help. But their approach was that it was life. And that they had no other choice but to accept what had happed to their mother and consequentially to them. They said they were trying to learn how to cope with it.

Margarett's only concern was that her father would honor her mother's wish of not having an open casket ceremony. But they still ended up having an open casket funeral. She was lying there in her beautiful silk dress, as if she was already in heaven.

My Dear God:

They faced their mother's death as a fact of life, as an unfortunate act of nature. It has happened to everyone for millions of years, and it will continue to happen to all of us as the world goes around. They handled with maturity and grace. While they were deeply hurt, they accepted no pity.

I kept in touch with Margarett for years. She had two beautiful boys from the professor she married first and they had a beautiful girl. The only thing she was missing in her life was her mother. She was still seeking to somehow reconnect with her mother.

Dezireh pursued nursing after she graduated from college. She earned her master's degree, and shortly after married a young man she fell in love with.

As for Dr. Mehrabian, he started a relationship with an American lady after some time. She had three children. Her youngest boy, who was ten, was still living with her. Since Dr. Mehrabian never had a son, I think he was feeling good to be a father figure to the boy. They moved in with Dr. Mehrabian, and they tried to fill out the empty place of Shafizeh.

The more I thought about Shafizeh's death, the more I realized that how we sometimes waste our lives, by finding things in life that we think they all are meaningful. Shafizeh was born in a very comfortable Armenian home. She played piano, and dance ballet before she got married to Dr. Mehrabian. She was raised by strict rules. Despite possessing multiple talents, she was at the same time very limited. Therefore she was expecting her daughters to be and act the same way, the way they were taught.

She had great passion for sewing, which she used for making incredible clothes. She had love for antiques. And she always made sure to keep them safe and secure.

Now that she was gone, everything that she has treasured and diligently taken care of was in the hands of people who never recognized their true value. What a shame! What a waste of time and life! To give up the simple joys of life!

That lady was expecting that Dr. Mehrabian would eventually marry her. But I didn't think Dr. Mehrabian was ready to go through marriage again. He took her all around the world. He spent lots of money on her, and her family. But he never had intentions of marrying her.

It looked as if Dr. Mehrabian's respect for his deceased wife was only increasing with time. He did not want to be alone, but at the same time he was not willing to replace Shafizeh by filling her place with another woman.

My Dear God:

Dr. Mehrabian's girlfriend lived with him for many years, but when she finally realized that he was not going to marry her, she decided to take him to court. This respectful and proud doctor was now facing charges for the crimes he had never committed. She was after his house, his antiques, his furniture, and his money.

The death of these two close friends made us realize that death can take you when you are young and healthy. They were both in a good shape and a good spirit. She watched her diet, and she didn't know that death was near.

She was the proudest woman on earth to celebrate her husband's sixtieth birthday. She threw his birthday party at a hote1, where she invited hundreds of guests. She was thanking to God for allowing her husband to be around for as long as he has been. She was hoping that they will live a long life together.

Although Dr. Mehrabian and I were not considered to be close friends, he became a close friend during my sufferings. He had a lot of respect for me, and he always said that Iraj had made the biggest mistake of his life. He never left my sight when I needed him. He even threw a good-bye party for me in his house in Michigan. He prepared the food, and invited our mutual friends.

At this time we all were so close to Badri's family that they had become part of our family. My children and I wanted to keep them happy at all times.

Aghdass Barkhordari, Naheed Soltanpoor, Badri and I took Mojgan and Rozan out for ice cream one evening. On our way back we started talking about life in general. Naheed brought up the subject of sex. We each expressed our opinion I was the only married woman among them. I said, "Sex and intercourse are fine, and I am sure everyone enjoys the right sex. But sometimes it becomes too much, especially if it happens during the period. Iraj on the other hand believes that it is the best time for sex, since women does not get pregnant". I was just trying to make a point that sex is good in our house, but sometimes it is natural that women don't want to have it. I had no intentions to be badmouthing my husband. Then all of a sudden Badri said, "Oh no, I did it all the time. And I did it any way and shape he wanted: oral, back, front. I did it anywhere at any time".

I found some time later that my comment about our sex has been discussed with Iraj. He was told that I said he had to beg sex, and that I never enjoyed having sex with him. Boy, oh boy Badri, shame on you, and a big shame on you! Unlike you, who was involved with other men, regardless of the fact that you were married or not, I was solely involved with my husband. As a matter of fact there is no sex better than the sex based on pure love. People like you, are very popular among men who just seek instant pleasure if you know what I mean.

My Dear God:

Little by little I started to see everything more clearly. One evening Iraj and I went over to Fassihils to pay a simple visit. As soon as we got there, Badri appeared unannounced. She told Sara, with that smile that Azeez always hated, "I left Rozan's shoe here last, and I came to get it". Sara was wondering why she didn't call first to make sure they were home.

And oddly enough, when they couldn't find the shoe anywhere, she said, with that same smile on her face, "Oh well, I thought I had left it here". By then Sara had no other choice but to invite her to stay.

I had to pick up Mojgan from school. She said to me in Farsi as I was leaving, "Either your place or mine". Everyone took her comment as a joke. At the time we had no idea what she was suggesting. But when I returned, once again she gave me her infamous smile, and said, "I didn't mean it that way. And I am sorry".

Yes, Badri, that was exactly what I had told his first mistress in Iran. He was trying to leave that prostitute, and come back to his family. I told her then, "I refuse to lower my values, and remain in the same place with you". And I left.

Iraj had destroyed everything in order to rid himself of that first affair. But he couldn't get away from you because you had the support of many other doctors. You were absolutely right; I would never sit where you sit. After all, you were providing sex for him as much as ten women altogether if not more, without loving him. But I only loved him. Obviously, he deserves you and only you.

Sara and I were certain that Iraj had asked her to join him at Fassihi's that night. So Badri decided to show up unannounced, and she made up the story about Rozan's shoe.

It was a custom that we went out to lunch on Saturdays together with our children. But on that one Saturday, while we were ordering our food, Badri appeared with her children. Because of Maseeh's and Roshanak's friendship, it was only natural for us to ask them to join us. But they didn't have a table for ten, so Iraj helped get a table close to us. I could not believe my eyes. That was not a coincidence. For the first time after his first affair, I started shivering, stricken with suspicion. I didn't know what to do. I knew no one would understand me. Iraj noticed my reaction. My children did not know what was going on. I kept shaking; I looked pale and nervous. Once again Iraj tried to make me look bad in front of my children. He said, "It so happened that they came at the same time to the same restaurant. Is there anything wrong with that?" Maseeh was very happy to see Roshanak, and so were others. While those two were having fun and enjoying their lunch, I sat there like a stupid, angry woman. I did not have any room in this world. Instead of screaming and breaking dishes at them, and instead of ending the beginning right there, I answered to Iraj's question, "I have a headache".

My Dear God:

You were there, my dear God. You saw what had happened to me. Oh, my dear God. Was it happening to me again? Were all my destructive emotions back? How can I even start this war? How can I even begin to explain to my children? So after I calmed myself, we finished our food, and left the restaurant.

During all those happenings, Iraj was trying to assure me that everything was fine, and that there was no need to worry. He was telling me that some incidents took place coincidentally, and others were just business.

Badri, on the other hand, was trying to awaken my jealousy, and make me mad at Iraj and the rest of the world.

There was another evening that we were in Tally Hall having dinner. And again she appeared there, this time accompanied by Roozbeh. We stopped to talk. They were acting like two shy lovers that couldn't look in each other's eyes. It seemed like they couldn't wait to be in each other's arms.

My past started to haunt me again. Iraj had dedicated all his life to making me forget about it. And now I was lost again. This time it was completely different. I didn't want to believe that it was happening again. I was able to cope with Iraj's affair with the help of my sister-in-laws when we were in Iran. But how about this time?

This time the involvement was different. Legally they were partners. Even if I stopped seeing her, Iraj still had to have contact with her. He didn't really have to, but he did it to look good in front of other doctors.

We have practically been inseparable since the day Dr. Malakuti passed away. We spent every weekend together, and we played blot three or four nights a week. And in the daytime they were together supposedly seeing lawyers and other people. She would appear at any place we went to. She just became my shadow.

Once I was supposed to go somewhere with Badri. I kept calling her, but her phone was busy. I tried to reach her for more than half an hour. I finally decided to call the operator, and I said that it was an emergency call for Mrs. Malakuti. The operator promised me to interrupt the conversation. The operator soon called back to inform me that Mrs. Malakuti was talking to Dr Rafani, and that she would hung up in ten minutes. I almost fainted.

I couldn't confront him, because I knew he would say it was about Azeez's business. I couldn't talk to anyone, including my own children. He had already made everybody believe that I had suspicious mind, and that I was jealous of poor Mrs. Malakuti, who had lost her husband. So you see, my dear GOD, I was trapped.

My Dear God:

When I finally got hold of her, she said, "I was talking to Dr. Rafani regarding the lawyer, and the property sale". I started questioning in my mind, "He was on the phone for over an hour during the busiest time in the office? Isn't it strange?" But I didn't tell her anything.

Kamal, my brother-in-law was having dinner with us that night. I casually asked Iraj, "Were you talking to Badri today?" He said. "Oh, was it you who interrupted our conversation?" I said, "Yes". He said, "She had a question about Roshanak". I noticed him turning red when he said that. I just told him, "I believe you".

I was no longer myself. My head was feeling heavy. I was felling nauseated. Because I couldn't talk to my children, they thought their mother was going senile. I was depressed and I was losing weight rapidly. I was sure that there were having an affair from the beginning, but because of the circumstances I was not able to detect it.

Parveen's advice came to my mind. After he was sorry and came back to us, she said to me after Iraj and I got back together, "Wouldn't it be better if we had kept it quite?" I knew by then that Badri was after him. And it was up to me to somehow handle it.

I did not want to challenge Iraj. I didn't want to bring the truth out in the open. I didn't want to push him towards something I was horrified would happen.

As I said before, according to Iraj I was a suspicious wife. And thanks to him all our friends were starting to believe in that myth as well. While I was conditioned to keep quite, Iraj continued his humanitarian voyage. I was also aware of Iraj's self-destructiveness. I

knew I was better off avoiding stepping on his tail. Plus I was trying to consider all the difficulties that surrounded him. And he was challenged by midlife crisis as well.

I was once browsing through "Human Sexuality" magazine, to which he was subscribing. I came across a story written by a doctor about his own menopause and midlife crisis. I recognized many similarities with Iraj's behavior.

The doctor's story brought tears to my eyes. He was talking about depression and thoughts of suicide. He had three children and a very loyal wife. He started doing things he never thought of doing before. He slept with many women. He even picked up prostitutes on his way home. Because he was able to write prescriptions, he had access to various drugs. Little by little he found himself addicted. It got to a point that he couldn't fall asleep unless he used some kind of drug. His performance at the hospital became very poor, which upset the faculty. He soon lost his medical license, and he was not able to practice any more.

My Dear God:

By that time his wife, who had become an alcoholic, was hospitalized. His only son had committed suicide. And his two daughters, one was in France, and the second one had dropped out of the school, and was working at a nearby restaurant.

This doctor wrote about himself, "A doctor, who has had everything: money, prestige, a beautiful wife, a nice house, and three most innocent children in the world, and everything he could have possibly asked for, ended up losing his job, his family, his health, and he almost became homeless".

The frightening part about his life story was that he said, "I didn't know what I was doing. And without knowing it, I was doing things that always hated. When I opened my eyes after seven years, and regained my consciousness, it was hard to realize that it was I who did all those destructive things. I had lost everything. I had nothing to go back to. There was nothing I could have done to bring my son back".

Then he proceeded with explaining his disease, "More than seventy percent of men will be faced by extremes of midlife crisis or male menopause around the ages forty and above. Many, before they know it, commit suicide. Some become depressed form fear of impotency, and are ashamed to talk about it. Some will become alcoholic or drug users, or both. And many throw themselves to the hands of women. This period usually lasts seven years. Some come to their senses before it is too late. And some, like me, will loose everything that they worked so hard to gain".

Reading these magazines and books I realized that Iraj fell into that category. I began to notice that he would wake up several times during the night for a shot of alcohol.

I was even more concerned, since his father was an alcoholic. I was scared. I was feeling helpless. I didn't know what else to do except to pray to GOD, "Please, God, don't let it to be true. Please help Iraj to regain his consciousness before it is too late".

I had many good reasons to pray for him. The memories of his sorrowful letters, and his remorseful acts were coming back to me. I couldn't bear to see him like that again. Oh, please God.

To me, the institution of marriage is based on truth, loyalty, trust, love and respect. If one partner breaks the structure of trust, and demolishes the respect and togetherness, the other partner cannot, and will not survive the devastation.

After his first affair, I was determined to rid my heart of him. I wanted to proudly start a life without a man, as if Iraj was only a dream. But he was capable of making the whole world cry for him. I still get emotional when I read those letters from thirty-five years ago. I feel really sorry for him.

My Dear God:

How could this man go back and put himself back to where he did not want to be? If he was sorry, and he returned to us with pride and happiness, and if he did everything in his power to become the best husband, the best father, and the best provider, then why was he going back to what he considered to be wrong? Why, my dear God? Was this man really phony? Does he ever know what he wants?

What was his promise about, that after our children were gone we would sell the house, and would travel the world? Why did he have to promise such a thing to me if he didn't love me? I had not pressured him into doing anything for me. He didn't have to make me love him, because I already loved him for the kind of a person that he was.

I thought I never knew Iraj. And I was so afraid to come face to face with real Iraj. No matter what I write or I say, I am not capable of describing my feelings during those days. I have no way of expressing myself. I was so afraid of finding out the truth.

We had become so connected with Badri that if we went somewhere without her, everyone would ask how come she wasn't with us. I knew that I might be able eliminate Badri at home, but I could never separate them during the office hours. They were entitled to handling legal matters together.

One evening I had a few of our friends over for dinner. Although I didn't want her to be there, at the same time I wanted to make sure that they didn't suspect anything. They kept asking me all night why Badri was not there. I had to come up with an excuse. And so I lied to them that she had company, and that she might join us later. But when they agreed to wait for her, I decided to ask her to come over before they started spreading rumors.

While I was caught in a battle between life and death, Badri was working on Iraj's emotions. Rozan gave a gift to Iraj one Christmas. We were at Neel's house. She also wrote him a card, which said, "You are not getting older, you are just getting better". When Sara Fassihi said this after she read it, "This was dictated to her by her mother. She is only nine years old. How could she think of such a sentence? Nine year old girl telling

something like this to a man of a middle age; it's impossible!"

Iraj always needed to be needed. He appreciated people who didn't know much, he appreciated people who depended on him, and followed him every step of the way. Badri recognized that need in Iraj. She also recognized his weakness for wishing to looking young. And from there she knew how to work on his weaknesses. She used her children as a shield. This way she looked innocent.

My Dear God:

One night we were having dinner in Mahajer's house. While we were around the dinner table, Roozbeh came in, and he quietly asked Iraj to follow him. He took him to another room to talk about his problems. Iraj put his food aside, and followed him. Everyone watched them, and then everyone started looking at me. Then Minoo said, "Oh my God, They have such a great relationship! Iraj is such a great friend! He really is a good father to them".

People were admiring Iraj for what he was doing. They tried to make the circle of our friends tighter and tighter. I was the one who did so much for them for the first eight months. Why did these people refuse to see my problem? Why were they trying to close their eyes and pretend that there was nothing wrong? Was it possible, my dear God, that they were all dumb? Who was supposed to come to my rescue except for you, my dear God? I begged you to show me the way. Losing my family would be equal to losing my life. My family was the only purpose for my living. I'd rather die than loose them that way. Why was I to lose my life, when all that I ever wanted was to bring comfort to that family? Was I guilty my dear God?

I couldn't sleep at nights. My weight loss was becoming very noticeable. I had lost my appetite, and most of the time I was feeling nauseated. Because I was very unhappy, I began acting edgy and irritable with my children. They couldn't understand my strange behavior or me.

One day Jalal Panah asked me, "Shamci, is something wrong? I noticed you have lost a lot of weight. Please let us know if there is something wrong. You don't try to hide it. Talk to your friends".

We were at Barkhordari's house. I refused to answer his questions. I just said, Thanks, there is nothing wrong with me". I pulled myself away from him lifelessly. And I went back to my house. I was shivering and at the same time perspiring. My heart was literally bursting out of my chest.

I was almost sure that if people heard anything from me, Iraj would once again start accusing me of having suspicious mind. And because of the humiliation, he would pull himself closer to Badri, more than before.

I knew that it was Badri's dream that I make a big scandal in front of our friends. She was hoping that I humiliated Iraj, and made him decide one way or another. So I

didn't want to talk to anyone. I was hoping they would realize that tightening the circle of friends, with Badri in the center of circle, they were destroying my family life. And the only answer to solving that problem was that they let go of Badri, and they made her realize that she must be on her own.

My Dear God:

This was very possible if that group of so-called friends had a little understanding, and they were not on a mission to get me.

Badri's entire family lived in California. She had inherited enough money from Malakuti to be able to live comfortably. She was still young, and she could remarry in no time. If all our friends boycotted her visits, and stopped treating her like a queen, she could have moved to California, and everything would have been fine.

But no, none of them were friends. They needed a subject to amuse themselves with. They needed to protect their own family life, while they were destroying a life of someone who didn't seem to be important. They all pretended to be blind. They were aware that Badri would eventually get somebody's husband. But as long as it was not their husbands, and it was only Shamci's, it was ok. Let it be. They needed their laughter after all. So I tried to deal with my problems on my own.

Once, Mahmood and Sara Fassihi were in our house. They were discussing Badri's life, and what she should do now that her husband was gone. Mahmood was at most meetings, and had paid some money to help the family. They were suggesting to Iraj that it would be wise for Badri to sell Azeez's Mercedes, and just keep the station wagon. They were suggesting that she tried to spend conservatively, and that she moved to California to be with her family. Iraj showed no interest in their ideas and as always he remained quiet.

They immediately stopped the conversation. But I am sure that made them wonder, "How come it was our duty to help that family emotionally and economically, but we are not allowed to guide them now?"

I knew by then of Iraj's affair with Badri, but I was not sure if they knew. Obviously I did not say a word.

I knew that in order for Iraj to snap out of his confusion Badri had to move to California. And it was so obvious that Badri could have gotten remarried within a month or so. And the only thing to make it possible was if all our friends made it clear to Badri that she has no other choice but to move to California. But unfortunately they were not my friends. Most of them tried competing with Iraj throughout all the years of our friendship. They were awaiting this opportunity to destroy him and his name.

I know that it was Iraj who chose to get involved in an affair with Badri. But if those so-called friends, who already knew what was going on, would stop associating with her, I would have had my family together like everyone else did. But in their eyes I was way too lucky, and I was way too happy. They couldn't stand to see that for me. What better way

to destroy it all than to let Badri get hold of Iraj? Like a poisonous snake, she sunk her teeth into his flash, and never let go. They did all this in the name of friendship.

My Dear God:

Meanwhile all of our lady-friends were very intimidated by Badri's presence around their husbands. They went as far as keeping their family trips a secret to insure she never tagged along.

I remember Badri calling me once. She knew I would do anything to comfort her. She was crying, and she told me, "Now that they know I have lost my husband, they go on a trip without me. And they kept it a secret all along". She certainly knew who to talk to. I began crying with her, and I asked her, "Who would do such a thing to you?" She continued, still crying, "Last week I was in Rohan's house. Every time I asked her about her plans for the Christmas, she either ignored me, or she changed the subject. Now I know that she was trying to keep it a secret. She did not want me and my children to go with them".

I, as stupid as I was, felt so sorry for her. I tried to comfort her, while I was trying to defend Rohan, "You are just assuming all these. Rohan is your friend, and I don't think she had any intention of hurting you".

After a long conversation I was able to convince her that no one was trying to hurt her. I promised her that we would go to California for Christmas. I told her, "You could come with us. Don't worry about things like this". Oh God, how stupid I was!

You see, my dear God. Today I have to refer to that as stupidity. Those days I felt obligated to help out a young friend who had just lost her husband. Weren't we taught to reach out and touch someone, especially the ones in need? Weren't we taught to be kind, and help others who need you? Then why did you create such devious creature?

When I look back, I see that those who didn't follow the rules of humanity those who always thought of themselves first, were the ones who were smart. They didn't give a damn about humanitarian acts. As millions of times before, it seems that rules are not for everyone to follow. Even in the judgments of the nature, we will find double standards. You'll never know whether you are heading in the right direction. That is why sometimes you will run into people who believe in taking law in their own hands, regardless of the consequences. Just like the case of that one woman who killed her husband and his new wife in their bedroom. This woman had helped her husband to become a successful lawyer. They had three beautiful children. Then eventually she became a victim of her husband's physical and emotional abuse for years after years. No one ever came to her rescue. Not only he was able to use his charm and power to take everything away from her, but also he was able to take away her children. So she decided to take the law in her own hands. She ended the life of those who had taken away her life and happiness.

My Dear God:

Okay, my dear God, where were these people to listen to her side of the story, to make the right judgment, and to defend her rights as a person, a woman, and a wife? Where were these people to stop her from becoming a murderer? I don't think she ever intended to kill anyone. And then the saddest part of the story was that all the twelve jurors unanimously voted for her conviction. What power and money cannot buy? I just wonder.

They made a movie of her life. They showed the whole world how much she suffered during her life with that husband. She was convicted with “life in prison without parole”. What kind of a person does come up with such a harsh conviction after seeing her life story? I really don’t know.

They held an interview with her while she was in prison. She showed no remorse, and she said, “I don’t care what people did to me. For the first time after many years of suffering, I feel free. I was in prison while I was living with him, and after that”.

You see, my dear God, I don’t know how you see it. But I think that not only she was not a murderer, but the court must have also rewarded her for getting rid of two dirty, scandalous, disgraceful creatures.

Although Malakuti was discussing the typical behavior of widowed women shortly before he died, and although he mentioned that they would try stealing their friend’s husband, yet I never allowed myself to doubt Iraj. After his regrets for having an affair, even if I saw him in bed with another woman, I wouldn’t believe that he was capable of doing such a thing.

So, here we go again. Didn’t I say that everything that took place in my life was interconnected as a series of chain? The events were connected like convicts chained together that made the escape impossible. Regardless of my preferences, it was an unavoidable chain reaction. No matter how I tried to approach it, there was something for me to reconsider.

I have talked about my life, and about his life. And I talked about how circumstances brought us together, and things that happened afterwards, up to the time that we met Azeez’s family. How these two became partners and how the revolution in Iran made it possible for Azeez and Iraj become close, while they did not have that much in common. And how Azeez’s death had enforced all the responsibilities of the well being of his family upon us! Everything that we did was already preplanned for us to do. Many of them we did not have our hands on, and if it were up to us, we would rather avoid them.

My Dear God:

I had blamed you many times, my dear God. I believed you were the one who planned those circumstances, the one who created those events. If you are the greatest power in the universe, and if you are in charge of all those events, how come you did not stop my sufferings, and how come you let me handle everything by myself?

Badri had already made up her mind. In the beginning I thought their affair began after Azeez's death. But as time went by, I came to realize that they had been planning this long before Azeez's death.

She used to tell me, "Azeez believes that as soon as he is gone, I will start fooling around, or get married right away". Her mother did, her three sisters did. There was no reason for her not to do exactly the same.

At that time Susan was my next-door neighbor. She asked me in many occasions, "Shamci, what is wrong? Why don't you tell me what's been bothering you?" But I just kept quiet. I knew that rumors traveled around quickly. And I also knew that Iraj couldn't stand to be humiliated. I knew he would give everything up, and make Badri's wish come true. So I was determined not to say a word to anyone. I knew the results would be devastating.

Meanwhile I was loosing my mind. I cried every time I was alone, which it was most part of the day. And at nights I was feeling so weak that at times I even fainted. I went down to get milk one morning, and I fainted right in front of refrigerator. Maseeh came down to the kitchen then. I had to pretend I was just resting there. I made an effort to get up after he left, and I went back to bed.

He had finally referred me to a neurologist at Beaumont Hospital. He performed many tests, including cat scan, but he found nothing significant. He did mention though that it might have been due to some kind of childhood epilepsy. So he prescribed a pill to be taken once a day. The first day I took the pill, I felt so dizzy that I had to stay in bed all day. I did not take the pill the next day. I thought to myself, "I'd rather die than be asleep all my life". So that was the last time I took that killer pill.

Once, prior to the fainting episode, I had to go in for breast biopsy. I couldn't think of a single person among that circle of friends that I could ask to come along. I didn't like showing weakness at any period of my life. So I went by myself, and I had to wait for three hours at the hospital before I could drive. Generally, I would break into pieces without having someone to share my problems with, or get help from. But that circle of people around me was just for having fun together, while you are happy and successful. Those people were not for the time you were in need.

My Dear God:

I used to have severe migraines, which would practically paralyze me. I had to lie down and cover my eyes with a black shawl in order to sleep. If after I slept for two hours, and I opened my eyes and the pain was gone, then I was okay. But if the pain lasted after the nap, it would become so severe that I would get nauseated and throw up, until eventually I got better the next day.

One morning Kayvan was in our house. Iraj had a delivery the night before, so he

was sleeping in. I was so sick that Kayvan wanted to call a doctor for me. He thought I was dying. But I stopped him by saying, "I will be all right".

Meanwhile Badri was crawling all over Iraj. She was poisoning my home, my children, my family, my friends and everything around me. Just like a quiet, colorful, and beautiful cobra, she was hypnotizing them with her eyes, and her innocent smile.

She was using everyone to make her dream a reality. She made everyone feel so sorry for her that they all forgot about poor Azeez, the real victim. Guided by the example of her mother and sisters, she knew exactly where she was going, and what she was doing.

Anywhere in the world when someone dies, there will be funerals, and other ceremonies. Then after a few months of mourning, everyone will go their own way, and survivors will have to learn to live again. And life will be as it did before. But Badri made sure that no one forgot Azeez's death, until she got what she wanted.

One day Bijan, her nephew, was with us, while we were discussing Badri's future. We were considering different options. He immediately interfered, when we started discussing the possibility of moving to California. He said, "It is out of the question. My aunt and her children would be more comfortable where Dr. Malakuti is buried. Besides, they are being watched, and they have been well taken care of by friends in Michigan, whereas if she moves to California, there would be no one to watch over her or her children. Everyone's busy with their own problems, they don't have time for them".

It seemed to me that they all had conspired together to grab Iraj. They had chosen her future husband, and now they had to work on it.

I did not want to start the war between us. While he was with Badri, he was still trying to hide it from the children, and me, as well as form his friends. I was thinking, given the possibility he would be with her for as long as I don't voice it, and then God knows what would happen.

My Dear God:

But Badri, with every chance she got, tried to demonstrate to me their love affair. One day, after dinner she wished us farewell and left. I followed her to the laundry room to make sure she left. I found Badri resting her head on her arm, and when she said good-bye, she had tears in her eyes. I realized that she must have had a conversation with Iraj before she said good-bye.

I fell apart, after she left. I kept walking in circles like a beheaded chicken. I didn't know if I should cry, and shout and scream, or get an object and slash my heart with. I felt trapped, very badly trapped. I no longer had hope.

Now, I heard those friends of mine talking about me, "Something is wrong with her. It must be depression. She must be going through menopause". Those were the words of the infamous Rohan Panah. Since I was no longer happy, they had to diagnose me with an incurable disease. Oh my God, what a pity that I had these people for friends for so many

years! What a waste of time to be associated with such a ruthless, no good people! She was nothing but a nuisance.

Toolu Avaregan was the one person who really wanted to help me. She knew that they were talking about me, and she advised that I must open up and start talking to someone. She said, "You should trust one person at least, and not let it pile up inside you. It is really going to destroy you".

Toolu was the first Iranian lady I met in Michigan. She kept busy with her own activities, and she always minded her own business. I always felt comfortable around her. We used to go to gym, to symphony and other places together. That would help me take my mind away from all my problems. There was a big difference between Badri and I. She married Azeez without loving him. Her main concern was to be in the arms of a man who gave her money to spend, and a home to live, and a bed to have sex on. While she was married to him, she considered having flings elsewhere.

It was completely different in my case. To begin with I was against marriage, unless I found a person whom I loved so much that I would give my heart for. And so it happened, with my open eyes I picked the only man I could ever be married to. Even though there were many who didn't approve our life, still we believed we had it made. I was happy without money, and I never dreamt of being in bed with another man.

So, when her husband died, I thought she had the same feelings about Azeez as I had for Iraj. Not knowing that she was very happy to loose her husband. I didn't know she couldn't wait to get into bed with my husband. In all reality it was my husband who had died. And it was my husband, whom we had buried instead of her husband. If she didn't cry for Azeez, it was only because someone else took his place in bed. She had no feelings for Azeez whatsoever. And I was mourning for such a long time because I knew that I had lost Iraj. So I tried to bury him.

My Dear God:

I knew they would never understand my feelings; therefore I didn't want to discuss my problems. I knew that as soon as I told them they would suggest that hired a lawyer to divorce him.

For the thirty years that we had been together not even once, even in the most crucial times of our lives together, Iraj had pronounced the word divorce. Not even once, ever. I would rather die than divorce him. So I knew that people could not ever help me, unless they all got together, and boycotted Badri's visitations and invitations, and sent her away to California. This was the only way to end Badri's desire for stealing Iraj.

Day after day they continued asking me, "Shamci, what is wrong? Why are you unhappy? Why don't you tell us?" One day, when Susan asked me, "Why don't you tell me what's wrong?" I decided to talk to her. We decided to go to movies, and then we came back to her house to talk.

She told me, "It was very obvious to all of us. One day Rohan, Minoo, and I tried to talk to Badri, and we advised her to leave Iraj and his family alone. We were positive that was the only thing that was bothering you".

I made sure to let her know that I did not wish to start a war with Iraj. And I let her know that I knew if Iraj set his mind on doing something, he would more likely do it when he was under pressure. Since he had the load of Azeez's legal work on his shoulders, he had to have connection with Badri outside of our social life. "I do not want to humiliate Iraj in front of his friends just because he was trying to fulfill his duties". Then I added that the only way to stop Badri from stealing Iraj was that all of us started to ignore her. "Do not invite her in your houses; do not go to her house. And make sure that she understands that she would be better off moving to California, where all her relatives lived". And I tried to assure her that nothing else would work. "As long as she has these many friends supporting her by inviting her to their houses, she will never leave Iraj alone". I continued, "Badri is trying her best to make sure that everyone knows that Iraj is after her. But I don't want to let this happen".

Okay, my dear God. You know everything that took place afterwards. It seemed that Susan, Rohan, Minoo, and others were on a mission to find out if their husbands were off hook. Although all three of them assured me that they were thinking of talking to Badri, and asking her to leave Iraj alone. But in reality they were pretending while looking me in the eyes. The same way they broke their promises to Azeez to back him up in the fight with Reza, the same way they turned their backs on me when they found out that Badri was not after their husbands. They only wanted to make sure that Badri had already found herself a husband, and she would not go after theirs.

My Dear God:

They knew everything, and after they had discussed it among themselves, they decided to deny all the facts and stay away from Shamci's problems.

Susan came over literally next day, and in our conversation she said to me, "I don't know, Shamci. I don't think Badri would do such a thing. And to tell you the truth, I don't have the heart to get involved with this kind of heartache".

You see, my dear God, for a long time I did not open my mouth, just because I knew that these people were the worst kind of friend on earth. I got to know them by their actions towards other friends. I had heard their stories behind other peoples' backs. There was no reason for them to act nice towards me. I knew that for sure. But they actually tricked me with their artificial kindness, just to be on the safe side.

My dear God, they thought they could harm me. But they were wrong. These unkind people, and their merciful grace, helped me learn how to cope with the situation.

I believe I was the only one among all these women who did not care to be the wife of a doctor. I married Iraj when he did not have enough money to pay for his journey to

America. I loved him and his success more than myself. I cared for him and his well being to a point that I treated him like my child. I wasn't there to be called Mrs. so and so. I just loved that specific person, and I just wanted to be with him. I was not defending a house, a title, or money. It was just he and my three children. It was a matter of saving them from the destroyer, and keeping my respect and stepping aside. Those who don't know what a real love is will never understand my words, or their meaning.

That day I realized that I had made the biggest mistake ever. I gave them a reason to laugh at us, and I helped Badri move forward, closer to her dream.

You remember, my dear God, how many times I stood by the pool to drown myself. But the thought of my children, especially Mojgan, who was only twelve-years-old at the time, stopped me from doing it. I had to put myself together before my children came home. I did that. I cooked their favorite dinner, and I dressed up nicely so that they didn't hate me.

My Dear God:

One day Iraj decided to do Mojgan a favor, and drive us to Cider Point. He asked Rozan and Badri, whom Mojgan didn't favor much, to join us. I was hesitant to go with them, and at the same time I didn't want to allow them to go by themselves. So I decided to go after all and asked Susan to come with us.

She could not see them in the mirror. They behaved the same on the surface. Meanwhile I was on fire, I was the only person who knew the reason why we were at Cider Point. My main concern was to keep control at all times. I was practically watching their love affair here and there, and there was nothing I could have done about it. And because we had become so close even before Azeez's death, no one else saw their love affair except me.

It was during this time that Badri's brother-in-law had a surgery done. Like always we went together, everywhere. When we went to visit him, her parents were there as well. Iraj was paying so much attention, and he was concerned about all of them in general. I noticed that her father smiled at Badri happily, and he blinked at her.

If a great writer was there, she could retell it exactly how it happened. But anyway, that blink meant, "Bravo, Bravo, continue what you are doing. Indeed, you are my girl". And to me he was trying to say, "It is too late for you to do anything. Forget it".

One night we were at Ozra and Dr. Salehi's house. As always I was talking and had fun with those whom I felt comfortable with. After we left the house I noticed that they were arranging something that Naheed was involved too. It was dark and they didn't know I was right behind them. They were chest to chest, as soon as Iraj saw me; they pulled away from each other.

You see, my dear God, I did all my duties at home. I supervised my children, I put on my make-up, I dressed very well, and I socialized with them, while my heart was bleeding,

and my soul was crying each minute during those days.

As I said before, Mary was probably the first person to notice their relationship, even before I did. And she had discussed it with Masseh and Mojgan. I knew that they were watching their father carefully.

One night we were getting ready to go to Malakutis. All three of them were ready waiting for us in the family room. After I got ready, I went downstairs and joined them. I was very well dressed, and it seemed like nothing was bothering me.

I noticed that they were discussing something over a piece of paper. I wanted to see what it was. But they refused to show me the paper. But I kept insisting, and I promised that I would give it back to them. It was a caricature of us drawn by Mary. I was amazed with her artwork, and the beauty and depth of her understanding. She drew Iraj in the middle, with his head down, looking confused. She wrote under him, "Poor guy does not know which way to go". She had drawn Badri pulling Iraj's hand, and with a look of a sensual woman, who was trying to please Iraj. And under her, she wrote, "I need you. Come on honey, I am the one who needs you". And she did such a nice job on me. She drew me with my head up. Very well dressed, with nice make up, walking with elegance. And under me she wrote, "She doesn't give a damn about any of them, and she is trying to deal with the situation". I kept that paper in my wallet for a long time. My children were trying to tell me, "Mother, we know who is who, and we know what is going on. You are not alone. We understand everything". That was what I felt then, and I meant to keep that caricature for the rest of my life. Unfortunately I had lost it somewhere, and I really miss it.

My Dear God:

Two weeks before Malakuti's death, my cousin Lili came to our house. We were working on her green card with the help of a friend. One night we went to Malakuti's house together. Although it was the first time she met Azeez, they had great time teasing each other. She too was very sorry for Malakuti's family. But she was shocked to hear how Badri had turned things around.

Iraj started to show more interest in his health. It seemed more than usual. He told me, "I got an appointment with a plastic surgeon to operate on my nose. It is necessary to help to get rid of my snoring". He was hospitalized for three days. I was there every day.

One day, while Maseeh and I were at the hospital, Susan came to visit too. Badri showed up soon after. She greeted everyone, and she walked towards Iraj's bed. She had her back to Susan, when she gave Iraj a long kiss on his lips. I was the only person who saw that. I started shaking and sweating. I left the room quietly. After I was able to calm myself down, I returned to the room with a big smile.

Badri did all those things in such a clever way that I could never make a sound. As a matter of fact she was doing all that, hoping that one day I would lose my cool and would

make a fool of myself. She would look in my eyes with that smile, hoping that I started screaming, crying, or even attacking her. But that never happened.

Iraj was never interested to watch TV shows, except for "I love Lucy" and "Red Skilton". We would always watch those shows together. Normally he was in bed reading Wall Street Journal, or we watched the news together.

My Dear God:

But when "Dynasty" started, he was so anxious and eager not to miss even one episode. He really thought he was the husband character on TV. Many times he would applaud for him, and he would get excited like a child. I used to follow that show, and I watched it every Wednesdays. But after I figured out that it was the story of my life, and Iraj and Badri were the main characters, I refused to continue watching it. Not only that, but they made me hate that show. To me my own life was just another episode of a Soap Opera.

My dear God, You know how badly I needed to talk to someone. You know how badly I wanted to scream, and at time hit my head against the wall. You know that I was embarrassed to talk to my own siblings. You know that my father wasn't alive to witness Iraj's behavior this time around. So please, my dear God, tell me what to do. Tell me where to go. Tell me how to deal with this ordeal.

Because I had witnessed how many religious leaders had started wars against humanitarian people in the name of God, I never wanted to accept any kind of religion. But I always believed and had faith in that super power that I call GOD.

At this time of my life to be able to have control of myself, I used to hold GHORAN in my arms, and I talked to you, my dear God, and I asked you show me the right way to find peace within me. I would press my back against the wall, while tears were rolling down my cheeks and onto my lap, I pressed the Ghoran to my chest, and started talking to my GOD. Through God I talked to my father. I talked to my mother and Iraj's parents. I asked them to come to my dreams, be with me, and tell me how to handle my problems. I was begging my parents for forgiveness for all the wrong things I did, and the way I disobeyed them. I talked to his parents, and I told them all about his first affair. I told them how sorry he was when he returned to us. I talked to them about the letters he wrote to me, asking for my forgiveness. I told them how he cried behind his dark eyeglasses asking for mercy from his children and me.

Night after night I did this to be able to put myself in your hands, my dear GOD. I needed you to guide me what action I should take the next day, and the days after, so that I didn't destroy me or anyone else. I wanted you to tell me what to do, and what not to.

You know, my dear GOD, my love for Iraj was so deep that I couldn't see what I was doing to myself. I remembered his past letters, and I did not want to see him in that position again. I knew that he didn't want to be this man that he was becoming. I believed

those letters were genuine. I thought no man ever would humiliate himself like that in front of his wife and his children to just make himself look good. I thought he meant it. He was very sorry, and he never wanted to do it again. I never wanted to see Iraj cry in his life again for doing the same thing over and over again.

My Dear God:

I knew that he was trapped in the hand of sneaky snake called Badri. I knew she would never let go of him. I just wanted you, my dear God, to help me to be able to help him before it was too late.

I wrote him few letters to remind him of his sorrowful letters to me. I wanted to let him know that the time that he has to save himself from that stormy destruction was now. "The time to see yourself and your actions is now".

I was hundred percent sure that the same way that on his first affair he was the big loser, the same way this time he will be the one who loses his name, his prestige, his respect, and above all, his dignity.

He never approved or praised those men, who betrayed their families for their own sexual desires, and he never gave credit to that kind of fathers.

The way that he acted towards me and his children up to Azeez's death was to prove to us that his dream was to be a great father and a great husband, until he died. These were the reasons that I was begging God to help me, and to help him before it was too late.

I knew for Badri and her sisters it didn't matter who they slept with, as long as they had money. Obviously most women follow this idea. But for me that was completely different. I believed in what I believed. I might have been odd in the way that I had chosen my dreams. But that was perfect for me, and I was very happy with my selection. And because I knew Iraj was for my ideas, I loved the way I was thinking, I thought we might be able to make it to the end.

While I was struggling to find a way to deal with all these problems, my so-called friends were entertaining Badri more and more. They were helping her succeed in her one desire, to get closer to Iraj. While they were trying to find out who will be the one who wins Iraj, at the same time they kept their husbands away from Badri's desires to go to bed with them. They were having lots of fun by having Badri in their group.

Four of us were once in Susan's house. Susan, Badri, Aghdass, and I were sitting around the table, playing Blot. Badri was talking about her children, "Rozan has been after me to get married. They want me to find my own life, and leave them alone. But my mother would always tell us, "If you find a man that you love, never let go of him, or you will be sorry for the rest of your life". And so I am waiting for that day".

My Dear God:

You see, my dear GOD, Susan and Aghdass were completely aware of what was

going on. And I knew what Badri was trying to tell me. But those days I still believed in Iraj's loyalty towards his family. I was so sure that he would never humiliate himself twice. I was hoping that with the help of GOD, he would probably be able to become strong enough to overcome all her temptations. I was hoping that he would use Badri the same way that he used other mistress.

But I did not realize that other mistress did not have as many supporters as Badri did. Most of member of our Blot group were trying so hard to save their own necks by pushing Badri and Iraj together so I give the credit for earning this privilege to those Iranian friends.

Badri was a walking newspaper among all Iranians. She would elaborate on many of their stories. I am sure that she was aware of Iraj's first affair. That was how she knew that she would only be able to get Iraj if she uses all those friends.

My Dear God:

I started to hang out with Toolu Avaregan more than with others. She was very faithful, and she dedicated most of her time to her husband's practice. Toolu would often encourage me to talk about my problems instead of keeping them inside. She would tell me, "It's the same as having a tumor. If you don't talk about it, it is going to burst open and it will eventually destroy you".

Sally Khodadadeh was one of our blot group members. Her husband was a pediatrician. She was American, and I always felt comfortable talking with her. She told me in one of our conversations that her mother-in-law believed that Badri had already stolen somebody's husband. "GOD helps the wife of her target". It was the first time that Sally and I had a conversation aside from the card game. But she was a Baha'i, so she had more reasons to be closer with Rohan and other Baha'is within our group. She was very appreciative of the fact that I had opened up to her, so she started sharing her own problems with me. She told me about Rohan's meanness, selfishness, and viciousness towards her husband, and especially her own mother. Meanwhile I kept wondering why and how would Sally retain the closeness with Rohan. She told me many things about Rohan that I never knew before. She also warned me not to ever trust Rohan's friendship. Sally tried to be sympathetic. Because she was working in her husband's office, she told me that Badri would bring her children to their office on daily basis with no apparent reason. I was sure she was worried that her husband was Badri's target. She felt relieved after I had told her of Iraj's involvement with Badri. And now she wanted to know everything about her and others.

My Dear God:

The only reason behind me discussing my personal issues with all those people was so that they hopefully would recognize the only solution to my misfortune. I wanted them to

pull away from Badri. I wished they could make her understand that the best for her and her children was to move to California to be with the rest of the family. It was the only way to separate Badri and Iraj. They might have continued their relationship, but it would give them a chance to hopefully come to their senses. I knew that as long as everyone was babying them, celebrating their birthdays, and pleasing her in one way or the other, she would never leave this State. And she would stay at it until she got what she wanted.

Finding a husband for Badri, her sisters, and her mother was as natural as drinking water. Even though I never thought they were any good, and in fact some looked quite unattractive, and they were not fashionable but they were promiscuous. And that makes all the matters easy. All they had to do was to pick a man.

All these people, who never gave a damn while Azeez was still alive, were now acting heroic. While my life was in jeopardy they were entertaining themselves mocking Azeez's death and my family's destruction. Believe it or not, those were my friends. They couldn't wait for me to loose control and ruin his reputation. That was exactly what Badri was after. She knew that would be the ideal solution for her to achieve her goals. But I was not planning to expedite her plans. I decided to stay quiet till the end. I was not planning on being destructive. I decided to go along with his lies, until he made the decision. And meanwhile I was hoping to survive through that ordeal. While he was pretending that he was helping Badri in her legal matters, I pretended that I believed him. Easy to say, because Iraj was trying hard to instigate confrontations among us as well. He made sure to draw a picture of innocent family man, who was forced to look for comfort elsewhere by his suspicious and scandalous wife.

My Dear God:

You see, my dear GOD, between you and I, doesn't it seem as if all these incidents interlock like series of connected chains? First, we met Malakutis. Then we formed the blot group. Next it was the revolution in Iran, and therefore more reasons for involvement. Then came the partnership in the weight loss clinic. And finally BOOM, a BULLET took Azeez's life. And no one still knows why or how it happened. They just took Badri's word for it. But as if that wasn't enough, my son Maseeh ended up in a love affair with Roshanak.

I had not done any wrong to deserve all this. At that time of my life I was under impression that both Iraj and I were looking forward to happiness in our later years together. Iraj's actions toward me were the evidence that we had it made after all. Please tell me then, my dear GOD, why me, and why my dear son? Why my poor innocent children? Why would circumstances bring so much desperation my way? Please let me understand what are the rules of life. Please let me know if there is GOOD and BAD? And are there such things as rewards and punishment? Are there?

I was only a step away from becoming a criminal. And then there were constant thoughts of suicide. But it was you, and your absolute power within me that helped me handle things the way I did. I learned to struggle through the swirling ocean of mud, and miraculously I made it a clean get away. Thank you, my dear GOD, for giving me the wisdom, the patience, and most of all my health to be able to overcome those destructive moments. Thank you for being within me at all times, and watching over me.

At the time I desperately needed to talk to someone. My niece Afsaneh called me from England. She said, "One of my friends, Ali Asghar Hushmand, is coming to States to continue his education. He does not have anyone there. I had asked him to contact you as soon as he arrives". I told her, "Don't worry. Your friend is my friend. I will make sure to watch over him like he was my own child".

Ali was offered a position of an assistant professor at the University of Michigan. When he finally arrived, I asked him to come and stay with us for the weekend. Ali didn't have a car, and so his roommate gave him a ride to our house. We had a nice visit. Ali's friend left shortly after dinner, so we had a chance to get to know each other a little better. He came from a family of very strong ties. He was one of ten children. My children and I connected with Ali from day one. He appeared to be an angel who brought hope back to my life. He immediately felt like family. He was a very humble and pleasant person. We insisted that he spent weekends and holidays with us. I knew he was comfortable around my children also. We would often talk about our families in Iran, along with many other subjects. But at first I was still hesitant to bother him with my personal problems.

My Dear God:

Eventually we became close friends. And he began talking about his personal life. I felt comfortable to open up to him as well. He told me he broke up with his girlfriend in England, and he was asking for my opinion about love and marriage in general.

Had this conversation taken place before Malakuti's death, I would have advised him to just follow his heart. But I was so disappointed with my love and myself that I felt I did not have the right to advise him. I did not know right from wrong. How could I give advice to someone else?

We went out to lunch at Tally Hall one day. We were discussing his future. He was dating a Brazilian girl, whose father was one of the high ranked government personnel. They were a very well off, contrary to his family's lifestyle. Ali's father was a blue-collar worker. He had worked so hard all his life to raise ten children. They basically had to learn how to survive by the minimum. And as always is the case they were very tight family. He always talked highly about his older brother David. He told me that it was David who watched over him, and recognized his intelligence. It was David who pushed him to go pursue higher education, and get his PHD in mathematics. He told me that his parents gave all of themselves to their children.

Even though he was very much in love with that girl, still he felt that the gap between the classes of the two families would not allow them to have a successful marriage. He also believed that he owed to his mother to marry a girl whom she had approved of. So he was completely confused. On one hand he wanted to marry the girl he was in love with, and on the other hand he felt obligated to his mother and the rest of the family to follow the tradition. He had to make the choice. And unfortunately I was not much help to him at that time. I was confused myself. I didn't know how to handle my own life, yet to be able to guide another person.

I remember one particular weekend when he came to our house. He seemed to be very distressed. He told me that he had a feeling that something bad had happened in Iran, and his family was trying to hide it from him. He said, "I think something happened to my father. I must go to Iran to find out the truth".

My Dear God:

He was right, his father passed away, and he did not even get a chance to see him. I didn't hear from him for a while. I tried to get in touch with him, and I found out that he went back to Iran. His mother made sure to introduce him to a girl in their family. She had just graduated from high school. At first it seemed strange that he never tried contacting me. I got hold of his address and phone the number. A young lady answered the phone. I thought I had a wrong number. But after I introduced myself and asked about Ali, she explained everything to me.

She introduced herself as Farahnaz Hushmans. She was very apologetic for Ali not being able to contact me. She told me he meant to call my children, and me, but he was too shy to tell them how he got married. They only knew each other for two weeks before they got married. Although they were related, and they even had the same last name, they had never met each other before. While Farahnaz was growing up in Iran, he was out of the country studying.

I wished I could have thrown a big party for them. But unfortunately my life was not in harmony. My life was in a jam. And I did not want to make a fool of myself.

Farahnaz invited me to their house. It was such a nice visit. She prepared various Iranian dishes, delicious Iranian drink, and sweets. She was only nineteen. She was beautiful, very out going, and full of energy. That visit was the beginning of a long lasting friendship.

We would talk of anything and everything. Among the topics were art, cooking, sewing, and sex. We talked about life in general, about our husbands, parents and children. I finally had someone to talk to. She made me feel so comfortable, I was no longer afraid of anything. She supported me fully. She never left my side. She was my angel of mercy, my savior.

Her father walked out on her mother when she was only two and a half. Her stories would make me cry. They had to cope with poverty, and deal with the death of her

This picture was taken when Farahnaz was at the hospital for her son's birth, Kasra. That day although we were supposed to go to Metropolis Airport to go to California and visit kamal and pari, I made it possible to go to Ann Arbor and see farahnaz while she was at the hospital.

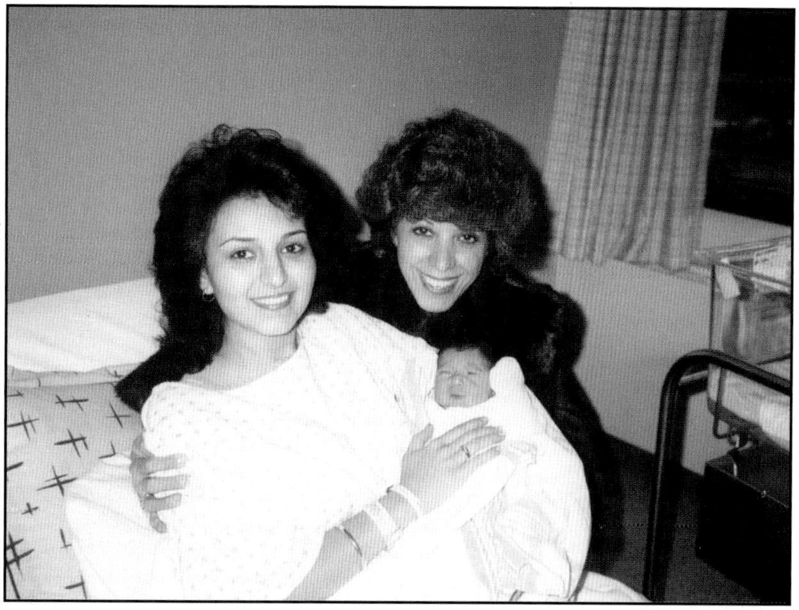

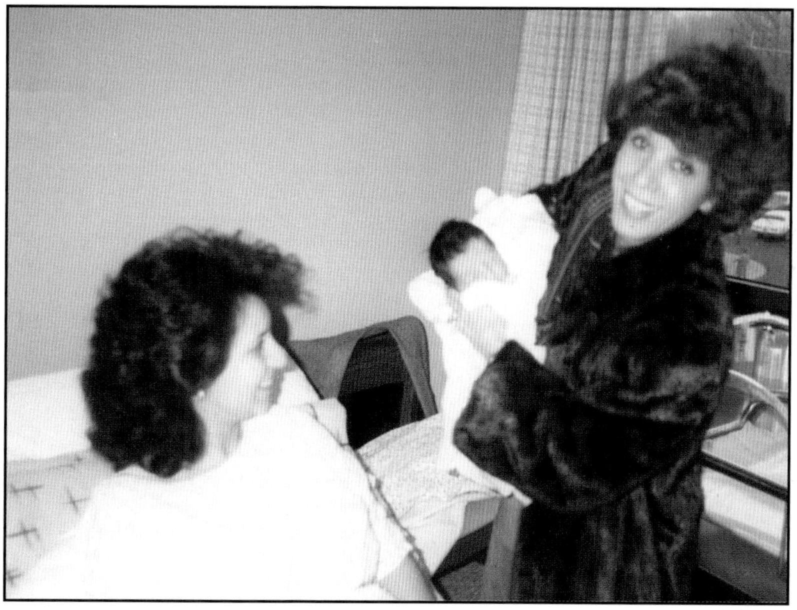

Here, I was enjoying her baby before I leave.

In this picture, Mary, Maseeh, and I were at Hushmand's house. Looking at these pictures and seeing my dear children unhappy and desperate in that age, makes me feel guilty and embarrassed. I told my parents I would make sure that my children never suffer in this world. Yet when I see them so confused, I realize how wrong I was, and how much my children suffered in an age that they needed their parents the most.

With Farahnaz in her dining room, watching the "Haft Seen" setting.

Here, I am holding Kasra at age one.

Farahnaz was my great supporter during the twilight zone of my life. I am at her house with Hosain Hushmand who was homesick then.

Mojgan and I were at Hushmand's house. Farahnaz was holding Layla. It was Norooz and we were around her "Haft Seen" (seven C's)

Me, Mary, and Farahnaz in her house.

Layla Ali, Farahnaz, and Kasra. It was a day that they were applying for a Green Card.

In London, someone somewhere took this picture of me. I really don't remember.

With Farahnaz and Kasra in her house; Again it is Norooz and we are next to the Haft Seen (seven C's) table.

in Farahnaz's bedroom in her new house
Layla and Kasra are with us.

brother. Iraj's behavior reminded her of the pain and sufferings of her childhood. So she did everything she could to heal my wounds.

Farahnaz has been living in Ann Arbor for almost a year when we first met. She was pregnant with her daughter Layla then. Despite her age, she appeared to be rather wise and mature. It was great to have Ali and Farahnaz by my side.

Nothing in the world hurt me more than watching Iraj getting destroyed. I knew from our experience in the past, and let his letters to me be my witness, that he was hoping to be able to keep his family out of harm's way. But he had many friends. And they were very competitive. They have always despised him for being so successful. They couldn't wait for him to slip, and somehow fall into a trap. Oh how much they would love to ridicule him. That was why Iraj has always kept his first affair a secret. He did not know that people talked. He did not know that they spread rumors just for the sake of entertainment.

My Dear God:

I knew that Iraj at that time was quite successful, and he had a good reputation among other doctors. Yes, my dear GOD, I am still convinced that Iraj could avoid that trap, if it wasn't for the assistance of those friends. In my opinion they were all pimps. Except for their incentive were merely the entertainment, and not the money. They were pimps with class, they carried doctorate degrees, and they resided with their wives in the upper class subdivisions of Detroit, like Bloomfield Hills and Wabeek.

Call me crazy, but I was feeling sorry for Iraj at that time. He had made us all believed that he despised men who gave up their homes and families. So I had all the rights to believe him.

I only had one advice for Ali before he went off to Iran to marry Farahnaz. I had told him that marriage, which is not based on true love, would be meaningless, and it would not last.

His girlfriend was once visiting from England. They invited me over for dinner. She was very classy, intelligent, and down to earth. She showed a lot of love and respect for Ali.

I got a chance to invite her to my house before she went back. She was very pleasant as usual. But to tell you the truth, my dear GOD, I couldn't help it not to realize that she deserved more than that. I never found out how she reacted to the news of Ali's marriage. I am sure that she was hurt.

My Dear God:

Now, don't be surprised that such licentious women would typically keep a close watch on their husbands. Meanwhile we, the society, allow them to carry on their playacting of a victim.

Personally, I can guarantee that a man will not pursue a woman unless he senses the interest on her part, despite, of course, rare forceful cases of rape. It is the woman who typically initiates flirtation, by means of body language, a potent form of non-verbal communication. She will farther try to intensify the relationship. Men are egoistic creatures. It is very seldom that they would approach a woman without the reassurance of her intents. It is quite effortless to get hold of a loose woman.

Yes, my dear GOD, I am a woman, and many men have tried to approach me. But they gave up on me immediately after they figured out that I was not interested. And even though they were always fond of me, they never belittled themselves by approaching me again.

You remember what Eve did to Adam? Many believe that men wrote this story; therefore it might not be completely accurate. But many years of life experience have brought me to believe that the story holds nothing but the truth.

While Badri was on a mission of starting a cold war between us, Iraj tried his best at acting normal. He pretended that everything was fine, and that his love for his family was as strong as ever.

He was always home on time. As always he called me when he was running late. He wanted to make sure to keep his name clear from any involvement with Badri. I think it was very important for him not to break his children's home.

Badri, on the other hand was sending me messages through her words and her acts. Like the time that she told me, "My mother had advised me that I never let go of a man I fall in love with, no matter the price". Or the time that she brought a crystal statuette to my attention. It was of two birds joining their beaks. It was obvious that she was letting me know that Iraj had given it to her.

My Dear God:

I plead you please, if you ever loved before, put yourself in my shoes, and you will feel my pain. All of you who loved truly and innocently like I did, you would understand me. You would feel the severity of my painful life.

GOD, please be with me. Please help me put those memories in writing, but please spare the pain. Please, GOD, help me write about that awful Sunday. Just help me please.

We got home very late that Saturday evening after playing Blot at Malakuti's house. So we were sleeping in that Sunday morning. We woke up happily in each other's arms. We made love, and stayed in bed for a while. He volunteered to make me breakfast and bring it to bed.

It was quite natural that I was feeling very happy. My husband woke up in a good mood, he made love to me, and he volunteered to serve me breakfast in bed. Just like anyone else would, I took those great deeds as acts of great love from my husband. Yes, I was very happy. I was very grateful that nothing was bothering him. I thought I must have

played my cards right.

So, after he went to make breakfast, I decided to call Rohan and friends to see if they could play Blot that night.

I am assuming that we both picked up the phone at the same time, because he was not aware that I was on the other end. He was whispering to her of the place of their meeting. It was to take place at some hotel. She agreed with a great laughter, and he hung up. So did I.

Ok, my dear GOD, there was no one else in the bedroom except you and I. You remember my reaction when I heard them. You remember that I was ready to kill them both. I rushed to the bathroom. I wanted to kill myself. I was feeling so hopeless; I wanted to end my life once and for all. The scenes of his first affair were coming back to me. I just sat there in the bathroom thinking. I realized that like always he would make me look guilty. He would tell everyone that I had made up the story. Besides, he never denied that he was seeing Badri. He told everyone, including his children, that he must see her for the sake of the partnership. There was no way out of it. He did it calmly, and he looked innocent. And even if everyone believed me, what was the use of violence? What good could come out of it?

My Dear God:

The fact of the matter was that he was lying to me. The fact of the matter was that he was betraying me for the second time. The fact of the matter was that he didn't love me to have respect for me. The fact of the matter was that even if the whole world found about his affair, it is nothing but a great humiliation for me and my family. The fact was that I had to open my eyes and find a way to deal with it. That woman was there to stay. Everyone was supporting her to overcome the loss of her husband by offering her my husband. I had to keep quiet.

He was willing to make me look crazy. He was willing to put me away in the mental institution. I remembered that he tried to do so in Iran. He knew he was capable of anything once he set his mind at it. I kept thinking, "I must beware before I go crazy". So as soon as he brought breakfast in the room I went and sat on the bed.

The realization was dawning that this was a major disaster. She had him firmly under her thumb. I refreshed myself, and I went back to bed, awaiting the breakfast. I decided not to say anything. I kept asking GOD to give me wisdom to be able to find a way to deal with the situation. I thought it was a good sign that Iraj was denying his involvement with Badri. I thought that I shouldn't make it bigger than it was? I decided not to push him towards her. So please, my dear GOD, hold my hand, and do not leave me alone. I need your help. Please tell me what to do.

He happily came back to the bedroom, carrying the breakfast. But I no longer was the same person. I had lost all my love for him; and now I was full of hate and anger. I kept reminding myself that I must learn to pretend that nothing had happened. While he was in the kitchen making breakfast, I was sick in the bathroom. But I made myself enjoy my meal, while pretending that I was stupid. I started a conversation with him, and thanked him for the delicious breakfast.

I thought of following him, but I forgot the name of the place and the time. Besides, I wasn't ready to face the ugly reality once again. I felt lifeless and so desperately lonely. After he left, I cried and cried, until I couldn't cry any more.

And I started a big fight with my dear GOD. I kept asking him: "Why did you let me pick up the phone at the time that he was talking to her? You know that I am not able to do anything about it. Why did you put me in a position that I could have committed crime? What if I killed someone? How do I commit suicide? Why did you put me in such position that I do not know what to do? How should I deal with it now? Please tell me what to do. I am so hopeless. Please help me, help me".

My Dear God:

I thought that if I stayed quiet, Iraj would probably find a way out of it. He would hopefully recognize his own value and prestige in the society, and stop destroying them before it is too late. I was convinced that he was sorry after his first affair. I could not believe that he would ever allow for it to happen again. He was really embarrassed, and humiliated when he returned to us. I thought it would be foolish to be repeating the acts of embarrassment and humiliation.

I was lost in contemplation. I couldn't help grieving for my life. The final realization of the truth has had an enormous effect on me. I tried my best to keep calm, and I made an effort to conceal my pain. But it was useless. My desperation showed in my appearance. It was obvious in my interaction with my children and others.

It was right around this time that I came across a talk show on TV. There was a middle-aged, intelligent, and beautiful lady sitting next to a young, tall, gorgeous girl, her husband's mistress. The lady was trying to condemn the young girl's acts. She was saying, "My husband has done it twice before, and he has eventually returned to me and my two daughters. For someone like my husband, a mistress is just a temporary delight. I know that you are with my husband, but I also know that he comes to you to satisfy certain needs, just like he has to go to the bathroom. And when he is finished, he will return to his family".

Then she continued, "I am a well respected woman, and I had raised two beautiful children. They each have a great career. We are grateful and happy with or without my husband. So, if he has enough understanding to tell the difference between good and evil, he will come back to us. Just like what he did the two times before. He will come back with his head down, and he will ask for our forgiveness. And we will give it to him. But if he decided not to come back to us, he will be sorry for the rest of his life. And the most

Dearest Mom,

I feel so bad. You don't know how I feel. God knows I don't hate you. I love you so much you'll never ever know how much. I just can't deal with everything now like I could before. Before, I could always handle the bad things you said about me, and I always cherished those good things you said. I can't possibly think of any woman who's well-being I care for more. But I can't stay here while you're this way. You're not doing anything for yourself at all mom;.. not anything. You have such warmth and loving, believe me I know, that's all I've ever seen you give me and I appreciate it. But mom, you have to use your mind too. Love hurts too much to use all the time. You have to find a get-a-way; a place to think, or maybe even just sit and not think. Mom, (and damnit, no matter what happens,.. I will call you mother) you have to start to live for yourself; you've got such potential, and such warmth, just no confidence in any of it. Please don't let yourself rot away in a house the rest of your life, where you'll only get frustrated and terribly unhappy. You've got what you need; for once don't be so lazy and irrational. Don't think of any more dumb reasons. Go out and do something besides loving. I guarantee it won't hurt as much. I don't mean stop loving because I know it's what you definitely do the best, but now do something else. Don't take out your frustrations on your kids; We love you so much, and to hear someone you care about and have had respect for for your whole life point out to you as fact, that you're a failure really hurts. Mom we all, Mary, Mojy and myself care so much for you. Don't read our feelings wrong. What we do & say is not out of anger or hate.... only frustration, the same as you. I know you love me, I refuse to believe you don't, because, Oh God knows, if I ever really believed you didn't, I'd die. Mom, please continue to love me forever; I'll always love you & dad. Just don't stop loving me. I need you two too much. Especially now. I've still got so many unanswered questions. God I've never felt so lonely before. Please mom, help Yourself. I know it would bring this family close for good. Please. Oh please

Love always
your son
Maseeh [signature]

This letter shows Maseeh's frustration during my mixed up times. I myself did not know what I was doing, what I was saying, or how I was acting towards my children. I have been lost in time and place. All that time I had to fight the temptation of destroying Iraj, Badri, or me and my children. on the other hand, my children were believing that I did not love them anymore. They were frustrated seeing I frustrated with the whole world. Neither of us was sure what was becoming of us sooner or later. Although they all knew where my frustration had come from, yet they didn't know how to cure it. At such a young age when they needed the most support from their parents, they had to find a way to help their mother, to teach her how to get out of the mess that their father had made for her. When I read this letter for I get embarrassed for not knowing what to do.

important part is that he will be ashamed to admit to his mistake and his sorrow".

That lady's point of view was so strong that the mistress, despite all her beauty and youth couldn't argue it. People applauded for the lady. She was applauded for her intelligence, and her courage.

Oh my GOD, I just needed to hear these words from someone like her. I needed to know that I was not alone. I thought if this American, professional businesswoman could think of her husband and her marriage this way, why couldn't I. I didn't think I would get better results from aggression. I just had to keep my mouth shut, and try to find a way to deal with it intelligently.

My Dear God:

I was under mistaken impression that it was only in such countries as Iran that women were bound to tolerate their husband's affairs. I thought it was mainly contributed to the economic factors. But after watching that program, as well as reading of similar stories, I realized that marriage was not based merely on money. I knew now that it is based mainly on morals and principals. The marriage institution is based on togetherness of a family. A home is like a nest, which requires a lot of policing and patrolling. One can observe such patrolling in the animal world. A human being is just one of the species, whose survival is mainly based on raising a good family in effort to provide better life for the next generation. In order to fulfill this dream the women must, and they will police and patrol their homes and families. Love for the family is based on trust, loyalty, truthfulness, and most of all respect for one another.

With all these in mind, I became more and more determined that I must find a way. I must stay put. I was not going to be assisting Badri in getting what she was after. I had to keep my eyes open; I had to study things more carefully.

I didn't want Iraj's love any more. I knew by then that his love for me has never been real, and it will never be. My main concern was my home and my children. I could not allow that woman to rob me off my happiness. I must find a way to deal with it, unless Iraj decided to move on. He was not worth fighting for, but I had to stand by my marriage, my children, and the principal of the importance of my thirty years of loving and caring. I thought that even if Iraj helped her win, I would still be proud and happy that I did my best to save my home, and my children's nest from that snake. After all, I didn't have anything to loose. Iraj had lost my love, my trust, and my respect, for him. In fact it would have been better not having him. But still I decided to stick to my principals, and let him to be the one who carried the shame and embarrassment for the rest of his life. He was the one to live with the guilt. Although he might not even known what guilt was. And he would definitely try to blame others for his own wrongdoings. He is the type that hides his head under the covers.

These thoughts were what had kept me going those days. Day after day, with GOD's

help I began my activities. And at nights I thanked him for helping me choose the right pathway to my survival. I wasn't sure of my own actions. I wasn't sure of what was going to happen next. Would something horrible happen? Or would one of us will get killed or commit a suicide? I considered days miraculous when everything went by safely.

My Dear God:

I was terrified of thinking criminal thoughts. I was trying to ignore all that I was seeing. I helped him make our children believe in his innocence. I felt that was the only way to make Iraj feel responsible to keep his word to his children. He was trying to prove to his children that, "I am innocent. There is nothing going on between Badri and me. These are all accusations made up by your mother's wild imagination".

I saw a benefit in his lies and pretense. He was now obligated to keep his promises. He was trying to prove his innocence to his children, so how could he not be embarrassed to act otherwise! I remained quiet, and I dealt with my problems my own way. I kept reassuring the children that their father was telling the truth, and that nothing wrong would happen after all. I was dreaming that Iraj might wake up one day before it was too late.

But it was so difficult for me to run my household, take care of my children, and entertain as I have always done before. Nothing was the same any longer. I tried to get involved with activities like volunteer work, classes, Bridge, and bowling. I even started looking for a job. And even then I couldn't cover up my sufferings. Everyone, including my children, knew that I was no longer the same Shamci. I was destroyed, and I was desperately trying to get back on my feet, and keep my sanity.

While Iraj remained calm through this entire ordeal, I would occasionally loose control. One day, while I was driving Mojgan to school, I just burst into tears. And I said to myself, "He does not love me any more". This sentence had a great effect on Mojgan. She always accused me of ruining her peace at the age of twelve. But could you blame me? I had no one to talk to.

My family has become ill fated after Malakuti's death. We each tried trying to deal with problems in our own way. We were afraid to talk to each other. It seemed that we were all afraid of facing the truth.

It was my habit to leave a note for my family if I had to run errands. There was one Sunday when Iraj promised Mojgan to take her to Red Lobster for dinner. He had to perform a surgery on Susan's grandmother that day. I was there, at Beaumont Hospital, to support Mrs. Froozan. He came to me after the surgery, and said, "I have to finish my rounds, and do some paper work. I'll be home soon to go out to dinner together". We went home in a few hours to get ready to go out to dinner. We found a note from Iraj, "I had to go to Malakutis' to fix their Alarm System".

Do you know, my dear GOD, what had happened to me then? Do you remember the

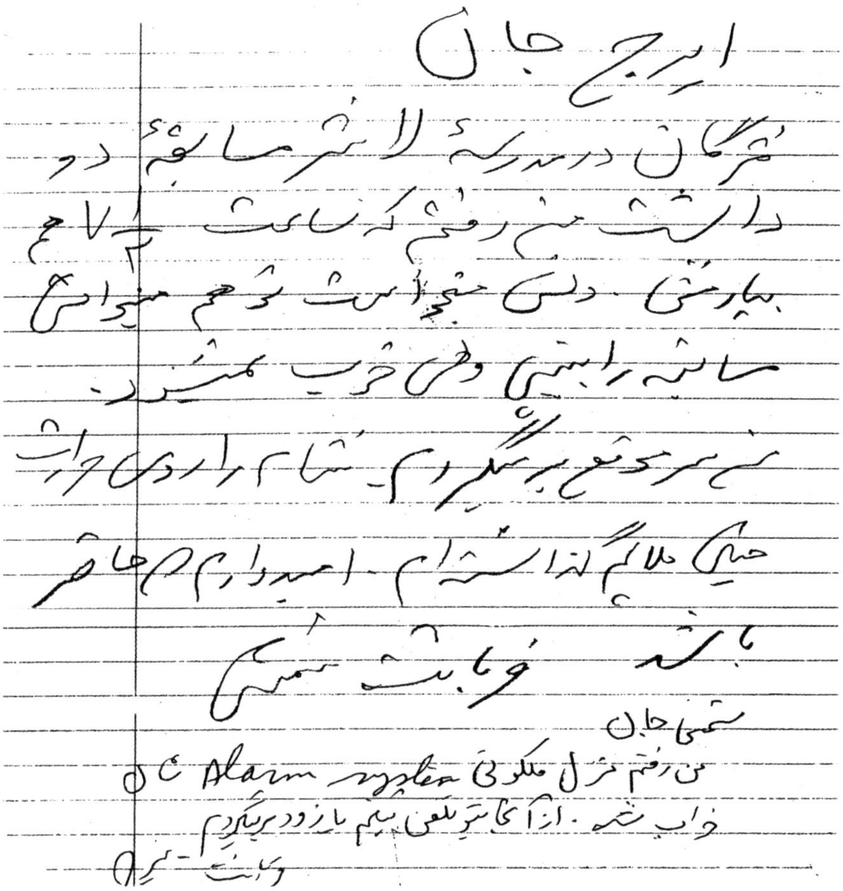
ایرج جان
مژگان در مدرسه لاشر مسابقه دو
داشت من رفتم که ساعت ۷ و ۱/۲
بیارمش.
شمسی جان
من رفتم منزل ملکوتی Alarm system شان
خراب شده. از آنجا تلفن میکنم یا زود برمیگردم

Dear Iraj:

I had left this note at home for Iraj telling him that, "I am taking Mojgan to Lahser School. She has a running race. I will be back soon. And remember, I have the food ready and warm in the oven." I signed it; "Love you Shamci."

When I came home, Iraj was not home yet. I went into the room and I found this note from him written under my note; "Dear Shamci, I have gone to Malakutis' to fix their alarm system. From there, I will call you, or I will be back soon. Love you, Iraj."

Right away, I recalled his first affair. I knew that he didn't know how to turn a switch, how could he fix her alarm system? I remembered when I was standing in my yard in Tehran, Iran. I saw Farkhondeh and Iraj were kissing, from the corner of the drapes. I died that night, when I saw them. I knew for sure this time was just like the last time. I was burning in hell. I had no one to turn to. When a mother goes through such a scene, what can she do? Do my children think that this is easy? Or do they think that I am made of stone? No, this is not it. I am a human. I have feelings, especially for a woman who is in love with her husband the way that I was. How can I control my emotions? How do I deal with this? Anyways, little things like this alarmed me and made me aware of what was going on.

shivering over my body? But I had to comfort Mojgan, and ask her to be patient. Naturally, I couldn't stand his home coming kiss to see his happy face. I was probably perceived as an ungrateful wife at the time.

My Dear God:

I am including his note in the book. He used the same piece of paper where I wrote a note for him. My note said, "Dear Iraj, I had to take Mojgan to Lasher High School. She has a running race. She wished that you could be here too, but unfortunately it is not possible. I will be back at seven thirty. I have the dinner ready on the low. I hope it is ready by then. Love, Shamci". This note was written in Farsi. So he wrote in Farsi, "Dear Shamci, I had to go to Malakutis' to fix their Alarm System. I will call you from there, or I will be back soon. Love, Iraj".

I could no longer stand up, my legs were shaking so hard. Iraj was never handy around the house. It was I who always tried fixing things. He wouldn't even know how to use a garbage disposal or the alarm system. I thought, "What a pity! He doesn't even know how to lie".

My children couldn't read Farsi. So I had to read the note to Mojgan, and I asked her to wait for him. She went back to her room, and shut the door with a slam. She called him from there. She was very angry.

He came back home in an hour or so, and we went to dinner. But he did not order anything to eat. He said, "Badri had made "sabzi polo mahi", rice with vegetables and fish. I knew what Mojgan must have been going through. I could not believe how spellbound he was by Badri. He was doing exactly the same thing he did twenty-five years ago. I can't recall my further actions; I just know that I hated the name, Red Lobster, for the rest of my life.

I started to give up all my hopes. I was getting more and more depressed. I just was hoping to die. But I kept reminding myself that my children needed me, no matter what. Being a mother is not a joke. It is a very big commitment. It was for their sake that I had to hold my head up, keep my cool, be alert, and keep my strength as a mother, who has been, and always will be the decision maker.

Thoughts of killing Iraj or myself lingered in my mind on many occasions. Many times I thought of killing Badri, or burning her home with all of them in it. Some nights I even walked out of the house to look for the way. Then one night I came down and held the Ghoran in my arms, and I sat in the corner of my kitchen. I discussed all my problems with my GOD, and my father. I asked them to help me to get out of this safely. I begged my father for forgiveness. I knew that if I committed suicide, my children would be never in peace. I knew that it would kill their souls, and destroy them.

My Dear God:

I took up all my responsibilities in the daytime, and at nights I thought of what I should do not to ruin my children's future. I knew that my children had only one mother and only one father. And even though their father was acting crazy, killing him would not end my problems. While they would loose their father, they would have a killer for a mother. And while that was worse than committing suicide, I didn't want to teach my children how to be cowards at the time of crisis by killing myself. All these, and many other thoughts were in my mind throughout the night. Then by morning time I was able to see things more clearly, and I was able to make the right decision for that day. Every night I asked GOD to show me how to walk, while my legs were broken. Many nights I woke up with Ghoran in my arms at the corner of the poolroom trying to destroy myself. I would then run back to my bedroom, and sleep till the next morning to continue my life.

Iraj was the only person that I loved dearly all my life. He was the only one I trusted with all my problems. He was the one I turned to when something was bothering me. Now that I had lost him, whom should I turn to?

I was always very close with my sister Ezzat. We shared the most important and personal secrets that we would never reveal to anyone else. She was the sister that I missed the most when we first moved to USA. I used to cry for her for months. I wanted to go back home. I wrote to Ezzat every day asking for her advice. When she realized that I am thinking of returning back to Iran, she wrote me a very powerful letter. That letter put me in my place, and cured my homesickness.

This was her letter, "You have been, and you still are in love with Iraj in such way that you were ready to join him in hell. But he took you to haven. America is considered the best place on earth. So, please, enough is enough. Open your eyes and see what you are asking. Forget about coming home, and start enjoying your life next to Iraj. That was your only dream. Do not allow your mind to go wrong. Do not make life hard on Iraj. Be with him, and come home when the time comes. And I do not want to hear from you again that you want to return to Iran. Please get it out of your mind".

This letter was like water on fire. I knew that I had no home to go to. My parents had disowned me, and I had to stay with my sisters-in-law for one whole year before I joined Iraj in USA. So I started thinking after that letter, and I started adapting to my new life.

So now, after twenty-five years, embarrassed and humiliated, I had to write to her, and tell her all about my life. I didn't know how to start my letter. I didn't know how she would react to my problem at this time of my life. I knew it would take at least one week for the letter to get to Iran, and then another week for her answer to come back to me. That was, if she wrote back to me right a way. But I decided to write to her anyway, and asked her to help me.

My Dear God:

My first letter was so sad and hopeless that seemed to her that I was suicidal. That letter helped me tremendously. Letter after letter, she gave me hope for being able to deal with it. And we kept writing to each other once, or twice a week. I received letters from her almost every other day.

I also talked to Pari, who was my best friend for more than thirty years. She shocked me with her reply, "He must have his reasons for not loving you any longer". Such comment from Pari, whom I have always considered a close friend, destroyed me. I couldn't believe it. Then, when I looked back, I started remembering Pari's strange comments about her sisters Parveen and Niya.

I wrote about Pari and her attitude towards my problems and me in one of my letters to Ezzat. And I wrote to her about her attitude towards her sisters. And was telling her, "I don't know why Pari, who was always my best friend, had turned her back on me at the time that I needed her the most".

Ezzat, being worried about my well-being, wrote back to me trying to calm me down. She wanted to make sure that I come to an understanding, and not act irrationally and foolishly to do something to myself. In her letter to me, she made sure that her words influence me effectively. And I heard her.

While she was talking about life in general, she said, "Many things in life are unavoidable. When circumstances arise beyond our control, we have no choice but to recognize them intelligently, and try to face them patiently with complete understanding. The difference between a smart, intelligent person and, not so intelligent person is just a little wall of understanding". Then she talked to me about Iraj and his personality. She talked about our childhood. She talked about our parents, their morality, and their faithfulness in their parenthood. And then she talked about Pari and her character. She wrote a lot about Pari and her behavior in the past. And then she said, "You know Pari better than all of us and talked about her reaction towards the kindness of her sister and many more."

My Dear God:

Her sisters obviously must be more important to her than you are. You are not any dearer to her than those sisters. Please think about it. Especially now that you have a very comfortable life, even much more than she has. True that she is your best friend, and you love her a lot, but this does not mean that she had to feel the same way about you.

You must pay attention to neither her good side nor the bad side. Just try to discover her more and more. And do not get emotional about her friendship". The significance of that letter was equal of Ghoran's. I kept it in the book I was reading. I would reread it at least once a day.

I kept in touch with Pari, and I continued our friendship as it always has been. I

چهارشنبه ۲۰/۱۲/۶۵

شمسی جان، سلام. روی زیبایت را از دور میبوسم. با آرزوی اینکه از سلامت کامل و روحیهٔ بسیار بالائی
برخوردار باشی. و مثل گذشته همهٔ سختیهای زندگی را آنچنان بسازی بگذری که در پیش قدرت تو بسیار ضعیف و کوچک
بنمایند. نامهٔ بسیار مهرآمیزت چند روز پیش بدستم رسیده. منهم همزمان با رسیدن نامهٔ تو، نامهٔ خودم را برایت پست کرده‌ام
با امید اینکه تا حال بدستت رسیده باشد. و اینک در ساعت حدود ۸/۵ صبح چهارشنبه ۲۰ اسفندماه است. فرصت مناسبی است
تا با زیبای باهم گپی بزنیم و جواب نامه‌ات را بنویسم. خیلی متأسفم از اینکه در این چند روز موفق به نوشتن جواب نشده‌ام. همهٔ مشغله‌
فکری زیاد و ناراحت کننده، و هم کارهای بدنی فوق العاده که در این سن و سال و وضع نامساعد روحی در قدرت من نیست، مانع
از اینست که هر کاری را درست و بموقع انجام دهم. در هر صورت مرا از بابت این تأخیر معذور بدار. هرچند که این روزها
نامه‌های بیشتری نسبت به گذشته برایت میدهم، ولی تمایل زیاد دارم که خیلی بیش از این بتوانم با تو گفتگوئی داشته باشم.

از اینکه نامه‌های من میتوانند در بالا نگهداشتن روحیهٔ تو تأثیر مثبتی داشته، و ترا به پیش بردن و ادامهٔ زندگی بهتر،
بهتر ملزم سازند بسیار خوشحالم. این سعادت بزرگی است اگر من بتوانم تا این حد در تو گرمی و وسائل لذت و رفاه فکری
و در همان آرام تو را فراهم کنم. اما به اینکه این من هستم که ترا زنده نگه میدارم، خود تو هستی که با تلاش و کوشش بی مانند سعی بر فائق
آمدن بر مشکلات نموده و راه صحیح و درست ادامهٔ زندگی را هم خودت هموار میسازی. من فقط در این راه همراه و همقدم با تو
و همبستگی تو بوده و هستم، و تا هستم و جان در بدن دارم هرگز نباید احساس تنهائی بر تو غلبه کند. علاوه من مطمئن هستم که روز
دیدار ما، هرچند کمی دیر ولی بالاخره فراهم خواهد شد، و آن روز ما میتوانیم اوقات و زمان زیادی را در کنار هم زیسته و باهم سر کنیم
و سرشار از لذت و ذوق دیدار یکدیگر به باز زندگی ادامه دهیم.

از اینکه بچه‌ها را همواره مورد محبت قرار داده، و رابطهٔ تنگاتنگ خود را با آنها حفظ میکنی بسیار خوشحال و بخصوص از تو
ممنونم. البته آنها در انتخاب راه زندگی همیشه مستقل و آزاد بوده، و هیچ محدودیتی از جانب من نداشته‌اند. و این خود باعث
مشوق باید بتوانند به خواسته‌ها و اهداف خود نزدیک شده و برای آنها جامهٔ عمل بپوشانند. هرچند که راه آنها متفاوت با دیگران
باشد. مهم اینست که جهت آنها سالم بوده و از زندگی واقعی و سعادت دلخواه برخوردار باشند. سعادت و لذت واقعی
زندگی تنها در ادامهٔ تحصیل و انباشت ثروت و سرمایه بدست نمیآید. باید دید هر کس چه دیدی نسبت به زندگی دارد.

از من و خودت بگذرم اصلاً زندگی را نشناخته‌ایم، و در راه انتخابی ما کاملاً به بیراهه منتهی شد! خیال نکن اگر این زندگی را در سایهٔ تحصیل و کسب مدرک بدست آورده! (هرچند همین خوشی و سعادت هم غیرواقعی و تظاهر است!) او باید سوء و پلید خود، و با تکیه بر محبتها و ارزشهای والای انسانی تو به چنین موقعیتی دست یافته! و حال هم دیگر خود را محتاج تو نمی‌یابد و چنین بی پروا و وقیحانه رفتاری غیرانسانی با تو در پیش گرفته و آن ارزشها را نادیده گرفته و حتی میتوان گفت کمترین آگاهی و شناختی از آنها ندارد! اگر افراد بوئی از انسانیت و شرف و خصائل والای انسانی برده باشند هرگز تا این حد دچار پستی و انحطاط اخلاقی نمیشوند! مرا ببخش که اینگونه سخن میگویم. وقتی دنائت و پستی در خون کسی ریشه دواند با هیچ شخصیت ظاهری مالی و تحصیلات کلاسیک و مدرکهای رنگارنگ قابل پاک شدن نیست! مهمتر از همه اینکه طبیعت انسان از لحاظ غرائز جنسی، و روابط عشقی و شهوانی و غیره و غیره، از بدو خلقت انسان، اگر تعمق کرده باشی، همیشه باین شکل بوده و هرگز نتوانسته قابل کنترل، و قرارداد باشد. افرادی مثل من و تو فقط خود را فریب میدهیم، و باعث پایمال شدن حقوق طبیعی و مسلم خود میشویم. در اینجا لازم به ذکر مطلبی است که هر انسانی در هر حال مطابق طبیعت خود عمل نموده و بدون توجه به اجتماع و محیط اطراف خود هرطور که مایل باشد زندگی و رفتار میکند. و تو نیز جز مطابق طبیعت و تربیت خود عمل نخواهی کرد و از جادهٔ خود منحرف نمیشوی. بنابراین هرگز نخواهی توانست آنطور که ایرج عمل کرده، خالی از ذره‌ای احساس و عاطفه! عمل کنی. و با توجه باینکه ایرج شناخت بسیار از روحیات و رفتار تو دارد، اگر روزی هزاران بار بگوئی که از این ببعد چنین عمل خواهی کرد و در راه او قدم خواهی گذاشت، نه تنها از تو باور نخواهد کرد، که همین گفته تو را بعنوان وسیله‌ای برای کوبیدن و خراب کردن تو بکار خواهد برد! که آنوقت مشتی آشی نخورده، و دهن سوخته!! بنابراین از من بشنو و دیگر هرگز چنین سخنانی بر زبان نیاور. مثل ایرج باید کار خود را کرد، و در انتظار لباس تقوی پوشید! و قیافه‌ای حق بجانب و منزه از آلودگیها بخود گرفت! برو برای خودت زندگی کن و از آن هرطور که شایسته است کام در فرصت مغتنم لذت ببر. لذتی که ضمن اینکه زندگی تو را پر میکند، احترام و حیثیت تو را نیز حفظ خواهد کرد. در هر حال شمسی جان، سخن در این مقوله بسیار است و قلم ناتوان. بامید اینکه فرزندان من نیز در زندگی راه و روش را پیش گیرند تا سرنوشت آنها موافق و مساعد با آمالشان باشد. درست است که باید بتقدیر و سرنوشت عقیده داشت، ولی باید دانست سرنوشت خود را در محدودهٔ اختیار خود، خود رقم میزنیم. پس اول باید خود و زندگی را بشناسیم.

و اما شمسی جان، از احوال ما بخواهی، بحمدالله همگی تا این لحظه سالم هستیم، اما روزگار را بسی سخت میگذرانیم! از خبرهای تازه اینکه، با احتمال ۹۹٪ پس فردا جمعه احسان هم ایران را بقصد دیاری دیگر ترک خواهد کرد! البته او بهمراه آقا کمال شیرازی خواهد بود، و اولین مقصدشان آلمان است، و ساعت یک بعد از نیمه شب پنجشنبه برای مشایعت آنها بفرودگاه خواهیم رفت. چه بهتر برای تو! همه پر و پاپیش ها دور و برت جمع میشوند و دیگر فرصت سر خاراندن هم نداری! در هر حال در نامه های بعدی ترا در جریان کلیه اخبار و رویدادهای خانوادگی و فامیلی قرار خواهم داد. بیش از ۹ روز دیگر به عید باقی نمانده.

همانطوریکه در نامه قبلی نوشتم درباره دوره های خانوادگی برقرار شده و هر پانزده روز یکبار همگی با هم در خانه یکی از اهالی جمع میشویم و ترا نیز با یادت و صحبت است در جمع خود داریم. البته داداش جان هنوز وارد گود نشده! ولی بالاخره او هم ناگزیر خواهد شد و خواهد آمد! منتظر خبرش باش.

راجع به جریان پول و ارتباط با آذر، همانطور که از قبل خودم گفته بودم هیچ مسئله ای نبود و با صلح و صفا با هم کنار آمدیم. در حال حاضر در مورد پولهائی که نزد هر یک از ما داری، خودمان شخصاً طرف حساب تو خواهیم بود، و آذر دیگر هیچ دخالتی ندارد. و تو از این بابت خیالت کاملاً راحت باشد.

و اما در مورد اوضاع خودم و ارتباط با افراد، خواهر جان درست است که مشکل گرفتاریهای من با تو متفاوت است، و در حال حاضر مراد ظاهراً از طرف من آمده و از کرده های خود پشیمان است! اما در وضعیت فعلی این چه مشکلی از صدها مشکل مرا حل میکند؟ نمیتوانم بلاهائی را هم هر روز در شکل تازه ای بدنبال عملکردهای آنان شست خود بر سرم نازل میکنند برایت تصور کنم! نمیدانم بالاخره روزی از این وضعیت خلاص خواهم شد؟ من فکر میکنم اگر زن بخواهد در زندگی زناشوئی شکل مثبتی در تو ضربه نخورد باید تسلیم روابط اجتماعی «مردسالاری» شود. البته مردی که حد و مرز و مدبر و مسئول باشد، نه هر کسی صورت داند و هم داشت! دل از یک بچه متعصب افتاده دست و پا چلفتی تر است! اگر در اینجا من با او نسازم و خرابکاریهایش را ماست مالی و رفع و رجوع نکنم! خدا میداند که چه بدتر از اینها بر سر من خواهد آمد! در هر حال این سرنوشت است که طبق گفته خودم، برای خودم رقم زده ام و در حال حاضر گریزی از آن نیست! اما برای اینکه خبر خوشی هم برایت داشته باشم، خوب است بدانی که با احتمال زیاد، دگوش شیطان کر! و اینبار اگر مانع تازه ای بر سر راهمان ایجاد نکنند، ظرف همین چند روزه قبل از عید بسند مالکیت ساختمان شهرک

هم هنوز تمام نشده، تمامی اش انتقال داده خواهد شد، ولی از بزرگترین موانع بر سر پیشرفت کارها از میان برداشته خواهد شد. می بینی هم من با همهٔ اینها هم غرق در گرفتاریها و مشکلات بزرگ هستم، چگونه روحیهٔ خود را حفظ کرده و امیدم را از دست نمیدهم؟! تنها همین نیروی نهانی است هم مرا نگه میدارد و نمیگذارد یکباره از پای درآیم! تو نیز هم از این نیروی نهانی بخوبی برخورداری، مثل من به بهترین اوضاع، به هر شکل هم تو را از این وضعیت و تنهائی بیرون کشد امیدوار باش. موفقیت با تو خواهد آمد. اگر ایرج در مورد فروش منزل و پول و وسائل و غیره هم، هر کاری میکند، تو بی تفاوت باش و واکنشی از خودت نشان نده. تو فقط مثل یک فرزند کار به هیچکار نداشته باش و رفع نیاز مادی خودت را با استفاده از هر موقعیتی بکن. مواظب باش هرگز او را عصبانی نکنی تا تصمیم بگیرد حق از تو ضایع کند. او یک غیر انسان لجباز و یکدنده است! فقط باید مواظب باشی و با سیاست حقوق حقهٔ خودت را هم در دست او دست حفظ نمائی. خیلی حواست جمع باشد. مبادا یک وقت بی گدار به آب بزنی. دیگر سفارش نمیکنم، چون میدانم تو عاقلتر از آن هستی هم بگذاری کارها خراب شود.

خوب شمسی جان، گفتم هم چند روز بیشتر به عید نمانده. رسیدن بهار دل انگیز و شروع این فصل آغازگر را از صمیم قلب به تو تبریک میگویم، و از تو میخواهم حتی در شرایط ناخوشایند، همواره لبخند بر لب داشته، و خود را خوشحال و سرزنده نگه داری، تا کور شود چشم آنهائی که برای تو دام نهاده اند. مطمئن باش در اعماق وجود آنها آتش حقد و حسد همیشه شعله ور خواهد بود، و بالاخره آنها را از پای درخواهد آورد. با قبول اینکه تمام این اعمال در روابط طبیعی و غریزی انسانهاست آرامش را بر مکر و حیله حقوقت مسلط کن. انسانها تنها میمانند، و هر روز بر تعدادشان افزوده میشود. دیشب به دلیل یکی از بیماریها درد جانب ادرار سراغم نازل شد، ساعتی بیدار هم تا صبح راه رفتم و آن درد به پهلوهایم عوض کرد و آزارم داد. هیچ احدی نفهمید هم من تا صبح چه کشیدم و در چه تنهائی کشنده ای بسر بردم؟! پس تنهائی چه در جمع و چه غیر از آن، هیچ فرقی نمیکند. تو هم اگر از محدودهٔ خود بیرون آئی و ارتباطاتت را با مردم بیشتر و بیشتر کنی، قطعاً یاران موافق و همفکر خود را پیدا خواهی کرد و لااقل در حد من قرار خواهی گرفت، منهای مسائل و گرفتاریهای کلی ما. دیگر وقت آن است هم نامه را به پایان برسانم و تا نامهٔ بعدی با تو خداحافظی کنم. رویت را از دور هزاران بار میبوسم و آرزوی بهروزی و شادی و شادکامی برایت دارم.

قربانت عزت

یکشنبه ۱۶/۱/۶۶

شمسی جان، خواهر بسیار عزیز و گرامیم، سلام. روی ماهت را از دور میبوسم و آرزوی سلامتی و موفقیت ات را دارم. نامه بسیار محبت آمیزت دیروز رسید. امروز یکشنبه ۱۶ فروردین است، و ساعت نزدیک به یک بعد از ظهر. یک ساعت و نیم دیگر بقصد تماس گرفتن با آقای ... به مناسبتی آقای شمیم ... به تلفنخانه بروم. بنابراین این فاصله را به گفتگو با تو اختصاص میدهم.

قبل از هر چیز باید بگویم که اینبار نامه ات بیش از همیشه مرا متأسف و نگران کرد! من انتظار نداشتم تا این نامه های عریض و طویل که برایت مینویسم، بجای ... بر واقعیت زندگی ... و بیش از هر زمان دیگر وسایل خوشی و بهتر زیستن را برای خودت فراهم کنی. در حالیکه نامه هایت چیزی غیر از این را بمن میگویند! آخر عزیز دلم چرا اینچنین با حسرت رفتار میکنی؟ و از امکاناتی که در اختیار داری استفاده لازم را نمیکنی؟ مگر دنیا را چند بار به انسان میدهند! فکر میکنی فقط تو یکنفر توی این دنیا تنها و بیکس مانده ای؟ پروین رفعتی چند سال است که تنهائی زندگی میکند؟ سعیده از چه سنی و چه مدت است که ناگزیر به تنهائی و زندگی فردی تسلیم شده و با این حقیقت رسیده که بعد از دوران شوهرداری خرابه تر است و وسایل خوشی و راحتی معقول و سالمی را برای خود فراهم آورده؟ هزاران نفر تنهای دیگر هستند که راه تنها زیستن و بهتر زیستن را پیدا کنند. پس تو چرا اینکار را نمیکنی؟ مگر چه از دیگران کم داری؟ مگر فقط شوهر، و یا یک مرد است که به زن زندگی میبخشد؟! نه عزیز من، نه جان من اتفاقاً این مرد است که هیچگاه قادر نیست بدون زن زندگی خود را به پیش ببرد! در مورد تو، آنچه از همه مهمتر و قابل تعمق است، اینست که، تو او را از اول هم اصلاً نداشتی! و در تمام طول زندگی مشترکتان او فقط توانسته ترا فریب داده! و از خصائل انسانی و محبت و صمیمیت تو بیشترین سوء استفاده را کرده و حالا هم دیگر به ادامه آن بازی نیازی ندارد و یکباره دست از تو و زندگی گذشته اش کشیده، و ماهیت پلید و فریبکارانه خودش را هویدا ساخته! اشکال اینست که نمیخواهی این واقعیت را بپذیری، که او از اول هم همه اش فقط بخودش ... بوده و نه به هیچکس دیگر! اگر قبول کنی که تمام سالهائی را که ظاهراً با ایرج و در کنار او گذرانده ای، همه یک دروغ بوده، و تو هیچوقت او را حقیقتاً در کنار خود نداشته، و همیشه در تنهائی مطلق زندگی کرده ای! پذیرفتن تنهائی امروزت، و ادامه هر چه بهتر زندگی، برایت بسیار سهل و آسان خواهد شد. فرق تنهائی امروز تو با تنهائی دیروزت اینست که تو آنموقع از وضع خود غافل بودی! ولی امروز بر آن واقف شده ای! شمسی جان تنها راه خلاصی تو از این کابوس اینست که دیگر سعی بر فریب خودت نکنی، و این واقعیت را که ایرج هیچوقت برای تو نبوده و نخواهد بود را بپذیری

منیژه، و هیچوقت همراه خود در کوله رخت منیژه نیندازی، و با بیرون راندن او از فکر و زندگی خود برای همیشه، راه تازه زندگی کردن
در این سالهای زندگی را بر خودت هموار سازی. مشکل حالا میدانی هم در کنار مسائل و گرفتاریهای خودم، لحظه‌ای از فکر و نگرانی تو بیرون
نمیروم، و شبانه‌روز با خود میگویم چه کاری از من ساخته است! اگر در کنارت بودم دستت را میگرفتم و بزور میکشیدم! اما از این همه فاصله
چه میتوانم بکنم! خودت هم در غربت کمکی نمیکنی! تا نامه را میخوانی و هنوز حرفهایم در گوشت صدا میکند خوبی. یکی دو روز از آن گذشت
دوباره فراموش کرده و باز به لاک خودت فرو میروی! ترا به جان فرزندانت بچه‌ها و حال غمخواهی که آنها در این میان ناراحت شده‌اند
از زمانی که به کالیفرنیا میروید زندگی جدیدی را برای خودت شروع کنی، و اسم و فکر و خاطرات ایرج را بکلی از خودت بیرون کنی.
در کالیفرنیا دیگر وضع بی‌پولی اینجا نیست. هم دور و برت جای شلوغ است، و پر است از ایرانی. مگر نه اگر شغل پیدا کنی دوستان
تنهائیت را چگونه پر میکنی، پس همه بیکار را در آغوش بکش. مطمئن باش هر مردمی ... هرگز دشمنی را هم چنین خشونتهائی
در حق زنانشان نمیکنند. در حق آنها نخواهند کرد. لااقل اگر دوست نباشند، دشمن هم نخواهند بود. و مهمتر اینکه برای تو میتوان از آنها
کناره گرفت و به دیگری پیوست. لااقل بعد از عمری فریب خوردن و خون با جگر، تا این حد تجربه بدست آورده‌ام دیگر مثل ایام شباب
و جوانی مسطور چشم و گوش بسته خود را در دام فرصت‌طلبان و فریبکاران نیندازیم! خلاصه خواهر خوب و نازنینم هر لحظه از فکر
تو و مسائل تو بیرون نمیروم و دائماً بدنبال راه حلی برای خلاصی تو از این وضع هستم، نمیدانی چقدر سخت است که دوستی با
خواهرانم از تو یاد میکنیم که هر روز بعضی از روز و پیش، من باید راجع به آنچه از وضع تو شنیده‌ام مهر سکوت بر لب زده و همانند آنها راجع
به تو سخن نگویم! و یا احیاناً با وانمود کردن به بی‌خبری از تو به سکوت و بی‌تفاوتی برگزار کنم! در هر حال هیچ راهی به نظر من نمیرسد جز
آنکه واقعیتی را که گفتم بپذیری و همچون زنان تنهای دیگر دنیا به زندگی خودت ادامه دهی. فقط این خودت هستی که مسئله را برای
خودت بزرگ کرده‌ای! و من فکر میکنم علتش اینست که برخلاف آنچه درباره‌اش میگوئی هنوز تا اندازه‌ای مهر ایرج را از دلت بیرون نکرده‌ای!
البته این در مورد کسی که متقابلاً مورد مهر قرار گرفته باشد جای تعجب نیست. اما در مورد تو به خاطر اینکه بیش از مهر و محبت نرجه و معنی و مفهوم
آن را نمیدانی و فقط دیوانه شهرت و شهوت است، و حقیقتاً روا نیست؟ حال خود دانی و آنچه باید بکنی. این در حال حاضر
تنها کاریست که از دست من بر میآید. بقول معروف «من آنچه شرط بلاغ است با تو میگویم» در این نامه بیش از این فکرم کار نمیکند!

و اما امروز از افسانه نامه‌ای داشتم که معلوم شد که بزودی به سراغش خواهی رفت. خیلی از این بابت خوشحالم. چرا که واقعاً
بسیار فرصت مناسبی است. سعید و هم را درس اش را تمام کند ... تهران ... چقدر به شما خوش خواهد گذشت. جای من خالیست
تمام غمم کارهای من تا آخر ماه درست نمیشود. خدا کند قبل از آنکه ویزا از آمریکا بیاید برسد کارها رو براه شود و من بتوانم چند روزی نزد تو

بیائیم. فعلاً چون وقت رفتن شده با تو خداحافظی میکنم، و ادامهٔ نامه را به فرصت بعدی موکول میکنم.

خوب شمسی جان مجدداً سلام. الآن ساعت ۱۱ صبح پنجشنبه است. حال به ادامهٔ نامه میپردازم. از اوضاع ایران در حال حاضر کم و بیش اطلاع داری. جای کمی خوشحالی و آرامش خاطر است که از حدود یکماهی قبل از عید تا بحال از طرف جباران خبری نبوده و مردم ایام عید را در آرامش نسبی گذراندند. اما مسائل دیگر نه تنها کاهش پیدا نکرده بلکه روز بروز دست و پاگیرتر و نگران کننده‌تر شده‌اند. اگر خدا به این ملت بدبخت رحم نکند، معلوم نیست عاقبت کارشان بکجا خواهد کشید! از اوضاع خودمان و کار ساختمان و غیره و غیره، گوش شیطان کر! اینطور که از قرائن پیدا است، امکان دارد تا پایان فروردین موفق بگرفتن وام از یکی از بانکها شده و مجدداً کار ساختمان را شروع کنیم و کار را بیک جائی برسانیم. ضمناً انتقال سند هم تمام شد قبل از عید انجام شد و حالا دیگر از این بابت هم خیالمان راحت است که خانه بنام خودمان است. اگر بدنبال اینها مشکل مالی مان هم تا حدی رفع شود دیگر برای یک ماه مدتی میتوانم نفسی براحتی بکشم و از آنهمه غم و غصه و نگرانی تا اندازه‌ای خلاص شوم. در مورد خانهٔ کرج هنوز موفق به پرداخت آن باج نشده‌ام تا بتوانم آن اراذل را از خانه بیرون بیندازم! خودت میتوانی تصورش را بکنی که این باج چقدر برای ما تمام میشود! خوب از اینهم بگذریم.

در مورد روابط خواهرها و برادرها، در نامهٔ قبل شرح تجدید روابط و برقراری مجدد آنها را داده‌ام. و اینک حامل خبر تازه‌ای هستم، و آن اینکه برادر بزرگ هم بالاخره تصمیم گرفت بجمع بپیوندد! پنجشنبه شب همین هفته یعنی سه روز دیگر قرار اولین دیدارمان در خانهٔ سعیده گذاشته شده. شرح دیدارمان را در نامهٔ بعدی برایت خواهم داد. باین ترتیب میتوانم بگویم که عید امسال برای ما خوب بود و عیدی بسیار خوب و جالبی دریافت کردیم که البته تو نیز در این موارد از ما جدا نیستی و در میان ما و در کنار خودمان قرار داری. فقط دیدارهای ما با تو در کشورهای دیگر میسر خواهد شد که اینهم خود لطف دیگری دارد. از اوضاع سینا خبر داری که احسان را هم فرستاد و الآن او هم در بلژیک با بچه‌ها زندگی میکند. آقای شیرازی هم مدت ۱۵ روز با آنها بوده و ما خیلی خوشحالیم که این کارها هم هر چند برای همه بسیار سخت بود، ولی بخیر و خوشی انجام شد. بعید نیست که اگر وسائلی فراهم شود، سینا هم بزودی به علی و احسان بپیوندد که در اینصورت تو خیلی راحت خواهی توانست با او دیدار کنی. من شروع خوب این سال را بفال نیک میگیرم و برای تو و همهٔ ما، همین امیدواری میتواند ما را در جهت دستیابی به خواسته‌هایمان رهبری کند. از تو میخواهم که تو هم مثل من این امید را در خودت تقویت

کنی تا بتوانی در جهت موفقیت کارهای خودت را پیش ببری. امید زیادی دارم هر نامه بعدی‌ات برای من بسیار خوشحال کننده و امیدوار کننده باشد. فقط باید این فکر را در خودت تقویت کنی که از اول هم ایرج را نداشته‌ای، و تمام این سالها را در تنهائی مطلق گذرانده تا آنجا که او همیشه مورد حمایت و پشتیبانی تو بوده. بنابراین تحمل تنهائی امروز برایت خیلی سهلتر خواهد بود. با این معنی که زندگی فعلی‌ات خیلی بهتر از گذشته باید باشد. در اینجا من یک سفارش مهم را بتو ضروری میدانم. و آن اینکه از لحاظ مالی خودت را حسابی بپائی و هر زمان هر مبلغ که میتوانی برای خودت کنار بگذاری. ضمناً رفتارت باید طوری باشد که او هرگز فرصت نکند از لحاظ مالی ترا در مضیقه قرار داده و کمترین حق از تو را پایمال کند. مطمئن باش که اگر اینکار را با دقت خاصی بکنی، دیگر از هیچ لحاظ مشکل و مسئله‌ای نخواهی داشت. زندگی برای تو خوب خواهد شد. یک زندگی جدا از دشمن و فرو رفتن بین مردم و اجتماع. یادت نرود.. من این را از تو میخواهم..

خوب دیگر وقت آن رسیده که نامه را بپایان برسانم، و سری به آشپزخانه بزنم تا برای ظهر ناهاری درست کنم. البته در تنهائی. چون مراد برنامه مشخصی ندارد و اگر هم دارد دیر وقت دنبال کارهاست. فقط شبها یک شام را حتماً با هم میخوریم. که نه همدلیم و نه همزبان. جبر زمانه ما را در کنار هم قرار داده! و ناچار به تحملش هستیم! و این نیز بخاطر فرزندانمان هست. تنها رشته‌ای که ما را بهم وصل میکند! همین و همین!

از کارهائی که در دست انجام دارید، و تغییر محل سکونت و آدرس جدید و شماره تلفن جدید، همه چیز برایم بنویس. کاری که ایرج قصد دارد بان دست بزند خیلی درآمد دارد، یعنی خیلی بیشتر از گذشته. پس مراقب باش که سهم خودت را از چنگش بیرون بکشی. هر چه بدست آورده از همت و گذشت تو در سالهائی که گذشت بوده است. مواظب خودت باش. منتظر خبرهای خوش از جانب تو هستم. بچه‌ها، مریم و مسیح و بزرگان عزیز را با تجدید زیاد ببوس و سعی کن آنها را با خودت موافق کنی و حتی الامکان برنامه‌هائی، البته در صورت تمایل خودشان، با آنها ترتیب دهی. فقط بایستی تلاش کنی که لحظه‌ها خوش بگذرد. بقیه دیگر هیچ است. روی مهربان و زیبایت را از اینجا میبوسم. با امید اینکه شرایطی پیش آید تا تو بتوانی سفری به ایران بیائی. و با امید اینکه روزی باز همه خانواده از کوچک و بزرگ دور یکی با هم جمع شویم و از گذشته‌ها یاد کنیم. همیشه و در هر حال بیادت هستم و هیچگاه از تو جدا نخواهم بود.

راستی یادم رفت بگویم، مبادا یک روز تو برای طلاق پیش قدم شوی، هر که این پیشنهاد را داد   با محبت زیاد - قربانت عزیزت

[illegible] نیست و داشته، تو فقط باید زندگی خودت را بدون طلاق از ایرج جدا کنی و اصلاً کاری بکارش نداشته باشی. بگذار اگر میخواهد خودش پیش قدم شود.

شنبه ۵ر۲ر۹۶ بازهم عیدت مبارک

خواهر بسیار عزیز و گرامیم، شمسی جان،

سلام. امیدوارم حالت خوب باشد، و که زیاد مسائل و مشکلات را پشت سر گذاشته باشی. پس روز پیش نامهٔ عزیز و مهرآمیزت رسید. امروز هم پنجم اردیبهشت ماه است، و از مشغله و گرفتاریها تا حدی خلاص شده‌ام، نشسته‌ام تا باز گفتگوئی با هم داشته باشیم. شب جمعهٔ پریشب باز برای اولین بار کلیهٔ خواهران و برادرها در خانهٔ داداش با هم جمع شدیم. ترمه از همان اول در جمع ما بود و ترتیب بازیها را میگیریم. حقیقتاً شب بسیار خوشی بر ما گذشت. موسیقی‌های اصیل را شنیدیم و با هم حالی کردیم. قصد این بود هم شب را همانجا بخوابیم و صبح دیگ آش را برداریم و به دشت و صحرا رویم. ولی چون ستیده شرکت داشت، و آذر هم بایستی به اداره میرفت! (این‌ها تا اغلب روزهای جمعه را هم بایستی کار کنند!) این بود هم برنامهٔ شب بهم خورد و برنامهٔ صحرا و صبح، و بدون آش اجرا کردیم. البته جواد و زری هم نیامدند چون منزل تقی‌زاده بودند. در هر صورت بعد از ظهر شنبه به تهران مراجعت کردیم و تا حدود دو ساعت و شب باز با هم بودیم، و بعد از آن هرکس به خانهٔ خود رفت. و حالا تو نمیتوانی از این برنامه‌ها با عزیزان هم از ما جدا شده و با تو بسیار نزدیکترند ترتیب داده تا از این لحاظ احساس کمبود نداشته باشی همچنانکه گاهگاه سراغ واقا به ما رفته و میروی، حالا دیگر نگین و علی و احسان هم هستند. خلاصه دیگر جای آن ندارد که از دوری ما بیش از حد اظهار تأسف و دلتنگی کنی. چون دیگر همه دارند نزدیک میشوند. اما از بابت مسئلهٔ خودت با ایرج، همانطور هم در بهار نامه‌ها گفته و باز هم میگویم، این هم مسئله از نسبت هم خاص تو نبوده و تو تنها زنی نباشی که شوهرت با تو قهر کرده و به دیگری پیوسته باشد. این موضوع حتی مبتلا به ... درصد زنهاست، و مسئلهٔ جدیدی هم و تازه‌ای نیست. این خود تو هستی که مسئله را آنقدر بزرگ می‌بینی، و زندگی را چه عبث بر خودت سخت میگیری! اگر بجای آن زنانی بودی که شوهرانشان هم سنخیتی با آنها نیست که با هم معشوقه خانگی میآورند و زن خود را رنجه میکنند و همکارانه‌ها و هم از لحاظ مالی آنها را از رفاه و رشد به قرار میدهند تا آنکه هم لقمه نانی را از آنها دریغ میکنند! و خیلی بلاهای دیگر! آنوقت چه میکردی؟ تو الان در خانهٔ خودت پول داری، رفاه داری، اختیار هر نوع رابطه و هر کاری را داری هر معاشرتی داشته باشی، هر خرجی داری، به هر صورت ولی هیچکس نیست مانع و مزاحم تو شود. تنها چیزی هم بنظر من، تو در حال حاضر نداری یک شریک زندگی با اسم شوهر است؟ هم این را در حال حاضر بیشتر زنها ندارند؟ پس چرا تو نمی

مثل آنها زندگی خسروت را نمی‌سازی؟ چرا اینقدر عرصه را بر خسروت تنگ می‌کنی؟ اصلاً مگر چه اتفاق افتضاحی برای تو در افتاده، که اینگونه خسروت را با فاجعه‌ای تا آنجا که بعضی اوقات با کمال تأسف اسم خودکشی و اینجور چیزها را بر زبان می‌آوردی! تو نباید کاری کنی که دشمنانت را خوشحال سازی. تو در حضور آنها هرگز نباید قیافه مغلوب و منهزم بخسروت بگیری. تو باید طوری رفتار کنی که آنها را به اندازه پشیزی هم بحساب نیاوری و بر ضعف و زبونی شان تأسف بخوری. شخصیت والا و قدرت و توان خسروت را در هر کاری به رخ آنها بکش و آنها را خیلی دست کم بگیر. مبادا هم از ترس اینکه مورد سرزنش و تمسخر آنها قرار بگیری با آنها ترک معاشرت کنی، بلکه بعلت ضعف شخصیت و حقارت و پستی شان ترکشان کن. این را به آنها نشان بده. آنها فقط هم جوجه تازه به دوران رسیده‌ها و اصل خود گم کرده‌ها هستند و لیاقت پول و مقام ندارند. لایق محبت و احترام نیستند. لایق دوستی و همنشینی با تو نیستند. خلاصه تو خیلی بالاتر از آنی که بخواهی در مقابل این کثافتها، شخص ضعف از خسروت نشان دهی! نمیدانم چقدر از این حرفها باید بزنم تا در تو اثر کند؟ و بشنوی و مطمئن شوم که زندگی خوب و در خور مقام و موقعیت خسروت را شروع کرده‌ای؟ چرا بخودی داری خسروت را از بین می‌بری! و این چیزیست که او و آنها میخواهند. بیا و این آرزو را به دلشان بگذار. کاری کن که برتری قدرت و شخصیت خسروت موجب غبطه بخورند. الان هم دیگر تعطیل جشن عید و با محیط و مردم تازه‌ای آشنا میشوید. بیا و از همین ابتدا به درون اجتماع برو و با افرادی در خور روحیه و شأن خسروت آشنا شو، و با آنها مبادله دوستی و محبت کن. خواهی دید که زندگی چهره روشنی بخود خواهد گرفت و خواهی فهمید که چه بیهوده عمر و جوانی خود را در کنار این سفلگان و دور از خصلتان سپری کردی! و از اینکه موفق شدی همین چند روز را در مابین، غرق در خوشی و لذت خواهی شد. باز هم میگویم، بزرگترین اشتباهی که تو در این ماجرا کردی، تأمین وضع مالی توست که از آنها با اینکه ترتیب آنرا خودت بدهی. یعنی بدون اینکه هیچ دخالتی را با ایرج شروع کنی. و یا تظاهر به کمترین غصه و ناراحتی بکنی، و یا لب به شکوه و شکایت از وضع موجود بگشایی، زندگی مستقل و دلخواه خسروت را شروع کن و ایرج را فقط مثل برادری ناموافق و مزاحم همیشه در کنار خسروت داشته باش. او با اسم شوهر از اول هم نبوده، حالا هم نیست. فقط با این فکر و بیرون کردن او از قلب خسروت خواهی توانست موفقیت لازم را بدست آوری. فقط سفارش من بتو اینست که از موضع قدرت و بالاتر با او و آنها برخورد کنی. در مراسم عیدشان شرکت کن و در هر مهمانی و جشن و بزم شان شرکت کن. بخند و برقص و شادی کن. اما نه آنطور که مصنوعی و ظاهری جلوه‌گر شود. مراقب باش که بهترین و مفیدترین غذاها را بخوری تا از سلامت کامل جسمی برخوردار باشی تا بتوانی بخوبی با آنها مقابله کنی. خدا را چه دیدی، یک دفعه مرض تضعیفشان کند که نتوانند از جاشان بلند شوند. خلاصه آنقدر از این حرفها دارم که تو خود حدیث مفصل از این مجمل خواهی خواند.

شمسی جان، بعد چیزی هم خانم صاحبخانه آمد و دو ساعت وقت مرا به حرف زدن گرفت. سه ساعت دیگر هم
باید آماده شوم و شبانه به منظوره بروم. بنابراین در این وقت کوتاه تا هرجا موفق شوم مینویسم، و بعد ادامهٔ نامه را به وقت
دیگری موکول میکنم.

در مورد لطف و محبت فوق العاده ای که کرده و هدیه ای برایم فرستاده ای تشکر بینهایت دارم. البته هنوز
بسته نرسیده. ولی من بهیچوجه راضی بزحمت تو نبوده ام. ازت خواهش میکنم هیچ چیز برای من نفرستی، چون در حال
حاضر اصلاً امکان جبران ندارم. در عین حال در جواب سؤالهای مکرر تو در نامه های قبلی هم پرسیده بودی برای من چه چیز بخرد
زیاد احتیاج دارم تا برایم بفرستی، گفته بودم فقط یک چراغ قوه هم با برق برای چند ساعتی شارژ میشود برایم
بفرستی هم انگار این نامه بدستت نرسیده؟ وگرنه بجای پیراهن همان را میفرستادی. در هر حال آنهم سالم رسید
و هیچ فرقی نمیکند. فقط من آن چراغ قوه را برای این خواسته بودم که وقتی برق قطع میشود اولاً بلافاصله بطور
اتوماتیک روشن میشود و مانع از صدمات ناشی از برخورد با وسائل در تاریکی میشود. در هر حال نمیدانم چه بگویم
و چگونه تشکر کنم. و بمحض رسیدن ترا مطلع خواهم کرد. بستهٔ آذر هم رسیده و دو هفته پیش حتماً تا حال رسیدنش را
اطلاع داده. ضمناً مطمئن باش هم راجع به فرستاده های تو با هیچکس صحبت نخواهیم کرد.

شمسی جان، با عرض معذرت، بعد از یک تأخیر ۲۴ ساعته دوباره شروع بنوشتن میکنم. باید اینکه
همین امروز تمامش کنم و به صندوق بیندازم.

و اما نمیدانم بالاخره امسال با رسیده افسانه و ما خواهی رفت یا نه؟ و اگر بروی زمانش را با او
تطبیق داده ای؟ سعیده هم هنوز وضعش معلوم نیست. خدا کند ویزایش به تأخیر برنخورد، وگرنه امسال به سفر
نخواهد رفت. تو نیز احتمالاً زیاد مدتی را مشغول جابجائی و تغییر منزل خواهی بود. آرزو میکنم تصمیم درست
را گرفته باشی تا در محل جدید برنامهٔ تازه ای برای زندگی خودت ترتیب دهی. خود این تغییر محل در تغییر وضعیت
تو بسیار موثر و مفید خواهد بود. و این تو هم باید بتوانی از این موقعیت به بهترین نحو استفاده کنی. میدانم
هم در سنین من و تو درس خواندن و کار کردن کار دشواری است. اما برای پر کردن وقت و بودن در اجتماع
و شناخت زندگی مردم و روابط آنها با یکدیگر و باز هم آموختن و تجربه اندوختن، بسیار خوب است و از اهمیت
فوق العاده برخوردار خواهد بود. در همین کشور خودمان، با همهٔ محدودیتها و گرفتاریهای بیحد و حساب هستند

پیر زمانی هم در کنار فرزندانشان به ادامه تحصیل و اشتغال دادند. حالا این تلاش برای ساختن آینده آنهاست،
یا گذران امروز به نحو مطلوب و رضایتبخش؟ حتی دست زدن به کار و شغلی هم در گذران انسان یاری شده، نه برای کسب درآمد،
هم برای پر کردن روزهای زندگی، و البته جلوگیری از احساس بیهودگی و بی‌ثمری، بسیار صحیح و منطقی خواهد بود. حقیقتاً میخواهی
آدم ماست، خوب است، ولی آدم میتوانی به نحو شایسته و رضایتبخش بگذرانی. بگفتن این حرفها از زندگی سیر گشته‌ای، و یا فقط منتظر مرگ!
هستی و از این قبیل، خراب کنی و بهر روی! در مورد بچه‌ها هم مگر ابر طور میخواهند فکر کنند. بگذار باید برشان موافق باشند
همهٔ گناهان را بگردن تو بیندازند. بیش از این چه ضربه‌ای به تو میتوانند بزنند؟! تو هم از ره رفتار معمول خود را نسبت به آنها
ادامه بده، و حرفت را کاملاً بی توقع و بی نیاز به آنها بشان بده، خواهی دید هم حرفشان سراغت خواهند آمد. همینکه او مایل
هر قدر محدود با آنها بگذرانی برای تو کافی و خوشحال کننده خواهد بود. بچه‌ها تقصیری ندارند هم اینطور بار آمده‌اند. وقتی ما هم
پدران و مادران آنها هستیم، اینهمه ترکیب خطا و اشتباه شده‌ایم و هنوز هم میشویم! آن طفل معصوم هم دیگر جای خود دارد! کسی هم
زندگی آرامی نداشته، چیزی از آرامش نمی‌فهمد. در هر حال منهم مثل تو آنچه را در ذهن پرورانده‌ام با تو باز گویم، بمحض نوشتن چند مطلب
بقیه از ذهنم خارج میشوند و باز همه گفتنها روی هم تل انبار میشوند! از اینکه مرتباً با بچه‌ها تلفن، علی و احسان تماس تلفنی میگیری
بسیار خوشحالم. همین خود در تقویت روحیه تو بسیار مفید است. ضمناً خبر بودن علی پای تلفن، برای ما هم خیلی جالب است. او همیشه
و با همه، حتی اضافه هم نازدانه اولیه او برای ابو سرافیش هم باز رفته همینطور خبری است! اما از اینکه با برادر بساط هر دو اکبر و خصوصاً از
به میدان هم برایش فرستاده‌ای بسیار ابراز خوشحالی و تشکر کرد. نمیدانی با چه خوشحالی به سینما گفته میرود، مثل جوان با چه علاقه
در هر حال همهٔ اینها زندگی انسانها را تشکیل میدهند، و ما خیال میکنیم زندگی چیزی غیر از اینست هم بعدها خواهد آمد! کدام بعدها؟!
(می نویسم هم بعد از این پس خواهی گفت، بی حوصلگی وقتی رفیق و همدم و همدرد و جفت) مثل گفته بیت بعدش را فراموش کرده‌ام!
در هر حال زندگی همین لحظه است، آن را دریاب، و اصلاً فکر فردا را مکن چون فردائی وجود ندارد. هر چه هست همین امروز است.
دیگر ناگزیر نامه را تمام کنم. دوباره سفارش میکنم: طوری وانمود کن که انگار هیچ اتفاقی نیفتاده و هیچکس و هیچ یک از این اعمال برای تو
کمترین اهمیتی ندارد. امکانش هست که چند روزی بسراغت بیایم. هر چند هم با بودن ایرج در خانه تو جائی ندارم. در هر صورت
برایت روزهای خوش و موفقیت آمیزی را آرزو میکنم. باشد که کارهایمان هر چه زودتر بجائی برسد، و دیدار خوشی با هم
داشته باشیم. روی تو را هزاران بار میبوسم. هر چند فرسنگها از تو دورم، ولی دلم همیشه با تو است. دستت را در دستم و صورتت را
برشانه‌ام احساس میکنم. اشکهایت را با تمام وجود از دیدگانت پاک میکنم، و اشک شوق جایگزینش میکنم. فقط این قول
را به من بده، یاری کنی و دستت را از دستم جدا نکنی. همه چیز درست خواهد شد. مواظب خودت باش. قربانت بهجت

thought, she has been my good friend, and she has done many nice things for me. I could never forget that, so I decided to let it be. Meanwhile she continued showing me that she was my friend.

I was still happy to see Pari, or spend time with her family. Every year we used to go to California and stay with them during the holidays. And they came to visit us in Michigan summertime. I enjoyed both visitations equally.

Once they came to visit us, when Iraj was completely involved with Badri. She asked me if I had any Persian books to read. I happened to be busy, and so I asked her get one from the bookshelf. I didn't realize that I still kept Ezzat's letter in that book. She read the letter, but she didn't say anything at first. And then right before she left for LA, she confronted me, "I was very mad when I read the letter. First, I am mad because you discussed Iraj's involvement with Badri with Ezzat. Second, I was very hurt that you judge me as a superficial person. I didn't show the letter to Iraj not to make him madder than he is".

My Dear God:

I told her, "First of all, that letter was confidential, and you had no right to read it. Second of all, she had spoken the truth, and only the good about you all. It was your own gossip that was bad. And I really don't care if Iraj saw it or not. It is not important any more, so let it be".

When Pari went to Iran a few years later, my sisters went to visit her. I had pleaded with my sisters, especially Ezzat, to be nice to Pari. I said, "They are not guilty of anything". So assured me they would, and they went to visit and welcome them.

But that night Pari attacked my sisters, in front of everyone. She put all the blame on my behavior and me. At this time, Ezzat's husband Moosavi, who was with them during the visit, asked Pari sarcastically, "Do you mean that all our wives are bad, and Shamci is the worst?" No one had anything else to say, and they all got up and left.

They all were mad at me for asking them to be nice to Pari. They wished they could tell her off the way she deserved it.

Surprisingly Pari call Ezzat the next day, and apologized for her behavior. She said, "I don't know why I allow myself to get involved with other people's business. It was not my business to talk to you, or treat you the way that I did. Shamci is my friend, and you all are my friends. I am sorry that I lost my control, and said the things that I am so ashamed of now".

When my sister told me that Pari called to apologize, I was proud of myself that I had asked them not to get emotional, and not to react harsh towards them. Her apologies were worst than any severe punishment.

My Dear God:

And then, Pari, supposedly my best friend, went to Iran and humiliated me in front of my sisters by giving them the shocking news of Iraj's affair with Badri. What a fiasco! How embarrassing! Well, at least nobody said, "I told you so".

Fereshteh came to Michigan once. She stayed with me for a whole month. I was trying so hard not to reveal my sadness. Then one day she said to me, "Shamci, you don't have to hide it from me. I know what is going on between you and Iraj". She refused to reveal her source. I found out later that Mary wrote about everything in her letter to her cousin Nazi. I was shocked to find out that this took place long before I got to find out about their involvement. She was trying to start the conversation with me to obtain more details. She noticed the coldness between us. We would go to parties together, and she noticed Badri's behavior. She said to me, "It seems that Badri is afraid of what she is doing". I couldn't understand what she meant by that. I thought she wanted to prove her innocence by showing the superficial curtsy towards me in front of other people.

As I have mentioned before, Fereshteh had married her husband Morteza for love as well. She even got married by proxy in Iran, and then she moved to East Lansing, Michigan.

By then they too were divorced all for the same reason. The only difference was that she had no children. We spent one happy month with Fereshteh in my house. We had something going on for us every day. We took walks to the lake most every day. We cooked together, and we partied together as often as we could.

At that time the relationship between Maseeh and Roshanak concerned me the most. I have almost given up the thought of Iraj and Badri. Fereshteh was trying to comfort me by promising my worries were unnecessary. I cried, and I asked GOD to save my son from destruction. There was nothing else I could have done but pray to GOD to solve my problems.

My Dear God:

As I said before, Sara and I were good friends. One day I thought I should talk to Mahmood about Iraj and Badri. Probably he could help me. We went to a restaurant with Mahmood. He assured me that Badri might think that Iraj might give up his family for her. But Iraj is not that stupid to get fooled by her. Your worries would be essential if she was an intelligent and noticeable woman. But how can he even think of Badri when he has you and his children. He might be having an affair with her. But to take Iraj away from his family, I don't think so. He does not seem to be so naive as to go after someone like Badri. He then continued, "Go home, and try to put your mind and thoughts together. And believe me, Iraj will not destroy his happy family for Badri". He was basically telling me that I must learn to deal with their affair in a wise way. I must learn and not let it bother me.

But when I talked to Sara, she told me, "I had sensed it long ago, and I am sure that every one else knows about it". She remembered the day that we went to her house, and Badri came over looking for Rozan's shoes. She remembered many times like that, and she was very mad that she was paying off my help by stealing my husband.

My Dear God:

I remember once I was so confused, I was suicidal. I decided to talk to Sara, "Sometimes I feel like leaving my family, moving into a hotel, and just divorcing Iraj". But she was able to talk me out of it. She said, "It would be an act of an immature person. Badri is trying hard to take your place. This way you would be assisting her. You must never think of leaving your house, or committing suicide. You must think that Iraj is in need to have an affair. So let him have it, and try to deal with it in an intelligent way". Then she talked about our so-called friends, who were trying to put these two together.

One night Mahmood and Sara came to visit. Sara mentioned that her assistant was gone and she badly needed help in her office. She asked me if I could help her for a while. Although I did not have any experience, I immediately accepted her offer right then. And I started my new job the next morning. I was to do filing, and assist with her patients. Sara showed me around the office, and she went over my responsibilities. I was supposed to be a temp employee, but she decided to hire me.

Mojgan was the only one who lived with us then. I made sure to handle my duties as I always have, so that there were no questions about my work.

My Dear God:

I drove to her house every morning, and we carpooled to her office. Although all the problems were still there, I thought, once again I was saved by a bell.

We talked and discussed all our problems every day. We went shopping together, cooked together, and helped each other tremendously.

She was the only one who would ask Badri to stay away from Iraj, and leave his family alone. She was so sincere about her feelings towards me that many times she got into fights with Mahmood over my family and me. She wanted to help me, but with the presence of those "friends" it was impossible.

For nearly one year that I worked in her office, we tried to be there for each other. We went to lunch together every day. She would even take me along to the hospital when she had to visit a patient. Many times people thought that we were sisters. We thought it was funny.

One evening Mahmood and Sara came to our house. When they were leaving, Iraj was giving them a big lecture about fighting and talking about separation. He told them, "I think no one in a right mind will ever talk about separation. No one in a right mind, and having such beautiful children, should ever talk about divorce. No one in a right mind

should allow anyone to endanger your family life. As parent we have a duty to try to solve the problem that may occur in our lives. Please go home, and think about it. Give it up, and never allow your madness get to a point that you mention the divorce". I am confident that Sara and Mahmood were as shocked as I was.

My Dear God:

The fight had started between them over the relationship between Iraj and Badri. Sara started to condemn Iraj's involvement with Badri, and Mahmood felt that Iraj would not do such a stupid thing. The conversation got deeper and deeper, to a point that they got into a big fight, each wanted to prove their own point, and it ended up with the subject of divorce. This was what Sara told me the next day.

I felt so bad that my problem was causing them such a serious argument. I asked Sara not to discuss my marriage with Mahmood any more. I did not want them to fight over a subject that did not have anything to do with them. I knew that they were concerned about my life, but their life was as important to me as mine.

My Dear God:

Then it was Christmas time. And as always we were planning our annual trip to California to visit Pari. When Sara found out that Badri and her children were going to come to California with us, she took her aside, and she told her, "If your family is good enough to welcome you and your children now, why don't you go and stay with them for good? And if you are not going just because of Iraj, why don't you go somewhere else and leave Rafani family alone. It is not fair that they baby-sit, just for the sake of not hurting your feelings. Sooner or latter you must find your own ways in life".

Many times I would feel bad that she had to get involved with my problems. But on the other hand I was thinking that if other friends were as sincere as Sara, if only they would back me up, then she would have to leave Michigan.

My Dear God:

Rabbanis were going to Island for Christmas that year. Badri's response to Sara's question, "Why don't you go with Rabbanis?" proved that she was not going to give up easily. With the help of friends she was going to destroy Iraj.

Since we practically spent all of our time together, Sara was now a witness to all of Badri's actions. She has made every effort to help me. When I told her that I wasn't able to sleep for three nights in a row, she gave me a tranquilizer pill to help me fall asleep, and deal with depression. She suggested that I took it daily. But I was afraid to take any pills that would take my powers away. I just kept the pills in my purse at all times. Believe it or not, I didn't use them even once. I believed that I must handle my problems on my own.

My Dear God:

While I was searching for an escape from my cancer-causing problem, I came across an advertisement about a class at Oakland Community Collage. The class was about a bestseller, "Women who love too much". I signed up immediately. You had to read the book, and then have a group discussion in class. I felt that it was very important that I knew what other people think of Love.

There were fourteen of us: young and old, both man and women. We came from various life styles, backgrounds, and cultures. We had different characters. There were six more students that joined us in midway. Day after day I got to learn more and more about life by just listening to twenty different ideas about that book. The main subject discussed was "Why so many of us are more eager to give more than to expect more?" Many of the ladies were trying to find out why they were looking for the same kind of man that they tried so hard to get rid of? Many of them talked about the mistakes they had repeated over and over again. It was very interesting to realize that until I opened my eyes and saw the world, with all the matters around it with the naked eye; I would not be able to find peace in my life. I had to figure out what my life was all about, and try to do things that were good for me, try to find that what satisfied me. Mainly I learned all about love and its dependency. I learned not to get fooled by the word "LOVE" again. I learned a lot in that class. I enjoyed listening to everyone's life story, while gaining from each and every one of them.

My Dear God:

Meanwhile I was playing bridge with the ladies in my neighborhood. They have been playing together for more than twenty years. I had to take up a course in bridge at Birmingham, Bloomfield Community House, BBCH, in order to keep up with them.

That class was very valuable to me. Not only I learned enough to play and compete with the ladies in my neighborhood, but also I got acquainted with another group of ladies, who were taking the class for the second time. Fortunately they needed one more person in order to have two tables. I gladly volunteered to join the group. I couldn't be happier. I played with both groups till I left Michigan. These activities, along with volunteer work occupied most of my spare time. At the same time they kept my mind occupied. I had no time for thinking nonsense, and making my life miserable. I had to learn how to deal with myself before it was too late. I needed strength. At this time the most disastrous fact was Maseeh's involvement with Roshanak. Besides loosing my husband to Badri, I was losing my son Maseeh, who meant so much to me, to her daughter Roshanak. Please tell me, my dear GOD, was this a disaster? Was I supposed to lose my mind and commit a crime?

This was the time that animosity of my so-called friends taught me a lesson. I turned my back at every one, and I just turned to GOD. I thought, "When I open my eyes in the

This was the group of bridge players in Bloomfield Hills, Michigan, who lived in my neighborhood.

At a wedding I am with Vickie and Mary's family. I am sitting between Vickie and Mary.

We were at Suzan Farah's wedding. I am standing next to the bride.

Mojgan, coming back from water skiing

I was playing bridge with these ladies from my neighborhood.

morning, I will ignore everything, and I will wait to see what will come to my mind, and then I will do exactly that, no matter what happens". I knew that was the guidance from God, and I knew that I must do it as it came to me. I was not scared any more. I had the sincere faith.

One night when we had Blot game in our house, I was ready ahead of time. I went in the bedroom to get a book to read. It was a book translated in Farsi, "Cheshmhayash, (Her Eyes). I've seen him read it. When I didn't find it between the books, I asked Iraj, "Do you know where "Cheshmhayash" is?" He looked at me doubtfully, and after a few seconds he said, "I think I gave it to Dr. Darian". It was so obvious that he was lying.

My Dear God:

That book was one of the revolutionary books, which we read together when we first started going out. I knew that Dr. Darian was not the type to read those books. Nevertheless I called Dr. Darian to ask him to bring it back. Poor Dr. Darian had never heard of the book. He couldn't understand why I would be asking him to return it. I was embarrassed, and I said, "I am sorry, I must have given it to someone else".

The thing that bothered me the most was that the book was from the most romantic period of our lives. No one else was into those kinds of books. My GOD, did he give it to Badri? She didn't even know what book is, and yet she read the revolutionary love story? I was going crazy. I was no longer myself. When people came to play cards, I had a hard time putting myself together. I think most of them, especially Minoo Panah, read the story in my face. But I tried to pass that night just laughing things off. I wanted to remain in one piece. I had promised myself that would never blow my top off. I was planning for Iraj and Badri to blow theirs instead.

I asked him about the book again when everyone left. This time he did not have anything to say. He just stayed quiet. I got really mad. I remembered his first affair in Iran. When we were in the bed, I asked him, "Iraj, are you cheating on me again? Are you doing the same thing all over again? Have you forgotten how sorry you were? Have you forgotten how you cried and asked for my forgiveness? Weren't you ashamed to face your children? Didn't you beg for their forgiveness, while you were crying behind those black eyeglasses? Didn't you admit that you were your own destroyer?" Then I started crying. And I couldn't stop. I didn't know what was happening afterwards.

It was Sunday morning. My children heard me, and they came in the room. Mojgan did not know about Iraj's first affair until that time. No one would ever bring it up, just because he was trying to make it up to all of us. So there was no need to bring it back. While she was crying, she was asking Mary and Maseeh, "Why didn't anyone tell me before about my father's affair?" Mary and Maseeh who had a very bad memory of their father's affair, were going crazy. I was almost dying.

The one thing that I was dreading was happening right in front of my eyes. I put my

children in the middle of a nasty situation. Although they could sense their father's behavior, I still did not want them to be in the middle of the disastrous life of mine. It was a sad scene. Everyone was crying and screaming. Each one was at the other person's throat. Each wanted to soothe the situation, and put an end to the argument. I snapped out of my state of insanity as soon as I realized that my poor children were involved with something they should not be involved with to begin with. I said to them, "I am very sorry that I lost control, and started the argument. I must have known better to deal with the situation myself. I am so sorry". I thought it could be the beginning of a new era with my children being involved. I must not let my children get hurt.

My Dear God:

He started telling my children, "Your mother is lying. She had never trusted me, and she had always blamed me for something I have never done". Then he continued with his lies, "These are all your mother's speculations. I have never done anything wrong, and I don't intend to do wrong". I realized that I was right. He has planned already to put the blame on me, and make himself innocent in the eyes of my children. I must have avoided confronting him. I must go along with him, and let my children to believe in him. This way he might feel obligated to them, which might ultimately stop him.

I knew I had lost the battle after that day. I promised my children that nothing was wrong, "Nothing that we can't handle by ourselves".

After that day everything was falling apart. The children were ruined emotionally. It was much more difficult for Mary and Maseeh than Mojgan. That day brought back the horrible memories of their childhood. The memories of uncertainty, loveless existence, and bitterness were coming back.

At that time Mary was majoring in History at U of M. Maseeh was at Center for Creative of Studies in Detroit. And Mojgan was attending West Hill Junior High.

They were all going through the stormiest period of their lives. They all needed love and sincere guidance. They needed someone who could show them the way, someone who had enough wisdom to make their problems go away, someone with a good head on his or her shoulders.

Iraj was going through his mid life crisis then, and he possessed no wisdom what so ever. He did no concept of what was going on in his children's minds. He was falling in love, and he didn't know how to get around it. He had completely lost his mind. To get to his love, he had to make up as many lies as possible. He was refusing to remember what had happened in the past, and he didn't know what would happen to him in the future.

My Dear God:

So, the only person who had to think of everyone, and stand by everyone, was I. While going through tremendously painful life, I had to make sure that I could be there

for each and every one of them. I had to evaluate their needs, and support for them accordingly. I felt this was my duty, and I must not turn my head away from them. I must become stronger to be able to deal with my problems in a more tolerant and intelligent way.

It was very difficult to think that way at that time. Every woman's dream is that it is much more tolerable to see your husband dead, than to find out he is cheating on you . That I had in mind. Especially when I loved Iraj so much that I was imagining that every cell of my children's body has been woven together with a bundle of LOVE. I just didn't have a man to go to bed with. I loved everything about him, and I suffered for seven years to make it possible.

When we got married, we were together only for two weeks before he had to leave for USA. During those two weeks he was insisting that I became pregnant. His reason was, "If I go, and something happens to me, I would like to have a child left of me. I, on the other hand, did not agree with him. My reason was that I would like to raise my child under supervision of both parents. "If GOD forbids, you are not going to be around, I do not want to raise a child without a father".

Now, at this time of my life, I ended up raising my children under supervision of a father, who does not even care for his children's well being. What a pity my dear GOD, what a pity!

After that night I decided to approach the whole matter in a wise and mature way. I thought, "I must think of my children and their happiness first. My children's future was in danger, and Maseeh's life especially, was in Jeopardy". I thought, "I have to deal with the situation in a positive way".

So with Maseeh's support, I decided to go and talk to Badri. I asked Maseeh to come with me to Badri's house, in case she decided to make up things, and then deliver big lies to Iraj. It was safer to be with Maseeh.

So one evening Maseeh and I finally went there. I told her in a very polite and caring tone, "No one knows as much as I do that your life has been very painful lately. I have been practically the only one who really had felt for you. It must have been awful to loose your husband the way you did. We all felt sorry, and we all know that you are going through a very hard time. That is why we did what we could to help you stand on your own two feet".

My Dear God:

And then I continued, "For almost a year I held your hand every step of the way. I was with you wherever or whenever you needed me. I cleaned your house, while your sisters, who were staying with you at the time, did not feel responsible to do so. I was present with you at court, and we took you with us on all our trips. My children did the same thing, and so did my husband. We thought it was our duty to help you and your

children. We thought we should not leave you alone at such a difficult time of your life. We are not only helping you at this time, but it has been our habit to help our friends at the time they needed us. Iraj has been helping many of his friends.

And then I continued, "If we did not leave you by yourself, like many of your friends did, is just because of our concerned nature. Those who left you were probably thinking more logically. They knew that sooner or later you have to be on your own, and start life allover again.

Then I said, "You are a young woman. You have three children. You have a long life ahead of you. Your parents, your sisters and brothers are living in Los Angeles, and you often have gone to visit them. You must go and join them. Soon you will find a young rich husband, and you will forget about the past. Then I continued, "I know and probably you know that my husband is under tremendous pressure. The house, the office, the hospital, the clinic, and plus all of Malakuti's businesses are on his shoulders. One person can only take so much. I do not want to see my husband to be played around with, or taken advantage of, or worst of all to be destroyed. This is not fair to my children, who are being destroyed along with their father. Don't take Iraj wrong. His help to you is as great as to others. He is a nice person and a good father. We worked so hard to make it up to now. Iraj has been, and is a respectful man, and I wish for him to continue that way.

Then I said, "Badri, please embrace your children, and move to LA, where your family is. They would love to be with you, and help you. Soon you will find a right husband for yourself, and you will be able to live happily ever after".

As if what I said was not for her to hear, or she had made up her mind already. She said after listening to me, "If two people are not comfortable with each other, the best is to separate, and divorce each other. I don't think divorce is a bad thing. It was many times that my husband told me and my children that he wanted to divorce me. So many times in front of my children he asked us to get ready for it. So divorce is not bad for two people who do not get along".

My Dear God:

I realized that she had made up her mind. I told her, "My dear Badri, it seems that you are not hearing me. First of all, not only we do get along well, but also we love each other more than before. Second, the reason that I am here and talking to you is that you and your business is coming between my husband and I. If Azeez had been willing to divorce you, and he told you that many times is because you were not good for him. So he wanted to divorce you just because you deserved to be divorced. But for Iraj and I the word divorce never existed. Even last time that he had affair on me, he never mentioned divorce to me. Instead he returned to us with embarrassment and sorrow. I was and I am a woman that Iraj has too much respect for not to allow himself to ever mention divorce. And for myself, I must tell you, you forget about it, because I will never, I mean never

divorce him. I will leave it up to him. No heart feelings. I love Iraj and I will never leave him".

Then I said, "We were having the happiest and loveliest time together, until you came along. I am sorry if there was no love between Azeez and you. But that does not mean that you should be playing around with my husband's emotions, and make a wrong person out of him. If he is helping you is because he owes it to his partner Azeez and his family. You do not interpret it in a wrong way. Iraj is in his mid-life crisis, and he just needs a woman like you to be destroyed".

I continued, "Even at this time that you are playing with his emotions, he still loves us, and he tries so hard to fulfill his responsibilities. He loves me very much, and he wants me to believe in his love. Only if you would leave him alone".

Then again she said, "I am not doing anything. I just have a kind of feeling for him. It is not my fault that we have special feelings for each other. And besides, everybody gets divorced. If you are not happy with him, there is nothing wrong with divorcing him".

I repeated myself calmly, "My dear Badri. It seems that you do not understand me. I know that he has been, and he will be kind to you and your children. But he has been this kind of a person all his life. He had done the same thing for other friends. He has provided this kind of help to those who were not even friends or partners. But none of them took it wrong, and started playing with his emotions. None of them claimed have special feelings for him. None of them wanted to destroy my children. I am telling you, you leave my children, and my husband alone. Don't try to repay his and my kindness by destroying us. If you are smart, take advantage of the opportunity, move to California, and marry a young rich man, and let your children start a happy new life".

My Dear God:

At this time Maseeh, who was all ears, started talking. And then to my surprise he said, "Yes we all must know where we stand, and try to be responsible for our actions". And he made a point, "We all must live a life that none of us regrets in the future". And he announced his love for Roshanak who was sitting there at all times. Although I felt good about his statement, his love for Roshanak was something new to me. I tried not to react to the news.

When we left her house, Maseeh turned to me and said, "Mom, I am so proud of you. It was fantastic the way you handled that conversation. I was expecting something very harsh and unpleasant. But you handled it with so much wisdom and class. I am really proud of you". And then he said, "I was expecting a fight, but you not only showed her your support, but you made her realize that she was not dealing with any ordinary person. You put your foot down in an intelligent way. To tell you the truth, at first I was scared to death. But now I realize who my Mom is. Now I am comfortable that Roshanak and I can continue our friendship without any interruption".

While I was so glad that I had made my dear son happy, I was so sad that he was speaking of love for Roshanak. I felt like I have lost my battle no matter what. This was the same Maseeh, who laughed at me two years ago, when I told him about Roshanak's love for him. He was the same person that said, "That would be the day that I love someone like Roshanak".

My dear GOD, do you remember that night? Do you remember the things I told you? Do you remember my tears? Why me? What have I done to deserve this? How do you want me to deal with this one? Are you there to hear me? Can you help me, or am I going to end up in an asylum? What should I do? Where should I go? Oh GOD, oh GOD, oh GOD. Help me, please help me.

What Maseeh had told me was something, and then I realized that Badri told me the same thing, only in different words. What could "special feelings" mean other than LOVE.

You see, my dear GOD, the reason that women like me become murderers is that the other women don't give up. The other women do not have any sense of understanding. They will push you to a point that there is no choice. No one ever punishes these women. The world is ready to put all the blame on the murderer. Isn't this really awful? Isn't this painful? Oh well.

My Dear God:

In front of her daughter Roshanak, and my son Maseeh, she admitted that she was in love with my husband. This was exactly what Azeez had told us. He said, "The moment I am gone, she will start celebrating, and she will find another person". He was absolutely right. Only he didn't know that this relationship was established long before he was gone.

I was the mourner at Azeez's funeral, and Badri was the happiest person. At that time the only worry she had was that he was still married. "How do I get rid of Shamci? But it is nothing to worry about. With the help of all of my friends I will be able to do anything. Not to worry".

My Dear God:

She knew what to do to grasp Iraj's attentions. The more she made herself incapable, and helpless, the more Iraj would be drawn to her. Iraj loved dependent and helpless women. So she was sure that she would succeed no matter what. Badri knew very well how to bolster the ego of a man in mid-life crisis. She made sure to chant her mantra to him daily, "You are young and handsome". She even used her children for that purpose. Will I ever forget the birthday card from Rozan? "You are only getting better". Am I supposed to believe that a nine year old could come up with such statement all on her own? Sara was convinced that Badri must have been behind it.

One of Badri's main goals was to create tension between Iraj and me. She was very

diligent about exposing her affair with Iraj. She made sure that I knew all about it. She wanted me to turn my back on him and our marriage. She was hoping that my jealousy, anger, and frustration would draw them closer.

I was to fight this battle by myself, and it was up to me to decide if I could cope with it.

But that wasn't it. I had to find the strength to deal with all my so-called friends: Rohan, Susan, Aghdass, Louise, Nayer, and others. I wasn't even questioning their animosity towards me. Among those who knew them well, they were known for their viciousness. Why should I even bother? I have learned about the meanness of their characters. They didn't need a particular reason to dislike people. They just wanted to be entertained by mocking others. Cruelty was a big part of their nature. I knew that in my case they could not stand the sight of our prosperity and happiness.

And so they waited out for the perfect time to make me into a target. Iraj was very vulnerable after Malakuti had passed away, drowned with his business and emotional affairs. They immediately started arranging parties more frequently, so that they secured interaction between Badri and Iraj.

It almost seemed as if they were daring Iraj to go after Badri. And there were only two reasons for their persistence: as I have mentioned before, they lived to be entertained by other people's misery and misfortune, and they wanted to ensure that Badri wasn't lusting after their husbands.

I found out that night that Maseeh had developed deep feelings for Roshanak. And I realized then that my son was being lured into a dangerous trap. I knew I had to stop dwelling on my own situation. I had to be alert, and protect my son from the upcoming disasters. I had to come up with an intelligent plan.

My Dear God:

I knew that divorcing him was not an option then. That was the most crucial period of my children's life. That was not the time to be concerned about my husband's love and faithfulness.

I had to concentrate on my children's future and their happiness. I was completely aware that I might not be able to achieve my goal completely, but at least I knew that I had tried.

I was also willing to try to understand Iraj's difficulties, and all the circumstances around him. I knew he didn't have it easy. Along with the enormous expense of our house, he had to provide for the expense of Mary's house in Ann Arbor. He had two offices, and a clinic. He was part owner of a nightclub. He had payments of college tuitions, the two hospitals and his patients. And above all those, the death of his partner had resulted in the responsibilities of his estate, and his family. But most of all there came the incapable, sneaky leech, sensuous Badri, who had kept insisting that Iraj was in love with her.

And even with all those, and the probability of having affair with Badri, he never forgot to show his love to me. And he tried to cover it up from his children. He always wanted them to believe that he was only in love with his family. And with that mission on his mind, he was always home on time. He made a point of spending all his free time with his family. I was happy to see that he was making an effort to act innocent. I thought the more he pretended to be innocent, the more he would be obligated to stay innocent. He could have Badri for his mistress for as long as it would last. I didn't want to divorce Iraj. Let them have their fun. I have other things to worry about.

Oh, how much fun our friends were having now. What a perfect case scenario! I was living a painful life, I was unhappy. They couldn't wait to see me cry, begging them to save my life from disastrous Badri. I bet they were wondering among each other, "Why is Shamci not talking? Why is she not divorcing Iraj?"

Our friends knew of their involvement. But instead of trying to prevent it, they arranged more and more parties, just to witness my sufferings.

I couldn't help not to think that those friends were walking all over my children, and me. I could hear them say, "If you are not happy with your husband, why don't you divorce him?" That was the exact same thing Badri had asked me once. They wanted me to fail; they couldn't wait to celebrate my unhappiness.

Those friends made it possible for Badri, who was never allowed to speak up while her husband was alive, to become somebody, or at least to think that she could be somebody.

Many times I blamed myself for helping her so much, while everyone else was minding their own business. Then again I remembered that it was the partnership, and the agreement signed had made me go as far as I did. It wasn't my stupidity that allowed them to have an affair. They already had something cooking behind Azeez's back and mine. And Azeez's death provided a solid ground for their affair to flourish.

My Dear God:

Many times I remembered Azeez's comments about Badri. He always said, "Badri might come in the room with a big smile at the corner of her crooked lips, and you will never believe that she had just killed".

It sounded like a joke then. But I came to realize later that he was not joking. It was very possible that she killed Azeez. And no one ever suspected her. No one knew that her husband wanted to divorce her. No one ever suspected that she was having an affair with Iraj long before Azeez had passed away. And because of the way everything was planned, no one even questioned her. And no one knew that Badri hated Azeez so much that killing him was a long lasting freedom for her.

Many times she spoke of Azeez's patients, and that she could easily handle them. She knew of that phone call on Friday. She knew that one of Azeez's schizophrenic patients

was coming to see him at eleven o'clock. She also knew that he was suicidal, and very disturbed.

So when questioned, she told the police, "I went to the office to pick up my station wagon, and leave his car for him. I needed a larger vehicle car to be able to take my parents around. That was the last time I saw him".

And then they accused Azeez's patient of killing his doctor. He wasn't ever in a right mind to explain what had happened. He was charged with murder, and sentenced for life in prison. The case was closed. And the whole world cried for Badri.

You know, my dear GOD, my dear friend and teacher, you were the only one who was there. You were the witness to all that happened. Do you remember what her husband said? He believed that she was capable of killing someone and get away with it.

She wanted to marry a person that she fell in love with. Remember what her mother always preached, "Make sure to marry the person you fall in love with, and never let him go". And she listened to her mother like a good girl. My dear GOD, you are the only one who knows that what happened in that office that day. You were the only witness.

I had to find a way to survive. My best remedy was writing to you. And then I awaited your response. I would hear, "You will be Okay, Shamci. Don't be afraid. Proceed with what you have planned. I am watching you. Give yourself some time, and believe in yourself. Do not allow wrong thoughts to interfere with your decision-making. You must believe in yourself". My dear GOD, thanks to you I began to believe that regardless of the outcome, it would be to my benefit. At the end it would be me, who would be very happy with the decisions I had made.

My Dear God:

It took me eight months after Azeez's death to realize that Iraj and Badri had been together all along.

My dear GOD, it is ironic how little we know ourselves, or how little we know about our future. One day I was so attached with Iraj that I thought I would never live without him. And he was almost sure that I would kill myself then. But the times had changed. I had different feelings and responsibilities. I would rather kill Iraj and Badri.

I thought they deserved to die because what they did was wrong. And then I realized that killing them would not solve my problems, and it would create trouble for my children and me. I knew there was another way.

God knows how many times I thought of revenge. How many times I thought of killing every member of Malakuti family, hoping it would put an end to my sufferings. How many times I thought of killing Iraj or myself. But at the end you, my dear GOD, came to my rescue. You showed me a better way to handle the situation. You made me think of myself first, and you helped me realize that they were not worthy of even killing. You made me regard myself so highly, while I thought of them so little. They became less than the dust under my feet. And only then I was able to continue to live my life.

I never found out if Iraj knew that Badri had asked me to divorce him. I knew that he was always against divorce. He never mentioned it to me, and he never expected to hear it from me. Iraj never gave up his responsibilities. He never forgot my birthdays or mother's day. He never went anywhere without me, or did anything without informing me. And while he was lying to me, he kept up the pretence that nothing could separate us.

I was so confused. I felt like I was in the middle of the ocean, hanging on a free log. I didn't know where to go or what to do. I was trying to keep floating atop that huge body of water. I was hoping to find the right solution. I didn't want to hurt my family.

Then came the first year anniversary of Malakuti's death. We were all at the graveyard. While everyone was standing around his grave, I wasn't myself. It was very difficult to watch Badri and Iraj play their roles. I was feeling nauseated. Then everyone proceeded with putting flowers on his grave. I did it too. When Badri, in her black dress, and her black lace scarf, put flower on her husband's grave, everyone started to cry. I felt like Mafioso surrounded me. They had done all the killings, and now they pretended to mourn. Then Iraj gave one of his speeches to commemorate Azeez. And when he started to talk about his poor children, he was so excited and nervous, that he confused ROOZBEH's name for BEHROOZ. I was so embarrassed. This was the man that one day I was proud of. He was the father of my children, and I always wanted them to be proud of him. Now, he was making a fool of himself in front of a crowd of people. I wished I could detach myself from those filthy liars. I wished I could scream, "Please, people, these two are lying. They are not crying for Azeez, they are celebrating his death. She was the one who got rid of Azeez, so that she could have affair with Iraj. People, please listen to me. These two have been sleeping together from the moment Azeez got killed. You've seen them in hotels. Please do not believe their mourning.

My Dear God:

I realized all of a sudden that all those whom I considered friends were impatiently awaiting this moment. They have been long anxious to witness my insanity. I knew I must stay cool, I knew I had to try and forget about Iraj and Badri. True that those two are liars, cheaters, and traitors, but I had to figure out a way of dealing with them. I still had a long way to go. I knew I could not let all those people delight themselves with my sufferings. I was not going to give them a chance to witness my humiliation. I no longer had control over my life circumstances.

I stayed behind at the cemetery, after everyone left for a dinner at Malakuti's. I stood there over his grave, and I damned him for marrying such a woman. "I just wish you were here to witness their behavior. I just wish you were here". Then I went to pay my respects to Shafizeh Mehrabian. Her grave happened to be only a few yards away. I told her, "I am glad that you did not live to witness what I have witnessed. I am glad that you

did not suffer and that you left this world peacefully".

Malakutis dinner party was starting to unravel when I got there. Everyone was having a wonderful time. My physical presence didn't mean much, because my spirit wasn't really there. I was alone with my thoughts. I tried to stay around those who would not bother me. So I decided to play Blot, to keep my mind off of what's been eating me up.

My dear GOD, as always I turned to you at times of disparity. And I pestered you, "My dear GOD, first you brought our families together. Then you brought the revolution in Iran between us, a possibility for them to get closer. Then you made them business partners. And you put the burden of the family of deceased Azeez a legal responsibility for Iraj. Next you took my son's love away, and offered Roshanak instead. Please, my dear GOD, if at this time I decide to kill them both, I will be considered guilty. How do you expect me to handle all these, when you are the one who carried them all out? How can I cope with it? Why would I be considered a murderer? What can I do, my dear GOD? What can I do?"

My Dear God:

There came a day when I came to terms with their affair. I realized that I had lost all my respect for Iraj. I started to ignore him. I became an emotionless observer; he could no longer upset me. I have detached myself from the reality, and ugliness of their relationship. It was the only way to prevent suicidal or homicidal thoughts. I made myself believe that my husband Iraj was dead, and this person was just his impostor. And his actions should not be one of my concerns.

I was terrified of the thoughts of killing them. How would I live with myself after that? What would happen to my children? I remembered the story of a lady who had murdered her ex-husband and his new wife. I knew then that the poor woman must have been emotionally destroyed by her ex-husband. But no one care to understand her, not even her own children. Until one day she had enough, and killed them both.

My Dear God:

We used to get together most Friday and Saturday nights to play Blot. I bumped into Rohan one Friday afternoon. She asked if I could play that night in their house. She said it was going to be just the four of us. I agreed. I was happy that Badri wasn't going to be there. This was around the time that I commiserated with Rohan. She knew that I was trying to avoid Badri's company.

I told Iraj that we would be playing at Rohan's, when he called to inquire about our plans for the night. Rohan pulled me aside shortly after we arrived. She said, "Shamci, I am sorry. Badri had called, and she wanted to come over. I couldn't stop her".

I started burning inside. I could feel fumes coming out of my ears and my eyes. But I put a smile on my face, and I said, "No worries, Rohan-jon. I understand".

It was obvious that Iraj had called Badri, and asked her join him at Rohan's. On the other hand, I was convinced that Rohan did not even try to stop her. She wanted to witness me suffer. She could have asked her to visit some other day. She could have explained to her that we were going to play cards, and that it was only four of us. It was very easy to find an excuse. Badri wasn't going to break into her house. Rohan had no problem hiding her Christmas trip from Badri. But if Badri didn't come that night, how else was Rohan going to see my sufferings? How else could she entertain herself? I just wonder.

My Dear God:

I did not give Rohan the pleasure of hurting me. I put myself together, and I acted as a lady that I always was, as normal as possible. I bet she was expecting that I left, or that I started arguing with Iraj, or that I would be rude and unpleasant that night.

I was completely aware of what was going on around me. Iraj was waiting for me to loose control under pressure, and become wild and crazy so that he could prove to everyone, including his children, that Shamci's jealousy and suspicion have always been a problem. And if I was angry with him, it was only because I was crazy. And as far as my friends, they were happy, first because their husbands were safe, and second that lucky Shamci is no longer so lucky.

So you see my dear GOD, I was not ready to make them happy. I knew I had to be strong, alert, and clever in order to deal with the situation. Thank you my dear God that you stood by me all the way through.

I have told Badri, "You will not see the day that I divorce Iraj. My happiness was destroyed when you came along. I will wait for Iraj to make the decision". I think this made Badri think of ways of making Iraj to consider divorce.

Meanwhile I told Iraj, "I will never divorce you. I am not the one who wants to destroy our home and my children's nest. You will have to do it all by yourself. Good or bad, I have to continue living, until you find a way to end this intriguing plot. I am going to leave it up to you, either you will make it, or break it.

I was not going to give up. I was ready to walk the most painful path of my life. I didn't feel any pain or sorrow. I had a plan to keep my place, and face the consequences.

The gatherings were getting numerously larger. Because of Azeez's death, we got to know more and more younger doctors and their wives. Everyone felt obligated to entertain Mrs. Malakuti, and her associates. Azeez's death made her the center of attention. I was the first person to push this idea. We all felt so sorry for her. Due to the loss of Azeez, every one of Iranian doctors tried to become friendlier than ever.

Iraj was trying so hard to convince everyone that he was a good friend and a humanitarian. He wanted them to believe that everything he did for Malakuti's family was strictly to fulfill the sense of his responsibilities towards his friend. To tell you the truth, at first I used to applaud him for his actions. And I was hoping that others could see it the same way. So people were applauding him by arranging dinners and praising him.

My Dear God:

I am not sure when people realized that he wasn't what he pretended to be. But for a while I was so naive and stupid. Since I was going to bed with him, adultery was out of question. I used to believe that intimacy was only based on ultimate feelings of love. And now, how could I sleep with someone who was cheating on me? It got to a point that I didn't wish to be in the same room with him. How could I make myself to be intimate with him?

He wanted to be with me regardless of his involvement with Badri. We've had a great relationship for as long as I can. He was gentle, and always cared for my feelings. He always made sure to make me happy first, and then he would enjoy himself. I don't think there are that many men who praise their wives after the intercourse. I do not remember that even once he got out of our bed unhappy. Neither did he let me be unhappy. And to my amazement, he still acted that way.

But after the day that he brought breakfast in my bed, while he made a date with Badri, I was completely lost. Many more things happened after that. Now that I had decided to stay put and try to stop Badri from destroying my house, I must get ready to act differently. I could not let her win so easily. He was my husband first, he was my lover first, and by law he was more mine than hers. I must train myself to be able to sleep with the person that I hate, and I must try to enjoy him as well. After all the more I tried to distance myself from Iraj, the more I would open the door of pleasures for Badri. I tried not to ignore Iraj's desires as long as Badri was in the picture. So, when he approached me at night, to my own surprise, I went for it, and I enjoyed it. Iraj has always been the one who initiated the desire for sex. I didn't even know that a woman could approach her husband first. I always thought that it was man's duty to ask for sex, and not a woman's.
On one hand I thought, in reality he is playing the role of husband in "Dynasty", the TV show. He created a scene where his wife gave in to his sexual desires just to get rid of his mistress. While in my wildest dreams I never wanted to be that wife.

Little by little I noticed that his sexual activities were changing. The circumstances around him, all those heavy responsibilities, Mid-life crisis all and all were affecting his performance. He was getting rough, and he paid less attention to my feelings. He was trying different methods, but still he was not happy, even though I did not reject him. I allowed it to happen. Many nights I felt like my own husband has raped me. He was completely crazy. Many nights he couldn't sleep. After tossing and turning he would get up, and go downstairs to the family room. He would have a drink, but still he couldn't fall asleep.

Dear Mom,

I don't quite know how to tell you just exactly what it is I've been feeling lately. I feel very proud of you.

There was a time when you were so upset and angry with certain people that you're complaints were very upsetting to me; Because it showed to me that you were hurt, and worst of all, that you had lost confidence in yourself. It seems to me that only a person who feels that they aren't lovable would ever _truly_ feel unloved.

Now I know you not that way. I have not heard a single complaint out of you in months. That leaves only the "others" complaining and playing games while you lay back, look in their face, and shine the truth directly at their eyes in a way that they cannot overlook.

Mom... You _are_ strong!

You _are_ very respected and looked up to,

and I would Imagine that best of all,...
You are very deeply loved by your son.

You have proven to me over and over again in the past years that you are a great woman.
I don't think that at this point I shall ever forget it.

You have my love + respect always

Your Son,

Marcel

This is the second letter of Maseeh to me. The first letter was written to me when I was still struggling to find a way to handle Iraj and his affair with Badri. I was completely lost at that time.

Then I made up my mind and decided to live my life and let them suffer. After finding my way to deal with them, and giving Iraj all the freedom that he wanted, I was able to see things more clearly. So, I started to change my behavior. As a result, my children who were very absorbent, realized that their mother was not who they thought she was.

I received this letter from Maseeh. He was proud of me for the way I was bringing shame into Badri and Iraj's life. He was glad that his mother could stand up straight. He was happy that his mother was not weak any more. He was glad that "his mother can look in their eyes and let them become embarrassed of their acts."

All right, I received this letter from Maseeh and I read it. I was sure that Maseeh knew everything by then. I was sure that all of my children knew what was going on in our married life. So by having this knowledge, I was expecting that they could understand me better. I was hoping that they have respect for my wishes. Not only did I not receive any support from any of them, but also they put me in the corner. They forgot what I had gone through during that awful nine years that their father had Badri as his mistress. Every minute of those nine years was torture for me. Then you wanted me to forget as you three had forgotten? Oh, no way. Not me. I was the wife. And I was a mother who gave up all her rights to defend her children's happiness. I could have done wrong. I could have gotten my revenge, but I played it safe. I let them do what they wanted to do. Although I was tortured every second of my life, I didn't fight this man whom I had lost my family for. How can you have respect for people who destroyed me and stabbed me the way they did? How can you even say hello to them? You wanted me to be alert and do something about my life. But, when I needed you, you, my children, turned your back on me, and paid me back the way you did.

I am glad that I was able to continue loving you. I am glad that I didn't hurt anyone. And I am glad that I was able to come to the conclusion that my children must have the right to love themselves first. And if there is no love in their heart for me, I'll let it be. I am glad that I have come to a point of my understanding to believe that there is no love after all, and I personally do not need it, not from you, not from anyone else. I must do right, say right, and act right. If I do all these, then I love myself, and this is what I need.

Loving your father was something that I wanted you to do. But to accept Badri and have respect for my stabber is just pure betrayal to me. The way that you include them into your lives and exclude me from the most pleasurable events of my life, is disloyalty to your mother. If not as bad as Iraj's disloyalty, to me it is worse. This was worse because it happened at the time that I was becoming a new Shamci. This killed me for the second time.

My Dear God:

I was very concerned that he would not follow his alcoholic father's path. I tried to figure out how to stop him. So instead of being mad at him, I tried to love him more and more. I thought I had to love him more when he was in need of love. Anyone can love you at good times. If I could love him, and help him then, it meant something. So most nights, I put myself to sleep with those thoughts so that I start all over the next day.

I started gathering newspapers and magazines like "Human Sexuality", which was published by doctors. I read about men in their mid-life crisis. I could see that Iraj was going through it. I felt more hopeless when I couldn't help him. I would look at him as a helpless child. I wished I could kiss him, and make him feel better. But that was an impossible dream.

I learned how some successful doctors had committed suicide, and many others ended up in mental institutions. Many lost their jobs and families.

That one doctor from Beaumont Hospital was one of them. He was happily married, and had six grown up boys. They all graduated from college with great success. And still that doctor shot himself in his bedroom.

There was another doctor among our friends, Dr. Limia. He was from Italy. He did his residency with Iraj at Beaumont. Dr. Limia had a beautiful wife and children. But for some reason he managed to become such a wrong person. He eventually lost his job, and actually, his license was revoked. He left his wife, and ignored his family.

I remembered the times when Iraj would talk to me about him. He seemed to be very worried. I knew now why he was so worried. But at the time he must have known things about Dr. Limia that I was completely unaware of.

Limia's wife, just like myself, never wanted to divorce her husband. She stood by him and his infidelity throughout their marriage. And the irony of it all was when Mary and I ran into Dr. Limia at a restaurant. He sat down with us, and started telling us lies about the course of his misfortunes. He told us, "If only my wife was more understanding. If only she could have coped with my behavior, she wouldn't have to divorce me".

I knew that he initiated their divorce. I was convinced that they revoked his license because they knew he was not in the right mind to practice medicine. And now he didn't even remember that he was the one who destroyed his own life, and that he was the one who asked for divorce.

My Dear God:

Iraj was the one who told me about Dr. Limia, and the other doctor who committed suicide. And each time he talked about them, I saw deep fear in his eyes. I think he was afraid that he would end up falling into the same category one day. No kidding. No one has ever done what he did to his own reputation. Therefore he had all the right to be constantly worried, and fearful. He could not have possibly forgotten what he had done to himself while he was in Iran. That was the most embarrassing time of his life. No wonder he was afraid of falling into the same trap.

Meanwhile, I kept on reading books about men in Mid-life crisis, which is almost the same as women in menopause. Both periods could be very destructive if one doesn't seek help.

Iraj was the star of nearly every story I had read. I was seeing so vividly that he was getting destroyed. I also saw that he was trying to fight it. I was his wife, and I could tell what was on his mind through many of his acts. There were many little things that he did or said that were indications of his eternal love for us, and that he was going to defeat the temptations.

It made me very happy when he tried to prove to his children that he was an honest man, who never intended to destroy their happiness. I would then recall what Dr. Limia had told me once, "If only my wife stayed quiet for a while, I might have been okay later on". If I could take it for a little longer, he would probably be able to keep his promises to his children, and he would come to his senses one day. I just was hoping.

On one hand I was trying to find the way to deal with Iraj and his mistress. And at the same time I was watching my son falling in love with a girl whom he never really cared for. It was right after he was separated from his high school sweetheart Beth. And he was suffering to be away from her. Now Roshanak had found a perfect time to make her dream come true. She has always been in love with Maseeh, but she could not have him. He was never interested in her. But the separation from his real love, and Malakuti's passing made it possible for her to attract Maseeh. She put herself in Maseeh's hands in order to forget about her father's tragic death. And Maseeh, being eighteen, felt good to be able to help her. That was the most appropriate time for Roshanak to grab Maseeh.

Although our children came from different backgrounds and culture, yet American life style had immense influence on them. I had heard through the grape vine that she was a very troubled girl. But one thing was certain, and that was that they had become very close. And they were not only lovers, but Maseeh had become a father figure to her.

My Dear God:

Meanwhile Badri was playing her own game, and she put the winning card down. You see, my dear GOD, please pay attention to her cleverness. She was an Iranian woman, who was having an affair with her friend's husband, right in front of her children. And yet she would not allow her daughter to go out with an Iranian boy. Her reasoning was that Iranians would gossip, and they would make her daughter look bad. She was insisting that they must get engaged to be able to go steady.

When Maseeh approached me for advice, I knew that he would get Iraj's approval. So I told him, "I will be with you all the way. Do what you want to do. I will support you to the end".

I saw his face lit up, and that all his worries were gone. I knew that I shouldn't make a fool of myself by speaking nonsense. I told him, "They know you are a student. They should know you don't have money. Go ask your father to buy a ring for her, and I will arrange the announcement party and the rest".

Isn't life ironic? My dear GOD, it was barely a year ago that I found Maseeh very upset in his room. He was just pacing around complaining, "These girls are crazy! They think that if a boy asks them out a couple of times, he should marry them the next. This girl is asking me to marry her only because we have gone out a few times. Don't you agree that they must be crazy?"

He was smart enough to know right from wrong. He knew better to stay away from trouble. And now, a year later, he fell into a trap with the assistance of his father and his mistress. I could not let my son get hurt.

My dear God, I used to be so proud of my son. I always thanked him for the way he dealt with brainless girls. But he was so helpless then. I knew that he was with Roshanak only because he thought she needed him.

So he talked to his father, and they decided to buy a ring for her. And I decided to throw a big party, and announce their engagement. I just wanted to make life easy for my son.

PLEASE GOD. PLEASE.

You remember me, and my feelings during those days. Do you remember how confused I was during the day, and how much I cried every night? Do you remember how I had to do all the preparations for that day? You remember how many times I asked you to take my life. I could no longer bare all the sufferings.

My Dear God:

I invited the usual group of friends. There were almost forty of us. I did not tell anyone about the occasion of our gathering. So they all were caught by surprise.

The house looked immaculately beautiful as always. The table was beautiful, filled with colorful and delicious meals.

When everyone gathered around the table, I called for everyone's attention: "Ladies and gentlemen, dear friends, as you know, since Dr. Malakuti's death Maseeh and Roshanak had become very fond of each other. So, I found it appropriate to announce their engagement today. I hope their friendship grows stronger with this ring, and they find happiness together. For better or worse, till death do them apart". And then I said, "Please help yourselves before the food gets cold".

I noticed while I was talking that Rohan told Louise, "Didn't I tell you Shamci has something on mind?" They all started to congratulate Maseeh and Roshanak. Badri approached me and kissed me. Her kiss felt like a bite of a snake. I could feel the venom running through my body.

Iraj was quite shocked and surprised. He stood there at the table with his head down. He looked like a thief embarrassed and humiliated in front of his peers.

You see, my dear God, until now I cannot understand why I loved and cared so much for Iraj. I never wished to see him feel bad or sad. I never wanted to see him sorry and regretful. I cared so much for his name and reputation.

We both worked so hard for our happiness. And he always tried so hard, and he always put all his efforts into bring happiness to our lives. Why should he be feeling embarrassed at the time that he should be feeling the proudest father of all. Why?

I could not help not to think of all those competitive friends of his. I could sense that they all were happy to see Iraj unhappy. They didn't have to say anything. And Iraj knew it too. That was why his head was down. How could he possibly justify his own actions? He was having an affair with the mother of his daughter in-law.

After dinner Maseeh and Roshanak both thanked me for the fine ceremony. Unfortunately it seemed like I wasn't even there. I didn't know what I was doing. It felt as if someone else was in my body, and that someone else was taking care of everything in a very exquisite order.

You see my dear God, Rohan and her friends were waiting for my downfall every day. They were waiting for me to break down, and ask for their pity. But they were witnessing that I was up on my feet, I had a smile on my face, and I was capable. They were waiting for the day that I became mad, and threw a scene in front of them. But thank you God, thank you for not letting it happened. Thank you for being with me all the way.

My Dear God:

Even when I was dealing with those horrible circumstances, I never failed my children. I was aware that my children did not have anyone in this country except their parents. They were at the most crucial age, and that was when they needed guidance the most. Meanwhile we were so busy with our own problems. How could we direct our children, when we needed guidance ourselves?

For years and years we blamed Mary's complexity and rebellion on her age. It has never occurred to us that it might be something else. I knew that Iraj's affair in Iran had the greatest effect on her. No one ever, not even Mary herself, could remember how much she had suffered during those years. I knew that her behavior was the result of those years. And probably in her own mind she was trying to take revenge.

Mojgan was only twelve at the time. And she went through tremendous sufferings, the extent of which even I was not aware. It wasn't until I discovered her diaries after we sold the house.

Oh God, I cannot conceive how Iraj was able to do what he had done. And I don't know how I was able to make them who they are today. She had all the right to feel the way she did. She went through such agony. I was doubtful that she would ever be able to survive.

My Dear God:

It was on her twelfth birthday, just one year before Malakuti had died, that Iraj took Mojgan and I to Four Season hotel in Canada on our birthdays. He treated us like royalties. It was fantastic. At nights we were dressed up to go out to restaurants, and during the days he dressed like a teenager, and he took Mojgan to Theme parks and rides. That was the first time that he celebrated our birthdays that way. I even think that he was more excited than we were.

There was something very eerie under all his calm. I came to realize later what it was. He doubted himself. He was not sure that he could be that kind of a father, or that kind of a husband eternally. There must have been a reason behind his doubts. He must have known then where his involvement was going to take him.

That was the first, and the most beautiful birthday celebration he had given us. Alas it was also the last.

My dear GOD, how do you think Mojgan must have felt after she realized that her father didn't love her any more? She wrote in her diary, "My father started hating me after Dr. Malakuti died".

It was so difficult for me to read her diaries. I had turned all our books and magazines to the local library. And then one day I got a call form the library, "We found a diary among your magazines. Please come and get it". I didn't know whose diary it was. So I rushed to the library to get it. My initial reaction was to return it to Mojgan. But then I thought that she would have taken it with her if she needed it. My curiosity was overwhelming, so I decided to read it. I was furious. I don't remember what the emergency was that I gave up the idea of burning them. I thank God over and over again.

I am including a copy of that page in her diary. And I wish that other mothers could relate to how I felt reading it at that moment. How do you think innocent people become murderers sometimes, even though they had never hurt anyone in their entire life? Why, no matter how much Mojgan tried, and no matter how much she screamed at her father and tried to rebel, she could not get his attention.

And finally Mojgan had to replace her father's love with the love of a young man from her school. His name was Glen. Although they both were very young, I appreciated their friendship. Mojgan at that time of her life needed to have happy feelings. It was a good thing for both of them to have each other. Mojgan's life was in shamble at the time. She needed something to hang on to. She needed someone to give her hope. I was hoping to meet his mother.

My Dear God:

One day I called his mother and invited her out to lunch. She accepted my invitation,

Oh wow. My dear husband was so happy with his life and his wife. When I told him that we were so happy together, he said, "I didn't know any better." I must leave all the comments to those who read this book.

We are at Four Season Hotel's restaurant. It seems that at the time he was wondering how to get rid of his family. I am glad that like some murderer, he did not decide to kill all the members of his family. That is the one positive point regarding our divorce.

Enjoying her birthday, Mojgan is sitting next to her father in the lobby of the Four Season Hotel. It was the next year that she would write in her diary, "My father hates me after Dr. Malakuti died." That was the last happy birthday with her father.

Mojgan on her thirteenth birthday in Toronto, Canada. She is eating her last happy ice cream with her father who gave up her love to loving Badri, his partner's wife. I wonder what he was thinking then. I just wonder.

In this picture, he was playing with Mojgan as if he was also thirteen.

Mojgan, Kaveh, Pari and I are in Disneyland.

We are on a trip with friends. Left to right: Iraj, me, Rohan, and Dr. Jalal Panah.

We were at the Four Season Hotel in Toronto, Canada. Actually, he was so nice to us and he wanted to celebrate our birthdays in a big way. Although he was in his midlife crisis, there was no Badri to occupy his mind. Any occasion he found, he would try to show us his love. And in return he got lots of love back.

Iraj treated Mojgan like her best friend and took her anywhere she wanted to go. He arranged the best birthday for both of us,not knowing that exactly in one year Malakuti would die, and Mojgan would write in her diary, "Since Dr. Malakuti died, my father hates me." And this is our life story. And yet I am the guilty one. Their father and mother have to pay for it. As Mr. Armstrong sang, "What a wonderful world!"

On Mojgan's twelfth birthday in Toronto, Canada in front of Four Season Hotel.

On the same trip in Toronto, Mojgan was taking pictures at the museum, but they forbade us to take more pictures.

In this picture, we are at Eaton Mall in Canada. For some reason Mojgan was mad and did not want her picture taken.

These were the days that Iraj was happy and loved his wife, his children, and his life. He wanted to show his children, sisters, and friends that after all, he had made a happy life. Believe it or not, these pictures were taken before the Malakutis appeared in our lives. When Azeez was alive, Iraj did it to make sure he does not suspect anything regarding Iraj and Badri's relationship. What a phony man!

He was actually kissing me. Mojgan was happy to take this picture of us. She was the one who tried so hard to stop her father from running away from us. She even stopped going to school for a while to follow him to LA, thinking that she might be able to change his mind. Unfortunately, her wish did not come true. She returned to Michigan after three months, and she went back to college to earn her degree.

Nazy, Pari, and I were having fun in Disneyland. On that day all of them wanted to go on a high ride, but I refused to go with them. Then, when they returned from their ride, Pari saw me talking to a nice gentleman. She teased me and said, "No wonder you did not come with us. You wanted to have fun in our absence."

and we ended up going out to a nice restaurant.

We really got to know each other that day. I found her to be a very nice lady, who was concerned about her children, just like all the mothers from different cultures. We talked on various subjects. I found out that she has been playing piano all her childhood, and that she has been very good at it. But she told me that she couldn't play any more. "I have neither desire, nor patience for my piano". And yet she was very interested in keeping herself busy and independent.

Those days, we, the mothers, thought that we had to devote our time solely to our children. We were in denial that there would come a day when they would eventually leave us. And then that emptiness will create uncertainty. But there was no one out there to help us cope. So we had to somehow get through, and we had to get ready to face the upcoming difficulties. I understood her completely. I had an idea what she was suffering from. Once we were somebody, and now we are nobody. If this kind of feelings does not make you suffer, then what will?

I just wanted to get to know her and let her know that. At this time of their lives it was very important that they had a great and loving relationship. They both had to face many difficulties. And I believed that having a sincere friendship would help them overcome their fears and uncertainties. I couldn't complain; our visit went well.

Glen loved Mojgan very much. His father took them out to dinner every once in a while. I knew it meant a lot to Mojgan. But As much as Glen loved Mojgan, his mother did not. She made life so difficult for them. Glen preferred to come to our house to spend time with Mojgan.

My Dear God:

Their relationship even improved their grades. Mojgan's influence on Glen was very obvious.

While I made sure to provide only the best for our children, his mother did just the opposite. But the more she disliked Mojgan, the more Glen fell in love with her. I always treated Glen like my own son. And at the same time I tried to be his friend.

Although there were many things that I disagreed with, I was still thankful to God for creating this relationship between them. I supported all their decisions I made sure that they felt safe in my house.

I believe that taking that PTE, parents teaching effectiveness, class when Mary turned thirteen had helped me a lot. Coming from a different culture made it more difficult to adapt to new ideas. I learned that the same rule would never work for all my children. I must learn who they are first, and then treat them accordingly.

Their togetherness really benefited them. Mojgan had felt great and acted more responsible seeing that Glen was doing well at school. Glen used to buy the most expensive gifts for Mojgan. I hated seeing them argue.

Mojgan was a Leo. She always proceeded with her decisions. And word "No" meant nothing to her. I had to be very careful with her; I had to watch what I said, and when and how I said it.

My dear God, I get the same fear and nervousness just thinking about those days. I used to watch her sufferings, and I couldn't do anything to help her.

Ah, my dear GOD, how many times I questioned you about my abilities as a mother. How could I fail my baby? What was the point of creating me, as the mother of three beautiful innocent children, if I didn't possess the ability to bring them happiness? How could you introduce the viciousness of her parents to my twelve-year-old daughter? How would you explain her father's irrational behavior? How would you reason with his love, and would you reason with his hatred for his own daughter, all within one year?

As I have mentioned before, I took up some volunteer jobs. And one of them was for Mojgan's school. I thought it would be appropriate to talk with her counselor in private, and make her aware of what Mojgan was going through.

I knew that Mojgan would have killed me if she ever found out. So I asked the counselor not to reveal it to her. I asked her to spend more time with Mojgan, and to keep an eye on her. I asked her to give Mojgan some responsibilities to make her feel important. I wanted her to talk to her as a friend, and not a counselor. I begged her to help Mojgan to regain her self-confidence. I asked her to help Mojgan understand that at times life would put us in very awkward situations. And that would be the time to use intellect to overcome the difficulties. And hopefully continue living with positive attitude. I wanted her to help Mojgan understand that no one is ever able to control or predict his or her family's future. And when things go wrong, we must find strength to move on. Life must go on regardless.

My Dear God:

The counselor was very nice, and she kept her promises to me. I just wanted to make sure that Mojgan graduated from school. And most importantly I wanted to make sure she never got involved with drugs.

The animosity and tension between parents will inevitably have an adverse effect on children. They will immediately loose respect for both their mother, and their father. And they will turn into pitiful manipulators.

My dear, dear God, I saw my children drown in front of my eyes. Meanwhile I remained standing next to them helplessly. I could not believe that was happening to me. I thought it must have been a nightmare. And I was hoping that everything would be back to normal when awoke up.

But I was drowning myself. And yet I was the only one who thought of saving my children from drowning. My dear God, you are the only one who knows what I had gone through those days. And if it wasn't for my writing, I would never be able to make it. Every day I went to the library to write to you, so that I could continue my existence.

By then my children knew that I began to ignore everything, and that I was trying to keep control of my life. They all were furious, and disappointed. They made every effort not to let Badri win.

My children were happy as long as Iraj kept the pretence that he was honest, and that he had nothing to do with Badri. And when I realized that his lies brought hope and happiness in my children, I just let him be. I was ready to continue our co-existence that way till the last day of my life. I was planning on letting Badri be his mistress eternally.

The more I ignored their affair things, the harder Badri pulled on Iraj's reins, threatening him to make a choice. She had planned from the beginning to get rid of me. She couldn't wait to take my place. I will never forget when she told me "Either your place, or mine", while in Sara's house. Or the time that her older sister kept hinting to me, "She got him, and you can't do anything about it".

My Dear God:

So Badri wasn't ready to give up that easily. Especially that she had all the support of her friends. It was not impossible to fulfill her dream.

While I tried to stand up to all the challenges, she kept influencing Iraj to make it even harder on me.

Many things happened those days that I never dared to discuss with anyone. And until today I still don't know the reason.

One day Mojgan told me, "I am going to lunch with my father". I was so glad that he was going out with her. Such incident kept me somewhat hopeful. But when Mojgan came back home, she was no longer the same Mojgan. She was so mad at me. I didn't know what to do. She wouldn't even talk to me.

There was no need to be questioning her. I knew that Iraj must have told her something that made her so mad at me. I decided to wait till she was ready to talk to me. But she never did. And until today I haven't asked her what had happened during that lunch. I tried to avoid confrontations. I knew that I wouldn't be able to change her mind by just trying to reason, so I just let it be. I was not willing to make it any worse then it already was.

Then years later, during one emotional conversation, she tried to put the blame on me by saying, "I was so mad at my father that the day that we went to lunch, I wanted to kill him. I actually wanted to murder my father". She was trying to rid herself from her anger by making me feel guilty.

Ok my dear God, was I supposed to cry, or scream, or kill anyone? Was I supposed to howl at you for what you were putting me through? What was I supposed to do at that time? Well, I just sat there quietly. I felt where her pain came from. I knew that talking in my defense would only make her pain worse. So I let her cry. And I only cried later, when I was alone.

It was Mojgan who wrote in her diary, "After Malakuti died, my father hates me". She was right, after Azeez's death no one, not even Mary had sensed anything. How could I be blamed for what their father did mainly to me, and then to them? Why was everyone repeatedly beating me? And I could never defend myself. But again writing to you, I had learned that by becoming mother, I had signed an agreement that when it came to my children, I must give up all my rights, including the right to my children.

A story of two women came to my mind, one, the biological mother and the other, the adoptive mother. They brought their matter of who gets to keep the child in front of a judge. But the judge was not able to get the truth out of them. Both women claimed they were the mothers of that child. The judge decided to end the argument, and cut the child in half. That way each woman would get their half. At this time one of the mothers shouted, "Stop, I am not the real mother, give the child to the other lady".

My Dear God:

The judge was then able to determine who the real mother was. He said, "You were the one who gave up your right, just for the sake of your child's safety".

Yes, my dear God, I had to get beaten by my children. It was their mother who gave them that father after all. It was that mother who had sworn on Iraj's loyalty, and fidelity, and truthfulness. It was my time to face the consequences.

Mojgan's confession was so shocking to me. I would never suspect anything of that source. I was speechless, and at the same time I felt relieved to have found out that her plans were somehow destroyed.

All this time I worked hard on not committing a crime. Now, I found out that Mojgan, among my children, who had thought of killing him? Oh my God, thank you for not letting it happen. Thank you for not letting my beautiful daughter to become a murderer. Thank you for supporting me all the way. I just can't thank you enough.

As I look back, I see that you had made me into a rock. I had absolutely no emotions. But you gave me wisdom. I could differentiate right from wrong. It was a blessing.

I am sure my children were not fully aware of everything that I was going through, and how much I was suffering. I don't think they knew how much, and how hard I was trying to protect our family from harms.

They obviously loved their father. They were the students in my class, where loving Iraj was my first priority. I did not want them to know what was going on between Iraj and Badri. I was afraid that if they found out they might think of committing a crime.

So, not only I didn't want them to be angry with Iraj, but also I always, in my own way, persuaded them to believe in their father. I wanted them to trust their father. And deep inside I was hoping that Iraj might one day come to his senses, and remember that it was his children's dignity that he was taking away. I sincerely believed that if that day came, none of us would have lost anything. Life would be as sweet as it was before Badri's

times.
So I never discussed my daily activities with my children. After her engagement with Maseeh, Roshanak was trying to become my friend. She had always been against her mother's involvement with Iraj. I don't think I have mentioned this before, but once she tried to confront Badri. They get into a big fight. Roshanak basically gave her mother an ultimatum. Badri got so mad that she grabbed Roshanak, and knocked her down on her back. She then squeezed a soap bar down her throat, trying to suffocate her. Fortunately at that exact moment the mailman showed up.

My Dear God:

That evening Maseeh called me to his room, "Mom, Roshanak is in my room. She barely got away from Badri. She wanted to kill her. I don't want anyone to know that she is here, until we find a solution". I was shocked. Could this be happening to them? I agreed to keep it quiet.

I remember one day Roshanak and Maseeh came home for lunch. We were talking, while making sandwiches. Roshanak was telling me that her mother was always out, pretending she had some legal work to take care of. She was telling me that she knew what she was after. She was not going into details, but in general she was confirming all my suspicions. I didn't feel comfortable discussing his father's affair in front of Maseeh.

Then Maseeh said, "I swear, if I see them together, and it is certain that somehow they are involved, I will get rid of them both".

With laughter I jumped in the middle of their conversation and said, "Are you crazy? What nonsense to say. No one in a right mind talks this way. Please put yourself together, and never, I mean never again get involved in any kind of wrong doing".

I knew then that many people have seen them together in hotels. One of those people was Tuloo Avaregan. And she decided to make me aware of what was going on. So one day, when we were going to a fundraising luncheon, she warned me, "Shamci, please pay attention to what I am telling you. People had seen them everywhere. They had seen them in hotels, in motels, in cars. This time take it seriously. Before he takes everything away from you, and before he puts you on the bare floor, divorce him. It is not too late to start the process today. I am only telling you this because I am your friend. Don't let him destroy you completely. It is not right. It is not fair".

Tuloo probably did not know that I already knew everything she was telling me. She wanted to make sure that I didn't get out of it empty handed. But I had already made up my mind, and wanted Iraj to destroy everything by himself and not me.

So hearing all these from people, I was sure that one day Maseeh would end up seeing them in a wrong place. Then what if Maseeh got mad, and did something drastic? How can I help if he sees them? How do I control this? Please, God, help me. So I would always talk against silly thoughts of killing them, while many times I was so close to doing it myself. I tried to pretend that I was just a passive observer of all those unfortunate events.

My Dear God:

Roshanak was taking Farsi at college. One day she was sitting next to Maseeh and me at our kitchen table doing her homework. She would ask for my help every once in a while. Then all of a sudden she started reading out loud, "Modare man be namooss ast. Modare man be namooss ast". And she kept repeating it loudly. She wanted to make sure that I knew what she thought of her mother. She wanted to make sure that I understood that she hated her mother's actions. She wanted to let me know that she was just the opposite of her mother. And do you know how I knew this. It was because the meaning of that sentence was, "My mother is a prostitute". Can you imagine my dear God? Even her own teenage daughter was ashamed of having such mother.

But I laughed, and pretended that I was not listening. While I was telling myself, "Yes, my dear, I feel the same way about your mother. Indeed she is a prostitute, and probably a good one too".

While my children knew that they had me under their thumbs, they never had to worry. He was the one who was ignoring them, and he chose a new love over them. They had to try to listen to his lies, and give him a chance to come back to them. And because deep down they knew the truth, they had to take their anger out on someone who never would give them away. And that person was their mother. As long as she was able to take the punches, let's give her more. And so they did.

Mary was the one to discover that her father had a relationship with Badri. She had even called Iran to inform Nazi. She was the one who drew that caricature with her father and Badri. And then later she shared it with Maseeh and Mojgan. So they knew from the beginning what their father had in mind.

Roshanak, and I am sure Roozbeh and Rozan, also knew what their mother was after.

And then there was Mojgan. She sensed it by herself that after Malakuti's death, her father started hating her. How dare they blame me for what their father has done?

Years later, when the divorce was final, Mojgan and I had a quarrel on the phone. She blamed me for many things. I wrote her a letter after, "My dear Mojgan, I am sending copies of pages from your diary. They are dated shortly after Malakuti's death. You had sensed that your father started hating you after Malakuti's death. You had sensed that your father's attention was elsewhere. Whereas I was completely unaware of what was going on then. I started noticing their relationship after eight months. I know that you are angry. I know that you have to have someone to take your anger on. But please, I am the one who had lost the battle to two promiscuous, dirty people after long time of fighting and trying. I think it is more difficult for me than anyone of you. You have the right to

September 18, 1981

It seems ever since Dr. Malikutiz died my father hates me. but I know thats not true. I'm just not going to think about it. Now on more important things, my new school!

Even though im in 7th grade im in a 9th grade french class!

[illegible]

till tomorrow.
Mojgan

September 22, 1981

Life sucks! I keep thinking my mother or father is going to die. One of my mom's friend's had an heartatache and died. Whenever I think about it I start to cry. I don't know what I do without them. I Love them so very much. I just never realized it. I prey that they don't die, but they're going sooner or later. I hope later.

till Later
Mojgan Rafani.

I hope I die before I get old. But without pain.

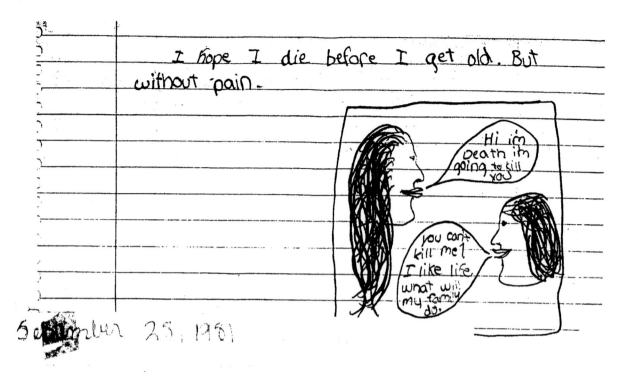

September 25, 1981

Death! I hate death. I'm so scared of it. My mother and father threaten me with it and everyone else warns me about it. And lately it seem every body's been dieing. I hope I die before anyone else dies. Because its hard to cope with it, but when you die your dead. The whole reason I started this diary was because everyone is dieing. I couldn't cope with it and I needed a friend that would [illegible] listen. Death was always there [illegible] ever saw it. Now that I see it I want to forget it.

This is another note from Mojgan's diary. She writes about life and death, her fear of dying, and much more. At this time of her life that she was in need of having strong and wise parents, her father was having fun with his mistress Badri. He left her all alone with her fears and unknowns.

think what you want to think of me. But what I did during those eight miserable years was defending my children's rights and mine. It was my right to stick to my home, and wisely protect my family from the unexpected. I just need your acknowledgement to judge fairly. Your happiness and success have always been my dream. No matter how you will judge about me, I'll be that same mother who loves you always".

My Dear God:

I wrote many letters several times to all of them. No matter what they said or did, I still was there to protect them. My only objective was to save my children and me from getting demolished.

Every time I thought of Iraj's promises to me about the time that our children would go away to college, tears rolled down on my cheeks quietly. He said time and time again, "When they are gone, we will sell the house, and we will travel around the world". The house that once was the sign of our happiness now was the cause of my family's sadness. We wanted to sell it in happiness then. And we had to sell it because of lack of happiness now.

The more complicated his troubles grew, the more he got involved with Badri. He was acting like a complete fool. It was not enough to be dealing with one weight-lost clinic; he opened another one in Southfield. Now he had many more people on his payroll. He was more in debt that anyone could handle. All and all he had trapped himself in the stickiest web. And then to escape from all his problems, he had found Badri's arms to go to. And he believed that it was the only way to cure his Mid-life-crisis. He had nothing else in mind, except promiscuous, sensual Badri.

Okay, my dear God, people get married to be part of each other's lives at the time of desperation. They become intimate to have someone to comfort them, and relief their aching agony. People want a partner in life for better or worse, till death do them part. If that was not the case, why would anyone get married? What is marriage anyway? If you don't need that shoulder to cry on, why bother? If you can't have someone to be with you through your sadness and happiness, why bother?

I was there for Iraj when his mother died. I did anything in my power to make him comfortable. I was there when his father died, in a strange country, far away from his family. I did not sleep, until I saw him sound sleep. I sat in bed while talking to him; I made him fall sleep. I made sure that he survived through it.

My Dear God:

While I was going through that heart aching situation, I had received the saddest news, since my brother Jalal died. I heard that Reza, my nephew, who was only twenty-two, died in a car accident.

Oh, my God, just one month prior to the accident I was talking on the phone to my

sister Azar in Iran. She was crying so hard that Reza had decided to join the army. The universities were closed because of the revolution at the time. Young men like Reza were doomed to stay home, and do nothing for years. Or they had to join the Islamic army, and fight for their country.

After Nader, his cousin and best friend moved to England, he was left alone, not knowing what to do with his time. He was tall and handsome. He was a talented poet, writer. He had a great sense of humor. His hobby was collecting books of knowledge, reading, and rewriting them.

While he was forced to stay away from college, he decided to learn a musical instrument, Dulcimer, a symbol of Iranian music. In less than two years he was able to achieve so much that he became master in that art. His teacher believed that he was a natural born genius. He completed his learning to a point that he was able to teach others.

Nader, his cousin, was into music since he was a baby. But he never learned how to read notes. Reza started taping dulcimer lessons on a tape for Nader, and he decided to send it to London, where Nader was going to school. He was planning to send it with Ezzat, who was going to London to see her children.

It seemed that it took a long time, and a great effort to record that tape. Every day that he was working on that tape, he repeated this sentence, "I don't know if I will ever be able to finish this piece". He had repeated that sentence many times. And you know what, my dear God, he was never able to finish it. He was in the car with four of his friends. They were on their way to a social gathering, when the car rolled over. Only one person died. And it was Reza.

Once, when I was talking to Afsaneh, she mentioned, "My Mom had to postpone her trip, because something came up. Then I also changed my ticket to be able to be with her.

We met each other with an extreme happiness. When Ezzat started crying, I thought it was out of excitement. But the next she told me during lunch of the reason that she had to postpone her trip. She told me she had to be there with my poor sister Azar to bury our most beloved Reza. And even now, after twenty years, still when we listen to his tape, and we hear his beautiful manly voice repeatedly saying, "If I ever could finish this tape". Sad enough he never did.

My Dear God:

My dear God, was it you who took away the pick of the litter, our most beautiful, young, innocent, the most knowledgeable one among all? Was it you who decided to take away the only son, the only hope, the only dream that Azar had in the world? Was it you who left all his cousins without a role model and a leader? Was it you who decided to leave a family of twenty-five people in mourning for the rest of their lives? Wasn't death of our dear brother Jalal enough? Then after twenty-two years you took away one more? Or are you going to claim that you didn't have anything to do with it, and like everything else this

رفتی و من ملازم این منزلم هنوز
زآب مژه بکوی توپای در گلم هنوز
راندی چو برق محمل خودراومن چوابر
باناله و فغان زپی محملم هنوز
امروز که پس از یکسال در غم ازدست دادن شمع محفلمان، تنها عشق و امید و مایه زندگیمان ، تنها نور چشم و خنده لبهایمان تنها صدا و فریاد رسمان و آخرین هستی وجودمان یگانه پسر و برادر عزیزمان ، جوان ناکام رضا غروی که چون حبابی آب شد وجمع پروانگان را دراین تاریکی شب تنها گذاشت بسوگ نشسته ایم زبان و قلبمان از ستایش او عاجز است و گذشت زمان نیز هیچگاه نمیتواند از سنگینی بار اندوه و غممان بکاهد تنها، گذشت لحظه لحظه یکسال جدائی و بی او زیستن نور ازدیده و قوت از زانوانمان ربوده است و با تنی رنجور و ناتوان بار سنگینی این لحظات را تازمان پیوستن به او ناچار تحمل می نماییم. بهمین مناسبت مجلس شب سال آن عزیز از دست رفته را برای گرامیداشت خاطرات خوب زندگی کوتاه و پربارش ازساعت ٥ (پنج) بعد ازظهر روز درشنبه ٢٤ر١٠ر٦٣ در منزل واقع در میدان آفریقا خیابان بیهقی خیابان چهاردهم شرقی پلاک ١٤ برپا میداریم وبااشك چشم وخون دل پذیرای مقدم مهمانان عزیزش خواهیم بود.
قبلا از حضور همه سروران گرامی دراین مجلس سپاسگزاریم.
مادر و خواهر همیشه داغدارش : آذرمیدخت غروی ـ رخند غروی

Reza and Maryam

This is his picture and the invitation to his one-year death ceremony. I can never write the extended meaning of their heartbreaking invitation on his one-year anniversary. Each time I read it, I cry. I now know why Azar cannot still believe that Reza is dead. Sometimes words cannot bring out the complete meaning of what we feel at the time. I think Azar was not able to believe that her son would never come home. She still keeps him in her heart as close as she can.

Azar, Shahb, Reza, and Rokhand Gharavi

Sina and Hosain Chirazi

Reza and Nader, before he went to London

Left to right: a friend, Reza, another friend, and Mr. Moosavi

These pictures were sent to me from Iran so I would know what was going on since I was not there for all those years. First row, in the front: Maryam and afriend. Second row: Mrs. Taghizadeh, Mamanjoon, Negin, Negar, and Layla. Third row: Sina, Saideh, Afsar, Rokhand, Ezzat, and Ehsan. In the back: Reza and his mother, Azar

All alone in London, England.

Afsaneh decided to come in the picture and watch the birds with me.

Afsaneh, Hosain and I are at a party in London.

Nader, his friend, and me.

سلامی گرم از سوی نادر　　که دارم آرزوی روی نادر
سلامی پر محبت عرض کردم　　جوابش را علیکم عرض کردم
رسید آن نامه نامی که دادی　　ولی نادر عجب تو کون گشادی
پس از یک عمر دادی نامه‌ای را　　که تا راحت کند بیچاره‌ای را
ولی بر هاشم مایه خود دری　　از آن نامه نبردم بهره سودی
الا ای مردک رند قرمدنگ　　برای ما نمی‌گردد دلت تنگ
نویسی یک از گرما و سرما　　و یا بنویسی از اینجا و آنجا
برو آقا کمی شرم و حیا کن　　کمی هم فکر ما بیچاره‌ها کن
تو پنداری مرا برگشته تنگلیت　　که بنویسی برای من اراجیف!؟
نه در آن گفتی از احوال جو شیف　　نه از افکار درویش و پریشیف
نه از دنیای غربیها نوشتی　　نه از آلام شرقیها نوشتی
نوشتی چار خط از ابر و باران　　ببین هم زشت زیبا با توفان باران
برو مردک گشادی را رها کن　　کمی هم فکر خواهشهای ما کن
تو هم بنویس هم یک خبرها　　گرفتی دفتر و کاغذ بریدی
قلم بگرفته و جوهر نمودی　　ورق را چون دُر و گوهر نمودی!!
هزاران مطلب زیبا بدیدی　　چرا از عاقبت اینرا گزیدی؟
تو با هنرهایت بگفتی از سر شب　　و یا آیا نمایی در محل مطلب!
ولی با این اگر این نامه دیر است　　به جایش عشق آن بس دلپذیر است
اگر این نامه را پس دیر دادم　　بدان متهم چو نادر کون گشادم
بگویم با تو این نامه‌ام را　　به نزد همچو مشتو حوشی زیبا

باد آمد و بوی می برآورد
یک نامه ز نادر خر آورد

This is one of Reza's poems who wrote to Nader when he was in London. I beg my children to find a way to read and understand this. A revolution was taking place in Iran and the universities were closed. He explains his everyday life in Tehran to Nader. You must know Farsi literature to be able to judge the value of his poem and his talent in his writing, his poem, and his music.

نامه نامی شما را حسب تیک بر ملاج علاج خورد دیدم (البته مهربانیت را پسندیدیم)
در نامه‌ات نوشته بودی ! دو صفحه‌ها نامه می‌نویسید فقط برای آنکه به وظیفه‌ای هم دارید
عمل کرده باشند و حاوی نامه چند خط را حبیب بیست ؟ الحق هم نامه‌ام از همین ردیف
(انگلیس هم یاری مضاعف است) به همین دلیل خیال دارم مستمری از نامه را به سبک خودت بنویسم تا لطیف
الان ساعت ۸ شب و خورشید مثل همیشه در وسط آسمان دیده میشود (معتقدم است
بخدا عیب از خورشید هم !! هوا آفتابی و گرم و طبق معمول باران نم‌نمک داره رگبار میباره
و تولاک شدید تا مریا بست !! و به گزارش اداره هواشناسی هوا خیلی پیسه ! از امروز
روز یکشنبه است تا روز جمعه که روز انتخابات است همینطور رگبار خواهد بارید !!
از بحث هواشناسی بلد دارم : نوشته بودی هم دارای کتاب پیرزنا و جمعه هم دارد میبارد چه پاک سیل
خانه هم که رفته اینشترن زیس کی داره نامه می‌نویسه ؟! (سبحان الله) و آقا در باره خود
(اصل مطلب) یادت هست هم دو هم از اینجا رفتی - من رفتم سرکار و جابری شدم ! از
هفت ماه ادب کالاکر رم وا زاد کاملی به بنیاد مستضعفان !! معرفی کردند و شوراهد جابری
بجا می‌کردم تا اینکه در اوایل [illegible] در یک جریان کمکی - وشیرین برایم آب عمویی باز کرده و مرا
حمام سونا بردند و خیلی خوشحال دادند که نگو و نپرس ! بعدهم از کار جابری کار شده و بقول معروف
خیالشان آسوده و مغرورم کرد سر سه آدار، و [illegible] برایم کرد
بله سه ماه تابستان را به بیکاری گذراندیم و امروز شما شرکت آقای شیرازی با ماهی
...۵۰ (پنجهار) ریال حقوق مشغول کارم در شکرگاه محبت بی حد و شمار آخر شده و اینجا
(یعنی تهران) صبحها با صدای روحیه در [illegible] بیدار میشویم در بین راه مردم را می‌بینیم که دم در
اول دنیا بهم تعارف میکنند! و شبها با صدای دل انگیز گربه تا به خواب میرویم (آه چه زندگی زیبا
است !) چند وقت هم هست هم هوس عشق و عاشقی به سرم زده و فیلم یاد هندستان
خبر ندارد بجوان گر تنها بید اما واقعا در این زندگی لذت دارد و یا هم جای یک دلدار خالیست
تا ز... عدار... [illegible]

This is one of Reza’s letters to Nader. He shows his talent in writing and his comic attitude in his daily life. We miss you my dear Reza. I wish I was able to get to know you more.

نامه ای از رضا عودی به نادر

سلامی گرم از این سوی نادر / که دارم آرزوی روی نادر

سلامی پر محبت عرض کردم / جوابش را علیکم عرض کردم

رسید آن نامهٔ نامی که دادی / ولی نادر عجب تو کون گشادی

پس از یک عمر دادی نامه ای را / که ناراحت کند بیچاره ای را

ولی بر ما تو هم سالم نبودی / از آن نامه نبردم بهره سودی

الا ای مردک رند و زرنگ / برای ما نمی گردد دلت تنگ؟

نوشتی یک از گرما و سرما / و یا هیچ نپرسی از اینجا و آنجا

برو آقا کمی شرم و حیا کن / کمی هم فکر با بیچاره ها کن

تو پنداری که بر تو گشته تکلیف / که بنویسی برای ما اراجیف؟

نه در آن گفتی از احوال خویشت / نه از افکار درویش و سرنیشت

نه از دنیای غربی ها نوشتی / نه از آلام شرقیها نوشتی

نوشتی چار خط از اهر و یاران / نپرسی هم "ترت زیاد" قربان یاران

برو مردک گشادی را رها کن / کمی هم فکر خواهشهای ما کن

تو که هم کیف و هم پاکت خریدی / گرفتی دفتر و کاغذ بریدی

قلم بگرفته و جوهر کمی زدی / ورق را چون دُر و گوهر نکردی!!!

هزاران مطلب زیبا ندیدی / چرا ای عاقبت این را گزیدی؟

تو با هر یار بگفتی از سر نیک / و یا آنجا بود قحط مطلب!

ولی باری اگر این نامه درست / بجایش شش آن پس دلپذیر است

اگر این نامه را پس دیر دادم / بدان منهم چو نادر کون گشادم

بگویم باز هی این نامه ام را / به شعری همچو شعر خویش زیبا

یاد آمد و جوی صبر آورد / یک نامه ز نادر خبر آورد

was simply the work of nature.

How can I even come close to try and describe my feelings? It was just one month before the accident that Azar was worried about him joining the army. She was worried she would lose her son forever. I tried so hard to calm her down. And I told her, "Azar-jon, Reza is a young man now. You must not kill yourself over every action he is going to take in his life. God forbid, if joined the army, and he got killed. What can you do to change things around you? Please Azar, it hasn't happened yet. Why are you mourning for him now? Please stop it. Let him live as long as he is able to live. You must not think that you are losing your son, and what you can do to stop him. Don't hurt yourself or him by crying and mourning for him while he is alive. If it happens, which probably never will, there will be plenty of time for mourning and crying".

My dear God, how do I face Azar now? How do I show her my sorrow and grief? How can I suggest to her to continue living? I was embarrassed to talk to her. It seemed to me and everyone else around her that she knew that Reza was going to die. But she wasn't sure of exactly how or where. She was just thinking that if she could stop him from joining the army, she might be able to prevent his death. Oh my heart, Oh my aching heart, what do I do now?

Azar died with Reza. How could she continue to walk, or talk, or work, or even breath again?

I was just an aunt, and I felt dead inside me. What could Azar do to survive this tragic event? Is it possible for her to watch her only love her only heart; her only hope and dream to be buried under tons of dirt? God please help her. Please help her.

Ezzat was going to London to visit her children. And I was going there to be with her and her children. We bought tickets, and setup a date to be in London at the same time.

When Ezzat told me the news, we had all the time to mourn together. Now we had to find the right way to break the news to Afsaneh and Nader. Afsaneh seemed to be more reasonable, but what about Nader? Those two were closer than brothers.

My Dear God:

Nader was impatiently waiting to receive the Dulcimer and the tape. His Farsi literature was excellent. His poem was even better. I would like to include one of his poems dedicated to Nader, although I know that my children cannot understand it. But if they are interested, they can get help from a Farsi person to translate it for them. His death left a tremendous pain in our hearts forever. His music, his poems, his writings, and the energy that he deposited in all his cousins, all are the symbols of his existence among all of us. He will never be forgotten.

The day that we had finally decided to break the news to Nader was very challenging. We were concerned that he might not be able to survive through it. While in the car we started discussing subjects in general. We talked about the revolution in Iran,

and about how many lives have been lost. Then I turned the subject to Iranian's tolerance during the unwanted war, which was forced on our country. And that almost every family was facing the losses of their children, without any mercy or forgiveness. And then I said, "What would you do if someone told you that Reza is dead?" And we continued the conversation. At first he didn't get it. Then again in the middle of our conversation I repeated the news. He still did not believe that I was giving him the news of Reza's death. Then I asked him again, "What if I told you right now that Reza is dead? What will you do?" He looked in my eyes, and he turned his face away from me. Then he looked at me again. I said, "Yes Nader-jon, we have 1ost our dear Reza. The reason that your mom had to postpone her trip was the unexpected death of Reza".

Everyone was quiet till we got home. He lay down on his back in the middle of the living room, with a glass of whisky next to him just staring at the ceiling. Tears were flowing over his cheeks down on the carpet. He drank himself to a point that his body looked lifeless.

My sister and I sat by him, and watched him experience the painful death of his only and closest friend.

After that Nader was never himself. They were the same age. They grew up together. They shared many laughs, they cried together. They were inseparable.

There were times that we thought that if Reza had the opportunity to get out of Iran with Nader, he would have probably still be living today. But how can we be sure? He would have probably end up joining the Islamic army, and get killed in the war.

Afsaneh mourned in private at first, and then she joined us. We sat there and just cried for poor Azar. The scary thought of covering that handsome body of Azar's son with dirt had never left me, even up to now. God, how could she live after Reza was gone? How did you expect her to survive? That was when we all realized that every good thing comes to an end. And that this would pass too.

My Dear God:

When I returned from London, no one in my family showed any emotion except Maseeh. Maseeh and Reza were only one month apart. He was sad. But since they lived so far way from each other for so many years, he only had some slight childhood memories. Once in my parent's house he hit his head against the faucet near the pool in their yard.

Azar pressed her hand against the hole in his head to stop the bleeding, and barefoot she ran to the nearest clinic, six blocks away from our house. Even though he was only four years old, he was so nice and gentle that he didn't move even once while they were putting the stitches. Even the doctor thought that he was unconscious.

Azar has gone through a lot. When she was little she got sick with Tetanus. She remained paralyzed from waist down for some time. She eventually recovered, but she never really gained her whole strength back. I still can't believe that she was able to carry

Reza for the whole six blocks. But she did that to save him from bleeding to death. And there were many other occasions that she showed superhuman powers in order to save her son. But this time around she was not there to save her Reza. That car rolled over him, and there was no one there to save him. It was the time for him to go, and wait for us to join him.

Even though Maseeh did not have many memories of Reza, he still showed me his sorrow. Whereas Iraj, the one who was supposed to be there for me in good or bad, did not say a word. He said neither good, nor bad. He was so busy with his love affair that he did not have time to think. What a pity! What a shame!

It was very difficult for my mother to deal with Reza's passing. I knew that watching Azar mourning over Reza's death was a reoccurring scene of Jalal's death for her. It was way too much for her to be loosing two beautiful young men in her life. I was not there next to her, but I knew that she was wishing she could join them both in heaven soon.

Then in about four months after Reza had passed away, on one gloomy, desperate day, she got ran over by a car. They couldn't find her for twenty-four hours. They had finally contacted police, and went down to morgue to find her body there.

What a life! What a disaster! Shame on me, shame on me! How can I write about all these as if I am just writing a story? How do you make us my dear GOD? How come you don't prepare us for these awful events in our lives? How do you expect to just observe our dearest people disappear like that? Why didn't you give us a heart that would be able to take all the pain, and not get ruined? And is it okay that you give us the pain, and then you expect to deal with it on our own? Very well, I think I am managing.

My Dear God:

Long time ago I thought that if I separated from my loved ones I would die. I didn't die, and I am still here writing about those whom I loved the most. I was in USA when Jalal died. I was here when my father died. I was here when Reza died. I was here when my mother died. And then above all I have lost the love of my life, my Iraj, whom I gave up my family for. You tell me, my dear GOD, is it fair? Don't you think I should have gone crazy? Don't you think I should have become a murderer? Don't you think I had the right to kill myself? What is there left for me to be hopeful with? Does it really make any difference what I do, or say? Why did you let me fall in love with this person? I was naive and stupid. But you were above everything. You knew him. You had the knowledge of giving us what was good for us. You made me believe that he was the only one for me in the entire universe.

I am sorry, my dear GOD, I don't know what to think any more. When a leaf falls from a tree, it is part of act of nature. When an earthquake trembles the cities, it is part of act of nature. When a hurricane occurs, it is part of act of nature. Why then when we die and disappear from this life, must we not be able to think that it was part of act of nature?

Why should we have sense to sufferings? So much?

It has been proven scientifically that there is no difference between things in existence. Nothing disappears forever. After they seem to physically disappear, things will eventually be back in different shape or form. So why should we be any different from earth or leaves? Why should we have feelings, and suffer so much, when we know that the person that we lost, his or her energy will be with us eternally? I really am puzzled. What is this arrangement for our existence? I believe that if we didn't have feelings not only we would avoid sufferings, but also we would not have ever created wars. And that the world would have been eternally in peace. Oh well, my dear God, I should have given this theory to you before you created me. Unfortunately now it is too late.

I was raised to love others. I was raised to care for others. I was raised with a preconceived idea that family is the base of our happiness. I was raised to be able to feel and experience the pain and agony of others. I was raised to have respect for others, regardless of their color, religion, or ethnicity. I was raised to never doubt in helping others. I was taught that whatever we make of ourselves is what we must expect to receive later on in life, even if it just meant your forgiveness. So I always did what I have been taught. And I was hoping to be able to have a great life.

My Dear God:

Now I find myself to be river rock. I have been pushed around by a body of powerful water, I got hit by other rocks and pebbles around me. And in the same manner that rock has changed in its shape and appearance, I must change myself from what I was once to what I must be now. For if I cannot learn how to change wisely according to what life is preparing for me, then I better say goodbye to life, and close my eyes forever. And I must take everything as it comes to me because I don't know much. And I must deal with it in a wise way.

At this time of my life I am a woman in my sixties, away from those who were once my whole world, apart from the love of my life, the love that I gave up my family for. I am away from my children, all alone, and I have survived those painful days. Thanks, my dear GOD, for being with me during my absolute sufferings. Thanks for showing me how to find the way to live again. Thank you for being within me, and for being my best friend.

I knew that hundreds of people would show up for my mother's memorial ceremony. I also knew that this was the best opportunity to see our house for those who hadn't had the chance to see it first, to pay the respect and second, to see the house.

He never showed any sorrow for my mother's passing either. Not even one word of condolence. But he started rearranging the furniture to be prepared for a number of people who were coming. He was getting ready to show his house to those who had not seen it before.

As I said before, you had sent to me many angels in form of friends. One of them was

Ali Hushmand. He knew how to prepare Iranian tea, and how to arrange serving it. I had hired two schoolgirls to serve tea around. Maseeh was very concerned, and he was helping in the kitchen with Ali and the girls.

They made sure that each person received a hot fresh tea, fruit, cakes and cookies. They passed around the sweets and kept kitchen very well organized.

As I said before, Ali came into my life exactly when I needed him the most. He became part of my family, without any hesitation.

Thanks to Ali and Maseeh, and the two beautiful hostesses everything went so well. All around the living room, and downstairs in the family room people were served. Halva and dates, which are customary in Iranian ceremonies, were served promptly. Ali did not mind to put all his work aside that weekend, and help me with the ceremony. That day he made me feel so comfortable. I will never forget it. Thanks again Ali. Thank you for being such a wonderful friend.

My Dear God:

That day people came and left, but none of them knew what was going on in my mind. Dressed in black, with lace scarves, they came to condole with me.

Please God, let me have enough strength to be able to talk about that day. How do I explain my heart, and the hatred for Badri within it? Everyone came forward to kiss me, and express their condolences. I was supposed to act nice to everyone. I couldn't act rude to Badri, who had lost her husband, in front of all those people. They would have thought that I was a rude and crazy woman. But when she approached me to kiss me, I wished that I could have slapped her face, threw her down on the floor, stood on her chest, spit at her in front of all those people. I wanted to tell her, "Don't even you dare come near me, you slut. If you want to be nice to me, stop going to bed with my husband. Stop destroying my family." But instead I just sat there, I said nothing, and I did nothing.

I wished to tell her, just like Azeez used to, "Please people do not believe her innocent smiling face. She has been in bed with my husband just a few hours ago. Please people, she has been sleeping with my husband since the first night her husband was killed". But instead I just sat there quietly, and I let her steal my husband. I was practically helping her to do so. And no, I did not let my voice be heard. I just kept crying for my mother, for myself, and for all the things that were forced on me by nature. I sat there quietly, and I thanked people for sharing my sorrow. I thanked my children, especially Maseeh, for all the help.

So, my dear God, I passed another important and memorable day in my life. And I didn't embarrass my family or myself. I didn't even go crazy. I was able to be a lady, a daughter, and a mother. Quietly, from far away I said goodbye to the most precious person in my life. She never found out what I was going through here in the USA, away from her. I said goodbye to my dear mother, who had worked so hard to raise nine children. I said goodbye to my mother, who had experienced so many difficulties in her life. God blesses her for passing her enormous strength to all of us.

You see, my dear GOD, looking back now I can understand people who had never done wrong, but sometimes they loose control and become criminals at shocking moments of their lives. I am willing to share those moments with you. And you tell me if I had the right to feel that way.

We continued getting together to play Blot regularly. But as if that was not enough, many ladies from our group insisted on arranging even more parties to comfort Badri. Her own family never celebrated Badri's birthdays. And now, after Malakuti's death, all of a sudden she had become so dear to some of Iranian ladies. They knew that those gatherings brought Iraj and Badri even closer. But they did it anyway just to see how I would react.

My Dear God:

There were many signs for me to know that something was going on. One of them was the day at the fairground in Birmingham. It was a Sunday. I had asked Iraj if he would like to come with us but he refused. When we were at the park, I noticed that Badri got on the phone, and left the children with me. I watched her while she was on the phone. And I realized that she was talking to a lover, just by her body language. I laughed, and agreed to what she was doing, not even knowing that her lover was Iraj. At the time he was lying on bed talking to Badri, who couldn't stay away from him even for a few hours.

My Dear God:

What a stupid woman I was! I was trying to entertain her, and her daughter, while she was having a love affair with my husband. How naive could I be? There was another time that Badri and I went shopping for plants, anticipating springtime. When I got home, I started telling Iraj about my day. And, of course I had included Badri. But he had mentioned something that it just made me wonder. He already knew where we shopped, and what we bought.

When I asked him, "How come you know everything?" He said, "Well, it is so obvious. I know you, and your taste".

I was so happy that he knew me well. I didn't suspect anything. I did not know that Badri had already told him about our day. What a dumb woman I was!

Iraj never cared to go to movies with us. On that one special Sunday he volunteered to take us to see a movie. Then he said, "It would be nice if Rozan could join", which consequently meant that Rozan's mother would be joining us as well. But we still thought that he just wanted to be a good father, and a husband. Once again, how dumb I was! This was the first time ever that he volunteered to take us to a movie on a Sunday. What a shame!

Mojgan was turning thirteen that summer. I had asked Iraj to give her part time job at his office to keep her busy, and therefore out of trouble. So she began working in his office couple times a week.

And then one day Mojgan asked her father at dinner table, "Dad, who did you bought that Fiat for? I saw the title papers with your name on the table". Poor girl, she probably thought that he had bought it for one of them. He said, "It was for Roozbeh, and I didn't buy it. Mojgan insisted, "But I saw your name and your signature on that title".

I realized then the reason why Roozbeh had been so quiet about his mother's behavior. That Fiat must have been the price to keep him quiet. She couldn't keep Roshanak quiet, but it worked in Roozbeh's case.

I said to myself, "Shamci, don't be surprised to find out that all of your family's wealth has been spent on Malakuti's family. Congratulations Mrs. Shamci Rafani! How do you feel now?

Well, those incidents were so many. And it is only now that I realize that having trusted Iraj had made me a fool.

This time around we decided to celebrate mother's day over a brunch gathering at a restaurant. There were fifteen couples, along with all the children. We decided to play Blot right after brunch. And we decided to get together at my house. I asked everyone to come to my house, but I did not ask Badri. I wanted her to know that she was not welcome in my house.

My Dear God:

Dr. Kashef rode with us. While I was getting ready, Iraj confronted me in front of Dr. Kashef, "How come you didn't ask Badri to come? I knew that she must have complained to him. I tried to explain to him that I didn't really formally invite anybody, and that everyone just decided to meet at our house. And then I made a phone call to Badri. I told her, "Listen, if you have any understanding you must know by now that I do not want you in my house. I am not going to announce this to the world. But if you have something up there to be able to distinguish right from wrong, please understand that this is my house, and you are not welcome here".

Families were arriving one after the other. I had prepared some food, and set the table for dinner and the game.

Then the doorbell interrupted our festivities. I rushed to the door. She was standing there smiling, surrounded by her children.

Dr. and Mrs. Mansoor Froozan, who were sitting in the living room saw her, they were so happy to see her. They got up to welcome her. I was forced to do the same.

Please tell me dear GOD, how could she be so worthless, that promiscuous woman? How come you, of all these beautiful families in the world, had decided to introduce Malakuti's family to us in particular? And most of all, how did you expect me not to be

homicidal? How was it fair? Was I supposed to just take the abuse from that sluttish woman? I was in a position where I couldn't say anything; I had to think of my husband's reputation, for he had worked so hard to earn it. Oh well.

But overall many, including Dr. and Mrs. Froozan, were not aware of Iraj's affair with Badri. And the ones that knew would love to see me suffer. But again I did not let that happen, I was a great hostess. Badri was the last person to leave my house that night. And I didn't even bother to say goodbye to her. I figured if she liked to be Iraj's mistress, let her be.

I had separated myself emotionally from Iraj at that time. I had lost all my respect for him. I could foresee my future, and I just wanted to preserve my dignity and pride, while I did everything to protect my home, and my children. Let them continue their love affair!

But there was this other time when I was very close to committing a crime. It was on that Wednesday that I had gone to visit Rohan's mother at Pontiac General Hospital. She broke her hip. Badri showed up while I was there with Rohan.

We all were at a party that same week. Jila Mohtadi was at our table. We were planning to take a trip to California then. Iraj was talking to Jila, and he asked if they would like to join us. He said he had bought four extra tickets. I don't know his reason for having four extra tickets. Jila said, "We are not planning to go. But you should ask Badri. I am sure that she would like to go".

My Dear God:

Now Iraj had a great reason to sell those tickets to Badri. He was following Mrs. Mohtadi's advice. It is so ridiculous that he thought that no one knew what was going on. So he gave those darn tickets to Badri. He said she was going to pay him later. That incident alone was enough to make me go crazy.

Dr. Vaziri was the psychiatrist that Iraj intended to take Mary to. But he was afraid that he would find out about Iraj's affairs back in Iran. He wanted to avoid the embarrassment. Dr. Vaziri was the one who had helped Azeez when he came to Michigan. He eventually got fed up with Azeez's jealousy, and his big mouth. Dr. Vaziri had a great name and reputation among successful psychiatrists. Every Iranian envied him.

Dr. Vaziri's office was near a high-rise building. I was a few minutes early for my appointment, so I decided to wait out in the car.

I knew Iraj's schedule on Tuesdays, or at least I thought I knew. He was supposed to be at the hospital attending surgeries, and after lunch he was supposed to be back at his office.

While I was waiting in my car I thought I noticed Iraj's car parked just four rows ahead of me. At first I thought that maybe it looked like his car. I got out, and started walking towards the car. Yes, it was his car. It was approximately two o'clock. What was

he doing there? I had a spare key. I opened the door, and I sat there for a while. I was shaking like a leaf. My fingers were numb. I broke the mirror on the right hand side. I took his umbrella, and all his Iranian tapes, and I put them in a large trash container. Then I locked the door, and went and back to my car. And I waited for him.

I was right. I saw Badri's brown Mercedes Benz pull by his car. Badri came out first. She had a blanket, which she folded and put away in the trunk. Then Iraj got in his car and drove away. He looked like a thief, keeping his head down.

My dear GOD, remember that day? Remember how I was crying? Remember how I was screaming? I kept hitting myself. I wanted to kill myself. Then I went to my appointment with Dr. Vaziri. I took the mirror with me. And I told him everything. He asked me to listen to him. He said, "Shamci, you already knew about this. Only you haven't witnessed it until today. You saw them. There is nothing left for you to find out. You and I both know all these Iranians. Why do you think that I try to stay away from most of them? There are only two things for you to do. You must decide to either divorce him, or you must close your eyes, go home and continue living with your children. You must then try to make it their problem. You will actually be doing them a favor, trying to destroy yourself. I think it is time for you to give yourself some credit for what you have done until now. You are a smart lady, and you know what you want. Put yourself together. Go home and decide one way or another. I know that you will be able to bring shame in both of them. No matter what, this will become your win. The way I see it, Iraj's loss would be a great win for you. You must know this".

My Dear God:

I went back and sat in my car. Motionless, thoughtless as if hit by a lightning. I wondered why I loved that thief for years. And I wondered how I could be proud of having a husband like him. Was this my Iraj? Was this my prestigious Iraj who was now acting like an escapee from prison? Who was this man? Did he really deserve to fall into this trap? Was he aware of what he was doing to himself and his family? Was Badri really worth it?

For a minute I thought I was having a nightmare. I opened my eyes and touched myself. I was alive. It was daytime. I wasn't dreaming. It was real. It was after three, and I had to go home to my children. I drove home, and I made the best "ghormeh sabzi" with rice and enjoyed my children's company that evening.

Now imagine, the following day was the Wednesday that I went to visit Rohan's mother.

Before Badri appeared, I was talking, laughing and listening to their stories. When she came in, I felt the weight of falling sky over my head. I could hardly breathe. It took me a few seconds to snap out of it. I kept telling myself, "Shamci, this is Rohan. You must not make a scene. Just pretend that you don't know this woman. Try to stay cool".

But, my dear God, you must remember how our visit ended that day. You remember her viciousness. You remember her infamous smile, always trying to act innocent. She said to me, "Here is the money for the tickets that Dr. Rafani had given to us. Please give this to him. Thank you very much".

Oh my poor heart! I had to hold on to it with my both hands not to let it jump out of my chest. I lost it. I started screaming, "You, sneaky slut. Why didn't you give him the money yesterday? Weren't you having a picnic with him? Or were you too busy entertaining him with your breasts? Wasn't three hours enough to both entertain him and give him that check? " But no voice came out of my mouth.

I wished I could break chairs on her head. I wished I could stab her million times, for as long as I could breath. But again no, don't do that. This was your voice my dear God, who came to my rescue. You said to me, "No, she is not worth it. You are above all these. She is a slut and you are not. She is a prostitute, and you are not. She is a poisonous snake and you are not. She is not worthy. You must not waste even one breath over her. Let her be".

My Dear God:

These words of wisdom came from you, my dear God, through me to stop me from criminal acts. These words of wisdom came to me to provide me with a greater happiness later in my life. These words of wisdom came to me to make me a woman of high intelligence. And these words of wisdom came to me to make me a woman that I am today. I thank you my dear God, for being with me every step of the way.

The funny part of all this was that almost two weeks later, one evening Iraj started talking to Maseeh at the dinner table. In a surprised tone he told him about the broken mirror and stolen tapes and his umbrella. When Maseeh asked him how that could have possibly happened when he always locked the doors, he had no answer. I just sat laughing to myself, "What a worthless and stupid person!"

That day I just kept driving, while screaming my head off. I drove, and drove, and I screamed to a point that I could scream no more. I was conscious enough to worry about getting into an accident, or harming someone. That was one of the worst days of my life. Today I am glad it is over with. I thank you GOD over and over again.

I knew that there must have been millions of other women like myself, who surfed through their lifetime the same way I did. We all had one thing in common; we were the victims of promiscuous women like Badri. I had to learn how to handle my life. I knew I must start doing what other women did.

Inside I was tormented, but I made sure to look good and project happiness on the outside. I did not wish to drown in my agonizing life circumstances. I had to fight back; I had to survive.

And even then the thought of divorcing him had never occurred to me. But there

finally came a point that I had to start at least researching into it. Sandy Froozan had divorced her husband a few years back. I heard she had a very good lawyer. So I asked Sandy for his contact information.

I found out through Sandy's lawyer that the "No-Fault Divorce" law had been effective in Michigan for some times, which meant that I couldn't use adultery against him. But the lawyer advised me not to lose any more time. He said, "Since men like your husband will typically try to conceal all the capital from you. Unless you take action now, you might lose everything. Right now is the best time to go after him, and make him split everything you had together".

I paid him two hundred dollars for ten minutes of his time. I left his office saying, "I have to think about it". And again he said, " it might be too late".

I still trusted him that he wouldn't break his children's hearts. I never thought he was capable of breaking his promises to his children. After all wasn't he the one to salute his family, and announce that he was proud of them? He made every effort to preserve the image of his innocence in front of his children. He always valued family traditions. Unfortunately he had fallen into Badri's hands, and he didn't know how to get out. I was still hopeful that he would wake up, and realize that it was not worthwhile to destroy his family.

My Dear God:

To be sure where I stand, one Saturday morning I asked Iraj to join me for breakfast at a restaurant. I wanted to talk to him in private. Right away I sensed Badri's intentions. I recalled speaking to her one day about my intimacy with Iraj. I had mentioned to her that day, "Sometimes I am not in the mood for it". She had turned our conversation around, and catered it to Iraj as if I made it sound that he had to beg me for sex. That was it! I was not going to divorce Iraj just because she wanted to have him. No! I must not pay attention to her behavior. She was not going to upset me any more!

During that cold meeting of ours Iraj made sure that I knew that his sex life was plentiful. And I recognized that there was nothing left between us. I realized that Badri was able to satisfy what he desired the most at that point of his life. There was nothing else left for me to do but to stick to my plan. And my plan was not to ever divorce Iraj. I decided to just live my own life apart from them and their affair.

I knew Iraj for thirty years. I will never forget his pitiful confessions. I knew that no matter what happened, at the end of the day it would be his loss. I loved the person that I was, and I was not going to change. Many might judge me for giving up my husband so easily. But you are not I. A husband like Iraj, whose brain was in his pants, did not deserve me.

Besides I was never ready emotionally to divorce Iraj. I have always believed that the impact of parents' divorce on their children is irreparable. To this day I believe that

divorce means destruction of love in a child's heart. It is not even a matter of their age. Divorce is as inconceivable to me more than a death in the family. So I was not planning on making Badri's wishes come true. And by no means was I planning to divorce Iraj. I was not going to take my children's love and happiness away.

I knew that I still had a long way to go. I knew that I would never be the same person again. I knew that I had to be able to close my eyes on many things. I was prepared that he might be planning on leaving me with nothing. But at that time I couldn't think about that.

Sandy's lawyer was furious when I announced to him, "I will not be perusing divorce". He said, "Then you must not expect that he leaves you anything. You are giving him the freedom. He might sell all the properties, and take away your share of money. You will not be able to go after him". But I said to him, "That's okay, I would like to take a chance".

My Dear God:

I knew that I would end up paying most of my money for the attorney fees. And I knew that if I did not have enough, they would sell my house in order to get their money. So I preferred my sufferings to becoming homeless.

The day that I broke into his car, he came to me to make love to me at night. At first I was worried that I would break into tears. I was worried that I would lose control, and tell him that I saw them. I locked my self in the bathroom, where I cried. But then I put myself together, and I started thinking, "He still is my husband. He has been the only man, whom I have enjoyed intimacy with. He has been with many other women before whether I liked it or not. So I should only treat and think of Badri as one of them. It is not new to me. So I better go and enjoy him". And so I did. I kept thinking, "If Mrs. Malakuti could sleep with my husband, while she knew that he made love to me every night, I must be able to do better than her". And I did indeed.

My dear GOD, I couldn't believe it myself! How did I do that? When I found out that it was doable, I decided to do it for as long as Badri was in the picture.

I knew that he wanted to be the husband from "Dynasty". But at the time I didn't care who he wanted to be. I was over him; I had lost all my respect for him. I let him do whatever he pleased. I just had to get rid of that nasty love in my heart. That was the most difficult part. I never thought that one day I would be able to live without him. I wanted only the best for him. How could I see my world without him? If I only knew that one day I would be able to live without him, and that my heart would eventually stop aching. Or if I knew that just the simple mention of his name would no longer bring tears to my eyes, it would have been so much easier to get through. But it was very difficult. Because I knew him since I got to know myself. And although that love was damaged for sometime, still he worked so hard to bring it back. And it became even stronger after. Even during all these

agonizing years I could sense that he felt horrible for what he was putting me through.

My Dear God:

His first affair ended up to be somewhat like a scene from "Fatal Attraction". She put gasoline all over him, his clothes, and his house. Only I don't know how he managed to stop her from lighting up a match. I guess I wasn't lucky enough to lose him that way. He stayed alive so that he could do it again.

On the other hand, thank you my dear God for the rest of my life with him. I was able to have my dear Mojgan. She has always been, and still is the joy of my life. Although we had caused her lots of grief, she has been a blessing. Thank you GOD.

It was so sad to witness Iraj's downfall. He was striving to be in the most undesirable place, a place where as he said it himself, "I have lost my good name. I have lost people's respect, even among my own family. I have lost my success, and I have lost my home".

He escaped from Iran, and came here to start all over again. He needed my help, and I happily gave it to him. He started to do very well. He became successful again. He had his good name and prestige back. That was his dream. It was not easy for me to come back to my first love, but I was able to do it after all thanks to all his efforts. I thought he had made it, I thought we had made it. He was indeed at the peak of his success. How could I be indifferent? Even then, back in Iran his name wasn't ruined this bad. This time he had become the subject of nearly every joke at Iranian gatherings. I didn't think he was envisioning becoming this kind of father. There is his letter, right in front of me. He wanted to be good, and he always wanted to have a good reputation. In fact he always dreamt of having a reputable life. And he worked hard for it. I was the wise one. I was the smart one. I loved him way too much to just sit around and watch his self-destructive behavior.

He was questioning himself in one of the many apologetic letters to me, "I don't know who put me through this. Why is this happening to me? How could I get ruined like this?" He was either lying back then trying to win me back, or he was lying to himself this time around. In any case, I loved him too much to see him being ruined like that. I believed he was too good to be destroyed. This time he got his own answer. He was the sole destroyer of his own reputation. There was no one else to be blamed.

My Dear God:

Now that it was clear to me about everything that went on between Iraj and Badri, I made a point to keep myself busy with various activities. I took a speech course at night at OCC. I volunteered both at the hospital, and at Mojgan's high school. Dr. Avaragan and Tuloo convinced me to become a member of the Bloomfield Birmingham Symphony Orchestra. I also volunteered for Red Cross. I got involved with activities at the local Senior Citizen Center.

I took a bridge class in Birmingham Bloomfield Community Center, where I met a new group of card players. They were looking for extra person to be able to play once a week. We were able to arrange two tables to play one night a week. Most of the members of B.B.S.O., the newfound group of players, were ladies. Most of us resided in the same neighborhood. So we were able to get together once a week. We each took turns hosting the games. We would get together at lunchtime, and we played for three hours.

This was the only way to keep my mind off of my miserable existence. At the same time I was always there for my children. I knew what they were going through.

Except for the nights of Blot games and a few other parties that I was willing to attend, I had disassociated myself from the Iranian community. I would not allow them to talk to me about my life, or guide me in any way. They seemed so valueless and low. I was sorry for knowing them to begin with. I had planned to be handling my life in my own way, no matter the outcome. As Frank Sinatra said, "I did it my way".

I wanted to do it my way. I had started my life my way, and I wanted to end it my own way.

On one of my trips to Iran, my sister-in-laws and I once we went out for dinner. I kept contemplating on how to pull my life back together, while we were waiting for our food. I noticed a frame on the wall. It was two lines from a poem.

That writing brought tears to my eyes. I knew it was meant by God that I went to that particular restaurant, and read the excerpt from that particular poem. It translates, "Please God, don't make me weak and needy in front of those who know me. Please don't try to test my strength and me by making me a subject to greater pains. I don't have anything against being bothered by my enemies. Please don't let me to suffer from my friends' pity on me. Please God".

That was a good lesson. I knew I wasn't afraid of those who were not my friends. I only feared those who were my friends for many years. They tried to mock me, and then they would pity me. So I tried to stay away from Iranians.

My Dear God:

Sara Fassihi was the one Iranian whom I turned to. She had a great understanding and she really wanted to help me. She was the one who decided to give me a job at her office when her receptionist was away. For eight months that I worked in her office, I felt so safe. We drove to work together, and we discussed all our problems, and we tried to solve them. We were always there for one another. She would frequently get into arguments with Mahmood over my rights.

Then there was Dr. Habeeb Vaziri who helped me a lot in his own way. I appreciate that he was there to just listen to me. And I appreciate his guidance. He was so helpful to put my mind in peace.

My dear God, I really think that you wanted me to be able to pass all my tests by

یارب به در خلق ناتوانم نکنی
در بوته صبر امتحانم نکنی
از طعنه دشمنان مرا باکی نیست
مستوجب رحم دوستانم نکنی

این دو بیت شعری است که در رستوران روی
دیوار نوشته شده بود و سبب شد که من بتوانم در
مقابل سختیهای زندگی هر چه بیشتر مستحکم و استوار
باشم.

On one of my trips to Iran, during the darkest times of my life, this poem caught my eyes while I was eating at a restaurant with my sister-in-law Parvin.
It translates like this:
"Please, God do not make me needy of people
Do not test my tolerance and patience
The sarcasm of my enemies does not worry me
Do not make me need my friend's pity."

bringing new people into my life. You allowed each and every one of them help me survive through those awful years. When I look back, I see that I wouldn't be able to do it without them.

Meeting Tilda Arnoldi at the center was like opening the doors to Haven. She was eighty-two. She was living with her daughter, her son-in-law, and their daughters Lisa and Tina. She was a dentist from Vienna. At age sixty-two she decided to move to America to help her daughter Lucciana with her children, Tina first, and then Lisa second. When Lisa was older she wrote a poem for her grandmother. They had framed it, and hung it on the wall. She had described her Nona as a beautiful angel from heaven. That poem brought tears to everyone's and anyone's eyes. And I realized exactly what Lisa was described about her. She had become my savior during the most awful time of my life.

I think they were from Italy, and Lucciana was her only child. I think Tilda had lost her husband soon after Lucciana was born. And again I think because of her love and respect for her husband she never remarried.

I know this because whenever I discussed my marriage life with her, and I would tell her, "This has never happened to you". She would answer, "I can't tell. Just because he didn't live long, we don't know what he would have done, had he lived longer. She was the only person who through her words of wisdom, made me understands what life was all about.

She was four feet eleven; her hair was absolutely white. She was very educated, and multi talented. She was working on a different project each time I saw her. Everything she did was very unique and special. She made beautiful dolls and beadwork. She cooked creative delicious food. She made me feel richer with every minute I had spent with her. I had always thought her to be my guardian angel. She had embraced all my problems and me from the first moment we met. It seemed as if she was expecting me.

My Dear God:

Despite Tilda's age we still went for walks every time I visited her. Sometimes we walked to the restaurant nearby. We spent many hours reading cards. We always found interesting subjects to discuss. I would frequently invite her to the bridge games at my house. Once I invited Tilda and her family to our new apartment for dinner. It was very comforting to be in her company. I was having Tilda withdrawals; I had to see her at least once a week.

She was so amazingly understanding. She never refused my visitations. And on the contrary she would arrange for my weekly visits. She knew I needed her badly. Although she lived with her daughter's family, still she would either arrange dinners at the house, or we would all go to movies together.

She knew that Iraj was off on Wednesdays. Iraj always made sure to spend that day with me. We would often go out to lunch together. He always tried to make me an

Ezzat, Sina and I with our Islamic uniforms and scarves, are in front of Tajreesh Bazaar in Tehran. What a sight! People were eager to finish their shopping.

I think we are in Nasreen's house. Left to right: Hajikhanoom, Nasreem with my hat on, Mehdi Agha, Maryam, and me.

The lady with gray hair, who is standing next to her daughter Luciana, is Tilda Arnoldi. She was my mentor, my life saver, my role model, and my rescuer during the time that I was in the twilight zone of my life. The lady with gray hair was a fantastic leader.

My dear friend and my supporter in any way held my hand and walked me through my suffering times. She watched me day and night and anytime in between. Her name is Dr. Chitra Amladi. She had two children who were the cause of our friendship. Yes, Mojgan babysat for them after school, and one day I had to cover for her. After we met, because of our similar circumstances, we were so supportive of each other that we became inseparable.

This picture was taken in Harlington, Texas with the two girls who were roommates with her, while they were seeking justice for refugees.

This lady was my neighbor when I lived alone in our rented house. He was in California, in quest of becoming a millionaire on that Hollywood Live in LA, Ca. Her name was Silvia and she was from El Salvador, in Central America. She was one nice lady and I can never forget her kindness. We got along very well. Together, we even drove to Chicago to Parveen and Parveez Tehrani's house. She was in love with her husband and two children. I wish her the best, always.

This card was made for me on my birthday, by two beautiful children of Dr. and Mrs. Amladi, Amita and Amol Amladi. They must be mature young men and women now.

important part of his life. I might have been naive thinking this way, but I have never seen anyone else do that for their wives. Everyone was amazed that he would spend his days off with his wife.

So knowing this, Tilda arranged that we spent our Wednesdays together. It got to a point that if Mr. Carponti didn't find my car parked in their driveway, he would ask everyone worriedly, "What happened? Isn't Wednesday coming this week?" They always welcomed me with gracious attitude, and made me feel at home.

They celebrated Tilda's birthday every year. They never forgot to invite me I remember one year that I was in Farahnaz's house in Ann Arbor. Lucciana insisted that she would drive all the way to Ann Arbor to pick me up for dinner. They later took me back there again. How would you explain such kindness from a family that I had barely met that one day at the center? Tilda must have been an angel sent to my rescue by you, my dear GOD, at the time when my friends of more than twenty-five years had betrayed me. No, they didn't just betray me, they had arranged for a new wife for my husband. Wasn't it miraculous that people like Tilda and Lucciana came into my life? I was so lucky. Shouldn't I believe that you, my dear God, whoever you are, or wherever you are, have been supporting me to just tell me you love me?

It was almost as if they knew I couldn't be alone. They came into my life to fill it with affection, attention, care and understanding. Tilda has become my best friend. I had never before enjoyed anyone's company more than I did hers. Her beautiful happy face, her intelligence and wisdom, her caring and attentive nature have made me the person that I am today.

My Dear God:

She has become my Psychotherapist. We used to take walks, and just talked. Actually, I was the one who did most of the talking, and she just listened holding my hand. She would never interrupt me.

I often blamed the whole world but Iraj for my misery. I always defended his innocence. I wanted to believe that he was trapped. She told me once in a very soft voice, "But my dear Shamci, Iraj was the one to take the first step. No one forced him to take that first step. He is a mature person. He knows very well how to distinguish between bad and good. He might have been as nice as you think he is, still he was the one who had initiated the destruction of his family. And until you allow yourself to accept that he did take that step willingly, you will be hurting. I wish you would understand what I am trying to tell you. Everything that had happened was only by Iraj's desires. It was his dishonesty and betrayal that allowed Badri to take advantage of the situation. She is no dummy, she knows exactly what Iraj needs, and so she is catering it to him. Yes, this is the way to trap a man. But not just any man. Only the one who shows interest, and initiates the possibility of being disloyal to his wife. Therefore my conclusion would be that he took the first step, and he allowed Badri to go as far as she has".

She knew that if I could rid myself of the love for Iraj I would be able to survive. And she also knew that if I kept hoping, and making excuses for his behavior, I would be destroyed when he eventually left me. She wanted to relate her wisdom to me. She wanted to make sure that I understand that I was the core of the family, and not Iraj. She always told me, "When the day comes that you would free your heart from that love for Iraj, you will be thanking God for taking him away from you forever".

I have no doubts that she was my guardian angel. I would have not been able to make it without the help of Tilda, and her family, and families like Farahnaz and Ali, and Sara Fassihi.

I still keep in touch with all of them, and I visit them every time I am in Michigan. I love them all, and I always wish them the best.

I got to meet Dr. Chitra and Mr. Presad Amladi around the same time. Mojgan was attending Andover High School. She had inquired about a job as a baby sitter, and so she was referred to Amladis.

Mojgan called me once from school and said, "Mom, I have an appointment, and I am afraid I won't be able to pick up Amladis' children from school". I told her not to worry, and that I would do it for her.

My Dear God:

When Dr. Amladi and her husband came home, they were delighted to see that their children were in good hands.

Amladis were from India. They were a very handsome couple. She was a doctor, and Persad was an engineer. They both were very ambitious. They had two children, Amita and Amol. Amladis dreamt of providing a great future for their children.

They were married in India according to their traditions. They both had walked the most difficult paths of their lives, getting ready for better future. I guess they were yet unaware that things are not always going the way they were planned.

I invited them to my house first. Then we began spending time together. My life was full of uncertainties at the time. We became close with Chitra, and I felt comfortable talking to her. It wasn't too long after we became close friends that one day she took her children out to dinner. While they were ordering the food, she fainted right there at the front counter. Paramedics took her to the emergency room, where she was diagnosed with Multiple Sclerosis. She went through the whole phase of denial first. She didn't want to believe that she would possibly get sick at the age of only forty "No, not me. I am here to help others. How will I be able to help them now?"

I was very disturbed when I found out about her illness. Amladis turned for second opinion to many other professionals and clinics. They even took a trip to New York. But her diagnosis was confirmed.

I didn't know how else to help her, other than by just being there for her, especially that she didn't have her family here in U.S. Together we often went to libraries seeking comfort in books.

Chitra's daughter Amita was diagnosed with attention deficit disorder from early on. That responsibility alone had become a great burden on Chitra's health condition.

I had become Chitra's sister, her best friend. Just like she had always been there for me to help me cope up with my pain, I was there for her at any time of the day or night. I drove her children to school, and I helped her with the chores. Amol, Chitra's son, was a very good student. He was a participant of nationwide mathematics competition. Chitra and Presad were very proud of him and they always encouraged and supported his extraordinary abilities.

The whole family, including Presad, had accepted me as own family member. Especially the children were very happy there. We cooked together, we read together.

My Dear God:

Amladis had a tradition of weekly family meetings. They had asked me to participate in them as well. That was where each member of the family discussed their daily activities and interactions. That was when they opened the discussions to complaints and criticism. And in the end justice was served to everyone's concerns and needs. I enjoyed attending those meetings, even though at times I had to serve as a mediator.

I had made it my responsibility to support Chitra when she was feeling vulnerable. And she did the same for me. Together we started researching on books that could help us gain inner strength. We traveled together, and we celebrated our birthdays together. It felt like having my family alongside with me.

When Chitra's disease started progressing, she decided to stop working at the hospital. It was an enormous sacrifice. I attended her farewell party at the hospital. And I believe I was the only one moved by her emotional speech. She was too young to be giving up career, the career that she worked so hard on for the past forty years. How was it fair my dear GOD?

Chitra attended that fatal court-hearing day with me. Yes, my dear GOD, that day I received and signed my divorce papers. Yes, my dear GOD, I had no choice. My husband in his mid life crisis had fallen in love with that woman.

I didn't cry that day. I said nothing that day. I only added my sarcastic opinion on the back of the divorce paper. And I finally thanked him for destroying our home. I thanked him for burning our house, and ruining our children's happiness. I am including a copy of that letter in this book.

So, my dear God, both Chitra and I had lost our hopes, and everything that we had gained in prior years. We both lacked an enormous aspect of physical and emotional lives. My existence was inconceivable at the time since I had lost my family and the love of my life. And loosing health, successful career, and most of all her dreams was very distrustful for Chitra. Nevertheless we decided to be strong and not to loose hope.

We were already involved in various activities. And we started joining even more classes, seminars, and volunteer groups.

My dear God, after leading the critical department of Sinai hospital for years, she was now demoted to nobody. It was as if she was never educated, or worked in medical field. One day Amita asked her, "Mom, are they going to refer to you as Dr. Amladi, or just Mrs. Amladi?" I saw tears in Chitra's eyes. She wouldn't answer. But I came to her rescue, "Amita, the disease might get to you mother physically, but it will never take away her achievements and her title as a doctor.

My Dear God:

Losing Roya Rabbani's daughter was very painful for me when I heard it. Not only was she young and beautiful on the outside, but she was even more beautiful on the inside. To tell you the truth, she was number one.

I know, my dear GOD, that their loved one was dead, whereas my love was leaving us. But the absence of my love felt equally painful. Would it be appropriate to tell them, "Well, now that she is gone, go and do your own thing, the same thing that Dr. Rabbani told me after Iraj divorced me".

Not only nothing happened to Iraj or Mohammad, but also they are living better than ever after these many years. Yes, they have to find a way to live after her loss. But I am asking you, my dear Rabbanis, do you think it is going to be the same as before you had lost her? Do you think you can forget loving her for that many years? Did you think it was easy for me to give up my family after thirty years and not suffer for it? I don't believe so. I do not believe so!

You know, Dr. M Rabbani, I never was a religious person. But you were Muslim, and your father was the leader of Islam. Both you and Nayer have been pretending that you didn't have anything to do with bringing Iraj and Badri together. You didn't even know what you had against me personally to dislike me to a point that it didn't bother you if I lost my family. If you were that innocent, and if you really had nothing to do with it, you could have boycotted their visitation after they got married. Just to prove that you have been innocent, and that you were not involved with their wrongdoings. But instead, you have welcomed them with open arms, and accepted their friendship with warmth and enthusiasm. You really don't know where God is standing, do you? Did you think that as long as you tried to cover up for them, and never talked about it, then GOD wouldn't know what your plans were? Do you really think that God is not in all our actions? I never thought you were that naive. Oh well.

I was at a stage of my life that I had to kill Shamci within me, and I gave birth to a new person with new character and personality. Since all my feelings were gone, I had created a new, wise and practical person. I had no idea what kind of a person I would end up being, but it didn't hurt to try.

Thanks to all my guardian angels my survival had become imminent. While I was trying to figure out what had happened to my life, Parveen and Niya were trying to visit from Iran. But since it was during the time of the hostage crisis, they were denied. Parveen had problem with her bladder, and Iraj tried applying for their visas through medical reasons. Still they were denied. So Iraj took some time off. He met them in Turkey, and they went to Europe together.

My Dear God:

That was the time that we put our house for sale. It was on the market for five years, but we were not able to sell it.

I had packed everything in boxes, and I labeled them all. Everything was ready to go. As always, everything was well organized and under control. The house was sold on his absence. With his power of attorney, I carefully checked all the papers and signed the deal.

Although I was aware of the fact that Iraj had been taking money out of our joint accounts, when I received the five hundred thousand dollar check, I just signed the back of it, I gave it to him upon his return.

I had many reasons for doing so. First, I could never see myself acting dishonest with Iraj. Second, the "No Fault Divorce" law was still enforced in Michigan at the time. Third, I knew that for hiring a lawyer would have cost me all of that money, and more. So I decided to stay calm. I signed the check, and gave it to him. I knew that if he tried to steal from me, it would have been easy for the authorities to trace the money. So it was much wiser to just leave it untouched, and wait to see what would happen.

I was sure that his sisters knowing our life history, wanted to find out more about what was happening then. They always wanted him to be a good man. I didn't want to intervene while they were in Europe.

You know, my dear God, he shocked me again when he returned from Europe. He had bought me a light chocolate color satin dress with a beautiful imitation diamond buckle by a Swiss designer.

Usually when people receive gifts as such from a person that they are in love with, they will naturally become happy and excited. Where in my case, I did not know what to feel. Did he still love me? His effort was obvious. And it was obvious that he had been thinking of me. He couldn't have possibly hated me. It would be stupid of me to think that way. Then again, it took me twenty-five years back, when he had his first affair. He would buy me more gifts than any husband ever did for their wives. Why, if he loved me so much, and he thought of me even when he was so far away from me, was he having an affair? Why, when he knew how cruel and dishonest Badri was, he would allow her to destroy his family? Why couldn't he think before it was too late? It brought back the memory of the night that we were in Iran at Froogh's house. Froogh was selling his artwork. No one else bought gifts for their wives, except Iraj Rafani, who at that time was having an affair with his nurse. God, please help me to understand him. Who was he? Why did he act this way? I loved him more than he could ever conceive. And I knew that he appreciated my love. I adored him. He knew that I worshiped him. Why would he act the way he did at times? Did he love me or not? God, please let me know what he expected from me?

My Dear God:

He gave me the gift in front of all those so-called friends. And everyone said, "Oh, how beautiful! What a great husband!"

As I have mentioned before we once scheduled full check-ups for him at the Cleveland Clinic. He wouldn't tell me why, but I had a felling it had something to do with impotency.

Even though I knew of his involvement with Badri, I had decided not to reject him in bed. And I tried to understand him.

But slowly he started pulling away from me. He rejected me even when I approached him. And eventually we stopped being intimate. I believe that he was struggling with impotency, and that Badri was his only cure. He was so wrapped and confused in lust for her.

My dear God, you had made me so strong so that I was able to take anything that came my way. You gave me the energy to enable me to perfect just anything I touched.

After we sold the house, we had to move to a three-bedroom apartment. While I was fighting for my life, I was experiencing enormous amount of energy all throughout. With your help my dear God, I was able to retain my dignity, and I was capable of performing miracles. I was supposed to downsize from a seven thousand square feet house with eight bathrooms, to a small three-bedroom apartment.

Not only I succeeded, but only a week after I was able to throw a dinner party for some friends. My lady-friends were shocked, "How did you manage to unpack, and arrange such a wonderful dinner all at the same time?"

Being familiar with Iraj's tendency for self-destruction, I was expecting a big shift in our lives. His brain was taking orders from the lower part of his body, instead of his head. The opening of his first clinic was almost immediately followed by the second one. In less then a year he sold that second clinic with great lost. Next he got involved with opening a nightclub on Six Mile Road in Detroit, the most dangerous part of city. He was so eager to become a millionaire, he didn't hear my advice. And to top it off, to prove his innocence to his children, he blamed me for being a negative person.

I got dressed for the opening of that nightclub. I was supposed to feel good about

Boy oh boy. What should I write about these pictures? It is much better not to say anything. These are the people whom Iraj started his partnership with, for a nightclub in Detroit. Iraj, Kamal, Hossainy, Naheed-Hossainy's sister, and obviously me.
What a memory!

The same group at the table. When I look at these pictures I get a bad headache. Who were we, and who did we become?

Mojgan and I walked around the shore for a long time. We talked and we fought and we fought. Then we sat on that stone and I asked a gentleman to take a picture of us. It turned out beautiful. It seems as if we were having fun all day, and we probably did. Moji screamed at me as loud as she could and that way she might have found herself a little comfort.

being part of a big money making project. Many important figures, like the mayor of Detroit, were present. The media and photographers were there too. But I wasn't there. I had strange mixed feelings that I couldn't explain. I was feeling out of place. I no longer knew who I was, and I didn't know what I was doing there. It felt like I was involved with Mafia. I didn't have this kind of life in mind for my children and me.

My Dear God:

What happened to the hospital parties and medical conventions? Supposedly I was a teacher, and he was a doctor. We were here to raise our children in good morals, and a dignified lifestyle.

I married Iraj to be able to raise my children with honesty, within a healthy and strong family structure, supported by the love I had for him. I wanted them to learn about life and happiness, and I was hoping they would find it within themselves. I wanted them to learn to work hard; I wanted to make sure they never sold themselves or their reputation for money. How could I explain to them what was going on? How could I teach my children something that I was not practicing myself? How could I make Iraj understand that he was leading my children in the wrong direction?

After his first affair, and until Badri came into his life, he always made sure to discuss his decisions with me. And for the most part of it he took to my advice. He believed that since we had joined our lives, we had to make our decisions based on mutual respect, trust and understanding. He sought my support for his new ideas. He went along with my ideas. Our children even accused him at times that he wasn't able to make his own decisions.

Like in the instance of Maseeh asking for a very expensive camera, my objection was that if he did not have good grades, he was not supposed to receive anything from us. I believed that we were not to reward our children unless they applied themselves. Meanwhile his father's answer to his request was, "I will have to ask your mom. I will have no objections if she agrees". Maseeh knew very well that I would not approve of that. And so he told his father, "Do you always have to ask my mom. Can't you ever make your own decisions without asking my Mom?"

While Iraj was quite amused by the incident, "These kids are so smart. He was planning to instigate a disagreement between us so that he could get his camera. This way he wouldn't even have to work hard for it".

It seemed that after his first affair he had plans to do it right this time. He was considering our togetherness an essential factor for their developing age. We both were thinking this way, and we tried to do our best before Azar's death.

There are many instances in marriage life that husband and wife stop thinking and re-evaluate their partner's character.

My Dear God:

Before Malakuti's death the kind of love and attention that he gave to his children and me was such that I would have bet my life on, "If all the men in the world turn their backs at their families, Iraj would be among those who would never do such a thing". He had bought my trust to a point that my love for him had tripled. He was so considerate in his actions for us, and especially for me, that sometimes I thought of him to be the most innocent man on earth.

My readers might judge me for being so stupid. They might wonder how could I have put the past behind us so easily. How could I forget what a con artist he was? And that the real reason behind his amiability was merely his guilt. He knew no other way of bearing my sincere love.

And then all of a sudden, after his involvement with Badri, the same person who always sought my advice didn't wish to hear me at all.

I knew that with the name of nightclub, there comes the mafia. There comes the drugs and alcohol. There come the prostitutes. And with all that there eventually would have come the involvement with law enforcement. I was against that business. But all that got out of my caring efforts was the accusation of being negative. This still makes me laugh, because in his letters to me or in person he always told me, "You have been the only one who pushed me towards my achievements. You have always been my lucky charm".

But now that he was trying to impress Badri, he ignored my advice. And he even told me, "Your lack of knowledge is and has been creating unhappy situation in my work environment, and it has been crippling my achievement". And he made sure that my children believed him. He told them, "Your mother's lack of knowledge and her negativity is damaging my goals". But he was not man enough to admit that every business that I disapproved of, he either lost money, or went bankrupt.

I agree, he was a doctor, and I was just a simple teacher. True that he read the Wall Street Journal and I didn't. But what's all that reading worth if you didn't gain enough common sense to collect common knowledge about things around you.

It was too bad that he never dared to admit his own mistakes. It was much easier to be blaming Shamci. What a sad story!

I never tried to defend myself. There was no need for that. If he ever analyzed his own actions, then he would see that not even one of his decisions that I was against turned out to be the right one. Not even one. That by itself is the proof of who had knowledge, and who did not.

My Dear God:

Regrettably the nightclub did well in the beginning. And pretty soon they started thinking of expanding the business to California. Even with the gloomy relationship that we had, still he was discussing his decisions with me.

Years ago he had passed the California's bar, in case we ever decided to move to California. But when we brought it up to Maseeh and the girls, they just laughed at us, and they disagreed. Moving away from friends, and not being able to ski was not very desirable for them. So we completely cross out the idea of moving to California. Although, now that I'm thinking, we would have never gotten to know Malakutis had we done so? And we would not have end up having this life that we were experiencing now.

So before we sold the house, he convinced me that we had to go to Los Angeles, and research about the possibility of opening another nightclub there. Dr. Hossaini was there as well looking for possible locations.

Neither of us ever resided in Los Angeles. And therefore it was hard to decide on the right location. But again, had we only used our common sense. If the place was a nightclub before, and if it was doing well, why would the owner want to get rid of it? So it was obvious that the previous owner would never tell the truth about the business, and how bad it was. The only thing he cared for was to sell his business for as much as he could. And if the seller was a good businessman, all he had to do was to come with a logical reason.

I had a solid proof, and as good reason as to worry about the nightclub in Los Angeles. In one of my conversations with a gentleman, I had mentioned that Iraj was going to expand his business in Los Angeles.

The gentleman happened to know the area very well, and he was familiar with that night club. For as soon as I had mentioned the name and the location of the nightclub, he said, "Oh wow, that location gave them such a hard time. We would always hear that someone was hurt, or they had to close down the nightclub for some time". So I knew all those facts long before I found out the truth about that area.

So we went to Los Angeles together to see the place that was supposed to make us millionaires. The building was located in the heart of Hollywood. At that time none of us knew anything about the history of that nightclub. It was a huge building with many different shops, restaurants, bars, and various rooms for dancing and entertainment.

My Dear God:

Dr. Hossaini gave us a tour of the building, and promised Iraj that in no time we would all become millionaires. He also mentioned that some minor remodeling was required to make the building more presentable.

Meanwhile life went on, and we were husband and wife. I was on the verge of going crazy. I decided to take two weeks off, and went to England to visit my niece Afsaneh and her husband Hossain. I talked to him only once while I was in England. And I felt as if I was talking to a stranger. Many people thought that considering the circumstances it was not right for me to leave Iraj. But I knew by then that I had no power to prevent them from seeing each other. It didn't really make a difference that I was gone. By the agreement of the partnership they had the right to see each other to handle Malakuti's affairs. This was what they were feeding to all our friends, and to our children, and I didn't have a chance to change anything at all.

Maseeh knew that because of Badri I was not very enthusiastic about his relationship with Roshanak. Although I truly wanted to believe that not all mothers and daughters are alike, still I couldn't help it when I saw Badri in Roshanak.

Once Roshanak ended up at the hospital, I couldn't find out what was wrong with her. But as the mother of her fiancé, and out of respect for Maseeh, I had to go and visit her. Badri was in the room with her. I tried not to look at Badri, or even talk to her. But she kept talking to me with her superficial smile, as if nothing happened, and as if her affair with my husband must not be any of my concern. I cut that visit short. I couldn't wait to get out of that room.

While I was in England I found out that Badri had invited everyone, including my children, for dinner. I heard that Mary had realized then that Badri had taken her mother's place. So she lost it, and she left the party after making a few humiliating remarks. I actually was surprised. Knowing Mary and her attitude toward me, I thought she would be the last person to criticize them. But as it happened in the past, Iraj was too involved, and too blind to see what Mary was going through. He had a great sex partner, the cure for his impotency. He could care less if Mary was mad at him, or she couldn't see Badri taking the place of her mother.

Again, while I was in England, Iraj had Malakutis over in our house one evening. The kids were playing in the TV room. While they were sitting under the Korsi, they felt something burning. They removed the blanket and the table to find our Persian rug on fire.

They were able to put out the fire. But it still made a big hole in the middle of the rug. I had to spend five hundred dollars to repair it. They told me later that Rozan was playing with the heater, which eventually caused the fire.

My Dear God:

Ironically when I returned from England, I found out that Maseeh and Roshanak were separated. I didn't ask any questions. I really didn't care to know why.

At that time Roshanak was attending U of M. And Ali Hushmand was one of her professors. He had heard from other students that Roshanak has been fooling around. This might have been the reason that Maseeh broke their engagement.

Everyone came to say goodbye when I was going to England. At the time of my departure it was so obvious that I was unhappy. While we were waiting to board the plane, a young gentleman approached me. He noticed me earlier when I was saying goodbye to my family. His name was Ali Elhaj. He happened to be a professor at U of M, and he was traveling to London to attend a convention. He was from Lebanon. We sat

Me, Maseeh, Mojgan, Glen Acaraxian, and Ali Elhaj whom I met once at the airport. He became friends with Mary, and once when we were away, he stayed in our house. I was hoping that Mary doesn’t fall in love with him.

together on the plane. When I found out that he did not know anyone in London, I gave him my niece's address and phone number, and I asked him to call me.

Ali called one evening, and came over to visit me at Afsaneh's. I gave him my address and phone number in Michigan then, and I asked him to feel free to contact us. He did call us, and he got to meet my family. He took special interest in Mary. He was handsome, intelligent, and very outgoing. Everyone liked him. Mary and Ali had a lot in common and they immediately hit it off.

I knew that Ali was apart from his family, and to that fact I sympathized genuinely. I wanted him to feel comfortable with us. He started to come to our house regularly.

It was Christmas time. And as usual we were getting ready to go to Los Angeles to see Parri and Kamal. Ali offered to stay at our house for the two weeks that we were going to be gone. When we came back, I found out that he had invited a couple of his friends over to our house. I realized that they slept in my bedroom. I did not confront him about it, since I didn't want to embarrass him. I thought that maybe he wanted to show off the house to his Lebanese friends, and show them how much we trusted him. So

Eventually he introduced that couple to us, Amira and Khadar Hossain. They were teachers, and beautiful people. I became friends with them, and I introduced them to Farahnaz and Ali Hushmand. I stayed friends with Amira even after I left Michigan. She would always invite me to her children's birthday parties. And she was always very respectful. Like my own family she cared to contact me.

My Dear God:

At the time that they were friends, I found out that he was lying to Mary. After he had told Mary one night that he had to work at the university, I found a note that he went to see a movie with another girl. I knew immediately that he was another con artist. And it became more obvious when he borrowed money from me to supposedly visit his parents in Lebanon. The only thing I could have done was not to let Mary fall in love with him. And thanks God it didn't happen.

Once he made Mary believe that he couldn't keep his room at the university for whatever reason, and that he desperately needed a place to stay. Mary told us about it, and she asked us to let him stay in our house until he found a place. At that time we were in the process of selling the house. Besides, no one was using the room downstairs. So we agreed that he moved in until he found a place.

He stayed with us for six months. Many times he would invite friends from university and they worked till late at night.

For some reason he sought my attention. One afternoon when I came home, I saw Iraj with some strange people. Then Ali came up to me, and only after he got my coat with amazing courtesy, he introduced me to his Lebanese friends. Again I realized that he was trying to impress that family. They were an older couple from Florida. I offered them to

stay for dinner to make him happy. I had previously prepared various dishes. We had a nice time together, and Ali was delighted.

He would always tell me, "My mother had asked me to give her a grandchild. So I have to get married to be able to make her wishes come true". And I think he ended up marrying the daughter of those older folks from Florida in order to give his mother a grandchild. He came to say goodbye to me when he was moving to Florida. He even gave me his address and phone number. Although I liked him, I didn't find him to be truthful.

While we were still in the big house, Maseeh was attending the Center for Creative of Studies. He shared an apartment with another student in Detroit. He used to smoke then. And he had a few pets. One of his pets was a snake that he kept in a cage.

So one evening I received an alarming phone call from him. He said his house had caught a fire. And even though no one was hurt, Maseeh sounded quite nervous. He kept saying it was a miracle that they were able to put out the fire. I was hoping that the accident would teach him a lesson, and that he would give up smoking. Alas, he was not ready to give up that awful habit.

It was during those awful times that Mojgan was graduating from high school. While we were supposed to feel the happiest then, we were sad. At least I kept my laughter, whereas Iraj looked depressed, desperate, and confused. I couldn't quite get it. Wasn't he the one who was having fun with Badri? It must have been his guilt conscious. He knew that he was destroying his beautiful family. He knew he was not worthy of being called a father.

My Dear God:

Mary used to smoke then as well. Despite of all the warnings about the danger of smoking, she still refused to quit smoking. But when she was studying Law in Detroit, she was rooming with another girl. One of her roommate's conditions was "No smoking indoors". So Mary had to smoke in the hallways. That made her realize how worthless, and dependent she had become for the sake of a smoke. So she gave it up.

It was before we sold the house that Fereshteh came to visit. She was my friend, the one who never wanted to get married. And just like me she fell in love with Morteza, and she married him by proxy. They moved to Madrid, and after many years they too got divorced. The reason was obvious; he too cheated on her. Although Fereshteh had the letters from his mistress, he still denied it.

I arrived at the Metropolitan Airport long before Fereshteh's flight was scheduled to arrive. And while I was waiting for her, I guess I got carried away sorting out all my problems, when I realized that I did not see Fereshteh among the passengers. I was sitting right in front of the entrance, so I don't know how she didn't notice me. I was getting worried, I looked all around, but I couldn't see her anywhere. I went to the information desk, and asked them to page her. And still she did not show up. I went to the luggage pick

Oh, when I look at these pictures and see that the person I loved so much is in trouble and I cannot help, it makes me cry. We had worked so hard to be there. We had gone through a lot together.
I would have died if he got a simple headache. Now I see he was suffering for something that I was not able to cure.
I was reading his letters which he wrote to me after he had his first affair in Iran, and I felt sorry for him. I thought I would help him this time before it is too late. But it was he, who wanted to destroy. It was he, who pushed it to the end. I just felt sorry for his dreams which didn't come true.

Please look at this picture. Was this man healthy to be able to make a decision to open a night club in the heart of LA in hopes of becoming a famous and rich millionaire?

Down here you see a sick and dying person. When I look at this picture, my heart aches for him. He didn't deserve to be destroyed this way.
He was so hopeful to make a good life for his wife and children. After all I made it, and he was the only loser in this battle. He lost his good name, his prestige, and his reputation. I am sure these thoughts were killing him then.

What a memory! What an awful picture! These pictures were taken by Dr. Kashef. I don't know what he looks like in this photo. I was trying to bring laughter to him, but the way he is laughing is worse than crying. I did what I could to help him put his life back together. But with Badri around and those so called friends, there was no way that he could see straight.

I was losing weight rapidly.

He was looking sadder and sadder all the time.

up area, but I didn't find her there either. I came up again to ask for the list of the passenger, when I spotted her. She was looking for me. I was so glad to have found her. I kept asking her, "Ok, I missed you, but how could you not see me sitting right in front of the door?" Anyway, we got her luggage and we drove home.

Well, life was completely different from the time that we used to be happy with our husbands. I didn't want to talk to her about my difficulties. I didn't want the word get around before our final decision. I was not aware that Fereshteh already knew everything.

After a few days that I stayed quiet, she attempted to start the conversation. She told me, "You don't have to be hiding it from me. I had heard it in Iran". She refused to reveal her sources to me. But I knew that Mary delivered the news to Nazi.

She stayed with us for one month. We attended parties together, and I gave a few parties at my house. And of course we discussed everything, and of course she noticed the change in Iraj's behavior. We talked about the times that he was having an affair in Iran. She told me about the times that Morteza would see them driving around the town with his mistress. She said, "I used to get into arguments with Morteza over him not opposing Iraj's betrayal".

My Dear God:

Once we were in Badri's house. She noticed that Badri acted so courteous to me in front of people. One might have thought she was afraid of me.

We went everywhere together; we took walks. I made sure to make her visit memorable. She realized that I was even more concerned about Maseeh's relationship with Roshanak. I knew that Fereshteh had always been very superstitious. So I listened and followed her advice just to make her feel good.

I will never forget that once when I was in Iran she insisted that we went to see this fortune teller. We had to travel to a very poor neighborhood. You could see barefoot children coming out from each room, all dressed in rags. We were seated on the floor in this gypsy woman's apartment. She sat in front of us, she reached out for our hands one by one, and she told us things that we knew all along. However Fereshteh thought that she was very good. I told Fereshteh then, "If this woman knows us so well, why doesn't she know anything about her own future? Why can't she change her own lifestyle? Why can't she change the world for her children? Anyway, we had a lot of fun that day.

I was shocked to find out that my friend Dr. Sara Fassihi was also very superstitious. We went everywhere together those days. She told me one day that she had an appointment with a fortuneteller. She said she had heard many nice things about him. She told me while we were driving there, "He does not want to see anyone else near his room while he is talking to his client", and many more rules that made me think twice. Obviously I didn't go near his room. When Sara came out, she was very happy with the outcome. Again I saw no logic in all that. And I told Sara, "You might be right to believe

in his words. But I think these people are simply very smart. And by just one look at you, and from hearing just one sentence from you they are able to buy your trust with delivering a few facts about your past. And who knows about the future anyway. There are certain events which are unknown to all of us".

While we were still in our old house, Maseeh graduated in college. He thought it was time to help his father with his new nightclub in Hollywood. And he thought it was time to move on to a new life in California.

It is believed that cats have nine lives. To tell you the truth, I think I had more than one life. The news of Maseeh moving to California was one thing, but to become involved with that nightclub was another thing. I was completely lost. Something was burning and screaming inside me, and crying for help. But I couldn't say anything. I had learned to talk only if others heard me.

My Dear God:

Iraj was so eager to go after that multi-million dollar business so that his name would be among the rich and famous that he did not take any time to stop and think.

I bet he kept visualizing himself among the rich and famous with his new wife Badri in his arms. I bet he was hoping to be cured from his impotency, and I bet he dreamt of being young again. How could he be paying attention to anything else? Whenever I looked at him, I laughed inside and asked myself, "Who is this man? " Or no, I am sorry. I have to say, "I have never allowed myself to see the true identity of this man". It was me who had made him up. I created this marvelous character for my husband, and tried to cover up his true identity. Meanwhile he had been that person all his life. But in my heart I wanted to see him as my imaginary husband, who he could never become.

He was acting like a gigolo rather than a youthful man. He used to tint the few hairs left on his bald head, he used to tint his mustache. The worst of all he used to pull up the sleeves of his suits. I thought that was the most embarrassing of all. Anyway, my twenty-two year old son, full of energy, ambitions, and optimism was looking forward to doing something good for his father's business. He packed his suitcase, and he decided to drive to California for an adventure.

Many times I had difficulty dealing with his multiple personalities. I wished I could find the real Iraj in him. I am sure that my children felt the same way. That was why they believed in him. That was why Maseeh felt that, "Hollywood Live" was his father's business first, and only then Dr. Hossaini's and Kamal's. That was why he put all his efforts into working there with his absolute honesty.

When Maseeh left, my heart was separated from me. Farzad Barkhordari accompanied him on that trip. It took them four days to get there. I knew that I would never find out all the details of their trip, nevertheless, he kept in touch periodically.

After several months of sleepless nights and hard work, there came the opening night of the Hollywood Live, located at the heart of Hollywood. As always we were staying with Parri. As far as I knew there were Dr. Hossaini, and ten other siblings, Iraj and I, and Kamal and Parri who were the partners in this business. Those who worked there were supposed to get paid by the regulations of the club. But as we found out later, it was so wrong to leave a profession in the hands of the unprofessional. And that was exactly what those people did.

My Dear God:

As I said, I didn't know how to handle Iraj's complexity. Everyone was excited at the opening night of the club. All the stores were busy working. All the restaurants were full, and they were running well. Some of the dance rooms were full. One of the rooms was scheduled to have music and dance, which was organized by a group from Greece. It was supposed to bring large audiences.

At the time that I wasn't even talking to him, I saw that he was looking for me. I had my black mink coat on, I had put on makeup, and I was very well dressed.

When he found me, he said happily, "Shamci, where have you been? I was looking all over for you. I want to introduce you to this lady who is the producer of the Greek show".

Then he grabbed me by my arm, and took me to that lady, that I forgot her name. Again happily he said to her, "This is my wife Shamci". And he introduced that lady to me. She was very nice and beautiful. After we were introduced, she asked Iraj, "How come you didn't tell me that you have such a young and beautiful wife?" And she turned to me and said, "You are a very beautiful lady". Although we were not more than two years apart, he had aged much more than I did. It must have been his guilty conscience.

He did nothing to surprise anyone. He always did this. But to do it at the time that he was having an affair with Badri and supposedly he wanted to divorce me at that time. I didn't know what to think of him any more. Still in all gatherings he pretended to be my good and faithful husband. He pretended to be honest, and loving and caring when he was with his children. One would never guess he was having an affair with Badri. He was very good at playing innocent.

If a person is in a right mind, at the time that he is having an affair, and at the time that he is trying to divorce his wife, he will stop paying attention to her all together, be that in private or in public. He would try to show his hatred towards her. And not show people that he was still proud to have Shamci as his wife.

Another time we were at Dr. Mehrabian's house. There was a group of doctors there. The only Iranian couple was Almass and Dr. Shahideh. They hired photographers that night. That time, out of nowhere Iraj came to me, he reached for my hand, and he held it happily. He then asked me to take a picture with him. I was really mad at him. Again I did not want to tell him off in front of people. So I asked Almass and her husband to take a picture with us. I have that picture now, and we look like a loving couple.

In Dr. Mehrabanian's house, while I was mad at him for having an affair with Badri, he came and asked me to take a picture with him. I did not want to make a scene, so I asked Almas to come also. Left to right: Almas Shahideh, Iraj, me, and his other two partners with lots of stories.

Whenever he acted that way, I felt that he must be with Badri just for the fun of it. I didn't think that he would be able to destroy his family after all. Otherwise, what was his reason for him to want to take a picture with me? No one else asked their wives to do that. He didn't have to do that, unless he had feelings for me. So that was the case.

My Dear God:

Then one night, while we were in a French restaurant in Hollywood Live, he did something so childish that even his sister Parri, and her husband Kamal were wondering about his state of mind.

He used to be so affectionate, and he used to express his love for me in such a way that I believed that he thought of me every second of the day. Because he always brought me candies, or a single rose with just a simple kiss, those were more valuable to me than billions of dollars.

There was a beautiful girl selling roses that night at the restaurant. If that incident had taken place before Badri's times, he would have happily bought me flowers. But that night he bought a rose, he looked into my eyes, and then he gave the rose to Parri. I don't think that Parri was pleased with such behavior. She started whispering something in Kamal's ear. I tried to ignore him, and I tried to keep a smile on my face. But when Kamal bought a rose for me, although at that time of my life I stopped caring for his attention, and I knew he wasn't worthy of my love, it still brought tears to my eyes. At that point of my life I was just there to do what I was supposed to do, and what I was the best at, take care of my children. I had stepped aside, and let him make a decision to destroy his family.

It was ironic to be hearing people complimenting Iraj on my appearance, "Your wife is so young, and she is so beautiful. You must be very happy". My dear God, it was because of the energy that you had provided me with. I faced all the challenges in life with a determination not to let go, and crumble down. Whereas Iraj was looking sad, depressed, he even aged sooner than others. I knew he was tormented by feelings of guilt.

The fact that Iraj was being thoughtful with me had led me to believe that his involvement with Badri was temporary. I had also convinced myself that the main reason for their involvement was their business affair. And if that was not the case, then why was he showing interest in me? And if he really was planning to end our marriage, then why would he care to be pretending? He wouldn't have made a point of introducing me to everyone. But I know now, my dear God, that my beliefs were just speculations.

The most difficult part of co-existing with Iraj then was that while I knew everything about Iraj's affair I had to pretend that nothing was wrong. And at night I had to make love to him. That was so torturous. It still gives me nightmares. Thank you, God, for taking him away from me.

My Dear God:

When people get married, they are expected to stay with each other for the rest of their lives: "For better or worse till death do us part". And when one becomes ill, the other must stand by him or her. And I began to believe that Iraj had become mentally ill. Therefore it was my duty to stand by him till the end. And so I did.

The day that I had to say goodbye to Maseeh, I felt like part of me had died. It was one loss after the other. After I gave up my family in Iran, Iraj was the one to replace them. Then there came my children, and they filled my life with joy. My life felt complete. I would never imagine that one day I might be in a position to be separated from them, or lose any one of them. But I had lost Iraj, and I had lost my home. My children had to leave their nest to be able to build their own nests. I knew that it was going to happen one day. But I never knew what it would feel like.

That was the first time that Maseeh was separated from me for an unknown period of time. When he held me in his strong arms, and looked at me with those beautiful brown eyes, I just smiled and thought, "This is the beginning of the end".

Oh GOD, it felt like yesterday when the nurse put him in my arms, and we brought him home. I didn't know what happened to those years. How soon he flew away from my arms. I had no one to share my feelings with. I remembered the times that I saw my parents crying when I was leaving Iran. I knew then how they must have felt. Because I felt exactly the same way, except I didn't have anyone to talk to.

I felt so happy when my children came back home for their school breaks. Maseeh was very athletic, and he had many interests in life. His friends always came to our house. They would usually work out, and swim together. Sometimes they went for walks, or worked on his car. Although I was busy with my routine work, still their presence was very comforting.

Maseeh usually took up summer jobs during his break. One of his jobs was to care and photograph old cars for an old gentleman. Maseeh was very interested in those cars. He even took me along to the garage one day.

He also worked in our yard. And the rest of the time he was either working on his car in our garage, or he would spend time with his friends, siblings, or cousins.

Although it was nine of us, I don't remember us fighting. We were not allowed to fight with each other. So I had raised my children with the same belief, they also were not allowed to fight physically or verbally.

My children naturally loved each other very much. Maseeh has always been funny and very sociable. And Mary and Mojgan were very fond of him. It was very strange for them to see siblings or cousins fight, and try to be mean to one another, or hurt each other.

My Dear God:

This took place on one summer day that their cousins were in our house. I had briefly left the house to take care of some errands. When I came back home, Maseeh came into my room. He looked quiet puzzled, and he wanted to talk to me. He started by saying, "You will never believe what happened today while you were gone". And then he said, "Arman and Kayvan got into a big fight out in the yard. They tried to kill each other. They were punching, throwing, and kicking each other and swearing in Farsi. Masseh's cousins in Iran have taught him a few bad words. So he was able to understand their swearing. And he was very worried that our neighbors might have heard them too. He thought they too understood the bad words. He was very shocked.

I calmed him down, and I told him, "Maseeh jon, "anyone who would allow himself to act this way towards his family or siblings, they are only belittling themselves. Now you understand the reason why I never wanted you to get into a fight".

That incident took place before my children were in high school, and soon after they became quite proficient with profanities. I still do not conceive how it had happened.

While we were moving from one house to the other, Maseeh was living in California. He was sharing an apartment with one of his friends. He knew nothing about my life at the time, and I didn't know what he had to deal with. It was only after I moved to California that he told me all about his sufferings. And again it made me think that I was responsible for all his pains. If I did not bring him into this world for my own pleasure, he would not have to go through all the sufferings.

My Dear God:

So young, Maseeh had left Michigan to help his father's business. He was building up a wealthy future for all of us, not knowing what his dear father had planned for us.

During the opening of Hollywood Live I was staying with Parri. Maseeh asked me to come and meet some of his friends at his apartment. There was a girl named Anna among them. She was hired to work at Hollywood Live. I knew that Maseeh would like me to make some Iranian dishes for that night. So I went shopping with Parri, and I bought everything that I knew he liked, and I made a few dishes. He absolutely loved it, and so did all his friends. Even now Anna remembers the Olivieh salad, and she likes to make it herself.

My children were raised to be honest, humble, polite, and respectful to elders and their superiors. Maseeh didn't really know his father. He did not know Kamal, Kayvan, Kaveh, and the rest of the group, when it came to the subject of business and partnership. He was not familiar with their Iranian tricks, and the games they played with one another.

All that Maseeh cared for was to make his father proud by working hard. But others, including his father, were after robbing each other, the business, and mainly Maseeh, who did not know their games.

As Maseeh was explaining it to me years later, every one of them got paid at all times. But when it came to Maseeh, they claimed there was no money to pay him. Many times the money was stolen from the office. They blamed it all on poor, innocent Anna. She knew that they all had the access to the vault.

At that time Iraj was planning his future with Badri. And while he thought that he was in charge, they were all robbing each other. Since I was back in Michigan, I was not aware of what was going on. The only thing that I could do was to stand by my children, and pretend that everything was going to be fine.

But I was very concerned. I was concerned for one reason that Iraj, supposedly the great father, and supposedly a role model for his children, had now turned into his real self, the liar, the betraying, and disloyal thief. He was supposed to be there for them during the most sensitive years of their lives. My children often heard of other awful fathers. I bet they would never imagine their father could be even worse. They were forced to believe his pretence, they chose to believe that he would never do them wrong. And I supported their beliefs, just to let them to be hopeful.

All those years he locked his real self away. My dear God, do you see it now that it was all my fault? Had I not been covering up his affairs then, my children would not be holding me responsible today. And even in the end I never stopped trying to convince my children in Iraj's innocence. I never stopped hoping that he would come to his senses one day, and that our life together would go on.

My Dear God:

My children were completely aware of everything that went on during those days. They were waiting to see what would eventually happen to me, while I kept quiet, and pretended that I was in control of our situation. What they did not see was what went on within me.

Mary was studying law at Detroit University. She was seeing a young lawyer at that time. They knew each other since high school. By then he was married twice, and he had a son from one of his previous marriages. They were living together in a house in downtown Detroit area. It was not a very safe place to be.

Although Mary made sure to keep me out of her life, still she asked me to visit her once in a while. He had three dogs, a few cats, and other pets. His son stayed with him most of the time. Mary loved that child. I knew from his behavior that he was involved with drugs. And knowing Mary, it was obvious to me that their relationship was not good news. Nevertheless I was never able to intervene with Mary's decisions.

Mary had told me years later that he used to abuse her both emotionally and physically. What could I have possibly done, my dear God? All I could do was to let her know that I was there for her. And I tried to convince her that things would eventually get better. I knew that she was in love with him, but I still believed that if Mary had a stable

home, and loving, loyal parents, she would not have to stick to a person who had no values. If she had loving parents, she would have had a kind and loving home to go to. And that would have made it easier for her to start her life allover again.

I was feeling responsible for her sufferings. I blamed myself for giving them that father. My poor kids, they did not choose their parents. They were stuck with the ones who gave them life for their own selfish pleasures.

And the worst of it all was that if I created scandalous scenes, while Iraj retained his calm, my children would blame me, and not Iraj for the family destruction.

How can I ever forget the day when I found Mary down on her knees crying? She was begging her father to reconsider his behavior. He remained laying on his side on the bed like a statue, while she was telling him, "Please do whatever you want, but do not undermine our dignity".

I couldn't recall the last time that I saw Mary cry. We always gave her so much love. She always acted so strong. She approached life and its challenges with intelligence and power. Bad or good, she made her decisions, and she carried them out without hesitations.

My Dear God:

There are certain occurrences in life that are beyond repair. Once again Iraj had humiliated himself and those who loved him.

He had already lost his reputation, name, and dignity once before. He ran away from Iran hoping to build a new life for himself and his family. I wondered where he was planning to escape to this time around. How was he planning to get his dignified life back? How could he avoid people's mockery?

He was acting like an ostrich. He kept his head in the sand thinking that no one could see him. Last time he cried for forgiveness, and luckily he got it, but what about this time? How are you going to gain your respect back? You have made people feel ashamed to even mention your name. And those who don't mind to have you around, they do it just for laugh. What a pity Iraj, what a pity! Your children might learn to live again. But how could they possibly tolerate a father like you?

My dear GOD, if I wasn't so stubborn to believe in Iraj's love, and if I didn't try to make my parents believe that they were wrong about Iraj, my children would not end up blaming me for everything that happened in their lives. And then I knew they were right. I am the one to be blamed.

At this time Mojgan was still friends with Glen. They claimed to love each other. I was glad to see that Mojgan had someone to rely on.

We moved into a town home after we sold the house. And then a year later we moved into an apartment. I met a family from Argentina while we lived in that town house, Sylvia, her husband, and their two children Maxi and Gigi. I went knocking on their door the first day we arrived at the house. I dreaded loneliness. I had to get to know

my neighbors. Sylvia's parents were visiting from Argentina at the time. I introduced myself, and they immediately asked me in. They told me that Sylvia was out. They assured me that she would come see me soon. Sylvia was very young, and she was very beautiful. We connected instantly. She was very talented and full of energy. She enjoyed cooking and baking, and she also designed art works. She was very much in love with her husband Tony. Tony was tall and handsome. He was an electrical engineer.

They were very warm, and affectionate. I often invite them to my house, and they always offered that I joined them when they went out. They decided to take a drive to Chicago once. They asked me if I could join them. I was glad to accompany their family. I loved their kids. They were very beautiful and well mannered. We kept in touch even after I moved. I went to visit them in their new house. It was a nice house. I remember she always talked about going back to Argentina. Then I did not hear from them for a while. I tried to find them, but I was unsuccessful. I hope that they are happy wherever they are. And I hope they have a wonderful life. My memories of them, and their sincere friendship at the time when I needed it the most will always remain with me.

My Dear God:

Iraj was getting ready to retire. But before anything he took care of Malakutis welfare. He began with listing their properties. And he sold the office for a very high price. Next he sold their house for an unbelievable price. So in no time he had made Mrs. Malakuti a millionaire. Wouldn't you think that must have been a good motive for killing Dr. Malakuti? Don't you think this price was greater than keeping a husband who did not love her? Please, you be the judge.

Iraj was living half of the time in California, and the rest of the time with us. I had lost the reason for living. I felt like a spinner. I was lost in time. My existence then was constrained to a day-by-day life. At any instance I was expecting something awful to happen. My entire body was numb. I couldn't even feel pain. I only wondered when discovered bruises or cuts on my body. I even wished to get some fatal disease. I was hoping it would end my sufferings and pain.

Once my doctor found it necessary to refer me for a biopsy on my breasts but I refused to follow his advice. He got pretty upset with me, and he asked me to sign a waiver stating that I had denied his request. He told me, "This is not the way to destroy yourself. If you get sick with Cancer, your death will not be instant. Your sufferings will get to a point that you will be sorry you ever wished for it." I realize now how stupid I have been.

The saddest part of my life was that my children refused to understand how I felt at that time. Just because I never complained, or for that matter even expressed my feelings, they never found out what I was going through. And besides, they were away most of the time.

It is very common that the ones among us who have been divorced and/or widowed

tend to break away their old environment. But thanks to her involvement with Iraj, Badri had made sure to attend every event organized by our Iranian Community. She even left her children at home to attend late night events and parties.

There was one night that we were all invited in Dr. and Maliheh Zamiri. It was snowing that night, and the roads were covered glazed ice. Driving on those hilly roads was almost impossible and dangerous.

My Dear God:

We left their house at four in the morning. Everyone was having difficulty getting their cars out of the driveway. Dr. Zamiri and others were trying to help Badri get her car out. She was stuck only a few steps farther, right in front of our car. Iraj finally got out of the car, leaving me in the middle of the road. And he walked to Badri's car, and drove her out of the subdivision. Then to everyone's amazement we drove home.

Obviously that night all his friends considered his actions heroic. He was the most humanitarian among all of us. Did I have the right to question him? Should I have been complaining then? No way. He was helping his friend's widow.

My Dear God:

Once we got together in my new apartment with friends from my old neighborhood for a game of Bridge. Susan Barkhordari was among us that day. Susan was the first person to approach me about my family problems. But after she heard out, she tried to deny the truth, and she refused to take part in my affairs. Now that years had passed, and now that they had even made plans for their future, she approached me after the game.

She reached out for my hand, and she said to me in a very concerned voice, "Shamci, I am your friend. Let me help you. Tell me what I can do for you. Don't sit there and do nothing. We all are here to help you. All you have to do is ask".

I started laughing so loud. I was so angry. I asked her, "What? Are you the same Susan who did not believe me, the one who did not want to have anything to do with my problems? No thanks Mrs. Barkhordari. It is too late for anyone to help me. You have all allowed for this situation to reach to this point. You have all pushed it to the end. All of you provided them with safe haven. Do you think that now that I had hit the rock bottom, I will crumble down, and plead for mercy and your help? Forget it. Just forget it. Your evil deeds are done. I don't need any help, and especially yours. I no longer care for Iraj. The only thing that I strive for is to remain the same person I've always been, Mrs. Shamci Rafani. I still have my home and my children. I will wait until you help her take this title away from me. I do not need your help. To tell you the truth, I consider the person that I was married to dead. I needed your help seven years ago. That was the time, not now. No thanks. Go and help them, they might still need your help".

Even though I was very mad, I did not loose control. I talked to her, and I told her

how I felt. And then she left.

Because I had involved Susan with the neighborhood group of bridge players, we used to see each other more often. One evening when Iraj was in California, I was in their house. Susan's mom was there too. I liked her a lot, and by the way she was a good bridge player. It was snowing that day; it was very cold and icy. Since Susan was busy, we started talking. I was sure she knew what was happening with Iraj and I. This was after we had sold our house, and we were living in the apartment. I did not want to talk to her about my life. I did not want to show her my weakness. We started talking on many subjects in general. But she was smart, and she read my mind. So she tried to make me comfortable, and she told me, "Mrs. Rafani, you must believe that anyone who interferes with another family's life, and helps break up their happy home and marriage, they will pay the price one day You must know that people will pay for their actions right here in this world. God will either punish them, or God will punish their children to make the punishment more severe".

My Dear God:

I realized then she was not aware of Susan's involvement. Otherwise she wouldn't have wished for their punishment, or her grandchildren's punishment. I told her, "Mrs. Froozan, God must be fair and merciful. Why should he punish someone's child who is completely innocent and unaware? I don't believe that God will ever think of such a thing. Coming from God, it is not really fair".

But she insisted, "No, when God punishes their children, he is trying to make them understand that breaking someone's heart by breaking their marriage could be as bad as a loss of a child". Still, until today I do not believe that God will destroy one innocent child to teach their parents a lesson.

It was around that time that I heard that their youngest son Roozbeh was diagnosed with Cancer, and that he underwent a major surgery. I was very sad, I had never wished for that. That child was very innocent; he was very well behaved and polite. But I heard that they were talking behind my back, "That's what Shamci has been wishing for. She is so rootless".

How could they ever say that? Alas I always knew how primitive and naïve they all were. They lacked a simple ability to make a judgment.

We went everywhere together, and we did everything together for as long I could remember. We spent our weekends with our children. And we spent every Wednesday, his day off, going places and having lunch together. It has never occurred prior to Badri that we spent our evenings apart from one another.

But now when someone invited us, and Badri was not able to go, he refused to go. And even if I wanted to go, he decided not to anyway. And when they invited us with Badri, and I decided not to go, he went without me. This had never happened before.

Although I felt very uncomfortable in Badri's presence almost everywhere we went, I still thought I should accompany him. I am still shocked about how much abuse I took from them.

Tally Hall was a big shopping center on Orchard Lake Road. We often took the kids there in the evenings, or on weekends. They had various ethnic restaurants that we all liked. The children would always bring their allowances along so that they could bye whatever they liked. Iraj would usually ask me what I wanted, and he would bye it for me. We then would sit down at a table, and enjoy our food.

My Dear God:

This particular time, and again by mere coincidence, Badri appeared with her children. Such a scene you will only find in classical movies. When they came toward us, Badri and Iraj both turned red as beets. I wish I could have videotaped them then. The way that they both tried to avoid eye contact, the way that they held their heads down, and never dared look at each other, the way they both started stuttering, took me back thirty years. He did the same thing when he was lying to my father.

My dear God, you were there, and you kept me from falling apart. Can you imagine what went through in my mind? I was so in love with my husband for so many years, and now I was witnessing his feelings for this other woman. And I wasn't able to say even one word.

Soon I realized that it must have been me. I should not ever let myself break down. I thought love was not something that we could beg for. It was either there, or it wasn't. And if it wasn't, I would never beg for it. I must learn to forget loving him. That was the only thing that would keep me alive. No more loving Iraj. And I must make it happen.

Those two were melting away from the heat of their love right in front of my eyes. It was so obvious that I noticed Roozbeh was feeling uncomfortable. Would you consider this torturous? Was I entitled to loosing my mind and sanity? Could my homicidal/suicidal acts be justified? My dear God, thank you for supporting me that night. Thank you for keeping me away from becoming a murderer.

Thanks to his involvement with the Hollywood Live in Los Angeles, his office practice was neglected. The income has become scarce. He had to sell both clinics. Those were the businesses that were supposed to bring us plenty of money based on Iraj's great economical wisdom. But instead everything was collapsing. If the books didn't show that business was doing well, he would not be able to sell his business for a fair price. Those were all the proofs of lack of wisdom on Iraj's behalf. What happened to all his Wall Street Journals?

He had lost one business after the other. And somehow it was all Shamci's fault. He told my children, whenever he got a chance, to blame me. The nightclub in Detroit was not doing well, and we were losing money. The Hollywood Live in L.A. had extremely high

rent, and they did not have enough income to pay the rent each month.

Since Parri and Kamal had sold their house to join the nightclub business, I always felt obligated not to stop their actions, and just let it be.

My Dear God:

For many months he transferred money from our personal bank account to pay the rent. There were ten Hossainis, five Kamoonehs, and two Alavinejads, who had moved to L.A. from Madrid. They became shareholders, hoping to become millionaires once again. Then finally it was us. Meanwhile our bank account was only being emptied.

One day Kamal called asking me to transfer fifty thousand dollars. He said they needed money to pay the rent. I asked him why they couldn't pay the rent out of the revenues of the nightclub. To my dismay he said, "What income? We are on the verge of bankruptcy here. If you don't send us the money now, we will have to close the business". I asked Kamal, "Why doesn't Iraj get the money himself?" Kamal said Iraj thought that you should have approved of that payment first.

I was jumping up and down, and burning up like popcorn in the machine. I was not there to see what was going on. I knew they were stealing from each other. There was no honest management in control of the business. There were more than enough partners involved, and yet we had to go deep into our personal bank account. He was actually digging into my children's pockets and mine. I t came down to that if I gave them the money, we would be losing our savings. But I already knew that if I didn't, I would have been blamed for their bankruptcy eternally. Why did he always set me up?

At that time I still didn't think that he was planning to divorce. Neither did Kamal and Parri. I would never want Kamal and Parri loose their house over our personal issues. I was so confused. I had no idea what to do.

It would not be as vital if my marriage was not at stake then. But I was afraid that if he ever decided to leave me, there would be nothing left to divide. God, please help me.

I see it clearly now what Iraj was planning. He was thinking ahead, and he knew that if I released the funds out of our account personally, he would not be held responsible for reimbursing me that money later. He had a solid proof, my signature.

So although he was swept off his feet by his new found object of sexual desires, and at the same time he had to overcome his weaknesses of a man in mid-life crisis, his vicious mind was still working well. Otherwise I could not see why he couldn't get the money from our account himself. It was already known that he didn't care about me, and he did not care for my approval.

So I resisted my selfish feelings and thoughts. I knew I couldn't have done that to Parri and Kamal. They gave up their house with hopes for better future. I wasn't going to allow for a disaster to happen to them. How could I not get the money for them? I wasn't thinking of my future. So I decided to get the money for them.

My Dear God:

I went to the bank first thing in the morning, right after my walk, and I sent fifty thousand dollars to them. I was not thinking what might happen to me next.

I kept contemplating why he had asked Kamal to talk to me about the money. Why couldn't he call himself? Maybe he was too embarrassed to admit that his business was going down. He knew I would question many things. He figured it would be easier to get Kamal involved.

It feels ridiculous now that I think I was in love with this absolute stranger. And it is funny to admit that I realize now that he hid himself behind a mask. I realize now that for other people, who were not blinded by love, it must have been easier to recognize the real Iraj.

We were all at Badri's sister's house one night. It was the Azzez's first year memorial. Maseeh was still engaged to Roshanak back then. Parri and Kamal were joined us as well. We all were sitting in the living room in a circle. Badri's nephew, Bijan, was sitting in one of those armchairs. He was no longer a child at that time. He was a doctor, and he actually had his pregnant wife with him. All of a sudden, in front of all those guests, his mother charged at him, pointing at the armchair he was sitting in. She said out loud, "Stop scratching the chair. It is only to sit on and not to play with". Bijan turned red of embarrassment. Iraj gave me a puzzled look, "What kind of people are they? Haven't they got any manners? Couldn't she pull this young doctor aside, and talk to him in private? How embarrassing"!

That same night Azeez's bachelor brother was there too. And of course no one then knew of Badri's relationship with Iraj. He kept complimenting, and admiring Badri's behavior after her husband's death. And they were admiring Iraj for helping her without any expectations. And again Iraj was watching me from the corner of his eyes. While Badri was acting so innocent, trying to charm everyone with her crooked smile.

No, if you want to know that if I did or said anything, the answer is no. They had no idea that Badri had sex with my husband the first day that Azeez died. My son was engaged to her daughter. I was not going to embarrass my son like that. All this time Parri, who was sitting next to me kept complaining and commenting about their acts. Badri's sister, I can't remember her name, was supposed to serve Halva for the diseased. But the way she was talking, and acting, it seemed that she was serving Halva at her wedding.

I am sure that Badri's family knew about her trap for Iraj. As a matter of fact they were the ones who pushed her to finish the job successfully. But Parri, who did not know that much, she was angry at the way they were treating their dead. She whispered to me "They talk of him as if he is an underground potato". I tried to stop her, but she did not listen. She said in my ear, "Shamci, I think I am going to get sick". I told her with

laughter, "Please let go before you make a scene". Almost immediately after that she collapsed on my arm. She seemed very exhausted. She nearly fainted right there on my shoulder. Iraj made her sniff kind of gas, and after a few seconds she regained her conscience.

My Dear God:

No one found out why Parri became so fatigued, not even Iraj. She was so upset with that family and their rootless acts that she got sick from just being in the same room with them. She kept asking me, "Who are these people? Where were they raised? I pity Azeez that he had to put up with them". But what a good fortune it was for me, and how unfortunate for them that they ended up becoming relatives. And they had to go through everything that Azeez went through for the rest of their lives. To my astonishment I have never heard of Parri fainting in their presence in later years. I am sure they had to adapt to their brother's creation. They must have been just like those drug addicts who fake to enjoy the drugs, while being destroyed by them.

Each time he went to California, he took some of his personal belongings. And sometimes he took some of Maseeh's. My children and I were still hoping that when the storm will pass, our life will be back to normal, and the Sun will shine again.

All I know is that Iraj was carrying out his role of an innocent father and husband so smoothly. No one knew what he had planned for us. I believe that even Iraj was unaware of his own plans, whereas Badri was so determined. She was so aware, and calculative of every move she made. Badri, who's husband believed that she was capable of killing a person, then wash off her hands, and appear in front of you as if nothing happened. That was their Badri.

As I had already repeated times and times again, I really don't know what had happened. I really don't know who did what, or what went wrong. I didn't know this Iraj, who was many people at once. In my writings I am merely the observer. It is you my dear GOD, and only you, who knows what had really happened. You know all about who did what, and how. In my writings I simply stated, or at time I interpreted their daily actions and performances.

It feels so good, my dear GOD, to be able to talk to you, to be able to write to you about anything, and everything. The best part of it is that I could talk the truth, feel the truth, and hear the truth. Because you know everything yourself, I know that if I fail to remember the truth, you, by being there, know the exact happenings. I wish I knew the truth as much as you did. But then the world would lack commotions, disturbances, and uproar.

My Dear God:

By talking to you, I just try to put my life together. I want to make my life bearable, and I would like to be able to function among my peers.

My dear God, you have been my mentor, my psychiatrist, my rescuer, my best listener, and my very best friend. From the time that I had been writing to you, my path of life had changed completely. I was never afraid of anything or anybody. I learned that no matter what happens, it is to my benefit. I learned not to get excited when I received something extraordinary. Neither do I lose my faith when something bad occurs in my life. I don't know if I ever lost this opportunity to sit by my typewriter, and write to you, how would I survive? When I write, I feel you so close to me that I could jump in the fire, and not be afraid of anything. I don't think anyone knows what a good feeling it is. Thank you for coming into me, thank you for always being around me. Whoever you are, or, wherever you are, you have been my rescuer. Thank you.

With our intelligence, knowledge, and understanding we should be able to distinguish between good and bad, between right and wrong. Otherwise if we don't have that absolutely necessary ability, we will not survive.

After his first affair he did everything to bring back my love for him. He built that house for me. I say "He built a house for me" because he tried to do everything to my taste and satisfaction. He bought me many beautiful, and expensive rings. I wouldn't have enough fingers to wear them all at once. And at times I was embarrassed to wear them. To me those were all signs of his love for me. What else would you call it? He always celebrated my every birthdays, and he would get me funny and beautiful cards, and gifts. He always demonstrated to me that he enjoyed spending his money on our children and me. We always traveled together with our children. And we dined in best restaurants. When it came to intimacy, he always was happy and fully satisfied. We did go through a challenging period with our teenagers, which is very common for every household with children. And we did our best, tried our hardest to keep it under control. There were never signs of major discrepancies between us.

My Dear God:

One night we were invited to Dr. Amirikia. After dinner we all went to their basement to listen to music. Badri was sitting on one of the bar stool having a drink. Iraj was sitting by himself on a cushion by the piano in the dark. He leaned his head on the wall. The Persian music was crying for love, "How can I find you in my arms, and I will die without you in my arms", and so on. I was sitting with other ladies pretending that I was paying attention to their gossips, while I kept my eye on Iraj. He was moving his head back and forth, looking into Badri's eyes, and repeating the word of the singer to her. You could tell he was ready to cry. To begin with Iranian music is very depressing. And makes you want to cry, either for your lover or other matters. No one else could see what was

going on between these lovers.

We were at Minoo Panah's house. After dinner some guests started dancing. Single dance is customary in Iran. Everyone would usually push Badri out in the middle to entertain us. She and Mrs. Aghdass Shushtari were the entertainers among our group. I just sat there observing, being amused by the dancers. Badri was moving and shaking her shoulders and chest, gazing at Iraj. She had her infamous smile at the corner of her crooked mouth. That night she didn't hold back when she saw me watching her, and she went on right in front of my eyes. And if anyone saw Iraj at that time, his mouth was watering; he looked as if he was aroused.

I tried not to show any emotions. I had no intentions of belittling myself. I treated him as a stranger then, and not my husband. I had told myself that I was simply being amused by a dancer. Her only duty was to entertain men, including my husband.

This took place before Ali Houshmand got married. We were invited to a wedding dinner ceremony. I asked Ali to accompany us, and he was so nice to accept my invitation.

Iraj followed Badri everywhere. They were taking pictures together. Minoo Panah and Sara noticed their behavior. They told me, "Why don't you stay next to your husband? Can't you see she is with him everywhere?"

But I just laughed at their concerns. And I said, "No thanks, I am not used to begging. And besides I have better things to do". And I went back to my children, who were sitting with Ali. I noticed they were talking before I approached them. Somehow I knew that I must have been the subject of their conversation. And we started dancing, just to show them that I didn't care.

My Dear God:

But you were there, my dear God. You knew what was going on inside me. You knew that many times I even thought of burning down her house along with her and her children. I don't remember how you stopped me. I really don't know.

No one was aware of what was going on with me. I did not discuss my feelings with my children. They never saw the fire burning within me. They didn't know who I was at that time, or why I did what I did. They witnessed my sadness; they witnessed my depression. They knew what had caused that, but they never judged me with fairness. They didn't know our history. They had come into our lives after we each had formed our own personality and character. So they had to judge us by what they absorbed around us, not knowing what we were really made of.

This husband was the same husband that even my friends envied his love and kindness to me. He was the one who bought me those beautiful, expensive rings, while we were in San Francisco. Nazi Mahajer told him jokingly that day, "What is Shamci doing to you that you buy her this many rings? You know that she does not have more than ten fingers".

And it was all an act. He did his job well indeed. He did make me forget all about his past affairs. Once again I made me trust him. My speech in his honor at his fiftieth birthday was very sincere; it came straight from my heart. I praised him for being the greatest husband and father. I believed genuinely that he was one of the best human beings on earth.

But what about now? Who was this man now? He had become a disgrace for our family. I was lucky that my children never joined our Iranian gatherings. I knew they would have been annoyed and humiliated.

Iraj was traveling. I was stock in a state of confusion and uncertainties. I decided to take a trip to Canada with Mojgan. My cousins Lucy and Fred were residing there with their families. We have never been really close, but they were still my favorite cousins.

Lucy and Mr. Taymoor Safari, and their children moved to Toronto first. And then Fred and his family relocated to Toronto from England. Lucy had four children. All four of them were college graduates, and two of them were married. Last time I saw my nieces and nephews was when they were still in Iran, and when they were very young. Mojgan was not even born then. So she was to meet everyone for the very first time.

My Dear God:

We drove to Toronto from Detroit. We found Lucy's house with ease. Lucy turned out to be a gracious hostess. The following night after our arrival Lucy invited Fred's family and her children over. That was the first introduction for both sides. Fred had four children. Some were married, and they showed up with their spouses. They were all very good-looking. I was surprised to see that my cousin's kids turned out to be much taller than their parents.

I have been away from these families for almost thirty years. The children have matured into adults. Everyone seemed to be excited to meet us.

After we had a delicious dinner, we all gathered in the living room for tea and desserts. We had a lot of memories. Some were funny, and interesting, and others were shocking. Mojgan was having a blast. She didn't realize she had that many first and second cousins.

I had heard a long time ago many stories about my uncle, Lucy's father. I was told he was too sophisticated for his family. He studied in India, where he had mastered English language. Eventually after his father had passed away, he returned to Iran.

I had also heard the story of his marriage many times. But that night Lucy started to tell the story to all our children. Some of them have never heard it before. Naturally Mojgan was one of them. Mojgan's eyes were fixed on Lucy. She couldn't believe the story.

Lucy's father, Mr. Nasser Saleh, a young and handsome man, had just returned to Chirazn from India. Almost immediately a well-known priest hired him as an English

teacher for his three children. The priest's wife fell in love with Nasser. She left her children, and married Nasser Saleh, Lucy's father.

Such behavior was considered a crime in Chiraz. The priest's wife leaves her husband and children for another man. And besides these two were like night and day. Maryam, the priest's wife, was Armenian Christian, whereas Nasser was born Muslim. The difference in their appearances was even more drastic. Maryam was a very tall woman, and Nasser was considered to be short among men.

After they got married, they had to live in my grandmother's house. The city and that neighborhood were known for extremism. It was very disturbing for the ignorant population to see a Christian woman, who was taller than most men, walking in the public places, wearing a veil (Chador). Some even threw rocks at her, and called her names.

Then Iran-England Oil Company employed Nasser. They were transferred to city of Ahvaz. Maryam had left her three children behind, and left the city of Chiraz to be with her new love. She had four children with him, Eliez, Lili, Lucy, and Fred.

My Dear God:

At the time this story was being told, we were at the presence of Lucy, and Fred and their families. Lili lived in North Carolina, and Eliez was living in Australia with her family. We never had a chance to meet Eliez. She had her own family before we became teenagers.

Such actions were not only forbidden eighty years ago, they are still forbidden now, and they will be forbidden in centuries to come. Mojgan, who had never heard of such incidents, was quite shocked. How could she believe that Lucy's mother had left her children for her lover?

I remember seeing Maryam only a few times when I was a teenager. It was hard to believe that she would be capable of doing that to her children. But to my surprise she always talked about her past. She often blamed herself for the things that went wrong with her children from her first marriage.

Her son Aslan died from tuberculosis at the age of eighteen. She could never forgive herself after that. She believed that she was the cause of his illness. She used to cry, and begged him to forgive her. Although they became wealthy, and she lived a very comfortable life, I found her unhappy and regretful. I believe I was deeply affected by this story. It made me realized that your children must always come first.

The following day Lucy's daughter Nelly took time off her tight college schedule to drive us around the town. We had a great time.

My cousin Fred was a Pastor in that town. We joined him for the Mass in the morning. Fred treated us to a dinner at a restaurant before we left. Fred tried to comfort me by placing positive thoughts in my mind.

While Fred and I were talking, Mojgan started complaining about me. She was

This picture has a great big story behind it. Among the two ladies who are sitting, the one on the left is my Uncle Saleh's mother and the one on the right is his wife Maryam. Standing from left to right: my Uncle Khalilpoor, Eliz, Lucy, and Lily. My Uncle Saleh, standing above his wife, married someone who looked like his mother. And there is little Fred.

telling Fred, who did not know much about our life, that she was tired of my distrust, and suspiciousness. Fred and I agreed with her, and at the same time told her that it was the duty of a mother to protect her child from unfortunate events. Fred was telling Mojgan, "You might not like it now, but you will come appreciate your mother's constant attention later".

We spent a great weekend with my cousins and their families. I was very happy that Mojgan had decided to join me on this trip.

It was puzzling to me that although my children had always witnessed us treating our guests and relatives with warmth and great hospitality; they were not willing to do the same. But when Nelly took time off to drive us around the town, and she was a gracious hostess, I was happy to show Mojgan that not all Iranian children reject their parent's guests. Some really make themselves a part of their family. If it wasn't for Nelly's warmth and kindness, we would probably never get to see the town. Although Nelly had never met us before, she still agreed to help her parents. She treated us as her own guests. I think it was very nice of her.

My Dear God:

My children on the contrary never wanted to associate themselves with our guests. They were trying to be more American than American kids. They always excused themselves by making remarks such as these, "It is not my job. It is not my business. I don't even know them". Their most favorite line from early on has become, "It is my life, and I know what I want to do with it".

I must have been too liberal in my ways of raising my children. Since I never liked to be forced into making decisions, likewise I never forced my children. I never pushed them, when they refused to do something. But the adverse results of my tactics were obvious. My dear father, who he had warned me righteously, "I really don't know about the way you are raising your children. And you let them make their own ways. One day, when someone rejects them, they will get hurt. And they will blame you. You will see".

Even now, when you visit someone in Iran, you will see a little girl have enough sense of responsibility to invite you in when the parents are not home. And they will serve you tea until the mother gets back. In any Iranian household it was customary that children shared the responsibility of household chores. We were accustomed to having maids around us.

Anyway, my trip to Canada turned out to be very soothing for my injured soul. In my desperation, and confusion I was searching to connect with people. I realized with that visit that I had close relatives in Canada. And it was comforting that they were close enough.

Please don't forget that at the time my only friends were people like Rohan Panah, Louies Neel, Susan Barkhordari, Nayer Rabbani, and Aghdass Shushtari. Those were my

so-called friends for the past twenty-five years. They had betrayed me; they had traded me in for Badri, and they became my enemies. For many years these people had caused harm to other friends of ours and now it was my turn.

I had to find ways of surrounding myself by reliable people. Knowing the vicious nature of my friends, I could not let them win. I never wanted to break down in their presence. The damage was done. My separation from Iraj was inevitable by then. I had to find strength.

My Dear God:

I think I know what happened. When I told Susan, "I am just trying to remain Mrs. Rafani", they made sure that Badri kept insisting that Iraj divorced me.

Up to that time she was not able to instigate scandals. Up to that time she had made every effort to make me look crazy. Up to that time she has intruded into our intimacy. However she had yet succeeded in her efforts to make Iraj divorce me. Now she got to a point that she simply gave him an ultimatum.

Again these are all my speculations. My dear God, now that it is all over with, I am asking you, "Was I right? Don't you think that they have been encouraging her all along? Or do you, just like everyone else, believe that, it was all just a coincidence?"

By this time we all were getting ready to move to California. I knew that I was hitting for a disaster. I was moving to a strange city, to embrace my insecurities and my vulnerability, and my uncertain future. Iraj never mentioned our divorce. And since I had decided not persuade the divorce, I was planning to stay put, and watch how far he could go with his ruthlessness? I did not believe for a second that he might think of divorcing me. I could still hear his cracked voice, and I could still see his tears, when he returned to us after his first affair. I couldn't believe that he would go ahead with it. I was planning to establish a way to run my life while we were living together, but without him. Nothing in the world could have convinced me that he was going to do it.

I remembered how crushed Mary and Maseeh were by his first affair. Since he was calling himself a man of intelligence, he should have been remembering it as well. Otherwise I really doubt his intelligence.

This time it was our precious Mojgan, and Mary and Maseeh who were being destroyed. How could he possibly forget the promises he had made to his two children? I think I gave him more credit than he deserved. I did so with hopes to forget his ruthlessness.

Unfortunately my children were still battling the complexities and confusion of their adolescence. They needed their parent's guidance the most then. They were neither ready, nor aware of the approaching storm.

At that time Mary was still attending Detroit Law School, Mojgan had just begun her studies in college, and Maseeh was helping with his father's nightclub in Los Angeles.

When he was in Michigan, we did everything like husband and wife. Neither of us had ever brought up the subject of divorce.

Although I had access to anything and everything we possessed, and although we always had joined bank accounts, I started noticing that he was hiding something from me. He bought a new briefcase with a combination lock. I was not able to open it any more.

My Dear God:

We used to never keep secrets from one another. And it was very disturbing to see that now he was hiding things from me. I couldn't figure out what it was. I kept wondering why he always kept his new briefcase locked. He would still talk to me about business. And I still had our checkbooks in my possession. He started talking about selling his office to some lady doctor.

You remember, my dear God, my grief for the loss of our trust for one another. Do you remember the emptiness within me? Do you remember how I used to just drive around seeking answers to my problems? You remember how I was hoping to die in a car accident? Do you remember how I was shouting at you? Remember how much I blamed you for all my misfortunes? I get emotional just thinking about those days. I wish that no one went through what I went through.

He was acting rather strange. He drove like a maniac when we went to parties together. I was worried about my safety. I even thought that he was willing to get rid of me. He always acted so innocent that no one would ever suspect him. It would have been much easier for him to get rid of me that way than to divorce me. My children would never question their father, because of the trust they had for him. I am still puzzled that he didn't do it?

The hospital gave a goodbye party for us. We were there at the party acting like a happy couple. I was wondering that night, while observing all those doctors and their wives, if any of them had a relationship similar to ours. I didn't know if they knew anything about Iraj and Badri. I know that he had made everyone believe that he was helping out Badri just as a business partner.

I remember when our divorce was final Dr. Mehrabian swore to me that he knew nothing about their relationship. There were only some, like his clinic partner's wife, who knew what was going on. She had even asked me one day, "Why don't you divorce your husband?" I realized that she must have seen them together, and now she wanted to make me speak. I knew that she used to be her husband's secretary. I was sure that she too was the cause for his divorce. So seeing another woman like Badri, I told her, "I don't see any reason for divorce". And I tried to end the conversation.

This was when we lived in that town house. He came back from California. I always drove him to and from the airport. This time he seemed unusually depressed. He went for his regular evening walk. Then he went to his room, where he stayed for a long time. Mary and Mojgan were home from college then.

I was downstairs working on something when I heard him calling Mary and Mojgan to his room. I didn't know what was going on there. In only a few minutes, which seemed hours to me, I heard lots of noise coming out of Mojgan's room. That noise was Mary and Mojgan screaming and crying. I ran upstairs to see what was wrong. When I opened the door, I saw them crying in each other's arms. They almost looked like they were mourning somebody.

My Dear God:

I knew right a way that he must have given them the bad news. I also knew that it was best to leave them alone, so that they were able to absorb the devastating news.

You see, my dear God, even my children didn't have anybody to share their problems with. It would have been so comforting for them to have their cousins, or aunts and uncles around during those times. Alas they had to deal with the pain on their own. Even Maseeh happened to be away then. They had each other and you, and I had only you to help me.

I just stood there by the door until they eventually stopped crying, and I could hear them talk. I heard them mention the word "divorce" a few times. I should have expecting that. I must not act surprised. I was so afraid to get close to them. I didn't know what to do. I saw the two most important people in my life being destroyed in front of my own eyes. I remembered when I told my father, "I will never let my children get hurt, ever". How am I doing now? Where is my poor father to tell me, "I told you so"? Who can I turn to now? What should I tell them to make them feel better? When will I learn to be able to take my children's pain away, once and for all?

I remembered the story of the priest who killed his five children, his wife, and his parents just because he did not want to see them hurt in this world. My God, if you don't help me, what will happen? Who else is going to help my children and me from this disastrous life? If you don't help me, and helplessly I commit a crime, I will hold you responsible for it. I need your help now. I need you to save my children and me from this agonizing life.

I kept walking across the hall. I wanted to be there when they open the door. I figured it must have been very painful for them to be the messengers in that instance. I was feeling guilty for being the cause of their pain. I kept wondering when would we, the parents, become decent enough to realize our duties towards our children? Please my dear God, wasn't this man the same man who cried for my hand and forgiveness twenty-five years ago? How could he not be ashamed now? Please God; please explain to me who I've been dealing with? What actions must I take to relieve my children of pain? Please God, help me, please.

My Dear God:

I was blaming myself for coming back to him. And I blamed myself for forgiving him, and for bringing Mojgan into this world, and make her suffer like that.

I was feeling numb. I knew that whatever they had heard, it must have been something very much unexpected.

I was thinking that all those years I stood my belief of not ever breaking my children's home and togetherness. I believed I should fight for my home, and my children's dignity until the end.

All those years he acted so fatherly. And he accused me of being suspicious. Could my children see now that I wasn't making it all up? Could they judge their father? Is it right for me to even mention that? Should I hurt my children even more, and try to prove my innocence to them?

Just before Iraj left for Los Angeles, he took Mojgan and I to a beautiful restaurant. He bought nice gifts for us. I saw so much happiness in Mojgan's eyes that day. Her eyes were telling me, "See how much my father loves us? See how he remembers our birthdays? Isn't he a great father? Please Mom; don't blame my father for not loving us. He is not the person that you believe he is. Please Mom; love him as much I do. He is really a great father. And he loves us all". I had no other choice but to thank Iraj that day just to show my appreciation of her father's kindness to Mojgan and I.

I had left my family in Iran, and came here for Iraj, and only Iraj. He was my husband, my lover, my friend, my mentor, and my whole world. Anywhere I went, I saw him. Anything I did, I asked him. Any place I went, I was with him. Now my whole world was gone. Parri, who used to be my stamina, my support, now that she found out that Iraj was serious about Badri, was no longer there for me. My heart was beating so hard, and so fast that it felt like it was in my hands. I don't remember how I was able to keep myself together for that time. I was waiting to find out what had happened.

They had finally stopped crying, and I could hear them discussing things among themselves. I found courage to knock on the door, and asked if I could come in. I think they were ready to give me the news. Their eyes were red, and their faces were crushed and lifeless. With a sad look on their faces they said, "Well Mom, he did it. He is going to divorce you, and that is that".

Although I was expecting something awful to happen, and although that meant the end of my life, I really didn't want to hear it. I acted as if I was neither hurt, nor surprised. I began by saying, "Well my dearest, please look around you. Every other family is divorced nowadays. You must know many kids that come from such families, and there is absolutely nothing wrong with them. And when parents decide to get divorced that does not mean that the love for their children will change. They are the same parents, and they love you the same. People will change, but life must go on no matter what. And it

doesn't mean that either of your parents is bad. The only thing that has happened is that one of them had changed, and they could no longer be dealing with one another. We don't ask about the reason, but this is the way it is". And then I said, "And we will get through this the same way others did. We are not the first, and we are not the last".

My Dear God:

By this time they were calm. I thought I did a good job bringing back some hope to them.

I really don't remember what I did that night. I don't even remember if I cried. I just remember the first thing I did was to call my cousin Lucy in Toronto. And I asked her about housing, and living arrangements in Canada. I asked her about the possibility of obtaining Canadian citizenship? I didn't even know why I was asking her all those questions. I knew that problems would not be resolved by moving there. She provided me with some information, and then she asked me to get in touch with the Canadian Embassy.

I called her because I had no one else to talk to. I had absolutely no one to turn to. Parri was the only close friend I had. But at that time she chose to stay bias, and sometimes I don't blame her. He was the only brother, and the only relative she had in this country. He was a doctor, and he could help her and her family. So although I didn't approve of his decision, she decided to stay out of it. She has probably told herself, "I like to have my comfortable life, and I am not going to willingly give it up for Shamci's sake. These matters must not concern me". So the only friend I always counted on was no longer there for me. I felt lucky that I could at least talk to Lucy.

I contacted the Canadian embassy the following day. I found out that it was not that easy for American citizens to obtain Canadian citizenship. Besides I did not have money, yet to buy a house. I felt like I was sleepwalking. I remember asking myself, "What about my children? What about their future? How can I leave them? What about my little Mojgan? Why would I make irrational decisions? Why don't I first give myself some time? Just think".

My dear God, those who had experienced the feelings I had would understand what I was going through. They say, "Accepting death of a husband is much easier than divorcing him". My GOD, it is so true.

His passing becomes a physical matter, whereas divorce is the end of love and feeling that they once had for one another for years. If one ever knew the true meaning of love, that would mean the end of his or her life.

My Dear God:

That was the end for me. Yes, I was still alive, the blood was circulating in my veins, and I was still able to breath. I was able to walk, and talk. But all my hopes, and love for life were gone. While I was absolutely crushed emotionally, still I was experiencing an

uncontrollable amount of physical energy.

I knew then that Iraj had lost to Badri. I knew that he fought himself for more than seven years; I knew he tried to pull himself out of that mess. I knew that neither Badri, nor her family were his type. I knew that he could never feel comfortable with them. And I knew so because he often talked to me about them, even more so before his involvement with Badri. I was convinced that he tried getting out of it many times. Or maybe it was that he just played his role well. I knew him well, and it made me realized that his loss was greater then mine. He was proud of having that family. He was the one who had betrayed his family. He was repeating his self-destructive act of twenty-five years ago. My poor beautiful Iraj! He had become the big loser among all those competitive Iranian friends of his. Poor Iraj, he had become a big joke. And he was now known only for his disloyalty. What a waste, I feel so sorry for him. He had lost his great name.

As long as marriage continues to be part of our society, the divorce will be the necessity as a correctional, and binder of marriage. But to do it so ruthlessly, and to become back stabbers the way they did, was nothing but a hateful act. I don't think anyone was expected to survive through that.

My dear God, here we go again. From the moment that we met Malakuti's family, it was no secret to Iraj, and everyone else for that sake, that Badri had never been in love with her husband. So Iraj felt that she must be an available woman. He also knew that because of Badri's body language. I think he had no doubts that all he had to do was ask. Next Iraj found a way to get close to Azeez, and the rest is history.

All right, my dear God, did you plan all those things, or was it just a coincidence? The whole world believes that, "GOD is the sole owner, the creator, and the organizer of the entire universe". If so, then why would we want to believe that God had also given us choices? And if choices had anything to do with our lives, then I can swear that Iraj and Badri had planned the whole thing from the beginning. And I can swear to you that Badri had planned Azeez's death the way that he always spoke of her. I don't know, but I believe that you were there, my dear GOD, and you know what had happened that day.

True, the police report stated, "He was scheduled to see one of his patients that day". And then they found Azeez's body in a pool of blood by the door to his office. They said he was trying to escape the gunshot. But no one had ever questioned Badri about the time that she went in his office to exchange keys. She played her role so well. So the young man presumed guilty, and he was put in prison for life.

My Dear God:

That night was the end of my life. All those thoughts and memories kept passing through my mind just like scenes on a TV screen. I was not living any more.

I truly believe that those two ruthless people were capable to do it all. Together they arranged the whole thing. How quietly, and smoothly they arranged for the partnership to take place. How candidly they enjoyed their lives together, while everyone thought it was just a regular friendship. Meanwhile they masterminded the completion of their project by throwing their last winning card at the end. So quietly and peacefully that no one to this day knows what had really happened.

My mind started going wild. I remembered years back in Detroit I was once waiting for my car to be serviced. While waiting, I started reading the Detroit News. I came across a crime story. I was shocked. I could not believe it.

A family of five lived in a small, quiet neighborhood in Berkley, Michigan. Their neighbors loved the parents, and their three girls. They were a happy family; all the neighbors had trust in them. The houses were built very small, and close to each other in that neighborhood. Until one day the family goes boating, and the mother drowns. The poor father, and his three girls try so hard to look for her. The police, and the guards were not able to recover her body. After three days of searching the heartbroken father and his three girls returned home without the mother. With much sadness the father started to care for his children. He dressed them in the mornings, and he fed them. He drove them to and from school. All the neighbors pitched in to help out in any way they could. The whole neighborhood was sympathizing with the poor father. After thirteen years they moved away from that house. The new owners decided to entirely redo the landscaping. They found a skeleton under the front stairway.

All right, my dear GOD, you already know whose skeleton it was. But even after the police captured the father, and he admitted to the crime, still all the neighbors sworn on his innocence. He had been so nice, and he had acted so innocently that even after he had admitted to his crime, they still could not believe that he had murdered his wife.

All kinds of thoughts went through my mind that night, I couldn't think straight. I thought if criminals looked like criminal, then all the problems of the unjust world would have been solved in no time.

My Dear God:

One would have never guessed what was on Badri's and Iraj's minds. I know now that they took time to mastermind their project. And with the help of their friends, they finally got what they wanted. Who killed Azeez? Who was more likely to pull that trigger? No one has ever suspected Badri. She was too pretty for a killer. But what about that poor young patient? He was mentally ill. How could he defend himself? He was accused of murder, and he had to accept it.

You know, my dear GOD, if that family didn't decide to move out, no one would ever find out who had murdered that woman.

I was feeling dizzy. I felt my blood was getting freezing in my veins. I held my heart in my hand going down in the kitchen. I prayed to you, "Please GOD, come to my rescue. Don't let me get destroyed in front of my children. Please help me, you are my rescuer".

I wasn't sure if that horrible night would come to an end. It felt as if all this time I was hanging of a cliff by only one strand of hair. But now that the last string of hair was cut, I had fallen on my face. My body was aching. I wasn't sure what to do next. "I should sit down, should I go to sleep, should I walk, or maybe I should just scream". I didn't think that there was voice to scream. I just kept repeating, "He did it after all. He did it. He did it. It really happened".

My heart was full of hate and anger. I feared myself. I didn't know how to put myself together. "What now? What could I do now? How do I face him? How do I talk to him?"

I didn't take the lawyer's advice, "You must divorce him now". But, my dear GOD, what should I do now? It was the end of our happiness. My children were officially the children of a broken home.

At the time when everyone else was helping their children through the rough times of their college years, my husband was busy concentrated on his mid-life crisis.

What about my poor innocent children? What about their hopes and dreams? All these years they tried so hard to bring their parents back together. But it didn't work. They didn't know that their father had an incurable disease. There is a good saying in Iran, "ESHGHE PEERY GAR BE JONBAD SAR BE ROSVAIE ZANAD". It means, "If an old person falls in love, he or she will bring shame and embarrassment for him/herself and the entire family".

It was true; their father took my children's happiness away from them, at their prime age.

There was a time, a few months earlier, that Dr. Mohammad Rabbani for some reason asked Iraj and I to go to his house one afternoon. Apparently he had decided to become a mediator. Iraj, just like during his first affair, sat down, he crossed one leg over the other, and he started to talk. Without mentioning any names, he said, "You know, I am tired of this life. I can't take it any more". And he went on and on.

My Dear God:

I was so humiliated. I stopped him right there. I refused to take abuse from this ruthless betrayer. I told him, "Obviously you had made up your mind. You know what you want, and you had decided to go after it. Then what we are here for? I feel sorry for you that you didn't find out that you were unhappy with your life before Azeez's death. So we have nothing to discuss".

This person was the same person who once cried and begged for my forgiveness. What a ruthless person indeed.

It is acceptable among Iranians, and especially among the Muslim population, to have more than one wife. So was the divorce. In Islamic marriage women are considered half a person, and they have right equal to only half. Women do not have the right to take the custody of their own children, even if the husband was guilty of adultery and/or

domestic violence. And because women were not allowed to have a job outside of the house, economically they were not prepared to take care of themselves after the divorce. So they had to take all the abuse, and continue living in that environment.

Despite my father warnings about the law in Islamic marriage, and the lawyer's advice, I decided to neglect my rights. I considered my children's rights first.

The reason that I wanted to marry Iraj so badly was that I always thought that he was against those laws. Coming from a Muslim mother and a Bahai father, he was able to form his own opinion about life. It was the same with me. I had my own opinion about life. I found Iraj to be more intelligent than others. I never dreamt of marrying an abusive adulterer. The one who would tell me, "If you ever mention the divorce, I will take your children away from you. You will never see them for the rest of your life".

I was glad that I wasn't married to a Muslim family. But I was wrong. He was the wrong person. He was exactly the opposite of what I thought he was. The Rabbanis who have never been in love, the Rabbanis whose marriage was arranged were still living together respectfully. This was a solid proof that Iraj and his pretentious lies have fooled me. I allowed myself to think of him as the greatest man in my life. Well, stupidity has different shapes and forms. At this moment of my life I think I had collected all.

My Dear God:

Now, after twenty-five years of marriage, that I thought we had made it, we were sitting in front of Dr. M Rabbani, who was Muslim. He was trying to have him as a mediator between us. What a shame! What a great humiliation! What an upside down world!

The thought of my children, and how they had to face the world after the divorce was killing me. I felt so sorry for them. They did not get to choose their parents. I was sure that if they had a choice, they would never pick us as their parents. Dishonesty, disloyalty, betrayal, adultery, cheating, stealing, and many other characteristics such as these were the personal treasury of Iraj. True those children must forget and forgive, but who could be proud of such an inheritance.

It was only a year prior to Azeez's death that we all were proud of being part of that family. I always showed my best possible love for Iraj. And I expected my children to do the same. How could I deal with my new feelings? How could I reveal to my children the kind of father or husband he has been? They must be able to love their father no matter what.

To tell you the truth that night I was shocked by Mary's reaction to the news of divorce. She was always so much against my authoritative motherhood that I thought that the news of our divorce would not bother her. But to my complete surprise she was experiencing enormous pain and agony. I was ashamed of myself to see her going through the same pain she had experienced twenty-five years prior to this. I helped her to the best

of my ability to survive through it then. What can I do now that she is a young lady? I knew from my past experience that no matter what I did, I would still be the guilty one. But I didn't mind it as long as they could come out of it without problems.

I was afraid to loose my children to either drugs or suicide. My children never saw or felt what their father's adultery did to me. The only thing they saw was my sadness and unhappiness. Naturally, it was a great back draw for me. I was able to make myself strong. But I was not able to be happy. That was my only fault, the only one.

My children had no idea what went on inside me, while on the outside it seemed as if I kept my sanity. I had to be the role model for my children.

There is a lot of truth is the saying, "It takes two to tango". But in marriage it is always only one of the partners that breaks the marriage vows, while the other one reacts out of anger, and tries to get even.

The plot of the movie "Burning bed" is a great example. The husband went so far that the wife had no other choice but to burn him in his bed. At that time of her life she did not care any more to be found guilty, or even executed for doing so. She just wanted to free herself from all the abuse that she had to take for that many years. But no one could understand what she had gone through, for if they did, they would have found her not guilty. The two hours of the movie was about physical abuse, and the destruction of that woman and her children during her marriage. She never intended to hurt him. But his violence got to a point that she had to make a decision to either get rid of him, or let him continue destroying her and her children. So she decided to finish the abuse once and for all.

My Dear God:

During those years I have been in a similar situation. Many times I was so close to harming the Malakutis' family, and Iraj, and even myself. But I was rescued by a power beyond my imagination. That power within me came to my rescue, and stopped me from wrongdoing. I was hoping that the same power would come to my children as well. I was hopeful that it would stop them from doing harmful acts to themselves, or anyone else.

I remember one particular Wednesday afternoon. We went to his office after lunch. He was talking about a patient of his from India. He was so amazed by her beauty. He could not stop talking about her. Then he started to talk about relationships, "What brings back a husband home to his own wife is not just good sex. It is not even if the wife is the most beautiful woman on earth. It is not the money or the job. The only thing that brings that man to his wife day after day is that sincere connection and the love and trust between them". The way I had interpreted his monologue was that "Although I see many beautiful women daily in my office, and I could have sex with many of them, still no one will be able to take your place in my heart".

But it was either my poor English, or my hopeless romanticism. According to the way he introduced Badri to me, the only thing that he had achieved in this affair was sex. Iraj had lost what he had always feared to loose. He lost his priceless prestige. And if he was telling the truth, and if sex was not what he was after, then he better accept the fact that Badri is nothing but a "good sex" and if that is what he needs, so be it.

You see, my dear God, it feels so strange that I am talking about all these things so calmly. Every moment, and every second was full of humiliation and torture for me. I am glad in a way that my children are not able to read Farsi; otherwise they would have felt even more humiliated.

Dr. Shahideh and his family were the only ones among Iranian doctors that I still visited frequently. We lived in the same neighborhood, and he was mine and my children's alergist. He would even give me my shots at his home, the same way he did for his own family. They always tried to comfort me by entertaining me, and talking about the past.

My Dear God:

Once after Iraj had decided on divorce, Almass seemed very uncomfortable to give me the news. But she finally told me after I insisted, "Some anonymous person wrote a sarcastic poem about Iraj and his behavior. I know that it will upset you if I show it to you. That was the reason that I did not want to bring it up. I didn't want to hurt you more than you have been hurt already". I showed no emotions when I read it. I only said, "What a rootless person! Who could have been so cruel to dedicate the time to destroy a family?" The letter was sent to every doctor in Michigan. I will enclose a copy of it in this book.

We talked about the possible author. The only person that we could think of writing it was DR. Naser Barkhordari. He was the only one who could write a poem with Turkish accent. Years ago in his house he had read many of his poems to us, and we admired him for it. But why? Was it really possible that he would have done that? Was he really that low and obtuse to do such a thing to his friends of thirty years?

Anyway we were unable to make sense of who might have done it. After dinner I went home, and in my lonely room I started to read it over and over again.

I cried for my lovely Iraj. I cried for the person I had lost. I cried for his foolishness and his naivety. I cried for his ruined name, for his demolished prestige and respect among his peers. I cried for the sincerity of his effort to help others. And I cried, and cried, and cried.

I kept wondering who might have done it. I didn't know any other poets among us except Naser and his sister Aghdass. I was convinced that Aghdass was not the one. I couldn't think of Naser to be so ruthless and cruel to do such a thing. But then I still suspected him to be the author.

I had mentioned before about how competitive Iraj, Naser, and M. Rabbani have always been. It didn't end at earning money and material possessions. But it was also about their popularity, name and prestige. They had always chased one another.

I had lost hope, and all my dreams. I kept thinking of the times when all of us, doctors and their families, had become as close as sisters and brothers. We were looking forward to a happy and great future in this part of the world away from rest of our families. Look what has become of us now. Look how we got separated and destroyed by the death of one person among us. And it was all because of his promiscuous wife. I was looking for his motive. And then I remembered one incident that took place right after Azeez passed away. Those were the times when everyone was trying to help out Badri in any way they could. We were all at Naser's house, when Badri mentioned that she wanted to go somewhere. When Naser asked her if he could help her, Badri answered, "Thank you, Dr. Rafani is helping me".

My Dear God:

At that time no one suspected anything about them. I was happy that Iraj was helping her. But I had noticed that Naser was disappointed.

If he was the one who wrote that poem, that would have been the best motive to destroy Iraj. And to make sure that he never recovered. That was the best way to show Iraj that he had lost the chase, and therefore proclaim his own victory. He made him the subject of mockery at every gathering. Iraj was out for good. What a shame! On the other hand I still was not convinced that Naser was that cruel. The more I read the poem, the more I was curious to figure out who was behind all those, and why.

I remembered that once Badri mentioned that her brother was the publisher of an Iranian newspaper in Los Angeles. Naturally he employed many talented poets. They usually wrote sarcastic poems about our country, and its politics.

I knew that all throughout those dreadful eight years, Badri had made every effort instigate my jealousy scenes in public. She would come up with thousands of scenarios just to let me know that she was having an affair with Iraj. She even had the audacity to ask me to divorce Iraj.

But when she realized that I was not going to make her wishes come true, and when she realized that I was not planning to initiate divorce, she thought of humiliating him anonymously.

I had decided that for as long as Iraj was keeping it quiet, I would be doing the same. I believe that Iraj was trying his best in dealing with all those circumstances, in the same manner that I was hoping for a miracle to reverse the situation. But Badri was determined to ruin us.

She was not going to reveal her plans to Iraj, "I am going to humiliate you in front of the whole world if you don't divorce Shamci and marry me". She didn't want to ruin her loving image. So the best way to put Iraj in a "do or die" situation was to find a way to bring their affair out into the open. Then she could comfort Iraj, and sympathize with him for being humiliated in such a harsh way at his age. She would tell him next, "Well, now

that the whole world knows that we have been lovers for years, it is only wise to go ahead, and do it after all".

She talked about her brother on many occasions. She made a point to mention, "If my brother ever finds out that someone is harassing his sister, he will kill him". And she would tell us about the incident that he was arrested for stabbing one of his co-workers.

My Dear God:

At the time that the anonymous poem was mass mailed to the entire Iranian community, Iraj had realized that it was time to stop playing around. He was in a position that he had to decide one way or another; otherwise Badri's brother could have killed him. And this was exactly what Badri was after.

It was obvious that the anonymous author was not fond of me. He made sure to make his message clear: the only reason for Iraj's kindness for Azeez and his family was to get to Badri. He made sure that Iranians recognized Iraj's ruthlessness. He put Badri on the pedestal, while he brought Shamci low.

My Dear God:

All in all he introduced Iraj as a scandalous and disgraceful person, whose only desire was to have fun with Badri. And while he did that, he fooled people around him to believe that he was protecting Azeez's family from further disasters".

Meanwhile he made fun of me. He mocked me for grieving over the loss of my family, and he laughed at me for trying to cope with the situation.

He announced in his poem, "Iraj is trying to move to California, while Badri is also moving to California". He did not mention anything about their plans for future. But at the end he mentioned sarcastically, "Now that these two families are leaving Michigan, and their friends, we all are saddened. Their absence among the Iranian community will be a big loss. They will be missed indeed".

This was what Badri wanted me to do for years. Humiliation was the only thing that could work for Iraj. I was running my life just as I always have before. I did not want to interfere with their affairs. I intended to continue what I was doing to the last moment. We attended parties together, and I continued entertaining in my house. When I did not invite Badri, she appeared regardless. I had become strong enough to be able to deal with those ruthless ones. And I though that I had succeeded.

Where were my children throughout all those times? Could they see what I had to deal with? I wouldn't want them to know anyway. They were not there when I made the decision to marry their father. Why should they be involved now that I realized that I had made a bad choice? Haven't they suffered enough already, yet to be sharing my problems with them? I was glad that they were not around. I was happy they could not read in Farsi. I knew that the poem would have crushed them.

The anonymous author was very familiar with Iraj's background. He was no stranger. He must have had a Turkish accent, since he used it in his poem. His viscous jealousy of Iraj's success was very obvious in every sentence he wrote. And he made it clear that he disliked me. He made me look very low in his comparisons with Badri, whom he regarded highly. He compared our appearances, mainly praising her for the size of her breasts.

My Dear God:

With your permission I would like to say a few words to the ignorant anonymous writer. After all, he deserves to get his recognition for all the hard work he did. Only he was so ruthless and vicious that he was ashamed to introduce himself. Not only he was worthless, but also he was even more ruthless than Iraj. What a shame that we had to have people like him among us, Iranians. I don't know who he is. And I think that no one else knew who he was. I am sure that he comes from a dirty background, for he is the most scandalous, and disgraceful person I have ever known. He was such a coward; he never dared to show his face to his friends.

And Mr. Anonymous, you must know this secret; it is not the size that makes the intimacy pleasant, because as far as I remember my husband praised and admired me every night. And all throughout my marriage I was praised for being the best in everything I did.

And Mr. Anonymous, the truth is Iraj never considered Badri to an outstanding woman. She did steal my husband because of her promiscuous nature. But just because she won my stupid husband's heart, she should not be considered superior. She will never be able to reach the pace where I was standing. It should be very obvious for those who appreciate the meaning of a true value of a woman. And I am very aware of the admiration for me from hundreds of our friends, which makes your poem and your opinions about me absolutely worthless.

Mr. Anonymous, I dare you to come forward and reveal yourself to me. I just want to show you that despite all your devilish expectation, you only did me a favor. All I have to say to you, "You are a dirty, the most scandalous and shameful person I have ever came across. Shame on you, and your behavior!

After all the research and investigation, I came to the conclusion Badri was the only one to benefit from that poem. Badri was the one who always wanted me to humiliate Iraj in front of his friends. She always manipulated my emotions, to make me go crazy. She had Iraj wrapped around her finger. She knew him well. And she was convinced that humiliation would assist her in reaching her goals. And if the anonymous poem was not one of Badri's doings. And if Nasser Barkhordari was the author, his purpose would be to help Badri first, and then to humiliate Iraj among his peers.

My Dear God:

As I said before I don't think anyone knew who was behind that awful act. But I know that he opened the door for Badri. He made it possible for her to complete her husband hunting. And she hunted Iraj down.

Okay, my dear GOD, why do you think it is that someone becomes so vicious and jealous, to a point that his/her enjoyment is destroying other people? I have never harmed anyone among our friends to deserve such a harsh punishment.

At that point I had no further doubts that Badri had laid out her winning card. And she was able to force Iraj to divorce me without even getting involved directly. There was no reason to believe otherwise.

My dear GOD, obviously these were all my speculations. To tell you the truth, I don't know why would anyone go so far as to write such a destructive poem, and then send it to the entire Iranian community. Why would anyone want to destroy an innocent family? It is still a big mystery to me.

If this anonymous person was completely aware of my struggles to keep my family together, why did he want so badly to destroy us? Please God; tell me who that person is. Please God; punish him. Please take his happiness away from him. Please.

The funniest of all was that Rohan Panah, the queen of ugliness, accused me of writing that poem. As always she wasn't capable of using her brain. Because if she did she would have realized that if I wanted to humiliate my husband, I wouldn't wait for that many years. I could have done it when they first started their affair. Secondly, I wasn't stupid to talk highly of Badri, and make myself look rotten. She wasn't anybody until her husband died. It was right after Azeez passed away that she became a celebrity among Iranians like Rohan.

Iraj loved his family so much that he was willing to die for us. He had great respect for me. He retained it even during his affair with Badri. He was embarrassed about breaking his children's home. At least that was my understanding. But the poem let him off the leash. He brought the news of divorce to my children. He ruined their hopes and happiness.

Just like the anonymous person described in his poem, we were planning to move to Los Angeles. He was pretending that after he retired, and because he started the nightclub business, we would move to Los Angeles. I was planning to go along with his fault pretense; I was prepared to treat Badri just as another prostitute in his life.

My Dear God:

While Maseeh was in Los Angeles working in Hollywood Live for his father, and Mary was studying law at Detroit University, Mojgan thought it would be great if she started college in Los Angeles. But the humiliating announcement of our divorce, and Iraj's affair was spreading fast. There was still the issue of Badri's brother, and her

infamous slyness. So Iraj had no other choice but to divorce me.

Iraj used to tell me, "You think Azeez is a psychiatrist? You are wrong. Badri is the real psychiatrist". Badri's plan from the beginning to the end, from killing Azeez to marrying Iraj, was a well-organized plan. I think besides being a classy call girl, she could serve as a valuable member of FBI or CIA.

Before we received the news for divorce, my children were still hopeful, whereas I gave up hope of our reconciliation. I knew all there was to know about their affair. I was no longer there because I loved him. I was there to protect my children's home. And at the same time I wanted to make sure that I wasn't the one who destroyed the family. This time he couldn't justify his behavior by blaming others, "Who made me do it?" If he had a brain, he would have recognized who made him to do it. If only he had a little brain!

At that time I needed all the strength I could get. I had to be able to stand on my feet. My family's happiness was shattered like a piece a glass. We had become so distant. Our hopes, our dreams, and love have disappeared from our hearts. We tried to hang on to each other as far as our emotions would allow us.

The reality was showing its bitter taste to us. There was no time for acting foolish, or thinking of revenge. No time for thinking about my rights. Instead I had to start teaching myself to believe that the life that I was living in was just a dream. I had to learn that there was no right or wrong in this world. I had to teach myself that both GOOD and BAD are there for all of us, they just occur at different times of our lives.

When we bring a baby into this world, it is a good happening to us. That is the time of celebration. So we congratulate one another, and we are happy for the person who had the baby.

And at the same time when one of our loved ones is diagnosed with a fatal disease, or if one of us had died in an accident, it is a bad thing to happen to us Then we will be sad for each other, and we will communicate our condolences to one another.

Divorce is the same thing. It needs condolences. Because it is the death of love, hopes, dreams, and happiness. None of us, who steps into this world, is exempted from these rules of nature.

I had to clear my mind from unhealthy thoughts to be able to bring peace into my life, and to prevent myself from getting involved with destructive activities. Those thoughts were not only destroying me, but my condition was affecting my children.

My Dear God:

I had read that before in many books. But I never paid attention to it. This time I studied the importance of the meaning of the statement. "(Yesterday which is gone is history. Tomorrow is a great mystery. Today is a valuable present. Be careful how you handle it.)"

I said to myself, "I must learn to practice this in my daily life. If only I could do

that!" It is true that we cannot change yesterday. But we can make our present days meaningful by learning from our experience, and by trying to correct ourselves. If only we could put our intelligence to work, and recognize the beauty of that quotation.

But as they say, talk is sweet. How could I put myself together, while my husband had given my children the news of our divorce? How could I make myself face the death of my hopes, my dreams, and my future? How could I start walking when I had lost my legs? How could I continue breathing when I had no heart? How could I think straight being in that state of mind? "Are you with me, my dear God, to hold my hand, and show me the way? Are you with me, my dear God, to lead my way to success?" Without you, my dear God, I wouldn't be able to survive. "You must come to my rescue, before I commit a crime, before I loose my mind, and before I find my children in a bad shape".

The library was the only place where I could let my thoughts go wild. I found my place refuge there. That was where I looked for solutions to my problems. I sat there for hours, and studied my past. I was looking to find out what were my mistakes? I wanted to find out that if that was my reward for sincere love and care for my husband and family, then what would be the reward for committing a crime?

It is true that our future is unknown. We will never know what will be there for us the next hour, or the next day. But we all know all of us have to die one day. If we live one day, or if we live one hundred years, still the day that we die seems like a moment. In reality it doesn't matter.

We know the truth about our mortality. We now that death can occur at any second. But we do not preoccupy ourselves with such thoughts on daily basis. We do not allow ourselves to be bothered by that truth. We keep living, and we keep hoping, we plan for future.

So I was planning to be my own teacher. I had no one to share my sadness with except my GOD in my heart. And it was because I was consulting him that I did what was right for me. I was trying to find enough strength to show him that he could never destroy my children or me. I was so determined to prove to him that he had only destroyed himself, and no one else. I wanted to be able to show him that he was no longer my GOD that I worshiped. The GOD that I was worshiping was in my heart, and my GOD was trying to help me survive.

My Dear God:

I decided to think clearly what was best for my children, and me. I decided to only trust to my instinct. I was planning to continue my existence guided by my instinct.

I thought Iraj had caught a disease of a "seven year itch". I assume that it might have been contagious for men in their mid-life crisis. Now it had reached to its peak, and there was nothing that anyone could do about it.

Badri knew how to target Iraj's weak points. Remember Rozan's card for Iraj's birthday, “You are not getting older, you are only getting better”? Remember Sara’s reaction when she read that greeting? She kept insisting, “This is not the act of a nine year old girl. This is Badri who wants to awaken Iraj’s sense of aging, so that she could then comfort him at the most vulnerable time of his life”. Indeed, that was the only insecurity that he had at that time.

Exactly one year before Malakuti’s death if everyone in this world came to me and told me in unison, “Iraj is going to leave you for Badri”, I still would not believe them. Because he acted like the best husband, and the best father. And I thought that I had it. That is why we say, “Tomorrow is a mystery”. What mysterious life!

Now, after eight years of struggle, and after I tried to protect my family, and Iraj from the huge tornado, I was standing where none of us could have imagined I would be standing. Badri had finally reached her goal with the help of her family and my friends.

Thanks to that sarcastic and humiliating poem she was able to get what she wanted. It was right after that poem was circulated that Iraj had decided to proceed with the divorce.

Even though I was expecting it, but I was still shocked because in all those years Iraj tried to make his children believe that their mother was making everything up. He always tried to comfort them that there was nothing to be concerned about. And I went along with it, since I wanted him to be obligated to his children. I was hoping that we would wake up one day from that awful nightmare.

Not knowing that he was more ruthless than I thought. Not knowing that one thing he did not care for was his family and his children. I wish that someone was there to witness my daughters’ grief on the night that he gave them the news of our divorce.

My Dear God:

I was shocked to realize that he really did not care about his children. The fact that he had no emotions about his children was more devastating for me that the news about our divorce.

At that time I had to be very clear about my plans. I witnessed that Iraj was destroyed and demolished by those friends of ours who always wanted him destroyed. Iraj’s disloyalty and his betrayal was the subject of laughter at every Iranian party. Iraj might have had a promiscuous woman in his arms, but what about his reputation? What about his prestige? What about his good name? Those so-called friends were finally able to destroy Iraj. They put him out of the race forever. All in all Iraj had dug his own grave.

It is true that I tried for eight years to save my home from burning down. But in reality the loss was his. He could no longer be qualified as a good doctor. He might be able to walk, talk, and have plenty of sex. But this was not what he was expecting from life. And if that was what he was expecting from life, I wouldn’t know it.

Today, when Iraj looks in the mirror, he will see a thief, a betrayer, and a dishonest

crook according to that anonymous poem. I am so glad that he will never be able to clear his name from these qualities. I am sure of that. The only reason that those doctors would invite him to their houses would be to ridicule him. They dared you to do it, so that they can be entertained now. If you are happy Iraj, I could be happy too.

After the news of our divorce, it was now all up to me to decide, and to arrange my life accordingly. I could not believe that I would ever survive this divorce. I had no one to turn to. His sister Parri, who was living in California, was my best and only friend. I realized that she had the right to support her only brother, and prefer him to me. First of all he was her only brother, and secondly he was a doctor. Her reasoning was very obvious. As far as my family, except for my older sister Ezzat, no other siblings of mine knew what was going on in my life. I chose not to tell them anything. I was so embarrassed to admit to them that they were right after all.

My connection with Ezzat, who was living in England, was via mail correspondence only. Her letters were my only source of comfort. She helped me prepare for my new life. She wrote to me frequently to keep me alive. She wanted to make sure that I didn't do something stupid.

It was in one of those letters that she talked to me about Parri. She asked me to ignore Parri's involvement with Iraj's decision. Her letter took almost a week to arrive. So I reread her letters, and I memorized all that she was expecting from me. I kept the letter inside one of the books, which I was reading at the time. One day, when Parri was in our house, she got hold of that book, and she found the letter. She obviously did not like Ezzat's comments. And when she went to Iran, she made a big deal about the relationship between the two families. But eventually she was very apologetic about her behavior.

My Dear God:

I realized after speaking to my cousin Lucy in Canada that I had no other choice but to stay in the U.S. I realized that I must learn to act civilized. I put myself together to be able to face Iraj. I wanted to find out what he had planned for us.

As always he had thought of everything to his own benefit. He broke down all my expenses, and he had it all in writing. And he believed that was what I needed, not more and not less. He agreed that I must start looking for a house, and he offered me one hundred fifty thousand dollars for the purchase of the house.

As I mentioned before, he was traveling when I sold our last house. I signed the papers with the power of attorney that I had from him, and I received the checks for almost half a million dollars. I deposited all the money into our joint account, and prior to that I consulted a lawyer. I knew that the law of divorce in Michigan was "No Fault Divorce". It meant that all the properties and the belongings must be divided in half, no matter who was the guilty. But the lawyer warned me then that many smart husbands know how to make their wealth and money disappear before the time of the legal divorce.

That was the reason that he was after me to move forward with the divorce.

But I have never been corrupt. I knew that regardless of what was going on, and how I handled the money at the time, when it came to legal divorce, I would have to give him his share. And I didn't know any way of hiding that. I was aware that after he pays off what he owed to the bank, the rest must be divided in half. But I also knew that all those checks that he asked me to write for the payment of the "Hollywood Live" for fifty thousand dollars a month, it was my money going down the drain.

My dear GOD, do you remember that evening that I sat at the corner of the bed to talk to him? Do you remember how hopeless and how lost I was? I was sitting in front of a person who used to be my lover, my admirer, and my supporter. There was a time when this person would have given anything to make my children and me happy. This person used to want the whole world for us. Now I had to ask to pay me enough to purchase a ticket to Iran to visit my family. And still he denied my request.

My Dear God:

I was sure that if I hired a lawyer, and took the case to court, with all those high attorney and court fees, I would have lost even the little money that I was receiving from him. I decided that having a little was better than have nothing. If I wanted to fight with him and take him to court, I should have done it right after Azeez's death. It was too late. He had done all that he needed to do. And he had spent as much of my money as he could. I didn't want it to get to this point. Now that we were there, I had to take it and move on.

My life was in a shamble. I was trying to remember who I was before I married Iraj. I wanted to bring that other life of mine back. I was hoping that I didn't have to talk to Iraj about money. I always wanted the whole world for him. Now he had chosen to be away from me, and I had to let him free. After all I only wanted him if he loved me like before. Otherwise he was not worth anything to me. I must be able to say goodbye to him forever. I must know that it was Iraj who died in the year 1981, and not Azeez. He died for me, and I had to try to burry him, and say goodbye forever.

All those years not only I did not want to divorce him, but I did not have that kind of power in me to be able to ruin the great love that I had for some years in my life. I could never see myself sitting opposite him in a courtroom, or blaming him for not loving me. It was too obvious that he didn't love me. Otherwise he would have never started that affair with Badri. Why would I even discuss that in any court? I never wanted to make him love me by asking him for more money. We were poor when we fell in love. Or I must say I fell in love. If his love was true, we would never end up where we are today. I wasn't able to make up false stories about him, like he was able to make up stories about me. Why would I humiliate myself? What was I asking for by hiring a lawyer? He already took everything away from me. And the rest had to be divided in half. So I was not willing to spend the rest of my money to prove to the court that Iraj didn't love me. I would never do such a thing.

At this time I must say, "You didn't deserve my love. You need to love a person just like yourself, and I am glad you found one".

During all those troubled years Maseeh had graduated from college, and he had moved to California. After some time that his life was in a shamble, he was able to share a place with two roommates. That was the time that he had met Anna. It was while she was working at the "Hollywood Live". I got to meet her on one of the trips to California. It was the night that Maseeh had asked me to prepare dinner for his friends. Later, when we became friends, Anna told me many stories of all the abuse that Maseeh used to take from his father, Kamal, and others.

Mary had graduated from U of M, and she was studying law at Detroit University. She made a point to keep her distance from me. She was living with a young lawyer, whom she knew from high school. He used to be married twice before, and he had a son from his first marriage. The boy was three years old, and he lived mostly with his father. His ex-wife still had him under her thumb. Mary loved that little boy very much. She enjoyed spending time with him. She used to invite me in her place every once in a while. One can only imagine their lifestyle. They lived in downtown Detroit, with five dogs, cats and other pets. While I visited, I could sense that many things were wrong. His behavior was not of a gentleman. And I was suspecting drugs as well. After the news of our divorce, Mary embraced the wrong relationship. She felt so scared, so lonely, and hopeless and crushed that she belittled herself, and became very weak. Because of the fears, and the lack of confidence, she consequentially took all the abuse from her boyfriend.

My Dear God:

She needed so badly someone to turn to that she actually thought she was in love with him. She was even planning to marry him despite all the abuse. She was assuming that their marriage would turn him into a better person. Okay, my dear GOD, what if you were not with me at that time? What if you did not pay attention to all the tears I shed day and night? What if you didn't come to my rescue? I was demolished, and my children were demolished just for the sake of one person's sexual desires.

Is it fair, my dear GOD that people go through such abuse? This man pretended that his entire life was for the sake of his children. He was willing to give his life for his children. Now he had destroyed them to such extent that I didn't know how to put them back together again.

After he had his first affair in Iran, and he was forced to escape the country with shame and embarrassment, he wrote to me from U.S.A., "When I see other children with both their parents having fun, I ask GOD, why shouldn't my beautiful dear innocent children be with both of us, and why shouldn't they have fun with us at this time?" You see, my dear GOD, hasn't he been the biggest liar?

Didn't you, my dear GOD, give him his life back with my complete help? Didn't you

gave him a second chance to make it up to his children, and try to bring happiness into their lives? Didn't you give me enough strength to be able to forgive him, and to start loving him again? Do you think that he was blind, and he could not see what his children were going through? Did he have enough sense to feel other people's pain, but not his own children's? What can I say or do to make my children feel better? Where do I begin?

He wrote to me, "Dear Shamci, I keep promising myself that with you, and only with your help I will be able to recover from this disaster. And I could bring happiness into my children's life once again".

My Dear God:

My dear GOD, this was the same man who was begging for my hand and my forgiveness to be able to build our happy home, and bring back the happiness that we lost. True, he was able to build a house. But even the house was build to destroy all our happiness.

Mojgan also graduated from high school at this time, and she was ready for college. She was still friends with Glen. It was a blessing for me. At the time that her father left her, his friendship with her was a reward to me. She had someone to talk to, someone to laugh with, someone to get angry at, and someone to count on. I needed him in her life at that time. Although I was wishing that my children did not think of marriage before they were done with their college, I was hoping that they could have someone in their life to be able to trust and rely on. She was experiencing the roughest times of her life. I was the only one, regardless of all my problems, who had to understand my children's position. I was the only one to comfort them at the time when they were in need.

Mojgan was going through the age of uncertainties. Plus she was facing the divorce of her parents in a most horrible and humiliating way possible. She was so confused that she didn't know what to do, or which way to go. She was trying to live each day as it came.

I knew by then that all of my children were involved with some kind of smoking. I wasn't sure what it was exactly, or up to what degree. I tried to watch them and walk with them according to the circumstances. They already were under so much pressure. They were trying to mingle with their peers. And at the same time they tried to escape the embarrassment of their parents' behavior. We had no idea of what the future held for us. Each in our own way we were searching for solutions to a happier life. And naturally "a happier life" had a different meaning for each of us. I never thought of turning to drugs or alcohol, because the clarity of a mind was of vital importance to me. But my children were not raised in an environment that promoted drug and alcohol free lifestyle. They were part of a society, which allowed young people do whatever they desired. The use of drugs and alcohol consumption were fashionable.

My children were smoking. I considered cigarettes the most harmful. My resistance

to their habits never appealed to them. Neither did they have enough love in their hearts for me to pay attention to my requests. The only option I had was to stand by them, and reiterate my opinion about their behavior. Even though my persistence made them hate me even more, I never gave up. I was hoping that one day they might realize that I was right.

My Dear God:

How could I expect my children to understand me and my problems, when they were facing the challenges of both their age, and the stupidity of their parents? I was aware of their problems, but I was unable to help them. They knew how their father betrayed them. They knew how their father lied to them. They knew how he took their home, and happiness away from them. They knew of Iraj's affair with Badri even before I found out. How could I tell them what to do? How could I expect them to follow my advice? How could I ask them to be wise?

I knew that they were trying to bring some stability and tranquility back into their lives. Unfortunately the only way they knew was to join their friends, and imitate their behavior.

I also knew that if I tried to be harsh on them, the results would have been even worse. So I chose not to interfere, and I stayed away. I was so lost; I was desperately in need of help. I prayed to God day and all night, asking God to make them come to their senses. I could not think of any other way of getting through them.

I thought I was a perfect role model. They have never seen me smoking or drinking. I thought that alone would be enough to help them distinguish right from wrong. They were completely aware of my expectations. But how could I ask them to listen to me? I hoped to stay strong, and I gave them more love than ever. I wanted them to hopefully realize one day that I had nothing but love for them. I was not going to give up. And at the same time I wanted to make to clear to them that I would never approve of their involvement with smoking, drugs and alcohol.

I had heard from some psychiatrists and I had read in many books that parents must not try to control their children's life. It is common for American society to believe that the parents must not try to control their children. People who never had kids must have originated this kind of attitude about raising children. We all are witnessing what had happened to our new generation. Children of age of nine are bringing guns to school; they are using and dealing drugs. Do you call this a healthy society? Or maybe such attitude has been created with a purpose of raising millions of disturbed children. So that some psychiatrists will have their job security. So that they can charge the parents per hour and still not be able to secure our children's recovery.

We all know that if a parent does not control a child's action at the right age, they will eventually pick up bad habits from their surrounding. Later on no one, neither their parents, nor the best psychiatrists would be able to correct them. It is same case as a tree, which was planted crooked from the beginning. The only answer to straightening that tree would be to cut it down.

My Dear God:

You can see that this rule could be applied to all the children of the world. If you don't step forward, and if you don't tell them what is expected from them, your children will never learn to follow the right path.

I knew I was right. I had many uncles who were drinking and using opium. Iraj's father was an alcoholic. But my parents and the rest of my family never did anything of that source.

I remember clearly that we were not allowed to ever think about such things. We were prohibited from any wrong doing by the laws of the family.

Today I believe that it was only our upbringing that had made my siblings and me great human beings. Our family was blessed by my parents' true love and dedication. I wish I had admitted to this truth when they were still living. I hope they hear me now, because I want them to know that I am proud of being a part of them. And I know that if it wasn't for their hard work, none of us would have been where we are now. I can only say thank you for your hard work and effort to push us towards true living. God bless you mother! God bless you father! Rest in peace forever. You were great role models. Rest in peace that I am sending you my morning prayers every day, no matter where I am.

So with reiterating all these, I would like to emphasize the importance of parents' care for their children. I knew that it was my duty to supervise my children's activities. Especially when their cousins Arman and Nazzy lived in our house. I knew they supplied my children with drugs. I had no choice but to keep my eyes open at all times.

Obviously my children didn't like it. They accused me of being a controller. But I didn't mind being called names than to neglecting my children. I was hoping that one day they would recognize that their mother was only after their well-being. She never intended to hurt them. Unfortunately neither their age, nor the circumstances around them were helpful.

Their father was too busy with his own affairs. He could care less about their troubles. I was the only person who cared for their health and emotions. I was hoping that with all my efforts they would grow up to be decent human beings. It was not important what they thought of my tactics. I was responsible for their well being whether they liked it or not.

It seems easy when I am writing about those times today. But, my dear God, do you remember those long nights that my pillows were wet from my tears? You remember how I was trying to hold my head up in front of my children? Do you remember how I was questioning you about your justice? I was asking you why were you punishing me for the

crimes I had never committed. You gave me enough strength to follow up with my duties. And as always, time is a great healer.

My Dear God:

Although I never forget those awful days and nights, still I am thanking you God for giving me all the patience and tolerance Thank you!

Mojgan was very much like me. She always tried to keep busy, even while she was studying. Besides the part time job at her father's office, she occasionally worked as a babysitter She was a responsible girl, and she always wanted to do her job well. It was through one of her baby-sitting jobs that I got to meet Dr. Chitra Amladi and her family. Chitra had later become one of my rescuers.

Then in the summer of that year Mojgan and Glen started selling knife sets for a large company. And they started cleaning offices for doctors on the weekends. They were working so hard; she made me feel so proud.

Not only she was working hard, but also she was a motivation for Glen. She was always after him to do things, or study together. I had given them enough freedom to be comfortable around me, just to be able to be around them at all times. I was ready to settle for anything just to keep them away from drugs and alcohol.

Unfortunately, both Glen and Mojgan were under plenty of pressure from their parents. Mojgan's parents were getting divorced. While Glen's parents, especially his mother, could not understand the world that her children were living in. She put so much pressure on her girls that both of them ran away from home to escape all the restrictions. Glen was warned to stay away from Mojgan, and that was killing him. He started drinking. This had created a lot of complications in their relationship. They were both very angry.

The situation got to a point that I decided to intervene. I invited Glen's mother to lunch, and I talked to her on subjects in general. She was a very conservative Armenian lady. She could not see herself and her family living in Rock and Roll decade. I realized during our conversation that just like any other woman of her age, she was suffering from midlife crisis. She was depressed because her children were adults now, and they had to go their own ways. And then she would have nothing to hang on to. She did not have a job, or career. I say this because she offered me to go into some sort of business together. This offer was a proof that she thought herself useless.

I knew that she had been a pianist. But she was so depressed that she believed that she was no longer able to play. From what I gathered her children had labeled her as "emotionally sick". She was forced to see a psychiatrist. I tried to explain to her that sometimes when we put so much pressure on our children, they tend to rebel. And when they do rebel they make irrational decisions. For example we might push them into an impulsive marriage. And I tried to tell her neither one of us needed for something like that

to happen to us.

My Dear God:

I made sure that she understood that in my culture we were also against sex before marriage. But I told her that I also believed that the rules of our times were not the same as the rules of the 60's. The society of sixties was actually condoning the cultural family by pushing drugs and alcohol down our children's throats by the name of freedom. The society has been able to get rid of morality, devotion, loyalty, and the love for the family. Behind these are the rules of capitalism. We could not fight it. We had to study those issues carefully, and try to deal with them.

In my own mind I was trying to make life easy for my children. I wanted them to know that no matter what they did, or how many mistakes they might make, I would still be there for them. I knew that they had to experience things, and learn from their experiences. I never pushed my children to get married. At the time marriage meant the end of freedom to me.

Mary told me once, "Mom, please don't worry so much about us. Drugs are so accessible to us. They are sold at the school library. How do you plan to stop us from getting them? So please just teach us, and leave the rest up to us. Meanwhile you can pray for us so that we use our heads". And she continued, "Stop worrying and crying. Stop following us, you are not going to accomplish much".

Mary was very smart. Everything that she said made a lot of sense. When drugs were easily exchanged between teachers and students at a private school, how could I prevent my children's wrong doings?

This reminds me of Mr. Art Linkletter's book. He was writing about his daughter's overdose. I made sure to read it twice not to miss anything. In short he was saying, "I wanted to find out who is responsible for the availability of drugs in the hands of our children. I started from little people, and up to the higher ranks of our society. As soon as I reached higher levels, like senators, or FBI, and CIA all the doors closed on me. I was prohibited to go any farther".

He was trying to tell us that we could get the little people, punish them, and put them away for the rest of their lives. But we will never be able to remove the drugs from our children's life. It was not because our government can't do anything about it. But it was because in this country the drug trafficking is the biggest income for those powerful people. And to our amazement they are the ones who are screaming, "Let's get all the drug dealers. Let's try to get the drugs out of our children's hands".

My Dear God:

What a shame! If our leaders had a little sense of understanding, and if they tried to create a better world for our children, and the new generation, I am sure that all of us

would have the opportunity to raise our children in a healthy environment, and we would live in a peaceful world.

The same case is for the parents of the world. If they were good leaders, and a good example for their children, we would not have a society like this today.

Mr. Art Linkletter was trying to let us know that our society was a creation and a product of our government's leadership. Those people were trying to convince us to look elsewhere for finding the causes of destruction of our environment. While their greed and desire for wealth and money had been detrimental to our society. These people are trying to make us believe that we must look elsewhere to catch a thief, or to get rid of terrorists, while thieves and terrorists were all among us.

Who kidnapped Hafa and got rid of him for good? Who killed John F Kennedy? Who killed Robert Kennedy? Who killed Martin Luther King? Who killed Malcolm X? And who killed so many good and influential people in this country? Do you think they would ever allow us to question the high ranked officials, "Why don't you catch the terrorists and the criminals in this country? Why should our children deal with insufficient knowledge about the country they love and live in?"

Such facts had made me feel sorry for our children and myself. My life was so awful at times, I didn't know how to save my children from falling into trap. I believed that we could only be saved by a miracle.

Please, my dear GOD, tell me how are we supposed to create a good future for our children when we don't have a good foundation for them to rely on? The only way for my wish to come true was to teach my children, and then leave it up to them to figure out the rest.

After he gave me the news of the divorce, and after I talked to him, I knew it was the time for us to put our agreement in writing. I was aware that without a lawyer I would not be able to get more money out of him. In the meantime all I could do was hope that he would follow our agreement, and that he would not rob me at the end.

My dear GOD, I get shivers just writing about his dishonesty and disloyalty. He was supposedly my best friend; he was the only person I trusted with my life for thirty years. How could I ever trust again, when I had to watch out for my best friend, the love of my life not to rob me or stab me? Don't you think that this feeling alone was enough to destroy me?

My Dear God:

I knew that if I had hired a lawyer, with his present income my minimum alimony would sum up to five thousand dollars per month. But I knew that I would have to deal with emotional suffering, which I was not prepared for. And I also knew that I would encounter high attorney fees. At that time I was barely able to breath, yet to get involved with court judgments and all the humiliation that would follow. I wanted nothing more

than to gain back control over my life. I had started my life with great love, and I was left with nothing.

We followed the rules of "No fault divorce". He put together the list of the things that he was interested to keep. Since he had moved to California, he decided not to claim any furniture. I asked for the half of everything else that we had earned during those years. I was supposed to receive half of the sales of the office, the clinic, and other properties we had together, and obviously half his share of the nightclub in Detroit, and half of his share on Hollywood Live in LA.

Being aware of the things that were happening around those clubs, and the scandalous activities that went on, I decided to make sure that he didn't hold me responsible for any of his losses. I was convinced that due to his involvement with wrong people and their wrong doings the success of those businesses was very unlikely. I made sure that the lawyer wrote me off of any kind of his losses.

My dear GOD, don't you think that this idea came to my mind by your will? How could I possibly be so wise at the time when I was almost out of my mind? I think you were trying to save me from the agony created by Iraj. You knew I had no one to defend me, or support me, or guide me to be able to survive. From the first moment you came to my rescue, and you showed me the way. I thank you sincerely. This way although I have only received a small amount of money, but I was able to avoid the humongous debts after our divorce was final.

The alimony he was willing to settle for was not even enough to pay for the rent of a house. I couldn't possibly afford to pay for health insurance. I knew that he wanted to destroy me. But even after I hired a lawyer, and spent $250.00 per hour, there would be no assurance that he would let me get what I had asked for. Plus I did not find enough strength in me to take him to court. To begin with I had never trusted any courts. And I believed that there was no justice in the world anyway. The one who made up better, and the most emotional stories would win no matter if he or she were guilty of the crime.

My Dear God:

So after his lawyer wrote the agreement between us. He gave me one month to look for house. He did not want to pay for the rent of my apartment after that month.

I contacted the same real estate agent who sold our house. In a way she was in the middle of our conflicted life. She was familiar with my taste, and she knew my lifestyle. I told her what I wanted, and I made sure that she got to work. I told her I had only one month to find a house. She was a very nice lady. She had two daughters. One of her daughters was a friend of Roxana, Rohan's daughter. She liked me a lot, and one day she told me the story of her own divorce.

That day she drove me to her house, and we had lunch together. After lunch she talked about her life, and she cried for at least one hour. After so many years her

memories were still fresh, and very painful.

She found me a house with big yard in Birmingham, Michigan, and a condominium overlooking the Cass Lake in the city of Waterford, Michigan. The city of Birmingham was a more reputable city. Even at this time of my life he was trying to influence me to look for something that could make me more money in the future, and not something that I liked. But I wanted something to give me security, and happiness now rather than later. The way that my life turned out there was no future to think about. Where were all my dreams, my happiness, and my struggle for keeping my family together? Why did I try to save so much money for our future?

Why should I even think of future? I had had enough. At that time I couldn't see myself living in a house with a big old yard all by myself. And taking care of it all by myself was impossible. I didn't even bother to look around, and inside the house. She told me, "I know what you want. And I know what you like, and what you need". She took me to the condo. It was on the third level, and it was not overlooking the lake, it was looking into a big beautiful swimming pool. There was a gazebo in the front yard, surrounded by trees and flowers.

The view from the balcony was fantastic. I didn't want to leave. The building had a subterranean parking with assigned parking and storage spaces. We took the elevator right from the paring lot. It was a key operated the elevator. This was the only way to access your home. The hallways reminded me of a hotel. The doors to each condominium were spaced not too far apart. The security factor appealed to me more than anything else. No yard work, no solicitors, and no possibility of burglary.

It was three bedrooms, and two baths condo. It had a spacious living room, a large kitchen over looking into the living room, and over looking the lake. There was a space for a dining room.

My Dear God:

The master bedroom was connected to a spacious mirrored closet area. There was a separate washroom. The master bath had a two-door shower, and a big sized marbled tub, all mirrored. It was just enjoyable to look at, and many other advantages.

Obviously my agent knew me well. I loved that condo, and I had to have it right away. But there was a huge problem. I only had one hundred and fifty thousand dollars. The owner, who did not need to sell his house fast, was insisting on selling it for one hundred and sixty five thousand dollars. I knew that Iraj was not willing to give me any more money. What was I going to do?

I knew it was my right to ask for that money. But knowing Iraj I did not want to talk to him about my rights. Instead I told him about the space for a boat, which would give our children the opportunity to use the lake whenever they came to visit me. This made him to pay ten thousand dollars more, and nothing above that.

This is the backside of my condominium in Waterford, Michigan. I was on the second floor. It was beautiful, but those days I was so afraid to live alone that after one year I rented it out and I tried to live with another friend. I had to find a way to be able to learn to live by myself. So I did.

This is the front of the condo, which overlooked the Cass Lake. In the front, there were two big pools, a big shower and a dressing room for those who swam there.

I was still five thousand dollars short. The condo was so beautiful, and so convenient for me at that time of my life that I thought that I would die if someone else bought it. This was the only hope for me, and the only security that I could have at that time.

I knew that if Iraj gave me the extra five thousand dollars I would be able to pay him back little by little. But he wasn't thinking at all. Or probably he wasn't able to think at all. His reason was that he did not have money at that time.

Since I knew that Iraj was close friends with Dr. M Rabbani, I thought I must get help from him. I was able to save some money from the work I was doing then. But I thought it was not fair that I spent this little savings of mine, and Iraj could get away with it all.

So I talked to Dr Rabbani. And I asked him to lend me the five thousand dollars. Dr. Rabbani told Iraj that he was going to lend me the money, and that Iraj could give him the money back when he had it available.

But I paid Dr. M Rabbani back out of my savings before I bought the condo. I did not want to borrow money from anyone. And since Iraj agreed to Dr. Rabbani's suggestion, and he ended up repaying him the five thousand dollars, Dr. Rabbani gave it to me. Thanks God I didn't have to fight, or beg. And I was able to buy that condo, and have something to look forward to.

All right, my dear GOD, today I can write, "Finding that condo was something for me to look forward to". But did it really mean that I was looking forward to, or I was just scared to death?

Since I started my life in the USA, I have been always living in comfort with Iraj, and my children next to me. He has been pampering me like a baby. Now I had to start my life like a newborn person. I had to learn how to live by myself, and all alone, apart from all my loved ones. No hope, no dream, just merely driven by the instinct of survival. I was afraid to be by myself. I would rather be outside of the house, even if I had to sleep in the parking lot. Although I was putting so much effort into getting grip of my life, there was still something in the back of my mind testing me, "It is better to end my life". So many times I was afraid to stay home by myself. Although it was very safe to live in the condo, I didn't trust myself. I made sure to keep occupied. I felt like Humpty Dumpty putting it together again. My dear God, where do I begin? Who do I turn to? Why me, why?

My Dear God:

The thought of not having anyone by my side would always give me chills. God please, how do I handle this? The though of committing crime was always in the back of my mind, and it scared me to death.

Before I got married, my huge family surrounded me at all times. But afterwards I only had Iraj and my children. What had happened to all of them? Where did they all go? How could I adapt myself to this new life? How was I supposed to survive all by myself in this strange city after living for more than fifty years surrounded by my family? God please, where were you planning to take me from here? Was there an end to my misery?

At this time Maseeh was in Los Angeles working at Hollywood Live, moving from one place to the other. He had become very distant from me. He didn't know what was happening in Michigan, or what I was going through. Mary was at law school. And she was trying to establish a relationship with that young lawyer, who in reality was destroying her. She was too mad and too sad to be able to get involved. And Mojgan was still undecided on her choice of college. She was working hard, and she had a great relationship with Glen.

I had arranged one bedroom for Mojgan. I tried to provide her with all her necessities. I put two double-sized beds in her room to accommodate for her friends. She had her own full shower next to her bedroom. Because I only had one car space in the garage, I made sure to park outside when she stayed over at my place. I made sure she had the parking space. I felt it was safer that she accessed the building through the garage.

Although I tried to give her the most comforting place, and I provided her with everything she had asked for, still I never saw her happy. Every time I looked at my young girl, who was then in her prime, I expected to see happiness and not sadness. I was so ashamed.

I told my parents, "I will build a loving home for my children, and I will make sure to sacrifice myself to achieve the ultimate happiness for them". Now I found myself in a situation that my children had no concept of happiness. Each apart from the other, far not in a happy arrangement. But by the force of circumstances, and angered by having useless parents, they didn't care who started it. And they didn't want to know which one of us was guilty. One thing they knew was that they were without that "home security", and that the home, which they hoped to come back to when they needed, was broken.

My Dear God:

To children both parents are alike. Therefore their happiness was demolished by our divorce. Watching Mojgan's desperation burned my heart in flames. But the worst of all was that they all took it against me. I wished I could have a power to be able to reverse the time to the times when I was not married. Then I did not have to witness my children's sufferings, caused by my so-called love and me.

My main objective in life became to lessen their sufferings, regardless of my own wounds. I never blamed Mojgan for acting like a firecracker. She was ready to pop or explode at any time. I had to watch myself, and pretend that I wasn't hurt.

I reserved a boat space so that my children could use their jet boats without any hassle, or difficulty when they visited. In effort to help my children fit in their society, I arranged for them to celebrate Christmas every year. Just like every other kid they found gifts, good or bad, big or little, under the Christmas tree every year.

That year in the condo Mojgan wanted to celebrate Christmas just like during all previous years. I bought a huge manmade tree, thinking that I could use it every year if they visit. I bought many beautiful ornaments for her to occupy her mind by arranging the Christmas tree. Although she was happy to do so, she still was not able to clear her unhappy heart, and to replace her sadness with happiness. Many times I suspected that she was not getting along with Glen. I could hear them arguing in her room. It seemed that they had difficulty communicating. This made me very worried. I was hoping that she could be with him, because he was the only person from the past that she was happy to be around him. I was afraid that if she lost him, I might lose Mojgan. Since she was a very strong-minded girl, I could never interfere with her decision-making. Besides, at that time I felt like a failure, and I thought that my advice would be useless.

One day I heard her scream when they were arguing. When I came to check what was happening, she showed me my Lalic figurine broken in pieces, and she said, "It was pulled by telephone cord and broke into two pieces".

I calmed her down by saying that there was still a possibility to repair it. I asked her not to worry, and that it wasn't a big deal.

My Dear God:

She felt better, and they stopped arguing. Accidents like this happened quite often. She was so disturbed, and ready to explode. We were all like that, because we didn't know what had happened to us. None of us knew about that sarcastic poem which was delivered to all Iranian homes. I still believe that it was the only force behind Iraj's decision on our divorce.

With my struggle to keep the family together in one piece, my kids were hoping that their father might not break his promises, and destroy the family. But at this time of their life they were facing the truth. It was a fact, and it was there now. After eight years of struggle, still their father left them. But they did not know how to deal with this bitter fact.

We were unable to communicate without loosing our temper. Every one was ready to put the blame on the other. No one wanted to talk about the family. This word made us mad every time the subject came up.

Since Maseeh was away from us. I did not know how he was dealing with the situation, until I moved to California. Mary was very angry, and whenever she came to visit, I had hard time to know how to handle her moods and emotions. Nothing that I said or did was right. And nothing made them happy.

But Mojgan, who was preparing to go to college, was hoping to bring her father back to the family, where she thought he belonged. She was desperately looking for a way to cling to her father, and bring him back. Not knowing that like the poet said, "Iraj has made up his mind about Badri long time ago".

My kids never needed to try to earn my love or me. I was always available for them.

So although they tried to hurt me, they were trying to attract their father's attention if they could.

Only a few months after Iraj moved to Los Angeles, Mojgan started her college at Western University in Kalamazoo Michigan. She came home one day looking quite puzzled, and she told me that she decided to move to LA. When I asked her, "What about your college?" She said, "I will arrange the transfer"

Please my dear God; help me describe my feelings, and my desperation at that time. All of a sudden I felt my blood freezing in my veins, and my heartbeat was out of control. I felt like my heart was going explode in my chest. I don't think there was a right word or a sentence to be able to describe my feelings.

I knew how desperate Mojgan was about trying to bring back her father. I was very familiar with her nature. I knew that when she had an idea, she had to make it work. She was determined to get her father back.

My Dear God:

After I put myself together, and I was able to once again cover up my emotions, I put a smile on my face, and I said, "Good for you". I didn't allow myself to question her.

After Iraj fooled his children for eight years by constantly keeping them hoping, and by blaming me for having a suspicious mind, Mojgan assumed that by moving to California, and by following her father she might be able to make him feel deeply loved. She was hoping that he would change his mind. She was unaware of the truth, or their arrangement. I just felt ashamed of myself, and I felt sorry for Mojgan. Now, after Mojgan leaves to LA, I would be all alone. But there was nothing that I could do to change things around me. Probably if I was in Mojgan's place, I would have done the same thing.

Since she always kept in contact with her father, I assumed that she would be staying with him. I never asked her about her plans, unless she wanted to tell me herself. She told me, "Glen and I are driving my car to LA, and then he will fly back to Michigan by himself". I didn't want to ask her any questions. I didn't want to make her frustrated.

We went shopping together, and I helped her pack. I did not allow myself to cry. I knew that my children had lost that essence for love, and for life in general, and that I must not play with their emotions any more. I was lost, confused. I was feeling empty. I didn't know when it was appropriate to laugh, or when it was appropriate to cry. For eight years I was preparing myself for this disastrous moment. But still I wasn't sure how to I face it. I knew I had to find a way to cope with it.

Mojgan knew that I would be left all alone, without a single sole to turn to. But she needed her father, and she had to try to get him back. I would not dare to question her, or give her my opinion. I was hoping that Mojgan's decision to move to Los Angeles would benefit her emotional state. I was hoping that she could at least bring love back into her life. That was all that mattered to me then. Just because Iraj stopped loving me, he

shouldn't stop loving his children. It was in a way that she would be close to him, and possibly regain her lost love. Even after all the damage that Iraj had done to his children with his lies and pretence, I still supported Mojgan's crazy idea. I wanted her to live her life with a positive attitude. I also wanted her to figure things out on her own.

Meanwhile I was getting ready for my loneliest times of my life. It was going to be just me, with no friends, no job, no family, no husband, and no children living by myself in a neighborhood. There was going to be no one else but I in my condominium, with my great superpower, which I referred to as "my own GOD".

My Dear God:

I was glad that before Mojgan moved to Los Angeles, they decided to come home. They brought their jet boat. They had so much fun on the lake. Many liked the view of my condo even more than the view from our big house on Wabeek Lake.

Mojgan loved my new place. I would always invite a few of our mutual friends whenever they visited. I would usually cook a big meal, and made sure that everyone enjoyed the weekend. Many times Mary visited together with her friends.

I was very sad on the day of Mojgan's departure. But I never showed my sorrow to her. I helped her pack the car, and I made sure she had everything she needed. I kissed her good-bye, and wished her a safe trip. I followed her car to the corner of the road, waving. I was not sure how long she would be gone for.

As soon as they left, I went back home, and cried and cried and cried. My dear GOD, do you remember that day? Do you remember how desperate and hopeless I was? Do you remember my tears? Do you remember how I talked to you quietly, hoping for a miracle? Do you remember how lonely I was feeling? Is there a way to express my feelings at that time?

While I was lying in my bed, I was reviewing my life. I remembered how my father had predicted this life for me. He had warned me about Iraj many times. He knew that while I was deeply in love with Iraj, his love for me was nothing but a need for someone to love him like a mother, and worship him as a lover. He had succeeded in fooling me; he had it all. I was having a very difficult time to face the truth. I thought I had a happy life.

Why should Malakuti move to Michigan? Why should we get to know them? Why would they form such partnership, if Iraj and Badri were not behind it all to begin with? And many other whys.

Alas I had no answers. Now that everyone was gone, I had to bring myself back to the times before I was in love. I must try to adapt myself to a life of a single woman. I must think as if I was never married, or had children. I must find a way dilute myself in some sort of activities to keep my mind occupied, and away from thoughts about my past. I figured that was the only way for me to survive. I had to do it all by myself. I must go back to being eighteen-year-old Shamci. The one who knew no love, no husband, and no children.

After all, children must go their own way. They will build their carriers, they will get married, and hopefully they will live happily ever after. Children are not supposed to stay by their mother's side for the rest of their lives.

One thing I was determined to do was to bring shame into Iraj's life by not allowing myself to be or feel like a loser. He was the one who had done wrong, and therefore he must feel ashamed. I had to go on with my life holding my head up. I had to remain the same authoritative mother I had always been. I always ran that household, and I will continue to do so. I haven't done anything wrong, and I had no intensions of doing so.

My Dear God:

I would have never believed that he might marry Badri. I still remember the way that he used to speak of her, and her family. I never thought he might get that low. I knew that by marrying her he would disgrace himself for the rest of his life. I would be happy to see him suffer from his own actions, without being able to admit to his own mistakes.

After having his first affair, when he came back to us with apologetic sorrow, all his sisters and I forgave him. And we allowed him to make a better life for himself. He was able to have a great come back, and create a loving atmosphere around us. But this time around he was completely destroyed. With that sarcastic poem in the hand of every Iranian, he would never be able to hold his head up high. And I must be happy. He did not have any value to begin with. And I am sorry I did not recognize it when my parents were insisting on informing me.

One thing I did not want to happen to me was to end up in a mental institution. I preferred death to insanity. I had started many activities to occupy my time wisely. But it was not enough. I added bowling to my bridge game, the best medicine for my clouded mind, was activities. I was bowling at a club with other members. I was working as a volunteer at the Saint Joseph hospital at Pontiac, which was near my condo. I also started volunteer work with the Red Cross in that area. I joined a mature mingler group, and participated in most all their activities. It was during those activities that I got to meet my angels. It is so funny; I used to laugh at those who believed in angels. Now I can feel the existence of these angels around me. They came to me without me looking for them. And they left me in the same manner.

Working at the hospital, although it was very rewarding, brought more sadness to my life. I couldn't afford to do that. I had enough sorrow and fear in my life.

So I started to look for a job that required with longer hours. The only job I ever had been teaching. I only worked for three years, and that was in Iran. Except the eight months that I worked for Sara Fassihi. I had many abilities like tailoring, alterations, cooking, hairstyling, and more. But to start something at my age was not easy. I wanted to find a job to fill up my time from morning till night, until I collapsed and fell sleep.

I started to search for a job through newspaper adds. But I was either not qualified, or I had to drive for two hours just to get to the job. I was feeling hopeless.

My Dear God:

My condo happened to be near Pontiac Mall. One morning I decided to walk to the Mall, and talk to someone about a job there. I walked into Hudson, and I asked for the person in charge of hiring. They guided me to her room. She was a lady in her forties. She seemed very nice. She apologized for being fifteen minutes late. Those fifteen minutes seemed to me like two hours. I was so nervous; I kept shivering. Somehow I found courage, and I told her what had happened to me. I told her all about my activities, and I told her that I needed a job to occupy my mind away from my problems. Without a job I don't think I could survive.

After listening to me carefully, she looked at her book and said, "Although we are not hiring at this time, I think I can make it possible for you to get a part time job here. How about you start this Friday? Take this letter to such and such person in such and such room. Tell her which days would you like to work. She will schedule you for the orientation this Friday. We don't have any full time positions at this moment, but I will make sure that you get more hours eventually. This is just to get you started. Make sure to be there on time".

I thought I was dreaming. How could I find a job so easily? I didn't know where to go, or what they were expecting from me. I had never worked in retail. I had never worked with any machinery. I was so scared, and so nervous.

The lady was so nice that she wanted to make sure I survived. She told me that on the day of the orientation they would introduce me to the new machinery, and they would teach me how to work with them. She asked me to hang in there. Hopefully they would be able to give me additional hours soon.

What a nice lady! What a warm hearted beautiful lady she was! I never knew that I was so lucky, yet to be able to find a job in my own neighborhood. The only thing that worried me was, "What if I fail? What if I was not able to pass the test?"
I realized that I was lucky also to live nearby the Mall. If I ever had car problems, I would be able to walk to Hudson.

I went to the orientation that Friday. To my surprise I learned how to work with those machines. I studied the book, and the signs carefully. And I was able to pass the test just as good as all other younger applicants.

I started my new job at the houseware department in the bed and bath area. I was to work for three days a week for half a day, rotating from morning to afternoon shifts.

Although I was very glad that I found that job, it was too slow for me. It did not include enough activities to keep my mind away from my problems. I was expecting my days to fill up my time like a spinning wheel. I wanted to get so busy, and so tired that I

STORE EXECUTIVE STAFF Security 9222

STORE MANAGER Darin EXTENSION ________

PERSONNEL MANAGER ________ EXTENSION ________

OPERATIONS MANAGER ________ EXTENSION ________

CUSTOMER SERVICE MANAGER ________ EXTENSION ________

AREA CUSTOMER SERVICE MANAGER ________ EXTENSION ________

MERCHANDISE MANAGER ________ EXTENSION ________

AREA MERCHANDISE MANAGER Elaine Halcomb EXTENSION ________

In the book, I have talked about all the activities that I tried to find for myself to be able to face the world I was living in. This page and the next are the examples of my hideaway places. I tried to be among the people who were not going to hurt me anymore. I hated those Iranians who were around me for years, and we thought we were friends. To escape from them and to be with someone, I pulled myself towards people who were strangers to me. I was tired of having those friends in my life. So, I made friends with those who didn't know me, those who were not jealous of me and my happiness. If I was going to live away from all those people who once were my love, my husband, my children, all alone by myself in a country that I had no one else to turn to, I had to find these places to just hide myself in. And it worked.

appreciation

Certificate of Appreciation

Presented to

SHAMCI RAFANI

In recognition of faithful service to education and to the community, as a member of the

PERDUE ADULT ED CENTER

1st. PLACE-MATH ENRICHMENT

honor

Certificate of Honor

This Certificate is Presented to

SHAMCI RAFANI

As an acknowledgement of your outstanding achievement

in COMPLETION OF THE GED

at PERDUE ADULT ED CENTER

We congratulate you and have confidence that your future will be equally successful.

Signed this 4th day of MAY

19 88

This was also another hideaway place for me. When I was there, I felt safe. I was not afraid any more. There were people around me whom I could communicate with easily. And that was what I needed.

Diploma

State College of Beauty

This certifies that Shamci Rafani has completed the Course of Study and Training in

All Branches of Beauty Culture

Given at Bloomfield Hills

this 4th day of June A.D. 1979

Vice-President

Diploma

Be it known that

Shamci Rafani

Has successfully completed a course in proficiency in

Personality Development and Make-up Artistry

Given at Bloomfield Hills Campus this 31st day of October 1977

Supervisor

Vice-President

Michigan

State Board of Education

Lansing Michigan

SHAMCI

has successfully completed all the requirements prescribed by the State Board of Education under the General Educational Development program and is hereby awarded this

High School Certificate

JUNE 10, 1988

Phillip E. Runkel
Superintendent of Public Instruction

State Board of Education

Dorothy Beardmore, Carroll M. Hutton, Cherry Jacobus, Barbara Roberts Mason, Annetta Miller, Dr. Gumecindo Salas, Norman Otto Stockmeyer, Sr., Dr. Edmund F. Vandette, *Ex-Officio Members:* Governor James J. Blanchard, Phillip E. Runkel

DETACH ALONG P[illegible]RATION FOR FRAMING • FRAME SIZE 8 x 10

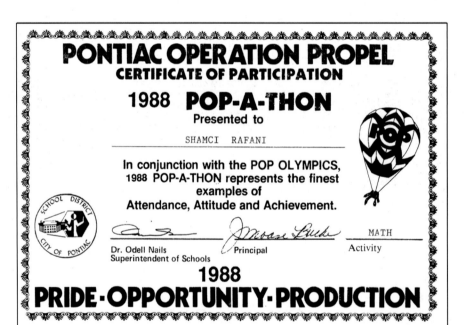

PONTIAC OPERATION PROPEL

CERTIFICATE OF PARTICIPATION

1988 POP-A-THON

Presented to

SHAMCI RAFANI

In conjunction with the POP OLYMPICS, 1988 POP-A-THON represents the finest examples of Attendance, Attitude and Achievement.

SCHOOL DISTRICT CITY OF PONTIAC

Dr. Odell Nails Superintendent of Schools	Principal	MATH Activity

1988

PRIDE · OPPORTUNITY · PRODUCTION

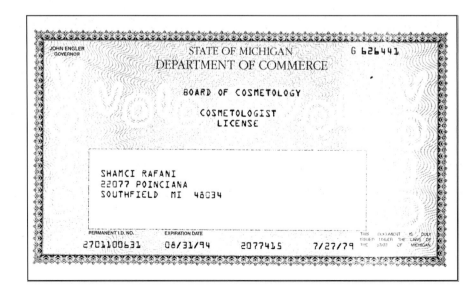

JOHN ENGLER
GOVERNOR

STATE OF MICHIGAN
DEPARTMENT OF COMMERCE

G 626441

BOARD OF COSMETOLOGY

COSMETOLOGIST
LICENSE

SHAMCI RAFANI
22077 POINCIANA
SOUTHFIELD MI 48034

PERMANENT I.D. NO.	EXPIRATION DATE			
2701100631	08/31/94	2077415	7/27/79	THIS DOCUMENT IS DULY ISSUED UNDER THE LAWS OF THE STATE OF MICHIGAN

I don't think this page needs any explanation. During my suffering years, I tried to connect myself with some activities which made me forget my problems. I didn't care what degree it was. As long that I could keep myself away from committing suicide, I was willing to do it.

had no time for thinking. I wanted to be able to work more than twenty hours a day, and to be able to sleep three or four hours a night. Otherwise I would have gone crazy.

My Dear God:

Meanwhile I took a speech class in the evening at OCC, Oakland Community College. Although that helped me keep my mind occupied, but driving by myself late at night was not an easy thing to do. I enjoyed that class, but I did not continue my studies there.

I signed myself in a high school in Pontiac for morning classes. I just wanted to review my English, and keep busy during the day. The principal was a young lady, who was as nice as can be. We talked a lot, and we went to lunch a few times. So was the math teacher, who was nothing but a bundle of niceness. Before the end of the school year we went to lunch, and we talked about our life experiences. So all those, plus the bridge games three times a week along with bowling, volunteer work for the hospital and the Red Cross, and many more positive activities helped me to continue my life.

I knew that the same way that I was trying so hard to bring back peace and hope in my life, my children also were trying hard to be able to hang on to their lives by finding right answers to their problems.

I had very little contact with both Maseeh and Mary. And Mojgan called me after five days that they got to California safe and sound. Since I knew that she was with her father, I did not want to discuss anything with her. The only things that mattered were that she was going to college, and that she was healthy. Every time she called, we just said, "Hi, how are you? I am fine thank you. How about you?" And that was it, nothing more, nothing less.

Iraj bought a car for Mojgan as a graduation gift before he left to Los Angeles. I was glad that she had her own car, and she could commute on her own. And I was hoping that her father paid for her college. It seemed that she was staying with her father, so I never called her. I just waited for her to contact me.

After a week or so Glen returned to Michigan. I never found out what was the deal between them. He would often called me, and he came to visit me. I knew that both Mojgan and Glen were trying their best, while everything else around them was a big mess. I made sure that he felt comfortable in my house, and we talked of any subjects. He also comforted me, and said, "I will always be your friend, no matter what happens". I tried to contact him as often as I could at his college. I asked him to call me if he ever needed anything, or if he wanted to talk to someone.

I was okay as long as I was busy. But as soon as I was by myself, my past bothered me to a point that I couldn't stop crying. I never talked to anyone about my life. I felt like it was my life, my problems, and my feelings. Just like people who had to go to their important jobs, I was up very early in the morning. I took shower, applied my make up,

got dressed, and started my daily schedule. I never cried in front of anyone, especially my children.

My Dear God:

I knew from my past experience that people will either pity you, or they will find something to blame you for. As long as I knew that they couldn't help me, I did not see any reasons to talk to anyone about my life. Not to anyone at all. I was safe as long as I had my super power to watch over me day and night, and every second of my life. And I was hoping that he never leaves me.

When I was dressed up, and had a smile on my face at least no one ever looked down at me. And that was what I wanted, especially from my children. I would never allow myself to beg my children for pity. Instead I learned to cry and talk to GOD only. I talked to God every night, and I cried myself to sleep that way. When I woke up, I felt like I had more strength to face my problems. This way I didn't have to cry on anyone's shoulder.

The more I talked to GOD, I came to realize that it has been him, and it is him who is always with us at all times. There was no one else who has been helping us. Therefore, I was getting ready to face and deal with whatever was going to happen to me.

Some time went by. One day I ran to Nazi Mahajer, who always looked down, and belittled Badri and Iraj for the way they robbed my family. I had shown her and Reza my condominium while I was buying it. They told me that eight years ago when that complex was still being built the price of a unit was only eighty thousand dollars. They wanted to buy it as an investment. But they ended up changing their minds. Now I was paying double that price, plus five thousand dollars. And once she told me, "I am so surprised at Iraj. He had reached all his goals in life. He seemed to always be happy and successful. I wonder what had made him fall for that woman, and destroy all his happiness. Only a crazy person would do that. I just can't get it".

Anyway, after greeting each other, and after I told her all about my job, she advised me to talk to Farah Shushtari. They were in the process of opening their own restaurant. "You will have more hours with them. And you will surrounded by people that you like, and who like you". At that time of my life nothing could have made me happier than being around an Iranian family that I liked. That was such a great idea. While I did not want to be a burden on anybody, still I could be working with this family that I've known for many years.

My Dear God:

Mrs. Farah Shushtari was the sister-in-law of Aghdass Shushtari, whom I talked about previously. Farah was the one that I was introduced to by Aghdass as an "ugly, but lucky and rich woman". Because of her problems with Aghdass, I was always there for her. In return she always wanted to help me, and make me happy. When my family was

still one, we often dined at their restaurant. They served Italian food, and my children loved it. But every time we went there for dinner, they would not charge us, especially when Farah was at the restaurant. Many times I thought of not going there any more. I felt we were imposing on them. She was trying to be courteous to an Iranian friend. But I was embarrassed when they did not charge us. So the last time we went there, I asked Iraj to talk to Fariborz, and tell him, "We are here because our children and ourselves enjoy your food very much. Please make us comfortable by charging us". And so they did.

While we were dining there, we noticed an Iranian lady as a hostess, and a gentleman, who was working in the kitchen. When I asked Farah who they were, she said, "They are Khosrow and Simeen Tavakolli. They have three girls, and they are new in Detroit. They had a sister-in-law Mitra Tavakolly with them, and she worked as a waitress".

At that time I did not know that they were partners with the Shushtaris'. But later on I heard that one day Khosrow went to see an Iranian doctor. After talking about his family and his children, he had mentioned that he would like to find a job among Iranians. At that time Shushtaris' had a pizza place in Detroit. They offered him a delivery job, which he readily accepted.

From there on they got to know each other. Khosrow found out that Shushtariss were looking for a place to open a restaurant. And he also found out that they were short on money. Khosrow had brought some money from Iran. He offered them forty thousand dollars to become partners. And Shushtaris' grabbed the idea, and they get to work. Soon after they sold their pizza place, they opened their new restaurant called "Alfoccino". At that time all of them knew that their business would bloom in no time. So they became partners, and started working together very hard.

My Dear God:

Although Farah was officially the supervisor, and she was the decision maker, but the head of ordering and management was the big brother Fariborz. He was the leader, who was loving, fair, and considerate. He was tall, handsome, intelligent, fresh college graduate. He had that innate know-how quality. He cared for his employees. And at any time of need he would put on his apron and join the others in the kitchen. This act taught everyone else in the family to be available at all times. He was very organized, and he wanted to start his restaurant on the right foot. And he did.

My Dear God:

It was funny. Before Khosrow became their partner, Iraj, who was looking for a way to get into a business with money, had offered Shushtaris' to become partners. But Fariborz was not interested in just money. He wanted someone, who would not be afraid to make his hands dirty, or put on the apron and go in the kitchen. So they rejected Iraj's

offer. With Fariborz's knowledge their business bloomed in no time. I always thought that if that with Iraj deal ever went through, I would have been one of their partners. Oh well, that didn't happen. At the beginning everyone was skeptic about their success. I bet you they were all surprised at the outcome, including Shushtaris' family.

The whole family was involved with the business, from young to old. Besides the restaurant business, they also provided catering. Farah was in charge of the catering. Iranians generally like to order special Iranian dishes, and Farah was a very good cook. So many families had their parties catered by Shushtaris'.

Their restaurant "Alfoccino" was located in the city of Farmington Hills, Michigan. It was forty-five minutes away from my condo on a normal day. But on cold and icy nights, depending on the condition of the road, it would take from one to three hours of driving.

After a few months of working at Hudson my hours still were not increased. So I decided to talk to Farah. After being a teacher, and a wife of a doctor for thirty years, now I had to beg for a job as a hostess or a cashier. And still I did not know if they would hire me.

At the beginning Farah told me that Fariborz was the decision maker. But I already knew that Farah had the authority to influence Fariborz, or anyone else for that matter. When I talked to Farah, first of all mentioned that Nazi Mahajer had suggested that I look into this position. And then I told her, "You must know that I have enough money to live on. And right now I had a part time job in Hudson. But that does not satisfy my needs. I need to work as many hours as possible. Besides, being around your family takes away the pain of my loneliness". I wanted to be able to work as many hours as they could assign me for the lowest wage. Farah promised me that she would talk to Fariborz. She said he would be the one to make the final decision.

One day Farah and I went to the restaurant. After lunch we walked to the next-door vacant store, and I started talking to him. Before that day I never talked to him about anything. But that day I had to tell him everything. I told him about the job I found at Hudson near my house. I told him about the importance of wanting to work with them. And especially I told them that, I had to be able to have time off to go to Iran to visit my family. Otherwise I would die without them. And more, and more. He promised to put me on his schedule, and make sure to give me as many hours as he could.

My Dear God:

Although I did not find that job suitable for me, still that was the happiest news for me. To me it seemed to be the answer to my loneliness. I felt an open arm was holding me, and keeping me from falling.

My dear GOD, why do you come to our rescue? When do you know it is time to minimize our sufferings? How do you know that what seemed to be bad yesterday, is good today, and vice versa?

Everyday was a learning experience for me. I had to put aside all my habits, and replace them with what appeared to be suitable for that time. No one could understand my feelings of loneliness, and the need for being around a familiar Iranian family, which remind me of my own family. In effort to survive I had to do things that I had never thought I would do. Yet, I chose to do and act the way that brought calm and tranquility to my daily life, regardless of what other people thought or said about me.

When Fariborz agreed to hire me, I felt that a huge load of desperation fell off my shoulders. I knew that being with them would help me put my past behind me. And little by little I will find my way to the path of recovery.

But I did not know how to give up my job at Hudson. I was so embarrassed to face the lady who hired me. She showed so much special care and love. She was so concerned about my life at that time that she felt like I was her mother. She went out of her way to get me a job right away, and she insisted on getting me more hours. Every time she talked to me, she made sure that I was okay. She was a real angel. I didn't have the heart to tell her, "I prefer to work with an Iranian family in their restaurant". After all her effort and kindness she put into finding me a job, how would I make her understand that I was not phony, and that I appreciated what she had done for me.

So although I was not planning to go to Iran right that second, I had told her about how I was missing my family. I told her that I needed to go to Iran to visit my family. She was so concerned about my mental health. She suggested that I must think twice, and that I better wait until I get a raise and more hours. Then I could apply for time off. But I told her that was impossible for me emotionally, and that I had to go. She hugged me and wished me the best. She advised me to think optimistic. She was indeed a wonderful woman. I wish I could remember her name. But unfortunately I was in such a mess that I did not memorize her name. If she ever reads these lines she might know who I am, and who I am talking about. I just want to tank you for your kindness.

My Dear God:

So I started the job at "Alfoccino" restaurant with three dollars an hour, less than the minimum wage. In the beginning I was there for as many hours as they were there. I took Wednesdays off to do my banking and other governmental work. At this time I had scheduled myself with this job and other activities in a way that I had not even one free hour to waste by looking back at my past. I was trying to live comfortable without any memories.

Indeed Farah was the main reason for my recovery. She was there for me at all times, even better than a good sister. She treated me like her own family. If I was at the restaurant working that was okay, otherwise she asked me to spend my time in her house with her family.

As I said before, because of my fears I had to choose a different life style. The things that I had never done, neither when I lived in my parents house, nor when I had my husband, and my children around me, became possible and doable for me.

When Farah wanted me to be a part of her family, although I knew that I was imposing on them, still I never refused her offer. Not only that but I felt relieved whenever she asked me to go to her house to be with her family. I do not expect anyone to understand me at that time. Even when I overheard Farah's husband questioning my frequent stays at their house, it didn't stop me from doing what I had to do to cure my wounds. I didn't care for what people thought about me. I was welcomed in their family and their house, and I accepted the offer.

Many women in my place would have turned to drugs and alcohol. Many would have looked for a replacement of their husbands. Many would have had committed suicide to end their agony. But I had chosen to stand strong. I didn't want to show weakness. And I wanted to be a role model for my children. I wanted to send them a message life must go on with all its problems.

As long as I sensed the respect among those who wanted to support me, I was willing to follow my instinct, and continue it to the end.

Despite of what my friends of twenty-five years did to destroy and to hurt me, I was able to find many beautiful people. Those people went out of their ways to comfort me, and to bring peace and tranquility into my life. They did that without any strings attached.

My Dear God:

As I talked about her before, the first time I went to the senior center, I met a lady with white hair. Her manners, her attitude, her artwork, and her accent attracted me. I think it was love at first sight. I was not the only one attracted. In the room full of people she chose to be with me, talk to me. We spent the whole day together. Her name was Tilda Arnoldi. She was an Italian descent. I had spoken of her before. She was a retired dentist, who came to America at the age sixty-two to be with her daughter Luciana Carpanti.

When I met her twenty years later at the age eighty-two, she was so vibrant, and so delightful. I wish I knew enough English to be able to find words to describe her, and her presence in my life. I think the closest one would be, "She was a present from GOD to me". Although I have met many friends throughout my lifetime, she was the only one who with her words of wisdom and her loving ability had turned my life around. I loved her then. I love her now. And I will love her for eternity.

Lucciana was a scholar, who finished her education in America. She was married to Mr. Art Carponti. They had two girls, Tina and Lisa. Tilda had lived with them since their birth. On one of Nona's birthdays Lisa presented her with a poem she wrote. I wish I had a copy of that to include it here.

We used to spend lots of time together. Not one word of gossip. Although she was living with her daughter and her family, still she had invited me to her house every Wednesday. It had become a tradition. We used to go to lunch and then spend our time in bookshops with books and cards. We used to read the cards and discuss the writing according to our beliefs.

Tilda would usually prepare dinner, while I sat by her and talked to her. Some nights all three of us went to see a movie. I brought dinner to their house a few times, and afterwards we spent nice evenings together, always with love and respect. I still think that these people came into my life as angels, just to save me from drowning in my problems.

Before all that happened to me, if anyone mentioned the word "angel", I would probably laugh at them. Now, very vividly I see that people like Tilda, Lucciana, Chitra, and others came in to my life when I needed them. How this could happen, or why did this happen? How did I get to meet them? What was the reason behind it?

Another angel was Dr. Chitra Amladi, whom I talked about previously. Although she was not Iranian, we had become so attached to one another. We had a great friendship. We met when my problems just started. Shortly after she got that awful disease, MS. My problems, and her awful disease had brought us together. Because she had come from the same culture, she knew what I was going through. And in the same manner I knew how painful her life was. To get that disease at the age only forty-two for a young doctor with two little children, full of hope and ambitions, was not easy to accept. Just like Farah, she wanted to make sure that I was never alone. She even had given me her house keys, and the combination of her alarm so that I could go to her house at any time of the day or night.

My Dear God:

So I did have many real friends at that time, Farah, Farahnaz and Ali, Tilda and Lucciana, and Chitra's family, whose true friendship I could always rely on. But besides taking the time to attend all the activities that I had created for myself, it seemed that I chose to live like a gypsy. I had my suitcase in the back of my car, and landed in one of my friends' places. It wasn't because I had no place to stay, but it was because I didn't have a home to go to. So I accepted all of their invitations to spend the night eagerly. I had to forget my past.

I usually stayed with Farahnaz when I was free on the weekends. They used to live in Ann Arbor, Michigan. I didn't want to drive back and forth in one day. Farahnaz was like a daughter, who was also a friend.

Another person, who never left my side, was Mrs. Claudette Meier. She was Julie and Susan's mother. Julie married Arman, Iraj's nephew. And Susan was Mary's friend. They studied law together. She was such a truthful person that when I was with her, I completely forgot about my problems. Each time I was with her, I learned so much more

about humanity. Our main subjects were our families and our parents and ancestors. We knew what our husbands had done or what they are capable of doing, so we figured out that bringing it up does not solve any problems. We both loved nature. Sometimes we went to lunch; sometimes we just went for a walk at Cranbrook, which had beautifu1 scenery. We had discovered that while there were so many beautiful things in nature, we better enjoy them rather than ruining it for us by bringing Iraj and other worthless people up. Many times we went to Baseball games with Fred, her husband. Other times we went to foreign movies, which was introduced to us by Susan in their university. They were usually good movies about human rights. She also was my angel. Although Julie and Arman got divorced, and Mary's friendship with Susan didn't last, Claudette and I remained friends.

Because all those Iranians surrounded me for almost thirty years, and I never sensed any friendship among them, I used to believe that friendship does not have a real meaning. But once again I was wrong. These friends that I am talking about, the ones that appeared in my life as angels, their friendship was not based on material and superficial matters. All of them were true with their feelings. There had no string attached with their affection. When I was with them, I learned about life. I learned about universe. I learned about value of art, music, education, work and workers. And I learned that their friendship had made me a richer person.

My Dear God:

These friends were the ones who turned my life around, and made me realize that I must not waste my time on remembering what he did with me. They were, they are, and they will be my valuable magnificent friends.

It was during this time that Farah was trying to bring her daughter Gazaleh and her family to the USA. She brought her first grand child Alireza a few years ago. She sent him to school in their neighborhood. She was a very responsible grandmother.

While she was working at her own shop, she also ran the catering business. And in reality she supervised the whole restaurant business. She used to tell me, "I always wanted my husband to be an ambitious person. When it didn't happen, I dreamt for my children to become ambitious, and go after achieving their ultimate goals. Now I am happy to see my dream came true, and my two sons are making it after all".

But just like herself, she made her daughter marry at a very young age. As I heard her husband Mohsen Ameen Lari was a young engineer, who was in love with Gazaleh. He was after marrying her no matter what. They had money, prestige, comfort, and family and friends to enjoy it with. They had two boys, Alireza and Abdi. Both were handsome, talented and well mannered. After they moved to Michigan, they had a girl called Rana.

Not only Farah was trying to make me part of her family, but Gazaleh, Mohsen and their children were so close to me that I felt wanted when I was with them. They treated

me like a real friend and family.

Among Iranians I had a lot of respect for Gazaleh. Just like her name in Farsi, she was tall, beautiful, dedicated, loving and very considerate about everyone around her. Her beauty was glowing more when you got to spend some time with her, as I did. I have never heard one word of gossip, or criticism. Not once I heard her talk down to her husband, her children, her brothers, her sisters- in-law, or any one else for that matter. Even with many things that went wrong around her, she made you so comfortable when you saw her. You would have never guessed that something was wrong.

Although they had a big and comfortable house in Iran, they stayed in her parents' house, like Fariborz and Farsheed before her. The only difference was that they had three children. Talking about knowing your duties, having respect for one another, and living under one roof peacefully and happily. This was the case with this family. I admired Gazaleh for her personality and the character. She was a unique individual, who never wanted to hurt anybody in her entire life. I formed my opinion about her after spending many years around her.

My Dear God:

While the husband and wife were happily married, they were not very compatible by appearance. She was tall, beautiful, blond, and lavishly sexy. Mohsen was short, balding, with a very average face. To most people, who talked about them, including her own parents, Gazaleh deserved a much better looking husband. But to my surprise I had never heard one word in this regard from her. It was as if she was completely unaware of his appearance.

While they were living in Farah's house, he was diagnosed with lymph cancer. At first it took sometimes to be diagnosed. Some people even thought that he was making it up. Some thought that he was depressed being away from Iran. Meanwhile he got worse and worse, until an Indian doctor discovered his disease. By then he was in and out of the hospitals. It had become everyone's concern. It got to a point that they gave up their hopes.

The restaurant's work and responsibilities were enough to occupy all of their time. Still they had to do something about Mohsen's illness. They had only one hope, and that a bone marrow transplantation. He was so sick that some were considering buying a property at the cemetery. The whole family got to work to be able to earn money for bone marrow transplant. They gave a big fund raising party at the restaurant. They invited mostly Iranian doctors, who could afford to spend money. They were able to collect enough money to start the procedure.

I went to the hospital with Farah or Gazaleh more than a few times. One night after her work at the restaurant, which was almost 10:00 PM, she rushed to the hospital. He was not in a good shape. She was so caring and nice that it brought tears in his eyes. I was really amazed. I thought, how could she be so caring, so patient, and so loving after all the hours of hard work, and never complain. How could she go against the odds, and still believe that he would survive? That night I thought she was an extra ordinary woman. I had more respect for her than ever.

Fariborz and Farah handled the management. The rest of the family was holding different jobs like book keeping, accounting, purchasing, some were cashiers, and hostesses. Some of them would get involved with the cooking when necessary. The family consisted of Farah and her husband Mr. Shushtari, who was in charge of making garlic sticks. Fariborz and his wife Marjan, Farsheed and his wife Sudabeh, Gazaleh and her husband Mohsen. And they had a cousin, Masood, who worked as a waiter. Then there was their partner Mr. Khosrow Tavakoli and his wife Simeen. Khosrow's sister-in-law, Mitra Tavakoli, was a waitress as well. Tavakolis had two daughters, who helped out once in a while. So did Gazaleh's sons Alireza and Abdi.

My Dear God:

At this time I had put all those Iranian friends aside. I never wanted to see them again. I only kept in touch with those who were faithful to me. With my new job, and all the new faces around me, I felt like I was born again. I had to make myself forget the past completely, and I had to adapt to new people and my new surroundings. I didn't know any of these people before, now some of them were assigned to be my rescuers. It is amazing how our lives can turn around in no time, and make a complete different person of us. Wow, what an experience! I just don't know how to explain it. No wonder why so many people give up and commit suicide. It is not easy.

You see, my dear God, I am just sitting and writing these sentences. But how can I explain my feelings at that time? How do I even describe that person who was in me? Who was she? I did not know her. That Shamci, who was married to Iraj was dead. She did not exist any more. While she was dead, the new person within her was trying to establish a different environment for herself to be able to continue her life. Why? I even don't know it myself.

For nine years I tried to struggle to swim against the stream, not in the sea, but in the ocean. I acted like a huge rock being thrown around by large waves again and again. Each time I tried to get up, another huge wave came along, and demolished me allover again. As I was hit harder, I lost more of my sensitivity, and more of my feelings. And yet I was trying to live. Not only Iraj was surprised when I didn't commit suicide, but I was surprised myself. My love for him was endless. Without him I was supposed to be dead. How come I was struggling to live? For me life without him did not exist. And yet, while I was numb, and emotionless, I took the bad and the good, the ugly and the beautiful, whichever came to me, and I continued to live.

You see, my dear God, those days that I used to go to Farah's shop to talk and to

comfort her, was before Malakuti's death. I was a lucky woman then. She loved to have me around, and she would tell me all about Aghdass and others. She was desperately looking for a close friend to listen to her, and I was there for her. I never knew that one day I would need her so badly. When Farah was complaining to me about Aghdass and her behavior, I had to listen to her, comfort her, and stay quiet. I never talked behind her back. I realized that although they had a big fight, they would eventually forget about their fight one day, and they would reconcile. So I just listened to her until she was calm and happy.

My Dear God:

I am not sure of the reasons, but Farah did a lot for me. She tried to make me forget about my past, and she involved me with her own family day and night. She had me in her house every chance she got. All her children were obeying her in this case. They invited me as often as they could. They all were very respectful to me till the end. If I ever looked for the right words to describe them, "They were beautiful".

At the beginning I had to deal with Fariborz only, who was the top manager. But as the time passed, other partners like Khosrow and Simeen, and Farsheed and Sudobeh came in to take over some responsibilities. Because they were not exactly behaving like Fariborz, many times I had trouble adjusting to their desires. But still I knew that they had the position, and I had to try to understand them, only to a point that they didn't lose respect for me.

To begin with I am a very responsible person. And I did my job at the restaurant as it was expected from me. Although every one knew why I was working there, I never tried to discuss my personal life with them. I was trying to do my best for two reasons. One was that Farah was responsible for hiring me. So I wanted to make sure that I didn't cause any disagreement between the members of the family. Second, I needed that job because I was feeling so supported and so safe that I felt like I was in Iran, and among those who loved me. I was so dependant on that job, Farah and her family, and their kindness. I was thinking that if I ever lost that job, and stayed away from that family, who had embraced me like my own family in Iran, I might end up committing suicide.

As often I spoke to myself, and I tried to reason with myself to avoid depending on anything or anybody, still the thought of being by myself alone, and not having their family around me was bothering me. Although I was trying to be my own teacher, and teach myself what was good or bad for me, still it took a long time for me to train myself to start thinking positive.

I was there from nine o'clock in the morning, until the time of closing, which was between ten and midnight. Most nights that Farah was there, she took me home with her. Probably even she didn't know how happy she had made me. Some nights I tried not to bother her family. But she promised me that not only it was not a bother for them, but also they were

very happy that I could come home with them. Some Wednesdays I had bridge games in my house. We got together for lunch. So on Tuesday nights, when I left the restaurant around midnight, I would stop at the supermarket to do my shopping for the next day. I was happy that I had something to do to keep my mind occupied till three or four in the morning. Then I only had a few hours to sleep. And in the morning I started cooking for the bridge group. With such schedule I was able to live my life, and carry a happy smile on my face.

My Dear God:

I remember one morning after I had received the news of divorce; I had to go to the bank. I don't remember how sad and depressed I was that it showed on my face. I guess it was so bad that a gentleman standing next to me looked at me, and said, "What is wrong lady? It is not the end of the world yet. Come on. Whatever it is, it is going to pass in no time, before you know it".

That comment of a person, who didn't even know me, made me realize that not only I must forget about what had happened to me, but also I must bring back my happy face. Looking back and feeling sorry for myself would not solve my problems. I must wake up before it was too late.

My dear GOD, is it possible for a person like me at that time to be able to put myself together, and survive? You were the only one who was with me at all times. I disowned my family to be able to be with the love of my life, Iraj. Now he was gone. My three children were gone. My teaching job in Iran was gone. My home, which we build together, was gone. All my so-called friends were gone. Don't you think it would be wiser for me to commit suicide? You know that sooner or later I have to die. Why didn't you help me to commit suicide? Why did you make me believe that with all the things that had happened to me, still I was the one who deserved to have a better and happier life than he could have? Were you trying to make me one of your favorites, and prove to me that there was a better life for me without Iraj? Was that my ultimate test to see if I could make it successfully? Whatever it was, I can swear to you that it was the most difficult time of my life. And how did I make it? I think it was you behind all these.

After I bought the condo, I was so upset with all those Iranians that I wanted to talk to them about what each and every one of them did to me. I had planned to invite them to my condo, and in an intelligent way introduce them to themselves. And instead of talking behind each one of them in private, tell them each off in front of each other.

A few of them had asked me to visit them like nothing had happened. One of them was Aghdass Shushtari, who called me one night when I was working at the restaurant, and invited me to her house. I told her, "I will come only if the whole group of Blot players is there. I would like to talk to all of them, either in your house, or Nayer Rabbani's house". But they never arranged such gathering. That was the time that I decided to invite

them to my condo. When I called them, everyone agreed to come. It was only one day before their scheduled visit that I had realized that with this act I was giving them the pleasure of seeing how they were able to destroy and demolish me after all. I was better off calling off the party. But I failed to do so, just because I had already prepared all the food. I thought to myself, "Instead I should just act like I invited them to have fun. I changed my mind about confronting them. I did not want to show them any anger or frustration. I decided that those people were not worthy. They already knew perfectly what they had done. Except that I would end up creating an ugly scene. What can you possibly achieve when you are dealing with ugly people?

My Dear God:

I had provided many Iranian dishes. I had called the same girl that usually helped me at the parties to help me that night. I tried to keep my cool at all times, while I felt miserable being surrounded by a bunch of betrayers. Some came on time, and some were late. It was a very cold party. Some were talking about their work; others were talking about their children. Once in a while, when I turned my back someone mentioned something about me, and then they all laughed. This was not new to me. They always did it to each other without any apparent reason. Obviously now they had a reason to laugh. They had that poem about Iraj and my family on hand. I thought maybe it must have been a cultural thing. But still I don't think it might have happened among people who know the meaning of ethics and moral principles.

This group of people, who had gathered around each other in Michigan by the name of doctors and doctors' wives, were all made at the same factory. Although their parents were different, and they were raised in different classes of the society, I was shocked how they complemented each other. While in reality they all hated each other, they still loved to be with one another. And they continued hurting each other.

I started off as a cashier at the restaurant. Sometimes I worked as a hostess. Because I was older than most of them, and they knew that I was Farah's friend, most of them had enough courtesy and respect for me. I had a good relationship with all of them. Little by little I got to know more about them. The eight or nine workers in the kitchen were mostly Arabs or African American.

Mitra Tavakoli was a young married woman with a son, who had left her husband in Iran, and fled to America. I really don't know the details of how and why she could come here with her little boy. But I knew that she was trying to divorce her husband in Iran. There were many stories about her that people often gossiped about. She was working hard to be able to take care of her son and pay her rent. Many times I went to her house and spend time with her. She knew some other young Iranians that I didn't know. Her brother in-law, Mr. Tavakoli, and his wife Simeen were nice family people. Since they were partners with Shushtaris', everyone had respect for them. And they liked to keep it

that way. It was because of them that she was able to work at the restaurant. So she was supposed to obey the rules of the management, and follow the orders.

My Dear God:

One morning I heard a scream in the kitchen. I saw everyone was running in that direction. I knew that something was going on between Khosrow and Mitra. But I didn't know what it was all about.

Then I heard that she was having a relationship with one of the African American cooks. This had been bothering Tavakolis' family. That day he saw them kissing, or doing something else in the kitchen. Khosrow got mad, and threw her out of kitchen. Then Mitra, without even thinking, slapped Khosrow. She quit her job and left the restaurant.

I thought it was a daring act from Mitra. She didn't know the language; she didn't know anybody. How did she dare to quit? She had to pay the rent, and feed her son. How was she planning to do that without a job? I was very concerned about her. Since she did not have a job permit, it would be very difficult for her to find a job. Luckily one of the Iranians she knew owned a bakery. She started working there after a month or two.

As she explained, her husband was an alcoholic and a drug addict. There was a time that they had everything. But because of his addiction they had lost everything. Then she explained that these two brothers had a very sad and unhappy childhood. Once on a snowy night Khosrow did not have any place to stay. He did not even have a warm coat. So he thought of something. He decided to cuddle with a dog. That dog kept him warm till morning. I heard this from Khosrow himself.

There were many stories like that. I doubted them sometimes. But it was true, and neither of them was able to finish their education. But both of them were very smart, and they were able to get into business.

These people fled Iran after the revolution. He had three children: two girls, and a boy. Five of them came to United States without knowing anybody, or knowing the language. To me such acts take a lot of courage. True that he had money to survive on, but it was a very big step to be taken at that time of their lives.

They were very family oriented. And they liked to live at the respectful level of the society. Both Simeen and Khosrow were working very hard. And they were trying to do their best for their children. Khosrow was a gentleman. I am sure they knew about my life. At the beginning some nights that we used to close very late, and it was icy and stormy outside, it was also very dangerous to drive. He asked me to stay in their house, which was only few minutes away from restaurant. Obviously I accepted with happiness. If I had to drive home in that kind of weather, it would take me three hours. I timed myself one night, and I remember it clearly. It wasn't only the road. I would be so frightened that I pressed my fingernails into my palm, until I started bleeding.

My Dear God:

Although I was embarrassed to bother them that often, but the fear of loneliness, and the fear of driving to my house that late at night convinced me that it was better for me to stay with them, and deal with the embarrassment.

It was during that time that I heard Mr. Shushtari talk to others about me staying in Tavakolis' house at nights. He had condemned my sleeping in Tavakolis' house. He told them, "Why is Shamci staying in Tavakolis' house? Doesn't she have her own house to go to? Doesn't she think that she is bothering them?"

After hearing this comment from Mr. Shushtari, I tried to understand his point of view. And it made me think twice to go to their house whenever Farah invited me. I did not want to discuss his gossip with Farah, and make her mad at him. But I tried to minimize my stays.

I tried to make myself understand that depending on other people to cure my fear of loneliness was not going to be the right way to my survival. This disease must be cured from within. As long as I depend on people to make me feel good, I might not ever find the cure, and learn to live by myself without fears.

But at that time of my life it was much easier to say than it was done. Someone like me, who was born and lived all her life in a crowded house. A person, who married into another crowded house. A person, who raised three children, and spent all her life with them. How could I be expecting to be able to be by myself all the time? I had to expect a miracle to happen to make me into a different person. No wonder people who become single try to replace their partner as quickly as they can, without knowing what would be the outcome of their actions.

I just was trying to look for an opportunity to be able to either find a housemate, or find a family that I could live with. Because I had a beautiful condo, and I had a bedroom and other comfortable facilities, I was ready to start looking for the right person. I would then go ahead with it, and save myself the agony.

When I first started to work at the restaurant, it wasn't crowded at all. I remember one day when Farsheed was talking to Khosrow. He was telling him, "If there comes a day that we could make two thousand dollars, I will be happy, and I will thank God for making it possible". But shortly after I started, they started making two thousand dollars just during the lunchtime. And at nights it doubled, and sometimes even tripled.

My Dear God:

By then they hired another young Iranian lady, Ida. She came to the restaurant with her boyfriend at the time. He was a young man called Mehrdad. Mehrdad knew Shushtaris'. So he was hoping to find a job for her in their restaurant. Ida didn't know any English, and she couldn't communicate with customers. So after a few days of working as a waitress, she was demoted to a bus person. She was a very pleasant girl. It

didn't take too long for Ida and Mitra to become friends. And as always is the case they got to know all about each other's lives.

Ida was very funny, and she talked about any subject very openly. She talked sweet, and because I liked to listen to her, she talked to me about herself, her family, and her marriage and their divorce, which was a long story.

She was married to a young man called Massood, in Iran. Their love story was widely known in every household in Shiraz. Like her father, who was alcoholic and smoked opium, her husband and her brother Bijan were both into alcohol and drugs. Ida was not too far from them either. So after a long story their nine-year marriage ended up in a romantic divorce. They both were hoping to return to each other, and start allover again.

Judging by her lifestyle I never thought that one day I might become friends with her. She was exactly the opposite of me. They were five sisters and a brother. They were all here from Iran after the revolution.

My Dear God:

Before I met Ida, I had seen Ziba and doctor Jahal at some Iranian parties. After I got to know Ida, they invited me more often. And I used to spend more time with all the members of their family. Each and every one of them was nice in their own way. There is no one in this world that is perfect. Each one of us has a few mental or physical handicaps. I would think it is appropriate to find out about our handicaps and pinpoint it first, before we try to bring up other people's handicaps. This way, not only we could find wrongs in others, but also we might be able to get rid of our own handicaps.

I found this family deserved applause for their kindness and togetherness. Although each one of them was a different individual in their acts and characters, still they were trying so hard to mingle and do things for each other. Every one of them worked different jobs. To be able to spend a pleasant and peaceful time with the whole family, usually one of them shopped and cooked and cleaned, and invited all of them in her house.

My Dear God:

I was introduced to Ida and her family as a doctor's wife whose husband fell in love with a psychiatrist's wife. The psychiatrist was killed by his patient's gun in his office. Ok, my dear GOD, Am I writing a story about someone else, or it is about me? This was me, who they were talking about. At the beginning they talked about my luck and my fabulous life. Now they are talking about my bad luck, and my runaway husband. This was and is the story of my life. It was mine and no one else's.

Do you think I had any kind of senses in me to be able to feel anything at all? Do you think with the numbness that I had in me; I could feel a thing whatsoever? Do you think that at that time I had choice to do anything about it? I don't think so. My life consisted of just a few sentences.

As the time passed by, Ida was getting closer and closer to me. The whole family made me a part of their socializing hours. Each and every one of them had enough respect for me to be able to talk about their personal problems with me. I was invited to all their parties when they wanted my opinion regarding their problems.

I didn't think if I was eligible even to notice anybody's problems, yet to be able to introduce the right solution. Was an unlikely thing to be asked to do. Or probably it was just me who thought of myself having lack of right judgment and wisdom. Others still thought of me as a wise woman. Otherwise they wouldn't ask me such an important question.

My Dear God:

When I met Ida, she acted like she had found her dream friend. She was trying to be with me all the time, and that was my dream also that someone be with me at all times.

Ida few times came to my condo and spent the night with me. Then in the morning we drove to work together. The good thing about it was that, when she was with me, she never drank or did anything else.

When she started her work at the restaurant, for sometimes she did not have a car. Since her house was almost on my way, I decided to give her a ride, until she got her own car. Even for that little favor that I was doing for her, some people were questioning me why was I doing it. It seems that people can never rest without gossiping, or interfering with other people's lives.

I started giving her a ride. At least I didn't have to cry all the way to the restaurant thinking about my past. So, not only it was bother for me, but also I didn't mind it at all. It was a blessing.

When Ida was with me, she always talked about her past, her father, her family, her love and marriage, and many other things. Just like me, she loved to play backgammon. We played so many rounds, and the winner would get one dollar to buy a lottery ticket. We had so much fun that we wanted to continue playing forever. It stopped us from thinking of our horrible past. Ida was getting to be very comfortable with me. She was telling me everything, including all the unspoken material.

My Dear God:

Mehrdad and Ida decided to get married.

They arranged the party at Ziba's house. Everyone did their best to help in any way they could. She bought a nice dress, with nice hat and gloves. They had setup for her wedding (sofrehaghd). It was arranged very nicely. I had sent a large bucket of roses. And everyone was ready for clergy to come.

At this time Syrous, Mehrdad's son, was three years old. He was well dressed, and he knew exactly what was going on. He never, even for one moment, left his father's side. Until that day I had never seen a three-year old boy so smart, so alert, and so observant. Even at the time that clergy announced, "Now Mr. Zonooz kiss Mrs. Zonooz", Syrous tried to stay between them. And he was quietly repeating, "No one is Mrs. Zonooz. No one is Mrs. Zonooz". I cannot forget that night. I realized that he had a great bonding with his mother. He was not acting like a child. He was like a grown up. With smile on his face, he never left his Dad's side.

So you see, my dear GOD, I don't know how you arranged all these nice people to come my way, and hold my hand when I was in need of someone holding my hand. I just don't know. It happened just like a dream. Yes Ida and Mehrdad soon became another angels in my life.

My Dear God:

Farah was one person, who always thought of me and never left me alone. It didn't matter what time of day or nigh. She always welcomed me. She made me feel at home.

Then it was Farahnaz, who was like a great daughter to me. She was watching me, like it was her duty to take good care of me. With the experience that she had from her own parents, she never left my side. For a long time I was hers on weekends.

Then it was the existence of Tilda in my life, which was like a miracle. She and her daughter Lucciana made me forget what had happened to me. They welcomed me to the last day of my staying in Michigan.

Then there was Chitra and her family. She made me feel her house was my house. She wanted me to be there any time of the day or night. She was a fantastic woman.

And now Ida, always kind, polite, warm, and very respectful. She believed that I was a miracle in her life. She was an exciting Backgammon player. She liked to drive in the rain with me, sitting in her front seat, listening to music, talking about her past.

You see, my dear GOD, these people did not come to my life to replace my lost family by my arrangement. I wasn't that kind of powerful person to be able to bring all these different people from different countries into my life to rescue me from my disastrous life. It was your arrangement, and only yours, to make me survive through that ugly ordeal.

When I moved into my condo, and after a while Mojgan left me to go to California to be with her father, I felt so empty, so alone, so afraid, so depressed, and so desperate that I didn't know how to live another day. I was so afraid of being alone that I would rather stay in my car at night then come home to be alone. I don't know what was in me, or why was I so afraid of myself. I am sure no one could ever understand me, or my need to be with others. Obviously they haven't been in my shoes to be able to understand my feelings.

No one ever knew what I was going through. No one ever witnessed my tears from the time that I got behind the wheel, until the time that I got home. And no one ever saw me crying till morning, except you my dear GOD. I never let anyone to see my tears. I

didn't want anyone to watch me crying. And I never cared why they were talking behind my back and complaining about me staying at my friends' homes. It was not enough what they did to my family. I could care less for them and their opinion about me.

My Dear God:

You see, my dear GOD, as long as you are watching over me, and as long as you are supporting me, and as long as you are trying to secure my safety, I think I handle everything that comes my way. I will not be afraid any more. And I will be forever thankful.

Ida's house was nearby the restaurant. They furnished their house little by little. They were planning minor remodeling. Some nights she asked me to go to her house after work. She always called me to make sure that I was going. And I was very happy to know that she was waiting for me. Mehrdad used to work evening shifts. So he usually got home after midnight. We waited for him, while we were talking and playing Backgammon.

It became a routine that I stayed at her house. Ida was very happy and excited to have me over. She would give a bath to Syrous, put him to bed, and wait for me. Some of the nights she was either cooking or baking, or she was doing something else by the time I got there. She shed away from letting me know how happy she was that I was staying with her. We both felt secure being next to each other. And I was glad that because of me she didn't drink or smoke. I was hoping to keep her away from cigarettes also.

While Mehrdad was working two jobs, from six in the morning to midnight, he still decided to start the construction by himself. Both Ida and Mehrdad talked about their problems with me, and I always tried to act as their mediator. It was not my place to carry their words to one another. In private I tried to make them understand how the other person's desires must be important to each one of them. I tried to make them see what they were doing to each other. And luckily many times it worked.

They were both very respectful with me. Many times they listened to me. But both had something that the other one disliked. As far as I knew, Mehrdad was not into drinking or smoking, and he was against Ida's drinking habit. Mehrdad liked to watch news when he was home. This would make Ida very mad, and it created many problems between the two of them.

When they started the construction around the house, they both worked very hard. For me was unbelievable and unfair to see that Mehrdad came home after midnight, and still started working on the house. I was wondering when he had time to sleep.

Before starting the addition in the attic, they rented out that room to Mitra and her son for some time. It was a great deal for both sides. Ida had earned a little money, while Mitra paid very little fee for rent. She was out of job at the time. After Mitra got a job, and she then had enough money to rent a place of her own, they though of making the attic into a separate area, which they could potentially rent out. That was a great idea, and

both of them got to work.

My Dear God:

While they were working on the addition, I was there most nights. Then Ida came up with the idea that it would be nice if I could move into her house. Since I didn't like the attic, she thought that they could move Syrous up there, and give me the room downstairs. In the beginning this was just a talk. But the more I thought about it, it was a great deal for me. I would be living with a family, close to the restaurant, and I didn't have to be a burden on that nice hearted family. So the best thing to do was to rent out my own condominium. I had to start looking for a tenant.

Okay, my dear GOD, when I lived with my parents, we had learned to share our rooms. When I married Iraj, from a little house we moved to big one, and then the bigger and the biggest. From seven thousand square feet house I moved to two different places, each almost two thousand five hundred square feet. Then I moved to my condominium of three thousand square feet. Now I had to move back into one room with a small closet. And as we all know, our last stop in this world would be not more than 6 by 4. This is in case that we get buried in a cemetery. Not in my case that, I would like to be cremated into ashes. And I want my ashes to be thrown in the ocean. So knowing all these, I didn't mind to move into a small room, and feel the pleasure of being a housemate with a nice young family.

At this time Mitra had returned to the restaurant, and got her old job back. She had rented a nice house near Ida's. She had two bedrooms, and a full bath upstairs. One room was her son's, and the second one was available. Mitra Tavakoli had an Iranian boy friend, named Siamac, at the time. He was an engineer, and he had a nice job from what I had heard. Mitra was hoping to marry him one day.

Mitra and I were getting very close. She talked to me about her parents, her husband, her family, and every thing else. She invited me to her house with her friends, and we shared passion for cooking. She was trying to make a good life for herself and her son. She worked hard, and she was able to pay the bills by herself.

By getting to know many different families and finding out about their past and their background, I realized that Iraj's family and his upbringing, and my family and my bringing up was very different but beautiful. There were many positive aspects in both, which meant to make a better persons out of us. But instead he got destroyed in a worst possible way, while others who didn't have a good background were still living together, and they made it. I just wonder why.

My Dear God:

While I was struggling to find the way out of my fear and loneliness, Mojgan called me from California. All I knew was that she was going to college. I didn't know where she

lived, or what was happening with her father. I didn't want to ask her any questions that would make her mad. I didn't want to interfere with what she was doing. As long as I knew that she was going to college, I didn't want to know about anybody or anything else. I knew that Mojgan was on a mission to move to California. I felt that she wanted to try to get her father back. Or at least she was hoping to be able to get close to him, and find solutions to her problems. And I knew that she was too naive to know what her father's plans were.

When she called and said, "I am returning to Michigan", I was so sad for her. I knew that her mission had failed. I realized that the sentence, which she wrote in her diary after Malakuti died, "My father hates me", was being proven to her for the second time. I felt like the world came to an end, and my baby had lost all her hopes. My right judgment clicked in a fraction of a second. I said without further hesitation, "Very well my dear. Have you been taking care of your college?" She said, "Yes, I had transferred my records to Western University in Kalamazoo, Michigan". I felt as happy as I could get to hear the news. I didn't care to know what had happened, or what went wrong. I didn't want to remind her, or bother her by questioning her.

For eight years Iraj fooled his children by pretending that his affair was their mother's imagination. He played the role to make them believe that he was a good father, and he would never destroy his children. The reason that she went to California was to make sure that her father was honest to her. Now that she was coming back disappointed, I must stay quiet and not bring up any questions about her reasons for returning to Michigan.

I knew that her return was bad news for me. I was getting ready to face her harshness. This time she had lost her hope completely. This time she was going to be even angrier than before. But as long as she continued her education, I didn't mind to face the difficulties, and make her feel at home.

Since I had no one to talk, after I hung up the phone I cried and I cried in private. I kept pacing around the room. "What should I do now? How do I comfort her now? How can I put myself together again, after being so destroyed emotionally? God, please come to my rescue again.

I still was a little hopeful. I knew that having Glen around her would reduce her pain of the loss of her father. At least I was hoping that this would be the case. Until one day I heard that she had broken up with Glen. This was sad news for me. She had been away from Glen for nearly seven months. They seemed to be fine when they came to my condo. I was so happy that she at least had him. I didn't know what had contributed to their separation. It must have been that they were going to different schools. I was completely shocked, especially I knew that Glen loved Mojgan very much.

My Dear God:

When Glen called me, he was very upset and angry. He was crying so hard that I did not know how to comfort him. We talked a lot. I asked him to count on me, if he ever wanted to talk to someone, or if he ever wanted to come to my house to talk. He seemed very concerned about Mojgan, and was worried that she was involved with wrong group of students.

When I saw him acting that way, I thought he must know something that I didn't. I always heard about student's activities at colleges and during their vacations. For me it was not only scary, but I didn't have anyway to reach Mojgan emotionally. Please God help me. When their cousins were living in my house, they provided my children with some drugs. At least at that time they were near me, and good or bad I had a way to react and show them some emotions. But what about now? She had lost her last hope with her father. She had broken up with her boyfriend of almost five years, who she loved a lot. She was away from me, in the middle of the environment with no control and no boundaries. What was I supposed to do my dear God? Who could I turn to? "Are you listening to me my dear God? Can you tell me what are my duties at this time? Except to be there for her, talk to her, and just pray and pray and pray".

While I was working at the restaurant, one afternoon she came to visit me. She was with a friend. I offered them lunch, and we talked for a short time. She introduced him to me as Joe Scheidler. He was in his third year at the Western University. He was involved with water ski club at the university. He seemed nice. He was not very tall, blond, with a fair skin. He was wearing a cap. One very noticeable thing about him was that his teeth seemed to be stained yellow. I couldn't think of a reason for that.

How could I judge a person in such a short time, that what kind of a person he was? How could I value him, or not value him during such a short visit? It is difficult to know a person even after thirty years. So that day he seemed like a nice person to me.

Mary was living with that lawyer, and once in a while she came to visit me. Once she came, and brought her painting stuff. She sat out on the balcony, and started to draw the view of the lake and the pool. She was always very depressed, and not talkative at all. There was a few times that I asked her if she would be comfortable to move in with me. Her answer usually was, "No". She thought my lifestyle did not suit her very well. Living on the lake, in a secluded area, being isolated from normal people was not for her.

My Dear God:

During all those years I witnessed how my children were thrown around, and they had to stick with whatever came their way. I used to think back, and remember our dreams for our children. What a life! And what an uncertainty! How could I know that I would create this kind of life for my children? Maseeh in California, Mary in Detroit, and Mojgan in Kalamozoo, all living with others if they could even find anyone.

Being a mother, I couldn't sleep at night knowing that my children were living in crummiest places. One day I asked Mary, if she was willing to buy a small house with my money. I knew that she was in such an unsecured position that she was afraid to take any responsibility, and I still offered her. But her answer was, "No". She not only disagreed with my offer, but when I offered it to Mojgan, she really got mad at me. I know that she didn't have anything against giving my money to Mojgan. But I am positive that she was worried about me losing my money. I know this because there was a few times she visited, and we went out to dinner. She was so upset with that idea, that all the way to the restaurant, in the restaurant, and back from restaurant, we did not say even one word to each other. I didn't know how to deal with her at all. I knew that losing her family, and her security had made her loose her trust in herself. She was always sad and mad, and confused. I always wondered if it was all because of her parents' stupidity. I didn't know how to explain Mary's behavior towards me, except crying at night, and praying to God during the day. I have been concerned about her the most from the beginning to the end. One day she made me believe that she actually loves me a lot. And the next day she made me feel that she never hated anyone as much as she hated me. I had to figure out what mood she was in during each and every visit. The more I saw her like that, the more I blamed myself for creating that kind of atmosphere for the greatest love of my life. "Please God, where do I turn to? How do I deal with her?"

At this time Mojgan was living with Joe. When I offered Mojgan, in the beginning she refused my offer. Then after a few months, and I assume that it was after she discussed it with Joe, they all of a sudden loved my offer. They started looking for a house on the lake in Kalamazoo. At that time Joe graduated from college, and he was looking for a job.

Although I didn't have much income, I was able to put together twenty thousand dollars for the down payment for a small house for them. I thought this would have saved one of them from being homeless.

My Dear God:

True that I was hoping that my daughter had a place of her own. But I was thinking of my future also. So when I talked to Mojgan, I made sure that she understood me. Then I asked her to buy the house as joint owners. Since I didn't have any support for my future, I wanted to help them in a way that I didn't lose my money. And the only way to insure that was to put my name on the title.

The main reason that I wanted her to buy a house was that I watched them pay a lot of money for such crummy houses. I thought if I came up with the down payment, they would at least be paying for their own house. And above all, she would find herself capable of taking the responsibility.

I realized that they were serious about their relationship. I didn't see anything wrong with that. Especially when I realized that they shared many interests. Mojgan used to like

skiing. Then she got involved with the water ski club. They both liked to keep active. I was hoping that Joe's presence in Mojgan's life would bring her happiness.

They were very happy with my offer, and they started to look for a small, affordable house on the lake. The reason that they wanted their house on the lake was that Joe and his two brothers were born and raised on the lake. And Mojgan was raised on her indoor pool. They both enjoyed activities in, on, and around the water.

First time I met Joe's mother Ruth, I liked her a lot. She was a teacher as well. She was very intelligent and nice person. His father John was an engineer, also very nice and likable person. His brothers, the older one Andy, and the youngest John Jr. were both beautiful people. I was very happy to see Mojgan being among them. Family was and is very important to me. It is the family that produces good or bad.

They took me to see every house they liked. After seeing many houses, they finally chose one in city of Portage. Joe had asked his father to become the co-signer for the loan. Everything was going smooth, until his father rejected our co-ownership. I couldn't figure out their reason. But I did not want to disappoint Mojgan at the time that I was trying to bring hope back into her life. After all Mojgan's happiness was worth much more than my twenty thousand dollars. To back-up on the deal was not my style, or my intention.

As I have spoken all throughout this book, from the beginning to the end the only person who I had trusted and loved, was only and only Iraj. After what he did to my children's life, and me, it seemed to me that no one else could ever hurt me as much as he did. No one was as much of a crook, a thief, and a mugger as Iraj had been. It seemed to me that after I lost him that way, I was safe, and no one would ever hurt me or rob me any more. I was so angry at him that I did many stupid things just to prove to myself, and the rest of the world that no one else was ever going to rob me.

My Dear God:

My banker, who knew me, was shocked. She started telling me stories about mothers, who gave away their money, and they regretted it later on. She was trying to awaken me to the unexpected possibilities. But although at that time I had sensed many possibilities, I still believed that giving Mojgan hope was worth more than my future. Because it had never happened to me before, I couldn't believe that my children were that kind of children. And when the day came that they had to pay the money back, many of them would not remember the day that they received the money. Anyway, I got the twenty thousand dollars in cash, and I took the bus to Kalamazoo. I had to change the bus in Detroit. I had twenty thousand dollars in my purse, and I had to wait in the crowded bus station in Detroit for two hours.

In the conference room at a bank, where the closing was taking place, more than ten people, including Joe's parents, were present. After everything went through nicely, and I had the cash in my hands, everyone started to feel uneasy. They started whispering to each

I am at Mr. Mehdi Gangi's house on one of my trips to Iran. Back row, left to right: Mr. Ghazvini- his son-in-law, Mrs. Gangi, Mrs. Hormozi, Homa Hormozi, Mr. Gangi and Nasreen- his daughter. Front row, sitting by the table: me, the birthday boy, and his sister Daryane.

At Mojgan's wedding, Kaveh and Kasra Kamooneh make me look shorter I was.

Mojgan and Maseeh were ready to ski, and T was ready to go and read my book.

Mojgan and Joe are snow skiing.

Mojgan and Joe are waterskiing.

Mr. & Ms. Kamooneh
and
Ms. Aldashi
Cordially invite you to attend
the wedding reception of
Rojiar & Kaveh

Saturday the 13th of May
Two thousand
at half an hour after seven

Walden on Lenox Road

Please RSVP by April 30th
(404) 659-8228

No gift please

As you see, this is the invitation to Roji and Kaveh's wedding. Kaveh is the middle son of Pari and Kamal Kamooneh. I always loved him and kept contact with him as much as possible. I think this picture is one of Maseeh's works. Both Roji, and Kaveh look much better in real life.

other. I also had a certified check, in case they were not comfortable with cash. So to end the confusion I wanted to say, "Don't worry. I knew exactly what I was doing. I just wanted to prove to myself it is never the strangers who rob us. The only person, who has a privilege of robbing us, is the one whom we trust the most, love the most, and most of all, depend on. You see I am speaking from experience. As you see, I took the bus here with the poorest and the most unfortunate people having all this money in my purse. But no one thought of robbing me, just because they didn't know me. They don't love me; neither do they care for me". It was obviously a stupid act. I must have known better that wasn't an act of a smart woman. But I did it just because I was mad at myself for loving, trusting, and depending on a person, who was not worthy of any of the above. But I didn't.

I was very happy to see Mojgan and Joe sharing that house. Her father already had bought her a brand new Toyota. Joe had a Jeep. They were young, athletic, energetic, intelligent, enthusiastic, and creative kids. I was hoping with all the activities that they were involve, they could stay away from drugs. The way that I saw it, I thought their involvement was very minimal.

Mojgan still had two more years of college. She was studying, working part time, and helping Joe to build furniture for the house. Joe was working, and together they were responsible for paying all the bills. To me that was a sign of maturity. Although they were not married at that time, their understanding and cooperation was great. They learned how to work side by side, and have the pleasure of love and respect for each other. I enjoyed witnessing their togetherness.

My Dear God:

When I thought of her buying a house, I had in mind that she could mature at a young age, and learn how to cooperate with others. Any successful step that I took towards my children's success and happiness, gave me a boost to believe in myself more than before. I wanted to be able to help them to get out of that ugly past, and look forward to a happy future for themselves. I knew that no matter what their father did, still they will blamed me for everything had happened to them. So I wanted to do my share of helping them.

I don't care if they realized, but my main goal was to help them survive. While we all were broken into millions of pieces, we were trying to hang in there. After all, life must go on no matter what.

For starters I gave Mojgan my dining room set: a round table with four chairs. I also gave them a few Persian rugs, many picture frames, my sewing machine, and all other necessities for kitchen, bedroom, and bathroom. I had even given them some of my artwork from Iran, and many other items that she wanted to keep. The more things she wanted to keep, the happier she made me. Because I thought this way she was trying to keep the memory of the family alive. I was feeling so sad and guilty to see my daughter

had to have the leftovers of the family to be able to survive. Oh well, that's life for you. There is no way out of it.

While Ida's house was in the process of renovation, Mitra offered me to be housemates with her. I thought that was a great idea. If it worked I would stay with her. And if not, as soon as Ida's house was ready, I would move in with her. But Ida was hurt by my decision. She thought I turned my back at her, and that I preferred Mitra to her. It took me a long time to convince her that I had to move at that time, and that my stay with Mitra was only temporary, until they finish the construction. But for some reason she wouldn't buy my story, and she was still hurt by my act.

As the time passed, my children and I became farther apart emotionally. After the news of our divorce, I did not want to ever to discuss my feelings with my children. I didn't want to remind them that they were wrong in trusting their father. I didn't want to make them feel guilty. So except that I wanted to be there for them, and help them, there was no other communication between us. If I chose to communicate with them, I would have many questions for them. I could have asked them, "If you told me your father was not involved with Badri, what about now? Where is my home or my certainty now?" And such questions would have brought more pain and agony to their lives. So in order not to hurt my children, I had to stay quiet, and not bring up any negativity in their lives. Eventually our communication had become very brief just, "Hi and How are you". We had become very distant, until we became strangers. On the other hand, he had a chance to get close to them, and he made them believe that their mother was guilty of causing all his actions.

My Dear God:

Again it reminded me of the story of two mothers, one biological, and the imposter who went to court to fight for the custody of a child. When the judge realized that none of them was willing to tell the truth about being a biological mother, he decided to find out the truth by creating a strange situation. He said, "I believe both of you are telling the truth. You both are biological mother of this child. Therefore I will order to cut the child in half, one half for each of you". At this time the silence of the courtroom was broken by a weak, but loud voice, "No, no, don't do that. I am not the biological mother. The child is hers". The judge was now relieved. He realized that the mother, who did not want the child to be cut in half, was the biological mother. After that it was easy for him to give the custody of that child to the real mother.

I thought of myself as of the real mother in that battle. For my children's sake I had to forget my rights, my love, my emotions, and especially owning my children. I not only did not own them, but their freedom of choice was my main concern. I did not want them to be forced to do anything against their will. So while I always was there for them, I pulled myself away from them so that they could find a happier life for themselves. I was

the one, who wanted my children in a happy, healthy place.

One thing that made Iraj's stupidity so obvious to me was that in one of our telephone conversations, he told me, "My children love me". He didn't know that, first of all, by nature, they had to love their father. Doesn't every serial killer's children love their father? Secondly, I was the one who always made sure that I loved him. I wanted them to keep their connection with their father. I was the one, who was there for them no matter what. I was always at their reach, no matter what. While he was there only physically, and never emotionally. He was the one who traded his family for sex. He destroyed our home. So I had to make sure that at that time nothing ever hurt them. I tried not to show any sorrow by not questioning the past. This way although we did not get into fights and disagreements, we grew farther and farther apart. There was nothing else to discuss among us except anger and disappointment.

My Dear God:

I had heard that most children, who come from divorced homes, usually feel guilty. So in effort to lessen their pain, I had minded my own business. I made a decision not to ever talk about the past. It was done and over with. There was no return or come back. We couldn't erase the hurt, and the painful memory of being robbed by the ones, whom we helped and comforted for eight years.

I don't know about my children, but I was not able to erase those painful moments then, and I don't think I will ever be able to erase them. I might be able to teach myself how to live again but to forget, is just impossible.

When Iraj had his first affair in Iran, and before I decided to separate from him, on one of his birthdays I wrote him a letter from Mary and Maseeh's perspective. I had been witnessing their sufferings all along. And especially I had witnessed Mary's destruction. I was the one who suffered with my children while he was spending his time in bed with another woman. I will include my original letter written in Farsi. There is nothing wrong that my children find out how much I loved them, and how I tried to keep my family together for such a high price. And how I tried to change Iraj's behavior by loving and caring. And especially I want them to know that I never tried to use the power of courts. This wasn't because I was afraid. I did not do it that way because I knew that what I had lost in my life, I could not bring it back, even if I went to court, won the case and got rewarded millions of dollars. I had a very meaningful life by loving my family the way that I did. I was not able to put a capital value on that. And I wanted to keep it that way.

The way that I raised my children, and what I did to fulfill my loving promises in our married life was overwhelming. It was to a point that he made me look like the most authoritative person in our household. Everything was running under my supervision. The things that I did, and we both were happy with it at that time, turned around and became a devilish behavior on my account, right after Malakuti died.

تبریک و تهنیت

به تو ای پدید آورنده زنده. به تو هم چنین شیرین‌ترین آن تشکیل پر سعادت ما خشت نخستین گذاشتی. به تو هزاران فرشته علیهای کوکب‌ها را با عمیق‌ترین آن ساختی. به تو هم آفریننده وجود مادر سازنده خانه دل‌ها هستی. به تو که مهربان‌ترین مردان و مهربان‌ترین و نیکوکارترین پدران هستی

به تو هم به موجودی که سازنده دنیای ما و موجود آورنده کاخ آمال و آرزوهای ما هستی. روز تولد تو را با بهترین تبریکات و صمیمانه‌ترین [illegible]

در حین [illegible] و ظرافت [illegible]. در روزهایی که همه [illegible] سناجی [illegible] را با خاطره‌ها [illegible] شادی‌ها افروزند. از [illegible]. از یاد [illegible]

[illegible] و دیگر شنیده. تو ای پدر عزیز [illegible] ما با عرصه وجود دل‌دادگی. در آن روز تو بیش از هر چیز به دل آنچه تو خواسته باشی به یاد آمد

دل‌هایی که [illegible] و زندگی را با [illegible] خودت [illegible] داشتی که زندگی چیست و کمال انسانی از چه خصوصیاتی باید برخوردار

[illegible] یاد داشته را هم [illegible] بیان فرزندانش نشنیده‌اند [illegible] و برای او جان و زندگی در [illegible] و راه خوشی [illegible] کرده برای

[illegible] ارزش یک انسان کامل بودن را چنین تو و دامان او تربیت شده بودی که انسان کامل بودن و [illegible] از خنده گذراندن

سعادت و شادی‌های زندگی خودت را با دیده گرفتی تا کاخ آمال و آرزوی دیگران را از نو [illegible] باشی و اینها همان سرنوشت است

که [illegible] معتقدند [illegible] در جریانات ادامه زندگی تو به دوام [illegible] ایم [illegible] اجتماع [illegible]

[illegible] است که [illegible] دور در [illegible] هم [illegible] [illegible] که [illegible] برادر [illegible]

خواهد آمد. این جز سرنوشت چیز دیگری نیست یعنی اگر تمام دنیا هم جمع شوند [illegible] نمی‌توانیم این [illegible] را هم

[illegible] باید تنها آن روزها را سعادت و خوشبختی و خوشی تو [illegible] زیرا در هر حال به [illegible] و [illegible] از جان خود [illegible]

داریم [illegible] نمی‌توانیم بگوییم [illegible] به خاطر اینکه وجود دیگر [illegible] آورده‌ای زندگی خودت را [illegible] فقط [illegible] هم [illegible]

[illegible] هم [illegible] [illegible] زیرا [illegible] در زندگی [illegible] چه [illegible] خواهد کرد [illegible]

معصوم هستیم [illegible] طوفان‌های سهمناک زندگی بدون هیچ [illegible] [illegible] بالاخره این [illegible]

[illegible] طوفان‌ها را [illegible] ما [illegible] [illegible] این [illegible] از [illegible] توجه [illegible]

[illegible] اگر از همسر [illegible] [illegible] از این [illegible]. [illegible] آخر [illegible] گناهش چیست؟

[illegible] و حال [illegible] کیست؟ روز خواهان و جشن [illegible] [illegible]؟ [illegible] عروسی [illegible]

[illegible] [illegible] جان پدر. از سر لطف [illegible] آور. خواهش صاحب فرزند [illegible]

[illegible] عیب [illegible] است. [illegible] گر چه تو [illegible] و [illegible]. باز [illegible] پدر [illegible] جان [illegible]

[illegible] شرح [illegible] آهسته. [illegible] دل و جان [illegible]. [illegible] زن و [illegible] هم [illegible]

[illegible] آینده [illegible] از فرزند. پارسال [illegible] دیگر [illegible] برگزار کردیم. امسال [illegible]

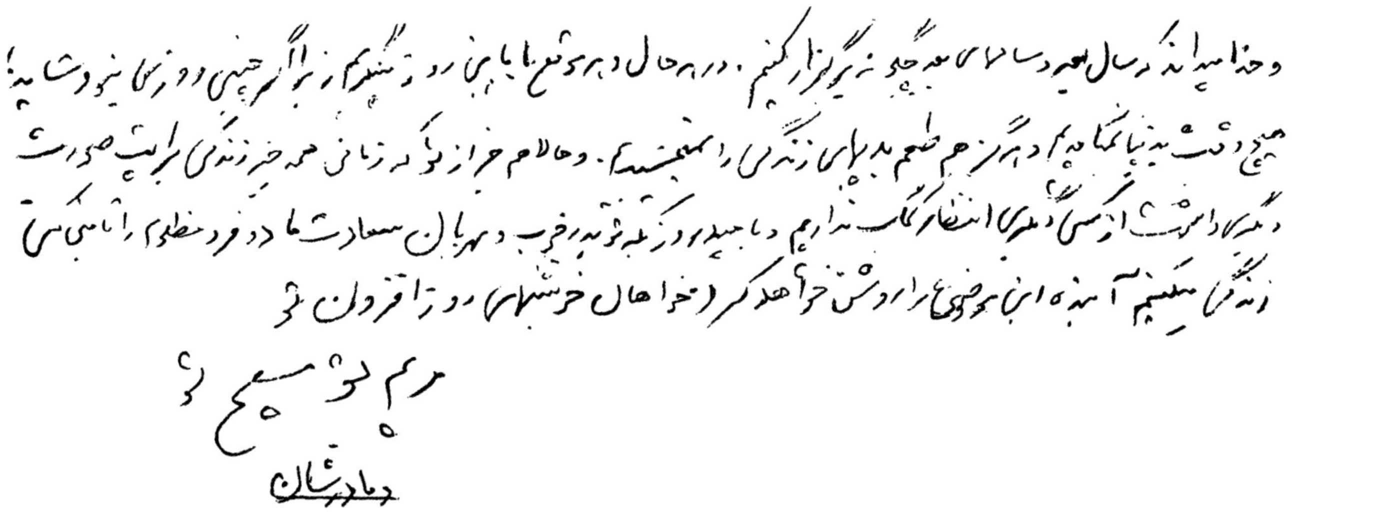
مریم تو مسیح تو
و مادرشان

This letter was written from me, Mary and little Maseeh to Iraj, on one of his birthdays, while he was having an affair in Tehran. From the beginning, I always wanted to get to him in a peaceful manner. I thought right words on a piece of paper would be more understanding than standing in front of each other and calling each other bad names. So I wrote this letter to him to let him know that Mary, Maseeh and I have some words to tell him, before he goes any further with his attempt. In the letter, I talked about our destiny, how we were born, why we met, where we came from, and why we made these children. I talked to him about our love for each other and our duty to recognize our responsibilities towards our children. I wrote it as if Mary and Maseeh were talking to him. Then I signed it, "Your Maryam, your Maseeh, and their mother."

But to a man whose life was full of dishonesty and disloyalty, nothing really mattered. He let Farkhondeh come and make a huge scene in our neighborhood to a point that she was running after him in our house to put gasoline on him and his house to burn him to the ground. If hadn't been for the neighbors to come to his rescue, he wouldn't be here today to repeat his act again. At that time, I was at my mother's house. He called me and said, "Shamci, come soon, come right now, she is trying to burn our house." I left right away with Mr. Moosavi and when we got there, he was already saved by the neighbors. I was embarrassed to find my husband in his pajamas running to the fourth floor of our house. And then, I came to the conclusion that when a man is bad, you must only burn him. Too bad, I didn't do it, and allowed him to destroy me, my children, and his sister's dignity.

If only Malakuti was still alive, and only if Iraj was not in his midlife crisis, and only if Badri wasn't a promiscuous woman, who had found Iraj as the most vulnerable man. And, if and if and if we were able to have a successful ending at this time. But no, after all these happenings, those acts of Shamci, which were love and care, have turned out to be Shamci's wrong approach to raising her children.

Isn't this painful for a woman whose only fault has been to love too much? How could a woman in such circumstances reverse the situation? While he was trying with all his power to attract my children's love towards him, I did nothing to stop him. I let it go to make my children happy by giving them freedom of choice. Not that I was happy with it. But I preferred my children's well being to mine. They knew that I would be there for them no matter what. It was only his love for them that I was concerned about. So I allowed to say whatever he pleased in effort to buy their love. After all it was my love and life, which was gone and destroyed. And I believe that when the love is gone, nothing else matters. And a love with no truth is not worth crying for. It is not easy to get rid of that feeling, but it is worth a try.

My Dear God:

You see, my dear GOD, Iraj has been a disloyal person all this time. It was only my love for him that allowed me to believe in his goodness. I don't want to believe that if Malakuti was still alive, he would have stopped fooling around, and became monogamous. I am sure he would have continued his infidelity. But like always, without having any knowledge, we would have continued our lives, thinking that every thing was fine. Then Badri would not be insisting to take my place. If Malakuti was alive, his wife would not dream to stick to Iraj like a tick. And obviously He would have never gotten divorced.

Unfortunately Malakuti had to die the way he did. Badri had to stick to Iraj the way she did. My children had to love the father I had given them. And I had to desperately look for a way of survival. I had to choose a way of living in order to teach my children that no matter what happens in our lives, we have to remain hopeful, and continue living with peace in our hearts.

In all these interactions taking place in my household, I was the one who stepped forward and demanded reasonable behavior from my children. Before Badri's appearance in our lives, Iraj was very supportive of all my actions. And at the same time I had respect for Iraj's attention to our children's behavior. But after Malakuti died, Iraj started disagreeing with my supervision of children to attract his children's attention. He tried to go against my will, and he made me look like a bad and mean person in my children's eyes. What a waist of my time, and what a pity! What a lack of self worth! Indeed he was not the guy that once I was married to. I just felt sorry for him. He didn't want to be this way.

Mary, who had more difficulty at youth, and she was the first fruit of our love, was

my main concern. I was willing to do anything to help her. Although in some of her actions she made sure to show me her love, but on many more occasions she purposely made me believe that she did not want me around. Very vividly she wished that I wasn't around to make her life difficult by watching her actions.

I have many apologetic letters from her. When she was not using anything, she had the understanding and recognized our love for her. She had thanked me for my patience, forgiveness, and loving her the way I did. I will include a few of her letters in this book. Many times, without any reason, she gave me gifts, which said what she had in her heart for me.

My Dear God:

Once she gave me a canvas with the following writing on it, "GOD could not be everywhere, so he created mothers". That gift was so meaningful to me. Every time she made me cry, and showed me her hate, I remembered that precious gift, and I continued loving her.

She was visiting San Francisco once. I knew that she had mo money, but she still sent me a dozen roses with a very loving card for my birthday from there. Since I was not expecting it, I was even happier.

Mary tried to burn me most of the time. She purposely did and said things to hurt me. While I wasn't as good as her in any subject, she seemed to be competing with me. I just could not understand her. Sometimes she did things that even Maseeh, who was her younger brother couldn't stand. Once she did something in his car that made Maseeh so mad. Many times he questioned me, "Why do you allow Mary to get away with everything?" He didn't know that I had to find a tactic with Mary to be able to reach my goal. Since they had different characters, I had to treat them accordingly.

What Mary was crying for, and what she feared of at the age of five was now becoming alive, and it had taken everything away from her. As she said once with her father's behavior, we all had lost our dignity. They were all in a shocking stage of their lives. Since their father had decided to run away from them, and destroy our home, while they had no power to stop him or question him, I was the only person to be blamed. I was abused and destroyed by my husband, and I was under attack by my children. I was being blamed and questioned, "Why did you do that? Why didn't you do this?" I had no choice but to take it all. After all I was the one who gave them life, and brought them into this world. They had all the right to blame me for the things they were going through.

I felt guilty twice as much for the way I raised Mary, and my two other children. From the beginning of their lives I made them believe that they could get anything they pointed at. I made them believe that just like myself, everyone will be at their service, and do everything they asked for. I made them believe that no matter right or wrong, I would agree with whatever their little hearts desired. So they expected this from everyone else.

Dear Mom and Dad,

sometimes it is hard for me to say some things straight out so I thought I would write this letter. I'm cleaning up my act, I guess you could say. I think that now I really know what I want and what I am going after, I don't think I ever was so sure of myself in my whole life. I was unhappy last year, always trying to be popular - that didn't work. I also was unhappy getting high all the time - I threw all my pot out (I did not have that much), I threw my pipe away (I still have Mark's pipe in my glove compartment & I will give it to him the next time I see him). I'm going to quit smoking pot for a while - until I'm sure I can keep it under control, it could take anywhere from a month to a year but I will know when or if I should start again (I will know it when the time comes). I also threw out my birth control pills and I doubt if I will go back on them before I turn eighteen, so you know that I will not be having much sexual activity on dates, of course you will have to take my word for that but you will also notice that in the future, things I do will not appear sneaky, like in the past, and I will be spending more time at home, with my family. I am very grateful to both of you for the way you've raised me. You gave me the freedom to learn from experience and those are the best lessons anybody can learn because the lesson learned is permanent. I think that if you had been like other parents and dictated rules to me all the time I still would not know who or what I am because I would not have had the experience to know what I enjoy doing or how often I enjoy doing it. I hope that makes sense to you. I haven't decided all of this just for you. I'm doing it for me, but I am telling →

you so you will be as proud of me as I am. I know me now. I don't know exactly what it is I want but I think I'm so close I can almost touch it. I feel great. Well, not great, just very, very, very, very good. [redacted] I feel good about myself, about my parents, and about my family.

Love,
Your Normal Daughter,
Mary

FOR MOM AND DAD

This is the second page of a two-page letter that Mary had written to her parents after realizing that she could not continue rebelling against her parents anymore. She wrote to us to inform us that the mixed-up days are over and she is coming back to be her good old self. She was looking for her parents' open arms to love her and give her their support. This was the time that I was praying for. This was the best time that I was hoping for. She was beautiful, intelligent, smart, and was willingly coming back to the world of adulthood with the help of her parents. Unfortunately, at that time her father was busy having an affair with Badri Malakuti, his mistress. And her mother was desperately searching for a way to find a solution to her family's problem, Badri and her desires for sex. So, Mary was not able to join the adulthood life in a normal way, instead she got more confused than she was ever before. This father after his first affair had promised his children to become the best father anyone could have. But, instead he became a sex maniac and the subject of laughter among all Iranian doctors and everyone else for that matter. He not only ruined his own image, but he also caused my children and I to lose our dignity.

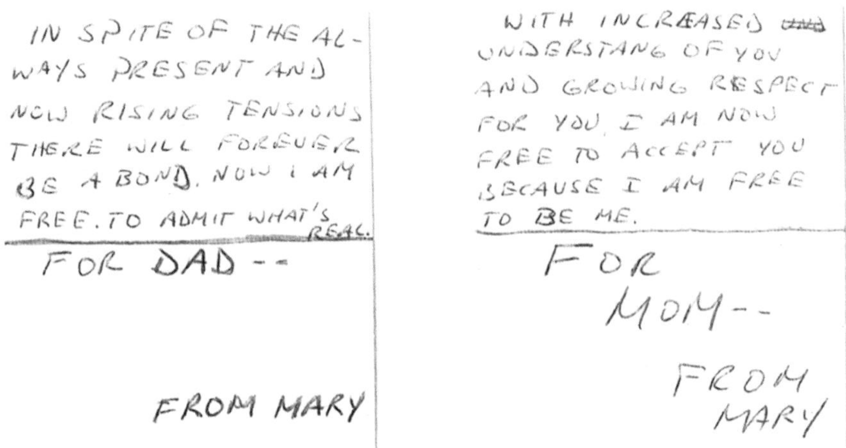

IN SPITE OF THE AL-
WAYS PRESENT AND
NOW RISING TENSIONS
THERE WILL FOREVER
BE A BOND. NOW I AM
FREE. TO ADMIT WHAT'S REAL.
FOR DAD --
FROM MARY
WITH INCREASED
UNDERSTANG OF YOU
AND GROWING RESPECT
FOR YOU, I AM NOW
FREE TO ACCEPT YOU
BECAUSE I AM FREE
TO BE ME.
FOR MOM --
FROM MARY

Please pay attention to these two cards from Mary to her parents. One is for me and the other one is for Iraj. It was around the time that she had given up her rebellion against her parents. She had found herself, and was happy to admit that she could love and respect our parental authorities. This was the time that I had been waiting for, for a long time. I tried to learn how to deal with rebellious teenagers. I joined classes, I read books, and I talked to parents who were in that situation with their children. And after we got the good results and Mary had found her way back to us, Iraj was not there for her. He was playing with his mistress Badri, and he had no time for understanding his children who needed him so badly at that time. At his mid-life crisis, he was acting like a rebellious child more than his own children.

And yet, I had to pay for all his mistakes. It was my fault that I was not able to cure his mid-life crisis disease. I have to say to my children, "I am sorry. I was not a veterinarian to have a cure for your father."

All these cards speak for themselves. While he was having an affair with his mistress Badri, he did not forget Mother Days, or my birthdays. What a loving person!

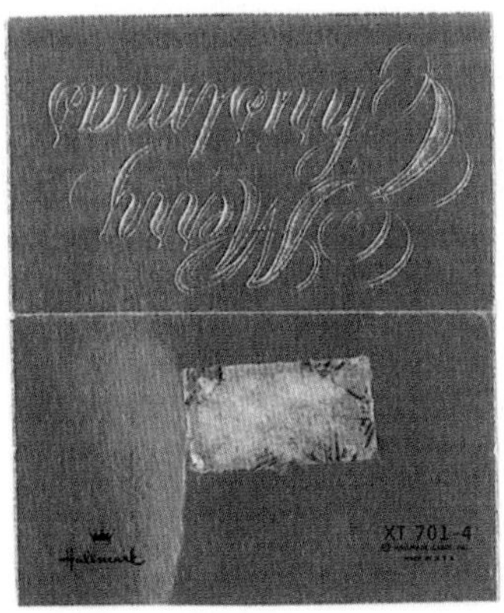

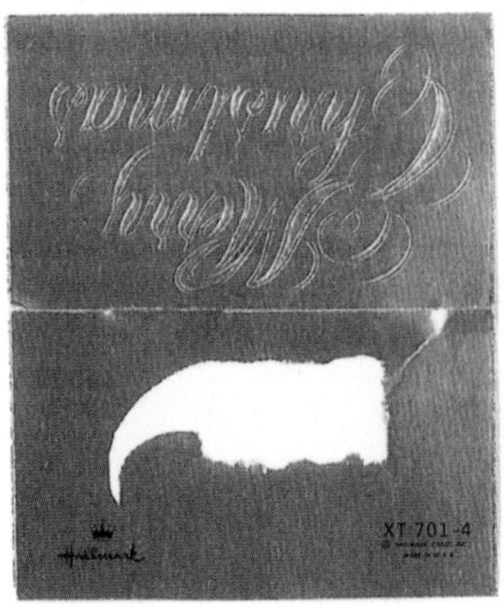

DUNSTAN-IVORY FLOWERS
7120 HIGHLAND ROAD
PONTIAC, MICHIGAN 48054
666-9596

So Mary especially was expecting from the whole world to agree with her on anything she said and did. If someone went against her will, she thought it was the end of the world. So she took her space from those who did not follow her ideas. Just like my father had warned me, I was her first target. As soon as she became a teenager, she started to rebel against us. And when she realized that I was against her wrongdoing, she started hating me. That hate never stopped no matter what I did to correct it. She didn't like her mother, and her interfering with her wrong doings.

My Dear God:

When Iraj and I were still together, there was one voice against her actions. Now that Iraj was apart from me, and he was trying to clear his name and dump all his guilt on me, he made them believe that because I had been insisting on rules and regulations, I was the guilty one. I, on the other hand, did not want to prove my innocence. I didn't even want them to love me, if they didn't see a point in loving me. But I was always there for her. I just wanted show her my love. I wanted to bring out the best in her, for her sake. Nothing she did stopped me from loving and caring for her.

I don't remember if I already talked about this poem in Farsi story, which describes the love of a mother for her son. The story goes like this, "Her son had fallen in love with a girl, who does not like his mother, and his love for her. Every day when they saw each other, she complained about his mother, 'She does not want me around. She does not like me. She fights with me. And as long as she is alive, I cannot love you the way you want me to. Unless you go and bring her heart for me, I cannot love you enough'. The son, who was madly in love, and wanted the girl so badly, went home and killed his mother. He took his mother's warm heart in his hands, and rushed to his lover. But he slipped and fell on his way. At this time a soft and concerned voice came from that warm heart saying, 'Oh, my son fell. Oh, my son's leg got hurt'." Possessing such feelings of motherhood, I was never able to let of my children go, even if they didn't want me. I felt it was my duty. I was persistently tried to make them, and not break them.

Sometimes when I look back I don't know how it was possible to make it. How did I do it day after day without breaking myself? Or how can a person become so tolerant to be able to put two and two together during those suffering days? Anyway it was my duty, and I had to do it. It didn't matter if I was hurt.

When Mary was living with that lawyer, I did not let her know that I did not like him. I knew that if Mary knew that I didn't like him, she would probably push herself even closer to him. So I just tried to stay quiet, and I let her do her own thing. Mary at that time was surrounded by many uncertainties. She didn't keep contact with me. We had become like two strangers.

My main concern was her involvement with those who liked drugs. While their father was not around, I was there to let their aggression out on me. When they needed to

مادر ایرانی

عیش آن نازنین همی داشت او — با جهانی هم‌نواست او
نامه‌ای ناخوانده با خطی کهن — قصه‌ای تازه که ننوشته‌ست او
درد دارد؟ گو که پیدایش نی — هی هی هر درد تنهاست او
کار و بارش سوختن، آموختن — آنکه در کارش فروماست او
دوستش دارم که در سرمای عمر — همچو گلهای زمستانست او
بی حضورش عشق را مفهوم نیست — عشق را هم باعث و بانیست او
لحظه‌ای از غم گذاری دور نیست — گریه پیدا مرد بارانی است او
از زمانی تا ابد عاشق است — عشق اول عشق پایانی است او
بوی گیسوی سفیدش محشر است — بهتر از هر گل که میدانی است او
روح او پایان نمی‌گیرد به مرگ — ماندنی در عالم فانی است او
این شگفت نازنین دانی که کیست؟ — مادر پرمهر ایرانی است او

These are two Iranian poems; one is titled "Iranian Mother", and the other, "Mother's Heart". There is no way that I could translate these two poems. Even if translate them to English, the meaning is hidden between the lines. And also, I don't think that this poem fits all the Iranian mothers. No way. Some are like Badri and the rest of her family, and some are like my mother in these poems. Since my children and I could not find time together so they would get to understand my culture, my feelings about motherhood, and my way of thinking, I am just hoping that after I am gone, they find a right Iranian to read these poems for them and make them understand what it means.

قلب مادر

داد معشوقه به عاشق پیغام — که کند مادر تو با من جنگ
هر کجا بیندم از دور کند — چهره پرچین و جبین پر آژنگ
با نگاه غضب آلود زند — بر دل نازک من تیر خدنگ
از در خانه مرا طرد کند — همچو سنگ از دهن قلماسنگ
مادر سنگدلت تا زنده است — شهد در کام من و توست شرنگ
نشوم یکدل و یکرنگ ترا — تا نسازی دل او از خون رنگ
گر تو خواهی به وصالم برسی — باید این ساعت بی خوف و درنگ
روی و سینهٔ تنگش بدری — دل برون آری از آن سینهٔ تنگ
گرم و خونین به منش باز آری — تا برد ز آینهٔ قلبم زنگ
عاشق بی خرد ناهنجار — نه، بل آن فاسق بی عصمت و ننگ
حرمت مادری از یاد ببرد — خیره از باده و دیوانه ز بنگ
رفت و مادر را افکند به خاک — سینه بدرید و دل آورد به چنگ
قصد سرمنزل معشوق نمود — دل مادر به کفش چون نارنگ
از قضا خورد دم در به زمین — و اندکی سوده شد او را آرنگ
وان دل گرم که جان داشت هنوز — اوفتاد از کف آن بی فرهنگ
از زمین باز چو برخاست نمود — پی برداشتن آن آهنگ
دید کز آن دل آغشته به خون — آید آهسته برون این آهنگ
آه دست پسرم یافت خراش — آه پای پسرم خورد به سنگ

get mad, and they wanted to break things or wanted to scream, I had to be there for them. Sometimes in all those scenes I saw the signs of their concern for me. I was there if they ever needed me.

My Dear God:

I heard that Mary had moved into her own place in Detroit. She obviously was separated from Tom, and she was living with her dog. Once I was in Kalamazoo visiting Mojgan, when she came to visit us. We had a good and quiet time together. But although it was a long weekend, she did not stay long. She insisted to return home. I noticed that her dog was not trained, and was giving her hard time. Once I took him for a walk. He started running, and pulled me after him in a way that his leash cut my fingers. He seemed to be wild.

As I mentioned before, Mary loved to write. Although she knew that my English was not good enough to be able to appreciate the level of her writing, she still read her poems and her writings to me. She gave me a copy of everything that was ever printed. She knew I loved to read her writings and her poems. Many times we communicated through the books or her writings by discussing the subjects. I didn't know what was really happening in her life at that time, but I knew that she was covering her true feelings from me. Just looking at her I knew that she was suffering. But I never wanted to irritate her by asking. I knew that if she wanted to talk she would do it herself. She had isolated herself from everyone, except Sue, Arman's ex sister-in-law. I was sure that she was doing wrong to herself. But I didn't dare to guide her. Who was I to lead her to a better way of life? She would have said to me, "If you knew right from wrong, why didn't you do it yourself? Why are we in this mess now? Where is our home and happiness now?" And when she asked me all those questions, how would I answer her? How could I clear her sensitive heart from all the pain that she was suffering from?

I was in a situation that made some people say to me, "If you did this, or if you had done that, you would be with your family now. If you danced to his tune, you might have had a better life". So who was I to guide or lead anyone, including my children? How could I tell my children what to do or not to do? Although in my heart I knew that I had given enough love and attention to my family, and I even read books to do my best. But in reality, while he made me believe that I was a great lover, a great wife, and a great mother, I was the one who lost the battle. I was the one, whose children were left without family. I was the one who lost to a couple of sex maniacs. I forgot to mention that I was always praised in bed, and yet I had lost to a promiscuous woman, whose husband certainly was aware.

My Dear God:

In any culture, especially our culture, the word woman describes the gender and the sex of a person. But the word lady describes a woman with all the qualities of being a great person. It describes a lady who is loyal, who is trustworthy, who is beautiful, who is humanitarian, and most of all, who is clean and clear from every vicious act on earth. And among many Iranian women, Badri was the only woman as far as I knew, that the word lady never fit her whatsoever. So was it my fault if I couldn't be like her? To tell you the truth, although I lost my family to her, I preferred to be a lady like me, rather than a woman like Badri, that even Iraj knew what kind of a dirty woman she was.

In a way GOD knew that Badri and Iraj were made for one another. That was why he got rid of Malakuti at his young age, just to save him from agony of knowing more about Badri. And in a way he separated Iraj from me to show me what would be the happiness without living with a crook.

So with all these, I couldn't advice Mary one way or another. During those troubled years I was not able to hold my children's hand or help them, while I was witnessing they were melting in front of my eyes.

Mary always loved her father a lot. Unconsciously she would be drawn to something he liked. For instance, he wanted Mary to go to a medical school. Since she found it too difficult, she chose to go to the next best thing, and that was a law school. She majored in history. She was a writer, a poet, and she was never fit to become a fighter like lawyers.

When she refused to accept money from me to buy a house for her, I knew that she was afraid of taking the responsibility. She preferred living in a slum to having the responsibility of managing a house. She teased me for living in the upper class society condo, and refused to share it with me.

As far as I can remember Mary had never done any oil painting. She always thought that she was not as talented as Maseeh. One day she came to visit me, and she brought all her tools for oil painting. She sat at the balcony the whole day, and she finished a beautiful view of the lake, and the pool, and the whole scene. That day I cooked her favorite Iranian dish "Abgoosht". She wanted to be by herself to be able to finish that painting. I read in her act, and those beautiful green eyes of hers that she was trying to get rid of her aggression by using the paintbrush over that canvas. But I was afraid to open my mouth. I did not want to hurt her feelings by reminding her about the things that bothered her. So I left to leave her alone. When I came back, and I saw what she had done, I was totally surprised. In amazement I told her, "You are nothing less than Maseeh. This is fantastic". But she was never satisfied with anything. She didn't think it was great.

My Dear God:

Usually artists do their best when their sensitivity becomes greater. They do their miracles at greater sadness. That day I witnessed Mary's great emotional sadness. But I

was not allowed to ask any questions. She did not want anybody's help. I packed her some of that "Abgoosht", which she liked a lot. She did not stay over night. She left her painting stuff, said goodbye to me, and left.

GOD, I wished you were a mother to be in my shoes that night. You remember how I cried hopelessly and helplessly after she left. It was like the time that she was only five years old in Iran. Then, in Iran, I could hold her in my arms, and kiss her head to toes to make her feel better. But what about now, my dear GOD? You were the only witness to see what was going on with my children emotionally. What could I have done to make her feel better? Don't you think that I cried a river during those years?

While she was pursuing her law school, she was earning her living at the Neighborhood Legal Services in Detroit. I had gone to her office sometimes, and also I have gone to her apartment.

I cannot even describe her apartment, or the furniture and dishes she had. She had some things I had given to her, and she had agreed that I make drapes for her room. There was a small bed in the corner of her room. She would never let me get her anything. She was against watching TV, so there was no TV in her room. She was influenced by her father that, "Your mother watches too much TV", and she felt that TV was unnecessary. She had no friends, no family, and she was separated from Tom and his son, whom she loved a lot.

I couldn't believe that my beautiful, gracious, intelligent daughter, who was the apple of my eye, was living in such a slum, in such loneliness. I don't believe that her dear father ever had time to witness how, and where his beautiful daughter was living. He was too busy with his mistress Badri, that he didn't give a damn about his child. He gave her a brand new car on her sixteenth birthday. Don't you think that gift was for his own ego, and not for the love for his daughter? He wanted to be number one among Iranian doctors, who gave his daughter a brand new car on her sweet sixteen. This was completely an American act. Even in America this was the act of people with lots of money. He only was trying to put himself among rich and famous.

Otherwise, why at this time of her life, he was not around? Why was he ignoring their existence? Why didn't he visit her in the house she lived with Tom in Detroit? And why hasn't he been at her new apartment in Detroit? Was it because he was ashamed of himself? Or was it because he never loved them to begin with?

My Dear God:

Please tell me, wasn't my duty to cover up the truth from my dear children? Didn't I have the right not to tell them that their father didn't love them? Weren't they suffering enough, that I allowed myself to break their hearts after they had been broken million times? Didn't I have to sit and just watch what life was going to bring us next? Please, you just tell me.

When I saw her loneliness, I decided to buy her a television set. First I talked to her, and it seemed that she was not against it. So one day, with plenty of hope in my heart, I went shopping. I bought her a 21-inch TV, I carried it in my car, and I drove to her apartment with such excitement. I was thinking that at least some of the shows on TV might take her mind away from her problems, and bring some laughter to her. At least I was hoping for this to happen.

I did not found her in a normal state when I got there. As always I tried to ignore her cold greetings. She asked me to leave the TV there for now. We finished her cooking in the kitchen together. We had our dinner in silence. I was afraid to open my mouth, not to trigger the fire, which was piled in her ready to burst. After dinner we opened the box. We removed the TV, and we found a place for it. After we hooked it up, we started to watch the news. After a short while, she tried to go to sleep.

As I said before, she had a small room, small bed, and very tight living area. As soon as I opened my mouth to ask her, "Aren't you going to watch TV?", she was ready to attack me. I can never forget that night. She started attacking me for being a TV lover. She said many things that writing it would not be appropriate. She asked me to pack my TV, and take it back.

It was just before midnight. No one in a right state of mind would drive through that part of Detroit in the daytime, and yet to be driving that late at night. I was afraid to get out of her unit. I could not even think of getting out of the apartment building. I realized that she must have been on some kind of drugs. I started to put TV back in its box. But I couldn't make myself carry that big box all the way down from the fifth floor to the street level. How did I know that my car was still there? How was I sure that no one would mug me in the stairway? Anyway, although I was afraid to stay with Mary in her apartment that night, I had no other choice.

Judging by her behavior, I wasn't sure if she would open the door and throw me out of her room that night. I certainly did not know whom I was dealing with. She had a big cage for her dog in the corner of the room. There was nothing, and no room for me to lie down on the floor. I had to stay there that night, no matter what. I did not have the heart to take that TV back at that time of night. I said to myself, "Even if she kills me in this room tonight, it is much better than going out of her apartment". So after I decided to stay, I said quietly, "But I cannot take it back tonight. I have to stay and take it back first thing in the morning".

My Dear God:

When I did not hear a word from her, I started to find a blanket or something to lie down on. I found a small space behind the door, where I was able to lie down. I kept staring at the ceiling, I don't remember if I ever went to sleep.

Although this was happening to me, I wasn't able to feel it, or think about it. I kept

thinking about what had happened to my beautiful daughter. I was praying to God to take her misery away. How could I believe that she was the same daughter of mine, who was loved by everyone for her innocence, her beauty, and intelligence? To me she was just an angel. How could I explain this to anyone?

Because I avoided contact with Iraj, I had to talk to someone I could trust. The only person that I could trust at that time was his friend Dr. Edward Mehrabian. He was my best and only friend, who was concerned about my family and me. He always told me, "You might not believe me. But this man is a big loser after what he did. He might pretend that he does not know it. But Shamci, believe me, that he knows it by all his heart. Don't you ever feel sorry for yourself. You must feel sorry for him, who had built a great name for himself, and yet he was not capable of keeping it". So next day after I returned the TV, I called Dr. Mehrabian. I told him what was happening to Mary. I begged him to contact Iraj, and inform him about what Mary was going through.

I was aware how much Mary loved her father. I was sure that without him, she might loose the battle for life. I remembered the reaction that she showed at the age of five, after his first affair. But so many relatives surrounded her then. They loved her, hugged her, kissed her, and bought her everything she had asked for. And took her to see Mary Poppins for more than ten times. If that was not a cure for her, it was good enough to keep her mind away from her father's acts. "But what about now? Who can I talk to?" Just crying did not help, even if I cried day and night. So I had to turn to Dr. Mehrabian for help. I even asked him to call Mary to see if he can do anything for her.

I knew that because of the property, and the office that they shared Iraj was in contact with him almost every day. I asked Dr. Mehrabian to inform Iraj of Mary's possible nervous break down. I asked him to make sure that Iraj came to see Mary, or introduced her to a well-known psychiatrist. I was so embarrassed to find myself sitting in Dr. Mehrabian's kitchen crying. It was not about the loss of Iraj, but about the troubles that my children had to experience. I didn't know how to help them, so I cried and cried.

My Dear God:

So after DR. Mehrabian talked to him, between the two of them they arranged for her to go and see a psychiatrist. While we were struggling with our scratched emotions, Mary was studying hard to finish her law school at Detroit law school. She informed me of her graduation day. This is usually the day for a family to celebrate with excitement and happiness. This was actually my dream day to celebrate Mary's graduation. How foolish I was to depend on Iraj's promises. Where was he on the day of our beautiful daughter's graduation? Where was he to show his appreciation to his hard working daughter? If he wasn't just a sex maniac to prefer his mistress to his daughter's graduation from law school, wouldn't he be present for that occasion? Or, am I stupid to think that way?

He was never there for his children on various occasions that they needed him. He

always had excuses, "I was on call, or I had a delivery". Obviously those were good excuses. No one could blame him for working so hard, and making money for his family. Especially that he had a wife like me at home who always covered for him. He was always on certain duties, or buried under the Wall Street Journal searching how to become a millionaire. I wonder whom he wanted to become millionaire for. Don't you think, my dear God, that he had planned this life for himself from the day that he thought of marrying me?

Now that I said that, I remember from the first day that I met him. He would always say, ""I am like my so and so uncle". Previously he had spoken about him, "He was a nice guy. He married his made, while he was married to his wife and had three children". He repeatedly mentioned, "I have the same character". Someone must remind me that it was my stupidity that I didn't get his massage. He has been trying all his life to tell me what kind of character he had. But I was not smart enough to get his message, and expect from him the stupidity that he was showing now. It was too late to think back forty years now, and wish to start all over again. There would be nothing I could have done to reverse the history of my life.

Like every proud mother, I dressed up in my regular manner. I always wore conservatively. Since it was a very cold day in Detroit, I wore my long black mink coat. I parked my car at the parking lot of Neighborhood Legal Services, and went inside to get Mary to accompany her to her graduation ceremony. After I introduced myself to her co-workers, I asked for Mary. From the moment she saw me, I noticed that something was bothering her. Without introducing me to her co-workers as her mother, we left the building. I realized later that my mink coat and my expensive purse have been an embarrassment to her in front of her co-workers. All day she kept that attitude towards me. I acted normal and did not want to bother her for something that she believed in strongly. I was by myself, and she tried to ignore me all day.

My Dear God:

During the ceremony and the swearing with all my excitement I took many pictures. While I was very happy for her, I was very sad that her father and her sister and brother, the only family members that she had, couldn't be there to celebrate that important occasion in her life. And I knew that part of being mad at me was created by our family problems. Since she didn't have anyone else to take her anger out on, she found me as the only available person to show her anger to. Even at lunchtime I took my space away from her thinking that she could associate more with the other lawyers without feeling obligated to introduce me to them. While I held back my tears, I was glad that I was there for her so she could take her aggression out. I was glad to be able to have enough understanding to recognize her needs, and I continued to be tolerant.

All other lawyers had their parents, their grandparents, their aunts and uncles, and

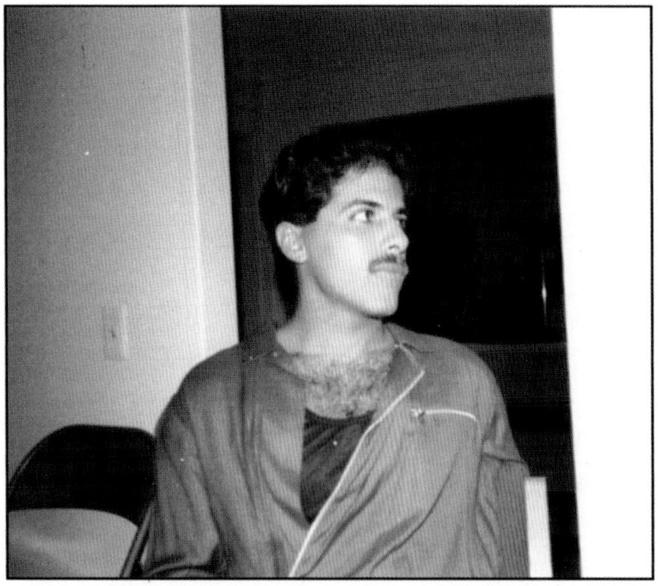

My son Maseeh, is wondering what the unknown would bring him.

Mary is at the swearing stage. I wonder what she was thinking when everyone's parents and all their families were there. I was so sorry then, and I am so sorry now. I don't blame all of you for hating me the way you do. It was I who gave you this father after all.

Mary is looking as lonely as she could get, among the graduate students. What awful feelings she might have had! I am so sorry for all the troubles you had gone through. Now I know why I could take all the abuse and not say a word. It is because I feel guilty. I feel guilty because I was not able to give you what you deserved.

My dearest and beautiful Mary, on the day of her graduation from University of Detroit, is getting her law degree. On that day, the day that was supposed to be the best happiest day of her life, I was the only one there to celebrate the occasion with her. On that day, no matter what I did, she was not happy. Now, when I put myself in her position, I realize that if I were she, I would not even be able to attend the ceremony. She was graduating while her father was in California with his mistress, Badri Malakuti. How could she forgive him? What an ugly father!

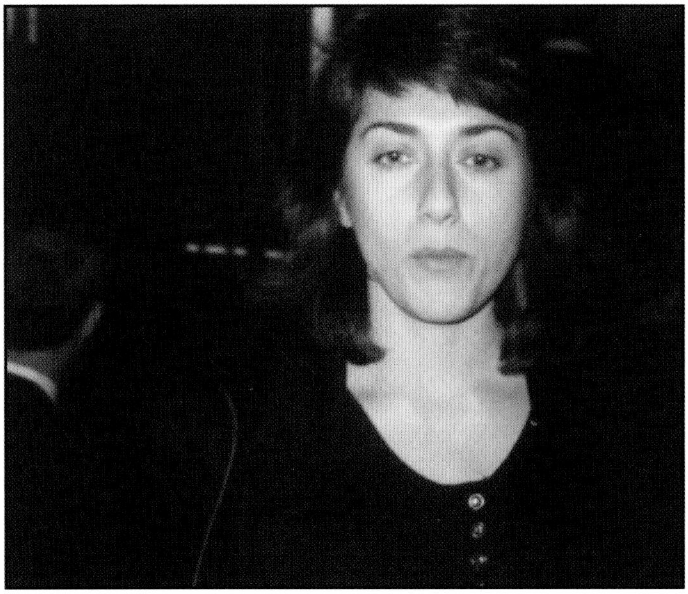

Here, she is at the swearing stage.

ATTORNEY AT LAW

MARY RAFANI

P.O. BOX 263
VISALIA, CALIFORNIA 93279

TELEPHONE (209) 636-1445
FACSIMILE (209) 636-9462

their nieces and nephews. But she didn't have anyone, and she had her mother, who was not dressed to her approval. I thought she had right to be mad.

Anyway that day I tried to cheer her up. I congratulated her sincerely, and I made sure that she realized how proud she had made me. Although paid no attention to my words, but I knew that deep down she was glad that at least I was there with her to celebrate the most important occasion in her life. When she left me, she did not thank me, or said anything else. She just left me with all the sadness in her heart.

Since I had no one to talk to, I cried in my private, discussing my problems with my dear God. And I asked him for guidance. Many times I took my problems to Dr. Mehrabian to contact her father, and let him know that Mary's life was in jeopardy.

While all these were happening, and I was still living in my condominium, one day Mary called to talk to me. She sounded completely different from all the other times. She was mumbling. It seemed that she had something to tell me, but she was hesitant.

She started talking about Maseeh and Mojgan. She asked me if they had called to talk to me. I started to sense that she called with bad news, and she was afraid to say it. My sixth sense was preparing me for something bad. Most of the time I was able to read between the lines. Before I tried to make a fool out of myself, I put myself together. Obviously Mary was okay, since she was talking to me. She must know about Maseeh and Mojgan, that they were ok too. As long as these three were okay, no news could have been bad news.

My Dear God:

After a short period of time, which seemed like the longest time to me, Mary started this way, "Maseeh and Mojgan had been willing to contact you, but they didn't know how to tell you that My Dad and Badri got …" I didn't let her finish her sentence. I knew that they couldn't bring me the news, so they had decided that Mary called me with news of their marriage.

I changed the subject of our conversation. I asked her about herself, and I told her, "I am going to rent out my condo, and move to Mitra's house temporarily. I did not allow her to see my sadness, and sounding absolutely happy I told her, "Don't worry at all. I am fine. Tell Maseeh and Mojgan that I am okay". She said, "Good bye", and I hung up the phone.

Obviously the last word of Mary's sentence was "married". No matter what language I choose to be able to explain my feelings at that time, it would be impossible to express myself to anyone, especially to my children. After eight years of struggle, and hoped that one day he might start thinking of his children and their dignity, he brought shame and embarrassment into our lives by humiliating all of us once and for all.

After I put the phone down, I lay down on my back in the middle of my bedroom for two or three hours and just cried. I was so numb that I thought I was dreaming. I was

alone. I was hopeless. While my tears were rolling down my cheeks, I was staring at the wall in front of me. Suddenly my eyes caught the big frame on the wall. It was the first letter that sent me from the ship to New York. I had enlarged it, and framed it to be able to remember who I once was in his life. He left me after two weeks of our marriage. In that letter he said, "I wish I never took this trip. I didn't know that this separation would be so difficult for me; otherwise I would have never attempted to go away. Now I understand that without you next to me, my life is worthless. I cannot live without you. If right now I had a chance and money, I would have bought a ticket, and I would have returned to you as fast as I could. Without you my success means nothing to me. Now I know that it was you, who persuaded me to take this trip. Not even once you stopped me from going, but it was you who encouraged me to take this trip", and then on and on. Then he said, "Now that it is no longer possible for me to come back, you must get to work. You, without any hesitation must go and contact the person who got my visa for me, and ask him to get your visa as soon as possible. This must be done today, and not tomorrow", and he went on and on.

My Dear God:

I was reading that letter, and I couldn't stop sobbing. That moment and that day was certainly the end of my life. Until that day I was counting on Iraj's love for his family, and especially his children.

Those who read those letters might think that for sure it has been my stupidity, which brought me this life. Yes, I admit that I was that stupid to frame that letter, and keep it in my bedroom. But I was hoping to be able to survive that disaster.

I wasn't able to move. After hours went by, I touched myself to see if I was still alive. I was glad that no one, especially my children were not there to see my reaction to that humiliation. On the other hand I needed to be with someone who could understand my great pain. I kept thinking, and I was wondering why did he have to lie to me in such loving manner for thirty years? I was wondering why it hurt me more now, while he had started his affair with Badri right after Malakuti's death, in the year 1981. I was wondering why I must feel this way, while I had already mourned for him for eight years. True that Badri and other friends pushed him to that situation, but after all the person who took the initiative was he and only he. I had tried so hard to kill him in my heart for eight years. I should have known that as ruthless as he was, this was coming. Why was I so hurt now, after I had tried so hard to give him up? Neither Dr. Malakuti, nor I were the right pair for these two ruthless people. Luckily for Dr. Malakuti he died before he got to know his real friend, and his real wife. Gladly he didn't have to deal with their disloyalty. Only it was me, who had to learn to recognize that the loss of a man like Iraj, must be a blessing to me. I must let my children know that their marriage had not harmed me any more than it had already harmed me eight years prior to this. I must show my children

that no matter what happens life must go on. I must make them understand that as long as they have themselves to depend on, loss of anyone, or anything should not bring enough sadness in them, or destroy them. I wanted to be their role model of strength and tolerance.

I lay down there until morning. There was no one to turn to. As usual I got up, took a shower, put my make-up on, and got dressed to go to work. As always I cried all the way to work, and then I cleaned up my act, put a smile on my face, and made myself lost among the other co-workers. No one ever saw me cry, or witnessed my sadness.

The next day was Wednesday, his day off that we always went places and had lunch together. Since I had substituted his presence with the company of Tilda and her family, I got dressed and went to Tilda's house. She greeted me with her dog Tasha with much love and attention. We walked to the restaurant nearby her house, and we talked of various subjects. In the evening, when Luciana came home, we had dinner. After dinner the three of us decided to go see a movie. These people were the angels of mercy, who had appeared in my life out of nowhere, and their love and attention was keeping me together in one piece. For as long as I shall live, I will owe my peace of mind at the most disastrous time of my life to Tilda.

My Dear God:

You see, my dear God, I know that millions of people become victims of someone's dishonesty, disloyalty, and unfaithfulness of their life partners. Some of them will end-up becoming murderers, while some will end-up becoming drug addicts or alcoholics, and others will end-up in a sanitarium. If these nice people did not appear in my life to share their wisdom with me and save me from my destructive thoughts, I would not be able to survive the way I did.

You see, my dear God, with all these happenings, it was I, who found a way to save my children's life and mine from falling apart. It was my choice to show my children that I could survive without depending on drugs, alcohol, or jumping in another man's arms. It was I, who tried to overcome that disastrous life that Iraj had created for me. And it was I, who made sure that my children understood the meaning of the right way of life, as opposed to the wrong way of life. By then they had enough intelligence to differentiate right from wrong. It didn't matter if they were near or far from me. They were aware of all my actions. I just was hoping that they could turn around and convince themselves that they, at troublesome periods of life, should not turn to alcohol or drugs for cure. There are people, like their mother, who search for wiser ways of facing their troubles.

Unfortunately my children never really got to know their mother. They never knew that my father has belted me many times to stop me from the idea of marrying him. They never knew what I had gone through to save them, and also save myself from emotional scars left from humiliation of their father's first affair. And they never knew what I was

going through since 1981, the year that their father started his affair with Badri. And didn't know what I was going through after our separation. They thought they had it hard. They never felt my pain and desperation. They had never seen my tears I didn't expect them to see me at my weakest moments. I wanted to discuss my problems with God only, and receive his merciful wisdom in me. This was my only way to deal with my problems.

My Dear God:

Since I was a liberal democrat in my ways of raising my children, I allowed them to follow their own intelligent choice in their religion, choice of sex partners, political views, and any other aspects of life.

When our life ended up in divorce, my main concern was my children's relationship with their father. All my life I fed them love of my husband and love of their father. I knew how desperately they loved their father. I had always encouraged their closeness with their father. Unfortunately getting close to him had strings attached. They had to act civilized if they were smart, and should have not made themselves a "sore thumb" in public eye. So in the end result I had to deal with that situation by pulling myself away from my own children to be able to stay away from enormous hate in my heart for Iraj and his live-in mistress.

I do not expect anyone to understand my feelings, or judge me. I just believe that my three children need a strong, rocky, firm, solid earth to be able to walk on, and continue their lives. I am standing there to be able to be there for them at the time that they need me. I feel I have no other duty in this world, but to just be there for my children.

No one could believe me, my dear God, except you, who are in me, and you are guiding me towards the possibility of making my wish come true. Otherwise, I don't know what is the purpose of my living.

I remember during his first affair, when my father advised me to reconcile and go back to him, he said to me, "You are not alone any more to just leave him. You have children, who depend on you and your decisions about their lives".

His words and his voice still are in me. I know that until I die, I must feel the responsibility of parenthood, no matter what. It was for my own pleasure that I gave them life, so I had to stick by them. "How I will be able to continue? I really don't know".

Suddenly I remembered something. Before our divorce became final, Iraj came to Michigan to finish up the legal work. He stayed in my condominium. I had to work at the restaurant. During that week Mrs. Shushtari had invited us for dinner. As I said before, I never talked directly to anyone, unless they got it first hand from his mistress. The night of the party Iraj came to get me to drive to the Shushtari's together. The next day everyone who watched us, were talking about our reconciliation. It was all because they saw that Iraj politely opened the car door for me, and we drove away. When Farah asked me if it

was true, I answered her, "This has always been his usual behavior. It was nothing new".

At that time my feelings for him were still very strong. His birthday was my dream day. I was always looking forward to getting him a gift with a loving silly card. Before he came to Michigan, I had purchased a beautiful chocolate rose in a box. I added a good-bye card in it to symbolize that it was my last birthday gift for him. At that time I still did not believe that he was going to marry her. How dumb I was! What a stupid, naive Shamci! With this dumbness, you deserved what you got.

My Dear God:

I prepared myself to move into Mitra's house, and rent out my condo. I thought since I was so afraid of being alone, and since I was spending most of the nights with either Farah, Simeen, and mainly Ida, why not move in with one of them, pay them some money for the rent, and feel comfortable, while living with a family. Since I had lost my own family, I could bring joy into my life by living with other families.

I had already given away most of my furniture. I had no time to wait for the right buyers. Places that I called from the yellow pages, they either did not want any furniture, or they were not willing to pay the price. Particularly no one was interested in my piano, or the billiard table. So I had to beg some of my friends to convince their friends that it was a really good deal. Hossain Houshmand, Ali Houshmand's brother, found me a buyer among his friends.

When we moved out of our house I had to pay eight hundred dollars to move that billiard table, and reassemble it. Now that I was trying to sell it, people wanted to charge me for removing it from my house. So when this family expressed interest to pay four hundred dollars for it, I could not refuse their offer. They had to go through disassembling it, moving it to their house, and then reassembling it again. Since I had to remove it from that house before we moved out that was the only answer to my problem.

I had to do the same thing with my piano. Since none of us had a home at that time, I had to get rid of it for practically nothing. What a shame! What a hopeless life! Whoever thought of Iraj putting us in this kind of situation, after he spent most of his life to please us. Whoever would believe that Iraj would play and destroy his success the way he did. And whoever could imagine that Iraj could do such a stupid act after crying and apologizing twenty-five years prior to this time. But he did it. And he thought he did the right thing, and he was proud of it. Well, let it be.

I gave many of my clothes, and some of my furniture away to Salvation Army. Some of my stuff was packed, and were stored in Mojgan's house. And many of my belongings were packed and ready to go to Mitra's basement. So one weekend with the help of Mr. Hossainy, who was working at the restaurant, I moved out of my condo, and I started to live in one of Mitra's bedrooms, which was on the second floor.

My Dear God:

Although I left some of the stuff, which I didn't really needed in my locker at the condo, and I paid six hundred dollars to Mr. Hossainy for carrying one load on his truck, at the end he was not satisfied. He was probably thinking, "This woman is in need, and I should take advantage of the moment". But I let him think that way, and I did not pay him any more.

While I was waiting for Ida and Mehrdad to finish their house, I became housemates with Mitra, her boy friend Syamac, and her son Ideen. I started my living in their house as a member of their family. They were like my children, and we did our own things, and were very respectful to each other. Since I was not that kind of person, who allowed my problems and my sadness stay on the surface, and destroy other people's happiness, we tried to create a happy living together.

You see, my dear GOD, those days that I was caught in the middle of those situations, it felt so long and so painful to just pass a day that at times I thought it would never end. But now that I am writing about it, and I realize that all those had happened to me, and they were not ever going to come back, I feel relieved. It was as I was born again and had become a new person. I can just imagine that this is just a story that I am reading. Sometimes I laugh, sometimes I cry, and sometimes I tell Shamci, who had the top role, "Good for you that you were able to make it. Good for you that you did not allow Iraj to destroy you and your children. And good for you that you still can live with your head up, and let Iraj figure out for himself what he had done right or wrong.

Anyway, Maseeh was in LA, and our contact was very scarce. We never talked about our family, usually we would talk about some unrelated to our family matters. Sometimes he talked about himself.

Mojgan, had her own house, was now living with Joe, and she was still at Western University in Kalamazoo. She used to call me often, and once in a while I went to visit her, or they came to visit me.

You remember, my dear GOD, that from the beginning my children were aware that right after Malakuti's death, their father was having an affair with Badri. They even knew much more than I knew. But because of the severity of the pain that they were going through, and their father was not available to take the blames, they found it easy to attack me, and blame me for something, which was not my fault.

Nothing surprised me more than one evening when Mojgan called me at the restaurant. It was after her father's marriage. She was full of sadness and anger. It was the busiest time of the night, and I wished I could be with her to be able to hold her head on my shoulder, and let her talk to me and cry. But since that wasn't the case, she said to me angrily, "Why did you let her win? Why you did not try harder? Why should you let her win?" She was sobbing, and she was ready to kill someone, or break the telephone.

My Dear God:

You tell me, my dear GOD, this was my girl, who wrote in her diary, “Since Dr. Malakuti died, my father hates me”. She wrote this in the year 1981,right after his death. They knew that I fought the situation for eight years. They knew that my life had been upside down during all those years. But one thing they did not know about their father was that how ruthless he was. How cold and emotionless he was, when it came to the subject of his loved ones, like his mother, when she died, and his children, when he killed their emotions without feeling their sadness and their unhappiness.

If she was able to tell me, “Why didn’t you try harder, not to let her win”, now, after my struggle for eight years, what would she had done to me if I had divorced him right after I found out about his affair with Badri? If she could find me guilty now, after fighting for eight years to be able to keep my family together, what would she had done to me if I didn’t try at all? At that time for the first time I felt good for what I did during all those years. I realized that if they think about it, they would know that I had done my best not to let it happen.

After what she told me that night, I got so sad and emotional that I couldn’t concentrate. There was no one to understand me. I never talked to anyone, because I didn’t want to make anyone involved in my private life.

After I got home, I walked and cried all night. I felt guilty again. I thought my children are hurting all because of my mistakes. For me marrying Iraj was a big crime. They are in this world, and suffering so much, because I did wrong. There was nothing for me to be able to correct it. What have I done to my children? What could I do to make them feel any better? “God, please let me know how do I get rid of their pain”. But I did not have any solutions. So I just took their attacks, each time they had to get rid of their anger.

After a month or so that I was living in Mitra’s house, one day Mary called me. For a change she was not in a bad mood. She asked me if she could come over to visit. It made me very happy to see Mary was actually accepting my stay with Mitra. She came over a few times, and I made her things that she liked the most. One Sunday she came over and brought her dog with her. We had lunch together with Mitra and Syamac that day, and for the first time after a very long time, I saw Mary having fun with me. We talked of many subjects. After lunch she washed her dog on the grass in their backyard. We had a very good time together. She was happy for me that I was living with Mitra’s family. For me, who knew Mary very well, I was surprised to see her in that mood. But Mitra and Syamac didn’t know anything about our lives and our differences. They didn’t know how much trouble I had to be able to see Mary happy.

My Dear God:

I had always believed that my problems were my own, and that I should not involve others with my family problems. Obviously because I saw her very happy, I asked her to visit me more often. I thought since I was paying them rent, there would be no problem if my daughter wanted to visit me. I had even told her that we go to movies together, like we always did. My purpose was to show her that I was comfortable, and there was nothing for her to worry about. I was hoping that she could do something about her own life, and start living a happy life again. I was hoping that she could forget about the past.

I really didn't know what was going on between her and her boy friend Tom. I knew that by losing her home, her security, her family, and her boy friend she was desperately looking for some miracle to rescue her from all the pain and agony. I thought that maybe by seeing me, looking forward to a happy life, she could convince herself to do the same. But I was not sure if she could do that.

My dear God, this was my beautiful Mary, who was my heart, my eyes, and was adored by everyone, especially the love of her father. This was the same Mary that her father was pleased to buy her a new car on her sixteenth birthday. This was the same Mary, whose father built a seven thousand square feet house, with an indoor swimming pool for her. Her own complete suite with her own bath and shower, her own stereo, intercom, telephone, and all that she had ever asked for. Now she was far away from those whom she loved. She was living in Detroit, in an apartment, barely big enough to fit her bed and a dog cage. She was living in a dangerous neighborhood, where people got killed daily. How could I expect her to be okay, and forget all about the past? Where was that father, who wanted to do everything for his family? I guess he did it only to be able to make a big name for himself. I never wanted to bring more pain to her by asking her, "What happened to that father, who you thought was innocent, and was not after Badri? Where is that nice father who was always buried under the Wall street Journal searching for ways to make more money for his family?" I never allowed myself to get nasty with my children. They were absolutely destroyed by his act; there was no need for me to remind them. I just wanted to find a way to her heart to bring her some hope.

It had been several months that I lived in Mitra's house. Ida's house was still under construction. They had to enlarge the closet in my room, and add a new door. Meanwhile I was feeling comfortable in Mitra's house. One Saturday Mary called me to let me know that she was coming over, and again she brought her dog along. That afternoon Mitra had to go to work, and stay there till late. When Mary came, she thought of washing her dog again, since it was a nice day to do that. She needed some kind of dog shampoo. She asked Syamac for a place where she could get it. Since she was not familiar with the neighborhood, Syamac offered to go with her. The place happened to be close by. They got the shampoo, and Mary washed her dog. After we played with the dog, we decided to go and see a movie.

My Dear God:

I thought I better ask Syamac, and invite him to come to movies with us. I thought first of all he was home by himself, and secondly, because he was so nice to help Mary. I didn't see anything wrong with it.

Since I had a very respectful relationship with Mitra, Syamac and Ideen, I thought inviting him was a polite thing to do.

At first Syamac did not want to accept my invitation, but after I insisted, he agreed to come with us. We chained the dog to a tree in their backyard, and went to see a movie. It had never occurred to me that I was doing something wrong. Before we left, a couple of their friends stopped by. We asked them to accompany us. They did, and we went to see a movie together. It seemed that everyone had a good time. For me to be able to see Mary happy was an exciting time. When she left, I thought that maybe God was rewarding me after the eight years of such a painful life. I asked her to come and see me again soon. And she agreed to that.

Next day I told Mitra all about what we did and where we went, unaware of knowing that other people might have interpreted our movie outing in a wrong light. Two days later Mitra, who had obviously been talking to her friends came to me, and started accusing me for trying to trap Syamac, for my Mary. You know my dear God, that the only thing that had never even come closed to such a fatal thought in my mind was that accusation. I was getting close to finding some light in my life being able to see Mary laughing again. Neither Mary, nor I had ever considered such a ruthless act. This was the time that I got mad at you, my dear God. I questioned you, "Aren't you the most merciful, the kindest, the most powerful, the most intelligent, and the most knowledgeable? Why did you let me invite Syamac to that movie, while you knew perfectly what was becoming of it? Why did you want to take that little hope in me, and test my pain resistance to such an extent? If you knew what was in my mind, why didn't you give this power to Mitra so that she too saw the genuineness of my thoughts? And why, why, why? I just wanted to be human. Wanted to be polite and courteous to a friend, who was a gentleman without having any wrong ideas in my mind. How could I explain to Mitra that she was wrong? Was it worth it to discuss my life and my situation with her? No, it obviously wasn't. I was not going to let anything bother Mary. Mitra was a woman with a young son, who had found a young educated man to hopefully marry him soon. So to herself she might have thought that a beautiful young lady lawyer might have been more suitable for Syamac. After she gave it a possibility in her mind, she thought, "I better stop the action right from the start". I thought Mitra was so far away from the reality. I did not even want to try convincing her, or explain anything to her. I wasn't that kind of a person to think or act in that category of people. I just informed Mitra, "I think you are talking to a wrong person. After the month is over, I will move out of your house, and you will be safe forever".

My Dear God:

Once again I was in a life and dead situation. Since I didn't want to hurt Mary more than she had already been hurt, I did not want to tell her the truth. She already knew that because Ida's house was ready I was going to move there. The next day I informed Ida that I was ready to move to her house by the end of the month.

Mehrdad and Ida were so nice and excited that right away they got to work, and finished my room. Although Ida still hesitated to believe me that I had planned to move into her house right after they were done with the construction, still she was happy that I was moving to her house. And I didn't even want to let her know what Mitra had accused me of.

Ida and Mehrdad got to work to be able to make my room ready for me, especially that my condo was rented out, and I did not have any place to stay if their house was not ready. I will never forget Mehrdad's and Ida's kindness to me. Not even my own family could have been that nice to me. They both tried so hard to make me feel at home. Their son Cyrous also was very happy to see me there. I have never seen anyone working as hard as Mehrdad did. During the day he worked at an electrical company, and in the evening in another company, and then, when he got home he had to carry all that wood upstairs, and he worked till dawn. I don't know when he slept during the night. I was so worried for him. I kept reminding him that this way he might create a big problem for his health. But he always said, "I have to. I have no choice".

Right after their wedding, when they moved into that house, the upstairs was just an attic. That was the time that they had rented out that part to Mitra and her son Ideen. After she moved out and started her life with Syamac, Ida thought of making that attic into a second floor. And so they did. With non-stop hard work they made it to a full suite, with a full bath, and everything for Cyrous. So with moving to Ida's house, I didn't let Mary know that her visit in Mitra's house had caused a big jealousy scene. And I just had to speed up my move to Ida's house.

My Dear God:

Although at that time the relationship between Ida and Mitra was not a peaceful one, still Mitra had warned Ida from the possibility of Shamci's wrong plans. She talked to her, and how she had accused me of planning to make Mary and Syamac close to each other. But luckily, Ida was smart enough to know that neither I was that kind of person, nor Mary was ever thinking of such a thing.

Mary was my only concern. I was trying so hard not to involve her with that kind of nonsense. She didn't have enough room in her mind to deal with this kind of discrepancies. I wanted to keep her away from any kind of disputes.

You see, my dear God, step-by-step, day-by-day, what was arranged for us, took

place without being planned by me. I felt exactly like a balloon on the water. I was being pushed away, and thrown from side to side without knowing where I wanted to go. But the important thing that I must mention is that you have never left my side. You were the one, who was moving our balloon in the right direction. So I didn't need to bring my problems to anyone. I didn't have to show weakness to anyone in order to gain something. I don't know who you are, or how you are watching over me at all times, but I know one thing, and only one thing, that it is your support that has been keeping me together. You always were the one who patched things together for me. Thank you!

True that things were falling into place for me, just enough to be able to keep my head up. But the loss of my family, home and children was always in my mind, and there was no way to get rid of it. At nights I either couldn't sleep at all. Or if I was lucky to fall sleep for only few hours, I had nightmare. The things, which had happened to me during all those years, were reoccurring to me, and made it look real. Sometimes, to avoid those kinds of feelings, I went to bed with my clothes on, so that I could jump out of my bed as soon as I woke up with in sweats. I wanted to get out of my conscience, and that was only possible if I had the courage to put a gun to my head. But since that was not an option, you have brought these nice families my way, and they made my life a little more tolerable.

These people never left me alone. Regardless of where Ida was invited, be that her sister's, or her brother's house, I was invited too. If sometimes I had to visit my other friends, Mehrdad teased me, "First of all drive carefully. Second, you must know that your curfew time is nine o'clock, and you must be home by then". And I promised them that I would be home on time. And we all laughed.

My Dear God:

Every morning Mehrdad was the first person to leave the house to go to work. The city's rule was not to park cars on the main street at night. Some nights, when I came home late, Mehrdad would wait for me to park my car at the end of the driveway, just because he did not want to wake me up to move my car. Many times I was so embarrassed from so much respect and kindness. Most of the times when the snow was above our knees, Mehrdad got my key to be able to do both cars by himself. He didn't want me to go through trouble. He was a real gentleman. I always thought it was because his mother had been away from him for a long time. He might have been thinking of his own mother, which I thought was very nice of him.

Ida and I went everywhere together. We cooked together, sew together, cleaned together, and we played lots of Backgammon together. Although people were talking about Ida's drinking and other stuff, I personally had found out that she was a good girl. And she wanted to do right. So by me living with her, she was trying to do right according to the family standards. People, who always look for something to gossip about, had been questioning the reason behind me living with Ida's family. But I never paid attention to

those gossips.

The way that Ida was talking about herself, and the way that her family agreed to that, she had been a troubled girl. And still she was not an easy person to deal with. But with me she was a completely different person. She loved to be with me just because I made her stay away from trouble. She knew it herself, and her family knew it too.

One Sunday her mom Letafat, and her sisters Ziba, Shahla, and Panny were having dinner in our house. We all had a good time. When they were leaving, her mother turned to me and said, "I would like to thank you for coming here and living with Ida. She has been a changed girl, and she seems very happy. Thank you from the bottom of my heart". I was happy to be there, and I wanted to be of any help to them. But unfortunately I couldn't be as helpful as I wanted to.

I always felt that I owed Ida and Mehrdad for the way they treated me. They both did their best to make me feel comfortable while I lived with them. They were very polite, very courteous, very respectful, and always tried to be there for me. I wish that wherever they are, and whatever they do, they could bring peace and happiness in their lives and their hearts.

Unfortunately, neither Ida, nor Mehrdad tried to live peacefully together. Whatever he liked to do, be that watching TV, especially the news, and not being very affectionate to Ida at all times, was not acceptable by Ida. On the other hand Mehrdad did not appreciate Ida's drinking on many occasions. And many little things, which created long lasting quarrels between them. And the responsibility over taking care of Cyrous did not help the matters to become any easy on both of them. So the more arguments they had, the more distant they had become both physically and emotionally.

My Dear God:

Despite of how many times I tried to talk to them, it didn't work, neither one of them tried to change. But as long as I was there, I kept them away from violence. But when I was away for a month or so, I heard that they did nasty things to each other, and they involved the police in their affairs. Too bad I couldn't be of any help to them, and at the end after all the hard work that have done together to make that house look like a home, they ended up with a violent divorce.

From the moment that Ida and I met at the restaurant, she had the greatest respect for me. Little by little she became inseparable from me. When she didn't have a car, I gave her a ride to work every day, since her house was on my way to the restaurant. She could talk so sweet for hours, and I never got tired of her talking. She was into poems and Farsi literature in general. She knew many famous poems familiar to both of us. She loved to drive in rainy days, and talk about her family and her past, and the love between her and her ex husband.

Before I moved into her house, every night without any exception, she called me at

the restaurant to remind me that her house was open to welcome me to sleep there. This person, who forgot many things most of the times, she never allowed herself to forget to call me. Since Mehrdad was working very late, she wanted to make sure that at the end of the day I go there, and we could have fun by playing Backgammon. Most of the times she was the winner, and she collected the one-dollar award. That was the best fun for us, and made us both forget what was going on around our lives. She was very happy that I was there every night, and I was very happy that I was invited to her house.

This was the main reason that she decided to offer me to move in with them, and meanwhile I paid rent for the room that I had. Existence of Ida and Mehrdad was a miracle to my loneliness. The only thing that I was afraid of was to be alone. God had introduced this family to me to help me rid myself of my biggest fear, without getting involved with any emotions. This was a blessing for me, to help me rise above my only weakness, which was, and could be very destructive to me.

How could I explain this to anyone? That it was only the power above me, or in me, which helped me day by day, and how to start my day, and how to get prepared for next day to come. If, it wasn't GOD, then who was that power that made things possible to bring me peace of mind? And who was that power that was helping me find the right way to be able to deal with my problems? I just don't know.

My Dear God:

While I was learning to live my life, I was concerned about both Mojgan, and especially Mary. She was the one who always worried me. By calling her more often, I realized that she did not want to be bothered by my telephone calls. Most of the time she was rude to me. She wanted to hurt me, and shut the door of our communication.

One day I thought that I must not let her be so isolated from the outside world. I called her to talk to her. The way that she sounded did not make me very happy. I smelled a severe depression. I asked her to let me see her. With complete hesitation, and after a lot of thoughts she agreed that I go see her one evening. When I got there, she just said, "Hi", and sat there. The house looked untidy. I started to wash her dishes, and tidy up the room. She was not in a mood for anything. I didn't know how to start a conversation. After we ate, and I started to talk to her, I realized that her father had been in town, and he had sold our condo we bought for Mary In Ann Arbor.

Obviously I was very shocked. Our agreement was to split in half whatever we had. How dared he come to Michigan, and sold a property without my knowledge. Most of all, that property was bought for Mary. How ruthless can he get to come and get Mary's signature, and take his daughter's money out of her hand? As soon as I opened my mouth to say, "That apartment belonged to both of us, and half belonged to you. He did not have any right to sell it without my consent", all of a sudden she raised her voice at me and with anger she said, "It was his apartment, it was his money. Everything is his. He doesn't want

to give it to you. Why don't you leave him alone?"

I realized that with the condition that Mary was in, and the way that he had poisoned her mind, I better stop talking to her about the matters, which could complicate her mind more than before.

Soon I realized that he had been able to turn my children against me. I had no choice but to leave it as it was. My children were not guilty of any wrongdoing. If he was capable of making them like a football in the middle, and play with their emotions to be able to save his head, I let him do that. Until now I had given up everything else, so let him take as much as he could. It was not me, who needed to prove my love for my children. My love for them has been there, and will always be there. It is him, who had to destroy their minds to be able to buy their love for him. I don't love my children in order to take their love back. It is my duty to love them without any in return. So I am not going to let him to destroy my children with my help. What he had done was already enough to destroy them.

My Dear God:

When I went home, again I couldn't fall asleep. All night I cried and talk to God to help my baby from farther disasters. I knew that something was very wrong with Mary, but I didn't know how to help her. Day after day she was getting more and more depressed, and moodier than before. I never wanted to talk about my children to anyone. I knew that people would use your words, and they would try to make a big case out of it. I wanted to look for the right answers, and not make them the subject of gossip.

So as always I talked to Dr, Mehrabian, and I mentioned that Iraj had sold the apartment in Ann Arbor, half of which was Mary's, and the other half was ours. And he had left me out of my share. But the only thing that I wanted to make sure to happen was that he gave Mary's share back.

The only person that Iraj had respect for, and he wanted to make himself look good in his eyes, was Dr. Mehrabian. So after he talked to him on the phone, and demanded that, "Mary's share of money must be deposited in her bank account", Iraj assured him that he had deposited five thousand dollars into her account. But I knew for sure that he didn't do it. Because if he had deposited that money into her account in California, she would have had a good credit to be able to buy a cell phone, when she was in California. While this was not a case, and because she did not have a good credit, she had to use my name, and buy her cell phone with my credit.

Again I didn't bring up this matter to Mary, and did not ask her about the five thousand dollars in her account. I knew that she couldn't help it if she had a crooked father, and by mentioning it I would have only made the matters worse. So he made Mary's share disappear, and he never gave me my share. Yes, I didn't have a lawyer to defend me. The reason was that I did not want to pay any attorney fees. I am sure if I had a lawyer to defend me, I would have had more money right now. So I let one crook steal my money rather than two.

This Mary, who was rude and hostile to me under the influence of her father, was in reality such a loving and caring girl. One day before she started law school, she had been planning to get her PHD. That day she had appointment with an advisor. We drove together, and we planned to go out to lunch afterwards. After she had her interview with her advisor, she was upset that she had scared her about the difficulties of getting PHD. I was mad to find out that the advisor instead had discouraged her. I questioned Mary, "Why didn't you ask her how she did it? You should have told her that you are going to achieve it the same way she did". Here is my point. That day at lunch she was completely herself. We discussed many subjects. She was concerned about Mojgan's future. In a very positive way she said, "I wish I could work hard to afford to open up trust fund for Mojgan's higher education. And I would like to be able to take care of you and my father when you are older". And many more statements like that.

My Dear God:

Look now. What did we do to this innocent and loving girl? Would anyone please interpret the meaning of crime? Look what we had changed Mary to! From that loving, caring, innocent girl we have made her mad and angry, emotionless, unstable, and rude girl. Between the three of them, she was the only one who showed me her concern about her family. If it wasn't her father's actions, and mine what was the reason behind all her madness? Why would she be destroying herself? Why do we bring these children into the world for our own pleasure, and soon we forget what our duties are? Without any knowledge about parenting we only create monsters. Why was my beautiful Mary no longer the same nice girl?

Iraj not only took all our money before our divorce, and hid it or spent it on other people, but he continued to do so after even our divorce was final. As I said before, I was not familiar with any legal matters, and tax papers. I used to take all the papers, which he sent to me to be signed to Dr. Mohammad Rabbani. He was his ex-partner in some of the properties, and he knew exactly what I should do and what I shouldn't. Many times he would inform me of Iraj's discrepancy over making me signing the tax papers, which he was supposed to pay himself. He always deducted the money from my monthly alimony, before I had a chance to ask him for the reason. Each time, when Dr. Rabbani asked me, "Why does he have to take this money away from you? This must be paid by him", I answered him that since I didn't have a lawyer, and he had the money, I could not fight him. Besides he had robbed me so big that these little things were not worth fighting.

I never talked to my children about these matters that he often did to me. I never wanted to make their minds even more clouded. They were not responsible for my life anyway. Therefore this information would only hurt them more. How would I benefit from involving them with our affairs?

ESPLANADE OB-GYN MEDICAL CLINIC, INC.

Iraj Rafani.

June 29, 1995

Today I deposit $3000 to your account with Coast Federal Bank

$1000 for 1/2 July Payment
$2000 for August Payment

I have sent you check 5-5-95 for $5000

$1000 for 1/2 July Payment
$4000 for May and June Payment

Beginning Sept 1, 1995 I will deposit $2000 every month for your account at Coast Federal saving

No matter how many different ways I found to deal with him so he would pay my money and not wait for me to call him and remind him, he would not understand me. He kept deducting from my share here and there, and I never tried to challenge him. I knew that he was there to hurt me and possibly send me to a mental institution. I, on the other hand, decided to let him do what he wished to do. I knew that he was ready to destroy all of us to show that he can do what he wants to do. Neither had I wanted to take him to court to prove that he does not love me. By then, it was too obvious that not only he didn't love me, but he didn't love his children either. There was no way for me to take him to court to prove that. So I let him take away as much money as he wanted out of my checks. For me, everything was over. I didn't need to spend so much money on lawyers to go after a little money from Iraj. And, when once Dr. Rabbani who was supervising me on some of my paper works told me, "Shamci, these taxes are not supposed to be deducted from your check." I answered him, "I'd rather not fight with a rootless person like Iraj. I don't want to pay lots of money to lawyers to be able to get a little back. I need my spending money, and I think I better let him finish destroying us."

P.O.Box 6029 • Oxnard, California 93031 • (805) 983-2226

ESPLANADE OB-GYN MEDICAL CLINIC, INC.

Iraj Rafani.

چک سپتامبر و اکتبر را هم هفته پیش پست کردم.
نامه شما دیروز رسید - چک جدید ضمیمه است.

همانطور که می‌بینید مبلغ ۳۳۹۱ دلار است زیرا ۱۲۱۸ دلار که مالیات
زمین ۵ ساله آ درنز دیا است یکجا پرداخت کردم که نصف آن سهم شما می‌شود و البته این مقدار را
شاید بتوانید از Tax کم کنید به هر حال مدارک مربوط به پرداخت این Tax را با نامه قبلی که
شکوفه نرسیده فرستاده بودم و حالا دو سر نسخه کپی آنها را ضمیمه میکنم

As you see I am sending you the check for amount of $ 3391,00 for the months of Sep and oct 1993. The rest which is $ 609 was paid for the t[illegible] property.

NBD **Transaction Receipt**

This is your receipt for the transaction described below.

First Line Shows: Bank # — Branch # — Teller #, Process Date, Serial #, Internal Bank Code

پول ماه سپتامبر و اکتبر
۶۰۹ دلار از آن مالیات
زمین الکساندریا برای ۵ سال هم کرده است

6914 3 9[illegible]

032-085-07 10/01/93 ( ) TC-18
DDA 165107407 3,391.00 CL 1220

Second Line Shows: Account Type, Account Number, Amount, Transaction Type, Sequence No.

[illegible] Reverse Side)

FHP
A Health Maintenance Organization

Iraj Rafani, M.D.
Obstetrician and Gyencology
F.A.C.O.G.

June 21, 1989

Correction and amendment of divorce settlement dated 2-27-89 between IRAJ RAFANI and Slamci RAFANI.

Both IRAJ RAFANI referred to as the "Husband" and Slamci RAFANI, thereafter referred to as the "wife", that Paragraph 3 to be changed as following (according to prior verbal agreement)

Paragraph 3 - It is acknowledged by the parties that wife is the sole owner of an unencumbered, fully paid for Condominium in her name alone, located at 3565 Port Cove Drive #76 Michigan 48054, and that under no circumstances does husband have any interest therein. Wife alone shall be entitled to any federal, or state Tax deduction or Credits attributable to her ownership of this Condominium and her payment of the real state Taxes. Wife hereby indemnifies and will hold husband harmless from any liabilities or claims against him for any indebtedness incurs after the date of divorce Judgment [illegible]

Witness to the signature of IRAJ RAFANI

[signature]

IRAJ RAFANI

witness to the signature of Slamci RAFANI

Marie C Juba
Postal Clerk

[signature]

Slamci RAFANI

PLAZA MEDICAL CAMPUS
2925 NO. PALO VERDE AVENUE, LONG BEACH, CA 90815 (213) 429-2473

What can a wife in my condition and the way he robbed me, think about this letter? In this letter, he was trying to play it safe. He got my signature under this letter to make sure that later on I would not have anything to say. What a clever man!

I wish I did not need to get any money from him at all. But, I had spent half of my life with him to make him rich. To be able to destroy whatever we had made together was one thing, and to be able to steal everything from me and my children was something else.

I haven't asked him what happened to the night club in Detroit. I haven't asked him what happened to Hollywood Live, the night club in Hollywood, California. I haven't asked him what happened to all those checks you made me write for Hollywood Live for fifty, sixty thousands of dollars as often as it happened. But, I am hoping someone questions you once and asks you, "Iraj, do you know how much money you owe Shamci and her children? Don't you think you are one of the best professional thieves who have ever lived on this Earth? Don't you?"

I survived the best possible way that a woman in my condition could survive. I managed to help my three children to purchase their beautiful houses. I was able to be there for them with love and understanding as many times as they turned to me. Not only did they not hurt you for destroying me, but they learned to love you. These are indeed the children whom I raised.

ESPLANADE OB-GYN MEDICAL CLINIC, INC.

Iraj Rafani.

I have translated this letter on the back. But I wish, I could write his real explanation for getting all the money which was mine. The person who wanted the whole world for me, now is stealing from me left and right, and he believes that he has right to do so. Just shame on you, man.

در پاسخ نامه ژانویه ۱۰-۱۹۹۸

۱- یک نسخه کامل از حساب‌های Profit Sharing Fund و Pension Fund ضمیمه این نامه است و این همانطور که نشان میدهد آخرین Statement است.

۲- چندین دفعه سعی کرده‌ام که با نماینده بیمه در شیکاگو تماس بگیرم و نسخه بیمه‌ای که مربوط به شما است برایم بفرستد که بعداً ارسال دارم. هرچه زودتر برسد خواهم فرستاد

۳- راجع به زمین Troy چون شرکت است نسخه اصلی آن در دست محمد ربانی است و حالا هم مدتهاست که برای فروش گذاشته‌اند متأسفانه مشتری پیدا نشده است. و مشخصات دقیق آنرا از اداره شهرداری City of Troy بگیرید.

۴- راجع به فروش اپارتمان Ann Arbor - همانطور که با موافقت خودتان بود که باقی مانده بود که حدود ۱۰۰۰۰ دلار بود به اسم مریم در حساب جاری او گذاشته‌ام و این پول از اول برای او بوده و بابت خرج تحصیل او بوده است و حالا هم که مرخصی است باید برای روز مبادا در اختیارش باشد. و اگر شما اصرار دارید اگر خود مریم موافقت کرد نصف آنرا برداشته و به شما بدهد.

۵- چکی که بابت Tam باسم شرکت بود با موافقت خود شما بخاطر ضررهای فراوانی که در کلاب متحمل شدیم و تمام اثاثیه زندگی و آپارتمان Pontiac را برای شما خریدیم باسم خودم دریافت کردم و البته در این مورد چندین نفر شاهد هستند که خودتان با این کار موافقت کردید.

هر موقع نامه بیمه رسید خواهم فرستاد.

با تقدیم احترام - دکتر ایرج رفانی

P.O.Box 6029 • Oxnard, California 93031 • (805) 983-2226

Answer to the January 1995 letters.

1 Enclosed I am sending a copy of penssion and profit sharing plan statement. these are the last statement I have recived.

2 I have been trying to reach the New york life insurance agent, in Michigan. as soon as he sends me a copy, I will send it to you.

3 The toy property, has been for sale, long time now, and the original copy of the lease is with Dr. Rahbani, the other partner.

4 The Ann arbor APT was sold, and 10.000 $ is in Mary's account.

5 the income tax return check was cashed by me because of the lost on the Clinic.

with all due respect

Dr. I Rafani

(this rootless man was expecting me to have a big party for his wedding with Badri. Since it didn't happened, he is angry)

FHP *From the desk of* IRAJ RAFANI, M.D.

شمسی گرامی

لطفاً پشت چک ضمیمه را

امضا کنی و برایم هرچه زودتر

پست کنی. البته هزینه زیادی

هزینه های فرم های Tax را داده ام

که با تو حساب نکرده ام.

ممنونم. ایرج

ضمیمه بود که با چک [در یک صفحه] برای ایرج فرستادم.

This one is really for laugh.

Honorable Shamci: (No Date)
Kindly sign on the back of this check and mail it to me as soon as possible. Of course, I have spent excessive amounts of money on tax forms, which I haven't charged you for.

Isn't this really funny? Doesn't it really make you cry for me? And then, he signs, "I am grateful, Iraj."

July 31, 88

شمسی گرامی

پاکت ضمیمه حاوی مدارکی است که باید کامل کنی و هرچه زودتر پست کنی. این مال حساب Stock Market است که در سفر اخیر باسم مشترک من و تو شد.

۱- روی کاغذی که شماره ① گذاشتم باید امضاء کنی و دو نفر در محل Witness امضاء کنند. هرکس شرایط بعنوان شاهد امضاء کند.

۲- روی کارتی که شماره ② گذاشتم باید زیر اسم من امضاء کنی و شماره social security خودت را در محل این بنویسی

۳- روی کارتی که شماره ③ گذاشتم باید زیر اسم من امضاء کنی

امید سعادت و موفقیت ترا دارم - ایرج

July 31, 1988

Honorable Shamci,

As you see, he is sending me some papers regarding some kind of stock market, which is supposed to be under both of our names. He had given me the directions of how and what to do, and he wanted me to sign that paper and send it to him as soon as possible. And he signs it, "Wish you all the success and happiness, Iraj".

What a joke! What a phony man! If you think I was able to receive one penny of all these, you are mistaken.

From the desk of
IRAJ RAFANI, M.D.

Mi 1040 1988

شمسی گرامی

لطفاً این فرم ۱۹۸۸ Tax

سال State Michigan

را امضا کنی و هرچه زودتر پست کنی

ممنونم، ایرج

Mi 1040 1988
Honorable Shamci,
Please sign this 1988 form and send it to me as soon as possible.

Thank you,
Iraj

FHP

From the desk of
IRAJ RAFANI, M.D.

198,

540 N? Cali non resident tax

شمسی گرامی

لطفاً این فرم Tax 1988
را امضا کن و هرچه زودتر Mail
کن. ممنونم.
ایرج

Mi 540 N …
Honorable Shamci,
Please sign this 1988 form and mail it to me as soon as possible.

Thank you,
Iraj

Since I didn't want to divorce him and I did not take him to court, he wrote an agreement for both of us to sign. At this time I did not have anything, including health insurance.

FHP

From the desk of
IRAJ RAFANI, M.D.

۱۹ ژانویه ۸۹

شمسی گرامی

امیدوارم که سلامت باشی. کپی Agreement

ضمیمه است و اصل آنرا برای Mr. Michael Stein

فرستادم لطفاً برو پیش او و در صورت موافقت

آنرا امضاء کن و برایم بفرست. در صورت سؤالی

داشتی تلفن کن. راجع به Health insurance

همانطور که بارها به تو گفتم این نوع بیمه را که من

گرفتم و کاملاً از جیب خودم بهای آنرا می‌پردازم

همه دکترها و بیمارستانها آنرا قبول می‌کنند امیدوارم

که رفع نگرانیت شده باشد

ایرج

1/19/1989
Honorable Shamci,
I wish you good health. I am sending this agreement and a copy of it to Mr. Michael Stain's office. Please go there and if you agree, sign it and send it to me. If you have any questions, call me. Regarding the health insurance, as I have told you repeatedly, this insurance that I am paying for from my own pocket, is valid anywhere, and in any hospital. Don't worry.
Iraj.

To tell you the truth, these letters bother me as if it was happening right now. I am hoping that this book finishes one day, and I don't have to see any of his words or his handwritings again.

As you see this date is supposed to be 1990, but he had written 1970. Keep dreaming. I think he had lost his memory because he had had too much sex. Oh well.

July 30, 1990
Honorable Shamci,
Please sign this tax return check, and send it to me as soon as possible. But, of course I owe IRS for 1988 and 1989 and this refund that I am keeping is to pay the IRS. If not, I have to pay it with your share of money and mine. I have sent the money for August and September on one check, and after this, I will mail your checks to Dr. Rabbani. I wish you good health and happiness.
Iraj.
PS: Let me know if you are going to Iran, and when you are coming back.
I have sent a copy of this and the check to Lora.

اشتباه در تاریخ را ملاحظه کنید؟ 1990

FHP
From the desk of
IRAJ RAFANI, M.D.

۳۰ جولای ۱۹۷۰
شمسی گرامی
لطفاً این چک که مال سال ۱۹۸۷ است امضاء
کن و برایم زودتر بفرست. البته برای سال ۱۹۸۸ و
۱۹۸۹ مقدار زیادی Tax به IRS بدهکار
هستم که باید بدهم. و این در پرداخت آن Tax ها
کمک خواهد کرد و الا مجبوریم که از حساب خودم و تو
Tax این سال را به IRS بدهیم.
چک ماهیانه ماه آگوست و سپتامبر را برایت یکجا
فرستادم البته از ماه اکتبر اگر خواستی به دکتر ربانی
خواهم فرستاد.
امیدوارم که سلامت و خوش [باشی].
ضمناً بنویس که کی به ایران میروی
و کی برگشت مرا مطلع کنی.
ایرج
یک نسخه و چک را هم برای لورا فرستادم

Please pay attention to this man who thinks everyone is dumb except for him. I had asked him to send my checks to Dr. Rabbani, to make sure that he witnesses Iraj's activities, but he does not send this one that shows he was clearly cheating. When I showed Dr. Rabanni the letter and the refund check, he was totally against it. He told me, this amount must have been divided between you two. Besides, it is not your duty to pay any of them." The person Iraj has become now, is a person whom he hated to be, or talk about if he knew any. He hated any men or husbands who cheated on their wife and children. Now that is what he had become, and his name had become the subject of teasing and laughter. Oh my god! What happened to the man who was so honest, so reliable, so trustworthy, and so beautiful? What happened to that man that I was proud of being with? Why did you become a man that you never wanted to be? Well, even at the end of his cheating letter, he is showing concern about the fact that I was going to Iran and coming back.

FHP

From the desk of
IRAJ RAFANI, M.D.

4-6-90

شمسی گرامی

چک بمبلغ ۲۰۰۰ دلار ضمیمه است
این ماه دکتر Sarma پول نفرستاد بعلت
اینکه گویا دو ماه اضافه پول داده اند بنابراین
تا روشن شدن حسابها که همین ماه خواهد بود
پول نخواهد فرستاد البته از روشن شدن
حسابها با خبر خواهم کرد

ایرج

4/6/1990

Honorable Shamci,
Here is a check for 2000.00 dollars. Because Dr. Sarma thinks that she has paid two months' payment ahead of time, she will not send it this month until everything becomes clear, which is this month. So until then, we have to wait. If anything comes up, I will let you know.

Iraj.

FHP

From the desk of
IRAJ RAFANI, M.D.

سپتامبر ۳- ۱۹۹۰

شمسی گرامی

لطفاً چک ضمیمه را که صورتحساب Tax سال ۱۹۸۷
است امضاء و هر چه زودتر برایم بفرست. البته همانطور که
قبلاً نوشتم برای سال ۱۹۸۹ باید نزدیک ۱۳۰۰۰
دلار تاکس بدهم و علاوه بر آن هر ماه مقدار زیادی
از جیب خودم برای آپارتمان Ann Arbor
و بقیه تاکس زمین های که در میشیگان داریم میدهم و هرگز
از تو طلب نکرده‌ام. بنابراین فکر نمیکنم که محل سرزنش
و ملامت باشد و خیلی در این جریان باصطلاح Fair
بوده و همیشه طبق شرط ماهانه سر وقت پول ترا فرستاده‌ام
از مسافرت خودت به ایران که کی میروی و برمیگردی
مرا اطلاع بده امیدوارم که سلامت و موفق و خوش باشی
[illegible] ایرج

For those who can read these letters, it will be a lot of fun. Wouldn't it be nice if one good lawyer could come forward and find a way to teach him a lesson? If I am lucky, I might find one, just one lawyer who wants to prove to himself that he could really make a difference.

September 3, 1990
Honorable Shamci,
I am sending the tax refund of the year 1987 for you to sign and send back as soon as possible. As I have said before, for 1989 we must pay almost 13000.00 dollars in tax. On top of that, I must pay every month for Ann Arbor's apartment and tax on properties in Michigan out of my own pocket, but I have never asked you for any money. So, I think there is no need for you to condemn me at all. As far as I know, I have been fair, and I have paid you monthly and on time. Let me know when you are going to Iran, and when you are coming back. I wish you health, happiness, and success.
Iraj.

Well, these are all in the past. I am glad that my life ends like this, when and how it does. I was a lucky woman. I found my way of life. Now I know what happiness means. When you look at all the pictures, you will agree with me.

FHP

From the desk of
IRAJ RAFANI, M.D.

۱۹ ژانویه ۱۹۹

شمسی گرامی

لطفاً فرم ضمیمه را امضا کن و حتماً
به تصدیق یک Notary public رسیده باشه
و هرچه زودتر تا دیر نشده برایمان بفرست
این مربوط به وصل کردن آب شهر برای
منزلی که در Crooks Rd داریم میباشد
خواهش میکنم که این کار را هرچه زودتر انجام بدی

ایرج

1/19/1990

Honorable Shamci,
I am sending you this form. It has to be signed by you and the notary public. This is regarding connecting the city water to our house in Crooks Rd. Please do it as fast as possible.

Iraj.

FHP

From the desk of
IRAJ RAFANI, M.D.

3-1-90

شمسی گرامی

چک ماه March را ضمیمه برایت فرستادم

از این ماه یکی از قسط‌های دکتر شرما Dr. Sharma

که 1388.88 دلار است تمام میشود و فقط

چند ماه دیگر قسط 833.33 دلار ادامه خواهد داشت

بنابراین چک این ماه مجموع ۲۰۰۰ دلار ماهیانه

با اضافه نصف 833.33 که 416.60 $ میشود

میباشد. امیدوارم که سلامت و موفق باشی

شماره تلفن من در office می‌توانی زنگ بزنی.

805-983-2226.

ایرج

3/1/1990
Honorable Shamci,
I am sending March's check for 2000.00 dollars. From this month, one of Dr. Sharma's payments will be over. The other one that is for $833.33 will also be over soon. I am sending your share of 416.60 dollars. I wish you a healthy and successful life. You can call me at my office number: 805-983-2226

I never called him. When Mary was living in my house, I asked her to get her own line of telephone to be able to answer those who called her. I made a mistake once in my life. I do not want to repeat that mistake ever again. Marrying you was one thing, but coming back to you is another. Now, I would like to say that I must wash my ear if I ever hear your nasty voice.

FHP

A Health Maintenance Organization

Iraj Rafani, M.D.
Obstetrician and Gyencology
F.A.C.O.G.

پنجم مارچ ۱۹۹۰

شمسی گرامی

امیدوارم که سلامت باشی. Tax return سال ۱۹۸۷ ایالت میشیگان

لطفاً امضاء کن و هر چه زودتر آن را برایم بفرست. بچه‌ها را از طرف من ببوس.

ایرج

March 5, 1990
Honorable Shamci,
I hope that you are OK. Please sign this Michigan tax return of 1990, and mail it o me as soon as possible. Kiss the children for me.
Iraj.

On the back he had written:
July 11th, 1991
Honorable Shamci,
I am sending the copy of our legal divorce paper. You must sign it and send it to me as soon as possible with a copy of your birth certificate and this request. We must get to it, in order to finish the process of our divorce. If you have any questions, write to me or call.
Iraj.
PS: Of course, you must sign the enclosed letter.

I don't know what to comment about this man and his character. Obviously, millions of women had a man like him in their lives. I am not the first one, and I will not be the last. But, it hurts so much to find out that the only man who was my love, my supporter, my mentor in many ways, my heart, my family, and my only friend turn out to be the ugliest person and the most disloyal, dishonest, and by all means the most clever crook.

PLAZA MEDICAL CAMPUS
2925 NO. PALO VERDE AVENUE, LONG BEACH, CA 90815 (213) 429-2473

FHP

From the desk of
IRAJ RAFANI, M.D.

1988

1040 US. IND Incom. tax

شمسی عزیز

Federal Tax لطفاً فرم

۱۹۸۸ را امضاء نموده فوری

پست کن.

قربانت - ایرج

Honorable Shamci,
I am sending you this 1040 federal tax form. Please sign it and send it to me as soon as possible.

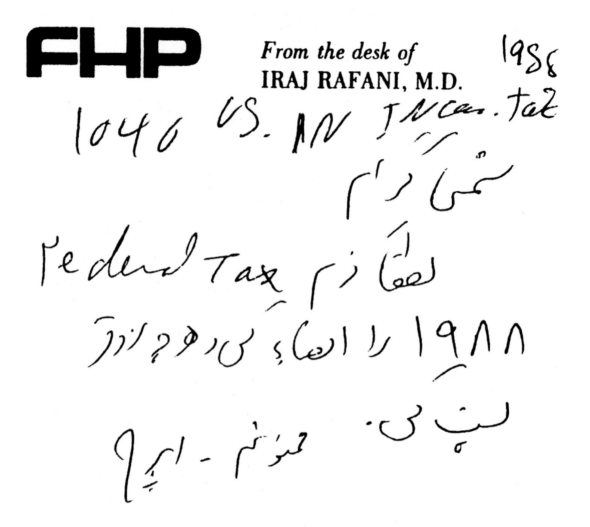

Thank you,
Iraj

FHP

From the desk of
IRAJ RAFANI, M.D.

۱۲ ژانویه ۹۰

شمسی گرامی

لطفاً فرم Tax ۱۹۸۷
را در محلی که علامت X قرمز دارد امضاء
کن و هر چه زودتر با Certified Mail
به آدرسی با پاکتی که توی آن هست با چک
ضمیمه بفرست. خیلی ممنون میشوم.
امیدوارم که سلامت و خوش باشی

ایرج

1/12/1990

Honorable Shamci,
I am sending this form of tax return. Please sign where I have marked red and make it certified mail, and put it in the self-address envelop which is there. I wish you good health and success. I thank you very much.

Iraj.

ESPLANADE OB-GYN MEDICAL CLINIC, INC.

Iraj Rafani, M.D.

۱۵ اکتبر ۱۹۹۲

شمسی گرامی

لطفاً Tax Return سال ۱۹۸۷ را امضاء کنی و با نامه
Power of attorney که برای دریافت چک IRS میباشد و باید به تصدیق
Notary public برسد برایم بفرست. متشکرم. سلامتی و موفقیت را خواستارم

ایرج

oct 16 1992

Dear Shamsi

Please sign the tax return of 1987, and enclosed Power of attorney. make sure to notarized them.

This has to be done for me to be able to cash the I.R.S. Check- wish you a good hea and success.

IRAJ

P.O.Box 6029 • Oxnard, California 93031 • (805) 983-2226

ESTRADERM®
estradiol transdermal system
0.05 mg and 0.1 mg

Jun 27, 90

شمسی گرامی

چک ماه جولای ضمیمه است. این آخرین
ماهی خواهد بود که از بابت فروش office
پول میگیرم. ربانی به من تلفن کرد که چک را هر ماه
برای او بفرستم. لطفاً به من خبر بده اگر
میخواهی برای او بفرستم. امیدوارم که سلامت
و خوش باشی
ایرج

CIBA
Closest to the ovary for estrogen replacement

June 27, 1990
Honorable Shamci,
I have sent the check for July which is the last payment from selling the office. Dr. Mohammad Rabbani called me and asked me to mail your checks to him. Please let me know if I must do so. I hope you are happy and OK.
Iraj.

Yes, at that time of my life I had lost all of my trust for him. He was not of any value to me. I wanted to be able to receive that little money which he had to pay me monthly. I knew that he wanted his friends to think of him as a nice and honest person. So, I had asked Dr. Rabbani to receive my checks from him every month. Otherwise, I was afraid that little by little he got rid of my money.

Feb 1, 1990
Honorable Shamci,
Because we were behind on the 1987 tax payment and I had paid 215 dollars, I am not paying the money from Dr. Sharma, and I will start sending you money from next month. Also, the furniture we have agreed to have them sent to me and the company said it was only 6 or 7 pieces. When I was in Michigan, we agreed on 25 pieces. You made me spend two thousand dollars for nothing. I hope you get to it and send me the rest as soon as possible. Of course, I have not received them yet, but I will receive them next week. I have tried to go through this divorce very peacefully and with both our agreements so we would not need to go to court or get a lawyer. Be aware of that. I have written my office address and telephone number on the back of this letter.

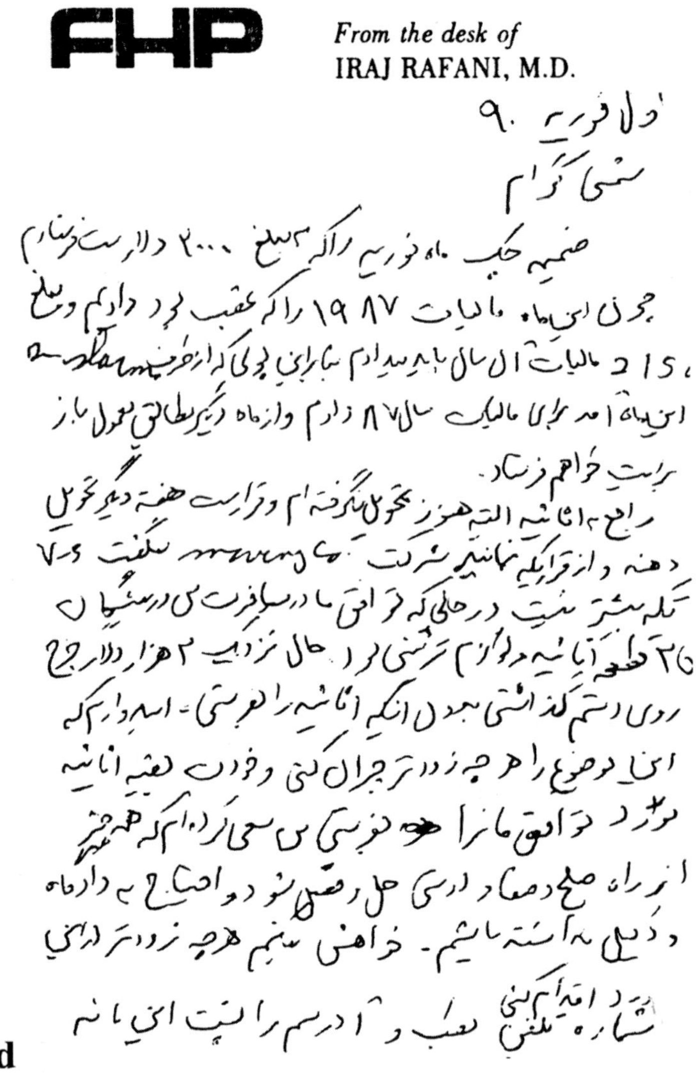
FHP

From the desk of
IRAJ RAFANI, M.D.

اول فوریه ۹۰
شمسی گرامی
ضمیمه چک ماه فوریه را که مبلغ ۲۰۰۰ دلار است می‌فرستم
چون این ماه مالیات ۱۹۸۷ را که عقب بود دادم و مبلغ
۲۱۵ د مالیات آن سال باید می‌دادم بنابراین پولی که از دکتر شرما
این ماه آمد برای مالیات سال ۸۷ دادم و از ماه دیگر طبق معمول باز
برایت خواهم فرستاد.
راجع به اثاثیه البته هنوز تحویل نگرفته‌ام و قرار است هفته دیگر تحویل
دهند و از قراری که نماینده شرکت movers به من گفت ۶-۷
تکه بیشتر نیست در حالی که توافق ما در مسافرت من در میشیگان
۲۵ قطعه اثاثیه و لوازم [illegible] بود حال [illegible] ۲ هزار دلار خرج
روی دستم گذاشتی بدون آنکه اثاثیه را بفرستی. امیدوارم که
این موضوع را هر چه زودتر جبران کنی و بقیه اثاثیه
مورد توافق ما را بفرستی. من سعی کرده‌ام که همه چیز
از راه صلح و صفا و درستی حل و فصل شود و احتیاج به دادگاه
و وکیل نداشته باشیم. خواهش می‌کنم هر چه زودتر اقدام کنی
شماره تلفن [illegible] و آدرسم را پشت این نامه

You see, when I say Iraj was and is really rootless, I am not mistaken. Because I knew him, I asked Dr. Rabbani to accept the responsibility of receiving my checks, just to put him in a do-or-don't situation. And I did the right thing. I also made sure that he cannot lie regarding the furniture. In front of the movers, I had made a list of the stuff that he had asked for, in English since they couldn't read Farsi. I asked them to write what they had received from me to take to California, and sign their name on it. I have a copy of it in Farsi and English which were signed by the movers on that date. I had chosen the wrong person for a husband. What a crook I had chosen to be my children's father! And what a happy and lucky woman I am to be able to live completely without him, his name, and his memory.

۱۱ جولای ۱۹۹۱

دفتر حفاظت منافع جمهوری اسلامی ایران - واشنگتن

اینجانب ایرج رفانی لطفی فرزند داودقلی در تاریخ ۲۸ June ۱۹۸۸ از دادگاه امریکا در میشیگان و در تاریخ ۱۱-۳-۱۳۷۰ توسط آقای کله داری در لوس انجلس از همسرم خانم شمسی السادات عزدی طلاق گرفته ام. موضوع مهریه و اموال ما با رضایت طرفین تعیین شده است و بچه های ما بالای ۱۸ ساله هستند و مستقل زندگی میکنند و بر علیه همدیگر هیچگونه ادعای و شکایتی نداریم

دکتر ایرج رفانی لطفی

ایرج رفانی

Dated july 11, 1991
This is his original letter to the embassy of the Islamic Republic of Iran in Washington. It is regarding our divorce, telling them that we have agreed to get a divorce without any disagreements, and that our children are above eighteen, and they are living independently.
Signed, Iraj Rafani

FHP

From the desk of
IRAJ RAFANI, M.D.

۱۱ جولای ۱۹۹۱

شمسی گرامی:

کپی ورقه طلاق شرعی را برایت فرستادم. همین
ها که دیروز از سفارت ایران بدستم رسید که امضاء کرده
و با اصل شناسنامه و اصل گذرنامه ات
را برایم بفرستی تا با مدارک دیگری که میخواهند
برایشان به دادگستری بفرستم و ترتیب موضوع
داده شود. اگر سئوالی داشتی بنویس یا
تلفن.

ایرج

البته ورقه ضمیمه را هم باید
امضاء کنی.

Honorable Shamci,
I have sent you a copy of the legal divorce papers. Sign it and send it to me with your original birth certificate. I will take care of the matter. If you have any questions, write or call me.

Iraj.

This is the sarcastic letter I wrote to him which I enclosed my divorce papers to. I thanked him for destroying our lives, just to bring shame on him. It is too bad that he does not have the intelligence to recognize the meaning of "shame". There are some people like Iraj who have to provide their own hell in this world, when they can have a heaven instead.

Once Dr. Mahajer's wife, Nazy asked me, "What was it that Iraj didn't have in his life that he tried to go and get? He had everything that any successful and happy man could ask for. Why did he have to destroy everything which he had worked for so hard to get? Why are some men so stupid?"

I am sure Nazy was not the only one who was puzzled by his stupid actions. Even he will ask himself, "Why did you do it? Why did you forget your first humiliation? Why did you let your stormy emotions destroy you when you were at the peak of your success and happiness?" well, I am not puzzled any more. I know for sure that he was not lucky.

On your fiftieth Birthday, my only dream-day, at Hilton Hotel, I told my friends : " my husband has been a very good husband, a very good father, and a very great person ";
and I meant that, because you really were.

With the kind of love you had for your family and your home, I never thought it will come to an end.

Now after seven years of struggle, I find myself having no choice, but signing my Death Certificate, meaning my divorce paper.

I thank you for killing my sole, destroying our family, and burning our home.

I will sign this paper without any fight or disagreement just to let you do all the destruction by yourself alone.

I am wishing someday you will realize what you have done to thirty years of the very best of our lives together. Yes you destroyed our very respectable life and made my children to loose their dignity

I don't have any power to do anything but Thank you

Shamci Rafani
2-27-89

Kidder, Peabody
Premium Account — Statement

10 Hanover Square, New York, N.Y. 10005

ACCOUNT	TAX I.D. NO.	PERIOD-	PAGE
5OE 41371 258	38-1986194	08 26 88-09 29 88	1

OFFICE SERVING YOUR ACCOUNT
3290 W BIG BEAVER RD STE 444
TROY MI 48084

REGISTERED REPRESENTATIVE
THEODORE WALTER KILAR
TEL 313 649-5700

IRAJ RAFANI MD PC PROFIT
SHARING PLAN U/A/D 7/24/85
IRAJ RAFANI MD TTEE
6840 HOLLYWOOD BLVD
HOLLYWOOD CA 90028

****SUMMARY OF BALANCES****

OPENING BALANCE	$.00	AVAILABLE CREDIT	$47,625	OPENING KPPA FUND	.00
CLOSING BALANCE	$.00	SECURITIES MARKET VALUE	$3,625.00	CLOSING KPPA FUND	.00
OPENING GOVERNMENT FUND	47,291.16				
CLOSING GOVERNMENT FUND	47,625.47				

****PORTFOLIO SUMMARY****

NET VALUE OF MONEY MARKET FUNDS	$47,625.47
PLUS LONG MARKET VALUE OF PRICED SECURITIES	$3,625.00
PLUS NET CREDIT BALANCE	$.00
NET PORTFOLIO EQUITY	$51,250.47

****SUMMARY OF INCOME****

DESCRIPTION	** THIS PERIOD	-- YEAR TO DATE **
GOVERNMENT FUND DIVIDENDS -	$334.31	$2,255.64

****ACCOUNT ACTIVITY - THIS PERIOD****

T	DATE	TRANSACTION	QUANTITY	DESCRIPTION	PRICE	AMOUNT	BALANCE	FUND SHARE BALANCE
	08 26			OPENING BALANCE			$.00	47,291.16
0	09 29	SHARE DIVIDEND	334	GOVERNMENT FUND	334.31	$.00	$.00	47,625.47
	09 29			CLOSING BALANCE			$.00	47,625.47

****SUMMARY OF INVESTMENT ACTIVITY****

T	DATE	TRANSACTION	QUANTITY	DESCRIPTION	PRICE	DEBIT	CREDIT
				****DIVIDENDS AND INTEREST****			
0	09 29	SHARE DIVIDEND	334	GOVERNMENT FUND	334.31		$334.31
				NET TOTAL			$334.31

As you see, I have added these pages to the book just because I didn't receive one penny form it. Where did the properties in Michigan go? Where did these accounts go? What happened to the club at Six Mile Rd. in Livonia, Mi? What happened to the stock market money that was in your name? If I can't find a lawyer to defend me, I hope that you can't steal them with good health.

Kidder, Peabody
Premium Account

Statement

10 Hanover Square, New York, N.Y. 10005

ACCOUNT	TAX I.D. NO.	PERIOD-	PAGE
50E 41371 258	38-1986194	08 26 88-09 29 88	2

CUSTOMER NAME
IRAJ RAFANI MD PC PROFIT

******SECURITY POSITIONS******

T			POSITIONS IN YOUR ACCOUNT	PRICE	MARKET VALUE
O	LONG	1,000	BUTTES GAS &OIL CO	.125	$125.00
O	LONG	2,000	TIGERA GROUP INC	1.000	$2,000.00
O	LONG	500	TOSCO CP	3.000	$1,500.00
			TOTAL OF PRICED SECURITIES		**$3,625.00**
O	LONG	47,625	KP GOVERNMENT MONEY FUND	1.000	$47,625.47

******KIDDER PEABODY MONEY MARKET FUNDS YIELD SUMMARY******

MONEY MKT FUND	EFFECTIVE ANNUAL YIELD	LATEST 30 DAY AVERAGE YIELD
PREMIUM ACCOUNT	7.92%	7.52%
GOV. MONEY FUND	7.78%	7.39%
TAX EXEMPT	5.17%	5.00%
CALIF TAX FUND	5.12%	4.89%

YOU CAN NOW GET CASH FROM "AUTOMATED TELLER MACHINES" USING YOUR PREMIER VISA CARD. CALL PREMIUM ACCOUNTS NEW TOLL-FREE NUMBER 1-800-KIDDER-P FOR DETAILS.

YOUR AVAILABLE CREDIT LIMIT OF $47,625 DOES NOT REFLECT DEPOSITS NOT CLEARED, CHECKS NOT PROCESSED OR PENDING AUTHORIZATIONS FOR VISA PURCHASES.

**** PLEASE RETAIN THIS STATEMENT FOR YOUR FUTURE REFERENCE ****

Kidder, Peabody
Premium Account Statement

10 Hanover Square, New York, N.Y. 10005

ACCOUNT	TAX I.D. NO.	PERIOD-	PAGE
5OE 41370 258	38-1986194	08 26 88-09 29 88	2

CUSTOMER NAME
IRAJ RAFANI MD PC PENSION

CONTINUED ******ACCOUNT ACTIVITY - THIS PERIOD****** ***CONTINUED***

T	DATE	TRANSACTION	QUANTITY	DESCRIPTION	PRICE	AMOUNT	BALANCE	FUNDS SHARE BALANCE
O	09 27	SOLD	132	DLRS AMOCO CDA PETE CO SER-A SEP 2013 7 3/8% SUB PEND CASH PAYMENT DATED 09/01/88 FC 03/01/89 VS EXCHANGE	95.000	$125.40CR	$188.17CR	98,680.96
O	09 28	SHARE PURCHASE	274	KP GOVERNMENT MONEY FUND	1	$274.88		
O	09 28	SHARE DIVIDEND		KPPA FUND 0.61		$.00		
O	09 28	SHARE SALE	86	KPPA FUND	1	$86.71CR	$.00	98,869.74
O	09 29	SHARE DIVIDEND	697	GOVERNMENT FUND 697.04		$.00	$.00	99,566.78
	09 29			**CLOSING BALANCE**			**$.00**	**99,566.78**

******SUMMARY OF INVESTMENT ACTIVITY******

T	DATE	TRANSACTION	QUANTITY	DESCRIPTION	PRICE	DEBIT	CREDIT
				******DIVIDENDS AND INTEREST******			
O	09 28	SHARE DIVIDEND		KPPA FUND 0.61			$.61
O	09 29	SHARE DIVIDEND	697	GOVERNMENT FUND 697.04			$697.04
				NET TOTAL			**$697.65**
				******SECURITY TRANSACTIONS******			
O	09 09	DELIVER	1,000 –	DOME PETROLEUM LTD PROCEEDS OF EXCHANGE			
O	09 09	RECEIVE	1,000	AMOCO CDA PETE CO S/D SER-A SEP 2013 7 3/8% MS EXCHBLE PROCEEDS OF EXCHANGE			
O	09 09	RECEIVE	132	DLRS AMOCO CDA PETE CO SER-A SEP 2013 7 3/8% SUB PEND CASH PAYMENT PROCEEDS OF EXCHANGE			

Kidder, Peabody
Premium Account

Statement

10 Hanover Square, New York, N.Y. 10005

ACCOUNT	TAX I.D. NO.	PERIOD-	PAGE
50E 41370 258	38-1986194	08 26 88-09 29 88	1

OFFICE SERVING YOUR ACCOUNT
3290 W BIG BEAVER RD STE 444
TROY MI 48084

REGISTERED REPRESENTATIVE
THEODORE WALTER KILAR
TEL 313 649-5700

IRAJ RAFANI MD PC PENSION
PLAN UNDER AGRMT DTD 7/24/85
IRAJ RAFANI MD TTEE
6840 HOLLYWOOD BLVD
HOLLYWOOD CA 90028

****SUMMARY OF BALANCES****

OPENING BALANCE	$.00	AVAILABLE CREDIT	$99,504	OPENING KPPA FUND	85.34
CLOSING BALANCE	$.00	SECURITIES MARKET VALUE	$71,540.50	CLOSING KPPA FUND	.00
OPENING GOVERNMENT FUND	98,594.86				
CLOSING GOVERNMENT FUND	99,566.78				

****PORTFOLIO SUMMARY****

NET VALUE OF MONEY MARKET FUNDS	$99,566.78
PLUS LONG MARKET VALUE OF PRICED SECURITIES	$71,540.50
PLUS NET CREDIT BALANCE	$.00
NET PORTFOLIO EQUITY	$171,107.28

****SUMMARY OF INCOME****

DESCRIPTION	** THIS PERIOD	-- YEAR TO DATE **
REPORTABLE DIVIDENDS - - -	$.00	$256.33
KPPA FUND DIVIDENDS - - - -	$.61	$2.51
GOVERNMENT FUND DIVIDENDS -	$597.04	$4,741.08

****ACCOUNT ACTIVITY - THIS PERIOD****

T	DATE	TRANSACTION	QUANTITY	DESCRIPTION	PRICE	AMOUNT	BALANCE	FUNDS SHARE BALANCE
	08 26			OPENING BALANCE			$.00	98,680.20
O	09 09	DELIVER	1,000	DOME PETROLEUM LTD PROCEEDS OF EXCHANGE		$.00		
O	09 09	RECEIVE	1,000	AMOCO CDA PETE CO S/D SER-A SEP 2013 7 3/8% MS EXCHBLE PROCEEDS OF EXCHANGE		$.00		
O	09 09			AMOCO CDA PETE CO S/D SER-A SEP 2013 7 3/8% MS EXCHBLE CASH-IN-LIEU OF EXCH		$.76CR		
O	09 09	RECEIVE	132	DLRS AMOCO CDA PETE CO SER-A SEP 2013 7 3/8% SUB PEND CASH PAYMENT PROCEEDS OF EXCHANGE		$.00	$.76CR	98,680.20
O	09 12	SHARE PURCHASE		KPPA FUND	1	$.76	$.00	98,680.96
O	09 27			INT ON SHS DOME PETE		$62.77CR		

Kidder, Peabody
Premium Account **Statement**

10 Hanover Square, New York, N.Y. 10005

ACCOUNT	TAX I.D. NO.	PERIOD-	PAGE	CUSTOMER NAME
50E 41370 258	38-1986194	08 26 88-09 29 88	3	IRAJ RAFANI MD PC PENSION

CONTINUED ****SUMMARY OF INVESTMENT ACTIVITY****

T	DATE	TRANSACTION	QUANTITY	DESCRIPTION	PRICE	DEBIT	CREDIT
CONTINUED				****SECURITY TRANSACTIONS****			
0	09 27	SOLD	132	DLRS AMOCO CDA PETE CO SER-A SEP 2013 7 3/8% SUB PEND CASH PAYMENT DATED 09/01/88 FC 03/01/89 VS EXCHANGE	95.000		$125.40
				TOTAL			**$125.40**

****SECURITY POSITIONS****

T	POSITIONS IN YOUR ACCOUNT			PRICE	MARKET VALUE
0	LONG	200	BANKAMERICA CORP	16.375	$3,275.00
0	LONG	500	DIASONICS INC	2.375	$1,187.50
0	LONG	500	GULF STATES UTIL	7.625	$3,812.50
0	LONG	500	HECLA MINING CO	14.500	$7,250.00
0	LONG	500	LAC MINERALS LTD NEW	10.250	$5,125.00
0	LONG	1,000	LAMSON & SESSIONS	19.000	$19,000.00
0	LONG	500	MCI COMMUNICATIONS CORP	19.875	$9,937.50
0	LONG	150	MAGNA COPPER CO NEW CL B	6.000	$900.00
0	LONG	1,000	OAK INDUSTRIES INC	1.000	$1,000.00
0	LONG	500	PAN AM CORP	2.625	$1,312.50
0	LONG	1,000	PILGRIM REGL BK SHS INC	8.250	$8,250.00
0	LONG	276	PLACER DOME INC	12.375	$3,415.50
0	LONG	1,000	RANGER OIL LTD	5.625	$5,625.00
0	LONG	1,000	TEXAS INTERNATIONAL CO	.500	$500.00
0	LONG	1,000	AMOCO CDA PETE CO S/D SER-A SEP 2013 7 3/8% MS EXCHBLE	95.000	$950.00
			TOTAL OF PRICED SECURITIES		**$71,540.50**
0	LONG	99,566	KP GOVERNMENT MONEY FUND	1.000	$99,566.78

Kidder, Peabody
Premium Account

Statement

10 Hanover Square, New York, N.Y. 10005

ACCOUNT	TAX I.D. NO.	PERIOD-	PAGE
50E 06891 258	493-46-3480	08 26 88-09 29 88	3

CUSTOMER NAME
DR IRAJ RAFANI

CONTINUED

****SUMMARY OF INVESTMENT ACTIVITY****

T	DATE	TRANSACTION	QUANTITY	DESCRIPTION	PRICE	DEBIT	CREDIT
				****SECURITY TRANSACTIONS****			
3	09 09	DELIVER	1,000	DOME PETROLEUM LTD PROCEEDS OF EXCHANGE			
3	09 09	RECEIVE	1,000	AMOCO CDA PETE CO S/D SER-A SEP 2013 7 3/8% MS EXCHBLE PROCEEDS OF EXCHANGE			
3	09 09	RECEIVE	132	DLRS AMOCO CDA PETE CO SER-A SEP 2013 7 3/8% SUB PEND CASH PAYMENT PROCEEDS OF EXCHANGE			
3	09 27	SOLD	132	DLRS AMOCO CDA PETE CO SER-A SEP 2013 7 3/8% SUB PEND CASH PAYMENT DATED 09/01/88 FC 03/01/89 VS EXCHANGE	95.000		$125.40
				TOTAL			$125.40

****SECURITY POSITIONS****

T			POSITIONS IN YOUR ACCOUNT	PRICE	MARKET VALUE
3	LONG	500	DIASONICS INC	2.375	$1,187.50
3	LONG	500	GULF STATES UTIL	7.625	$3,812.50
3	LONG	200	LAC MINERALS LTD NEW	10.250	$2,050.00
3	LONG	150	MAGNA COPPER CO NEW CL B	6.000	$900.00
3	LONG	500	NAVISTAR INTL CORP	5.250	$2,625.00
3	LONG	1,000	OAK INDUSTRIES INC	1.000	$1,000.00
3	LONG	276	PLACER DOME INC	12.375	$3,415.50
3	LONG	500	SUNSHINE MINING CO	3.750	$1,875.00
3	LONG	1,000	TEXAS INTERNATIONAL CO	.500	$500.00
3	LONG	1,000	TIGERA GROUP INC	1.000	$1,000.00
3	LONG	500	TOSCO CP	3.000	$1,500.00
3	LONG	1,000	AMOCO CDA PETE CO S/D SER-A SEP 2013 7 3/8% MS EXCHBLE	95.000	$950.00
			TOTAL OF PRICED SECURITIES		$20,815.50

Kidder, Peabody
Premium Account

Statement

10 Hanover Square, New York, N.Y. 10005

ACCOUNT	TAX I.D. NO.	PERIOD-	PAGE
5OE 06891 258	493-46-3480	08 26 88-09 29 88	4

CUSTOMER NAME
DR IRAJ RAFANI

****KIDDER PEABODY MONEY MARKET FUNDS YIELD SUMMARY****

MONEY MKT FUND	EFFECTIVE ANNUAL YIELD	LATEST 30 DAY AVERAGE YIELD
PREMIUM ACCOUNT	7.92%	7.52%
GOV. MONEY FUND	7.78%	7.39%
TAX EXEMPT	5.17%	5.00%
CALIF TAX FUND	5.12%	4.89%

YOU CAN NOW GET CASH FROM "AUTOMATED TELLER MACHINES" USING YOUR PREMIER VISA CARD. CALL PREMIUM ACCOUNTS NEW TOLL-FREE NUMBER 1-800-KIDDER-P FOR DETAILS.

YOUR AVAILABLE CREDIT LIMIT OF $8,785 DOES NOT REFLECT DEPOSITS NOT CLEARED, CHECKS NOT PROCESSED OR PENDING AUTHORIZATIONS FOR VISA PURCHASES.

** PLEASE RETAIN THIS STATEMENT FOR YOUR FUTURE REFERENCE **

Kidder, Peabody
Premium Account — Statement

10 Hanover Square, New York, N.Y. 10005

ACCOUNT	TAX I.D. NO.	PERIOD-	PAGE
50E 06891 258	493-46-3480	08 26 88-09 29 88	1

OFFICE SERVING YOUR ACCOUNT
3290 W BIG BEAVER RD STE 444
TROY MI 48084

REGISTERED REPRESENTATIVE
THEODORE WALTER KILAR
TEL 313 649-5700

DR IRAJ RAFANI
355 E BIG BEAVER
TROY MI 48083-1225

****SUMMARY OF BALANCES****

OPENING BALANCE	$2,373.35DR	AVAILABLE CREDIT	$8,785	OPENING KPPA FUND	.00
CLOSING BALANCE	$2,210.71DR	SECURITIES MARKET VALUE	$20,815.50	CLOSING KPPA FUND	.00

****PORTFOLIO SUMMARY****

NET VALUE OF MONEY MARKET FUNDS	$.00
PLUS LONG MARKET VALUE OF PRICED SECURITIES	$20,815.50
LESS NET DEBIT BALANCE	$2,210.71
NET PORTFOLIO EQUITY	$18,604.79

****SUMMARY OF INCOME & CHARGES****

DESCRIPTION	** THIS PERIOD	-- YEAR TO DATE **
REPORTABLE DIVIDENDS - - -	$.00	$39.69
KPPA FUND DIVIDENDS - - - -	$.00	$156.61
MARGIN INTEREST CHARGES - -	$26.29	$66.76

****ACCOUNT ACTIVITY - THIS PERIOD****

T	DATE	TRANSACTION	QUANTITY	DESCRIPTION	PRICE	AMOUNT	BALANCE	FUND SHARE BALANCE
	08 26			**OPENING BALANCE**			$2,373.35DR	.00
3	09 09	DELIVER	1,000	DOME PETROLEUM LTD PROCEEDS OF EXCHANGE		$.00		
3	09 09	RECEIVE	1,000	AMOCO CDA PETE CO S/D SER-A SEP 2013 7 3/8% MS EXCHBLE PROCEEDS OF EXCHANGE		$.00		
3	09 09			AMOCO CDA PETE CO S/D SER-A SEP 2013 7 3/8% MS EXCHBLE CASH-IN-LIEU OF EXCH		$.76CR		
3	09 09	RECEIVE	132	DLRS AMOCO CDA PETE CO SER-A SEP 2013 7 3/8% SUB PEND CASH PAYMENT PROCEEDS OF EXCHANGE		$.00	$2,372.59	.00
3	09 14	INTEREST CHG		20 DAYS - 08/25 THRU 09/13 $2,373.16DB AVG DEBIT BAL AS OF 09/13/88	11.50%	$15.16	$2,387.75	.00
3	09 27			INT ON SHS DOME PETE		$62.77CR		

Kidder, Peabody
Premium Account — Statement

10 Hanover Square, New York, N.Y. 10005

ACCOUNT	TAX I.D. NO.	PERIOD-	PAGE
5OE O6891 258	493-46-3480	08 26 88-09 29 88	2

CUSTOMER NAME
DR IRAJ RAFANI

CONTINUED ****ACCOUNT ACTIVITY - THIS PERIOD**** *CONTINUED*

T	DATE	TRANSACTION	QUANTITY	DESCRIPTION	PRICE	AMOUNT	BALANCE	FUND SHARE BALANCE
3	09 27	SOLD	132	DLRS AMOCO CDA PETE CO SER-A SEP 2013 7 3/8% SUB PEND CASH PAYMENT DATED 09/01/88 FC 03/01/89 VS EXCHANGE	95.000	$125.40CR	$2,199.58	.00
3	09 29	INTEREST CHG		5 DAYS - 09/24 THRU 09/28 $2,320.11DB AVG DEBIT BAL AS OF 09/28/88	11.37%	$3.67		
3	09 29	INTEREST CHG		10 DAYS - 09/14 THRU 09/23 $2,387.75DB AVG DEBIT BAL AS OF 09/23/88	11.25%	$7.46	$2,210.71	.00
	09 29			**CLOSING BALANCE**			**$2,210.71DR**	.00

****SUMMARY OF INVESTMENT ACTIVITY****

T	DATE	TRANSACTION	QUANTITY	DESCRIPTION	PRICE	DEBIT	CREDIT
				****DIVIDENDS AND INTEREST****			
3	09 14	INTEREST CHG		20 DAYS - 08/25 THRU 09/13 $2,373.16DB AVG DEBIT BAL AS OF 09/13/88	11.50%	$15.16	
3	09 29	INTEREST CHG		5 DAYS - 09/24 THRU 09/28 $2,320.11DB AVG DEBIT BAL AS OF 09/28/88	11.37%	$3.67	
3	09 29	INTEREST CHG		10 DAYS - 09/14 THRU 09/23 $2,387.75DB AVG DEBIT BAL AS OF 09/23/88	11.25%	$7.46	
				NET TOTAL		**$26.29**	

BETTER LIVING MEDICAL CENTER
BALANCE SHEET
SEPTEMBER 30, 1987

EQUITY

CURRENT LIABILITIES

Notes Payable	10,411.56
FICA WH	282.42
Federal WH	336.00
State WH	151.72
Loan from Stockholders	5,636.00
TOTAL CURRENT LIAB.	16,817.70
LONG TERM LIAB.	
Notes Payable	0.00
TOTAL LONG TERM LIAB.	0.00
TOTAL LIABILITIES	16,817.70
OWNERS EQUITY	
Capital	20,000.00
Capital Surplus	42,000.00
Retained Earnings	(75,947.12)
Earnings - YTD	9,533.29
TOTAL OWNERS EQUITY	(4,413.83)
TOTAL EQUITY	12,403.87

BETTER LIVING [illegible]
BALANCE SHEET
SEPTEMBER 30, 1987

ASSETS		
CURRENT ASSETS		
Cash		6,977.21
Loans to Stockholders		0.00
Other Investments		
BLMC - Mehrabian		716.66
Citation Laboratory		3,330.00
Security Deposits		1,380.00
TOTAL CURRENT ASSETS		12,403.87
FIXED ASSETS		
Equipment	19,893.00	
Less: Accum. Deprec.	19,893.00	
		0.00
Leasehold Improvements	11,941.00	
Less: Amortization	11,941.00	
		0.00
Organizational Costs	1,363.00	
Less: Amortization	1,363.00	
		0.00
TOTAL FIXED ASSETS		0.00
TOTAL ASSETS		12,403.87

BETTER LIVING HEALTH PRODUCTS, INC.
BALANCE SHEET
SEPTEMBER 30, 1986

ASSETS		
Cash		9,571.71
Furniture & Fixtures	460.00	
Less: Depreciation	460.00	0.00
TOTAL ASSETS		9,571.71
EQUITY		
Accounts Payable		2,500.00
Capital Stock		2,000.00
Retained Earning		5,182.00
YTD - Profit & Loss		(110.29)
TOTAL EQUITY		9,571.71

BETTER LIVING MEDICAL CENTER
BALANCE SHEET
SEPTEMBER 30, 1986

ADJ. 10/27

ASSETS

CURRENT ASSETS

Cash		8,011.96
Loans to Stockholders		0.00
Other Investments		
BLMC - Mehrabian		1,793.00
Citation Laboratory		3,330.00
Security Deposits		1,380.00
TOTAL CURRENT ASSETS		14,514.96
FIXED ASSETS		
Equipment	19,893.00	
Less: Accum. Deprec.	19,893.00	
		0.00
Leasehold Improvements	11,941.00	
Less: Amortization	10,306.00	
		1,635.00
Organizational Costs	1,363.00	
Less: Amortization	1,363.00	
		0.00
TOTAL FIXED ASSETS		1,635.00
TOTAL ASSETS		16,149.96

ADJ. 10/27

BETTER LIVING MEDICAL CENTER
BALANCE SHEET
SEPTEMBER 30, 1986

EQUITY

CURRENT LIABILITIES

Notes Payable	23,272.01
FICA WH	465.64
Federal WH	461.00
State WH	262.43
Loan from Stockholders	5,636.00
TOTAL CURRENT LIAB.	30,097.08
LONG TERM LIAB.	
Notes Payable	0.00
TOTAL LONG TERM LIAB.	0.00
TOTAL LIABILITIES	30,097.08
OWNERS EQUITY	
Capital	20,000.00
Capital Surplus	42,000.00
Retained Earnings	(89,538.38)
Earnings - YTD	13,591.26
TOTAL OWNERS EQUITY	(13,947.12)
TOTAL EQUITY	16,149.96

INCOME STATEMENT
OCTOBER 1, 1985 THRU SEPTEMBER 30, 1986

INCOME	AMOUNT	%
Sales	118,823.21	100.00%
TOTAL INCOME	118,823.21	100.00%
COST OF GOODS SOLD		
Purchases	73,472.67	61.83%
TOTAL COST OF GOODS SOLD	73,472.67	61.83%
GROSS PROFIT	45,350.54	38.17%
OPERATING EXPENDITURES		
Rent	0.00	0.00%
Taxes	7.41	0.01%
Management Fees	3,000.00	2.52%
Legal & Accounting	555.00	0.47%
Office Expense	0.00	0.00%
Commissions - Rafani	38,140.00	32.10%
Commissions - Charlton	2,400.00	2.02%
Travel & Entertainment	872.32	0.73%
Bank Charges	236.10	0.20%
Miscellaneous	250.00	0.21%
Depreciation	0.00	0.00%
TOTAL OPERATING EXPENDITURES	45,460.83	38.26%
NET INCOME	(110.29)	-0.09%

INCOME STATEMENT
OCTOBER 1, 1986 THRU SEPTEMBER 30, 1987

INCOME	AMOUNT	%
Sales	129,642.75	100.00%
TOTAL INCOME	129,642.75	100.00%
COST OF GOODS SOLD		
Purchases	85,492.77	65.94%
TOTAL COST OF GOODS SOLD	85,492.77	65.94%
GROSS PROFIT	44,149.98	34.06%
OPERATING EXPENDITURES		
Rent	0.00	0.00%
Taxes	6.33	0.00%
Management Fees	3,250.00	2.51%
Legal & Accounting	140.00	0.11%
Office Expense	0.00	0.00%
Commissions - Rafani	29,500.00	22.75%
Commissions - Charlton	1,300.00	1.00%
Commissions - Zaworski	800.00	0.62%
Travel & Entertainment	656.00	0.51%
Bank Charges	674.81	0.52%
Miscellaneous	0.00	0.00%
Penalty	52.78	0.04%
TOTAL OPERATING EXPENDITURES	36,379.92	28.06%
NET INCOME	7,770.06	5.99%

BETTER LIVING MEDICAL CENTER
INCOME STATEMENT
OCTOBER 1, 1986 THRU SEPTEMBER 30, 1987

INCOME	YTD	
Fees	94,683.97	49.76%
Insurance	53,259.74	27.99%
Rent	14,700.00	7.73%
Citation	21,600.00	11.35%
BLHP Management Fee	3,000.00	1.58%
BLMC Mehrabian	3,023.66	1.59%
GROSS INCOME	190,267.37	100.00%
EXPENDITURES		
Payroll	49,313.93	25.92%
Outside Services	61,840.00	32.50%
Taxes - Payroll	4,399.10	2.31%
Medical Supplies	6,131.72	3.22%
Repairs & Maintenance	1,055.54	0.55%
Meeting & Conventions	581.74	0.31%
Equipment Rental	0.00	0.00%
Dues & Subscriptions	204.98	0.11%
Advertising	0.00	0.00%
Entertainment	0.00	0.00%
Insurance - Employees	1,016.29	0.53%
Insurance - Others	893.25	0.47%
Utilities	1,923.88	1.01%
Legal & Accounting	1,680.00	0.88%
Office Supplies	2,985.52	1.57%
Taxes - Other	3,308.58	1.74%
Rent	35,190.00	18.50%
Telephone	4,208.98	2.21%
Interest	4,365.56	2.29%
Depreciation	0.00	0.00%
Amortization	1,635.00	0.86%
TOTAL EXPENDITURES	180,734.08	94.99%
NET INCOME OR (LOSS)	9,533.29	5.01%

BETTER LIVING MEDICAL CENTER
INCOME STATEMENT

ADJ. 10/27 OCTOBER 1, 1985 THRU SEPTEMBER 30, 1986

INCOME	YTD	%
Fees	106,178.65	49.95%
Insurance	59,341.76	27.92%
Rent	14,676.26	6.90%
Citation	26,847.00	12.63%
BLHP Management Fee	3,000.00	1.41%
BLMC Mehrabian	2,525.00	1.19%
GROSS INCOME	212,568.67	100.00%
EXPENDITURES		
Payroll	61,217.14	28.80%
Outside Services	65,060.60	30.61%
Taxes - Payroll	5,511.19	2.59%
Medical Supplies	6,889.57	3.24%
Repairs & Maintenance	1,186.00	0.56%
Meeting & Conventions	653.64	0.31%
Equipment Rental	0.00	0.00%
Dues & Subscriptions	230.32	0.11%
Advertising	0.00	0.00%
Entertainment	0.00	0.00%
Insurance - Employees	1,141.90	0.54%
Insurance - Others	1,003.65	0.47%
Utilities	1,832.27	0.86%
Legal & Accounting	2,460.00	1.16%
Office Supplies	3,354.62	1.58%
Taxes - Other	3,717.51	1.75%
Rent	29,659.43	13.95%
Telephone	4,008.55	1.89%
Interest	4,905.12	2.31%
Depreciation	2,028.00	0.95%
Amortization	4,118.00	1.94%
TOTAL EXPENDITURES	198,977.41	93.61%
NET INCOME OR (LOSS)	13,591.26	6.39%

TUESDAY

1st	band	pre-sell	100	tickets	@	$5.00	each	.............$	500.00
2nd	"	"	"	130	"	"	"	....	650.00
3rd	"	"	"	130	"	"	"	....	650.00
									0.00

WEDNESDAY

1st	band	pre-sell	100	tickets	@	$5.50	each	.............$	550.00
2nd	"	"	"	130	"	"	"	....	715.00
3rd	"	"	"	130	"	"	"	....	715.00
4th	"	"	"	100	"	"	"	....	550.00
								TOTAL	$2,530.00

THURSDAY

1st	band	pre-sell	100	tickets	@	$6.00	each	.............$	600.00
2nd	"	"	"	130	"	"	"	....	780.00
3rd	"	"	"	130	"	"	"	....	780.00
4th	"	"	"	100	"	"	"	....	600.00
								TOTAL	$2,760.00

FRIDAY

1st	band	pre-sell	110	tickets	@	$6.50	each	.............$	715.00
2nd	"	"	"	130	"	"	"	....	845.00
3rd	"	"	"	130	"	"	"	....	845.00
4th	"	"	"	110	"	"	"	....	715.00
								TOTAL	$3,120.00

SATURDAY

1st	band	pre-sell	120	tickets	@	$8.00	each	.............$	960.00
2nd	"	"	"	140	"	"	"	....	1,120.00
3rd	"	"	"	140	"	"	"	....	1,120.00
4th	"	"	"	120	"	"	"	....	960.00
								TOTAL	$4,160.00

JULY 1988

5 Sundays X $1,840.00 =................................	$ 9,200.00
4 Mondays X $1,840.00 =................................	7,360.00
4 Tuesdays X $2,300.00 =...............................	9,200.00
4 Wednesdays X $2,530.00 =.............................	10,120.00
4 Thursdays X $2,760.00 =..............................	11,040.00
5 Fridays X $3,120.00 =................................	15,600.00
5 Saturdays X $4,160.00=...............................	20,800.00
TOTAL FOR MONTH..........	$ 83,320.00

SIX MONTH PROJECTION $83,320.00 X 6 =................. $499,920.00

ONE YEAR PROJECTION $499,920.00 X 2 =................. $999,840.00

POWER OF ATTORNEY

Shamci Rafani

hereby appoints Iraj Rafani the right to cash the Internal Revenue Service refund check made payable to Iraj Rafani and Shamci Rafani from their joint tax return.

The filing of this Power of Attorney automatically revokes all earlier power(s) of attorney pertaining to this matter.

Shamci Rafani
Name

Ex spouse from 1988

october 21st 98
Date

my new address is
22077 Poinciana
Southfild, MI. 48034

I added my address hoping he would send my one-half of the check. But he never did.

Some might ask me why I signed it, why I allowed him to do these things to me. I have just one answer for them; because there is no justice in the world. I had to pay what little money I had, to the lawyers and in the end, the results would be the same. Because I didn't want to become homeless, I decided to go along with him and let him do whatever he could and want to do. This way, I kept that little money, and saved myself the agony of running after him. True, he did all this, but my freedom and my peace of mind were more important to me than his dirty money.

Form **1040X** (Rev. October 1990)

Department of the Treasury—Internal Revenue Service

Amended U.S. Individual Income Tax Return

▶ See separate instructions.

OMB No. 1545-0091
Expires 10-31-93

This return is for calendar year ▶ 1987 , OR fiscal year ended ▶ , 19

Please print or type

Your first name and initial: IRAJ	Last name: RAFANI	Your social security number
If a joint return, spouse's first name and initial: SHAMCI	Last name: RAFANI	Spouse's social security number
Home address (number and street) (If you have a P.O. box, see instructions.): 2207 INVERNESS CT.	Apt. no.	Telephone number (optional) ( )
City, town or post office, state, and ZIP code. (If you have a foreign address, see instructions.): OXNARD, CA 93030		For Paperwork Reduction Act Notice, see page 1 of separate instructions.

Enter name and address as shown on original return (if same as above, write "Same"). If changing from separate to joint return, enter names and addresses from original returns.
IRAJ & SHAMCI RAFANI, 333 FIRST ST. #K315, SEAL BEACH, CA 90740

A Service center where original return was filed: FRESNO

B Has original return been changed or audited by IRS? ☐ Yes ☒ No
If "No," have you been notified that it will be? ☐ Yes ☒ No
If "Yes," identify IRS office ▶

C Are you amending your return to include any item (loss, credit, deduction, other tax benefit, or income) relating to a tax shelter required to be registered? ☐ Yes ☒ No
If "Yes," you MUST attach Form 8271, Investor Reporting of Tax Shelter Registration Number.

D Filing status claimed. (**Note:** *You cannot change from joint to separate returns after the due date has passed.*)
On original return ▶ ☐ Single ☒ Married filing joint return ☐ Married filing separate return ☐ Head of household ☐ Qualifying widow(er)
On this return ▶ ☐ Single ☒ Married filing joint return ☐ Married filing separate return ☐ Head of household ☐ Qualifying widow(er)

Income and Deductions (see Instructions) (*Note: Be sure to complete page 2*)		A. As originally reported or as adjusted (see Instructions)	B. Net change—Increase or (Decrease)—explain on page 2	C. Correct amount
1 Total income	1	161,024	<108,099>	52,925
2 Adjustments to income	2	186	-0-	186
3 Adjusted gross income (subtract line 2 from line 1)	3	160,838	<108,099>	52,739
4 Itemized deductions or standard deduction	4	25,098	-0-	25,098
5 Subtract line 4 from line 3	5	135,740	<108,099>	27,641
6 Exemptions	6	9,500	-0-	9,500
7 Taxable income (subtract line 6 from line 5)	7	126,240	<108,099>	18,141
Tax Liability 8 Tax (see instructions). (Method used in col. C TAX TABLES)	8	31,594	<28,995>	2,599
9 Credits (see instructions)	9	420	<181>	239
10 Subtract line 9 from line 8. Enter the result, but not less than zero	10	31,174	<28,814>	2,360
11 Other taxes (such as self-employment tax, alternative minimum tax)	11	-0-	⌀	⌀
12 Total tax (add lines 10 and 11)	12	31,174	<28,814>	2,360
Payments 13 Federal income tax withheld and excess FICA and RRTA tax withheld	13	29,024	-0-	29,024
14 Estimated tax payments	14	-0-	-0-	-0-
15 Earned income credit	15	-0-	-0-	-0-
16 Credits for Federal tax on fuels, regulated investment company, etc.	16	-0-	-0-	-0-
17 Amount paid with Form 4868, Form 2688, or Form 2350 (application for extension of time to file)	17			-0-
18 Amount paid with original return, plus additional tax paid after it was filed	18			2,150
19 Add lines 13 through 18 in column C	19			31,174
Refund or Amount You Owe				
20 Overpayment, if any, as shown on original return (or as previously adjusted by IRS)	20			
21 Subtract line 20 from line 19 (see instructions)	21			31,174
22 **AMOUNT YOU OWE.** If line 12, col. C, is more than line 21, enter difference. Please pay in full with this return	22			—
23 **REFUND** to be received. If line 12, column C, is less than line 21, enter difference	23			28,814

Please Sign Here
Under penalties of perjury, I declare that I have filed an original return and that I have examined this amended return, including accompanying schedules and statements, and to the best of my knowledge and belief, this amended return is true, correct, and complete. Declaration of preparer (other than taxpayer) is based on all information of which the preparer has any knowledge.

▶ X ______ Your signature | X Date | ▶ X Shamci Rafani (Ex Spouse) Spouse's signature (if joint return, BOTH must sign) | Date

Paid Preparer's Use Only
Preparer's signature ▶ Siamak [signature] CPA | Date 10/19/92 | Check if self-employed ☐ | Preparer's social security no. 572 55 9310
Firm's name (or yours if self-employed) and address ▶ | E.I. No. | ZIP code

consents that the holder may extend the time of payment of any part or the whole of the debt at any time at the request of any other person liable.

This note is secured by an Assignment of Purchaser's Interest in Land Contract of even date herewith, made by the undersigned to the above payee, which Assignment covers real estate in Detroit, Michigan, described as:

> Land in the City of Detroit, Wayne County, Michigan, described as Lots 348 and 350 of Assessor's Plat No. 22, according to the plat thereof, as recorded in Liber 75, Page 837, Wayne County Records.
> Commonly known as 14345 Livernois

WITNESS:

_______________________   _______________________
JAMES H. HOSEYNI

Subscribed to and sworn before me this 4th day of June 1987

____

RACHEL S. SHORE
Notary Public, Wayne County, Michigan
My Commission Expires [illegible]

I would like to know what happened to this deal, Dr. Rafani.

SECURED NOTE

$200,000.00 Troy, Michigan, June 1, 1987

FOR VALUE RECEIVED the undersigned promises to pay to the order of IRAJ RAFANI, TRUSTEE OF THE IRAJ RAFANI, M.D., P.C., EMPLOYEES' PENSION PLAN, the principal sum of TWO HUNDRED THOUSAND AND 00/100 ($200,000.00) DOLLARS, with interest from the date hereof at the rate of Eleven (11%) percent per annum, until all sums are fully paid. Said principal and interest shall be paid by the undersigned in lawful money of the United States of America as follows:

a) Payments of principal, in the amount of Fifty Thousand ($50,000.00) Dollars, together with interest, shall be made on the following dates:

1) June 1, 1988

2) June 1, 1989

3) June 1, 1990

4) June 1, 1991

Both principal and interest of this note are payable at Troy, Michigan, or such other place as the holder hereof may direct.

Should default be made in the payment of any installments of interest and/or principal due hereunder for a period of thirty days, then such default shall mature the entire indebtedness evidenced hereby, without notice, at the option of the holder thereof. Every person at any time liable for the payment of the debt evidenced hereby, waives presentment for payment, demand and notice of non-payment of this note, and

Scotiabank THE BANK OF NOVA SCOTIA — **TERM DEPOSIT**

RECEIVED AT: 71852 WINDSOR

☐ DUPLICATE ☐ RENEWAL

ACCOUNT NO. 21276-79 — PLEASE REFER TO THIS NUMBER WHEN INQUIRING ABOUT YOUR TERM DEPOSIT

DEPOSITOR'S: MR IRAJ RAFANI

AMOUNT: ***********21,444.44 CURRENCY CAD

ISSUE DATE: MAY 11,1987

TERM: *** DAY(S) ** MO(S). 1 YEAR(S)

INTEREST RATE PER ANNUM: 6.7500%

MATURITY DATE: MAY 11,1988

INTEREST PAYMENT FREQUENCY: X ANNUALLY / SEMI-ANNUALLY / MONTHLY ($5000 ONLY) / AT MATURITY

IF ALL OR PART OF THE DEPOSIT IS WITHDRAWN BEFORE MATURITY, INTEREST WILL BE PAID ON THE AMOUNT WITHDRAWN FROM THE DATE OF ISSUE TO THE DATE OF WITHDRAWAL AT THE FOLLOWING RATE(S).

EARLY WITHDRAWAL RATE(S) (% PER ANNUM)

1 TO 29 DAYS	N/A
30 DAYS UP TO MATURITY	3.50

Receipt Only

WHEN DENOMINATED IN A CURRENCY OTHER THAN CANADIAN DOLLARS, THIS IS NOT A DEPOSIT INSURED UNDER THE *CANADA DEPOSIT INSURANCE CORPORATION ACT*.

This Deposit is subject to the above terms and to the additional terms set out overleaf.

AUTHORIZED OFFICER

1461818 (12/85)

Scotiabank THE BANK OF NOVA SCOTIA — **TERM DEPOSIT**

RECEIVED AT: 71852 WINDSOR

☐ DUPLICATE ☐ RENEWAL

ACCOUNT NO. 23556-71 — PLEASE REFER TO THIS NUMBER WHEN INQUIRING ABOUT YOUR TERM DEPOSIT

DEPOSITOR'S: MR IRAJ RAFANI

AMOUNT: ***********14,922.86 CURRENCY CA

ISSUE DATE: MAR 02,1987

TERM: *** DAY(S) ** MO(S). 1 YEAR(S)

INTEREST RATE PER ANNUM: 7.2500%

MATURITY DATE: MAR 02,1988

INTEREST PAYMENT FREQUENCY: X ANNUALLY / SEMI-ANNUALLY / MONTHLY ($5000 ONLY) / AT MATURITY

IF ALL OR PART OF THE DEPOSIT IS WITHDRAWN BEFORE MATURITY, INTEREST WILL BE PAID ON THE AMOUNT WITHDRAWN FROM THE DATE OF ISSUE TO THE DATE OF WITHDRAWAL AT THE FOLLOWING RATE(S).

EARLY WITHDRAWAL RATE(S) (% PER ANNUM)

1 TO 29 DAYS	N/A
30 DAYS UP TO MATURITY	3.50

Receipt Only

WHEN DENOMINATED IN A CURRENCY OTHER THAN CANADIAN DOLLARS, THIS IS NOT A DEPOSIT INSURED UNDER THE *CANADA DEPOSIT INSURANCE CORPORATION ACT*.

This Deposit is subject to the above terms and to the additional terms set out overleaf.

AUTHORIZED OFFICER

1461818 (12/85)

PWK F.H.P. LONG BEACH, CALIFORNIA 90815 — ADP Pay Statement

Co. Code	Department	File No.	Clock No./ID.	Name	Pay Period	Pay Date
PWK	51130E	4700		RAFANI, IRAJ	091988-100288	100788

Hours/Units	Rate	Earnings	Type	Deduction	Type	Deduction	Type
8000	412696	412696	REG	2950	L T D	11099	INDEM
		5538	AUTOAL				

	Gross Pay	Fed. With. Tax	Social Security	State With. Tax	City With. Tax	SUI/SDI	Net Pay
This Pay	418234	105444	31409	29201		5019	233112
YTD	501879	116231	37691	30646		6023	

What about this? How come didn't you add the title "Dr." to your name? These kinds of accounts did not need my signature obviously. The divorce lawyer that I talked to said to me, "Be aware of the time that he pulls the rug from underneath you. He will take all of your assets and make them lost in a way that no one will ever find out."
I see how true his statement was, and how naive I was.

abank
K OF NOVA SCOTIA

TERM DEPOSIT AGREEMENT AND RECEIPT

TERM DEPOSIT ACCOUNT NUMBER 16963718 ◀ PLEASE REFER TO THIS NUMBER WHEN MAKING INQUIRIES

BR/

MR, MRS, MISS, OTHER	INITIALS	FIRST NAME	SURNAME
MR.		IRAJ	RAFANI

R(S) NAME OF ACCOUNT

▶ 18175709

CURRENCY: 0 (0-CDN. 1-U.S.)

TERM: Y 1 MOS 00 DAYS 000 OR MATURITY DATE: M M D D Y Y 05 09 86

NSTRUCTIONS

INTEREST WILL BE PAID 2 — 0 - SEMI-ANNUALLY, 1 - MONTHLY, 2 - ANNUALLY
*AT MATURITY IF TERM UNDER ONE YEAR

MATURITY INSTRUCTIONS 1
0 - RENEW PRINCIPAL AND PAY INTEREST AS INDICATED BELOW
4 - RENEW PRINCIPAL AND PAY INTEREST AS INDICATED BELOW AND ISSUE A RECEIPT
3 - RENEW PRINCIPAL AND INTEREST AND ISSUE A RECEIPT
2 - RENEW PRINCIPAL AND INTEREST
1 - PAY PRINCIPAL AND INTEREST AS INDICATED BELOW

INTEREST RATE PER ANNUM 8.5000 %

INTEREST TO BE DEPOSITED TO ACCT. OR P+I ANN INT

PRINCIPAL TO BE (COMPLETE ONLY IF DIFFERENT THAN INTEREST) DEPOSITED TO ACCT. OR

THIS DEPOSIT IS SUBJECT TO THE ABOVE TERMS AND THE FOLLOWING ADDITIONAL TERMS

F THE DEPOSIT IS WITHDRAWN Y, INTEREST WILL BE PAID ON THDRAWN FROM THE DATE OF ATE OF WITHDRAWAL AT THE E(S):

WITHDRAWAL RATE(S) % PER ANNUM)

7	DAYS	090
1	DAYS	490
	DAYS	
	DAYS	
	DAYS	
	DAYS	
	DAYS	
	DAYS	
	DAYS	
	DAYS	
	2 YEARS	
N	YEARS	

ADDITIONAL TERMS

1. RENEWAL:
Unless the Bank is otherwise instructed by the depositor one full business day before maturity, the Bank will renew the deposit (principal and unpaid interest, if applicable) in accordance with the above Maturity Instructions. In the absence of Maturity Instructions, the Bank will renew the deposit (principal and unpaid interest) if the term of this deposit is less than one year, or will renew the deposit (principal only) and pay unpaid interest to the depositor if the term of this deposit is one year or more. All renewals will be for the same term as this deposit at the Bank's then prevailing rate of interest and early withdrawal rates for like deposits and subject to the Additional Terms applicable on such date.

2. WITHDRAWALS:
Canadian Dollar Deposits:
Full or partial withdrawals may be made by the depositor at the receiving Branch before maturity upon giving the Bank 24 hours' notice provided that,
(a) in the case of a deposit of less than $100,000, the amount of a partial withdrawal is not less than $1,000 and the balance remaining on deposit after the partial withdrawal is not less than $1,000, in the case of a deposit of less than $5,000, and not less than $5,000 in the case of a deposit of $5,000 or more, and
(b) in the case of a deposit of $100,000 or more, the amount of a partial withdrawal and of the balance on deposit after the partial withdrawal is not less than $100,000. (If a depositor wishes to make an early withdrawal of less than $100,000, inquiries should be made at the Branch.)
Cheques are not permitted.
Foreign Currency Deposits:
Withdrawals may not be made before maturity.

3. INTEREST PAYMENT DATES:
Canadian Dollar Deposits:
(a) On deposits of less than one year, interest will be calculated and paid only on early withdrawal and at maturity.
(b) On deposits for one year or more, interest will be calculated and paid
(i) on April 30th and October 31st of each year, or
(ii) if requested by the depositor, annually on each anniversary of the date the deposit is made, or
(iii) if requested by the depositor and the deposit is an eligible Scotia 59er deposit, monthly,
and on early withdrawal and at maturity. (Whether a deposit is an eligible Scotia 59er deposit can be determined by inquiring at the receiving Branch.)

Foreign Currency Deposits:
Interest will be paid only at maturity.

4. JOINT DEPOSITS:
If there are two or more depositors, the Bank may act on the instructions of the deposit, including without limitation all withdrawals and payments of int NAME OF ACCOUNT above. If there are two or more depositors and each is a the deposit and any interest shall be held by the surviving depositor or, if th surviving depositors, subject to the terms of this paragraph.

5. INTEREST ADJUSTMENTS:
Interest payable on early withdrawal will be calculated at the appropriate
(a) If the amount so determined is greater than the amount of interest pr which it is greater will be paid as interest on the early withdrawal da
(b) If the amount so determined is less than the amount of interest previous it is less will be deducted from the principal amount of the deposit.

6. PAYMENTS:
All payments of withdrawals and interest will be made
(a) by transfer to a designated account maintained by the depositor at the as the depositor may request in writing or,
(b) if no such designation or request is made, by a bank draft sent by fir of the depositor recorded at the receiving Branch or at such other addr or if requested by the depositor, by a bank draft delivered to the dep

7. EXTENDED MATURITY DATE
If the term of the deposit expires on a day that is not a business day at th will be extended to the next business day and interest will be paid to that

8. NON-TRANSFERABLE:
This deposit is not transferable or assignable.

9. LAWS:
This deposit is governed in all respects by the laws of the jurisdiction in w

TIAL

AUTHORIZED OFFICER — CUSTOMER SIGNATURE — DATE OF ISSUE May 9/85 hereof pursuant to a certain Promissory Notes dated June 1, 1987 and August 1, 1987, and made by the undersigned to the above payee, which Further Assignment covers real estate in Detroit, Michigan, described as:

> Land in the City of Detroit, Wayne County, Michigan, described as Lots 348 and 350 of Assessor's Plat No. 22, according to the plat thereof, as recorded in Liber 75, Page 837, Wayne County Records.
> Commonly known as 14345 Livernois

This Note is further secured by two quit claim deed conveyances, by the Payor and ROBERT HOSEINI, respectively, of their respective one-third (1/3) interests in certain real estate situated in the City of Detroit, County of Wayne and State of Michigan and described as follows:

Land in the City of Detroit, Wayne County, Michigan described as:

> Lots 123 to 131 inclusive, Roycourt Subdivision, as recorded in Liber 49, Page 62 of Plats, Wayne County Records. ALSO including a parcel of land of part of the Northwest 1/4 of Section 25, Town 1 South, Range 10 East, City of Detroit, Wayne County, Michigan, which is more particularly described as beginning at the intersection of the South line of Schoolcraft Avenue, 93 feet wide (as now established) and the East line of Abington Avenue (as now established); thence Easterly along the South line of Schoolcraft Avenue a distance of 131.69 feet to a point on the West line of McErlane's Schoolcraft Subdivision; thence Southerly along the West line of McErlane's Schoolcraft Subdivision, a distance of 93 feet to a point on the North line of a public alley; thence West along the North line of public alley a distance of 131.69 feet to the East line of Abington Avenue; thence North along the East line of Abington Avenue a distance of 93 feet to the point of beginning. AND Lots 1, 2, 3, 4, 5 and 6 of McErlane's Schoolcraft Subdivision, of part of the East 1/2 of West 1/2 of East 1/2 of Northwest 1/4 of Section 25, Town 1 South, Range 10 East, City of Detroit, Wayne County, Michigan, according to the plat thereof recorded in Liber 58, Page 23, Wayne County Records.

WITNESS:

[signature] KAMAL KAMOONGH

[signature] JAMES H. HOSEYNI, a/k/a JAMES HOSEINI, a single man

I would like to know what happened to this property. I would like to know where the money has gone. All this money which you robbed me must have been collected from somewhere and somehow. Not only did you rob me, but also you robbed your good children. We were planning to make a home for them to come back to and be happy. You did not even let them see or feel that happiness. Then you tell me that you have been fair. You must be out of your mind.

SECURED NOTE

$50,000.00 Troy, Michigan, November 25, 1987

FOR VALUE RECEIVED the undersigned promises to pay to the order of IRAJ RAFANI, TRUSTEE OF THE IRAJ RAFANI, M.D., P.C., EMPLOYEES' PENSION PLAN, the principal sum of FIFTY THOUSAND and 00/100 ($50,000.00) DOLLARS, with interest from the date hereof at the rate of Eleven (11%) percent per annum, until all sums are fully paid. Said principal and interest shall be paid by the undersigned in lawful money of the United States of America as follows:

a) Payment of principal, in the amount of Twelve Thousand Five Hundred ($12,500.00) Dollars, together with interest, shall be made on the following dates:

1) December 1, 1988
2) December 1, 1989
3) December 1, 1990
4) December 1, 1991

Both principal and interest of this note are payable at Troy, Michigan, or such other place as the holder hereof may direct.

Should default be made in the payment of any installments of interest and/or principal due hereunder for a period of thirty days, then such default shall mature the entire indebtedness evidenced hereby, without notice, at the option of the holder thereof. Every person at any time liable for the payment of the debt evidenced hereby, waives presentment for payment, demand and notice of non-payment of this note, and consents that the holder may extend the time of payment of any part or the whole of the debt at any time at the request of any other person liable.

This note is secured by a Further Assignment of Purchaser's Interest in Land Contract of even date herewith, said Purchaser's Interest having already been Assigned to the Payee

July 8, 1988

Dr. Iraj Rafani
Hollywood Live
6840 Hollywood Boulevard
Hollywood, CA 90028

Dear Dr. Rafani:

This letter will confirm our interest in the management and/or investment in the Hollywood Live Pravilion.

At this point, our intentions are to start dialogue along the lines mentioned above. These will be rather candid responses to your request to have us submit to you a tentative proposal which would involve a financial investment on our part. We would be interested in investing a minimum of $50,000 in the renovating aspects of this endeavor. Details of the investment can be discussed later.

Our investment would be contingent on a management contract tied to gross income. Our fee would be $15,000 per month or 25% of the profit, whichever is greater.

As a further inducement for us to invest our time, money and expertise, we would want an option to buy the lease in twelve (12) months. We would want first right of refusal should another party show interest in either the purchase of the lease or the facility.

If these points can be negotiated in good faith, we will have our attorney start drafting the necessary contracts.

Should you have any questions, please feel free to call us.

Sincerely yours,

Sally

TO: Dr. Iraj Rafani
Maseeh Rafani
HOLLYWOOD LIVE

FROM: William J. Thomas
Sally Mishkind
Creative Image Associates

DATE: July 6, 1988

SUBJECT: Proposal to manager and/or invest in Hollywood Live

****

PROJECTED GUARANTEED INCOME FROM SOUTH WING MAIN FLOOR (500 Capacity Room).

TYPICAL MONTH - JULY 1988

Using July as a typical month, we would book four (4) local bands on each day of the month. Each band would be required to pre-sell tickets ranging in quantites from 100 to 140 tickets. The ticket price to the band would range from $4.00 to $8.00 per ticket, depending on the time slot and the day of the week.

The shows would start promptly at 8:00 PM. and each set would be 45 minutes with one-half hour between sets for breakdown and setup of the next band's equipment.

SUNDAY

1st	band	pre-sell	100	tickets	@	$4.00	each	.............$	400.00
2nd	"	"	"	130	"	"	"	....	520.00
3rd	"	"	"	130	"	"	"	....	520.00
4th	"	"	"	100	"	"	"	....	400.00
							TOTAL		$1,840.00

MONDAY

1st	band	pre-sell	100	tickets	@	$4.00	each	.............$	400.00
2nd	"	"	"	130	"	"	"	....	520.00
3rd	"	"	"	130	"	"	"	....	520.00
4th	"	"	"	100	"	"	"	....	400.00
							TOTAL		$1,840.00

These seven pages and a few more that I found in his papers bring up many questions. One of them is: what happened to my share of money that you made me sign for? If you are fair, what happened to my money, Mr. truthful?

But the more I tried to give my children peace of mind, the more he took advantage of the situation. When they didn't know what was going on, how could they possibly judge me to who is the guilty one? He told them all about my bad acts, but I never talked to them about his. Again, this looks like the story of the two mothers, when only the biological mother agreed to give up her rights in order to save her son from being cut in the middle. Because of my children I had to either take it or leave it. "This is all you get".

My Dear God:

My children did not know what I was going through. There was no need for them to know anything about my life. I didn't want to put that responsibility on their shoulders. But I knew absolutely everything that they were going through. And I felt responsible to ease their pain, to lessen their problems, and bring hope into their lives.

So I didn't know how to deal with Mary. That same Mary, who sent me the frames canvas with the writing, "GOD could not be everywhere, so he created mothers". What had happened to her that she must act so rude to me? This person, who used to love me so much, why was she trying to hurt me purposely? The thing that hurt me the most was that I noticed that she was suffering herself. God, what an ugly situation I was caught up in! Why should I be feeling so helpless that I had to cry endlessly? I could not see Mary in that condition. I thought that all her problems were because of my existence. I took all the blame, and left her to GOD to watch over her. I had no other choice but to continue being there for her. And that was it.

The way that Mary was treating me, I thought that she had been emotionally injured and damaged in a way that she needed GOD and medicine combined together to help her get out of that horrible situation. I just prayed for her to be able to come to her senses. My only hope was to hopefully put myself together.

Sometimes life is so sad that we even cannot imagine it. When I was still in my condo, Iraj once came to get the share of his belongings. This person, who one day wanted the whole world for me, was now here to divide our belongings. After he robbed us completely, stole our money, and sold the property without my knowledge, he was there to ask for more. What a shameful and sad life! To begin with I never wanted to keep anything that reminded me of him. His name and anything that reminded me of him was poisonous to me. I wished that I could give everything to him, and get rid of all his belongings at that time. But I realized that after all those years we only had three large Iranian rugs, and one of them was purchased with my teaching money when I worked in Iran. And I felt that those are for my three children. Why should I give up my children's belongings to this thief, who was completely out of his mind?

While he was standing there, talking about what he should get, and what he must leave for me, I remembered who this man once was in my life. I remembered days that he promised me his life was mine. I remembered the times that he hated husbands and wives

who were fighting over their household items. I remembered how he was happy with the way that we never mentioned yours and mine. I saw myself standing next to a person, who once was my love, my GOD, my heart, my eyes, and my whole life. How could that possibly be happening to us? Was it even true? Did I see right, and this man was once my husband? It was really sad.

My Dear God:

Who was that man; standing there negotiating pots and pans? Was he even worth talking to? I didn't think so. After I mentioned to him that I was hoping to give the three Persian rugs to my three children, I told him, "Go ahead, get what you think you want. Make a list with a complete description of things which belong to you, and I will send all of them without any objection. By the way, I do not want the Ivory set, which we bought at the antique auction. I would only like to keep the Laliques, which I liked a lot".

He looked around. He wrote the list in Farsi, which no American could read. I asked him to keep a copy of that list for himself, so that later on he would not accuse me of wrongdoing. And I asked him to write the list also in English, and sign it. And he did.

Please my dear GOD, you tell me if this man was crazy? Right after this act, he took Mojgan and I for lunch to a restaurant. And he had bought Mojgan and also for me birthday gifts, since it was our birthdays. When he gave me the gift, I saw a glow in Mojgan's eyes. I was so lost; I didn't know how to react. On one hand I hated the charades that he still was playing to make Mojgan believe that he was a nice father and husband. I had to thank him, and show happiness just for Mojgan's sake. And on the other hand, I was so mad that if it was possible I could have killed him. He was a shrewd, scandalous person that no one could imagine.

As I said before, his birthday was the greatest day in my life. I always made fuss about his birthdays. Not only I had never forgotten his birthdays, but also he never forgot my birthdays either. So when it was his birthday, he was in California. I was so attached to the idea of his birthday that it seemed to me that if I didn't do anything for him, it would be the end of the world for me. So that was the reason that I had bought that chocolate rose for him, and I was planning to send it to him. But after I thought for a while, I realized that enough was enough.

A strong voice within told me, "Shamci, when are you going to realize that everything is over and done between you and Iraj? Let him send you whatever he wants, and give you as many gifts as he wants. But you should stop doing it once and for all. It is time for you to put the end to this masquerade. It is time to put an end to all the humiliation, and emotional abuse. Shamci, wake up, and open your eyes, and see what he had done to you and your beautiful children! Look what he had done to your dignity. Love or no love, there is no more Iraj for you. He is gone, he is vanished, he is dead, and he has disappeared from the face of the earth for you from now on to eternity. So stop right here.

No more Iraj, and no more celebrating his birthdays. Enough is enough".

My Dear God:

Whoever this voice belonged to, it did me some good. At least it has stopped me from sending that rose to him. But I gave it to him when it was long past his birthday, and he was there to divide our belongings. I gave it to him for two reasons. One was to let him know that it was all over for me. Second was to remind him about the beautiful side of me.

I believe that there are different ways to punish a person, who had hurt you emotionally for a while. One of them is to punish him with soft love and kindness. This way if he ever becomes conscious of his guilt in his private time, probably, and only probably, he would feel ashamed of his own act. And that was my reason to possibly embarrass him in front of his own conscious, only if he had any. That was my way of saying good-bye to my greatest love I had ever experienced in my whole life. That was the best way to tell him that, "You didn't hurt me at all. You hurt yourself by losing me forever:. That was to tell him that, "You couldn't destroy me. You just destroyed yourself". And that was my way of telling him, "You are completely dead for me, and this is the only rose that I have ready to put on your grave". All these were written on the card, which he received along with my rose.

When he received the rose from me, before reading the card, he looked at me with his smile and said, "Oh, it is not real. It is a chocolate rose". I don't know what were his feelings after he read my card.

Or the time that our divorce was final, I added a sarcastic letter to our divorce papers, thanking him for the things he did to us. I will add a copy of that letter in this book.

Obviously, these kinds of punishments will hurt much more if the punished one has sense of awareness to his acts, or consciousness. Otherwise punishment will be useless to that person, except being killed. And because I wasn't allowed to do that to me my way was the best.

So, by me handling everything in my own way, my children never knew what was going on in my life, or what kind of abuse I was getting from their father. They neither knew me, nor they knew their father. And I knew that I must not expect from them to take my side, or his side. For any parent to put their children in the middle of their dispute is an ugly move.

I thought, I would do my own thing, and I let Iraj do his own. If my children were not able to find the truth, I could not blame them. Whatever they choose to do or act, I must not let it bother me. One thing I was never able to hide from them was my pure hatred for Iraj, and especially Badri. About that one case, I didn't want to lie to them, and I never will.

My Dear God:

The funniest thing was that when he sent the movers to pack his stuff for him, still he was planning to cheat on me again. I felt so good that I asked him to write the list in both English and Farsi together.

In that case I had a signed copy of him in my hand, and he couldn't prove me wrong. I actually knew him more than he knew himself. And at the end I made sure that the movers identified, and marked each item separately, and signed for them at the bottom of the list. I also kept a copy of that signed list, so that he could not accuse me of any wrongdoing.

Again with all the cautiousness that I showed for sending his stuff, he dared to blame me for causing him thousands of dollars in moving expenses at the time that he was going broke. I just laughed at him. As if he was expecting me to buy a house for him and Badri in California, and pay the movers to take his stuff, and furnish the house for them as well. What a funny and stupid person! What a changed and strange person! Boy, oh boy. I am so glad that he is not any part of my life any more. What a life!

My dear GOD, thanks a million for all the tolerance and enduring awareness that you had given me. Million thanks for giving me such mind, and intelligence to be able to overcome all kinds of painful and destructive problems at the right time. And a trillion times thanks for making me proud of all the decisions I had made with your help during those horrible, horrible, painful years.

I wish my English was good enough, and my vocabulary was strong enough, and my sentences were rich enough to be able to put you, the readers of these pages, exactly were I was, and make you feel exactly how I felt during those awful days, months, and years. But for you, my dear, dear God, it doesn't matter how I write, or what language I use. You know them all yourself, because you were with me all the times in every step of the way. So you are the only one, who understands me completely.

Because Badri had asked me so shamelessly to divorce Iraj, and free him for her to marry, I was determined to stay married to him for as long as it took. So I was trying to live like those women, who knew their husbands had mistress. Only they didn't know their husband's mistresses, and I knew her so perfectly. I even tried to sleep with him for the six years out of those eight years. And I enjoyed him, while I knew that he was sleeping with Badri as often as he could. While he was pretending that he loved my children, and me I tried to pretend to him that I believed him. And I feel the same way about him. While I was doing that, I was hoping that if one day he woke up and returned to his family, I would have been able to keep his prestigious reputation from being ruined. And above all that, all his friends would have admired his strength and loyalty to his family by fighting against Badri's temptations.

Susan
N. Am Van lines
837.8581
Pick up
Jan 16, 1990

قالی بزرگ ایرانی رنگ آبی
قالیچه نائینی گلدانه
قالیچه دورو گلدانه
لاک با Figure
عاج‌ها
نقاشی کار ایتالیا سایز بزرگ نگیرد
سینی بزرگ مسی پرطاووسی
کاسه مسی بزرگ دکمه دار
کاسه نقره کوچک
عکس بزرگ منبت کاری دور عکس
بشقاب Rosenthal نگیرد
مجسمه Bronze نگیرد
نقاشی رستم
شمعدانی آویز بلوری دراز
قاب منبت کاری با عکس دو عدد
ترشکاری چوبی

This is the list of the furniture and his other belongings which he had asked me to send by his movers to California on 1/16/1990. Since the movers couldn't read Farsi, I translated the list on the back of this sheet and showed it to them one by one, and made them sign it. But this man, the person whose wife I was proud to be, wrote to me on some of his notes, "You made me spend 2000.00 dollars to move only 6 or 7 pieces of my furniture." He had written these notes prior to receiving the furniture. I don't know what he did after he received his belongings including his list which was signed by his movers.

What can I say? The more I talk about him and his stupidity, the more I realize why he did what he did. Obviously, no other man among the Iranian doctors was as dumb and as Iraj was. Otherwise Badri would not have been able to finish her job on him the way she did. She witnessed his stupidity, and she just jumped in. And I witnessed a husband who used to be so eager to spend lots of money on me trying to even pull the rug from underneath me. Doesn't this prove that there is no real love? Doesn't this tell us not to trust anyone's love? Well, I believe so. I don't care if no one else does.

1 Big Blue Carpet
2 Smal Naien carpet
3 Small two sided Carpet
4 Sabe with Figure
5 Ivory s. 9 of them
6 Black & white Painting
7 Big Coppr tray
8 Big Bowl with stone
9 Silver fruit Bowl
10 Picture of Darvish
11 one Rosental plate
12 Bronze Statue
13 Rostam painting
14 Red old Shandleer
15 two monolibat Carey frame
16 wooden ashtray

Recieved on 1-16-90
[signature]
North American
Items above for DR. RAFAAT

My Dear God:

But obviously my dream did not come true. And since Badri had gotten her answer from me, "I will never divorce my husband". And it was too obvious to her that Iraj was not planning to divorce Shamci, she found a way to trap Iraj in her webs so that he could never move again. It was the creation of that sarcastic poem that was sent to all Iranian doctors to humiliate Iraj once and for all, and force him to divorce Shamci.

I never talked to my children about that poem. And I don't believe they had ever heard of the poem, or that ugly act. I felt that even if I showed them the poem, first of all they might not even understand it. And second of all, they had been hurt and humiliated by their father's act enough, that I decided to keep it a secret. I am not sure that if they heard it from others. Only because it was never discussed between us, I thought that they might have not been aware of it at all.

Among her children only Roshanak was against her mother's act. That was because she was engaged to Maseeh, and meanwhile she wanted to prove to me that she was not like her mother. That was why once she got into a big fight with her mother. And after Badri tried to suffocate her by pushing a bar of soap down her throat, she was lucky she was able to escape. She was hiding in Maseeh's room for a few days.

But at the end they all gave in because of the benefits involved. The more that time passed, the more I realize that the damage done to my family, especially to my children was so enormous that there was not much hope for fixing it. We never became the same family we were before. There was a time when they had so much fun together. I could not see the slightest sign of that togetherness any longer. True that each one of us had to learn to live again, but it was far away from being the same family again. We had been shattered all along the way, that there would not be any possibility for repairs. We had become so distant. The meaning of love had completely disappeared from our lives.

My Dear God:

True that civilization and modern living had allowed divorce among more than fifty percent of the families. But what they did in reality was to get rid of all the love and emotions among those families also. It has been proven that death of a parent brings more love and togetherness in the family. And it does exactly the opposite in the case of divorce. It creates the loss of love and friendship, and it will destroy their affections for the rest of their lives.

Well, I must mention that there were also many marriages like Badri's, which were not based on love. And as Badri explained to me, "My husband many times had asked me in front of my children to end our lives together, and he wanted to divorce me". Unfortunately he did not survive to be able to divorce Badri. But families like theirs must get a divorce. It would have probably helped them to love and care, but not my family. My children cannot and will not remember even once that my husband wanted to divorce me.

Even when he had his first affair, it was me who was looking for right solutions, which meant divorce. But my father stopped me from that thought, and he asked me to forget about it. So here we were after thirty years of loving and caring, a woman like Badri had destroyed us. This proves that we know nothing after all.

While I was creating more and more activities for myself to be able to forget my problems, the problems were there, and they refused to just disappear. One day, when I still was in Mitra's house, when Mary called me. It seemed as if she had million things to talk about, but she didn't know how to begin. I was waiting for her, while she was waiting for me. So after a few seconds she said, "Mom, I have written a poem, and if you have time, I would like to read it to you. Happily I said, "Well, yes. What could be more important than to listen to your poem?"

She always read her writings and poems to me. Sometimes some of them were too strong for my weak English. But with her help, I tried to understand most of them. When she started reading her poem over the phone, from the beginning I started to recognize the bitterness in all her sentences. The more she read, the more it sounded like a dead-end street of her life. My heart started pumping so loud that if someone was near me, they would be able to hear it. I almost felt as if I was where she was in her poem. I felt the confusion, the depression, the fears, the uncertainty, the lost love and hope, the ugliness of people, the darkness of the world, the noise of the useless crowds, the cruelty of human beings, the betrayal of friendship, the humiliation of existence, and above all, the pleasure of getting rid of this humiliation by ending this dark life of living in a big black hole of crawling warm …

My Dear God:

She still was half a way when she refused to finish reading. I asked her to continue, But she said, "I have to go somewhere" She left me shivering like a leaf. For the millionth time I felt the dead-end of my life. Please GOD; don't let her do this to me.

In that moment I remembered my poor mother, and the loss of her son Jalal. With no one to turn to, I ran upstairs to my room, and started crying, talking to GOD, and praying and praying. I was thinking of committing suicide, before she could destroy herself. To me it sounded that she was gone. How could I reach her, while she did not want me? How should I save her, if I didn't know how? Why her, my GOD, why her? What have I done to deserve this? "OK. I have to contact Dr. Mehrabian no matter how much trouble I cause him. I have to get help for her before it is too late. I don't care if she loves me. I don't care if she loves her father. But I have to continue loving her, and find some kind of help for her before she does something wrong.

First, I had to put myself together. With what Mitra did and said about Mary, I had to hide my desperation. And most of all, I did not want to allow people find a subject to talk and laugh about.

I got dressed, and I ran out of the house to be able to talk to Dr. Mehrabian in private. Luckily he was at home when I called him. I told him all about Mary. I told him that she has been in love with her father all her life. I told him that this was the second time that Mary had lost her father in the same manner, but this time there was no hope of his return. I told him that since she didn't want to see me or talk to me, there was no way for me to be able to get to her. The way that I saw her, tomorrow she might be on the streets of Detroit, among those homeless people, or the crazy ones. I begged Dr. Mehrabian to contact her father immediately. And I asked him to let Iraj know about Mary's condition, and that he come to her rescue. If he could not come, he must make up a story, and invite Mary to California for a week or so, to be able to find out what was wrong with her. I told Dr. Mehrabian to stop what he was doing, and make sure that Iraj was listening to him. Since we both knew that Mary was seeing a psychiatrist, I wanted him to contact her psychiatrist to inquire Mary's condition. I wanted to find a way to Mary's recovery. I was hoping to die before I found out that something was very wrong with her. Please GOD, help me, please.

Meanwhile I called her office to talk to her, and I found out that she was not at work. When I found her, she told me that she had a medical excuse. It was too obvious to me that, at work they might have recognized some disturbance in her. I was right. She had left her work, and she was staying with her friend Sue Meier.

My Dear God:

It was very cold and snowy time of the year. Although it was bad news for me, but I was very happy that she was staying with her friend Sue, and that she was not alone. I was so worried that she might do something to herself in that dark, lonely apartment in Detroit.

The next day was a Saturday. I was invited in Mrs. Claudette Meier's house for lunch. I am sure that she knew about Mary staying in her daughter's house, because, she had invited both Mary and Sue to come over also. In the morning of that Saturday, Mary had an appointment with her psychiatrist. With the forceful help of Dr. Mehrabian, Iraj had contacted her psychiatrist, and between them they decided to immediately send her a ticket. He asked her to come stay with him for only one week, and then return back to Michigan. This arrangement was to take her to LA, without letting her know why she was going. If it was up to her she might have never agreed to that trip. And as long as my name was not involved, she couldn't have any objection to going.

I was there, when Sue came in. She told me, "Her father called the doctor and arranged to send her a ticket to go to LA for one week". I was so happy that I could kiss the ground, and I did not show any involvement at all. In my heart I thanked Dr. Mehrabian more than million times.

When Mary came in, she told me about her sudden decision to go to LA. When I

asked her, "What can I do in your absence?" she told me, "I have nothing for you to do. My car will be in Sue's driveway, and I will return in one week. The only thing that you can do while I am gone is to get rid of old food in my refrigerator".

While she was talking to me about her decision, I discovered that deep down she was sorry for leaving me alone". I made her understand that not only I was glad that she had decided to go, but also I thought she needed to take this trip after all the hard studying.

At that time, while I knew that I was giving up my Mary to her father forever, deep down I was happy for her to be able to get medical help from her father. I preferred for her to be healthy and happy away from me, than being near me, but unhealthy and feeling miserable. So I held her in my arms, when she was saying goodbye after lunch. And while I knew that her separation was for indefinite time, I kissed her, and wished her the best possible visit in LA.

I knew that Mary was not in a right mind to make the right decision at that time. And I did not want her to know that we wanted her to go to LA to seek a psychiatric evaluation. In that case she would have never agreed to go. I knew that we were not talking about a broken arm or a leg. That would have been an easy fix. But we were talking about Mary's sanity, about her mental awareness. There was not a subject of "let's wait and see". It was very urgent, and had to be taken care of immediately.

My Dear God:

I cannot thank you enough for giving me such strength to be able to make such a decision, at the most miserable time of my life. Mary was a beautiful, pure, naive, and innocent girl. The way that I knew her she did not have one bone of viciousness or gimmick in all her body. She was too good to be destroyed like that. What did I do to her? How did I manage to ruin her life like that? Where did I go wrong? I always wanted the best, and did my best for them. I stood by them every minute of their lives. I served them. I watched them. I followed them everywhere they went. I read many books to be able to become one of the best mothers ever existed. Please, my dear God, tell me what was my fault? Where did I go wrong? How could I, or, was it ever possible to be corrected at all?

The only fear I had was that what if she changed her mind, and wanted to stay and take care of her dog. At that time we had to arrange a forceful medical trip for her that would have caused a disaster for us. Luckily Sue had offered her to take care of her dog in her absence. Her car was safe in Sue's driveway. And I made sure to make her feel good about her trip to LA. It seemed that my complete approval of her trip meant a lot to her. Or this was my belief. So again and again, God helped me to be successful in my decision. I never wanted to label my daughter as mentally ill. And I was able to send her without any struggle. She left with a knap sack, thinking that she would only stay for one week. But in my heart I knew that it was not the case at all. After all what I had gone through those years, my first sweet fruit of love had to leave me for an indefinite period of time.

Although she had separated herself from me emotionally for many years, but she was counting on me being there for her any time she needed me. So I said good-bye to her, and she left.

Okay, my dear God, you have been, and you are the only witness to my life, and the complete cycle of it. Just thirty years prior to these events I left my parents, my sisters and brothers to come to my greatest love on earth. Then you witnessed what happened to my greatest love. Now you were witnessing how my children one by one had to leave me. If Mary had left me the same way that Maseeh and Mojgan did, it would not be as difficult on me as it was in this situation. The lack of knowledge and certainty about her health was destroying me completely.

Now I realize that those, who love too much, are the only people who suffer too much. How could I take all these happenings lightly, and continue living as before? How could I call this life living? How could I end this life, while I knew for sure that they needed me? How could you, my dear God, expect me not to commit a crime and not to go crazy?

My Dear God:

My gorgeous, beautiful, loving daughter must be taking away from me to an unknown destination, where my two greatest enemies were. I had to send her to two betrayers, cheaters, promiscuous sex maniacs, and continue to live like a normal person. But I had to do it for Mary's sake. So not only happily I arranged this trip for her, but also I was able to bring some hope in my heart, for seeing Mary happy and healthy again. I knew that I had to work on bringing hope back in her, and make her understand that no matter what life brings us, we have to take it from there, and continue living. I had to find a way to train myself to the loss of my family, and then go on with working on Mary's emotions from far.

I was trying to accept the idea of making it possible for my children to be near anyone who can bring them happiness. I must give up myself completely, and think of their happiness only.

I got to know my strength after all those years of suffering. I was aware of my condition, and I knew that I was able to come to my senses, and logically deal with my circumstances. But I wasn't sure about my children. How they were going to bring back normality in their lives? The only way that I knew was to let them free of me, and my thoughts completely, to be able to find their happiness.

Maseeh was with his father in LA anyway. Mojgan was at Western University in Kalamazoo, Michigan. And now I had to send Mary to her father for hopefully farther treatment.

The only thing that kept me hopeful was that they were not little any more. I was glad that they were able to defend themselves, and they were able to choose their own

destiny according to their own acceptance and desires.

After eight years of struggle, when Iraj had left me, and I broke into million pieces, I got up again and tried to stand up against all the odds. But when Mary had to be separate from me the way that she did, I wasn't able to put myself together again. I wasn't sure what was happening to her in California. I didn't know anything about her health. She was living with the two disloyal people that I would never have allowed myself to contact. I didn't want to disturb Dr. Mehrabian every day by asking him questions. Maseeh did not contact me often enough to let me know what was going on with her. So I left her in the hands of my powerful GOD, and I asked him to watch over her for me. I knew that it has been him, who watched over us until now, and I felt it was him who would continue doing it for all of us.

My Dear God:

Although I did not want to have any contact with the house that she was living in, still I felt responsible to have my contact with Mary in writing. And I knew that she was not happy to receive letters from me, which sounded like a lecture to her. So one day I thought of something. I went to a card shop, and I found some hopeful and encouraging prints, which could boost up her hopes and confidence. It was one whole page of hope and brightness. I thought that was the answer to my problem. I bought the whole set of cards, thinking I might not be able to find something as effective as those lines.

I mailed one for her every week. I didn't have to write to her myself. Those writings said it all for me. I only signed them, "With lots of love, Mom". That was it. That was my only connection with her. No answer, no nothing. I was completely helpless. I felt so numb and feeling less. Many times I noticed cuts or bruises on my legs, arms, or knees, which I didn't remember how, or where, or when I have got them. I was in many places, while I didn't think I was there. I didn't remember the name of the people, whom I had met. I didn't care for bad or good, which came my way. I thought for sure I was going to lose my mind. There was nothing to be able to put a smile on my face. I kept wondering how I was walking or talking to people. I had nothing to look forward to. One day, not too long ago, I was among the luckiest woman on earth, having the best of everything. And now, I was one unlucky woman, who had nothing to look forward to. The one who had no life to live for. "God please, let me know where am I going to end up after all? Is this going to continue before I see the light?"

When Mary didn't return after one week, I understood the complexity of her health condition. Maseeh called me, and said, "Mary is under observation. Hopefully there is nothing wrong with her, or at least nothing seriously wrong". But he didn't tell me the whole truth.

Every night when I went to bed, I held her in my arms in my dreams. I told her, "Don't worry. I have you in my arms whether you want it or not. You will be in good

hands. Just stop worrying please". I thought she might have a brain tumor. I thought of as many bad diseases possible. I had no choice but to wait and see.

Soon she called me. She told me that because she was under observation, and she had to be on some medication, she must remain in LA. I felt like God had given me the second life when I heard her voice. She seemed happy. I gave her all the support that she might need, and persuaded her to stay in LA. I told her, "To begin with, the sunny and nice weather will have a deep effect on everyone's mood, and it will be very good for you". I told her that, if I didn't call her in his house, instead I would send her those cards every week to be able to communicate with her that way. So she promised me to call me and talk to me.

My Dear God:

When I apologized, "I hope you are not bothered by my cards" she replied, "No, no those are fine. I am enjoying them". Then I realized that there had been a change of mood in her that she noticed the beauty of those cards. I really thanked GOD for that. I felt happy that I sent her sooner and not later.

After some times that she was there, she called me and said, "Mom, I have decided to move to California". Although she was going away from me, it still brought a great deal of happiness to my life. I felt that it was the right decision to send her to her father. After all she loved her father a lot. And she also loved Maseeh a lot. And they were both living in LA. And besides, the weather was the main factor to keep anyone out of depression. I told her, "Mary jon, this is just great. You should have thought of this long ago. I am very happy for your decision. If I can be of any help, please let me know. I will be glad to do it for you. Please don't hesitate to call me, if you need anything". So I kept sending her those cards. And she kept calling me if she wanted to talk.

You see, my dear GOD, if I tell people that those days I actually was not in my body, no one could understand or even believe me except you. If I tell them that it was not I, who was walking or talking, going places and making decisions, no one would see it except you. And if I tell any one it was not I, who handled everything with a great deal of power and strength, without me being there no one would believe or understand me at all. The strength, the power, and the capability that I found in myself were shocking to me. I was able to handle things around me with great deal of thoughts, which later on surprised me. Obviously, I wasn't that smart or knowledgeable about things, which were happening around me. So I had to believe that there was some mental power coming into me, from some unknown sources, which people called it GOD. I know it was within me, and it never parted from me. At the most miserable times of my life, I was able to do, say, and act right. As if it was written for me what to do, or not to do, I wish I had more knowledge to find out who was behind all those to open the door of possibilities for me.

So when I was so confused that I didn't know where I was, or how I got cuts on my

hand, or why I got bruises on my legs, I had the right to be that way. Which reminds me of 0J Simpson's trial. When they asked him about the cut on his hand at the time that he heard the news of his wife being murdered, he didn't exactly remember where, when, or how it had happened. I completely sympathized with him, because I had been in that kind of confusion. The only difference was that no one had to ask me anything about my cuts or my bruises. It was I, who was asking myself where, or when, or how I got them. And I never found an answer for it. When I look back, I see myself so lucky that did not get involved with any wrongdoing.

My Dear God:

Every day I woke up, got ready, went to work, and after long hours I came home to Ida and Mehrdad and Cyruse. The way I was able to hold my head up, they thought everything was all right with me. Every day I walked five miles to be able to meditate, and clear my mind from things that were bothering me. It was important for me to get in touch with the reality. I was trying to keep my sanity before it was too late. I was trying not to make myself the subject of teases, and laughter of my so-called friends by becoming insane. I was trying to convince myself that I was not the first wife, who was destroyed by her husband, and I will not be the last one either.

I was thinking that if I wasn't able to have complete control over my actions, then the only answer was to commit suicide. Then I thought, "What if Mary called to talk to me, and she heard that her mother had committed suicide?" I wasn't that good of a mother for them when I was alive. Now with my sudden death I would cause them more pain and agony. Not only that, but for the rest of their lives they would have to carry the shame of having a crazy mother. Especially after sending those hopeful cards to Mary at least once a week to give her hope and boost her confidence, such an act from me would have been overwhelming.

Many times when I talked to Maseeh, I read between the lines that Mary had been hospitalized, but she is okay now. Mary herself talked to me, and did not mention anything about her hospitalization. She sounded happy and I did not want to dig any farther. I knew that no matter what, being near her father must be to her benefit. I thanked GOD, when I realized that she did not have a brain tumor, I was able to feel a little calmer. I was just hoping that soon she would recover from her nervous breakdown, and by being near her father; soon she will be back to normal.

Before I explode under tremendous painful life, I decided to make a trip to Iran. I wanted to be among my siblings to be able to bring some comfort into my life. Although I knew that I was not able to talk to them about my problems, and especially my divorce, still I rather be there among them, and feel the warmth of my family. Since they had been away from me nearly thirty years, there was no need to put them in the middle of my life, which none of them had any part in it. Besides, I was not planning to open up my shameful

life to them after thirty years of "happy" marriage. The only person, who knew about my life, was my sister Ezzat. With her letters she was my guide during those miserable eight years. I loved those letters, and I was sure that without them I would have been lost completely. But I was not so brave to talk to my other sisters and brothers. I didn't want to hear them nag that "I told you so".

My Dear God:

Then, one day Mary called me to let me know that she liked to move to California. We didn't go into detail. She sounded all right, and was happy with her decision. And I was happy to see she was well enough to be able to take such a big step, and move to LA, where her brother and her father, those whom she loved the most, lived. At that time nothing made me happier.

After I gave her my complete approval and support, I asked her what could I do here for you? Tell me anything. I will be glad to do it.

It was almost three months after she had left. It was a cold, snowy winter of Michigan. Her car was parked in front of Sue's house in the same spot for those three months. And her dog was staying with Sue as well.

She asked me to pack all her stuff, get rid of her bed, and some other things. She asked me to sell her car, which was leased with an option to buy. She still owed eight thousand dollars for it. She thought I could sell it for that amount. And she asked Sue to find a nice owner for her dog. And that was it.

Soon I got to work. So did Sue, and she found a nice person for her dog. The next day I put an ad in the newspaper to sell her car. It would have been wrong to list the number for the restaurant, so I gave my home phone number, and asked to call after the working hours. But I was not successful. I paid lots of money for advertising, but no one was interested. Then after repeating the ad for a few times, I decided to bring her car to the parking lot in front of the restaurant.

One day I discussed the matter with Mr. Tavakoli. He offered to help me. We scheduled one morning to bring the car to the parking lot. That day was one of the coldest winter days. The windshield factor was reading minus 20. It was so cold that even in the car our fingers were frozen.

Sue was at work, but she knew of our plans. When we got there, we couldn't open the door. It had not been used for three months, and due to the weather, we had difficulty getting in to it. After trying for a while, we finally were able to open the door. After the attempts to start the car for ten minutes, he realized that the wheels were frozen. No matter what he did, or as many tricks he used, we were not successful. The point was that we were not ready for this kind of challenge. We both had to be back at the restaurant to attend to our jobs.

While snow was above our knees, and we both were freezing, I volunteered to go

door to door, and ask the neighbors to give us hot water so that we could defreeze the wheels. But we had no luck. It was a working day, and most people at that time of the day were at work. I was so embarrassed I didn't even know how to apologize to him. I wasn't expecting this.

My Dear God:

Although Mr. K was very knowledgeable about cars, he still could not think of anything at the time. My fingers and my toes were completely frozen, I wasn't able to stand or walk, and so was Mr. K. We almost were going to give up. While he was trying to push the car, I decided one more time to walk farther to neighbors and find someone to help us. To my surprise one gentleman was home, and he came to our rescue. His house wasn't that close to us. So we had to carry as many buckets of hot water at once as it was possible. After half an hour or so the wheels started to roll. He drove Mary's car, and I drove mine to the restaurant's parking lot. It was a big ordeal, and we were happy that we were able to succeed.

We left a sign "For Sale" on it. We did not receive too many calls. And if they called, they did not show any interest. Time was passing without any results. If it wasn't sold on certain time, the Bank would have auctioned it. Then Mary would have to pay a large amount of money, which she did not have.

Ali Hushmand's brother Hossain, was into buying and selling cars. When I talked to him, he promised me to find a buyer among his friends. I was in a position that I had to get rid of that car. So the offer was very low. I never met the buyer, but Hossain was my contact. No matter how hard I tried, they didn't pay more than three thousand dollars. Mary had to pay eight thousand dollars to the bank to be able to free her credit.

I was aware that Mary was sick first of all. She was out of job, second of all. And last, she was staying in her father's house to remind her what a good father she had. So I didn't want to reason with Mary about her financial situation. And her father was a smart aleck crook, who was ready to take advantage of any in upcoming situation.

The funny part of all these was that, when he told me on the phone, "My children love me". Obviously they love you. When I tried so hard to minimize their pain and agony, which all was created by your promiscuity, and not let them go through much more pain which they had experienced only by your existence, what do you expect? I did all these things only to be able to minimize their pain. Not that I had plenty of money to spare. Not that I was a big shot doctor whose main purpose was just looking good, and not doing good. No, I just was a responsible mother who had lost all her dreams, and now, she was only trying to do what she could to bring back sanity to her children. By the way serial killer's children still love their father. That does not mean that he was a good person. If they love you, it is because they are in need and only they have to.

My Dear God:

I was very thankful to Mr. K. He worked two hours on that icy day that I will never forget it. He was a real gentleman. Then to show my appreciation, I bought them a big crystal tray for their house. Besides, they opened their door for me as many nights as I was afraid to go home. They were a nice family.

After I cleared up her car situation, it was time to clear up her apartment, pack her stuff and send it to her. For a few weeks every morning before I went to work, I stopped at some grocery stores to collect number of boxes: little, medium, or large needed for her packing. After I collected enough boxes, then I scheduled myself one-week end to go to her apartment, and started packing. Does anyone understand at all what I was going through at that time? Or I must say, did anyone care at all? How could my children ever understand the pain that I was going through? How do they know what I did, or how I did it? How do they want to judge me for things, which they are not aware of? And how these kids dare to put me at the same level that they put their crooked father? Or should I ever tell them, or just let it be.

You see, my dear GOD, I even don't know how to begin to write about that weekend. When I used to watch some soap operas, I always thought to myself, "How could one person always run into most disastrous situations, which no one else could stand even one of them?" And yet I was watching myself one by one going through the things, which I never dreamt of. Even if it happened in my dreams, I couldn't possibly take it. Now in my real life, one by one it was happening to me, and still I got up, shook myself, and walked towards the new stuff ready for me again.

Except you, who were with me through this entire ordeal, who could ever feel or experience the pain that I was going through that day? Who could ever feel my loneliness, which I had never felt before, in my entire life?

From the moment I started cleaning and packing, I cried and cried and cried. What happened to those dreams that we had for Mary, the beautiful. She was the most beautiful girl among all our relatives' children. How did I go wrong? Where did I go wrong? It is sad but normal if somebody dies in the family. If someone gets a disease it is by nature, and it is nobody's fault. But a person, who still does not know what he had done to his family, had created this life of my children's and mine without any regret whatsoever.

I cleaned, and packed all her books in small boxes. I wrote a letter of congratulation on starting her new life in a new place. I told her that the sunshine of California would brig the brightest days in her life. I teased and joked to be able to bring laughter in her face. And while my tears were dripping on those letters, I put one on each box and wished her happiness. Then again and again I read the letters myself to be sure that I didn't say anything to provoke her anger. The letters went like this, "My dear Mary, every change in our lives is the beginning of a greater happiness. Only we have to allow ourselves to find that happiness by looking for it, and recognizing it. What you are doing today is another

step towards success and happiness. I am very happy for you that you took this step. You must be happy and proud of yourself for taking this positive action, and bringing the real sunshine in your life. With lots of love, Mom."

My Dear God:

These letters with my tears on them accompanied every box. I packed, I cried, I walked, I cried. And once in a while I sat and reread her little notes. I went through all her belongings. I hated Iraj more than ever. Mary was his favorite girl. We named her after his mother Maryam. He wanted the whole world for Mary, and for all of us. Where was he to see what kind of a place his beautiful daughter was living at? Where was he to see what Mary had in her house? He had bought a brand new car for her sixteenth birthday. He built a big beautiful house for his children. "Why don't you ever come, and see what you have done to your children's life after promising them that you would never do it again. Have you ever thought that you need to look in the mirror to be able to see the real Iraj? Shame on you man! Shame on you, you ruthless man! Just shame!

Where were my children to see that he was never any part of their lives? They had seen me getting involved with every affair, which concerned them. They had seen me following them everywhere they went to be able to help them. Even for Maseeh, who was his only son, he had never paid any attention to know where he was living, or what he was doing. I was the one, who did all the fatherly care for him. I was the one, who ran after his first bicycle. I was the one, who played ball with him. I was the one, who took him to swimming lessons. And I was the one, who was always available at their school when there was a difficulty. Now, while he was sitting and entertaining the leftovers of Dr. Malakuti, he was telling me, "My children love me".

My dear GOD, how come you did not let me know this man when my poor father was trying so hard to make me understand that he was no good, and that he would destroy me one day. And then it would be too late for me to do anything about it. Now was that day. I was lost. I was nothing. I was dead. I didn't know where I was, or who I was. I wished my father could have killed me then, and never let me go through this life at all. I wished I was never born at all, and that didn't bring these three innocent children into this ugly world.

My Dear God:

I just cried, cleaned, packed, walked, and talked to myself. "What else? What is next?" Where were my children to see my pain and agony? Was there anyone that I could put my head on her or his shoulder, and cry myself to death? "GOD, do you hear me? Do you?"

No, there was no one but I, myself, and my thoughts. I had to go through it. I had to finish her packing, and arrange to send it to her. I had to be glad for her, to see that she

was starting a new life. Hopefully she could forget the loss of family, and create a happy life for herself.

This was Saturday. I separated her stuff, which she needed to be sent to California from the things, which weren't worth sending, or she didn't need them at all. I labeled every box, which was ready to go, and I left a letter of encouragement in them. It was getting late, and it was dark outside. I thought I must leave the rest for next day, which was Sunday. Then I washed up, put a smile on my face, locked the door, and left her apartment to go home to Ida and her family.

Not one word about my desperation or sadness, or anything like that. They knew that Mary had moved to LA, and I was sending her stuff. So like always we sat, and chatted, and spent a nice evening together. And then we watched a movie on TV. When I went to bed, although I was very tired, I could not sleep at all. Then I sat on my bed, and started knitting till I don't remember what time I fell asleep.

Next day was Sunday. I got up early, went for my walk, and got ready to go to Mary's apartment to finish her packing. During all these times neither Maseeh, nor Mojgan called me to see how I was, or what I was doing. I started packing, and crying, and talking to GOD again. I was not in the mood or any condition to see anyone or even talk to someone. All of a sudden Mojgan called me. She had called home, and they told her where I was. Not only I wasn't happy that she called me on such a day, but she also insisted that she and Joe wanted to see me. No matter how I tried to explain to her that I was not in a condition to see anyone, she refused to hear me. She wanted to see me, and she wanted to see me that Sunday.

She insisted that she needed me, and she must see me. I knew that she must need money. Otherwise, she never wanted to see me this badly to show me that she cared for me. This had never happened. She started with her routine behavior, and started crying and accusing me of loving Mary more than her, and I never paid enough attention to her needs. It always worked. She got me right there. I agreed to come. She drove from Kalamazoo to come and see me. That never happened if she didn't want to ask for something big. So I had to stop my work, and see what she had to say.

My Dear God:

She has never been to Mary's apartment before. She took her address from me, and she came in the afternoon. Okay, my dear GOD, how should I talk or complain about her visit that day? Is it proper to complain about my daughter's reaction towards me? People would say, "This is your own creation, why are you complaining?" Didn't my father warn me of such day? Didn't he tell me that the way I was raising my children, their first target in life would be me, their mother? Didn't he tell me, "The way you raise them, you make them believe that the whole world must be under their command, and do what they asked"? Wasn't I naive enough not to hear my father, or not listen to him? So there was no space for my complaints at all. Without having any feelings for me whatsoever, without asking me how was I doing, she commanded that she must come that day in the middle of me packing. And she came.

At that time she was living with Joe Scheidler. They came in. They saw me in that ugly shape, but she didn't even ask to give me a helping hand, or say anything that showed her concern for me. I was right. I knew her very well. She was in a hurry to return to Kalamazoo.

The way she explained it to me, she said, "We had spent the money, which we were not supposed to. We are loosing our credit in the Bank. We need your help. You must give us four thousand dollars to payoff the Bank. And I promise you that we will pay you back as soon as we have money".

I was shocked. I thought I was asleep, and I was dreaming. Who did she think I was? Did she think that I was printing money? Did she know that the amount that she was asking was ruining my credit? Did she know that I wasn't a doctor, and she could ask the parent who was a doctor?

At that time I had already spent five thousand dollars on Mary's car to clear her credit. Now she was standing in front of her boy friend, asking me for four thousand dollars. What were these kids trying to do to me? What if there came a day that I had become homeless? God, please. First their father emptied our pockets, and now these kids were putting me in a situation that I lose the little amount, which I had received. "What can I do? Where should I go?" This was a trap that I had made for myself with my own hands.

I tried to talk to both of them, and make them understand that that was not the way to overspend the money, and come to me and ask for help. But it didn't sink in. She started blaming me, screaming, and crying in that little apartment in front of Joe, whom I had seen only a few times. At this time Joe started to be a mediator. He stopped Mojgan from screaming, and said, "Shamci, Mojgan loves you very much, but she has been so hurt that most of the times she is out of control. If, she tells you, 'I hate you, and I want you to die', she does not mean it. She is hurt, and she is concerned about you. Please try to understand her". And then he continued, "We will pay the money back to you as soon as we can".

My Dear God:

I knew that there was no way for me to escape her desire. I didn't want her to make a scene in the Detroit apartment, especially in front of Joe. There was no way out of it. I never wanted to hurt my children by telling them, "If you love your father so much, and you know that he robbed us first of all, and second he is the one, who is a doctor. Why don't you ask him for money, and anything else?" No, I didn't want to bring more pain to their lives by questioning them that way. So after Joe took the responsibility of paying

Shamai

Life has been so busy, we haven't had much time to talk lately. Moj & I are both working M-F full days. We both would like to see you but the weekends are really the only time when we have much free-time.

The weekends of the 15-16 and 22-23 are open because we leave for Breckenridge CO. on Fri the 28th and will be gone through the Sunday the 8th

We will give you a call this week about it.

Love

Joe & Moj

Shanci

Here is March payment on your generous loan. Just knowing your there when we need you is a very comfortable feeling.

We love you very much and want you to know that you always have an open invitation to visit at any time.

Hope to be together soon

Love Joe

back my money, I asked him to write on a piece of paper that he admitted first to borrowing four thousand dollars from me, and second his promise to pay it back to me. But because I knew that Mojgan always spent her money before she got it, I asked him to arrange a payment of two hundred and fifty dollars per month to me, just because I did not want to make it hard on them. He wrote this agreement on a piece of paper, signed it, and gave it to me. And I wrote a check for four thousand dollars, and postdated for one day later. I had to go to the Bank and transfer money from my saving to my checking. That was her visit. They left. They did not ask me if I need anything. They did not ask if I had lunch or not, which I didn't. They didn't ask who had helped me with all those boxes. They just said, "Good bye", and left me with my own miserable life.

The day that I was going to Mary's apartment, Sue was supposed to meet me in front of her house. When she saw me carrying those boxes up the stairs, and washing and cleaning by myself in that place in Detroit, she seemed surprised. She told me, "I had never seen any mother, who does this much for her children, and they never appreciate her love and attention". Even then I didn't like to see someone seeing my children this way. This was a friend of Mary, who paid attention. But my own daughter not only didn't see what I was doing, but she also accused me of being a bad mother, and for loving Mary more then her. What a pity!

Okay, my dear God, you were there with me. I don't have to explain any of those events to you. You remember how I felt after they left me by myself in that dark, lonely, and empty apartment. I never talked to anyone except you. I knew that people, who heard it from me, they would have laughed at me. Or they would have not believed me. Or they might have thought those were the results of my own actions. Probably they were right. Probably I was being punished for what I did to my parents. But then I remembered that they had forgiven me, and they sent their blessings for me many times.

My Dear God:

I watched Mojgan, and her behavior towards me. I asked myself, "Is this the same innocent lively girl who was the joy and laughter of our family? Is she the same girl, who had a great sense of humor, and made Mary and Maseeh laugh all the times? Was she the same girl that was supposed to be "the apple of my eye"? Was this my true life, or was I just dreaming? Who was she? Why didn't she ask me if I needed anything? Was she really my sweet Mojgan? Why should I live to take this much abuse from my husband, and now from my children? God, if you were not bringing the darkness upon me, then who was? If everything goes well, they say you did it. And when everything goes wrong, then they say I did it. "You tell me what I should say. What should I do? Where should I go? Who should I talk to, except you? Help me. Help me please". I was crying, and loudly speaking to God. I was walking, packing, and loudly talking to my poor parents. I wished somehow I was able to commit suicide. I thought that was the best time to do it. But what about Mary?

What about Mojgan when she called me and needed me? Why were those people blaming me for a crime, which I did not commit?

If she hated me, and she wished me dead, why did she contact me when she needed something? I made it possible for all of them to go to their father, since I knew that I couldn't solve their problems. But she figured out that her father was not who she thought he was. After only a few months she decided to come back to Michigan. Why didn't those people open their eyes to see that whatever had happened in our lives was only because of their father, his promiscuity? Every one of them knew when, and where, and with whom he started his adulterated affair. They knew it even before I knew anything about it. Did they expect me to welcome their affair, and celebrate it by giving a party for them? What did those people want from me? Didn't they know that I had the same blood running in my veins just like everyone else? Why should I have suffered like that my dear God? Why? Why? Why?

After an hour or two, I started to come back to my senses. I realized that when she went to California to capture her father's attention, she was at least hopeful to be able to buy her father's love back. But not only was she unsuccessful, but also she had to return empty handed. I never asked her what had happened. And she never mentioned one word about it to me. When he was not available for them to take their anger and frustration out, they had to find the one who could take the abuse, and still be able to help them and comfort them. With the life that their father had made for us, we all needed a punching bag to be able to let out our frustrations. While I did not have any, my children had found it easy to make me into their punching bag, and they struck me whenever they needed to scream at some one. I was the mother, who gave them this life. So I had to be able to take it, weather I liked it or not. I thought this was their way to survive through the whole ordeal. So I had to let it happen. That was what it was for me. I better take it or leave it. Because I didn't have a way out of it, it was better to take it, and see what would happen next.

My Dear God:

All day I packed and cried. I just kept talking to myself. I talked, and talked like someone else was with me in that room. Who else, except their mother, could be the right target for them? Who else, except their mother, could stand by them? Who else, except their mother, could forget and forgive? Who else, except their mother, could spend the whole weekend in a dark and smelly room, packing one daughter's stuff, and listening to another daughter's screams for the crime, which she had not been any part of? And yet, she stood up, thanked God for the tolerance, and capability to take all that pain, and get stronger to continue supporting them times and times again. I cried, and talked until I couldn't cry any more. I cleaned up myself, and started thinking.

I realized that she had many big pieces of furniture, which were big, and she didn't

need them in there: her bed, her mattress, and more pieces, which I had to give away to be able to clean the room. I wanted to finish the job, and then give the key to the manager. After I put myself together, I started to go neighbor to neighbor to find out if anyone needed that stuff. Luckily some families needed some of her stuff. The ones, which they did not want, I had to get rid of to be able to clean her room.

Since there was no one to help me, I decided to take everything one by one, from fifth floor to the big garbage containers, which were located behind the apartments, near the parking area. I had to take them at least more than twenty times, each time more than fifty steps down and up again.

That Sunday by itself I lost a piece of my mind to a newer and more tolerant piece. This Shamci had much less feelings, and was becoming a completely different person. She was someone else, whom I didn't know her before.

Everything was safely packed, and ready to be shipped to her. I had to call some moving companies to find a safe and reasonable price. And then give the key to the manager, and end her rental agreement.

I drove home when it was really dark. My car had been my best loyal friend. In it I had screamed, I had cried, I talked about everything. This car had seen me going through things that no one had seen. In my car I was safe. I loved it because I was able to trust it. It was my only joy. So I sat in it, I put a happy face on, and it seemed that I had a great day.

My Dear God:

When I got home, they were ready to eat dinner. We talked, we laughed, and we joked around like we had no difficulties whatsoever. Then again, when I went to bed, it was different story.

Next day I called, and after researching for the right price, I found a reputable company. I talked to them about the price, the size of the boxes, and we made arrangements for next Thursday to come and take her furniture.

Since I had spent so much money, and paid five thousand dollars for her car, I arranged to send her stuff COD, I thought her father, being a doctor, could have the decency, in case Mary was not able to pay for it, to put his hand in his pocket, and spend some money for his beautiful daughter. But I was shocked when the bill came back to me, and I had to pay three thousand dollars for her stuff. I couldn't talk to Mary because she was not in a condition to be reminded what kind of father she has. And I didn't want to give Iraj any value, by questioning him about the payment. So this was their father who they loved so much. What can I say? Again it was my fault that I gave tem this father. To tell you the truth, they haven't asked for this father. It was my choice. So now I had to pay for it. No question about it.

The movers were supposed to be by her house between nine AM to five PM. Since Mary's apartment's doorbell was out of order, and for some reason was not working, to be able to see them when they arrived, I had to stand behind the door, or sit in my car, and watch when they were coming. I didn't want to miss them because they had a busy schedule, and probably if I missed them I had to wait for another month to reschedule me.

There was three feet snow on the ground, and the wind was so strong that going to my car in her parking lot from her house was a real challenge. I was by her house at eight thirty. While I had a very heavy coat and warm boots on, still I was very cold sitting in my car in that weather. Since I was not familiar with that neighborhood in Detroit, I didn't know where to go. I went inside her building, and stood behind the door. Still it was so cold that my toes were frozen. Consequently, I had to wait in my car or in the hallway all day for the movers. There was a public telephone at the corner of the street. I once called them around noon to find out if my name was on their list or not. They said, "Yes, we will be there before five PM". Walking to the telephone and back was a challenge and made my face crack. I wrapped my shawl around my head and my face to be able to walk back to my car. I had some thing with me to munch on for lunch. After I ate, I was getting impatient. I was cold, tired, lonely, and I didn't know what to do. It was almost four PM, and still they were not there. While it was pouring snow, and wind was blowing things around, I decided to go once again call the company to find out, if they forgot about me. But they assured me that their people were on their way. At least I felt good that I knew they were coming. The fun part was that coming back from public telephone to my car was two steps forward and one step backward. I was trying to push myself forward, while the wind was pushing me backward. With a lot of struggle I made it into my car, and I started warming myself until they come.

My Dear God:

While I was waiting in my car, I was paying attention to people's activities. I saw many homeless people walking around, looking for food or something else. I put my thoughts into work. I thought everyone of those homeless people once in their lives were very dear to someone. I tried to go through their lives, from the beginning. I thought not all of them could be alcoholic. I thought not all of them could be drug addicts. Not every one of them was born homeless. Every one of them must have had a mother, and a father, and obviously a home for some time in their lives. Someone at some point of their lives had loved most of them dearly.

I watched a middle age, very handsome man with beautiful gray hair that when I dressed him in a nice suit, he would have looked as handsome as Jimmy Stewart. I started to look for a reason, which had created the homelessness for them. Why was he there? Who pushed him there? Again I found a reason to question GOD, "If you are the creator of man, how can you let these people down by not helping them to choose to take the right path in their lives? Was it them? Was it the lack of having good parents? Or was it the system, which pushed them into this trap? Then I realized that all of the above took away their dignity and self worth, and when circumstances arise, they gave in, and simply they stopped caring. Obviously each and every one of them did not mind to have a warm home, good food, or someone who really cared for them. Otherwise on that cold windy day in Detroit, they wouldn't be walking around the city with long sticks in their hands, going through the garbage cans, looking for food. Obviously, circumstances around them were inevitable to a point that they lost their resistance, and here they were.

At this time I started thinking about the poem that Mary wrote, and read it to me on the phone. I felt that she must have been at her dead end of the rope. My God, what if me, or Mary could not find our way out of these awful circumstances? What if she could not continue, and gave up? What if I go crazy, and I would not be able to help her? What if each one of us became like those homeless people? And without noticing where I was, I started screaming and crying. For a moment I thought I was losing it.

My Dear God:

I checked the time on the watch that I wanted to take to K-Mart to be fixed. It was four thirty. The movers were still not there. The cold weather and hunger stopped me from crying, and I started to move around and think of possibility of something good happening to us. I started seeing Mary happy, healthy, and successful. I wished for that day to come, and give me second chance to live.

It was almost five PM that the truck appeared from far. I was in that car from eight thirty AM to five PM, in and out of the car, and the building until they arrived. My fingers were numb. I was so glad to see them that I was ready to kiss them.

I took them upstairs to the fifth floor to Mary's apartment. I had packed everything already. They only had to take them down in the truck. He identified the quantity of parcels on the statement, and we agreed on the payment to be COD. I signed the paper, and got a copy for myself. The condition was that if the other side did not pay, I would be responsible for the payment. And I never thought that her father was that ruthless not to pay for his daughter's stuff, and return the bill to me. Well, he was my own choice after all.

That whole ordeal was unbelievable. I had sent Mary away from Michigan without saying proper good-bye or kissing her. I sent her, and I sent her stuff to her like she never existed. My first fruit of love, who always was concerned about me, in very small words, had to leave me without any trace. I was hoping that she could have a close contact with her father to be able to get rid of all her desperation, and by getting back her good health. This was the only bright hope in my mind

After the movers left, I just sat there in that empty place. I cried as hard as it was possible. I felt that there was neither energy, nor life in me. I said to myself, "Is that all there is?" I did not have anywhere to go. I did not have anyone. I made myself look presentable, and wrote a note for the manager of the apartment. I enclosed the key and

put it in her mailbox, where I was supposed to put it. I went in my car, and started to talk to God. I put all the blames on him, for not stopping me from marrying Iraj to begin with. But then I realized that I was not the first wife, who had been destroyed by her husband, and I will not be the last one. I might have been married to another man, and he might have been worst than Iraj.

At that time I had no sense, no life, no conscious, and most of all no place to go to. I felt completely lost, and didn't know where to go or what to do. I didn't know if I went home to Ida that I would be able to control myself, and not cry.

My Dear God:

I started driving home on Orchard Lake Road. When I passed K-Mart, I turned around and came back. I thought that was a good place for spending some time. After I parked the car, I walked slowly towards the K-Mart, like a person without a purpose. While I was talking to myself, I started walking round and round K-Mart. I didn't want anybody to think I was crazy, so I stopped at different places to look at some merchandise. Then I stopped, while I wasn't planning to buy anything, I felt to buy something to show people I had a purpose. I don't exactly remember what I picked up. I think it was a pair of socks, underwear, and some hairpins, or something else.

I soon remembered that I had my watch in my car, and I thought it was a good idea to go and get it from my car. Without any hesitation I walked towards my car to bring my watch to be fixed. When I reached my car, a policewoman stopped me and said, "You have to come in with me". All of a sudden I woke up from my dream. I saw many people gathered around me. They didn't give me a chance to explain to them that I was going to get my watch from my car to bring it in to be fixed. I even didn't know where I was, or what was happening. Few policemen, and some salesmen took me to the office. The salesman, who had called the police for me, explained to them this way, "I was watching this lady since she walked in. She was acting very strange. Sometimes she walked, sometimes she talked, and sometimes she ran. She got all this stuff, and she ran out of K-Mart like it was all hers. From the beginning I knew that she was up to something no good". And they asked me to put all the stuff that I had picked up on the table. At that time I realized that they caught me for shoplifting. I had nothing to say. He was right about everything but the part that I was just going to go to my car to get the watch, and bring it in. They didn't know what I had in mind. I just cried and said, "You are not listening to me. I was in a condition that I can't explain".

At this time the salesman, who had reported me, was on the phone talking to another person telling him, "I knew this Christmas would bring me luck. Now that I got this shoplifter, for sure I will receive the raise that I was expecting. This time it is for real. I must be rewarded, and from now and then, I must be put on a pedesto1". I realized that there was no way out of it for me. He was looking for a target, and I was the right one.

They handcuffed me, and took me to the police car. I was so confused that I didn't know where I was, or who I was, or even if I was alive, and this was happening in my real life. I started talking to God, asking if he was my friend or my enemy. "Is this an awakening for me? Are you supposed to give it to me as far as I can take it? Don't you see what is happening? Don't you want to do something about it? Is this really happening?" The police lady took me in a room for fingerprinting, and to take a picture. I was like a piece of rock. No feelings, no emotions, no life at all in me. I was completely numb. I thought I was watching a movie. I didn't know what to expect next. No one was talking at all. They were doing their job, and were ready to deal with me. After half an hour one of the policemen came to me and said, "We have to keep you, unless you call someone to come and pay three hundred dollars to be able to release you for tonight. Then you have to wait for your court date. If they find you innocent, we will refund your money".

My Dear God:

I told them, "I have no one to call. But I could pay three hundred dollars myself". When I started to write a check, they said, "Check is not acceptable. It must be paid by cash". This time I realized that GOD was with me. That day I took some cash with me in case of emergency. Then I realized this was that emergency, which was put in my head by the power above me. Otherwise I had to call someone to come and help me. And that was something I never wanted to do. I preferred to stay overnight than to ever talk to anyone about it, especially to my children. I always tried to teach them honesty and respect for themselves by choosing to do right. Now they would see their own mother had been caught for shoplifting. What a shameful life would it be for them! No one ever could understand me. No one ever could believe me. Even if I went free, still people would think, "Shamci had done it for sure".

So little hope came into my mind. I told them, "I could pay you cash". When they agreed it was the most rewarding thing that ever happened in my life. At that time I knew I was innocent. I knew that the security man at K-Mart would receive his raise, and I knew that having that cash with me was a blessing. I didn't mind to go to court, or pay more money. But I was relieved to hear that I could go home without any more disturbances.

When the police realized that I had no one to come and get me, they offered me a ride to my car. The same lady, who drove me to the police station, asked me to wait for her after she was done with her work. She drove me to my car, and said good-bye to me.

Exactly like a dream I sat in my dear car, I closed my eyes and opened it. I slapped my face to see if I was awake. I asked myself, "Shamci, do you know what had happened just an hour ago? Do you know that by losing your mind you will only create more difficulty for yourself? Wake up, Shamci, wake up before it is too late. You better accept the loss of your husband, your children, your home, and anything you had lived for in thirty years. You must stop crying and mourning before you find yourself in a sanitarium. This was an awakening call for you. With mourning and crying you will make the matters much worse than making it easy for anyone. You must think that you had no one in your life to love or depend on, and still you don't have anyone. They were yours once. But now they are all gone. Accept it, and deal with it. If you do not help yourself to open your eyes, and see the reality of life, you will never be able to overcome your sadness, nor will you be able to help your children".

My Dear God:

With these thoughts in my mind I sat in my car, and cried a river. I felt I was lucky again for having that cash in my purse. I started driving home. I screamed at least for five minutes. I felt people were hearing me in their cars. I wished I could have killed those who stole the carpet underneath me. While I was getting close to home, I put myself together again, and life continued just like before.

Okay, my dear God, you were there, and you saw everything. Didn't you think it was enough punishment for me that you let me go through that? Haven't you studied my tolerance, yet you put me in such a situation that I got lost completely? If I was suppose to die, why didn't you get rid of me at once, and instead you were torturing me? Why didn't you remind me to take my watch with me to the shop to begin with? Was this for me to learn another lesson to be able to calculate my own ability to cope with my destiny? I felt like a cat with nine lives. Once in a while one of them gets taken away from me. Then I get up, and start allover again.

Until that day I was happy that during the crisis, I was able to stay away from destroying myself, or anyone else for that matter. I was glad that I could stay away from wrongdoing. I was happy with the direction that I was going. And yet I didn't know about this awful and ugly event, which was waiting to happen to me. This was one thing that I wished never happened to anyone, and it happened to me. Was there going to be a day that I would become free from this disastrous life? How long should I continue living in shamble? Then I realized how lucky I had been to have three hundred dollars cash with me to be able to get my freedom back. The more I thought about it, the more I saw clearly that I was blessed by a superpower.

I thought of those innocent people, who had lost their lives for a crime they have never committed. Those unfortunate people, who had to spend all their lives in prison for conviction, which they were never involved with! I thought of those many people who are suffering daily from our justice, and our court system. Then I realized that, it was time for me to think positive and thank God for leaving that cash in my purse, to be able to survive the ordeal all together. It could have been much worse. Now I must wait for the court to see if they would listen to me, or how they would judge me.

My Dear God:

One week after the incident I received a letter from K-Mart that had charged me one hundred dollars for the attempt to shoplifting. I wrote a check right away, and sent it to the company. Each time a letter came in the mail, I was going to get heart attack. I was worried if Ida or Mehrdad received it they might have questioned me.

It took six months till they set up a court day for me. You can see how miserable my life was during that waiting period. In the letter they asked me if I preferred to have jury, or just the judge to decide on my case? Without any questions I answered, "I prefer the judge".

I cannot explain my feelings during those six months. Each night I had nightmares that I was hanging upside down by my feet, or I was put to sleep by injecting drugs in me, or things very similar to those awful punishments. And during the day, I was so scared that if someone wanted to talk to me, I thought they were going to discuss the matter of my punishment. Oh boy, oh boy. I thought for sure I would die.

On that day there were many people in that room. My heart was pumping so hard that, the person next to me tried to comfort me. Some had lawyers with them, and some did not. I was there by myself.

The judge asked me to explain what had happened. I told him the exact truth. And I told him that, "While I left all the objects on the table, still K-Mart had charged me hundred dollars". Then with a loud voice he said, "This is not even a case to bring to court. K-Mart did not have right to continue this case, and bring it to the court. I think even they have to return your hundred dollars to you, and although you did not receive the merchandise, only charge you for the price of merchandise, which comes to five dollars". And then he dismissed the case.

When I got out of the court, I kissed the ground, and I thanked God for being there and defending me. After one month I received an apology sending my three hundred dollars back, including all the fingerprints, and anything else regarding my arrest concluding that, "This file has been erased from our files".

My dear God, you remember how many times I thanked you, and how this incident changed my attitude throughout the rest of my life? I lost all my fears after this incident. I became hopeful again. I knew that I had become invincible. This incident was the most difficult, and the scariest thing in my life. It made me forget about my other problems. It put me where I wanted to be, a fearless person.

My Dear God:

For six months of my life I felt like I was waiting for my execution. The thought of going to court, or going to a police station gave me shivers. I had never been involved in a situation like that. I wanted to raise my children in the same way that we were raised. So now I had to face an impossible event, which was destroying me by all means.

I remember another time I was at a clothing shop to purchase a suit for myself. After I tried many of them with the help of the saleslady, I decided on one of them. I asked the lady to wrap it for me. She did it very nicely, and I paid the money and started to walk out of the store. As soon I stepped out, the alarm went off, and I froze in the middle of the door. Everybody's eyes turned to me, thinking that I hid something in my bag. Immediately I returned to the counter to be checked. There was nothing in that bag except the suit that I had paid for. The only problem was that the lady had forgotten to remove the alarm activator from my suit. When she started apologizing, I was ready to kill her. I told her, "Apologizing to me is not enough. You must announce to all the customers that this was a false alarm. Otherwise those, who saw me coming back to the store, do not know that this was a false alarm. And wherever they see me, they will remember me as a shoplifter". I was so mad at that lady that I did not want to buy that suit any more. I wished this time I had a proof like that to be able to proof to the judge. Unfortunately my proof was not there to hand it to the judge. Only I asked God to make him understand me. It was a painful six months that I will never forget. I am only glad that it ended the way it did.

While I had this killer thoughts in my mind, one day Mojgan called me to remind me of our birthdays, which were coming up. She had never been in Mitra's or Ida's houses to visit me. Either I went to visit her, or we arranged to see each other at a restaurant. This time she wanted to kill two birds with one stone. Since she was taking a course at Wayne State University, and she had an exam at eight o'clock in the morning, it was too far to drive that early in the morning to the university. So she decided to come to Ida's house the night before, and then she would spend the night with me, and drive to the university in the morning. Although I wasn't happy that she would see me in that little room, still I was very glad to see her and spend a night with her.

Remember that this was both our birthdays. She got there late in the evening. She tried to go to bed early to be able to get up on time in the morning. Probably my room was only ten by twelve feet, with only one small bed in it. I gave my bed to her. And while she was insisting that I must take my own bed, I made her sleep on my bed, and I slept on the floor on a sleeping bag. I was embarrassed to entertain her in that room. The next day she went to university for her exam. She decided to take me out to dinner, and then go to the Mall. I didn't know what she had in mind by going to Mall. I was going to give her a gift anyway. But she told me that she needed to borrow money from me. So I decided to give her two hundred fifty dollars as a gift. I thought that would make her happy. After I gave her the money she took me to an expensive clothing shop. She made me sit, and give her my approval on her selections. She tried on suits, blouses, skirts, and very expensive ones. I was wondering if she was in need to borrow money from me, how come she was trying to buy these many clothes. I knew that she had one room full of never used clothes. I started to worry. In no time she made me realize that I was supposed to pay for those clothes as

her birthday gift. I told her, "The money I gave you was your gift. Besides, you have so many clothes that you are not using all of them. What would be the urgency to spend so much money on something, which is not needed?" She paid a lot of money, and bought some clothes, which she had tried on.
Not realizing that it was my birthday too, and I needed something to be happy with, she started doing her own routine acts. I became a bad mother, a worthless mother, a person, who ruined the family, and more and more and more.

My Dear God:

This was the visit of my dear daughter, who remembered my birthday. Again the voice of my father started ringing in my ears, "You will raise these children in a way that they will believe that the whole world owes them something. If they don't get what they want, they will make you their first target". Oh so true, so true. She made me feel unwanted more than before. She made me feel guilty more than before. She made me wish for my early death.

I remembered her twelfth birthday that Iraj took us to the Four Season in Canada. That was the year before Malakuti died. He treated both of us like queens. We had a great time together. Although now when I look back, I see that sometimes he was watching us in a strange way. Probably at that time he knew something that we didn't know. But now, after nearly nine years of suffering and struggle, he took our happiness completely away. While he was having fun, I was the one, who was paying for it. What a life! What a miserable life!

I thought since I had given her life, and I had caused this unhappy life for them, so I have to take all the abuse. Hoping that some day this pain would go away, and life would change for all of us.

The more these kind of conflicts appeared between us, the more I lost my motherly worth. I realized that I could not bring back my children's happiness. I thought Iraj was right when he said, "People, according to their own selfishness and comfort try to forget the truth around them. They will go after the powerful, the rich, and the one who brings them more pleasure". He was fully right.

My Dear God:

At this time of their lives, he was not there to listen to them. They knew he didn't ever pay attention to their teenage attitude. He kept himself out of their reach, and he wouldn't allow himself to be disturbed by their problems, or by their demands. And especially they knew that their father because of his own interest not only does not support or defend their mother, but he would be completely glad to dump all the guilt on her. And he will be very happy if they could abuse their mother. At this time he was trying to be accepted by his children. So to be able to achieve that, without knowing what he is doing to

their emotions, he tried to make himself look innocent in their eyes, and put all the guilt on their mother. No wonder one day he gave me the news and said, "My children love me". Please don't make me laugh. I am the one who pushed them towards that. I am the one, who they could depend on all their lives. They knew that they never should come after me to be able to get my love. It was you, who was never available for them. They had to beg you not let them to lose their dignity.

So, please my dear God, don't you think I must take their abuse, and not make them madder than they were? Don't you think someone should be their punching bag? Don't you think that they need to scream, and destroy the one person who listened to them? So that person was I, the mother, who went wrong.

Mojgan left me with a lot of anger in her, and no feelings for me. Maseeh was in California with very minimum contact. Mary was in California in her father's house, and being hospitalized for sometimes that I didn't know of. And Mojgan in Kalamazoo was trying to destroy her and me both.

Whenever I looked at other children, who still were under their parent's supervision, and were becoming adults gracefully, I cried for my children, especially Mojgan. I cried for her, because I read in her diary, "Since DR. Malakuti died, my father hates me". This sentence by itself was enough for me to be able to take all her abuse, and never say one word. Didn't her father prove to her by his actions that he hated his children, especially Mojgan, after Malakuti died? Weren't his actions louder than thousands words?

When I look back and see a seductive woman like Badri had seduced Iraj, who was supposed to become one of the best fathers among all those fathers, I feel sorry for all mankind. If this was not the story of Adam and Eve, then what should we call it? I felt sorry for my dear son, if he wanted to be prisoner in the hands of a seductive woman. Until men were showing weakness in their sexuality, women like Badri will go after them, seduce them, and destroy their homes and their reputation. I just feel sorry for men like Iraj. Until I die I will believe that Iraj hated men like himself in his entire life. He could fool everyone else. He could fool himself, but he will never be able to fool me. He hated men, who did what he did to his family. I just feel sorry for him. And I allowed my children to take their aggression on me as long as they needed it. And if Iraj was not ashamed of his own actions, he would have never looked so old and ugly. I am sure that his premature aging was the result of his shame and embarrassments. I have the right to feel sorry for him, and all men like him. Seductive women like Badri put a trap for hungry men like Iraj. If they were able to seduce them, and keep them under their sex power, everything was fine. But if with all their seduction they couldn't capture their prisoners for themselves, then they would scream their heads off, and blame the man for attempting to rape them, or use the newest tactic "sexual harassment". There has not been one good man, who had destroyed his family for a seductive woman, and had been happy with his act at the end of his life. Remember I said, "All the good men". Since any brainless woman

like Badri was able to take advantage of sexual weakness in a man with brain, intelligence, success, and most of all dignity, and bring him to a level that he only could make decisions from his pants and not his scalp, I really feel sorry for men. Women had abused them in general, and they were the blame for whatever went wrong in the world. Not that all men are good. But the good ones had been played around, and abused by women like Badri. The only thing that they are proud of is their breasts, their sexual part, and how to be able to sell it in the market. Until Badri came along, I thought this was only the act of a prostitute. But now I realize that this kind of women had given a bad name to prostitutes. The police will go after them to stop their work, and put them in prison, and yet we were watching most of them on TV, and we applaud them. What an upside down world! What a crazy world! Either this act was bad, or we must stop everyone from it. Or it is good, so then allow everyone to be able to do one like animals. Why were there restrictions by law for some, and there is complete freedom for some other people?

My Dear God:

Anyway, my dear God, I have so much to talk to you about. But then I see myself talking too much as if I wasn't. I know that I am not able to correct any of the wrong acts in the world. But when I discuss them with you, I feel someone is listening. And that is important to me

My Dear God:

Well, as they say, "Life must go on no matter what". I was trying to live, and be there for my children the best way if I could. I was trying to work more, get active more, read books more, and wait for the next disaster to come to my way. When I realized that Mojgan had interest to be near me most of the times, although she was always hurting me, and fighting with me for very little reason, I decided to look for a house in her neighborhood. She had in mind to get into a business like catering, or baking with me. But I knew that business needed a peaceful relationship between the partners to make it work. Not only that but trust and respect for one another are the principal factors in any partnership. Which at that time I couldn't find it between us. So I contacted a Real Estate lady who knew Mojgan. Any weekend that I was there, she showed me few houses. After seeing many houses big or small, expensive or not very expensive, we found one a few blocks away from Mojgan's house. It did not have a garage, and it was not right on the lake. It was a right size house for me. It had a very big and open kitchen, which attracted both Mojgan and I. It was not possible to build a garage for it, so that was a minus for me. And at the same time I was trying to make a trip to London and Iran to visit my family.

After I paid money to Mojgan to buy her house, I felt very good seeing Mojgan and Joe having their own house. They were very compatible. Then I realized that if I could do the same thing for Maseeh, I was sure that it would give him a boost in his life. So we

discussed it with Maseeh. At that time I did not have enough money for him to be able to pay for the premium of the house that he wanted. The houses in LA were very expensive, and we were planning by my payment for the premium, and mortgage and insurance and other expenses by Maseeh. I could move with him and Anna, his girlfriend at that time. We had this idea, but the premium was too high for me.

At the same time I was planning to go to Iran. The thought of living with Maseeh, stopped me from farther search for a house in Kalamazoo. And it was at this time that, Ida and Mehrdad were not getting along. I could see it clearly that soon they would separate, and I would have to move out as well.

With all these things happening at the same time, I was planning for a long trip to Iran. Since I did not want to be a burden on my children's shoulders, I started to look for a house in Southfield City, away from the suburb. I wanted to have a next-door neighbor to be able to see them and talk to them. I wanted to see children laughing and playing together with laughter, or sometimes cry. I wanted to live like a human being, not like a rich snob, so-called higher-class society. I hated my mink coats and my jewelry. I hated that untrue and superficial life. I was looking for the truth, and I wanted to find it. It was possible to find it away from those phony Iranians.

My Dear God:

I thought I would buy a house to be able to share it with a housemate. The same way that it was possible for me to live with a family like Ida's, the same way I could find a housemate to live with me in my house. This thought made me start looking for a house in Southfield area.

The way that I saw my children, I realized that this was a great idea. I thought I would travel to Iran and England for six months, and live the other six months of the year in the U.S.A.

When I was almost putting my thoughts into actions, Maseeh started to take the subject of buying a house together seriously. Anna was the one, who promoted the idea. I was caught between the ideas of buying a house in Southfield Michigan, or going into a partnership with my son. I was very honest with Maseeh. I discussed my feelings about the advantages and the disadvantages. Sometimes he didn't agree with my ideas. And sometimes I didn't like his.

I didn't want to lose the little money, which I was able to earn from Iraj by force. How did I know what kind of a son he would become later on? My accountant was against giving my money away, and DR. Mehrabian warned me from the time that I would be homeless. Plus if I was going to share the house with them I would have disturbed their privacy, and I was obligated to lose my freedom and privacy also. So if I wanted to share the payment on the house with him, I had to make sure that my rights were protected as well as theirs.

Maseeh, who rarely called me, with the idea of having his own house, was calling me every day, even more than once. The thought of bringing happiness into his life by giving him my money for the payment of the premium of his house was overwhelming for me. He was new at his work, and he had no credit to be able to borrow money from banks. The more I thought about it, the more I realized that Maseeh's happiness was first, and the rest would be easy to handle.

I had met Anna, his girl friend, many times. She seemed very nice. I knew that Maseeh was in a life and death situation when he met Anna. He had moved from Michigan to California for the first time to start his life separate from his family. He had no job, no one to take care of him. To help his father's club business, he started working at Hollywood Live, not knowing what was going on between the partners at all. He was used and abused by his father, and his other partners to a point that they did not pay his money, while they were stealing money from the club left and right. Meanwhile his father's affair with Badri had brought up the ugliness of divorce upon him. For the first time he was living away from his mother, who had never left his sight before. At such an important and young age, he was facing what he was always afraid of: the separation of his parents with a lot of bitterness and embarrassments among his peers. A young man, who used to have a good home, good parents, good education, and came from a good background, and thought he had a dignified life, now he must face the impossible, and sadly cried for his lost happiness.

My Dear God:

He was in such a mixed up situation when he met Anna. She had applied for a job at Hollywood Live, and was working for the group. First time when I met her, it was the night of the open house for the club. We were staying in Parri's house as always. Maseeh was sharing a house with two other friends. He wanted to invite his friends for dinner. So he asked me if I could cook for them. He always appreciated my cooking, and I went shopping with Parri and cooked a few dishes, which Maseeh approved of, and we took them to Maseeh's house.

Anna was one of the guests in Maseeh's house that night. When I met her I was in a life and death situation. My husband was having affair with Badri, and I had to deal with it. She was his mistress for as long as Malakuti was dead. So I don't remember how I was reacting in that meeting with Anna. I liked her, and she seemed like a nice girl. But I don't know how she felt about me after that first meeting. I thought that by just looking at me in such a pain, everyone could see my heart bleeding. Although I always was trying to keep my cool, still I don't remember how I acted, or what did I said.

The funny part was that when I look at the pictures from those days, I look happy and cheerful in them. It seems like I was having the time of my life. That first meeting with Anna, I didn't realize that one day she will be living with him, and I never thought of me

living with her in one house. Life is so strange.

Maseeh's painful life at that time, and Anna's separation from her ex boyfriend of nine years, had brought them together. The way that I heard the story, Maseeh had been having such a rough life at that time that Anna offered her house to him, and Maseeh moved in with her. As they say, "The friend in need, is a friend indeed". She was five years older than Maseeh, and she had a way of comforting him. They both cared for each other's friendship. Maseeh always talked highly of her to me. He talked about her talent in art, her neatness in general, and her responsibility towards her work. Times and times he told me, "She reminds me of you". I think he wanted to make sure that I was approving of her. He wanted me to accept her the same way that he was accepting her.

My Dear God:

When I went to LA, and stayed with them for a week or two, I realized that Maseeh was right. She was pretty, talented, active, and very meticulous all together. She had inherited her artistic talent from her father. He actually earned his living by selling his paintings. Anna and I got along very well. And I realized that their living together at that time of their lives was a great thing that happened to both of them. Among all Anna's sisters and brothers, none of them were college graduates. Maseeh tried so hard to persuade Anna to go back to college. He tried to make her believe in herself, and raised the level of her self-confidence. He told her that, "It means wasting your mind and your talent, if you do not take the opportunity, and prove to yourself once and for all that you are capable of doing it".

Meanwhile he was climbing up the ladder at his job at Warner Bros., located in Burbank. It seemed that he was doing an outstanding job that each year he received one or two awards. Although he did not talk about it much; but I was very proud. Maseeh is one of the unique men in my life. He is my dream son. He is very handsome, very well mannered, very loyal, very respectful to the opposite sex, and altogether he is a real gentleman. You might think that I, as his mother, must talk about him this way. But it is not only I, you can hear the same things from all his friends of many years, and all his past girlfriends.

I will never forget the day that he explained to me why he had to forgive his father for his behavior in his midlife crisis. He had such a strong and intelligent point that I became proud of myself for raising such a young man. Although I hated Iraj, and anything about him, still I felt proud of Maseeh. He explained it to me this way, "Recently one of my friend's father, who had committed the same act that my father did, had gotten Alzheimer's disease, and had been hospitalized. He does not recognize his own son when he goes to visit him. It is very painful to my friend. The father does not understand or remember anything. Although he did not do any thing wrong during their fights or divorce, yet he is sorry for the rest of his life why he neglected his father, and why he did

not make peace with his father before it was too late. So although he is not guilty of any wrong doing, still he blames himself for not being able to be with his father when he was fine". Then he turned to me and said, "With all due respect for you, I don't want the same thing to happen to me. I am completely aware of what my father had brought upon us. But he had done it. And there is nothing that we can do to correct by punishing him. Hopefully one day he will become to his own senses, and realize that what he did to destroy his family was not worth it". At that time I did not say anything. I just thanked GOD for making my father's wish come true. He always wished that would be able to raise his children as a great human being. And also wanted that his children's children become someone to be proud of. Too bad he was not there to see what a gentleman I had raised. I saw he was right. He was not willing to continue living with guilty conscious for the rest of his life. I wished my father was there to see what kind of a son I raised, while he had a father like Iraj, disloyal, dishonest, crooked betrayer, and the most scandalous man of all times. I hoped he could continue to be the same person that I saw him that day.

My Dear God:

Anna thought of Maseeh the same way I did. But because of the love and intimacy that they had for each other, she put him more on the pedestal than I did. Obviously it should have been that way. But one thing about Anna that I realized was that deep down she did not want to believe that Maseeh had to be part of Iranian culture. What I had seeded in my children mostly came from my background and my upbringing. The intelligence, the manners, the control, the patience, and the perfect humanitarian belief at such a crucial time and period of their lives was just what my father expected from his children and his grand children.

I met Anna's parents at Maseeh's house. I cooked Ghormeh Sabzi for them, and they loved it. They were very nice people. Besides their own six children, they had adopted a few more, and loved to have a simple life. Her father, who was very well known for making portraits, made a nice portrait of me. They both were talking so highly about Maseeh. Often they congratulated me for raising a son like Maseeh. They lived in Oregon, and many times had invited Maseeh to their house and had gone fishing together. Something that Maseeh liked a lot, and not even once his dear father made himself available for him to go fishing together. Maseeh had a lot of respect for their family, and thought that Knutsons were the best. And still till this day, they are very good friends.

Whenever Maseeh's friends, neighbors, or those who had associated with him at some time or other, talked so highly about him, I felt like a proud mother. And when I say Maseeh is handsome, is not just because I am his mother. It is because of the facts, and what I heard from people around us.

Once I had to go to a dentist when I was in their house. He drove me to the dentist's office. The young lady at the counter did not know that he was my son. She looked at me

after Maseeh left, and told me "Wasn't he handsome? Oh he was handsome". I smiled at her and I said, "I know, he is my son".

Anna was very sensitive about Maseeh's attractiveness; to a point that most of the times she made her own life miserable. One evening we were going to dinner with another couple of his friends. The restaurant was a walking distance from their house. Boys were walking together, and us, the three girls were following them, or vice versa. As usual we had a very nice evening. When we were going into the restaurant, the girl behind the counter, who took our coats and hats, started talking nicely, admiring Maseeh. Well, Maseeh was not rude to her; he obviously answered her with a smile. After dinner, when we walked out of the restaurant, again the same girl greeted Maseeh in a pleasant way. He said thanks, and we walked out of the restaurant.

My Dear God:

Walking home, Anna was very upset, and all the way home she was talking about it. Although we all knew that Maseeh did not have to do anything with it at all, still Anna couldn't let go of the subject. Both girls were bothered why their men never become jealous like they do. By that kind of reaction from her I realized that Anna was planning to have control on every movement of Maseeh. The way that I knew Maseeh, he was not happy to be under anyone's command or control, even if that person was like a GOD to him. So I never interfered with their way of relationship with each other. I thought it was their business to know how to deal with one another.

Anna had bought my trust, and she was comfortable to talk to me about her personal feelings. Late at nights, when I sat by her to finish her homework, or her paintings till three o'clock AM, we talked of any subject possible. She even talked to me about their sexual habits. Although I was trying to let her know that I was not ready to love anyone any more, still she wanted to prove to me that I was wrong. She could love me as her mother, and I could love her as my daughter. I must put my past behind me and forget about those people, who came in my way wrongly, and start seeing people as they really were.

When I heard their conversation about their men in lives, who did not show any jealousy towards them, I knew that their men were very secure, and sure of themselves. There was no need for them to feel jealous at all. But the girls, although were sure of their men, they were not sure of other women. This subject made them uneasy whenever they were around other women. It is the other woman, who is not ever trusted. When she has her eyes on your man, she will make it possible to grab him, and hide him under her deceitful web, which was woven in her mind for him. So by knowing this, women in general cannot ever feel secure or safe. Any woman can be afraid of another woman, who pays too much attention to her man.

For generation after generation society had put the blames on men, and their natural

behavior towards their sexualities. But the society had not been fair to men in general. For years and years women had fooled them without knowing it. Such a shame! Those men had been our fathers, our brothers, our sons, and our husbands. Women did it throughout centuries to satisfy their sexual desires.

My Dear God:

I have always been a liberal woman, and I always will be. But if we study the history of both sexes relationship during the centuries, we will see the truth, and save our men from being destroyed. If it wasn't for another woman, who allowed herself to come forward and seduce a married man with temptation, that married man does not dare to destroy his family life. And if by nature he needed extra marital affair, he only goes to prostitutes. In that case he had satisfied his thirst for sexual desires, and meanwhile he had kept it away from his home and family. And better yet, that prostitute never goes after his wife and his home. Not that I agree with this kind of act. But at this time that I am writing these lines, ninety-five percent of married men are going after prostitutes. And more than half of these men are still with their wives, and are living happily ever after. I believe that those years that I thought Iraj was clean and honest with me, he was with others, and he used to pick up prostitutes. Only I didn't know. And so were many of his doctor friends. Without any questions those couples, who are still together, if they read these lines in their hearts will agree with me. So the reason that women in general are always jealous and insecure is because they know their own gender. They are the ones who are not trustworthy. If a girl likes your husband, she will go after him without any hesitation or fear.

Anna had kept Maseeh's picture above her artwork. She loved him dearly, and so did her parents. Maseeh was the same with Anna, and called her from work four or five times a day to see if she was doing fine. And I was very happy to see they were truthful to each other. Maseeh was trying so hard not to make Anna jealous for any reason. He made sure to do his loving duty towards Anna by all means. I remember one Valentine's Day that I was in their house. He rarely sent me a flower. That day, as a routine, he wanted to send flowers for Anna. Not to make me feel left out, he had ordered two similar flowers for both of us. They were most beautiful and expensive orchids in two different pots, one for Anna, and one for his mom. Obviously I was very excited to receive a flower from my son on Valentine's Day. Anna was happy and excited also. But I felt that something was missing for Anna, because I heard them quarreling in their bedroom after dinner. I thought Anna had been broken because Maseeh's love for her had been divided in her eyes. Obviously the subject of quarrel couldn't be that. But that feeling in Anna had created a different subject for quarrel.

My Dear God:

Maseeh was not used to calling or talking to me often on the phone. But after I offered him the possibility of giving him the down payment for purchasing a new house, he called me often.

I couldn't understand him why was he against joint ownership. He wasn't sure that having my name on his property was a good idea. On the other hand I wanted to make sure that I didn't lose my savings. I knew that no matter what happened to me, my money was his money, and my property was his property, dead or alive. But if God forbid something happened to him, I couldn't have a proof that I shared the house with him, and I was a part owner of the house. So when he did not agree with my decision, we dropped the subject for a while, until we come to the right solution. Anna was the one who loved the idea of sharing home with me. She made herself a mediator, and wanted Maseeh to think wisely.

The fact was that I had been stupid all my life, because I loved too much. This time I did not want to become homeless, just because I wanted to help my children. I wanted to find a legal way to be able to protect and defend my rights if necessary. Although Anna was insisting that this matter was only between Maseeh and I, and she didn't want to have to do anything with it, still she was the one, who wanted Maseeh to go ahead with his decision and buy a house with me. So although Maseeh was not used to calling me often, for this purpose he started calling me every day as often as he thought it was necessary. And if we couldn't come to any agreement, I wrote him a letter to make him understand why I was trying to have a proof of giving him my savings to him for the purchase of his house.

I was aware of advantages and disadvantages of living together with Maseeh and his girlfriend. I knew that no matter how much money I gave him, still it was his house and I did not have any right to say or do anything. I knew that by living together they were giving up their complete privacy. After all, there was a third person living in their house at all times. For a young couple that was not fantastic news. Somehow they were obligated to have respect for the third party's needs. And to me that was a little awkward. On the other hand I would see myself obligated not to do things, which I was allowed to do in my own house. For instance, I was obligated not to invite some people in my house, because they preferred not to see them. So in all there were many advantages and disadvantages to be considered. But again thinking that Maseeh would have his comfort in his new house with the two women he loved the most, Anna and his mother, gave me a go ahead. Especially when I heard from Anna later on that one day she had to look allover for him. It was the time that he was so fed up with his father's and the partners' behavior that he actually was suicidal. She found him in a cave like by the ocean.

My Dear God:

The more I heard those stories about Maseeh's uncertainty and sadness, the more I realized that I must do something to bring hope and liveliness in his life. Obviously the first step was to find a way to make the purchase of the house easy on him. He must have something to make him look forward to the future. When he left Michigan, we were still living in that big house. He wasn't with us when we sold the house, and we were moving from one apartment to another. After he said goodbye to that house and the people in it, he did not know what life was going to bring us soon after. While we were wandering from place to place, he was wandering from a room to an apartment in order to bring some stability in his life. Although I was not stable myself, still I felt responsible to take the biggest step by paying the twenty percent down payment for his new home, whatever it cost me.

At that time I had my condominium on Cass Lake in Pontiac, Michigan. And since it was giving me rental, and I was working on the side too, I was able to save more, and I did not have to sell my condo.

By now Mary was in California under treatment. Since I didn't want to discuss any kind of family matter with my children, my only connection was Dr. Mehrabian. I was trying to stay far away from Iraj and Badri. I never allowed myself to hear their names, or their voices. The hatred that I had for them made my voice shake, and it made my body tremble. I was trying to cut them, and that period of my life out of my memory. I was trying to pretend that I have never been married, nor did I have any children. Although the only thing that I had in mind was to think about my children's happiness, and find a way to bring hope in their lives, still I did not want to involve them with any of my affairs. I made decisions by myself, and I received all the necessary information through Dr. Mehrabian, and sometimes from Dr. Mohammad Rabbani regarding my legal papers. And that was it. So I was only trying to be there for my children when they needed me, but not think of them as of my children. I couldn't have that bond of motherhood with them, while I knew they were his children, and they had to love him with strings attached. I knew completely that it was not their fault. It was me, who gave them this father, without being aware of his character.

My Dear God:

However, those kinds of feelings, and this way of thinking were out of my control. I tried so hard not to become a criminal. And with the wisdom that I found in me I was able not to kill any of them. But until I am alive, and I can breath, I will hate them and anyone, who had any respect for them. The only problem was that in my children's case I was the guilty one. I introduced them to that father. I gave them that father, yet I had to love them, be there for them, when they needed me, and stay away from them as much as is possible. Many times I have said it, "Anyone, who has respect for my stabber, is my

stabber, even if they are my own children". This belief was in my heart, and it will be in my heart until I die.

The reason that I had chosen those families to live with them, and substituted my own family with them was to be able to learn how to live without my own children. I knew that they didn't belong to me any more. I knew that they had to save themselves from falling apart, rather than thinking of their mother's need and desires. So I had to let go of what my desire was.

Dr. Mehrabian was my only connection with Iraj regarding my children. He was a faithful friend, and had a lot of respect for me. Although Iraj was his partner in some properties, and he was working at his hospital, I thought he might have known about Iraj's affair with Badri and their plans for marriage. But he told me that he was not aware of his plans until he left Michigan. He was not even on the list of that anonymous Iranian, who sent the famous sarcastic poem to all Iranians. He thought he didn't know Iraj at all. I told him, "You are not the only one, my dear. Welcome to my unknown".

With new friends and supporters around me I was able to get to know my way to life. With the help of each and every one of them I was able to see more clearly that the faster I got rid of those destructive feelings called LOVE, the sooner I would find peace.

I was preparing for a trip to Iran and the partnership with Maseeh to buy a house in California. It was too obvious that soon I had to give up the job at the restaurant. But I couldn't see myself staying away from that job if I was still living in Michigan. Being with their family all day, and working non-stop was the only cure for my desperation. There were a few times gossips created some difficulties at work for me. Each time after I discussed it with Farah, who was the leader of the group, she talked to her children, and the problem was solved, and I continued working there.

My Dear God:

As I said before there were many Arabs and African American workers in that kitchen. As my nature is, all my life I have been a supporter of underdog. There was another Iranian partner, whom I didn't know before. But they were nice, and we got along well. They were Mr. K and Simeen Tavakoli, whom I talked about before. Just prior going to Iran, one day Mr. K allowed himself to attack my integrity for supporting one of the co-workers. Actually they had this attitude towards me from day one. The reason was that I was there by the decision of the most powerful partner, Farah Shushtari. But I knew that they were a nice, hard working family, and I had respect for them. We even became friends, and they did many nice things for me.

That day was not like any other day for me. In front of the waiters, who were standing there, he wanted to show me the equal power of his partnership with Shushtaris. He didn't know that even if Shushtaris allowed themselves to talk to me that way, I was not the kind of person who would take it and not react to it. I realized that it was time for

me to end that job right there. I was aware that from day one Tavakolis did not want me there, but they did not have the power to do anything about it. Now he was working on the floor, and not only in the kitchen, and he had gained equal rights of partnership. So to prove that he had equal rights with Shushtaris, the best way was to insult my integrity in front of my co-workers, and show them who was the boss.

He didn't dare to fire me, so he tried to hurt me in a way that I gave up the job. And that time was the right time for me to quit. I knew that Tavakolis were able to get the support of Farsheed and his wife Sudabeh. And, by all means, I did not want to cause any difficulty between Farah and her children. So the best thing was to say good-bye to everyone.

As soon as Mr. K finished his sentence, without any hesitation, I said good-bye to those who were standing there, and I left the restaurant, where I started working right after their opening. And I have been with that family, and the long hours of work brought more peace in me than the strongest drugs.

When I got home, I called Farah to talk to her. I thanked her for all her friendship, kindness, and the opportunity she had given me to be able to work so many hours, to be able to take myself away from my problems. Without of those long hours of work I don't think I would have been able to survive the way that I did. And I apologized for not going back to work.

I am sure that she knew how important that job was to my survival. So after researching about the situation, she asked me to go back to work, and that she would try to make them understand that they must behave differently towards me. But I told her, "I think it is time for me to stop working there. First, because I do not want to cause any problems between the partners. And second, if it wasn't for Mr. K, I would probably still want that job, and I would not allow myself to see clearly. As a matter of fact, probably Mr. K was the sender of GOD to wake me up, "Hey Shamci, enough is enough. You must wake up now, and find a different lifestyle. You had enough time to come to conclusions. Open your eyes, while the opportunity is there, find the right way to start your new life without those who once belonged to you. That time of your life was not real, and neither is this one. Find a life free of attachments, and go on with your new life. You are the decision maker and a winner. Mr. K was here to shake you and bring wisdom to you. Be happy".

My Dear God:

Being with Ida was a blessing for me. The couple was so nice and respectful to me that I will never forget. I was so attached to the full time job that after two days staying home, I was going crazy. I thought until I got passport, I would have to find another job. Without working elsewhere, I would have gone crazy. One night, when we were invited in Dr. Jalil Farah's house, I thought it would be nice if he could get me a job in the Radiology Department, where he was the chief of staff. He already had hired another divorced

Iranian lady, and it made a huge difference in her life. Obviously it was a more prestigious job than working in a restaurant. Not only that But Dr. Farah himself was nearly thirty years chief of staff of the Radiology Department at Beaumont Hospital, and at that time his son was working with him at the same department. He was somebody very important and prestigious, not like some other Iranian doctor, whose name was spread all around the town with a sarcastic poem to prove that he was scandalous man.

When I told him about my need for a job to be able to keep me away from wrong thoughts, he gave me a number and the name of a lady to contact. He told me he was going to talk to that lady, who was in charge of hiring for his department, and told me to just go there, "You don't have to talk about your life at all. Just fill out the application, and give her all the information that she needs". I told him, "I had applied for my passport, and any time I might receive it". He still asked me to go ahead with it. He cared and had a lot of respect for me. After Iraj was gone, there was no party in their house that I was not invited. Also Mrs. Elizabeth Farah bought me tickets for occasional luncheons, and invited me to go places, which we were not going before my divorce.

So I contacted the lady. She was very warm and understanding. She started working on my application. It took sometime to arrange the interview. Right before my interview I received my passport and I was ready to take-off. When I called the lady to apologize for the inconvenience, and told her the importance of my trip to Iran, and not being able to go on my interview, she accepted it with an open mind. She wished me a safe trip, and reminded me to call her when I came back from Iran. I promised her that when and if I came back, I would call her immediately.

My Dear God:

I called Dr. Farah and apologized for not being able to make it to my appointment, and at the same time I thanked him for his care and friendship, and I said good bye to them.

You see, my dear GOD, this was the first time that I was going to Iran with such bad news. I didn't know how to face anyone. I was embarrassed to look at anyone, or talk about the outcome of my marriage. Since I was away from my country and my family, I was able not to bring up any subject about my life or my family. I knew that they might have heard about it from other people, but I didn't want them to hear it from me. I didn't want them to tell me, "We knew what Iraj was capable of. We knew how ruthless he was". Or probably some of them felt sorry for me, and wanted to have pity for me. I was planning to stay away from any conversations regarding my marriage. I didn't want to show any weakness to anyone, especially my brother Jamal, who was Iraj's friend to begin with. It was their friendship that introduced Iraj to me. But he got to know Iraj to a point that when I married Iraj, he threw me out of the house and said, "Now, you go to hell. If you want him, we don't want you any more".

I was wondering how to face people, who knew Iraj so well. I still was in the stage of shock. What I was doing here, I just was spinning around to be able to find escape from going crazy, or become a murderer. I knew that what happened to my life was like dying. The same way that there was no prevention from dying. The same way there was no prevention for me to be able to save my marriage, unless I was able to kill them both, and leave my name on the list of murderers. Thanks God that didn't happen to me! It wasn't worth ruining my name killing two promiscuous dogs. I was too valuable and too important to get my hands dirty with the blood of two worthless people. I am glad I was able to keep my mind away from that ugly act.

So I tried to adapt myself to the idea of going to Iran, and play it by ear. I wanted to adapt myself to go with the float of water. If they see that I was not discussing my life with them, they would find out that they were not allowed to ask anything about my private life. I figured out that there was no time for sadness or unhappiness.

Previous to this trip, when I went to Iran, it was in the beginning of Iraj and Badri's affair. The only person who knew about it was my sister Ezzat. She was the one who kept me alive with her letters. At that time I thought no one else knew anything about them. But later on I found out that Nazi Forghani knew everything through Mary's letters. And she had spread around the news. Only I didn't know it.

My Dear God:

Obviously, this time everyone, who knew us, must have heard the news of our separation. Anyway, I had prepared myself for an excremental trip to Iran. Everyone, my sisters, nieces, nephews, cousins, with flowers in their hands was greeting me at the airport. For me, after a long time of suffering, it was an exciting and a delightful moment. The flowers, the tears of happiness or sadness, the warm welcome, their hugs and kisses made me feel like a queen. But only my dear GOD knew what was beneath my laughter. There was a great deal of emptiness in my heart that I was trying to hide. While I was crying for the great loss of my family, they assumed that I was crying from happiness. This time I did not have my most wonderful husband any more. I didn't have my beautiful children any more. I didn't have that great love of life in me any more. I didn't have my security and sense of belonging any more. But they didn't have to know that. We all were crying, laughing, and looking at each other to see if it was true that we were sitting next to each other. Was that happening that we were all under one roof again? Was it real? How much each one of us had changed during those years!

They had arranged a big party for that day. My brothers, their wives, and their children came. Little by little I started to feel right at home. But what they were seeing in me was not what I had in me. I had lost thirty great years of my life, and now I had to be able to go back and connect myself to the age that I wasn't married, and I had no children, while everyone there had their families, and thanks God, they had their health also. While

In Sina's kitchen after we ate, we sat to relax. We talked about any subject.
Left to right: Hosain, Azar, Rokhand, me, Sina and Saideh

We are in Azar's house. She worked too hard that day.
Left to right: Azar, Negar, Javad, me, Saideh, Jamal
Front row: Layla, Rokhand, Afsar and Azar

In London, England with Hosain and Afsaneh at their house

In London, England, at my Sister Ezzat's house. I was bugging Nader that day like always. Left to right: Ezzat, Sudabeh, me, Nader, Ali, and Sudabeh's husband who is a dentist in London.

Ali, Farnaz, and I are in their new house.

With Sina in Shiraz

In my house; Mary, Maseeh, and his canine

In London with Ezzat

In London with Ezzat

Sina, Shamci, and Ezzat at their friend's coffee shop, getting ready to leave. We were in Belgium, and the owner of the shop was Ali, Ehsan's friend.

This good-bye party was given by Sadegh and Rokhand for me. Left to right: Afsar, Rokhand, Hassan, Saideh, Javad, Zari, her mother, Fereshteh, and the waiters with their uniforms on.

Here, I am with some of my good friends in Fereshteh's house, in Iran. Being exactly the opposite of my so called "friends" in Michigan, there was not a single time that I went to Iran and they didn't invite me to welcome me to Iran and to their house. Something is very nice about nature that has not created all the human beings the same. Few of these ladies are friends with Fereshteh. Others are: Naheed Naghsineh, Fereshteh, Farideh Pazandeh, her daughter Partow, Fereshteh Attaran, me, and my role model, my mentor, and a great example of a lady: Shahnaz Toosi, that without her our group would be apart.

Here, we are sitting around the lunch table in Farideh Pazandeh's house. Her daughter Partow had come to visit from Chicago, and some of her friends were there that day. Among us were: me, Parveen Rafani, Shahnaz Toosi in the middle, Farideh, and Naheed Naghshineh. Farideh's daughter-in-law and her daughter Partow are the two standing. As you see the table is so colorful. The foods were so delicious that I get hungry just by looking at them.

Here, we are in Shahnaz's yard. What a day! What a beautiful group! I wish them all great happiness. From left to right, sitting: Shamci, Naheed, and Partow. Fereshteh, farideh, and Shahnaz, our gracious host and companion are standing.

I was thankful for that, I was embarrassed that I had failed to keep my family together. I had no choice but to put my past behind me, cut out that period of my life out of my memory, and ignore that it was ever part of my life. As long as no one brought up the subject, I would be fine. And that was that.

I thought if everyone knew about my life; let them keep it within themselves. There was no need to discuss it with me. And those who haven't heard the story of my life, they can't help me by knowing it. So I started to live my life as if I have never had any past. The idea worked very well for me. I had planned to stay for four months in Iran and two months in London. It seemed that they took the insecure and scared Shamci out of my body, and replaced her with a jolly, cheerful, and pleasant person that I was before my marriage. I felt confident, dignified, and powerful enough to be able to face the world again. I became the old jolly good fellow that nobody could deny. My heart that was empty of any feelings, returned to a heart with lots of love, care, and happiness. I learned to laugh again. The muscles of my face, which were not able to open to a smile, started coming back and perform as they always did. As the time passed, my laughter became louder being among my family. We talked about our childhood, and the things we did to one another.

My Dear God:

My sister Azar had lost her son Reza only a year ago. She wasn't able to remove her black, or see the light after that loss, which was as heart aching for each one of us as it was for Azar. With me being there, I tried so hard to make her get lost at the moment and be able to act like her normal self. Before I go there, she was completely numb and emotionless. After I got there, she was moving along with us, and sometimes she forgot that she was dead. One night, after telling many jokes and laughing our heads off, I saw her doing her old routine self. She was doing her old silly dance, which was making everybody laugh. I felt so good that I really cried. It was the first time that anyone saw Azar actually laugh.

So as you see, my dear GOD, with that visit to Iran, I was able to go back to my routine silliness, and brought back happiness in everyone's life, including Azar. I was really proud of myself. When we were teenagers, Azar was the joker among siblings. She and Parri, my sister in-law, were the comedians, and they put on shows whenever the two families were together. Our mothers were specially amused by their acts.

I think I had talked about Azar and the death of her son, Reza. It happened at the beginning of my crisis with Iraj. Whenever I was very sad and depressed, I tried to put myself in Azar's shoes, and see that the loss of her twenty two year old son Reza was greater than the loss of my husband. Then I realized that nothing could ever be more painful than the sudden death of the most handsome, the most talented, educated, beautiful twenty two year old son. Whenever I thought of her, I thought my problems were nothing. The thoughts of Azar's unexpla1nable pain were so deep and strong that I felt shameful thinking of my own pain. I realized that if Azar, with such a great loss, still she must walk, talk, work, breath, and continue living, I must be able to do the same thing. Life must go on no matter what.

Whenever I compared the severity of her pain over mine, I realized that her pain would never end for her, even if she learned how to laugh. But my pain would disappear as soon as I could get rid of my past love and my past memories. The day that I made Azar laugh and dance for the first time after Reza's death, I thought that was the beginning for both of us. I had three children to look after, and Azar had her only daughter Rokhand, who had lost her only brother to look up to.

My Dear God:

Rokhand's parents were divorced when they were six and four years of age. They had such a hard time growing up, sometimes with mother, and sometimes with their father and his new family. Azar was a respectful teacher and a principal of a high school. Her life was her two children. Reza was not only dear to all of us, but he was the only man, and the only love in Azar's and Rokhand's life. He was the only support for both of them. He was a son, a brother, a lover, a husband and a father to both of them. I have heard that, "GOD is great". I wish I could have asked you my dear GOD, "What was the reason behind taking Reza away from these two women at such a young age? Why are you supposed to act like an Indian giver? If you wanted to take him away from them so soon, why did you give him to them to begin with?" Well, I don't think we have the right to question you. Obviously there was and is an important purpose behind all these happenings. Time will tell, and time will heel. Then, when it comes to this point, we must find out the definition of the word "faith". We must learn that each coming has one going. When we understand this, we would not allow ourselves to question the length of the life, or existence of anybody or anything for that matter. So I was just happy to remind Azar, and also myself that, while we are still living, we must be happy and we must be able to bring happiness into the lives of those who need us and love us. We must stop asking, "Why me, why me?" All and all we have to learn to love life again. Sadness and giving up hopes does not help anybody. The best solution is to be able to keep the best memories from them in our hearts, and continue adapting ourselves with new opportunities, which will become available for us just by nature.

While I was in Iran, my children called me to see if I was okay. I wrote Mary once or twice a week. I just asked her to hang in there and be happy. I was trying to make my children forget the past completely, like what I was trying to do. There was no reason to dwell on something, which was out of our control. I believed that if we didn't try, we were not able to put the painful past behind us. And to be able to show my children that life must go on no matter what, I myself started to bring many changes in my life, which created the happiness that I wanted. Some people might have been happy to bring another man in their lives to give them the happiness, that they were looking for. But for me the happiness was to find my own self, the happy-go Shamci that I was before my marriage. And that trip to Iran was a complete turning point for me.

I had many friends, and sisters and brothers, who filled up my life with happiness, including my sisters-in-law and their other relatives. Many times, when my children called, I was not home so they had to find out where I was and call me there. This way they were sure that I was not destroyed, and I was having plenty of fun with my siblings, who had once disowned me for marrying Iraj. Many times I wanted to set up one specific time for them to call me. But it didn't work. So many times they had hard time finding me. Sometimes I called them the next day. And it was difficult finding them also. I never called Mary, because she was still living with her father. I wrote her twice a week to be able to keep my contact with her. As long as I knew that they were okay, I was happy and okay too.

My Dear God:

Life was great for me, and I was coming back to life. One day we were in my brother Jamal's house. All sisters and brothers and their families were there. I was having such a great time that, it seemed like a dream to me. Those were the ones who disowned me one day for marrying Iraj. Now they were the only hope that I had. I never gave up loving them, although they did not want me any more to be any part of their lives. But when my parents forgave me, everything went back to normal. Their love was there for me as strong as before or even more. While we all were talking and joking and laughing, we received a telephone call from Mojgan, who has been trying to reach me three other places. I was very happy to hear from her.

First happily she gave me the news of Joe's cousin's wedding. She said that the whole family was there. And then, all of a sudden, she started crying.

Since nobody had talked to me about my personal life, I didn't know how to talk to her in front of all those people. And I didn't know how to react to her sadness. They all knew enough English to understand the conversation between Mojgan and me. I was going crazy. My heart was pumping so fast that it was coming out of my chest. I just kept asking what had happened, and what I could do for you. I wished I could hold her in my arms, wipe up her tears, and comfort her. But I was thousands miles away from her, and I didn't know what to do. When I asked her what had happened for so many times, while she was crying she said, “It was a beautiful wedding. Both the bride and the groom had their parents with them. They were the luckiest people in the world. Why should I be the only one who has nobody to care about me? Why should this happen to our family and us? Why can't I have my parents together like they were before? Why do I have to come from a broken home?”, and on and on and on.

I felt I was losing control. I was hoping that I could get rid of my heart not to be able to feel that much pain. I went in the kitchen to be able to talk to her in private. I tried to calm her down, and gave her all my support for her wedding when it comes the time. I told her, "Until now I have been yours, and I promise you I will do my best to bring all the happiness in the world into your life. I had done my best, and I will do my best to bring happiness into your life, and Mary's, and Maseeh's. The love that I have for you in my heart is immeasurable. You are my heart. You are my whole life. How can you say that nobody loves you?" After listening to me while she was crying, angrily she asked me, "Why did you let her win? Why did you? Why didn't you fight more? Why, why? Why did you let her win?" I knew that her pain was greater than what I could imagine. How could I tell her the reason that I stayed with her father, and did not apply for divorce was to not to let her win? How could I tell her that as much as I tried to prevent our divorce from happening, her father was the one who made it possible? How could I ask her, "Wasn't eight years enough to take the abuse from two ruthless people?" But, it was not the right time, or the right place to tell her all those. So after I calmed her down, I told her, "If you promise me to be happy and think of my love for you, I will call you tomorrow and will be able to talk more about this. Now everybody is here, and I don't want to talk in front of them. Please promise me to stay happy because I know how much I love you".

My Dear God:

When I finished the conversation with her, and I went in the living room everybody had sensed that something was wrong. But I told them, "Everything is fine, only she was missing me".

That night when I went home I couldn't sleep. Again and again I thought it was me who made this kind of life possible for them. Unfortunately there was no way to reverse the existing situation. I just prepared myself to talk to her and give her as much support as possible.

Because of a nine and a half hours difference in time, I made sure to find her at the right time at home. She repeated the whole thing that she told me the night before. At least this time she was not crying. I thought it was better to talk to her on the phone, rather than being face to face. She always made it impossible to communicate. At the end of each conversation she made it into a big fight, and then no more talk. She was not able to hear the truth. For a person who wrote in her diary, "Since Dr. Malakuti died, my father hates me". And she, Mary and Maseeh had discussed their father's relationship with Badri, blaming me for the affair of their father. It was a torture. So it was my duty to comfort them, and take their abuse the way that made them feel good.

I told her, "Mojgan jon, you were not around when your father had his first affair. At that time, when he was sorry and after three years he decided to come back to me and apologized to us, every one including Parveen, my sister-in-law told me that it was much better to keep it quiet, and wait for him to come back without hassle. This time I decided to take their advice, and hope that he gave up, and came to his senses. Eight years of abuse was not enough, yet he was the one who initiated the divorce. When I didn't invite Badri in my house, your father invited her. He was the one who bought the ticket for her and her children to go to California with us to visit her family. I didn't want to create a fight to ruin your father's reputation. If I lost to her, it was because of your father's determination to destroy his family. You don't know what had happened to me in those eight years. I just did what I thought was right for me to do. But you must know that you are not the only one who had lost her family. If you look around you will see that there are millions of children whose home come apart every day. Not many of them are as fortunate as you are. You have a mother, who loves you enough to pay the premium of a house for you, and your boyfriend to live comfortably. You have a nice boyfriend, whom you can count on. You are a beautiful, and a hard working girl, who is capable of doing anything you wish. How many girls your age could have this many blessings? The day that I carried twenty thousand dollars cash in my purse to come by bus from Detroit to Kalamazoo for the closing of your house, I was not crazy to do that. Only I was so mad at your father, who betrayed his family the way he did, that I wanted to prove to myself that no one in the world could cheat and empty my pocket as your father did. I changed a bus in Detroit. I had a two-hour wait in that bus station among all poor, homeless people, and yet nobody robbed me. Didn't you believe that your father hated you after Malakuti died? Think about it. See what he had done to me, and my trust on him for thirty years? If that wasn't disloyalty and hate, then what would you call it?"

My Dear God:

After I said all these, I asked her to forget about the past. It is not possible for us to bring back what we all had lost. To look back only creates depression for us. We have to look forward and be hopeful for the better future. Crying does not solve any problem. Life must go on no matter what. Those who can learn from their sufferings are very fortunate people. No matter how much we cry we would not be able to mend our suffering hearts. We have to be able to rebuild our hearts with new hopes and new desires

I knew that all what I did was just a talk. She was the one who did not know anything about her father's affair in Iran. She was the one who was starting the age of puberty, and she had to learn that her father hated her. She was the only child who had it all so perfect, and lost everything at the most sensitive and difficult time of her life. The only thing that I could repeat and repeat and repeat was to say, "Shame on you Iraj. Shame on you millions and millions more. Too bad I did not have the video of you crying and apologizing to us after your first affair. I am sure you would have died just seeing that scene. Shame on you all. You never deserved to be a father to any child, yet to be the father of my children. Shame on you and more shame on you. Shame on you for bringing

endless pain and sufferings to my children's life and mine. Shame on you till eternity!

My Dear God:

Finally I was able to calm her down. She started talking in a confident voice. It seemed that she trusted my words and was ready to look forward to a happier life.

One week later she called me. She was in a good mood. After talking about everybody or different things, she gave me her good news. She said, "Joe and I are going to plan our wedding for the time you are here with the help and support of Ruth and John Scheidler. We are planning to arrange an outdoor wedding party in Scheidler's backyard on the lake".

It was like a dream come true for me. I completely approved of their idea, and I offered them my complete support and a helping hand of any kind. Ruth and I were in constant contact by letters. She put me on every little detail, and assured me that everything would be taken care of. Also she will leave my share of duties for the time when I get there.

Another good news was that her father had agreed to pay some money for her wedding and her honeymoon in Hawaii. That news made me a little more secure. The other news, which made me surprised, was that Mojgan, who never liked any kind of Iranian food, was asking me to cook for their wedding dinner. She wanted all Iranian food. To make Iranian dish by itself was a difficult task to begin with. Yet to make many different dishes for two hundred people was an obligation of a cook who wanted to stay in the kitchen all night. And I was not willing to do that. Instead I offered her to cook the rehearsal diner.

I asked her to avoid inviting any of Malakuti's family or any Iranians, whom we knew for that matter. Otherwise I would not be involved with her wedding at all. She promised me that she would consider it done. She even had thought of a menu, which she thought Joe and his family might like to have. The menu was combined of zereshk polo with morgh, (barberie with white rice and safron, with chicken,) salad olivieh:(chicken, eggs, carrots, green peas, pickles, green onions, potatoes, all chopped finely with salt, pepper, lemon juice and mayonnaise, mixed well,) dolmeh badenjon, felfeleh sabz, gojehfarangi: (stuffed bell peppers, eggplant, tomatoes,) tahcheene morgh: (yogurt, safron rice with chicken or lamb,) shish kabab and chicken kabab with white rice, green salad and shirazi salad and many more. I just was wondering how a person like Mojgan, who had never tried any of those foods, was asking me to make all those Iranian dishes for group of Americans. Then I realized that with the loss of her family she was trying to bring back the memory of the culture and background that she came from. So I promised Mojgan that I would be there, and I would do my best to make it an excellent and memorable dinner. Meanwhile I was in contact with Ruth to make sure that everything went as well as was Mojgan's and Joe's dream.

2-21-92

Dear Mom,

Hi. I miss you a lot. I have been so busy lately, I have not had time to call. I am sorry about that. I hope you have been well. I think I told you that Joe & I were going to Colorado for spring break. Well anyhow we are. I am so excited to ski in the mountains. I remember when we went to Colorado when I was too little to ski. Mom, I love you so much, I hope you know that. I wish we could see eachother more often but your just as busy as me. But I would really love it if we could start writing eachother regularly.

Mom, you know that you are always invited to come stay with us for a visit. Anytime!! I feel uncomforable going to your place to stay with you because it's not your house. But don't worry I will definately come down there as soon as I get back from spring break.

There are so many things I want to tell you about but I don't know where to start. First of all I am starting a waterski school for kids this summer. I am so excited, It has been a lot of fun planning. I am hoping that this will give me experience for starting my own business, some day.

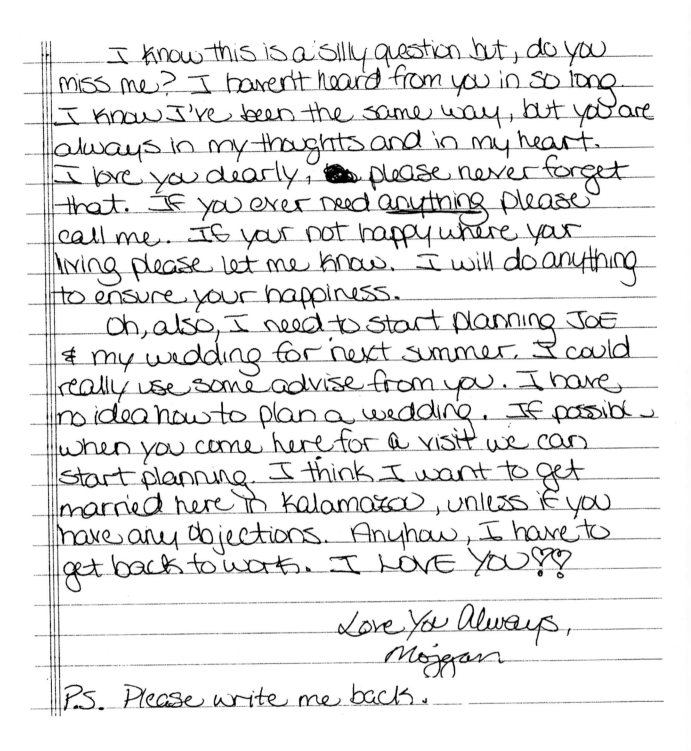

I know this is a silly question but, do you miss me? I haven't heard from you in so long. I know I've been the same way, but you are always in my thoughts and in my heart. I love you dearly, please never forget that. If you ever need *anything* please call me. If your not happy where your living please let me know. I will do anything to ensure your happiness.

Oh, also, I need to start planning JOE & my wedding for next summer. I could really use some advise from you. I have no idea how to plan a wedding. If possible when you come here for a visit we can start planning. I think I want to get married here in Kalamazoo, unless if you have any objections. Anyhow, I have to get back to work. I LOVE YOU!!

Love You Always,
Mojgan

P.S. Please write me back.

Although I was with Mojgan most of the time, she thought I was not at her house regularly enough. Once she told me, "My friend believes that I am lucky to have my mother around me as often as I do." But another friend of hers had said to her, "How can you have your mother with you as long as you do?"

Dear Shamci, 1

I have planned to write you this letter, but just didn't get it done with the busy stuff that goes on during the last of a year teaching. But now you can read it with Moj and Joe there to add more details. It is probably all stuff you already know, but I want to share it with you just to make sure.

I'm delighted that not only will we have this great day together, but that we could kind of trade some of the usual responsibilities of the wedding. I can't TELL you how happy I am that you are planning that dinner the night before. And it will be far more special if the food is Iranian. Not only will I get to eat it, I'll get to watch/help you make it Thur. and Fri. Friday you and I can assemble those baskets of flowers and candle holders for on the tables. I really think they'll be lovely, and the colors will soften the white table cloths. I have ordered Baby's Breath, greens, and the statice and Japanese Iris that will be in Moj's bouquet. If my father's Peonies are still in bloom we can use them too, and if not we'll just get more flowers by the bunch. Peonies look kind of like large, soft cabbage roses. They are mostly white and light pink.

All 3 of you had to let me make a lot of arrangements that you might have wished to do yourself, but because the wedding is here, and I am here, and you are all away, I made the best choices I could find in this area. I think you will be happy with them; I sure hope so! I almost wish I had kept a count of how many phone calls it took! Fortunately Moj realized that we had to make reservations as soon as possible. You weren't back from your trip yet, and Moj was absolutely right. People were starting to get booked up. But I did get my first choice in both caterers and rental.

I'm sure Moj and Joe have told you the menu. I think it sounds elegant, easy to eat (no bones), and special. Irma is a local caterer, and I have eaten COUNTLESS dinners from her crew, and they have been excellent. She wisely steered us away from choices that would not work well considering the fact that they will be transported out of town and served outside. Dinner will be lovely, and you and I won't have to do a SINGLE THING. That is as it should be; we can be busy as bees the day before and the morning before, but we should just get to sit down and eat with everyone else.

The cake is also being made by a woman I have known for years, and she was recommended by SEVERAL co-teachers when I asked. Moj chose a beautiful combination of flavors and fresh fruit. I think it will be the classiest wedding cake ever. Vi will come set up the whole thing, and we ordered plenty of cake. I'm glad Moj chose to add an extra sheet cake because so many of us will be there into the evening and the next morning - it will get eaten. Moj and Joe will take the top small layer home with them for their first anniversary.

They will be married either by Judge David Coyle, or his Magistrate, Betty Walkup. They are both friends, and extremely kind, friendly people. Since they usually do not marry people outside of the courthouse itself (they're busy people) we lucked out. It is not legal to pay them. I baked homemade cinnamon bread for them, and offered our house to them when we go out west this summer. Before next week I will know which one is coming, and I will let them know how special the rehearsal dinner will be.

The tents, tables and chairs will be delivered on Friday, and the man will help us set the tents in place. John, and probably Johnner, Andy and Joe, will be there. Because our yard is large, the tents can be in the side area towards the drive, while the ceremony can take place under the trees next to the deck. That works out amazingly well. John is building a lattice frame for the flowers where Moj, Joe and the judge will stand. That will make it easier to hang the flower arrangements.

Flowers are being taken care of by a business in town called Neitzerts, and that too is run by people we know. Plus the fact that they now have a man who is really talented at arranging flowers. Kathy Neitzert was a lot of help- she thought of things that didn't even occur to us. This is a bit new to all of us!

IF the weather doesn't cooperate we have several plans. If it is only mildly sprinkly, we can move the entire ceremony under the tents. If it is really HORRID (I'm hoping we have used up the rain for awhile) we would hold the ceremony inside our house, and move the dinner to a Lake Association Building at the other end of the lake. It has long tables and chairs, a kitchen and bathroom, and parking. It isn't lovely, it is plain. But if we have to use the space it will work well enough. And when we add people, food, cake and flowers, it will do just fine. Oh- and the tents are brand new, white, and look elegant. I have rented two "walls" that can block off one end and part of a side, just in case it is windy.

Friday night I have you and Moj sleeping at our house. Joe and his friends will stay 3 houses down at a friend's cottage. Moj's girls may stay with friends around the lake if they want to stay over. That's all set. There are 2 rooms in town for Mary, Masseh, etc. (the LAST TWO IN TOWN - there are some big races that weekend and all the motels are full).

Saturday night we have reserved a room for Moj and Joe (they know all about it). You will stay with us again. That night everyone else is figuring out their "own thing" except for those two rooms in town, and the cottage, which will be used by John's brother and their family. We have sleeping mats for 5 on the porch, and many of Joe and Moj's friends plan to camp out in the yard or the field behind (which will be our parking lot on Saturday). Sunday morning there will hopefully be a lot of people around for whatever breakfast there is. I have had several friends offer to help, and I tell them we need two things. Snack stuff for what I expect will be a late party Sat. night, and any kind of breakfast stuff for Sun. morning. I'm not going to worry about it one way or another. We can make a gigantic pot of coffee, lots of juice, and go to town for a couple boxes of donuts. They'll be fine. And we can all just relax at that point. I am REALLY glad that this party will carry over through Sunday morning. I think it is simply going to be too much fun to just stop Sat. night. I like the idea that we can all relax together and enjoy, and laugh about the days before. It will probably do us all a lot of good. This is a big event, and I don't want to hurry the ending. I'm really glad they won't leave on their trip right away.

There is a Polish term for a 3 day party, and I can't remember it but will try to find it. That is what this sounds like to me, and I think it will be terrific. My job right now is stuff that I want done in our house, stuff that I couldn't do until school got out. Right now I am writing this at school early in the morning. I had to drop John off to keep the car (my sister and a friend are here from Denmark and they have our other car on a camping trip up north). Anyway, the stores don't open until 9:00, so I am typing this until close to 9:00.

Hope all that sounds okay. I have plenty of dishes and stuff for the dinner the night before. If you bring whatever ingredients you need (we can go to the grocery Thursday or on the way here Wed.) I have lots of pan sizes and baking dishes and serving dishes. The only thing that would be a problem would be unusual ingredients, or that special rice, if you need it. There is a real limit on what you can buy in a small town like this! That's partly why I felt so fortunate that Moj had us start making reservations early, and that we GOT the stuff we need for this wedding, with few exceptions. I think they have made lovely plans, and plans for a wedding that will be uniquely theirs. I am always pleased when people have the courage to set their own, perhaps new, traditions, within the framework of what they want to keep from the "old." It will truly be THEIR day. I like that a lot. And people could see that coming when those beautiful, original invitations arrived. They are truly special. I have heard LOTS of compliments about them.

So I'll see you soon. Your bedroom is nearly ready. Today I'm doing odds and ends in town, then working on the beach and the steps. The good long run thing about all this is that I'm getting stuff DONE that I really want done. This just gets me going. And there will be plenty of work yet to do when you get here. Plus this is a beautiful place to walk. I need to either go back to morning walks or start going to town to swim laps. I'm certainly not any skinnier. And I just ate a LARGE apple fritter with my coffee while I wrote all this!

It's now 9:00 and I must scoot. Call anytime, and see you soon.

Fondly,

Ruth

From the moment I met Ruth Scheidler and her husband John and the rest of their family, I liked them a lot. We saw each other once in a while. After Mojgan bought the house, we invited them to her house, and so Ruth invited us to their house. They were all very nice people.

When Mojgan decided to marry Joe, it was great news to my aching heart. At the time of her decision, I was away overseas. When she called me in my brother's house, although I got very excited, I was the person who had lost all her dreams and hopes.

My beautiful Mojgan, at the happiest and most important time of her life, was all alone by herself, deciding on her own marriage. Where were her parents who were supposed to help her and accompany her at such a sensitive time of her life? Where were her parents who were supposed to hold her hand and comfort her? Her father was married to his mistress of eight years, Badri and he didn't know what was happening to his precious daughter, Mojgan. Shame on you. With this letter from Ruth to me, you will see how fortunate I have been to have her near Mojgan like a mother. Wasn't I lucky? Wasn't I blessed by my God? Thank you.

R.S.V.P.
3822 Lake Drive
Coldwater MI 49036

Joe
&
Moj

Two Lives, Two Hearts
Joined Together in Friendship
United Forever in Love

Please R.S.V.P. on or Before

May Twelveth

Adult Children Only Please

By Postcard or Phone.

Miss Mojgan Rafani
Daughter of
Shamci Rafani and Iraj Rafani
with
Joseph R. Scheidler

Request the Honor of Your
presence on our
Joyous Wedding Day

Three O'Clock Saturday
June Nineteenth at the Home of
Ruth and John Scheidler

Dinner and Reception following the
Ceremony

Hi Mom,
Hope you like the invitations
we picked out. Missing you.
Keep in touch.
Love,
Moji & Joe

Number Planning to Attend: ____

Sorry, ____ Of Us Cannot Attend.

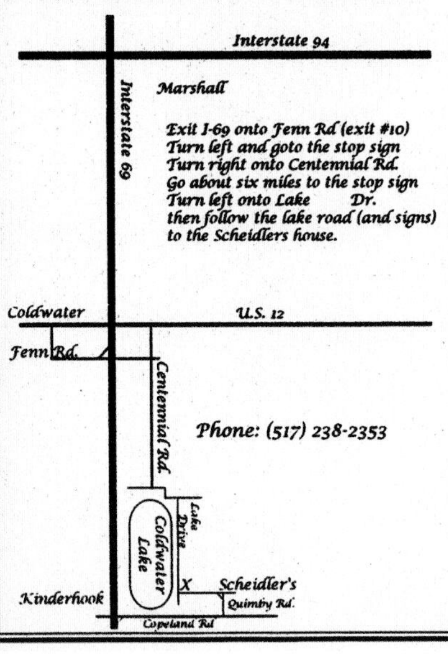
Interstate 94
Interstate 69
Marshall
Exit I-69 onto Fenn Rd (exit #10)
Turn left and goto the stop sign
Turn right onto Centennial Rd.
Go about six miles to the stop sign
Turn left onto Lake Dr.
then follow the lake road (and signs)
to the Scheidlers house.
Coldwater
U.S. 12
Fenn Rd.
Centennial Rd.
Phone: (517) 238-2353
Lake Drive
Coldwater Lake
X Scheidler's
Quimby Rd.
Kinderhook
Copeland Rd

Mojgan's Junior Year

Joseph Scheidler and
Mojgan Rafani

Oh, what a beautiful scene! They were all beautiful. The bride, the groom, the bridesmaids, and the gentlemen were all beautiful. After the wedding, I stayed at the Scheidler's for the cleanup. Ruth and I were talking about the pleasure we had had in that period of time. I was especially happy to see that my baby had found her love and it could bring some hope and happiness into their lives.

This is Mojgan's wedding which was held in the Scheidlers' house on the lake. Left to right: Andrew, John J., me, Mojgan, Joe, Mr. Scheidler, Mrs. Scheidler, and Maryam. Thanks to Mr. and Mrs. Scheidler who worked so hard to make it that beautiful.

It went so well that neither I nor mojgan had expected. Everything turned out all right. I loved Mojgan's dress which she had purchased from Chicago.

One of the guests was Kaveh Kamooneh.

At Christmas time we were in their hot tub inside Mojgan's yard at Tahoma City, CA.

Ezzat, Afsar, Joe, and Mojgan are at her dinner table.

We were ready to serve those who were invited to Mojgan's house.

My Dear God:

You see, you always were my supporter and my rescuer. While I was away, you brought forward Ruth to take my place for Mojgan, and actually mothering Mojgan, when she needed her mother to be close to her. You were always one step ahead of me. You felt I needed that trip to be able to rejuvenate and bring a new life in me. When I felt good about Mojgan, I was able to enjoy the rest of my trip, and let myself free from the painful past.

One thing I had planned was to get rid of my worst disease, which was the LOVE for Iraj in my heart. That wasn't easy, unless I pretended and believed that he was dead. Being among my people and his people helped me a lot to be able to do so. That trip to Iran was a great experience for me. It made me to get to know my real self. In addition to all my siblings and their families, I had my sisters-in—law, Parveen and Neya, who did their best to make me comfortable in Iran, and also the rest of his family, who were aware of my love for Iraj. They accepted and greeted me in the best way possible. All these gave me more confidence, and I realized that life without Iraj not only was not bad, but it would be beautiful too. It seemed to me that they all knew the ugliness and cruelty of Iraj's act, and among themselves they thought of me very highly. This made me proud. While I never talked to anyone about my life, they had heard it from Iraj's family, and they were trying to show me their disrespect for Iraj and his disloyalty towards his family. They all went out of their way to please me one way or another.

Once his sister Parveen, who was a midwife in Gazveen, a city near Tehran, invited Neya, Fereshteh, and I to go to her house for a long weekend. She had arranged to take us to North of Gazveen on a riverside. While she had her own car, she decided to rent a limousine to drive us around. Since the roads were narrow, she preferred that a driver drove us, while she herself was enjoying the views also. That day we spent a nice day together.

Although I never discussed my marital situation with them openly, still one day Parveen asked me if I needed any help not to ever hesitate to call on her. And I promised her that if I ever needed help for sure I would go to them for help. While she was busy with her midwifery at her office, which was located at the first floor of her house, still she invited my friends and me to her house often, and cooked us very delicious Iranian food.

My Dear God:

Neya did the same thing. If I ever mentioned that I like to do something, or to go somewhere, she made it possible for me, and went out of her way to make me happy. Although they never told me, “I love you”, yet their acts were more than saying, “I love you”.

At the same time that I was in Iran, her daughter Baharak was in Iran for a visit.

She was studying in Switzerland. I was friends with Zahra, Neya's sister-in-law, who was living in Bandar Pahlavi. Neya and I used to go there and visit her any chance we got. This time I suggested going to visit them by bus instead of Neya driving on those high mountains. Although she never liked to take a bus, and preferred driving herself, still she agreed to buy tickets to go to Bandar Pahlavi. Not only that, but in the bus, which was very cold, she removed her coat, rolled it and made a soft pillow for under my head. I was embarrassed from that kind of kindness. She did it quietly and lovingly.

Although I knew that Parri and Neya had been attacking my integrity in front of my family a few years ago, I still did not take it against Neya. I knew that they had only one brother, and the embarrassment of his act was too much for them, so they were looking for a way to put the blame on me to be able to minimize their brother's guilt. Besides, Neya was not the one who started the attack. She was trying to support Parri, who was attacking me behind my back. She didn't want to leave Parri alone at the scene of battle against me. So she accompanied her in her attack.

Although Parri's embarrassment was to a point that the next day she called my sister Ezzat, and apologized to her and every one else for interfering in a business, which wasn't hers, I didn't take it against them. I was confident and sure of myself that I had done everything in my power to protect Iraj's name and dealing with the whole situation in an intelligent way. However Neya's kindness and her loving towards my children and me were and is a reason to appreciate and be thankful to her all the times. The same goes for Parri, who always was my best and only friend. I will remember them as my very favorite people. Not that they didn't say or do anything to me, but in comparison to others, including Iraj, they were beautiful angels. I will always have respect for them.

Not only my sisters-in-law were making me welcome and accepted, their aunt and their cousin Mehdiagha and his wife Hoji khanom and the family of their uncle Mr. Hormozi, Hormoz and his wife Homa, Masoomeh and her family, and all the others had treated me so nicely that I will always deeply appreciate their friendship. I must talk about some of their serious support for me.

My Dear God:

At the beginning of my arrival to Iran once we were in Parveen's house. Her aunt was there too. Although I didn't want to talk about Iraj at all, any chance she got, she whispered in my ears, "This bastard, this despicable coward did such an unmanly act that I am embarrassed to think of him as my nephew". As many times she said it to me, I told her Khaleh jon, auntie, don't worry. I am glad that he showed his true self to me and everyone else. Now I am able to live happily, without him being around me.

Not only his aunt talked to me about him in that manner, but also every one else did it in that manner. Once we were picnicking at a park. Parveen, Fereshteh, and I were sitting around a table talking. Parveen was talking to Fereshteh about men in general.

Then she emphasized on this sentence, "Men in general are bastard, especially the ones who are from Beerjand, the city which was Iraj's home town. And she said it loudly and repeatedly for me to hear it out. She never wanted to criticize her brother's act to me, but she said it in a way that I get her message.

But Parri was the one who surprised me with her actions. On one hand, when Iraj had left me, she called me from her friend's house Faranak, with an angry voice telling me, and insisting that, "This bastard, I could never forgive his act. If I was you, right now at this moment I would find a boy friend, just to show him that I can do it too". On the other hand, she goes to Iran, and behind my back she criticized my acts and me in front of my sisters, who were very hurt by it. I couldn't understand her point of view one way or another. Obviously she was embarrassed by Iraj's act at that moment, and she never allowed herself to talk bad behind me to my friends in Iran. I heard from them that in front of them she always criticized her brother's act.

Many funny things had happened in Iran that until today when I think about then, I laugh. As I said before, I made sure that friends and relatives think of my visit in Iran as a joyous, pleasant visit and nothing else. So friends and relatives came to visit me, and we never talked about anything else other than all happy occasions. Even if some of them knew what was going on, they kept it to themselves. Until one day Azar's neighbor, who was living on the first floor, came to visit. Because of the way that Azar had talked to them about my visit, they were not expecting anything but the happy and good news

It was my older sister Ezzat, who was leaving to go to London. It was Azar, Sina, and I, who were gathered in the living room. We were talking of any subject, and we were laughing our heads off. At this moment the husband out of nowhere asked me, "Where is your husband?" I wasn't expecting this question at all. As I had trained myself to believe that Iraj was dead, I answered him, "He is dead". Oh boy, Oh boy. You must have been there to see the pail faces of my sisters, and the shock in our visitors. All of a sudden it seemed like an electric shock to everyone. The atmosphere of the room had changed completely. The guests were questioning, "If he is dead, how come you are celebrating? I realized that my sisters were speechless. So I said, "No one knew until now", and I changed the subject.

My Dear God:

But the scene couldn't go back to what it was before. We talked of other subjects, and after a while they decided to leave. They left in a great confusion. While I was laughing hysterically, for the unusual answer that I gave them, my sisters, especially Azar were hurt and upset with me. And it made me laugh even harder. She was very concerned that either they might think that we had made fun of them, or might think that we were so stupid that we didn't know the difference between sad and happy occasions. At this time my sisters remembered the face of our guests when they heard the shocking news from me, and they started laughing with me. I didn't have any answer for my stupid comment. I just was laughing uncontrollably. And they were completely confused.

While I was laughing like that, I remembered that the neighbor was very fond of me. He had told Azar, “Your sister Shamci is a big time teaser”. I thought of that sentence for a moment. While I still was laughing, to be able to solve the problem and bring peace in Azar’s mind, I suggested that since he believed that I am a big teaser, I will go downstairs and tell him, “This was all a joke. There was a bid between Azar and I to see who could make up the biggest lie of the day that could be more believable. And now that I saw you had believed my lie, you made me win hundred dollars”. When I told Azar of my decision, although she was not very fond of it, still they continued to laugh with me.

So I went downstairs and told him about our bid. He embraced me and said, “I must have known that this was one of your practical jokes. This time was on Azar. I am glad you won”. When I came upstairs my sisters still were in shock. They wanted to know how I did it. And I had no answer for them, except laughing and laughing. With my laughter, they laughed with me, also. The more that time passed, the more it seemed funnier to me. Even at night when I went to bed, I laughed so much that they thought I was going crazy. To this day, whenever I think of that scene, automatically I laugh. It was the silliest tease I have ever done.

My Dear God:

Cases like this happened so often. In every gathering we laughed, we teased, we joked, and we made fun, and laughed and laughed. It was a great therapy for me and Azar, and everyone else. After eight years of sufferings, and not knowing what laughter was, now I was becoming my own self again. I was free at last, free at last.

Every little nice act from family and friends helped me to give me a boost towards the recovery. One of those little acts, which seemed very important to me, was a night that we were invited in Iraj's cousin, Assad's house. There were other guests there, who have not met me before. Neya and Mohandess Forghani drove me to the party. When we got there, Neya introduced me to the new group, “This is my sister-in-law Shamci. She is here from USA to visit the family”. She said all this before I opened my mouth to introduce myself as Shamci Gharavi. I was almost shocked, and yet grateful to Neya, who still was thinking of me as her sister-in-law. I knew that Neya was aware of everything that had happened between us. But I felt that she didn't want to hurt me. I don't know if she even remembers that incident, but I remember it so clearly, because it was the word of love to me. The way that I see it Neya was a silent lover to me and to her sisters. She was and she is a nice sister-in-law. I must say that three of them were nice, each in their own way, and I was pleased to have them around any time it was possible for them. I wish them the very best all through their lives.

After spending four months in Iran, I went to London to visit my sister Ezzat and her

Left to right: Maryam, Layla, Zary, and Javad.

Left to right: Afsar, Jamal, Ezzat, me, Javad, and Zary. Sina, Hosain, Saideh, Azar and Hassan who is holding Ahmadreza are standing.

Those trips that I made to Iran were very stimulating for me. We never discussed Iraj and his whereabouts. I was aware that everyone knew completely what was going on. But since I have done it my way, I didn't allow anyone to ask me about Iraj, or what had happened to him. Left to right: my brother Jamal, my sister Ezzat, my sister Azar, and my brother Javad. Saideh, I, and Sina are standing. With all our differences, we were always happy to get together and talk about good days when we were bothering and teasing one another the best we could.

in Iran with
Chirazi and Sina
in Mellat Park,
Tehran

the beautiful
Mellat Park

a statue located in
Mellat Park,
Tehran

We are having dinner at Cherry Restaurant in Velenjak, where Sina and Chirazi live. We are having as much fun as we can. Left to right: Hosain, Zary, me, Sina, Afsar who was having pain in her legs, and Ezzat.

In a cave in Hamadan, left to right: Shamci, Hosain, Sina, and Ezzat.

This place has a view over a lovely river. This was found by Ezzat and Sina when Iraq was bombing Iran. They wanted to save their families by hiding in some hidden area. They rented one large room in Nargess's house in Gachsar and furnished it. Since then, it had become the getaway place for the whole family. That night we were having fun, sitting in front of the river, smoking hookah and watching the fire burning in front of us. Left to right: Afsar, me, Hosain, Jamal, Ezzat, and Nargess.

Here, we were in Sina's house. As you see, Hosain is lying down on the bed, recovering a stroke. Neither Ezzat nor I wanted to go to the bedroom to take a short nap. So we decided to lie down on the sofa, as you can see us. Obviously, Sina was the photographer.

This statue was in the Mellat Park as well.

Sightseeing with Sina and Chirazi in Iran

Sightseeing with Sina in Shiraz, Iran. We were able to get rid of our scarves for a moment to take a picture.

We are in Javad's house. Left to right: Saideh, Layla, Afsar, and Azar. Standing in the back: Maryam, me, Zary's mother, Zary, and Negar. How much fun we had when we gathered together! It was really fun.

Here we are, left to right: Azar, Maryam, me, Negar, and Layla. Sina, Rokhand, Afsar and Zary are sitting. We had so much fun together in front of the camera.

Here, Sina and I are in Shiraz. Thanks to Farhad Mozaffar who drove us around and spent one whole day with us. Thank you, dear Farhad.

Looking at this picture you can tell how much fun we were having at that time. It was my birthday and my cousin, Khosro Mozaffar was teasing me by giving me a silly gift which made everyone laugh. Maryam, Azar, Saideh, Layla, and Zary are seen under our hands. Khosro is shaking hands with me to make sure that I receive the gift.

When the whole family is together, the children will most likely behave very well to prove that they are the best child in the family. Even those who do not usually behave well, compete against each other to be number one. Left to right: Saideh, Negar, Khosro, Layla, and Azar. Sitting down, left to right: Rokhand, me, Sina, and Maryam.

Here we are in Shiraz, in one of my cousins' house. As you know in many places, they still serve food on a tablecloth which is called "Sofreh". Left to right: Azar, Rokhand, me, Akbar, Javad, Khosro, and Farhad.
I don't know the rest.

In sina's house, from left to right: Sina, me, Azar, and Saideh

Someone took this picture from Mary at a party, and gave it to us. Isn't she beautiful? Isn't she?

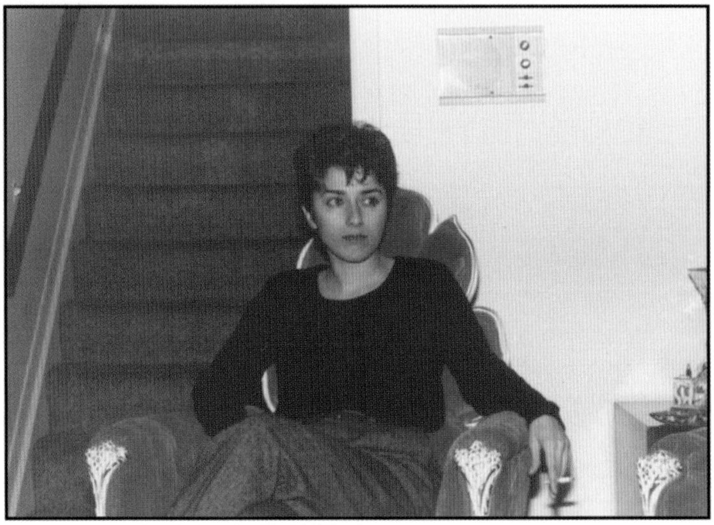

Maryam, Zari, and Layla

In Tehran at Azar's house, Rokhand was ready to say goodbye and go to a party. Left to right: Rokhand, Sadegh, Saideh, and Sina.

Left to right: Mary, Mojgan, Samantha, Joe, and I are at a restaurant before I leave for Iran.

children Afsaneh and Nader. As always it was a great experience. Their warmth and attention kept me going. We spent a great deal of learning time together. I was born again, and I had to adapt myself to a brand new great expectation.

When I returned to USA, everything was different for me. I was more grown up, and much more positive about myself. I almost had found the Shamci before she got married. I was looking at things completely differently. After eight years of struggle, I almost knew who I was. And I was very pleased with who I was.

Right after I arrived, Maseeh called me to see if I had enough money for the down payment for his house. And he asked me to make a trip to LA to seriously look for a house.

Meanwhile Mojgan was preparing herself for her wedding on June 19th 1993. I had been in contact with her and also Ruth at all times. We had decided that I would go to Kalamazoo in Scheidler's house one week prior to the rehearsal night. I needed to go shopping, and prepare everything for the rehearsal dinner. I talked to Mojgan and Ruth about my trip to LA, and I asked them if there was anything for me to do before I left. They both said, “There is nothing for you to do now but we will have plenty when you get back”.

My Dear God:

When Maseeh called me and said, “I put an offer on a house, and I want you to come and see the house”, I immediately bought a ticket and flew to LA. When I saw the house I didn't like it as much as he did. His purpose was that since I was paying the first payment, and he took the responsibility of mortgage payments and other expenses, we would live together comfortably. But that house was very small and did not have a private section for me to live in. It had no storage, or any other facilities.

I knew that because of all the hard times that he had been going through those years, he was trying to rush into that decision. But I didn't want, and didn't have the right to interfere with his decision. After all it was his house and his choice. He knew that the house was not roomy at all, and I went along with his opinion. We decided to look for more houses that weekend, while he had the opportunity to back off the deal without any loss. I agreed, and especially Anna agreed to look for more houses. I just wanted him to be happy, no matter what his decision would be. Now that he had made his hopes up, I must help him with his decision. I knew that the reason that he had put an offer on that house was that he was afraid not to be able to find a bigger house with his budget. With the high property prices in LA, I didn't blame him to be worried.

That weekend we were able to go to many open houses. Maseeh drove me to as many places as he could. On Sunday we went without our agent. One of the last houses we saw was thoughtfully made and designed for us. The house was perfect, and the price was not much higher than the other one.

Most houses in LA were not built with a basement. But this one had a complete

London, England in front of my Sister Ezzat's house

We are doing sightseeing with Ezzat in London.

Mojgan, my second cousin and I are sightseeing in Toronto, Canada.

We are in front of Dr. Shahideh's house with his wife Almas, me, and Sara Fassihi.

My nephew Nader, was playing the piano to entertain us.

**We are in Nader's house in London, England.
Left to right: Ezzat, Ali, me and Said, my sister's son-in-law.**

In Nader's house, I was braiding his long hair.

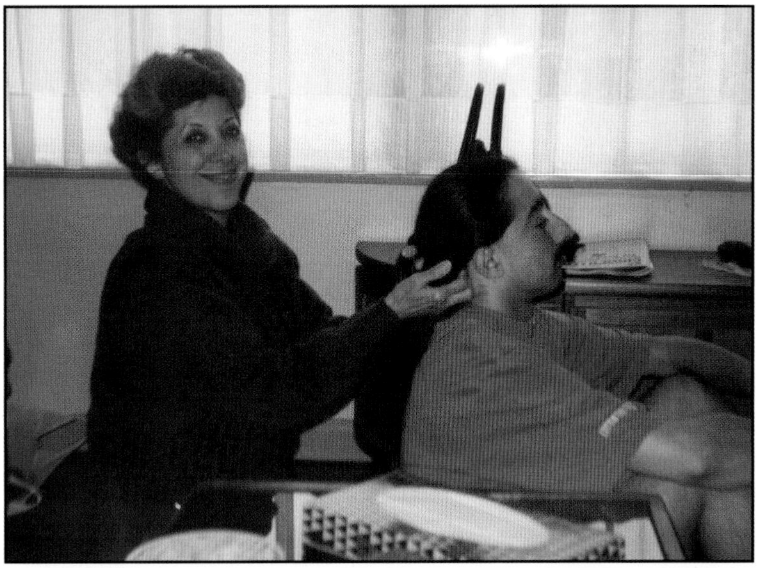

This was one of the meetings regarding the night club. I don't know why Iraj is not happy.

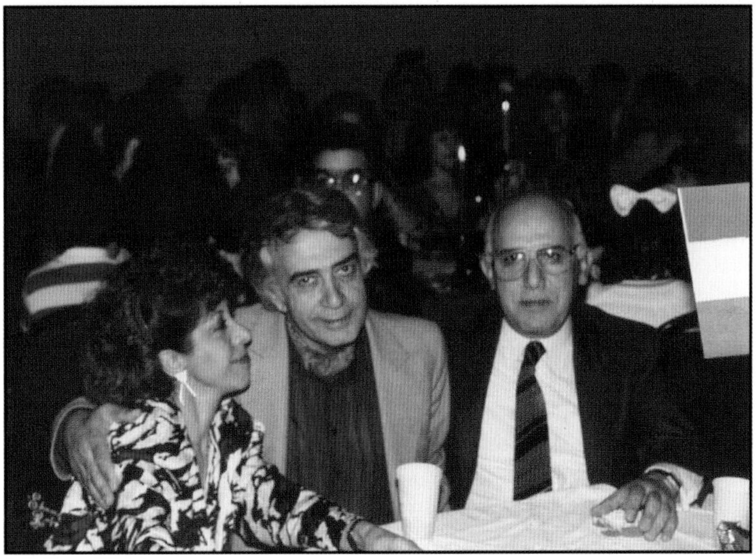

**When Ehsan visited me from Belgium, we went together to visit Mojgan and her husband Joe. We were saying good bye to them, to leave Sacramento and go back to Visalia.
Left to right: Shamci, Joe, Mojgan and Ehsan**

**Here, we are in Belgium.
Left to right: Sina, Ezzat, Shamci and Hosain Chirazi**

**Here, we are at Ehsan's house.
Left to right: Said, Hosain, Ehsan (who seems unhappy), Sina, Ezzat and me**

finished basement. One section was established for an art studio with many spacious closets. The other section was made for sport activities with lots of closets covered with mirrors. The main floor had a large foyer, spacious living room and dinning room, a big kitchen, a bathroom and a big pantry. The backyard was tri-level, beautifully landscaped with many fruit trees. The original bedroom area upstairs had two bedrooms, which one of them was very big, with a big bathroom and many closets. There was a new addition to the bedroom area, which was designed to Maseeh's taste. It was completely separate from the original section. It had a large bathroom, walking closets and many more. To me it seemed that they had designed it for the taste of three of us. There was a big garage with lots of storage spaces, and many more qualities to be able to talk about. The best part of that property was the location. The house was located in Studio city. While it was in the suburb, it was very close to town also. It was great for me to be able to get to know the city.

My Dear God:

The original bedroom was so big, and had a terrace overlooking the road. The room had a great view from three sides, which made me feel that I was outside, two large closets with sliding mirror doors, and lots of windows. I liked that room so much that I called it my room. Although I liked it so much, still I told Maseeh, "These are the advantages, which this house has over the other one. Still it is up to you to decide which one you would like to buy".

The next day I was leaving LA to go back to Michigan. The time that we looked at the house, Anna was not with us. I explained the whole house to her, and I insisted that she must go and see the house before someone else put an offer for it. I told Anna to make sure that Maseeh used his right judgment in selecting the house. Before I left I wrote a handwritten agreement between us. And they agreed to my proposal, which we had talked about before. They both signed the agreement, and each one of us kept a copy to remember what we had promised to each other. At that time Maseeh did not have any credit to be able to borrow money from banks. I agreed to withdraw the amount of eighty-five thousands dollars from my savings account, which at that time I was receiving 8% interest on. And gave it to Maseeh for the down payment for his house. In return, starting after six months, if his income was more than hundred thousand dollars, he would pay me $250.00 per month. And if his income was higher than that, he would pay me only up to $500.00 a month, so that I did not lose too much interest of that money.

At the same time Maseeh has the responsibility of mortgage, insurance, tax on property, and all other responsibilities of a homeowner. In addition I asked him to write the Deed on a joined account that if God forbid something had happened to Maseeh, I had a chance to get my money back before it went into his father's pocket again. There were no questions about after my dead. Obviously the money was his. So I wanted him to understand my point of view. We all agreed on that in writing. Maseeh gave me his account number to deposit the 85,000.00 dollars as soon as I got to Michigan.

I left the next day, and I was hoping that they decided on the second house. As I understood, Maseeh and Anna talked it over, after Anna had seen the house. They had realized that the second house was just perfect, and it was an offer they couldn't refuse. Fortunately he didn't have to lose any money on the first offer he had made. The address was 4001 Van Noord Avenue, Studio City, CA 91604. In the morning of the next day, I went to my Bank to transfer the money to his account from my annuity. I found out that for the early withdrawal, I would lose $650.00. Obviously that did not stop me from my action. I thought we must not waste any time in approaching the deal. The thought of Maseeh's happiness being in his own new house after long years of sufferings, made me very anxious and eager to do it, even if I lost that much money on it. I thought at least I could take one step to my son's success and happiness. And that made me very proud to be able to take the first step.

My Dear God:

While I was in LA, they asked me about the interesting incident that happened to me. Among many incidents that I talked about, I remembered a very interesting one that I had to mention. At that time for a person like me, who was traveling to Iran after losing all her hopes and her family, I needed something like that to happen, and bring back my confidence. The story happened when I was going to Iran. In the Heathrow Airport I had nine hours transit before I take another plane to Tehran. It was an hour or two that all the passengers for Tehran gathered in front of the gate waiting for the boarding time.

While I was walking with my handbag and my black mink coat on my shoulder, a gentleman among the passengers approached me, and offered his help to carry my bag. I thanked him, and we started talking, walking, and waiting. He seemed very polite, very well dressed, and good-looking. He was an Iranian, who was going to Iran from England for business, which he had in Iran and in England, with his two sons, who were residing in London. In a very kind manner he showed me he was interested to be with me. Neither of us talked about our marital stages. Although I was in a stage that I hated all men on earth, still he bought my trust, and did not allow me to ignore the conversation with him. When they started boarding, he carried my bag, and walked behind me to be able to help me. We went in, we each found our seats, and took our places. After the plane took off, he came to me and said the seat next to me is not occupied. Please come and seat there".

The passenger next to me was a heavy, very serious Englishman. So I didn't mind to move away from him. After five minutes, the gentleman came back and asked if he could carry my bag to the seat next to him. At that time I agreed, I gave him my bag, and after he left, I followed him to the seat next to him. In a very respectful manner, he tried to please me. We talked of any subjects. He gave me his card, and he talked about the soap

business, which he was sharing with his sons in England. Meanwhile some other young Iranians, who were going to Iran after almost twenty years, started talking to us. They all were very excited to see their families after such a long time. The gentleman was insisting that I go to lunch or dinner with him. He asked me so many times, "Please give me a call to see each other, and have lunch together". Since I didn't want to be rude, or hurt his fillings in any way, I told him, "I am staying in my sister Azar's house. I don't know anything about their schedua1e. I am sure they had arranged parties for me that I could not separate myself from them. But if I get a chance I will call you for sure. Until the plain came to stop, he asked me over and over again not to forget to call him". The plain stopped. We had to consider our Islamic coverage. I went my way, and after he took my promise to call him, he went his way also. As always everyone was waiting for me with flowers in their hands. When I discussed this passenger with my sister, she offered that we could invite him on the day that all sisters and brothers came to visit me.

My Dear God:

Actually that was my idea. Since I did not want to see any man in private, I thought it was a good idea to invite him in our family gathering. This way I had done two things at the same time. First, I had kept my promise to call him. Second, I would find out what he meant by asking me to go to lunch together. If he agreed to come and join my family for dinner, he might be looking for a simple friendship. And if he refused my invitation, that would be another story, which I was not looking forward to that kind of relationship.

When I called him and asked him to come to our family gathering, he thanked me first and said, "Just like you, there is another engagement arranged for me that I cannot cancel it at this time. But if the party doesn't last long, I will try to join your party". He took the address and the telephone number, and the exact date and time. We said good-bye and that was it. I didn't think he would come.

The morning of the party, the intercom rang, and they asked for me. When I answered it, the voice said, "We have a delivery for you. I was wondering what could it be that it would take long to bring it up? After twenty minutes two young men carried a huge plant pot, three feet in diameter, beautifully arranged with an indoor palm tree in the middle, and twenty of the most beautiful orchids around it. I was totally shocked. "Who is this from", I thought. I was embarrassed that those two men had to carry that big pot all the way to the third floor. I had to give them a very big tip, which I did. When I looked at the card attached to it, it was from him. He had apologized for not being able to join our party. Well, to begin with, not any man and woman could keep their friendship, if there wasn't some kind of sex involved. I had this in mind. And I knew that not now, and not ever I was ready to fall for that kind of relationship, even if it had a great deal of money involved. Not for a million years. So I was happy that I handled it that way. I kept my promise with respect for him, and he appreciated in his own way. That worked well for

both of us.

My Dear God:

Although I still have his card, I never contacted him again. Everyone, especially my sister-in-law Parveen and Fereshteh, were teasing me why I didn't call him back again. They asked me, “If you don't want to call him, give his phone number to us. We will call him”. And I always laughed, and said, “No thanks. One relationship was enough for me. Let's leave it as is”. Well, we laughed and we made jokes about it. But it was a big thing for me. It made me feel wanted. It made me believe in my attraction after all those years.

You see, my dear GOD, when I tell you that you have been always one step ahead of me to bring comfort into my life, I am not lying. Iraj was the one who gave me big gifts, which made people's eyes pop out. Yet at this time of my life you showed me that it was my value and intelligence, which made a man in only six hours of conversation becoming so attracted to me to send me such an expensive gift, which shocked everyone. Isn't true that, whoever you are, or what kind of power you are, you have been, and you are watching over me? Indeed whoever you are, or what kind of power you have on all of us, I sincerely thank you with all my heart. It was not that pot of plant that was important to me. It was the proof of my value to myself to open my eyes and see the things more clearly.

After my friends saw that gift, and discovered who gave it to me whenever they saw me cheerful and happy, they teased me and said, “Well, no wonder Shamci is so happy. This gift can make anyone happy for that matter. We don't blame you to be happy and cheerful at all times." But it was not the gift that made me happy. It was the concept behind it.

This was not the only time, which gave a boost to my ego. There had been many times that I ran into such cases. Although I was getting old and had gray hair, still I had that kind of attraction and liveliness to make people around me happy, and bring pleasure in their lives.

Since I always had associated with all those so-called Iranian friends, normal people rarely surrounded me. It only happened when I was traveling, at the airport. Prior to the last incident, once again I was going to Iran, and I had to transit in Heathrow Airport. While I was waiting, an Iranian gentleman as young as my son approached me, and started to talk to me. After we talked about our families and other subjects, I realized that he wanted to spend all his time with me. He even said something that made me think twice. While I was talking about my children, he said, “I don't believe that any woman, who becomes a mother must lose her freedom and privileges of doing what they want to do”. I thought there was more meaning underneath that one sentence. I kept him occupied with talking, till the time was there for me to fly. I said goodbye, and left the scene.

My Dear God:

Another time I was leaving from LA airport to go to Iran. While I was waiting a young gentleman, who was sitting behind my seat started talking to me. He was living in Texas, and was going to Rome Italy. We both were on the same plain till London. Again he found a double seat and asked me to join him. I did, and we talked of any subject regarding our families and the country and the revolution, and many more. When we got to London Airport, we both had some time to waste before our next flight. We walked, we talked, and we ate until it was near our departure. I told him. " I better go find my gate, and find out what was going on". He gave me his address and his phone number on his card in Texas, and asked me to make contact with him when I get back to the States. But I didn't know that if I passed that border, I was not allowed to come back again. So without saying goodbye to him, I left. I tried to find a way to tell him what had happened. But there was no way to reach the other side.

Anyway, it seemed that I was an interesting person to them that they were willing to be with me, or have contact with me. This case happened when I still was married to Iraj. Many times it came into my mind that I contact him in Texas, and be friends with him. Then again I changed my mind. I thought I should not allow my weakness to win over my strength. So I did not ever call him.

Anyway, after I returned from Iran, Ida and Mehrdad were at the end of their ropes, meaning that their divorce was becoming final, but not in an easy way. Before I went to Iran, the fight between them was very ugly. They had pulled knives at each other, and called the police, and many more. So because my life situation was not stable yet, I just begged them to just hold everything, and sleep on it for a few months until I came back. And I talked to Ziba, Ida's sister to talk to them, and make them understand that neither of them could win with the ugly and nasty fight.

I think I mentioned that before I went to Iran, after what I went through sending Mary to her father, and I packed all her stuff and sent them to her, one day she called me and said, "I am trying to come back to Michigan. It was like the sky came down on my head. I felt numb and immobile. I didn't know what, or how to answer her. After giving up her apartment, after sending her belongings with so much difficulty, after spending so much money on her move and on her car to be able to bring peace into her life by being near her father, now she wanted to come back.

My Dear God:

I didn't want to make things difficult for her by showing my sadness on the phone. I didn't allowed myself to sound upset and make her feel guilty. I didn't know if she wanted to be with me, or she was missing her boyfriend Tom, and his son, whom she loved a lot. I knew that to Mary word no did not mean anything. I tried to control my emotions, and not to aggravate her towards her hopelessness. That was the time that I had to find the right

solution to her uncertainty. I was sure that if she came back to Detroit, her life would have been ruined even more than before, and she probably would need to be hospitalized. So the only thing that came to my mind was to tell her, "Okay, but I am leaving to go to Iran soon. Where you are now, you are near your father. The weather is sunny and beautiful. Maseeh is in LA, and you can be with him when you like to. But when I am away for six months, I wonder what you would do with this nasty weather. Just think about it, and do what you think is good for you".

My dear, dear God, you remember that day so perfectly. You remember how I was drained and exhausted. You remember that I even couldn't fit in my own body. Even now, when I think back and remember it, I get chills and numbness of that day's desperation.

So, when a week later she called me and said," I decided to stay here and find a job", suddenly I felt alive again. I figured out that after talking desperately to Maseeh about her and her decision, he might have talked to her, and influenced her to decide to stay in LA. God was with me again and again and again.

So to be able to have contact with her all the time, and not use my own words to her, to sound like a lecture to her, I bought plenty of meaningful cards, which were all about hope and happiness. I signed all of them, and mailed them to her one or two a week. I even asked her if my cards were ever bothering her to just let me know, and I would stop sending them. But when I was in Iran, she called me more than the other two, and talked to me about herself. That made me very happy.

My Dear God:

I think the only reason that I was continuing my life was to show my children that, "If I can go through all these and survive, so can you". But I never realized that my children didn't know what I was going through. I didn't know that if they don't see me, and if I don't talk to them about my feelings, they would never know my desperation and hopelessness. But I never wanted to involve them. They had plenty of their own to be worried and concerned about. When I was in Iran, and I was so concerned about Mary, none of them told me anything about her. Even when I got back, they still did not tell me what had happened to Mary when I was in Iran. But I heard that she had been hospitalized for some time. When Maseeh told me all about it, I just wept, and wept.

My thoughts were that all those family problems had given her a nervous breakdown. So I put all my efforts to make sure to send her to her father. At least I knew that even if it was to save his own name, he had to help his daughter in that situation. At the beginning they thought that she might have had a brain tumor. Then they thought she might have been some chemical imbalanced. So after putting her on medications, she had improved, and thanks God, she was out of the hospital.

You see, my dear God, writing to you was the best and only cure for me. When I was living with Iraj, many times, as I should say so, many times I felt as lonely as it could be.

But since I started witting to you, I had never felt lonely again. I knew that as long as I put myself in your hands, you would make me think right, and act right, and decide right. Writing to you, and having complete faith in you not only I never felt alone, but also my life had turned around one hundred eighty degrees. Sometimes, when I am away from my writing, even though I was among friends and family, I needed to write to you. The trip to Iran, although interrupted my writing, still you were the one that I listened to me. And you were the one that I depended on strongly. Yes my dear God, I had seen, and I am seeing your footprints behind me wherever I go, or whatever I do. I thank you if you are light, if you are power, or if you are just nature. You had done a lot for me. Thank you!

After Maseeh had bought that house in Studio City, I was sure that I had a place to move into. So I started packing to move to LA, and live with my son and his girlfriend Anna under one roof.

At the same time, Ida and Mehrdad got divorced, and they had to put their house for sale. Prior to the sail of their house Mehrdad had rented an apartment in a nice area of Southfield, with outdoor swimming pool for himself and his son Cyrous. Since I had a good relationship with them, I bought a gift and I went to visit them.

My Dear God:

I don't know if I mentioned that the house that Mehrdad and Ida had, was under the name of Ziba Jahan, her sister. So when their marriage ended in divorce, which she had suspected that, she did not have any difficulty with them. She decided to put the house for sale, and whatever the house was sold, after she paid whatever they owed on the house, she divided the rest between the two of them. So after I sent my furniture to Maseeh's house, and since Mehrdad was out of the house, she asked Ida to move out of the house and stay with her mother and Panny. Then she changed the lock, and put a "For Sale" sign in front of the house. How good my timing was! The way that things worked out for me was just a miracle.

My main concern was Mary, who at that time seemed very happy. I had sent my furniture to California to Maseeh's house, and prior to that I was getting ready to go to Kalamazoo for the preparations of Mojgan's wedding. Everything like a puzzle board fit perfectly. I don't think I was smart enough to be able to arrange all these things the way that it happened. The power that was supporting me and helping me did all the arrangements for me. That was the reason that I realized that I had to leave everything to the source of power, which was handling my life.

To be able to make my life comfortable and to minimize my belongings, I got rid of much stuff. Every box was labeled with the name and the number of items. All was ready to go. Then I started to research about the companies and the prices to move my furniture. I found one reputable and reasonable company that I decided to hire. When I talked about it to Mojgan, she suggested that her friend, who was the son of her neighbor, was willing to help me. If I could get a U-Hall truck and send the furniture with him, it would have been safer for me, and it would give a chance to her friend to experience this hard task.

When I called U-Hall, their rental price, the money for gas, and food for him and his friend, who was going to accompany him, and other expenses was more than the price of my selected company. I just thought that it might have been safer to send it with her friend. Besides, they would have agreed to take some of my furniture to Mojgan's house with me, and then left the next day from Mojgan's house. Some furniture like love seat and some chairs, which I did not want to keep, I gave them to her friend Brigit, who was going to be Mojgan's bridesmaid. While staying with Mojgan, I also made curtains for Brigit's apartment. They also arranged to move my car with the U-Hall to California, which helped me a lot.

I said good-bye to all those friends who helped me during my disastrous years. Many of them gave good-bye parties for me. One of them was Dr. Edward Mehrabian, who made me grateful to him. He had invited all the doctors whom we used to associate with for more than twenty years. He did all the cooking himself, and made me highly respected. Farah Shushtari and her family did so much for me that there is not enough words to be able to show my appreciation to her. She simply was there for me every minute of the day or night. She never left even a moment for me to think of my losses. She actually babied me. She actually filled up all other times, which I was not working, or I was not busy elsewhere. She was my rescuer.

My Dear God:

I said good-bye to Ida, Mehrdad, and her family. She was very nice and so was Mehrdad. They both were very respectful to me. They treated me much better than their own mothers. I realized that although people were talking behind my back and criticized me for choosing to live with Ida and Mehrdad, I felt that I had done something right at least.

Meanwhile I asked Maseeh to welcome Mark and his friend to his house, and let them spend few days in his house. He did, and he made them feel good about staying with him. Then they took back the U-Hall truck to the U-Hall station.

When things were going so smooth for me without any interruption, I was becoming hopeful. It was almost three or four weeks before Mojgan's wedding, and I was there to help her. With the help of my savings, Maseeh was able to buy a beautiful house for himself. I had sent my furniture to my son's house, where I was going to reside. I was thinking that living six months in Iran and England, and the other six months in the U.S.A., I would be the happiest woman alive.

My Dear God:

Can you believe my dear GOD how lucky I was? Do you see how everything was taking place like it was prescheduled? When I believe in that supper power that made it possible for me to survive through this ordeal, I have all the right to believe so. I was neither that intelligent, nor I was that smart to be able to put all the pieces of puzzle together so wisely. There was no reason or time for me to worry about anything. Things were happening so smoothly that I was seeing the light in my life, and I was looking for a happier future.

Mojgan had selected the most beautiful wedding dress when she was in Chicago. Her selection was so beautiful that I felt I had ordered it myself. So simple, so elegant, and so presentable that I felt comfortable by seeing it. She had put so much effort into her wedding, and she expected that her parents do not ruin her wedding day with their stupidity. And I respected that. I had promised her that if Malakutis and those vicious Iranians were not invited, I would make her wedding night a night to remember.

You know, my dear GOD, I wished my children could have felt my feelings after their father had married Badri. True that Badri was delighted to see her husband dead. But I was emotionally dead after my husband was gone. How did they expect me to see him and feel happy? They never felt my pain. They never saw my tears at night. But I tried so hard to make her wedding night so happy and so good that the end of the night she whispered in my ear, "Thanks Mom, I can't believe it. Everybody is happy and having a great time. I can't thank you enough". I danced very rarely, only once or twice in some occasions.

That night I danced for five consecutive hours. I danced with Mary, with Kaveh, with Kasra, with John, and many others, and I never got tired. Because of all the excitement and energy in me, they thought that I might have had too many drinks. While I never used to drink, and especially that night, I did not have even one drink. I just was happy to see Mojgan happy. Even Mary noticed it, and said, "You have all the right to be happy and dance all night tirelessly".

My Dear God:

First she promised me not to invite anyone, whom I disliked. Then she asked me to cook Iranian dishes for her rehearsal dinner. She had arranged for me to stay one week in Scheidler's house prior to the rehearsal night to be able to do all the shopping and arrangement for cooking easily. Although it was difficult to do all the cooking in a kitchen that I was not used to, still my children thought that it would not be hard for their mother. They were right. I did it, and I did it perfectly. Ruth had agreed to make several great desserts for the party.

Her cousins Kaveh and Kasra each came on a different day and at different times. They had to go and pick them up from the Metropolitan Airport, which was ninety

minutes away.

Two weeks prior to her party Mojgan had asked Maseeh to play his guitar and sing at her wedding accompanied by Andy and John, Joe's brothers. They had also arranged a band on her wedding day. Surprisingly Maseeh, who had never played guitar or sang in front of live audience, had agreed to Mojgan's request.

Ruth had arranged rooms in some of their neighbor's houses for some of the guests to stay, and for others she had arranged some cozy and beautiful hotels. Everything was very well thought of. All of us had tried to put all our efforts to make Mojgan's and Joe's dreams come true. We had hopes for our children to get married under our wings, and come back home to us with their children.

But guess what my dear God; Joe had his parents sitting next to each other around the table. And Mojgan had her parents each one at each end of the table. At least I was able to go along with it this far. Not only that, but the forecast for that afternoon was strong winds and a storm. Families and friends from both sides were there for the rehearsal night. Ruth and I prepared everything, and Joe was in charge of fire for shish kebab. The band was placed near the kitchen door. Once in a while I came out to check on the grill. I was trying so hard not to become face to face with Iraj. I didn't want to face him at all. After he had arrived, once I came out and he was standing there near the band. As soon as I stepped out, loudly he said, “Salam”. I pretended that I did not hear him, and I turned around and went inside to look for something I didn't need. After that we both got lost in the crowd.

Until then everything had gone so well. Young and old were having the time of their lives. Everyone was enjoying the food, and Mojgan was happy to tell them all about those foods. It was a very beautiful night. Most of their friends took their sleeping bags and their blankets to any place of the house where they found room. It looked like camping grounds. I was the happiest of all among them that was the rehearsal night.

My Dear God:

Ruth had rented a hot tub for those who enjoyed using the hot tub in that cold. Ruth and I used it more than others. Ruth had put up a huge tent, which easily could sit two hundred people. We made all the centerpieces with Ruth, and all the gifts and candies for individuals. The chairs were set up in front of the house, and the tent behind the chairs, in case it started to rain. They had catered very delicious food for that night.

The ceremony was supposed to start at three P.M. sharp because of the forecast for that afternoon. The band had practiced all day, and they were ready. Guests were gathering one by one, and all the seats were taken. The bride was ready, waiting anxiously in her room. And the groom was waiting in the neighbor's house, because he was not supposed to see the bride in her wedding gown before the ceremony. The clock was showing after three. It started to get very windy, and everyone was waiting for the father of bride to come and walk the bride to start the ceremony. No one was as impatient as I was. I knew him and his careless attitude about things like that. With the wind, which was getting stronger, everyone else in the yard was getting impatient. Everyone was getting uneasy. Some were questioning Maseeh, "Where is your father? Is he coming?" He explained to them that it was all Kasra's fault. They had gone to town shopping. But he never mentioned that it was his father, who listened to Kasra and kept people waiting in the storm for more than thirty minutes. Too bad they couldn't do it without him.

Finally, after people were getting up and walking, the news arrived that, "The father of the bride is here". In the film you can see that he was stuttering to explain to the father of the groom why was he late, and why he had to go shopping at that time. Until that time everything was fine and everyone had done their best to make it a pleasant wedding for Mojgan and Joe, until he came along. Even in that moment the storm stopped, and the sun came out, and the ceremony went well. Again GOD came to my rescue and answered my prayers.

Among the guests from our side I had only invited Claudette and Sue Meier, who were sitting around our table, and Kaveh and Kasra their cousins. I had invited another two good friends of mine Farahnaz and Ali Hushmand. They decided not to come because they were afraid to face him, and not be able to control themselves. So they decided not to come.

In all this time the respect that I received from everyone was so encouraging that I couldn't imagine. Yet all the times in the back of my mind I was thinking, "If I didn't marry Iraj, right now Mojgan would not have to go through the most important day of her life with her parents hating each other. Again I felt guilty, while it was possible that the same thing happened if I had married another guy. How could I tell what would have happened if I have never been in that position? I just don't know. I think I am ready to make excuses to find myself guilty for our broken home. True that we learn to continue living. But when a home is broken this way by hate and anger, none of us could go back to the original feelings that we had before. We will be like a broken diamond, which needs mending. But never and never will we become the same as original. That is how I felt. And that is how my children will feel for the rest of their lives.

My Dear God:

You see, I write these things and pass by it as if I am talking about someone else's life. It seems that I am not talking of my life and me. The dreams that I had for my children, the hope that I had for our future, the plans about our retirement, the hope that we had for our children and their children's future, and the dreams, which had kept me happy and dependent on Iraj's love for his family all those years, all were gone. While I kept busy doing things, I felt like an empty hearted stranger to the whole thing. Although Mojgan's wedding turned out to be very unique and genuine, I felt like an outsider to the

whole thing. I felt like I was watching a movie, which I had to be part of it. Nothing was mine. And I did not belong there.

I did my best to make it possible for my children to be happy by keeping myself happy as much as I could, while at night in my bed I cried to be able to keep my sanity and do well the next day. The truth was that at that time of my life I was homeless. I had sent my furniture to Los Angeles to Maseeh's house. After two more days that I stayed with Scheidlers to clean up the mess that we had made in their yard, and since Maseeh was still painting the house, I had proposed to my friend Chitra that I stayed with her for few weeks. So I got ready to go back to Michigan, and then flew from there to my destiny, which was living with my son and his girl friend Anna. Meanwhile the next day Mojgan and Joe took off to Hawaii for their honeymoon.

Before I forget I should mention, before Mojgan's wedding, when Mary was feeling much better, one day when I was staying with Chitra, at seven o'clock in the morning she called me. She wanted to give me the good news that she had passed the California Bar at her first attempt. She made me so happy that I started crying. I was so proud of her. With all the hard ache and difficulty, which was surrounding her, still she was able to pass it with success. I was very happy. And knowing Mary, God forbid, if she was not able to pass it, she would have become so depressed that I just would be worried about the outcome. So I had my reasons to be really happy.

I mentioned this to bring up the subject of the toast at Mojgan's wedding. As I said around our table, besides my children, their father, and their cousins, were Claudette and Sue Meier. Since Iraj was so embarrassed that he was hiding himself from the crowd, I started to toast to the bride and groom. Since many people in that group did not know us, I started this way, "Hello and welcome. I am Shamci, Mojgan's mother. I always had this dream that my children one day could find their true love, without which no one can ever survive. And I think Mojgan did. I am so proud to be part of Scheidler's family, and I am more proud to have Joe as my son-in-law, whom I love very much. Indeed I am a lucky woman. Thank you all for coming, and may GOD bless you all". Then I continued and said," To my daughter Mary, who recently had passed a very difficult exam, the California Bar exam, I congratulate you Mary. And to my son Maseeh, who is indeed one of very few good men, 'SALAMATIE', which means to your good health".

My Dear God:

They gave me a big round of applauds. Then Ruth started toasted the couple. She started this way, "What can I say after your beautiful toast?" Since she did not have a daughter, and she had only three sons, she ended her toast this way, "With my son's marriage, not only I am not losing my son, but I am gaining a daughter". Then all their friends toasted to them, and the wedding became more like a cozy, friendly party. Joe's elementary school teachers, who were also his neighbors, told many funny stories about

his childhood. Some of their friends said teasing stories that they couldn't stop laughing. The party turned out so friendly and warm that no one wanted to leave. That was the time that Mojgan kept thanking me for making it possible to become such a good party. She said, "Mom, I was hoping that my celebration be a good one. But I never expected it to be this good. Thanks Mom!"

When I sent the video of the wedding to some of my friends, they agreed that poor Iraj looked embarrassed and guilty. The way he walked, the way he was talking to Mr. Scheidler why he was late for the ceremony, and he was trying to hide himself from his guilt. Instead I was the happy, and jolly. I kept my head up, and I was walking straight. I knew that I had done nothing wrong. It wasn't only my dream to raise our children together, and make a good future for them. To tell you the truth, it was as much his dream as it was mine. It was more his dream because he always was believing that his personality was like one of his uncle's, who left his wife and his children, and married his maid. His lack of confidence had made him more anxious to be a good father and not destroy his family. And at that time, although he was trying to deny his mistakes and guilt, still deep down he knew that he had done it all wrong. He had destroyed all and every one of us. He couldn't be proud of the things that people said about him, even his own family. To be able to continue his life, he must try to put all the blame on someone else. But no one, and no one knew better than him what he had done to his own name and his children. And no one will ever know more than him that he has to take it to his grave. I stood by him for eight years. I watched his love affair with Badri for eight years. I allowed him to take all the money away from us, and yet I did not apply for divorce. I was so tolerant that one day, when he was having affair with Badri, I told him, "I am not going to allow you to break and crush me. I will try to make you bring so much shame and embarrassment in your life that you wish you never did what you did to my children and me. If words such as liar, cheater, disloyal, dishonest, betrayer, promiscuous, and more, which come after your name, make you proud, then be it".

My Dear God:

But after people got to know me, even those who were not friends with me before, but they knew me, they tried to become my friend, and they had a lot of respect for me. This was hundred percent true. Many families became closer friend with me after they received that sarcastic letter about him. Two of them were the two sisters from Shiraz, my mother's hometown. They were friends with Dr. Jalil and Elizabeth Farah. We used to see them only at Dr. Farah's parties. After they found out about Iraj's disloyalty, they started inviting me more often in their houses.

Mary was the younger sister, who was married to Dr. Enrique Boqin. She had two boys and one girl. All of them were very advanced at school, and had earned scholarships from good universities. I always felt comfortable talking to her, or being at their house.

Because her husband was not Iranian, the atmosphere and guests were international. It was much more enjoyable to be with different cultures, and associate with more intelligent people.

Her older sister Viki was married to Casimer Zacharek, who was not Iranian also. She had one set of twins, a girl and a boy, and two more boys. They were also very advanced at school, and her older son became a doctor. They were so nice and so respectful to me that I could never forget their kindness and their attention for me. I still have my connection with them, and I remember that it was their respect and their attention that made me more tolerant and more hopeful. I thank them from the bottom of my heart.

Another lady doctor, who was going through divorce at the same time with me, was Dr. Zahra Khademian, who was married to Dr. Kashef. I met her at Dr. Shehideh's party one night, when she was pregnant with her second child. She was a psychiatrist and very nice lady. We got to know each other, and few times we went to lunch with her and Sara Fasihi. I enjoyed talking to her. Although she lived far from me, still we were able to keep our contact until today.

My Dear God:

Among non-Iranians there were many people, who were more respectful to me after my divorce than before. One of them was Dr. Chitra Amladi and her family. Just like Farah Shushtari, she had practically made her house mine. She even had given her house key, and their alarm code to me in case I needed to come to their house late at night. They welcomed me to their home at any time of the day or night. Although I did not have to use it, still their trust, their respect, and their acceptance of me was one more step towards my recovery. Such friendships were especially important to me at the time that those Iranian so-called friends of mine were acting like I had committed crime. They pulled themselves away from me if they saw me at any gathering. And they started whispering about me, and showing me to others. The people, whom I had entertained every week for twenty years, were treating me like I had a rotten smell. Many of them turned their heads away from me, and pretended that they did not know me. They reminded me of the stories of hundred years ago, and the way people were treating a divorcee in their communities. This proved to me how I had wasted my thirty years associating with them and socializing with them. At the beginning it was awful to think these people were once my friends. Then, when I realized how fortunate I had been that I was able to lose them, I thought of myself as a really lucky woman.

Unfortunately Iraj was so busy with his affair with Badri that even until the end, and after the sarcastic poem, still he couldn't see the truth. Or maybe he was so happy with what he got, that he did not want to bother to even recognize the plot that carefully was planned by his friends. As I said, they were very competitive. When Iraj was on the top of

his success, this was the only way to bring him down and put him out of race forever. They were able to put his name in the category of despicable cowards, and a no good man, a category that they were not in. So after they broke Iraj into millions of pieces, they were able to live happily ever after. Iraj was out of the race for the rest of his life.

When the wedding was over, Mojgan and Joe left for their Honeymoon in Hawaii. After two days of cleaning up, I left to stay with Farahnaz and Ali for one week. They were the only couple that I always depended on. There was not even one time that they did not welcome me. They always invited me with open arms, and they always greeted me with love and care. True, that I had entertained them in my house before. But I had entertained those Iranian so-called friends hundred more times than I did Farahnaz. The difference was that they were my enemies and not my friends. That was why they helped Badri in stealing Iraj. That was why they found the opportunity to destroy Iraj, and then had fun with his destruction. But Farahnaz and Ali were not phony; they were genuine friends. They had roots. They believed in good name and good family. And most of all, they both knew how I loved my family. They both knew the ugliness of Iraj and Badri's acts. They hated them to a point that, they didn't come to Mojgan's wedding, not to face Iraj after what he had done to his family. They sent their gift and their congratulations to Mojgan and Joe, and wished them all the happiness.

My Dear God:

As much as my children couldn't think of my problems, and me, God introduced Farahnaz and Ali to me to become like my children. They were behind me hundred percent, and they never left me by myself. So I went to Farahnaz and Ali to be able to see them before I go to LA. Although she was always busy with her schoolwork and her two children, Layla and Kasra, still she made sure that I had a great time, while I was staying with her. We did everything together, like a mother and daughter who were friends. And we went everywhere together as a family. Our relationship still is going as strong as before.

After Farahnaz's house, I had promised Chitra to go to her house and stay with her for three weeks. She wanted me to stay longer, but I had to go to LA to my son's house and unpack my stuff. I felt very comfortable when I was with Chitra. I actually was part of their family. Her children, Amol and Amita, were happy to be with me like they were with their grandma. They did their homework with me being around, and they cleaned their rooms with me being around, although they hated to do that. Then we cooked together, we ate diner together, we cleaned up together, and we watched TV together. Many times Chitra and I took the kids to movies. They were giving me the family that I had lost. And then Chitra, who had MS, was happy when I was able to spend time with her family. Her husband Mr. Presad Amladi was an engineer, who graduated from Berkley in California. He was one of the nicest men I have ever met. He loved his wife and his children very

much. Because of his wife's MS, each day after he got home he cooked, he washed the dishes, he went shopping, he cleaned the yard on weekends. All together he was very helpful to his wife and the children.

Chitra was very sensitive about her disease. After few years still she was shocked of the way that she was the one who got it. We used to talk for hours and hours about her disease. She was an internist, and she was aware of what was going on with her. That made it more difficult on her. She was very close to me, and she discussed with me any private subject that she liked. Many times we slept near each other after we finished watching a movie, or finished talking about a book, which she had offered me to read. Even a few of my friends came to her house, when they wanted to visit me. Once Kaveh came over, another time Tilda and Luciana came over.

My Dear God:

And the day that I was leaving to go to Metropolitan Airport to go to LA, Dr. Mehrabian volunteered to drive me to the airport. He came in and got to know Dr. Amladi and her family.

The same way I was with them wherever they went. We took short trips together. We went to restaurants together. Both Chitra and I tried so hard to forget what had happened in our lives. I thought at that time both our diseases were incurable, while I think I was mistaken. Mine was curable, if I put my effort to forget about my lost love. But hers was there forever, even if it went into remission, it still was there, and it still worried her. I did whatever I had in my power to make her feel good and forget about the upcoming hard times. She felt worse when she saw what was coming to her. No book, no movie, no story could stop her from worrying. Her children were teenagers, although they were very good academically, still she added to her worries. She always helped them with their schoolwork. She never stopped helping them for one moment. While she had difficulty driving, still she drove them everywhere: to the library, to their different classes, and to their schools every day. Mr. Amladi helped them with their homework, and never let go of one moment of attention to them.

So because of my promise to Chitra, and the care and attention that she gave to me while I was desperately in need of attention, I decided to spend some time with her and her family to be able to pay my dues to her. Meanwhile not to waste my time while I was there, I sewed covers for her living room furniture. We went together and bought the fabric that she liked, and I tried to make her happy by making it exactly the way she had it in mind.

When that trip was over, and Maseeh's house was ready for me to move in, I tried to buy a one-way ticket to California, and say good-bye to Michigan and my memories for more than twenty-five years. I called a friend of mine, whom I had met at Bridge class, and she was a travel agent to buy me a one-way ticket to LA. My friend Rosita Accasta bought me a ticket through Southwest Airline. This was the first time I was traveling with this airline. I had no idea that they did not serve any meals. I never checked my itinerary to find out what was going on in that airline. I think I was so anxious to leave Michigan forever, that I lost track of what was going on altogether.

My Dear God:

Ok my dear God, how should I explain all these? Whenever I watched a soap opera, or I ran into a person whose life was full of disappointments, I thought how could all that happen to one person consecutively? And now, I see myself exactly in that same position. Things came my way consecutively. And it was so strange that I did not know how to explain it even to myself.

Rosita got me one-way ticket to LA with Southwest airline. Dr Mehrabian drove me to Metropolitan airport from Chitra's house. I thanked all my friends who had helped me all those years, and said bye to them and bye to Michigan forever.

I became very disappointed when I realized that they were not serving food. The reason was that I had to eat a lot to keep my stomach full to prevent myself being nauseated. That was why I always carried different kinds of snacks with me in my bag. But to eat only snacks did not help me at all. I had to have a full meal, and then I had my snacks when my stomach asked for it. My problem in this trip was that I was so confused and so lost that I didn't study my ticket whatsoever. I sat in the plane, and I thought it would take me to my destination, where my son Maseeh was expecting me. Not knowing that the plane had a few stops before I reach LA.

Because they did not serve food, I kept munching on my snacks to be able to sleep. It worked, and surprisingly I fell asleep. When I woke up, and I saw everyone was leaving, I thought I must be in LA. So I got off the plane also. Not knowing that I got out where I must not get off. The point was that the staff of that plane was acting completely different from other airlines, which I had traveled with for many years, such as American, United, British Air, Iran Air, or many others. The lady who introduced herself as the wife of the pilot, and another girl who was assisting her to put up a show to entertain passengers were trying to bring smile on everyone's face by teasing their own crew for not serving meals. It was their useless talk and act that put me to sleep.

When I got off, I followed the crowd to the luggage pick-up area. I waited and waited until the last luggage was gone. When I did not see my son there, and I did not find my luggage, I went to the information desk to find out what was going on. Only when I talked to them, I realized that I was in the wrong city. I was worried about my son, who was supposed to pick me up from the airport in Los Angeles. I was exhausted, hungry, nauseated, and still half asleep. I was so disappointed at myself, and the crew that I wanted to throw up. That was the worst feeling.

At that airport they tried to help me. They scheduled me for the next plane to LA. Through them I contacted my son, and explained to him what had happened. While I had

to wait nine more hours for the next flight, I had something to eat. But because I was so nervous and worried not to miss my plane again, I couldn't fall asleep. I was in the most miserable state that anyone could be. I made sure that I had enough food in my bag to avoid vomiting.

My Dear God:

Finally the plane was there, and they started boarding. Everyone found their seats, put on the seat belts, and the two stewardesses gave all the required instructions. As always that I kept my handbag under the seat and near my feet. I kept it there to be able to reach for it as often as my stomach acted funny. The younger stewardess came to me and asked for my bag to put it in the overhead compartment. I told her that because I get sick in the plane, and I have to have my snacks within my reach, I preferred to keep my bag under the seat.

The plane already was in the runway, and on its way to take off. I was at a point of throwing up. I was trying to close my eyes not to see the movement of the plane. In no time I realized that the plane was slowing down. The passengers were wondering what was going on. The passenger, who was sitting in front of me said, "I think they are talking about you". I couldn't believe it. There was no reason that they stopped the plane to talk about me. After the plain stopped, the younger stewardess showed me to the pilot, and said, "This lady". At this time I was feeling sicker than I was before. I wanted to eat something to stop me from being nauseated. The pilot asked me to step out of plain. He said, "I understand that you are disturbing the peace in the aircraft". I tried to explain to him that I always get sick in the plane, so I asked to keep my bag within my reach, under the seat, which I have always done in any aircraft. But they did not listen to my reasoning, and they carried me to the exit door. And they asked me to leave the aircraft.

I had never been this humiliated in my entire life. Sick in my stomach, and humiliated in front of hundreds of passengers, I sat on the floor. While crying I said, I haven't done anything wrong. What have I done to disturb the peace of the aircraft? My son is waiting for me at the LAX. Why should you treat me this way?"

If at that time I wasn't that weak and sick, probably I would have done something to disturb the peace of that aircraft. But I was so sick and so disable to do anything that I couldn't move at all. At this time they tried to make a condition, and in a very humiliating and embarrassing way they asked me, "If only you promise that you will not disturb the safety in the plane, you can go back to your seat".

All right my dear GOD, you were the witness there. Have you ever heard that an aircraft crew started the plane on the runway, ready to take off, and then they would bring the plane to stop to ask a lady, who just wanted to keep her bag of food under her seat only to avoid vomiting to get out of the plane? Until today, have you ever heard such a thing? If it were possession of drugs, a knife, a weapon, or any other dangerous object,

they would have the right to act that way. But for a small bag of food to keep it under my seat, they acted so vicious and animalistic that until today when I think about it I get nauseated.

My Dear God:

I sat on my seat, closed my eyes, and tried to sleep. You were my witness, my dear GOD. I felt like burning down the plane. I didn't know how to face my son. I couldn't think that he might believe me. It was even harder for me to believe that the pilot and his crew took off on the runway, and then came back and stopped the plane to ask a passenger to leave the plane because she had asked to keep her bag under her seat and not in the overhead compartment. Who would believe such a thing? They might have thought that I hit someone, or I had a fistfight with someone, or I was trying to burn the plane, which after that humiliation I wished I was able to do. I was so angry that I think I had fainted. I was hoping that when I got to LA airport, I must and I will do something about their behavior.

Until that day, whenever something went wrong in any airline, the pilot and the crew blamed it on poor passengers, and we all believed it. But what about now? If no one was with me, my dear GOD, you were the one who was with me, and you witnessed the whole thing. Now I know what goes inside a plane when I hear about a fatal accident. The crew made a person like me so made to make a criminal out of him. What an experience! I was so disappointed and disturbed by that Southwest aircraft that I thought I would never travel with plane.

When I got to LA, Maseeh was expecting me. But I was a zombie. I just asked Maseeh to allow me to sit for some time to be able to restore my strength. I was not able to say hello, or talk for a while. When I told him what had happened, he too became furious. He asked me to sit down, and he went to look for the airline management to report the incident. At that time of night there was no one there.

When Maseeh returned, and he wanted to take me to the luggage pick up, the crew was coming out. I showed the stewardess to him, and at the same time I wanted to attack her. I wanted to wrap her hair around her neck for the vicious thing she did to me. But we decided to go home, and write a letter of complaint through my travel agent. What an experience! What a cruel crew! What a ruthless staff!

After I went home, for days and days I thought of why she would have done such an act. Then I came to a conclusion that there might have been a romantic relationship between the pilot and the stewardess. When I did not give my bag to her, and did not obey her order, she got mad at me, and asked the pilot, who already was on the runway to throw me out of plane. And the pilot, being a man who would do anything to satisfy his lover, without further questions stopped the aircraft, and asked me out of that plane. Just to tell his lover, "My dear love, I would do anything for you. You just tell me what you

November 1, 1993

To whom it may concern at SouthWest airlines management:

My name is Mrs. Shamci Rafani. I n the past year alone, I have traveled world wide on nearly six or seven occasions. I have done so with many different airlines except for SouthWest Airlines. My decision to choose your airline for my last cross-country trip was the single worst travel decision I believe I have ever made.

As a 33 year resident in the state of Michigan, I had made the decision to relocate to Los Angeles, California. I purchased my ticket with your company through Royal International Travel; A travel agency with which I have been dealing a long time. My agent, Mrs. Rosita Accosta, has never steered me wrong in all the years I've dealt with her. For this reason I am quite certain that it was through no fault what-so-ever of Mrs. Accosta that my flight was so dreadful. She could not have known what she was getting me into.

The ticket I purchased was for a flight that supposedly had only one stop between my place of departure and my final destination(Detroit-St. Louis-Los Angeles). As it turned out SouthWest has a policy off adding stops without informing their passengers. When I arrived at my second stop I assumed that I was In Los angeles because no one had informed me otherwise. It wasn't until an hour later when my luggage was still nowhere to be found and my son, who was to pick me up, was not there to greet me, that I found out I was in Phoenix, Arizona...............................PHOENIX , ARIZONA!

No mention on the ticket, no mention on the plane. I was stranded at this point, my connecting flight having left some time ago for Los Angeles. I was also several hours late because I had to Endure a Minimum 1 hour delay at each of my stops.

At this point I was highly agitated and beginning to feel quite nauseous.I had not eaten anything of substance for several hours. After having secured a seat on the next SouthWest flight to Los Angeles, I boarded with my single carry-on hand bag; In which I carry the only cure for my queasiness when I travel by air, A package of Ritz crackers . As I sat in my seat with my bag between my legs and at my feet, A flight attendant came to advise me to slide my beg beneath my seat before take-off. While trying not to get sick, I attempted to communicate to this attendant that I needed my bag handy and that I would like to keep it where it was. This response so ruffled her feathers that without so much as a word she reached down, grabbed my bag , and only as she was walking away behind me, mumbled some thing about my getting the bag back later. I protested quite loudly that I needed what was in my bag. I received no response at all.

I then proceeded to feel so ill, I had to close my eyes to regain my composure.It was then that I heard the voice of the flight attendant trying to explain her actions and to advise me of when she would allow me to have my bag back.

With my eyes closed and a waving gesture of my hand I told her to please get away from me and that I had no desire to listen at that point to a single thing she had to say. My hand had touched hers as I gestured in the dark cabin and this obviously offended her for she then began a pattern of treatment toward me not befitting of the worst of criminals.

The plane was stopped from approaching the runway for take-off , the doors were opened, I was escorted outside by members of the crew and treated in such a humiliating manner that I could only sit on the floor in disbelief over the the threat that I had become to the safety of this flight because I wanted my Ritz crackers and modicum of respect.

I simply kept my mouth shut; To keep from getting angrier and to keep from getting sick. The crew, all the while, acted as though they were completely within reason to treat me in the manner they did. This attitude I attributed solely to the briefing that I'm sure the flight attendant afforded the crew in my absence.

I knew my son was still waiting for me in Los Angeles and probably still had no idea when I would arrive. I conceded my dignity only to get myself to Los Angeles as soon as possible.

Once I arrived at my destination I tried vehemently to find a SouthWest official to whom I could file a complaint. I was told, however, that it was too late in the evening and that there was no such official present to help me. I told myself then to just go home and deal with this in due course.

With-in the next few days I contacted my travel agent to complain and was advised to write SouthWest a letter.. In the time that it has taken since to find someone to accurately record my thoughts (English is not my first language , and I wanted to be certain to communicate as clearly as possible) I am certain that the somewhat emotional tone of this letter is still a major dilution of the feelings that I experienced that evening. I continue to feel ill every time I think that I payed hard earned money to be treated in such a horrible manner.

I await impatiently for your response to this letter before I take any further action.

Your extremely dissatisfied customer;

Shamci Rafani

These two pages are the letter that I wrote to Southwest Airlines. Although they apologized and sent me one free ride inside the United Sates, I was so sick and afraid of flying that I did not use the ticket and it expired after one year. I was so disappointed that I thought I might never be able to travel again. But like everything else, I completely forgot it after a while and started my journeys again.

want, and I will do it for you, my dear love". If that was not the case, then what else could it be?

My Dear God:

Now, you tell me, my dear GOD, has this happen to any other person? Or if it had happened, was the case just like mine? Has it ever happened that a pilot after he started half way on the runway with nearly two hundred passengers in the plane would come back, stop the plane, and ask a lady out of the plane just because she was sick and wanted to keep her bag of snacks, which already she had shown to the stewardess under her seat to be within her reach? I am sure that many cases like this had happened to many more people. And I am sure that the crew of that aircraft was able to put the blame on the poor and innocent passengers.

When I believe that the strangest incidents had come my way without asking for it, my dear GOD, you must believe me. If no one else was there to witness the incident, you were there. You saw it. And I think you are the only one who knows why it had happened. If after many years, still I am wondering why, or how it happened, I am sure that no other person who reads this, would believe that I was innocent, and that there was no reason for that crew to act in such way towards a passenger, who actually needed their help at that special time. Thanks GOD that time is a healer; otherwise I would have been giving up plane rides altogether after that incident.

Although the letter of complaint made them understand that they were guilty of ruining the life of a woman, who at that time was under their care, and needed their help. Yet they did not have any explanation why they did what they did. If I was okay, and healthy enough to fight, or if I was vicious enough like them, I would have brought a lawsuit against the Southwest Airline to teach them a lesson not to do such an act to anyone else. And I am sure that I would have won. In a country that the lady burns her leg with hot coffee bought from McDonalds, can sue the company and win millions of dollars, there was no way that I wouldn't win that case. But as I said, I was too tired and too weak to be able to run after money. I was looking for a peace and tranquility after eight years of struggle, and I was planning to find it in our new house. That was my ultimate dream and nothing else.

Yes, my dear GOD, that one-way ticket from Metropolitan Airport to LAX, with that strange and ugly experience was the end of thirty years of my happy and unhappy life. My happy times were the greatest that not many people could have experienced the kind of love that I did experience. And the unhappy and strange period of my life also was so ugly and so catastrophically dreadful that I don't think that too many women had experienced it like I did. That one-way ticket was the end of all my good memories, and all my bad memories. That one-way ticket was the mourning for the loss of thirty years of my young life that I was planning to bury it under a ton of forgetfulness. That one-way ticket

was the end of my life with all my feelings and whatever memories I had from the beginning to the end. That one-way ticket was the beginning of a new life. A new life with no memories, a new life with no feelings whatsoever, a new life to start all over again, a new life to teach me from A to Z without planning to repeat my past mistakes again. I was planning to make a life with no life in it whatsoever. There would be no more loving, no more trusting, no more depending, and no more expectation from anyone at all. I had to learn how to arrange my life as if I was the only person on earth. I had to learn to see no people, hear no people, and learn to live a life that GOD had given to me to enjoy, once and for all.

My Dear God:

Anyway, the Southwest Airline sent us an apology letter, and a one-way ticket to anywhere in the United States, which expired after one year. But at that time I was so afraid of flying, or it is better to say that I hated all the airlines that I didn't want to get near any plane, yet to use Southwest Airline again. That was not permissible for me, not even if Southwest gave me plenty of money. The name of Southwest Airline made me feel nauseated.

That was the end of thirty years living in Michigan, and the start of many years in California. I was starting another, unknown part of my life in California. Not knowing what to expect, and I didn't know what life was going to bring me at this time. The only thing that I remember was that I was planning to stand still, and show my children how a person could become strong and fight the negativities, which came his or her way to destroy them. I had only one thing in mind: to stay strong, and not to let anything to bother me whatsoever. Nothing made me happier than to leave all those insincere, phony Iranian friends behind in Michigan, and never see them again. That by itself was a blessing to me. Their evil intentions and viciousness towards me is not even describable. I was fortunate to be able to get as far away from them as I did. That by itself brought happiness into my life.

So I sat in the car next to my son Maseeh, and closed my eyes to be able to bring peace in me, and tried to fall asleep. I had neither strength, nor life in me to be able to talk or do anything. I knew that I had lost thirty years of my young life, and I had nothing in me to back me up to be able to build a happy future. No one, especially my children, could understand what was going on in my mind. They didn't feel my feelings after losing all my past memories and my happiness. I never discussed my pain and sufferings with them, thinking that they had enough of their own to deal with. But in my heart I was expecting them to know what their father had put me through during those nine years. I knew that they were aware of what they did to me, and I was expecting that sometimes they showed some reaction to their father's behavior. I had heard, and read books about children who punished the parent who had done wrong. But we don't always get what we want. So we

have to learn how to deal with it. My mind was full of anger, hopelessness, and most of all dead tired that I slept on our way home.

My Dear God:

When we got home, Anna and their big Akita were waiting for us. They introduced me to Kane, hopefully to get to know me more. He had seen me before, but this time was different. This time I was going to share the house with him. I had to learn his liking and disliking. After we brought the luggage in, we sat and started talking about my long and painful one-way trip with Southwest Airline. Both Anna and Maseeh were so upset and angry that started to write the complaint at that moment. And they demanded a serious action by the Southwest Airline Company.

But the person inside me was a person I didn't know at all. She was a hopeless, emotionless, a newborn adult who had to start to learn from A to Z allover again. I had to learn not to be fooled by trusting anyone else in the world except myself. I had to learn not to love anyone except myself, which was the hardest thing to do for me. I had to learn to stay away from those who needed my help desperately, like Badri, and tell them to go to Hell.

There is an expression in Iran, which translates, "If you see a blind person is falling into a ditch, if you stay quiet and ignore seeing her, and let her fall into the ditch, you will be considered a sinner in the eye of God". But I changed this expression to, "If you ever see a blind person falling into a ditch, if you don't push her to speed up her fall, then you are considered a sinner". This was my belief, and it still is. If I did not stepped forward to help Badri at the time that her husband was killed, just like other Iranians who got her children a box of doughnuts and kept their distance from her, today I would still be with my family. And my children would not be apart as they are today. Helping Badri was like helping a snake, and then she turns and bites your hand. I will feel her venom in my children's blood stream and mine for as long as we all live. So if I believe the way that I do about helping a needy person, I have all the right in the world.

Maseeh and Anna were very excited being in their new house. They had the whole house painted inside and out. They did some modifications here and there. They had waited for me to move my furniture from their garage to my room. They already had thrown my Persian rug in my room, and put my bed and some other stuff in there. To me my room was the best part of the house. This room was the master bedroom. The new addition bedroom, which was much bigger with walking closets and beautiful bath area, now was Anna and Maseeh's bedroom. My bedroom was surrounded with extra large windows on three sides. And I had a little balcony in the front that made it even more pleasant to watch the view. The way that the house was built on the hilly road, overlooking all the beautiful scenery around that area. It was heavenly beautiful. I had lots of mirrored closets that made the room much larger than it was. After ten years of struggling with life,

that was the first night that I wanted to feel secure. I wanted to put my past behind me, and start a different life with different person in my body. I wanted to close my eyes, and sleep like a baby.

My Dear God:

But this will never happen if you are a concerned mother. How could I put my past behind me, while I didn't know what was happening to Mary? I sent her a meaningful card every week, and she called me once in a while to say hello. We never discussed anything else, but hello and how are you. Since she was with her father, I wanted to think that she was okay. Although I was trying to put my past behind me, still the thoughts of past were dancing in front of my eyes.

I was asking myself, "What had happened to me? Since I came to America, I had a comfortable life. I had the love of my life, my husband, my support, my friend, and my family next to me always. He always did anything and everything in his power to make me happy. He always looked happy when he put a smile on my face. He held my hand, and tried to show me his true love by buying the best and most expensive gifts to prove to me that I was the only one whom he loved and cared for. He kissed my hands and thanked me for loving him the way I did in our privacy. He was an example of a good husband among all our friends. On our twenty-second anniversary he gave me a gift with a card. On it he wrote twenty two times "I LOVE YOU". There was not one time that he forgot my birthday. How could this person after the death of Malakuti change to a completely opposite person? The torture and anguish that he put me and my children though for ten years is not even describable". I kept opening my eyes to be able to let go of those thoughts, but it didn't work. I was too tired to fall asleep, and I was so attached to those memories to be able to let go. During those ten years I had learned how to keep busy all the time to be able to stay away from the memory of my past. But now that I was comfortably lying down on my bed in my bedroom in my son's house, I was not able to let go of all those miserable and frustrating ten years. That night it was like I had just started to feel the pain of the past.

My Dear God:

My life was so painful to me that a day lasted like a year. It seemed to me that I had been chained and beaten vigorously for ten consecutive years, and all my body was black and blue, and all my bones were crushed. I had been spinning around and around for ten years. That night that I was supposed to forget my whole past and sleep comfortably the painful past did not want to leave me alone. My mind couldn't be away from Mary and her life situation. I didn't know her health status or anything else about her. I was anxiously waiting to find out if she was okay or not. I was asking myself, "When will my tortures be over? Either in my daily life, or at night I had to face the thought of their

Saks Fifth Avenue

Dear Shamci,

I love you
I love you
I love you
I love you
I love you
I love you
I love you
I love you
I love you
I love you
I love you
I love you
I love you
I love you
I love you
I love you
I love you
I love you
I love you
I love you
I love you
I love you

Iraj

This is a card Iraj gave me on our twenty second wedding anniversary. I think it speaks for itself. There is no need to explain it. Many people might have done the same thing and not mean it. It doesn't mean anything at all. I don't remember what the gift was that came with it.

May 26, 1976

Dear Dr. Rafani,

Thank you for many months of patience and one evening of encouragement!

Enclosed find a terrible view of me (my mom the amateur photographer) but thought it was an ok shot of you - anyway, good for a laugh!

I'll see you soon with more questions, I'm sure!

Thanks again,
for everything,
from both of us!
Steve & Elaine
Weicker

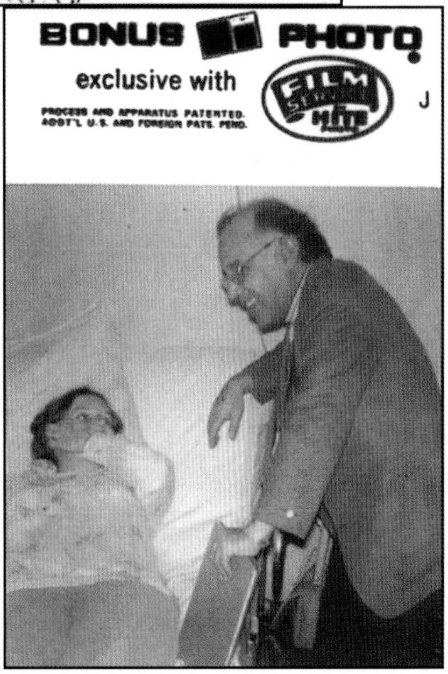

You can tell that when I say he was good in many ways, I am right. He was a good doctor, he was a good husband, he was trying to be a good father, he was a good brother, and he was a good friend, but the only thing is that he was not loyal to me and his children. He betrayed me and my children. He cheated on us and he left us with a sad memory of him. It is painful having someone who is good and finding out that you have been in the dark all your life.

cruelty. I had to fight and struggle with horrible nightmares, the results of my torturous past. Please GOD, please end it here. End it and bring a kind of peace in me that I could put my past behind me. Please".

The next day with great happiness I started to unpack. My room looked so comfortable and beautiful. I was trying to live again. Maseeh was so happy to see me full of life again. He was working very hard every day, and the time that he was home we were together. Sometimes we went out to dinner and sometimes to a movie. The rest of the time everyone kept busy with their own personal activities.

Anna was very sweet, and she tried so hard to become closer and closer to me. She wanted to make me happy no matter what. She did and said things, which were my favorite. She used to get the mail, and bring mine in my bedroom. By knocking on my door, I knew that it was she. Many times I mentioned to her, "Please this is your house, you don't have to knock to come in". I welcomed her by saying, "My beautiful mail lady", and she liked it. Many times she stayed with me and talked about her childhood, and how once she had to wear a ripped shirt to school, and after all these times still she remembered the humiliation of that event. She talked to me about her parents, her siblings, and those children who were adopted by her parents. While she remembered every little hurtful event in her life, she was trying by giving me love and attention to make me forget what had happened to my life and me.

As I mentioned before, Maseeh had persuaded Anna to go back to school to get her degree in Arts. She was the only one among her siblings who applied for a degree. She was very good at it according to Maseeh, and she was very talented. She was motivated by Maseeh's influence, and she was working very hard on it.

What was very shocking to me was that these two young friends did not go to bed at the same time. Anna used to work on her projects until two or three in the morning. Most of the nights I would sit by her, and while she was working, we talked of the very unusual events, which had happened in our lives. She had many stories from her childhood about her siblings. This way I was listening more than talking. I didn't want to bring up the unhappiness in me by remembering them.

My Dear God:

Anna talked to me of any subject. She felt very close to me, and she wanted me to feel the same way about her. Many times I told her, "Please Anna, I want to stay away from loving and trusting other people. Don't make me love you. I have no strength to face more disasters in my life". She used to laugh and say, "Don't worry. This is not going to happen. I love you dearly like my own mother". She was as sweet as she could get. We had our closeness and our distances. Sometimes I cooked the food that they liked, and Anna was the one who loved and appreciated it the most. We invited her parents, and cooked "ghormeh sabzi" for them, and they loved it. They loved Maseeh, and Maseeh loved them back dearly. It was a loving and peaceful atmosphere that I loved to have around me. Each one of us knew the other person's rights, and we respected that. I was the same way that I lived with my father-in-law and three sisters-in-law during the first year of my marriage, peacefully and respectfully. That was when my parents disowned me for marrying Iraj. My God, how life plays jokes on us! How we survive through each ordeal one by one!

After long suffering time, it was the first Christmas in that house with my excited son and creative Anna. And I was having a ball. Anna was very organized, and she had all the ornaments, old and new, ready. Many of her ornaments were hand made by her friends or her relatives. Maseeh and I bought the tree, while Anna was at school. There was nothing more rewarding and more pleasant than seeing my son Maseeh so excited, so happy and so full of pleasure and satisfaction with his new house. He loved the fireplace, and any chance he got he burned wood in that fireplace. I was very happy for him that he decided to buy this house, and not the one that he had put an offer for. In comparison to that, this was three times bigger and much nicer. We all were enjoying the house.

It was in that room and in that house that I started to organize my writings. I would sit on my high bed at the corner of my bedroom, while I felt like I was sitting in the middle of a meadow; I reviewed my life from the beginning to the end.

When I started my conversation with my "own" GOD, it seemed that all the doors of heaven were opened to me. I had found someone to trust, to talk to, to laugh with, and to cry on his shoulder. I had found a dependable supporter, who was always with me at all times. Who was listening to me, while he knew perfectly what had gone with my life, and knew what I was expecting to happen to me in future.

My Dear God:

The funny thing about my writing was that until I started typing my letters, I did not have knowledge that I was dyslexic. As I continued typing, and automatically the letters were placed in the wrong place, or my eyes read them in the wrong place. The more I studied myself and my writings, and the more I studied about this disorder of brain, the more I realized that I have had it without knowing it. Then I realized that the reason that I had been a slow reader, it might have been the cause of this disorder. I couldn't recognize it in Farsi language. I think it was the character of writing, which was cursive. So I hadn't had a chance to find out that I had a disorder, called dyslexia. That was the reason for my slow reading and slow writing. But this will pass also, like every other thing that had passed and got forgotten.

Anyway, at nights the happy dreams of my good times, and the nightmares of bad times never left me alone. The more I wrote, the less I slept, and the less I had nightmares. I started to find my way around the house. The house was located in a way that it seemed we were living in town and out in the suburb. I was able to walk to the shops, the post

office and other places within five to ten minutes.

I did my routine walking every morning, before anyone got up. Maseeh and Anna were trying to warn me of dangers on the streets of Los Angeles area. They warned me of strange and unfriendly people around us. They wanted me to stay away from strange people and homeless. Anna was especially concerned. But after living there for some time, and finding my way around, and talking to some homeless people, I realized that they were wrong. I not only did not find it unpleasant, I found it very enjoyable instead. I found a banker in Bank of America who not only she helped me wisely as a consultant, but also she and I became friends, and we talked about our family life. I searched and found out about the Bridge club, and joined some of them. I was feeling so safe and so happy that I thought my GOD knew that I deserved this happiness after such an ordeal: lonely nights, and falling sleep with my tears wetting my pillows. After ten years of being thrown from one place to another, and after being apart from my children physically and emotionally, now I was safe and feeling great. All those years I was expecting that either I would go crazy and become institutionalized; or I would lose one or all my children to a suicide. Those thoughts destroyed me more than anything else. Now that I was with my happy and successful son, and Mary had passed her Bar Exam, and Mojgan was on her way married to her love, Joe, I thought that miracles could happen. As they say, "Time and patience will payoff". How true it was for me! At last ten years of every day sufferings was paying me a reward: a peaceful mind, and a comfortable life. Thank you my dear GOD. Forever and ever thank you.

My Dear God:

But this was not the end of my struggle. It was just a beginning of learning and adjusting myself with my new surroundings. I must try to find a comfort for everyone. I had a long plan ahead of me. I had to find my place, while my children had to live their own life.

My Dear God:

Many times I felt sorry for Maseeh. He was trying so hard to be fair to his girlfriend Anna, and his mother. Actually I knew that he must pay more attention to his girlfriend, and not me. But he was always afraid that he might hurt Anna's feelings one way or another. Like the time that on the sweetest day he bought us two beautiful Orchid plants and sent them home to us. They were both in the living room to beautify the house. It didn't matter which one belonged to whom.

I don't know what had happened in their private bedroom, but I felt that something was bothering Anna. I don't know if it was my assumption, or she had other things in her mind. Many times I noticed that in their bedroom, they were trying to resolve their differences.

So life was going great for me. I was happy, and I tried to write to you, my dear GOD, for as many hours as I could. When I wrote, I laughed a little, I cried a little, and I was able to think much better every day.

It was nearly three months that I was in Maseeh's house, when one night around four AM, I felt that my bed was rocking back and forth with me on it. Before I find out what it was, I heard Maseeh calling me, "Mom, Mom, don't move. There has been an earthquake. I have a flashlight in my hand. I am coming to get you". Anna and Maseeh were so scared that they did not know what to do. As we were talking, still the place was shaking.

My Dear God:

Maseeh came into my room, and asked me to grab my medications and all my basic necessities and run out of the house before we feel another quake. First I had to find out about Mary. I dialed Mary's phone number, which she had given to me. She was okay, and they didn't feel it like we did. When I heard that I picked up my stuff, and got out of the house. At the same time the telephone rang. Anna jumped in and answered it. It seemed that Iraj had called to see what had happened to them. But to my shocking surprise Anna swore to me that the first person he had asked about was I, Shamci. For some special reason I had doubts to accept that. But remembering his past behavior, I could convince myself that it might have been true. That person, who while was having affair on me, bought the most expensive gifts, while other husbands didn't, could commit such an act. Anyway, we were all standing in the middle of street in the darkness to see what would happen next.

Anna's sister, Coleen, was living in an apartment nearby. Anna couldn't find her through the phone. She thought she might have been destroyed. So although we knew that it was dangerous to drive, we took the car and started to look for her. Until we got to Ventura Boulevard, we did not know the extent of the earthquake. There was not one building, shop, or street, which was standing still. The more we drove, the more we found that we were just lucky. We drove in front of Coleen's apartment, we found no one there. We asked some people around her apartment, they didn't know what had happened to them. Everyone was on the street because of the after shocks, which were bringing down more homes and buildings than the original quake itself. They were trying to contact her on their cell phone. But no matter how many times they tried, there was no answer.

I was freezing, and also needed to use the bathroom badly. I asked one of the neighbors if I could use their bathroom. It was too dark to be able to go by myself and find the place. So the poor young man, while he knew that it was very dangerous to go into the building, guided me with his flashlight, and showed me the bathroom. It was so nice of him to come with me and put his life in danger, while the ground was still shaking. Later we found Coleen. She too had been out looking for us.

Little by little daylight started to show itself to the world. We were able to see the

results of that earthquake more clearly. The year was nineteen ninety-three, 1993, the Northridge quake, which was read 7.3 on scale. Or at least this is what I remember. When we drove home, it looked like the city was bombarded with explosives. When we got home, we found all the books and bookshelves were turned over, and all the china and their cabinets were down. Many dishes were broken.

My Dear God:

The top part of the walls around the house was cracked. The living room, dinning room, bathrooms, kitchen, upstairs, and downstairs the cracks were like a belt all around the house.

It was until the next day that we found out the whole fireplace, right above my head, had been moved and ready to fall with one little shake. Maseeh was so relived when he found out that the fireplace had not fallen on my head, and didn't kill me. He kept talking about the possibilities if the fireplace had fallen over my head. The garage and the storage room behind it, and the whole driveway were cracked and completely damaged. The yard's pavement was all cracked.

Although everywhere in the house were damages, still it was nothing near what we saw all over the Ventura Boulevard. The house was standing there, and none of us was killed. But every minute we were expecting a big fall from after quakes. We all were expecting that the house came down on us now or then. None of us were sleeping in our bedrooms. Everyone was lying down on the sofa or sleeping bags in the middle of living room. Every one of us, especially Anna, was horrified to see another big after shock. The media, TV, radio, and newspapers were not only making it easy on people, but they stretched and extended the stories to a point that they were able to make the whole population terrified from the aftermath.

Many stores were down and closed. Some were half open, and part of their stuff on the ground. The market for batteries and first aids were high rocketing. Medicine and other necessities became more expensive, or there was shortage on many of them. As if it was the end of the world. It really was too scary, but not as scary as media had made it. Meanwhile life must go on no matter what. Insurances were busy selling earthquake insurance, and everyone was finding a way to bring back their lives to a norm. To be ahead of earthquake, Maseeh and Anna purchased everything, which was mentioned on TV or radio. They bought more water, more food, more flashlights, more batteries, and emergency kit with all the mentioned objects, which were advised by media. Everything was kept near the entrance door. With every aftershock, we all jumped out of the house with some stuff in our hands. This was the advice of media, who made us believe that our house, damaged and cracked all around, had a possibility to come down with one little aftershock.

As always I looked at the bright side. I was very happy that we had the opportunity

to celebrate the Christmas month before. I brought that up to them many times. I wanted to make sure that we have been lucky to be able to see the light again, and see our house was still standing up.

My Dear God:

The relationship between Anna and I was growing stronger than ever. We had love and mutual respect for each other. Although she was busy with her school, work day and night; still her main goal was bodybuilding and her daily exercises. While she was underweight, she was on those bodybuilding machines every day for four or more hours.

My main concern still was Mary. When she told me, "I got my own place, and have my own telephone number", I was very delighted. But when I asked her to go and visit her, in a regretful voice she told me, "But I rented my place in Badri's mother's house". I was aware that she knew that I would never want to see that family. So I said nothing to her, and I changed the subject. I think I talked about the way that I sent Mary to her father's house before I come to California. I was hoping that he had decency to watch and pay attention to his sick and needy daughter. But I was wrong about him again.

My Dear God:

After she was able to pass the Bar exam, she was able to look for a job. After having the nervous breakdown, I was glad to hear that she was coming back, and was becoming the same active and ambitious girl that she was before. I was glad that she got a job at an insurance company. And I was happy to see that she was able to have her own place, but to know that her father had agreed to let her live in Badri's mother's maid quarters. All those years I struggled not to see my children be second-class citizen in their own parents' eyes. Now, I saw that Dr. Rafani had sent his beautiful daughter to live in his mother-in-law's maid quarters to be able to help her with some money. Shouldn't I be mad at him and his ruthlessness? Shouldn't I look at him as the same father who sold his sperm for the price of only seven Tooman, Iranian money? Didn't he have knowledge that each one of his sperms had become a child like Mary or Maseeh or Mojgan? Did he even care for those babies? Why should I expect from him to care and love these three children? Even if he did something for them, it was not because he had love for them. One reason was that he was responsible by law, and second reason was that he liked his own name, and he wanted to show people that he was a caring and loving father. Otherwise these three children were the same as the other sperms that he sold for nothing. And yet with all the anger that I had for him, I saw myself responsible for what had happened to my children. It was I, who didn't listen to my father's advice, and I though I was doing the right thing by marring Iraj. Yes, it was me, who destroyed my children's happiness by giving them this ruthless father. Shame on you Iraj! This was your beautiful girl that at the age sixteen you bought her a brand new car to prove to your friends that you were somebody. And

now, after recovering from her sickness, you put her in your mother-in-law's maid quarters, again to show your family and friends that you were a real ruthless bastard. By this act of yours, you proved to the world that nothing in the world took the place of sex and money for you. You proved to those who knew you that there was no father lower than you.

But could I ever tell my children what he was doing to them? He was lowering them to being second-class citizens. Could I remind them that their father is a sex maniac and money hungry? No, I preferred not to let them know the truth about his feelings for them. If I did, I would have made it harder on them. Knowing that their father didn't love them, they had seen it all. There was no need for me to remind them of their father's lack of love and fatherly care and affection. I wanted to make sure that the same way that they loved their father, he loved them also. But I knew in my heart and trough all his actions that he was treating my children the same way that he treated his other sperms. I had to let them hate me, and never find out about their father's real feelings for them. I was strong enough to take their anger and hate. But with all what he did to us, he was ruthless enough to turn my children more and more against me. He didn't have enough knowledge to know that making them hate me would destroy them emotionally and physically.

My Dear God:

She came to visit Maseeh's house once in a while. Sometimes we went to movies together. She always chose the movie. But it wasn't like a mother and daughter that once we were. I never talked about the past and my feelings, and I didn't want Mary to talk about her father, or what was happening in his house. So our conversation was very limited. The subject was her work, her success, or the weather and things like that. Although I let my children know how much I hated their father for what and how he did to me, I never talked to them about his lack of love for his children, or I did not want them to see the ugliness of his fatherhood.

My Dear God:

For me not to get hurt more than I was hurt before, I tried to ignore their closeness to their father, and more and more I stayed away from their business. I knew with what I did, I had lost the love of my children for me. And knowing that love was not something one could earn by force, or as a duty, I never tried to beg for their love. I thought either it was there, or it was not. If it was there, it was fine with me. And if it was not there, I was not a kind of mother who begged for it. Let it be as it was. No matter if they loved me or not, I would be there for them as long as they needed me. It is my duty to support and love my children for as long as I am living.

Rafani upped to WB sr. VP

By BENEDICT CARVER

Warner Bros. has promoted Massey Rafani to senior VP of creative advertising.

He will report to Brad Ball, WB prexy of domestic theatrical marketing. His responsibilities will include strategy, supervision and application of WB's theatrical advertising campaigns.

Rafani

Rafani joined WB in 1991 as senior art director at the Idea Place, WB's inhouse creative advertising division.

He became VP in 1996 and has worked on such pics as "Grumpy Old Men," "Space Jam," "Conspiracy Theory" and "The Negotiator."

The Hollywood Reporter

Rafani

Continued from page 6—

advertising campaigns.

"Massey has a clear creative point of view that he has used to create advertising materials that cut through the clutter and resonate with impact," Ball said. "This promotion recognizes the key role Massey plays as part of the domestic theatrical creative group."

Rafani joined Warner Bros. in 1991 as senior art director at in-house creative advertising division the Idea Place, where he was later named director of print creative advertising in 1992.

Rafani

In 1996, Rafani was named vp creative advertising for Warner Bros. His campaigns include the "Grumpy Old Men" franchise, "Space Jam," "The Negotiator," "Practical Magic" and the rerelease of "The Wizard of Oz." □

Winners:
Walt Disney Studios' Fred Tio and Warner Bros.' Maseeh Rafani

Maseeh might not like to see these pictures in my book. But Maseeh jon, I am very sorry. I had to do it to show the people who read this that I am telling the truth about my son being handsome.

These are all the awards that he has received during his job, working with WB.

WARNER BROS.
4000 Warner Boulevard
Burbank, California 91522
(818) 954-6287
Fax: (818) 954-5457
E-Mail: massey_rafani@warnerbros.com
A Time Warner Entertainment Company

Massey Rafani
Senior Vice President
Creative Advertising

My son Maseeh is on the phone. My God, what a handsome young man!

This is my portrait which was drawn and painted by Mr. Knutson, Anna's father. He made me look so good. Thank you. I was looking at it while I was watching Jeopardy on TV in LA.

My Dear God:

Although we did not discuss any family matters, I was able to read between the lines. I was ready to come to their rescue, even if they never saw it, and they never appreciated it.

I remember once Maseeh said to me, “I am not he. Don't look at me like you had seen Iraj”. I knew that I was hurting my children by showing my hatred for their father. But it was out of my control when their love for him took me back to his ruthlessness and his bastardly acts. After all, this despicable coward had ruined my life by taking away whatever I lived for. I was thankful to my dear GOD, who saved all of us from destruction. Although separate from each other emotionally, but they were healthy and successful. That was enough to make me happy.

But knowing that Mary had been treated like a second-class citizen with her father’s decision, made me crazy to a point that I hated him and his family more than ever. If I was not afraid of causing my own children an everlasting pain and agony, I would have been a murderer by killing all of them. My hate for them had reached to the level of extreme. But again, because of Mary's health situation, I had to remain quiet, and not let them know what was going on in my mind. Unfortunately they had to love their father to be able to function in their own society.

My Dear God:

By ignoring their closeness to their father, and not allowing them to find out about my real feelings, they forgot what had happened to me, and my feelings of thirty years. Promiscuity and having multiple lovers, like their father, became something normal to them. Little by little they forgot the ugliness of their father's act. In their eyes I became the person who was weird and abnormal. To be able not to show them my anger and hatred towards their father, the closer they got to him, the farther I made my distance from them. I was happier when I couldn't see what was going on.

You see, my dear GOD, you think my children could understand what had happened to me? Do you think they even wanted to understand what had happened to me? Do you think they even cared? I don't think so. They wanted to find a way to be able to live dignified. They wanted to become free from that twilight zone. So they had to ignore my feelings. To tell you the truth, at that time nobody could help it. Everyone had to follow his or her own path of life, in their own way. I only had to sit and watch.

Little by little to be able to earn their father's love and attention, they forgave him for ruining their adolescent life. And not only that, but they took it one step farther. In their mind to be able to live guilt free, they made their mother the one who caused the misery in their life, who ruined their life, and destroy them completely. They believed that she was the guilty one. She was the one who peacefully did not throw the red carpet for their father's mistress. I knew that in any court of law every one is innocent until proven

guilty. In my case, while my children from the beginning they knew that their father had started the affair with Badri, and they knew that that was the reason of my sadness and depression, they closed their eyes on their father's guilt, and they tried to put all the blame on me. They found me the cause of their unhappiness. And as a crazy mother like me, I chose to empty their aggression on me. I thought after all my children's well-being was in jeopardy. It was my duty to forget and forgive them, since I was not able to change anything. Something had happened, and was done and over with. I stayed quiet, and let them do their own thing meaning loving and respecting their father with his ugly string attached.

My Dear God:

As long as Mary seemed happy, I did not show her any emotions about things which happened. And when she talked to me, she sounded happy. I didn't complain about his behavior towards Mary, and I promised her that everything would be all right in the near future.

While in Maseeh's house, I was getting ready to travel to Iran and England. I was planning to stay for six months in Iran and England. After I received my passport, I bought my ticket, and flew to Iran in March of 1994. Maseeh and Anna were happy to drive me to the airport. We said the warmest goodbyes to one another, and Maseeh held me up in the air, he kissed me and wished me a safe trip. It was the beginning of a new life for me. Things were looking good.

In Tehran Airport everyone was waiting for me at seven o'clock in the morning. Their greetings and excitement made me cry. Each time I saw my siblings around me I felt guilty and embarrassed of the outcome of my marriage. I was very happy to be with them, and they were pleased to see me happy.

Fereshteh Alavinejad, whom I talked about in previous pages, was in Iran also. We partied almost every night, and traveled together in Iran, as many times as it was possible. We did volunteer work for the senior homes, where one of our mutual friends Froogh Azimi was involved. One day of the week we were there from ten o'clock in the morning till three or four in the afternoon. We made everything from sewing, knitting, painting, drawing, or building objects to prepare plenty of materials to sell for collecting donations. They had arranged one week each year for fundraising for Kahrizak homes. These homes were established for people who did not have home or money, or they were retarded. Ladies prepared many different dishes of food for buyers. The workers or other people donated most materials. Froogh made lunch for those ladies who volunteered in her house once a week. Fereshteh and I were the entertainers who brought laughter on everyone's face. We had many funny stories from our past, married lives that made the day pass by faster, and made a more productive day.

My Dear God:

Another positive point about being in Iran was having old friends, whom I talked about before. Unlike the Iranians in Michigan, they were among the nicest people I have ever known.

Before we return to US, we had a few couples of friends who we partied with. Some of them we had met when we were in Michigan. Now all of them were back in Iran with their families. Froogh was one of them.

Although Fereshteh and I were divorced at that time, not only they didn't treat us any less, but also they went out of their ways to welcome us with their warmth and great hospitality. It made me wonder who were that group of Iranians in Michigan, or where were they raised that they were the most vicious of all human kind. How was this group able to gather together in Detroit Michigan? As if they were handpicked to be together. But on the other hand they all disliked each other and talked nasty about each other. As if they were made for each other.

My Dear God:

I visited all my friends in Iran, and they treated me like a queen. Each one of them invited me for dinner among other mutual friends. Neither of them bothered to ask a question about my fortunate, or unfortunate life. Exactly the opposite of Iranians in Michigan, who did whatever they could to hurt and destroy me. This group went out of their way to comfort me. Nothing in the world made me happier now that I was far away from the group of Iranians in Michigan. More and more I believe that what comes our way is always for the best. It seemed that the battle for getting rid of me was between Michigan's Iranians rather than between Iraj and I. The more they found me happy, the more they pushed Badri into Iraj's arms. When the final stroke happened, there was a reason for them to celebrate. But one thing they didn't know was that they caused me to find greater happiness in my life. You see, my dear God, this happened to me because you gave me the wisdom to understand life in general. I gave love to those who deserved it, and stayed away from those who were not worthy of loving.

So in Iran everyone welcomed me. I felt wanted, needed, respected, and found the real love after all. I enjoyed my friends' attention, and my siblings' support and care. We partied and took tours with friends and relatives. In Ghazveen's tour, which I took with Saideh, she lost her expensive camera. And I lost my eyeglasses with its case. But in all we had a fantastic time together.

Meanwhile I was in contact with my children, and I knew that every one of them was doing fine. That was my goal to be able to hear my children were doing fine. With me being away, they had a chance to get closer to their father. I had plans for them to be able to have their father's support to be able to have someone to turn to. My children were in the picture from beginning to the end. They didn't need any explanation from me. They

were adults and intelligent to be able to distinguish between their father's behavior and their mother's reaction to their father's behavior. If they had decency to choose their father respectfully over me by his influential act I had nothing against it. After all, they had to love themselves before they had any love for me. Love is not something we can buy or force someone to give it to us. It has to come from within.

My Dear God:

The same way that I allowed them to find their own religion, and I did not force my religion on them, the same way I allowed them to continue their relationship with their father the way that they chose to do it.

The four months that I spent in Iran was awakening time for me. It was during that time that Mary had been hospitalized. I was not aware of it until I returned to LA. I was sending her those meaningful cards, and she would call to talk to me often enough to make me happy.

From Iran I went to England to stay with my sister Ezzat and her two children who were residing in London. I was there for two months. Again my children were in contact with me. I had as good times in London as I did in Iran. Ezzat not only was my older sister, but all my life she had been my best friend. This was the sister that when I was living in Iran, she took care of Mary and Maseeh, who were three and five years old most nights that we were partying till one or two o'clock in the morning. Although she had to go to work early in the morning still she never refused to take care of them. Those nights she stood up for me to come home and helped me to carry my children from their second floor to the car, while they were sound asleep. She was a great supporter and a wise adviser to me. Just like our childhood that we slept together, we did it again when I was in London. We felt safer to cuddle in each other's arms like the times that we were little. I remember one night, while we were getting ready to sleep, Afsaneh came in our bedroom. After she hugged each one of us, she covered us with a blanket, and sung a nursery rhyme for us. We laughed so hard; we couldn't fall asleep till the middle of night. Since she has never been in my house in USA, I asked her to accompany me on my return to LA. It was my dream to be able to have Ezzat in my house to be able to repay some of her love and attention to me. I wanted to be able to serve her, and entertain her as she deserved it.

My Dear God:

After discussing it with her children, she agreed to come with me. I was able to buy her a ticket with the same airline, which was British Air, one seat next to mine. This way I was happy to see that the lack of speaking English was not a problem for her.

Although it was not my own house, still I was the part owner, and I had the right to invite my sister for two months in my house. My living section was completely private, and was possible to give complete privacy to Maseeh and Anna and their dog Kane. I talked to

Maseeh, and I told him about our decision. Since Maseeh had been raised in my house, and had been familiar with our custom of welcoming someone in our house I didn't think it was necessary to remind him how to prepare himself to welcome his aunt, especially for the first time, in his house. The least I was expecting was that he had their own dinner ready. And I was expecting to see him at the Airport welcoming us.

As much as I was excited about our trip together, Ezzat was very uneasy to come to my house, which wasn't all mine. Besides she hasn't seen Maseeh for twenty years. And she didn't know Anna at all. And because she couldn't speak English, she was shy to meet Anna. But I promised her that Anna was very nice girl and has a similar character to Ezzat's. So I made sure that she felt comfortable, and did not worry about anything.

In any trip I take I must prepare some food for myself not to let myself get sick in the plane. It was the same for Ezzat. We prepared a delicious meat cutlet, made many sandwiches to take with us in the plain.

When Maseeh called me to find out about exact time of our arrival, I was sure that he would be at the Airport waiting for us. But when we came to the luggage pick up area we saw Mary instead. When I asked where Maseeh was, she replied "Something urgent came up for him, so he asked me to come and get you".

I knew that Mary hasn't been feeling good. And I knew that her house was more than an hour away from Maseeh's, and nearly two hours from the airport. I just wondered why Mary should go through this trouble to drive us home. But I did not mention anything.

Ezzat was so excited to see Mary after twenty-five years. She was almost in tears. They hugged each other for a long time. I was so happy to see Mary happy and healthy that I cried.

On the way home she told me that she had found a job three hours away from LA. And soon she would be moving. We offered her our help if she needed any. We asked her not to hesitate to call on us any time of the day or night. She thanked us and promised that she would call on us if she needed help. After driving us home, it was late at night. When I asked her to stay and spend the night with us, she said, "I have to go home". We thanked her many times, and she drove away from our driveway.

My Dear God:

Ezzat was so delighted to see Maseeh was such a handsome man. Both were so excited that Maseeh hugged and held Ezzat in the air, and squeezed her that later on Ezzat felt a crack on her rib. She remembered Maseeh's love for a long time. Ezzat with such excitement kept asking Maseeh, "Is this our Maseeh? My God, you are a handsome guy". She kept kissing him so often to be able to make up for the lost time.

Anna was not home. She was still at school. After Mary left, and we sat there to relax, I thought to serve my sister something to eat. When I asked Maseeh what he had for

These pictures speak for themselves. In a trip that Ezzat made to LA, California while I was still sharing a place with Maseeh, she stayed with us for almost two months. Although I was new in LA myself and I did not know my way around, I made it possible for us to go many places, and see as many tourist sites as we could.

To me it was all fun although I was at the peak of my decision making to find the right way to continue my life. Staying with my son for a long time was not what I had in mind. Coming to LA was the beginning of finding a right way, not becoming a burden on my children's shoulders. I was planning to find the right time and the right place to give his freedom back to Maseeh.

In Baghe Gilass (Cherry Garden), left to right: Saideh, Ahmadreza, Ezzat, Fali, me, Zary, Fereshteh, Sadegh, Javad, and Azar. I think we had a nice visit with Fali that night. It was her first time she met many members of my family.

In Fali's house, she had invited my sister, Ezzat who was visiting me from San Jose, CA. Left to right: me, Ezzat, Fali, Foster, and Mary. Shila, and Dr. Hakimipoor are standing. What a colorful table!

We are in Mehdi and Shila's house. This is the morning before we left their house. We had a great time. Left to right: Fali, Mehdi, Shila, and me.

One night I met this lady at Straw Hat Restaurant. Her name was Shahpar and she was the mother of a young man in that group. One day I invited Fali and her to come to my house. And once we drove to her house in San Jose.

We were invited to Maseeh's house. It was a cold day. Here, Fali and I are sitting in front of the fireplace and eating marshmallows. Hameed and Mojdeh are on the right, and their baby is sitting on the floor.

With Ezzat and Maseeh at Georgia's restaurant by the ocean. What a beautiful place! What a nice view!

me to offer Ezzat, he told me they had nothing ready. I went and looked in the refrigerator, and I found not even one thing for me to be able to prepare something for us. I not only was shocked, but I was so embarrassed in front of my sister that I wanted to cry. Soon I remembered that there might have been a reason behind all that. To change the atmosphere I said, "Maseeh jon, it is not important at all. We had dinner already in the plain. Besides, we have still some more cutlet sandwiches that if we get hungry we will eat".

At this time Maseeh said, "Oh good, we can leave some fore Anna. She likes cutlets very much". Happily we wrapped the sandwiches back, and we put them in the refrigerator for Anna to eat. They always had cooked food or frozen food in the house. I was so hurt that I cried at night in my bed. My son had seen me million times that how I had treated my guests in my house. Many of those guests were Maseeh's friends. He knew that we did it to show our respect to our guests. How could he do this to my sister, who was coming to my house for the first time? What was happening to him? Should I even ask him why didn't he think of preparing some food? "No", I said to myself. We had the food with us. Besides, we were not that hungry. And we were so sleepy that there was no time for dueling over something that might not have been as important to them. And I was glad to see that Ezzat didn't make a big deal of that.

When Anna came home, she came into the room and welcomed Ezzat. They both got to know each other with the little English that Ezzat knew. Even Kane, after he saw Maseeh holding Ezzat in the air, he realized that she was someone he had to respect and be nice to. So after that night, he greeted Ezzat as one of the family, who had the right to be there.

One thing, never clear to me was that Maseeh always had a lot of money, and he bought very expensive things. I couldn't figure out their reason for that behavior on our arrival night. Later on I explained it to myself this way. They might have had a fight or disagreement before that day that caused them to act that way. Anyway, their behavior towards us on the first night marked my heart to believe that they not only didn't think of our arrival to be important to them, but I took it as an insult to us. More than that I was shocked from Anna. She was a thirty-seven year lady, who had seen how I treated her and her family at the first time they came to our house. She had heard me talking about my sister Ezzat, and how important she had been in my life. She knew that I wanted to do my best for her. How come she acted so carelessly? How bad the fight between them had been that it made them forget about us? First, Maseeh didn't come to the airport to pick us up, and then they didn't have anything at home to offer us.

My Dear God:

But my mind was set up to make Ezzat's visit in my house a pleasant one. I didn't even bring up the subject. As always I thought something should not have happened and it had happened. I must forget it and get to find the right way to make everyone happy.

After a day or two that we rested completely, I started to learn and research about places that were important to visit. Since I myself was new in LA area, I had to learn how to find my way around the town.

When Mary left she promised that one day next week she would come and take us to Venice beach in LA. She came early in the morning, and drove us to Venice beach. It was very interesting for Ezzat to see that unusual crowd on the beach. We had lunch in one of the restaurants near the beach. It was especially very nice for me to see Mary was doing fine. In the afternoon we returned home, and Mary left again.

I scheduled us to be busy every day visiting different places. Every night we had diner together, and Maseeh and Ezzat talked about the old days and the rest of the family. I cooked sometimes, and Anna and Maseeh cooked some other times. We all were happy to be together like that.

Some nights we went out to diner, and some lunches Ezzat and I went to an Iranian restaurant called "Shiraz". For us was just like being in Iran. Every night we sat in the living room to have tea and dessert after dinner. We enjoyed talking about everybody's childhood, especially Maseeh's. It felt so good to be free of any kind of headache.

One Sunday Maseeh drove us to Pacific Ocean. We had a great time, and I took as many pictures as I could. We were there till evening, and had diner and back home again. During all those times Anna was busy studying, or she was at school, or she was exercising on her machines.

My Dear God:

Because everyone was busy with their own activities the family atmosphere was nothing like in Iran. Most of the time Ezzat and I did our activities apart from Maseeh and Anna. We wanted not to take too much of their privacy away from them. I was planning not to involve Maseeh's time with us, in case Anna was not comfortable with it. After all, we were in their house, and I wanted to make sure that we were not there to bother them. Especially knowing how Anna was sensitive about sharing Maseeh with someone else, especially his mother. I had to be very careful not to create fight between them. When we were at home, mostly we spent our time in my room. Only in the evenings for dinner or after dinner we spent some time with Maseeh. Most of those times Anna was studying, or she was finishing her paintings. In the evenings after diner usually we went for a walk at the high school near the house. We walked a few times around the track. It was a dream life for me. Any time I thought of Ezzat's departure, I felt a funny feeling in my stomach.

Ezzat wanted so badly to see Mojgan also. But she was in Michigan, too far away to reach. But she talked to her a few times, and she mailed her the cups and saucers with cream and sugar dish to her. That set of teapot was hand made clay with very artistic

design. I think Mojgan liked it.

While Ezzat was with us, Mary moved to her new place, which was in the city of Visalia. When I asked her how come she didn’t ask us for help, she answered that there were people to help her. I was glad that she had enough help, and she didn't need us after all. We were in contact all the times, and she had asked me to go and visit her. To make me interested to go and visit her, she described her house to be located in a beautiful area. She was working with four other lawyers, and she seemed to like her job a lot. For me that was a dream come true.

When insistently she was inviting me to go to her house, I was wondering what would be different now from then if I went to her house. With the memory of the past experience, I was afraid to go to her house even if it was for one day. But she seemed healthier and happier. I was hoping that she had put the sad past behind her. The memory of the time that I stayed with her in Arizona, and the memory of the time that I visited her in her apartment in Detroit that I bought a TV for her, brought chills allover my body. But I knew that I was her mother, and I must be able to forget.

With Ezzat we went to as many places as was possible for us to see. We went to Disneyland two or three times, to Venice beach, more than twice to Universal studio, to Beverly Hills, where all the movie stars were living. Each day we went to different shopping centers. One day I drove out of my way to go and visit Afsaneh's friend Charlotte in a different city. We went to the Olive Garden restaurant. Coming back my car didn't start in front of their house. Thanks God, her cousin was home and he did something to it that I was able to drive back. Many nights we walked up and down Ventura Boulevard, and had dinner in one of the outside restaurants, and then we walked back home.

My Dear God:

I had the greatest time of my life. But knowing Ezzat, I don't know if she had a great time or not. Probably she was missing her children, or there was something else that was bothering her. I know that she wasn't happy with many pictures as I took. But I didn't listen to her, and I took plenty of pictures that I still am very happy to look at them once in a while. And then, one day in October 1994, after two memorable months, Maseeh and I drove her to the LAX. And that was the end of her trip to my house in LA. After we had lunch, Ezzat said goodbye to us and flew to England. We returned home, and Maseeh went back to his work. And life became the routine task.

While I was in Maseeh's house, once Parri and Kamala came to visit me. Since Parri had been bad mouthing me behind my back in front of my sisters in Iran, I couldn't feel and act the same way that I always loved her. I didn't have much to talk to her. I welcomed both of them very nicely, and tried to keep them company. I was very respectful to her. We talked about the families in Iran. We laughed and said jokes. For the first time

I felt like a stranger to her. I remembered that as long as I knew her as my friend, she was always on my side. She was an honest and genuine friend. Then how come all of a sudden, when I needed her friendship, she turned her back at me? Once when we were eating at a restaurant she told me, "Well, you must have done something to cause his lack of love for you". After that day I couldn't think of her as my friend. I knew that to be able to keep her friendship with her brother, although she knew it was completely his brother's fault, still she preferred to put the blame on me. That was the time that I lost my trust of friendship on her. My feelings towards having relationship with friends has been damaged.

That day we had lunch together with Anna. We served them tea and Iranian sweets after lunch. Kamal and I had a great friendly relationship since we met the first time in Iran. We always joked and teased around. Since he accepted Iraj's behavior the way he did, I thought of him just another man like Iraj. I didn't find it necessary to have the same respect for him as I did before.

In one of their visits that they came to Maseeh's house, Parri gave me very bad news. The news was that one of her cousins in Iran, called Masoomeh, had been diagnosed with a kind of fatal cancer. That news was so shocking to me that still after so many years I cannot accept that.

My Dear God:

She was as young as my daughter. She was married to her cousin, and had two children. She gave a big party for me when I was in Iran. Her husband Homayoon Tahery and other cousins, including Kamal, were there. They seemed to have wonderful life going for them. She was so upset with Iraj and his behavior that she couldn't stop talking about his past and his family. To comfort me for what he had done to me, she talked about Iraj's father and how he treated his sister, Ammeh.

When I heard the news about her health, I was very disappointed. When I asked Parri how much hope we had, she answered, "None. After doctors in Iran refused to open her, they took her to Germany, where two of her brothers and her sister and her brother-in-law, who was a doctor himself, were there. For her surgery the brother-in -law was there also. But unfortunately they had to close her because it had been too late. Her cancer had metastasized all the parts of her body. So she returned to Iran with a body full of cancer.

Since I was planning to go to Iran again after Parri, the only thing that I could ask God was to save this girl from dying in that young age. I was hoping to go and find her well.

As I mentioned before, I always was in contact with my children whether they wanted me or not. And as I mentioned, my Mary had spent many difficult times in her life. It was mainly because, just like her father, she was looking for it, and she was self-

destructive.

When Ezzat was in LA, we went for one week to Helen and Arman Afsaneh's friend. One night after diner I received a telephone call from Mary. I was in San Jose far away from her to be able to reach her.

She sounded so scared and so hopeless that I started to panic. I didn't know how to talk to her. She was the one who always hated me and wanted the worst things to happen to me. And sometimes she showed me so much of her hidden love that I wasn't sure how to deal with her. I was afraid to open my mouth to say anything, good or bad, to her. I had to study her face, her act, and her emotions to be able to find a word to talk to her.

My Dear God:

That night she was so unhappy and so depressed that she kept telling me, "I love you, Mom". She started begging me to love her. She kept telling me that there was no hope in her life. She just went on and on with her hopeless life. I let her finish her talking, and then calmly I started to talk. "My dearest Mary", I said "There has not been one person in this world that I always loved more than you. I have never given up loving you, even if it was for one minute in my life. The things that you did during your growing years were not only wrong, but also they were part of growing up. Everyone in this world had done it, so you were one of them. You were not only loved by me all your life, but everyone in our family loved you, and they still love you the same. I never thought that you might doubt my love for you ever. Even when you hated me to love you, I still continued to show you my love by supporting you in anything you wanted to do". Then I told her, "I sent you million cards to just tell you how lucky you are that you have been able to succeed in your life the way you did. You must be proud of yourself that you have been able to choose the right path in your life. We all made mistakes in our lives. There is no one who grew up without being mixed up sometimes in their lives. Why do you have to beat yourself for something that had not been your fault? Everyone in this world will change after a period of time. This happens physically, emotionally, or psychologically. This is not just about you. It happens to everyone, and you have been one among the rest of the world. You are a beautiful girl, who was born with a silver spoon in your mouth. You were always an ambitious girl with having a goal to achieve. You tried to pass the Bar, and you were able to pass it at your first attempt. You must, and I insist you must, stop punishing yourself for things which you didn't have control on. You have so much to be thankful for. What would you have done if you were in Rokhand's shoes? She lost the only brother, the only support, the only friend and the only person to be able to turn to all her life in a car accident at the age of twenty-two. Not only that but she had to watch her mother, because with the loss of her brother her life was in danger also. Don't you think that was a real disaster in their lives? Don't you think that coming out of that is almost impossible? What had happened to you is not considered a problem. In America more than fifty percent of families go through divorce. Most of those families will survive and learn something good from it". Then I asked her to leave the worrying to the birds, and start looking for all the good fortune and good qualities within herself. "I am sure they are as many as you cannot count them with your fingers Please stop attacking yourself for making wrong decisions, if you had made any. Even if you did because of the changes in you, still you are not the only one. If some decision we made was wrong, we have the ability to learn from our mistakes and not repeat them again. You are too good and too beautiful to get mad at yourself and destroy yourself the way you are doing it. You must recognize your capabilities, your values, your determinations, and your intelligence that is loaded in you. Not everyone can have what you have in you. You must be proud of yourself and see the sunshine in your life. Negativity will kill your spirit. Please don't let this happen to you. Get to know the beautiful, sincere, honest, hard working Mary that you are. I am sure if you do this, you will be as happy as you have ever been". I talked as long as I felt that her tone of voice has changed. At first I thought she was suicidal, and I couldn't reach her by any means. I thought my words must get to her somehow. For the first time in her life she was begging for my love. Something that I always gave to her, and she refused to take it in a bitter manner. I knew that she was at the end of her rope. After I talked to her for a long time in a room away from my sister and everyone else, I realized that she became a different person. She agreed to whatever I told her. She agreed that I had never failed to love her in any condition that she had been in. Then she promised me to follow my advice and call me and talk to me whenever she needed me. When she asked me that the only thing that might help her was to be able to hold me in her arms and feel my love, I promised her that that would happen sooner than she thought. But because at that moment it was not possible for me to be near her, I asked her to continue her conversation for as long as she needed me. We were able to talk to a point that she was laughing and joking, and altogether was a different person from that Mary who called me an hour ago. I was thankful to God, and I felt relieved.

My Dear God:

When I hung up, I felt completely motionless. I didn't know what to think any more. I was very happy with the way that our conversation ended and she became happy Mary again. And then I was sad again and again and again. I was sad that if I wasn't the one who brought Mary into this world for my own pleasure, she would never had to go through whatever she was going through now.

I was the naive and inexperienced person that I believed that I would be able to protect my children from the heat and cold of the world. I was the one who thought with the kind of love that I had for my husband and my children, I could be the most powerful to keep my children away from any harm.

Now that I saw they had been harmed all through their lives, I was just embarrassed and ashamed of myself. No one was there to tell me, "Shame on you, Shamci". But I had the right to tell myself, "Shame on you Shamci for choosing this man for your husband. Shame on you for not listening to your father! And shame on you for believing wrong people".

My Dear God:

Why should I be so naive to believe that I could turn the world upside down for my family and not let them to be harmed by the world's disasters? Why shouldn't I know that I was not the only person in this world that my children had to deal with uncertainties? Why shouldn't I let my children to discover that the world was full of good and bad, happy and unhappy, rewards and punishments, and most of all let them learn to deal with all of them and be able to survive going through it? Why, and many more whys? Why shouldn't I have the vision to teach my children the ability to adapt themselves to any circumstances? Then when I heard they were calling my name from the other room, I woke up from my dream, I got up, put a beautiful smile on my face, because I was happy that I was able to get to Mary, and shake her from whatever was bothering her. After that we talked every day. And I was glad that she wanted me after all those years.

Anna was preparing for her finals. Most of the times, Maseeh helped her with her homework by taking it in the office. He wanted to make sure that she did her best, and did it professionally. He even went to the office on weekends to speed up her work for her finals. Not only he was helping Anna with her homework at his free time, but he was helping Kasra, his cousin, also.

Since Kasra's parents were in Iran and away from him, Maseeh was becoming his big brother.

Interruptions, interruptions, interruptions! I don't know when I will be able to finish this book. This time it was a trip to Iran. We had arranged that all five sisters get together in Iran from all over the world. One sister was in Iran. Ezzat came from England. Sina had come from Belgium. Saideh had come from Montreal, Canada. And I had come from USA to have a meeting to be able to bring peace into this crazy world. Guess what, my dear GOD, except having fun, we were not able to do anything else. I will talk about this trip and others in my next book probably. After six weeks I returned to Visalia, and again after one week I had to go to Lake Tahoe, where my daughter Mojgan is living. I had to stay for another six weeks, which I have plenty to talk about in my next book. Today, I am glad that interruption is over, and I am able to talk to you freely and with great pleasure.

So Maseeh who was very busy with his own job, he was helping Anna and Kasra at the same time. Many times he got frustrated with Kasra, whose foolishness was going above their head. Kasra was studying Architecture, the same profession that his father had. Since his parents often were in Iran, and he did not have a close relationship with his brothers, he always was clinging to Maseeh for anything and everything. Maseeh was a big

brother to him, or sometimes he felt like a parent to him. Although he used to get mad at Kasra for his wrong behavior, still he never left him without a support. Maseeh loved Kasra since he was a little baby. That love stayed in him till now. And I think since Maseeh had never had a brother, he always treated Kasra as his own brother. I noticed that he watched him carefully not to go wrong. Besides being in his house, Maseeh spent long hours on the phone with him to make him understand that he was doing wrong.

My Dear God:

Once when I was in Maseeh's house, Kasra came over with his Japanese girlfriend, who was a medical student, a very bright and beautiful girl. They spent the night, and I got to know her too. But Kasra wasn't treating her the way he should have. I even questioned him many times for his misbehaving. But soon I heard that she left him for good. For some reason he had some visible hatred for women in general, and he wasn't afraid to show his hatred.

Anna was very worried and nervous about her finals. To prepare herself, she stood up most nights. Plus that she was a kind of person, who always worried about her parents, Kane's health, earthquake, and the society in general. Although she was very skinny, she always felt that she was overweight. She was very sensitive and concerned about what other people thought or said about her.

One night after she got home from school she was very bitter and uneasy. When Maseeh asked her what was the reason, nervously she answered, "Someone was trying to kidnap me, and if it was not for Kane being with me in the car, I am sure he could have been successful in his attempt". Maseeh became worried, and he was very scared. He didn't know how to help her except that he advised her to be more careful and avoid going through quiet roads.

Every day he called her four or five times to see if she was okay. Sometimes I wondered how Maseeh had this much extra time to be on the phone for that many times. He was very concerned about her. I knew that he wanted to make sure that she was okay, and that nothing was bothering her.

One day a bird flew in through the window and got hurt. I couldn't believe how these two adults reacted to this accident. She took the bird to the Vet. Then they made sure to take turns to feed the bird by hand. I was one of the caretakers who had to feed the bird hourly. I was worried; what if the bird dies while it was under my care. She was so sensitive and worried about things, which we didn't have any control on.

Both Maseeh and Anna were worried if Kane ever attacked anyone. They had believed that they were the ones who could control his behavior. And they got panicky when someone came by the door. They thought, since he was a big dog and I was small, probably I was not able to control him when they were not home. Not knowing that I was able to control the dog with out getting panicky.

My Dear God:

Since I was living with them, I had learned how to deal with him. As soon the doorbell rang, I showed him something that he liked, and then I kept him in the bathroom and closed the door on him. After I answered the door, and took care of the business, I opened the bathroom door and let him out without any danger or panic. Above all those, they were worried if I invited a friend who had children. Once I was talking about inviting one of my friends from Michigan. They had two children. Since they were my only supporter in Michigan, I needed badly to be able to see them. But I knew with all my heart that they were not able to make it, no matter how many times I called them and invited them. But I realized that Anna was making a big deal about inviting my friends to my house. This way she made Maseeh to become uneasy about the subject.

I didn't want to quarrel with them about the subject, since I was sure that they couldn't come. But I realized that they were trying to control my coming and going. I didn't like it one bit. With action and attitude like that I started to think that was not my house. I must think of getting back my own privacy, and give their privacy back to them. I wasn't a kind of mother who had to take orders from anyone, especially my children. The same way they wanted to live free from other people's influence in their lives, I had the right to have the freedom of choice under any circumstances. I was paying attention to see when and where I could find the best solution.

When I paid a big check to them to buy a house on his name, I was hoping to have equal freedom in that house. I wanted to feel at home completely. I wanted to be able to go anywhere I wished, and invite anyone I wanted. People, who have dogs, do not live under such restricted rules. Having a dog is like having children. The owner must know how to tame and control their dog, and not close their doors and not allow anyone to come to their house.

So after a while I started to think of other options, if there was any or not. When I shared my house with Maseeh, my plan was to spend six months of the year in his house, and the other six months in Iran and England. Although I was very happy to be with Maseeh, I felt that it wasn't my house. They did their best to make me feel comfortable, and I was doing my best to give them their privacy by either staying in my room, going out to movies, or traveling. I knew that young couples like and need their privacy. So I tried to do my best to leave them by themselves as much as I could. This way I had more chance to be able to write and talk to you my dear, dear GOD. By talking to you, and bringing all my problems to you, I became a little wiser every day.

My Dear God:

I remembered my poor mother's quotation, "I hope to be able to live on my own till the last moment of my life. And not be forced to live with anyone of my children". That

time of my life I realized what she meant by that. Life was comfortable and beautiful for me. After a period of nine to ten years of suffering and nightmares, I was free at last.

Mojgan had called me many times, and invited me to go to her house. And the Hushmands had bought a new house in Cincinnati, so I arranged a trip to Michigan first, and Cincinnati second. But since I did not have health insurance at that time, I had arranged the trip to Michigan for a complete checkup under supervision of doctor Mehrabian. Meanwhile I wanted to pay my dues to Dr. Chitra Amladi, who had been one of the angels for my survival.

Dr. Mehrabian drove all the way to Metropolitan Airport to drive me to his house. The next day he had scheduled me at his hospital, Medical Community Center, for a complete checkup. He spent all his office hours that morning to be with me, and followed me from room to room to make sure that no one created any problems for me. Since I had no insurance, he wanted to make sure that the hospital handled that with no charges to me. He was one gentleman.

They did everything from blood test to mammography, x-ray, liver, you name it. Everything was done in one morning. Dr. Mehrabian liked my "ghorme sabzi" so much that he always said, "No one ever makes ghormeh sabzi like Shamci does". Coming home we stopped at the store, we bought the stuff for making ghormeh sabzi, and we went home. That night his girlfriend was there also. She also liked the ghormeh sabzi, which was made of vegetables, beef, and red beans, plus some herbs from our country, served over white rice. We ate some of it that night. And I filled up a few containers with the rest of ghormeh sabzi, and I put it away in his freezer. I realized that his girl friend was too shy to spend the night. So after two days I asked him to take me to Dr. Amladis house. I knew that she was expecting me to go there.

While I was with Chitra, some of my friends invited me to go and visit them. It was a good opportunity for those friends to see me happy again. All of them had helped me tremendously. I will always remember their kindness.

Then I went to Kalamazoo to stay with Mojgan. As always she asked me to go there, yet she always created an unhappy scene for all of us that I felt sorry that I accept her invitation. I always took her abuse, believing that she had the right to take out her anger and aggression on someone. And that someone was always her mother.

My Dear God:

After spending three weeks there, I was happy to go to Cincinnati to be with Farahnaz and Ali Houshmand. Because Farahnaz was at school, Ali and his children came to the airport to welcome me. Happily we hugged and kissed, and drove home in their new car. With her care, attention, and courteous Farahnaz had captured my genuine love for her. Whenever I was with them, I felt like being with my friends and family.

My Dear God:

So when I returned from Iran, and Mary gave me the news of moving away and working with a group of lawyers, it sounded like good news to me. Although she was moving three hours away from me, still I jumped up from happiness. Probably both Mary and Ezzat in the car were surprised why was I so happy to see her move much farther away from me. But they didn't know what was going on in my cluttered mind. It didn't bother me if my children got mad at me and took their aggression on me. It didn't bother me if they forgave their father's polygamy. It didn't bother me if they decided to make me the guilty one. But I was hurt and destroyed when I witnessed my children being demolished by their father. Since he was busy with his midlife crises, and his extreme sexual desires, I was the one who had to open my eyes and see the reality. There was no other way to cure my children's wounds, unless to ignore what was happening to me. Hoping that one day my children would open their eyes and think back to see that besides being their mother, still I was a human being. I had feelings. If I didn't kill anyone, or I didn't destroy anything, it was just to be able to save them from disasters.

Mary was aware of her father's affair with Badri since the first week after Malakuti's death. That was why she drew a caricature of the family with Badri sticking to Iraj, while I was very sad.

Maseeh knew that his father was having an affair with Badri because Roshanak had told him. That was why one day they both were discussing it with me. And Maseeh said, "Only if I see them anywhere together, I will kill both of them". And Mojgan wrote in her diary, "Since Dr. Malakuti died, my father hates me". Poor girl, she was not able to connect her father's hate with his love for Badri

Yet three of them, to be able to live guilt free, and to be able to continue loving their father, they started to ignore everything, and not make it their business. In a way I actually pushed them to their father. I wanted to make sure that they were able to get their share too. But I never expected my children to turn their backs at the truth, and not be concerned about their mother's feelings, and have respect for people who vividly stabbed and destroyed me for the rest of my life. But no matter what happened, I had to wake up, and be aware that my life was my life, and I had to watch over myself, even if my children couldn't see my point of view. I needed to get special strength from my God to be able to start a different life without my children's care and attention.

When Ezzat left, I felt her empty space. I had made it a custom not to duel over anything that we didn't have control over. She must go back to England to be with her children, and live happily ever after. And I was supposed to continue my life without making myself depressed about anything.

My Dear God:

At this time Mary had moved to her new place and started her new job. When I asked her, "Why didn't you call us to help you?" She said, "There were some people here to help me". I was happy that someone had helped her. She called me often to talk to me about her job. This was her first serious job after she passed the bar. She seemed very happy with it. That was my dream come true.

Then she started asking me to go and visit her. To tell you the truth, my dear GOD, I wasn't sure what would have happened to me if this time I went to her house. The last experience that I had with her was not a pleasant one. But I knew that she was sick, and she was on something that made her that way. I didn't know how I should handle her.

Each time she talked about her place and promised me that it was my kind of lifestyle. It seemed that she liked to see me happy in her place. And yet I thought she didn't want to be alone in that apartment. She seemed anxious and hopeful. Then one day, when she said, "If you come to visit me, you will give a chance to Maseeh to breath", I realized that it might have been of Maseeh's concern that he liked to live sometimes without his mom in his house. At that moment I promised her that I would go to her house to visit her, and I did, only for a week or two.

Okay, my dear GOD, you know how worried I was if she had not changed. You know I was praying to let her be the healthy and happy Mary. You know how I was sad why I should be at Maseeh's house that he could feel that he was trapped. And you know many more things, which were coming into my mind. But I decided that I had to go to her house anyway.

I left my car in LA, and took a bus to Visalia, which I had never heard of. She anxiously picked me up from the bus station. With lots of excitement the second night she took me to an expensive restaurant in Visalia town. She spent lots of money, and we talked about the good things that had happened to her, and more to come.

She was very happy. I thought I made it. My sufferings had paid off. My report card was beginning to show me an excellent result. While I was watching her, I thanked God for making me understand which way to chose to go with Mary. I felt that she had come back. At that time I felt that the whole world was mine. She talked about the four lawyers who she was working with. Although it was too early for her to get to know their true personalities, at that time she felt comfortable working with them. That was a great welcome to me. I realized that she had suffered tremendously. I thought this was just a miracle. After nearly fifteen years of challenge, Mary and I were peacefully living under one roof, lovingly. This was the Mary that I had given up on her, and just sent her away for some kind of force to cure her. It was just a miracle to see her being herself again. Was it possible that she had found peace with me in her heart? Could she be the same girl that she was once before? Was it really happening or was I dreaming?

My Dear God:

Anyway, I was happy and delighted to see Mary doing well. She had rented a one-bedroom apartment nearby her office. The entrance to her apartment was beautiful and inviting. There was a pool in the middle of the circle of apartments surrounded with palm trees, and well designed landscaping. Mary's apartment was on the second floor, which had a greater view from the yard. That yard with all those palm trees reminded me of my childhood. It is amazing how we can picture the past so vividly. I was very amused by the place, and I felt that Mary's description was very accurate. It was just like she told me on the phone.

But when I went inside, I saw what I never wanted to see. Iraj had done it again. With the chilling disappointment, I saw Badri's old furniture in Mary's house. All right, my dear God, those who read these pages probably think, and ask themselves, "What could be the disappointment? What could be wrong?" I will tell you what could be wrong. That was the furniture, which Iraj and Badri had sex on for eight years. I had to sit on it, smell them, and see them having sex in front of me every time I looked at it. It makes me throw up. How could I deal with this one, my dear God? Please help me.

That was one aspect of looking at it. How about the other one? How could Iraj treat our beautiful daughter as a servant of Malakutis? First he sent her off to Badri's mother's maid quarters. Now he gave the old, ugly, dirty, smelly, broken furniture to a girl who was once the apple of his eye. How could I explain this to Mary? The way that I saw it, she wasn't even thinking of home, furniture, clothing or anything like that. She had gotten her health back. She had found a nice job. She has passed the bar exam successfully. And now she wanted her mother near her to put her head on her lap again, and not ever think back. I must cover up all my feelings. I must not let her suspect what or how I was thinking. If she didn't know the things that her father did to her was to show her his love, let it be. If she didn't know that with this act her father belittled her and treated her as a secondary person in his life, let it be. And if with being there and looking at that furniture I would have suffered every second of my life, so let it be. I must find a way to forget it and put that thought out of my mind.

My Dear God:

I had to encourage Mary about whatever she thought, or whatever she did. That time that I did not have the power to have things under my control had passed. I must be a new person. And this was a brand new life. "Shamci, you must be able to deal with it. This will pass also".

I realized that was Mary's house, she was happy with the things in her house, why should I aggravate her life with something that she was not aware of. I didn't even believe that she knew that it used to be Badri's furniture in Michigan. Or if she knew, she didn't see it the way I did looked at it. She couldn't understand my feelings. So quietly I passed

through it, and pretended that I didn't know were that furniture came from. I was her guest only for two weeks. So I would be able to adapt myself to the situation by passing time. Again I knew that time will heal everything. I not only stayed quiet about it, but until now I have not mentioned it to anyone. I didn't think that it would do Mary or me any good to even bring up what kind of a ruthless father he had been.

Then I remembered that first when I came to USA, we bought our furniture from Salvation Army. It was so bad that I had to make covers for them, and we had to paint them black and gray. How did I know where that furniture had come from? We lived with it until we went back to Iran. So I made myself come out of that ugly feeling, and started to live happily ever after.

One thing always amazed me my feelings for my children and myself. No matter what they did to me, or how they treated me, still I remained loyal to my love for them. Although Mary had done unbelievable things to me, and she hurt me the most, yet when I came to LA and shared the house with Maseeh, she was trying to be nice to me. She called often, and some days she came over to go to a movie with me. Some nights she stayed in my bedroom, and I pampered her like before. This was after she had her nervous breakdown, and I was very careful when she was around me.

At that time she was working for an insurance company. One day, after she explained to me that she would earn money only if she could sell high amount of insurance. And when I found out that she had difficulty selling it, I volunteered to buy insurance for a large sum of money before I even read the contract. Next day, when she brought me the contract and I read it, I realized that I was signing a paper, which confirmed that there was no guarantee for the return of my money. And in many cases I might lose the principal also. Soon I realized that the deal was not right for me. Although I was trying to help Mary in some way, I could have lost my only remaining security money. When I read it to Mary, and she agreed with me on understanding the contract correctly, then I changed my mind, and stopped buying it. For a long time I was sad that I couldn't help Mary. But since I didn't want to become homeless one day, I had to decide wisely, and I did.

My Dear God:

In Mary's apartment we were getting along very well. She was working hard, and doing her best to make up for the past. She was cooperative and agreeable most of the times. We went to lunch, to dinner, to brunch, and many times to movies in the town of Visalia, which reminded me of old Tehran and Pahlavi Avenue. The Fox Theater on Main Street made me fall in love with that city. That historic theater had appealed to me immensely. It reminded me of the streets of Tehran. After watching a movie and having popcorn, we walked on Main Street hand in hand, and with laughter and happiness we went towards ice cream, and then home.

It was a dream come true to see Mary that happy, living under one roof with me, and no disagreement whatsoever. That was just a miracle. Every day I thought that I had been rewarded by God to know that I had been doing right, and I must continue to do so.

Since I liked to cook and keep busy, I kept myself busy by cooking, cleaning, and the rest of the time I spent at the library. I went there in the morning, and came back at closing time. I read, I wrote, and I went to lunch when I felt like it.

So Mary was happy with her work, and she kept asking me to go and visit her as often as I was with Mojgan. Now she wanted me to be with her. She wanted her mommy to comfort her and cuddle in her arms. I couldn't believe that was really happening. This was the same Mary who hated the love that she had for her parents. Because she was afraid of losing any one of them, she tried so hard not to love them at all. She rebelled, she fought, and she was destructive to herself. After that many years of challenge and struggle, and after getting that unexpected sickness, now she was coming back to life. Now that her parents were divorced, and the whole family was apart, and there was nothing more to be afraid of, she was trying to come to peace with herself after all. Now she felt the need for wanting them. She was feeling the need for wanting all of them, including me, her mommy. She had decided to come out of her shell, and live peacefully. That was what I thought of her, and interpreted to myself.

After fighting for fifteen years, now she wanted to live a normal life. She was trying to fit to the norm of society. She tried to accept people and their behavior if they seemed odd to her. The girl who once told me, "Mom, you are suffocating us with your love", now she was asking for that crazy love. Now she wanted to drown herself in my loving, and put her head on my knee and cuddle in my arms. She actually was asking for all of my attention, and not only some of it. Just like when she was three years old, she wanted me all for herself and nobody else.

My Dear God:

At this time of my life I didn't know what to think. I didn't want to be dependent on anybody's love, especially my children's. I knew that no matter what they belonged to their partners and not me. I had learned that no matter how strong their love would be, they must leave me one day and follow their own lifestyle with their own partner. Yet I had to give her as much love as I possibly could.

I was thinking, my dear God, how you had managed to remove all the darkness from my life, and open all the doors to a lighter and brighter life. How did you manage to bless me with such strength that nothing seemed impossible or difficult to me any more? You handled my life in a way that there was no need for me to worry about anything. For anything I had asked one day, I was receiving today.

Mary was very happy to be on her own. And she was happy to be with me. Time and time she asked me to go and stay with her for more than two weeks. She was asking me to

reside in Visalia, and move away from LA. With loving Main Street, and seeing Mary in such a happy mood, and especially knowing that Maseeh seemed to be trapped under some obligation to live with me, it didn't seem like a bad idea to me. I started thinking about it seriously.

While in Mary's apartment, when I looked at that furniture every day, I remembered an incident, which once happened in Michigan.

As I said before, because I didn't know anything about taxes or any papers regarding taxes, I used to take them to Dr. Mohammad Rabbani, since he knew what was going on to help me. One day I made an appointment with him to take my papers, which I received from Iraj, and find out why he had to deduct some money from my alimony to pay for taxes. We were sitting in the kitchen. After he looked at those papers, he told me, "These taxes must be paid by him. It does not have anything to do with you". And I told him, "I have no hands on that. He always deducts the money, and sends the remainder to me. I can't do anything about it. If I want to fight with him, I will have to have a lawyer to defend me. So this way it will cost me much more than what he is deducting now". At this time his wife Nayer joined us with hot tea on a tray. To get free from guilt Dr. Rabbani said, "I really never suspected that there was anything going on between Iraj and Badri. When I did, and I mentioned it to Nayer, she assured me that, "I don't think there is anything going on between them. Just yesterday Badri talked to me and said, 'I really like Shamci, and I am willing to help her if she needs me".

My Dear God:

I felt so angry. I thought to myself, "Either these two are stupid, or they are trying to play stupid". I exploded like a firecracker, and I said to them, "It would be only over my dead body to let myself being needy of Badri. Yes, the best help was to leave my husband and the father of my children alone, and go and live with her family in California. That was the only help she could have done for me. Not to seduce him into betraying his family and tempt him into destroying himself and his family".

In reality I knew that both Mohammad and Nayer were in it from the beginning. Mohammad always was in competition with Iraj, and that was the time to destroy his good name. And Nayer, she never had a close friend to do all her chores for her, including babysitting for her. So, while Badri was bribing Nayer with being close to her, The Rabbanis threw a red carpet for Badri, telling her, "Go ahead, this is your chance to find the right husband for yourself, and stay among us to watch over you".

Those so-called friends, if they didn't know anything about their relationship, and as they pretended they were fooled by Badri, after Iraj and Badri got married, they would cut their friendship with them, put them away, and, boycott visiting them for the rest of their lives. And not that right after they got married, they accepted them as if nothing had happened.

Now I was sitting in Mary's apartment, looking at that furniture, and thinking that, "My God, she has been helping my daughter with the furniture, which she has been having an affair on it with her father for more than eight years. And now, to keep the memory alive for me, they gave it as a gift to my poor daughter, who innocently was enjoying them. God, what a punishment! And yet Dr. Rabbani and Nayer, and the rest of the crowd were trying to play a role of innocent people in front of God's judgment. They must know, the only power that never gets fooled is GOD himself that no one ever is able to hide something from him. For sure he acts on it on time.

So after spending two weeks of happy time with Mary in her apartment, I returned to LA. Anna was done with her finals, and she was looking for a job. Both Maseeh and Anna were trying to find something to do with a popular magazine. Anna was very proud of herself, since she was the only one among her siblings who had graduated from collage. She used to bring her work into my bedroom, and explained to me what was each drawing all about. She liked to put me in what she had in mind for her next project.

Once, when I was with them in their old apartment, she did a big drawing for the senior center in Studio City, and donated it to them. I watched her closely when she was working on it. I thought it took a real talent to be able to finish such a painting. The day that she delivered it to the center, we went together. She always showed interest to spend her time with me. And I was very pleased to be with her, and listen to her ideas. Some nights, when her younger sister Kaleen came over to visit, we sat till two or three in the morning and talked about world around us. One morning Anna thanked me for being a good listener and entertainer for Kaleen.

My Dear God:

Anna enjoyed working late at nights. Many times I wondered why Anna did not go to bed at the same time that Maseeh did. It seemed very odd to me for a young couple that loved each other not to go to bed at the same time. Maseeh met Anna while she was working in Hollywood Live for his father and the rest of the group. That was a suffering time for Maseeh, since it was the beginning of the separation of his parents. Anna had found it easy to get close to him and comforted him. After a while they felt comfortable being together, so Maseeh moved in to Anna's apartment, which was located in North Hollywood. By that time Anna was aware of what was going on between Iraj and me.

Although I did not want to talk about my past, yet she always tried to condemn Iraj and Badri, just to see me happy. She knew how high the level of my hatred and anger was for them. My anger was to a point that I didn't want to get close to anyone, or love anyone. Since Anna was very nice to me, and she tried to comfort me all the time, one day I told her, "Anna, please don't try to be so nice to me. I have been so hurt that I can't love anyone any more".

Living with them was great. They both were trying to make me comfortable, and

bring me back to life again. But many times I saw them having long discussions quietly in their own bedroom. While we had a great relationship between us, I was wondering, "What if I was a burden on their shoulders? What if they couldn't tell me in my face?" I knew that I was trying so hard to stay away from all their affairs. Yet this was always in the back of my mind that what was really going on between them?

When Mary called me again and asked me to go and stay with her longer, this time I wondered, "What if this was a decision made between them? When she told me, "I feel so comfortable with you being next to me", I forgot completely what was the reason that was behind her asking. I felt if she really was happy with me being near her, I must leave immediately, and not waste any time.

She was delighted and happy to see me. For many years she had suffered enough, that she wanted to have peace in her life for a change. I thought she was tired of fast running, and rebelling against everything in her way, including her mother. For her it was time to be nice to herself for once, and clean up her act. So she tried to be a close friend to me, and have me by her side as long as she liked.

My Dear God:

After the age of ten I have never seen Mary this happy and full of life. It seemed that she was anxious to do well and make it all right. She introduced me to her friends and her co-workers. We went places together. We went to lunch, dinner, movies, theater, walking and hiking together. I cooked Iranian food and invited any of her friends that she wanted to. It didn't matter if they were black or white, or man or women, homosexual or lesbian, with any kind of job, from doctor to a garbage person, if she wanted to invite them, I did it for her. I did anything for her that her heart desired. We went shopping together. And, if she wanted to get one gallon of milk at night, we walked together to get it. She trusted me by all means, and most of the times she talked to me about the things which had happened to her, and made her think of committing suicide. Most of the nights, when she wanted to use the lawyer's library, I went with her, and I read my own book or magazine. There were times that she had court hearings outside of Visalia, and she had to leave at four o'clock in the morning to take a small plain, I was there to accompany her. Many times when she had to drive to LA, or Riverside to follow a case, we drove together; we made the business combined with pleasure. When she had a seminar to go to, we went together. While she was at work, I spent my time reading or writing. We both enjoyed the trips on the road together. At night in the hotel we ordered pizza, and we ate it with laughter.

Since I had never done this kind of simple and fun loving things with Mary for a long time, I always thought I was dreaming. I always did these simple loving things whenever I was with my siblings. Now I saw that Mary was becoming alive, and she was trying to enjoy her life. I was so happy I didn't know if I should believe it was true or not. For me it was just like a dream. Mary was acting like a mother, who had found her lost child. She

was as happy as a person should be. Sometimes she slept on my arms, or put her head on my lap. When it was cold, she liked to cuddle under a blanket with me, and fall asleep.

Since she had gained a lot of weight, I, with a political act, persuaded her to eat healthy and fat free. I made our food completely healthy. When we went to restaurants, I ordered just a salad, trying to show her she could do the same thing that I was doing. But she couldn't skip a good meal for a salad. I was walking more than an hour every day. Once in a while she decided to walk with me. We walked and talked together.

My Dear God:

One day she told me about the incident that happened to her just before I came to LA. She said, "One evening I was so depressed that I couldn't help myself any more. I was at the edge of committing suicide. I was so scared of myself that I called the police to help me. They came and talked me out of it". Oh GOD, I didn't know how to punish myself for what I had put her through. It was me who brought her into this world to be able to give her the best life possible. But not only I was not able to do that, I gave her a life that she hated, and she wanted to get rid of it. What a stupid person I was! What a naive person I was!

Then another day she talked to me about a friend, who committed suicide. She was a writer and an unhappy person. She always felt that she didn't have anybody to turn to. I thought I must think of something to make her understand it was only her friend's loss. I was against glamorizing the act of suicide, and I wanted to explain to her that no matter what we choose to do, life must go on. So I started talking to her, "You know, Mary, there is not one person who comes to this world and has no problems. And there is not one person who comes to this world, thinking that he or she might live forever. So with these thoughts in our minds, we must know that the person who chooses to commit a suicide must be a real coward. Life has its ups and downs. We have to be able to understand that everyone will go through it, no matter what. A person who chooses to commit suicide must know that after she or he is gone, and the mourning for her is over, everyone will continue their lives, and soon will forget about her. Everyone will start their own routine activities, as if she was never born. So you see Mary jon, no one ever can stop anyone from committing suicide, except if that person wizens up one day, and realizes that we all had come to this world to find our way to live a happy normal life. And this takes a challenge, it takes getting hurt, it takes suffering, and meanwhile it takes getting up in the morning and looking forward to the day ahead of you. If you make that day happy, and work hard for it, it will be to your benefit. And if you waste your time by being lazy and feeling sorry for yourself to a point that you believe it is better that I take my life because I am not worthy of anything that would be your own complete lost". And I continued, "Now your friend is gone, while the rest of family, each and every one of them are doing their own living. What a shame! If only she had a little courage, and understanding that she was as good as everybody else in this world, and that by killing herself she made herself the only loser in this world. Too bad she is not here to see it for herself that everyone else is living happily, and no one even remembers her name. It's just too bad!"

When I finished talking, she looked at me with a puzzled face, thinking how true my statement was. Then she said, "You are right". Knowing that Mary had been thinking of committing suicide, and knowing that she knew about my brother Jalal's suicide, my statement was just to remind her that the same way that we all lived after Jalal took his life, the same way that I survived the loss of my husband and my family, the same way life would continue if you ever decided to attempt a suicide. This way I wanted to let her know that you must love yourself, get active, be hopeful, and not let anyone feel sorry for you. "It is you, and only you, who must help you that you are beautiful and worthy of living. No one else can put this in your mind. You must know that you are a valuable person, and not only your family, but the whole world needs you and wants you. Put away the thought of sadness, and start a happy new life. Because no one else is as worthy as you are for all of us. And I think to a point she was able to grab my point, and she started feeling good about herself.

My Dear God:

Both Mary and I were trying to look forward, and never allowed ourselves to think of our past. We would never be able to reverse things, which had happened before. Actually it was I, who had become so strong as a rock, to show my children that I was able to survive. I had to be a role model for them. After Badri and Iraj ran away together, I tried to put myself together for the sake of my children. There was no other way of communication, except showing them in action. And I did it.

Mary was badly injured emotionally from the age three to six, when her father had his first affair. Since we never talked about it, and nothing that happened became clear to her, the scar of that injury left a mark on her, which never healed. Still to this day no one ever talked about it. In my opinion, and understanding of Mary that incident and the thought of losing her father, who she loved a lot, took her life, her hope, her security, and her trust away from her. She never recovered from that, till the second one destroyed her completely. And the way that she rebelled during her teenage years, and she became a self-destructive person was the cause of that.

So I always felt that it was my duty to recognize my children's needs, and act or react according to their needs and desires. At that age to tell my children what to do, or not do was out of order for me. The best possible way to show them what was right for them to do was to act upon it myself.

To show her what was the right way to lose weight, when we went to brunch most Sundays, with long buffet full of different meats, eggs, breads, different kind of omelets, cooked vegetables, and so many fresh fruits, plus all kinds of cakes and delicious pastries,

I did not order from the buffet. I ordered from menu just egg whites and vegetables. She watched me every Sunday. I wanted to show her that was the way to control my weight. I walked more than one hour every day religiously. I exercised thirty minutes daily. But I never told her you must loose weight. Saying no to Mary had a complete opposite effect.

My Dear God:

So this way we were getting along very well. To a point that I was worried to become so attached to me, like the time she was a baby. If she was invited to go anywhere, I was with her. Any involvement she had with different groups, she asked me to go with her. For Christmas parties she wanted to take me as her date. Even at her work out of Visalia, she asked me to go with her. One day I went shopping, and after that I went to the library. While I was writing, I saw her shadow above my head. She had come to take me home. Another day, after library I went shopping, thinking that I was at the library, she had come to the library. When she didn't find me there, she started walking around the library to find me. At the same time I was walking home, and we ran into each other. She held me in her arms and said, "Where were you Mom, I looked allover for you". When we started walking home, with a very passionate voice she said to me, "Mom, I don't know what could I do without you". I thought that was the time that I say something to her. I said, "Wait Mary jon, I am not doing anything for you. It had been you all along that did everything by yourself. It had been you who went to the university, and lived all alone by yourself. It was you who went to Ann Arbor by yourself. It was you who studied for Bar just by yourself. Although I was hundred percent behind you, yet it was only you who helped yourself to make it to here. And I know the day that I won't be here; still you will be as ambitious as you always have been. Please, you must believe that, it is the strength in you that pushes you towards achieving, and it is only you who must hold your hand and pat you on your shoulder, and make you run. It hasn't been me, it is not I now, and it won't be me in the future. The same way that I am making my own life, the same way you are making your own life with your own powerful intelligence.

We were living peacefully together and tried to make it fun. Yet here and there I saw sadness in her. Sometimes when she cuddled in my arms, and she asked me if she was doing something wrong. I told her, "Don't even think about it. In Iran most families are accustomed to be passionate together, especially a mother and daughter. This is nothing out of ordinary. Hugging your mother, kissing her, and talking to her about whatever is bothering you is the best therapy for not letting you fall into depression. That is why going to psychiatrists is not part of our lives. Before somebody falling into a bad depression, the loving family will help him or her to get out of it. Actually this is the best, and only medicine that could help sadness or depression. Don't you ever condemn this passionate love among us, which is coming only from our hearts".

My Dear God:

But I knew that she was still thinking of her old boyfriend Tom. Tom had a young son from his first or second wife. Mary loved that little boy. She took care of him, and drew a portrait of him. She kept it with her at all times. No matter how badly I tried to make Mary understand that if a person did not care for you, or never thought of you, you must get rid of his love in your heart, she never wanted to hear me. She kept him in her heart, and allowed herself to suffer for it. I didn't know how to convince her that this way she only would destroy herself. From her mood I knew when she had called him. She seemed more depressed, and more into herself.

I had to learn how to deal with her, when she was in different moods. God forbid if I did, or acted, or said something at a wrong time, or in a wrong place. Here we go with three or four days of depression. I had to find a way to get her out of that mood. But as I stated before, she had to be left alone with her decision-making. She didn't take any guidance whatsoever. She wanted to follow her own aspirations.

Okay, my dear GOD, can you make me understand why Mary did what she did to me from the age of ten? Can you make me understand what our life is all about? As soon as she started her puberty it was the beginning of a cold war between her and me. The person, whose only love was her mother Shamci till the age ten, she started hating her mom after the age ten. It wasn't clear to me what she had against me. One moment it was plenty of love, the other time it was just pure hatred. How could I understand her language, except loving her and helping her no matter what she did?

Now, after twenty-five years, she was giving me the love that she gave me when she was under the age ten. How could I adapt myself with her new mood, except loving her, and believing in her love for me? I could never find out what was going on in her mind then and what is going on now. I just had to do my duty and wait and see what future brought us.

My Dear God:

At that time I just knew that she wanted me badly. She wanted all of me for herself only. And I was glad to be able to give her as much love as she needed. That was my dream to see my children happy, and now my dream had come true. I just knew that Mary, who was my main concern, was showing a sign of improvement. I knew that there was a power behind all these blessings for me. I felt great.

I had nothing to complain at all. Maseeh was doing great at his job, winning awards one after another. He had his beautiful house, with a private section for his mother, living with Anna his girlfriend. Mojgan had her husband, the love of her life. She had her own house, a car, and she was finding work in different places. And Mary had her job with a group of lawyers, and seemed to be looking forward to a better and happier life in future.

Little by little I realized that helping my children to be independent and live happy has paid off my hard suffering life. This was my goal, and I saw it happening. All three of them, each in their own way were active, athletic, healthy, sociable, and opposite of their father, they were very trustworthy. At that time I had the whole world in my hands. Obviously I had no hand in that, except that a blessing power was supporting my children and me. All of us could have been destroyed with many wrong doings in front of us. But none of us turned to be somebody like Iraj, who not only he ruined his name and his prestige, but he ruined all of us in the family also. Too bad for him, he turned out to become a man who he always hated to be. Luckily I could say, "It is no longer my business. If he was happy to be in the category of bastards, let him be".

Nothing worried me as much as the subject of drugs among the teenagers, especially for those who had the tendency to experiment. My children were caught in the middle of dealing drugs easily. As Mary told me once, "Do not worry about us mother. At my school drugs are handed from a teacher to a student in the safest place, the library. If anyone of us wanted to do it, no one could ever stop us". This was at the school that we used to pay five thousand dollars per student. And the other place was my own house. My children's cousins, who used to come to America many summers, and stayed in our house, started going to Cranbrook, another private school, and during the summers and weekends they were in our house. By the way that Kayvan, the other cousin was giving me reports of their activities at school, not only they were using drugs, but also he has been involved with dealing them. And he made it available for Mary and others also. While I was burning to death every second of my life and I couldn't do anything about it. So with raising my children in such atmosphere, am I not the luckiest mother on earth? Shouldn't I believe that there was a blessing power supporting my children and me? Shouldn't I feel great and be happy? Shouldn't I thank you GOD for saving them from disasters? Even millions and millions thanks still is not enough for what I am receiving now. At this time not only I am not sad for losing Iraj, but also I am very glad that with losing him I was rewarded with having nice children without being involved with any wrongdoing. And I am hoping that none of them inherited disloyalty, dishonesty from their father.

My Dear God:

When I was living with Maseeh and Anna in LA, I thought I must do something about my pension and profit sharing before Iraj got rid of it, and made it disappear. Since I never had a lawyer to defend me I thought I must find a good lawyer to help me without charging me too much. I researched around, and realized that lawyers do not work as contingency on a divorce matter, so each one had their own system for charging me.

One day I was walking on Ventura Boulevard. I ran into one of Mary's and Maseeh's teachers from Michigan. I couldn't believe my eyes. What are you doing here?" I asked him. He was surprised to see me too. He was Mr. Ronnie Clemmer, who was their English teacher. He was friends with Mary, and we had invited him for dinner a few times

in our house. He asked about Mary and Maseeh, and they had seen each other a few times. He told me, "I have a movie production in Studio City, called "Longbow Production". He wasn't surprised about my separation, because I knew that Mary must have talked to him. When he told me that he had been busy dealing with his divorce, I asked him if he had a lawyer. He said he was very happy with his lawyer, and that she was a family friend, and she was very good. I got her number from him, and I thanked him for being a big help to me. This way I found a lawyer to follow my wish to be able to get something from Iraj. Otherwise if I didn't ask for it, he would have made it disappeared like everything else.

By that time I was able to find my way around Los Angeles, and I could drive anywhere that I needed to go. I called Laura's office, and I arranged a meeting with her. She was young and beautiful lady, just like Mary. She was married, and had no children. When I told her the story about my life, she felt for me because her own mother had gone through a sad divorce. We hugged and kissed, and she promised me to do her best to make me happy. Lawfully she thought we could go after him to get my share of Hollywood Live, plus other things, which he refused to pay me. But after exchanging two or three letters, and accusing me of things, which were unheard of, I asked Laura to forget what he must have done, or by law what he owed me. She agreed with me and said, "You are right. You don't want to spend the money of your pension and profit sharing, to fight for something that he ruthlessly will fight for". So she went only after my pension and profit sharing, plus the security of the life insurance, which he had bought for me. It took us a long time, but I was happy that I did not let him eat up the rest of my money.

My Dear God:

Laura Meyer treated me like her mother. She cared for me, and watched over my rights. After a year or so she got pregnant and had a beautiful baby. At that time she was the happiest woman, and I was very happy for her.

Living with Mary in her apartment became more frequent. Because I was staying there longer each time, I needed more of my stuff with me. I wasn't happy to live temporary in a place. This time I stayed with Mary for more than two months. It was around Christmas that Mojgan called and asked me to go to her house. Since I needed some of my stuff from Maseeh's house, I had to go to Maseeh's house first, and then fly to Michigan, and from there to Kalamazoo. It was hard, but I was happy to do it.

Maseeh and Anna were happy to see me. After sometimes I got my ticket through my friend in Michigan to go to Portage and be with Mojgan. Maseeh and Anna drove me to the LAX. We hugged and kissed, and they said their warmest goodbye to me. They were happy together, and I was happy for them.

I stayed for one week in Detroit with Chitra to be with her family. Meanwhile I set up time to visit Dr. Mehrabian, who invited me to dinner. And I visited Farah Shushtari and all of her family. I visited Mary and Vickie, the two sisters from Shiraz. And I visited

Tilda and her daughter Luciana. They all accepted me with lots of love and respect, and treated me to lunch or dinner.

From there I flew to Portage Michigan, where Mojgan was living. For Christmas dinner everyone was supposed to go to Joe's parents' house. Ruth's parents, who lived in the same neighborhood, baked the big turkey and brought it to Scheidler's house. All the gifts were under the Christmas tree, and everyone was excited to find out what they got after exchanging the gifts. Being among their family, feeling the warmth and their togetherness, made me forgot my sufferings.

My Dear God:

Each person volunteered to take the responsibility to do some thing. Mama baked the turkey, Ruth made bread, vegetables, and stuffing, Mojgan made bread and a few desserts. It was a very nice gathering, and everyone enjoyed it. It was very valuable to me to see Papa and Mama taking the place at the head of the table, just like the Norooz time in Iran among my own family, which seemed so far away.

After three weeks that I spent in Mojgan's house, I had a ticket to go to Cincinnati to visit the Hushmands. As always Farahnaz, Ali, and her two children Layla and Kasra were welcoming me at the airport. My feelings about them were that they were my children, and their children were my grandchildren. What they did for me during my suffering years was the reason to bring me back to life. Farahnaz was from the same culture and the same upbringing. Since her own parents had an ugly divorce when she was only three years of age, she treated me like her own mother. She felt for me. She tried to make me forget what had happened to me. Not only Farahnaz, but also Ali was the same way with me. Opposite of my own children, who accepted their father and his wife, and forgot about my feelings, Farahnaz and Ali hated them, and even didn't come to Mojgan's wedding just to avoid seeing him. What they did to me had not been and will never be acceptable in any rich and moralist society. In books we read, at movies we watch, in any court of judgment, they are and they were guilty as hell. Any person, who had just a little understanding, could see the ugliness of their act. Yet my children chose to close their eyes on what went on, and they decided to treat that no good pro…….. as a clean woman. No one with a right mind can do that. So I had the right to admire Ali and Farahnaz, and others who turned their backs at them.

I was supposed to stay with them for two weeks. But as always she made me exchange my ticket for one more week. When I called Maseeh to let him know of my delay, he didn't sound like the same person. I got worried, and didn't say anything. Then the night before my flight to Los Angeles Maseeh called me. I thought he wanted to know the time of my arrival. But to my surprise I found out that something was very wrong with him. In short he explained to me that he and Anna broke-up, and he needed some more time to be by himself. I realized that he wanted me to stay longer with Farahnaz. And I realized that he did not want anyone to interfere with his decision at that moment.

For a short time something clicked in my mind. Was Maseeh asking me to stay out of my own house? Oh Shamci, what a pity! You must put the end to this charade now or never. I knew that he was in pain, and didn't want me to see him in that condition. I realized that he needed his privacy so badly that he was asking me to stay away from him. Although it was partially my house, still he had the right to wanting to be alone. I knew that there were times, and there were times. That was the time that he needed his privacy, and I had to respect that.

My Dear God:

After I calmed him down, I told him that because I had already exchanged my ticket once to extend my stay, I didn't want to pay more to exchange my ticket. I had to come home anyway. But I promise him that I would stay out of his way, and after two days I would go back to Mary, since she had been asking me. He agreed.

When I got there, I found out that Anna had moved out of his house. But I was puzzled. What might have happened between them to cause Anna leave Maseeh, whom she loved so dearly. She had his picture above her desk, where she was painting or studying. I offered Maseeh to allow me to talk to Anna and ask her to come back. But Maseeh suggested that it was not going to work. He told me that she had moved with her boyfriend, and it was late to do anything about it. My eyes became so wide open that I thought they were coming out the sockets. How could she have a boyfriend ready in her hands with the kind of love that she had for Maseeh? What kind of world did I live in that I was not familiar with what was going on in it? Then I asked Maseeh if I could call Patricia, Anna's mother, and talk to her? Since he didn't mind I called her to see what was going on. Talking to Patricia, I realized that this has been Maseeh's idea. And she said to me, “I don't think we can do anything about it”. But the way that Maseeh was acting, I thought it must have been Anna's idea. I found Maseeh very hurt, very depressed, and I didn’t have any way to get to him, or comfort him, or even find out what had happened that Maseeh had come to making that decision. The next day I left to go and stay with Mary.

Although Mary was very happy to see me, and to be with me, it was the time for me to make my big decision, and start looking for a house for myself. If Mary liked to live with me, I would welcome her with all my love. And if she wanted to live apart from me, still it would be okay for me. The only thing that I had in mind was to find a house in the city of Visalia, and make sure to have a separate section if I ever was forced to have a housemate. I must follow my own destiny, and plan to have my life in my own hands. There wasn’t going to be anything for me in the future, except I would gain my independency. I taught and pushed my children to live independently, now it was time for myself to show them how easy it would be when you live independently.

Living in Visalia with Mary for sometimes now, I had become very fond of the city. It reminded me of my childhood in Iran. I felt happy and comfortable there. Since I did not have a job or a good income, I was worried that I might not be able to fulfill my dream. But I thought, I would be able to sell my condo in Michigan, and pay for a house in Visalia.

My Dear God:

With living in that big house in Michigan, and watching movies with huge dining rooms with extremely long dining tables in them, that husband and wife needed a telephone to be able to talk to each other from one end to the other, I completely was fed-up with any kind of luxury which was separating me from the norm of living and the real people. I wanted a small house in the city of Visalia, and I made up my mind that where and how I wanted to live in future.

So without any delay I called the real estate agent from Century 21, Jordan-Link & Company. They introduced me to a lady named Betty Grant. In our first meeting that she picked me up to show me a house I told her all about myself, and what I had in mind. I explained to her that I had had it all, and I had seen it all. I just wanted a small comfortable house in the town of Visalia, near the Main Street, close to the library, the post office, doctor's offices, and a place to be able to see my neighbors, and talk to them, and be able to walk every day. I wanted to be able to do my daily needs without the use of car or any other thing, which would limit my freedom. I told her that I had lived in a world of pretence, and I was fed-up with it. No more pretence. I wanted to live like the majority of the world's population. I like to live like Europeans and people from the rest of the world. To tell you the truth, I wanted to live as a human being. I was so upset with living thirty years of pretence with Iraj that I wanted to get rid of that feeling once and for all. I wanted to be free at last, free at last, and free at last.

We became friends. I invited her for lunch or dinner, and she liked to try Iranian food of any kind. She promised me that she would find a house for me exactly like what I was looking for.

Since Anna and I had a good relationship, I wrote her a letter and expressed my sorrow over their separation. And I asked her if my presence in that house, or any of my acts were the cause of their separation. I asked her to let me know if my moving out of the house would help them to get back together again. In return she wrote to me, "I have never been happier with anyone as much as I was happy to live with you. Our separation didn't have anything to do with you. It was time for Maseeh to move on with his life, and I moved on with mine. You were like a close friend and a mother to me. I have nothing but good memories from you, Mary, or Maseeh". She wanted me to believe her that our friendship would last forever, and that it didn't have anything to do with what had happened between them. She wanted me to believe that Maseeh still was her best and

closest friend.

My Dear God:

Her letter made me feel good. I didn't want to see her being hurt. And with exchanging letters with Patricia, her mother, I realized that they were happy for both of them. Meanwhile they loved Maseeh as before, and had continued their relationship just like before. So did I. We sent Christmas gifts and cards to each other, and I invited them to come and visit us if they could.

No matter how many times they all told me that I wasn't the cause of their separation, I was determined to move out of that house as soon as possible. I wanted to live by myself, and teach my children that there was nothing wrong with living alone. It was possible to live by myself and still enjoy my life. Until they saw me in act, they would not believe it. So I was almost in a hurry to buy my house and move out of Maseeh's house.

At this time I was so bothered with having my furniture in Maseeh's house that I wanted to rent a storage area, and let Maseeh live without a headache. But I thought it wasn't a good idea. I must wait to find a house, and then move out my furniture.

We were looking for house periodically. With me being in three different places all the times, the house hunting was not that easy. I was either in Mary's, Mojgan's, or Maseeh's houses. If I wanted to have my own house, I had to be there to be able to take care of physical and financial part of it. I couldn't just buy it, and then let go. So I was in the middle of a debate within me and myself what to do. Especially that Betty had warned me that finding a house in the historic area of town was not that easy. Usually houses were passed from generation to generation. But there were times that some from the new generation wanted to get rid of the old house, and that would be the time that we would get lucky. After waiting for some time, and we did not find any of those historic homes, and with Betty's comments I was almost giving up. Not because I thought I couldn't find a house in town, but because I wanted to hurry my moving out of Maseeh's house. I wanted to give him his freedom and his privacy back as soon as I could. So with this idea we started to look for houses out of town and in the suburbs.

We looked at many houses, which were new, and nicely designed, and I didn't think they were overpriced either. But they were not located in town, and I was thinking that we might lose the opportunity to find the right one.

One day Betty showed me a house on the same street that I am living on now, but she wasn't very enthusiastic about it. The price was low, and it needed a lot of repairs to be able to live in it. With a good architect and a good builder it would have come to be a nice house. Especially that its picture was in the Visalia's historic homes book. The only back draw about it was that it was located between some out of shape, and dirty and broken houses. And I was new in this town, and I didn't know anybody to guide me or help me. With the money that I had it was not easy to start to construct a new home. But I don't

Dear Shamci,

This letter is long over-due but very necessary. I'm so sorry for the way I left with no goodby's or explanations. I really didn't know how to explain everything nor could I. To look at the faces of the people I loved and grew so fond of over an eight year span was more than I could bear.

I know Maseeh tried to explain the situation and it was probably better than I ever could have. I wanted you to know from me that our decision had little to do with you or anyone else.

I loved you dearly Shamci and always will and hope some how you can find understanding from this but most of all, find it in your heart to forgive me. My intentions were not to hurt you or belittle our friendship. I felt helpless and didn't know any other way to handle things.

I love you dearly as well as Mary, Moji and especially Maseeh. I always will till the day I die. When I left all of you, some of me died. Your son is a good and decent man and was, is and always will be my dearest friend. He helped me in more ways than anyone in my life ever did or will do. He gave me strengths and courage and helped me to be a better human-being. Maseeh and I were good for each other over time but couldn't make each other truely happy or peaceful. Emotionally, it was/became detrimental and we were holding each other back.

Maseeh needed room to breath and grow and I guess I did too. I think I was too settled and grew lazy in my career goals which I blamed Maseeh and lashed out at him, holding him back.

I have no idea what the future holds for any of us but I have a feeling Maseeh is going to make us all very proud. Please support him and know how good he is and how much he loves you too.

It's important you know how special you are and how much I valued what you did for me and the love you shared with me. I will always hold you in my heart.

Life is a gift and how we choose to accept what it brings to us will determine how happy we will be.

(4)

My time with you, Mary, Moji and especially Maseeh has given me my most precious memories. You were always a friend to me and I love you like my own mother.

Please open you heart and find forgiveness knowing that my love for you is undying. I will always love & think of you. You're in my prayers Shamci.

Forever,

Anna

As you see, this is Anna's letter to me after she and Maseeh broke up. With this letter, I realized that in reality it was not my actions that had created difficulty between them. I loved Anna dearly and I was aware of her love for me. That was the reason that I always told her, "Dear Anna I have been accused of loving too much. Please don't make me love again." And I wanted to let her know that loving is great. But it is difficult to love and give it up. I am glad that I could keep the memory of loving Anna in my heart, and I will always think of her as "the best".

Patricia

Dear Shanei,

How are you, my dear friend!?

This has been a really hectic two years for me, but all is well now. My mother, Ina, spent her last year with us so that I could care for her. (she was 88, on oxygen, and heart disease, so I was so glad to have her. She died last December 8, 2000.

The two boys we've been raising moved in with their father 2 months ago, so Emil and I are <u>alone</u>! Now we're

This is another letter from Patricia Knutson, Anna's mother. I felt very well each time she sent me a letter like this. With me being apart from all my siblings, this kind of friendly and affectionate letters meant a lot to me. Besides, this proves that I have always had a way of loving nice and special people.

(2)

Patricia

more than ready to have you come and visit us!! Except the weather is lousy right now. Rain, rain, days on end. We really needed the rain, so I'd better not complain.

Think of you often — especially during the Holiday Season. We had such a good time, those few years ago.

Emil says "Hello", too —

Much love,

Pat

January 30, 1998

Dear Shamci,

Well, my dear friend, the Christmas season is over and I have yet to send a card. I can't believe how quickly these days pass and how little I accomplish. It certainly isn't because I'm getting older!? Ha!

Anna told me that this was the first Christmas that you had your family all together. How very happy you must be. I would like to see you all! Tell Mujgan and Mary "Hi" for me! when you see them - or write.

After such a terrible season last year, I am so glad for Maseeh that he's found his "love", and that he and Anna are still such good friends. Emil and I were so afraid that we'd lost you

(2)

all, as part of our family, but now we're closer than ever! I am so eager to meet Mary. As long as she loves Maseeh as he deserves, we will love her, too!

Is Mary still working in LA? And does she still like her job?

Does Mujgan still live in Michigan?

Did you get to visit Iran this (last) year? I know how much you miss all of your friends, And I wonder if the touchy situation over there, makes it difficult for you to visit.

Our family keeps growing. You've probably heard that Cliff and Velda had another daughter, Cassandra Grace. Christianna is 2½ now! And Kolleen is doing great, working in a photography studio. She

(3) is still with Jim and his mother, Betty; healthy and well!! Thank goodness!

Age 40 Steve is still fishing, working at the mill, and playing a lot of golf. He is also training for competition "dead-lift", a form of weight-lifting. He is so very strong. And still no steady girl. He dates three different girls a lot, one who is an outdoor person and likes to fish; one that plays golf; and one who is a homebody that likes to read! Steve is a voracious reader and likes to discuss books. Now if we could put all those girls into one! Ha!

Age 37 Ken and Debbie are busy all the time. They both work. Ken is still regional director for Primerica, and Deb at the bank. The kids, Nick, Kyle, and Kaylyn,

(4)

are all soccer players, so we go to their games when possible.

Age 33 Norma has a new boy-friend (for over a year now), named Rick, and he has two 12 year old twin boys, so we add to the progeny!!!

Age 31 Karin, John, and the three children, Danny, Francie, and J.R., are happy living in Vancouver, Washington.

My sorority, Beta Sigma Phi, has a big Valentine Ball every year. Ours is Feb. 14th this year, so I'm getting excited. Emil and I love to dance, so once a year we do it! Ha. I'm president this year, so really busy!

Thanks for your invitation to visit you. We would love it. Don't know when, though, as Emil is so busy with portraits, now, and for some time to come. He's supposed

(5)

to make another trip to San Diego, too, but can't find the time. I didn't get to go last time!! Its too hard to leave with the two boys here. They're 10 (Dwight) and 7 (Timmy) now, Dwight plays YMCA basketball, and Timmy's a Cub Scout.

Jan 31, 1998

Looks like this will take longer than I thought. Can't seem to sit down and finish!

Feb. 2, 1998

Well - here I am again! Just put the boys to bed, after 1 1/2 hours of homework. Emil is still out in the shop, working. He has so much to do, he says "there's just not enough hours in the day!"!

My dishes in the sink are calling to me - "Come wash our messiness, please!"

Much love, Pat

This letter is from Patricia Knutson to me after I had invited them to our house in Studio City, CA. If you read the letter, you will see how friendly she is. We were able to write to each other even after Maseeh and Anna broke up. I have always been the kind of person to cherish this kind of affection. Although Anna and Maseeh broke up, they were able to remain friends, and so did I.

know where I got my strength and my fearlessness? Although Betty didn't want to go along with me, I decided to show the house to Mary and get her opinion too, since she was willing to live with me.

My Dear God:

When Mary saw the house, she liked it. When she find out what my plan was for buying that house, she offered that one of her friends who was architect, could give us advice, or any kind of help. Mary arranged an appointment with her friend Betty and I to see the house together, and find out what our possibilities were.

He said the same thing that I thought. He liked it a lot, and believed that after a good fixing it would be a beautiful home. But he did not have any idea about the houses next door or in front of the house. Him being in that business and knowing that my idea was doable, I decided to put an offer on the house. It was near the library, near the bus station, and near the main street. And most of all, Mary liked it and was happy to move in with me.

That night I was worried a lot. I didn't know how to start, or how to finish. The only thing that I was happy with was that I would move my furniture from Maseeh's house, and put it all in one room, like a storage, and while we were still living in Mary's apartment, I would be done with the construction, and we would live happily ever after. But something inside me couldn't deal to stand seeing the broken and dirty houses next door to me. While I put down a deposit and signed the papers, still in my heart I was not satisfied. Not only me, but also I read it in my agent's eyes that she was not happy to get that house either. The only hope that she had was that another offer had been made before us. If theirs did not get approved, we would be next in line.

At that time I couldn't understand why Betty did not like the house for me. To be a bad person, I thought she had in mind to sell me the more expensive house, so she didn't want me to go ahead with that little amount. Not knowing that at that time she knew me, she knew my style, she knew that I was rushing it just because I was desperate. She knew that to construct and remodel that house would be the biggest headache of all for me. And I think that was the truth behind her actions.

When she gave me the news that they had accepted the first offer, and I was free to go house hunting again, in many ways I was relieved. After I got my deposit back, we started to look for more houses in that neighborhood. But it seemed that there was no chance. She started to show me some other houses in the suburb. She thought I might like it anyway.

My Dear God:

During one of those showings, a house caught my eye. It was new, with a nice plan. It had spiral stairway that took you upstairs to the bedrooms. It had one bedroom downstairs and two bedrooms upstairs. It had three baths, and big and open kitchen. Altogether I was taken, and I was tempted to forget the inner city, and research more about that house.

It was almost Christmas time, and I was planning to go to Michigan again. Mojgan wanted me to go there. Not paying attention to my plan, I felt that I could put an offer on that house since I liked it, and the price was not too high for me. So I asked Mary to go and see the house, and let me know how she felt about the house. She didn't have anything against it, but she was not very enthusiastic about it. So I arranged with Betty to come over one night, and I put an offer on the house, and signed the papers.

My dear GOD, I don't know what was about my life that always something happened on time to stop me from wrongdoings. My daughter Mary, who saw the first house, and agreed to move in with me, now about this house she said, “I don't know. I am not ready to move with you”. It was right after I had signed the first page of our agreement. That was an alarming sign for me. I opened my eyes, and I saw that I was planning to go away for two months in just one week, and Mary was not even going to move in with me. How could I going to deal with everything if I was not going to be there? Not only that, but I didn't have anyone to cover for me. How would that work? Someone needed to be here to handle the deal, and be able to take care of the house, cut the grass, water the plants, and many other things, which I didn't think of.

I turned to Betty, and I said to her, “Betty, if she is not ready to move in with me, and if I can't be here to finish the deal, I think it is not the right time or the right place to go ahead with this deal. I apologize for the inconvenience, but I wasn't looking at it clearly. This house is nice, and I might have been happy with it. But I think this is a wrong time for me to make a deal as such. Forgive me please for wasting your evening. I owe you a dinner and a movie. Probably there is another house for me in the city, in near future”. She tore apart the first page of our agreement, and I ended up owing her a movie and a dinner.

When I was living with Mary in her apartment she had many bills to pay each month: the house rent, the utilities, her car and its expenses, and the daily expenses like any other family. When she decided to move in my house, I was thinking to find a way to make sure that she could have some savings for herself. And because I was aware of her way of spending money without counting her budget, it always worried me. For instance, she bought her girl friend's daughter a three hundred dollar Atlas. She bought expensive gifts for people, who were not worthy. She spent money like she was a rich person, who didn’t work hard to make that money. If indeed she didn't have to work so hard to earn that money, it wouldn't have bothered me. But I was living with her. And I saw her how hard she worked for that money. So I was thinking to find a reasonable way to make her save some of her money for the rainy day.

My Dear God:

The group of lawyers that she was working for had two offices. Mary was hired by the one that had an office in Visalia. The other office was in Hanford, and the other two lawyers were there. At the beginning the relationship with that lawyer, his wife and their son were great. I got to know them, and I became friends with his wife. She was a very nice lady, and she wanted to be a good friend with Mary. Away from the office work she called to talk to Mary, to go to lunch, or just be together somewhere. Sometimes she was working in the office also.

Little by little I realized that, there is some tension between Mary and her boss. First I didn't know the seriousness of their dispute. But as time passed, it became more serious and even dangerous for Mary. During all those times his wife did not get involved with what was going on between her husband and Mary.

To begin with, Mary was always vulnerable. She did not fully recovered from a sickness, and she needed a peaceful place to work at. She did not deserve those of difficulties. I was worried to death for her. Each time when she got home, she told me how he was hurting her by belittling her with words. I had no choice but to calm her down, and ask her not to let it bother her.

One day she came home, and said, “He had reduced my salary to half”. I comforted her by saying, “Give him a chance, probably he will change his behavior”. Not knowing what really was going on in that office, I couldn't go any farther with my judgment. But Mary was uptight, upset, and very mad at him. And most of all, she wanted to stay away from his wife, who had nothing to do with him.

I was running around with Mary, and the only thing that I could do was to hold her, kiss her, comfort her by words, which sometimes she wasn't much happy with it.

I myself was in a condition that I couldn't see Mary's sadness. With the high blood pressure, and high cholesterol that I had, and I was taking medication for it every day, I thought it was the end of me.

My Dear God:

Mary had chosen that city because of her job. She was expecting to find a peaceful life there, next to her mother. With all the expenses that she had around her, how could she deal with that man? How should she get along with him? One day she came home in the middle of the day. She said to me, “Mom, I was fired”. For a moment, I went numb as if my blood was frozen. While I didn't want to make the matter worse for her, in a way that she did not get more upset, I started to talk to her. I had to make her believe that it was not the end of the world. She was not the first person who had been fired from her job, and, she was not the last either. There were always ways to handle things, and the only way to do it was to do it in a calm and collective way. I told her that we would put our minds together to see what way we could go.

Just like me, who decided not to hire a lawyer to fight Iraj, Mary didn't want to fight with that lawyer. To get involved with the lawyers' dispute normally is a very difficult situation. Yet to be sick and weak, especially emotionally, was a very difficult task to follow. We both were not capable of handling that feud.

That day she was too upset to be able to think of anything. I made her believe that we would survive no matter what. After she took a nap, we were able to review all the options available for her. Because of the existing contract between them she wrote him a letter. With the exchange of the letters, he had to hire her back. But he made it clear that she had to work at the Hanford office with the two other lawyers. For the time being she didn't mind it. But emotionally she was destroyed and demolished by his act. My main concern was that what if that complication pushed her back to the hospital. What if she did not have enough strength to fight it physically and emotionally? "What can I do to help her, my dear God? Let me know how I deal with this disappointment. Please God, do not leave me alone. Please help her to be able to put her mind together, and do the best that she can".

Mary might not have been an aggressive lawyer, but she was a good lawyer and a hard working one. I remembered at the beginning she was concerned about how well she would do at the courtroom. Many nights before her court day she practiced her opening statement, and the closing statement in front of me, and she wanted me to point to her if she could do better than that. Many nights we laughed a lot because it seemed to us that it was like acting in a movie. One night, after she practiced in front of me, and we talked about different sentences, which might have been more appropriate, she went to her room to work on her case for the next day. While I was sitting there, I thought of completely different closing statement, and I wrote it down on a piece of paper. I liked it so much that I took it to her and read it to her. She was amazed. She took the paper from me, she read it again, and she said, "Mom, this is fantastic. I really like it". And I remembered many more occasions, which were very amusing for both of us. What could I do to make it like before?

My Dear God:

She knew that the new position was not promising either. She bought a computer, and started working at home.

I was standing behind her hundred percent. I was promising her that there was no way that we couldn't overcome all the obstacles, which came in our way. I was even willing to find any kind of job to be able to pay the rent. I didn't have my car in Visalia, whenever I was there to visit her. One of those Saturday mornings that she was so confused about the situation, she called me and said, "I have locked myself in the bathroom, and I can't get out". I got worried. I told her, "I will walk to the office, and we will find a way. Just don't panic please. I will be right there as soon as I can". I left

immediately to go to the office to rescue her. I went around the office, and there was no way of getting in. She didn't know anybody's number by heart to tell me, and I could contact them. While we were talking, and discussing what to do, one of the secretaries, who needed to get something from the office came in. I was relieved. Soon I opened the bathroom door, which someone pressed the wrong button accidentally, and freed Mary. We both stayed till she finished her work, then we went home.

I knew that Mary was suffering by that lawyer's act. And I knew that she was not happy to drive to Hanford every morning in thick fog, and work for half the amount of her contract. She started to write to other lawyers in Visalia and the neighboring cities to introduce herself, hoping for referral cases. To do this many Saturdays or Sundays we went to the office. She wrote the letters, and I put them in envelopes, which I stamped and addressed. And then we went to the post office to mail them. Usually we spent six to seven hours on those papers.

After her contract was over, she even applied for unemployment. But she was rejected for some reason that I couldn't understand. Little by little the referrals were rolling in. It was too early to be able to rent an office. So she started to work at home.

At this time I went different places to apply for a job. I never worked in this country, except the time in Michigan as a cashier for my friend. So it was difficult to find a job, especially at my age. Yet I went to the meat department of Albertson to get an application. I thought they might need someone to do a good job for them, and I knew for sure that I could do it well. Before they called me, Mary's work picked up, and she was able to rent her own office. I knew my Mary. I knew she was my ambitious girl. I knew that with all the physical and emotional sufferings, still she would be driven to find her goal. She never thought too much about money, but she knew that she had to have enough to be able to pay her bills. She worked very hard to get it, but she was never an aggressive and ruthless lawyer, who would forget her morals. She was my daughter after all, what else could I have asked for?

My Dear God:

My dear God, when was the time of need that you did not come to my rescue? When was the time that I asked you to do something for me, and you didn't do it? When was the time that you left me alone? Never, never my dear God. Thank you!

Mary was getting her confidence back. Even at the time that a lawyer told her, "This city has plenty of lawyers, and it will be very difficult for us to survive". She did not take it as hard as before. I made sure that she believed in herself to a point that she could challenge any other lawyer. I told her one day, "Mary jon, tell those lawyers that since you work hard you expect something good to come of it". And it did happen.

Mary and I were living together so peacefully that I couldn't believe it. During the years of suffering I had learned to use the reverse psychology with Mary when it was needed. Sometimes I had to stay quiet, while she accused me of wrongdoing, and I let her come to her senses and wake-up. Arguing with Mary was not the right way. Soon she would withdraw herself from you, and pull herself into depression, which I never wanted to happen. I always tried to leave the door open for her to be able to come back and start communicating with me. I knew that I was the mother, and mothers are always the guilty ones. So there was no reason to defend myself for the price of her sadness. I had worked all my life to be able to bring happiness in her life, and I should never stop that. The only disagreement, which we had once in a while, was over cleanliness of the house. Then I realized that it was her house. She must have freedom to do what she wanted. If things like that bothered me, I must do the cleaning myself, and never argue over it. To my surprise she loved to see her house clean when it was done.

At that time of our lives we were like two lovers. Together we worked to get rid of all the problems, and together we tried to feel optimistic about our future. We were both honest and truthful with our feelings. We both did things together. We went to movies, restaurants, and parties together. And we invited her friends to our house for good Persian dinner. We were having the times of our lives. It was to a point that I was worried that what if Mary became dependant and attached to me. That wasn't good for her. I must think of something to make her understand that it was not right that she thought of me as the partner of her life. But I never wanted to endanger her trust in me, or cause anything to ruin our good relationship. Not that I was thinking of separating her from me, but we could never have control over nature's act. What if nature decided to take me away one day soon? She must be able to take it from there, and continue her life. Anyway, we had become two people, who lived as one, thought the same, ate the same, and wanted the best for each other. And that was great.

My Dear God:

Although everything was fine for me, it was very funny, meanwhile sad in reality. I was homeless at that time. I had part of my stuff in Maseeh's house, some part of it in Mojgan's house, and I was living in Mary's house with just one suitcase. Even when I was in Iran, I had more clothing with me than I had in Visalia. I thought I must be able to do something about it.

So it was Christmas time, and Mojgan was insisting that I spent the New Year with them. I packed my suitcase again, and I flew to Michigan. Mojgan and her husband Joe had spent many long hours to make some changes to their house. They had extended a big porch to the back of their house, looking towards the lake. They had built another bathroom on the second floor. They had changed the carpeting, and had built wooden outdoor chairs and a big table. They made their house so beautiful, and it was done so professional that I couldn't believe my eyes.

Knowing Mojgan I knew that she must have something on her mind. I soon find out that she had in mind to sell her house, and move closer to the rest of the family. But at that time still everything was up in the air. She did not know where or when she would be able to put her plans to work. But I was very happy to see that young couple was doing so well, and both of them had been creative and smart about the whole thing. This was what I had in mind for them when I decided to give them money to buy a house for themselves. I was glad to see that Mojgan had been thoughtful, and just like me, she was planning to go after her dreams very wisely.

Sometimes things become so strange that it makes us wonder. Now that the whole family was apart both physically and emotionally they were trying to move near one another. Well, probably we don't know anything about life. Why are we doing strange things at different times of our lives, we really don't know. Only GOD must know the philosophy behind all these. When they had the most comfortable house, all of them were eager to escape from it. Now that they were all apart, they wanted to become closer. Isn't this strange my dear GOD? I really think it is.

I didn't know whom exactly she wanted to be closer to. But she was thinking of it, and she was studying it carefully. She was researching all the possibilities available for them. Since Anna's family was from Oregon, and she had discussed the matter with Anna, she made a trip to Oregon to find out if she liked it. But she was not happy with what was available for her there.

My Dear God:

My main concern was that both Mojgan and Joe were interested to live on the lake. They loved water-skiing snow skiing. So finding a house on the lake was very expensive, and I was afraid that if they sold their house, and meanwhile they wouldn't be able to find a house on the lake in California, they might spend the house money elsewhere, and owning a home would become secondary to them. It was important to me to know that my children owned their homes. That was why I gave her the twenty thousand dollars, although at that time they were not married yet. I made sure to make my children responsible individuals. So to make sure that my money did not disappear in the middle of that transaction, I asked Mojgan to put my share of money in my bank account until they were ready to pay for their new house.

Although as usual she did not like my idea, and she started a big fight with me, accusing me of not trusting her, still I insisted on keeping my money in my account until they were ready to pay for their new house. I made sure to make her understand my point of view. I wasn't a rich woman who could throw away money like that. I had given her my only savings for her to be able to own a house and live a comfortable life. So with the money in my account, as long as they were looking for a house, that money would be saved with out any attempts to spend it.

While I was at Mojgan's house, her cousin Kaveh came to visit also. Kaveh was planning, while he was near the Canadian border, to go to Toronto and visit his Iranian childhood friends. At the same time I was going back to Michigan to spend some time with Chitra, and visit my other friends. And because my cousins Lucy and Fred were also living in Toronto, we decided to take the trip together. Since Kaveh was aware that I was against his smoking, it was on that trip that he gave me the news of quitting his bad habit of smoking. At this time, just for laughs, I told him, "I had never had a bad habit to be forced to give it up. But I had a very destructive habit that luckily I was able to give it up". As soon as I opened my mouth to tell him what my habit was that I gave up, he laughed and said, "I know, it was loving my uncle". And we both laughed.

The funny thing was that when we got to Detroit, I realized that I did not have my passport with me. We were very disappointed. We stopped at the American embassy near the Canadian border in Windsor. But there was no way for me to be able to get a pass. So he drove me to Chitra's house. He met her and her children. Then he said good-bye and drove away to Canada. After he left, I called my cousin Lucy, and told her the news. She was also disappointed because she was expecting us.

My Dear God:

Since I had a plain ticket from Kalamazoo to Cincinnati to spend some time with Farahnaz, I had to return to Kalamazoo with Kaveh. So, after his visit was over, he drove back to Chitra's house, and then we drove back to Kalamazoo together. As always, staying in Farahnaz's house was delightful. Unfortunately this time Layla got sick. She was at home from school one week with high fever. Again they made me extend my trip, and before I left their house Layla was feeling much better.

It was almost a month or two that I was back from my trip to Michigan. One day Betty Grant called me and said, "I have a nice house to show you. It is something that I think you might like. Get ready; I will come pick you up to go see it". The way she sounded, I felt that she might have found a house in town for me. I was ready when she was at my door. As I sat in her car, surprisingly she told me, "I didn't think that this soon there will be a house for sale in downtown Visalia. I certainly think that this house has been made for you". I became so excited that I couldn't wait to see it.

The house turned out to be just like she said. It was of a size that I wanted, very well kept, located at 616 N. Encino Street, between many beautiful historic homes, and the price was affordable for me. I couldn't have asked for more. There was a winning prize plaque posted on the wall next to the front door from the city of Visalia for keeping the house well after more than a century. Just the plaque itself impressed me. It was December 1996. If I wanted to do something about it, I had to do it before Christmas, before the holidays started and Banks and offices were closed.

This time I was not sure if Mary was interested to move in the new house with me. I asked her to go and see the house with Betty. When we entered the house, Mary looked around and said, "And this will be my room". I realized that she was all for it.

After researching about all the legalities regarding the house's background, which did not take long, I asked Betty to go ahead, and put an offer for the house. But I made sure that it must be my house, and we must do whatever it took to make it mine. Even if we had to pay for whatever they had asked.

The house was in excellent shape. Its owner was a young painter, who had painted the house recently. The owner before him had changed and updated the entire electrical system in the house eight years prior to that date. Inside the house and the garage it was nice and clean. It was newly carpeted, and painted, and very well kept. In the backyard there was a whirlpool, which seated eight people. It had grass and some fruit trees, like peaches, figs and others. It was located between many big historic homes. It was near Main Street, where Mary and I used to go to see movies and walked hand in hand. It was only five to ten minutes to my doctor's office, to the bus stop, to the banks, and everything I ever needed. It was just a dream house for me. I couldn't believe that God was answering to all my wishes. Was I one of his favorite creatures, who was trying to bring happiness in my life? To me it was so visible that some powerful hand always was on my shoulders. How could I explain this to anyone? Even if sometimes I was ready to make a mistake, it was exactly like an invisible hand would stop me right there. It made me change my mind, and guided me in the right direction. What a lucky person I was! And what a fortunate person I became!

My Dear God:

The Main Street, which I fell in love with reminded me of the streets in Tehran. Together with Mary once or twice a week we went to movies, and walked to have ice cream, and talked and talked. We teased each other, and laughed and laughed. She used to put her head on my shoulder and talk about her future. There were times that she was worried about her future, and I tried to comfort her by promising her that as long as I was around and she was doing her best as always, and she was doing everything in her power to succeed, nothing in the world could have stopped her from succeeding. I told her, "You are young, smart, beautiful, intelligent, knowledgeable, enthusiastic, and very hard working girl. You passed the Bar exam at your first attempt, while many other recent graduates were not able to do that. You must be very proud of yourself". That way I wanted her not to ever doubt herself. I just wanted her to believe in herself to a point that even for some unknown reason if she was not able to make it the way she was expecting it, at least she must know that she had applied herself to the extreme. Just the fact that she had applied herself to her full potential must make her always feel like a winner. Always, after I talked to her that way, she held my hand and showed me her sense of security. And then she said, "Oh Mom, I am so glad you are with me".

Many times because I was afraid that she got too attached to me, like when she was a little girl, I made sure that she knew that she had always been successful by herself, without me being around her. It hasn't been me, who made things happening for her. Instead it had been her own intelligence, and independence that made her succeed.

This Mary was the same Mary that hated loving her parents only because she was afraid to lose them one day by divorce or by death. She was practicing not to love them at all, while she loved them dearly. She wanted to get used to the feeling that if the separation ever happened, or when it happened. But now, after the divorce, she had come back to me with full love. I really don't know if it was love or fear of the unknown. But the way she was acting, it was the sign of loving. It didn’t make a difference to me whether she loved me or not. I was her mother, who loved her regardless. I always loved her, the same whether she loved me or not. And I was very happy to see her happy and secure. That was my ultimate goal.

My Dear God:

There were times that she felt like sleeping in my arms. Then after a while she moved herself away from me and asked if she was doing something wrong. I assured her that there was nothing wrong with that, “In our culture in Iran people, especially mothers and daughters do it often. That is why not very many people go to psychiatrists when they have someone to love them dearly, and advice them on the right solution to their problems. This kind of love and affections were and are very normal between the members of families. Holding, kissing, and caring are very common at all ages. So don't you ever worry that you are doing something wrong. It is not true at all”. Obviously in America it might be a different story. And that is why psychiatrists are trying to put a nametag on normal behavior, just to be able to have more clients. I still am very close with my sisters and my sisters-in-law. Talking to them is the best therapy for me and for them also.

Unfortunately, because Mary was not born in our culture, and she had not witnessed this kind of kissing and loving and caring in her daily life, and she was not very amused by my motherly attention, which most of the times she tried to stay away from it, if sometimes she felt like getting close to me affectionately, she stopped herself from doing it, thinking that she was doing something wrong. And then I had to remind her that giving pure love to your mother or your daughter was not a crime. And those, who could have it, were the luckiest people on earth. At least it would keep people away from psychiatrists. That by itself was a blessing. We had to be thankful to have had that opportunity. Not everyone's mother was alive or could be that closed to her daughter. This was a gift, which we had received.

Anyway, that Main Street, which had made me fall in love with the city of Visalia, and by walking up and down the street, Mary was able to show her love to me more and more every day, now was to become our own Main Street.

The funny thing was that the owner, who was a young newly married man, with his bride had left for their honeymoon to go hiking on some mountain. They did not have any idea that as soon as they put their house on the market for sale, there was a person standing there to finish the deal.

Betty called him on his cell phone. She told him the news. But we had to wait till they came back from their honeymoon. Meanwhile I had asked Betty to collect all the information regarding the deal, and prepare all the necessary papers, which might have taken time, before he got back.

My Dear God:

His name was David Dobson, and his job was painting and wallpapering. When I asked his wife, "What was the reason that you wanted to sell your house?" she answered me, "He wanted to move to the area so that I went to college". They both were very nice, and they knew exactly what they wanted to do. But I don't know how happy they were when they found out that they had to move out of their house right after they got back from their honeymoon. Obviously it was a shock to them that their house was sold only in one day. In a way it was good for them, but to move out right after their honeymoon might not have been what they had expected.

Again and again I must thank you GOD for making the impossible possible. This was my only dream come true, at the right age for me, and at the right time of my life. Again thank you!

Since I didn't have any income, except the little alimony, it was very hard to apply for a loan. But between Betty and her Banker friend, they made it possible. And because of many reasons I made sure that if I wanted to pay off the house after six months, I would be able to do so without any penalties. Everything was going very well. The closing date was scheduled on December 24th 1996. If we lacked even one piece of information, or if we had to contact any of the governmental offices on that day, which was the day before holiday, it would not have been possible to finish the deal before Christmas. I was planning to move in there before the end of the year. I had already ordered my refrigerator, washer and dryer, garbage disposal, and many other fixtures for the new house. I was ready to move in the next day. This was and is my habit to take precautionary measures before entering any act. So as always I took all the necessary steps to make it happen. I think we were among the last group of people, who left the bank on the evening of 24th of December 1996. We closed the deal, and I was ready to move in right away.

We moved in the house on the 26th of December 1996. At that time I was living with Mary on and off. She was living in Barcelona Apartments, located at 715 S. Demaree Road. Lynda and Charles Cook were the managers of the buildings. They were very nice and Charles helped us move Mary's furniture with his own truck. Since it was not a long distance to drive, it did not take long to load the truck or unload them in the house. Although the carpet was brand new, still I had it washed professionally prior to moving in.

Mary had a client, who was a trucker commuting to Los Angeles. When he found out that I had my furniture in LA, he volunteered to do the job for me, and get paid as other movers. I agreed. The next day we moved my furniture from Maseeh's house, and the day after, while he had his niece and her daughters help us, we moved all my furniture from Maseeh's house to my own house. It was five days before the New Year of 1997 that I removed everything from Maseeh's house. Maseeh was home, and helped us to carry the big sofa and chairs.

My Dear God:

Mary was very happy and excited. Although I had given each one of my children whatever they needed, from rugs to dinning chairs, still I had enough furniture to be able to furnish my room, and Mary had enough to furnish her room. After I had my furniture all in one place, it was easy to take care of the rest.

As I said before, Mary was paying more than five hundred dollars for rent. She was paying for her telephone, her utilities, and everything else. I thought, before we move into our new house, it would be better to make it clear who should spend on what. And to be able to remember what we had agreed on, I wrote the agreement on a piece of paper. That way we both knew our duties. And as I mentioned this before, because I knew that Mary would spend extravagantly at a wrong time on the wrong people, I asked her to put the five hundred dollars, which she was paying for house rent into a joint Bank account, to be able to save that money for the rainy day. Although she agreed to do that, but most of the times she insulted me, and thought that I was getting rent from her.

Since I was aware of Mary's behavior and her changing moods, I tried not to take it personal. I was paying a high mortgage, and the taxes, and I was spending lots of money on the remodel of the house. I was doing the landscaping, the sprinkler system, the air-conditioning, the alarm system, and whatever were needed to update the house. I did the aluminum and iron fencing all around the house. I never thought of that house to be only mine.

I thought it was Mary's first, and it was mine as well. I wanted her to have the best of everything, like she deserved it. I asked her to get her own telephone line so that I didn't have to answer when the people, whom I didn't like, called. But she never believed me that I was trying to keep her money in the bank only for her own use. I even advised her in case that I became deceased, she must remove the money from our joint account, and not to let it to be combined with my trust. Still she wasn't happy, and she thought that I wanted to make her money disappear.

Another thing that I knew Mary would not remember was to accept the responsibilities of the house chores. I wrote on a piece of paper the responsibility for each one of us, and I wanted her to see and feel the equality between us for taking care of the house. But since she never followed the rules, I stopped nagging at her, and I learned to do

everything by myself. That way there weren't any disagreements.

My Dear God:

I don't know if it was other people's influence on her, or if it was her own mind that she couldn't see that I was trying to collect some money for her. When I realized that she was unhappy about depositing the five hundred dollars in the bank, I asked her to just put three hundred dollars, and I would pay for the utilities also. And we did that. I even offered her to see if she was not happy to live with me, I would be willing to help her in any way or shape.

It was true that I liked to have a house in the city. And it was true that I wanted to live in a neighborhood where I could hear the laughter and crying of children. But I also wanted to live in a very beautiful house, which reminds me more of the houses that I used to live in Iran. So after moving completely in, I started to think what I should do to the yard to remind me of my past.

Mary was not ever in the mood to find out what I was planning to do to the house. Most of the time when she heard that I was planning to make changes to the house, she would get angry or upset. She was thinking that because I was new in town, and it was difficult to find a good contractor who would finish the job without any complications, I might have lost my money, and then I would get mad and become sick over renovating the house. In a way she was right. Anyone that we talked to starting from neighbors to construction people, or anyone who had done a similar job, they had doubts that it was going to be easy and with no head aches. This kind of talks scared her, and she was trying to stop me from thinking of it. But the reason that I bought that house was to be able to bring some changes in there, to make it a cute and comfortable house for me. I did not want to have a show-off house. I just wanted to make it pleasant enough to remind me of my past.

But to find people to understand my plan and me was not easy. Mary knew an Iranian gentleman. His name was Yusoph, and I think he was in construction business. I had met him once, and he had given me the list of names of many Iranians, who were living in Visalia. He was planning to show me a way to get in touch with them, and make friends with them.

I asked Mary to invite him for dinner one night. I thought it was wise to talk to some knowledgeable people, and listen to their point of view. He actually didn't have much idea about the things that I wanted to do in the yard, but he mentioned that I could use the Yellow Pages, or adds in newspapers to find the person that I was looking for.

My plan was to change my yard to a completely different yard from all other houses. I wanted to get rid of all the grass covered, and replace it with stone and bricks. I wanted to plant roses and fruit trees, which I had memories with. I wanted big fountains in both front and back yards. I wanted eight to ten foot high fence all around the front and back

yard. And many more things had to be done here and there. Obviously it was a big step to take. Many times I didn't know where or how should I even start the project.

My Dear God:

I started calling people, and researching. Talking to some of contractors made me to forget about renovating the house. The way that they talked to me, it seemed that I had no luck to go after such a thing. "What to do now, what to do?"

First I wanted to keep the hot tub, and just move it to the corner of the yard. Since I didn't know that Mary might move out of my house, I was willing to go through as much trouble to be able to keep Mary happy. But when I realized that she was not showing any interest on using the whirlpool, I decided to completely get rid of it, and not to bother with it at all.

Although I didn't want to ask for any money for it still getting rid of it seemed impossible. Every day I was into Yellow Pages to find out who would like to get a hot tub, which seated eight people and it was in a good shape for free. Sometimes people referred me to another person, who they thought might like it. They gave me phone numbers, and asked me to try them. And I did. Finally one gentleman accepted to come and see it. He liked it, and decided to come back with a few helpers the next day. Luckily I did not have the fence up yet. So they drove their big truck through the neighbor's driveway. They dismantled it, and put it piece by piece in the truck, and drove away. That was a big headache, which we were able to get rid of. It wasn't easy, but I did it.

Every day I had pencil and paper in my hand to draw and measure my plan. I wasn't an architect or a contractor, but I wanted to do it right. Since I was planning to travel overseas for almost half of the year, I wanted to make my yard completely care free. No grass cutting every week, and no watering every day. I wanted to have my yard covered with bricks and concrete with different colors and different designs. And this had to be done only by my own constructive creation, which I was familiar with. The only problem was how do I go with it, or how to find a person or persons who could understand me hundred percent. I had to make it my goal, and thoughtfully go after it step by step regardless of what it took.

Since I was my own contractor I had to find an electrician, a sprinkler contractor, a mason to lay out the bricks, and the concrete job, a welder to make my fence, and many other trades. They all had to work together, while they did not know one another. Then I wanted to paint the outside, and get rid of the old paint, which was done very badly and was peeling off.

My Dear God:

I already had found my electrician through the yellow pages. His name was Richard Rivera, and he lived two streets away from our house. He seemed very nice. He installed

my garage door opener, which I had purchased from Sears. And he did my sensor lights. So I had him to do all the electrical work inside and outside of the house. And because he lived nearby, there was no problem to contact him.

Then through newspapers and the yellow pages I ran into the name Jerry C. Quair, who advertised cement and grading work. Since he was giving free estimates, I called him to arrange an appointment. He was a well-built young man, who would make you believe everything that he said. He had another gentleman with him, who seemed to be his assistant. His name was Danny Trijo, and he wrote his telephone number on the card also. After we came to an agreement, he decided to start the job, and we agreed on the price also. After I wrote the agreement for him to be signed, he never showed. And when I got him on the phone, he told me, "There was a death in the family, and I have to go to LA for a few days". Since I didn't hear from him after calling and calling him, I realized that he was not the kind of worker that I wished to deal with. Then I called his friend Danny to find out what had happened to him. Talking to Danny made me believe that first of all Danny had been doing most of the jobs; second Jerry had lied about everything, including the story about the death in his family. He had a huge fight with his wife, and he decided to disappear. But he volunteered to take the responsibility, and do the job with even lesser money.

My dear GOD, as I have said this, more and more I still believe that the bravery, the strength, and the self confidence that I found in myself in any action that I took, was only because your power was all around me without letting anything go wrong. Otherwise how could I have jumped to such a brave action, and ask Danny to sign the agreement between us, which I had written for him, and ask him to start the next week? Something inside of me must have been telling me, "Go ahead, there was nothing wrong with what you are doing. I will stand behind you, and help you to succeed in all your actions. While you have my support, you must not be afraid or be weak. Just open your eyes, and watch everything carefully, the rest will be with me". Yes, this powerful voice in my ears was the cause of my success. Otherwise I would have been demolished by now, and anything that I touched would have been destroyed.

My Dear God:

Danny had an assistant, Eddie. He was young, skinny, and full of ideas and plenty of talent, of which was completely unaware of. Since Danny agreed that as we went forward I would have the right to change some of my plans as long as I notified him ahead of time, I agreed.

While I was looking for a person to handle my sprinkler system, Danny volunteered to do it himself for additional money. Again we agreed on the plan and the price, and he signed the paper. Things were starting to go well until one day when I came home from my bridge game, I found out that Eddie and Danny had a big fight in front of the

neighbors, and Eddie had quit the job. I became furious. He was the one who had good ideas, and knew how to get to my design. Obviously I wanted him back on the job. Soon I called him to come over. He explained to me that Danny did not pay him the share of his money, while he was the one who did the most thinking and work. And he mentioned that it was his birthday that day. After I talked to him, I paid him one hundred dollars for his birthday gift, and I asked him to come back and finish the job. I complimented his talent and his know how on his work to bring him back in his working mood. So he agreed, and the next day he came back to work.

Meanwhile he introduced a fencer to me, since I had some misunderstanding with the person who was supposed to make my fence originally. His name was Mario Helo, who was working for a company, and he was working for himself as well. The story behind my fence man was unique by itself. I had been calling many fence men; they all came to my house to give me a free estimate. None of them were suitable for me. My neighbor from across the street, whom we had a very nice relationship with had an antique shop. At the same time his brother, who was a fence man was working with him, and it seemed that they were partners.

Prior to all these projects he always advised me that his brother was good, and he could do a nice job. On the other hand, when I was thinking of buying a few antique lampposts for my front yard, he asked me to look into buying them from him. And to make me more interested or more obligated, he brought up the subject of a high tuition for his two girls, who would soon be going to college, and that my contribution would be a great help to him. So I not only liked him, but also I wanted to do something for him.

The same way that I asked other fence men to give me a free estimate, I asked his brother to come and see my plans, and give me an estimate. After he gave me an estimate, and told me the price per foot, I mentioned to him that those were not my final measurements. "I might change it, and I might have to ask you to give me a different price". He agreed and we were waiting for the time to come.

My Dear God:

Meanwhile one day Mary and I went to his antique shop to look at the lampposts. Between all what he had, I just liked the one that I was interested in before going to his shop, and he had given me such a high price that I started bargaining for it. He was asking two thousand and five hundred dollars for that lamppost. And I thought it was too high for me. So when he didn't come down on the price, I told him, "I have to think about it".

Now that Mary and I were standing under the lamppost, I tried to convince myself, "I must have this lamp, because it was a copy of my house, and it would match my house". But Mary turned her eyes at me and said, "You want to pay this much money for one lamp? What a waste of money? Do you know what you are doing?"

While I knew that she was right, I asked the neighbor, who was at the shop, about that lamppost. She told me that it was sold. Since it was the only one there, I felt like talking to her husband, and find out if it had been a final sale? When I talked to him, he said, "Oh no, it was not sold. I still can sell it to you for three thousand dollars". I was shocked. "At first it was twenty five hundred dollars, which I was not happy to pay for, and I was bargaining with you. Now that you see I am really interested to buy it, you change your words and say "I told you it was three thousand dollars from the beginning." How can you say such a thing? How can you change your words like this?" So I told him, "I have a lot of thinking to do. This is not a little money that I can decide on it so quickly. I have to wait a while." And I dropped the conversation.

Later on I called him again, and asked if I could ask his brother to come and measure the front and the back yards together, and give me another estimate.

Without discussing it with his brother or wasting any time, as if he was mad or had fight with someone, with a voice that was very new to me he said, "I don't know Shamci. I don't understand your English, and my brother's time is valuable to him. The same way that doctors do not give a free estimate to anyone, he is not available to give free estimate."

I was surprised, shocked and very hurt. From the time that we moved into our house, he was always very friendly, and we even invited each other to our houses. I couldn't find a reason that he would talk to me in that manner. But after I was introduced to Mr. Mario Helo, and he gave me his price, and showed me the album of his work all around Visalia, I realized that dealing with my neighbor, was not actually a good idea. And because GOD did not want me to be sorry, or get hurt, he made it possible that my neighbor himself pulled himself away from my job. This is why I believe that God never left me alone. He made sure that something came up and break the wrong deal for me. With the new measurements all around the house, the neighbor's price was twenty thousand dollars more than what Mr. Helo's price was. You see, my dear God, if it was not your power behind this transaction I would not be able to finish the fence, and neither I would be able to finish the yard and my landscape in such a peaceful way that it happened.

My Dear God:

Since I was confused from neighbor's act, and meanwhile I did not want to see my neighbor hurt for any reason, the next day when the whole family were in the yard, I crossed the street first to say hello to them, and second to apologize to them for any inconvenience that I had caused him or his brother.

When I got there the older brother was there also. While he didn't have a smile on his face, I said hello to all of them, and I asked them that if they did not understand my English to please ask me to repeat myself. And I said to him, "I am very sorry if I asked your brother to come and give me estimate for the fence around the yard. Since everyone else wanted to do it for free, I assumed that his estimate would be free also. If you had told me before I asked him, I would have never asked him to come and do my job. Because a person who charges for an estimate as much as for a doctor's visit, his price would be too high for me, and I would never deal with such a costly fencing contractor. If you had told me before, you obviously could have made it much easier on my decisions.

After I said this, his brother turned to me and said, "My dear, this is not a kind of English that people cannot understand. I can understand you more than I could understand others." At this time I apologized again for wasting their time, and told him, "You are a nice family man, and I like you and your family. And I don't want anything to jeopardize our good neighborly relationship".

When I left them, everybody was happy. Before this incident I always asked him for his opinion on things, which I wanted to do around the house. After that conversation I was willing to do it again. Since we lived across each other, we stayed friends.

So I became a contractor, who was on job at six o'clock in the morning. Through Yellow Pages and referrals I found some sincere workers to do my job. Since they knew that I was there every minute of the day, they were following my instructions step by step. One day Danny told Mary, "When this job is over, you should find your mom another full time job. Otherwise she will be bored". One of the lazy workers, who did not like my discipline, called me a "Hulk" behind my back. I didn't mind it as long as he was doing his job.

My Dear God:

I had a group of professionals like an electrician, a fencer, a mason, and a landscaper. They each had a crew of three or more workers. I had to make sure that each trade communicated with each other before they started on the job. For instance, the electrician must run some wiring through the whole yard before they poured the concrete. It was the same for the Gas Company representative, who would have to run the gas hose through the yard, before they could start the concrete work. So if they didn't communicate, most likely things would have gone wrong, and we might have had ended up opening the concrete afterwards. And in that case not only it would have been very costly, but also it could have been a real disaster, which I was not looking forward to.

In the middle of pouring concrete I realized that the way that Danny was handling the job, spending two thousand dollars on the concrete and the workers, pretty soon we would run out of his contract money. And then I would end up with an unfinished yard, or I had to spend extra from my own pocket. So I decided to take over completely. I learned how to measure and order the cement for each section of the yard, and I paid them with a check right away. And I paid the workers every day, as it was schedules. Thanks God everything went well, and with many more problems, which we had with many of the workers, still we finished the job, and I was able to breath. But this was just a part of it. To deal with the city of Visalia, the painter and the fencer was yet to come.

Between all other things, which had happened during the construction, this one was

sticking out to show my real stupidity. I knew that it had been my soft heartedness, which had caused me all the miseries throughout my lifetime. When I look back, I see that if from the beginning I stood firm, and if I didn't listen to my heart, the things that came upon me could have been avoided.

One of the concrete workers, who was a young, skinny, ugly and almost crippled man, captured my feelings. I felt he needed more attention than others. Some days I made them lunch. I offered them hot or cold drinks. And I always paid attention to see what he needed. I was shocked when I found out that he was married. I was wondering who could his wife be. At the time that I was paying their daily checks, one day a woman came at my door, and introduced herself as Alex's wife. While she was shivering and almost crying, she told me, "My daughter has been murdered. I have no money to bury her. Alex told me you might be able to help us. Please do something for me. I don't know who to turn to".

My Dear God:

I sympathized with her, and I asked her how it had happened. While she was crying she said, "She had a boy friend. They were both into drugs, and they killed her". I didn't even know that Alex was married, yet that he had a daughter that age. It did not sound right to me. When I asked other workers, they agreed with her, and they said the reason that Alex had been off for a few days was that he was trying to help his wife. And they added that the girl was from her previous marriage. At that time I started believing her. Not only that, but I felt, "What if this had happened to my daughter, and I did not have anybody to come to my rescue. I asked her, "Why don't you ask your family or his family? She said, "I had, none of them had money to spare". I thought and thought. I realized that if she was not in need, she would not have been at my door. I must help her somehow. Then I told her, "I will write you a check for two hundred dollars. And because I know that you need money at this time, I will not deduct it from his daily checks. But he must work for me extra when I need his help". She agreed, and I gave her the check. But not only he refused to return my favor, but he was the only one who asked for more money, and he asked other workers to quit the job if I did not accept their proposal. Even after the completion of the job his wife kept calling me asking for the money, which she thought I owed them.

Another important part of this renovation was to follow the City codes of conduct and their requirements. I had to have a permit for extending the gas pipe to the end of the yard for the BBQ grill. I needed the permit for the height of the brick pillars around the house. And I had to have a permit for positioning the gate 10 feet away from the edge of the road, which I was not aware of. As I discussed it with the workers, they knew that it had to be only 10 feet. I measured the distance between all the neighbor's gates to the edge of the road, and they were all 10 feet. So I thought we were on the right track since everyone agreed to 10 feet.

After the concrete work in the front yard was finished, and we were ready to start the iron fence, I scheduled an appointment with the City to check the plans, and obtain the permit.

When the city inspector came and said, "You must have 12 feet away from the road" I almost fainted. I thought, "I had done my best to study every step, and I asked the workers, who knew the city rules, and I had measured every neighbor's driveway, how did I manage to go wrong? What can I do to talk to city and let them know that I had followed the City's rule by measuring the neighbor's driveways and talking to my construction crew?" But I had no idea what to do, unless I go to the City and explain my yard plan to the higher ranked personnel. Otherwise I had to remove the concrete in the front yard in its entirety, and move the plan three feet farther away from the driveway. Not only it was very costly, but also I couldn't ask the workers to come back and finish that job again. I ran into plenty of heart aches to be able to finish that part. How could the city ask me to have wider driveway than other people on my street? This was not fair at all. The city had to follow the same rule for everyone on one street, rather than different rules for each one of them. I couldn't sleep that night. I couldn't wait to go to the City the next day and find out what was that all about.

My Dear God:

Before I go into details, I must mention that since my house was one of the historic homes I knew that I had to have a permit prior to even touching the house. So after my plans for renovating were complete, I mailed it to the Historic Preservation Advisory Committee, HPAC #98-02, and I enclosed this letter to the staff representative, Mr. Andy Chamberlain:

City of Visalia
315 East Acequia Ave., Visalia, CA 93291

Community Development
Planning Division
Tel: (559) 713-4369 Fax: (559) 713-4814

October 11, 2002

Shamci Rafani
616 N. Encina
Visalia, CA 93291

RE: Historic Structures Recognition

Dear Mrs.Rafani:

This letter is in recognition of your house located at 616 N. Encina. The house located at 616 N. Encina is listed on the Local Historic Register as a "Background Vernacular Structure," and is also located in the Historic District.

If you have any questions please call me at (559) 713-4348.

Sincerely,

Jason Pausma
Assistant Planner

When I started to renovate my house, this letter was sent to me that I have proof that my house is recognized by Historic Structures. This was needed for the changes I was making to the house.

GIFT LETTER

DATE: 3-23-2000

TO WHOM IT MAY CONCERN:

I, (We), Shamci Rafani

am (are) giving my (our) daughter, Mary Rafani

the amount of $ twenty five thousand dollars 25,000

The property is located at

This is an outright gift from me (us) and does not have to be repaid. There is not repayment expected or implied, written or verbal, in the form of cash or by future service or services by the person(s) receiving the gift, the mortgagor(s).

This gift (will be) (was) made on paid on the closing date.

from the funds on deposit as follows:

Name of Institution: Bank of America

Address: 212 E Main street Visalia CA. 93291

Acct No.: ______ Type of Acct Money Market

Shamci Rafani
(signature)

(signature)

616, N. Encina, Visalia CA. 93291
(address, city, state, zip code)

559) 636-6254
(phone number)

If additional accounts are needed to verify total amount of gift, please provide similar information on reverse side of the letter.

Contact mr. Jon Haskins at BA (559) 739-3787

"I (We) the mortgagor(s), acknowledge that we have received this gift under the term shown above."

Mary Rafani (daughter)
(name & relationship)

Shamci Rafani (mother)
(name & relationship)

This letter was prepared for tax purposes. It shows that this amount was a gift to Mary from her mother to purchase a new house.

We are at Cedar Point, Michigan. The person whose hand was always on my shoulder or in my hand, and looked happy, was unhappy to do so after Malakuti's death. In this picture, he is the only husband who did so. Left to right: Naheed, Louise, Susan, Aghdass Shushtari, me, Iraj, Naser, Aghdass Barkhordari, and Dr. Shushtari

Please pay attention. In the next picture everyone is happy and laughing except Iraj. If I truly write about how I feel when I see these pictures, you will probably laugh at me. But you do not understand my feelings for Iraj to know that even then I was upset to see him that way. I always wanted the best for him. How could I sit and see him suffer this way? He was as dear as my children to me. I had given up all my siblings and my parents to be with him and make him happy. Why must he suffer like this? Why? This was a New Year's Eve party in Dr. Panah's house. Left to right: Nancy Neel, Roshanak, Badri, Louise, Mojgan, me, and Mary. In the front: Partow, Farzad, and Masseh. In the back: Roshanak, Roozbeh Malakuti, Iraj, Aghdass Shushtari, Dr. Shushtari, Jalal, Rohan, Lisa, Dr. Neel, Roozbeh B., Susan, and Marjon We had become so Americanized that on this night Iraj kissed Badri on her lips, who then said, "Can't Iranians learn?"

Reza Mahajer, Susan, Rohan, Jalal, me, Iraj, and Nazy. I wonder what happened to the days that we didn't know the Malakutis. Those days the people were all nice. No one was after anyone's wife or husband. Why did they come to Michigan? Why?

These pictures are so valuable to me. The short person in the middle is my father. He got married at the age of twenty. He had a son at the age of twenty one. This is the time that he was working for the government at the beginning of his parenthood. He was the president of his department and the people next to him in the picture were his co-workers.

He is standing next to the people who were in his room.

Happy
Sweetest Day
You're our sweetheart
Always.
Your men,
Iraj & Maseeh

This was the card that I found on beautiful flowers in a big vase, which was delivered to my neighbors, the Barkhordaris. I used to receive many gifts on many different occasions, but never on a Sweetest Day. I had never received it from anyone, especially not from Iraj. Please pay attention to the writing on the card. My children were completely aware of Iraj and Badri's affair. As you read in the book, you will see that they tried to bring their father to his senses. Maseeh had made his father order the flowers with a card that said, "You're our sweetheart. From your men: Iraj and Maseeh." This is from 1993. Iraj and Badri's affair was already out of hand. I was desperately searching for an answer to my problem, when my poor children were trying to cheer me up by doing things like this. I really am so sorry for them. I wish their father was dead, and he could never put them in such emotional situations. What is strange about this gift is that it was the only gift I received for this occasion, and it was also the last gift from any of them. On the day that I received this gift, we were having lunch with Mrs. Aghdass Barkhordari who was living with Naheed. Mrs. Tabatabaii was entertaining us by telling our fortune by reading our coffee cups. When it was my turn she told me, "Right now you will go home and you will receive a gift that you have never received before, or you will never receive in the future." I didn't believe it then. All those years I have been wondering how she knew it. Was she there or what?

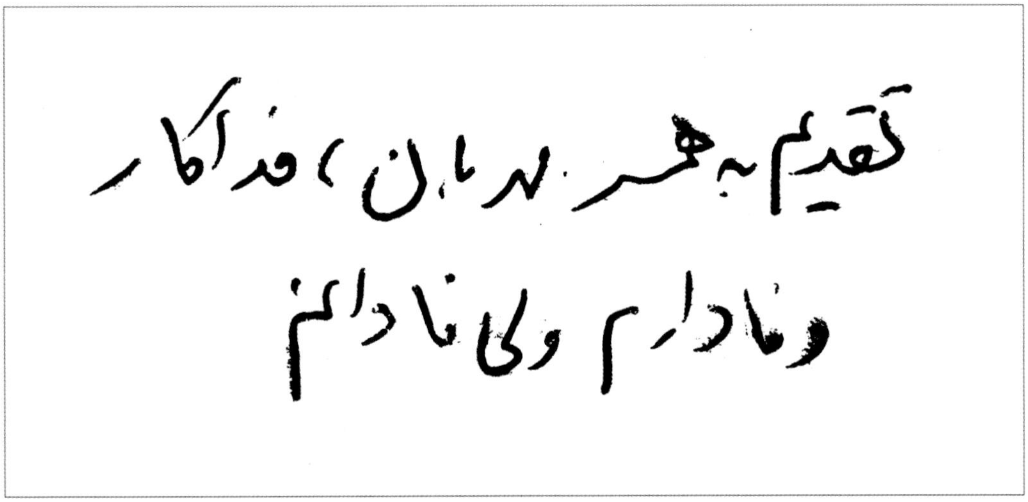
تقدیم به همسر مهربان، فداکار
وفادار ولی نادانم

On the back of the card he had written, "To my kind, forgiving, and faithful but naive spouse."

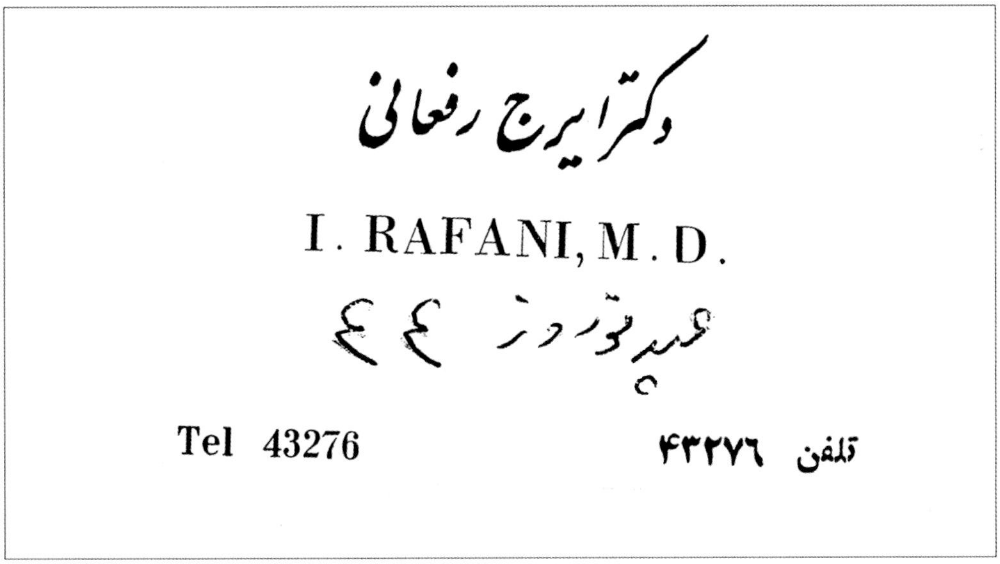
دکتر ایرج رفعانی
I. RAFANI, M.D.
عید نوروز ٤٤
Tel 43276
تلفن ۴۳۲۷۶

This was Iraj's business card that he gave me with his gift for Norooz (our New Year) in Iran at the time of his affair.

...we're flocking together
to wish you
a wonderful
Mother's Day!
LOTS OF LOVE

He had signed the name of my children on this card as well.
Oh, I wish I could write what I felt when I received the card.
Well, it is not important now.

Americard

AMERICAN GREETINGS

100M 1613-1C

From All of Us

Like birds of a feather...

Wishing you happiness...

...not just for today,
but always.

نوروزت مبارک
قربانت - ایرج

سال ۱۹۸۳

This card was sent to me on our New Year's Day which is the first day of spring. March, twenty first of each year is our Eaid (New Year). Although we had talked about it and the whole world celebrated the beginning of spring, my children would not remember that this day was as important to me, as their New Year was to them.

AMERICAN GREETINGS

75M 0202-1B

On Mother's Day

Sometimes I wonder why I kept these cards to begin with. Did I know that he was not who he said he was? Or did it happen so I could write about them and publish them? Whatever the reason, they always remind me of that time. They make me hate whatever he had done for me with the name of love.

With warmest wishes for a happy day!

Love
[illegible]

1986

May it be yours
on your birthday
and always.
1985

Many of these cards speak for themselves.
There is no need for me to try to explain them.

AMERICAN GREETINGS

100B 396-78A

Happiness is the best gift
anyone could have...

Iraj Had bought a gift for me from Bonwit Teller. The writing on it was as simple as it could be. At this point of his life, he was so confused and lost in his own world that finding the right way was impossible for him. If he wasn't able to see his children's suffering, what could I expect from him?

BONWIT TELLER

Dear Shama

wish you a very

Happy Birthday

Love - Tiaj

1986

Happy Birthday,
Honey!

Have I told you
lately, Honey
That I love you very much?
Have I mentioned
that you give my life
A brighter, happier touch?
If I haven't,
let me tell you now
That no matter where I go
You're always
in my thoughts and dreams
Because I love you so!

with lots of love and happiness

This is the kind of card I used to receive from Iraj before Malakuti got killed by an unidentified person in his office. What could have happened to him? In all other cards after that murder, Iraj's words changed from a loving husband to an outsider who is forced to send a card to his loving wife. He used to tell his wife, "Honey, have I ever told you how much I love you?" But after knowing what kind of a woman Badri was, he lost the control of his behavior and changed to a person he never wanted to be. Maybe, he was lying to me to make himself look good in my eyes, so his children and I would believe his words and his love for us. I am sure this was the case. He was neither a truthful person to himself nor to his children. No wonder Mojgan who was thirteen at the time wrote in her diary, "After Malakuti died my father hates me."

With Love, Honey

On Your Birthday

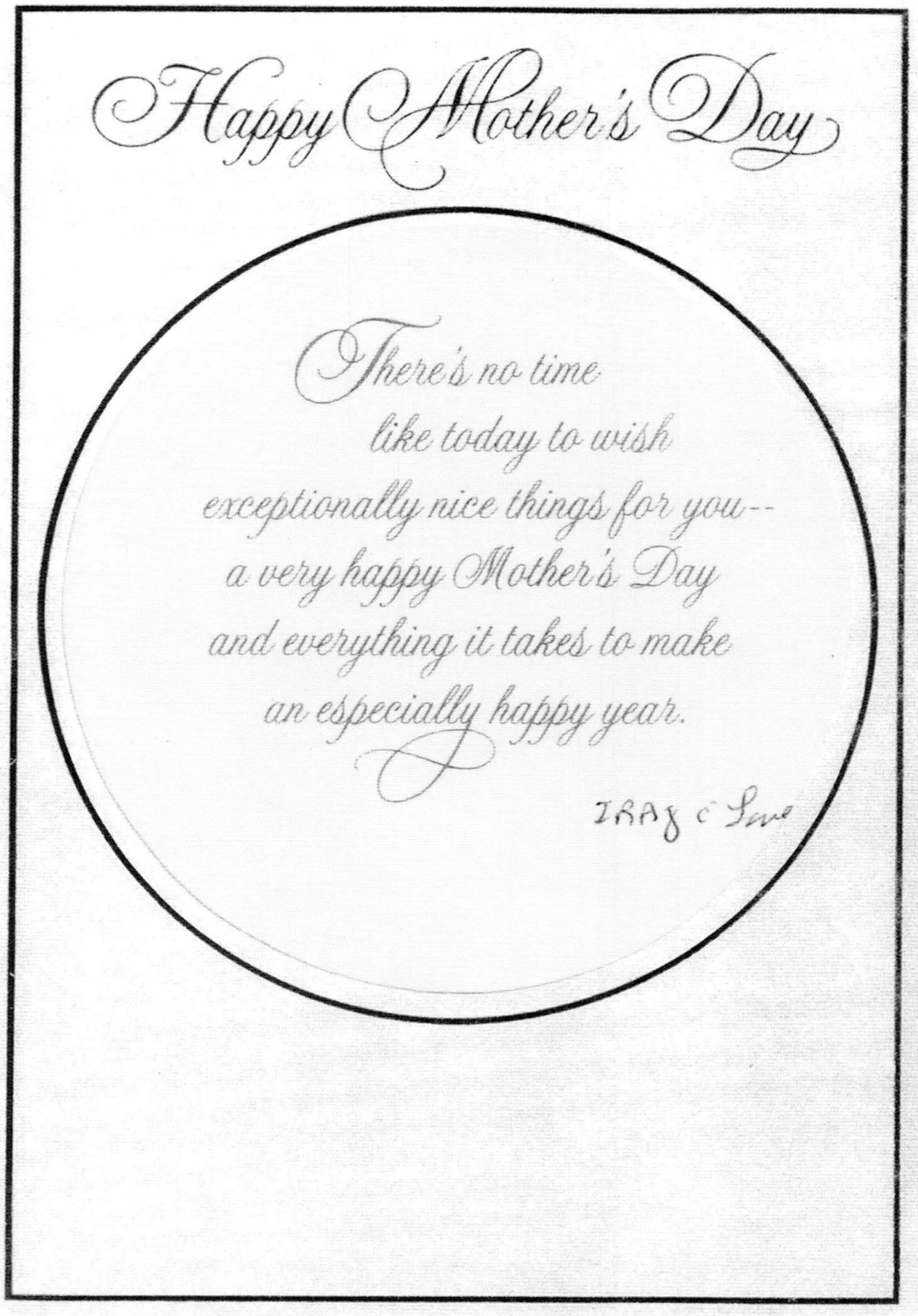

Happy Mother's Day
There's no time
like today to wish
exceptionally nice things for you--
a very happy Mother's Day
and everything it takes to make
an especially happy year.

Some of his cards do not need any explanation; they speak for themselves.

"A wish for joy is a joy in itself."

Hallmark

Happy Birthday

Life's Best Always

For today...
hours of sunshine
and wonderful things,
For tomorrow...
bright, blue skies,
and nice happenings,
For every day after...
a heart filled with laughter,
and all the contentment
that happiness brings!

Best wishes
[illegible]
1987

My comment to the writing on the back is, “Yes Iraj, you brought laughter to my heart years later when I laughed at you, not with you.”

AMERICAN GREETINGS

Genuine Parchment

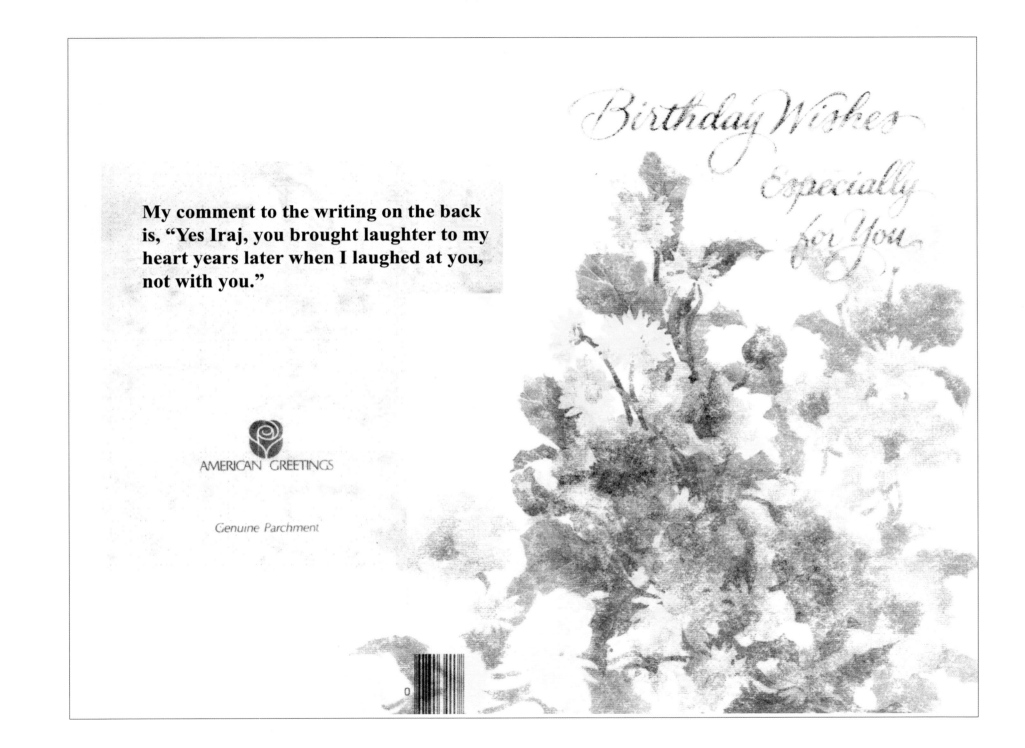

Birthday Wishes
Especially
for You

AMERICAN GREETINGS

75M 0201-2A

I have asked myself many times that if I was so good, what caused you to do such a humiliating thing. Didn't you hate men who went your way? Or were you trying to keep me in the dark as long as I was in love with you?

A wish for every happiness
This day can bring to you
For you deserve
the best there is
And plenty of it, too!

Happy Mother's Day

wil Love
IRAJ & Kids

PX 76F

Ambassador Cards

How beautiful! He always wanted happiness for me, especially for putting up with his mistress for eight years and inviting her to my house since I wouldn't invite her among our friends.

Have a bright and happy holiday season.

Dear Shamsi
wish a very happy
& successful new year
with love - ZRDJ.

AMERICAN GREETINGS
Americard

From all of Us Mother

on Mother's Day

There is
no love more beautiful
than a mother's love –
no word more beautiful
than "Mother"

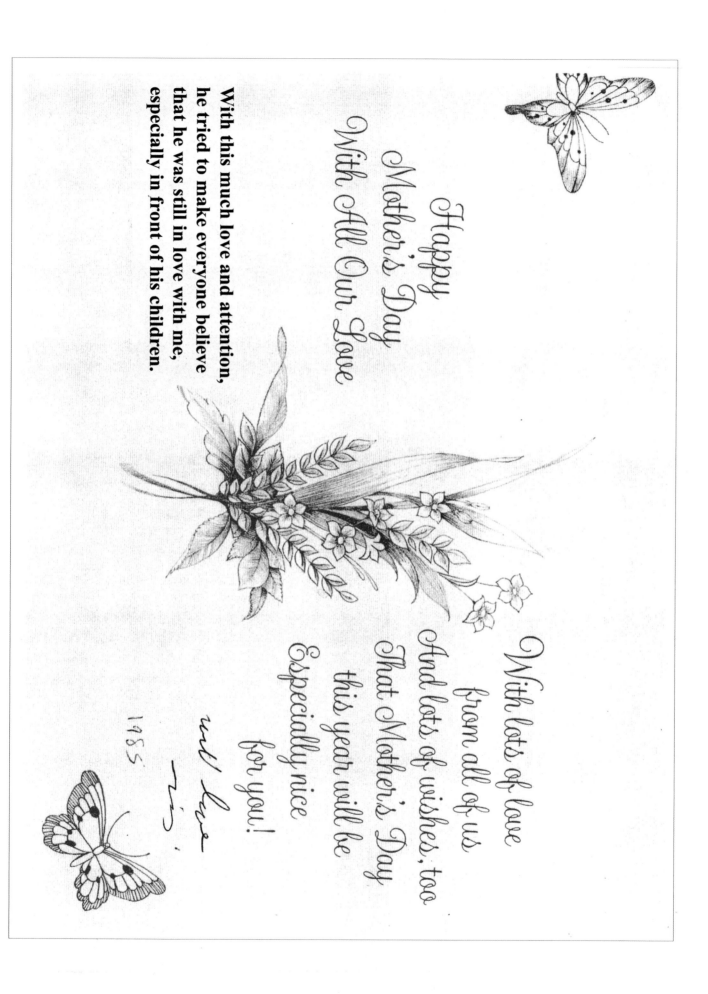

Happy
Mother's Day
With All Our Love

With lots of love
from all of us
And lots of wishes, too
That Mother's Day
this year will be
Especially nice
for you!

with love

1985

**With this much love and attention,
he tried to make everyone believe
that he was still in love with me,
especially in front of his children.**

AMERICAN GREETINGS

+ C 8013T +

This is from a loving husband to his loving wife. Don’t you think I had the right to get mad after I received it?

Many good wishes
for a wonderful
holiday season!

Best wishes for the New Year

—[illegible]

On
your birthday,
especially...

AMERICAN GREETINGS

Touch

75STB 396-77K

Wow, this is a card from a husband who used to write four-page letters to his loving wife. What can I write about my feelings when I received this card? I just put it away and pretended that I never received it.

. . . may you be blessed
with happiness
and contentment.

with Love
AZUL — Ming & Kids

Mr. Andy Chamberlain:
11-06-97

I am Shamci Rafani from 616 N. Encina Street. As I talked to you on the phone regarding renovating my property, I will enclose the plan and the description for you to see that my plan is only working on the yard, and I am not planning to bring any changes on or inside of this historic home. If you have any questions understanding the plan, please don't hesitate to call me at (209) 636-6254 between 9~11 in the morning. If you think that I need an approval for this renovation, please send me one, I will be glad to start beautifying the street of our city.

Sincerely

Shamci Rafani

Shamci Rafani

After a week or so I received this letter from the city:

HISTORIC PRESERVATION ADVISORY COMMITTEE
HPAC # 98-02
STATEMENT OF ACTION

APPLICANT:
Shamci Rafani

LOCATION:
616 N. Encina

PROJECT:
Brick and wrought iron fence in the front yard.

On March 25, 1998, the Historic Preservation Advisory committee of the City of Visalia reviewed and approved application HPAC #98-02 subject to the following conditions:

1. That the project be developed in substantial compliance with the site plan Exhibits "A" and "B", and that any significant changes be brought before this committee for review prior to their occurrence.

2. That the maximum height be 4 feet, except the light fixtures, which may be slightly higher based upon staff approval.

3. That any gates will need to be sliding gates that go to the sides or fold back onto the property only, no gates may swing out over the public right-of-way.

4. That all other city codes and ordinances are met.

This approval was based on the finding that the proposal conforms to the spirit and intent of the Historic Preservation Element of the Visalia general plan.

A building permit may not be issued and construction may not begin until 10 days after the committee's decision. This is to allow appeals to be submitted as prescribed in Article 26, section 7712 of the city of Visalia Historic Preservation District Ordinance.

Andy Chamberlain Staff Representative

We exchanged this letter and many more letters regarding the installation of the iron fence and the pillars. In none of these letters were mentioned the width of the driveway. So as everyone else assumed it was to be the same width as the other parts of the street.

My Dear God:

So the day that inspector came to my house and did not approve the plan, I just went crazy. I was sick till the next morning that I went to their office. While I was trying to explain the whole ordeal to the lady at the desk, I was crying. I asked her to take me to a person who could do something for me. I wanted to talk to her superior. When she noticed that I was very upset, she asked me to sit down and wait for him. When Mr. Chamberlain came and talked to me, he was very nice and apologetic, why he had been late to see me. After a lengthy time that he listened to me, I insisted that he had to come to my house and judge by himself. I insisted that he gave me an appointment to come to my house and tell me what I should do. He agreed.

The day that he came to my house, he was very pleased with the whole plan. And he thought that it was done in a good taste. But there was only one problem, and that was that thirteen years ago the city of Visalia's Historic Committee had approved that the width of the driveways must be twelve feet instead of ten feet.

In a very positive voice, I told him, "From the beginning I had tried to get permit for whatever change I was going to bring into this house. Now that I had finished the concrete work in the front yard, and I ran the electric conduits, constructed the pillars, installed the lights, and the water fountain, I would not touch them in order to move the whole plan two feet farther. As a matter of fact, if from the beginning that I applied for permit of any kind it was mentioned to me the exact width of the fence to the edge of the street, it would have had a better view of my house. Now, with the amount of the money that I had spent, I was not going to redo it. You must find a way for me Mr. Chamberlain. Please do something for me".

He knew that I was not going to change the plan whatsoever. And he was happy with the way the yard was. After some thinking he told me, "I think we can do something for you. Since this width is uniform with the rest of the houses in this street, there is a way to deal with it. You must write a letter to the City of Visalia, and assure them that in case of necessity, the city will be allowed to push your pavement back with your own expenses".

I was very happy that he found a solution to my problem. I agreed to go the next day and write that letter to the City, and sign it. I thought whatever the City wanted to do to other houses was okay to do it to mine. The next day I went to the office to sign that paper. Here is the paper, which I signed:

The City of Visalia
315 East Acequia
Visalia,CA 93291

April 13,1998
Shamci Rafani
616 N.Encina Street Visalia,CA 93291

Dear Mrs. Rafani,

The City will allow your wrought iron fence with brick pilasters to be located along Encina Street under the following conditions:

1. Your homeowner's insurance names the City as additional insured with regards to at least the area in the right-of-way on Encina Street where the fence is being built.

2. Mrs. Rafani agrees to remove the fence as the City determines the fence is in the way, including conflicts with City or utility projects in the City's right-of-way.

3. Shamci Rafani signs below with notarized signature, signifying agreement with all conditions of this letter.

Sincerely,
John S. Dutton,
City Engineer

Signed signifying agreement with all conditions above:
Shamci Rafani and I signed above the line.

And this was the story of getting permit to be able to finish the renovating my beautiful house. There were many more cases like this, which brought tears in my eyes, but none of them was like this that I had to stand in the office and cry my real tears.

At this time of my life I was finding my own self again. Things were going well, and I was ready to start the construction on the house. Mary had her own office which was only ten minutes walking distance from our house. The relationship between Mary and I was just beautiful. She was doing her best to get to know the city, and she tried to make herself known by involving herself with many different volunteer works. Meanwhile she got a job at the City Defense Department by the advice of a good friend. The job was very heavy for her, and it took many long and hard hours of her time. The hours that she was spending on that job were so many that after she calculated her income, it came down to almost three dollars an hour. She had accepted that job to be able to defend the kids, who she thought were abused. So with that heavy load of paperwork she decided to hire a secretary in the office.

My Dear God:

She hired an African American gentleman, who used to be her client. He was very nice, well built, good mannered. He was working as a security officer prior working for Mary. Although he was almost Mary's age, he had five children: two from his first marriage, and three from his second one. We became friends. He invited us to his house, and we invited them to our house once in a while. He was a Black Muslim with a strong faith, and was practicing it at home and his daily life. I admired him for his courage and faithfulness. To me it seemed that he was a nice father and a nice husband. His wife also was working with the Humane Society in the City of Visalia. At that time he was thinking of going to school to become a paralegal. Since after a few years of working with Mary he was able to change his job, I don't know if he was able to pursue his dream.

My Dear God:

During that time one day, Mojgan called me and said, "Mom, please get ready. On such a day I will be in Sacramento. I already have contacted a real estate agent to show me a house. There are several houses available for sale. Since we sold the house, it is best time to find another one. I have rented a room for both of us at the Youth Center, and I will pick you up in front of the bus station on such a day. Please be there, we wil1 have fun together". I agreed, and I was there on the appointed day.

The Youth Center was in the city of Sacramento, and was very cultural since people who came over were from countries all around the world. Some of them couldn't speak English. There was a big kitchen for as many students as they wanted to prepare their food, and there was a refrigerator for them to keep their food in it. There were few stoves to make it easy on students. It was a multi-cultural place. The only drawback was that everyone had to leave their room before ten o'clock in the morning. The reason was that they had to use the house for different purposes, like meetings or other occasions. Although the place was mainly for students, older people could be there as well.

The first night there was an older lady at our table, who loved the place enough to come there most every year. We had dinner together, and we shared some thoughts about the world in general. Since we were not allowed to come back before five o'clock in the afternoon, we had enough time to go and look for houses, go to lunch, and at night we went to dinner and movies.

We were there for several days. Between the houses that we saw there were two of them that appealed to us. They both were located on the lake. One was good for my lifestyle since I was looking mainly for a beautiful view and a great landscaping. It had an extremely long lake frontage and a beautiful garden in the back. It was very well and expensive built. But since the lake was a manmade one water skiing was not allowed there.

And this is the view from my backyard after it was completed.

This is the view of my house after it was completed.

This is the sidewall.

As you see all of them are tired of me taking pictures of them. Left to right: Maseeh, Maryam, Afsaneh, and Said are sitting in my backyard and enjoying teasing me.

I am sitting on the stairs to my entrance.

This is the view of my backyard fence at night. As you see, some of the lights are off. The reason is that I was away. One neighbor said, "If you want to know if Shamci is here or not, just look at these lights."

I am enjoying my son's gift for Mother's Day. What a nice feeling! But, oh God when they forget to even call you, you feel unwanted and forgotten.

While I was feeling good that day, I tried on one of Mary's hats. It didn't look bad on me at all.

By myself sitting on my backyard patio. It was a nice weather.

Look at this picture please. Look at my three most beautiful children. They were visiting me in my new house which I was sharing with Mary in Visalia. In my mind, we were celebrating my freedom from homelessness. I was able to establish a place of my own without being a burden on anyone, specially my children.

In one occasion, we are at my house. Since I was the one taking this picture, I was in a hurry to sit with the rest of the group. Left to right: Arman, Helen-Afsaneh's friend, Maseeh, Afsaneh, Said with Helen's son on his lap, and Mary.

This is the night that I had invited some of my neighbors and Bridge players to come and meet my sister Ezzat, my sister-in-law Afsar, my niece Negin, and her daughter Yasamin.

Here we are in my house again. Left to right: Mojgan, Mary, Joe, Maseeh, me, and Afsaneh.

The top picture was taken of Shila, Arsham, and Mehdi for Norooz, our New Year. Isn't it beautiful? They all look good, especially Arsham.

Left to right: Mojdeh Orandi, me, Fali, and Shila. It was a hot day and the kids were impatient.

Here, we were sitting and enjoying Lake Tahoe. We were staying in Mojgan's house. It was a lovely day.

There were times that my children fussed about Mother's Day, and sent me beautiful flowers. These flowers are from one of those times. I took a picture with them so I could remember them on the days that they either forgot my birthday or Mother's Day.

Here, we were invited to Anna's brother's wedding. Someone took this picture from us.

We first visited Belgium when Ali and Ehsan were studying there. Since their parents were not able to go and visit them, we decided to go there after we had visited Ezzat in England.

So, that one was out of order for Mojgan, since they were only interested in water skiing on that lake. And the price was much lower than the second one.

The second house was located on Combi Lake in Auburn city near Sacramento. It was located in a wooded area, almost three stories above the lake, with wooden steps that took you to the deck. The house was tri-level, and the first level was a finished and complete building by itself and had a separate entrance. It had a bath, a nice sized kitchen, and a comfortable place to live in. The second level was their main living area, with a huge kitchen, and a connecting room with standing bed on the wall and a big balcony across the whole living area. The kitchen took you down to the lake by steps. The house was beautiful and very well kept. Its residents, who had rented the house, wished that they were able to buy that house. It was perfect house for Mojgan and Joe. I think it was five thousands square feet, which was very big for two people. But if we remember Mojgan was raised in a seven thousands square feet house with an indoor pool and eight bathrooms. So it was nothing new to her. I liked the house and so did Mojgan. After looking at it again and again, it was the time for Mojgan to calculate her budget and find out if it was doable for them. Since Joe was at his job and couldn't be there with Mojgan, she faxed him all the pictures and talked to him about the financial part of their purchase. It was obvious that they could not come to a conclusion because Joe was flying to Sacramento on the weekend.

My Dear God:

At that time my job was done, and after spending fun time together I returned to Visalia. Being the mother that I was I was worried that what if they had not calculated their payments for each month correctly. What if they became short on the mortgage payment, car payments, boat payments, their insurances, and not to forget their monthly expanses, which were never little? So as soon as I got home I wrote her a letter. I explained to her all the payments, which she had to pay every month without exception. I calculated all her expenses, which could have come up to seven to eight thousands dollars a month. Joe's job in Sacramento still was up in the air. Mojgan herself did not have a steady job. "What if you buy this house and things do not work out as they were planned? It is so easy to lose a house or a car if you cannot pay the mortgage on time. It had happened to many people, and it might happen to you if you don't handle it with care and thoughtfulness. One thing I don't want to happen to you is to see you hurt over losing your house and your money". And I mailed the letter to her right away. I thought there are times that we can take our chances, and things will go great. But what if once it didn't? God forbid, I did not want that to happen to Mojgan, because if it did happen to her there would be nothing to back her up. It would have been the end of Mojgan's happiness and also mine.

I don't know if this letter hurt her or helped her. I just tried to let her know that any step she took in her life must be taken with thoughtfulness. Wasn't this beautiful my dear GOD? At the same time that she bought this house, she was done with selling her other

house. I was able to sleep all through the night. But this was a great deal of worrying on my mind. Now I was ready to go and help her in her new house. I don't know if she thought of that house as of her dream house. I certainly thought it was a dream house. Just like I did when I wanted to move from one place to the next, Mojgan had done it also. She had packed all her stuff into big or small boxes, and she had labeled them all. She had sent her furniture, her cars and her boat with a moving company. They were in the house before the movers arrived. I was there a few days later.

My Dear God:

It was just two weeks before Christmas of 1997. We cleaned up and we placed every piece of furniture and the dishes, and other things in their places as if we had moved in long time ago. Mojgan was surprised of the way things were happening so fast. Many times she told me, "Mom, I just don't know how you did it. And I can't thank you enough. I was thinking that it might take a few months to put the stuff away. Thanks so very much Mom".

She had planned to have her family over for Christmas dinner. We did the shopping and prepared the turkey and the rest of the things, plus the great pumpkin pies and other desserts like someone had catered it for us. The family was Maseeh, Mary, Mojgan and I. And she invited one of her neighbors with his wife to have dinner with us. It was a wonderful feeling to be able to manage the whole thing successfully. Before the year changes to 1998, at 4:00 PM we served our Christmas dinner in a very happy atmosphere.

Now please my dear God, nature, or light, or power, whoever you are, shouldn't I believe that you were with me all these times, and that it was you who made it possible for me to get whatever I had asked for? Don't you think that it was you who gave me the courage, the strength, and the wisdom to decide right and receive a good result? I know that no matter how many times of the day I thank you, still I am short in thanking you. So many thanks for your support. I just hope that you stay with me all the times. Thank you!

After the earthquake of 1993 in LA, and the damages to Maseeh's house he was thinking of changing the house rather than fixing it, and especially because he bought his house to satisfy my way of lifestyle rather than it being his own taste. Not that he did not like his house, but now that he had to re build it anyway, and I was not living with him any more, he liked to make bigger changes. He always mentioned. "This house is just right for you Mom! It is located in the suburb, and yet it is close to the city, which you like to walk and see people." He was right. It was behind Ventura Blvd., and yet walking across this Boulevard was nothing but fun for me. All the shopping, all the restaurants, lots of activities, it really was plenty of fun for me. But obviously his mind was elsewhere. Although at that time I had my car with me, and I could drive places that I needed to go still I preferred to walk to most places like post office, or book shops or many more. It was even more pleasant when my sister Ezzat was staying with us. And besides all the though I have Joe. I need my family, I need my mother who was once my closest friend. Remember when I was very young and we did everything together, I do.

I hope this letter was not upsetting to you in the least, because it was in no way meant to be. I just wanted to convey my feelings in a way I never have before. Mom I am so sorry for all the pain you've gone through. Please understand that I am still having much pain myself. I hope that you listened to this letter with an open mind, then maybe we can begin again with a close relationship. I love you so much, you have no idea. Please write me back and tell me how you feel.

Your Forever Loving Daughter,

Mojgan Schmidt

P.S. We now have a fax # if you want to send me a letter that way.

FAX #: (616) 327-5384

My dear God, please pay attention to this letter of Mojgan. I cannot explain my feelings when I received this letter from her. Although I was there for her all the time and I stayed at her house as many times as she wanted me to, every time she started a big fight and we ended up getting nowhere by not being able to communicate peacefully. I knew that it was not possible for us to go back to where we were before. She had the right to attack me for the loss of her family the way she did. Since she was not able to reach her father by any means and I was not able to get rid of my hatred for Iraj's actions, we were not able to communicate without fighting. I knew that she had the right to be mad. I knew that I had done my best to support my children in many ways for more than eight years. For a wife who sees her loving husband with his mistress for eight years and not divorces him just to defend her children's home was not enough? Her father's act of betrayal killed all the love in all of our hearts. I was and I am sorry to see my children being destroyed by their own father after he had promised them a great future together. Yes, she is right. When she needed us the most, her father was wrapped up with his mid-life crisis, Badri.

Dear Mom,

Hi. How do you like my new computer. You always siad to type my letters so they would be easier for you to read. I hope your trip abroad went well. I think about you a lot. I know you may not think so but I do. I feel like our relationship has been on a roller coaster for the past few years. Honestly I long for a close relationship with you. But we've gotten in so many terrible fights and said so many horrible things that it makes it difficult. I know your just tring to get your life back on track but I sincerely hope that we don't continue to let this go on this way. I truely want a mother who is my friend, and a mother who won't judge every move I make. I know I am guilty of exactly what I am asking you not to do.

I am really beginning to believe we both hold the same anger but aren't willing to admit it. You've always been angry at me for not being there enough for you and not being your protector. And I have been angry for feeling so alone because of your & Dad's troubles. I other words I have been angry that both you and Dad were so wrapped up in your anger for each other you **both** forgot about me. And its not that you didn't provide for me or care about me but I just feel like my childhood and adolesence was riddled with adult anger and adult nonsense. But I am beginning to realize the past is the past. That is why I am writing this letter.

I would really like it if we could try and forget about the past and concentrate on our future together. I **love** you dearly. And I would like more than anything for you to be a BIG part of mine and Joes life. We are beginning to think seriously about having children in the next few years and I am terrified. I think that if we were closer and I had your support having children might be easier. I still have such a feeling of being alone, even

First Christmas at Mojgan's house in Sacramento. We all helped to make it beautiful. Mary, Maseeh, Joe and I are in the top picture.

Here, Maseeh is preparing a delicious breakfast for us.

Mary, Mojgan and I are preparing the turkey, and Joe is enjoying it.

Mary and I were at the Law Library at night. I read my book while she was working.

First Christmas at Mary's new house. Mary, Foster, Maseeh, and me.

We were sightseeing with Fali.

Here, we had lunch with Mojgan who was pregnant, and Joe before coming back home. I like the statue above us.

These Iranian ladies had rented Mojgan's lower level apartment. On that night, we had a potluck at Mojgan's patio. Doesn't Mojgan look so beautiful? Doesn't she really?

It is Christmas time in Mojgan's house. We are sitting around the table with dear Samantha. Samantha, joe, me, Maseeh, and Mojgan.

Mojgan, Joe, me, Maseeh, and Kristina. Samantha enjoys some milk.

In Mojgan's kitchen, Samantha is entertaining Fali and me.

sightseeing, which we went together: every evening we went to the school, which was behind the house, and we walked around the track yard. Some nights we walked to the restaurants and enjoyed our dinner sitting at the sidewalk café, and watching people pass by. There was an Iranian restaurant called Shiraz, which was not too far from the house. Many times we went there and had Shish Kebab and rice, which gave us the sense of being home. After being in this country for almost forty years, and being away from all my siblings, if being with my sister to go to a Persian restaurant and order Iranian food was not a pleasure, then what could be pleasure for me?

My Dear God:

So Maseeh was planning to change his house and buy a new one. As always the year was over and I was going back to Iran. I have gone to Iran so many times during writing this book, and I had kept myself away from writing that I will be surprised if I ever finish it. And each time that I went to Iran, because of the care, respect, love and attention of my family and his family I returned with a greater will and desire to live.

This time when I returned from Iran, Maseeh took me to his new house. The first time I saw the house I was surprised. When we lived in our house in Bloomfield Hills, he was questioning the style of the house being too modern and contemporary. So when I looked at his house it was almost as contemporary as our old house. It was beautiful. It had a large swimming pool outside, and next to it was a whirlpool, which by itself was of a size of a small pool. It was a very beautiful house, standing on the top of the green hill, with a fantastic view overlooking the city. It was located at the same city, which was his first house, Studio City. It looked to me that it was more than five thousand square feet, but I really didn't ask him. Everything about it looked beautiful. There was beautiful marble all over the house. His bedroom area was very spacious and nicely designed. I felt so happy to see Maseeh living so comfortable in his house, having a great job, and working so hard. Yet again it was another dream come true for me. Thank you!

As the time passed and I saw the improvement in my children's lifestyle, I was glad that I was able to put in their mind that owning their house was one step towards success. I not only put the idea in their mind, but I volunteered to pay the down payment on their houses. That made it very easy on them. In America without having a credit no one can own anything. Although they had lived in a seven thousand square feet home, to me their own houses were more practical, more beautiful, and more cultural. They had many more advantages over the house that did not bring our family any happiness, but it rather brought insecurity and misery for all of us. It was now Mary's turn to have her own house. But because when I bought the house there was not any subject of hers, or mine I never wanted to tell her that if she liked it she could buy her own house. I felt that if I ever brought up that subject with the kind of sensitivity that I had seen in her, she might have interpreted it as if I wanted to ask her out of my house. With Mary I had to be very

Sara Fasihi came to visit me in Maseeh's house. At the top, we are in front of Maseeh's motorcycle, and in front of his garage. At the bottom, Maseeh, Sara, and I are sitting in his backyard. Isn't this a beautiful view? Isn't my son handsome? Well, I am only a mother.

This picture was taken on a night that all these people were teasing me. Me, Joe, Mojgan, Maseeh, Marie, and Mary.

Mary and I are at a restaurant in Monterey, CA. I remember we had a delicious clam chowder soup.

At Mary's house, Foster, Mary, me, Maseeh, and Kristina.

Sara, Maseeh and I were having lunch at a restaurant in LA. After lunch, we went to his house and talked about old days. She was a nice lady, only sometimes she would listen to people's gossip. I always thought she had more class to bring herself down to the level of those gossipers.

This is the most beautiful picture I have ever taken of my children. As I said, they always teased me for taking lots of pictures of them. On this night, they all decided to act this silly. I took the picture and they loved it. Left to right: Joe, Mojgan, Maseeh, Marie, and my Mary. Later on, they couldn't stop laughing about it all night.

Mojgan's and my birthday
at Maseeh's house.

Maseeh and I were going to
Kathy Fasihi's wedding.

Eating turkey at Mary's house. Foster, Mary, me, Kasra, and Maseeh.

Maseeh held Mojgan's and my birthday party which are both in July. He had ordered two cakes, but not enough candles. We had a great time.

Here, we were having lunch in a restaurant in LA. Left to right: Marie's mother, Marie- Maseeh's friend, Maseeh, me, Fali, and Marie's father.

We are at Homa Hormozi's house. Her brother Mehdi Agha and his wife Haji Khanoom, her daughter Nasreen, her granddaughter Daryaneh, and Homa's child were there. Look at this table. What a feast! Isn't this yummy? Mrs. Hormozi, her mother-in-law who is sitting at the top of the table must be proud of Homa, indeed.

Ezzat and I are in Maseeh's backyard.

I invited Fali and her son Keyan to go to Mimi's Restaurant for his graduation. These girls around our table were cheering for him.

careful whenever I talked to her. I didn't know when it was the right time to bring up a subject. So I was waiting for her to come forward with the idea. Then I would take it from there, and I would follow it up.

My Dear God:

If our house was on the lake, which we were never able to use it, now in their own houses they had lake that they water-skied. They had pools, they had spas, they had steam rooms, and most of all they owned those houses, and their father couldn't steal it from them, and use it for Malakuti's family. My children might not have seen it that way, but I was proud of myself to be able to push them towards buying their houses, and I was even more proud of them that they were able to take the responsibility and show me their commitment to become achievers. By acting so responsible they were able to fulfill my wishes for them. To hell that their father ran away with a pro…..! To hell that he robbed us to a point that nothing was left for us! Instead I earned happiness that I always dreamt of. This was my reward, and in my opinion there is no greater reward than having happy, healthy, and successful children.

In the year 1978 I did not go to Iran. I was busy renovating my house. Instead I spent more time with my children at the time that they needed me. I made myself available for them at any time they wanted me for any reason. While I made myself useful to them, we went places together, we partied together, and we had fun together.

In March 1999 I arranged another trip to go to Iran and Europe. I just can tell that the trip was one of the best trips I had ever made. From our nine siblings seven of us still living and well. All of us had gathered in Tehran at the same time. My sister Sina was in Iran getting ready to go back to Belgium. My sister Ezzat came to Iran from England two weeks after I got there. Saideh's house was next door to Sina. Sina's house was on the top of the mountain overlooking the lights of the whole city. We decided that I stayed with Saideh in her house, and Ezzat stayed with Sina in her house. This way we were all together without overcrowding the place. Every day we were together. We cooked together, we ate together, we went to parties together, and we invited all others to our houses together. Days and nights, nights and days we stuck together as if someone was trying to take away the time away from us. The best part of this visit was that we, the four sisters, didn't need any transportation to get together. It was only Azar who was a little away from us. And still in no time we made it possible to be with each other.

My Dear God:

Every morning I got up and got ready to go for my morning walk on the top of Velengac's mountains. Sometimes on weekends Sina or Saideh and her husband Hassan also came with me for the walk. Sometimes we went to the coffee shop and we had breakfast. To be able to breath fresh air around that beautiful mountain, and walk with my sisters after living away for forty years, to be able to talk about our bad times and good times in those past forty years was a blessing to me and all others. We had so much to talk about that we didn't know where to begin.

Also we were blessed by having Rokhand's baby, Ahmad Reza, among us. After Azar had lost her son Reza, she never lived in our world. The whole world was dark and lifeless for her. Now with Ahmad Reza coming into this world, Azar was becoming alive again. Her whole world was Ahmad Reza. A person who was always very outgoing, very sociable, principal of a school, a big help of any kind of work like sewing, cooking, decorating, and many more, now she only devoted herself and her life to taking care of Ahmad Reza. That was her only reason to live for. He was her dream come true. We all were happy to see Azar was finding her place in this world again. I was the happiest since I had been concerned about her after her divorce from Shahab. In my heart I had a close bond with her, probably she didn't know it, but I was feeling responsible for bringing life into her heart and watching her live again. This was that time that I was waiting for. It had become too obvious to me that no matter what I ask from God soon he brings it to me. No wonder wherever I went and whatever I did people around me realized that I was celebrating of some kind or another. I always had something to be thankful for. I kept telling everyone around me that, "Today is the last day of my living life. So I am trying to make every minute count, and not waste even one minute on sorrow or sadness. I intend to celebrate my life everyday, since I was able to get rid of that distrustful, disloyal, dishonest, disgusting, and "dis" everything in my life, and make my disengagement from him the biggest celebration of my life".

It was funny when some friend like Fereshteh kept asking me, "Well, you just keep talking about it that 'This is the last day of my life', why don't you finish it? Why don't you let it be the last day of your life? And then everyone laughed and had a good time.

My Dear God:

Having a good time, yes, but we never were free from the very painful moments that had come through our way during those forty years. When we were walking towards the mountain of Velengac, we talked about how every one of us undergone disastrous eras. Azar among us was the one who got hit the most. She was my father's favorite, very lively, very talented, and very beautiful. She really did not deserve what she got in life. Since I was not in Iran all those occurrences, mainly Sina was the one who talked about it to be able to release her own pain, and to put me in the middle of those events as they were in it.

The more we talked to each other, the more we realized that the things which come in our way in this world must have something to do with other things. When Ezzat brought up the subject of possibility of it being hereditary, I almost was shocked. Philosophically we had learned that most diseases were supposed to be hereditary. But to see that the death pattern, which happens in families, might be based on being hereditary

In Azar's house, Sadegh is holding Ahmadreza. Rokhand, ready to put on her uniform is next to Saideh.

Javad and I are waiting for our table at the restaurant.

Sina, Ezzat, Shamci, and Chirazi are doing sightseeing in Belgium.

We are again at the "Baghe Gilass" restaurant. Left to right: Azar, Rokhand, Sadegh, me, Sina and Mrs. Hormozi. Ahmadreza is sitting in the front.

in the same restaurant, left to right: Nasreen, Hormoz Hormozi on the phone, Mr. Ghazveeni, me, Dr. Assad Khorram-nejad, Ezzat and Mr. Gangi

On this day Rokhand was in the hospital for her heart problem. We had gathered together in Javad's house; actually we were invited. Left to right: Saideh, Maryam, Ahmadreza, Javad, Ezzat, Afsar, Hassan, Mrs. Taghizadeh, Sina, Azar, Zari, Sadegh and me on the floor. What a beautiful group!

I was at Rokhand's engagement party. I remember she was very happy but tired that night. Left to right: Rokhand, me, Sadegh, and my sister Azar.

Here, we are at Sina's house. As always we were teasing each other and having a good time. Left to right: Afsar, me, Rokhand, Negar, Layla, Maryam and Zary.

That day in Hushmand's house, Mary was not happy. Something was on her mind. I knew what it was, but I didn't want to question her. I knew she had enough to deal with.

At Fereshteh's house. It was always nice and very colorful. Look at the table. Look at her artwork. As you see most of the houses that I have been to, did a great job on cooking and entertaining. Left to right: Sadegh, me, Saideh, Fereshteh, and Azar

Again at the same table, from left to right: Sadegh, Sina, Saideh, Mr. Mehraban, Rokhand, happy Fereshteh, and Azar

We are in Azar's house. Left to right: Sina, Ezzat, Saideh, Azar, and me. As you see I have tried to put the pictures in a sequenced order.

Ahmadreza, my niece Rokhand's son, and the love of my life in Iran whose visit brings me all the happiness I could get.

In Tehran, Sina, Ezzat, Hosain, and me.

Here we are at the dinner table at Rokhand's house. Sadegh was holding me on one side and Negar and Maryam on the other side.

We are in Rokhand's living room, with Ahmadreza in her arms.

Sadegh, and Rokhand are holding one-year-old Ahmadreza.

As you see we are all very happy at Helen-Afsaneh's friend's house. Left to right: Ezzat, me, Helen's mother, her cousin, her father, Helen-the host, and Afsaneh.

Ezzat and I are at the Stanford shopping area. Afsaneh is on the phone.

Mojgan, Shamci, Margoneh, and Fall at Mojgan's dining room

I was in Florida with my beautiful children, Maseeh next to me, and Mary next to her father. Both Mary and Maseeh were very happy.

My lovely son Maseeh at the age of eighteen was a grown man. We were vacationing in Florida. He was drinking to our health and happiness. I don't know what happened to the happiness.

was questionable for all of us.

According to Ezzat, who was older than us, my great grandmother lost a young boy near the age of eighteen. My grandmother lost a young son at the age of twenty. My mother lost her son at the age of seventeen and a half. And now my sister Azar lost her twenty two year old son. How could it be? Was coincidental maybe? It was almost the same as marriage in Badri's family. The mother and her four daughters' husbands died in different ways, and then all of them found new husbands shortly after their death. I know that their mother chose her second husband even before marrying the first husband. This was obviously the same thing that Badri did, except that she found the second husband when she was married to her first husband. I don't know about the other three. And I don't want to know anything about them either. I am just wondering how many more things are in this world that we don't know and we can't have any knowledge of. I am sure that there are millions that are not known to us. If these subjects in our lives could be hereditary, then it is possible that no matter what we do or what we learn, still it will follow us everywhere, and take over our actions. But I really doubted that.

If this was true there would be no way that people could change their true identity. No matter what we do or what we study still we are trapped in the hands of our heredity. Then it brings to my mind that from the beginning of starting our relationship with Malakutis every action was connected to the other one just like a chain reaction. For me there was no way out of it except, the way that I had to take it as it came just to be able to save my children, and to be able to save myself from the agony of becoming a murderer. Probably being a murderer has not been registered in my hereditary file.

My Dear God:

The way that they explained Azar's circumstances to me was that more than three months prior to Reza's death, Azar was worried like it had happened already. With the new Islamic Republican Government, and the war between Iran and Iraq all the universities were closed. Reza had been taking music lessons to be able to occupy his time wisely. He has been teaching his cousin Nader in England whatever he had learned from his teacher on playing Dulcimer. As many times as he found free time he started typing and recording those lessons for Nader. While he was talking to Nader he would repeat this sentence, “I don't know if I ever will be able to finish this tape”. Azar once called me from Iran, and while she was crying she told me, “Reza is going to army. He will be joining the troops and I am sure that I am going to lose him”. It seemed that not only Reza had sensed his own destination, but Azar also had sensed that something bad was there to destroy them. The loss of Reza after the loss of Jalal, our brother, was a tremendous pain for all of us, especially the children, who were mesmerized by his knowledge, his care, his love and attention, and by his comedian character. He was his cousin's idol. They not only loved him but they worshipped him.

The loss of Reza not only was the end of Azar's life, but it was the most disastrous thing that ever happened to his little cousins around him. Most of them wanted to follow Reza's footprints. Ali followed his footprints, and just recently got his PHD in metaphysics. Just like Reza he deeply believes in God, and until now he had never let himself to be involved with any wrongdoing, even as minor as smoking a cigarettes. All those kids, who were near him, they made him their role model, and they followed his footpath.

We were walking and talking, sometimes laughing and sometimes crying. We all needed to open our hearts to each other to be able to comfort one another therapeutically, and get rid of the past disasters memories from all of our hearts by just talking about them. They talked about the time of my mother's death. That happened at the time that I was burning in hell, meaning that I was in the middle of Iraj's and Badri's love affair. She passed away six months after Reza's death. For more than two years she sat and watched Reza suffering from the so-called revolution, suffering from lack of a job, lack of education, lack of right activities, and most of all the lack of having a worthy father at the time that he needed him the most. My mother watched her dear Reza's declining years emotionally and physically. And as if those were not enough, then she had to watch his burial, while she was watching Azar's declining day after day after day. Iran was not Iran for them any more. No one knew which way the country was turning to. There was a mother who had lost five of her children under the law of execution by the new Islamic Republic. She watched her grandson dye, her daughter Azar's health was declining, and her granddaughter Rokhand was almost lost in the crowds. She witnessed that Rokhand had lost her only brother, her only friend, and her only supporter at such a young age. Reza's death brought up the memory of her own son Jalal. No one to turn to and no way out of that political situation, this had caused all the stress, uncertainty, confusion, and depression. Even if some families did not have problems of their own, other people's problems were so excessive huge that they were not able to turn their face the other way, and not make it their own. My poor mother could not survive going through all these heartache and confusion. One day while crossing the road, a car hit her, and she died at the hospital. She really couldn't take it any longer. She was ready to go and join Reza.

Actually when the police found her body, she did not have anything with her that they could identify her. When she did not come home after a few hours, my brothers and sisters, and the whole family, especially Azar were looking for her. At the end they were sent to a morgue. After spending nearly seventy years of her life on her nine children, after devoting all her life only and only to her children, and after working so hard to raise all of us in her best way possible, she died on the street of Tehran unknown, and her children had to go and identify her at the morgue. What a life! What a joke! What a sad ending! Being away I just cried and cried. There was nothing left for us except talking about her life and how unfairly she was treated by life by nature and by her children, who she gave up all of her life for them. The only thing that she needed from her children was to love her enough to be able to spend time with her. She was not able to live away from her children. But her children could not understand her needs. They thought it was okay to leave her alone for a day or two. Not knowing that she was addicted to be with and see her children every second of her life. She didn't know any other way of living except spending all her time with her children. So if she wasn't able to see them one day, she would get depressed and didn't know what to do with herself. And those who were living with her could not understand her emotions at that time. I felt the most guilt, since I was away from her as far as USA, for as long as she remembered.

My Dear God:

Probably even if I was in Iran like others, still I would not understand her needs just like others. This is correct. Because those three and a half years that I lived in Iran, not only I had time to visit my parents every day but I became the biggest problem on their shoulders when Iraj was having an affair with his mistress Farkhondeh for two years. And then he had to escape Iran with the biggest humiliation for himself and for his family. After he escaped Iran, my children and I had to follow him right after seven months. So I never did my share of duties to my mother. And neither did the ones who were living near her.

My Dear God:

We talked about how our lives were destroyed after the revolution in Iran. Sina had to send her two sons Ali and Ehsan away from her to go to Belgium to be able to continue their educations, and to be able to stay alive at the ages of seventeen and fourteen. Since she was not able to understand and communicate with the newcomers, she retired herself from her teaching at high school, she sold her first time new house to be able to pay for her children's departure, consequently she became severely depressed to a point that she was almost giving up all her hope, and was under complete supervision of a psychiatrist. She was thinking that she might never see the light again.

Now her both sons were educated with respectful jobs, and were able to bring their parents to Belgium near themselves. With all the heartaches, which all of us went through, at that time that we were talking about our past times we found out that all of us were able to make it because we just were lucky. Our main concerns were our children, and that all of them were doing fine physically and emotionally. They all had become well educated and successful in their own way. None of us had plenty of money, but we all had good names and good reputation. And I think this is what it counts.

But at that time we didn't know how the things might change in future. We didn't know even what would happen to our children. I think after God examined us one by one, and realized that we had enough tolerance to be able to deal with pain, and then he

decided to change our fortune to a good luck. But at the time of sufferings we couldn't believe that one day things might change for the better.

It was on that trip that I found out Azar was becoming alive. With her grandson she was living in a different world. Her night was Ahmad Reza, her day was Ahmad Reza, and her whole world was Ahmad Reza. She cleaned him, she fed him, she bathe him, she changed him, and she put him to sleep on her skinny legs, while rocking him at all times, as if he was the reason for her breathing. Whenever I watched her doing those tiring works at the age of 55, I felt that she smelled Reza through Ahmad Reza. It was too obvious that in her mind she was giving love to her Reza through Ahmad Reza. She was willingly doing all the work, and did not want to share him with anyone. There were times that while everyone was dancing and laughing, quietly she was watching everyone with tears in her eyes. I knew that Azar never got over Reza's death. She always was missing her Reza.

My Dear God:

The trip of 1999 to Iran was just fabulous. Each time when I looked at all my seven sisters and brothers being together I saw healthy, respectful citizens. My parents were there with us in our minds and our hearts. We wished that they could be there to see that all their hard work had been paid off. They both wanted for their children to become dignified and honorable not by means of money, but by morals and manners that at the time we all were. God bless their souls. They will be always remembered in our hearts.

My brother Jamal and his wife Afsar were both teachers. They had two girls Negin and Negar. Negin was a pharmacist in Canada, and Negar was studying pharmacy in Tehran University. My older sister Ezzat had two children Afsaneh and Nader. They both were in London. Afsaneh was in teaching, and Nader was into computers. My sister Azar had two children Reza and Rokhand. After Reza's death she put all her efforts to save Rokhand's life from destruction. She emphasized on Rokhand's education. She got her master in Art and Directing. My sister Sina was a teacher, and her husband Hosain Shirazi who got his degree in Mine Engineering in Germany, had two children Ali and Ehsan. They both were studying in Belgium. Ali was working on his PHD in Physics, and Ehsan was entering the university. My brother Javad and his wife Zari both were educated in England. Javad had got his PHD in economy, and had two girls Layla and Maryam. Layla became an electrical engineer and Maryam went to a photography school. Layla got accepted to go to Finland on scholarship to continue her education. Saideh had no children, yet she had become a very knowledgeable lady, who spoke four languages fluently. She did secretarial work, and translated books. Not only she was very self-sufficient, but also she was helpful to others. This by itself could be an honor. And I, Shamci Gharavi Rafani, am known to all of you readers at this time. My son Maseeh went to Art and Directing, my daughter Mary had become an attorney, and Mojgan got her

degree in business and marketing. I just wished that my parents were there to see the results of their hard work.

You see my dear God; it was more difficult for me to raise my children away from my family and my culture. You were the only one who was with me during all the hardship. You were the one who witnessed my cries, my worries, my begging to you, my constant attention, the walking and watching day and night, the insisting and enforcing, which came only from the great love that I had for them. You were the one who supported me while I myself was being used and abused by my life partner. I never thought that my children one day could come out all right. Thanks to you they did. The impossible became possible. Mojgan was only twelve when her father's affair with Badri started. It was then that she wrote in her diary, “Since Dr. Malakuti died, my father hates me”. Mary had worst experience of losing her father to another mistress, Farkhondeh, at the age of five. And so did Maseeh. How would I be able to heal these wounds in my children if I wasn't that kind of mother to watch every move of theirs at every second of their lives? Each one of them had to be watched separately, according to their characters and personalities. Yet because I was the enforcer, I was the guilty one. Because I loved them unconditionally, I was the guilty one. Because my children were my only business, then I was the mother who could not understand her children. At this time I really don't care what they are thinking of me, or what kind of mother they think I was. I am only happy that they turned out all right. That was my main goal and nothing else.

My Dear God:

The more I think about all our siblings and their families, the more I remember the sentence that our father was repeating to us each time that something went wrong. He always said, “It is easy to get a degree to become a doctor. But it is not easy to be a human with great understanding.” In our family Iraj proved my father's saying. He was the only medical doctor among us. And he was the only inhuman among us. He was the only one who lacked normal human qualities. What a pity! What a disappointment!

My dear God, life is beautiful. Today is March first 2000. I am sitting in my bedroom surrounded with all the soft and comfortable cushions, which I had made myself, in the most comfortable position listening to music, and while looking out of my windows watching all these beautiful roses in my house, which I planted myself, and I am talking to you. No one ever can see my real happiness that I am feeling now except you. How did you made it possible for me to be able to be this happy again in my life? I don't know.

March first was the day that I used to worship. It was Iraj's birthday. This day always gave me more excitement than any other day in the calendar. Yesterday I had time to go through fifty-five letters, which Iraj wrote me from DePaul Hospital dated 1957 and 1958, before I came to the USA. The more I read them, the more I questioned how could that love had been untrue? How could a person like him become a person that he turned

out to be? Since I loved him so much, and I knew that he loved my love for him, I gave him as much love as it was possible to give to someone. In all those letters there were promises of loving, caring, giving, and looking forward to the great future in a loving home with a beautiful family. I thought, "He didn't have to write those letters if he didn't meant it. He was in America and I was in Iran. Easily he could have stopped writing to me, and forget about me. There were no forces behind him. Or he could have written to me once a month, or once every other month. But despite his busy schedule at the hospital, he wrote to me once or twice a week. Since he didn't like writing letters, in his last letter before my arrival he wrote, "I am very happy that you are joining me and I don't have to write to you any more". It was very funny. Then I realized that he believed in love in the family. And he was in-love with my love for him. But on the other hand he was willing to have extra marital affairs. And since I did not accept this, he is where he is today, and I am where I am now. So I was glad to put the letters away and think about my real happiness now. No more looking back, and no more feeling sorry for the loss of the love, which was never real.

My Dear God:

After many years of desperation and uncertainty, I can see myself not being homeless after all. Not only I made sure that my children has their own homes, but I had my own home, and no one was able to take it away from me. Actually, this was the only house that I was able to fix it my own way. From the beginning to the end, "I did it my way". What a nice feeling!

You see my dear God, this comfort and this happiness that I am having today in a peaceful home is what I have dreamt of my entire life. My dream came true only with one, exception. The kind of life that I am having right now is the kind of life that Iraj was promising to me in his letters. And he tried so hard to make his dream come true. But at this time I found my peace and tranquility, while I have my head up, and I am proud of whatever actions I took to make it possible. But again and again I will say this, and I will repeat it, "I really feel sorry for Iraj. His dreams never came true. Because I knew him and his dreams, I had patiently waited for him to recover from his midlife crisis for eight years. Unfortunately he never was able to recover. And he is not able to join me in my great happiness. As he said it over and over, "Whenever I am at the peak of my success and my happiness, somehow a very rocky storm hits me. And it destroys all that I have accomplished". I wish I had kept all his letters to me after his first affair so that you could see for yourself how sorry and sympathetic he was for himself, for reputation, and the prestige he had made for himself among his family and friends. With all those apologetic letters he was begging for my forgiveness, and he was promising me a happier life in future. He always dreamt to be a good father, a great husband, and a prestigious person. According to him he loved me to a point that he hoped to sell our big house, and take me

with him around the world. He had dreams that words such as "good person, great doctor, nice family man, and a loving husband" followed his name. Too bad, not only was he unable to bring those adjectives after his name, but also he deserved words like dishonest, disloyal, polygamist, disgraceful, and many more. I don't believe that he have ever dreamt that, his name would be followed by those adjectives. No matter how long he can fool himself and pretend that this was the life that he wanted, I personally cannot believe him. He always hated men who were in this category. And he talked so badly about them. How could he be happy and proud of himself now that his name is exactly in that category? I think it is impossible. If he was able to review that anonymous poem, written by one of his friends, and not become embarrassed of his own judgment, then I am wrong, and he had been this person that he is right now all along. Otherwise, he must be an unhappy man inside, who is pretending that he is a happy person.

My Dear God:

By the way, I never found out who was that anonymous poet, who wrote that sarcastic and taunt remarks about him, and then mailed it to all Iranians in Michigan. I hope at least he had been able to find him and ask him or her, whoever he or she was, "How did he or she know him so well? And ask him or her why he or she was Shamci's enemy. I have no doubts that it was Dr. Barkhordari, or someone from Badri's family. Either one did not like me, and had something against me. Obviously, whoever that person was, he or she was not an honorable person, and did not have high regards from anyone. Otherwise, he or she could have contacted me, and talk to me why he or she was so against my happiness. Therefore he was a chicken, a coward who did not have courage to come forward and tell me why he or she did it. It would be nice for me if he could come forward and tell me what his or hers reason was that he or she hated me so much. At least I would have found out what have I done to him or her that I have created such hatred.

Now, after ten or twelve years, he can come forward like a man, and open his heart to me. I will have no hard feelings against him any more. I have been able to put my past behind me, and start a new life. Nothing can bother me any more.

I still remember the day that Sara was trying to explain to me why those doctor's wives were pushing Badri into Iraj's arms. It was not only to be able to laugh at me. They did it to be able to stop Badri from going to bed with their own husbands. And when they didn't see Iraj getting serious about marrying Badri, someone thought of that poem to make Iraj angry enough to move fast, and decide on marrying her. I stood in their way quietly for more than eight years, but being just a mistress was not satisfying for Badri. So humiliating Iraj with that poem was the only way to make Iraj angry and smoothen out his way towards marrying Badri. It was either someone from Badri's family, or Barkhordari, who also was very interested to go to bed with Badri, or he hated my guts enough to speed up their marriage. Anyway the purpose behind writing that sarcastic

poem and mailing it to all the doctors in Michigan was to push Iraj towards marrying Badri. And for sure it had been the creation of her smart-alecky family. They probably all got their second husbands the same way.

My Dear God:

Good or bad, it is nearly twenty years after Malakuti's death. My life had turned out to be the most satisfying and happy. The most beautiful and happy and peaceful life that Iraj had been promising to me for thirty years! In his promises he always insisted on, "You and I together." But, thanks God, I was able to achieve that all by myself. When I was in love with him, it was the greatest, one of a kind love for me. I loved every minute of it. And when he left me, I was able to hang on to the best and most positive part of it, and let go of the hateful and ugly times. With the kind of love that I had for him, I was, and I am very fortunate that I didn't make my hands dirty with a crime, which was a big possibility.

I had the greatest love and the most comfortable life that any woman could dream of. I gave life to three of the most beautiful children in the world. While he was destroying my life, I learned to become stronger and more tolerant. And to those who knew something about family culture morality and respect, I had gained more respect and acceptance than ever before. I can assure those who tried so hard to help Badri in marrying Iraj that I have greater love and happiness in my life than any of them could ever have. As they say, "When you dig a hole for someone, beware, you might be the first". From far I had heard the troubles and unhappiness that most of you had to deal with. I was neither shocked, not I was surprised. The consequences of your mean actions will bring your way much more than before. God's action does not talk; only it becomes visible sometimes. You must be aware of it.

Those of you, who played a role of a pimp, and made Badri, the pro......., available for Iraj you will never be able to find real peace within yourselves. Having big houses, yes! Living by the shore in exotic places, yes! Showing off to each other and enjoy talking behind each other's backs, yes! But real happiness and peaceful life, I can assure you, never! Just watch, it is coming.

As for me, God had given me every brick for building peace and happiness in my life. God, you continue to hold my hands, giving me good health, taking away the painful things in my life, like very bad migraines that I used to have. It had disappeared from my life forever. As people tell me, I am getting younger every day. I am the life of the places I go to, be that to socialize or play bridge with some groups. I am happy, and I can bring happiness to others also. The bad chapter of my life is gone, and I am looking forward to the new and happy life. I will never be homeless any more. Not only that, but after going ahead and helping Mary to buy a house, now three of them have their own homes with my help. I am very fortunate to be able to arrange for this to happen.

GIFT LETTER

DATE: 3-23-2000

TO WHOM IT MAY CONCERN:

I, (We), Shamci Rafani

am (are) giving my (our) daughter, Mary Rafani

the amount of $ twenty five thousand dollars 25,000

The property is located at

This is an outright gift from me (us) and does not have to be repaid. There is not repayment expected or implied, written or verbal, in the form of cash or by future service or services by the person(s) receiving the gift, the mortgagor(s).

This gift (will be) (was) made on paid on the closing date.

from the funds on deposit as follows:

Name of Institution: Bank of America

Address: 212 E Main street, Visalia, CA. 93291

Acct No.: ______ Type of Acct Money Market

Shamci Rafani
(signature)

______
(signature)

616, N. Encina, Visalia CA. 93291
(address, city, state, zip code)

559) 636-6254
(phone number)

If additional accounts are needed to verify total amount of gift, please provide similar information on reverse side of the letter.

Contact Mr. Jon Hoskins at BA (559) 739-3787

"I (We) the mortgagor(s), acknowledge that we have received this gift under the term shown above."

Mary Rafani (daughter)
(name & relationship)

Shamci Rafani (mother)
(name & relationship)

This letter was prepared for tax purposes. It shows that this amount was a gift to Mary from her mother to purchase a new house.

My Dear God:

Right after my return from Iran, I had noticed a house for sale across the street. I thought it would be nice to buy that house for Mary. However, I didn't want to bring it up to her, thinking that she might take it wrong, and interpret that I wanted her out of my house. So while I was thinking about it, I came to the conclusion that I would go see the house. And if we were able to agree on the price, I would buy it for myself. And if Mary liked it I would give it to her. And, if she didn't like it, I would keep it as a rental house.

The next day I called the neighbor, whose name was Maryline, and asked her if I could go and see her house. After her daughter died in that house, Maryline was living there with her sister. When I went there, both of them welcomed me. When we sat and started talking about their house, she told me that her neighbor, who owns the Bed and Breakfast next-door, had already given her an offer. And if that offer got accepted, it would be sold to them. I felt bad that I didn't apply for it first. It was a small beautiful house, which was opposite my house. And I could be living near Mary, if not in my house.

When I talked to Mary about it, and told her "I wish it could be mine." She told me that since one of her friends bought a house in the same area, she would like to look at the house near to see if she could buy a house in that neighborhood.

I was glad to hear that from Mary herself. She needed to have her own private place. Although I was worried to leave her by herself, yet I thought that she was a mature lady, and she must live her own life, especially that whenever I was home, she couldn't invite her other side of the family. Even though in my house she had her own phone so, that I didn't have to answer the phone for her. Only when I was out of the country, she invited those that I did not like to see in my house.

One night Mary asked me to go to a potluck to one of her friends from church. We met many people, including the lady minister of their congregation. The subject of the house for sale in that neighborhood came up. Two days later Mary asked me to go with her to see that house. Since it was for sale by owner, she had gone to see, and she liked it a lot.

When I saw the house, I liked it also. The only objection that I had was that there was a narrow alley behind the house. And it had been broken into in the past. That subject worried me a lot. But since Mary liked it, and I liked it, we decided to do something about it.

My Dear God:

I had an Iranian lady friend, whom I met in Visalia that I will talk about in the next few pages. I asked her to research about the house, since she was in real estate business, and she knew how to go about it. We knew that the present owner had bought this house six months ago. They were building a big house in Visalia. For them it was more practical

to buy this house, while their house was under construction, than to rent a house. After they bought the house, they did many nice things to it, including installing an alarm system, a good answer to the previous burglary. The house was the right size for Mary. It was in good shape, and it had a nice back yard. The most important advantage was that it was only seven minutes walk from my house.

Well my dear God, could you have ever arranged it any better than that? Could I have asked for more blessing than that?

Mary was the one that I could never dictate to her what was good for her or what was bad. And she was the one whom I worried about the most. Now coincidentally her office was ten minutes walk to my right, and her house to be was seven minutes walk to my left. Could I have asked for anything better than that my dear God? Shouldn't I believe that you loved me immensely, and you will always continue loving me the same? This was not only great for me, but it must be one of your miracles. Thanks again!

At this time of our lives the relationship between Mary and I was just fantastic. According to her we were friends, we were lovers, we were mother and daughter, and most of all we were each other's companions. Anybody, whom she was friends with, regardless if they were man or woman, whether they were African American or white, gay or straight, lawyers or a rubbish collectors, and even those that I knew were using some kind of drugs, were always welcomed in my house, just because I wanted to give Mary a loving home to be able to feel good about herself and her life. By welcoming all her associates in my house, I was trying to stop her and her friends from wrongdoing. Even if she asked me to go to a Bar with her to listen to her favorite band, happily I did it. And although I do not believe in any organized religion, when she wanted me to go to church with her on Sundays, gladly I accepted her invitation, and I accompanied her. I never left her sight for a single moment. Except her work, which took most of her energy, and sometimes made her mad, everything else around her seemed to be satisfactory. By making fat free brunches or dinners, I made her to be conscience about her weight, without telling her directly. I was happy to see her being focused on doing the things she liked to do. We used to walk to movies at Fox Theater. We would buy a big bucket of popcorn, while she let me eat the most of it. Since she enjoyed having ice cream after the movie, we got our ice cream, and walked up and down the Main Street. And some weekends we sat outdoors to enjoy watching some kind of performances. I was willing to bring to her as much happiness that she had missed during our troubled years.

My Dear God:

With all that we were doing together, still I had to watch her moods and act very carefully. Sometimes in the middle of laughter and happy times, she would jump into her strange mood. That was very unexpected to me. Sometimes she hurt me so badly that I needed some time to recover.

Ok my dear God, here we go again. Mary was thinking of buying that house to live on her own. Not a bad idea at all. The only problem was that she did not have any credit to be able to borrow money from a bank for the down payment. When I saw her worried that bad, I volunteered to pay money the same way that I did for the other two. But for her I was willing to go even farther. I thought, "I will remove my retirement money from the bank, pay cash for her house, and close the deal". That way she did not have to ever pay mortgage.

My Dear God:

As soon as Mojgan heard about this deal, she talked to Maseeh about it. Both of them tried to convince me that not only it was unwise for me to do that, but also Mary would have to pay a great amount of taxes, and they brought up many more reasons that made sense to me. They also talked to Mary to make her understand my financial situation. At first she was a little unhappy, since she had to pay mortgage every month. But when I told her that I would pay the first payment anyway, she started looking into it.

At this time I reminded her about the money, which she had been depositing into our joint account for that rainy day, and that today was that rainy day. I told her I would use those savings, plus my own money to pay for the premium. Although I wasn't expecting a "Thank you" from her, I don't recall that I heard such a thing from her when we went together to the bank, and I wrote her a big check.

After the decision was made, and I gave her a check for twenty five thousand dollars, out of which the six thousand dollars were the savings money in our joint account. She always thought that I kept her rent money for myself. I introduced her to the lady banker, whom I got my mortgage from. Soon everything fell into place, and within two weeks they closed the deal. Since Mary wasn't picky about the condition of her house, she was ready to move in immediately. She was satisfied with a basic, thorough cleaning.

I have to remind you that when Mary brought her furniture in my house, it was a reminder of Iraj's and Badri's sexual activities. I hated looking at it. Since I couldn't discuss it with Mary, to make her feel good I volunteered to reupholster her furniture. My reason was that it was dirty, and either they needed cleaning or reupholstering. Obviously, since I was in charge, and I was paying for it, she agreed without any hard feelings.

I found a gentleman from the Yellow Pages who sounded like a good worker. He brought many samples of the fabrics for upholstery, which I had plenty to choose from. My selection was a complete off-white striped pattern, which seemed very elegant. So for moving into her new house, I didn't have to look at that ugly furniture, which reminded me of Iraj's adultery. Once and for all I closed the book on that depressing subject.

My Dear God:

Her house is located at 742 Highland Street, Visalia, CA 93291, just a few streets

north of my house. It was time for her to start buying furniture, and giving parties. The house had a character that fit Mary so well. It had a warm atmosphere that anyone could feel comfortable there. I was happy to see her happy in her own place after many years of sufferings. I thought she deserved that happiness, since she had lost her happiness for many years.

Right after she moved to her new house, I wrote her a very powerful letter. I wanted to congratulate her on being able to buy her own house. And I wanted to make sure that she recognized her own values on achieving whatever she set her mind on. I wanted her to know that she had done everything by herself, thanks to her own ambitiousness. I talked about her puberty, and that if she made mistakes; it was part of her growing. I told her, "I did it, your father did it, the president did it, and the whole world did it". It has been and it is part of growing age. At the end I apologized for becoming her mother without her knowledge and her invitation, if she thought that I wasn't a mother that she expected to have. I did my best to be a great mother in my own way not knowing what kind of a mother my children wanted me to be. And I gave that letter to her along with a gift to welcome her to her new house.

She liked the letter so much that she said, "I will frame this letter and keep it on my wall so that everybody can read it and see how lucky I am". But until now I have not seen it anywhere. Probably it fell in the trash. Although Mary was the one that wanted to hurt me the most, she was the one that many times she praised me on my talent, my strength, my capability, and my tolerance. So I never knew how she perceived me.

Ok my dear God, you remember that how I hated Iranians in Michigan, who played the role of pimps for Iraj and Badri. I never wanted to get to know any Iranian after I left Michigan. Although there were many other Iranians who did their best to support me, and they comforted me during my sufferings. Many of them stood by me day and night to make sure that I was okay. With all these, the harm that most of my so-called friends did to me was so great that I hated to hear the name of an Iranian.

My Dear God:

So when I moved to Visalia, most people who got to know that I was from Iran, tried to introduce me to other Iranians that they associated with. I never rejected their offers, since they were not aware what was going on in my mind. When they would give me the name and the telephone number, I thanked them, but I never contacted them. I knew that no one could ever hurt me more than how I was already hurt before. Yet in my mind I didn't want to get involved with another group of disorientated and dishonorable human being.

Mary had a friend who was working at the hospital. Her name was Sue. Every time she came to our house or we went to restaurant or a picnic, she talked to me about one Iranian lady she knew. She explained to me that she seemed to be a wonderful person, and she thought that we were good match. She gave me her name and telephone number, and she asked me to give her a call. And every time Sue asked me "did you give her a call?" I told her that I didn't have time. And that I would call her one day when I had more time. Meanwhile she gave her friend my name and number, asking her to contact me.

One day, while in the middle of the construction, I was busy dealing with the concrete worker, when somebody rang my doorbell. When I opened the door, I saw an Iranian lady at the door she said "Salam." Without any hesitation I invited her in. To tell you the truth, I don't remember what she said, or what I said during our first meeting that day. But it was as if I knew her all my life. Later on she told me that, "I had come to your house to sell you something, but the only thing we did not talk about was that something".

Since her life story was similar to mine, we had become close friend. Although from my past experience I have learned not to ever call anyone a "friend", yet we became close like two schoolmates, who just enjoyed being together. Her name was Fali Salehi. Coincidentally, Saleh was the last name of my mother and my uncle with the exception of the "i" at the end. Her own last name was Orandi, which made her Fali Orandi Salehi. She was in real estate business, and she had four children. First time I went to her house for a short visit, I had got to meet her son Syrous, his wife Marjan, and their son Bahador. Bahador was eight years old; he had Cerebral Palsy. I met her daughter Shilla, her husband Mahdi, and I think at that time they were expecting a baby, and her two younger sons Vaheed and Keyan. From that very first moment I liked the togetherness of the family.

My Dear God:

Syrous was attending a dental university, and he was in the process of moving nearby the university. Shilla and Mehdi, who was a medical doctor, were going to Iran for that summer. Meanwhile Shilla was working on her degree in architecture, and she got her degree from Iran.

She got to know my children, my siblings, and my entire family. I got to know all her family. We traveled together to her brother Hameed and his wife Mojdeh, and together we went to my son's house in Studio City. Once, when I was in Mojgan's house in Sacramento Fali and Marjan came to visit, and we drove back to Visalia together. Another time, when Mojgan was in Lake Tahoe, Fali and I drove to her house together and stayed there for one week. On our way back I drove all the way home for six and a half hours. Each time we spent a happy and peaceful time together. The only person that I considered to be my friend all my life was Parri Kamooneh, my sister-in-law. The same relationship that I was having with Fali now, I had with Parri then and much more. I was very close to her, and I loved her dearly. Now that my whole world had turned around, and there was nothing to look back any more, all of a sudden a person came at my door to introduce me to a unique and rare friendship that I was not ever expecting it. She was pure, she was innocent, she

We are at Mr. Hakimipoor-Mehdi's father's house in kerman. Indeed, Mehdi did his best to make me feel at home. He is the only child of Hakimipoors and he was preparing to take his last exam to enter the world of the United State's physicians. Left to right: Shila, Mrs. Hakimipoor, Dr. Mehdi Hakimipoor, Arsham, Mr. Hakimipoor, me, and Fali.

In 2004, Fali came with me on the same trip that I made to Iran. We are in Azar's house, eating, talking and laughing. Left to right: Fali, Azar, me, and Fereshteh.

We are around a warm and nice lunch table in Sakineh Khanoom's house in Kerman. Fali's sister and her family made me feel so comfortable. Left to right: Mehdi, Shila, me, Sakineh, and Fali, the rest are all their family who helped with preparing this lunch.

As you see, this is Azar's house. Her son Reza's photo and his poem about life and death are framed on the wall. Left to right: me, Mehdi, Azar, Fereshteh, Arsham, Fali, and Shila. We are all in Azar's house to say goodbye to them. They were leaving Iran before I did.

We are sightseeing in Kerman. What a nice view! Shila and Arsham seem tired, but Fali and I are OK.

I had lunch with Mehdi, Shila, Fali, and Arsham in the bazaar (mall).

Fali and I are on top of a rock, adjacent to Lake Tahoe. Fali wanted to take a picture somewhere with no one around. After we had taken the picture, we found out that a gentleman had been sitting behind us. Because of that, we had an excuse to laugh more and enjoy our day more.

In this picture we are in my house. Left to right: Me, Fali, Shila, Mojdeh, and Hameed Orandi. Their daughter is resting on the sofa.

Fali and I were sightseeing in South Lake Tahoe. It really was beautiful.

In Fali's living room, left to right: Shila, Arsham, Fali, and me. I think it was my birthday.

In Fali's living room, Cyrus, Marjon, Vaheed, Bahador, Fali, Keyan, Reza, me, and their cousin.

In my living room, Dr. Hakimipoor with three-month-old Arsham in his arms, Shila, and Fali.

Valley's Persian Community Keeps Nowruz Tradition Alive

TEXT BY AARON COLLINS

Beneath the surface of the general culture in the San Joaquin Valley lie many communities of surprising diversity and degrees of fidelity to their original homeland traditions. While many European cultures here merged as a single more-or-less general American identity and retain few original Old World social mores and traditions, other more recent immigrant groups keep their traditions alive for new Americanized generations growing up outside their country of origin – such as the Iranian American community that settled in the Valley in considerable numbers after fleeing Iran following the fall of Shah Reza Pahlavi in the late '70s.

One Persian tradition going strong in the region is the Persian New Year celebration known as *Nowruz*. As the Persian solar calendar begins with spring, so the event might be considered an equivalent conflation of Easter's paganish roots as a celebration of nature's return to fecundity and New Year's – two Western traditions as one.

Recently, the Persian community gathered at Woodward Park in Fresno, a city that is the focus of the Iranian community due mainly to Fresno's large population and its resulting base for three Iranian cultural groups: the Iranian Culture Society of Fresno, the Islamic Cultural Center of Fresno, and Kanoon, the Iranian Culture and Art Club of Fresno. (The kanoon is the predecessor to the harpsichord and piano, and is a lap-harp with approximately 72 strings, tuned in sets of three. It is plucked with finger-picks extended from each index finger held by a metal circular band.)

But south Valley cities like Visalia also have an Iranian presence, according to Fali Salehi, 61, an area realtor and pistachio farmer who came to Visalia from Iran in 1995, and who has close ties to the Iranian American community at large (her extended family, some retired physicians, brought pistachios to the Terra Bella area in south Tulare County more than 30 years ago). About the celebration, Salehi fondly recalls her home land: "Nowruz starts at the beginning of spring, and the Valley's spring is exactly like most parts in Iran, where spring starts so beautifully on the first day of the first month of the new year," she said.

The tradition was brought to America by the older generations of Iranians and other Middle Easterners who moved to the United States. (Nowruz, which means "new day," is celebrated throughout the near and Middle East, not just in Iran.). It is being kept alive through introduction to the younger generations that were born stateside. Families want them to learn about their cultural traditions, and Salehi says the Nowruz gatherings helps them to know who is from where and provides them a chance to meet one another.

The specific customs of Nowruz directly foster that knowledge, underscoring the social order with a series of 13 days of visits that are structured according to family and social relationships. →

PHOTO PROVIDED BY DR. AHMAD EMAMI

PHOTOS BY DAVID MENENDIAN

Planning for the custom begins in *Esfand,* the final month of the winter calendar. Spring cleaning is the first major ritual, followed by the purchase of new clothes for the new year and flowers – hyacinth and tulips being popular customary choices. The new clothes are worn on the first day of the 13, which marks the first day of the new year itself. Family gatherings begin the rite, followed by visits to other senior members of the family, then other relatives on subsequent days, then finally friends and neighbors. On the 13th and final day of celebrations, all convene on *Sizdeh-Bedar* (literally "13-out") in a picnic outdoors to enjoy the return of spring's warmth. Woodward Park was the site of Fresno's *Sizdeh-Bedar* event, a traditional gathering place for the occasion.

On the first day, family members gather around the table and await the exact moment when spring beings. Gifts are exchanged, then later that day the short house visits with relatives begin. It is customary for younger family members to visit the more senior members, who later reciprocate with what are typically half-hour sessions. Fresh and dried fruits and special nuts along with sherbet are traditional holiday offerings, along with home-baked pastries and cookies. For far-flung family members, families will often book a large facility to host the festivities in one central location, in lieu of some of the visitations.

The night before the last Wednesday of the year, *Chaharshanbe Suri,* is a festival of fire celebrated by Iranians and marks the return and victory of the light over darkness, symbolism that is rooted in Zoroastrianism, the world's oldest religion and once the dominant sect in Iran where it is rooted. Nowruz itself is ancient, thought to be around 15,000 years old, dating back to the time of King Jamshid of Persia.

Some who celebrate Nowruz believe that whatever one does and how one acts on the occasion will affect the direction of the year ahead. So if warmth and compassion are expressed, the year ahead looks bright. If strife or misfortune arise, that is considered a bad omen by celebrants.

Salehi says the Americanized version of Nowruz differs from Middle Eastern versions in that in the Middle East it occurs as a holiday with ample time off, which affords celebrants the opportunity to engage in all the home visits. The American version does not coincide with work time off, and therefore limits entertaining by necessity.

Nowruz is not the only evidence of the Persian culture in the Valley. The Assemi family of Fresno, owners of Granville Homes, a major Fresno developer, built and donated the Persian Center (Mosque) there, a community focal point that is known throughout the Iranian-American community in the Valley.

Reza Assemi, among the second generation, is noted as arguably Fresno's most progressive young developer, having introduced many so-called Smart Growth principles to downtown revitalization. Artist loft housing and studio facilities are among the strategies he has brought to one of the most troubled downtowns in the United States. This strategy is believed by many locals to effectively be undoing decades of neglect and bad Fresno urban planning decisions that favored unwise but profitable development over a vision that offered lasting civic benefits for all. Assemi is a co-founder of Creative Fresno, a civic professional group that aims to shape public policy to attract greater numbers to Fresno's nascent creative industries like advertising, computer programming and the arts. Consequently, the Assemis are among the highest profile and most successful members of the Iranian-American culture in the Valley, and prominent in the Fresno business community at large. They participate in many key Persian traditional and religious events, according to Salehi, but have also managed to integrate with the local dominant culture, as well.

And with the addition of Nowruz to our community's various celebrations, the melting pot of American culture has added another flavor. ■

was humble, she was hard working, and just like me, she was a victim of disloyalty and unjustifiable circumstances. The same way that I was comfortable with Parri, the same way I am comfortable with Fali now. I believe that the way that she entered my life was to awaken me from wrong assumptions about people, whom I haven't met. It wasn't right for me to assume that most Iranians were like the group of Iranians who I was associated with in Michigan. There was no proof that any Iranian that I talked would become a person Like Badri, her friends, and her family. God forbid, they are just one of a kind. Besides, I have no husband any more that someone would go after him while I still maybe wrong about knowing the real Fali.

When I met those people, although they seemed nice at the beginning, I never felt close or friendly with them. They were just associates to socialize with. Yet I got caught in the middle in such a way that there was no escape from it. Because of my past experience, when I was with Fali those thought would often come to my mind, "How do I know that if Fali was among that group in Michigan, would she be able to join them in destroying me?" Then I thought, "No, she couldn't be that type. Not in a million years". That way I was able to get rid of all the doubts in me, and enjoy her company as much as I could.

So it was Fali, the lady realtor, who did the investigation on Mary's house at the time of purchase, and it was Fali who at this time is a friend of mine. If the way things are going, stays the same way; I think both of us have been lucky to be able to find each other.

My Dear God:

You see my dear God, I don't believe in you like all other religious people do. I think of you as a light, as a power, as nature, as my within. I don't believe that you are found only in churches, mosques, or in synagogues. Those who think you are found only in those places, are the ones who do not feel you around them wherever they go. That is why they all pray in those special buildings, and then carry on with their forbidden activities elsewhere. Thinking that as long as they are not doing it in holy places, you do not see them or you cannot witness their thoughts or their minds anywhere they are, or anything they do. I see you as an organized and powerful disciplinary, who is in each and every one of us. You are not away or separate from us wherever we go or whatever we do.

So when I look around me, and study the things that happened to me step by step, I realize that the fulfillments that I received through my troubled times and after that were only because of the kind of faith I had within me. This faith, which consists of a special energy, strength, and willingness, brought another chapter in my life. It prepared me for accepting the harsher events, which I was facing in my older age. You, being with me at every minute of the day or night, have made me capable to be able to face the events with a calmer and smoother wisdom. I have been thanking you from the beginning of the book until the end. Not that this is the end of my writing to you. No, this is from the Shamci's birth, the happening of all the events from good or bad in her life. Obviously there is much

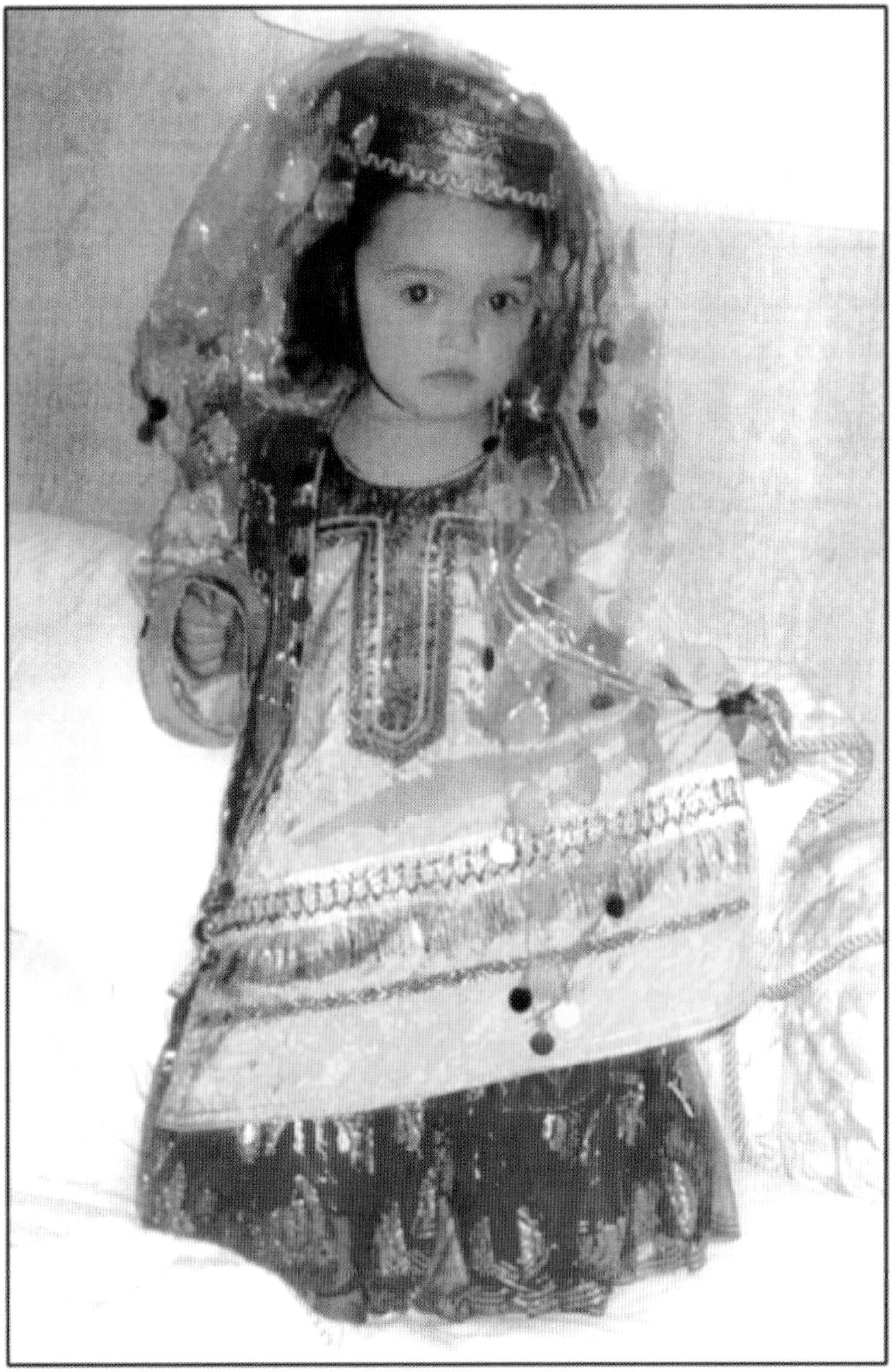

This is my beautiful Samantha, my precious grandchild who was born on December fourteenth, 2002. I was lucky to have been there before, during and after. She is in a dress from Rasht, a city in Iran. She is my whole life. With her being in my life, I learned to love again although I was planning not to love again. Loving her gives me the greatest happiness in the world. I would do anything to make her life happy. I LOVE YOU SAMANTHA, WITH ALL MY HEART.

Samantha on her ski

Samantha on top of her toys in her room

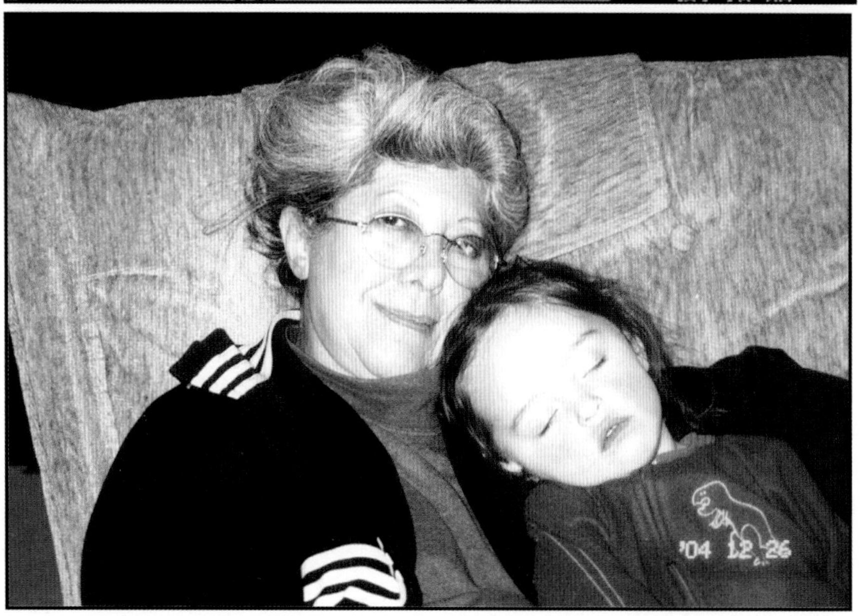

My love of life, Samantha had been sleeping on my chest for more than two hours.

My dear Samantha is discussing something very serious withher dad when she is not two yet.

Samantha is trying on her Hawaii outfit; with her mom Mojgan.

Samantha in a Ghashghaii dress from Iran

We are at a restaurant for brunch in Lake Tahoe. Kristina, Maseeh, Joe, Mojgan, Samantha, and me

Samantha on her daddy's lap

Samantha is kissed by her Uncle Maseeh.

Samantha is drinking her milk while comfortably lying down on her dog, Coco.

Samantha half naked, lets us enjoy her all together.

Samantha plays with me in her room. Have you noticed that she has her feet in a little box?

Samantha in a "Rashti" outfit from North of Iran

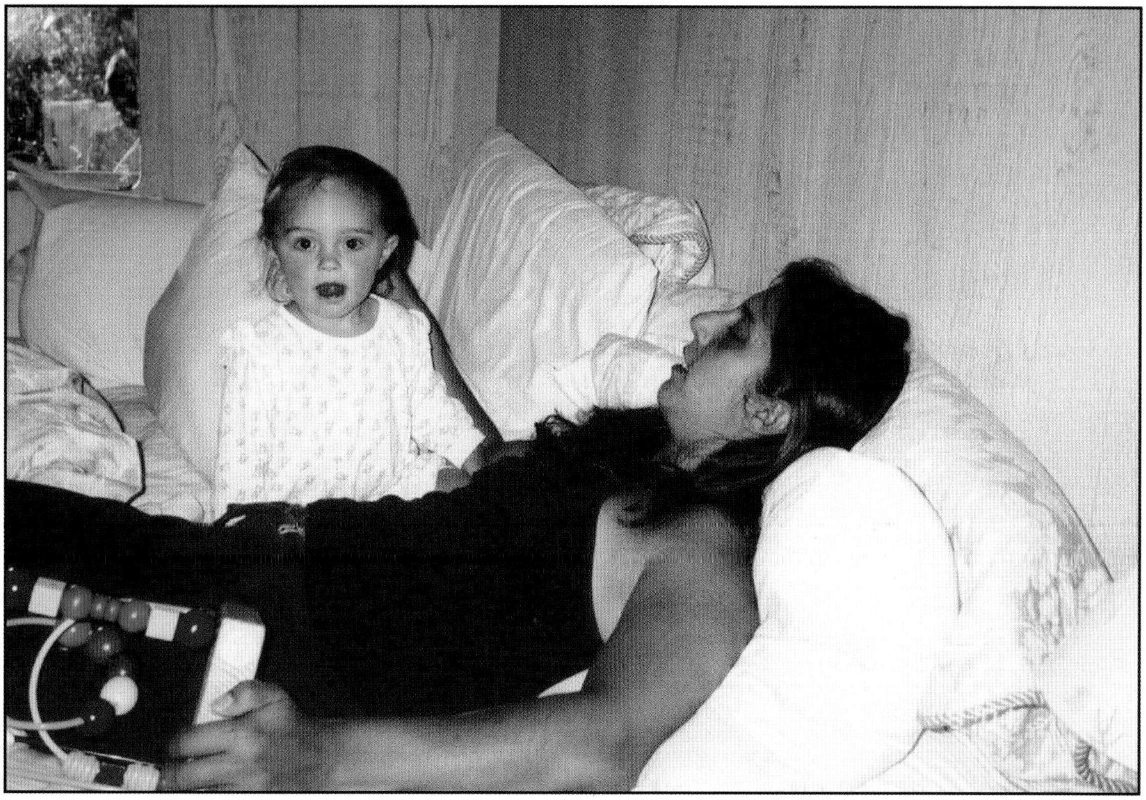

Samantha and her mom in bed, where she sleeps at night

In front of Mojgan's house in Tahoe City, California. We were celebrating Mojgan's and my birthday with my handsome Maseeh and my beautiful Maryam. My beautiful Samantha was in her stroller. I am glad that I had the chance to live long enough to be able to see my grandchildren. Left to right: Maseeh, Mojgan, Shamci, and Maryam.

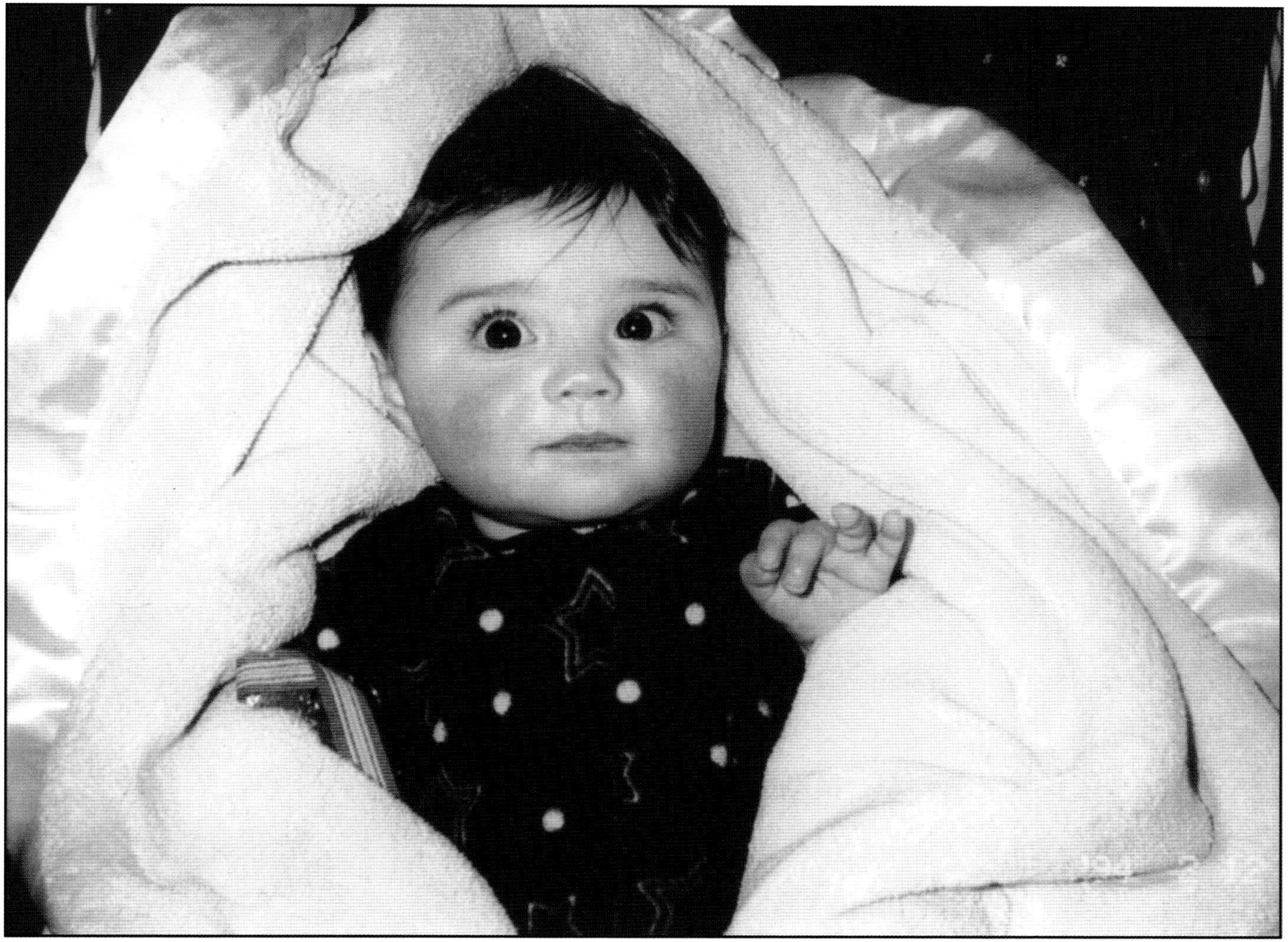

This beautiful, gorgeous and precious little girl is no one but my second grandchild, Hanna. She was born on July fifth, 2005 in Tahoe City, California. I was lucky enough to be there before, during and after her birth. My love for her is so huge that I cannot put a measure on it. I love you very dearly Hanna.

Mojgan is holding her beautiful children in her arms. I hope that she could be the best mother for her children and make a warm and happy home for them. I just pray to God to make these two precious little girls as happy as they can be.

Christmas 2006 on Santa's lap asking for a happy life and loving parents. I don't know anything about their future, but I am hoping that they could get what they asked Santa. I just wish for them to be able to have parents much better than Mojgan's. They deserve to have a happy and caring family. Dear Samantha and Hanna, I would like you to know that, I WILL ALWAYS LOVE YOU DEARLY. This is your Nana talking.

What should I write about these two beautiful and innocent children who came into my life after I had finished writing my book? There are no words to describe the love that I have for them. I made sure that they are in my book so they would, later in their lives, remember all my loving words on those beautiful cards I sent them almost every week. Samantha and Hanna are precious gifts from heaven to me.

These are ethnic clothes from North of Iran that I bought for them when I went to Iran for a visit. I had the most fun when I was trying to put the clothes on them to take these pictures. Their laughter, their giggling, their teasing and their happiness was worth more than billions of dollars to me. People might earn that much money, but to find this kind of love in your heart, one should be there to recognize the meaning of being wealthy. Dear Samantha and Hanna, you must know that I have loved you so dearly from the time you were born until the day I die.

April 11-08

Mrs. Slamci Calarami (RAFANI)

1- this is to inform you that your monthly Alimony payment will be mailed to you on monthly basis

2- In our settlement divorce it has been agreed when you receive social security payment, the exact money must be deducted from your alimony payment.

if you are receiving any social security payment, provide me the exact date and money that you have started to receive.

I must have to have these informations. within two weeks from today by April 25-008

IRAJ RAFANI. M.D

[signature]

Since there is no justice in this world,

and

Since I have no one who could defend my rights,

and

Since I don't know how or when I had agreed to such an unfair and stupid settlement, while with your income, even three times of this amount if not more, had not been enough to justify my rights,

and

Since I had read the book <u>A New Earth,</u>

and

Since I had to leave everything regarding my life to such a person to handle,

I think I had received $559 since 2005.

Y063865

Since this book will not be published until 2008, and I have received this letter from Iraj which is his new tactic to deduct money from my monthly payment, I have answered him on the back of this page as you will see.

Yes, I might have agreed to such an unfair and stupid settlement which I have no recollection of, or I had no other way of defending my rights since I had refused to divorce him altogether.

At the time that I was suicidal all the time; at the time that Mary was living in Detroit, Mi, working on her law degree and had no hope or certainty in her life whatsoever; at the time that Maseeh was living hopelessly in LA, working on his father's investment, Hollywood Live Nightclub; at the time that Mojgan was attending Western University in Kalamazoo, Mi, so hopelessly away from her father who was only occupied with his mid-life crisis, away from each other and me, probably and only probably at that time that I was not able to read or ignored reading anything regarding my divorce which I struggled for eight years to not let it happen; I might have had signed such a paper which I do not remember.

As usual, he sat on the corner of the bed to inform me of his new decision. He said, "I will pay you two thousand dollars per month, and that is it."

For many years I was not able to have health insurance of any kind. I had to travel to Iran to be able to find myself and put my mind together again if I wanted to continue living. I had to do it before destroying myself or others. So, I don't know how or when I had agreed to such an unfair and stupid settlement. At that time with his income, I would have been able to receive three times that amount at least, if not more.

Now, at the age seventy five, I must deal with more unfairness that I had created for myself just because I was trying to save the nest of my children from a poisonous cobra (Badri) and stop the breakage of my family, as it had been done in the past in my culture.

For those who might ask me why I did it, I must answer that first of all, you have not walked in my shoes. Second, I was not certain that I could win even if I wanted to pursue the divorce. When I asked a lawyer, "What if I lose my case and I do not have money to pay you?" he answered me in a clear voice, "You have your house, and we will be able to get it that way." That was the reason that I decided not to follow the subject of the divorce and allowed him to do whatever he wants to do. I did not want to become homeless. I thought to myself, a little is better than nothing.

Now, at this time of my life I wish one clever and knowledgeable lawyer who reads my story would be able to take my cold case, and represent me on contingency bases. I will be always grateful and appreciative.

I would like him to ask for my share of money from the Southfield Weigh Loss Clinic, my share of Chapel Hill apartment in Ann Arbor, Mi, my share of Hollywood Live Nightclub in LA, and to ask for those checks he made me write for the rental of Hollywood Live for the amount of more than fifty thousand dollars, as many times as he did. These were our money and the way that he made me pay it, looked like I did it willingly and I have no right to ask for my share. Also, I want my share of many more properties which I do not remember.

Only if there were a good intelligent lawyer who could get help from his heart and combine it with his cleverness to help one woman's wish come true. I hope, I hope.

May 1, 2008

Mrs. Hamci Glarani (RAFANI)

I received your note on 4-28-08. The information you wrote was not adequate and possibly not correct.

I want to have monthly or yearly payment you receive from social security also the year and date you started getting it, also any other financial assistance, including health insurance you are receiving

since you have not giving me the information I need to calculat the amount of monthly payment, and also to find how much you have received up to date.

I enclosed a check for $1000 (one thousand dollar for first half month of May payment. I will send you the second half payment on May 15 provided I get the necessary information I requested above.

As you see, he sent me this letter after I had mailed the information to him for the second time. This time I registered the mail, just like he did.

IRAJ RAFANI, M.D

[signature]

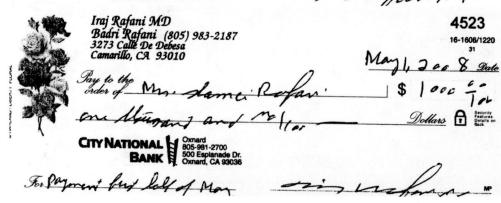

Iraj Rafani MD
Badri Rafani (805) 983-2187
3273 Calle De Debesa
Camarillo, CA 93010

4523

16-1606/1220
31

May 1, 2008 Date

Pay to the order of Mrs. Hamci Rafani $ 1000 00/100

one thousand and no/100 Dollars

CITY NATIONAL BANK
Oxnard
805-981-2700
500 Esplanade Dr.
Oxnard, CA 93036

For payment first half of May

[signature]

5/12/2008

According to my tax records,
I have received 528 dollars per month in 2005, equivalent to 6,330 dollars.
I have received 543 dollars per month in 2006, equivalent to 6,516 dollars.
I have received 559 dollars per month in 2007, equivalent to 6,708 dollars.
And, I have received 571 dollars per month from January 2008.
I did not know there are other ways to receive money from the government except Social Security. If there are any, I would like to learn about them. Except for prostitution and/or sleeping with married men, I don't know any other way, which are these things that I am not.
Above is the answer to his third letter. You will see what I told him. If only he could remember how poor he was when he married me. I had to pay his ticket to America. We used to live on furniture that we had bought from the Salvation Army. Iraj, I have to remind you that, I would rather die than to beg you for money. I will not bring myself down to your level. I'll survive. I'll survive. I'll survive.

Shamci Rafani

This is the copy of registering my letter to him.

SENDER: *COMPLETE THIS SECTION*	*COMPLETE THIS SECTION ON DELIVERY*
■ Complete items 1, 2, and 3. Also complete item 4 if Restricted Delivery is desired. ■ Print your name and address on the reverse so that we can return the card to you. ■ Attach this card to the back of the mailpiece, or on the front if space permits.	A. Signature X B. K ☐ Agent ☐ Addressee B. Received by (*Printed Name*) K Raffani — C. Date of Delivery 5-5-08
1. Article Addressed to: IRAJ RAFANI 3273 Calle De Debesa Camarillo, CA. 93010	D. Is delivery address different from item 1? ☐ Yes If YES, enter delivery address below: ☐ No
	3. Service Type ☐ Certified Mail ☐ Express Mail ☐ Registered ☐ Return Receipt for Merchandise ☐ Insured Mail ☐ C.O.D.
	4. Restricted Delivery? (*Extra Fee*) ☐ Yes
2. Article Number (*Transfer from service*	7007 2560 0002 5404 0701

PS Form 3811, February 2004 — Domestic Return Receipt — 102595-02-M-1540 more, which have not being said. This is the end of Shamci, who once was born and raised, and then got demolished by the hand of circumstances. Yet she could be born again as a completely different person. With your guidance I was able to save my children from destruction, and I found myself a home of great happiness, something I never thought I might be able to achieve.

But what will come in my next book, "My children and I", it will be much more interesting to read. I don't know what the saying "mirror has two faces" means. But in my new book there is more to talk about, and review the reason for our existence. My view of life is not the same as it was when I was younger. I see things completely different from when I was sensitive to oncoming disasters. Then my attachment was to people around me, thinking that they were my rescuers. As my life passed and I came across many harsh and disastrous misfortunes, I realized that I only needed to have faith in you to be able to survive through the hard times and turn around and make it look like an easy task.

Today, emotionally I feel like an iron creature or robot, which is not afraid of anything: fire, earthquake, mudslide, and loss of my belongings from loss of life or materials. If it happens, it happens. I have no hand in changing that situation. Even the most powerful people in the world had no hand on changing the act of nature. Yes, science might bring some changes to speed up or delay some of nature's activities. But in a long run things will happen the way that they must happen. People might be happy with delaying or speeding it up. But sooner or later they have to accept the oncoming fortune or misfortune. So today, instead of worrying about things, which might bring unhappiness in my life, with the faith that I have in you, I will look forward to the good first, and let the bad pass by me. Thanks many millions for bringing peace and real happiness into my life. No psychiatrist, no therapies, no tranquilizers, and no medication could have cured me, except my closeness to you by my writing. I was able to walk through the pathway of peaceful life and tranquility by discussing my problems with you, and I followed your guidance from the beginning to the end.

My Dear God:

This book is getting close to the end. But I have to tell you in my sincere word that the only time that I lived with happiness, comfort, and a leisure was the time that I started my day by sitting in front of my typewriter, and I spoke to you about my life. It certainly was the most pleasing time that I can remember. And if I die right at this moment, I have had experience of being in Heaven as long as I was able to talk to you, and found a way to be able to put all my troubles away and behind me. I sincerely thank you for giving me this opportunity to be able to survive, and save my children from destruction in a best possible way.

My dear God:

The Finishing Touch:

As I said before, I am not a writer, nor am I good in English to be able to express my feelings as I am truly in pain, or I am suffering from one event. And as I discovered while I started to write about my sufferings, I found out by myself that I have been Dyslexic. So I would like to apologize to those who read this book, and will recognize my many, many mistakes. I did not write this book to show anyone that I have enough knowledge to become a writer. I just wanted to show everyone how I started to cure myself by writing to an unknown power, who became the source of my strength, and my tolerance, who I called him my dear GOD. Whoever he was or, wherever he was at the time of my need, he came to my rescue. Now if this source was nature, or was light, or was power of some kind, whoever, or whatever he was, from our childhood we were raised to call him "GOD".

It worked for me to sit in front of my typewriter, and talk to him about all my problems. And in return I discovered some kind of wisdom and strength in me, which I believe it came from that unknown power.

Actually, he doesn't need language, he doesn't need English, because no matter how, or which way I talk to him, he was and he will be with me. That was what I needed to be able to survive, and take action to the best of my ability. That was the only thing to let me escape from the act of crime. That was the only way to stop me from committing suicide. And that was what I needed to show my children, who their mother was, whom they never knew.

Sorry if I was bad or if I was good, this was I, and this was the way that I was brought up. And this was the way that I tried my best to make three good and beautiful children from you.

All throughout the book, I took all the blames for what I had done wrong in your lives. But can you find out where did I go so wrong to deserve this kind of torture for as many years as I suffered for it? Anyway, all and all the purpose of life, especially a good one, is to learn to think right, to do right, and to say right. This has been Zoroastrians religion, which I truly believe in.

I did all my best not only for my children and for my husband, but for everyone else, who was somehow connected to me either by blood or by marriage. I was very lucky to find three most incredible sisters-in-law, who everyone could dream to have. They not only were like good sisters to me, but they were my best friends. That by itself had something to do with my inner strength. I wish them the best, and they deserve to have a happy and successful life. And when I had love in my life, it was the greatest any woman could dream to have. And for those angels, who came into my life when I needed them the most, I am not able to thank them enough. They all deserve the best of happiness.

My Dear God:

I know for sure that what good they did for me, it will be back to them somehow, somewhere, and at some time. If it wasn't for the care and the friendship of my sisters-in-law, and the kindness and efforts of those who went out of their way to help me emotionally, I would not have been able to survive the way I did. Thanks a million to all of you! This peace and tranquility, which is spreading over my life, I owe it to all of you and My Dear God.